ONE VOLUME
SEMINARY

MICHAEL J. BOYLE, LAURIE L. NORRIS,
AND KERWIN A. RODRIGUEZ (GENERAL EDITORS)

ONE VOLUME SEMINARY

A Complete Ministry Education
from the Faculty of
Moody Bible Institute and
Moody Theological Seminary

MOODY PUBLISHERS
CHICAGO

Unless otherwise noted, Scripture quotations taken from the (NASB®) New American Standard Bible®, Copyright © 1960, 1971, 1977, 1995, 2020 by The Lockman Foundation. Used by permission. All rights reserved. www.lockman.org

Scripture quotations marked (ESV) are from the *ESV® Bible (The Holy Bible, English Standard Version®)*, Copyright © 2001 by Crossway, a publishing ministry of Good News Publishers. Used by permission. All rights reserved.

Scripture quotations marked (NIV) are taken from the Holy Bible, New International Version®, NIV®. Copyright © 1973, 1978, 1984, 2011 by Biblica, Inc.™ Used by permission of Zondervan. All rights reserved worldwide. www.zondervan.com The "NIV" and "New International Version" are trademarks registered in the United States Patent and Trademark Office by Biblica, Inc.™

Scripture quotations marked (NLT) are taken from the Holy Bible, New Living Translation, copyright ©1996, 2004, 2015 by Tyndale House Foundation. Used by permission of Tyndale House Publishers, Carol Stream, Illinois 60188. All rights reserved.

All emphasis in Scripture has been added.

Edited by Kevin Mungons, Pamela J. Pugh, and Jeff Robinson Sr.
Interior design: Puckett Smartt
Cover design: Charles Brock
Cover illustration of Bible copyright © 2016 by gleb261194.gmail.com / Depositphotos (121545178). All rights reserved.
Cover illustration of line pattern copyright © 2016 by Marylia17 / Vectorstock (36755131). All rights reserved.

Library of Congress Cataloging-in-Publication Data

Names: Boyle, Michael J. (Writer on religion), editor. | Norris, Laurie L., editor. | Rodriguez, Kerwin A., editor.
Title: One volume seminary : a complete ministry education from the faculty of Moody Bible Institute and Moody Theological Seminary / Michael J. Boyle, Laurie L. Norris, and Kerwin A. Rodriguez (general editors).
Description: Chicago : Moody Publishers, [2022] | Includes bibliographical references. | Summary: "Moody Bible Institute and Moody Theological Seminary faculty authors combine pastoral wisdom, academic scholarship, and savvy street smarts from the church's frontlines to provide a one-stop shop for ministry training. One Volume Seminary contains sixty essays with practical advice for every aspect of church life-always grounded in God's Word-to help you succeed in ministry"-- Provided by publisher.
Identifiers: LCCN 2021044647 (print) | LCCN 2021044648 (ebook) | ISBN 9780802419422 (hardcover) | ISBN 9780802498014 (ebook)
Subjects: LCSH: Theology, Practical--Handbooks, manuals, etc. | BISAC: RELIGION / Christian Ministry / Pastoral Resources | RELIGION / Christian Ministry / General
Classification: LCC BV3 .O54 2022 (print) | LCC BV3 (ebook) | DDC 253--dc23/eng/20211022
LC record available at https://lccn.loc.gov/2021044647
LC ebook record available at https://lccn.loc.gov/2021044648

Originally delivered by fleets of horse-drawn wagons, the affordable paperbacks from D. L. Moody's publishing house resourced the church and served everyday people. Now, after more than 125 years of publishing and ministry, Moody Publishers' mission remains the same—even if our delivery systems have changed a bit. For more information on other books (and resources) created from a biblical perspective, go to www.moodypublishers.com or write to:

Moody Publishers
820 N. LaSalle Boulevard
Chicago, IL 60610

1 3 5 7 9 10 8 6 4 2

Printed in the United States of America

CONTENTS

SECTION 4: MINISTRY TO THE WORLD

SECTION 5: PROCLAIMING THE WORD IN WORSHIP AND PREACHING

SECTION 6: PRACTICAL CHURCH SKILLS

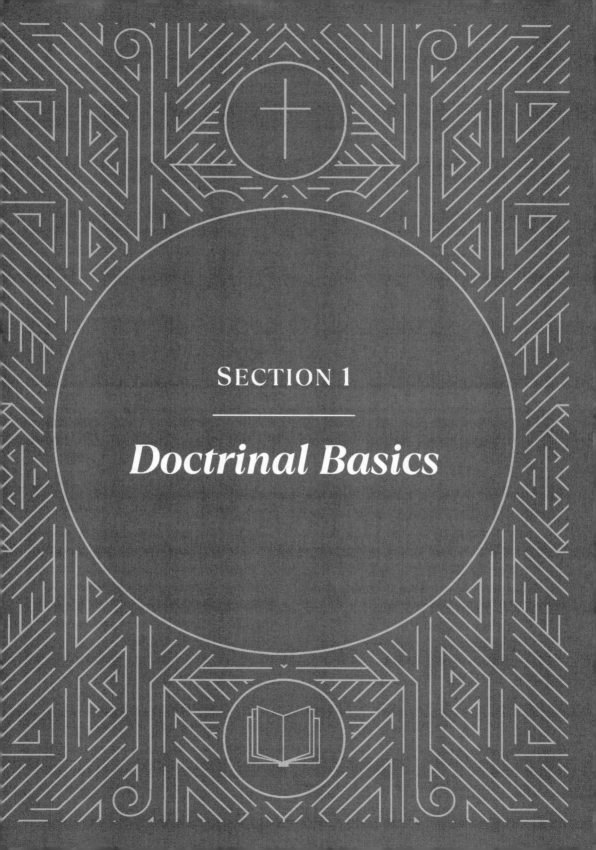

SECTION 1

Doctrinal Basics

Theology Is for the Church

LAURIE L. NORRIS

MISCONCEPTIONS ABOUT THEOLOGY

What is theology? And, more importantly, what does theology have to do with the pastor or church ministry leader? For many, the word "theology" refers to a lofty academic enterprise reserved for those with advanced degrees or who inhabit ivory towers. It describes an elite discipline pursued by professional scholars and seminarians, not a discourse aimed at the average person in the pew. Theologians purportedly work with abstractions, whereas ministry leaders deal in concrete matters of pastoral care and participate in the work of so-called practical ministry. In other words, ministry vocation is deemed more practical than theological. For many church leaders, theology is viewed as irrelevant to daily life or, at worst, even detrimental to personal faith and relationship with Jesus Christ. These conceptions, however, reflect a flawed understanding of theology and a tragic false dichotomy between Christian belief and practice.

CONFRONTING FALSE DICHOTOMIES

Theology most simply refers to the "study of God," that is, our beliefs and conversations about God. Every person operates—whether consciously or subconsciously—out of an underlying belief about who God is and what He is like. In this sense, every person is indeed a "theologian" and engaged in theological vocation; all of life is inherently theological. The real question, then, is this: Do our thoughts about God rightly correspond with His own self-revelation in Scripture and with the unified testimony of the Christian church down through the ages? Do we know God on *His* terms, or do we relate to Him more as a reflection of our own preferences, suppositions, and cultural influences? Do our convictions conform to God's revealed truth, or do we worship one created in our own image?[1]

A. W. Tozer wrote in *The Knowledge of the Holy,* "What comes into our minds when we think about God is the most important thing about us."[2] That is, our thoughts about God define everything about us, and they orient our life and worship. As Tozer rightly warns,

> The idolatrous heart assumes that God is other than He is . . . and substitutes for the true God one made after its own likeness. . . . The essence of idolatry is the entertainment of thoughts about God that are unworthy of Him. . . . Wrong ideas about God are not only the fountain from which the polluted waters of idolatry flow; they are themselves idolatrous. The idolater simply imagines things about God and acts as if they were true.[3]

In other words, we will enact what we truly believe, so what we believe really matters. True theology must be lived, and Christian practice must be rooted in our theology. Theology always has practical implications, and such practice inevitably reflects our underlying theology.

Knowledge in Scripture is never merely cognitive. It has as its *telos* a rightly ordered love for God that produces covenant faithfulness. Such knowing is never merely an abstraction. The Scriptures express a relational covenant between the Lord and His people. To know God in the biblical sense is to love and obey Him. Conversely, love of God in Scripture demands that we rightly comprehend the object of our worship. Genuine love cannot exist apart from genuine knowledge. Right knowledge of God cultivates our love and purifies our worship. Such growth in knowledge transforms our vision of ourselves and of the world around us, as we increasingly view all reality through the lens of God's own self-revelation and our participation in His redemptive story.

Theology invites us to respond rightly to the one who has made Himself known to us. This pursuit is both propositional and personal, for the inspired and inerrant written word of God also leads us to encounter the eternal word of God *made flesh* (John 1:14). Kelly Kapic says it beautifully: "Christians are called to enter into the chorus of praise that is true worship, responding in the Spirit to the revelation of the saving God in Jesus Christ. Theology is all about knowing how to sing the song of redemption. . . . But in order to enjoy the song and sing it well, we must learn the words and the music."[4] Or, as Kevin Vanhoozer aptly concludes, "Christians learn doctrine in order to participate more deeply, passionately, and truthfully in the drama of redemption."[5]

So then, whom exactly do we love, and what is He like? This is an inherently *theological* question, and yet how often we fall prey to false dichotomies that pit theology against personal piety or "practical ministry." Such divorce of theology from spiritual life often leads to its neglect. Perhaps such neglect of theology in some Christian circles reflects a form of anti-intellectualism or a disproportional emphasis on subjective personal experience. Perhaps it comes from lack of exposure to formal biblical-theological study, as some educational institutions set aside this study for subjects deemed more "relevant." Perhaps it comes from a negative past experience, namely, a dry and lifeless approach to theology that smothered joy instead of stirring love, that stimulated the mind but neglected the soul. Perhaps it comes from a tragic disconnect between theology and its lived implications. Whatever the reasons, as Grenz and Olson rightly counter, "The antidote to bad theology is not no theology; it is good theology."[6]

THE IMPORTANCE OF THEOLOGY IN MINISTRY

What we believe about God and the content of His self-revelation inevitably shapes our practice. Orthodoxy and orthopraxy, dogma and devotion, go hand in hand. One necessarily informs the other. Our belief about God informs our posture and practice. And our posture before God informs our belief. As it says in Proverbs 1:7, "The fear of the LORD is the beginning of knowledge." Genuine worship of our triune God cannot be compartmentalized. We worship holistically, both in spirit and in truth (John 4:23). We worship with our mind, our affections and our will. Theology, then, is not only an academic enterprise. Christian theology is, first and foremost, *ecclesial*. It is for *the church*. All members of Christ's body are called to grow in knowledge and love of God that bears the fruit of obedience.

How much more, then, does this calling extend to those appointed as leaders to shepherd Christ's church in sound biblical teaching and faithful application of that teaching to life! We observe this emphasis most strongly in the Pastoral Epistles, where Paul establishes clear qualifications for church leadership with respect to biblical knowledge, doctrinal fidelity, and instructional competency. This includes the ability to recognize and confront error. According to Titus 1:9, elders and overseers must hold "firmly the faithful word which is in accordance with the teaching, so that [they] will be able both to exhort in sound doctrine and to refute those who contradict it" (see "able to teach" in 1 Tim. 3:2; 2 Tim. 2:2, 24). Paul urges Timothy to present himself to God an approved worker who rightly handles the word of truth (2 Tim. 2:15). Through this divinely inspired word, Timothy will be equipped "for every good work"—able to teach, reprove, correct, and train in righteousness (2 Tim. 3:16). Elsewhere Paul warns of false teachers who would distort or jettison the faith, imploring Timothy to "protect what has been entrusted to [him]" (1 Tim. 6:20–21; see 2 Tim. 1:13–14; 3:10–15). The expectation is clear: Those called to shepherd the church of Christ must faithfully transmit and safeguard the teachings of Christ.

So then, theology is for those serving in the trenches of ministry, and it will determine the very shape of that ministry. It will drive the "why," the "what," and the "how" of church practice—from Sunday morning liturgy and order of worship to educational philosophy and church programming, from models of pastoral counseling to various expressions of communal life, from the nature and scope of mission to matters of church polity. Ministry competency entails theological competency, like the most basic of tools in a builder's belt. The pastor as theologian seeks to understand the entirety of God's self-revelation through the written word of Scripture and the incarnate word of Christ, in "conversation" with the voice of Christian tradition (that is, the community of faith past and present), the testimony of creation, human reason, and experience. He then applies this revelation "where he lives" in contextually appropriate ways, letting God's Word speak into every facet of life, not least in the context of church ministry. Such biblical-theological rootedness enables the ministry leader to address both the needs of the flock and the contemporary issues of the day with spiritual sensitivity, conviction, and authority. It offers sure footing to remain steadfast in the face of shifting cultural winds and pressures. It guides the church in faithful expressions of Christian thinking and living, but also in discerning what is *not Christian*—namely, those beliefs and behaviors that subtly distort or outright contradict the distinctive doctrines and practices of historic Christian faith.

The church cannot afford ministry leaders and pastors who neglect biblical-theological study. Such neglect produces anemic sheep who waste away for lack of spiritual nutrition and who wander in the wastelands of cultural relativism because they do not recognize the voice of their Shepherd. The church cannot afford ministry leaders who bypass the timeless authority of God's Word for the latest ministry strategy, or who jettison disciplined theological reflection for a results-driven pragmatism. The minister who dwells only in shallow waters cannot lead others into spiritual depths. What are we actually feeding the sheep? How are we forming them and, conversely, how are we being formed?

The stakes are high. Souls hang in the balance, and what we believe about God, about ourselves, about the church, and about the world, matters profoundly. Ministry leaders must be theologically equipped for the gravity of this task.[7] If not fed, the sheep may starve; if not led, the sheep may stray. For this reason, Paul urged

Timothy to keep vigilant watch over both his life and teaching for the sake of himself and his hearers, lest they fall into error (1 Tim. 4:16).

CONCLUSION

A minister must be equipped biblically and theologically to lead God's people into right understanding and right living. No leadership theory, innovative program, or growth strategy can replace this necessary foundation. We "exegete" all of life—ourselves, the church, our culture—in submission to God's Word, for we see our own reflection most clearly in the waters of God's own self-revelation.[8] So then, this volume begins in the proper place: by establishing the biblical and theological foundations for ministry practice.

The following twelve chapters will provide instruction for studying and interpreting God's Word and for synthesizing these biblical truths as faithful Christian doctrine. To that end, this section begins with a practical approach to biblical interpretation that addresses basic Bible study methods and hermeneutics in relation to the broader storyline of the Bible, the theology of both Old and New Testaments, and the historical-cultural worlds of the Bible. The remaining chapters summarize central Christian doctrines pertaining to the nature of God, humanity, Scripture, salvation, the church, and end times. This includes an overview of church history and its importance for understanding theology, along with an introduction to apologetics that considers how best to validate and defend these truths within one's present, historical-cultural context. The goal? To shepherd the church in bringing all of life into conscious submission to the knowledge of God. This includes even the most routine, ordinary, and seemingly mundane spheres of our daily existence that form us in the likeness of Christ.

NOTES

1. Stanley J. Grenz and Roger E. Olson, *Who Needs Theology?: An Invitation to the Study of God* (Downers Grove, IL: InterVarsity, 1996), 45.

2. A. W. Tozer, *The Knowledge of the Holy: The Attributes of God: Their Meaning in the Christian Life* (Lincoln, NE: Back to the Bible Broadcast, 1961), 1–3.

3. Ibid., 4–5.

4. Kelly M. Kapic, *A Little Book for New Theologians: Why and How to Study Theology* (Downers Grove, IL: InterVarsity, 2012), 22–23.

5. Kevin J. Vanhoozer, *The Drama of Doctrine: A Canonical-Linguistic Approach to Christian Theology* (Louisville: Westminster John Knox, 2005), 107.

6. Grenz and Olson, *Who Needs Theology?* 51.

7. See Gerald Hiestand and Todd Wilson, *The Pastor Theologian: Resurrecting an Ancient Vision* (Grand Rapids: Zondervan, 2015), 101; also Jason A. Nicholls, "The Pastor Theologian in the Pastoral Epistles," in *Becoming a Pastor*

Theologian: New Possibilities for Church Leadership, ed. Todd Wilson and Gerald Hiestand (Downers Grove, IL: IVP Academic, 2016), 151–62.

8. On the knowledge of God as necessarily preceding right knowledge of self, see John Calvin, *Institutes of the Christian Religion*, ed. John T. McNeill, trans. Ford Lewis Battles, 2 vols., Library of Christian Classics (Philadelphia: Westminster, 1960), 1.1.1–2.

Studying the Bible

ERIC C. REDMOND

*Man shall not live on bread alone, but man shall live
on everything that comes out of the mouth of the LORD.*

DEUTERONOMY 8:3

The words above were quoted by Jesus in Matthew 4:4 and Luke 4:4 during His temptation in the wilderness. They remind us that life consists of more than our physical appetites and corporeal existence. Food would have satisfied Jesus' hunger after forty days and strengthened his body, since the human body certainly requires "bread," i.e., physical sustenance, and Jesus acknowledged that. However, man is not merely a creature of physical existence. Made in the image of God, man reasons, creates, has language, and can make moral decisions. He "shall not live on bread alone," but his deepest needs are met by "everything that comes out of the mouth of the LORD." In this particular scenario, Jesus called on the Word of God during His battle with the devil. In feasting on the Word of God, the Lord Jesus experienced victory and blessings from God the Father.

This image of words coming from the mouth of God agrees with previous and later descriptions of the Word of God in Scripture (e.g., 1 Kings 8:15; 2 Chron. 35:22; 36:12; Ps. 36:3). All Scripture is inspired by God (2 Tim. 3:16), originating in His mouth before being penned accurately by the hand of the human author. The writer to the Hebrews describes the Scriptures as God *speaking*, having power greater than any earthly, human-made sword that pierces and exposes what is inside of a person (Heb. 1:1–2; 4:12–13; 12:25).[1] The assumption of the biblical authors is that God has spoken, that what they have written are the very words God has spoken, that these words continue to speak because they are living, and that God makes His person, works, and will known through these very same words.[2]

Therefore, becoming readers of Scripture with understanding is important to the task of hearing God speak. This chapter presents tools for reading Scripture well so that we might become discerning hearers of the voice of God. We will discuss the preparation for hearing the Lord speak from Scripture, focusing on the tools of spiritual orientation and background study. We will then examine hermeneutics, or interpretation, giving attention to various literary genres represented in Scripture, then move to discerning the message, and end with application.

PREPARATION: SPIRITUAL ORIENTATION

Spiritual orientation relates to the nature of the Word of God as a divine work, and our relationship to it as such.

God is a being completely different from us. The Lord is without beginning and end, having life within Himself, being the only completely independent being—one whose existence depends on no one and nothing else. He is the "I AM" (Ex. 3:14), the everlasting God (Isa. 40:28). His speech is divine and unique. It comes from an eternal being—the Creator Himself, who spoke all things into existence.

In contrast, though made in His image, as fallen creatures we are sinful, spiritually blind, ignorant of God, and darkened in our understanding of Him.[3] Our natural capacities allow us to obtain information in knowable areas such as math, science, literature, the arts, and history. But God is not knowable to sinners by means of our own capability, and we cannot force our way into knowing Him. Knowing Him must be something He initiates by His grace, on the basis of Christ's work of redemption for us (Eph. 1:17–19; 2:1–6).

Therefore, in order to hear God's voice from Scripture and in order to know the mind of God, one must be a believer (1 Cor. 2:14–16), a person who has placed his or her faith in Christ and has been redeemed by Christ from the fallen, spiritually blind state.

As believers, however, we are not then left to our own intellectual capacities to make sense of what we are reading or hearing the Lord say. Instead, Scripture portrays the need for the Lord to open our eyes in order for us to gain insight from His Word. We may pray with the psalmist, "Open my eyes, that I may behold wonderful things from Your Law" (Ps. 119:18). The psalmist does not lack in physical vision; instead, the psalmist is asking for spiritual insight into God's ways.

Therefore, because we understand the Word of God to be *living*, being the very voice of God, we must ask the Author of Scripture to make Himself and His truth known to us. We cannot barge into His presence and attempt to know Him by force of our will. The need for the Lord to open our capacity to understand His truth and its significance places us in a position in which we must seek Him and walk in humility in our own knowledge before Him. We must ask the Lord, in His mercy and grace, to reveal the truth of His Word to us.

PREPARATION: BACKGROUND STUDY

Background study relates to the Word of God as a human work written by, to, and within ancient cultures. Not only should we pay attention to the spiritual orientation of our hearts in preparing to study God's Word, we also need to orient ourselves to the world of the biblical text. That is, we must attend to its historical, cultural, and social context.

While reading the Scriptures, we should be cautious to avoid both *under-reading* ancient cultural understandings in our texts and *over-reading* the ancient cultural practices into the significance of the text. Under-reading implies not paying enough attention to the historical background of a text and thus missing some of the purpose or richness of a passage or book. Likewise, an over-reading of a portion of Scripture can result in treating it as of mostly historical significance than of the spiritual message it intends to convey.

UNDER-READING TEXTUAL BACKGROUNDS

We must first recognize that the original readers were aware of cultural ideas inherent in the text but unfamiliar to us. They understood practices such as a barren woman giving her handmaiden to her husband as a surrogate, so the story of Sarah and Hagar in Genesis 16 might seem to be a natural or common occurrence to them. They would be familiar with the hospitality customs of the first century that Simon the Pharisee failed to practice when Jesus commended the woman from the city who wiped His feet with her tears and hair (Luke 7:36–50). We cannot ignore that such a cultural literacy exists in the milieus of the biblical writers and their original audiences.

It is within the work of background study that one endeavors to discern the *occasion* of a biblical book.[4] "Occasion" connotes the historical circumstances of the writer and original audience in relationship to each other that prompt the writing. For example, in Habakkuk, the references to the violence in Judah (Hab. 1:2), the Lord's calling of the Chaldeans to bring judgment upon Israel (1:6–11), the three "Selah" insertions (3:3, 9, 13), and the note to the choirmaster (3:19) allow one to reconstruct an occasion for the writing of this book. Seeing the lack of judgment as promised in the law, the prophet Habakkuk questions the justice of God and receives prophetic oracles. The prophecies answer questions concerning justice for both the prophet and the people who are reflecting on the destruction of Jerusalem and deportation of the children of Judah. While Habakkuk spoke to a generation facing coming judgment, the writing of his prophecy gives evidence of reception by an exiled audience in need of explanation of the justice of God's judgment through their oppressors. That audience is invited to *sing* the words of Habakkuk with the same settled disposition the prophet has with the Lord's sovereignty in Judah's judgment.

Similarly, in 2 Timothy, there are references to Timothy's tears (2 Tim. 1:4), shame concerning Paul's imprisonment (1:8), the "last days" (3:1), Paul's coming martyrdom (4:6), the desertion of Paul's coworkers in the gospel (4:9–12, 16), and the coming of winter (4:21). Such references, and many like these, allow the reader to discern a tone of urgency. The writing of 2 Timothy is prompted both by Timothy's need to remain steadfast in the work of the gospel in the face of being without Paul, his spiritual father and mentor, and by Paul's desire to receive ministry from Timothy before his execution. In each of these examples, we observe the importance of identifying the historical occasion that informs the writing.

OVER-READING TEXTUAL BACKGROUNDS

Although understanding the historical situation behind a text is important, we should remember that the biblical writer is a prophet of the revelation of God, not simply a purveyor of his particular social and literary context. When a cultural allusion is found in a passage of Scripture, we may assume it is there to illumine the spiritual aspect of that text.

For example, salt had many uses in the first century, such as to flavor, preserve, fertilize, parch, heal, or repair, and even to reduce slipperiness over marble surfaces after a rain. Biblical writers do not need to communicate an entire cultural milieu within a single text that mention salt; they do not suggest that we must understand the full gamut of how salt was used. Instead, they draw from the culturally relevant aspect that transcends cultures.[5]

Having a recently published Bible dictionary and Bible encyclopedia (to benefit from the latest scholarship) will help an interpreter ascertain information about the various ancient cultures represented in Scripture. It is recommended that Bible study reference works come from a conservative interpretive stance that holds to the inerrancy of the Scriptures. This guideline is especially important about the dating of biblical books. For example, Exodus, Isaiah, Daniel, Mark, John, and 2 Peter, whose dates of writing strongly influence the interpretation of their works, are a few of the books receiving unnecessary skepticism due to misinterpretation of background-related data and the reconstruction of the occasion of these writings.[6] Fortunately, we have many excellent resources that hold to the truth of Scripture to aid our understanding.

HERMENEUTICS: GENRE, MESSAGE, AND APPLICATION

With a posture of humility before the Lord and background information in hand, one can move toward interpreting a text—a process often referred to as *hermeneutics*. Hermeneutics is the art and science of interpreting a text, so biblical hermeneutics is the art and science of interpreting biblical texts. We study a text both in relation to its immediate literary context, as well as in relation to the broader context of Scripture. In this chapter, our hermeneutical approach considers matters of genre, message, and application. These three elements will help us draw out the meaning of a passage and suggest how to put the passage into obedient Christian practice.

GENRE

Genre simply refers to a *type* or category of literary work and incorporates a recognizable pattern that has its own features and communicates its meanings to us in a manner different from other types. For example, *narrative* as a genre communicates meaning via the interactions of characters within the plot of a story. One recognizes this genre when the writer tells a story, such as the account of Joseph in Genesis or the beautiful book of Ruth. *Poetry* communicates through expressive language. One recognizes poetry when reading a psalm, proverbial statements, the speeches in Job, much of Old Testament prophecy, and the songs in Luke 1–2.[7] The biblical writers most often employ narrative and poetry within the canon of Scripture to communicate the voice of God.[8]

Given the different interpretative tools for just these two categories, we are reminded of the importance of respecting genre as we read. Proper interpretation involves reading according to the particular rules of a given genre, rather than imposing the rules of another. To ignore this would be to ignore the means by which the Holy Spirit uses the writer to communicate the revelation of God. We would not use the same tools, for example, to interpret the book of Romans as we would Ecclesiastes.

While some variation exists among scholarly designation of genres in Scripture, there is general consensus of these: narrative (which includes history), parable, poetry, law, letters, wisdom, prophecy, and subsets of each. We will examine these seven with a view toward approaching Scripture intelligently for greatest understanding.[9]

Narrative: As indicated above, at the most basic level, narrative literature is story. The narrative genre in the Bible encompasses the historical books, the Gospels, and Acts. These books tell of true events. Narrative consists of a sequence of events, tied around a *plot*, the intentional sequencing of the movement of a story from beginning to middle to end. The story revolves around a *goal*, a *conflict* or series of conflicts, and the *resolution* thereof. Every biblical story has a plot, whether in the Old or New Testament. Thus, all biblical stories work the same way at a macro level.

The *plot goal* is *the intended outcome of the story*. In order to identify the *goal* of a story's plot, one should ask questions of the passage such as "Where is this story going?" "What is at stake in this passage?" "Based on the opening verses or scenes of the story, how would one expect this story to unfold and resolve?" The plot goal invites us to consider what we would expect to happen if, without interruption, the character(s) in question achieves, completes, finds, or understands at the end of the story what the character(s) intends to achieve, complete, find, or understand at the beginning of the story. The plot goal sets the literary trajectory of the story, inviting a reader to anticipate or imagine how a story on this trajectory might travel and end in a perfect world.

The *plot conflict*(s) are the hurdles, obstacles, interruptions, or changes that take place in a story to keep the plot goal from coming to immediate fulfillment. In order to identify the conflict or conflicts, one may wish to ask about the passage, "What takes place here that prevents the plot goal from being achieved immediately?" "What do the characters in question need to overcome to achieve a positive outcome (or a negative outcome) to the story?"

The *plot resolution* is the outcome of the story and how it unfolds. In order to identify the resolution, one should ask, "How were the original tensions in the story resolved?" or, "What outcomes occur and how?" Everything in a story that is not part of the plot goal or plot conflict(s) is part of the plot resolution, whether that be dialogue, an unexpected ending or twist, narrator commentary, more story, or even the absence of any movement toward relieving the story's tension. The plot must account for everything in a narrative passage of Scripture.

The story of Abram in Genesis 15 is a good example of narrative. In this account, we find the plot goal: assurance for Abram that God's promise that he will have a son will be fulfilled. The plot conflict is Abram's lack of an heir in his household. In the resolution, the writer of Genesis resolves the tension between Abram's desire for assurance and the lack of an heir as God gives Abram a promise, Abram responds in faith, God provides a covenant with pronouncement, and Abram sleeps.

Parable: Parable is a narrative sequence that makes a comparison between common experiences and historical realities to clarify, exemplify, or magnify historical theological discourse.[10] As a narrative sequence, it is an interaction of setting, character, point of view, and dialogue revolving around a plot. Thus, parables need to be analyzed as stories. As literature that makes a comparison between the common experience and historical reality, parables draw from shared experiences of hearers such as sowing, baking, fishing, feasting, shepherding, building, squandering wealth, relations between the rich and the poor, canceling of debts, and the planting of vineyards. Common experiences, although drawn from realities, are not historical realities in their telling. The common experience is then related to something in the real (nonfiction) world of the audience and author of the parable. The parables themselves teach theological truth indirectly, like truth about forgiveness or truth about being a neighbor (e.g., Matt. 18:35; Luke 10:36–37).

Parables' correspondence to historical realities requires the interpreter to ask, "What issue does the parable raise?" No parable is told in isolation from the gospel account's history around the speaker of the parable. Consider Luke 10:25–37: The legal expert's question about the identity of his neighbor prompts the parable of the Good Samaritan. Only with the expert's attempt to justify himself—which is part of an attempt to ascertain the congruency of Jesus' teaching on eternal life with the law of Moses—does Jesus begin the parable.

One should approach this parable as a narrative, in which the plot goal is for someone to stop to help the man robbed and beaten. This goal comes into conflict with the priest's and Levite's apathy toward the man and his plight and is resolved when a journeying Samaritan provides abundant and sacrificial compassion to the man. Bandaging and providing medicinal help would have been common, but the progress to the inn and events thereafter reveal excess and sacrifice.

The characters and issues within the parable correspond to the characters outside of the parable. For example, the priest and the Levite, being religious experts in the Mosaic law, correspond to the legal expert who posed the original question about who was his neighbor. The man robbed corresponds to the "neighbor" in question. The Samaritan, as model neighbor, portrays one ideally following the law—as one who demonstrates possession of eternal life. The Samaritan proves himself a neighbor.

Luke 10:36–37 provides a common post-parable dialogue in which Jesus is able to commend the expert to do the same as the one who showed mercy. That is, the Samaritan's evidence of being a neighbor receives Jesus' commendation to be followed by the expert in the law. This idea then informs the resolution of the full narrative: *eternal life's relationship to the law demands those who know about the law to be a neighbor.*

Poetry: Poetry is highly concentrated language used to communicate the poems, prayers, prophecies, and songs of the people of God throughout the Old Testament and in some passages of the New Testament (e.g., Luke 1:46–55, 68–79; 1 Cor. 13; Phil. 2:5–11; 1 Tim. 3:16; 2 Tim. 2:11–13; 1 John 4:7–12).

Unlike English poetry, which functions largely according to the conventions of rhyme and meter, Hebrew poetry communicates via many literary devices, a common one being parallelism.[11] *Parallelism* is the sharpening or focusing of meaning in two or more lines of poetry.[12] For example, in Proverbs 16:32, there are two lines of poetry, and the lines have similar, parallel ideas in them. One can visualize by writing them out:

One who *is slow to anger* **is better than** the mighty,
and one who *rules his spirit*, **than** one who captures a city.

We can easily catch that the two lines together actually convey a singular idea. The broader idea, "slow to anger," is sharpened in the second line, "rules his spirit." The spirit of a person is ruled so that anger does not control. The imagery of someone conquering a city portrays this mighty person as a warrior who commands others en route to victory. The person with self-control over his or her individual anger proves to be one of greater might than the person who commands troops to rout a municipality.[13]

Job, Psalms, Proverbs, Ecclesiastes, Song of Solomon, and Lamentations are considered the books of poetry in the Bible, though poetic passages permeate Scripture. For example, Judges is classified as a historical book, yet Deborah's song, poetry, is recorded in chapter 5. As has been reiterated, the genres in Scripture do not fall within concrete boundaries. A book or a passage may contain more than one genre.

Other literary devices such as imagery, metaphor, simile, and personification are found throughout the Bible's poetic literature. Imagery is a poetic device that adds flavor to prose by creating a response. Song of Solomon is loaded with imagery that beguile the senses. In chapter 2 alone we have sweet fruit (v. 3), lovely flowers (v. 12), singing birds (v. 12), fragrant vines (v. 13). The rich imagery in the six short verses that comprise Psalm 23 evoke responses of peace, care, darkness, hope, assurance.

Metaphor and simile are techniques that make use of comparison. These techniques are illustrated in passages such as Psalm 23; Proverbs 1:8–9; 10:20; 25:11; Lamentations 4:2; and countless others. Personification is endowing nonliving or nonhuman things with human characteristics. Psalm 98:8 is a well-known example of this device. Proverbs chapter 1 through 9 is a tribute to wisdom and often speak of wisdom as a woman who should be heeded (e.g., 4:6–9, 13).

The student of poetic literature in the Bible will be greatly enriched by keeping an attitude of discovery of the various literary techniques employed throughout Scripture.

Law: The first five books of the Old Testament are considered the books of the law. However, because Genesis, Exodus, and Numbers are historical narrative, we will consider Exodus 20–40, Leviticus, and Deuteronomy as the major portions that present the law—the Mosaic law.

The Mosaic law covers civil, ceremonial, and moral matters. As Francis Turretin surmised, "The law given by Moses is usually distinguished into three species: moral (treating of morals or of perpetual duties towards God and our neighbor); ceremonial (of the ceremonies or rites about the sacred things to be observed under the Old Testament); and civil (constituting the civil government of the Israelite people)."[14]

Civil laws provide instruction for social relations between the people or between the people and their leaders, such as the kings. They instruct in matters of governing authority. The ceremonial laws instructed the Israelites on the prescribed system of religious sacrifices, holidays and feasts, offerings, and other rites. Moral laws intended personal piety based on God's holy character; the Ten Commandments are the epitome of the moral law.

As the civil and ceremonial laws were tied to Israel as a covenant nation, they seem to have come to an end in Christ's earthly work in redemption. The local church member does not need to provide a wave offering, make a pilgrimage to Jerusalem three times per year, keep the Passover, or give the land rest every seventh year. It would seem that these aspects of the law have passed away (Matt. 5:18; Rom. 10:4).

However, the stipulations of the moral law seem to be consistent throughout history and binding on all persons. Except for the command to keep the Sabbath, all the Commandments are repeated in the New Testament as instructions for believers.[15] Even so, it is Paul who writes, "Circumcision is nothing, and uncircumcision is nothing, but what matters is the keeping of the commandments of God" (1 Cor. 7:19). It is evident that no one principle governs the interpretation of the law, and neither is it possible to draw out any so-called universal principles from the law. Instead, faithful interpretation of each passage of the law should consider the relationship of a moral law to one of the Ten Commandments. Similarly, it should consider how as each civil, ceremonial, and moral law points to Christ and His work, and how the work of Christ has fulfilled that law in part or whole.

Letters: Another category or genre in the New Testament is the letters. Thirteen letters are attributed to Paul, with others written by Peter, John, James, and Jude. The authorship of the epistle to the Hebrews is uncertain.

Among the letters, "epistles" generally follow the form of Greco-Roman letter-writing of the time, beginning with the greeting from the writer to the recipient(s), a blessing, the body of the letter, and ending with a final exhortation and often personal greetings. In the body of the work, epistles offer readers logical structuring of their arguments, greater familiarity with the biography of the author, the historical setting of the audience, and many clues to the historical situation in focus. Without either a greeting or ending, "sermonic letters" like Hebrews, James, and 1 John share a similar content to the epistles. Therefore, interpreting the literature of the letters requires the reader to understand the characteristics of the audience and the historical occasion prompting the writing in order to accurately follow the flow of arguments of the writer.[16]

Various themes found in the letter include the preeminence of Christ and the joy of knowing Him, the priority of the grace in sanctification, justification by faith, works as evidence of conversion, correction of false teaching and its resulting false morality, encouragement in the midst of persecution, exhortation to remain faithful, future events, spiritual fruit and gifting, and church governance. The letters are replete with personal touches (2 Tim. 4:13) and emotion (Phil. 1:3–4; 2 Tim. 1:4). The entirety of the content of the letter stems from the gospel of the four Gospels; the letters are the outworking of the gospels in the life of the church universal and local assemblies, and the lives of individual believers.

A reader should approach the letters looking for the writer and recipients; clues to the historical occasion of the letter; any conflict, misunderstanding, or exhortation; and references to the death and resurrection of Christ. All the letters were written to address what was occasional to the original recipients, but their teaching is as relevant and practical to the church today as it was in the first century.[17]

Wisdom: Job, Proverbs, and Ecclesiastes are generally classified as books of wisdom, since all three works have complex literary designs of mixed subgenres. That is, Proverbs' large passages in chapters 1–9 and chapter 31 differ from the aphoristic and axiomatic statements of chapters 10–30. The observations in Ecclesiastes 1–2 differ from those in 4–6, the proverbial statements of 7–11, and the monologues of chapters 3 and 12. Very evidently the narrative portions of Job 1–2 and 42 differ from the cycles of dialogue in 3–42.

Therefore, focusing only on the proverbial statements of wisdom, two guidelines are important for reading wisdom.[18] First, wisdom literature is revelation from God about the sages' observations of people over the course of their lives. As revelation from God it is true and truth. But it is true in the sense that wisdom is true: *it speaks in generalities, not promises.* However, in the truth of wisdom, to ignore wisdom is to ensure one's own destruction.

Second, within the individual statements, clusters, themes and chapter-units of the proverbial statements, the statements with respect to wisdom and righteousness invite the reader to choose to follow their truths in order to be blessed by staying on the path of blessing. A whole chapter may lead to a choice (e.g., Prov. 5), or a smaller unit may lead to a choice (e.g., Prov. 16:1–9).

Third, specifically related to the Proverbs, but important for reading all proverbial statements, one discerns three types of purposes: (1) to give people skill for navigating the issues and events of life, (2) to give people discipline (training) for living the skilled life, (3) and to give people discernment for counseling and insight into the words and ways of others. Thus, one should attempt to discern if the statements in Proverbs are for gaining skills for living, for training that will lead to skillful living, for gaining discernment, or a combination of such.

Prophecy: Prophecy is revelation that reproves, pronounces judgment, and announces consolation to historical audiences in Israel through the composition of a prophet's sermons or oracles.[19] It is *revelation* from God as evidenced by a statement such as "the word of the Lord came" (Hag. 1:1; Jer. 14:1) or the word "vision" (Dan. 8:1; Obad. 1:1; Nah. 1:1). It reproves the sin of the nation or individual within the nations (Isa. 1:2–23), pronounces judgment upon such sins (Isa. 1:24–25), and announces consolation to such a one (Isa. 1:26–31). It is most often in poetic form, which allows one to analyze its meaning using the same conventions for analyzing the poetical literature.

The fulfillment of prophecy is a complex issue because a prophet often spoke of events of a near historical fulfillment in the same sermon or oracle as events of far futuristic fulfillment (Isa. 61:1 in Luke 4:18–19), or spoke of both in the same terms (Ps. 24:7–10).[20] We refer to the discerning of the differences in prophetic fulfillment as *historical fulfillment, first advent fulfillment,* and *second advent fulfillment.* Historical fulfillment refers to completion of a prophetic promise within the period of Old Testament history. First advent fulfillment refers to the completion of a prophetic promise within the time of the earthly ministry of Jesus and the ministry of the apostles. Second advent fulfillment concerns prophetic promises associated with the events of the tribulation period and Christ's earthly return.

Prophetic fulfillment also may be *partial* or *complete.* Partial fulfillment indicates that a portion or aspect of a prophetic oracle has been fulfilled at a point in history, but the fulfillment of the remaining aspects and/or portions of an oracle await later fulfillment. Complete fulfillment means that every aspect of a prophetic oracle was completed when its fulfillment was announced or revealed in history.

MESSAGE

Integrating spiritual orientation and background studies with hermeneutics, including consideration of genre, prepares the reader to discern the *message* of the passage. Each biblical writer intended to communicate one central idea in a passage, and that such an idea can be restated by the reader in one complete sentence. This sentence will be reflective of the cultural setting, genre, and structure of a portion of Scripture.[21] This sentence also is intended to reflect God's voice in the passage, if we understand that God is the one speaking through the human writer and has safeguarded the writing and transmission of the biblical text so that it is free from error.

The message of a passage consists of two parts: *subject* and *complement*. The *subject* is what the author is talking about, and will be stated as an incomplete sentence, as it will be *completed* by the *complement*. More specifically, the subject is *the most talked about idea in a passage that unifies all other ideas in a passage.*[22] The *complement* is what the author is saying about the subject, adding more detail.

Discerning the subject and the complement prepares the reader to hear, obey, and communicate God's voice. For what we are saying in this stage is that the Divine Author of the passage, speaking through the human author of the written work, has spoken one main idea to His audience. Recovery of the message intends to help the reader hear what God is talking about in a passage rather than allowing one simply to bring one's own ideas to and impose them on the passage. Faithful interpretation requires submitting oneself to the authority of the author and the author's ideas—the central idea of the text.

In order to discern the subject of the message, the reader should begin asking, "In general, what is the main thing this passage is talking about?" and/or, "What idea takes up the most space in this passage or unifies the ideas in this passage?" Using Matthew 1:18–25 as an example, we see that Joseph's response to the announcement of Mary's virgin conception is key to the passage. The focus on his response begins with "she was found to be pregnant" and carries through the remainder of the passage. The subject is not the birth of the Christ, the fulfillment of the promise of the virgin birth, or trouble surrounding the announcement of the birth of Christ. These are ideas in the passage, but they do not unify the passage or take up the bulk of space. *Joseph's response*, however, brings all these ideas together.

Once you approach a subject, ask six questions of the proposed subject: Who? What? When? Where? Why? How? The goal of asking these questions of the subject is to narrow down the nuances of the author's message so that the one-sentence meaning will be as accurate as possible.

You want to identify if there is a person *who* is the focus of the subject, *what* the action of that person is, *when* the action of the subject occurs, *where,* if location is relevant, *why* the subject happens, and *how* the subject happens. Every passage answers at least one of these questions, and some passages answer more than one.

The complement consists of everything in the passage that is not the subject. The complement is the commentary made on the subject by the writer, i.e., what the writer is saying about it.

In the example above, the commentary on Joseph's response to the announcement of Mary's virgin conception is that it honors the angelic announcement (1:20–21, 24), allowing Christ's birth to fulfill Scripture (1:22–23) in righteousness and without shame on Mary (1:19, 25), and naming the child Jesus (1:25). The complement gathers together the ideas communicated by all the other contents in the passage. The subject plus complement forms one sentence that communicates God's voice in this passage: Joseph's response to the announcement of Mary's virgin conception honors the angelic announcement, allowing Christ's birth to fulfill Scripture in righteousness and without shame on Mary, and naming the child Jesus. This is the *message* of Matthew 1:18–25. All passages of Scripture, regardless of genre, have a subject and complement, and work in a similar way.

APPLICATION

Application is the task of relating what God has said in His Word to a modern audience. It addresses concerns such as worldview, conviction and repentance, obedience, and service. The Scriptures must be acted on, not simply heard and learned (Deut. 12:28; Ps. 119:109–10; Acts 20:32; Col. 3:16; James 1:19–25), so the process of understanding ends in humble, obedient practice in response to the message of a passage.

Asking these questions begins the process of application: (1) Does this apply to me? and (2) How do I apply this? The first question concerns the *relevance* of a passage to a modern audience, and the second concerns one's *response* to the relevance of the passage. For a spiritual leader or teacher, these questions must extend to relating them to the congregation or group you are keeping charge over.

The authors of the Scriptures intended their writing to speak to an *original* audience. Therefore, a question we should ask of each passage of Scripture is, "Does this message relate to us in the same way in which it did to the original hearers?"

For example, do the instructions for building the tabernacle relate to the church in the twenty-first century the same way they related to Moses's recipients who lived centuries before Christ? If so, then why do we not assemble before the tabernacle three times per year to celebrate the feasts of Israel? If not, why not, and what then shall we do with the entirety of Exodus 25–40 as believers?

Or, as another example, do Paul's instructions concerning tongues and prophecy relate to us in the same way they related to the Corinthians? If so, should we have interpretation of tongues available when we assemble for worship, and should women in the gathering be silent during the speaking and interpretation of tongues? If not, then to what issue(s) should we relate Paul's instructions in 1 Corinthians 14?

Proper application of any passage of Scripture requires us to reconstruct the message of a passage into a contemporary applicational statement.[23] We employ two strategies to assist in this reconstruction. First, we must consider the message in light of what else the Lord reveals as He continues to speak in Scripture. Second, we must consider the message in comparison to how the Lord was dispensing His purposes in an ancient period versus what has changed in dispensing His purposes in light of Christ's entrance into the world.

Now let's briefly return to the sample passage from which we have already gleaned a message: *Joseph's response to the announcement of Mary's virgin conception honors the angelic announcement, allowing Christ's birth to fulfill Scripture in righteousness and without shame on Mary, and naming the child Jesus.* The three elements of the message—Joseph, Mary, and the naming of the Christ child—do not continue in the remainder of the revelation of Scripture. But this does not mean the passage only applied to Joseph and Mary. The believer will ask how this passage is relevant to him or her today—whether it is the presentation of a tenet of Christianity or how the faith is lived out. Likewise, a pastor in a corporate setting or a Bible study leader will guide in application of Scripture. Those of us reading Matthew 1 today are neither Joseph nor Mary, the historical figures. Can the pronouncement of the virgin conception be applied, since that was a one-time event in history?

What is gained by considering the message of Matthew 1:18–25 in light of the full canon of Scripture, and the changes in the dispensing of God's purposes, is that the passage invites a modern-day audience to live in response to the truth of the fulfillment of the virgin birth prophecy. That is, the relevance of this passage to a modern audience concerns the manner in which a righteous person responds to the completed revelation about the virgin birth of Jesus. A modern reader does not likely receive a divinely authoritative revelatory dream, meet a young maiden who is pregnant with the Savior via a virgin conception, or fulfill the related Isaiah prophecy (Isa. 7:14). All these concepts within the passage have been completed. However, the Scriptures continue to speak about the significance of the virgin birth of Jesus for the believer. Part of our Christian living rests on the fact of the virgin birth and God's faithfulness to His prophetic word, foretelling of that birth.

We need not use this space to analyze Matthew 1:18–25 in depth, but the reader or church leader can take a few principles of application in a way that will bear on application of other passages. The subject of this one—*Joseph's response to the announcement of Mary's virgin conception*—calls the believer to act in grace and righteousness in accordance with God's Word, following the example of Joseph. We can maintain righteousness, like Joseph, and be gracious—as gracious as it is for the Lord to give the Christ on our behalf and be faithful to His promise to do so. We can give grace because of the faithfulness the Lord showed to His promise. God's faithfulness and the power of God for us—power that was displayed in the virgin-born Christ—are both supporting us as we also try to respond righteously to another's sin or shame.

Unlike Joseph and Mary, we have not been called on to name the Christ, but to trust the name of Jesus—the Christ of whom fallen history has awaited and now has been revealed (see Col. 3:17; 2 Thess. 1:12; Heb. 1:4; 12:2; 13:20–21).

Having read a passage as part of all of Scripture and in light of the entirety of redemptive history—the story from creation to the kingdom of Christ, that is all of Scripture—we need to be obedient to what we have read. So now we want to put into practice the teaching, rebuke, correction, or training in a passage of Scripture. We need specific responses that tell us what to *do* with the truth of the passage in our daily walk with Christ—in our love of God and of our neighbor.

CONCLUSION

The goal of reading Scripture is to produce lives that honor Christ and experience intimacy with God. To live in this manner, we must first hear God speak from the ancient text. Once we have used our genre clues and discerned the message God is speaking through the terms of the text, we then also must discern how that message applies relevantly and practically to our own walks before the Lord. These are the first steps in cultivating Christian lives that do not live on earthly bread alone, but on the very words of God.

NOTES

1. See also Ephesians 6:17 and Revelation 1:16; 2:12, 16; 19:15, 21.

2. See Isaiah 40:8; Zechariah 1:6; Matthew 24:35; Romans 15:4; 1 Corinthians 10:6, 11; 1 Peter 1:23, 25.

3. See 2 Corinthians 3:12–4:4 and Ephesians 4:17–23 for a fuller discussion.

4. Space limitations do not permit a lengthy discussion of the reconstruction of the occasion of texts and the rhetorical strategy of the writer and/or editor(s) with respect to an original audience. Many individual commentaries on each book of Scripture will provide such discussions with respect to the biblical book in focus.

5. For more on discerning the meaning of terms based on a pattern of usage of terms—or "types"—also known as a process of "type-logic," see E. D. Hirsch, *Validity in Interpretation* (New Haven, CT: Yale University Press, 1967), 25.

6. For introductory matters related to the dating of Old Testament books, see K. A. Kitchens, *On the Reliability of the Old Testament* (Grand Rapids: Eerdmans, 2006); Tremper Longman III and Raymond Dillard, *An Introduction to the Old Testament*, 2nd ed. (Grand Rapids: Zondervan, 2006); Eugene Merrill, Mark Rooker, et al., *The World and the Word: An Introduction to the Old Testament* (Nashville: B&H Academic, 2001). For New Testament books, see Craig L. Blomberg, *The Historical Reliability of the New Testament: Countering the Challenges to Evangelical Christian Beliefs* (Nashville: B&H Academic, 2016); D. A. Carson and Douglas J. Moo, *Introduction to the New Testament* (Grand Rapids: Zondervan, 2005); Andreas J. Köstenberger, L. Scott Kellum, et al., *The Cradle, the Cross, and the Crown: An Introduction to the New Testament* (Nashville: B&H Academic, 2016); Peter J. Williams, *Can We Trust the Gospels?* (Wheaton, IL: Crossway, 2018).

7. Historically, the church refers to the four poetical passages in Luke 1–2 as "Magnificat" or "Mary's Song" (1:46–55), "Benedictus" or "Zechariah's Song" (1:68–79), "Gloria Patri" or "The Angels' Song" (2:13–14), and "Nunc Dimittis" or "Simeon's Song" (2:29–32). Yet it is evident that Zechariah's song is a prophetic oracle (1:67) and Simeon is offering a prayer (2:28).

8. "Next to story, poetry is the most prevalent type of writing in the Bible" (Leland Ryken, *How to Read the Bible as Literature* [Grand Rapids: Zondervan, 1984], 87).

9. For general instruction on interpreting the various genres of literature, see Robert H. Stein, *Basic Guide to Interpreting the Bible*, 2nd ed. (Grand Rapids: Baker, 2011).

   Space limitations for this submission do not permit detailed discussions of every genre used in Scripture. For more on interpreting the letters and epistles, see Lisa M. Bowens, *African American Readings of Paul: Reception, Resistance, and Transformation* (Grand Rapids: Eerdmans, 2020); Sherri Brown and Francis J. Moloney, *Interpreting the Gospel and Letters of John: An Introduction* (Grand Rapids: Eerdmans, 2017); John Harvey, *Interpreting the Pauline Letters: An Exegetical Handbook* (Grand Rapids: Kregel, 2012); Karen H. Jobes, *Letters to the Church: A Survey of Hebrews and the General Epistles* (Grand Rapids: Zondervan; 2011); and Thomas R. Schreiner, *Interpreting the Pauline Epistles*, 2nd ed. (Grand Rapids: Baker, 2011).

   For interpreting apocalyptic literature, see Paul Benware, *Understanding End Times Prophecy: A Comprehensive Approach*, rev. and exp. ed. (Chicago: Moody), 2006; and Richard A. Taylor, *Interpreting Apocalyptic Literature: An Exegetical Handbook* (Grand Rapids: Kregel, 2016).

10. For more on this theory of parable, see Elliott E. Johnson, *Expository Hermeneutics: An Introduction* (Grand Rapids: Zondervan, 1990), 173–74.

11. I use "Hebrew poetry" here rather than "biblical poetry" in order to contrast it with a form of Western literature. In doing so, I also recognize that New Testament poetry is largely spoken or written by descendants of Israel who had faith in Christ. Therefore, New Testament poetry reflects the conventions of Hebrew poetry, as the speakers and writers made use of the forms of the Hebrew culture. It is easy to see that the New Testament hymns of Paul reflect a Hebrew form rather than a Homeric form (e.g., Phil. 2:5–11; 1 Tim. 3:16).

12. Following Robert Lowth's *Lectures on Sacred Poetry of the* Hebrew (1753); an older definition of parallelism said that it is the *repetition* of meaning in two or more lines of poetry. The idea was that the second (and third, and fourth lines, etc.) only repeated the first line in different terms. However, works by Kugel, Berlin, Alter, and Garrett have advanced the discussion. See Robert Alter, *The Art of Biblical Poetry* (New York: Basic Books, 1985); Adele Berlin, *The Dynamics of Biblical Parallelism*, 2nd. ed. (Grand Rapids: Eerdmans, 2007); Duane A. Garrett, *Proverbs, Ecclesiastes, Song of Songs* (Nashville: Holman Reference, 1993); James Kugel, *The Idea of Biblical Poetry* (New Haven, CT: Yale University Press, 1981).

13. There are multiple types of parallelism in biblical poetry. Non-technical discussions on various parallelism types include George L. Klein, "Poetry," in *Evangelical Dictionary of Biblical Theology*, electronic ed., Baker reference library (Grand Rapids: Baker Book House, 1996), 615–616; T. Longman, "Poetry," *New Bible Dictionary* (Leicester, England; Downers Grove, IL: InterVarsity, 1996), 938; Tremper Longman III, *How to Read Proverbs* (Downers Grove, IL: IVP Academic, 2002), 39–42.

14. Francis Turretin, *Institutes of Elenctic Theology*, ed. James T. Dennison, Jr. (Philipsburg, NJ: P&R Publishing, 2007), 11.24.1.

15. In order of the commandments:

    1st—Luke 4:8; Rev. 14:7; 2nd—Acts 15:20; 1 Cor. 6:9–10; 3rd—1 Tim. 6:1; James 2:7; 5th—Eph. 6:1–3; Col. 3:20; 6th—Mark 10:19; Rev. 21:8; 7th—Matt. 5:27–28; Rom. 7:2–3; 8th—Eph. 4:28; 1 Peter 4:15; 9th—Matt. 19:18; Eph. 4:5; 10th—Rom. 7:7; Eph. 5:3–5; Col. 3:5.

    Some places in the New Testament will give many of the Ten Commandments in a group listing, as in Mark 10:17–19 and Rom. 13:9. In 1 Tim. 1:8–10, Paul refers to the bulk of the Ten Commandments implicitly: "We know that the Law is good, if one uses it lawfully, realizing the fact that law is not made for a righteous person but for those who are lawless and rebellious, for the ungodly and sinners, for the unholy and worldly [3rd], for those who kill their fathers or mothers [5th], for murderers [6th], for the sexually immoral [7th], homosexuals [7th], slave traders [8th], liars, perjurers [9th], and whatever else is contrary to sound teaching."

16. In addition to other resources mentioned in this article for interpreting letters, the student would do well to consult the works of John Harvey and Andreas Köstenberger to address specific concerns in the interpretation of letters: John Harvey, ed., *Interpreting the Pauline Letters: An Exegetical Handbook* (Grand Rapids: Kregel, 2012); Andreas J. Köstenberger, "Hermeneutical and Exegetical Challenges in Interpreting the Pastoral Epistles," *Southern Baptist Journal of Theology* 7 (Fall 2003): 4–17.

17. The basis of such a claim rests on believer's shared identity as "God's holy people" (aka "saints," Eph. 1:1; Phil. 1:1), "brothers and sisters" (Col. 1:2; James 1:2), "the church" (1 Cor. 1:2), "churches" (Gal. 1:2), "in Christ" (Eph. 1:1), and like terms. Consider the shared identity of contemporary believer with the original recipients of 2 Peter: "To those who through the righteousness of our God and Savior Jesus Christ have received a faith as precious as ours" (2 Peter 1:1 NIV).

18. The "guidelines" are not intended to suggest the student vanquish the *literal* (meaning of a term in its context), *grammatical-historical* (historical meaning of terms and the full implications of such terms), *literary* (consideration of the genre and structure in which meaning is communicated), and *theological* (revelation of God and His works) premises which guide one to the message (meaning) with a text or texts. They are the application of such premises to the book of Proverbs.

19. For more on understanding the various forms of prophetic speech, see Bill T. Arnold, "Forms of Prophetic Speech in the Old Testament: A Summary of Claus Westermann's Contributions," *Ashland Theological Journal* 27 (1995): 30–40; Al Fuhr and Gary Yates, *The Message of the Twelve: Hearing the Voice of the Minor Prophets* (Grand Rapids: Baker Academic, 2016); Peter Gentry, *How to Read and Understand the Biblical Prophets* (Wheaton, IL: Crossway, 2017); Walter C. Kaiser Jr., *Back Toward the Future: Hints for Interpreting Biblical Prophecy* (Eugene, OR: Wipf and Stock, 2003); O. Palmer Robertson, *The Christ of the Prophets* (Philipsburg, NJ: P&R Publishing Company, 2008); Gary Smith, *Interpreting the Prophetic Books: An Exegetical Handbook* (Grand Rapids: Kregel, 2014); Willem A. VanGemeren, *Interpreting the Prophetic Word: An Introduction to the Prophetic Literature of the Old Testament* (Grand Rapids: Zondervan, 1996); Clause Westermann, *Basic Forms of Prophetic Speech* (Louisville: Westminster John Knox, 1991); and Clause Westermann, *Prophetic Oracles of Salvation in the Old Testament* (Louisville: Westminster John Knox, 1987).

20. In Luke 4:16–21, Jesus only quotes Isaiah 61:1, not claiming to fulfill Isaiah 61:2–11 in His earthly ministry. However, the reader of Isaiah cannot tell that 61:1 would be fulfilled at a period different than 61:2–11. Similarly, the initial fulfillment of Ps. 24:7–10 occurs in Matt. 21:1–11. However, all that the psalmist describes in Ps. 24:7–10 does not occur in Matt. 21:1–11 but awaits fulfillment within the second advent.

21. My idea of "message" is very similar to what Haddon Robinson identifies as the "Big Idea" of a passage (Haddon Robinson, *Biblical Preaching: The Development and Delivery of Expository Messages*, 2nd ed. [Grand Rapids: Baker, 2001], 36–54). It also is similar to what David Helm calls the "Melodic Line" of a passage (David Helm, *Expositional Preaching: How We Speak God's Word Today* [Wheaton, IL: Crossway, 2014], 47–50).

22. For more on this concept of *subject*, see Elliot E. Johnson, *Expository Hermeneutics: An Introduction* (Grand Rapids: Zondervan, 1990).

23. Intentionally, the method of application I propose here avoids finding so-called timeless principles or universal principles, for such principles are highly subjective. I am offering a concept that seeks to ground application in the story of Scripture. Neither am I advocating for an analogy of faith or rule of faith, for such approaches intend to prioritize certain passages or genres of Scripture over others. While I believe Scripture cannot contradict itself, I do not believe any one place of God's voice in Scripture has priority or weight over another place. All Scripture is breathed out by God and profitable (2 Tim. 3:16).

CHAPTER 1.2

Survey of the Old and New Testaments

WILLIAM MARTY

The Bible is composed of multiple books written by different authors, in different places, and at different times; but it is not a random collection of stories. The Bible is a continuous story about God and humanity. Unfortunately, the story of God's amazing plan of redemption is often lost in a survey because the focus is on individual books rather than the overarching storyline. The emphasis in this survey is on the biblical story. I have divided the storyline into sixteen historical periods.

The Old Testament (Creation—400 BC)
Primeval
Patriarchal
Egyptian
Wilderness
Conquest
Judges
United Kingdom
Divided Kingdom (Israel and Judah)
Single Kingdom
Exile
Return from Exile (Restoration)

Between the Testaments—400 Years
The New Testament (5 BC—AD 100)
Expectation (Life of Christ)
Establishment (Birth of the church; Growth of the church in Jerusalem)
Extension (Growth of the church from Jerusalem to Samaria)
Expansion (Growth of the church throughout the Roman world)
Consolidation (Two Threats—Persecution and Heresy)

PRIMEVAL (GENESIS 1–11)

The story of redemption begins with the history of all humanity from Adam and his descendants to Abraham. The first eleven chapters of Genesis describe four major events.

CREATION (1–2)

Genesis 1 tells us why there is something rather than nothing. God created everything that exists in six days. Original creation was "good," perfect for God's intended purpose. On the sixth day He created male and female in His image; thus like God, Adam and Eve had intellect, emotion, and will.

The Lord placed Adam and Eve in the garden of Eden and permitted them to eat from any trees in the garden except one. They were warned that if they ate from "the tree of the knowledge of good and evil" they would surely die. The prohibition gave Adam and Eve opportunity to prove submission and loyalty to their Creator.

The Lord gave humankind dominion over creation. He permitted Adam to name the animals, and established marriage as an inseparable bond between one man and one woman by joining Adam and Eve together as one flesh.

FALL (3–5)

Without explanation of his origin, Satan entered the drama of redemption in the form of a serpent. He convinced Eve that she would become like God—able to determine for herself what is right and wrong. After eating fruit from the forbidden tree, she gave some to Adam, and both became sinners alienated from their Creator.

God pronounced judgment on all three; but in His mercy, He did not impose the death penalty on Adam and Eve. They died spiritually but not physically. As a preview of substitutionary sacrifice God covered their nakedness with the skins of animals.

The sin of Adam and Eve corrupted all of creation, including their descendants. Cain killed his brother Abel. Lamech boasted about getting revenge on those who offended him. The genealogy of death in Genesis 5 exposes the lie of Satan. Everyone died, except Enoch, whose bodily translation gave hope for life after death.

FLOOD (6–11)

It grieved the Lord that humankind had become hopelessly wicked, and He made the painful decision to destroy the world He had created. One man, however, found grace in the eyes of the Lord. God instructed Noah to build an ark for protection from the destruction of the flood. Noah demonstrated remarkable faith by doing everything exactly as the Lord had commanded.

PATRIARCHAL (GENESIS 12–50)

The focus moves from a general account of redemptive history to a specific focus on four individuals.

ABRAHAM (12–25)

While Abraham was living in Ur, God made an unconditional covenant with him. God promised to bless the patriarch, multiply his physical descendants, and honor those who by faith would become his spiritual descendants. The unconditional provisions are personal, national, and universal, and are foundational for the unfolding plan of redemption. God swore on His divine honor that He would keep His promises by walking alone between the animals Abraham had sacrificed.

The story of Abraham gives a paradigm of the faith journey of both Old and New Testament believers. Though at times his faith wavered, Abraham never abandoned the Lord. God blessed him and Sarah with Isaac, the son of promise. Abraham passed the ultimate test of faith when God asked him to sacrifice his beloved son Isaac. The patriarch obeyed because he believed God would raise Isaac from the dead (Heb. 11:19), and we see the concept of a substitutionary sacrifice in God's provision of an animal in place of Isaac.

ISAAC (26–27)

The covenant God made with Abraham was confirmed to Isaac not Ishmael, and God blessed Isaac with two sons, Jacob and Esau. Though Isaac favored Esau, God chose to bless Jacob, the second born.

JACOB (28–38)

After tricking his brother into selling him the family birthright, Jacob fled to Haran because Esau intended to murder him. Jacob married Leah and Rachel, and fathered twelve sons, who became the heads of the twelve tribes of Israel. Though a self-made man, Jacob surrendered to the Lord in a dramatic nighttime encounter with God at the Jabbok River.

JOSEPH (39–50)

Born to Rachel, Joseph was Jacob's favorite son, and was important because God sovereignly controlled his circumstances to protect the chosen family from destruction by the Canaanites. Joseph became a powerful official in a foreign land and relocated his extended family to Egypt. In Egypt, God's chosen people prospered and multiplied under the protection of one of the most powerful nations in the ancient world.

The patriarchal period concludes with uncertainty about God's promises to Abraham. His descendants are few and in a foreign land under the control of a foreign power. How will God fulfill His promises to make Abraham's descendants into a great nation, and how will God bless the world through Abraham's seed?

EGYPTIAN (EXODUS 1–12)

The book of Exodus continues the story of God's plan to rescue fallen humanity. Exodus can be divided into two main sections: (1) the redemption of Israel from slavery in Egypt (1–12), and (2) the revelation of the Law and instructions for the building of the tabernacle at Mount Sinai (13–40).

OPPRESSION OF GOD'S PEOPLE (EXODUS 1–2)

Four hundred years passed from the time the descendants of Abraham moved to Egypt. Initially the Egyptians considered the Israelites an asset to their nation, but that changed when a new dynasty came to power. Pharaoh, a title for Egyptian rulers, enslaved the Hebrews (Israelites). The term *Hebrew* was a derogatory name given to the Israelites.

But God had not forgotten His promises to Abraham and raised up Moses to lead His people out of bondage. To stem the population growth among the Hebrews, Pharaoh ordered the midwives to kill all the males at birth, but they ignored his edict. To protect her son, Moses's mother committed him to God by placing him in a basket on the Nile River when he was three months old.

In the providence of God, Pharaoh's daughter found the infant, and adopted him as her son. Though Moses was raised in Pharaoh's palace, he knew that he was a Hebrew not an Egyptian. When he killed an Egyptian, who was mistreating a Hebrew, he was betrayed by his own people and forced to flee to Midian.

DELIVERANCE OF GOD'S PEOPLE (EXODUS 3–12)

Moses could flee from the Egyptians but not from God. God appeared to Moses in a burning bush as the LORD (Yahweh), the eternal "I AM," and commanded Moses to return to Egypt.

Moses confronted Pharaoh in the name of the Lord, but Pharaoh hardened his heart and refused to release God's people.

To force Pharaoh to obey, Moses inflicted ten plagues on the Egyptians. Each plague was directed at the gods and goddesses the Egyptians worshiped, including the death of the firstborn because the Egyptians believed in the deity of Pharaoh. Before the tenth plague, the Lord instructed the children of Israel to observe the Passover. This redemptive event became an everlasting memorial to remember Israel's deliverance from Egypt and to preview the atoning death of Jesus Christ (1 Cor. 5:7).

WILDERNESS (EXODUS 13–40, LEVITICUS, NUMBERS, DEUTERONOMY)

Because the Israelites had lived in the environment of Egyptian polytheism for 400 years, they needed instruction on the nature of the true and living God. This period contains the divine revelation that enabled God's people to have a relationship with a holy and loving God, and traces Israel's wilderness journey from Egypt to Canaan (the promised land).

TO SINAI (EXODUS 13–LEVITICUS 27)

After the Israelites left Egypt, Pharaoh ordered his army to pursue them. The pursuit came to an abrupt end when the Lord destroyed Pharaoh's army in the Red Sea.

The Lord led the Israelites on a southern route to Mount Sinai, guiding them with a cloud by day and a pillar of fire by night, and miraculously sustaining them with a daily provision of manna, quail, and water.

At Mount Sinai, the Lord met with Moses and gave him the constitution for the incipient nation. Israel would become a theocracy—a nation governed by God through appointed rulers. The Ten Commandments served as the preamble and were elaborated in hundreds of laws governing Israel's relationship with God, one another, and other nations.

The priesthood was established to represent the people before God. Aaron was appointed as the high priest, his sons as priests, and the tribe of Levi as assistants. Leviticus gives the specific instructions for worshiping God and the necessity for holiness in every aspect of life. The fundamental principle is stated in Leviticus 19:2 (NIV), "Be holy because I, the LORD your God, am holy."

IN THE WILDERNESS (NUMBERS)

Numbers derives its name from the census Moses took to determine military strength before leaving Mount Sinai. From Sinai the Israelites traveled north to Kadesh Barnea. At Kadesh Moses sent out twelve spies to make a reconnaissance of Canaan. They discovered the land was fertile but occupied by powerful tribal groups who had built fortified cities. Though Joshua and Caleb encouraged the people to trust God, Israel rebelled, and were made to wander in the wilderness until the unbelieving generation died. After forty years, the new generation arrived on the plains of Moab, east of the Jordan River. They took a second census, only to discover that a new generation had entirely replaced the old.

ON THE PLAINS OF MOAB (DEUTERONOMY)

The Greek term "Deuteronomy" means "second law," and refers to the three prophetic messages of Moses recorded in the book. In a form resembling an ancient suzerainty-vassal treaty, Moses assures Israel of God's covenant love. He warns of judgment for disobedience, but promises that if they repent, God will restore His covenant people to the promised land. Before his death, Moses passes the mantel of leadership to Joshua.

CONQUEST (JOSHUA)

The book of Joshua records Israel's conquest of the promised land. The Israelites make a miraculous crossing of the Jordan River that confirms Joshua as Israel's divinely appointed leader and strikes fear in the hearts of the Canaanites. With God's help, Israel conquers Jericho in the center of the land, defeats a coalition of five kings in the south, and another in the north led by Jabin, the powerful king of Hazor. After taking control of the land, Joshua gives an allotment of land to eleven tribes, and assigns the tribe of Levi to live and minister in towns within the boundaries of the other eleven tribes. Before his death, Joshua leads Israel in a covenant renewal ceremony at Shechem, in which he challenges Israel to love and obey the Lord and warns of judgment for worshiping Canaanite deities and engaging in their pagan practices.

JUDGES/PRE-KINGDOM (JUDGES)

Judges explains Israel's transition from a tribal confederacy to a monarchy. Judges were charismatic leaders whose rule was limited to tribal territory and temporary.

The book describes seven cycles of judges with the rule of Deborah, a godly woman, and Samuel, Israel's king maker, as bookends on the period.

The book concludes with stories about idolatry and immorality that illustrate how incredibly wicked people can become when they do what is right in their own eyes (Judg. 17–21). The repetition of two expressions stressed the need for a king: "In those days Israel had no king," and "everyone did what was right in his own eyes" (Judg. 17:6, author's paraphrase; 18:1; 19:1; 21:25).

UNITED KINGDOM (1 AND 2 SAMUEL; 1 KINGS 1–11; BOOKS OF POETRY)

Samuel, the last of the judges, anointed Saul and then David as Israel's first and second kings. David designated his son, Solomon, as his successor. God blessed Solomon with wisdom, but his sins and the oppressive policies of his foolish and arrogant son divided the United Kingdom.

SAUL (1 SAMUEL)

The transition from a tribal confederacy to a monarchy began with the birth of Samuel. Because Hannah and Elkanah were unable to have children, they promised to dedicate their son to the Lord. God heard their prayer and blessed them with Samuel. They kept their promise and dedicated Samuel to serve in the tabernacle. After the death of Eli, Samuel became the high priest and judge over all Israel. Instead of limiting his ministry to one tribal area, Samuel was a circuit-riding judge, serving all Israel from Bethel to Gilgal and Mizpah (1 Sam. 7:15–17).

As Samuel neared the end of his life, the people pleaded with him for a king "like all the nations" (1 Sam. 8:5). Though Samuel interpreted the people's request as a personal rejection of his leadership, the Lord instructed him to grant their request though it was a rejection of His lordship over Israel.

Samuel anointed Saul as Israel's first king in a private and then public ceremony (1 Sam. 10:1, 17–24). Saul gained popular support to serve as king when he rescued the men of Jabesh-gilead (1 Sam. 11). Though the Lord would have blessed Saul's rule, he was foolish and disobedient, and quickly lost the right to serve as the Lord's appointed ruler.

DAVID (1 SAMUEL 16–31; 2 SAMUEL)

Samuel rebuked Saul and sought "a man after [God's] own heart" (1 Sam. 13:13–14). The Lord guided Samuel to anoint David to replace Saul (1 Sam. 16:1–13).

David was the youngest of Jesse's eight sons, and unknown in Israel. He gained recognition of all Israel when he defeated Goliath (1 Sam. 17:1–58). Though anointed king, David refused to overthrow Saul by violence, though he was ruthlessly pursued by the paranoid king for fifteen years. David became king when the Philistines wounded Saul, who took his own life rather than risk capture and torture.

Though the tribe of Judah recognized David as king, the northern tribes remained loyal to Saul's son, Ishbosheth. After a season of struggle and intrigue between the two dynasties, David became king over all Israel when two foreigners murdered Ishbosheth.

David captured Jerusalem, a Jebusite fortress, and made it the political capital and religious center for all Israel. David wanted to build a temple to honor the Lord, but Nathan, the prophet, said that his son was the one who would build the temple. Instead, the Lord made an eternal and unconditional covenant with David (2 Sam. 7). In his genealogy, Matthew traces Jesus' ancestry through David to Abraham showing that Jesus is the ultimate fulfillment of the Davidic covenant (Matt. 1:1).

Though the "ideal king," David was not perfect. He committed adultery with Bathsheba and had her husband killed to hide his sin (2 Sam. 11). After the prophet Nathan rebuked him, David repented, but suffered the grievous consequences of his transgression (2 Sam. 12:1–14; Ps. 51). The child Bathsheba conceived died, and she later gave birth to Solomon. There was continual conflict in David's household, and his son Absalom almost succeeded in taking the throne from David.

SOLOMON (1 KINGS 1–11)

Before he died, David made arrangements to ensure that his son Solomon would become king. Solomon is known for his wisdom, wealth, and fame. His greatest achievement was building the temple. At the height of Solomon's career, the Queen of Sheba traveled to Jerusalem to see for herself if what she had heard about Solomon and his kingdom was true. After questioning Solomon and seeing his accomplishments, she testified that indeed the Lord had blessed Solomon, and his people had much to be grateful for (1 Kings 10:8–9).

Though known for his wisdom, Solomon foolishly took wives from foreign nations, and worshiped their gods. Because his heart was not fully devoted to the Lord, the Lord announced to Solomon that his kingdom would be divided. The king with a divided heart left behind a divided kingdom.

BOOKS OF POETRY
(JOB, PSALMS, PROVERBS, ECCLESIASTES, SONG OF SOLOMON)

The Poetical Books or Wisdom Literature were composed during the United Kingdom Period by Israel's sages (wisdom teachers) and contain both practical and reflective wisdom.

The book of Job is a reflection on human suffering and the sovereignty of God. The story is from an earlier period (perhaps the Patriarchal) but was passed down from generation to generation and composed in its final form in the United Kingdom Period. Job is a theodicy taking on the age-old question: How are we to understand the suffering of the righteous if God is good and great (sovereign)?

The Psalms are quoted more times in the New Testament than any other book in the Old Testament. They record real life experiences in prayers, hymns, and meditations. Many are lament psalms, but there are also psalms of praise and wisdom. Some record experiences that anticipate the life and work of the Messiah (Christ).

Proverbs contains practical wisdom and not reflective wisdom as found in Job and Ecclesiastes. The individual proverbs are concise and memorable observations on life. They are generalizations, not absolute truths, intended to develop godly character and provide practical skill or wisdom for daily living. Many are formatted as a father's advice to his son.

Ecclesiastes, like Job, is reflective or philosophical wisdom. Though some think the author gives a negative view of life, the exact opposite is true. The purpose is to show the futility and meaninglessness of life without God. The author forces the reader to the conclusion: "Fear God and keep his commandments, for this is the duty of all mankind" (Eccl. 12:13 NIV). Then despite confusing and difficult uncertainties, life can be meaningful and fulfilling.

The Song of Solomon or Song of Songs is a poem about love. Though some interpret it as an allegory about God's love for Israel or Christ's love for the church, the book encourages and endorses a romantic and sexual experience between a man and a woman in the context of marriage.

KINGS OF ISRAEL (1 KINGS 12:1–2 KINGS 17; 1 CHRONICLES)

While Solomon was still living, Ahijah the prophet announced to Jeroboam, who was from the rival tribe of Ephraim, that he would become king of ten tribes. Ahijah's prophecy was fulfilled when Solomon's son, Rehoboam, imposed heavy taxes and harsh labor practices on Israel. Ten tribes revolted and organized the Northern Kingdom of Israel. The tribes of Judah and Benjamin remained loyal to

Rehoboam, Solomon's son, and descendant of David. Thus, the United Kingdom was divided into two kingdoms—Israel in the north and Judah in the south.

Though he was not perfect, David set the standard for kings in the north and south. The succession of the nineteen kings in the north was a spiritual disaster. They were all evil and were not faithful to the Lord as David had been. The Lord would have blessed Jeroboam, but he corrupted the worship of Yahweh by establishing apostate worship centers at Bethel and Dan and appointing non-Levitical priests (1 Kings 12:25–33).

Some of the kings were especially bad. Ahab married Jezebel, a fanatical Baal worshiper, and introduced Baal worship into the northern kingdom. To stem the tide of Baalism in the north, God raised up the prophet Elijah. He confronted Ahab and challenged the false prophets of Baal at Mount Carmel but could not stop Israel's slide into apostasy. Near the end of his life, he was taken to heaven in a fiery chariot, but passed his prophetic mantle to Elisha, who continued the struggle against Baal worship.

Hoshea, the last king in the north, was evil but not like the kings who preceded him; however, it was too late (2 Kings 17:2). The king of Assyria invaded Israel and captured Samaria, the capital, in 722 BC, and dispersed the northern tribes throughout the Assyrian Empire.

KINGS OF JUDAH (2 KINGS 18–25; 2 CHRONICLES)

Of the twenty kings who ruled in Judah, only eight were good. Second Chronicles provides the complete record of the eight good kings. We see the detrimental impact of Solomon's marriage to foreign wives in the rule of his son Rehoboam, the first king of Judah. He was undoubtedly influenced by his mother, Naamah, an Ammonite, and set up shrines to worship other gods and encouraged the detestable practices of pagan nations.

Asa, Rehoboam's son, did what was pleasing to the Lord as David had done (1 Kings 15:11). Though he did not remove all the pagan shrines, he led Judah in a national covenant renewal (2 Chron. 15:9–15). Asa made a tragic mistake when he accepted military help from Ben-hadad, king of Aram. He died from a fatal disease in his feet after ruling for forty-one years.

The seven good kings after Asa were considered revival kings because they reversed the evil policies and practices of their predecessors.

Hezekiah was the greatest of the revival kings. His father, Ahaz, was godless, closed the temple, and robbed it to pay tribute to Tiglath-pileser, king of Assyria. Hezekiah reopened the temple, organized a huge Passover celebration, and invited

Israel to join Judah in the celebration. When the Assyrians attacked Judah and Jerusalem, the Lord destroyed the Assyrian army, and Sennacherib was forced to return to Nineveh. When Hezekiah became terminally ill, he sought help from Isaiah the prophet, and the Lord healed him. One of his remarkable engineering feats was building a tunnel from the Gihon spring to provide a water supply for Jerusalem during times of siege. Hezekiah was known as "a second Solomon" because his scribes added to Solomon's collection of Proverbs (Prov. 25:1–29:37).

Manasseh was extremely evil. He rebuilt the pagan shrines his father had destroyed, practiced witchcraft, sacrificed his son, and persecuted the prophets. In a remarkable change of heart, Manasseh repented when the Assyrians took him captive to Babylon. His repentance and return to Judah previewed the return of Israel from exile. During the reign of Josiah, the priests discovered the Book of the Law when repairing the temple, and Josiah used the book as a guide for the nation's spiritual renewal.

Judah's end came in 586 BC when the Babylonians captured Jerusalem, and carried thousands into exile. As Jeremiah had predicted, God's people suffered seventy years of exile for abandoning the Lord and refusing to heed the prophets' warnings (Jer. 25:11).

THE EXILE (EZEKIEL AND DANIEL)

The exile was devastating. The unthinkable happened: God abandoned His chosen people. Everything was lost. The Babylonians destroyed entire towns, including Jerusalem; even the temple was sacked and burned. Thousands were deported to Babylon.

But God had not permanently abandoned His people or His plan to redeem the world. God was still at work preparing Israel for Messiah's coming. The prophets Ezekiel and Daniel inspired hope for both the near and distant future. Ezekiel describes the miraculous renewal of God's people and restoration to the land. Scholars hold different eschatological views about Ezekiel's detailed description of the rebuilding of the temple and the reinstitution of sacrifices (Ezek. 40–48). In the stories of Daniel and his friends in exile, the prophet emphasizes God's sovereignty over all nations and the panorama of history until the establishing of God's everlasting kingdom.

RESTORATION—RETURN FROM EXILE
(EZRA, NEHEMIAH, ESTHER, HAGGAI, ZECHARIAH, MALACHI)

The story of Israel's return from exile or the Post-Exile period is recorded in the three historical books of Ezra, Nehemiah, and Esther and the three prophetical books of Haggai, Zechariah, and Malachi.

God continued speaking through the prophets but was also at work through the rise and fall of nations. The Persians conquered the Babylonians, and Cyrus the Great allowed the Jews to return to the promised land. Isaiah named Cyrus as Israel's deliverer 150 years before he issued a decree allowing the Jews to return to their homeland (Ezra 1:1–4; Isa. 44:28–45:6). The historical books of Ezra and Nehemiah record the events of the return and the rebuilding of the temple. The book of Esther tells how God providentially protected the Jews who remained in Persia.

BOOKS OF PROPHECY

In the worst of times, God is often at His best. This is true in the years leading up to the exile. By worshiping other gods, Israel broke the covenant God had confirmed with them when He delivered them from bondage in Egypt (Deut. 29–30). God did not abandon His people; He raised up His servants, the prophets, to remind His people of their covenant obligations. They warned of judgment (curses) for rebellion but promised forgiveness and restoration for repentance (blessings).

The ministry of the prophets can be divided into three eras as indicated in the chart that follows. The prophets before the exile indicted Israel for rebellion but also promised that God would send a Savior to rescue them from their sins (Isa. 53). Some of the prophets, like Isaiah, looked into the distant future and anticipated not only the return from exile but the re-creation of all things including the new heavens and earth.

Ezekiel and Daniel ministered during Judah's exile in Babylon. In a series of bizarre visions, Ezekiel sees the departure of God's glory from the temple and the destruction of Jerusalem. But he also prophesied the defeat of Israel's enemies, the forgiveness of sins, and the restoration of Israel. Taken to Babylon as a hostage, Daniel became an advisor to the kings of Babylon and later to the Persians. His prophesies emphasize God's sovereignty over all the earth. God, not man, controls the rise and fall of the kingdoms of the world, and history is moving inexorably toward the establishment of God's eternal kingdom.

After the exile, Habakkuk and Zechariah encouraged returnees to finish rebuilding the temple. In rebuilding the temple, they were not only building for themselves but for the future. Zechariah, the most messianic book in the Old Testament, predicts that the Messiah who was rejected at His first coming, will come again as a conquering king and rule over all the earth in peace and holiness. Written after Haggai and Zechariah, Malachi uses a series of questions and answers to correct Israel's hypocritical abuse of their privileged covenant relationship.

BEFORE THE EXILE

To Judah	*To Israel*	*To Edom*	*To Assyria*
Joel	Hosea	Obadiah	Jonah
Isaiah	Amos	Nahum	
Micah			
Habakkuk			
Zephaniah			
Jeremiah (Lamentations)			

DURING THE EXILE

Ezekiel

Daniel

AFTER THE EXILE

Haggai

Zechariah

Malachi

BETWEEN THE TESTAMENTS (400 YEARS OF SILENCE)

The 400-year interval between Malachi and Matthew is sometimes called "The 400 Years of Silence" because the voice of prophecy ceased with Malachi and did not resume until the coming of John the Baptist.

Under the dynamic leadership of Alexander the Great, the Greeks conquered Persia and extended their empire south to Egypt and as far east as the Indus River. Alexander is known as "the Apostle of Hellenism" because he was a fervent proponent of the Greek culture and language in the countries he conquered. Through his influence Greek became the common language throughout the Middle East.

On his death at an early age, Alexander's empire was divided between his four generals. Israel came initially under the benevolent control of the Ptolemies in

Egypt. One of the rulers, Ptolemy II Philadelphus, had an interest in Jewish law, and authorized the translation of the Hebrew Old Testament into Greek. The translation is known as the Septuagint from LXX, the Roman numeral abbreviation for the number seventy, because according to tradition seventy Jewish scholars produced the translation.

Antiochus the Great defeated the Ptolemies in 190 BC, and Israel came under the control of the Seleucids (Syrians). The notorious Seleucid ruler, Antiochus Epiphanies, hated the Jews, and tried to destroy Judaism. He is infamous for sacrificing a pig on the temple altar, a sacrilege known as "the Abomination of Desolation," and which previews future abominable events by the Romans and the "man of lawlessness," or the Antichrist.

Antiochus' oppressive policies precipitated a Jewish revolt. By sheer determination and remarkable courage, the Maccabees won decisive victories over the Syrians, and eventually established an independent state. Named for Hashmon, an ancestor of the Maccabees, the Hasmonean kingdom ended when the Roman general Pompey captured Jerusalem in 63 BC. Therefore, when Christ was born in approximately 5 BC, Palestine was ruled by the Romans under the client king, Herod the Great.

THE NEW TESTAMENT (5 BC—AD 100)

EXPECTATION (FOUR GOSPELS)

When Christ was born, messianic hopes were high in Israel. Rome had extended its empire in the east, and had conquered Israel, making it a Roman province. Most Jews despised the Romans and were anxiously awaiting a Davidic king to lead them in a revolt against their Roman overlords. Israel's religious leaders were generally corrupt and were more concerned about money and power than godliness. Some, however, like the parents of John the Baptist and Jesus, were godly and recognized their need for a Savior.

The four gospels record the life of Christ. Though the Synoptic Gospels (Matthew, Mark, and Luke) are similar, they are not identical. The gospel of John is unique in its interpretive and theological perspective on the life of Jesus. Together, the Gospels give us a multifaceted portrait of Christ.

Most scholars opt for the priority of Mark believing that Mark was written first and that Matthew and Luke borrowed and expanded on Mark's shorter version of the life of Christ. Some, however, believe that Matthew was the first gospel. The unanimous view of the church fathers, the placement of Matthew in the canon, and the need for a gospel explaining Israel's rejection of their messianic king support the priority of Matthew.

MATTHEW

Matthew was a tax collector before Jesus called him to become a disciple (Matt. 9:9). Matthew responded immediately and invited Jesus to dinner at his house.

Matthew emphasizes that Jesus was Israel's long-awaited Messiah-King by focusing on how Jesus fulfilled prophecy. More than sixty times, he repeats the fulfillment formula: This was to fulfill what the Lord said through the prophet.

Despite the evidence, the religious leaders oppose and reject Jesus. They charge He was a false prophet, law breaker, and phony messiah. Their opposition culminated when they secretly arrested Jesus, charged Him with blasphemy, and turned Him over to the Romans for execution.

Matthew makes it clear that Jesus is Immanuel, "God with us," and the Savior of the world, Israel's Messiah. He traces Jesus' genealogy through David to Abraham and concludes his gospel with the Great Commission (Matt. 28:19–20).

MARK

Mark was not one of the Twelve, but he was a companion of both Paul and Peter. He started the first missionary journey with Paul and Barnabas but abandoned them and returned to Jerusalem when they began ministering to Gentiles. Paul and Barnabas ended their partnership in ministry when they sharply disagreed about taking Mark on the second journey. Later, when imprisoned in Rome, Paul wrote favorably about Mark's usefulness in ministry (2 Tim. 4:11).

After opening his gospel with a statement that Jesus Christ is "the Son of God," Mark holds his readers in suspense about Jesus' identity. Even His disciples are slow in recognizing Jesus as the Son of God. A Gentile centurion in charge of Jesus' execution makes the final and climatic statement about Jesus' identity when he testifies, "Truly this man was the Son of God" (Mark 15:39).

Mark focuses on Jesus' ministry to establish the kingdom of God. The greatest obstacle to God's kingdom is not the Romans but Satan. After announcing the arrival of the kingdom, Jesus begins His ministry in a synagogue in Capernaum where He is confronted by a demon-possessed man. With a stern command, Jesus orders the demon out of the man and continues to exercise His power over demons, sickness, and nature until His arrest and crucifixion. To settle an argument about who is the greatest, Jesus explains His mission to His disciples, "For even the Son of Man did not come to be served, but to serve, and to give His life a ransom for the many" (Mark 10:45).

LUKE

Luke, a physician, is the only Gentile writer of the New Testament. He traveled with Paul on his second and third missionary journeys and went with the apostle when Paul was transferred to Rome as a prisoner. Luke also wrote Acts. The two books were originally two volumes in a single work but were separated when the canon was organized.

Luke is the longest and most comprehensive of the four gospels. He begins with the birth of John the Baptist and concludes with Jesus' resurrection and ascension. Two major themes in the gospel are Jesus' compassion for the poor and disfranchised and the importance of repentance in the conversion experience. These two themes are graphically revealed in Jesus' interaction with Zaccheus, a despised chief tax collector. Zaccheus repents, offering to sell half of his possessions to repay those he has cheated and help the poor. Jesus commends him and declares, "For the Son of Man has come to seek and to save that which was lost" (Luke 19:10).

Luke focuses more on Jesus' humanity than the other gospel writers. He is a descendant of Adam; but unlike the first Adam, who failed when tempted by Satan, Jesus resists and is victorious. Though fully divine, Jesus needed to pray seeking His Father's guidance at critical moments in His life.

Luke offers proof of the resurrection through Jesus' surprise appearance to those whose hopes had been dashed by the crucifixion. The account of Jesus' resurrection appearance to the two disciples on the road to Emmaus is a classic short story (Luke 24:13–35).

JOHN

John, who was the son of Zebedee and was a fisherman, gives a unique theological and interpretative perspective on the life of Christ. He states his purpose in John 20:30–31. He wants to convince people that Jesus is the Christ and the Son of God and promises eternal life to all who will believe. He emphasizes that Jesus is God's unique Son and that the Father sent His Son into the world because He loves the world and is not willing that any should perish (John 3:16).

John begins his gospel with a simple yet profound statement. Jesus is the *Logos*, the preexistent Word. He has always been with God, and He is God (John 1:1). Jesus claims deity seven times by referring to Himself as "I AM," the divine name for God in the Old Testament (Ex. 3:14). When Jesus declares that He and His Father are one, the Jews attempt to stone Him (John 10:32–33).

John advances his gospel primarily through seven miracles, which he calls "signs," and seven messages (John 1:19–12:50). In John, Jesus does not merely fulfill Scripture, He exceeds Old Testament expectations. For example, Moses gave the people manna in the wilderness, but Jesus is the "Bread of Life" that has come down from heaven to give life to the world (John 6:32–33). John gives an extended account of Jesus' teaching in the upper room (John 13:1–26). His announcement about His departure is upsetting, but Jesus promises to send another "Comforter," the Holy Spirit. The section concludes with Jesus' high priestly prayer for Himself, His disciples, and all believers (John 17:1–26).

Jesus' death was not a tragic mistake but was His voluntary sacrifice for the sins of the world (John 19:28–30). Joseph and Nicodemus gave Jesus a burial suited for a king, but Jesus conquered death as He had promised. When Mary went to the tomb, it was empty. Later, Peter, John, and all the disciples saw the resurrected Lord. When Jesus appeared to "doubting" Thomas, he exclaimed, "My Lord and my God!" (John 20:28). The gospel concludes with Jesus meeting with His disciples on the Sea of Galilee and the reinstatement of Peter, who had denied Jesus.

ESTABLISHMENT (ACTS 1:1–6:7)

In his gospel, Luke wrote about the life of Christ; in Acts he continued the story of Jesus by tracing the birth and growth of the church from Jerusalem to Rome.

Jesus fulfills His promise to build His church on the day of Pentecost (Matt. 16:18). He pours out the promised Holy Spirit on all His followers (John 14:16) and empowers them by the Spirit. Peter proclaims that the resurrected Jesus is Lord and Messiah. The church is born when in response to Peter's message 3,000 believe and are baptized (Acts 2:36–41).

Luke describes how the church experienced supernatural growth in spite of external opposition and internal problems. He alternates between external opposition and internal problems ending each section with a statement of victory and continued growth. The pattern is as follows:

The arrest of Peter and John (4:5–31)
The deceit and death of Ananias and Sapphira (5:1–16)
The arrest and miraculous release of all the apostles (5:17–42)
The complaint over the care of widows (6:1–7)

EXTENSION OF THE CHURCH (ACTS 6:8–9:31)

To explain the growth of the church beyond Jerusalem, Luke focuses his inspired spotlight on three men. Stephen is arrested and becomes the first martyr when he indicts his countrymen for the murder of Jesus (the Prophet like Moses) and their callous rejection of the Holy Spirit. When persecution forces believers to leave

Jerusalem, Philip takes the gospel to Samaria. Paul, a fanatical Jew, tries to destroy the infant church, but becomes a zealous follower of Christ when the resurrected Lord appears to him on the Damascus Road and commissions him as the apostle to the Gentiles.

EXPANSION (ACTS 9:32–28:31)

Peter set a precedent for ministry to the Gentiles when he preached the gospel to Cornelius, a Gentile centurion, and his family. His conversion was validated by the same gift of the Spirit that was given to the Jews on the day of Pentecost (Acts 11:15–17).

Beginning in Acts 13, Luke focused on the ministry of the apostle Paul. His purpose was to give an account of the supernatural growth of the church and affirm Paul's unique apostleship to the Gentiles. He recorded Paul's three missionary journeys and concluded with Paul's arrest and transfer by ship to Rome. Between the first and second journeys, Luke gave a detailed account of the Jerusalem Council (Acts 15). Hardcore Jews, known as Judaizers, jeopardized the growth of the church by insisting that Gentiles submit to circumcision. After discussing the issue, the Jerusalem Council decided against imposing the Law of Moses on Gentiles (Acts 15). This important decision preserved the doctrine of salvation by grace and allowed for the universal growth of the church by the inclusion of all ethnic groups. Acts concludes with Paul under house arrest in Rome but with freedom to proclaim the gospel of the kingdom.

THE JOURNEY EPISTLES (IN CHRONOLOGICAL ORDER)

During the era of rapid expansion, Paul wrote ten of his thirteen epistles. After his first journey, he writes Galatians to refute Jewish legalists who tried to impose the Jewish law on Gentile believers. Paul insists that his message is the only true gospel for the salvation of Jews and Gentiles.

While at Corinth on his second journey Paul writes 1 Thessalonians to commend the new converts for their steadfastness in faith, love, and hope. They are a model (*tupos*) church. He assures them the resurrection of Jesus gives hope for both the dead and the living. Six months later, Paul writes the second epistle to refute misleading teaching about the day of the Lord.

On his third journey, Paul receives a report from Chole's household about chaos in the church at Corinth. He writes to correct and instruct the Corinthians because of their misunderstanding of the gospel, the ministry of the Holy Spirit, and the resurrection of Christ. Second Corinthians is the most personal of Paul's epistles because he defends his apostleship and hopes to convince the Corinthians that as a minister of the new covenant, his ministry is in every way superior to that of his Jewish opponents.

Romans is the most doctrinal of Paul's epistles. He argues persuasively that Gentiles and Jews need God's provision of righteousness, and all are justified by faith not the works of the law. Salvation is a three-part process of justification, sanctification, and glorification. In his sovereignty and wisdom, God has included Gentiles in the church, which Paul compares to a body. To promote unity between Jews and Gentiles, Paul emphasizes that all parts of the body are significant and needed in God's amazing plan of redemption.

THE PRISON EPISTLES

I take the view that Paul was imprisoned two times. During his first confinement of house arrest in Rome, Paul had the freedom to write the four Prison Epistles.

Ephesians was written to assure believers who had been involved in the occult that Christ was triumphant over all powers and authorities in heaven and earth. It also explained how this made Jews and Gentiles one in Christ and transformed their life and walk in the world.

In Colossians, Paul assured believers that Christ was their all-sufficient Savior and that they do not need to submit to Jewish legalism, Eastern mysticism, or any kind of self-imposed asceticism.

Paul assured the Philippians that he was not discouraged by his imprisonment; rather he was thankful and joyful because it had given him unique opportunities for ministry in Rome. He urged them to humbly serve one another even as Christ humbled Himself and suffered an ignominious death on the cross. Because He was obedient to a shameful death, God exalted His Son over all powers and authorities.

Philemon was related to the widespread practice of slavery in the first century. The apostle urged Philemon, an elder in the church in Philippi, to forgive and accept Onesimus, a runaway slave, as a beloved brother in the Lord.

CONSOLIDATION

The epistles written during the second half of the first century address two major threats: persecution and false teaching.

THE PASTORALS

Paul wrote the Pastorals, 1 and 2 Timothy and Titus, to instruct his pastoral representatives at Ephesus and Crete on the importance of sound doctrine, the management of the church, and their pastoral and personal responsibilities. Written from Rome during his second imprisonment, 2 Timothy was Paul's last epistle and his final instructions for the perpetuation of the Christian faith.

THE GENERAL EPISTLES

The unknown author of Hebrews emphasized the superiority of Christ over all aspects of Judaism and warned about the danger of turning back to the obsolete system of the law.

First Peter inspired hope for believers who were slandered and sometimes physically abused for their radically different and godly lifestyle.

Second Peter and Jude were somewhat similar. Both exposed false teachers and warn of severe judgment but assured true believers that their Savior was faithful and able to keep them from falling.

The apostle John wrote three epistles. First John was written to refute a heretical view of the person of Christ. John emphasized that true believers will live righteously, love one another, and recognize the full humanity and deity of Christ. Second John was written to an elect lady, possibly a church, commending her for her love of the truth but cautioning that she might be inadvertently giving hospitality to false teachers. In his third epistle, John commended Gaius for his love of the truth but criticized Diotrephes, an egotistical elder, for refusing to welcome John and his associates.

Written to the seven churches of Asia Minor, the book of Revelation gave assurance to believers, who were persecuted during the rule of Domitian, the Roman Emperor, that God was in absolute control of history. The book opens with John's vision of the triumphant Christ. John then includes elements of the vision in his letters to the seven churches. He described how the Lamb will pour out on the earth three series of judgments that culminate with the coming of Christ to cast Satan and all his diabolical forces into a lake of fire. John concluded with a description of the magnificence of the new Jerusalem and heaven where believers of all ages will worship and dwell with God and Christ forever.

THE GREATEST STORY EVER TOLD (FROM CREATION TO THE NEW CREATION)

The Bible tells a dramatic story of redemption. The drama begins with the creation of the heavens and earth and Adam and Eve in the image of God. But seduced by Satan, Adam and Eve rebelled against their creator. Their sin wrecked God's perfect creation, but instead of destroying them God initiated an amazing plan of redemption. His plan moved from a descendant of Adam to Abraham and his descendants.

The hope for a Redeemer burned bright through the eras of Egyptian bondage, the exodus, wilderness wanderings, the conquest of the land, the judges, and the establishment of a kingdom. But then, because of disobedience God allowed their enemies to defeat them. Though scattered among the nations, God brought His people back to the land, and was ready to make His most dramatic move to rescue rebellious humanity.

God the Father sent His one and only Son into the world as the perfect and final Redeemer. Jesus voluntarily gave up His life as a sacrifice for sins, conquered death, and was exalted to the right hand of His Father. As exalted Lord and Savior, Jesus sent the Holy Spirit to empower believers to tell "the good news" to the world. There was hope for sinful humanity. Anyone who believed on Christ would receive forgiveness of sins and eternal life. The dramatic story of redemption concluded with the destruction of Satan and his followers and the creation of new heavens and earth where believers would enjoy life with the Father and Son forever.

CHAPTER 1.3

Understanding the Theology of the Old and New Testaments

JOHN K. GOODRICH

When people define *theology*, they often describe it as the study of God, or more narrowly, as the study of Christian belief. While these definitions are quite standard, the truth is there are numerous valid ways of *defining* theology, and even of *doing* theology—that is, of studying God and the Christian faith. For this reason, theologians commonly distinguish between various branches of theology, most notably philosophical theology, historical theology, systematic theology, and biblical theology.

Unsurprisingly, each of these branches emphasizes the qualifier attached to its name. Philosophical theology prioritizes reason to infer truths about God and His nature. Historical theology focuses on the formation of Christian doctrine throughout the history of the church. Systematic theology seeks to provide an orderly and unified account of the major doctrines of Christianity. What, then, distinguishes biblical theology? After all, isn't all theology biblical insofar as it is based on the Bible?

Generally speaking, the answer is yes—all Christian theology is concerned with the Bible, though not all branches of theology draw on the Bible in the same way and toward the same ends. Biblical theology, thus, is a distinct branch of theology with its own methods and goals, though the very best biblical theologians do not consider themselves as competing with practitioners of other theological disciplines.

What characterizes biblical theology? What are its distinctive methods and goals, and why is it an important area of study? It is the aim of this chapter to introduce what biblical theology is, to demonstrate how it is practiced, and to explain how it benefits the church.

INTRODUCING BIBLICAL THEOLOGY

The following is our working definition of biblical theology: *Biblical theology is the study of God's Word that accounts for the unity, diversity, and historical particularity of the Bible's message and storyline.* While such a brief description omits important details, it gives us a starting place as we introduce and elucidate the discipline with greater specificity below.

Biblical theology has only been recognized as a distinct branch of academic theology since the late-eighteenth century. Some of the methods germane to biblical theology were practiced before this time. However, the majority of important pre-modern theologians prioritized what is known today as systematic theology, emphasizing less the discrete contexts and diverse contributions of individual books of the Bible and focusing rather on the united witness and timeless nature of the canon of Scripture.[1] But with the arrival of the Enlightenment and its accompanying sensitivity to the historical contingency of biblical interpretation, theologians began to use methodologies that treated the biblical books as individual compositions of literature whose respective meanings and messages were historically bound. Ancient languages, historical contexts, even literary theories became more widely used in biblical exegesis and as preliminary to the task of theological synthesis. To be sure, not all tools of historical criticism are conducive to a high view of Scripture, though there is indeed value to certain modern exegetical and analytical methods. Thus, evangelical practitioners of biblical theology have normally sought to employ the most reliable historical methodologies while maintaining the historic Christian belief that the biblical books are inspired, inerrant Scripture whose meanings are bound up with the message of the whole canon.[2] We will now unpack the key features of our brief definition of biblical theology before offering a test case.

UNITY

When we talk about *unity* as a defining feature of biblical theology, we mean the *inner theological coherence* of the canon that results from the Bible's divine inspiration as well as the use of shared historical, theological, and textual traditions by its human authors. Within Israel, each passing generation inherited an existing body of sacred literature and a common worldview projected by those available Scriptures. This worldview contained a single grand narrative about God's interaction with the world and was reflected in Israel's various religious symbols and practices. The biblical authors themselves, under the Spirit's superintendence, adopted this worldview with its attendant rituals and traditions and even added to this expanding account of God by retelling and recycling some of the histories, themes, and idioms found in the existing Scriptures. From a human perspective, then, we can explain some of the Bible's thematic coherence—the biblical authors swam in the same sea of ancient Israelite traditions as their prophetic predecessors, as they sought both to preserve and to develop those teachings.

Yet studying the Bible *theologically* only promises to be a fruitful endeavor when we appreciate that the canon, though containing two testaments comprising sixty-six books penned by at least forty different human writers, is in fact *one book* with a *single divine author*. Thus, when we confess that the one true God has inspired all Scripture, our minds should be alerted to the fact that the Bible's divine author intends for His literary, canonical masterpiece to cohere deeply and broadly in its fundamental narrative and message; and that is what one discovers when reading the entire biblical witness (see the previous chapter for a summary of this grand narrative). It is this essential harmony with respect to Scripture's primary subject matter, recognizable through the deployment and redeployment of a multiplicity of central stories and themes, that testifies to God's revelatory activity and invites close study. And this type of narrative and thematic analysis is what has become almost synonymous in evangelical circles with doing biblical theology.

In addition to emphasizing the unity of Scripture's theological message and themes, biblical theology also stresses *the singular plot and coherent framework* of the biblical narrative. In other words, when biblical theologians read Scripture, they are closely attuned to the history of redemption and to how the individual books of the canon contribute to, as well as derive their deeper meaning from, that overarching storyline. This requires from the reader an understanding of the chronological relationship between the biblical accounts and the ability to grasp the parts of the story in relation to the whole. But once it is realized that the canon is both projecting and being driven along by a coherent narrative of cosmic salvation (indeed, *a drama of redemption*, as some theologians say), then it becomes far easier to detect the discrete themes that are woven through the larger canonical story.

An additional byproduct of reading the Bible in light of its unified themes and narrative is the recognition of theological *continuity*. To observe theological continuity is to note how the various covenants relate to one another, especially the old and new covenants. Inherent to the notion of continuity is the recognition that despite whatever novelties are introduced in the New Testament, there is a significant degree of continuation from the Old Testament into the church age, especially with respect to how God relates to humanity, what God expects of His people, and which of His early (Old Testament) promises apply to them. One example of continuity in the Scriptures centers on God's grace. It is by grace that God entered into a relationship with Abraham, that He established a covenant with Israel, that He made promises to David, and that He sent Jesus Christ to inaugurate the new covenant. Although there are real differences in the stipulations of the various covenants, from the beginning to the end of the Bible God is shown to be gracious in how He relates to humanity, always taking the initiative to repair what is broken.

In sum, Scripture communicates a single grand narrative about how the sovereign Creator of the universe is actively pursuing His beloved creation. Practitioners of biblical theology not only recognize this unified message, they seek to demonstrate how that message, though articulated in various ways, runs seamlessly through the two testaments.

DIVERSITY

While biblical theology first emphasizes Scripture's theological *unity*, it is not at the expense of theological *diversity*. For in addition to studying the theological *harmony* of the canon of Scripture, biblical theology has an equally strong commitment to analyzing the *discrete contributions* of the various biblical books and authors. These contributions come in many forms.

Biblical theology is built on close exegesis of biblical texts, including the study of words, grammar, syntax, discourses, historical-cultural context, and more. Close readings of texts bring to bear historical and literary data that cannot help but expose the rhetorical tendencies and theological idiosyncrasies of particular human authors. This is not to suggest that there are direct contradictions within Scripture, but it is to acknowledge that in His supreme wisdom, God has allowed the various writers of the Bible to communicate in their own terms, to draw on their own preferred images, and to share from their own perspectives. This has resulted in some biblical authors, even some contemporaries of one another, making different yet complementary theological claims.

Many such distinctives can be attributed to an author's particular location in redemptive history. Biblical writers, while inspired to record authoritative texts, are limited in what they can communicate by the extent of special revelation God has disclosed to them. Biblical theology recognizes this progressive quality of special revelation and thereby seeks to give all parts of Scripture a voice while also appreciating how later portions of Scripture often bring greater clarity to the earlier parts. Other differences between biblical books can be attributed to their particular historical, cultural, and geographical contexts, as well as to the special circumstances of their respective audiences. Both the messages of the individual biblical books and the manner in which they were communicated were largely determined by such historical particularities. Biblical theology seeks to identify the rhetorical and theological emphases of individual authors, conditioned as they were by their contexts and the needs of their audiences, in order to showcase the multi-perspectival nature of the biblical witness.

HISTORICAL PARTICULARITY

Despite the continuity that exists between the various time periods in redemptive history, biblical theology also seeks to recognize the *plurality* of the biblical covenants and the *progressions and pivots* that occur between them. While there is indeed a large degree of carryover with respect to God's promises—from the Abrahamic covenant, to the Davidic covenant, to the new covenant—God has revealed His plan to His people in multiple stages, disclosing His redemptive program gradually and with greater clarity as the key periods of salvation history unfold one after another. Moreover, throughout this gradual revelatory process (known as *progressive revelation*), significant degrees of change have been introduced at important moments, especially as God's mode for relating to His people changed with the termination of the Mosaic covenant and with the inauguration of the new covenant. This is to be expected, as the new covenant was installed precisely because of the inability of human beings to comply with the demands of the old covenant expressed in the law of Moses. But what exactly has changed?

Some covenantal changes are more obvious than others. In both testaments the Holy Spirit is responsible for empowering people to accomplish noteworthy tasks for the Lord, though the Spirit's indwelling presence is somewhat transient in the Old Testament. He comes upon a person for a limited time or for a particular task as, for example, He did on Bezalel so he might design the tabernacle furnishings and priestly garments (Ex. 31:1–11); or as He did on Samson and Saul (Judg. 13:25; 14:6, 19; 15:14; 1 Sam. 11:6), only to depart at a later time (1 Sam. 16:14). In the New Testament, however, God's Spirit indwells individuals permanently, as a guarantee of God's pledge of salvation and as the first installment of His transformative work in their lives (see 2 Cor. 1:22; 3:18; 5:5; Eph. 1:13–14). This is a significant change in God's way of relating to His people and marks one of the key developments in God's progressive plan of redemption.

THEMATIC STUDY

Lest we give the impression that doing biblical theology always and only involves studying the entire message of the Bible from beginning to end (a nearly impossible task on any occasion), we should note that many practitioners of biblical theology content themselves with thematic case studies. Some biblical theologians select a single motif—covenant, atonement, temple, worship, or the like—and trace its development for as long as it surfaces in Scripture. Others focus on a singular concept within a particular biblical book or author—e.g., the theology of sin in Romans or Matthew's idea of righteousness. In other words, biblical theology need not always be exhaustive. Even by examining one theme, we can catch a glimpse of the unity and diversity of the scriptural witness.

Having outlined some of the defining features and emphases of biblical theology, we will now offer our own test case by analyzing a single major theme in the Old and New Testaments—the kingdom of God. We have not selected this motif at random. God's kingdom is one of the major topics of Scripture, one that develops over time as well as highlights and holds together many other significant themes.

PRACTICING BIBLICAL THEOLOGY

The Bible unequivocally portrays God as the everlasting King of the world. God is the one who created all things and rules all things, both in heaven and on earth (Isa. 66:1–2). Although the Bible affirms that God is omnipresent (Ps. 139:7–10) and that at certain times He reigns in particular terrestrial locales, Scripture normally depicts God as ruling from heaven, where He sits enthroned as King of the cosmos (Pss. 45:6; 47:2; 93:2; 103:19). Because God rules principally from heaven, His reign is invisible. God's prophets are occasionally afforded visions of His heavenly throne room (Isa. 6:1–13), but for the most part, God's cosmic kingship involves His unseen rule, which is characterized by certain inalienable attributes.

There are three main characteristics of God's kingship. First, as King of the world, God possesses unrivaled *power* (1 Chron. 29:11), and He therefore has the right and authority to demand obedience. Second, He demonstrated *justice* (or *righteousness*; Ps. 97:2). It is because of His just rule that God issues covenantal stipulations based on His own moral standard. And it is on the basis of His justice that God blesses the righteous and curses the wicked (Deut. 11:26–27; Pss. 1:1–6; 9:3–8; Rom. 2:5). Yet despite the disobedience of humanity (for all people disobey), God's rule is also defined by His *love* (or *generosity*; Ps. 89:14). On this basis, God takes the initiative to reconcile with His disobedient subjects, graciously providing means of atonement and forgiveness of sins (Ps. 103:1–14; Rom. 5:6–8; 8:31–32). Each of these attributes is true of God's reign throughout the Bible. Yet it is only when we pay close attention to the narrative dimension of God's kingdom, especially as the new covenant is inaugurated and replaces the old (Mosaic) covenant, that the Bible's development of this theme comes into focus.

GOD'S KINGDOM IN THE OLD TESTAMENT

This section will focus on three dimensions of God's kingdom in the Old and New Testaments: (1) the exercise of God's rule over a particular people in a particular place; (2) the mediation of God's rule by leaders and law codes; and (3) the challenge of God's rule by His enemies.[3]

God's Kingdom Established—The Creation of Humanity and the Birth of Israel

Despite the Old Testament's portrayal of God's rule as limitless, sometimes the Old Testament attests to God's rule in a narrower sense, as we see in His rule over a particular people in a particular place. The people whom God rules are consciously and willfully subject to His rule, and the place of this narrower rule has measurable, geographical limits. The *who* and the *where*, however, correspond to the *when*—in other words, the demographic and geographic scope of God's kingdom changes and even develops as the Old Testament narrative progresses.

God's rule in the Old Testament first manifests in the creation account. After powerfully bringing the heavens and the earth into existence, God conquered the then-chaotic cosmos by creating light, sky, oceans, land, vegetation, stars, sun, and moon (Gen. 1:1–19). He then populated the newly created world by calling animals into being—fish, birds, reptiles, mammals—and finally humans (Gen. 1:20–31). Thus, God's kingship initially extended to all creation, and all beings were subjected to His authority, with His rule over humanity in Eden being its particular focus.

With the sin and expulsion of the first humans, however, God's reign of the world began to regress. It was not that God became any less sovereign over creation, but at this time humanity grew increasingly rebellious toward its cosmic king. This resulted in several instances of regal judgment, including the punishment of Cain (Gen. 4:10–12), the worldwide flood (Gen. 6–8), and the destruction and redistribution at Babel (Gen. 11:6–9). This marks a low point in humanity's relationship to God's rule.

Yet through the installation of His covenant with Abraham, God began to implement His plan to reestablish His rule over humanity. Although He did not immediately make Abraham's family into a proper kingdom, God promised to Abraham that a nation would be established from among his descendants (Gen. 12:2), that kings would come forth from his lineage (Gen. 17:6), and that land would be secured for this family (Gen. 17:8), extending from the Nile to the Euphrates (Gen. 15:18), from the Red Sea to the Mediterranean Sea (Ex. 23:31).

These promises would not come to fruition immediately or in mundane fashion. Indeed, over four hundred years passed before God's regal program made any major advances. But the day eventually came when Yahweh, after having seen the affliction and hearing the cry of His people (Ex. 3:7), miraculously liberated Abraham's descendants (Israel) from bondage under Egyptian rule as their mighty warrior King (Ex. 15:3, 6, 18). God then guided His people to Mount Sinai, where He declared them to be "a kingdom of priests and a holy nation" (Ex. 19:6). Later, God led Israel militarily into the land of Canaan, where the Hebrews conquered the region's inhabitants and occupied nearly the entire territory for about seven hundred years. All the while, God reigned in the nation's midst, enthroned above the ark of the covenant (1 Sam. 4:4; 2 Sam. 6:2; 2 Kings 19:15; Pss. 80:1; 99:1). Thus, God's kingdom was established in Israel, as He possessed for Himself a particular people and reigned over them in a particular locale from the conquest of Canaan (ca. 1400 BC) to the Babylonian Captivity (586 BC).

God's Kingdom Mediated—Kings and Law Codes

Because ancient Israel was a theocracy, God served as the Israelites' ultimate King from the time of the nation's beginning (Isa. 43:15). However, throughout Israel's early history God's rule was exercised only indirectly, mediated as it was by human leaders and divine legislation. Tracing the development of Israel's mediated rule reveals important aspects of God's kingdom.

Once Israel was established as a nation, Yahweh governed His people principally through the law of Moses. Containing 613 commandments that reflected the very character of God, the law required meticulous observance in order for the nation to imitate and remain in right standing before its divine Lawgiver. The people were to be, as the law itself demands, "holy, for I the LORD your God am holy" (Lev. 19:2; see 11:44–45; 20:7, 26; 21:8). These commandments were not optional; the people's blessing and longevity in the land were contingent on their faithfulness to God's covenant ordinances. Deuteronomy 30:15–16 captures the obligatory nature of Israel's legal system well: "See, I have placed before you today life and happiness, and death and adversity, in that I am commanding you today to love the LORD your God, to walk in His ways and to keep His commandments, His statutes, and His judgments, so that you may live and become numerous, and that the LORD your God may bless you in the land where you are entering to take possession of it."

God's rule was at various times also mediated on earth through regal, judicial, and prophetic figures. As King over creation, God appointed Adam and Eve (epitomizing all humanity) as His vice regents over creation to represent Him on earth.

Hence, God said to the first humans not only to "be fruitful and multiply," but also to "fill the earth, and subdue it," that is, to "rule over the fish of the sea and over the birds of the sky and over every living thing that moves on the earth" (Gen. 1:28; see Ps. 8:3–8).

God's rule of Israel was also mediated by vice regents. Initially, the nation was led by the prophets Moses and Joshua, who spoke for God but did not possess the authority to govern the people absolutely. Later, judges such as Deborah, Samson, and Samuel were empowered by the Spirit of the Lord to lead Israel in various times and locales. It was not, however, until Saul was installed as king at the outset of Israel's monarchy that God's reign was officially mediated by an earthly ruler, marking a major advancement in God's kingdom on earth.

To be sure, Israel's development into a monarchy was no mistake. It is true that Israel's demand for a human king like that of the other nations—in which a human monarch would fight for his people (1 Sam. 8:20)—was in some respects a rejection of God Himself as King and thus was met with divine warning and rebuke (1 Sam. 8:5–18). Even so, Israel's monarchy was anticipated long before Saul rose to power. God promised Abraham that "kings will come from you" (Gen. 17:6), just as He promised that the "scepter will not depart from Judah" (Gen. 49:10). Moreover, Moses himself outlined in the Pentateuch the so-called law of kingship (Deut. 17:14–20), suggesting that from the beginning of the nation's history God had intended for Israel to become a monarchy. Thus, the installation of a vice regent over the nation was not a departure from God's plan or design for Israel. In fact, Israel's king was intended by God to serve as a model of humility and righteous obedience for Israel. For this reason, the king was to make a copy of the law for himself so that he might study and observe it throughout his reign (Deut. 17:18–20). Beyond that, Israel's monarch was expected to not multiply his army, his wives, or his wealth (Deut. 17:16–17), in order that his faith and focus might remain squarely on God rather than on earthly powers and pleasures.

Yet none of Israel's kings lived up to their high calling by executing their duties in accordance with God's law. In fact, even Israel's most celebrated kings disobeyed God's expectations by accumulating massive armies, numerous wives, and great wealth (1 Kings 4:26; 11:1–3; 2 Chron. 9:13–23). Some, to be sure, ruled more faithfully and benevolently than others. Yet on the whole, Israel's kings—from Saul, to David, to Solomon, through the divided monarchy—were marked by the same failures as the rest of the nation, and at many times were themselves responsible for leading the Israelites into moral and religious compromise.

God's Kingdom Contested—Israel's Political Enemies

Like many monarchic figures known to history, King Yahweh has had many enemies during His reign. Throughout the story of Israel, these opponents and the wars waged against them were among the defining features of God's kingship. The Old Testament attests repeatedly to the many foreign nations and kingdoms that opposed God's early rule in Israel. The Canaanites and the Philistines are among the most notorious peoples to have stood in opposition to God's kingdom. But Israel's most significant enemy is without question the kingdom of Egypt, which enslaved the nation and whom God subdued in order to bring His kingdom on earth into being. In fact, many of God's later enemies are compared to the Egyptians, and God's rescue of His people from foreign powers is often likened to the great exodus, with God Himself portrayed as a warrior King who defeats Israel's captors in the same way He did the Egyptians (Isa. 11:15–16; see Ex. 15:1–18).

Despite God's opposition to these foreign powers, He occasionally used them for His own purposes. Due to Israel's covenantal disobedience, Yahweh repeatedly disciplined His people, finally sending them into exile in two primary phases: the northern kingdom was captured and exiled by the Assyrians in 722 BC, and the southern kingdom experienced the same at the hands of the Babylonians in 586 BC. Although in a cosmic sense God remained sovereign over all people and nations (Dan. 4:25; see 4:17, 32; 5:21), during this time His special reign was removed from Israel.

God promised, however, that He would not allow His people to remain under foreign rule forever. God pledged that He would eventually liberate Israel at the hands of a future King from the lineage of David. At the time of this deliverance, the "good news" that God had returned to rule over His people Israel once again would be proclaimed to the nation (Isa. 40:1–11; 52:1–12; 61:1–3). Furthermore, at the end of days God's kingdom would be restored. The Son of Man (the Messiah) would be "given dominion, honor, and a kingdom, so that all the peoples, nations, and populations of all languages might serve Him. His dominion is an everlasting dominion which will not pass away" (Dan. 7:14; see 2 Sam. 7:12–16; 1 Chron. 17:11–14). Moreover, through this messianic figure God would make a new covenant with His people, forgive their sins, gather them back into the land, and pour out His Spirit on them so that they might be empowered to obey Him (Deut. 30:1–6; Jer. 31:31–34; Ezek. 36:24–28). God's restored people, in fact, would themselves take possession of the kingdom and reign with God (Dan. 7:22, 27). Surely, the prospect of the return of God's kingdom was the cause of great hope and anticipation.

God's Kingdom in the New Testament

When we turn to the New Testament, we find that God's kingdom is just as pervasive a theme as in the Old Testament. However, we need to approach the concept with caution, because God's kingdom is routinely described in the New Testament in highly enigmatic terms and in ways that are both similar to and yet different from its portrayal in the Old Testament. The New Testament teaches that, with the first coming of Jesus Christ, the kingdom of God has arrived (or better, has been restored), and yet God's kingdom is also still to come. Moreover, we find that the kingdom is a place in which a particular people will eventually reside with their cosmic king, but it is also already a sphere of existence for the church, a realm of power that has broken into the present world and through which God is currently redeeming and transforming people. Finally, God's kingdom is challenged by God's human enemies, though God's nonhuman enemies are even mightier, as they stand above and behind God's political opponents. All these aspects form part of the mystery of the kingdom about which Jesus and the New Testament authors taught.

God's Kingdom Renewed—The Restoration of Israel and the Birth of the Church

In the New Testament, God's eschatological kingdom is inaugurated at the first coming of Jesus Christ. As early as the commencement of the gospel of Mark, we learn that "Jesus came into Galilee, preaching the gospel of God, and saying, 'The time is fulfilled, and the kingdom of God is at hand; repent and believe in the gospel'" (Mark 1:14–15). In these verses, the nearness of the kingdom refers to its arrival. This is why Jesus at other times can say, "Behold, the kingdom of God is in your midst" (Luke 17:21), and, "If I cast out the demons by the Spirit of God, then the kingdom of God has come upon you" (Matt. 12:28).

In Mark 1:14–15, the arrival of the kingdom is also signaled by Jesus' proclamation of "the gospel" (good news). As seen in Isaiah, the proclamation of good news is nothing less than the announcement that God has acted decisively to restore and once again reign over His covenant people, Israel. Although both Jews and Gentiles are welcome in God's restored kingdom—provided they "repent and believe in the gospel" (Mark 1:15)—the message of the kingdom proclaimed by Jesus and the apostles is that which was anticipated originally in the Old Testament and concerns, in the first place, the restoration of Israel (Acts 1:6; 28:20). This does not mean that when Gentiles believe the gospel they become Israelites and cease to be Gentiles. Gentiles who are in Christ surely remain ethnic Gentiles, though when they respond to the gospel message they become fellow citizens of God's kingdom, along with Jewish believers, and they begin to share in "the commonwealth of Israel" (Eph. 2:12 ESV) as participants in God's covenantal blessings.

Despite the fact that God's kingdom has been inaugurated, it is not at this time a visible, political entity with a clearly demarcated earthly territory. The believer's citizenship remains in heaven until the return of Jesus Christ (Phil. 3:20; see John 18:36). Yet God's kingdom has broken into this world and forms a sphere of power that believers now inhabit. As Paul maintains, God has "rescued us from the domain of darkness, and transferred us to the kingdom of His beloved Son" (Col. 1:13).

In fact, God's kingdom will not be consummated and expand into an entity with firm geographical boundaries until Jesus' second coming. This is why the disciples asked the resurrected Jesus, "Lord, is it at this time that You are restoring the kingdom to Israel?" (Acts 1:6). Clearly, even the original disciples, who had heard Jesus' prior teaching about the kingdom, had seen His many miracles, and were witnesses to His bodily resurrection, did not regard all the Old Testament kingdom promises as having been fulfilled in His first advent. The full restoration of Israel and the consummated kingdom are yet to come (Acts 3:19–21). The New Testament repeatedly indicates as much, describing the kingdom as still future, as something yet to be inherited by believers (Matt. 25:34; 1 Cor. 6:9–10, 15:50; Gal. 5:21; Eph. 5:5). This still-future inheritance will be initially received during the millennial kingdom (Rev. 20:1–6) and then finally in the New Jerusalem, the New Creation (Rev. 21:7). During the millennial kingdom, God's rule will center on Israel, with surrounding nations enjoying or rejecting the blessings offered by God's rule (Rev. 20:7–10; see Zech. 14:16–19). However, in the eternal state, God's kingdom will span the (new) earth, with the land of Israel serving as the centerpiece of that rule (Rev. 21:24–26).

God's kingdom in the New Testament, then, has many facets—it is both here and not yet here; it is both a place and a power; it both centers on Israel, yet welcomes Gentiles. In all these respects, God's kingdom is an evolving reality that will grow and transform until God's rule encompasses the entire world (Mark 4:26–32).

God's Kingdom Mediated—Christ and the Law of Christ

Although we observed in the Old Testament that God's kingdom was mediated by various political and religious authorities as well as by the law of Moses, in the New Testament God's rule is mediated by Jesus Christ as well as by the law of Christ—the model of cruciformity ("cross-shaped" living) exemplified by Jesus and empowered by the Holy Spirit.

Unlike the kingdom of Israel in the Old Testament, in which various human kings were appointed to lead God's people as monarchs, God's restored kingdom in the New Testament is ruled initially by God's Christ, Jesus of Nazareth. The word "Christ" itself means "anointed one" and is the Greek translation of the Hebrew term from which we derive "Messiah." The Messiah figure in Old Testament prophecy principally occupied a regal position in the model of David's kingship: "When your [David's] days are finished and you lie down with your fathers, I will raise up your descendant after you, who will come from you, and I will establish his kingdom. He shall build a house for My name, and I will establish the throne of his kingdom forever" (2 Sam. 7:12–13). In Jesus, then, Israel's long-awaited Davidic King has arrived: "He will be great and will be called the Son of the Most High; and the Lord God will give Him the throne of His father David; and He will reign over the house of Jacob forever, and His kingdom will have no end" (Luke 1:32–33).

Although Jesus' rule is invisible from a human perspective, He reigns even now enthroned at the right hand of the Father in heaven (Acts 2:32–36; Eph. 1:20–23; Heb. 1:3). Moreover, Jesus' followers have been raised up and seated in the heavenly places with Christ and thus share in His mediatorial reign (Eph. 2:6). Jesus' reign will only become visible on earth when He returns to "strike down the nations", and "rule them with a rod of iron" (Rev. 19:15). At that time, He will establish His kingdom on earth, where He will co-reign with His followers for a thousand years (Rev. 20:6; see Luke 22:29–30), just as they will reign with God the Father forever in the eternal state (Rev. 22:5; see Dan. 7:22, 27).

Jesus' kingship is also mediated by a code of moral behavior among His followers that is marked principally by love of others. Although followers of Jesus are not obligated to keep the commandments of Moses as stipulations of covenant fidelity, their lives should reflect the core principles of the divine law as they seek to love God with their entire selves, and to love others as themselves (Matt. 22:36–40; citing Deut. 6:5; Lev. 19:18). This call to love others is modeled on the self-giving of Jesus Himself, and is thus labeled "the law of Christ" (Gal. 6:2; see 1 Cor. 9:21). Such other-regard will take many forms in the multicultural church, though its defining feature is self-sacrifice. For just as Jesus gave of Himself for all people, so believers should embody Jesus' generosity by giving of themselves for the sake of others (Rom. 15:2–3). The embodiment of this ethic is not the result of the believer's own willpower alone. Christians are recipients of the Holy Spirit and thereby divinely transformed into Christ's image as they are enabled to obey God and love others. It is for this reason that Paul can say that "the fruit of the Spirit is love" (Gal. 5:22).

God's Kingdom Contested—The Church's Political and Spiritual Enemies

In the Old Testament, we saw that God's rule is challenged principally by nations that opposed Israel, especially the Egyptians, Canaanites, Philistines, Assyrians, and Babylonians. Although less emphasized, evil nonhuman powers such as Satan and demonic beings were also considered God's enemies in the Old Testament. In the New Testament, human and national powers likewise oppose God, including the Jewish authorities, the Roman Empire, and various persons who stand in the way of the advancement of God's kingdom. In the Gospels, the Jewish authorities are skeptical of Jesus' ministry and seek to put an end to it. Ultimately, they arrest Jesus, put Him on trial, and call for His crucifixion. In Acts, they treat the apostles similarly. Peter and John are arrested in Jerusalem (Acts 4:1–3), Paul is stoned at Lystra (Acts 14:19), and Sosthenes is beaten before the Roman tribunal (Acts 18:17).

At times the Roman authorities also pose a threat. In the Gospels, a reluctant Pilate concedes to the will of the masses by having Jesus executed, and in Paul's letters the "rulers of this age" are credited with having "crucified the Lord of glory" (1 Cor. 2:8). Imprisonments are not uncommon in Acts, and in Revelation the Roman Empire is portrayed as a beast that blasphemes God and wages war against Christians (13:4–7, 15).

But beyond human opponents, in the New Testament the principal forces at work against God's kingdom are supranatural agents such as sin, death, and demonic beings. In the Gospels, demons plague humanity (Mark 5:1–13), and Satan himself opposes the gospel (Matt. 4:1–11). The sins of humanity are also a problem that need to be forgiven through the atoning death of Jesus Christ. But in Paul's letters, sin is not only a moral-religious infraction; sin (or Sin) is a power that reigns over all people (Rom. 3:9; 5:21; 6:12; 7:14, 23; Gal. 3:22). Death, likewise, is an oppressive power that imprisons humanity (Rom. 7:24). The death, resurrection, and exaltation of Christ, however, mark the initial defeat of these powers (Rom. 8:1–3; Eph. 1:20–22; Col. 2:13–15). Their final defeat still awaits Christ's future eschatological victory over all God's enemies. As Paul explains, Christ "must reign until He has put all His enemies under His feet. The last enemy that will be abolished is death" (1 Cor. 15:25–26; see Rev. 20:14).

APPLYING BIBLICAL THEOLOGY

Having provided a case study of a major biblical theological theme, we close with three brief implications that biblical theology has for the church. First, biblical theology encourages all Christians—not just pastors who proclaim the Word—to read the Bible carefully. As stressed repeatedly, although there is significant coherence in the message of Scripture, there is also considerable diversity among the contexts, perspectives, emphases, and rhetorical tendencies of the biblical authors. Much of this will be missed, however, if readers fail to appreciate the books of the Bible as individual literary works and to spend adequate time reading these works in their entirety. At the same time, students of Scripture should consider carefully how these individual works contribute to the message of the whole canon. Only when we recognize how the individual books relate to the Book (like chapters in a novel) can we say that we are doing biblical theology.

Second, biblical theology supports the expository preaching of pastors. This is because biblical theologians and expository preachers share a commitment to the historical-grammatical method of biblical interpretation. Both prioritize the original meaning of a passage within its immediate historical and literary context before actively engaging in synthesis with other passages of Scripture. For this reason, those who practice biblical theology will probably be drawn to the expository method of preaching, and those who preach expository sermons will have an affinity for biblical theology. Even so, because systematic theology is the branch of theology most familiar to the church, it is often tempting for teachers and preachers of the Bible to move immediately from exegesis to systematic theology, without giving due attention to the revelatory development of certain themes and concepts within a given biblical book, corpus of literature, testament, or the history of redemption. Although it might not always be the case that biblical theology serves as the intermediate stepping-stone between exegesis and systematic theology, Bible lesson teachers and preachers should consider the biblical-theological significance of a text as much as its relevance for systematic theology.

Finally, biblical theology invites Christians to participate in the drama of redemption. When unbelievers read Scripture, they probably view themselves simply as onlookers of ancient history or as students of an ancient philosophy. For slightly more invested readers, the Bible is a sourcebook of inspiration or a textbook on Christian ethics. But for Christians who read the Bible not only as the infallible story of God, but as God's inspired story of *us*, they should conceive of themselves as participants or actors within a cosmic drama of redemption that is playing out in the world in which they live.[4] We, too, are participants in the narrative that began with Adam, Abraham, Moses, David, Jesus, and Paul. We are the beneficiaries of their encounters with God and of the promises He established with them, but we are not thereby removed from the story, which has yet to reach its finale. Christ has not yet returned, the gospel must still be proclaimed, the Spirit must continue to transform lives, and the church must persevere as aliens and strangers in this world. Christians are actors in this story of salvation. We must therefore pay all the more attention to our script (the Bible) so we can more faithfully perform our roles in this divinely directed redemptive drama.

NOTES

1. See Craig G. Bartholomew, "Biblical Theology," in *Dictionary of Theological Interpretation of the Bible*, ed. K. J. Vanhoozer (Grand Rapids: Baker Academic, 2005), 84–90.

2. Biblical theology, however, is not a monolithic enterprise with only a single methodology employed by all its practitioners; indeed, nuances abound. Even so, the approach described here is followed by a majority of evangelical

theologians. For a taxonomy of approaches, see Edward W. Klink III and Darian R. Lockett, *Understanding Biblical Theology: A Comparison of Theory and Practice* (Grand Rapids: Zondervan Academic, 2012).

3. Here I am adapting and building on the definition of Patrick Schreiner, who says, "The kingdom is the King's power over the King's people in the King's place." *The Kingdom of God and the Glory of the Cross: Short Studies in Biblical Theology* (Wheaton, IL: Crossway, 2018), 18.

4. For the theater analogy, see Kevin J. Vanhoozer, *Faith Speaking Understanding: Performing the Drama of Doctrine* (Louisville: Westminster John Knox, 2014).

Understanding the Historical Background of the Bible

STEVEN H. SANCHEZ

Everyone is born into a context, and that context shapes how we understand the life of an individual. Formative experiences during childhood leave a lasting impression, which influences adult decisions. Understanding a person's context and background can provide insight into why they do what they do. The people whose lives are described in the Bible were, likewise, born into a context, one that in many ways is vastly different from ours. The authors of the Bible, in most cases, assume readers understand the basic historical context of the lives of the characters that grace its pages. The writers don't always take the time to explain why things are the way they are. Interpreting and teaching the Bible, therefore, requires some effort to understand the details of the historical background of this wonderful text.

The student of the Bible does not have to be a scholar to realize that life was different in ancient times. The cultures, customs, and implements of everyday life illustrate this plainly. Make no mistake, there are parts of the world where people experience life in a manner that seems unchanged over hundreds, even thousands of years; nevertheless, for most of us, times have changed since Moses met God in a bush that did not burn. It is important for students of the Bible to spend time understanding the historical and cultural background lest we make assumptions about the text based upon our modern experience.

JUSTIFICATION FOR THE STUDY

When confronted with a body of knowledge as vast as the historical and cultural background of the Bible, the task becomes immediately daunting. There is a lot to learn. Every year it seems a new volume appears on the market. Journals appear monthly with new discoveries, and changed opinions. What is the busy church leader to do? The first response is often to downplay the role Bible backgrounds play in interpreting the Bible. Are these details some sort of twenty-first-century gnosticism? Must people have secret, specialized knowledge to understand the Bible? The question is somewhat justified. Few people will take the time to gain any kind of comprehensive understanding of the ancient cultures. Fewer still will ever participate in archaeological excavations. For the Old Testament alone, one scholar suggests background studies should include "the entire Ancient Near East from roughly 10,000 BC down to the turn of the era, from Crete, to the Indus, from the Black Sea to Sudan and the Arabian Sea."[1] This is a challenging subject to learn and it can be tempting to dismiss it as unnecessary. Nevertheless, one does not need to be a professional archaeologist or an expert in Bible backgrounds to use available information to help people understand the context and message of a particular passage. There are many tools available that can help the pastor or teacher bring the word of Scripture to life in a fresh way.

BENEFITS OF THE STUDY

ACCURATE INTERPRETATION

To accurately interpret a text one should have some understanding of the context out of which it grows. For example, was Jesus being rude when He replied to His mother's request for Him to do something about the wine problem? "Woman, why do you involve me?" (John 2:40 NIV), He said to her. Or was He simply responding in the form of the day? Mary didn't seem offended. What are we to make of the Tower of Babel? What did its builders mean when they said, "Let's build ourselves a city, and a tower whose top will reach into heaven" (Gen. 11:4)? Was it a tower of the kind depicted in medieval paintings? Was it an ancient skyscraper? Or did it resemble a ziggurat, a stepped tower topped with a temple for a god? Answering these kinds of questions ensures that the reader interprets Scripture contextually, and therefore accurately. To presume that twenty-first-century readers can ignore background studies is to leave people at a disadvantage when it comes to interpretation. Not every text will require the same effort, but the Bible is a big book and there are many places where accuracy is improved by background studies.

INSIGHT AND CLARITY

Because ancient lives were different from our lives in many ways, background studies can clarify difficult texts by highlighting differences. For those who have become very familiar with the Bible, this study is helpful for reminding readers that the world of the Bible was quite different. We have a tendency, especially in the English-speaking world, to think that Bible times were simply a less-developed version of Western culture. This is not true, and a study of Bible backgrounds can help show just how different things were and as a result, force readers to engage the material with fresh eyes. As an example, consider that the temple in Jerusalem was the only place in the world where Jewish people could offer sacrifices for sin. Whereas the Christian can bow at any moment, confess, and find forgiveness, the Jewish believer was required to offer a sacrifice in a specific place (Deut. 12; John 4). Three times a year the faithful gathered in one specific place to worship. These would have been special times in a person's spiritual life! But for some the place was quite far, so the law of Moses included instructions to sell their sacrifices for money, and use the money to purchase a different animal at the distant place of worship (Deut. 14:25–26). This created a business opportunity for people to sell clean animals that would be needed for sacrifice at the temple. Sadly, it also provided an opportunity for abuse. Jesus called these vendors "robbers" and drove from the temple (Matt. 21:12–17). Their businesses were encroaching on the only place the faithful Gentile people could pray at the temple. Understanding the implications of a single point of sacrifice can be helpful for understanding why some events in the Old Testament and New Testament happened the way they did.

TO MINIMIZE DIFFERENCES

On the other hand, we must avoid the trap of believing that the world of the Bible is so different when compared to ours that it is not relevant. We must remember that people are people regardless of the time period. Clearly there are many, many similarities between then and now. People ate and drank, they bought and sold. They married and were given in marriage. They lived, died, and were buried. I recall participating in the archaeological excavations at Tel Shimron in 2019 and excavating a storage jar from the Middle Bronze Age (2100–1550 BC). As we removed the soil with hand picks and brushes it became clear that this jar had been used to bury the remains of a child who died in infancy! What must that have been like, to lovingly bury the lifeless body of a child? Are we so different from the ancients who cried out to their gods for deliverance from death? A sin nature resides in each of us. Young and old can behave foolishly. We still give in to sexual temptation. We are greedy and need to restrain our covetousness. Law is necessary to control behaviors that harm others now, just as they did then. Business owners are still tempted to exploit their workers, and workers are tempted to slack off while the boss is away. Studying historical backgrounds helps us see that we have the same drives and predilections as our forebears. As a result, the biblical wisdom, exhortations, rebukes, and counsel they received is still relevant for us! It prevents us from saying, "This doesn't apply to me," or "That writer lived so long ago, he doesn't understand."

To Defend the Trustworthiness of Scripture

Finally, this information can also have an apologetic use by establishing the reasonableness of the biblical setting so as to confirm its credibility. Some would suggest that to attempt to demonstrate the reliability of the Bible diminishes the need for faith. This does not have to be true. Faith will always be necessary to enjoy a relationship with God and to believe His Word. But nowhere does the Bible demand faith for things that can be demonstrated in the world. In fact, God designed the world so that physical evidence can create conditions for faith. Physically verifiable reality can be a catalyst for faith in that which is real but unverifiable.

When Israel gathered on the plains of Moab, Moses exhorted them to believe what God would do in the future, because, "The LORD your God, who is going before you, will fight for you, as he did for you in Egypt, before your very eyes, and in the wilderness. There you saw how the LORD your God carried you, as a father carries his son, all the way you went until you reached this place" (Deut. 1:30-31 NIV). They needed faith for the future, not the past! The past was knowable, and they were expected to learn from it. This would empower their faith in what God would do in the future.

No less than Jesus Himself said, "Do not believe me unless I do the works of my Father. But if I do them, even though you do not believe me, believe the works, that you may know and understand that the Father is in me, and I in the Father" (John 10:37–38 NIV; also 14:10–11). He argued that His works, which could be verified, were done so that people would believe the unverifiable things He was saying. In this same way, studying historical backgrounds should be done in a way that encourages faith. As basic doubts about the reliability of Scripture fall away with exposure to evidence about the Bible's historical background, a reader's faith in the many, many things that can never be physically verified can grow.

HISTORY AND CONTEXT

A broad study of Bible backgrounds must begin with a survey of the historical eras through which the storyline of the Bible takes place. Interpreters should consider the historical setting of each book. To do this we must place biblical events in chronological order and understand the time in which they took place. To do this we rely on the Bible as well as extrabiblical texts that provide details that help establish context. These texts are not inspired Scripture, but have value for setting the stage on which the events of the Bible took place. What follows is a historical survey of the broad contextual eras in which each book of the Bible took place.

THE HISTORICAL CONTEXT OF THE BIBLE

EARLIEST HISTORY (GENESIS 1–11)

Creation, the fall, the flood, and the construction of the Tower of Babel belong to what we might call the prehistory or earliest history of the Bible. This designation is appropriate for one reason: we have no written records from this time period. This is not to say the events of Genesis 1–11 did not happen, or that the accounts of Genesis are not historical. They did, and they are. We are simply acknowledging that we do not have written records from the time of Noah. Could Noah write? It would be difficult to build an ark of that size without the ability to write. The Bible, however, is the only source for some of the events recorded in Genesis. Although stories about floods are present in Mesopotamian accounts such as the Sumerian King List, Atrahasis, Eridu Genesis, and Enuma Elish, none of these ever mention Noah and his family. The Tower of Babel event is likewise not recorded anywhere other than in the Bible.

THE PATRIARCHAL ERA (GENESIS 12–50)

The stories of Abraham and his descendants occurred in the era known as the Middle Bronze Age (2100–1550 BC). During this time period, powerful cultures arose and expanded their reach in Mesopotamia, between the Tigris and Euphrates Rivers. These cultures developed writing systems, and as a result we have written documentation of their way of life, institutions, laws, and customs. These texts, recorded on clay tablets, reveal a sophisticated culture with a powerful temple administration at the center of a city-state system ruled by leaders who occasionally claimed divine status. Excavations at Ur, by Leonard Woolley in the early twentieth century, unearthed artifacts that illustrate wealth and sophistication.

The Bible suggests that Abraham, born ca. 2166 BC, was a Mesopotamian, either from the famous Ur mentioned above, in southern Mesopotamia, or perhaps another city of the same name in northern Mesopotamia. Clay tablets from the cities of Nuzi and Mari, although dated centuries later than the time of Abraham, may serve to illustrate the lives of the patriarchs. For example, cultural practices like long distance marriages, childbearing by surrogate, inheritance rights, etc., are documented.

Abraham moved his family from Mesopotamia to Canaan where he encountered fortified cities. Here the patriarchs also encountered the Canaanites, the inhabitants of the land who would prove to be a theological temptation to their descendants. Abraham's son Isaac (born 2066 BC; Gen. 21:5) lived in Beersheba, in the semiarid Negev region of Canaan. In the course of time Jacob (born 2006 BC; Gen. 25:26) moved his family to Egypt, the other end of the Fertile Crescent where his descendants lived for 400 years.

Egypt was a presence astride the Nile River long before Jacob arrived. The country was ruled by powerful kings, called pharaohs. Egypt's fortunes rose and fell and rose again in a series of phases known as periods as they were led by dynastic rulers. The Old Kingdom Period ca. 2686–2160 BC included the Third–Sixth Dynasties and was responsible for building the great pyramids of Giza. This kingdom fell into crisis during dynasties 9–11, the First Intermediate Period. Egypt reemerged in strength ca. 2055 BC in the Middle Kingdom led by dynasties 11–13. This was a time of cultural flourishing. During this period, Jacob and his twelve sons arrived in Egypt (1876 BC) where they remained first as guests, then as slaves for 400 years (Gen. 46). Egypt's power waned once more in a Second Intermediate Period during which the nation was ruled by competing dynasties 14–17.

THE EXODUS AND WANDERING (EXODUS, LEVITICUS, NUMBERS, AND DEUTERONOMY)

During the Late Bronze Age (1550–1200 BC) a powerful new ruler inaugurated the Eighteenth Dynasty in Egypt. This is the dynasty that included Pharaoh Tutankhamen. Egypt was part of a larger international diplomatic system and dominated the Eastern Mediterranean as never before. It was during this phase, when Egypt was at the height of its power, that the God of Israel rescued His people from bondage, entered into covenant with them at Mount Sinai, and led them through the wilderness to the border of Canaan in fulfillment of His promise to Abraham.

THE CONQUEST AND SETTLEMENT (JOSHUA, JUDGES, AND RUTH)

The stories of Joshua, the conquest of Canaan, and the accounts of the Judges also took place in during the Late Bronze Age. When they arrived in Canaan, Israel found the land inhabited by sophisticated and attractive civilizations, like the Philistines and Canaanites. Canaanite armies oppress the nation, but it was the attractiveness of Canaanite religion that was the greater problem. Documents from the city of Ugarit reveal a religious system whose goal was to ensure fertility of land, animal, and human. Focused on appeasing deities with names like Yam, Mot, Anat, and Baal, this religious system was completely antithetical to what God revealed to His people on Mount Sinai. But it was attractive, because it did not require moral change, but promised the same reward: security and prosperity.

Late Bronze Age civilizations in the ancient world collapsed around 1200 BC, perhaps as a result of earthquakes in the region, which caused a cascade of problems including displaced populations, famine, and war. In Canaan, when the dust settled, the major powers had retreated to their heartlands in Egypt and Mesopotamia, leaving room for smaller nations like Israel and her neighbors to vie for power in the land.

THE KINGDOM PERIOD (SAMUEL, KINGS, CHRONICLES, AND MANY OF THE PROPHETIC BOOKS)

It is in this period, the Iron Age (1200–586 BC), that Saul ruled as Israel's first king before being replaced by David the son of Jesse. Solomon replaced David, but upon his death the kingdom split into two independent nations, the kingdom of Judah and the kingdom of Israel. Because the larger, international empires were experiencing decline, the smaller nations that occupied Canaan and Transjordan were free to compete for regional hegemony. The frequent wars between Judah, Israel, Edom, Moab, Ammon, Aram, and Philistia described in the books of Samuel, Kings, and Chronicles illustrate the situation.

Israel abandoned God though He sent many prophets (Isaiah, Micah, Amos, Jeremiah, et al.) who urged them to repent (2 Kings 17:13). And in 722 BC, the Israelite capital city, Samaria, fell to the Assyrian Empire led by Shalmaneser V, who deported her citizens (2 Kings 17:6). As a result of God's commitment to David, Judah survived for over a century longer, but also endured invasion at the hands of the Assyrians. Eventually Judah was driven from their land in 58 BC by Nebuchadnezzar II, king of Babylon (2 Kings 25:8–9).

RETURN FROM EXILE (EZRA, NEHEMIAH, ESTHER, HAGGAI, ZECHARIAH, MALACHI)

In 539 BC, Cyrus the Great, king of a newly dominant Medo-Persian empire, conquered Babylon and inherited their territory, according to Ezra, Chronicles, and the Cyrus Cylinder (COS II, 314–15). He permitted nations who had been transplanted by the Babylonians to return to their homelands. In 538 BC, after seventy years in exile (counting from the first invasion of Nebuchadnezzar in 605 BC), many Judeans who survived the exile returned to their land under the leadership of Zerubbabel. Esther defended her people in Persia while Ezra, Nehemiah, and the prophets Haggai, Zechariah, and Malachi led the nation in a time of restoration and spiritual revival.

THE SECOND TEMPLE PERIOD (BETWEEN THE OT AND NT)

In 331 BC, the Greek and Macedonian forces of Alexander the Great defeated the armies of Persia led by Darius III. This victory had consequences for the Judeans, who lived in relative peace under the Persians, but Alexander did not trouble them. When Alexander died in 323 BC, his kingdom was divided between his generals. After a series of wars, the territory of Judea fell under the control of Ptolemy, who ruled from Egypt. His rival to the north, Antiochus, who ruled from Syria, coveted his territory. The dynasties they inaugurated, the Ptolemaic dynasty and the Seleucid dynasty fought a series of wars with Israel caught in the middle. Eventually the Seleucids gained control of the land, and when they did, they ruthlessly oppressed the Jews and sought to impose Hellenistic culture upon them by force (167 BC). The prophet Daniel prophesied about these events (Dan. 11).

The Jews rebelled at the imposition of Hellenistic culture, and under the leadership of the Maccabees, and their descendants called the Hasmoneans, established an independent kingdom for themselves in the land of their ancestors, Israel. They expanded the borders of the kingdom but the spiritual state of the nation declined. They may have been back in the land and out from under the thumb of the Gentiles, but they were not reaping the full benefit of God's promises.

THE RISE OF ROME (THE BOOKS OF THE NEW TESTAMENT)

Judean independence was short-lived because in the west a new power was ascendant: Rome. As the Roman Republic emerged victorious from the Punic Wars, they turned their eyes eastward to incorporate Greece, the Levant, and Egypt into their empire. In 40 BC, just a few years after the assassination of Julius Caesar, the Roman Senate became concerned about a Parthian invasion from the east, so they named Herod, son of Antipas, king of the Jews. Herod the Great was a lover of Greco-Roman culture. He worked hard to integrate his small kingdom into the larger Roman world. Although he ruled effectively (40–4 BC), his kingdom was divided among his heirs when he died. Herod Archaelus ruled Judea, Idumea, and Samaria poorly, and was replaced by a series of Roman employees, the most famous of which was Pontius Pilate (Matt. 2:13; 27:2). In the north, Herod's son Antipas had more success, and he ruled for over three decades. He had John the Baptist beheaded (Matt. 14:10), and Jesus Christ refused to speak with him before He was crucified (Luke 23:9). Religious life in Jewish society was influenced by religious authorities in the temple and synagogues. These groups, with the complicity of Roman authorities, persecuted Jesus, His disciples, and the early Christians in Israel, as did the emperor Nero in Rome.

Increasingly, the heavy hand of the empire offended Jewish sensibilities, and in AD 66 the nation revolted, plunging the region into war. Titus, son of the Roman emperor Vespasian, presided over the looting and destruction of the Jerusalem temple in AD 70. The gold and other riches from Jerusalem paid for the construction of the Colosseum in Rome, which opened a decade later. This Roman context forms the background of the early church and the New Testament.

GEOGRAPHY

In addition to the basic historical outline, preachers and teachers should become familiar with geography of the lands mentioned in the Bible. Consider that the text is full of geographic references that the authors assume we understand. If these references go unexplained, we are missing out on important details. While a trip to Israel is valuable, using a good Bible atlas can provide the necessary data. As an example, recall that Elijah, having defeated Jezebel's prophets of Baal and incurred the wrath of that wicked queen, fled from Jezreel to Beersheba and from there to Mount Sinai (1 Kings 19). A map, even the ones at the back of your Bible, reveals that Elijah traversed almost the length of the entire country to escape from Jezebel! Mount Carmel lies just south of the Jezreel Valley, while Beersheba lies in the extreme south. When John tells us that that Jesus "had to go through Samaria" we might be tempted to assume that He had to go that way because that's the way the road went (John 4:4). But an atlas will show that Jews in Jesus' day regularly avoided Samaria. Jesus went there because He had a divine appointment! Without an understanding of the location of these places, their names become just words on a page. Understanding geography is like understanding the playing board of the biblical world. Key to understanding Israel's position is realizing that it is a land in the middle: in the middle of continents, travel networks, clashing climates, and competing theologies.

A BRIDGE TO EVERYWHERE

Israel is a bridge to everywhere in the ancient world for a number of reasons. First, it is a land between continents. This strip of land, about the size of New Jersey, occupies a strategic place as part of the land bridge between Africa, Asia, and Europe. As a result, the empires of the ancient world always had their eye on it as a corridor for travel between population centers, or as a buffer zone for protection.

CLASHING CLIMATES

Israel was a land between the dueling weather patterns generated by the warm moist air of the Mediterranean Sea and the hot dry air of the Arabian Desert. These had an impact on the climate such that the year was broken into a dry season and a rainy season. With few large rivers in the land, inhabitants of Israel were forced to depend on the weather for the water they needed. Since no one can control the weather, Israel was forced to trust God, who promised rain at the right time as a blessing for obedience, and drought as a punishment for disobedience (Deut. 28:12, 23–24). Part of the attraction of the indigenous religions was that their gods could be manipulated to provide rain without the necessary moral component that Israel's God demanded.

TRAVEL NETWORKS

Another part of this land's importance lay in the fact that important roads passed through it. Along the coast ran the major international trade route through the country, sometimes called the Great Trunk Road or the International Coastal Highway, even the *via maris*. On this road traveled the chariots of Pharaoh as well as the legions of Rome. A parallel road, the King's Highway, ran east of the Jordan River (Num. 20:17, 22). Down the middle of the country, on top of the central ridge, lay another local road, which accessed the heartland of the country. These roads were connected to each other and the rest of the ancient Near East in a network that allowed people, goods, and information to spread from east to west and vice versa. But the trade network was not limited to overland travel. Although Israel was not blessed with deep harbors, her Phoenician neighbors to the north had them. Israel's proximity to this seafaring nation provided access to the entire Mediterranean basin (Ezek. 27). When Herod the Great became king, he built Caesarea Maritima with its artificial harbor to connect his nation to the Roman world through trade.

COMPETING THEOLOGIES

Finally, Israel was a land between theologies. The ancient world, not unlike today, was polytheistic. People believed in more than one god. Each nation had its own god or gods, and the general belief was that each god was a national deity. When two nations fought a battle, it was believed to be a battle between their gods. If I defeat you, it was assumed that my god defeated your god (1 Sam. 5:2). This of course is the key difference between Israelite theology and that of any other nation in the ancient world. The Jews believed there was only one God, and His name is Yahweh.

CULTURAL PRACTICES

Culture can be defined as the unique collection of behaviors and practices that describe life in a particular place. With this in mind, we may consider the various ways people cook and consume food. Some use forks, others chopsticks, still others clean fingers. When we approach the various people described in the Bible we should take note of the different ways their cultures accomplish important aspects of life. What was their homeland? Where did they come from? How was their nation organized? Did they have laws? Whom did they worship? How did they worship? What kind of dwellings did they live in? Was there a wide disparity between rich and poor? What did they plant? What did they eat? What were they forbidden from eating? What did they wear? How did they get around? What goods did they buy and sell?

Notice that these are the very same things that are important to people today! Take weddings as an example. Cultures vary widely on wedding practices. Issues of dowery and family involvement are all culturally normed behaviors. Understanding how these activities were carried out in the various biblical contexts can help us interpret more accurately. Clearly Jesus' parable about the wedding feast invokes a different culture than persists in many cultures today (Luke 14:8).

MATERIAL CULTURE

Another source of helpful information are the things ancient societies have left behind. Material culture refers to the objects a civilization leaves behind. These artifacts tell a story about the people who created, used, and disposed of them.

But how do these artifacts illumine the text? The implements of daily life are mentioned often in the Bible. Israel is told not to have separate weights in their bag (Deut. 25:13). David played a lyre (1 Sam. 16:23). Joshua circumcised the men of Israel with flint knives (Josh. 5:3). A group of young prophets cooked their food in a pot (2 Kings 4:40). A woman touched the hem of Jesus' clothing (Luke 8:44). Peter fished with nets (John 21:6). Eutychus fell from a third-story window (Acts 20:9)! These verses are a small fraction of the places where physical things are mentioned in the Bible. These artifacts can range from tiny things like beads, jewelry, coins, figurines and common eating utensils, to dining ware, luxurious ivory game boards, storage jars, and altars, to large architectural features like building foundations, city gates, and wall systems. The world's museums are full of artifacts that expose life in the ancient world and they are worth a visit. These details can serve to illustrate, highlight, and enrich our understanding and presentation of the Scriptures.

Archaeologists uncover these remains, ideally in a formal excavation, and interpret them to unpack the history of the people who used them. Since we don't have an ancient person standing next to us, we must make an educated guess about an object's purpose. If an archaeologist comes upon a cooking installation, he can reasonably infer that the inhabitants of this home cooked meals there. Flint knives suggest that someone in that place was cutting things. A large storage jar filled with decomposed grain can reveal the local diet.

SOME WORDS OF CAUTION

KEEP THE MAIN THING THE MAIN THING

Teachers of the Bible can at times leave their hearers with the impression that the only way to understand the Scriptures fully is to have access to the secret knowledge of Bible backgrounds. This must be avoided. Using Bible backgrounds should clarify the meaning of a text and leave the audience with a fuller appreciation of what it says. Like a well-dressed stage, or a finely appointed table, background studies should highlight the main point of the text in question, not detract from it. It is true that many simply do not realize that the stories of the Bible happened in a historical context, but it is the job of the teacher to introduce that context in a way that invites greater study. Jesus used a coin to teach about the one who has ultimate ownership of our allegiance (Matt. 22:19–21). It would be a distraction to include so much background about coins in the Roman world that people are distracted from His main teaching point.

DISTINGUISH BETWEEN THE OLD TESTAMENT AND NEW TESTAMENT

The time covered by the events described in the Bible is very long. Life in Israel changed significantly between the time Joshua invaded the land and when Jesus stood before Caiaphas. It is important to avoid oversimplifying the historical context by assuming everyone in the Bible did things the same way at the same time. For example, we would not use coins as an illustration of Old Testament worshipers making donations to Solomon's temple in Jerusalem since coinage was not widely in use until around the fifth or sixth century BC. (We find a couple of references to coins later; Neh. 10:32; Ezra 2:69.)

WE DON'T HAVE EVERYTHING WE WANT

The field of background studies relies on an incomplete body of evidence. We simply do not have data for every event, or historical figure, or custom described in the Bible. We must not leave our hearers with the impression that we know everything, or that everything is confirmed by evidence. As one Jehovah's Witness suggested to me with a wave of a hand, when I asked if the Bible could be trusted, "Yes, with archaeology, it's all confirmed." This is not true, and allowing people to believe this sets them up for a rude awakening when they discover that we have little to no direct evidence of Solomon's temple in Jerusalem, or the many miracles of Jesus. This is an unrealistic expectation.

Instead, we must understand, and teach, that we are building a plausible case for what the Bible describes. We may not have a tablet with Abraham's name on it, but the evidence we do have suggests that his world, as described in the Bible, is rooted in reality. It's not a fairy tale. Sometimes we have to wait for scholarship to sort through the data before the verdict is in. It takes patience. Consider the case of the argument that since camels were not domesticated until the first millennium BC, the Bible must be inaccurate when it mentions that Abraham had herds of cattle among his riches. This question has provoked people for decades but as time goes on and new data is discovered opinions change.[2] This is a field of study with a growing body of knowledge. Archaeology in particular is an ever expanding science. Year after year, teams of archaeologists uncover new artifacts that shed light on life in ancient Israel.

THIS IS A FIELD THAT CHANGES

Try to consult the latest resources. Publishing quality research is costly, and as a result encyclopedias and other texts tend to remain in use for a long time—sometimes too long; they can be out of date. Be wary of pounding the pulpit on a matter of cultural background if your source is 100 years old. Be skeptical about free tools as often they are significantly out of date. Take extra time to search for the latest conclusion about a subject rather than just quoting a commentary, which, no matter how theologically accurate, may be in error when it comes to history and cultural backgrounds. The latest resources will include the latest interpretations of the data.

DEALING WITH CONTRADICTORY EVIDENCE

A discussion about backgrounds would be incomplete if we didn't address the headlines that appear from time to time, suggesting that recent evidence does not support the historicity of the Bible. It is true that we do not have physical evidence for every single event that the Bible describes. In some cases, it would be unrealistic for us to expect to have anything. Peter, Jesus' disciple, was one individual in the entire Roman world. It is unlikely that we will ever find a title deed to his home in Capernaum with his name on it. This should not be a cause for significant distress; we know we don't have all the evidence we want. But this is not the same thing as finding positive evidence that contradicts the Bible.

When evidence does surface that causes us to question our understanding of biblical history, we must be humble. The Bible is a text that must be interpreted. Perhaps we have interpreted it wrongly. Likewise, artifacts must be interpreted. It is just as possible that our interpretation of those items is incorrect. Sometimes the headlines scream error when a close reading of the data suggests that presuppositional bias against the Bible is at work. In addition, we must recognize we continue to learn as new things are discovered. A few years ago new DNA evidence surfaced that suggested that the Israelites did not kill all of the Canaanite populations as God commanded them to. Headlines implied the Bible got the story wrong. But a close reading of Joshua and Judges reveals that these texts acknowledge that Israelites did not fully obey the command to destroy the inhabitants of the land. This is one of the reasons Israel fell away from their God. Based on what the text says, we should expect to find Canaanite DNA in modern populations who descend from those people groups. If you don't read past the headline, it's easy to be misled. When you encounter the suggestion that some detail disproves the Bible, be careful to understand just what claim is being made, and the evidence the claim is based on. Many a skeptic has doubted the historical accuracy of the Bible, only to be found incorrect in time.

In the end, studying the background of the Bible should enhance our understanding of Scripture, not distract from it. Our goal is to explain the details of God's Word against the backdrop of its original audience. Understanding this context can help clarify and illuminate our understanding by giving us a window into a different world.

RESOURCES

BIBLES AND COMMENTARIES

These present data in the context of the passages they discuss. Although they are designed to coordinate with a particular version of the Bible, they are valuable even if you prefer a different version.

NIV Cultural Backgrounds Study Bible. Grand Rapids: Zondervan, 2016.
ESV Archaeology Study Bible. Wheaton, IL: Crossway, 2018.
NIV Archaeological Study Bible: An Illustrated Walk through Biblical History and Culture. Grand Rapids: Zondervan, 2006.
The IVP Bible Background Commentary (2 vols.). Downers Grove, IL: IVP Academic (2000 and 2014).
Lexham Geographic Commentaries (6 vols.). Bellingham, WA: Lexham Press, 2019.

ATLASES

Every library should include a Bible atlas. Simply put, the maps in the back of the average Bible are not detailed enough for serious study. An atlas is the kind of tool that explains events with careful attention given to the role of geography and topography.

The New Moody Atlas of the Bible by Barry Beitzel. Chicago: Moody Publishers, 2009. Strikes balance between text and maps. Theologically oriented.

Crossway ESV Bible Atlas by John D. Currid and David P. Barrett. Wheaton, IL: Crossway, 2010. Designed to work with the ESV translation but good even if you prefer another version.

The Carta Bible Atlas (5th ed.) by Yohanan Aharoni, Michael Avi-Yonah, et al. Jerusalem: Carta Jerusalem, 2011. Heavy on maps and lighter on text. Comprehensively presented, generally avoids theological discussion.

The Sacred Bridge. Jerusalem: Carta Jerusalem, 2015. Comprehensive and technical. Full of primary source material. If you like details, this is the atlas for you.

Zondervan Atlas of the Bible, rev. ed. by Carl G. Rasmussen. Grand Rapids: Zondervan, 2010.

Ultimate Bible Atlas: revised & expanded. Nashville: Holman Bible Publishers, 2021.

HISTORIES

These are comprehensive presentations of the history of Israel in the context of the ancient world. They will explain how life in Israel was impacted by events in the Near East and Greco-Roman world.

Bible Dictionaries/Encyclopedias—These often multivolume tools are useful places to get a broad understanding of a topic. It's important to note that publishers sometimes reprint older editions without always updating the scholarship.

Ben Witherington III. *New Testament History.* Grand Rapids: Baker Academic, 2003.

Chad Brand, ed. *Holman Illustrated Bible Dictionary* (1 vol.). Nashville: Broadman and Holman, 2015. A well-illustrated Bible dictionary written with a high view of Scripture.

David Noel Freeman, ed. *Anchor Bible Dictionary* (6 vols.), New York: Doubleday, 1992. A comprehensive collection of articles on all things related to the Bible. Written from a critical perspective. Particularly useful in areas of archaeology, customs, and culture. Less trustworthy in theology or interpretation. Articles include bibliographies. Out of date in some areas, but still very valuable.

David Noel Freeman, ed. *Eerdmans Dictionary of the Bible* (1 vol.). Grand Rapids: Eerdmans, 2000. A one-volume Bible dictionary similar to the *Anchor Bible Dictionary.*

Kenneth Kitchen. *On the Reliability of the Old Testament.* Grand Rapids: Eerdmans, 2006.

Iain Provan, V. Philips Long, and Temper Longman III. *A Biblical History of Israel,* 2nd ed. Louisville: Westminster John Knox, 2015.

Journals/Magazines

The latest research shows up here. Well-illustrated with pictures and diagrams. Subscriptions required, but theological libraries usually have back issues.

Biblical Archaeology Review—The most popular resources on the subject for a semi-technical audience. It is not conservative, nor is it theologically oriented.

Biblical Illustrator—An excellent resource. Writers are conservative and hold a high view of Scripture. Articles are very well illustrated.

Websites

https://www.bibleplaces.com/blog/
https://holylandphotos.org

NOTES

1. K. A. Kitchen, *On the Reliability of the Old Testament* (Grand Rapids: Eerdmans, 2006), 498.
2. Mark W. Chavalas, "Biblical Views: Did Abraham Ride a Camel?" *Biblical Archaeology Review* 44:6 (2018): 52, 64–65.

Understanding the Basic Doctrine of God

MARCUS PETER JOHNSON

Theology is dedicated to knowledge of God, and with delight in God. That makes theological study unlike any other kind of knowledge, because knowing God is unlike any other kind of knowing. To know God is the highest possible human aspiration and blessing, the very pinnacle of human apprehension of truth. To know God is the most basic and essential form of human knowledge because God is the source and ground of all true knowledge. It is for this reason that theology has historically been referred to as the *Regina scientiarum*—"the queen of the sciences." All other forms of knowledge derive their basic foundations from the reality of God, who brought everything and everyone into existence by the sheer miracle of His loving and almighty will. When we know God, we possess the very best and highest form of knowledge because God is the foundation for all true understanding and wisdom.

KNOWING AND LOVING GOD

Theological study is also unlike other areas of study because in theology we attempt to know something (Someone) who transcends our intellectual abilities. Unlike almost every other kind of study, our study of God cannot be manufactured from within ourselves. Our knowledge of God is something that must be *revealed* rather than discovered. A basic principle of the knowledge of God must be emphasized here: Only God knows God and, therefore, only God can make Himself known (1 Cor. 2). God is the author and Lord of His revelation of Himself. We do not determine or define the nature and being of God. He does. We come to know who God is only because God reveals and defines Himself. The study of God, therefore, involves not so much the self-generated accumulation of human wisdom, but rather patient and faithful listening to God's revelation of Himself through Holy Scripture.

The study of the nature of God is also unique because it involves a kind of knowledge that, while it certainly concerns the intellect, is in reality grounded in an experience of God that engages the heart, mind, and soul. God is a personal being, and there is no other way to truly know Him than to experience Him as the living God that He is. Many other kinds of knowledge may be described as principally or essentially intellectual—but not knowledge of God. Theological knowledge is concerned with a God who makes Himself personally known, heard, and experienced in the depths of our being. There is, quite simply, no other way to truly know God than to know Him as the fullest meaning of our lives. It is no exaggeration to say that knowledge of God is the highest and best kind of knowledge available to human beings. J. I. Packer has put this truth wonderfully:

> What were we made for? To know God. What aim should we set ourselves in life? To know God. What is the "eternal life" that Jesus gives? Knowledge of God. . . . What is the best thing in life, bringing more joy, delight and contentment than anything else? Knowledge of God. . . . What, of all the states God ever sees man in, gives God most pleasure? Knowledge of himself.[1]

Is it really true that knowledge of God is what we were made for? Is it really true that knowledge of God *is* the eternal life that Jesus gives? It all sounds a bit too overstated until we listen to the words of Jesus Himself, when He prayerfully declares to His Father in the presence of His disciples, "This is eternal life, that they may know You, the only true God, and Jesus Christ whom You have sent" (John 17:3). Knowledge of God, according to the Lord Jesus Himself, is what eternal life consists of. If there were ever a reason to emphasize how important our doctrine of God is, this is certainly it. What we believe and confess about God has everything to do with our eternal existence.

To know God is to do far more than to merely entertain Him as an object of our mental reflection. To know God is to love and fear Him. To know God is to listen to Him and follow Him. To know God is to experience Him and delight in Him with all our God-given faculties. And, let us stress this point: to know God is to believe in Him as He has actually revealed Himself. Every true and authentic Christian doctrine of God rests on His revelation of Himself in the Holy Scriptures of the Old and New Testaments. It is there, in the witness of prophets and apostles, that God has made Himself known through Jesus Christ, through the inspiration of the Holy Spirit. Apart from this utterly unique and singular revelation, we have no confidence that we can know God. Conversely, through Jesus Christ, and by the inspiration of the Holy Spirit working through the Bible, we can have perfect confidence that knowledge of the Father (eternal life) is most certainly ours.

So, who is God? That question is the most important of all human questions. How we answer that question is crucial. Christians at all times and all places have insisted that God can only truly be known as He speaks for Himself. Here we must state clearly a basic theological truth: God is defined by Jesus Christ as He is revealed in the Bible. Therefore, any supposed knowledge of God that contradicts the revelation of His Son contained in His Holy Word is counterfeit. All true and authentic knowledge of God is governed and given by His Word.

In obedience to the Word of God, Christians of whatever denomination and tradition have always gladly and resolutely affirmed that the most important thing we confess about the nature of God is that God is one God: Father, Son, and Holy Spirit. This most glorious truth is enshrined and professed in the two most basic and significant expressions of Christian theology: the Apostles' Creed and the Nicene Creed. Together they bear witness to the faith held once and for all by the saints, from the very earliest days of the church's existence. In glad and joyful obedience to the Holy Bible, Christians have asserted the following unassailable realities about the nature of God.

"WE BELIEVE IN ONE GOD, THE FATHER ALMIGHTY"

The belief that God is "one God" is a testament to the repeated witness of the Bible: "Hear, Israel! The LORD is our God, the LORD is one!" (Deut. 6:4; Mark 12:29). To say that God is one is to say that God is perfect as He is, needing no addition to His glorious being to be exactly who only God can be. Pagan religions typically confess a multitude of gods, in the hopes that the worship of many gods is superior to the worship of one god; a multiplication of gods was thought to make human existence and worship more secure. On the contrary, and from the very beginning of creation, God declares that He alone is the subject of our worship: "You shall have no other gods before Me" (Ex. 20:3). This is a source of great courage and comfort to His people, then and now (1 Cor. 8:5–6). God is one, and so He needs no other existence of any kind to be exactly who He always has been, is now, and forever will be.

As a way of elaborating on the wonderful reality that God is one, Christians have always asserted that God is the Father Almighty. In other words, we do not believe in a generalized and abstract deity that can exist apart from being a heavenly Father. The God we confess as the one true God cannot be other than the Father that He is (Eph. 4:6). We are taught to address God as Father (Matt. 6:9) and to know that, from beginning to end, He is the Lord Almighty: "'I am the Alpha and Omega,' says the Lord God, 'who is and who was and who is to come, the Almighty'" (Rev. 1:8). God is the Father because He is almighty, and God is almighty because He is the Father.

The most important reason that Christians confess that God is Father is because He has always been a Father to His eternally begotten Son, who is the Word and Son of God. God has existed in eternal relation to the Son and Word of God from before time ever began: "In the beginning was the Word, and the Word was with God, and the Word was God. He was in the beginning with God" (John 1:1–2). God is our Father because He has never been other than a Father in His everlasting existence with the Son. God has not always been Creator—after all, He existed before He created the heavens and the earth—but He has forever been a Father to His eternal Son. It is the Father's eternal love for His eternal Son that determines God's being, and it also ensures that God can be, and is, our heavenly and almighty Father. If God did not eternally have a Son, then He could not eternally be the one God and Father in whom we believe.

Thus, when we confess that God is one, and that God is the Father Almighty, we are confessing a fundamental truth of the gospel: that the grace and peace of God—His almighty will to love and save us—is determined by His nature as Father to our Lord Jesus, as the writers often affirmed at the beginning of their epistles. The Bible undeniably, consistently, and repeatedly insists that God is none other, and can be none other, than the Father of His Son and our Savior, Jesus Christ. That is why all Christians confess with unbridled conviction and joy that "we believe in one God, the Father Almighty."

"WE BELIEVE IN ONE LORD, JESUS CHRIST"

The touchstone of all authentic Christian thought regarding the nature and being of God—the fundamental and essential basis for all true knowledge of God—is our belief that Jesus of Nazareth is God the Son incarnate.[2] When we confess that Jesus is the "Lord," we are confessing that He is the Lord God Almighty, the second person of the Holy Trinity. Jesus Christ is God Himself (John 8:58; 20:28), in whom "the fullness of Deity dwells in bodily form" (Col. 2:9). He is God the Savior (Titus 2:13), the one who is co-creator of heaven and earth (John 1:3; Col. 1:16). Jesus is the very Word of God, and is God as that Word (John 1:1). The Bible is crystal clear regarding the full deity of Jesus Christ: He sits on the very throne of God

(Matt. 19:28); He has the authority to forgive sins (Luke 5:20–21); all authority in heaven and earth belongs to Him (Matt. 28:18). Indeed, there is no other name except the name of Christ by which people might be saved, a prerogative that belongs entirely to God (Acts 4:12).

Jesus Christ is God, and He is fully God. He is perfectly, unreservedly, and unequivocally God. This biblical affirmation is the foundation for our belief that when we come to know Jesus in His Word, it is exactly and precisely God whom we come to know. Therefore, when we believe in Christ, it is God that we believe in. When we know the love of Christ, it is the very love of God Himself that we know. When we know the forgiveness of our sins through Christ, it is none other than the forgiveness of God that we know. When we receive the righteousness of Christ, it is none other than the very righteousness of God that is ours. When we have life in Christ, it is none other than the life of God Himself (1 John 5:20). In short, to know Christ is what it means to know God: "The one who has seen Me has seen the Father" (John 14:9).

Against a host of those who, in the history of the church's existence, sought to either deny or downplay the reality or significance of the full deity of our Lord and Savior, Jesus Christ, the early church stood in faithfulness with the Holy Scriptures by resolutely affirming that Jesus is God. The Nicene Creed includes a thunderous affirmation of authentic Christian faith when it says of our one Lord Jesus that He is "God from God, Light from Light, true God from true God, begotten, not made, of one Being with the Father, through whom all things were made." This sentence was calculated to repudiate and reject any reservations about the full deity of Christ, then and now. None of this could be said of Jesus if He were not fully who God is. The most important of these affirmations is that Jesus the Lord is "of one Being with the Father." This is perhaps the most important theological statement of the church since the time of the apostles. For what it affirms is that the essence of Jesus Christ is identical (Gk. *homoousion*: "of the same substance") with the essence of God the Father. In other words, Jesus is as perfectly God as God the Father is perfectly God. As Jesus puts it straightforwardly, "I and the Father are one" (John 10:30). When we declare our belief in "One Lord Jesus Christ," we are declaring that Jesus is the Lord God Almighty. Jesus Christ, to be precise, is the Son of God and not the Father, but He is every bit God as His Father is. Jesus is the Son of God, to be sure, but to be exact, we say that Jesus is God the Son.

"WE BELIEVE IN THE HOLY SPIRIT, THE LORD, THE GIVER OF LIFE, WHO PROCEEDS FROM THE FATHER AND THE SON. WITH THE FATHER AND THE SON HE IS WORSHIPED AND GLORIFIED."

Together with the Father and Son, all Christians confess and believe that the Holy Spirit—the third person of the Holy Trinity—is also Lord and God. The Holy Spirit is perfectly and fully God, and He is so because He exists in perfect communion with the Father and the Son. The Spirit is not the Father, and the Spirit is not the Son, but the Spirit is fully God. How do we know that the Spirit is fully God? First, the Spirit is continually the giver of life in Holy Scripture, which life God alone can give. He is present as life-giver at the point of creation (Gen. 1:2; 2:7). He is the One who gives life to Jesus of Nazareth in the womb of Mary (Luke 1:35). The Spirit gives believers new and eternal life in Jesus (John 3:5), and the Spirit raises Jesus from the grave (Rom. 8:11). Only God can do what the Holy Spirit does.

Second, the Nicene Creed indicates that the Holy Spirit proceeds from the Father and the Son. This means that the Spirit is so intimately related to God the Father and God the Son that God could not be who He is without the existence of the Holy Spirit. All the works of the Father and the Son depend entirely on the Spirit for their effectiveness. Believers are made one with Christ by the Spirit (Rom. 8:8–10), believers are only able to know God through the Spirit (1 Cor. 2:12), and believers are empowered to bear witness to Christ through the Spirit (Acts 1:8). The Holy Spirit, who is the presence of God in our midst, enables us to receive and know the gospel in perfect accordance with who God is in Christ (John 14:26; 15:26). Without the Holy Spirit, who is God, we could not know God or benefit in any way from who God truly and perfectly is. That is why to lie to the Spirit is the very same thing as to lie to God Himself (Acts 5:3–4).

Finally, all Christians believe that the Spirit is worshiped and glorified along with the Father and the Son. This is a completely idolatrous statement unless the Holy Spirit is truly and fully God, for God *alone* is the recipient of worship. Throughout the Bible, the threefold and holy name of God is the proper object of worship (Isa. 6:3; Rev. 4:8). God is thrice-holy and worthy of worship precisely and only because He exists as the holy Father, Son, and Spirit: Holy, holy, holy! If the Spirit were not the object of Christian worship and glorification, it would be entirely inconceivable that the Spirit would be included as the object of our baptism: "Go, therefore, and make disciples of all the nations, baptizing them in the name of the Father and the Son and the Holy Spirit" (Matt. 28:19). It would be just as inconceivable, and undesirable, that Christian prayer be addressed to the Holy Spirit if the Spirit were not God. Prayer is addressed to God alone. And yet, that is exactly how the apostle Paul directs our prayer to God in 2 Corinthians 13:14:

"The grace of the Lord Jesus Christ, and the love of God, and the fellowship of the Holy Spirit, be with you all." We pray, like Paul, in the fellowship of the Holy Spirit, because it is to God that we pray. When we believe in the Holy Spirit, "the Lord, the Giver of Life," we believe that the Holy Spirit is the Lord God Himself.

The most fundamental reality of God, the most basic aspect of His being and nature, is that He is one God in three persons. Christians do not confess the unity of God in spite of the fact that He is three persons. Rather, we confess that God is a perfect unity because He is three perfectly unified persons. The perfect communion of the Father, Son, and Holy Spirit is the precise occasion for God's unity. In other words, God is one because He exists as an everlasting union of the three eternal persons of the Godhead. The full deity of the persons of the Trinity are not a "problem" for our doctrine of the one God. Quite the contrary. The fact that each of the three persons of the Trinity are fully God is the very reason why we say that God is One. The everlasting fellowship and love among the Father, Son, and Spirit is the basis for our joyful belief in the only God there is, and the only God that could ever be. We believe in one God: the Father, the Son, and the Holy Spirit.

THE PERFECTIONS OF GOD

That God is a Holy Trinity of persons is the most wonderful and astounding aspect of His existence; it defines and determines what it means for God to be God. But that does not exhaust what we are able to say about God. Throughout the Holy Scriptures, God reveals a great deal about what it means for Him to be the triune God that He is. We shall refer to these aspects of His being as His "perfections." We do so because whoever God is, and whatever He does, He is and does perfectly. The astonishing number of ways that God refers to His perfect triune character are too many for us to number exhaustively. It is no exaggeration to say that our praise of God's nature is the subject of our eternal consideration and delight. Nevertheless, given our space constraints, we are right and confident to say at least the following about the perfections of God as we find them revealed though His Word.

1. God is **love** (1 John 4:8). When Christians confess that God is love, we mean that love originates in God Himself, that He is the source and foundation of love. Thus, although it is true to say that God "loves," or that God is "loving," we mean much more than that. God is loving because He is the love behind all that we can possibly imagine by the word—He is the very definition of love. God's love did not come into existence with the creation of human beings; His love has eternally existed in the love given and received by the Father, in the Son, and through the Holy Spirit (John 17:24). It is that very love of God that is shed abroad in the creation

of the world through the Son and by the Spirit (John 3:16). It is also important to emphasize that the love of God is always and everywhere self-giving and life-giving (Rom. 5:8; Gal. 2:20; 1 John 4:10), contrary to many modern notions of love. God's love is so great that He is entirely willing to give His Son as a sacrifice for sinners. God's love is so great that it conquers sin and death forever.

2. God is **omnipotent**, which means that He is all-powerful and almighty. Affirmations of God's omnipotence appear repeatedly throughout Scripture, accentuating that His power is indeed infinite (Isa. 46:10; Dan. 4:35; Eph. 1:19). Omnipotence speaks of God's power to perform His purposes, which is to say, God is able to accomplish all His holy will perfectly. God's purposes—and His power to accomplish them—are determined by His character, which His purposes and power cannot contradict. For instance, God cannot lie, or do evil (Titus 1:2; Heb. 6:18); God cannot be unfaithful, or deny Himself in any way (2 Tim. 2:13). God is perfectly powerful to carry out all that He wills, and He wills to conform all things in heaven and earth to His loving purposes. There is no one or nothing more powerful than God.

3. God is entirely **self-existent**, which means that God is non-created and noncontingent. God is not dependent for His existence on anyone or anything apart from Himself (Ex. 3:14; Job 41:11; Acts 17:24–25). In this crucial way, God is totally and utterly unique. All other life is dependent, finite, and contingent. But not God. He exists in perfection from before time began. This means that we can be completely assured of His will for us in Christ Jesus, for He is reliant on nothing and no one to bring that will to completion. God is the only being who is entirely self-existent and entirely able to be who He is. Therefore, we can depend on Him fully.

4. God is **immutable**, which means that God is unchanging. God's ways and purposes, His truth and character, His nature and promises, never change (Ps. 33:11; Isa. 40:6–8; Mal. 3:6; James 1:17). By very definition, every creature has a beginning and an end, and is subject to numerous changes in between. God, however, is the Creator, not a creature. He is from everlasting to everlasting, the first and the last (Ps. 90:2; Isa. 48:12). God alone is immortal, and God alone is not subject to change (Ps. 102:26–27; 1 Tim. 6:16). God always has been, now is, and forever will be nothing or no one other than Himself. That is why we sing with Holy Scripture that "Jesus Christ is the same yesterday and today, and forever" (Heb. 13:8). Who God is for those of us in Christ will never change. God can be completely trusted to be perfectly who He says He is.

5. God is **omnipresent**, which means that God is present in His whole being in all times and all places (1 Kings 8:27; Ps. 139:8; Jer. 23:23–24; Amos 9:2). Therefore, we can be assured that we are never alone, abandoned, or forsaken. We are never beyond the reach of God's blessing and consolation, or His correction, because

God is not limited by time and space as we are. To say that God is omnipresent does not mean that He is equally present everywhere in the same way, as if we might conclude that God's presence at the seashore is the same as His presence in the gospel. God's omnipresence in Scripture declares to us that there is nothing that can keep Him from relating to us in the ways He has ordained. There is no time, no distance, and no space where we can escape the perfect love and judgment of God.

6. God is **holy**. God's holiness has to do with His utter incomparability and uniqueness, the majesty and singular purity that the triune God is in Himself; He is the thrice-holy God (Isa. 6:1–3; Rev. 4:8). God's holiness is that perfection of His being that makes Him entirely trustworthy to judge the truth and beauty of all things in heaven and on earth. His holiness, therefore, demands that He oppose all that is contrary to His work as Creator and Redeemer. Because God's holiness marks out His sheer incomparability, uniqueness, and purity, it is no wonder that humans are "undone," so to speak, in their encounter with Him in His holiness (Isa. 6:1–5; Luke 5:8). The beautiful and perfect holiness of God stands in opposition to the unholiness of sin and sinners, exposing sin as a contradiction of His nature. And yet in Christ God gives us the gift of holiness so that we may be ever more like Him (2 Cor. 3:17–18; Eph. 1:3–7). The holiness of God assures that sin and evil will never have the last word.

7. God is **beautiful**, which is to say that God is the sum and perfection of all desirable qualities. God is beautiful in the sense that He defines all beauty, and His beauty is the ultimate desire of the human heart. This is why the psalmist declares, "One thing I have asked from the LORD, that I shall seek: That I may dwell in the house of the LORD all the days of my life, to behold the beauty of the LORD " (Ps. 27:4). All human striving after beauty finds its place in the unmatched, unequaled, majestic beauty of the Lord God, whose beauty will sustain our hearts forever. Beauty belongs to the Lord.

8. God is **glorious**. In the Bible, the glory of God is related to His honor, excellence, supreme worth, fame, reputation, and radiance. The glory of God belongs to Him alone (Isa. 42:8), and it calls forth from His creation praise and awe. Humans praise the glory of God (1 Tim. 1:17), and so does the rest of creation: "The heavens tell of the glory of God" (Ps. 19:1). God displays His unsurpassable glory and brightness in all that He has made, but He chiefly makes known His glory in the revelation of His Son, Jesus Christ, who "is the radiance of His glory and the exact representation of His nature" (Heb. 1:3). Through Jesus Christ, Christians come to know the glory of God (John 1:14) and even come to share in that glory (John 17:22). The glory of God is so amazing that humans are sustained and enriched by glorifying God in all things: "Therefore, whether you eat or drink, or whatever you do, do all things for the glory of God" (1 Cor. 10:31).

9. God is **wrathful**. God's wrath is His perfectly holy and entirely loving action against anything and anyone that would seek to thwart His purposes in creation and redemption. God's wrath is not the opposite of His holiness and love, but that very holiness and love in action against sin. There is abundant scriptural witness to God's wrath against sin and sinners (Ex. 32:9–10; John 3:36; Rom. 1:18; 2:5; 5:9; Col. 3:6; Heb. 3:11). Although God's wrath against sin is often misunderstood and even caricatured, Christians are glad to confess that God is set against all that opposes His mercy, love, righteousness, and purity. And His wrath is what assures us that He will never let sin and evil prevail, that righteousness will finally and ultimately be victorious. The righteous wrath of God against all that is sinful is made known in our Lord Jesus (Rom. 1:18; 3:21), who as God suffers that wrath finally and fully, allowing peace and reconciliation between God and sinners forever through faith.

10. God is **omniscient**. God knows all things, from eternity past to eternity future (Isa. 46:9–10). "Great is our Lord and abundant in strength; His understanding is infinite" (Ps. 147:5). There is no knowledge hidden from God, for He searches and knows the hearts of all those He creates (Ps. 139:1–3; Heb. 4:13). God is the beginning and end of all true knowledge, the Alpha and Omega of all true wisdom and truth. God's omniscience is gloriously good news for all who truly know Him, for He knows us better than we know ourselves (Ps. 139; Matt. 10:30) and directs our paths according to His unsearchable knowledge. The knowledge of God is inexhaustible by humankind, and yet is truly revealed to us in His Son, who is Himself the wisdom of God incarnate (1 Cor. 1:30). It is Jesus who prompts us to declare: "Oh, the depth of the riches, both of the wisdom and knowledge of God! How unsearchable are His judgments and unfathomable His ways!" (Rom. 11:33).

To this list we might add many more perfections of God. For instance, God is perfectly wise (Dan. 2:20), perfectly just (Deut. 32:4), perfectly merciful (Rom. 9:15–16), perfectly faithful (2 Tim. 2:13), and perfectly good (Ps. 34:8). Suffice it to say that God is perfect in His being as Father, Son, and Spirit. All that He is, and all that He does, is entirely perfect.

THE NATURE OF GOD AND THE CHRISTIAN LIFE

It would be all too tempting, as we study the nature and being of God, to forget that when we speak of who God is, and what God is like, this has *everything* to do with how we live our lives as children of our heavenly Father. God does not reveal who He is so that we might merely think rightly about Him. Far from it! God reveals who He is to us for at least three very significant and enormously practical reasons. The first is that God has created us for everlasting fellowship with Him. God reveals

Himself for the purpose of bringing us to share in His very own life. To know God, in biblical terms, is the exact same thing as to experience intimacy with Him, and therefore to have eternal life (John 17:3). God reveals Himself for the express purpose of creating an everlasting relationship with us that has been broken through sin. That is why God sent His Son into the world, to reveal fully and finally what it means—and what it cost—for God to be our God and Savior now and forever. The whole purpose of our knowing God is that we may come to truly experience who He is. As we do so, we also come to experience who *we* are. To know God is to be forever transformed by God by participating in His life through Christ.

The second reason why God reveals Himself is so that we may come to praise Him and delight in Him forever and ever. The goal of knowing God is to begin to experience in our daily lives the purpose for which we exist. The Westminster Catechism captures this biblical truth so very well when it asks and answers one of the most important questions a human being can ponder: "What is the chief and highest end of man? Man's chief and highest end is to glorify God and fully to enjoy Him forever." What does it mean to glorify God? It means to ascribe to Him the full significance of His perfect nature as He has made Himself known in His Son and through His Holy Spirit, attested to by prophets and apostles in Holy Scripture. *Soli Deo Gloria!* To the glory of God alone! What does it mean, then, fully to enjoy God forever? It means to experience the love the Father has eternally lavished on His Son. The prayer Jesus addressed to His Father on our behalf says it all: "I have made Your name known to them, and will make it known, so that the love with which You loved Me may be in them, and I in them" (John 17:26). To put it all too simply, we were created to experience the eternal love the Father has for His Son. This is the chief and highest purpose of our lives, and God grants it to us freely in Jesus. Our mission in life is to enjoy this love now, and to enjoy this love everlastingly. To know God never means less than to experience the love of God.

The third reason God reveals Himself—in such a way that we have true and real communion with Him, and that we glorify and enjoy Him forever—is so that we might be like Him. From the very beginning of time, God created us in His image, to reflect and echo His nature and being in our lives (Gen. 1:26–28). This inestimable privilege, given alone to human beings, was distorted and defaced through the fall of humanity into sin. And yet, by the pure grace of God, He has restored that privilege to us through the giving of His Son, Jesus Christ, who was and is the perfect image of God, "the radiance of [God's] glory and the exact representation of His nature" (Heb. 1:3). Jesus is the "image of the invisible God" (Col. 1:15), and in Him "all the fullness of Deity dwells in bodily form" (Col. 2:9). Through Jesus Christ, and in Him, we are being restored to the image of God. Through the power of the Holy Spirit, we who are in Christ are being are "being transformed into the same image from glory to glory, just as from the Lord, the Spirit" (2 Cor. 3:18). This means that knowing God is inseparable from being like God. One of the greatest gifts that God gives to His people is the honor of being like Him. That is why God created us, and that is why He reveals Himself.

CONCLUSION

This chapter began with the assertion that theology—"the study of the nature of God"— is dedicated to knowing who God is and, thus, delighting evermore in Him. Theology takes its true place in the life of the Christian, and in the life of Christ's church, when it is fully alive to this truth. Saint Augustine, one of the most significant and influential of the early church fathers, expressed the truth of the Christian life (and theology!) so very well when he said that "our hearts are restless till they rest in Thee."[3] How very true. God created us for fellowship with Him, and we are impoverished and incomplete until we find the true meaning of our existence in Him. We must never forget that when we commit ourselves to understanding the nature of God, we are joyfully obeying the commandment of God Himself: "You shall love the Lord your God with all your heart, and with all your soul, and with all your strength, and with all your mind" (Luke 10:27; see Deut. 6:5). Theology requires that we pursue knowledge of God with our mind, to be sure. But it requires no less the engagement of our heart and soul. To know God is to love God, and to love God is to know God. "Amen, blessing, glory, wisdom, thanksgiving, honor, power, and might, belong to our God forever and ever. Amen" (Rev. 7:12).

NOTES

1. J. I. Packer, *Knowing God*, 20th-Anniversary Edition (Downers Grove, IL: InterVarsity, 1993), 33. For other valuable resources exploring the nature of God, see Michael Reeves, *Delighting in the Trinity: An Introduction to the Christian Faith* (Downers Grove, IL: IVP Academic, 2012) and Gerald Bray, *The Doctrine of God* (Downers Grove, IL: IVP Academic, 1993).

2. On this point, see John C. Clark and Marcus Peter Johnson, *The Incarnation of God: The Mystery of the Gospel as the Foundation of Evangelical Theology* (Wheaton, IL: Crossway, 2015).

3. Augustine, *The Confessions of Saint Augustine*, trans. F. J. Sheed, 2nd ed. (Indianapolis: Hackett Publishing, 2006), 3.

Understanding the Basic Doctrine of Humanity

ANDREW J. SCHMUTZER

INTRODUCTION

This study of humanity considers the Christian understanding of the human being. It prioritizes what Scripture says about humankind in their origin, nature, purpose, and redemption. Ultimately, a biblical view of being human directly connects to the relationship people have with the God who made them.

The study of humanity has seen some significant shift in trends in the last generation. It is always important to know where one stands in any era of study. For example, biblical theologians no longer speak of "the doctrine of man," as such phrases are unsuitably gender specific and even offensive in some circles. Nor is "anthropology" the best term for a doctrinal study (as traditionally used with soteriology in the doctrine of salvation), since it risks confusion with a more biblically rooted theology. The subdiscipline of *cultural* anthropology draws on wider fields of interest, if the Bible even enters that discussion at all.[1]

Most significantly, however, the popular study of humanity has shifted away from a focus on the individual to the community. What drives definitions now is the *where*-of-location, rather than the *what*-of-personhood. Throughout our study, we will touch on some implications of this new metric. What comprises the "self" may be the focus of the social sciences, but in present theological studies, the focus is on the *interrelatedness* of humanity. In truth, these disciplines can be complementary.

As an illustration of such shifts, Bibles traditionally translated the key phrase in Genesis, "in the image of God He created him" (Gen. 1:27b; NASB, ESV), but this is now commonly rendered "in the image of God he created them" (NLT, NIV). Since the next phrase reads "male and female He created them" (v. 27c), this shift in translation reflects neither a liberal nor conservative impulse, but rather an attempt to sidestep gender confusion (Hebrew: singular "him"), while also emphasizing another contemporary value—*inclusivity* (Hebrew: plural "them"). To accomplish this, we need to look more closely at the creation passages.

HUMANITY IN CREATION

GENESIS 1 AND 2 IN STEREO

Any biblical doctrine of humanity is deeply rooted in the texts of Genesis 1 and 2. These two texts complement each other, highlighting different perspectives and roles of both the Creator and humankind, the most significant creative work of God. It is a misstep to pit these two chapters against each other, whether in academic study or popular teaching. Observe the following complementary themes between these two chapters:

- whereas God is the transcendent sovereign and Creator in Genesis 1 ("Elohim"), He is the immanent craftsman and provider in covenant relationship in Genesis 2 ("YHWH-Elohim");

- whereas the scope of Genesis 1 is universal ("heaven and earth"), it is essentially a local "garden" sanctuary in Genesis 2;

- whereas Genesis 1 focuses on sacred time and "seasons," Genesis 2 focuses on the sacred space of "Eden";

- whereas the human being is the sexually differentiated "male and female" in Genesis 1, they are majestically paired as "man and woman" in Genesis 2;

- whereas God speaks in priestly blessing of fertility in Genesis 1, the man speaks in poetic celebration of marriage in Genesis 2;

- whereas humankind is the climax of created acts in Genesis 1, humankind forms the center of Genesis 2.

So prized is humankind in Genesis 1, their appearance is given the longest address (149 words) on day six of creation, the eighth and final creative act of God (Gen. 1:24–31). In fact, in 1:27, the important verb *bara'* ("create") is used three times in one verse to highlight human creation! Further, it is only after the creation of humankind that God then declares that creation is beyond just "good" (1:10), but "very good" (1:31). God created the world "good" and innocent—not complete and perfect.[2] This declaration is part of the broader speech that God uses. The need for humankind was built into creation itself.

THE ACT OF SPEECH

The role of *speech* in Genesis 1 and 2 gives us great insight into both God and humankind. When God speaks, it fully and immediately manifests something (Gen. 1:3, 6, 9, 11, etc.). The speech of God is the efficient work of God—creation is worded forth! God is uncontested. Whatever Elohim commands appears. The Creator's mighty acts also include His repeated *evaluations* ("God saw . . . good," vv. 10, 12, 18, 25, 31). More than aesthetics, this evaluation is heard when creation stands ready to support vibrant life. Notice that God also speaks by "naming" the life-support systems of days 1–3. Rather, we are informed of God's words, but we do not actually hear them at this point. However, God's most colorful speech is reserved for the creation of humankind.

Of God's eight creative acts, humankind receives the most unique attention (Gen. 1:26–28). This signal of newness comes particularly through a change in God's speech. From the repeated formula, "Let there be," one now hears the relationally personal, "Let Us make" (1:26). Only with the creation of humankind is God's intent announced beforehand. Distant words now give way to the dearest of speech. No part of creation is placed as close to God as humankind (see Ps. 8). This scene of creation is like a "screenshot" from a far older era. With respect to the plural "Us," the Trinity was not a concept that the Old Testament audience would have understood at this point in revelation (recall that the first commandment intentionally addresses the danger of "other gods"). Acknowledging progressive revelation, most Old Testament scholars argue a more organic explanation, namely, that this plural addresses the heavenly court surrounding God, which is a standard picture of king and royal court in the Old Testament (see 1 Kings 22:19–22; Job 1:6; 2:1).[3] Much like the scene of God's royal throne room in Isaiah's call ("Whom shall I send . . . who will go for Us," Isa. 6:8), it is actually God who does the sending, and here, the creating ("So God created man," Gen. 1:27a). Yet as the cosmic King, God often directs speech to His heavenly court (1:26; see 3:22; 11:7), more to officially reveal His divine will than to request aid (yet, see 1 Kings 22:19–22).

In fact, it is God's speech that envelopes this important scene of human creation

(Gen. 1: 26 and 28). If 1:26 informs, then 1:28 blesses. Humankind is the "terrestrial counterpart to God's heavenly entourage."[4] God's own experience of community now spills over into a new arena, "deepening and broadening the community of relationships that already exists in the divine realm."[5] As we shall see, relationship is true of earthly creatures because it is true of God. Those who are modeled after the divine are now to serve their king by modeling the divine to the world (Pss. 8:4–5; 115:16).

At a canonical level, God's speech awakens and fuels human worship. In fact, initially death is viewed as the great silencer of praise: "If I go down to the pit . . . Will the dust praise You?" (Ps. 30:9). Highlighted in the praise psalms, Genesis 1 is likely a world-making liturgy that invites God's people "to respond in regular litany, 'It is good . . . very good.'"[6] While we have seen the climax of creation in 1:31 ("very good"), we have yet to hear its stunning conclusion. Our observations of speech are not yet finished. So, we turn our attention to Genesis 2, a "second exposition" of creation that focuses on the covenant intimacy with humankind, now using "LORD God."

Notice how the LORD God steps into the milieu of human need: "It is not good for the man to be alone" (Gen. 2:18a). If creation was "perfect," how could God observe such a profound lack? Further, why "subdue" and "rule over" that which is already perfect (see Gen. 1:28)? Then we hear it—the man now speaks:

> "This one is finally bone from [*min*] my bone,
>   and flesh from [*min*] my flesh;
>   This one shall be called 'woman' [*'issah*]
>   for from [*min*] man [*'ish*] was this one taken." (2:23, author's translation)

This is Adam's jubilant poetry, and for good reason! He uses a pun on "man" and "woman" to highlight their organic connection. One could say that nothing exists as an "individual," defined in isolation. Otherness is not added to person-hood from the outside; it is part of the constitution of selfhood.[7] So the man (*'ish*) only speaks when there is another like him to speak with—the woman (*'issah*). Following the pattern: 1 → 2 → 1, marriage is pictured as a reunification of an orig-inal unity. Only a woman, "built" from his body, could be the complement Adam needs, and this remains the benchmark of intimacy and celebration—the man for the unique presence of the woman. Adam's response illustrates what we could call the "sacrament of surprise." Infidelity (emotional or physical) destroys this sacra-ment. In other words, Adam's joy shows the sacramentality of marriage, because his ecstatic poetry illustrates the joy of particularity. Positively, his joy highlights God's design for marriage; negatively, it also explains how infidelity operates in a world of faceless individuals. The significance of God's solution to Adam's isolation is significant (2:18b). The Hebrew term "helper" (*'ezer*) is used almost exclusively for God's aid to Israel in the Old Testament. Far from demeaning, this "suitable helper" does not indicate a difference of essence, status, or value.

In the New Testament, this is precisely the creation standard of "male and female" pairing that Jesus refers to, when He cites Gen. 1:27 with 2:24, as foundational to the original blessed plan of God. In fact, when Jesus passed over the divorce laws of Moses in Deuteronomy for the creation account of Genesis, He placed the Creator's ideal will above God's concessionary will in order to curb the pattern of domestic abuses among Israel's leaders (Mark 10:6–9; see Deut. 24:1–4). Imagine that—the Creator's design was elevated above all legal exceptions and social protests!

Alone, one is an individual, but in another's company, we are fully persons— beings in community. Significantly, this time God allows Adam to make the evaluation! It is not surprising that God's image-bearer is necessarily an evaluator. The first human words that we hear declare what is good and timely, poised for new life.[8] As God made the animals, Adam assessed their nature and named them accordingly: God "brought them to the man to see what he would call them; and whatever the man called a living creature, that was its name" (Gen. 2:19). This is tender nobility, already at work. God names no living creature. Instead, He shares that power and assessment with humans. Clearly, God is the generous delegator. God even forfeits the right to reverse human decisions—"*whatever* he called" them. Ultimately, this underscores both the creativity and cooperation of their life as a couple: ruling, propagating, and working were never meant to be a solo enterprise.

So why this exercise in naming animals? First, humans must respect the fact that people and animals were made on the same day. This is the domain of human caretaking (Gen. 1:28). Noah's ark saved people and animals, not plants and land. Second, Adam could not cultivate alone, guard alone, or procreate alone. The woman is not just fitting in nature; she is a timely companion, a matching partner, and a needed coworker. Adam needed to grasp the uniqueness of his relational need. Only one "from his side" could stand next to him. This would be another person from his own body! In this way, "human beings are the only creatures capable of being evaluators as God has been throughout Genesis 1."[9] Human work is not merely passive maintenance or novel activity, but genuine engagement. The theological message of 2:15–23 teaches us that "God's creating is not done alone . . . *God chooses interdependence rather than independence*"[10] (emphasis added). By intention, God left the wider world "undeveloped," intending the splendor, fertility, and worship of Eden to shape the rest of creation. God works in *partnership* with humans. This meaningful relationship is possible only because the Creator made

Himself available.[11] Having considered the majesty of the Creator's design, we are now ready to explore the nature of the human being more closely.

TERMS FOR HUMANKIND

So what is a human being? There is a philosophical tradition in Western cultures that seeks to itemize the "parts" that make up the human being. This tradition has come up with two or three core parts. Some passages in Scripture portray a *trichotomous* (threefold) nature of the human being: mind, body, soul (see 2 Cor. 4:16; 5:1–9; 1 Thess. 5:23). Another view rooted in Greek culture sees a *dualism* between the soul (*psyche*) and the body (*soma*). While there may be room for a soft-dualism in the New Testament, a hard distinction between the body and soul is not warranted (see Matt. 6:25; 27:50; Luke 10:27; 2 Cor. 4:11). To better understand the constitution of the human being, we will note some important texts throughout Scripture.

The creation texts that form the backstory of humankind are rooted in the ancient Mediterranean world. In this backdrop, we do not find God going to war against evil forces or drawing humans from the blood of slain enemies. While some ancient cultures thought that way, the world of Scripture does not: matter and physical forms do not have an independent life of their own, nor are they inherently evil. Returning to Greek culture, this was the claim of Gnosticism, many Greek philosophers, and most pagan religions.

Unfortunately, many of these notions persist even today in elements of mysticism and the new age worldview, in which evil impulses can be contacted in sinister places or through mantras and figurines. However, in contrast to such worldviews that attempt to appease the spirit world, and even escape one's own body to take "trips," God created the human being for a *bodily* existence. Both the man and the woman were made from existing physical substances (Gen. 2:7; 2:21–22). This highlights intimate connections, defines fertility and family, and orients human work toward the same ground from which they were taken (Gen. 1:28; 2:15). These biblical truths are identity-making. The human being was not made to "escape" life in the physical world. Rather, *everything God made was created to participate in time and space.* For good reason, humankind is intended to look to God as Lord of both nature and history.[12]

Not surprisingly, some key terms from Scripture must be clarified and allowed to fill in the gaps of our own contemporary views of humankind. The biblical world reflected in Scripture held to an integrated relation of mind and body—a *psychosomatic unity.* We need a better grasp of this. For example, when the abstract word "soul" is used in Scripture—a whole life is in view! In fact, so holistic was the Old Testament notion of personhood that "living being" (*nephesh*, Gen. 2:7 NIV) could also be used of a person's corpse (Lev. 21:1; 22:4). *Nephesh* is distinct enough to be used in the psalms with the vocative of direct address: "Why are you in despair, O my life/soul?" (Ps. 42:5, 11 ESV). Similarly, the Greek word *psyche* ("life") is theologically general enough to refer to "life" or "human life" (only rarely used as "soul").

There are also significant terms for human capacities, such as "mind," "heart," and "flesh." While mind is crucial for Christian values, even used to describe maturity (Rom. 12:2), heart supports the value of emotions and will, and has implications for the unconscious. Flesh essentially refers to human weakness or frailty, but can also refer to self-reliance, more negatively. We will explore more of these terms in what follows. But generally speaking, the human "body" (*soma*) usually refers to the entire human being, the visible and tangible aspect. In the New Testament, Paul's concept of body can be described this way:

> [Our body is] that piece of the world, which we ourselves are and for which we bear responsibility, because it was the earliest gift of our Creator to us. Body is not primarily to be regarded from the standpoint of the individual. For the apostle it signifies man in his worldliness (i.e. as part of the world) and therefore, in his ability to communicate. . . . In the bodily obedience of the Christian . . . in the world of every day, the Lordship of Christ finds visible expression, and only when this visible expression takes shape in us does the whole thing become credible as gospel message.[13]

Practically speaking, the human body is a profound gift, necessary for determined discipleship, granting us the opportunity to serve others, showing an obedient life, and demonstrating credibility to the lordship of Christ. We should observe how both testaments use key terms, and so develop these concepts.

"Heart" (Hebrew, *leb*; Greek, *kardia*) typically expresses deep feeling (Gen. 6:6), such as anxiety (Gen. 45:26) and joy (1 Sam. 2:1). The most important use of heart for contemporary people is how the term even speaks of the unconscious that operates in *secret*—such as Paul's "secrets of [the] heart" (1 Cor. 14:25). Here, the Holy Spirit is poured into the believer's heart, prompting prayer in the heart, with "groanings too deep for words" (Rom. 8:26–7).

"Conscience" reflects the Greek *syneidesis*, with no Hebrew equivalent. It is not the same as modern ideas of the conscience. Rather, it is "self-awareness" (1 Cor. 8–10). For Paul, those who had a "weak" conscience were less confident in their convictions than those bolder members of the church.

"Mind" (Greek, *nous*) has more positive meaning than is often suggested. Paul exhorts the Thessalonians to think rightly (1 Thess. 5:21). He encourages believers to employ rational inference and deduction. All Christians are encouraged to reflect positively on the ethical conduct and quality of virtuous lives that make them an example worthy of following (Heb. 5:14; 13:7). Such redeemed people may be the closest example of what Adam was intended to become.

"Flesh" (Greek, *sarx*) is used in several ways. While it can be physical substance, it often refers to human weakness and fallibility. That said, one can distinguish between "flesh" and "body." Respected Greek scholar J. A. T. Robinson insightfully states, "While *sarx* stands for man, in the solidarity of creation, in his distance from God, *soma* stands for man, in the solidarity of creation, as made *for* God."[14] When Paul speaks of "the mind set on the flesh" (Rom. 8:6), it seems he has in view both humankind in their weakness, and in their sin. Here is humankind in their self-reliant attitude, with their trust in self.[15] But what did God intend in the beginning? There is a symphony of relationships that God has built around people. We now consider humankind in this theatre of relationships.

THE RELATIONAL ECOSYSTEM

Simply put, humankind cannot be understood apart from their relationship with God, their Creator. Any attempt to do so inevitably elevates the creature or demotes the Creator. For good reason, arrogant human actions in Scripture are viewed as some combination of hubris, rebellion, or blasphemy. The rebellion of Adam and Eve is not altogether different from the arrogance of King Nebuchadnezzar (Dan. 4:28–33).

Whether through the interests of various philosophies or the dictates of cultures long past, humankind can neither be captured in popular social trends, nor be simply confined by their traditions. Rather, humans are responsible agents and their actions have consequences, rather dire sometimes. Inside the faith, theologians have also struggled—verging on apologizing—to understand a God who moved beyond His own free, sovereign, and sufficient existence to create human beings, and we know how that turned out (i.e., "the fall," Gen. 3:1–19). Our own relational brokenness befuddles us, especially when we meet such a relational God.

The theologian Anthony C. Thiselton puts us on the right track:

> God chose to create the universe and other orders of created being *out of love*, and to go forth, as it were, out of himself to enter into relationships with the *other*. . . . God remains transcendent as well as immanent. . . . Creation is not only an act of the past but it also signifies the *present dependence* of all created beings and things on God. . . . He dwells within it, but is also beyond it.[16]

In other words, God did not create humans, animals, or any other order because He was lonely, liked a good joke, or realized He could cut corners on His sovereignty. In Thiselton's words, it was "out of love" that God chose to make and populate the world with many kinds of relational dynamics. He is also right to remind us that people live only in "present dependence" upon God. This multi-layered interdependence we can call the *relational ecosystem*.

We should not be surprised that our relational God built creation to function relationally. For His part, God remains transcendent over all creation, yet stunningly *involved* in His created order. God is as committed to redeeming it as establishing it. Contrary to all power-hungry deities of the ages, the Creator-God not only reveals Himself in dreams and visions; He also walks, converses, speaks, and even reveals His thoughts to the reader, on occasion (Gen. 8:21). God's immanence—that is, being personal—is evident in His patient and faithful relationships with human beings, even to the point of feeling profound sorrow in His heart over their sin (Gen. 6:6). This pain is God's first emotion ever mentioned! In fact, God is so relationally engaged, that His creation "might be called the beginning of the passion of God."[17] Clearly, God has a price to pay for His partnership with sinful and wayward humans. This should not sound strange, since this theme is fully developed in the New Testament, where Jesus willingly accepts the role of servant, and the heavenly King reigns from a cross. "Interaction with humans cost God dearly."[18]

In the creation mandate (1:28), God blesses humankind to rule and have dominion (Gen. 1:28) over all creation. God's blessing—often in His speech—accomplishes several things: (1) brings fertility and success, (2) grants authority and dominion, (3) provides protection and security, (4) and offers rest and peace. This is God's functional blessing, bestowing a vitality of relationship, status, and capability for both propagation and governance. Significantly, God's blessings assume an existing relationship between God and the one blessed (see 9:1). As we shall see, the image of God (1:26–27, see below) granted a royal authorization for humankind to rule over creation as God's "under-kings," a unique mission celebrated in Psalm 8.

Whether humankind is the climax of universal creation (1:26–28) or operating at the center of God's activity (2:5–18), we can identify five key associations that comprise this relational ecosystem within the divinely created order:

1. *God with humankind*—binding of royalty (Gen. 1:26; Ps. 8:5);
2. *Humankind with the ground*—binding of origin (Gen. 1:24; 2:7; Ps. 146:4);
3. *Humankind with the animals*—binding of domain (Gen. 1:28; Jonah 3:7–8);
4. *Man with woman*—binding of mission (Gen. 1:28; 2:23);
5. *Humankind with self*—binding of honor (Gen. 1:26; 2:25).

These are the core bindings in the relational ecosystem that also forms the backdrop for sacred marriage. Though somewhat distasteful to contemporary readers, in the theology of Scripture, one's place of origin and the nature of their birth inform their purpose, security, and general characteristics in life. Not understanding or disregarding these relational bindings has negatively shaped Western values. For this reason, the notion of an individual is essentially an autonomous self, constantly in search of personal meaning, as noted in the worn-out mantra, "What's in it for me?"

As the Bible defines these bindings, the "human" (*'adam*) was extracted from the "humus" (*'adama*, 2:7), as the "woman" (*'issha*) was extracted from the "man" (*'ish*, 2:22). This makes Adam uniquely bound to the fertility of the soil, just as Eve is uniquely bound to the fertility of the body. Even the animals are formed "out of the ground" (2:19) to move "on the earth" (1:30), but notice the same connection to the ground (1:30). Significantly, the biblical notion of self is a *relationally embedded* self, rooted in a web of extended relationships.[19] This is a sharp contrast with "unembedded" notions of individualism, popularized by Maslow's hierarchy of needs—culminating in self-actualization. Seeing the broader relational ecosystem and its relationship to personhood, it is vital to recognize how all these bindings were broken through the sin of Adam and Eve (Gen. 3:1–13), a rebellion that shattered the relational ecosystem.

The reality of rebellion more closely captures how the first man and woman react to God's command (Gen. 2:16–17). They did not trust their gracious Creator! Neither the word "sin" nor the phrase "the fall" are actually used in Genesis 3. At another level, these familiar terms are appropriate when we realize that Christian doctrine draws these concepts not from the dire consequences seen in Genesis 3–11, but primarily from the New Testament writings of Paul (Rom. 1:18–3:23; 5:12–21; 1 Cor. 15:21–22). The doctrine of the fall comes from the broader message of Scripture, with its persistent address of sin and the need of all people for Christ's redemption.[20]

The selfish decisions of Adam and Eve (Gen. 3:1–7) reverberate through history because they were the parents of all humanity. As Adam and Eve ate together, so together they feel a naked-shame, and make a desperate attempt to clothe themselves as they scramble to hide from each other and even their Maker. The results were beyond catastrophic—all the "bindings" that held creation together were broken. The new reality is one of torn relationships, which we all experience in our own lives. The consequences from their first sin set aflame in people a propensity for evil and the resulting moral alienation.[21] This has shattered the Creator's relational ecosystem.

So when we talk about humans and their sin, what brought Christ to redeem us in human form, we see that sin is not primarily a matter of personal acts that fall short of God's standards. Rather, "it more fundamentally denotes an *attitude toward God*, which is *other than worship, trust, obedience, and fellowship*."[22] As Paul writes in Romans 5:17, Adam has become the archetypal human who deliberately refused to obey God's single command given him (Gen. 2:17). Called *original sin* in Christian theology, contemporary readers may recoil at their connection to Adam's guilt and corrupted nature. However, "each of us has become our own Adam."[23] How sin relates to the image of God—even damages it—is important to understand.

IMAGE OF GOD

While vital to the unique status of human beings, "image of God" as a phrase is rarely even mentioned (Gen. 1:26, 27; 5:1, 3; 9:6; 1 Cor. 11:7; James 3:9), but it is as complex as it is important to theology. Classic Western interest in *what* the image is does not adequately capture the fuller picture. Human beings do not *have* God's "image," they *are* God's image. Image bearers represent God's royal presence on earth. As patron deities in the ancient world installed their statues (= images) in the temple and its beautiful garden surroundings, so God intentionally stations His image bearer in the garden-sanctuary of Eden, and gives this couple specific tasks to accomplish (see Gen. 2:15).

Like a stained-glass window, the image of God may best be viewed through its various facets that make up a larger "picture" we call the image of God. It is important to see that at the outset, humankind was made in dialogue for dialogue (Gen. 1:26, 28; 2:23). The biblical text highlights several key points: only with His image bearers is God found in dialogue ("let Us"). While plants and animals reproduce "after their kind," only humans are made after God's image. Only for image bearers does God uniquely breathe into their nostrils the "breath of life" (2:5–7). Only for humans does God utter a priestly blessing that we call the creation mandate (1:28). Finally, only human wickedness on earth causes the Lord to be "sorry that He had made mankind," filling His heart with grief (Gen. 6:5–6). All these elements comprise the special status and authority to rule God's creation as His royal vice-regents.

It is no surprise that Psalm 8 draws on this theology to call people to *worship*: "What is mankind that you are mindful of them? . . . You have . . . crowned them with glory and honor. . . . You made them rulers over the works of your hands" (Ps. 8:4–6 NIV). "Image of God" is not a needed phrase here because the creation mandate—the stewardship God gave man and woman—clearly speaks of the role given to humankind in their royal commission. Working, worshiping, propagating, and developing God's world was the stewardship given to humankind. So humankind is the earthly counterpart to God's heavenly entourage. God's experience of community now spills over into a new realm, broadening the community of relationships that already exists within God's realm.[24]

We must note some significant implications here for personhood. The human form is *theomorphic* (having the form of God), as "Our image" and "Our likeness" (1:26)—essentially synonyms—fix their point of reference in God, not in "him" or "herself." In practical terms, we are image bearers who have gender, not genders who have image. The mention of "male and female" (1:27) highlights two *expressions* of the same image (in Genesis 9:6, God commands not to kill an image of God, not a gender). God models a common humanity, not our gender specificity.[25] In fact, throughout these important Genesis texts, *God addresses humans as persons, not isolated genders—persons in a community of need.* There is no mandate for humans to rule each other.[26]

We can summarize this discussion of humanity as the image of God with several significant observations. First, the human person is an embodied spirit and a spirited body. Both in this life and the next, human existence is an *embodied* existence. As Miroslav Volf has stated it, "Paul's claim that in Christ there is 'no longer male and female' entails no eschatological denial of gender dimorphism. . . . The oneness in Christ is a community of people with sexed bodies and distinct gender identities, not some abstract unity of pure spirits or de-gendered 'persons.'"[27]

Second, because the image of God entails an embodied anthropology, we are also able to speak meaningfully about physical boundaries, sexual intercourse, physical violence, even mental health and trauma. In other words, because the image of God includes embodiment, the human being cannot be limited to the cognitive ability, spiritual aspect, creative capacity, or emotion-filled relationship—because each of these seeks to locate the image of God in the *interiority* of the person. It is best to think of the image of God as an *integrated psychosomatic relation* of mind and body. The words of Eugene H. Merrill are a helpful summary:

> The statement that the Godhead created man "in Our image, according to Our likeness" (1:26) delineates man's function (what he is to be and do) and not merely his essence (what he is like) . . . Man was created . . . to serve as the agent of God in implementing God's sovereign will and sway over the universe. God commissioned mankind, the crowning jewel of His creation, to serve as His vice-regent in the world.[28]

WHERE THE HUMAN STORY GOES

Sin may be pervasive, but our Redeemer has brought a persistent hope! Victims of a self-inflicted wound, humans are dying creatures. A greater "helper" is needed. Paul knew that the word *'adam* in the Old Testament was both a personal name and a term for all humanity, mired in Adam's sin (1 Cor. 15:21–22). Even in Paul's sermons (see Acts 17:24–26), he states that all nations stand in Adam's wake and need for salvation. Because everyone daily endorses Adam's attitude of sin,[29] Christ—the last Adam—has conquered death: "So also in Christ all will be made alive" (1 Cor. 15:22).

The first humans were given the privilege and responsibility of showing the glory of God and extending the beauty of His creation, and both Adam and the people of God failed in this task. So God took on flesh in Jesus Christ, as the *true image of God*, and fulfilled this vocation—"Christ ... is the image of God" (2 Cor. 4:4; Col. 1:15). Seeing what Christ accomplished, Paul's view of humanity is overwhelmingly *eschatological*. Paul grounds this theological climax in the "risen Lord"—the final destiny of redeemed humankind is "in Christ" (1 Cor. 15:20–28, 44–49; Eph. 1:9–10). The relational ecosystem is also slated for an upgrade. While creation is presently subjected to futility (Rom. 8:19–22) and humans to death (Rom. 5:12–14), we hear Paul shout in another sacrament of surprise about a coming "new creation" (Gal. 6:15; see 2 Cor. 5:17). Being united with Christ, according to Paul, brings the needed cosmological and anthropological achievement. We should not speak merely of salvation, but of the *restoration* of all creation. The first chorus in heaven praised God for His majestic control of the world (Rev. 4:11; see 10:6; 14:7).

This fresh impact on humanity is already experienced in a down payment by the Spirit (Eph. 1:12–14), partly realized in this "evil age" by eliminating distinctions between Jews, Gentiles, slaves, free, and male and female (Gal. 3:28; see 1 Cor. 12:12–13). This is part of God making the "former things" into "new things" (2 Cor. 5:17; see Isa. 65:17–19). Until we join such singing, being human means we live in a palpable tension of "already" experiencing gifts of the new creation and "not yet" completely realizing them, or being distanced from the full calamity of sin (Rom. 8:18–30; 2 Cor. 12:5–10).

CLOSING REFLECTIONS

Understanding the Christian doctrine of humanity prioritizes the teaching of Holy Scripture. However, such a study also seeks to engage contemporary society *with the truths of God's Holy Word*—in that order. In light of our discussion on humanity, several current issues are raised for the reader to consider a faithful Christian response.

First, the heightened attention to the issue of race has reemerged in our generation. Some contemporary writing and speaking has been helpful, but some of the discussion has become toxic and divisive. How should the biblical information on human identity—rooted in the image of God and renewed in Christ's resurrection—be applied to trends that "re-segregate" races and elevate new identities that attempt to define the "real self"? Since the complexity of living as people who struggle with sin is hard enough, it is important that the atoning work of Christ, the second Adam, be our focus, not the social atonements of our age, which can never bring the true redemption. Understanding the problem of human sin actually highlights the rescue of the God-man who stepped into our situation for us.

Christians must celebrate biblical diversity of "tribe, nation, and tongue" that Scripture speaks about. But this comes with a warning: exchanging the Creator's *designed* diversity in all life for a *political* diversity for "my life" recalibrates human worth along temporal lines and will not achieve the unity of heaven's new citizenship, drawn from all nations. Believers are called to live presently as the sole bride of Christ, with our core identity rooted in the Pioneer and Perfecter of our faith.

Second, we are besieged with gender issues and an odd commitment to sexual ambiguity. How can the doctrine of humanity respond to a culture that is increasingly committed to the *infinite malleability* of gender? Christian theology teaches us that our sexuality is a stewardship to God, rather than a project for "me." As such, sexuality reflects the design of our Creator. Practically, this means sexual expression is fulfilling within the boundaries made by God. Like a fire enjoyed in the hearth, or a train "free" on the tracks, believers must learn to submit their sexual expression to the Lord of our life. Of course, this is difficult, but as Christians we are called to holiness, not gratification. This principled life is actually part of the attraction of the gospel. Our contemporary lust for novel sexual expression must mature into the "old truth" of our created design. The beauty of man and woman—as Scripture speaks—is a God-thing. What are the implications for marriage, sex, and the theology of the church as Christ's bride? Among other things, we must embrace the *goodness* of boundaries. Whether as a single, a recovering sex addict, or a newly married couple—the Bible is requesting our moral ear. There is wonderful truth and powerful doctrine that informs our sexual expression, healing, and marital goals. But there are also sober warnings throughout Scripture. Redemption applies to every aspect of our life, and no area may be as powerful a witness for the gospel of Christ as sexual control. Whatever the season or state of life, as a single adult or a wife struggling with infertility, delay is not denial. Even our Lord was never married. Our redeemed identity is not advanced or diminished by any kind of sexual encounter, be that infidelity, faithfulness, or abuse. Thanks be to God, even our sexuality can find great healing in our Savior.

Theology must be fleshed out in complex issues like these. This is a Christian practice of thinking, studying, and living. May God grant us all His wisdom from above as we: honor our Creator in resourceful living, enjoy God's blessing in creative development, and faithfully serve our Lord who stooped to redeem a lost humanity. As God never abandoned His world, let us cherish the rich truths of God's Word, until we all join a new chorus—of redemption accomplished.

NOTES

1. See Brian M. Howell and Jenell Williams Paris, *Introducing Cultural Anthropology: A Christian Perspective* (Grand Rapids: Baker Academic: 2011, 2019).

2. On the philosophical notion of a "perfect creation," see William J. Dumbrell, *The Search for Order: Biblical Eschatology in Focus* (Eugene, OR: Wipf and Stock, 2001), 20–21.

3. Bruce K. Waltke, *Genesis: A Commentary* (Grand Rapids: Zondervan, 2001), 64; John H. Walton, *Ancient Near Eastern Thought and the Old Testament* (Grand Rapids: Baker Academic, 2006, 2018), 93–97. Following the initial "us" of human creation (1:26), Waltke observes, "It seems that in the four occurrences of the pronoun 'us' for God, God refers to 'us' when human beings are impinging on the heavenly realm and he is deciding their fate" (*Genesis*, 64). For further discussion of the views, see Waltke's excellent treatment (64–65).

4. S. Dean McBride Jr., "Divine Protocol: Genesis 1:1–2:3 as Prologue to the Pentateuch," in *God Who Creates: Essays in Honor of W. Sibley Towner*, ed. W.P. Brown and S.D. McBride, Jr. (Grand Rapids: Eerdmans, 2000), 16.

5. Dennis T. Olson, "Genesis" in *The New Interpreter's Bible: One Volume Commentary*, ed. Beverly Roberts Gaventa and David Petersen (Nashville: Abingdon, 2010), 4.

6. Walter Brueggemann, "Creation," in *Reverberations of Faith: A Theological Handbook of Old Testament Themes* (Louisville: Westminster John Knox, 2002), 40.

7. John Zizioulas, *Being as Communion: Studies in Personhood and the Church* (New York: St Vladimir's Seminary Press, 1997), 103, 108; drawing on Paul Ricoeur, *Oneself as Another* (Chicago: University of Chicago Press, 1992), 317.

8. Terence E. Fretheim, *Creation Untamed: The Bible, God, and Natural Disasters* (Grand Rapids: Baker Academic, 2010), 36.

9. Ibid., 32, n48.

10. Ibid., 37.

11. James McKeown, *Genesis*, The Two Horizons Old Testament Commentary (Grand Rapids: Eerdmans, 2008), 275.

12. Anthony C. Thiselton, "Creation," in *The Thiselton Companion to Christian Theology* (Grand Rapids: Eerdmans, 205), 263.

13. Ernst Käsemann, *New Testament Questions of Today* (London: SCM Press, 1969), 135.

14. John A. T. Robinson, *The Body: A Study in Pauline Theology* (London: SCM Press, 1952), 31.

15. Rudolf Bultmann, *Theology of the New Testament*, vol. 1 (London: SCM Press, 1952), 240.

16. Thiselton, "Creation," 263; emphasis original.

17. Terence Fretheim, *The Suffering of God: An Old Testament Perspective*, OBT (Philadelphia: Fortress, 1984), 58.

18. McKeown, *Genesis*, 275, n6.

19. Robert A. DiVito, "Old Testament Anthropology and the Construction of Personal Identity," *Catholic Biblical Quarterly* 61 (1999): 217–38.

20. Eugene H. Merrill, "Fall of Humankind," *New International Dictionary of Old Testament Theology*, vol. 4, ed. W. A. VanGemeren (Grand Rapids: Zondervan, 1997), 638.

21. John Kessler, *Old Testament Theology: Divine Call and Human Response* (Waco, TX: Baylor University Press, 2013), 138, n106.

22. Anthony C. Thiselton, *Systematic Theology* (Grand Rapids: Eerdmans, 2015), 151; emphasis original.

23. Ibid., 152.

24. Dennis T. Olson, "Genesis," in *The New Interpreter's Bible: One Volume Commentary*, ed. Beverly Roberts Gaventa and David Peterson (Nashville: Abingdon, 2010), 4.

25. Miroslav Volf, *Exclusion & Embrace: A Theological Exploration of Identity, Otherness, and Reconciliation* (Nashville: Abingdon, 1996), 172.

26. Patrick D. Miller, "Man and Woman: Towards a Theological Anthropology," in *The Way of the Lord: Essays in Old Testament Theology* (Grand Rapids: Eerdmans, 2004), 310–12.

27. Volf, *Exclusion & Embrace*, 184.

28. Eugene F. Merrill, Mark F. Rooker, and Michael A. Grisanti, "The Book of Genesis," in *The World and the Word: An Introduction to the Old Testament* (Nashville: Broadman & Holman Academic, 2011), 185.

29. Anthony C. Thiselton, "Sin," in *The Thiselton Companion to Christian Theology* (Grand Rapids: Eerdmans, 2015), 771.

Understanding the Basic Doctrine of Holy Scripture

MICHAEL RYDELNIK

My friend Larry Feldman has not missed a single day reading the Bible since he became a follower of Yeshua (Jesus) on January 15, 1972. As I write this, that is 17,645 days in a row. What makes this so extraordinary is that he is not a legalist nor is he spiritually proud. Rather, he is an incredibly faithful and extremely disciplined person. Larry's daily reading of the Bible is an amazing achievement of consistency. Even though I have been close friends with Larry for more than forty years, only recently did I ask him why he was so faithfully committed to reading the Scriptures daily. His answer was so simple it startled me.

Larry said that people everywhere are saying that they desperately would like to hear God's voice. Most people tell him that they would just like to hear God speak; that they long for Him only to give them some sort of message. Larry said he felt the same way. And almost immediately upon his coming to faith in the Messiah, someone told Larry that the Bible was God's inspired Word. It was explained that God had revealed Himself in the Scriptures and could and would speak to him through them. Larry concluded that since God had chosen to communicate to humanity through the Bible, it would be disrespectful to God and damaging to himself not to read God's message to him on a daily basis. So that is why Larry reads the Bible everyday—because it is God's inspired Word.

This chapter is about the very teaching that motivated Larry to read the Scriptures daily—what theologians call bibliology, or the doctrine of the Bible. What does the Bible teach about itself? In what sense is it God's Word? What is the guarantee that it is true? Is it truly without error? How did the individual books of the Bible get included? This chapter will address these issues concerning the doctrine of Holy Scripture.

REVELATION

The first part of understanding the doctrine of the Bible is to recognize that it is God's revelation to humanity. Both the biblical Hebrew and Greek words translated *revelation* mean "to uncover" or "to unveil." In that sense the Scriptures make it clear that revelation refers to God's self-disclosure (or the unveiling of Himself) to humanity. This is evident in Hebrews 1:1–2: "God, after He spoke long ago to the fathers in the prophets in many portions and in many ways, in these last days has spoken to us in His Son." God's self-disclosure or the revelation of Himself is usually categorized in two ways: general and special revelation.

General Revelation

General revelation (sometimes called *natural revelation*) refers to God's self-disclosure that is available to all people. It is evident in a number of ways:

The Creation of the Universe. The Bible discloses that God has made Himself evident to all people through the very creation of the world. In Psalm 19, David describes the creation as a means of understanding that there is a unique and glorious Creator. He writes, "The heavens are telling of the glory of God; and their expanse is declaring the work of His hands" (Ps. 19:1). Daily, creation speaks of God the Creator ("Day to day pours forth speech," Ps. 19:2a) and reveals His existence ("night to night reveals knowledge" [of God], Ps. 19:2b).

In the New Testament, the apostle Paul also claims that creation reveals God's existence in the New Testament. He argues, "That which is known about God is evident within them; for God made it evident to them. For since the creation of the world His invisible attributes, that is, His eternal power and divine nature, have been clearly perceived, being understood by what has been made, so that they are without excuse" (Rom. 1:19–20). These verses develop three ideas: (1) Humanity has evidence and knows about God; (2) The creation of the world is this evidence; and (3) This evidence leaves people, when facing God's judgment, without an excuse because they should have responded to God's self-disclosure in creation. This third idea is crucial: General revelation in creation is sufficient to condemn people but insufficient to save them. Paul also argues that people need more of the specific revelation of the Messiah Jesus Himself (the Living Word) and the Scriptures (the Written Word) for salvation. Although this may seem unfair, the point seems to be that people suppress the revelation they already have in creation. The Lord would have sent them further revelation as found in Jesus the Messiah and the Bible had they responded positively to the available evidence.

The existence of the universe reveals that there must be a Creator, a first cause who started it all. Not only that, but this Creator has made a world that is a perfectly designed environment for human beings. Some have called this *the anthropic principle*. Without using that phrase, Paul Enns describes it this way:

> Wherever man peers at the universe, there is orderliness. At a distance of ninety-three million miles from the earth, the sun provides exactly the right temperature environment for man to function on earth. Were the sun closer, it would be too hot to survive, and were it farther away it would be too cold for man to function. If the moon were closer than two hundred forty thousand miles the gravitational pull of the tides would engulf the earth's surface with water from the oceans.[1]

A world, perfectly designed and created for human life is God's self-disclosure to all, revealing that He exists and people are accountable to Him.

The Conscience of Humanity. It might be maintained that people need the Bible to know right from wrong and to realize that they are accountable to the Creator of the world. The apostle Paul says no, because even pagans, who never had God's written Law, "instinctively perform the requirements of the Law." This is because "the work of the Law [is] written in their hearts, their conscience testifying and their thoughts alternately accusing or else defending them" (Rom. 2:14–15). His point is that all humans have a sense of right and wrong. Their Creator instilled this sense in them by writing it on their hearts. C. S. Lewis describes this principle as "Right and Wrong as a Clue to the Meaning of the Universe." Lewis makes the moral argument for the existence of God in his book *Mere Christianity*. He maintains that humanity's intrinsic sense of right and wrong, the human conscience, points to a Supreme Moral Being who instilled it within them. This is all the more remarkable, because people fail to live up to their own standards of right and wrong.[2] Both the apostle Paul and C. S. Lewis are making the same point: Conscience in humanity is part of God's revelation of Himself to all people.

The Care for Humanity. God, in His goodness, has chosen to provide care for all people, even those who forget Him or diminish His greatness through idolatry. The book of Acts records the time when Paul and Barnabas came to a pagan temple in the city of Lystra (Acts 14:8–18). There they healed a lame man. Those who saw this miracle thought that Barnabas and Paul were the pagan gods Zeus and Hermes. Paul in turn reminded them that they should turn to the true and living God, not mere men (14:15). Moreover, even though God had allowed people to wander into paganism (14:16), He did not leave Himself without a witness to His own existence. Paul declared this was evident "in that He did good and gave you rains from heaven and fruitful seasons, satisfying your hearts with food and gladness" (14:17). The apostle's point was that God's common kindness and care for humanity was a means of His self-disclosure to all. Rain and bountiful harvests all point to the existence of a God who cares for the people He has made.

The famed architect, Sir Christopher Wren, who designed London's St. Paul's Cathedral and whose crypt is there, has these words on his epitaph: "Reader, if you seek his monument, look around you."[3] The idea is that one must examine Wren's cathedral, his masterpiece, in order to learn about Wren. This indeed would tell the observer much about Wren but not about every aspect of his life. What kind of husband, father, or friend was he? Was he caring or cold, greedy or generous? In a similar way, general revelation discloses much about God. Observing God's creation, the human conscience, and God's divine care of the world will reveal much about Him. However it will not provide all the answers that God wants humanity to know. Therefore, God has not left people on their own to discover Him only through observation of general revelation. He has also disclosed Himself to some through what theologians have called special revelation.

SPECIAL REVELATION

Special revelation refers to God's self-disclosure through His message to specific people (as opposed to general revelation, which is to all people). The book of Hebrews states that God revealed Himself "in many portions and in many ways" (Heb. 1:1), indicating that special revelation, has multiple forms. Yet, the most remarkable type of special revelation is that God "has spoken to us in His Son" (Heb. 1:2). God has revealed Himself through the *incarnation* of the messianic Son of God, Jesus.

God's revelation of Himself through the incarnation led the apostle John to call the Messiah Jesus "the Word." He further maintains that "the Word was God" (John 1:1) and states that the Word "became flesh, and dwelt among us" (John 1:14). Finally, the apostle declares that "God the only Son, who is in the arms of the Father, He has explained Him" (John 1:18). The incarnation of the unique Son of God revealed God the Father. The word *explain* (used in John 1:18) means "to set forth in great detail" or "to expound,"[4] indicating that God the Son, by becoming flesh, has made known God the Father in great detail. This is the concept in Jesus' words to Philip, "He who has seen Me has seen the Father" (John 14:9). Although Jesus the Messiah is the Living Word and the ultimate expression of God's special revelation, today all that can be known about the Lord Jesus is to be found in the Bible, God's written Word. No one can claim a distinctive or special insight into the Messiah Jesus beyond what the Scriptures indicate.

In addition to the incarnation of the Son of God, special revelation also took other forms. For example, God spoke through *dreams* to Joseph (Gen. 37:5–11), *visions* to Daniel (Dan. 7:1–28), and in an *audible voice* to Samuel (1 Sam. 3:1–14). He used *angels* to communicate with Lot (Gen. 19:1–22), a *theophany*[5] to Moses (Ex. 3:1–4:19), a *miracle* for a paralytic man (Mark 2:10–12); and a *prophetic word* to David (1 Sam. 22:5; 2 Sam. 7:8–17). God even used the mysterious *Urim and Thummim* to communicate with Israel (Num. 27:21). This list does not include *all* special revelation from God nor every kind. Rather, it shows the manifold ways God has spoken in the past. Today, however, all these forms of special revelation are only accessed through God's written Word, the Bible.

General and special revelation show that God cares for people so much that He freely discloses Himself to humanity. As such not every special revelation or spoken prophetic oracle the Lord ever gave was preserved in Scripture. Every miracle of Jesus was not included in the Gospels (John 21:25). However, God chose to preserve some of His revelation to humanity by putting it into the Bible. This was God's work of inspiration.

INSPIRATION

The second part of understanding the doctrine of the Bible is to recognize that God inspired His Word, the Bible, to give His revelation to humanity.

THE MEANING OF INSPIRATION

The Bible declares, "All Scripture is inspired by God and beneficial for teaching, for rebuke, for correction, for training in righteousness" (2 Tim. 3:16). But what does this most foundational text mean by the word *inspired*? The normal meaning of English word "inspired" has to do with "breathing in" but this is not what the Greek word *theopneustos* means. It is a combination of two words, *Theos* (God) and *pneuma* (breath), together meaning "God-breathed." This shows that inspiration refers not to God breathing into human writings, making them exceptional, but rather to God breathing out the Bible. Another way of saying this is that God produced the Scriptures.

This explanation of inspiration repudiates a mistaken view called *natural inspiration*. This approach sees biblical writers as men of great genius whose works were products of that divinely given genius, similar to other great writers in history, such as Shakespeare or Tolstoy. God breathing out the Scriptures demonstrates that natural inspiration is not what the Bible means by inspiration.

THE SIGNIFICANCE OF INSPIRATION

The claim that the Bible is inspired or produced by God demands clarification. What is actually inspired and to what extent? And what difference does inspiration make? Three principles explain the significance of the inspiration of the Bible.

First, inspiration refers to the written words of the Bible. The word for "Scripture" used in 2 Timothy 3:16 is *"graphē,"* which, in its simplest sense means a "writing."[6] The previous verse makes clear that Paul was speaking of the written Bible, calling it "sacred writings" (2 Tim. 3:15). In fact, throughout the New Testament, the word *graphē* takes on the specialized sense of "Scripture" (e.g. Acts 8:32; John 20:9; Rom. 4:3; James 4:5), indicating that it is speaking of the words written in the Bible. So, when the Messiah Jesus was tempted by Satan, He responded three times with the phrase, "it is written" (Matt. 4:4, 7, 10), an expression used more than ninety times in the Bible. Moreover, inspiration also pertains to the very words in Scripture, not just of the general writings as a whole. That is why Paul describes his epistles as *"words . . . taught by the Spirit"* (1 Cor. 2:13). Inspiration also applies to the tenses of the verbs, as evident in Jesus' defense of the resurrection from the dead. He maintained that when God said, "I am the God of Abraham, the God of Isaac, and the God of Jacob" it proved that the Lord was the God of the living and not the dead (Matt. 22:31–32). His argument turned on the present tense of the verb expressed in the words "I am." Inspiration also extends down to the letters used in a word as seen in Paul's argument hinging on whether the word used in the Bible is "seed" or "seeds" (Gal. 3:16). In fact, Jesus said that inspiration included "the smallest letter or stroke" of a letter (Matt. 5:18). This is why theologians often speak of the verbal inspiration of the Bible, indicating that inspiration extends to the very words of Scripture.

The Bible's claim of verbal inspiration demonstrates that the view called *conceptual inspiration* is deeply problematic. Conceptual inspiration affirms that the *ideas* taught in a biblical writing may be inspired but the words are not. Some hold this view in order to allow for alleged errors in the details of the Bible. The Lord Jesus clearly repudiates this lesser view of the Word of God by saying, "The Scripture cannot be nullified" (John 10:35).

Second, inspiration refers to the whole Bible. This is Paul's point in writing, *"All Scripture is inspired"* (2 Tim. 3:16). A few Bible translations have expressed this phrase as "every inspired Scripture has its use,"[7] seemingly indicating that only some, but not all, of the Scriptures are God-breathed. It is possible to translate the first word as either "all" or "every" emphasizing either the Bible as a whole ("all") or the individual parts of Scripture ("every"). However, it is incorrect to translate this as "every inspired Scripture" because it violates the natural parallelism of the text. The subject of the sentence ("all Scripture") has a predicate consisting of two adjectives describing it. These adjectives are connected by a conjunction, making the correct translation "all Scripture is inspired and profitable." To translate this as "every inspired Scripture" mangles the syntax and ignores the conjunction. Paul is maintaining a holistic approach, seeing all the Scriptures as God-breathed.

Some might object that when Paul wrote this, he was only referring to the Hebrew Scriptures, or the Old Testament. However, the Messiah Jesus promised that the Holy Spirit would teach and guide His apostles and even disclose the future to them (John 14:26; 16:13), indicating there was more revelation to come. Also, the apostle Paul, in 1 Timothy 5:18, quotes two verses, Deuteronomy 25:4 and Luke 10:7, calling them both Scripture. Clearly, Paul included the New Testament gospel of Luke in the Scriptures. Moreover, the apostle Peter says Paul's letters "are hard to understand" causing some untaught and unstable people to distort them "as they do also the rest of the Scriptures" (2 Peter 3:16). In this way, Peter included Paul's letters in the Scriptures. It is safe to say that once the New Testament was complete, its writings were understood as belonging to the Scriptures.

Understanding the whole Bible as inspired negates the incorrect theory called *partial inspiration*. This view says that certain parts of the Bible are inspired but other sections, such as the story of creation or predictive elements (which seemingly could not be known by a human author) should not be considered inspired. It is evident that this falls short of the plain statement that "all Scripture is inspired" because both Jesus and Paul cite from both the creation story (Matt. 19:4–5; 1 Tim. 2:13) *and* the predictions of the Bible (Matt. 24:15; 2 Thess. 2:3–4) showing they both considered all the Scriptures to be God-breathed.

The view that the whole Bible is inspired is called *plenary inspiration*. Combining the above two observations, this chapter is affirming the verbal, plenary inspiration of Scripture.

A third crucial observation is that it is the text of Scripture that is inspired. This is evident in Paul saying "all *Scripture* is inspired." One common but mistaken idea is to apply inspiration to the human authors of the books of the Bible. Certainly, the Holy Spirit used human authors in writing the Bible but the idea of being God-breathed pertains to the actual text of Scripture.

Seeing the text as inspired uncovers yet another common error. In addition to the text of the Bible, some also consider the historical events recorded in the Bible to be revelatory in and of themselves. As such, too often interpreters, using archaeology or ancient inscriptions, search for what "really happened" in a biblical event in order to discover all the revelation found in this event, even beyond what the Bible reveals. However, in actuality, God inspired the text of Scripture not the historical events contained in those texts. Therefore, the recounting of these events in the God-breathed Scripture makes their description historically true and accurate even without extrabiblical substantiation. Moreover, it is the text of the Bible that gives an accurate and true explanation with the divine perspective of those events.[8]

J. I. Packer rightly maintains that the meaning and significance of the historical events recorded in the Bible are found in God's revelatory explanation of them as found in Scripture, not in the historical events themselves. He says that the Exodus was one of many ancient people migrations and the crucifixion of Jesus was one of thousands of Roman executions. It is the Scriptures that interpret their significance, showing that through these events, God redeemed Israel as a nation and through the death and resurrection of Jesus, God redeemed humanity.[9] Simply put, readers of the Bible need to interpret the text of Scripture, not recover the historical events recounted in the Bible.

Accepting the idea that the text of Scripture is inspired negates the error of the *neoorthodox view of Scripture*: the claim that the Bible becomes the Word of God when a reader encounters the Messiah Jesus "in his own subjective experience."[10] This view places inspiration into the reader's perspective rather than the text of Scripture.

Understanding the God-breathed nature of the Bible begs another question: By what means were the Scriptures inspired or how did God use human authors to produce it? To that discussion we now turn.

THE MEANS OF INSPIRATION

The central verse describing how God used human authors to write the books of the Bible is 2 Peter 1:20–21: "No prophecy of Scripture becomes a matter of someone's own interpretation, for no prophecy was ever made by an act of human will, but men moved by the Holy Spirit spoke from God." According to this verse, the Bible is a theanthropic book, meaning a divine-human book, derived from the Greek word for God (*theos*) and human (*anthrōpos*). Here are three observations about Peter's words.

First, God is the source of the contents of Scripture. Clearly, Peter is using the word *prophecy* (v. 21) to refer to the Bible because in just the previous verse he speaks of a "prophecy of Scripture." His point is that the word from God did not originate in the human authors of Scripture (thus it is not of their own interpretation) but found their source in God. The prophet Jeremiah describes false prophets as those who "tell a vision of their own imagination, not from the mouth of the LORD" (Jer. 23:16). On the contrary, a true prophet receives his message from God.

Second, the Holy Spirit moved the authors of Scripture to write God's words. Just as David said of the psalms he wrote, "The Spirit of the LORD spoke through me, and His word was on my tongue" (2 Sam. 23:2), so Peter sees the Holy Spirit as causing human writers to communicate God's word. This is a supernatural superintending of human authors to write the words of the Bible.

The Holy Spirit did this by "moving" or "bearing along"[11] human authors to speak, and by inference, to write their words down. The word translated "moved" (*pherō*) is used in Acts 27:15 about a ship being driven by the wind. In the same way a ship is borne along by the wind, so the human authors were borne along by the Holy Spirit. This explains the varying writing styles and perspectives of biblical authors. Just as the same wind can bear differing ships with different kinds of sails along in different ways, so the Holy Spirit can move writers with unique personalities and styles to write God's words.

This is similar to the scene in the classic fairy tale movie, *The Princess Bride,* in which Princess Buttercup has been kidnapped and put on a sailing ship. Her rescuer Westley pursues her and her kidnappers in a different ship and is speedily catching up to them. Then, Inigo, one of the kidnappers ponders, "I wonder if he is using the same wind we are using." Of course, the answer is yes; but different sails are moved differently by the same wind. And different biblical authors express themselves distinctively, using their own personalities and styles, even though they are all borne along by the same Holy Spirit.

A third observation is that the human authors took an active role in producing the Scriptures. Peter writes that "men . . . spoke from God" (2 Peter 1:21), indicating these were not passive agents but active participants in the process. God really was the source of their message and the Holy Spirit truly moved them along, but these writers knew what they meant and intentionally communicated their message. They were not merely taking dictation from God, as the *dictation theory of inspiration* asserts. It is a mistake to read the Bible in a way that ignores the human author's intentions, as if he did not comprehend his own message. That the author's words originated with God and were superintended by the Holy Spirit becomes the guarantee of truth and accuracy of the biblical author. It does not eliminate the author's intention, method, style, or self-understanding of his own words.

THE DEFINITION OF INSPIRATION

Having examined the meaning of the main biblical texts about inspiration, here is a simple definition of this important theological concept. This definition is based on the work of Charles C. Ryrie: Biblical inspiration is God's superintendence of human authors of the Bible so that, using their own individual personalities, they composed and recorded without error His revelation to humanity in the words of the original writings.[12]

This definition indicates that inspiration, in a direct sense, only occurred in the original writings. Of course, the science of textual criticism provides readers with a transmitted copy of the Bible that is virtually and essentially identical to those original manuscripts. Moreover, this definition presumes that an inspired text is without error. This relates to the issue of inerrancy, to which we now turn.

INERRANCY

For many years, theologians who believed in inspiration affirmed that the Bible was infallible. Yet, in the second half of the twentieth century, some theologians began to claim that although the Bible was authoritative when it came to matters of faith and practice, it contained factual errors and contradictions. In response, other theologians affirmed that a consequence of believing the Bible to be the Word of God was the confidence that it is also without error. This is the position called *inerrancy*, and it will be defended and explained in what follows.

THE DEFENSE OF INERRANCY

Some have questioned whether the Bible claims inerrancy for itself. It does, but that claim must be deduced logically from Scripture.

First, the Bible teaches that God is always true. Numbers 23:19 declares that "God is not a man, that He should lie." Exodus 34:6 describes the Lord as "abounding in faithfulness and truth." Various passages call Him the "God of truth" (Ps. 31:5; Isa. 65:16). All the ways and paths of the Lord are considered true (Ps. 25:10; 86:11). Jesus, the God-man, calls Himself "the truth" (John 14:6) and He describes the Holy Spirit as "the Spirit of truth" (John 14:17; 15:26; 16:13; see 1 John 5:6). Paul says, "God must prove to be true, though every person be found a liar" (Rom. 3:4). So many more biblical passages proclaim the truthfulness of God that it can be considered one of His essential attributes.

Second, the God who is truthful produced the Scriptures. This idea is derived from the previous discussion of the inspiration of Scripture. Since God breathed out the Bible (2 Tim. 3:16) and the Holy Spirit moved people in writing the message of Scripture (2 Peter 1:21), then plainly, God's Word must be truthful.

Third, since the truthful God produced the Scriptures, the Bible is entirely true. This was the conclusion of the psalmist: "The sum [or entirety] of Your word is truth" (Ps. 119:160). Even more significantly, the Lord Jesus prayed to God the Father that His disciples would be sanctified in the truth and then He declared, "Your word is truth" (John 17:17). Clearly the Bible teaches that the Word of God is true. Based on this, it is necessary to define inerrancy theologically.

THE DEFINITION OF INERRANCY

Paul Feinberg has given a clear definition of inerrancy: "Inerrancy means that when all facts are known, the Scriptures in their original autographs and properly interpreted will be shown to be wholly true in everything that they affirm, whether that has to do with doctrine or morality or with the social, physical, or life sciences."[13] What follows will clarify some of the finer points of this definition.[14]

THE CLARIFICATION OF INERRANCY

Simply put, the above definition claims that the Bible tells the truth. However, in order to understand the doctrine of inerrancy, some clarification is needed.

First, inerrancy is limited to the original autographs of Scripture. Inspiration, and therefore inerrancy, only apply to the original copies of the biblical books. Since none of those are extant, some have questioned the necessity of even claiming inerrancy for the Bible. However, using the science of textual criticism demonstrates that the Bible, as available today, contains 95 to 99 percent of the words of the original texts.[15] And for those passages that have unclear textual variants, the variants are either inconsequential or the original manuscripts are readily evident through sound textual criticism. Therefore, the modern copies of the Bible can be safely said to be inerrant.

Second, inerrancy only applies to what the Bible affirms. There are many statements in the Scriptures that are accurately recorded but not what the Bible actually teaches. For example, the serpent, tempting Eve in the garden, quoted God inaccurately, claiming that God prohibited eating from any tree (Gen. 3:2). The Bible records his words accurately but does not affirm his statement. Similarly, the Bible accurately records the bad advice Job's friends gave him without affirming their mistaken ideas.

Third, inerrancy assumes the use of normal, ordinary language. When people speak with imprecise or nonscientific speech, they are still considered truthful. The same is true for the Bible. So when the Bible speaks of "the four corners of the earth" (Isa. 11:12), it is not claiming a square earth but using a figure of speech to describe the extremities of the world. When Jesus says that the mustard seed is "the smallest of all the seeds" (Mark 4:31), He is not using scientific precision, but merely using what was commonly understood in that day. Also when the Scriptures mention sunrise (Ps. 113:3), it is not denying a heliocentric world but merely using speech as a meteorologist does on a local newscast when giving the weather forecast. When Genesis 15:13 says that Abraham's descendants would be in Egypt for 400 years, it is merely rounding the precise number of 430 found in Exodus 12:40. Rounding numbers and ordinary speech do not deny the truthfulness of the Bible.

Some critics have cited a few grammatical errors found in the Bible or some of its loose quotations as objections to inerrancy. But a grammatical mistake or a free quotation would not cause a court to question the truthfulness of a witness. With the ordinary use of language, truthfulness is the core issue—not perfect grammar or verbatim quotations.

Finally, what the Bible affirms must correspond to reality. Some philosophers have questioned whether it is even possible for propositional ideas (as found in the Bible) to correspond to the reality of the world. Therefore, they have adopted an alternative coherence theory of truth, claiming that truth should be tested by internal consistency or coherence not correspondence to reality. John S. Feinberg has criticized the coherence theory of truth this way: Some may have "produced an internally consistent system (hence true in a coherence sense), but that doesn't mean that the beliefs affirm anything that matches the world." He illustrates the problem with coherence by listing five propositions about the Bible and then points out,

> Now, none of the five propositions contradicts any of the others. Hence, if coherence is our measure of truth, all five must be true. . . . Each claim affirms something about the universe in which we live. If what these sentences affirm doesn't match/correspond to states of affairs in our world, then these five propositions may be nothing more than fantasies—perhaps comforting ones, but fantasies nonetheless.[16]

As Feinberg makes plain, for a proposition to be true, it must not only cohere to other propositions in a text, it must also conform to the reality. Therefore, coherence as a theory is insufficient. Inerrancy requires the propositional affirmations of the Bible to correspond to the truth. Thus, the parting of the Red Sea or the resurrection of Jesus not only cohere with the rest of Scripture, they correspond to actual reality.

God has delivered His inspired Word without error to this world. However, how can people be sure that the correct books were included in the Bible? This is the next issue to be discussed.

CANONICITY

The Greek word *kanōn* literally means "rod, ruler, or reed," indicating it is the measure of something. Our term "canon" is generally used of the authoritative norm for a group of writings, for example, "the canon of Shakespeare" or "the Dickens' Canon." When it comes to the Bible, it refers to the authoritative writings of Scripture. The question at hand is how were the individual books of the Bible included in the canon?

Popular novelists seem to think that church leaders or church councils determined the canon of Scripture in some sort of conspiracy. In actuality, God determined the biblical canon via inspiration. The essential test of canonicity is inspiration. God inspired certain books and these were placed in the canon. So *God's role was to determine* the canon by inspiring the books while the role of *God's people was to discover* which books God had made canonical.

The people of God discovered the canon of Scripture using six principles.

1. The Reception Principle—God's people immediately received the individual books as Scripture. Even some disputed books were immediately accepted and only later were they questioned. The faithful remnant of Israel immediately received divinely inspired books as Scripture. With the New Testament, the churches immediately accepted, circulated, and copied the books because they were recognized as inspired. An example of this is in Paul's words to the Thessalonians, "When you received the word of God which you heard from us, you accepted it not as the word of mere men, but as what it really is, the word of God" (1 Thess. 2:13).

2. The Prophetic/Apostolic Principle—The books of the Bible were written by authoritative spokesmen for God. Israel's prophets were moved by God's Spirit to write the Old Testament Scriptures (2 Peter 1:21), and apostles or their prophetic associates wrote the New Testament books (Eph. 2:20). Of course, the authors of some books are unknown today (e.g., 1 and 2 Kings, or Hebrews) but the original receptors likely knew the identity of these authors and deemed them prophetic.

3. The Truthfulness Principle—In the Old Testament, prophets were tested by their words coming true (Deut. 18:22). Similarly, in the New Testament, teaching was determined to be true by its conformity to apostolic teaching (Gal. 1:8). The assumption was that true biblical books would correspond to reality and faithful doctrine.

4. The Attestation Principle—Whenever Scripture was written, God confirmed the truth of the message with signs and wonders. So, when Moses wrote the Torah, God worked remarkable miracles for Moses and Joshua to substantiate it. When Elijah and Elisha were used by God to elevate the prophetic office in Israel, God substantiated their work (and the books of the other prophets) through miraculous confirmation of their ministries. Also, with the Gospels and the apostolic writings, God authenticated those biblical books with the miraculous ministries of Jesus and the apostles (Acts 2:22; 14:3; 2 Cor. 12:12; Heb. 2:3–4).

5. The Dynamic Principle—The books of the Bible were not merely ancient books or considered spiritually helpful. Rather, the author of Hebrews identifies "the word of God" as "living and active, and sharper than any two-edged sword" (Heb. 4:12). The books of the Bible were discovered as canonical because they were dynamic in changing lives.

6. The Messianic Principle—One factor in discovering the Old Testament canon was whether those books had an ultimate expectation of the coming Messiah (Luke 24:25–27, 44–46). John H. Sailhamer is correct when he writes,

> I believe the messianic thrust of the OT was the *whole* reason the books of the Hebrew Bible were written. In other words, the Hebrew Bible was not written as the national literature of Israel. It probably also was not written to the nation of Israel as such. Rather, it was written, in my opinion, as the expression of the deep-seated messianic hope of a small group of faithful prophets and their followers.[17]

Similarly, New Testament books needed an elevated understanding of the Messiah Jesus. Whether telling the story of the God-man, the messianic King Jesus, as the Gospels do, or the apostolic proclamation of the exalted Jesus in Acts, or the depiction of believers being united with the divine Messiah in the epistles, or the victorious return of glorified Messiah Jesus in Revelation, the books of the New Testament were recognized because they were centered on Jesus with an highly elevated Christology.

Despite recent attempts to add or take away books from the canon, it can be stated confidently that the sixty-six books of the Bible are authentic and true. Intentionally, the last book of the Bible, Revelation, ends with the warning against adding or taking away from the words of this book (Rev. 22:18–19). Although this admonition applies directly to the book of Revelation, its placement at the end of the canon serves as an appropriate message for the whole Bible.

CONCLUSION

William Tyndale, the English Reformer, was strangled and burned at the stake on October 6, 1536. His crime? Tyndale had translated the Bible into English so ordinary people could read it. Both the religious and political leadership of his day were radically opposed to common people having access to the Scriptures. But Tyndale was fearless. He said,

> Let it not make thee despair, neither yet discourage thee, O reader, that it is forbidden thee in pain of life and goods, or that it is made breaking of the king's peace, or treason unto his highness, to read the Word of thy soul's health—for if God be on our side, what matter maketh it who be against us.[18]

William Tyndale translated the Scriptures into English because He believed in the absolute inspiration and authority of God's Word. That made him willing to give his life for the Bible.

The point of this chapter was to articulate what the Bible teaches about itself; that it is actually God's inspired and inerrant revelation to humanity. Most of us own an excellent translation of the Scriptures in our own mother tongues maybe even multiple translations. Unfortunately, even those who hold to the high view Scripture espoused in this chapter may be inconsistent Bible readers or even neglect it completely. Most likely, we will never be required to give our lives for the Bible as Tyndale did. But if we believe that God's Word is forever settled in heaven (Ps. 119:89) and that it will stand forever (Isa. 40:8), we will take some time to read it on a daily basis. The Bible is God's Word, freely given to us, and God will use it to transform our lives.

NOTES

1. Paul Enns, *The Moody Handbook of Theology* (Chicago: Moody Publishers, 1989), 156.

2. C.S. Lewis, *Mere Christianity* (New York: Macmillan, 1952), 17–39.

3. "Discover the Crypt," St. Paul's Cathedral, https: //www.stpauls.co.uk/history-collections/history/explore-the-cathedral/discover-the-crypt.

4. "ἐξηγέομαι," *A Greek-English Lexicon of the New Testament and Other Christian Literature* (BDAG), 3rd ed. (Chicago: University of Chicago Press, 2001), 349.

5. A theophany is a manifestation of the Lord in the form of "the Angel of the Lord." Since Scripture plainly states that no one has ever seen the Father (John 1:18), theophanies are preincarnate manifestations of God the Son. As such, they could also be called christophanies.

6. "γραφή," BDAG, 206.

7. The New English Bible is an example of this translation.

8. That is not to say that inscriptions and archaeological findings are useless. In fact, they are quite helpful in defending the authenticity and truth of the biblical record.

9. J. I. Packer, *God Speaks to Man, Revelation and the Bible* (Philadelphia: Westminster, 1965), 51–52.

10. Enns, *The Moody Handbook of Theology*, 162.

11. "φέρω," BDAG, 1051.

12. This definition is a conflation of two similar definitions written by Charles C. Ryrie. The first is in *A Survey of Bible Doctrine* (Chicago: Moody Press, 1972), 38, and the second one is found in *Basic Theology* (Chicago: Moody Publishers, 1987), 81.

13. Paul Feinberg, "The Meaning of Inerrancy," *Inerrancy*, ed. Norman Geisler (Grand Rapids: Zondervan:, 1979), 294.

14. Some have found problems in the text of Scripture and as a result have challenged the inerrancy of the Bible. However, there are helpful solutions to these alleged errors, seeming contradictions or text critical difficulties. The brevity of this chapter prevents addressing these but one good source for dealing with them is Gleason L. Archer Jr.'s *New International Encyclopedia of Bible Difficulties* (Grand Rapids: Zondervan, 2001).

15. See the excellent discussion of inerrancy as it relates to the original autographs in *Light in a Dark Place: The Doctrine of Scripture* (Wheaton, IL: Crossway Books, 2018), 307–17, specifically that the New Testament has 99 percent certainty and the Old Testament 95 percent, 313.

16. John S. Feinberg, *Light in a Dark Place: The Doctrine of Scripture* (Wheaton, IL: Crossway, 2018), 253. Feinberg's entire discussion of correspondence vs. coherence as a theory of truth is extremely helpful. See 251–56.

17. John H. Sailhamer, "The Messiah and the Hebrew Bible," *The Moody Handbook of Messianic Prophecy*, eds. Michael Rydelnik and Edwin Blum (Chicago: Moody Publishers, 2019), 59.

18. "William Tyndale: Translator of the First English Testament," Christian History, https: //www.christianitytoday.com/history/people/scholarsandscientists/william-tyndale.html.

Understanding the Basic Doctrine of Salvation

BRYAN L. O'NEAL

INTRODUCTION

"Soteriology" is the theological term for the doctrine of salvation; it is derived from the Greek word *sōtēr*, which means "to save or deliver." From a Christian perspective, salvation is the sovereign work of the triune God whereby fallen, sinful humans are conformed perfectly and finally to the likeness of Jesus, and everything that happens in all of creation is oriented to achieve this goal. This rich doctrine is developed throughout the Old and New Testaments, but is summarized beautifully in Romans 8:28–30:

> And we know that God causes all things to work together for good to those who love God, to those who are called according to His purpose. For those whom He foreknew, He also predestined to become conformed to the image of His Son, so that He would be the firstborn among many brothers and sisters; and these whom He predestined, He also called; and these whom He called, He also justified; and these whom He justified, He also glorified.

Several key observations from this passage will frame the study that follows. First, we observe that the ultimate goal of God's saving work is our "conform[ity] to the image of His Son." This is the "good" spoken of in the oft-quoted Romans 8:28—a far greater benefit than an improved job or an upgraded relationship, the sorts of things people often seem to have in mind when they claim this verse. What a comfort for Christians to realize that "all things" work together to make us like Jesus! This verse also implies that humans in their natural condition fail to conform to the image of Jesus and are thus in need of this saving work; our need for salvation will be the first topic addressed below.

Second, we see that the work of salvation is actually a complex and richly textured unified series of divine actions—this passage includes "foreknowing," "predestining," "calling," "justifying," and "glorifying." Notably, from a grammatical perspective, God is the subject of each of these clauses, indicating that He is the one performing the action. Salvation is a work achieved by God, not by us! Other passages include descriptions of adopting, sealing, and sanctifying. What these and other concepts reveal is that there is both a logical and temporal series, or order, of how God goes about securing our salvation (the Latin term for this is *ordo salutis*). These elements are often considered in a logical order, or cataloged according to the work of each divine person (the work of the Father, the work of the Son, the work of the Spirit); both of these treatments are fully legitimate. In the section below on the order of salvation, we will be exploring these components in a generally temporal order (which corresponds in large part to the logical and personal orderings), considering the past, present, and future aspects of God's saving work.

Nested in the salvific sequence of Romans 8:28–30 is the mention of justification, which points us to the pivotal event of Jesus' death on the cross. Though justification is not equivalent or reducible to the cross-work of Jesus, a proper understanding of this event and those surrounding it are obviously crucial to an accurate understanding of the Christian faith. When we speak of Jesus as a "sacrifice" or "dying for our sins on the cross," we are referring to the atoning work of Christ. Several theories, or accounts, of the atonement have been proposed; below we will consider several inaccurate or incomplete theories, as well as present the historically orthodox position of "vicarious penal atonement."

THE NEED FOR SALVATION

A discussion of "salvation" or "deliverance" implies peril that threatens us. That peril is reflected in verses asserting "all have sinned and fall short of the glory of God" (Rom. 3:23) and the "wages of sin is death" (Rom. 6:23). Though the doctrine of the fall is discussed in greater depth in an earlier chapter on the doctrine of humanity, a brief analysis of the fallen condition will motivate the exposition of salvation that follows.

Humankind originally was created not only without sin (a negative condition that applies just as well to animals and the rest of creation), but particularly "in the image of God," a positive characteristic applied uniquely to humans (Gen. 1:26–27). In the fall, people became sinful in deed and inclination, but perhaps worse, also suffered corruption of the divine image.

This poses a two-fold problem for mankind; and the salvation God provides, as described in the Scriptures, addresses both. First, there is a penalty for sin—death—as decreed in God's warning to Adam in Genesis 2:17 and reiterated in Romans 6:23. This death is a literal bodily death, as well as a spiritual death of separation from God. Further, though the divine image is not lost in the fall, it is corrupted, and as such we are repulsive in the presence of the Holy One. Jesus' parable of the guest at the wedding feast who is expelled for not being properly attired points to this (Matt. 22:11–13). Stated more explicitly in Habakkuk 1:13: "Your eyes are too pure to look at evil." So, the salvation we require must include a payment of just punishment, as well as the healing of our corrupted image and restoration to the unsullied image of God.

ORDER OF SALVATION

Paul declares, "For by grace you have been saved through faith; and this is not of yourselves, it is the gift of God; not as a result of works, so that no one may boast" (Eph. 2:8–9); this is rightly the core of gospel presentation. Marriage is a recurring biblical metaphor for God's relationship with His people, and the illustration is helpful here. A bride might view the marriage proposal as beginning the new relationship, initiated when she accepts the invitation. However, much has happened prior to that invitation, even if she is unaware, and much will follow afterward. It makes as little sense to reduce salvation to "receiving Christ" as it does to reduce marriage to "getting engaged," as crucial as that moment of decision is.

FOREKNOWLEDGE AND ELECTION

Salvation, we learn, begins in eternity past, when God "chose us in Him before the foundation of the world, that we would be holy and blameless before Him. In love He predestined us to adoption as sons and daughters through Jesus Christ" (Eph. 1:4–5). In the Romans 8 "golden chain" of salvation, we read that first God "foreknew" us, and "those whom He foreknew, He also predestined" (Rom. 8:29). Biblically, knowledge and foreknowledge are not matters of mere intellectual acquaintance, but instead an affirmation of deep intimacy. The King James Version accurately translates this in Genesis 4:1 when it reads, "And Adam knew Eve his wife; and she conceived," a fact obscured by more modern translations that read "had relations" (e.g., NASB). The sexual relationship is a mere expression of the much deeper knowledge relationship between husband and wife, or between God and human beings.

This illustration helps us understand some otherwise puzzling words of Jesus in the Sermon on the Mount: "Not everyone who says to Me, 'Lord, Lord,' will enter the kingdom of heaven. . . . Many will say to Me on that day, 'Lord, Lord, did we not prophesy in Your name, and in Your name cast out demons, and in Your name perform many miracles?' And then I will declare to them, 'I never knew you; leave Me, you who practice lawlessness'" (Matt. 7:21–23). Obviously, the omniscient Christ is not invoking His own intellectual ignorance as the grounds for rejecting these lawless ones, but rather, is indicating that He has never had an intimate relationship with them. If knowledge, biblically speaking, connotes deep personal intimacy, then *fore*knowledge speaks of an intimacy, a love, prior even to creation itself, before the foundation of the world. God is love (1 John 4:8), the relationship among the members of the Trinity is defined by love (John 3:35; 5:20), and it is the Father's love for the world that motivates Him to send Jesus to secure our salvation (John 3:16).

Election, and predestination, are inescapably biblical concepts and corollaries of God's foreknowledge. Our passage from Romans 8 above declares, "Those whom He foreknew, He also predestined . . . , and those whom He predestined, He also called" (8:29). Later in that chapter Paul asks rhetorically, "Who will bring charges against God's elect?" (8:33). "Election" connotes the idea of God choosing the object of His grace, and "predestination" literally means "determining the destination before."

Two common objections to this doctrine are that it makes our salvation arbitrary, and that it is a violation of our free will. However, this passage (Rom. 8) corrects both those misunderstandings. Predestination, we see, is grounded in the love of God—God elects, or predestines, those He has eternally foreknown, or foreloved. And God's love, while mysterious, is definitely not arbitrary, any more than the love humans have for one another is arbitrary. Second, as we will see below, God's acting out of this election is to "call" men and women to Himself—to give them new life by the regenerating work of the Holy Spirit and then to effectively call them to trust in Jesus. This does not override human will, but rather engages it to accomplish the purposes of God.

CALLING AND REGENERATION

Despite God's eternal love for us, in our rebellion we suffer from a distortion of His image, a commitment to rebellion, and an expectation of deserved condemnation. The gospel, or "good news," is that God in the person of Jesus has suffered that deserved condemnation in our place, and we can enjoy the benefit of His sacrifice by casting ourselves on His mercy and trusting in Him alone for salvation. The gospel call is both the declaration of our fallen condition and the invitation to turn to Jesus for salvation.

Though our salvation is grounded in eternity past, as those eternally foreloved of the Father, and is objectively secured at the cross through the atoning sacrifice of Jesus, our experience of salvation begins when we hear and respond to the gospel call to repent of our sins and put our trust in Jesus for deliverance. The problem, however, is that we are "dead in our sins" and as such cannot truly hear and respond to the call of God.

Given this reality, it makes sense to distinguish between the "general call" and an "effective call" whereby we respond in saving faith. "The heavens tell of the glory of God" (Ps. 19:1), and "For since the creation of the world His invisible attributes, that is, His eternal power and divine nature, have been clearly perceived, being understood by what has been made, so that they are without excuse" (Rom. 1:20). We are surrounded by the constant declaration of God's power and justice. And yet, though we know it, in our spiritual death we have no desire to respond or submit to this call. Though all see and hear it, it does not lead to the salvation of all. That is the point of Paul's rebuttal in Romans 10 to the hypothetical challenge "How are they to hear [better, how could they have heard] without a preacher?": all *have*, in fact, heard of God's character and the just demand for worship and righteous living through this general revelation, mediated to all through both nature and conscience. Though all have heard, the call falls on deaf (and dead) ears, and all naturally persist in unbelief.

If in our fallen condition we are dead and unable to respond to the call of God, what we need is new life, to be made alive and reborn ("born again"), that in our new life we might not only hear the call of God but respond in faith and in joy. This is precisely what Jesus describes to Nicodemus in the famous exchange of John 3.

This gift of new life is called "regeneration," which Jesus declares is a work of the Holy Spirit: "That which has been born of the flesh is flesh, and that which has been born of the Spirit is spirit. Do not be amazed that I said to you, 'You must be born again'" (John 3:6–7). It is only after having been made alive again by the Spirit through the new birth that we hear the same gospel call, to repent of sin and turn to Christ. And now, in our regenerated condition, we can see the truth and beauty of the gospel, and have the desire to embrace it. This is the testimony of so many believers—that for years they sat week after week in church hearing biblical preaching and evangelistic messages without effect, but one time, suddenly, they heard it differently and responded in faith. This is not because the message of the gospel was altered to be finally attractive, but it was the receptivity of the respondent miraculously transformed through new birth. Theologically, this is expressed by the assertion that "regeneration precedes faith." (Acceptance of this truth would help relieve the anxiety and guilt of those Christians who continually search for the perfect argument or "silver bullet" to convince and convert their unbelieving friends. We would be wise to remember the words of Paul in 1 Corinthians 3:5–9 that while some plant and others water, it is God who brings the growth.)

FAITH AND JUSTIFICATION

We have been "justified by faith" (Rom. 5:1), and "everyone who believes in [Jesus] will not perish, but have eternal life" (John 3:16). Faith, or belief, clearly is critical to the experience of salvation. This faith is of a special nature, however, and must be distinguished from reductionistic characterizations. One component of belief is intellectual understanding—we comprehend what it means to say that we are sinners deserving of death, that God offers His Son, Jesus, as a substitute on our behalf, and that we can receive the benefit of Jesus' punishment in place of our own by trusting, or accepting, that offer. This understanding (Latin, *noticia*) does not save us, however. Many atheists understand the Christian message as well as any believer, but they believe the message is false. Salvation requires that we believe this message to be true (Latin *assensus*, or assent). And yet, even such assent is not sufficient to save us. Satan and the demons likewise know the gospel message is true as James points out, "You believe that God is one. You do well; the demons also believe, and shudder" (James 2:19). Beyond understanding and affirmation, the kind of belief required for salvation is trust (Latin, *fiducia*)—that is, a declaration that we know the gospel to be true but also rely only on the work and faithfulness of God in Christ to save us. Trust, even more than belief, is the key to saving faith. And by the grace of God, when we are regenerated, we not only believe in God and His offer of deliverance, but we joyfully and wholeheartedly embrace the gospel and trust in Christ alone for salvation.

Justification, then, is the divine work whereby in response to trusting faith, God reckons, or regards, us as righteous. This reckoning is grounded in the sacrifice of Jesus on the cross and relies on an imputation in two directions. "Imputation" occurs when a quality or value is credited to someone; for example, in marriage the obligations and assets of each partner typically are credited to the other (at least in the age before prenuptial agreements). As already discussed at length, we are hopeless and condemned, lost in our sins. We owe a debt we cannot pay; and at the cross, He who knew no sin became sin for us (2 Cor. 5:21). Our sins are credited, or imputed, to Jesus, so that when He dies, He really is dying for our sins. It is objectively true, like a rich benefactor taking upon himself our crushing financial obligation and wiping it out by paying off all our creditors.

Jesus' act of bearing the sins of the world, suffering and dying for them on the cross, is sometimes termed the "passive obedience of Christ" (though there is obviously nothing passive about it). Jesus, through His work on the cross, receives the wrath of God in full measure and on our behalf. "This is love, not that we loved God, but that He loved us and sent His Son to be the propitiation for our sins" (1 John 4:10). "Propitiation" means "turning away wrath," and this is how God becomes both "just and the justifier" (Rom. 3:26)—just, in that God demands that the penalty for sins be paid, and justifier, in that God paid that penalty Himself in the person of Jesus.

However, as awesome as it is that our debt has been wiped out, that alone still is not enough for our salvation; the reckoning as described thus far only succeeds in getting us to neutral, or zero. This is comparable to a person who owns absolutely nothing and yet has an overwhelming debt (and negative net financial worth), whose obligations are graciously satisfied by another. After those debts are paid, the person still has nothing, no assets (a "zero net financial worth"). Though obviously a vastly superior position than remaining in crushing debt, this is still a condition of utter poverty. Thankfully there is a second imputation, in which God also imputes to us the riches, or moral righteousness, of Christ; it is as if the benefactor, after satisfying our debts, goes further and adds our names to his bank accounts and makes us co-owners of all his assets.

To enjoy the eternal presence of God and true fellowship with Him requires positive righteousness, achieved through conformity to the character and law of God. In this, the first Adam and all of Israel failed. Jesus Christ, the second Adam, in His incarnation and earthly sojourn, not only avoided sin at every moment but also actually fulfilled the law. He loved God with all His heart, soul, strength, and mind, and He truly loved His neighbor as Himself (along with satisfying the rest of the Law). That is, Jesus was not only innocent of sin, but also positively righteous—rich, if you will, with the righteousness of God. In the second imputation of the cross, this storehouse of Jesus' righteous richness, achieved through a life of perfect obedience to the Father (sometimes termed the "active obedience of Christ") is credited to us, even as our sin is credited to Him. This idea is captured in Jesus' parable of the wedding, which demands that those in attendance be clothed in appropriate garments—namely, the righteousness of Christ (Phil. 3:9).

Justification, then, is based on this double imputation—our sins to Jesus and His righteousness to us—and this divine transaction occurs in history on the cross. Though the ground of this justification is objectively accomplished at the cross, it is subjectively applied in the act of saving faith, in which we trust in the work of Christ and not our own ability to pay our debts or build up our assets. And it is a *reality*. This is not a case of God playing "Let's Pretend," in which He pretends we are righteous, but we really are not. That perspective is akin to a children's game of pretending to be married while all the while knowing it is not really true. This genuine justification and reckoning of righteousness, rather, is pictured in an authentic marriage, where the two become one, and that which God joins let no one separate.

Paul declares that Jesus "was delivered over because of our wrongdoings, and was raised because of our justification" (Rom. 4:25). By His resurrection, Jesus proves that His sacrifice was acceptable to the Father. Furthermore, He is the "first fruits" of a great resurrection, in which we will also one day participate, culminating in our own glorification (1 Cor. 15:20–23).

SANCTIFICATION AND GLORIFICATION

Salvation as described to this point has primarily focused on events in the past: the foreloving of God, Jesus' work on the cross, and that moment when we were born again, trusted Jesus for salvation, and were justified. Unfortunately, it is all too common to reduce our understanding of salvation to these past events. It would be a grave omission, however, to view salvation as only an historic event and to neglect its present and future dimensions.

Just as it makes sense to look back to when we "were saved" (objectively at the cross and subjectively at conversion), we should recognize that we "are being saved" in the present (sanctification) and we "will be saved in the future" (glorification).

Paul tells the believers in Philippi to "work out [their] salvation" (Phil. 2:12). As we have already seen, he cannot be telling them to work *for* their salvation, as that is accomplished through justification (we are saved by grace through faith). Rather, he is calling them to live a certain way in response to their salvation. "Sanctification" is the process of growing in experiential holiness, pursuing and knowing God more, being progressively conformed to His image in Christ by the Spirit. Though we have been objectively saved, we still live in a fallen world and are confronted by the triple enemies of the world, the flesh, and the devil (Eph. 2:1–3). The New Testament epistles are filled with instructions to believing Christians to turn from their ongoing sinful behaviors and to advance in righteous living. In the same letter, Paul can declare that the Corinthians are "saints"—holy ones—and also confront them for their particular actions of unholiness (1 Cor. 1:2; 4:14). In the face of our ongoing sin, as those who now are found in Christ Jesus (Phil. 3:9), we do not experience the critical judgment or condemnation of God (Rom. 8:1), but we do experience the mercy and sympathy of God (Heb. 2:17–18; 4:15–16) as well as the discipline of God as a loving Father (Heb. 12:4–11). In contrast to the other components of salvation we have considered, which are basically punctiliar, i.e., occurring at a specific point in time, sanctification is progressive, occurring over time. We grow in obedience and holiness, and as such are "being saved" in the present.

The scriptural passage that has served to frame this entire discussion of salvation is Romans 8:28–30, and we recall from there that God's goal in salvation—the "good" to which all these actions point—is that we be "conformed to the image of His Son." In justification we are regarded as righteous, truly credited with the righteousness of Christ, though we continue to sin in this life. In sanctification, we are undergoing a process of being made holy but will never achieve perfect obedience or perfect conformity in this life. However, the end of the "golden chain" of salvation in Romans 8 is glorification: when we see Jesus (at our death or His return) "we will be like Him, because we will see Him just as He is" (1 John 3:2). Then, we will be finally and completely saved.

It is sometimes said that in the past, at justification, we are delivered from the penalty of sin; in the present, through sanctification, we are being delivered from the power of sin; and in the future, when glorified, we will be delivered from even the presence of sin. While useful, this characterization is not precisely true. It is true that when we are finally in the presence of Jesus, we will be perfectly conformed to His image. However, glorified believers will be present ruling with Christ in the millennial kingdom, which will continue to include sin and rebellion against the lordship of Christ and will conclude with final judgment at the great white throne. Better, we should say that in glorification, in resurrected bodies, we are delivered from the proclivity to sin, as well as the corruption of our bodies leading to physical death. Before we were justified, we wanted to sin and we did sin; after conversion, we want to not sin but still regularly do. When glorified, we will be conformed to the moral image of Jesus and will not even want to sin, even as He does not sin, as the beauty of the divine nature will be so apparent to us that we vastly prefer to live in conformity to the character of Jesus than to any lesser model.

Two points demand clarification here: first, we will continue to be fully human through all eternity, and this will include exercising our minds and wills and bodies. Eternity will not be a boring time of bland passivity, with no meaningful action. Rather, we will spend forever knowing (and growing in knowledge) of God and His creation, worshiping Him, and exercising righteous dominion over the universe. "Heaven" is actually a place on earth—the new heavens and the new earth—a re-created Eden occupied by a redeemed and glorified humanity. In that place and time, we will not only fail to sin, we will persistently act in ways that fulfill the will of God and display genuine righteousness.

Second, glorification results in perfect conformity to the moral image of Jesus, but not conformity to His divine nature; we will always be human, with all that entails, including finitude. When confronted by a mystery or something we do not understand in this age, Christians sometimes console one another by saying we will understand or know these things in heaven, when we are glorified. Though I am confident there will be many things that will make sense in the presence of

Jesus that do not while we see through a mirror dimly (1 Cor. 13:12), it does not follow that we will know "everything" in glory. Omniscience—perfect and complete knowledge—is a divine attribute, and we will never be divine. When glorified, we will cast off false beliefs and will continue to acquire additional true beliefs and understanding, but we will never know or understand everything—and we will be satisfied with that.

ASPECTS OF SALVATION: UNION, ADOPTION, AND SEALING

Though not mentioned explicitly in the "order of salvation" in Romans 8 that is guiding our consideration, a few other aspects of salvation require acknowledgment here. These include our union with Christ, adoption as sons and daughters, and the Spirit's sealing of believers. Theologians differ as to whether these should be characterized as the result, or "fruit," of salvation, or regarded as the foundation of salvation itself. Regardless, it is clear from the Bible that these components are inseparable from salvation and thus merit our attention (and wonder!).

UNITED WITH CHRIST

One of the great metaphysical mysteries of the Bible is that we are declared to be united, or one, with Christ (and with one another). This mystery is so incomprehensible to us that God ordained marriage to help us comprehend this miracle, among other reasons. God declares that in marriage, a husband and wife become "one flesh"—they are united to each other (Gen. 2:24). This declaration informs the characterization—so much more than mere metaphor—that the church is the bride of Christ. This understanding entails and grounds all biblical instructions for marriage, including that the husband must sacrificially love and care for, and even if necessary die for his wife, even as Christ does for the church. Further, the wife must honor and submit to her husband in response to his sacrificial love, even as the church is called to be rapturously devoted to Jesus. As in marriage, these behaviors are not the cause of our unity with Christ but rather the outgrowth of that unity. We have been united to Christ, which means we are one with Him—we are credited with His righteousness and conformed to His image. This union with Christ, and in marriage, is why Paul finds the physically and spiritually adulterous relationships of the Corinthians so scandalous. When we participate in sexual immorality or any other sin, as those who are united with Christ, it is almost as if we were introducing unrighteousness into that very union. May it never be!

ADOPTION

This understanding of union with Christ also informs the doctrine of adoption. Paul and John repeatedly assert that we have been brought into the family of God (Rom. 8:15; John 1:12). In this as well, our human understanding of adoption is instructive but inadequate. Human adoption is a truly gracious act by which a family reaches out to one not related by blood and makes them legally and literally a part of the family. There is a sense in which God's adoption of us is similar, although in the new birth we are "born again" into the family of God through regeneration.

Union with Christ better informs even this. If Christ is our bridegroom and we are united with Him, then our adoption is effectively the consequence of our being united to Him. As He is a true Son of God, and we are truly united with Him, then we also are sons and daughters of God through this union. This is a great mystery, but even our access to the Father is mediated through our relationship with Jesus (as when we pray, "Our Father, who is in heaven"). The effect of our adoption is that we gain access to all the benefits enjoyed by "true born children," which includes access to the Father, His unqualified favor, and co-stewardship and co-regency of the inheritance of heaven. First-century Roman adoption practices bolstered this understanding, as displayed prominently in Julius Caesar's adoption of Octavian as his heir. Octavian ultimately inherited the riches and title of Caesar at his death. We know him more familiarly as Caesar Augustus, the Roman ruler who played such a pivotal role in the birth narrative of Jesus.

SEALING

This focus on adoption leads naturally to a consideration of the sealing ministry of the Holy Spirit. Paul admonishes us to "not grieve the Holy Spirit of God, by whom you were sealed for the day of redemption" (Eph. 4:30), and he assures us that "having also believed, you were sealed in Him with the Holy Spirit of promise, who is a first installment of our inheritance" (Eph. 1:13–14).

Several ramifications of the Spirit's sealing are evident here. In Roman times, a seal was a distinctive marker, indicating origin, possession, or approval; Paul uses the word in this sense when he describes his relationship to the Corinthians (1 Cor. 9:2) and the Romans (Rom. 15:28). A seal can also protect or impose a limit, such as when a letter is sealed with wax and can only be legally opened by the sender or recipient. This was the significance of Jesus' tomb being sealed by the soldiers in Matthew 27:66; rather than a line of solder running around the perimeter of the stone, this was likely a single blob of wax marked with the Roman signet, declaring that anyone who breaks the seal incurs the full wrath of Caesar.

Finally, we see in these texts a reference to the Spirit as a "seal" on the transaction of salvation—a pledge of a more complete salvation to follow. In this sense, the indwelling Spirit is a down payment or first installment on all future benefits associated with salvation. Just as no one willingly forfeits their down payment by failing to complete all future obligations in a contract, so also our evidence that God will give us all things, even heaven itself, is proven by the fact that He has already given us His Spirit to indwell us. So then, Paul summarily declares, "For you have not received a spirit of slavery leading to fear again, but you have received a spirit of adoption as sons and daughters by which we cry out 'Abba! Father!'" (Rom. 8:15). That is, in continuity with the doctrine of adoption discussed above, our adoption itself is actually a work of the Holy Spirit; the Spirit is the one who brings us into unity with Christ and thus makes us sons and daughters of God. It is Christ's work on the cross that makes it possible for us to be sons and daughters, and it is the Spirit's work that makes it actual. This adoption is the most forceful aspect of "sealing" and securing us that the Spirit could possibly perform.

BIBLICAL BACKGROUND OF ATONEMENT

We know that the cross of Christ is the time and place of our reconciliation to God, but what does this mean? How does the atonement work? To gain a fuller understanding of atonement, we examine the biblical background of what Jesus accomplished on the cross. The various feasts and sacrifices of the Jewish people, as prescribed in the Old Testament, point forward to the coming of Jesus as Messiah, the Anointed One who came to save and lead God's people. Two of those feasts are particularly foundational for understanding the cross-work of Jesus: the Passover and the Day of Atonement.

In the biblical account of the institution of the Passover feast, each household of the people of Israel was instructed to select a lamb without blemish, to kill it at twilight, and to take the blood of the lamb and paint the doorposts of their houses. When the Lord moved through Egypt that night, pouring out His wrath and striking down the firstborn in each household, that blood would be a sign of God's people and an indication that a death had occurred already, that blood had been shed; He would pass over those houses (Ex. 12). Jesus celebrates the Passover meal with His disciples the night before the crucifixion, and He interprets the bread and wine of the meal as His own body and blood given for them (1 Cor. 11:23–25). So Paul declares, "Christ our Passover also has been sacrificed" (1 Cor. 5:7).

After the exodus from Egypt, the Jewish people received instructions for an annual Day of Atonement (Lev. 16), on which once more the blood of animals would be shed to cover the sin of the people. Of particular importance is the instruction regarding two goats. One goat, the "sin offering," was to be slaughtered and its blood sprinkled about the tabernacle, the priestly garments, the ark of the covenant, and the altar of sacrifice. The writer of Hebrews comments, "Almost all things are cleansed with blood, according to the Law, and without the shedding of blood there is no forgiveness" (Heb. 9:22).

The second goat was the scapegoat: on this one the priest was to lay his bloody hands and "confess over it all the wrongdoings of the sons of Israel and all their unlawful acts regarding all their sins; and he shall place them on the head of the goat and send it away into the wilderness" (Lev. 16:21). The sins of the people were thus assigned to the goat, which was then ceremonially and symbolically cast out from the presence of God in His tabernacle. In his prophecy of the coming Messiah, Isaiah foresees that the Lord's "Servant will justify the many, for He will bear their wrongdoings" (Isa. 53:11).

Two themes persist through the various Old Testament accounts of atonement: first, there must be punishment, specifically death through the shedding of blood as the consequence of sin. Second, if it is not the guilty party himself who must die, there must be a designated substitute on whom the punishment falls. These themes of punishment ("penal") and substitution ("vicarious") must be included in any biblically faithful account of atonement.

In ways that specifically parallel the ceremonial atonement of the Jewish religious system, Jesus—the true Lamb of God—was presented to the priests, determined to be without flaw or sin, and killed on Passover with the rest of the sacrificial lambs. Though this sacrifice was administered by Roman governmental agents, it conformed in every way to the prescriptions of the Jewish systems by which the righteous wrath of God was satisfied and sin was atoned. In striking contrast, however, the atoning work of Jesus does not require annual repetition: "Every priest stands daily ministering and offering time after time the same sacrifices, which can never take away sins; but He, having offered one sacrifice for sins for all time, sat down at the right hand of God, . . . For by one offering He has perfected for all time those who are sanctified" (Heb. 10:11–12, 14).

THEORIES OF THE NATURE OF ATONEMENT

We know that Jesus died for our sins on the cross, but we may wonder how that actually worked to secure our salvation. "Atonement" refers to the work one does to satisfy a debt or offense and to the achieved reconciliation, or restored relationship. For us, this atonement or reconciliation was accomplished on the cross:

> But God demonstrates His own love toward us, in that while we were still sinners,
> Christ died for us. Much more then, having now been justified by His blood, we
> shall be saved from the wrath of God through Him. For if while we were enemies
> we were reconciled to God through the death of His Son, much more, having
> been reconciled, we shall be saved by His life. (Rom. 5:8–10)

Several inaccurate theories have been proposed to account for the nature of the atonement: ransom to Satan, Christus Victor, moral influence, governmental. We will now consider and assess the validity or adequacy of these varying theories, and follow with a brief discussion of the explanation that we regard as the most sound from an orthodox and historical viewpoint, vicarious (substitutionary) penal atonement.

RANSOM TO SATAN

On the cross, Jesus paid for our sins, which has overtones of a financial transaction. This naturally prompts the question, Payment to whom? The "Ransom to Satan" theory supposes that in the fall, humans have come to be the possession of the devil, and that if God wants them back, He must pay the price or otherwise compensate Satan for the exchange. In support of this view are verses that describe the devil as "the prince of the power of the air" and fallen humans as being "in bondage" (Eph. 2:2; Rom. 7:14; Heb. 2:14–15).

This view—though prominent in the early church, and in contemporary popular culture through cartoons that depict Satan and his legions brandishing pitchforks and lording over wretched humans in hell—reflects a serious misunderstanding of the natures of both God and Satan, as well as a mischaracterization of the sin debt. God the Creator is eternal, omnipotent, and independent; Satan and humans are created beings, temporal, limited in power and knowledge, and utterly dependent on the grace of God for their continued existence. Satan has no standing to negotiate with God, and God owes him nothing. Satan and fallen humans differ from one another only in their respective degrees of power and intelligence, and in these respects are far closer to one another than either is to God. They stand condemned under the same sentence of judgment before a holy God; Satan, at most, is a prison yard bully who dominates other inmates but is himself powerless before his guardians.

This view also misdirects the nature of the sin offense, and the one to whom the debt is paid. Humankind in rebellion has sinned against God, and it is the holiness and justice of God that demands satisfaction. The wages, or penalty, of sin is death, and the condemned sinner must pay that penalty through physical death and infinite separation from God. This is the payment Jesus remits on the cross to the Father. The transaction is an intra-Trinitarian one, and Satan figures nowhere in the equation. At the risk of offending countless devotees of C. S. Lewis's *The Lion, the Witch, and the Wardrobe*, the fundamental flaw of that narrative is its portrayal of Aslan owing something to the White Witch in order to redeem Edmund, as opposed to owing something to his Father, the Emperor-Beyond-the-Sea. This is a false account of the atonement, as there is no debt, or ransom, due to Satan.

CHRISTUS VICTOR

Literally "Christ the Victor," Christus Victor is the position that in the crucifixion and resurrection Jesus defeated the powers of Satan, death, and hell. Jesus is the one who enters the house of the "strong man," binds him, and then plunders his house (Mark 3:27). Jesus' resurrection is a victory whose benefits are extended to us (1 Cor. 15:54–57).

As a theory of the atonement this view is inadequate: it continues the fundamental misunderstanding considered above in the Ransom to Satan view, that the basic obstacle to our salvation is the dominion of Satan, which must be negotiated or defeated. In fact, our basic problem is that we have offended the holy God, and it is His wrath that must be satisfied through the blood payment offered by Jesus (Rom. 3:25). However, as an aspect of the atonement, it is appropriate to celebrate the cosmic victory of Jesus over death and the grave, which secured our freedom from spiritual bondage and deliverance from the domain of darkness (Col. 1:13–14; 2:13–15; Heb. 2:14–15), and indeed that all His enemies have been made a footstool for Him (Ps. 110:1; Luke 20:43).

MORAL INFLUENCE

The moral influence view of the atonement, propounded by medieval theologian Peter Abelard, is sometimes characterized as a "subjective" view, because it does not claim that the crucifixion produced any objective outcome like the payment of a debt or the turning aside of God's wrath. Instead, the voluntary death of Jesus should evoke feelings within us to recognize and appreciate the love of God, and should lead to a desire on our part to be similarly loving to those around us.

Certainly, Jesus is our moral example, and because of His life and death it is incumbent upon us to live as He did. As Paul instructs, "Be imitators of me, just as I also am of Christ" (1 Cor. 11:1). However, as a characterization of the crucifixion, it is woefully inadequate. First, this position denies that there is any moral or legal offense to be satisfied, or if there is, it leaves that offense completely unaddressed. This view presupposes a doctrine of God's love apart from wrath, and a distorted view of morality that allows injustice to persist without reparations to the offended party. Second, it is very difficult to see how Jesus' death is in any way loving toward sinners, or what about it should inspire similar behavior in us. Jesus said, "Greater love has no one than this, that a person will lay down his life for his friends" (John 15:13), but this makes sense only objectively—if the one who dies is actually taking the place of his friends, like a soldier jumping on a grenade to save his comrades. It is no act of love to jump on a live grenade when there is no one around needing saving.

The moral influence theory is an inadequate one, for the atonement is far more than described here. We certainly should live lives of self-sacrifice and consider others more important than ourselves, following the example of Jesus (Phil. 2:1–11) as part of our appropriate response to Jesus' crucifixion and resurrection. However, that response should also include heartfelt repentance for the sin that compelled Jesus to take our burden on Himself, and gratitude that we have escaped a just sentence of condemnation—reactions that make no sense from a mere moral influence or example perspective.

GOVERNMENTAL

The governmental view of the atonement is likewise subjective, in that the effect, or intent, of the crucifixion is to instill within us fear, or at least a hearty respect for God's rule of law, and to motivate us back to righteous living. On this view, initially propounded by Dutch lawyer/theologian Hugo Grotius, humankind's continued rebellion against God's rightful rule threatens the proper ordering of creation, and people must be taught that God will not be mocked. Lest we conclude that God is neglectful or apathetic in view of our sinfulness, He breaks into history and declares enough is enough, so that Jesus' execution reestablishes God's rightful authority. God is the legitimate governor of creation, and He can govern with an iron fist if necessary.

As a view of the atonement, this theory seems to be advancing claims that are true, yet also inadequate (and maybe irrelevant) for an understanding of the crucifixion. God declares that in His abundant mercy, He has often held off on punishing evil (Ex. 34:6–7), such that evildoers and believers alike might even begin to think God's judgment will be indefinitely postponed (2 Peter 3:9). Paul does say that for certain sins, punishment should be severe and public (Gal. 2:11–14; 1 Tim. 1:20). But it is difficult to see how this is adequate or even relevant to the specific historical act of the crucifixion. On this view, it seems that any victim would suffice as a target for the wrath of God. Indeed, it would not matter if the victim were himself guilty or innocent, as the point is not to punish any specific sins, but rather to demonstrate that the "sheriff is back in town," and God's wrath will be poured out on lawlessness. Such an arbitrary nature of the crucifixion counters any appeal to justice, the paying of debts, and the reestablishment of proper relationships, but serves only to instill a fear-based obedience. The work of Jesus on the cross assures us that "there is now no condemnation at all for those who are in Christ Jesus" (Rom. 8:1) and that we might "approach the throne of grace with confidence" (Heb. 4:16).

VICARIOUS (SUBSTITUTIONARY) PENAL ATONEMENT

Ultimately, we end where we began, with a faithful commitment to the biblical revelation and an honest reckoning with the desperate human condition before an awesomely holy and just God. In our fallen, sinful state, we confess that we are desperately wicked, alienated from God and richly deserving of His wrath. We are justly condemned, and there must be punishment: "The soul who sins will die" (Ezek. 18:4), and "It is destined for people to die once, and after this comes judgment" (Heb. 9:27). In that judgment we have no hope in our own merit; surely we must die and be cast eternally from the presence of God.

The wonder of the grace of salvation is this—that Jesus Christ, "who knew no sin," became sin for us (2 Cor. 5:21). At the direction of the Father, He willingly took our sin on Himself, like the bloody scapegoat upon whom was laid all the iniquities of Israel. Like the goat of the sin offering, Jesus died a bloody death on the cross to fulfill the demands of the Law (itself a reflection of God's character), that sin—rebellion against God—is a capital crime necessitating death.

Further, as Jesus is fully man and fully God (see the earlier chapter in this volume on the doctrine of God), Jesus is both suitable and sufficient to substitute for those justly condemned. As a man, He is the right kind of sacrifice (Deut. 24:16; Heb. 2:14; 10:4–6). As the infinite and eternal God, He is sufficient to take on Himself the infinite and eternal punishment rightly due us. Through His death on the cross, Jesus paid the bloody price demanded of us; and through His alienation from the Father ("My God, My God, why have You forsaken Me?"), He—as the infinite second person of the Trinity—accomplished in a finite moment what it would have taken us as finite creatures an infinity of time to endure.

Admittedly, the Penal Atonement view has come under intense scrutiny in recent times, even being likened to a form of "cosmic child abuse." The very idea that a father would pour out wrath on his own son is horrifying to us, as it should be. This horror is not a merely modern reaction, however. The gospel message was just as discomforting when it was first proclaimed, and, just as much, is evidence of the depths of our sin overcome by the love of God (Rom. 8:32). Beyond this, we must understand that although Jesus was a Son, He was no child, and He was no victim. Jesus said, "For this reason the Father loves Me, because I lay down My life so that I may take it back. No one has taken it away from Me, but I lay it down on My own. I have authority to lay it down, and I have authority to take it back" (John 10:17–18); that same Jesus is described as "the originator and perfecter of the faith, who for the **joy** set before Him endured the **cross**, despising the shame" (Heb. 12:2). The biblical witness is clear, that Jesus Himself determined to take on human flesh and suffer crucifixion to atone for the sins of His people, and now is highly exalted because of it (Phil. 2:5–11).

We see, then, that the biblical text and the logic of salvation require that the atonement—the work of Christ on the cross—be both "penal" (punishing) and vicarious (substitutionary). "Christ died for us" (Rom. 5:8). The "for" in this verse is the Greek preposition *anti*, which also means "in place of." Christ died (penal) for (vicarious) us. This is an objective account of the atonement, which holds that there was real offense that required a concrete payment. This payment was accomplished through the Trinitarian work whereby the Father justly demands punishment, the Son freely and graciously provides that payment in His own flesh, and the Spirit effectively applies that sacrifice to the undeserving sinner. This account allows us to understand the errors and/or limitations of the theories considered above. Of course, as recipients of unmerited grace, we should be impelled to likewise sacrifice ourselves and our wills in service to others (as per the Moral Influence theory), and the execution on Calvary demonstrates that God is not unjust or uncaring by allowing wickedness to go unpunished (Governmental theory).

In the resurrection of Jesus, God displays complete victory over death and the designs of Satan to lure us into sharing for eternity the condemnation due him and fallen sinners ("[He] was raised because of our justification," Rom. 4:25); contrary to the Ransom to Satan theory, our deliverance occurs not by God satisfying the demands of Satan, but through the Son satisfying the demands of the Father, and consequently demonstrating victory over His enemies (Christus Victor). Any account of the atonement that fails to affirm its vicarious nature in satisfying the justice due to God alone is unacceptable as a biblically faithful doctrine.

CONCLUSION

God's work in saving fallen sinners is a magnificent display of His grace. Of course, creation and revelation are also gracious works of God, as are simpler measures of His grace like an unexpected financial windfall or a change of heart that leads to a restored familial relationship. The richness of a focused study on salvation, digging deeply into a single theological topic, is offset by the risk of fragmentation—that is, viewing this and other doctrines in isolation from each other. As beneficial as this consideration might be, its value would only be enhanced by similar attention to the other foundational doctrines expounded in this volume, for the story of salvation is that of God (Theology Proper) saving humans (Anthropology) through the work of Jesus (Christology) by the power of the Spirit (Pneumatology), uniting them to the church (Ecclesiology) to dwell with Him eternally (Eschatology), as revealed in the Scriptures (Bibliology). A careful study of these interconnected and mutually supportive doctrines will do even more to impress upon us "so great a salvation!" (Heb. 2:3) as we enjoy the pursuing and perfecting love and grace of God in Christ Jesus.

Understanding the Basic Doctrine of the Church

J. BRIAN TUCKER

INTRODUCTION

In response to Peter's confession of Jesus' messianic identity in Matthew 16:16, Jesus said: "You are Peter, and upon this rock I will build My church" (Matt. 16:18). The significance of the phrase "My church" provides an entry point for our discussion of the doctrine of the church. The English word "church" in Matthew 16:18 translates the Greek word *ekklēsia*. The Septuagint (LXX) often translates the Hebrew word *qahal* with *ekklēsia*. A temporary gathering or generic assembly is indicated by the context (see Gen. 49:6; Deut. 9:10) and *qahal* without the limiter "of the Lord" or "Israel" does not refer to Israel (see Num. 20:4; Deut. 23:1–3; 1 Kings 8:14, 22). In the New Testament, there are several additional uses of *ekklēsia*, but "people with shared belief" becomes the dominant use for those who belong to Jesus' *ekklēsia* (see Acts 19:32, 39, 41; Eph. 1:22–23; 1 Cor. 12:13; Matt. 28:19–20).[1] The term *ekklēsia* is not applied to Israel in the New Testament in the sense of a "people with shared belief." When Luke wrote, "the assembly in the wilderness" (Acts 7:38), it refers to "a regularly summoned legislative body," another potential use of *ekklēsia*.[2] Israel and the church remain distinct. (This will be discussed below.) This chapter unfolds by a discussion of the images of the church via the four marks, its governance, dispensational issues, and its mission and ministry.

THE FOUR MARKS AND THE IMAGES OF THE CHURCH

The historic center for Christian teaching on the church is found in the Nicene-Constantinopolitan Creed of AD 381, which affirms that we believe "in one, holy, catholic, and apostolic church." These marks organize key images of the church found in the New Testament. These are literary devices designed to reveal important aspects of the nature of the church. Combining the marks and images, they offer insight into biblical pastoral practice.

ONE CHURCH

Body of Christ

The church as one brings to the fore its unity, which is based on the group's shared membership in the body of Christ. The church as the body of Christ is one of the more important images that describe the church. The image is used by Paul to highlight two different points. In 1 Corinthians 12:12–18, he highlights the way each member is dependent on other members in the body. He presents the image to instruct the Corinthians to recognize the need for diversity and interdependence within their shared unity in Christ (see also Rom. 12:4–5).

Head of the Body

In Ephesians and Colossians, a more cosmic orientation is evident as Christ is placed as the Head of the body (Eph. 1:22–23; 4:15–16; Col. 1:18). In these two letters Christ is the source of vitality for the group. The interpersonal nature of the relationship is evident in all of Paul's usages, though the particular contextual emphases should not be downplayed. The church as the body of Christ, however, is part of the mystery nature of the church (Eph. 3:1–6; 5:32).[3] Paul makes the connection between Christ and the church in light of his Damascus Road experience (Acts 9:1, 4; 1 Cor. 15:9). The mystery nature of the church, especially as it relates to the unity between Jews and non-Jews as members of God's family, was also proclaimed by other apostolic leaders (Acts 10:34–36; 15:13–17).

HOLY CHURCH

Temple of God

The church as holy suggests it is set apart from the world; two images are particularly helpful regarding holiness. First, the church as a temple of God builds on existing ideas of sacred space and holiness. Paul writes, "Do you not know that you are a temple of God and that the Spirit of God dwells in you?" (1 Cor. 3:16). The point of the image is that God dwells among the Corinthian Christ followers. Corinth was a Roman colony noted for its many temples and shrines. Paul takes an existing image and reuses it to remind them of core issues of belonging and holiness (1 Cor. 3:23).

More broadly, Paul draws on construction imagery to expand the temple imagery of the church as a building whose foundation is Christ (1 Cor. 3:10–11). Additionally, the role of the apostles is highlighted because the foundational agency is "the apostles and prophets" and now Jesus is "the cornerstone" (Eph. 2:20–21). These images blend conceptually together the grounding and unity within the church. From a practical standpoint, what might our day-to-day practice reveal about the continuation of temple imagery in ministry (e.g., sacramental versus non-sacramental approaches to theology)? How do we hold together the personal and communal temple symbolism in 1 Corinthians 3:16 and 6:19 as we navigate conflicts in the church?

The Bride of Christ

The church as the bride of Christ has been particularly important for dispensational interpreters as they seek to highlight the idea that the church differs from the kingdom (2 Cor. 11:2; Eph. 5:22–33; Rev. 21:2, 9, 10). The relationship between Christ and the church in Ephesians 5:26–27 relates to His ongoing sanctifying work on the Ephesian Christ followers' behalf as well as a future one in which the church is presented "holy and blameless." The bride of Christ image activates first-century marriage customs that are often unclear for contemporary readers. When discussing this metaphor, it would be wise to describe this cultural process.[4] It seems likely that the referent for the image is intimacy and commitment between Christ and His church (John 14:2–3). From the point of view of the bride, the focus is on dependence and obligation with an anticipation of a future together (Rev. 19:7–9).

CATHOLIC CHURCH

The church as catholic, or universal, brings to the fore a couple of ideas. The Greek word *katholikos* is built on two morphemes *kata* "according to" and *holos* "whole," when combined emphasizes "wholeness." This wholeness relates to Christ, Ignatius wrote, "Wherever Jesus Christ is, there is the catholic church" (*Smyrnaeans* 8:2). The universal church also highlights the shared connection and dependence with Jesus for membership; this is evident in vine and branches and sheep and shepherd imagery found in Scripture.

Vine and Branches

First, Jesus, as He was nearing the end of His ministry, highlighted the biblical symbol of the church as branches connected to a vine (John 15:1–8). Building on imagery from Israel's scriptural tradition (Isa. 5:1–2), Jesus makes it clear the disciples' ongoing spiritual vitality had its basis in their universal connection to Him as He calls them to abide in Him (John 15:4). This word picture should remind pastoral leaders of the necessity of staying connected to Jesus in the ongoing practice of ministry (John 15:5). This image also supports the larger contention that members of the church are those who are in Christ (i.e., believer membership), and functions as a reminder to think generously about those whose ecclesial practices differ from ours.

Sheep and Shepherd

Second, the catholicity and dependence of the church on Jesus is also seen in the image of the church as a flock of sheep and Jesus as the "Good Shepherd" (John 10:14–15; Luke 15:4–7). This imagery would have activated an existing cultural encyclopedia for Jesus' original hearers, one that may be missed for those living in an urban twenty-first century setting. Those who are part of Jesus' flock rely on Him for their existence since they are vulnerable to attack (Matt. 7:15; Acts 20:29). Regarding leadership within the church, leaders are "under-shepherds" with delegated responsibility from the "Good Shepherd" to lead in accordance with "the will of God" (1 Peter 5:1–4). This suggests that even the ongoing leading and feeding of a local assembly may be deficient if the "under-shepherds" do not practice ministry within the conceptual field of the sheep-shepherd imagery. Jesus is to be our shepherd daily enabling His under-shepherds to perform their tasks with integrity and compassion.

APOSTOLIC CHURCH

Shared Body of Beliefs

This mark comes from the Greek word *apostolos*, meaning "messenger." So, apostolicity points to the idea that the church has the apostles as its foundation. For the Roman Catholic Church this means apostolic succession, a view that claims unbroken continuity from the original apostles to contemporary bishops, who in turn function authoritatively within the Catholic Church. For Evangelicals, the idea of apostolicity points to the authoritative writings of the apostles. The church, in this view, proclaims and follows the teachings of the apostles written down in the New Testament. This apostolic witness of the church then connects to a shared body of beliefs that find their basis in the Scriptures. While the four marks are not designed to directly reflect aspects of the biblical imagery, they do serve as entry points into some of the images found there. One brief example is the priesthood of the believer since this one has direct relevance to the issue of church authority inherent to the mark of apostolicity.

Priesthood of the Believer

This suggests a functional aspect to this mark of the church. If that is the case, then the church as a priesthood, which also highlights a functional image aligns with this mark. This image builds on Peter's description of Christians as "a royal priesthood" (1 Peter 2:9). This imagery draws on Israel's scriptural tradition as well (Ex. 19:6) but brings to the fore the idea that all in Christ now "offer up spiritual sacrifices that are acceptable to God" (1 Peter 2:5). In the history of interpretation this imagery has been warmly debated under the label of the priesthood of all believers.[5] In maintaining this principle of the Protestant Reformation, leaders today can reinforce this imagery by reminding congregants of the call to "present your bodies as a living sacrifice" (Rom. 12:1) and their responsibility to "pray for one another" (James 5:16). These can reinforce the groups' identity as believer-priests and reconnect congregations with the earliest strata of Christ-movement doctrine and practice.

These four marks via the six images provide a framework for thinking biblically and practically about the relationship between Christ and the church. When one moves from imagery to significance, it becomes clear that there are differences as to the application of these word pictures. These differences can be seen in diverse church polities and leadership practices.

CHURCH POLITIES AND LEADERSHIP POSITIONS

There are three dominant church government structures historically: Episcopal, Presbyterian, and Congregational. Each draw from an array of scriptural and historical arguments for their practice, with some congregations practicing aspects of all three to form an eclectic governing structure.[6] This is a place for an acceptable level of diversity since Christianity is culturally flexible and there may be contextual reasons to highlight a certain set of texts over others.

EPISCOPAL CHURCH POLITY

The episcopal church polity comes from the New Testament word *episkopos* translated into English as "overseer." The Roman Catholic Church and the Eastern Orthodox follow this structure, as do many mainline denominations. This approach reaches back to the second century, and delegates responsibility to key leaders who are "guardians" for the whole group. The "guardian" idea shifted quickly to the "bishop." Philippians 1:1 may point to the meaning of "bishop" represented by the Episcopal tradition. These bishops then consecrate others who then form a hierarchical leadership structure, such as bishops, priests, and deacons. Often, these traditions place a high value on the proper administration of the Lord's Supper, baptism, and the preaching of the Word, restricting who may engage in these practices. There is also reflection on apostolic authority as a form of legitimation and an attendant bifurcation between the clergy and laity that is more pronounced than in the other two church government forms.

PRESBYTERIAN CHURCH POLITY

The presbyterian church government structure builds on the New Testament word *presbyteros* often translated into English as "elder." Reformed and Presbyterian denominations are generally organized around this structure. From a lexical standpoint, those who hold this view contend that their application of the *presbyteros* word group is the most consistent of the three polity options. The Jerusalem Council is Acts 15 is seen as a model for the type of delegated authority they have in mind. First Timothy 5:17 serves as a crucial verse for the presbyterian hierarchical leadership structure. Authority is given to the "ruling elders", chosen by the congregation along with "teaching elders," who are commonly called the pastor, and both together make up the session. The next level of authority is referred to as the presbytery which has regional jurisdiction. The presbytery is part of a synod that functions as a gatekeeper when doctrinal or practical challenges arise. The final level of ecclesial authority is found in the general assembly. This group has the ultimate approval for a course of action or doctrinal dispute.

Outside of the Presbyterian and Reformed denominations, this has been a growing choice of church polity for many nondenominational churches. The distinction of these nondenominational churches is that while they function with elders giving oversight to the congregation, they also function without any accountability to a presbytery or session. This governmental form gives more local authority than the episcopal one, but not as much as the congregational form.

CONGREGATIONAL CHURCH POLITY

The congregational church government structure oscillates between the use of terms such as "elders" and "deacons" but tends to use these differently than in the presbyterian form of government. The congregational form is seen most predominantly in baptistic churches, as well as the Anabaptist and Free Church traditions, and many nondenominational and fundamentalist churches. Central to congregationalism are ideas of democracy, independence, and the local church as the final authority. The theological framework for congregational polity begins with Christ as the head of the church and the priesthood of all believers. This suggests that all the members should be involved in all facets of ministry within the church. In practice, leaders such as "pastors," "elders," or in some settings "deacons" are elected by the congregation and are delegated with the implementation of the day-to-day aspects of the church's ministry. This form, in contrast to the previously mentioned two, allows for the move congregational involvement in ministerial and business decisions.[7]

CHURCH LEADERSHIP—ELDERS

Moving from the governmental polities to the church offices, the following should be noted. First, elders and deacons appear to be the most textually determined offices. Elders were generally synonymous with overseers, but the New Testament also reflects some variation in practice. The multiple "elders" (*presbyteroi*) approach to leadership was developed from within existing Jewish practice (Ex. 19:7; Mark 11:27). Elders were appointed in various congregations (Acts 14:23) and evident in Jerusalem (Acts 21:18); they led along with the apostles in the early Christ-movement (Acts 16:4).

The Johannine community adopted an elder structure (2 John 1; 3 John 1) but transformed it into a single elder configuration. Outside of the Johannine literature, elders are given an explicit leadership position in 1 Timothy 5:7 and a ritual function in James 5:14. There are no examples in the New Testament of women being referred to as elders, though the restrictions given in 1 Timothy 3:1–7; 1 Timothy 5:17–22; and Titus 1:5–6 result in the exclusion of many men as well.[8]

In the contemporary debate over the role of women in church leadership, complementarianism and egalitarianism serve as the dominant options. Complementarians argue that women are not elder eligible. They support their position based on 1 Timothy 2:11–15, especially v. 12, which reads, "But I do not allow a woman to teach or exercise authority over a man, but to remain quiet" (see also 1 Cor. 11:2–6; 14:34). Furthermore, the requirement that an elder be the "husband of one wife" in 1 Timothy 3:2 cannot be fulfilled by a woman.

Egalitarians contend that there are no restrictions for women's leadership within the church. They support their position by noting that in Christ gender distinctions have been erased: "There is neither Jew nor Greek, there is neither slave nor free, there is neither male nor female; for you are all one in Christ Jesus" (Gal. 3:28). Since these distinctions have been erased, the teachings mentioned by Complementarians no longer apply. Furthermore, Romans 16 details several women who are thought to be functioning as leaders. The tension felt between these views relates to Romans 16:1–16, which seems to highlight women engaged in what 1 Corinthians 11:2–16; 14:33b–36; 1 Timothy 2:8–15; 3:2 seem to restrict. Finally, there are differences between these two camps regarding the significance of the continuation of gender distinctions within the church and home (Gal. 3:28; Eph. 5:22–23).

Church Leadership—Deacons[9]

Deacons (*diakonoi*) as leaders in the Christ-movement are ubiquitous in the New Testament, though as in the case of the overseers, it is not clear when this term shifted in referent from a generic "servant" or "minister" to a "deacon." Mark 10:43 is a good example of the way Jesus' teaching influenced the development of a leadership position with an emphasis on serving as a measure of greatness. The serving aspect is most clearly seen in Acts 6:2–3 where the "servant" is one who waits on tables; perhaps here the development of this leadership position from the earlier generic meaning begins. Paul refers to himself and Apollos as "servants" in 1 Corinthians 3:5 and to himself (and others) in 2 Corinthians 3:6 as "servants of a new covenant." These may refer to a similar generic idea of servility.

A shift occurs in Philippians 1:1, where Paul refers to "overseers" and "deacons" who serve as an intermediate-stage group descriptor. By the time of the Pastoral Epistles, the term has further developed into an office since the congregation is given instructions concerning the way to identify those who qualify (1 Tim. 3:8–13). As with overseers, these individuals are also to have strong organizational skills and to exhibit blameless moral character.

The earlier debate concerning women serving as elders shifts when it comes to deacons since Romans 16:1 refers to Phoebe as a "servant" (*diakonos*) of the "church" (*ekklēsia*) in Cenchrea. The question is: Does this signify a generic position or a later leadership office? It is unlikely that this refers to the generic category; rather, it refers to the middle use, similar to Philippians 1:1. Though *diakonos* is used in the New Testament primarily in reference to men, deacons must have included mixed groups since at least in one case the word is used to refer to a woman and 1 Timothy 3:11 provides counsel to women who are associated with this leadership position, i.e., they are to model prototypical characteristics.[10]

Regarding church polities and offices, the textual base we have to work from likely contributes to the diverse applications we see in evangelical churches. Ecclesial differences are not only evident in the organization of the church but also in the theological systems that undergird them. This becomes evident as one considers dispensational issues.

ISSUES IN DISPENSATIONALISM

Several ideas that should be kept together in maintaining a dispensational doctrine of the church: (1) the church is the body of Christ (this was discussed above); (2) the church began on the day of Pentecost; (3) the distinction between Israel and the church; and (4) the church's mission as gospel proclamation.[11] A crucial theological position for dispensationalism is that the church began on the day of Pentecost. Jesus' teaching in Matthew concerning the church is a primary reason dispensationalists see the beginning of the church at Pentecost. Jesus says to Peter, "Upon this rock I will build My church; and the gates of Hades will not overpower it" (Matt. 16:18). Covenant interpreters see this as a promise that the church will prevail throughout the church age since for them the church was already in existence, reaching back to include all of God's elect. However, the use of the predictive future in "I will build," indicates something that will come to pass. This does not indicate the specific timing of the beginning of the church but Matthew 16:21 suggests it is after Jesus' death, resurrection, and ascension.[12]

PENTECOST AS THE BEGINNING OF THE CHURCH

Other Scriptures also teach that the church had to come after the earthly work of Christ. Ephesians 1:19–23 indicates that Jesus' death, burial, and ascension are crucial for the establishment of the church. Paul writes that God has "made [Christ] head over all things to the church, which is His body" (Eph. 1:22–23a; see 1 Cor. 12:13; Col. 1:18a). This is the first time *ekklēsia* is used in Ephesians and here the term has in view the universal church. Jesus' death was necessary for the "Helper" to "come" (John 16:7), the church's hope rests on the resurrection (1 Cor. 15:12–19), and the promise of Spirit baptism was given in the context of the ascension (Acts 1:5). The "body" into which believers are placed in Ephesians 1:23a, is the body of Christ and this only occurs through the baptism in the Holy Spirit, which first occurred in Acts 2:1–4, 41. In Acts 11:15, Peter refers back to the day of Pentecost as "the beginning" in connection to the outpouring of the Spirit suggesting that is when the church began.

SPIRIT BAPTISM

Further, Spirit baptism is that which brings a person into the church spiritually. This is a work of the Spirit during the church age, an era that begins on the day of Pentecost. In 1 Corinthians 12:13, Paul writes, "For by one Spirit we were all baptized into one body, whether Jews or Greeks, whether slaves or free, and we were all made to drink of one Spirit." Paul begins: "For by one Spirit," which is a reference to the Holy Spirit's work; "we were all baptized," the "we" here refers to all those in Christ and "baptized" refers to those who are part of the universal body of Christ. So, through the work of the Holy Spirit, all believers are incorporated "into one body."

This membership in the "one body" does not erase existing identities, Paul continues, "whether Jews or Greeks, whether slaves or free." The first pair is most important for the doctrine of the church for dispensationalism since it maintains a continuing covenantal identity for Israel, one that has not been taken over by the church. Members of the "one body" in 1 Corinthians 12:13 are in-Christ Jews and in-Christ Gentiles (1 Cor. 7:17–24). Paul concludes 1 Corinthians 12:13: "and we were all made to drink of one Spirit." The word "drink" here indicates that personal salvation is in view for membership within the church. Those in the one body of Christ are incorporated into Him as a result of God's prior election that is made evident in history by a person's faith response to Christ, which itself is connected to the baptizing work of the Spirit (Eph. 1:3–6).

DISTINCTION OF ISRAEL AND THE CHURCH

While the beginning of the church is on the day of Pentecost, the completion of it, or at least the church age, occurs at the rapture (this is area where dispensationalism and covenant theology disagree). The rapture (See Eschatology in this volume) is the time that all the members of Christ's body, both alive and dead, will be "caught up together" in order "to meet the Lord in the air" (1 Thess. 4:16–17).

The newness of the church on the day of Pentecost and the baptizing work of the Spirit of believers into the body of Christ, lead to the conclusion that the church in the new covenant is distinct from Israel in the old covenant. Covenantal interpreters discern in "the Israel of God" in Galatians 6:16 and an alleged division of Israel in Romans 9:6 a redefinition of Israel in a manner that Israel's covenantal identity has been given to the church. However, the referent in the Galatians verse is debatable and need not be understood to refer to the church. It is more likely that the "Israel of God" refers to historical Israel, as recipients of a blessing along with the nations. In Romans 9:6, Paul has in-Christ Jews in view and not the church (who has supposedly taken over Israel's identity). Paul consistently uses "Israel" to refer to the historic nation and does not use it to refer to the church.

Why should pastors maintain these dispensational distinctives? First, keeping the Israel and church distinction is crucial for the way one organizes the Bible's story. The metanarrative, i.e., the overarching story all too often gets truncated as creation, fall, redemption, and consummation. But this approach only needs the first three chapters of Genesis and then one can jump to Matthew 1. A better approach is creation, fall, Israel, redemption, and then consummation.[13] Israel is a vital part of the continuing and future story of God's work in the world. Maintaining the distinction between Israel and the church helps us be more virtuous readers of the whole Bible. It also gives us theological resources to overcome anti-Judaism and anti-Semitism in the contemporary context. The church is not Israel redefined.

MISSION AND MINISTRY OF THE CHURCH

A nexus of ideas and practices that animate the mission and ministry of the local church is evident in Acts 2:41–42, "So then, those who had received his word were baptized; and that day there were added about three thousand souls. They were continually devoting themselves to the apostles' teaching and to fellowship, to the breaking of bread and to prayer." These verses, along with Matthew 28:19–20, highlight six aspects that should be present in the ongoing mission and ministry of the church: evangelism, baptism, preaching and teaching, fellowship, the Lord's Supper, and prayer and worship. These components form the basis for what should regulate decisions regulating activities of a local church.[14]

Evangelism

Evangelism is to be understood in the narrow sense of verbal proclamation of the gospel that leads people into a salvific relationship with the triune God. It is an inference drawn from the emergence of the group of "those who had received his word" in Acts 2:41. While nonverbal practices are important, these are only a subcomponent of that which is crucial: the mission of the local church is gospel proclamation. In an era where there are many activities a group of believers might organize themselves around, evangelism must not be neglected since being a witness was an integral part an in-Christ identity early on (Acts 1:8). A wider perspective on evangelism would include making disciples (Matt. 28:19–20), planting new churches (Acts 14:21–22), and serving others (James 2:14).

Serving others is sometimes seen as controversial since it is thought to move churches in the direction of the social gospel. Serving others with a gospel focus can open opportunities for gospel proclamation (1 Thess. 1:5).

Evangelism Questions for local church leaders:

- Is your church too inward-focused?

- Are you replacing verbal proclamation with presence evangelism, a practice where unbelievers are only engaged relationally without ever explicitly sharing the gospel?

- Is there an appropriate number of resources directed toward missions?

Baptism

Baptism is another vital aspect of the local church's mission and ministry; the passage in Acts continues by noting that those who were converted "were baptized" (Acts 2:41). Baptism is the rite of initiation for those already in Christ that marks their entry into a local Christian community (Rom. 6:3–4). It is the individual's public testimony of their saving faith and should be done in the Trinitarian name: Father, Son, and Holy Spirit (Matt. 28:19). Since it is a public testimony, it is most properly reserved for adults who are capable of such a testimony. This is called "believer's baptism" or "credobaptism" from the Latin word *credo*, "I believe." It implies an act of conscious, verbal testimony in front of witnesses.

Infant baptism is called "paedobaptism" from the Latin prefix *paed-* referring to boys or children. While infant baptism is practiced by many Christians influenced by covenant theology today, there are no explicit New Testament texts that require this practice (see Acts 16:15). Often credobaptists wrongly accuse paedobaptists of thinking that infant baptism saves the child. It is true the Roman Catholic Church and Lutheran Church hold to infant baptism saving the child; that is not an accurate reflection of the Protestant Reformed tradition, which engages in this practice based on covenant theology with a typological connection between circumcision and baptism (Col. 2:11–12).

Baptism Questions:

- Is public testimony required for candidates for baptism (Acts 2:38)?
- Is it the case that infants were included in the household baptisms in the New Testament?
- Is the connection between circumcision and baptism at the ritual level or at the spiritual one (Rom. 2:29)?

Teaching

Teaching is another nonnegotiable aspect of the local church's mission and ministry. In Acts 2:42, Luke points out those in Jerusalem organized themselves around "the apostles' teaching." Today, apostolic teaching is contained in the Bible. The activity of teaching, a word broad enough in Greek to include all sorts of instruction like preaching, was central to the church's life early on (2 Tim. 4:2). The weekly proclamation of the Scriptures should be the focal point for the church's gatherings (1 Cor. 1:21).

The communication of the apostolic teachings through preaching the Word is central to the church's mission and ministry. That is accomplished primarily through the pastor or elder but teaching also highlights the importance of discipleship, a calling for all those in Christ (2 Tim. 2:2).

Members of a local group of believers are to embody a life of discipleship and that includes passing on the social implications of the gospel to others who can then teach others. The combination of preaching and teaching should result in the local church being formed into the image of Christ.

Teaching Questions:

- Is the faithful exposition of God's Word central to the weekly gatherings of the congregation?

- How can local leadership determine if faithful exposition is occurring?
- Is the local body of believers equipped, exercising their spiritual gifts, and engaged in making disciples and teaching others?

Fellowship

Fellowship is an often misunderstood but needed aspect of the local church's mission and ministry. Fellowship is not simply getting together with people we like. It is partnership, it is a shared communal life based in God's call and union with Christ (1 Cor. 1:9–10). It is participation in God's mission in the world (Rom. 15:26; Phil. 2:1–4). It is something that the Holy Spirit sustains within the group (2 Cor. 13:14). In light of these passages, the fellowship in view here is a fully Trinitarian sharing based on the outward work of the Father, Son, and Holy Spirit, expressed beautifully in the common life and identity of those who have been reconciled to God and to one another (Eph. 2:11–22).

Fellowship Questions:

- Is the fellowship in the local congregation shallow or based on cultural identities?
- How can thinking about fellowship in a Trinitarian framework deepen existing group involvements?
- How can we cultivate a sense of partnership and vulnerability in the congregation?

The Lord's Supper

The Lord's Supper is central to the mission and ministry of the church. Acts 2:42 refers to this as "the breaking of bread," and describes a practice of the earliest Christ-followers from the beginning of the church. There is an obvious connection between this meal and the one Jesus shared with His disciples before His arrest (Luke 22:14–20; 1 Cor. 11:23). With regard to the church's mission, the Lord's Supper is a social practice that declares the group's sharing with Christ (John 6:51). It is sometimes carried out in an overly individualistic way, but one of its main purposes is to reinforce the unity of a local group of Christ-followers (1 Cor. 11:27, 29). Sometimes churches will refer to this as Communion or the Eucharist, in light of Paul's descriptor in 1 Corinthians 11:20 it seems "the Lord's Supper" is the label most textually determined (although those calling it Communion will point to 1 Cor. 10:16 with its reference to "a sharing" and those calling it the Eucharist will highlight 1 Cor. 11:24 with its reference to "given thanks" from the Greek, *eucharisteo*).

Lord's Supper Questions:

- How often should we celebrate the Lord's Supper?
- Who should be allowed to participate in it?
- How do we make sure this time strengthens the unity of the congregation rather than reinforce individualistic tendencies (1 Cor. 10:16–17; Eph. 4:3–5)?

Worship

Worship is the final aspect of the church's mission and ministry, though the text describes only one aspect of worship, i.e., "prayer" (Acts 2:42). In some ways worship incorporates much of the previous discussion but its focal point is different. Worship is directed toward God; it is the veneration and adulation of God. In one sense, all of life is worship but here we are focused more narrowly on worship as the mission and ministry of the local church. Prayer, a key aspect of worship, should occur as part of the weekly gatherings, Paul makes it clear he wants people "in every place to pray" (1 Tim. 2:8). Praising God and singing together are nonnegotiable aspects of the church's mission (Col. 3:16). Giving money in offerings is also an unchanging aspect of the church's ministry (1 Cor. 16:2). This verse along with Revelation 1:10 forms a strong argument for gathering to worship on Sunday, "the Lord's day," the first day of every week.

Reflection on what should occur in public worship is best achieved through the regulative or normative principle of worship. If the group is oriented toward the regulative, then only what the Scriptures explicitly prescribe can be done. If the local church is more inclined toward including cultural aspects into their worship, then the normative approach is in order since it would require an openness to various expressions of worship as long as Scripture does not explicitly forbid them. Either way, ministry leaders should remember that worship is about God and must be gospel centered.

Worship Questions:

- What does our current public worship service indicate about our definition of worship?
- When organizing our public service are we free to include aspects of our culture context; if so, what are the boundaries?
- Can biblically defined worship occur in an online environment?

CONCLUSION

As pastors we are called to faithful ministry. Attending to our doctrine of the church goes a long way in helping us do that. We live in an era where far too many have begun to see their involvement in the church as something optional in their spiritual journey. This can often become a point of frustration for ministry leaders. Faithful ministry includes renewing our love for Christ and His church, as we model the importance of this in our own personal walk. Leaders who have a theologically informed passion for the church can be part of the vanguard of those who help resist the drift away from the church that is all too evident today. Faithful ministry will often be defined in ways that differ from the indicators of success evident in the broader culture. In this case, success may be defined as being faithful to your call.

The ability to be faithful, however, is something that comes from God Himself who remains faithful (2 Tim. 2:13). This can give us confidence as we recall that our faithfulness derives from God's faithfulness. Many of the topics discussed in this chapter are points of contention and call for a steady, empathetic heart; as we all navigate these different views, know that Christ will empower us to lead as we remind those to whom we minister of God's great faithfulness to each generation (Ps. 89:1–2).

NOTES

1. Walter Bauer, *A Greek English Lexicon of the New Testament and Other Early Christian Literature*, 3rd. ed., rev. and ed. Fredrick William Danker (Chicago: University of Chicago Press, 2001), 303.

2. Bauer, *Greek*, 303. This is one of the other options for *ekklēsia* given there.

3. Gary Gromacki, "Paul's Ecclesiology of Ephesians," *The Journal of Ministry and Theology* 19 (2015): 82–115.

4. Harold W. Hoehner, *Ephesians: An Exegetical Commentary* (Grand Rapids: Baker, 2002), 748–62.

5. Hank Voss, *The Priesthood of All Believers and the Missio Dei* (Eugene, OR: Pickwick, 2017), 247–68.

6. Gregg R. Allison, *Sojourners and Strangers: The Doctrine of the Church* (Wheaton, IL: Crossway, 2012), 205–317.

7. John MacArthur and Richard Mayhue, *Biblical Doctrine* (Wheaton, IL: Crossway, 2017), 769.

8. Adapted from J. Brian Tucker, "New Testament," in *The Oxford Encyclopedia of the Bible and Gender Studies*, vol. 2, Julia M. O'Brien, editor in chief (Oxford: Oxford University Press, 2014), 187–88.

9. The first three paragraphs of this section are adapted from ibid., 187.

10. Laurie Norris, "On Gender Roles," in *Standing Firm: The Doctrinal Commitments of Moody Bible Institute*, eds. John A. Jelinek and Bryan O'Neal (Chicago: Moody, 2019), 125–34.

11. Mark A. Snoeberger, "A Tale of Two Kingdoms: The Struggle for the Spirituality of the Church and the Genius of the Dispensationalist System," *Detroit Baptist Seminary Journal* 19 (2014): 53–71.

12. Charles C. Ryrie, *Dispensationalism* (Chicago: Moody, 2007), 143.

13. R. Kendall Soulen, *The God of Israel and Christian* (Minneapolis: Augsburg, 1996).

14. John S. Hammett, *Biblical Foundations for Baptist Churches: A Contemporary Ecclesiology* (Grand Rapids: Kregel, 2005), 219–56.

Understanding the Basic Doctrine of the End Times

DAVID FINKBEINER

Jesus is coming again, and that changes everything. Scripture tells us that a Christian waits with anticipation for the glorious return of our Lord Jesus (Titus 2:13). And no wonder, for when Christ returns He will complete His grand work of redemption, dwelling forever in fellowship with His renewed people, meting out final justice, restoring all creation, and more. For the Christian, therefore, eschatology—the doctrine of last things—is no mere addendum to theology. It focuses on the jubilant consummation of the Bible's grand storyline, the happily-ever-after for which we yearn. It thus repays further study. Toward that end, this chapter will explore the major elements of the doctrine of last things.

DEATH AND THE INTERMEDIATE STATE

Death is an inescapable reality in this fallen world. It was not part of God's original creation, but it entered the world through Adam's sin and since then has dominated human existence (Rom. 5:12). Scripture speaks of death in three basic senses. *Spiritual death* is our spiritual separation from God. Being alienated from, even hostile to Him (Rom. 8:6–7; Eph. 2:1–5), we are dominated from our very conception by sin's power and corrosive effects (Rom. 5:21–6:23). *Physical death* is "the irreversible cessation of bodily functions."[1] Resulting from our separation from God, it involves separation from relationships, activities, and opportunities of earthly life (Eccl. 9:1–10; 11:7–12:7) and separation of the body from the spirit (James 2:26; Gen. 35:18). *Eternal death* (or the "second death," Rev. 20:14) makes spiritual death permanent for those who are not redeemed when they are separated from God forever in the lake of fire (Rev. 20:14; 21:8, 27).

Clearly, the last two senses of death have eschatological import. Eternal death is the destiny of all human beings who have not been redeemed; only believers escape its clutches. The same could not be said of physical death. Since the fall and until Christ's return, physical death is inevitable for every human being, believer and nonbeliever alike (Heb. 9:27). Nevertheless, death's future is not secure. In the end, Christ will utterly destroy death once and for all (1 Cor. 15:23–26, 54–55; Rev. 20:14, 21:4). Believers redeemed in Christ, therefore, having already been delivered from spiritual death, will never face eternal death. Nor will physical death have the last word for them, for Christ at His return will resurrect their bodies to a body like His own resurrected body—glorious, powerful, and imperishable (1 Cor. 15:42–44).

Despite these grand prospects for the believer's future even in the face of death, the reality of physical death prior to Christ's return raises an important question. What happens to believers between their physical death and the resurrection of their bodies at Christ's return? This period of time is called the *intermediate state*. Because Scripture stresses the reality of the believer's final resurrected state, it says relatively little about the intermediate state. Nevertheless, it does address the intermediate state in passages like Luke 16:19–31, Philippians 1:21–26, and 2 Corinthians 5:1–10.

What does Scripture say about the intermediate state of believers? First, the souls of believers continue to exist apart from their bodies, which remain behind and decay. Paul thus talks about it as departing rather than remaining in the body (Phil. 1:23–24), as being "absent from the body" (2 Cor. 5:8), and as being "unclothed" (2 Cor. 5:4). This separation of body and soul is temporary, since we were designed as body-soul creatures and will be redeemed soul *and* body at the resurrection. Second, the believer's soul remains conscious. Both Luke 16:19–31 and Revelation 6:9–11 picture the intermediate state as involving conscious interaction and memory. Third, believers' souls will go to be "with" Christ in heaven (Phil. 1:23). Hence, we will be "at home with the Lord" rather than "absent from" Him (2 Cor. 5:6, 8). Fourth, believers will enjoy enriched fellowship with Christ. This is why the intermediate state is desirable and "very much better" (Phil. 1:23) than our current condition, and can even be seen as "rest" from earthly difficulties (Rev. 14:13). Fifth, while better, the intermediate state still falls short of perfection. Paul therefore says that ultimately "we do not want to be unclothed but to be clothed" (2 Cor. 5:4) with our resurrected body, and martyred saints in the intermediate state long for

Christ's return and His just judgment (Rev. 6:10). The intermediate state is better for us, but not yet the best.

Scripture indicates that there is an intermediate state for nonbelievers as well. The story of the rich man and Lazarus in Luke 16 is the central text (especially vv. 22–26). On his death, the body of the condemned rich man is buried, but his soul is sent to Hades. He clearly is conscious of his dire straits there. It is a place of torment, far removed from the blessed existence of the saints in heaven. Hades is not yet the final destination for the condemned, for it will be cast into the lake of fire after the final judgment (Rev. 20:14).

Not everyone has accepted the view presented above. Roman Catholics teach the doctrine of purgatory. This doctrine maintains that after death, the souls of all Christians (except for the holiest few) will need to be purged of their remaining sins in the suffering of purgatory before they can enter heaven. But beyond the reality that Scripture nowhere teaches that such a place even exists, this view also fails to recognize that through faith in Christ, believers' sins have been paid in full by Christ's atoning work on the cross (Rom. 3:21–26), and there is "now no condemnation for those who are in Christ Jesus" (Rom. 8:1).

In addition, some groups teach the doctrine of "soul sleep." Advocates maintain that in the intermediate state, the souls of believers continue in *unconscious* existence, only to reawaken to consciousness when their bodies are raised at the resurrection. This view is based on Scripture's use of the metaphor of "sleep" to speak of death (e.g., John 11:11–14; 1 Cor. 15:6). However, the point of the metaphor is not that believers lose consciousness in the intermediate state but that physical death for them is no more permanent than sleep. Furthermore, as noted above, Scripture teaches that the intermediate state is a time of enriched fellowship with Christ "away from the body" rather than a dormant state without consciousness.

What are some pastoral implications of a biblical perspective on physical death and the intermediate state? First, it gives us realistic expectations. Since physical death is inevitable this side of glory, we should neither deny it nor be shocked when it comes. Second, such a perspective acknowledges that physical death is grievous. It as an evil compatriot of sin, an outrage to God's created order, an enemy to be defeated. Grief is therefore entirely appropriate when physical death takes our loved ones or when our own death draws close. Third, a biblical perspective gives believers hope in the face of physical death. Christ has defeated it; it has been "swallowed up in victory" (1 Cor. 15:54). Grievously evil though it may be, physical death nevertheless ushers us into the presence of the Lord in the intermediate state, a desirable state that is better by far (Phil. 1:23). Believers therefore need not be terrified of death, and their sorrow over death will always be mingled with hope

(1 Thess. 4:13). Sadly, the same cannot be said for nonbelievers, as physical death ends any hope for escaping inevitable judgment.

THE SECOND COMING OF CHRIST

Two Basic Approaches to the Destiny of History

One's view on the nature of Christ's second coming is shaped by larger theological considerations. These considerations include one's understanding of the structure of the Bible's grand storyline, one's understanding of the relationship between Israel and the church, and one's interpretive approach to predictive prophecy. In contemporary protestant evangelicalism, two basic approaches to these issues are particularly prominent: covenant theology and dispensationalism.

Covenant theology usually understands the structure of redemption in terms of three covenants. First, the *covenant of redemption* was the agreement between the three Persons of the Trinity in eternity past to redeem God's people from among the human race, which would fall. Second, the *covenant of works* was instituted in the garden between God and Adam, who represented all the human race. Adam's obedience to God's stipulation would have confirmed eternal life for the human race, but his disobedience resulted in universal sin and death for us all. In response to human failure in Eden, God established a third covenant, the *covenant of grace*, in order that His people might be redeemed. Through faith in Christ, who as the second Adam graciously redeems those united to Him, God's people receive eternal life and are delivered from sin and death. The rest of redemptive history since the fall—including different eras and covenants—are manifestations of this one covenant of grace.

Typically for covenant theology, this single covenant implies a supersessionist theology of the relationship between Israel and the church. Supersessionism maintains that "the NT Church is the new and/or true Israel that has forever superseded the nation Israel as the people of God."[2] This supersession happens because Jesus Himself is the true Israel, and so, as a result of Christ's first coming, all who are united with Him by faith—Jew or Gentile—become part of "Israel." Consequently, the church as the New Israel becomes the recipient in Him of any promises to Israel not fulfilled in the OT. Israel *as a national entity* therefore has no future in God's eschatological plan.[3]

Supersessionism has significant impact on how covenant theology interprets Old Testament predictive prophecy. The heart of a covenantal hermeneutic is the priority of the New Testament in understanding Old Testament predictions about national Israel. Convinced that the New Testament teaches that the church is the New Israel, covenant theology interprets Old Testament predictions about Israel's national future as being fulfilled in Christ and the church. National Israel should be seen as a type, a shadow pointing to the greater reality of Christ and the church. This means that physical predictions about the nation (e.g., Israel's land) should not be interpreted in a strictly literal way, but in nonliteral, even spiritual, way.[4]

On these points, dispensationalism differs dramatically from covenant theology. Dispensationalism maintains that the Bible's storyline can be structured by a succession of different dispensations. A dispensation is "a particular way of God's administering His rule over the world as He progressively works out His purpose for world history."[5] To be sure, dispensationalists insist that there is only one way of salvation throughout these different dispensations. But unlike covenant theology, which also recognizes different eras in salvation history, dispensationalists stress greater discontinuity between dispensations than do covenant theologians.

The discontinuity between dispensations is exemplified in the relationship between Israel and the church. For dispensationalists, Israel and the church are distinct; the latter began at Pentecost and is not the "New Israel." While salvation is always by grace through faith in both Testaments, Israel is a *national* category in ways not true of the church. "It is not God's plan for all believers to become Israel, but for there to be ethnic diversity in the people of God as the people of God idea includes both Israelites and Gentiles without either losing their ethnic identities."[6] As a result, Israel as a nation still has a future in God's sovereign plan. He will restore them and, through Christ, fulfill in them everything He has promised them as a nation. This will happen when Christ returns and rules over the earth.

Dispensationalism's distinction between Israel and the church significantly shapes its approach to predictive prophecy. Because it denies that the New Testament teaches supersessionism, it approaches Old Testament predictions about Israel's future with what Vlach calls "passage priority." This means that "all details of the Old Testament prophecies, promises, and covenants must be fulfilled in the way the original inspired Bible authors intended," and the New Testament does not override that original meaning. Hence, if an Old Testament text in its original context makes physical and national promises to Israel, those promises will be fulfilled literally as originally intended rather than nonliterally or spiritually instead.[7] Any such promise not yet literally fulfilled will be so fulfilled when Christ returns.

THE MILLENNIUM

All Protestant evangelicals believe that Jesus Christ will return to the earth. His return will be personal (John 14:3), bodily (Acts 1:11), and gloriously triumphant (Matt. 24:30; Rev. 1:7). It will result in resurrection, final judgment, and ultimately, the eternal state. But evangelicals differ on when and how all the events associated with Christ's return occur. These differences center on the nature of the millennium and whether Christ returns before or after it. There are three major millennial views: amillennialism, postmillennialism, and premillennialism. Whereas covenant theologians can hold to any of these three views, all dispensationalists embrace premillennialism because this view alone allows for a future period in which God's promises to national Israel can be fulfilled.

MILLENNIAL VIEWS

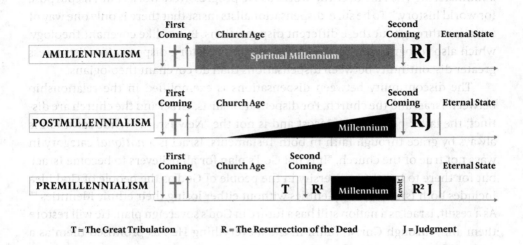

T = The Great Tribulation   R = The Resurrection of the Dead   J = Judgment

AMILLENNIALISM

Amillennialism maintains that Christ's millennial rule began with His resurrection and ascension and thus we are currently in the millennium. The millennium is not a literal 1000-year reign of Christ from the earth over the earth. It is rather an indefinitely long period of time in which Christ reigns spiritually from heaven over the church.[8] The millennium will end sometime in the future when Christ returns to the earth. At that time there will a general resurrection of all human beings and then the final judgment.

What are some arguments proffered by amillennialists? First, they start with the hermeneutical assumptions of covenant theology, that the New Testament is the key to understanding Old Testament prophecy. Consequently, Christ and the church fulfill Old Testament promises to Israel, and so there is no need for a future millennial reign of Christ to fulfill national promises to Israel. Second, advocates maintain that amillennialism best captures the "simple eschatological chronology" found in the New Testament as a whole (e.g., 2 Peter 3:10–13), that the "present age will climax in the return of Christ in triumph and judgment, followed immediately by the inauguration of the eternal state."[9] This simple eschatology is the framework by which interpreters must understand complex eschatological texts, like Revelation 20:1–10.

Third, amillennialists argue against the other two views. Regarding premillennialism, they maintain that premillennialists read too much into their central text, Revelation 20:1–10. Premillennialists, they believe, fail to appreciate that Revelation is highly symbolic and as a result read this passage too literally. For example, based on their reading of Revelation 20:4–6, premillennialists wrongly believe that there are two different resurrections, but Scripture teaches that there is only one general resurrection (John 5:28–29; Acts 24:15). In addition, amillennialists consider premillennialism's vision of the millennium problematic, for it pictures Christ returning in triumph but then not actually achieving *complete* triumph until a thousand years after His return. The millennium is thus only a partial, not a complete triumph; sin, rebellion, and death will not be defeated until the eternal state, after the millennium. Where else does Scripture teach a time of partial triumph after Christ returns?[10] Regarding postmillennialism, amillennialists maintain that postmillennialism is too optimistic this side of Christ's return. The golden age envisioned in postmillennialism cannot happen until Christ returns to establish the new heaven and earth. Until then, good and evil will coexist.

Postmillennialism

Postmillennialism is structured like amillennialism. So the millennium is an indefinitely long period of time at the end of which Christ returns, resurrects the saved and lost, and judges all in the final judgment. The major difference between amillennialism and postmillennialism is the nature of the millennium. True, in both views, Christ reigns from heaven. But in postmillennialism, His reign is not a spiritual reign alone, and the full manifestation of the millennium is still future. Christ's rule over the earth grows gradually as the gospel expands to the ends of the earth and triumphs. This expansion of Christ's rule through the exponential growth of believers ushers in a golden age where evil is mitigated and the world prospers. Righteousness will triumph throughout the world, shaping culture, politics, economics, and society as a whole, as well as spiritual life. At the end of His triumphal reign over the earth from heaven, Christ will return.

In addition to sharing several of the same arguments with amillenialism, postmillennialists make additional arguments supporting their view in particular. First, advocates maintain that postmillennialism best fits the picture in Scripture that the gospel will indeed go forth and permeate the world (see Matt. 28:18–20; Acts 1:8). In fact, several kingdom parables speak of the kingdom gradually growing until it permeates the world (see Matt. 13:31–33: the mustard seed and leaven). This, they believe, is a strong foundation for postmillennial optimism. Second, although postmillennialists agree with amillennialists (against premillennialism) that Revelation 20 is highly symbolic, they believe amillennial interpretation of the text is still inadequate. Because they deny that Revelation 20:1–6 follows chronologically from 19:11–21, amillennialists fail to see that 19:11–21 speaks of the triumph of the gospel leading to the establishment of the millennium in 20:1–6. Third, postmillennialists believe that the other two views do not adequately grapple with the significance of the statement in Matthew 28:18 that Christ has all authority in heaven and earth. If Christ is present with us until the end of the age (28:20), then His comprehensive authority is with us as well.[11] Fourth, postmillennialists believe their approach to Old Testament predictions of a future golden age (e.g., Isa. 65:17–25) is more balanced than either amillennialism or premillennialism. For they stress the spiritual fulfillment of these predictions (against premillennialism) while leaving room for some earthly, physical fulfillment as well (against amillennialism[12]). Finally, postmillennialists point out that the church history has demonstrated the amazing growth of the church as a worldwide movement far beyond its humble beginnings, which fits postmillennial expectations nicely.

PREMILLENNIALISM

Unlike the other two views, premillennialism maintains that Christ comes before the millennium and establishes it Himself. Before He returns to the earth to rule, there is a period (usually understood to be seven years) of intense evil and suffering on the earth known as the great tribulation. This period is identified with Daniel's seventieth "week" (a seven-year period) in Daniel 9:24–27. It is a terrible time in which satanic forces, led by the Antichrist (or the "Beast" in Revelation) and his henchman (the False Prophet) dominate the world and persecute God's people, while at the same time God pours His wrath on the world. Christ Himself ends the great tribulation when He returns to earth, crushes the forces of evil arrayed against Him, and imprisons Satan (Rev. 19:11–20:3). At this point, Christ resurrects believers martyred during the great tribulation (Rev. 10:4–5); this is called the "first resurrection." Premillennialists disagree about whether at this point all other believers are resurrected as well, or whether Christ resurrects other believers earlier in a "rapture" (to be discussed separately below). With His resurrected saints, Christ rules over the whole world for 1000 years,[13] a golden age of unprecedented blessing, peace, prosperity, justice, and righteousness (Rev. 20:4–6). For dispensationalists, this is when the Lord will fulfill all His promises to national Israel. Still, the millennium falls short of the perfection of the new heaven and earth, for there are those living under Christ's rule who have a rebellious heart. This is revealed when Satan is released from his imprisonment for a short time and rallies a vast multitude of rebels to take up arms against Christ, but this rebellion is easily vanquished (Rev. 20:7–10). At this point comes the final judgment, including the resurrection of unbelievers to eternal condemnation.

Premillenialists make several arguments in favor of their view, including the following. First, premillennialists point out that the structure of premillennialism is built directly on a straightforward reading of Revelation 19:11–20:10 in its narrative flow. For example, it explicitly says that there are two resurrections separated by 1,000 years. The other views cannot provide sufficient evidence from the text itself to justify not reading it straightforwardly. Second, premillennialists appeal to other texts in Scripture that reflect a premillennial eschatology. For example, Grudem points to texts that speak of a time "which is far greater than the present church age but which still does not see the removal of all sin and rebellion and death from the earth," including Isaiah 11:6–11; 65:17–25; Psalm 72:8–14; Zechariah 14:5–17; and Revelation 2:19–27.[14] Moreover, 1 Corinthians 15:23–28 suggests that, as there is a long time gap between Christ's resurrection, so too there is a time gap between the resurrection of believers and "the end" when death itself is defeated (as expected in premillennialism).[15] Third, premillennialists point out that the idea of Christ's return establishing a partial but not yet perfect reality is not so unusual as the other two views suggest. After all, throughout salvation history God has been working to redeem humanity progressively rather than all at once. For example, believers in this present age are already saved but also not yet saved. In a similar vein, the millennial reign of Christ is the penultimate step to the final consummation. Finally, for dispensationalists, there is one other critical argument. If national Israel has a future in God's plan because of His promises not yet fulfilled, then they can only be fulfilled during Christ's future millennial reign on the earth. A dispensational theology makes a premillennial conception of the millennium inevitable.

THE RAPTURE

Among premillennialists, there is another debate regarding Christ's second coming. It has to do with the rapture of believers as predicted in 1 Thessalonians 4:13–18. At the rapture, believers—both dead and living at the time—are "caught up . . . in the clouds to meet the Lord in the air" (v. 17). In particular, premillennialists debate whether the rapture is a distinguishable phase of Christ's second coming, and if it is, when it happens in relation to the tribulation period. The two most common views on the rapture today are the posttribulational and pretribulational views, but there are several other views as well.

RAPTURE VIEWS

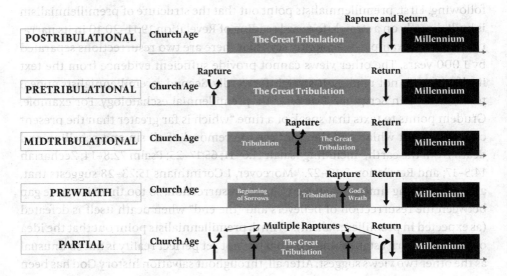

THE POSTTRIBULATIONAL RAPTURE

The posttribulational view does not believe that the rapture is a distinguishable phase of Christ's second coming. As a result, the church will suffer through the great tribulation, and then Christ will return. When He does, all believers will be resurrected, rise to meet Him in the clouds, and then immediately return back to earth with Him as He defeats the wicked and establishes His millennial kingdom.

Some of the arguments used by posttribulationalists include the following.[16] First, the Scriptures insist that the church should expect persecution and suffering in this present age, and so we should not expect to escape the great tribulation either. Passages like Revelation 3:10 only promise to preserve the church through times of trial, not to take us away from trial. Second, Scripture nowhere explicitly teaches that Christ will come in two phases; the other views are built on inferences from the text. The more natural reading of passages on Christ's second coming (e.g., Matt. 24; 1 Thess. 4–5; 2 Thess. 1–2; Rev. 3:10) is that it will be a single event after the tribulation that includes both the rapture and return to the earth. Third, belief in a separable rapture phase in Christ's second coming is a recent innovation in church history; the church throughout history has understood Christ's second coming to be a single event without separable phases.

THE PRETRIBULATIONAL RAPTURE[17]

Pretribulationalists believe that the rapture will occur before the great tribulation, and then Christ will return to the earth after the great tribulation to set up

His millennial kingdom. Hence, Christ comes in two phases: *for His* saints before the tribulation (rapture), and *with His* saints after the tribulation (return to the earth). The pretribulational view is typically held by dispensationalists.

Some of the arguments used in support of pretribulationalism include the following.[18] First, advocates argue that there are differences between the various passages describing the second coming, differences best accounted for by distinguishing the rapture from Christ's return to the earth.[19] For example, in John 14:1–3, Jesus indicates that He will come again and bring believers to His house in heaven, while in Revelation 19 He returns with His saints to rule on the earth. Second, pretribulationalists point to the purpose of the great tribulation. Its purpose is not only to pour God's wrath on the rebellious human world, but also to prepare Israel through trials to receive the Messiah (e.g., Dan. 9:24–27; Jer. 30:7; Rev. 7). The church has no role in either purpose. In a similar vein, third, advocates point out that, while the church certainly should expect trials, she is exempt from the coming divine wrath (1 Thess. 1:10; 5:9). Consequently, God promises the church in Revelation 3:10 that He "will keep you from the hour of the testing, that hour which is about to come upon the whole world, to test those who live on the earth."

Third, pretribulationalists argue that only a pretribulational rapture adequately accounts for the imminency of Christ's second coming. Scripture indicates that we are to be ready because Christ could come back at any time (e.g., James 5:7–9; 1 Thess. 1:10; Phil. 3:20–21; Titus 2:13; Rev. 22:20). At the same time, there is a tension here because Scripture also indicates that there will be signs before Christ's return.[20] The pretribulational rapture handles this tension well, for the rapture is imminent while the signs pertain to Christ's return to the earth after the rapture and tribulation.

Finally, pretribulationalists argue that, if a premillennial eschatology is to make sense, there must be a time interval between the rapture and Christ's establishment of His earthly kingdom. If all believers are raptured into glorified bodies at the end of the tribulation, and all Christ's enemies are excluded from the kingdom (Matt. 25:31–46), then who will populate the earth in non-glorified bodies during the millennium (as expected in premillennialism)? Pretribulationists believe they have the best answer to that: tribulation survivors who become believers during the tribulation, including Jews who turn to Christ, will do so.

Other Rapture Views

There have been several other, less common views on the rapture. They all share in common the pretribulational conviction that the rapture is a distinguishable phase of Christ's second coming, but they differ from pretribulationalism and from one another on the timing of the rapture. Midtribulationalists maintain that the rapture occurs at the midway point of the great tribulation, which helps explain why Scripture mentions or alludes to this midway point several times (e.g., Dan. 7:25; 9:27; 12:7, 11; Rev. 12:14).[21] The prewrath rapture maintains that the rapture occurs three-quarters of the way through Daniel's seventieth week. The third quarter of that seven-year period is the great tribulation, and so the church will suffer through that. However, the last quarter of those seven-years will be the time of God's wrath, and the church will be raptured before that (Rev. 3:10).[22] The partial rapture view maintains that the rapture itself occurs in multiple phases throughout the great tribulation depending on whether the person is prepared for Christ's coming and spiritually mature.

RESURRECTION

Although they will differ on its timing, all views presented above agree that Christ's second coming will usher in the resurrection. Scripture clearly teaches that the bodies of all humans, believer and unbeliever alike, will be resurrected (John 5:28–29; Acts 24:15; Dan. 12:2). We know very little about the nature of the unbeliever's resurrection, except that it will be a "resurrection of judgment" (John 5:29) that inexorably culminates in the second death (Rev. 20:5–6, 13–15). Instead, Scripture focuses attention on the resurrection of believers. Christ will raise what remains of believers' earthly bodies[23] and transform them into glorious bodies patterned after Christ's resurrected body (1 Cor. 15:22–23). This resurrected body will therefore be powerful and imperishable (1 Cor. 15:42–43), perfectly suited for living in the new heaven and earth forever. Believers' resurrection marks the completion of God's redeeming work in their lives when they will be finally conformed to the image of Christ (Rom. 8:23, 28–30). We thus have good reason to be "firm, immovable, always excelling in the work of the Lord, knowing that your labor is not in vain in the Lord" (1 Cor. 15:58).

JUDGMENT

As with the resurrection, the various eschatological views also do not agree on the timing of the judgment.[24] But they all agree that Christ will come to judge (Matt. 25:31ff; Acts 10:42), and He will do so with perfect justice (Isa. 11:3–5; Rom. 2:11–12; Rev. 19:1–2). Remarkably, Scripture indicates that believers will also participate with Him in some of this judgment (1 Cor. 6:2–3; see Rev. 20:4).

Who will be judged? First, Christ will judge all unbelievers (Rev. 20:11–15). No one will have any legitimate defense against His righteous judgments, and so all will be condemned (Rom. 3:19) ultimately to eternal punishment in the lake of fire (Rev. 20:13–15). Nevertheless, there will be degrees of punishment meted out depending on how sinfully unbelievers have lived (Matt. 11:22, 24; Luke 20:47; Matt.

12:36).[25] Second, Christ will judge fallen angels, including Satan (2 Peter 2:4; Jude 6; Rev. 20:10). This too will result in just, eternal condemnation.[26] Third, Christ will also judge believers (2 Cor. 5:10; Rom. 14:10, 12).[27] Notably, this judgment does not threaten our eternal life at all, for there is no condemnation for those in Christ Jesus (Rom. 8:1; John 3:16–18; 5:24). Instead, this judgment will evaluate believers' works (1 Cor. 3:12–15), including their faithfulness (1 Cor. 4:1–2) and hidden motives (1 Cor. 4:5). This judgment results in different degrees of reward for the believer (2 Cor. 5:10; 1 Cor. 3:15; Luke 19:11–27).

Grudem helpfully points out that the doctrine of final judgment has several practical ramifications. First, it demonstrates that there is ultimate justice in the universe, which is satisfying and comforting. Second, freeing us from seeking vengeance and encouraging us to trust in God as righteous judge, this doctrine "enables us to forgive others freely." Third, it also gives believers ample motivation both to live godly lives and share the gospel with others.[28]

THE ETERNAL STATE

After the millennium, Christ will establish the eternal or final state. As these names suggest, this describes the permanent condition of all human beings resulting from the consummation of God's work of redemption and judgment. There are two eternal states, that of the condemned and that of the redeemed.

THE ETERNAL STATE OF THE CONDEMNED

Those who have never been redeemed by Christ through faith in Him (and so are still in their sins) face hell as their inevitable destiny (John 3:18, 36). The term "hell" encompasses both the intermediate state of unbelievers in Hades and their final state in the lake of fire (*Gehenna*). The focus here is on the latter. The fundamental reality of the final state of all unbelievers is eternal death, banishment forever from the living God and the infinite joy His presence entails. Instead, they face the dreadful prospects of God's holy wrath (Rom. 2:6–8; 5:9; 1 Thess. 1:10; 2 Thess. 1:7–10; Rev. 6:15–18; 9:15), "a terrifying thing" indeed (Heb. 10:31). It is a place of ruin and suffering, being described as "eternal fire" (Matt. 25:41), "destruction" (Matt. 7:13–14; 2 Thess. 1:9), "outer darkness" where there will be "weeping and gnashing of teeth" (Matt. 8:12), and torment "with fire and brimstone" (Rev. 14:10–11). This suffering indicates that its inhabitants will be conscious. Worse still, they will experience it eternally (Matt. 24:41, 46; Mark 9:43, 48; Rev. 14:9–11; 2 Thess. 1:9).

The reality of hell reflects God's just punishment (Matt. 24:46); "God's punishment is not a vindictive but a righteous retribution for wrongs committed."[29] As a result, there will be degrees of punishment in hell (Matt. 11:21–24; Luke 12:47–48; 20:47). Yet for everyone in hell, the punishment will never end. For sin is an offense against the infinite God, calling for an infinite punishment, and in any case it is likely that hell's inhabitants will continue to sin throughout eternity.[30]

Because the prospects of nonbelievers are so horrifying, some try to minimize them. *Universalists* claim that eventually all human beings will be reconciled to God and end up in heaven. But this violates Scripture's teaching seen above that hell is an *eternal* reality for all unbelievers. In addition, *annihilationists* maintain that the condemned in hell will suffer for a time, but eventually they will cease to exist. They argue that Scripture's language of "destruction" and "fire" suggests annihilation, and this annihilation is "eternal" in the sense that it lasts forever. But in regard to hell, the language for "destruction" more likely speaks of ruin rather than annihilation. Moreover, Scripture's teaching about eternal *conscious suffering* seen above militates against the notion that the condemned cease to exist.[31] Sadly, then, Scripture does teach that the prospects of the unbeliever are as horrifying as described above. The believer's appropriate response to the reality of hell is sorrow for those condemned (e.g., Rom. 9:2–3), awe before God's righteous judgment (Rev. 19:1–3), a passion to share the gospel with the lost (2 Tim. 2:10), and thankful praise for God's redemptive work in our lives (Rom. 11:33–36).

THE ETERNAL STATE OF THE REDEEMED

The prospects of believers are far brighter, for heaven is their future. Like the word "hell," the word "heaven" similarly refers both to believers' intermediate state as well as their final state. Once again, the focus here is on the latter. Revelation 21–22 describe the eternal state of the redeemed as a new heaven and earth and the New Jerusalem. Sin in all its forms and effects will be forever banished, as will death itself, a place with no sorrow, no suffering, no pain. It will be a place of unspeakable beauty, resplendent in glory, Eden intensified and expanded. We will dwell there with our glorified, immortal bodies, perfectly suited to life in this wonderful place. But most important of all, God Himself will dwell there with His people, and so we will experience the unending bliss of unhindered fellowship with the living God. It is this for which we were made. Little wonder that that believers long for Christ's soon return. "Amen. Come, Lord Jesus" (Rev. 22:20).

NOTES

1. Murray Harris, "Death," in *New Dictionary of Theology*, ed. Sinclair Ferguson and David Wright (Downers Grove, IL: IVP, 1988), 188.

2. Michael J. Vlach, *Has the Church Replaced Israel?: A Theological Evaluation* (Nashville: B&H Publishing, 2010), 12 (original italics omitted).

3. Vlach, *Has the Church Replaced Israel?*, 89. This does not mean that God has no plans for Jews at all. In light of Romans 11, many covenant theologians today would affirm that a large number of Jews will turn to Christ in connection with Christ's return and be joined to Him and the church.

4. Ibid., 88. See also Kim Riddlebarger, *A Case for Amillennialism: Understanding the End Times* (Grand Rapids: Baker, 2003), 36–38.

5. Renald E. Showers, *There Really Is a Difference! A Comparison of Covenant and Dispensational Theology* (Bellmawr, NJ: Friends of Israel, 1990), 30.

6. Michael J. Vlach, *Dispensationalism: Essential Beliefs and Common Myths*, revised and updated (Los Angeles: Theological Studies Press, 2017), 90.

7. Ibid., 87–88. This does not mean that the NT may not *complement* or *expand* on the original meaning of the OT text.

8. Another version of amillennialism considers the spiritual millennium to be a strictly heavenly reality. See Paul N. Benware, *Understanding End Times Prophecy* (Chicago: Moody, 2006), 103–4; Stanley J. Grenz, *The Millennial Maze: Sorting Out Evangelical Options* (Downers Grove, IL: InterVarsity, 1992), 151–52.

9. Grenz, *The Millennial Maze*, 158.

10. See Ibid., 143–44 for a similar point.

11. Grenz, *The Millennial Maze*, 76.

12. Some amillennialists do allow for some physical fulfillment of those predictions, not in the millennium, but in the eternal state.

13. Some premillennialists would argue, like amillennialists and postmillennialists, that the figure of 1,000 years is symbolic of an indefinitely long period of time.

14. Wayne Grudem, *Systematic Theology* (Grand Rapids: Zondervan, 1994), 1127–30.

15. Ibid., 1130.

16. For a nice short summary of arguments in support of posttribulationalism, see Grudem, *Systematic Theology*, 1131–35. For a more detailed case, see Douglas Moo, "A Case for the Posttribulational Rapture," in *Three Views on the Rapture: Pretribulation, Prewrath, or Posttribulation*, 2nd ed., Alan Hultberg, ed. (Grand Rapids: Zondervan, 2010), 185–241.

17. Moody Bible Institute embraces a dispensational, premillennial, pretribulational position. For a brief articulation and defense, see John K. Goodrich, "On the Last Things," in *Standing Firm: The Doctrinal Commitments of Moody Bible Institute*, ed. John Jelinek and Bryan O'Neal (Chicago: Moody Publishers, 2019), 103–12.

18. A case for pretribulationalism is made by Paul Feinberg, "The Case for the Pretribulational Rapture Position," in *The Rapture: Pre-, Mid-, or Post-Tribulational?* (Grand Rapids: Zondervan, 1984), 45–86; Craig Blaising, "A Case for the Pretribulational Rapture," in *Pretribulation, Prewrath, or Posttribulation*, 2nd ed.; Benware, *Understanding End Times Prophecy*, 157–87; and especially John Hart, ed., *Evidenced for the Rapture: A Biblical Case for Pretribulationalism* (Chicago: Moody, 2015).

19. See Feinberg, "The Case for the Pretribulational Rapture Position," 80–86.

20. See Grudem, *Systematic Theology*, 1095–99.

21. For a more detailed case for this view, see Gleason L. Archer, "The Case for the Mid-Seventieth Week Rapture Position," in *The Rapture: Pre-, Mid-, or Post-Tribulational?*, 113–45.

22. For a detailed case for this view, see Marvin Rosenthal, *The Pre-Wrath Rapture of the Church* (Nashville: Thomas Nelson, 1990). See also Alan Hultberg, "A Case for the Prewrath Rapture," in *Three Views on the Rapture*, 109–54.

23. For believers who have physically died at the resurrection, Christ will resurrect whatever is left of the destroyed body, and for believers who are physically alive at the resurrection, their bodies will be transformed.

24. Most of the views maintain that all judgment takes place right before the final state. However, dispensationalists typically maintain that there are several phases of judgment: 1) a judgment of believers at the rapture; 2) a judgment of the nations after the tribulation and right before the millennium to determine who can enter the millennial kingdom; 3) the great white throne judgment at the end of the millennium resulting in the final judgment of all unbelievers. See Benware, *Understanding End Times Prophecy*, 269–77.

25. See the helpful discussion of this point in Grudem, *Systematic Theology*, 1142–43.

26. It is possible that Paul's statement in 1 Corinthians 6:3 that believers will judge "angels" includes righteous angels as well as fallen ones. In the case of the former, this obviously would not result in condemnation. See ibid., 1145.

27. This judgment is sometimes called the *bema* judgment (or the judgment seat of Christ; Rom. 14:10; 2 Cor. 5:10). In the Roman world, the *bema* was a raised platform from which a judge decided a case or officials issued athletic

rewards. For short but helpful discussions, see Benware, *Understanding End Times Prophecy*, 271–73; Grudem, 1143–45.

28. Grudem, *Systematic Theology*, 1147–48.

29. John Macarthur and Richard Mayhue, *Biblical Doctrine: A Systematic Summary of Bible Truth* (Wheaton, IL: Crossway, 2017), 845.

30. See the helpful discussion in D.A. Carson, *The Gagging of God: Christianity Confronts Pluralism* (Grand Rapids: Zondervan, 1996), 532–34.

31. For a very helpful discussion of annihilationism, including a good case against it, see Carson, *The Gagging of God*, 515–36.

Understanding the Basics of Church History

BRYAN M. LITFIN

THE BIBLE'S EMPHASIS ON HISTORY

The Christian faith is, at its core, historical. Its central event—the life, death, and resurrection of Jesus of Nazareth—took place on the stage of human history. Let that reality sink in for a moment. The eternal Creator of the universe, in the person of God the Son, entered the universe, which He had created long before. God permanently joined Himself to human affairs in the incarnation. If that does not count as an amazing affirmation of history, nothing does!

The earliest Christians continued this emphasis on history in their writings and practices. The gospel writer Luke tells us that he will rely on what has been "handed down" by "those who from the beginning were eyewitnesses." He has "investigated everything carefully" so that his "orderly sequence" will produce certainty in his audience (1:1–4). This excellent description of historical method could still be used today. Obviously, it was important for the first believers to record the momentous events of Christianity just as they had happened in the real world.

Of course, a historical focus did not begin with the apostles. The Old Testament had been demonstrating God's value for history long before the coming of Christ. The biblical God gets involved with earthly events. In the garden of Eden, God walked with Adam and Eve (Gen. 3:8). He often showed Himself in a *theophany*, or a physical manifestation of God. Sometimes, the figure known as the angel of the

Lord was not a mere angel but God Himself, visible to human eyes, such as at the burning bush (Ex. 3:2), or when Hagar spoke with the Lord about her son Ishmael (Gen. 16:11). We even have a divine wrestling match between God and Jacob! (Gen. 32:22–32). In all these biblical texts, we see that God is willing to enter into human history. Unlike the Greek view of the supreme deity articulated by Plato, the God of Scripture takes great interest in earthly affairs.

Even when God is not physically entering the human world, His divine hand can be seen guiding His chosen people. Beginning with Abram in Genesis 12, we read that God is calling a special nation to Himself. He leads them to the land of Israel, protects them in Egypt, and draws them back to the promised land. Although God chastises the Israelites by the hands of wicked nations or the foolishness of their own kings, He also preserves them by sending judges and prophets. After the Jews are taken into captivity in Assyria and Babylon, God brings them home again under brave leaders like Ezra and Nehemiah. The preservation of the Jewish nation to this day is proof of God's care and concern for His chosen people. So when the early Christians began to record the mighty works of God in history, they had long-standing precedent for this in the Old Testament.

One of the most important commands to church leaders in the New Testament is to "pass on" the true faith. In 1 Corinthians 15:3–4, the apostle Paul says, "For I handed down to you as of first importance what I also received, that Christ died for our sins according to the Scriptures, and that He was buried, and that He was raised on the third day according to the Scriptures." Similarly, the biblical writer Jude exhorts church leaders to "contend earnestly for the faith that was once for all time handed down to the saints" (1:3). The Pastoral Epistles urge leaders and elders to pass on a sound inheritance (e.g., 2 Tim. 2:2). And the epistle to the Hebrews gives the best reason for pastors to be church historians when it recites the mighty deeds of those who have gone before (ch. 11), then calls the contemporary generation to run its own race before "such a great a cloud of witnesses" (12:1).

In sum, the Bible tells us that being a faithful leader of a Christian congregation includes the important task of transmitting to subsequent generations a reliable account of what our spiritual ancestors have done. Church history—like Israel's history before it—is something about which God cares very much. Therefore, the pastor should too.

THE FIVE ERAS OF CHURCH HISTORY

It has been two millennia since Jesus of Nazareth walked the dusty roads of Galilee or the stone-paved streets of Jerusalem. We know from the Bible what happened next: He ascended into heaven, and the apostles spread the gospel message far and wide. The book of Acts ends with the apostle Paul in confinement. But then what happened? Did church history grind to a halt? Of course not. Although there is no inspired account of subsequent events, the task of the church historian is to use non-inspired sources (texts, artifacts, and architectural remains) to piece together all that happened afterward.

To describe the flow of Christian history, most church historians think in terms of four main periods, with a fifth that we are now in. The precise dates for the divisions could be debated, yet the periods are basically the same. They are: **Ancient** (birth of the church up to AD 500); **Medieval** (500–1500); **Reformation** (1500–1700); and **Modern** (1700–1950). Sometime in the middle of the twentieth century, people in certain parts of the globe, particularly in Europe and North America, entered the fifth period: the **Postmodern era** (1950–present). This five-part scheme works well for church history in the Roman Empire and Western Europe up to the twenty-first century. Because this is the historical trajectory that gave rise to modern evangelicalism, the present chapter will use this common five-fold periodization. Yet attention to global Christianity will be included as much as possible in this brief narrative.

ANCIENT PERIOD (ORIGINS TO 500)

The Ancient phase of church history coincides with the existence of the Roman Empire. The Christian leaders of the time are often referred to as the "early church fathers." Once the empire fell to foreign invaders, it gradually broke apart or morphed into other political structures. A new era of church history began, and the Ancient Period came to an end. The Ancient Period can be subdivided like this:

Apostolic Fathers (100–150)

After the first generation of apostles who knew the Lord, the second generation of writers were known as the apostolic fathers. These figures often knew the apostles personally, but not Jesus Himself. For example, **Clement of Rome** was an early leader in that city, who wrote an epistle to the Corinthians dealing with the problem of church divisions. Other texts included among the Apostolic Fathers are: *Epistle of Barnabas*; *Shepherd of Hermas*; the baptismal manual called the *Didache*; the seven letters of **Ignatius of Antioch**; and the *Martyrdom of Polycarp*, an elderly bishop in Smyrna who personally knew the apostle John.

Apologists (150–300)

After the apostolic fathers came the apologists. In the second and third centuries, Christianity began to be recognized as a religion distinct from Judaism—and it was not well-liked. Pagan opponents such as Galen, Celsus, and Porphyry attacked the church from outside, while heretics arose from within (such as Marcion, who taught that Jesus did not come from the Old Testament God, or the Gnostics, who taught that salvation comes through mental knowledge instead of the cross). In response, a generation of leaders rose up to defend the true faith through apologetics. These men wrote more advanced treatises than the apostolic fathers, who tended to be simple and pastoral. The Apologists borrowed concepts from Greek philosophy to express and contextualize their arguments, and in so doing, added a great deal more sophistication to the church's theology. Some important ancient apologists were **Justin Martyr**, **Irenaeus**, **Tertullian**, **Clement of Alexandria**, and **Origen**.

Theologians (300–500)

Although the apologists were certainly doing important theological thinking, the era that brought forth the greatest ancient theologians was the fourth and fifth centuries. This was the period after Emperor Constantine had proclaimed tolerance and favoritism toward the church (AD 313). With the end of Christian persecution, advanced theological reflection occurred, thanks to more frequent travel by bishops, a greater exchange of their writings, and the convocation of church-wide councils.

One of the most important councils was Nicaea (325), from which we get today's Nicene Creed (though it was slightly adapted in a subsequent council). Against the heresy of Arius who considered Jesus to be a creature made by God, the doctrine of the Trinity was put forth: that there is one God, eternally existing in three Persons, the Father, Son, and Holy Spirit. Each of these persons is consubstantial with the others, meaning they share the "same substance" (*homoousios* in Greek). A second important council was Chalcedon (451). This ancient council taught the full deity and true humanity of Jesus Christ. He is one person (*hypostasis*) who, after His incarnation by Mary, possessed two distinct natures (*physis*): a human nature and a divine nature. The Egyptian bishop **Cyril of Alexandria** popularized the phrase that we use to describe this truth today: hypostatic union.

The most noteworthy theologian from the early church is **Augustine of Hippo** (354–430). As chronicled in his autobiography, the *Confessions*, Augustine was a rebellious boy in North Africa who resisted God in his youth, but dramatically turned from his sins to the Lord in a Milanese garden in 386. He went on to be the ancient church's greatest theologian. Augustine taught many important doctrines, such as the doctrine of original sin inherited by all people from Adam, against the heresy of Pelagius, who said that humans had not fallen into Adam's sin but could earn salvation through good works. Augustine is also famous for his doctrine of predestination. His greatest work was *City of God*, which divided humanity into two "cities" of God or man, with a fundamental opposition between them, and two vastly different outcomes: eternal punishment or everlasting bliss.

During the century of the 400s, some dramatic events occurred that marked the end of the Roman Empire. Scholars today recognize that the transition to the Middle Ages was gradual. At the same time, the 400s were characterized by the invasion and/or immigration of Germanic people who settled in portions of the former empire, defeated the old Roman leaders, and brought new political realities to the lands that for so long had been under the sway of imperial Rome. By the year 500 (to give it a round number), we can definitely see that the Ancient regime had passed and a new future was dawning.

MEDIEVAL PERIOD (500–1500)

The Medieval Period is also known as the Middle Ages because these centuries stood between the Ancient and Modern eras. It may be subdivided as follows:

Early Medieval Period (500–1000)

During this historical age, Western Europe came under the religious sway of the Roman Catholic Church. Eventually a thoroughly Christianized society arose that is often referred to as Christendom. Yet outside of Europe, Christianity was spreading into other areas of the globe. Let us first mention this development, then return to Western Europe.

Although the Christian faith had traveled outside the Roman Empire during the Ancient Period, we know relatively little about these circumstances. In the Middle Eastern areas that are now Lebanon, Syria, Jordan, and Iraq, and then farther eastward along the trading route known as the Silk Road, Christian ideas began to spread through many parts of southern Asia, such as Iran, Afghanistan, Pakistan, the Central Asian republics, India, Mongolia, and eventually as far as the Pacific coast of China. Sometimes, these groups were affected by Gnostic doctrines and became a strange hybrid of truth and heresy. These congregations have mostly disappeared from history.

In contrast, the global communion known as the Assyrian Church of the East did not accept Gnostic heresies. Yet neither did they embrace the doctrine of hypostatic union taught at Chalcedon. Today, they hold the two natures of Christ to be separate (a teaching known as Dyophysitism, sometimes referred to as Nestorianism). Another group that is still prominent in the Middle East and Asia today is the Oriental Orthodox Church. Their origins, too, come from rejecting Chalcedon. They teach that the one divine nature of Jesus Christ has essentially swallowed up His human nature (the doctrine of Miaphysitism, sometimes called Monophysitism). Both of these still-existing churches expanded rapidly in the Early

Medieval Period. In this same era, the Eastern Orthodox Church (which *did* accept the Christological doctrines of Chalcedon) evangelized from Greece into Eastern Europe and Russia, eventually forming very large churches there. Obviously, the Christian faith had a major eastward trajectory from early times.

Meanwhile, back in Western Europe, many changes were happening in the Early Medieval Period. One was the rise of monasticism. This term refers to the practice of monks seeking solitude and embracing spiritual disciplines as a means of growing closer to God. The lifestyle had roots in the ancient church, when many people pursued ascetic practices such as fasting, chastity, and other bodily hardships. The goal of these devoted men and women was to "[put] to death the deeds of the body" (Rom. 8:13; Col. 3:5) and "discipline [the] body" (1 Cor. 9:27), so that God's higher spiritual purposes would come into clearer focus. The monastic lifestyle was codified for Western Christians by the *Rule of St. Benedict*, written sometime after 500. The Benedictine Order flourished during the Early Middle Ages as many brothers adopted the *Rule* as their way of life.

Another important event of the Early Medieval Period was the growing power of the Roman Catholic Church. The church in Rome had always been important because the city was the capital of the Roman Empire. At first, it did not claim authority over other churches, or at least it claimed only the informal authority of its doctrinal accuracy and long-standing prestige. But starting in the Early Middle Ages, the church of Rome began to assume a more formal position in the Latin-speaking world, since Western Europe was in chaos due to the social upheaval after the fall of the Roman Empire.

Early Medieval Christians began to use the title *papa* (a respectful term meaning "father," commonly applied to all bishops) in a new way: to designate only the "pope" who spoke with the living voice of Peter, the greatest apostle who had died and was buried on the Vatican Hill at Rome. Because Western Europe was in such disarray, the popes of the Early Middle Ages were able to consolidate power, not just over the bishops of other cities, but even over the new Germanic aristocracy, because Jesus had given to Peter the "keys of the kingdom of heaven" (Matt. 16:19). This power to control the pearly gates was something that every medieval person—from the lowliest serf to the loftiest king—had to fear. Their eternal destiny depended on staying in the good graces of the Roman Catholic Church whose head was the pope.

One king who certainly did find favor with the bishops of Europe was Charlemagne. Crowned by the pope in St. Peter's Basilica in the year 800, Charlemagne ("Charles the Great") reigned over a mighty empire that covered the whole continent of western and central Europe, except Spain and the southern part of Italy. (Some people considered this a revival of the Roman Empire, but in reality, it was not.) During this era, medieval society came to be divided into the three main classes of aristocrats, clergy, and peasants. The members of these classes were bound to each other by oaths of loyalty and reciprocal obligations, a system known as feudalism. Most people lived in small towns, or on farms called manors, while great cities were relatively rare. Though Charlemagne's stable reign led to a brief blossoming of education and literature, much of Early Medieval society was ignorant, backward, and squalid in comparison to the glories of ancient Rome. For this reason, historians have referred to this era as the Dark Ages. It was not, of course, completely "dark." Yet a tremendous amount of cultural capital was lost when the Roman Empire faded away.

High Medieval Period (1000–1300)

The so-called Dark Ages were followed by an era of noteworthy cultural achievement, the High Middle Ages. For the first five hundred years after the fall of Rome, the economies of Europe had not been trading many goods and services over long distances. Numerous farm fields had gone back to wilderness, ancient technologies had been lost, bandits often robbed travelers, and populations had drastically declined. Unlike the highly mobile culture of the imperial age—think of the apostle Paul's extensive journeys, for example—few medieval people ever traveled more than a couple of miles from their birthplace.

But now in the High Middle Ages, a new international economy was rebirthed. People banded together into traveling caravans of long-distance merchants, establishing a circuit of trading fairs across the landscape. To facilitate trade, a money and banking economy was reintroduced to supplement the barter system. Craftsmen began to form guilds and network with one another. Even the European climate changed: a long warming period began, and winters were less harsh. Populations at last began to rise again.

One of the strangest causes of the economic blossoming of the High Middle Ages was the unfortunate series of wars known as the Crusades. These wars, complex in origin, were fought in waves for about two hundred years (approximately 1100–1300). The energetic Crusaders—who were sanctioned by the Roman Catholic Church in concept, though not in all their deeds—were upper class knights (sometimes including the highest levels of the aristocracy) who traveled to the eastern Mediterranean region with their supporters to make war on Muslims.

The Arabian religion of Islam had arisen in the seventh century AD, and its adherents quickly captured Jerusalem and the Holy Land. Now the Crusaders were leaving Europe to recapture those "Christian" lands, as well as to gain spoils and establish kingdoms known as the Crusader States. Today, the Crusaders are often depicted as cruel invaders of a tolerant and peaceable society, but the situation was not that simple. There was plenty of bloodshed on all sides, and many knights were motivated by a desire to redress injustices against the helpless Christian victims of Muslim policies. That said, the rapacious behavior of the knights has left negative associations with the Crusades that live on today.

Contact during the Crusades with Mediterranean people—who were themselves in contact with the products and ideas of the Far East—helped Western Europe finally awaken from its economic and intellectual slumber. This new period of vitality led to the establishment of great schools, called "universities," in places like Bologna, Paris, Oxford, and Cambridge. The philosophical movement that established the climate in which these universities could flourish was known as Scholasticism.

The Scholastic outlook was characterized by a new willingness to ask questions. Prior to this, medieval intellectual life was carried out by monks who counted it a virtue to simply pass on truth in humble submission to their monastic superiors. Asking questions would have been viewed as a form of pride. But now, in the new universities, question-asking was encouraged. Knowledge gained from various sources—the Bible, church tradition, historical theologians, the liberal arts, ancient Greek philosophy (especially Aristotle), and even the insights of Islamic thought from Spain—could be marshaled on behalf of Christian theology. Thus, Scholasticism was highly synthetic. It put all forms of earthly learning into the service of the Catholic Church, and so of God Himself.

One of the most noteworthy of the Scholastics, because he was a foundational figure, was **Anselm of Canterbury** (1033–1109). Anselm is famous for two main contributions. One is a slogan that epitomizes his thought: *Fides Quaerens Intellectum*, or "faith seeking understanding." The slogan means that a thinker must start from a stance of faith. Only after having faith can he learn more about what he believes through the mental quest of philosophy. In this way, human reason serves the task of theology. The second of Anselm's contributions illustrates this point. His famous "ontological argument" (an argument from essence or being) is a philosophical proof of God's existence. For Anselm, philosophy and human reason can support what we already believe by faith.

The foremost Scholastic figure—and indeed, the most important theologian between Augustine and the Reformation—was **Thomas Aquinas** (1225–1274). He was a celebrated professor at the University of Paris, today called the Sorbonne. Aquinas epitomizes medieval Scholasticism more than anyone else. His greatest work was called the *Summa Theologiae*, a true "summary of theology." It put all topics of medieval theological interest into one great multivolume writing. Some of Aquinas's most lasting contributions had to do with the theological theories about how sacraments operate. Aquinas argued that sacraments transmit grace not because of the priest, nor because of the recipient, but because God had made them instruments of His salvation. Although Aquinas himself greatly appreciated the need to depend on God's grace, his views later developed into a rote understanding of the Catholic sacraments (especially penance and the Mass), in which the works themselves brought forgiveness, instead of a contrite heart and true faith.

One unfortunate development in the High Middle Ages was a corruption of the monastic movement, which was formerly marked by spiritual vibrancy. Over time, monasticism had become stale and the flame of ascetic fervor had grown dim. Instead of engaging in ministries of prayer and hospitality, many monks were immoral or lazy, living in comfort behind the walls of their now very rich monasteries. Because of this, the so-called Mendicant Orders arose. The word "mendicant" means that these new monks, who were simple brothers known as friars, did not possess great wealth, but had to beg for their everyday needs. They did not stay behind walls but wandered around preaching and serving the common people in exchange for their daily bread. The most famous Mendicant Orders were the Franciscans (founded by **Francis of Assisi** in 1209), and the Dominicans (founded by **Dominic** in 1215).

By the end of the High Middle Ages, the popes were extremely powerful, and their "power of the keys" made even the great kings and emperors of Europe fear for their immortal souls. With one command, the popes could make the sacraments invalid; and then the peasantry and aristocracy alike would be facing many long years in purgatory, or even hell. High Medieval Roman Catholicism had reached its apex of political and cultural influence. But its dominance was not to last.

Late Medieval Period (1300–1500)

This era of church history overlaps with what is often called the Renaissance, an age of intellectual, artistic, and cultural rebirth centered in Italy. The Late Middle Ages can thus be viewed as a period of both decay and rebirth (which is what "renaissance" means). On the one hand, the old medieval way of doing things had stagnated and was coming to an end. Exposure to new ideas and new products from outside Europe was bringing a growing awareness that things could change. Even a terrible tragedy had its benefits: the rat-borne plague known as the Black Death of the late 1300s greatly reduced Europe's population, forcing social changes and creating new workforce mobility through competition for scarce labor. It was a time of social collapse that cleared the way for new beginnings.

Of course, not everything was grim and dire in Late Medieval Europe, nor has everything from that time disappeared today. Some of the most enduring monuments of the Middle Ages are its great cathedrals. These mighty churches, usually placed on a main town square, were built in a style that has come to be called

Gothic, a term originally intended to insult it as barbarous, but which today is considered a sign of great beauty. Using the new art of stained glass for which Gothic architecture is famous, the multicolored light of heaven began to flood the lofty interiors of Europe's churches. Although the Gothic style began in 1144, the Late Middle Ages was its period of most intense creativity.

Cathedrals were built so lavishly (often taking hundreds of years to construct) because they housed the liturgy of the Mass, in which bread and wine were "transubstantiated" by the priest to become (supposedly) the actual body and blood of Christ. With such holy bread available to take away the people's sins, the Catholic sacraments became the all-important means of salvation. Another central sacrament was penance (the doing of good deeds to show one's repentance), which could include monetary gifts to good causes. Eventually, "indulgences" could be bought to cover one's sins. Huge revenue from the guilt-ridden population began to flow into the Catholic Church. The priests and bishops, with the pope at the top, became the powerful gatekeepers of everyone's hope for a good afterlife.

Prophetic voices began to arise to critique Catholic sacramental abuses, turning attention back to the Scriptures and the divine grace that flowed from genuine faith not meritorious works. In England, **John Wycliffe** (1330–1384) was an Oxford University professor who rejected transubstantiation and advocated translating the Bible into popular English. **Jan Hus** (1362–1415) was another reformer from Bohemia, which is today the Czech Republic. Like Wycliffe, Hus criticized the rich and powerful clergy, even daring to say that the Bible stands over the pope. For these views, he was burned at the stake in 1415. These men, and others like them, are considered forerunners of the Reformation.

REFORMATION PERIOD (1500–1700)

This era is sometimes referred to as the Early Modern Period; but because we are focusing on church history, we will use the term "Reformation." There were four main strands of the Protestant Reformation.

Lutheran Church

The Reformation is understood to have begun on October 31, 1517, when **Martin Luther** (1483–1546) nailed his famous 95 Theses to the door of the Castle Church in Wittenberg, Germany. The theses were points of contention about the use and abuse of sacraments and indulgences. Eventually, they sparked a continent-wide discussion about the role of human works in salvation. The Catholics viewed works as means of grace, as opposed to Luther's doctrine of justification by faith alone.

Martin Luther was a devout monk who did not set out to sever the German church from Roman Catholicism. Yet that is eventually what happened. Luther and his doctrines were condemned at a political/church council in 1529. Six German princes, speaking on behalf of many others, protested this decision. These new "Protestants" argued for ideas that came to be expressed in five slogans called the *solas* (Latin for "alone"): grace alone, faith alone, Scripture alone, Christ alone, and glory to God alone. The *solas* stood in contrast to human meritorious works that were understood to earn favor with God.

Reformed Church

The Reformed Protestant tradition is associated primarily with **John Calvin** (1509–1564), who took a pastorate at Geneva, Switzerland, in 1537. Yet the Swiss Reformed tradition had begun earlier, under **Ulrich Zwingli** (1484–1531) in Zurich. The various Reformed churches today hold to the doctrinal system known as Calvinism. It differed from the Lutheran churches by not accepting the "real presence" of Christ in the bread and wine of communion. In his *Institutes of the Christian Religion* and many other writings, Calvin taught a comprehensive system- atic theology that included the authority of God's Word and various Augustinian ideas about the sovereignty of God. The Calvinistic doctrine of salvation has been summarized by the acronym TULIP: the **t**otal depravity of humans; God's **u**ncondi- tional election or predestination of some people to salvation; the **l**imited intent of Christ's atonement for only those who are elect; the **i**rresistible grace of God that draws the elect to salvation; and the **p**erseverance of these saints in their faith, so that their salvation can never be lost.

Radical Reformation/Anabaptists

Both Luther and Calvin sought to pursue their Protestant theologies within the old Catholic system of a state church, which had its roots in the fourth century under Emperor Constantine. But the Radical Reformation or Free Church tradition sought to go even further: to emancipate the Christian church completely from government. Menno Simons (1496–1561) was a leader of this movement. Instead of a society in which Christians are baptized as infants into the official church of Christendom, the Radical Reformation advocated believer's baptism based on one's conscious profession of faith. Since most people at that time would have been baptized already as infants, these reformers came to be called Anabaptists, or "re-baptizers."

Often, this movement was so opposed to official church structures that they rejected any institutionalism whatsoever, such as liturgies and clergy, and focused instead on the freedom of the Holy Spirit. Because of their self-isolating and sep- aratist tendencies, persecution from both Catholic and Protestant authorities fell hard upon the early Anabaptists. Modern descendants of this movement include the Mennonites and Amish. There is also much overlap with (and probably some direct influence upon) today's Baptist denominations.

Anglican Church

In England, the Reformation came in a different way than on the European continent. Although English figures such as John Wycliffe had been advocating reforming ideas for quite some time, it was King Henry VIII who made a formal political break in 1534, taking the Church of England, also known as the Anglican Church, out from under the pope and his Roman Catholic hierarchy. Shortly after this, Catholic monasteries across the land were disbanded, and many church properties came under the control of the English monarch. **Thomas Cranmer** (1489–1556), Archbishop of Canterbury, developed the *Book of Common Prayer* that standardized the new English forms of worship. Often, the Anglican Church is portrayed as a *via media*, or middle way, because it retains some high church elements familiar to Catholics, yet it is a Protestant communion with a historic tendency toward Reformed doctrines. Later groups that separated out of the Church of England include the Puritans; the Baptists under **John Smyth** (1554–1612); and the Methodists under **John Wesley** (1703–1791).

Counter-Reformation

In the late 1500s, there was a concerted effort by the Roman Catholic Church to refute Protestantism and defend Catholic doctrines and practices. The Council of Trent in Italy was held during the years 1545–1563. It issued many decrees that reinforced traditional Roman beliefs, such as the primacy of popes and bishops, the authority of tradition alongside Scripture, the inclusion of the Apocrypha in the canon, the veneration of saints, the necessity of works in the process of justification, and the priest's power to transubstantiate the elements of the Mass.

Yet the Counter-Reformation was not just a defensive movement that sought to preserve the past, but a true reformation in its own right. The rote piety of former years was corrected, and Catholic spiritual or even mystical movements arose across Europe. Because the New World was being opened at this time, the Counter-Reformation also fought to establish Catholic missions in North and South America, though not without fierce competition from Protestant nations that were doing the same. The areas colonized by Spain and Portugal were particularly influenced by Catholicism.

MODERN PERIOD (1700–1950)

The European theological conflict between Catholics and Protestants led, unfortunately, to a series of violent religious wars, such as the Thirty Years' War of 1618–1648. Bloody conflict was almost continuous somewhere in Europe throughout the 1500s and 1600s. The trauma and destruction caused by these wars led to a severe distaste toward religion. Confidence was placed instead in man's reason, leading to many discoveries during the Scientific Revolution of the late 1500s and 1600s. Following this, a new movement arose that came to be called the Enlightenment, which flourished in the 1700s. Many Enlightenment thinkers were atheistic or hostile to traditional religion, such as **Voltaire** (1694–1788), **David Hume** (1711–1776), and **Immanuel Kant** (1724–1804). Yet rationalist thinking could also have Christian overtones, as seen in philosophers like **René Descartes** (1596–1650), **Blaise Pascal** (1623–1662), and **John Locke** (1632–1704). One significant principle that came from the Enlightenment was the separation of church and state, as implied by the US Constitution in 1788.

The Early Modern Period of church history was, as we noted above, a time of expansion into the New World. Yet we should not think that Christianity was only coming out of Western Europe. By the year 1600, many forms of the Christian faith had already spread across central, southern, and far eastern Asia, though not yet in any Protestant version. North Africa, too, had experienced earlier Christian conversion, although Muslim regimes had wiped out most of it until the great missionary movements rekindled African Christianity in the modern era.

Christianity had no way to cross the Atlantic Ocean until European explorers arrived in the Americas in 1492. Among the Roman Catholics, the Society of Jesus (the Jesuit Order), founded in 1534 by the devout Spanish priest **Ignatius of Loyola** (1491–1556), served as a primary catalyst of missionary expansion around the world. Many Asians, Africans, and Native Americans heard the name of Jesus for the first time from Jesuit missionaries, though the Franciscans and Dominicans contributed greatly as well throughout the 1500s and 1600s.

Protestant missionaries were less prompt to the foreign field but no less passionate once they got there. Gospel ministers penetrated the colonies of the Old World under the auspices of the British East India Company and the Dutch East India Company (both founded around 1600). The Moravian Church (the spiritual descendants of Jan Hus) began sending out missionaries in the early 1700s. Other evangelistic efforts came from Pietist Lutheran groups in Germany and Denmark; the Anglicans under **Thomas Bray** (1658–1730), who founded a foreign missions organization in 1701; and the Baptists under **William Carey** (1761–1834), who arrived in India in 1793.

With the European exploration and colonization of North America's east coast, Christianity finally reached the native peoples who had never encountered it. In the thirteen colonies, the great theologian and minister **Jonathan Edwards** (1703–1758) served as a missionary to the Indians of Massachusetts. He, along with

George Whitefield (1714–1770), preached fiery evangelistic sermons whose energy spread among the American colonists and led to the spiritual revival that came to be called the First Great Awakening. Spiritual enthusiasm continued to move westward as the American frontier progressed that way. The Methodists, in particular, sent "circuit riders" across the growing country to preach revival. The most prominent of them was **Francis Asbury** (1745–1816).

A Second Great Awakening occurred in the early 1800s, and this one included many black converts, both slave and free. The Philadelphia educator and church leader **Richard Allen** (1760–1831) founded the African Methodist Episcopal Church (AME) in 1816, and Christianity experienced a great expansion at this time among African Americans.

It is at this juncture in church history that scholars identify the emergence of evangelicalism in its contemporary sense. Various strands of British and American religion, influenced by continental pietism, converged in the 1730s to form a broad movement that was trans-denominational and bound by no central authority. Its hallmarks were the preeminence of the Bible; an emphasis on preaching and personal conversion to Christ; an inward and individualized piety toward God (often referred to today as a "relationship"); and zeal for missions and social work. The two Great Awakenings were foundational events that served as catalysts for the rise of the evangelical movement. Its period of greatest expansion came in the late 1800s and the turn of the century, when great evangelists like **D. L. Moody** (1837–1899) preached on both sides of the Atlantic. Other great missionaries of this era included **David Livingstone** (1813–1873), **Hudson Taylor** (1832–1905), and **Amy Carmichael** (1867–1951). But the two World Wars brought a temporary halt to this evangelistic expansion.

Evangelicalism is a theologically conservative movement, so it stands in contrast to the liberal theology that emerged in the European and American universities of the nineteenth century. **Friedrich Schleiermacher** (1768–1834) attempted to rescue Christianity from supposed irrelevance by reconciling its doctrines with the Enlightenment. In this way, he became the "father of liberal theology," which is always suspicious of traditional ideas from the past and tries to unite theology with secular, rational, or modern currents of thought. Other important liberals were the German history professor **Adolf von Harnack** (1851–1930) and American pastor **Walter Rauschenbusch** (1861–1918). Liberal theology attempts to meet the needs of modern times, often by focusing on justice issues (the social gospel). While these are laudable goals, the downside of liberalism was that it discarded essential doctrines like the substitutionary atonement of Christ and the inerrancy of Scripture. Higher criticism of the Bible allowed that the biblical text could have errors in it because it was produced by mistake-prone, non-inspired writers.

The early twentieth century saw the rise of two distinct responses to liberal theology. On the one hand, neo-orthodoxy, led by the Swiss theologian **Karl Barth** (1886–1968), refocused theological attention on the transcendence of God, not man-made ideas and rational innovations. Barth centered his theology on Jesus Christ, the true Word of God, who speaks authoritatively to us in the Bible. Although the biblical text might contain some errors in its minor details, it is nonetheless God's Word to the world through Christ who speaks in its pages.

The second response was fundamentalism, a diverse movement that had much in common with earlier attempts to defend biblical inerrancy, such as the Princeton theology of figures like **Charles Hodge** (1797–1878), or the biblical preaching of **Charles Haddon Spurgeon** (1834–1892). Beginning in the 1910s, the fundamentalists, through many books, conferences, and educational institutions (including Moody Bible Institute, Dallas Theological Seminary, and Westminster Theological Seminary) defended the doctrines of traditional Christian orthodoxy. Leaders included **B. B. Warfield** (1851–1921), **R. A. Torrey** (1856–1928), and **Lewis Sperry Chafer** (1871–1952). Like Karl Barth, the movement sought to preserve a theological posture in which God is preeminent and Jesus Christ is humankind's sovereign Lord. Yet the fundamentalists diverged from neo-orthodoxy by insisting on the inerrancy of Scripture and its literal interpretation in every word, a position which is still used to demarcate evangelicalism today.

POSTMODERN PERIOD (1950–?)

Although the scientific/modern worldview that goes back to Descartes is still very much in place today, at the same time, many aspects of twenty-first-century life can be described as postmodern. This term refers to a collection of tendencies across many fields and disciplines. It emerged in the 1950s as a critique of Enlightenment modernism's confidence in scientific progress, the powers of human reason, and the absolute nature of truth. Postmodernism recognizes that people perceive "truth" in different ways; and science, far from being an inevitable good for mankind, could be put to great destructive use (as evidenced by the two World Wars).

Therefore, one of the hallmarks of postmodernism is that everything must be interpreted. Universal meaning does not exist "out there" for human minds to access. Meaning is always being constructed by people who are pursuing their own selfish goals. No single narrative binds society or gives unified coherence to human experience. The relativism of postmodernism led to the rise of theologies that are grounded not in divine revelation, but in the experience of one's own particular group. Marxist, feminist, queer, and liberation theologies are harmful and false ideologies when taken as a whole, even if a few important truths can be gleaned within them.

Yet one of the helpful insights of postmodernism is that brothers and sisters in the worldwide church operate with fundamentally different perspectives, even as they worship the same risen Lord. The twentieth century gave birth to the ecumenical movement, a purposeful attempt to find common ground among all kinds of Christians. The World Council of Churches was founded in 1948 as an interdenominational umbrella organization. Although such efforts sometimes led to reducing truth to the lowest common denominator, an ecumenical outlook also allowed the evangelist **Billy Graham** (1918–2018) to achieve global respect. Graham was able to unite all evangelicals—and many other Christians with a generally "evangelical" spirit—around the essentials of the gospel.

Following World War II, evangelicals began to defend the faith as the modern world was changing ever more rapidly. **Francis Schaeffer** (1912–1984) developed an apologetic for young believers through his ministry of thoughtful communal living called L'Abri Fellowship. College ministries such as Campus Crusade for Christ (now CRU), InterVarsity Christian Fellowship, and The Navigators provided fellowship and training for college students in America and beyond. In 1956, Billy Graham founded the magazine *Christianity Today*, naming **Carl F. H. Henry** (1915–2003) its first editor. Henry was also instrumental in founding the National Association of Evangelicals and the Evangelical Theological Society. All three of these entities continue to influence evangelical subculture in the twenty-first century.

WHY PASTORS NEED CHURCH HISTORY

Perhaps we can picture church history like a great ship transporting its passengers into the future. Today's pastors stand at the ship's prow, scanning the distant horizon, looking ever ahead—and sometimes forgetting what is carrying them along! But a quick glance over their shoulders will remind them that they are part of something bigger than themselves or their congregations. Many others have crewed the ship of faith before today's pastors stepped on board. These brave sailors must never be forgotten. Pastoral humility demands that we remember them.

In the end, however, it was not the sailors themselves who propelled the Christian ship forward. Human energy can only accomplish so much. Ultimately, it is the wind of the Holy Spirit in the sails of the church that will bring this mighty vessel into the safe harbor of Jesus Christ.

Understanding the Basics
of Apologetics

SANJAY MERCHANT

At His arrest in the garden of Gethsemane, Jesus commanded Peter to sheathe his sword (John 18:10–11), explaining to Pilate, "My kingdom is not of this world. If My kingdom were of this world, My servants would be fighting so that I would not be handed over to the Jews; but as it is, My kingdom is not of this realm" (John 18:36). Meager weapons are useless within the kingdom of God, where the resurrection of Jesus from the tomb and the descent of the Holy Spirit from heaven reveal God's matchless power. Hence, Paul stressed to the Corinthians that "we do not wage battle according to the flesh, for the weapons of our warfare are not of the flesh, but divinely powerful for the destruction of fortresses. We are destroying arguments and all arrogance raised against the knowledge of God, and we are taking every thought captive to the obedience of Christ" (2 Cor. 10:3–5). And Peter urged believers suffering under Roman persecution:

> Do not fear their intimidation, and do not fear, but sanctify Christ as Lord in your hearts, always being ready to make a defense (Greek: *apologia*) to everyone who asks you to give an account for the hope that is in you, but with gentleness and respect; and keep a good conscience so that in the thing in which you are slandered, those who disparage your good behavior in Christ will be put to shame. (1 Peter 3:14–16)

The appropriate response to dissent from the gospel is a persuasive and peaceable answer concerning one's trust in Christ. In this vein, Christian apologetics is the theory and practice of (1) substantiating Christian faith by formulating reasons and adducing evidences for the central claims of Christian theology, (2) vindicating Christian faith by refuting objections to the central claims of Christian theology, and (3) critiquing the central claims of non-Christian belief systems. The tasks of substantiating, vindicating, and critiquing involve an appeal to reason and evidence, despite the frailty of human rationality. Winsome ministers of Christ are both generously reasonable and persistently respectful.

> The Lord's bond-servant must not be quarrelsome, but be kind to all, skillful in teaching, patient when wronged, with gentleness correcting those who are in opposition, if perhaps God may grant them repentance leading to the knowledge of the truth, and they may come to their senses and escape from the snare of the devil, having been held captive by him to do his will. (2 Tim. 2:24–26)

Courtesy and charity are integral to earnest apologetic ministry and honoring to Christ. Biblically faithful and philosophically incisive answers to vexing questions about Christian theology foster the faith of believers and promote the conversion of unbelievers. In submitting our philosophical, scientific, and historical conceptions to the lordship of Christ, we cultivate deeper insights, reap greater devotion, and satisfy our duty to worship God with our minds (Matt. 22:37). Sound apologetics enhances our confidence in the gospel as a means by which we are "transformed by the renewing of [our minds]" (Rom. 12:1–2).

The following sections outline the major topics of apologetic substantiation or *offensive apologetics*, apologetic vindication or *defensive apologetics*, and apologetic critique or *polemical theology*, with references to noteworthy works that flesh out the details.

Projects in offensive apologetics are classified into two related categories. The first category consists of philosophical/scientific arguments for God as the powerful explanation of the existence of the universe, the intelligent explanation of the physical order of the universe, and the good explanation of the existence of moral facts and duties. What is more, God is maximally great—all-powerful or omnipotent, all-intelligent or omniscient, all-good or omnibenevolent, and unreservedly free—barring a persuasive argument that the source of the world is arbitrarily powerful, intelligent, good, and free. The second category consists of theological/historical evidences that God has revealed His omnipotence, omniscience, and omnibenevolence in the person and resurrection of Jesus Christ.

Projects in defensive apologetics consist of philosophical/scientific defenses of the coherence of Christian theology and the historicity of Scripture against critical objections. Finally, projects in polemical theology consist of gospel-centered appraisals of non-Christian belief systems across a range of categories, including indecisive skepticism, decisive skepticism, singular views of God, and plural views of God. Cults of Christianity are particularly important targets of polemical arguments. The final section addresses a few questions of theological basis and methodology.

OFFENSIVE APOLOGETICS

In his sermon to the Epicurean and Stoic philosophers at Mars Hill (Acts 17:22–34), Paul modeled the offensive strategy, which encompasses philosophical/scientific arguments for the existence of God and theological/historical evidences for the resurrection of Jesus.[1] Paul identified common ground on which to reason with the Athenians by commenting on a local altar dedicated to an "unknown God" and citing one of their philosophers, arguing that God is the transcendent, self-sustained source of the world (vv. 24–25 and 29) who providentially orders our lives (vv. 26–28). As the cause of the world's existence and order, "God is now proclaiming to mankind that all people everywhere should repent, because He has set a day on which He will judge the world in righteousness through a Man whom He has appointed, having furnished proof to all people by raising Him from the dead" (vv. 30b–31). The resurrection is confirmation, therefore, of God's supremacy and Christ's lordship.

David sang: "The heavens tell of the glory of God; and their expanse declares the work of His hands. Day to day pours forth speech, and night to night reveals knowledge" (Ps. 19:1–2). And Paul declared to the Romans that "since the creation of the world His invisible attributes, that is, His eternal power and divine nature, have been clearly perceived, being understood by what has been made" (Rom. 1:20). Creation discloses its Creator.

The *cosmological argument* demonstrates that God is the transcendent and powerful explanation of the existence of the universe. Evidently, there either is or is not an answer to the question: What explains the existence of the universe? If there is an answer, then the universe is explicable, whether we ultimately ascertain the answer or not. But if there is not an answer, then the universe is inexplicable, and any attempt to probe the question is misguided.

Yet why would the universe be mysteriously inexplicable? The persistent intuition behind scientific inquiry is that questions about physical realities have answers, in principle. Indeed, theologians, philosophers, and scientists regard the question as worthy of serious contemplation. Either the natural world—including space, time, matter, energy, and forces—explains its own existence, under the purview of physics, or else something above the purview of physics explains its existence. Physicists can, nevertheless, coherently conceive of the absence of space, time, matter, energy, and forces. And the big bang cosmology provides convincing evidence that the universe began to exist. The universe is not inexplicable and does not explain its own existence. On the contrary, something beyond the natural world and above the purview of physics explains the existence of the universe: a supernatural being, under the purview of theology.

The *teleological argument* demonstrates that God is the transcendent and intelligent explanation of the physical order of the universe. As it turns out, certain fundamental conditions of physics—such as the mass difference between neutrons and protons, which enables hydrogen atoms to form and the triple-alpha process, which enables carbon-12 atoms to form, among other things—are apparently "adjusted" or "fine-tuned" for the existence of biological life. Unless the fundamental conditions occupy extremely narrow parameters, life cannot exist. Cosmic fine-tuning is not physically necessary because physicists can coherently conceive of universes wherein the fundamental conditions do not occupy life-permitting parameters. It is exceedingly improbable that the fundamental conditions should permit life, let alone produce life, by chance. As a consequence, cosmic fine-tuning is evidence that a supernatural being designed the universe.

Skeptics routinely ask whether God has a creator and designer, insinuating that proponents of the cosmological and teleological arguments must admit that either God requires an external explanation of His existence and order or the universe does not require an external explanation of its existence and order. First, whereas the big bang cosmology suggests that God caused the universe and cosmic fine-tuning suggests that God designed the universe, there is no indication that God_2 caused and designed God. And second, supposing that God_2 explains God's existence and order, we should ask whether God_2 also has a causer and designer: God_3; and so on, ad infinitum. Yet, given an infinite regress of explanations, nothing ultimately explains the existence and order of the universe. God is plausibly the uncaused cause and undesigned designer of the universe since something ultimately explains the existence and order of the universe.

The *moral argument* demonstrates that God is the transcendent and good explanation of moral facts and duties. Moral facts—for example, "kindness is right," "cruelty is wrong," "honesty is right," "dishonesty is wrong"—are objectively true, or true without reference to our conventions or preferences, and have corresponding moral duties—"one ought to be kind," "one ought not be cruel," "one ought to be honest," "one ought not be dishonest." Despite the doubts of a small contingent of moral nihilists and relativists, moral facts are widely acknowledged. To cite a controversial example: proponents and opponents of abortion do not disagree that murder is wrong. It is wrong to kill innocent persons. They disagree that fetuses are persons. The moral fact, however, is undebatable.

Atheistic moral realism holds that the world of moral facts, like the physical world, is either inexplicable or self-explanatory, effectively sanctioning the existence of moral facts by positing a mysterious divide between the natural and moral worlds. Moral naturalism grounds moral facts and duties in the natural world, without reference to God, usually in terms of biological evolution. The evolutionary account of morality removes the mysterious divide posited by atheistic moral realism, proposing that the process of evolution produced moral values in humans, just as it supposedly produced biological features. Even so, human moral values produced by evolution are not facts. Other species might eventually harbor diverse moral values as a result of their distinct evolutionary histories. And, despite the evolutionary emergence of human moral values, one is not bound to respect corresponding duties in an atheistic world. A psychopath might disavow his duty to refrain from committing murder by pleading that he lacks a sense of disapprobation of murder. So, if God does not exist then moral facts and duties do not exist; but if moral facts and duties exist then God exists.

Besides these three major arguments, there are other traditional philosophical/scientific arguments for God, such as the *ontological argument* from the very concept of deity and the *noological argument* from human consciousness. As Paul implied while preaching to the philosophers at Mars Hill, such reasoning is a prelude to the apostolic message that God raised Jesus from the dead.

The theological/historical *case for the resurrection* demonstrates that God is the providential explanation of the empty tomb and postmortem appearances of Jesus; and that Jesus is the victorious, risen Lord of the world. This argument has four main elements, which the apostle Paul himself enumerated when he relayed a terse creed regarding the resurrection in 1 Corinthians 15:3–5: "For I handed down to you as of first importance what I also received, that Christ died for our sins according to the Scriptures, and that He was buried, and that He was raised on the third day according to the Scriptures, and that He appeared to Cephas, then to the twelve." The repeated term "and that" (Greek, *kai hoti*) effectively gives us the four points: (1) Christ died, (2) Christ was buried, (3) Christ was raised, and (4) Christ was witnessed. Paul likely received the creed a few years after the crucifixion at his first meeting with Peter and James (Gal. 1:18–19).

Concerning point (2): the gospel of Mark, which contains the earliest record of Jesus' life, attests that a Sanhedrinist, Joseph of Arimathea, buried Jesus. The dependent gospels of Matthew and Luke and the independent gospel of John corroborate the burial account. Christian evangelists could not have broadcast a lie about a public figure like Joseph in Jerusalem. They would not have invented a story in which a member of the Sanhedrin, the Jewish authoritative body that condemned Jesus, delivered Him to Pontius Pilate for execution, and persecuted His followers, provided Jesus with an honorable burial. And they would not have portrayed Jesus' principal followers, particularly Peter and John, as craven deserters unless they had actually abandoned Jesus at His trial. For these reasons, the burial account was certainly not a literary invention.

Concerning point (3): the credal confession that "He was raised on the third day" indicates that the resurrection was a temporal, physical event and implies that the tomb was found empty, as the gospel of Mark attests. It is unlikely that Mark's narrative ends without a risen Jesus, as some critical scholars propose. The denouement is surely Jesus' final victory in the form of an empty tomb, not the abrupt defeat of His mission. Soon after, Peter publicly announced that "God raised Him from the dead, putting an end to the agony of death, since it was impossible for Him to be held in its power" (Acts 2:24), meaning that God had restored Jesus to physical life, in keeping with the traditional Jewish doctrine of resurrection. His audience would not have understood him to mean that God "raised" Him in a nonphysical form, leaving His corpse in the tomb.

Mark's admission that Mary Magdalene, Mary the mother of James, and Salome found the tomb empty (Mark 16:1–8) is surprising given the low value placed on women's testimony in first-century Jewish society. The Jewish historian Josephus expressed the prevailing attitude that neither women, "on account of the levity and boldness of their sex," nor slaves, "on account of the ignobility of their soul," were considered credible legal witnesses.[2] Mark's reliance on the testimony of women undoubtedly hampered evangelism by making Jesus' male disciples appear cowardly for failing to attend His burial or visit His tomb with the women. Like the burial account, the discovery of the empty tomb was not a literary invention.

According to the gospel of Matthew, the chief priest bribed the tomb guards to report that the disciples stole the body of Jesus after they fell asleep (Matt. 28:11–15). Matthew parenthetically remarked that "this story was widely spread among the Jews and is to this day" (v. 15). In other words, first-century Jews conceded that the tomb was empty but insisted that the body of Jesus was missing due to a conspiracy rather than a miracle. Even if Matthew invented the story, as some critical scholars allege, he expected that his readers were aware that Jewish opponents of the gospel accused the disciples of stealing the body. What is more, assuming the historicity of the burial narrative, it is notable that neither Jewish nor Roman authorities produced the body from Joseph's tomb in order to refute Peter's scandalous first sermon. The public, evidently, believed that the tomb was empty, otherwise the apostles could not have effectively preached in Jerusalem. Conversion was tantamount to treason. In light of the high social cost of joining the church, the empty tomb was a necessary precondition for conversion.

Concerning point (4): Luke and John confirmed that Jesus appeared to Peter (Aramaic: "Cephas") and the disciples (Luke 24:34–42; John 20:19–20). Paul reinforced point (4) with a supplemental list of witnesses: "After that He appeared to more than five hundred brothers and sisters at one time, most of whom remain until now, but some have fallen asleep; then He appeared to James, then to all the apostles; and last of all, as to one untimely born, He appeared to me also" (1 Cor. 15:6–8). The appearance to James, the younger brother of Jesus, explains his unexpected emergence as a leading figure in the early Christian community. Jesus' siblings had once scoffed at His teachings (John 7:1–10), believing He was insane (Mark 3:21). Still, James joined the church (Acts 1:14) and became a "pillar," with Peter and John (Gal. 2:9). Luke reported that James rendered an authoritative decision in response to the Judaizing controversy (Acts 15:13–21) and, in due course, independently headed the Jerusalem church (Acts 21:17–26). Josephus chronicled his martyrdom by stoning.[3] Luke also recorded Paul's zealous campaign against the Christians and dramatic conversion on the way to Damascus (Acts 7–9), which Paul recounted in his epistle to the Galatians (Gal. 1:13–17). Their conversions, ministries, and martyrdoms constitute evidence that James and Paul witnessed the risen Jesus.

DEFENSIVE APOLOGETICS

In observance of Peter's charge to "always [be] ready to make a defense to everyone who asks you to give an account for the hope that is in you" (1 Peter 3:15), defensive apologetics vindicates Christian faith by refuting objections to the central claims of Christian theology.[4] The two categories of objections mirror the categories of offensive apologetics: philosophical/scientific and theological/historical. Philosophical/scientific objections include the *stone paradox* for divine omnipotence, the *problem of theological fatalism* for divine omniscience, and the infamous *problem of evil* for divine omnibenevolence, among others.

THE STONE PARADOX

According to the stone paradox, God either can create an immovable stone or cannot create an immovable stone. There is no other option. Of course, if God can create an immovable stone then there is something He cannot move. Conversely, if He cannot create an immovable stone then there is something He cannot create. Ostensibly, God cannot be omnipotent, contrary to a central claim of Christian theology.

An utterly immovable object remains stubbornly unaffected by physical forces of any magnitude. Consider, for instance, the number 7: although it has numerical properties—being odd, being prime, and being greater than 6—it does not have physical properties. God cannot move the number 7 because it is not physical.

Immovable objects are not subject to physics. Stones, however, are physical objects. Divine omnipotence means that God can accomplish any logically possible act but giving substance to an absurd being, like a stone that is not subject to physics or a square circle, is not logically possible. For this reason, the stone paradox is an unsuccessful objection to God's existence.

THEOLOGICAL FATALISM

The problem of theological fatalism raises an apparent dilemma: either God knows the future and we act as we are fated to, or we act freely and God does not know the future. Imagine that, immediately prior to Jesus' arrest, John reasoned that "if Christ foreknows that Peter will deny Him three times then Peter will deny Him three times. And Christ foreknows that Peter will deny Him three times. Therefore, Peter will deny Christ three times, despite his oath to die rather than disown the Lord." John might conclude that Peter is fated to betray Jesus by divine foreknowledge.

The first horn of the dilemma, wherein divine foreknowledge precludes human freedom, is theologically untenable. Fatalism implies that God's foreknowledge causally determines our acts, which implies that our acts are not free, which implies that we are not morally responsible for our acts, which implies that we are not sinners, which implies that we do not need a savior, which implies that the gospel is false. Peter was, undoubtedly, morally responsible for his unfaithfulness and culpable for his sin.

The second horn of the dilemma, wherein human freedom precludes divine foreknowledge, is palpably unbiblical. So-called open theists suggest that God knows the past and present but not the future, since the future does not exist. They maintain that the future is unknowable, just as logically impossible acts are undoable. Notwithstanding, Peter's denial is just one instance of divine foreknowledge (Mark 14:31), as God is ever able to "declare . . . the things that are coming and the events that are going to take place" (Isa. 44:7). Assuming that future tense statements, like past and present tense statements, are either true or false, God knows all true future tense statements and believes no false future tense statements.

In the hypothetical pretrial situation, John mistakenly reasoned that Peter was fated to deny the Lord. Christ's past knowledge does not *cause* Peter's future, fated denial. Quite the opposite, Peter's future, free denial causes Christ's past knowledge. In that moment, if Peter will freely refrain from denying Him then Jesus foreknows that Peter will freely refrain from denying Him. God foreknows and foreordains (e.g., Acts 4:27–28; Rom. 8:29; Eph. 1:5) but does not causally determine our acts. Christian theology, thereby, navigates between fatalism and divine ignorance.

THE PROBLEM OF EVIL

The problem of evil is the most notorious philosophical/scientific argument against Christian theology. As per the *logical problem of evil,* the skeptic reasons that Christian theology harbors a contradiction between the assertions that God wills to prevent evil acts (being omnibenevolent) and can prevent evil acts (being omnipotent) but, nonetheless, permits evil acts. The *free will defense* undercuts the objection by emphasizing that, although God is omnipotent, He cannot causally determine our acts without precluding libertarian free will.

In addition, although God is omnibenevolent, He does not *immediately* will to prevent evil acts, but *ultimately* wills to prevent evil acts. As a prime example, He permitted the sons of Jacob and Potiphar's wife to persecute Joseph the patriarch for a greater purpose. Joseph said to his brothers, "As for you, you meant evil against me, but God meant it for good, in order to bring about this present result, to keep many people alive" (Gen. 50:20). The *soul building defense* undercuts the objection on the grounds that God providentially intends to bring about greater goods by permitting acts of evil.

Philosophers of religion generally grant that the free will and soul building defenses defuse the logical problem of evil. In response, anti-Christian skeptics advance the *evidential problem of evil*, which asserts that there are unnecessary acts of evil that have no providential value. Skeptics claim that God ought to be able to maximize good while permitting fewer acts of evil.

A helpful response to this argument can be illustrated in this way. Imagine that, after a woman tells her son to organize his bedroom, the boy procrastinates for hours. The mother is in a good position to accuse him of wasting time because she knows, through experience, the basic tasks involved in organizing his room and the time frame in which those tasks can be accomplished. We are not, however, in a good position to accuse God of permitting unnecessary evils since we do not know the complex tasks involved in realizing the goods of the actual world. While the evidential problem of evil has some traction, it is an unsuccessful objection to God's existence. We are not able to see the complex set of good things that arise out of what we perceive, in the moment, to be an evil thing.

OTHER ARGUMENTS AGAINST GOD

Theological/historical objections include the apparent incoherence of the doctrines of the Trinity and the hypostatic union, the apparent injustice of the doctrines of substitutionary atonement and hell, and a number of purported historical inaccuracies in Scripture. The Bible is composed in three languages (Hebrew, Aramaic, and Greek), containing several literary genres embedded within various cultural settings over 2,000 years. The historical authenticity of numerous biblical peoples, places, and events is well-established, while others remain uncorroborated by extrabiblical evidence. The flood of Noah, the exodus from Egypt, and the events of the book of Jonah are primary examples of historically disputed narratives. By consistently studying the major biblical periods and events—the patriarchal period, the exodus, the conquest of Canaan, the period of the Judges, the united kingdom of Israel, the divided kingdoms of Israel and Judah, the exilic period, the rebuilding of Jerusalem, the ministry and resurrection of Christ, and Paul's missionary journeys—the apologist develops expertise in certain issues of biblical historicity, which is essential for developing a holistic, biblically based apologetic, personally invigorating and edifying to the Christian community.

To very briefly vindicate the central claim of Christian theology that God is one divine being subsisting as three divine persons: the doctrine of the Trinity is not intended as a scientific description of God but an analogical, appropriate, and serviceable depiction of an ultimately incomprehensible Deity. Our ability to conceptualize His being is too limited, as "His greatness is unsearchable" (Ps. 145:3). By employing analogies, trinitarianism does not postulate a contradictory being; again, like an immovable stone or a square circle.

Scripture conveys three sub-doctrines about God's nature: (1) There is one divine being, God, or monotheism; (2) The Father, Son, and Holy Spirit are equally divine, or the maximal deity of the persons; and (3) The Father, Son, and Holy Spirit are distinct divine persons, or the individuality of the persons.

Early fourth-century theologians compared the Father to the sun, emitting the Son like light, God's visible representation, and the Spirit like heat, God's felt presence. Just as we see the sun by its light and feel the sun by its heat, the Son and Spirit reveal the invisible God. The divine persons are as individual as the sun, its radiance, and its warmth, while remaining one being. Where, after all, does the sun end and the sunlight begin? And when has the sun existed without its light and heat? God is always Father, radiating His presence into the world through His Son and Spirit. Still, the sun analogy is incomplete insofar as it underemphasizes the maximal deity of the persons.

Subsequent theologians compared the three divine persons to three human persons sharing humanness. The critical difference is that divine persons, unlike human persons, do not merely *share* divinity, they *are* divinity. The divine persons share being, like three torches coming together to form one light. The torch analogy is also incomplete insofar as it underemphasizes monotheism.

Finally, the fifth-century theologian Augustine likened the Father to a personal being with rationality, personified by the Son, and affection, personified by the Spirit. Consider your own self-concept: although you know nearly everything about yourself, you do not know yourself completely. God the Father, however, knows Himself completely, such that His self-concept is "evolved up" so as to constitute another divine person within Him: His Son. The Son is analogous to an internal conversation partner except that, in God, the other person is real, not feigned. Similarly, God's love is evolved up in the person of the Spirit, such that His knowledge and love are eternally distinct, like friends rather than personal properties. The person analogy is also incomplete insofar as it underemphasizes the individuality of the persons. Cumulatively, the models facilitate multifaceted and worshipful meditation on God's nature. As a result, the doctrine of the Trinity does not involve an explicit contradiction.[5]

POLEMICAL THEOLOGY

The task of polemical theology is to critique the central claims of non-Christian belief systems.[6] A serviceable belief system is a structured set of knowledge claims, beliefs, and values by which one formulates individually coherent, mutually consistent, and broadly explanatory answers to persistent questions about the world and human existence, and through which one interprets reality. Apologists must be familiar with the broad spectrum of belief systems. The following are some of the most common systems that non-Christians have today.

Skepticism

Indecisive skepticism is also called *agnosticm,* meaning that the fact of God's existence is impossible for humans to know. It includes *strong agnosticism*, the thesis that it is impossible to know whether or not God exists, and *weak agnosticism*, the thesis that, while it is possible to know whether or not God exists, the evidence is insufficient to warrant either conclusion. The burden for strong agnostics is to formulate a philosophy of knowledge that definitively excludes the possibility of theological knowledge. The burden for weak agnostics is to rebut the persuasive evidence for God.

Decisive skepticism is also called atheism, for it has become convinced that God does not exist. It includes *strong atheism*, the thesis that God certainly does not exist, and *weak atheism*, the thesis that someone may properly believe that God does not exist due to the absence of evidence for God. Nevertheless, atheism bears a burden of proof. Nonbelief in the existence of God (agnosticism) does not justify belief in the nonexistence of God (atheism). Naturalism, the doctrine that every being is material or reducible to matter and that every event is governed by the laws of physics, is the metaphysical theory behind atheism. Although atheists assert that naturalism encapsulates the simplest conception of reality, it cannot adequately explain the existence and order of the universe or the existence of moral facts and duties, logical facts, minds, rationality, and free will. The irony of atheism is that the universe sprang into existence from nothing without a cause, order emerged from chaos, and insignificant chunks of inanimate matter within a vast, purposeless physical order accidentally gained consciousness, only to realize that they are insignificant chunks of matter.

SINGULAR VIEWS OF GOD

Among singular views of God, *pantheism*, the thesis that God is the universe, is a brand of religious naturalism, conceptually similar to skepticism. Unfortunately, views that fail to distinguish between the world and God cannot provide a humane solution to the problem of evil. Other singular views of God include *panentheism*, the thesis that God pervades the universe as souls pervade bodies; *theism*, the thesis that God both pervades and transcends the universe; and *deism*, the thesis that God transcends the universe. There are, moreover, two types of theism: unitarian theism with one God subsisting as one divine person and trinitarian theism with one God subsisting as three divine persons.

As theistic religions, both Islam, the most recognizable unitarian religion, and Christianity, the only trinitarian religion, espouse that God is maximally great—omnipotent, omniscient, omnibenevolent, and unreservedly free. An omnibenevolent being plausibly expresses and experiences perfect love. And so, a unitarian deity must create objects of love in order to express and experience perfect love. But, if God must create then He is not unreservedly free. Islamic theology cannot assert that God is both omnibenevolent and unreservedly free. Christian theology, on the other hand, holds that the Father, Son, and Spirit eternally express and experience perfect love without sacrificing divine freedom.

PLURALIST VIEWS OF GOD

Pluralist views of God include *polytheism* and *henotheism*, according to which there are many gods. The difference is that polytheists worship many gods while henotheists worship one out of many. The Church of Jesus Christ of Latter-day Saints, a cult of Christianity commonly known as the LDS Church or Mormon Church, began promoting polytheism (or possibly henotheism, depending on the meaning of the term *god* in Mormon theology) in the nineteenth century. Joseph Smith, the founder of the LDS Church, declared that the Father, Son, and Spirit, along with all angelic and human persons, constitute a race of eternal, divine beings.

A cult is a theologically aberrant derivative of a primary world religion such as Hinduism, Buddhism, Judaism, Christianity, or Islam. The cults of Christianity purport to disseminate the gospel message while denying or significantly modifying certain central claims of Christian theology—typically the authority of the Bible, the deity of Christ, the Trinity, sin, Christ's substitutionary atonement, and salvation by grace through faith. Peter warned believers to beware of those who promote false gospels:

> But false prophets also appeared among the people, just as there will also be false teachers among you, who will secretly introduce destructive heresies, even denying the Master who bought them, bringing swift destruction upon themselves. Many will follow their indecent behavior, and because of them the way of the truth will be maligned; and in their greed they will exploit you with false words; their judgment from long ago is not idle, and their destruction is not asleep. (2 Peter 2:1–3)

Mormonism is a theologically aberrant derivative of Christianity on multiple counts: Mormon theology cedes the authority of the Bible to the prophetic and interpretive authority of the LDS Church; denies the maximal deity of Christ, monotheism, and Christ's substitutionary atonement; diminishes the doctrine of sin; and endorses salvation by works. Joseph Smith effectively invalidated the concept of maximal greatness within Mormon theology by denying monotheism. After all, if we are members of a race of eternal, divine beings, along with the Father, Son, and Spirit, then no one is the transcendent, omnipotent, omniscient, omnibenevolent, and unreservedly free source of reality. And, since no one is maximally great, maximal power is not required to overcome sin. The problem of sin must be manageable. In Mormon theology, Jesus provided an example of obedience that we must emulate in order to prove our worth to the Father and attain godhood. There is, thus, a direct line from Smith's denial of the doctrine of the Trinity to salvation by works. Mormonism is a remarkable example of a contemporary false gospel.

AN APOLOGETIC FOR APOLOGETICS

Critics of the practice of apologetics protest that appeals to reason and evidence undermine heartfelt devotion to God.[7] After all, the Holy Spirit reveals spiritual truths (1 Cor. 2:10–13), whereas the insights of philosophy, science, and history are too feeble to sustain a believer's faith or move an unbeliever's hardened heart. As Paul admitted to the Corinthians, "My message and my preaching were not in persuasive words of wisdom, but in demonstration of the Spirit and of power, so that your faith would not rest on the wisdom of mankind, but on the power of God" (1 Cor. 2:4–5). Put succinctly: one who believes God by faith does not need proofs and one who needs proofs does not have faith with which to believe.

Unfortunately, this blunt contrast between faith and reason is simplistic. Faith is not the foundation of Christian belief or a spiritual denunciation of mundane knowledge. Faith is trust proportional to knowledge. To illustrate: a young woman stranded on a dark highway would trust her loving, devoted, conscientious father to rescue her because she knows his character. Yet, for the same reason, she would not trust her selfish, lazy brother to come to her aid. We have far more *faith* that God will rescue us from sin and death because we *know* that He is infinite love, wisdom, and power. Knowledge of God, founded in Scripture and bolstered by philosophy, science, and history, deepens faith.

One's "heart" cannot be strictly divorced from one's "head." Jesus commands us to worship God with our entire being—heart, soul, strength, and mind (Luke 10:27). Applying tools of reason and evidence to revelation sharpens our perception of God's nature and acts in history, stretches our minds, and enlarges our souls. Small souls are spiritually immature, ruled by sensations and emotions, because they only know small things and harbor a convenient conception of God. (Very tiny souls worship anything that provides them with pleasure, which is the origin of paganism.) Big souls are spiritually mature, ruled by His Word and love, because they know big things and enjoy an increasingly accurate conception of God.

According to a more formidable objection, although faith is trust proportional to knowledge, saving knowledge is not communicated by means of theoretical apologetics. Reason and evidence fortify faith once the Spirit has renewed our minds, but cannot lead us to salvation because "a natural person does not accept the things of the Spirit of God, for they are foolishness to him; and he cannot understand them, because they are spiritually discerned" (1 Cor. 2:14). The Spirit alone, unaided by reason and evidence, communicates saving knowledge, which inspires trust in God. Critics insist that, since human reason and evidence cannot ground knowledge of God, let alone trust in God, we must not present philosophical, scientific, and historical arguments for God to unbelievers. They consider offensive apologetics, in particular, misleading, if not blasphemous.

Indeed, the testimony of the Holy Spirit, rather than apologetic argumentation, is the basis of saving knowledge. Apologetic argumentation is not, however, superfluous to conversion. Although the ministry of the Spirit, rather than pastoral teaching and care, is the basis of sanctification, the Spirit often uses corporate praise and confession, meditation on Scripture, exegetically sound sermons, and prayer to sanctify us in Christ. Similarly, the Spirit often uses sound reasons and cogent evidences to justify us in Christ. In utilizing well-structured argumentation, He converts the unbeliever's heart by redirecting his devotions to Christ and mind by restructuring his thoughts, such that they are consistent with his newfound devotions. God uses apologetics as a tool to facilitate conversion, ushering new believers into worshiping and thinking with the church.[8]

NOTES

1. For introductory readings in offensive apologetics, I recommend William Lane Craig, *Reasonable Faith: Christian Truth and Apologetics*, 3rd ed. (Wheaton, IL: Crossway Books, 2008); Gary R. Habermas and Michael R. Licona, *The Case for the Resurrection of Jesus* (Grand Rapids: Kregel Publications, 1998); and Lee Strobel, *The Case for Christ: A Journalist's Personal Investigation of the Evidence for Jesus* (Grand Rapids: Zondervan, 1998).

2. Josephus, *Antiquities of the Jews*, trans. William Whiston (London, 1737), 4.8.15.

3. Josephus, 20.9.1.

4. For introductory readings in defensive apologetics, I recommend Thomas V. Morris, *Our Idea of God: An Introduction to Philosophical Theology* (Downers Grove, IL: InterVarsity, 1991); J.P. Moreland and William Lane Craig, *Philosophical Foundations for a Christian Worldview* (Downers Grove, IL: InterVarsity, 2003), chapters 25–31; and Craig Blomberg, *The Historical Reliability of the Gospel*, 2nd ed. (Downers Grove, IL: IVP Academic, 2014).

5. See my chapter "On the Triune God" in John Jelinek and Bryan O'Neal, eds., *Standing Firm: The Doctrinal Commitment of the Moody Bible Institute* (Chicago: Moody Publishers, 2019) for a basic outline of the logic of trinitarian theology.

6. For introductory readings in polemical theology, I recommend Alan W. Gomes, ed. *Unmasking the Cults: Zondervan Guide to Cults and Religions Movement* (Grand Rapids: Zondervan, 1995) and the subsequent books in the series.

7. For a comprehensive discussion of apologetic methods, I recommend Kenneth D. Boa and Robert M. Bowman Jr., *Faith Has Its Reasons: Integrative Approaches to Defending the Christian Faith* (Downers Grove, IL: InterVarsity Press, 2001).

8. I thank the elders at Northshore Christian Church in Everett, Washington, for vetting this chapter and for their continued fellowship.

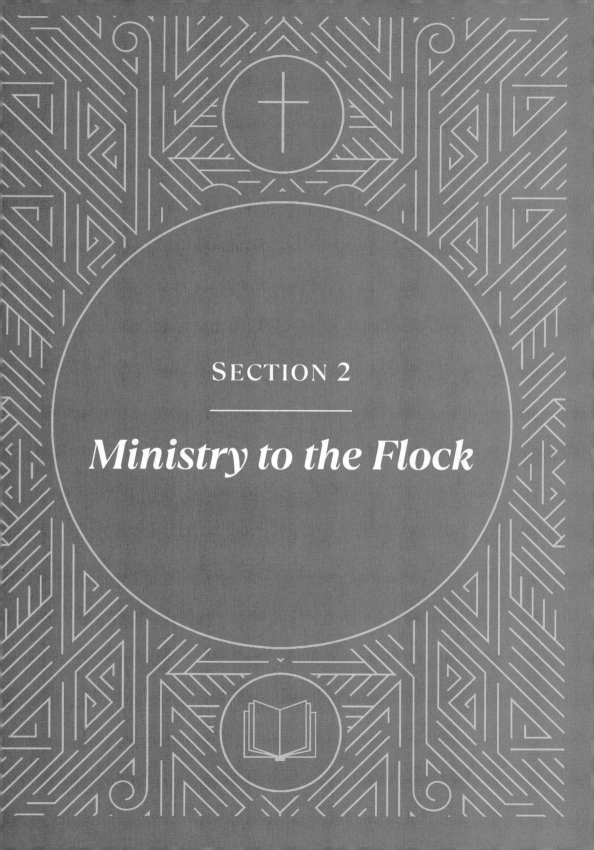

SECTION 2

Ministry to the Flock

INTRODUCTION

What Is Pastoral Ministry?

MICHAEL J. BOYLE

You might be called a lead pastor. Senior pastor. Solo pastor. Youth pastor. Discipleship pastor. Worship pastor. Associate pastor. Or assistant pastor. They all have one thing in common: they are all a pastor. But what is a pastor? There are many models associated with being a pastor. A business model with pastors being called a CEO, leader, or vision caster. A mental health model with pastors being called a counselor, chaplain, or caregiver. Or a religious model with pastors being called preacher, teacher, or evangelist. So many metaphors or titles! Where do we begin to understand what a pastor is?

This question is an important one, no matter what kind of pastor you might be. In Section 2 of this book, we are addressing various kinds of ministry that every pastor faces. The pastor develops in the follower of Christ their spiritual maturity, including victory in spiritual warfare against the Adversary. Then, each phase of life must be discipled and pastorally cared for: children, teens, young adults, adult women and men, and seniors. A pastor must be adept at caring for each of these life stages and demographics. This task will be helped by understanding exactly what a pastor is. What does this word mean?

THE MEANING OF "PASTOR": A SHEPHERD

Many pastors today have not been raised in a rural or agrarian society, in which taking care of sheep is a common practice. Instead, their leadership culture is drawn from business, politics, advertising, or secular administration. Today's

217

leaders often hail from an urban or suburban culture. But shepherds come from an agrarian culture, which focuses on the land, soil, crops, animals, water, and the weather. In most of these cultures, the common picture of a leader is a shepherd. So, let's try to understand it. What does a shepherd do? How do you pastor a flock in the church of Jesus Christ?

The word "pastor" comes from Old French *pastour*, which means "herdsman or shepherd," and this is derived from the Latin noun *pastor*, which also means "shepherd." The Greek word in the Bible is *poimen* and the Hebrew is *roi*. And that is the primary metaphor in the Scriptures for a leader of God's people: a shepherd.

The concept of spiritual leaders as shepherds is seen throughout the Bible. In the Old Testament, Yahweh is the shepherd of Israel when He declared, "I will care for My sheep" (Ezek. 34:12). Of David we read, "He also chose His servant David/ And took him from the sheepfolds; / From the care of the ewes with nursing lambs He brought him / To shepherd Jacob His people, / And Israel His inheritance" (Ps. 78:70–71). This is precisely what God commanded David to do. God said to him, "In times past, even when Saul was king, you were the one who led out and brought in Israel; and the LORD your God said to you, 'You shall shepherd My people Israel, and you shall be leader over My people Israel'" (1 Chron. 11:2).

In the Gospels, Jesus Christ Himself stated, "I am the good shepherd" (John 10:11). He is also called "the Chief Shepherd" (1 Peter 5:4) and "the great Shepherd" (Heb. 13:20). Some of the final words of Jesus to the apostle Peter were, "Tend My lambs. . . . Shepherd My sheep. . . . Tend My sheep" (John 21:15–17). The model of Jesus Christ is to be a shepherd of His people.

In the New Testament church, Peter commanded the elders to shepherd. "Therefore, I urge elders among you, as your fellow elder and a witness of the sufferings of Christ, and one who is also a fellow partaker of the glory that is to be revealed: shepherd the flock of God among you" (1 Peter 5:1–2a). And Paul identifies a spiritual gift of pastor/teacher in Ephesians 4:11. This is the only verse in the New Testament of the NASB where "shepherd" is translated "pastor." The ESV translates this as "shepherds and teachers."

Clearly, pastors are commanded by Scripture to shepherd the church. But what does that look like? Today's pastors must: (1) guard their motives, (2) adhere to biblical qualifications, and (3) faithfully carry out the many tasks of a biblical shepherd.

THE MOTIVES OF A SHEPHERD

Unfortunately, pastors can sometimes be **self-serving**. Ezekiel decries the self-serving shepherds of Israel, saying, "Woe, shepherds of Israel who have been feeding themselves! Should the shepherds not feed the flock? You eat the fat and clothe yourselves with the wool, you slaughter the fat sheep without feeding the flock" (Ezek. 34:2b–3). Peter likewise warns pastors against serving with wrong motives. He urges them to exercise oversight "not under compulsion but voluntarily, according to the will of God; and not with greed but with eagerness; nor yet as domineering over those assigned to your care, but by proving to be examples to the flock" (1 Peter 5:2b–3). Pastors can be tempted to shear the sheep for personal gain and benefit, "feeding themselves" but not feeding the sheep as Ezekiel puts it. It is for "greed," which is dishonoring, disrespectful, and disgraceful conduct that is carried out for the pastor's own financial benefit. The King James translation called it "filthy lucre."

Pastors who don't watch their motives can also become "**domineering**." They can abuse their authority so that they can bring the sheep under their manipulative control, exercising complete dominion over them. And according to Ezekiel, this can be done "with force and harshness." Pastors can be oppressive, powerful, and even violent in their shepherding.

Finally, pastors can shepherd "**under compulsion**." Pressure can be exercised from parents, family, or even the church itself to make someone serve as a pastor. He does not sense a calling or gifting for the task but serves as a pastor only to meet the desires and expectations of others.

In contrast to all this, Peter, who was instructed by Jesus to shepherd His sheep, identifies the right motives of a pastor. A pastor shepherds "**voluntarily**." He is deliberate and intentional with a **willing** spirit to care for the people of God. A pastor also shepherds "**with eagerness**." He is ready, willing, and able to give himself to the ministry with all his heart and mind. Finally, a pastor is an "**example to the flock**." The pastor is a model of leadership and basic Christian living. He sets the standard for what the followers of Christ should be. These are the motives which drive the heart of a true pastor to care for his sheep.

THE BIBLICAL QUALIFICATIONS OF THE SHEPHERD

At Paul's farewell to the Ephesian church leaders in Acts 20, he calls them elders (*presbuteros*) in verse 17, and then he calls them overseers (*episkopos*) in verse 28. This interchange of words means that Paul equates an elder and overseer as the same position of leadership in the church. And to these Ephesian elders, Paul gave the command "to shepherd the church of God" (20:28). This means that the elders and overseers of the church are also the pastors and shepherds of the church.

In 1 Timothy 3:1–7, Paul gives the qualifications for an elder, overseer, or pastor. First, the man called into ministry must **desire to lead**. This individual must "aspire" to the office of overseer. This is contrary to our culture in the church. Usually when someone wants to lead, we think they are disqualified because they lack humility. But Paul calls for someone to lead who wants to take on that job. The word implies that they eagerly want to lead and are stretching and striving to reach for the opportunity to provide guidance for the church. How often we have leaders who don't want to be leaders! And how frustrated we get with these leaderless congregations. Paul says churches need pastors who want to be in that role.

Second, pastors must have **the character to lead.** Paul walks through a whole range of descriptive terms and activities of a pastor. He doesn't list preaching or teaching or any specific gifting to be a pastor. He wants the pastor to have high moral character. The overarching term is "above reproach." The pastor brings no shame, dishonor, disgrace, or blame to his church through his conduct and behavior. This passage looks at the pastor's relationships with strangers (being "hospitable"); his family and household (he "manages his own household well"); and his flock (he is "gentle, not contentious").

Third, pastors must **not be a new convert**. Pastors are to be grounded in the Word of God, established in their walk with Christ, and growing in respect to their salvation. It seems there is a reason they are called elders and not youngsters! Young pastors and leaders may "become conceited." This is not just a case of being a little puffed up. The word entails an extreme and exaggerated arrogance.

THE MINISTRY TASKS OF A SHEPHERD

Assuming the pastor has the necessary moral qualifications that Scripture demands, what does he actually do? The Bible gives us five key roles of a good shepherd, who follows Christ as his example.

1. FEED THE SHEEP

Sheep are helpless animals who need to be led into the pasture or be provided with fodder. So too, pastors must feed their sheep. The Word of God is the sustenance for maturity and growth. Believers are likened to "newborn babies" who must "long for the pure milk of the word, so that by it you may grow in respect to salvation" (1 Peter 2:2). The author of Hebrews sees the Word of God as that source of food and spiritual growth. "For though by this time you ought to be teachers, you have need again for someone to teach you the elementary principles of the actual words of God, and you have come to need milk and not solid food. For everyone who partakes only of milk is unacquainted with the word of righteousness, for he is an infant. But solid food is for the mature, who because of practice have their senses trained to distinguish good and evil" (Heb. 5:12–14).

Pastors study God's Word to feed their congregation with the best tasting and most healthy food. Well-trained pastors have studied hermeneutics, theology, and the biblical text itself to understand the truth they share with their congregation. And when they do this, they are in good company. The shepherd of Psalm 23 brings the sheep to "green pastures" and "quiet waters." Or in another passage the Lord says, "I will feed them in a good pasture, and their grazing place will be on the mountain heights of Israel. There they will lie down in a good grazing place and feed in rich pasture on the mountains of Israel. I Myself will feed My flock and I Myself will lead them to rest" (Ezek. 34:14–15). When the apostles reviewed their responsibilities for the early church, they concluded, "But we will devote ourselves to prayer and to the ministry of the word" (Acts 6:4). As pastors feed the flock, their labors are "for the equipping of the saints for the work of ministry, for the building up of the body of Christ" (Eph. 4:12). The goal is to equip the saints to serve and minister to the people of God.

2. Lead the Sheep

The pastor also leads his sheep, following the pattern of the Good Shepherd. What a great truth it is when David prophetically says about Christ, "He leads me" (Ps. 23:2). He will lead us to watering holes and stations to give us food and rest. To think that pastors are to provide that same kind of leadership! We talk vision, mission, and values in our leadership, but how often do we consider the needs of the sheep? Does our leadership provide the guidance and help they need? Does it bring them into places of rest and refreshment? Does it help them to go in the right direction at this time in their life? Shepherds are leaders of the sheep. Leading sheep is to "rescue them from all the places where they were scattered" (Ezek. 34:12) and to "lead them to rest" (34:15). The result of good leadership is to have willing followers. Jesus said, "My sheep listen to My voice, and I know them, and they follow Me" (John 10:27). All good leaders should look over their shoulders to see if anyone is following them!

3. Care for the Sheep

The care of the sheep begins with a personal relationship with them. Jesus said, "I know My own, and My own know Me" (John 10:14). There is a mutual relationship of the pastor knowing the sheep and the sheep knowing the pastor. But the opposite can sometimes happen: pastors can neglect the sheep. Ezekiel brings this charge against the shepherds of Israel when he writes, "Those who are sickly you have not strengthened, the diseased you have not healed, the broken you have not bound up, the scattered you have not brought back, nor have you searched for the lost" (Ezek. 34:4). In contrast the Lord declared, "I will seek the lost, bring back the scattered, bind up the broken, and strengthen the sick" (Ezek. 34:16). Do not forget that in a high-tech world, people need high touch. Pastors care for God's people in their broken, weakened, and sickened states. Good and godly pastors need to come alongside these sheep and provide the same loving care that they have experienced from Jesus Christ.

4. PROTECT THE SHEEP

Paul's final words in Acts 20 are left ringing in the ears of the Ephesian elders: "Be on guard for yourselves and for all the flock, among which the Holy Spirit has made you overseers" (Acts 20:28). What an important calling it is for a pastor to guard the flock! A pastor is to be "in a continuous state of readiness to learn of any future danger, need, or error, and to respond appropriately—'to pay attention to, to keep on the lookout for, to be alert for, to be on one's guard against.'"[1] This means the pastor's eyes are open all the time, set upon the horizon for any doctrinal errors, or any wolves or dangers that could wound, injure, or kill the sheep, leading them astray from Christ.

When David confronted Goliath, he recalled, "Your servant has killed both the lion and the bear; and this uncircumcised Philistine will be like one of them" (1 Sam. 17:36). The courage of the pastor to guard and protect the sheep comes as he recalls the past victories and deliverances they have had in the spiritual warfare that they faced.

5. SACRIFICE FOR THE SHEEP

In today's pleasure-driven world, self-sacrifice is not what we immediately think of as a pastoral duty. The leading and feeding of the sheep are probably our first responses, but sacrifice is at the heart of a true shepherd. Jesus stated, "The good shepherd lays down His life for the sheep" (John 10:11). In John 10:15, Jesus repeated this statement, applying it directly to Himself: "I lay down My life for the sheep." Jesus then added, "For this reason the Father loves Me, because I lay down My life so that I may take it back" (John 10:17). Three times in seven verses, Jesus said, "I lay down my life." That is sacrifice for the sheep. And of course, He took that sacrificial commitment all the way to the cross.

Today we often talk about the cost of following Jesus. There is a cost of discipleship. Likewise, there is a cost of leadership. But we often forget, there is also a cost to "shepherdship." And that in turn means there is a cost that comes with being in the pastorate. As a pastor, you may be called to sacrifice money, education, a home, savings, land, opportunities, friends, family, or even your own life. The high calling of a pastor is a sacrificial life to serve the Good and Great Shepherd.

Indeed, you have one of the highest callings as a pastor. You follow the example of Jesus Christ, who gave Himself for His church, when you shepherd your God-given flock. And you do this this with the right motives and the right qualifications to carry out the right ministry. Why? Because you are an under-shepherd of the Lord Jesus Christ.

NOTES

1. J. P. Louw and E. A. Nida, *Greek-English Lexicon of the New Testament: Based on Sematic Domains* 2nd ed., vol. 1 (New York: United Bible Societies, 1996), 332 (electronic ed.).

CHAPTER 2.1

Developing
Spiritual Maturity

KIRK S. BAKER

Imagine for a moment the following situations where someone's spiritual maturity is put on display:

Consider a family where the mother and father possess a significant level of maturity in Christ. What does the atmosphere of the home feel like? What capacity or potential exists for children in the family to flourish and thrive? How do the parents as a team navigate the difficulties and struggles that life brings? What type of environment do they foster for their neighbors and those to whom they show hospitality?

Reflect on the workplace where a supervisor demonstrates a significant level of spiritual maturity. What type of office culture is created? How are employees cared for? How do they advance in their career? What is the emotional state of employees as they enter their yearly performance reviews? How are conflicts on the job handled? How trustworthy is the company's hiring process? How faithful and honorable is the release process?

Or think about a local church small group. The spiritual maturity of a group leader is very pronounced as you sit under their leadership. How does the group grow in intimacy with the Lord and with each other? To what degree is mission highlighted? How does the leader navigate tense and awkward moments in the life of the group to move toward greater growth and unity? How is respect, value, and honor demonstrated toward each group member? How is confidentiality maintained? Each of these points directly correlates with the spiritual maturity of the leader.

One could easily conclude from these scenarios that progress in our spiritual maturity is necessary for efficiency and effectiveness in our various spheres of life. The assumption may be that our vocational, relational, and familial systems will run much more smoothly if we just move the maturity gauge in the right direction. While this may be partially true, I believe God's purpose, mission, and agenda for our spiritual maturity is much grander than that.

WHY SPIRITUAL MATURITY?

In Ephesians, Paul says that we were "created in Christ Jesus for good works" (Eph. 2:10). The way these good works are accomplished is directly correlated with our spiritual maturity. The quality of our spiritual maturity determines the efficiency, capacity, effectiveness, capability, sustainability, and scope of influence of our good works. This is like the potential an athlete possesses as they pursue the success of their team. Their contribution to the team depends on their ability to consistently execute the tasks and roles they are called to play. God desires His followers to develop skilled and sturdy souls to partner with Him in His mission.

These good works for which God has created us do not function in isolation, but are to be put on display (2 Cor. 5:20). God is making His appeal to the world through us, His church. In Matthew's gospel we are told, "Your light must shine before people in such a way that they may see your good works, and glorify your Father who is in heaven" (Matt. 5:16).

Developing in spiritual maturity produces a stabilizing effect as well. As our so-called spiritual roots go down (Ps. 1:3; Jer. 17:7–8), we begin to possess a sturdiness against the storms of life (James 1; Eph. 4:14). This spiritual sturdiness displays itself through a stronger identity in Christ, ministry motivation and skill set, relational capacity, and emotional resilience. I believe this is the picture we observe in Galatians 6 of those who are called to help restore those caught in wrongdoing (v. 1).

Consider a hospital that is not passionate and aggressive in providing adequate medical attention for its patients. This would be contrary to its created design and purpose. Similarly, we as the church must pursue with intentionality and vigor a spiritual maturity that testifies to the divine image in which we have been made!

WHAT IS SPIRITUAL MATURITY? TOWARD A DEFINITION

Attempting to define spiritual maturity is no easy task. The concept is somewhat squishy and difficult to get our arms around. The words used for maturity in Scripture (such as *telios*) convey the idea of perfection, completion, and wholeness—with nothing lacking, left out, or out of place. That which is mature or perfect has fulfilled its intended goal. This is the central concept of maturity. Perfection accurately describes our present spiritual status in Christ, as those fully clothed in His righteousness (2 Cor. 5:21; Phil. 3:9), but it also needs to be actualized in this life. In other words, we must increasingly become who we already are in Christ, living more fully into that spiritual status and being progressively transformed into His glorious image (2 Cor. 3:18; Rom. 8:29; Col. 3:1–14). One day, we shall be fully like Him, but absolute perfection remains a future reality, belonging to the age to come (1 Cor. 13:10; Phil. 3:12–14). That future hope of our final state serves to inspire our present life.

We may address spiritual maturity from three different angles: theological, missional, and ecclesial. First, maturity that is both spiritual and Christian must be grounded in the life and reality of the living God: Father, Son, and Holy Spirit. Having God at the center of reality lays the foundation for our identity and our reflection of His likeness. It activates who we are in Christ spiritually, in an embodied way. Christ has pronounced upon us and over us exactly what and who a Christian is, that is, our spiritual identity. From this pronouncement, we receive our marching orders, so to speak. We acquire the map and the path we are to follow. Maturity in Christ involves the formation of our intellect, emotions, desires, will, and actions to display an accurate image of who we are in Christ. This image will testify in a holistic manner to our Creator, Redeemer, and Healer. We become a display.

Second, spiritual maturity involves demonstrating the missional and redemptive nature of God. Mature followers of Jesus understand the mission in which God is engaged and partner with Him in it. They learn how this mission addresses their personal context and how maturity determines much of their fruit-bearing within that missional context.

Last, spiritual maturity results in growth and unity in the body of Christ. Those who have acquired a high level of competence in which their gifts, talents, and power are being used for God's purposes and glory, for the edification of the church, could be characterized as spiritually mature. Maturity includes the church's corporate expression of unity displayed by faith and love. In Christ, the church already exists as God's new mature person (Eph. 2:15). However, it must pursue these virtues with the help of the ministers Christ provides (Eph. 4:16). Paul mentions that love binds and unites the gifts and efforts of the body. Pursuing love produces perfection and results in a Christlike ethic.

SPIRITUAL AND THEOLOGICAL FOUNDATIONS

The temptation in one's pursuit of spiritual maturity is the tendency for it to be driven by pragmatic motivations and methods—that is, simply to apply a set of "best practices." Of course, certain practices are definitely needed for spiritual growth, but any practices or behaviors must be founded on theological directives from God's Word. One such directive is the revelation and response dynamic woven throughout the canon of Scripture. Our Creator is a revelatory God who has and does reveal Himself to His creation. He has revealed Himself through specific (His Word) and general (creation) ways. He has entered this world physically through the incarnation, the Word made flesh, displaying the full revelation of God in the Son by taking on our humanity. He has entered human lives spiritually by sending us the Holy Spirit, allowing us to walk in faithfulness and carry out the mission God has initiated.

For those who have come to saving faith in Jesus, the indwelling of the Spirit continues to provide opportunities and enablement to respond to this revelation. Humanity is compelled to respond as a result of God's self-disclosing revelation of Himself, His mission, and His ways. This response is an act of sacrificial worship to our Savior (Rom. 12:1–2). But more specifically, this response takes the shape of pursuing growth and maturity in Christ. Hence, walking according to the Spirit and following His ways is an act of worship that translates to the mission of God being accomplished and His glory being put on display.

Throughout Scripture we see God pursuing and rescuing His people. Whether Noah and his family in the ark or the people of Israel under the oppression of Pharaoh—God hears the cry of His people, and in lovingkindness and mercy reaches out to secure their welfare. However, contrary to what we may think, God does not rescue simply to ensure our security and comfortability, but in order that His followers would testify to His power and faithfulness, and glorify the Rescuer by learning how to follow, obey, and grow in Him.

The pathway to maturity comes through our salvation and redemption in the Lord. He makes possible the means necessary to begin the journey toward maturity in Christ. Through Christ's sacrifice and atoning work, the Holy Spirit begins to have access and influence to develop our sensibilities and affections for growth in Christlikeness. The spiritual and theological reality of being "in Christ" through His atoning sacrifice creates the setting for new life and new birth to bear the fruit that God desires.

True spiritual maturity is not something humans can muster up or manufacture in and of themselves. It requires the in-breaking of the Spirit of God to cause the human soul to respond in faith, turning from self-governance to allegiance to

Christ, and placing full trust in Christ's finished work, righteousness, and lordship. Only the Spirit of God can produce in us the life and character of God.

Spiritual maturity also is rooted in one's worship. Worship is the activity that remains for all eternity, long after we become "complete in Christ" (Col. 1:28). Therefore, worship in all its aspects—keeping God's commands; loving and serving with heart, mind, and soul; walking in His ways; and fearing Him (Deut. 10:12–15)— should season the believer's life. A life of worship, integrated into everyday realities and routines, begins to ground our desires, affections, and disposition around the things of God. Over time, our heart, mind, and soul are conditioned in a way that produces spiritual maturity. Engaging in holistic worship develops a growing God-mindedness, as our awareness of Him and His economy begins to break into our faulty ways of thinking and living. Thought patterns are reconstructed, heart dispositions are exposed, and behavioral habits are recalibrated. These formative spheres, practices, and disciplines of everyday worship have the power to promote the process of maturity in a very substantial way. Such worship extends beyond singing on Sunday mornings to include those daily, formational disciplines and patterns that foster growth and God-centeredness.

SELF-KNOWLEDGE DISCLOSED THROUGH INTIMACY WITH GOD

An important part of seeing and hearing correctly includes how one understands the self. The pursuit of spiritual maturity is critically dependent upon how an individual sees oneself, God, and the world around them. John Calvin provided a helpful rubric for self-understanding when he wrote, "Though the knowledge of God and knowledge of ourselves are bound together by a mutual tie, due arrangement requires that we treat of the former in the first place, and then descend to the latter."[1] It is through our union, communion, worship, and fellowship with God that we begin to rightly see who we truly are. Worship, reflection, and meditation on God orient us to accurately comprehend our fallen state and God's redemptive mercy. From the beginning of the Christian life until we are fully in His presence, this way of knowing and being known shapes our existence. This interplay of allowing ourselves to be known by God and following His pattern of knowing us produces a manner of knowing that approaches the intimacy He desires and for which we were created.

One of the foundational principles undergirding spiritual maturity is one's new identity in Christ (2 Cor. 5:17). The Christian's identity is one patterned after the image of God (Gen. 1:26–27). Believers are adopted into the family of God as sons and daughters through their union with Christ (Rom. 5:6–21; Col. 2:6, 3:1).

It is through their participation in the work of Christ—that is, His death, burial, and resurrection (Rom. 6)—and their communion with His person that believers engage in the process of discovering their true selves and identity. Integrating Christ's likeness into all aspects of daily existence is the lifelong task of a vibrant Christ follower.

THE PROCESS TOWARD MATURITY

The process that brings about growth and healthy change in a person's life is complex. Several interconnected ingredients factor into the transformation Christ desires to produce. These factors include God's saving intervention, the truth of God's living Word, the work and ministry of the Holy Spirit, significant relationships with wise and spiritually mature people, experiences of pain and suffering, tending of the human heart, and prayer. Each of these influences could be discussed and explored at great length. For our purposes, however, we will only touch on them briefly, in order to see how they function in the process of transformation and maturation.

GOD'S INTERVENTION

First, God graciously initiates and enters your life to establish a relationship with Him. As previously mentioned, this is the initial catalyst that makes any true change, growth, or maturity possible. It is the life of Christ in us that activates this process. Without His redeeming grace and atoning work on the cross, we remain in our sin and fallen state. We are given sight and hearing to make sense of His truth and a new heart that has the capacity to follow His ways (John 3:1–8; 2 Cor. 5:17; 1 Peter 1:3).

GOD'S LIVING WORD

A second factor that produces Godward change in an individual is Scripture. M. Robert Mulholland describes the Word of God as "the action of the presence, the purpose, and the power of God in the midst of human life."[2] God says that His Word will bear fruit and accomplish the task for which it was created (Isa. 55:10–11). Abiding in His Word allows us as His disciples to embody and fulfill our true identity, to become that which He has pronounced upon us. As a result, we discover true freedom and the abundant life He has made available to His followers (John 8:31–32; 10:10).

Scripture uses the illustration of moving from spiritual milk to solid food in describing the progress of maturity (Heb. 5:11–14). If maturity is the standard to be pursued, then faithful and consistent engagement with the Word of God is the practice through which such maturity develops. According to this passage, you are spiritually mature if you have trained yourself in the Scriptures to discern between good and evil. If we consider some of the outcomes produced by maturity, such as being equipped for every good work, it is clear that the ministry of the Word has a significant role in bringing this about (2 Tim. 3:16–17). God's Word is compassionate and competent to meet us in the brokenness of our lives. God's Word is a gift of grace to guide and sustain us until we are finally in His presence.

THE MINISTRY OF THE HOLY SPIRIT

Another factor that influences change toward maturity in light of what Christ has made possible through our salvation is the ministry of the Holy Spirit. One of the primary roles of the Spirit is to testify to and make much of the Son. Therefore, it is through the Spirit's ministry in us and to us that we begin to appropriate our union with Christ. Our maturity hinges on our life in Christ and the empowering work of the Spirit to live out that same life. Since the Spirit resides in us, the apostle Paul exhorts us to pursue holiness and cleansing from unrighteousness (2 Cor. 7:1). The Spirit provides the strength and the means to pursue our training in righteousness (Titus 2:12).

In what ways does the Spirit enable us to pursue maturity in Christ? His work conforms us to Christ (Rom. 12:2): helps us resist sin (Heb. 12:4), walk in the Spirit (Gal. 5:16), die to self (Luke 9:23), and put to death the flesh (Col. 3:5). He fosters imitation of God (Eph. 5:1), promotes perfection (Phil. 3:12), and enables us to abide in Christ (1 John 3:6). Our sanctification in and through the Spirit could be categorized as a battle of the mind or beliefs that bears practical fruit (1 Tim. 6:12; 2 Tim. 4:7), a beholding of the beauty and majesty of Christ (Heb. 12:2), and a walking in step with the Spirit (Gal. 5:16–26).

GOD-HONORING RELATIONSHIPS

God also uses relationships to foster growth and maturity in His people. Peering into the nature and life of our triune God, we become aligned to God's ideal for how His image bearers also should relate to one another. Each member of the Trinity—Father, Son, and Holy Spirit—is fully complete in and of Himself. While one in essence, each member possesses a distinct identity. It is out of these respective identities that they give fully of themselves for the others' benefit and good. This is the process of *perichoresis* that has been highlighted throughout church history. Perichoresis is our way of describing how the life of each divine person flows through each of the others, so that each member of the Trinity infuses the others and has direct access to the consciousness of the others.[3] This mutual indwelling, interpenetration, and life sharing that we observe in the Trinity emphasizes the oneness of God. This oneness with distinction reveals each member relating for the benefit and good of the others.

As we reflect on this theological reality as image bearers, we come to see our own relational vulnerability and interdependency in a different light. We no longer view them as liabilities, but as assets—attributes to embrace, drawing us deeper into relationship with God and with others. Often our relationships can function based on ability and performance rather than on grace and true knowing. Our pursuit of maturity requires that we push back against this pattern of knowing, instead cultivating deeper intimacy, authenticity, and trust with one another.

Relating as an ecclesial being—that is, seeing ourselves as part of the interconnected body of Christ rather than simply as an individual—promotes spiritual maturity. Our tendency is to function individualistically in our relationships. Our historical-cultural context today in the West has positioned us to identify and behave as such. Spiritually, however, if we are in Christ, our primary identity is the church. We are part of the body of Christ, knit together spiritually through Jesus due to our union with Him. This spiritual reality can influence our embodied and social realities in a profound way. Relating to others becomes significantly different if I perceive these others to be brothers and sisters in Christ—as family!

The implication of the body of Christ being a "family" is that it thrusts us into the messiness of others' lives. We soon encounter details about one another that may cause relational friction, discomfort, or irritation. God may permit this dynamic to produce growth and maturity as we work through unpleasant tension. Oftentimes, overcoming relational difficulties forces us to rally around the gospel, to affirm who each one is in Christ, and to displace individual preferences. This significant growth opportunity demonstrates why church small groups and accountability relationships are so valuable. These structures provide the social setting and relational intimacy where individuals can be challenged and supported appropriately as they grow toward Christlikeness. So then, spiritual maturity is not simply a personal ("I") pursuit, but also a corporate ("we") pursuit, as we grow together in our unity and likeness to the body's head, Jesus Christ.

TENDING TO THE HEART

One of the perennial challenges with spiritual growth is the seeming disparity between our actual spiritual progress and the level of knowledge we possess. Living out what we know to be true is a constant struggle. A primary reason for this is how we navigate our heart. Typically, we define the heart as our feelings, attitudes, and emotional temperature toward something. When we consider the manner in which the Bible uses the word "heart" (*kardia*), we discover a much broader range of meaning. The semantic domain for heart, scripturally speaking, includes personality, intellect, emotions, desires, memory, and will. Attention to these areas is critical if we want to progress in our spiritual maturity. The following steps prove helpful in tending and navigating the heart:

1. *Discover the nature of the heart.* Given to its own devices, the heart naturally becomes hardened (Ezek. 11:19), is crooked (Prov. 17:20), and proud (Prov. 16:5).

2. *Allow our heart to be examined.* The Lord says He knows our heart fully (1 Kings 8:39), weighs it (Prov. 24:12), and examines and tests it (Jer. 12:3; Ps. 139:23).

3. *Recognize that brokenness is the pathway to growth.* King David models for us a heart in which God delights (Ps. 51:15–17; Isa. 66:2; 2 Cor. 12:7–10). His example of humility and repentance guides us toward a life of maturity and Christlikeness.

4. *Acknowledge the hiddenness of our heart, even to our own consciousness.* We are often surprised and disappointed by what we say and do. This proves that we do not fully know or recognize what is in our heart (Jer. 17:9–10).

5. *Understand that we live out of the impressions that are formed in our heart.* Words and actions often leave impressions on our hearts. Many of these remain for long periods of time, shaping the ways we respond to the world around us (1 Sam. 1:8; 2:1).

6. *Remain mindful of what we feed our heart.* Sowing either to the flesh or to the Spirit necessarily influences the condition of our heart (Col. 3:1–17; Gal. 5:16–26).

7. *Remember that wisdom and discernment are developed through tending our heart.* The author of Proverbs states, "Watch over your heart with all diligence, for from it flow the springs of life" (Prov. 4:23). Heart tending becomes the central task in our pursuit of wisdom and discernment.

Each of these principles and practices promotes our maturity, but greater fruitfulness will come as we saturate each of these in prayer. Praying through each step of this process moves us from a place of mere cognition to a place of deep-seated conviction. The ministry of the Word and Spirit work in concert with prayer to transform our thinking and behavior. Paul prayed for the church in Colossae that God would fill them with "the knowledge of His will in all spiritual wisdom and understanding" (Col. 1:9).

This ongoing process of spiritual growth works as a partnership between grace and effort. Grace has been provided for our transformation and growth (2 Tim. 1:9), but effort is required on our part for it to be applied (Col. 1:29). The Lord has established our life and position in Christ and has called us to participate in His divine nature, to walk in His promises with our whole being (2 Peter 1:3, 5–8). Growing in knowledge and grace requires lived experience over time. As John Koessler explains, "There is effort involved, but it is an effort that has been energized by the life of Christ. . . . The responsibility is ours but the power to comply comes from God."[4] By the Spirit, we diligently tend what God alone has graciously planted.

PAIN AND SUFFERING AS AGENTS OF CHANGE

This is the final factor we will consider with respect to spiritual maturity. Experiencing hardships in life has a way of exposing the heart in ways it would not otherwise be exposed. Stress and resistance have the potential to produce growth and create new pathways of understanding in our lives. The life and missionary journeys of the apostle Paul provide a great example of how maturity develops through struggle and suffering. Second Corinthians 6:3–10 combines a long list of things that happened to Paul while on mission—afflictions, hardships, difficulties, beatings, imprisonments, mob attacks, labors, sleeplessness, hunger—with qualities associated with maturity—endurance, purity, knowledge, patience, kindness, genuine love—and ends by contrasting faulty perceptions of Paul's mission with the actual corresponding spiritual realities: "having nothing and yet possessing all things"(v. 10). This is a great reminder that God's mission and the gospel work in which we are immersed can often result in difficult circumstances and trials. And the outcome of these hardships typically sees God's mission progressing and God's children being transformed increasingly into His likeness.

The Lord actually provides a language for His people as they encounter pain and suffering; this language is called "lament." Lament is a great gift to the church—providing space, articulation, and expression for those suffering. It functions as a spiritual discipline, helping the sufferer to reconstruct meaning after the disorienting effects of their experience.[5] We observe in the biblical psalms of lament a framework and pattern that expresses the pain of the people. This pattern includes the psalmist's opening address to God, complaint or reason for the lament, petition or request, and a closing vow of praise to God. Biblical lament does not deny pain, nor does it drown in despair. It is honest, but it also bows the knee in trust and submission to God.

A reordering of desires and perceptions often occurs as someone works through their trauma and pain. Theologian Todd Billings cites Augustine's thoughts explaining, "The Psalms are given to us as a divine pedagogy for our affections— God's way of reshaping our desires and perceptions so that they learn to lament in the right things and take joy in the right things."[6] This is an extremely personal and relational process with our Lord, taking us deeper into the intimate fellowship that He desires and that we long for.

As we encounter these challenging experiences and relationships within the framework of God's providence, embracing them with a certain posture and attitude proves helpful. This posture can be characterized as purposeful, participatory, and missional. As we enter into each relational or experiential situation, we do so aware of who we are (identity) and what we are called to do (mission). This follows the pattern that we observe in our Savior, as demonstrated in the moments leading up to Jesus' dramatic act of washing His disciples' feet. Declaring His identity from above and His mission from the Father, Jesus carried out that profound and intentional act of service (John 13:1–5). He lovingly leaned into this action, knowing His betrayal and arrest were right around the corner, and even washing the feet of His betrayer. Such moments highlight, as well as influence and enlarge, key aspects of our identity and calling. We move forward from these challenges with a potentially more solidified identity and clarified calling. This process is often unsettling, and not without struggle. But the spiritual benefit and fruit this process produces is ultimately worthwhile—namely, a portrait of the life of discipleship to which Jesus has called us (Luke 14:25–33; James 1:2–4).

A VISION OF SPIRITUAL MATURITY: WHAT DOES IT LOOK LIKE?

I once asked my kids, "Who's more effective in hunting for food, a baby lion or its mother?" Of course they answered, "The mother." Maturity is a trait that is innate and embedded in God's creation. Adult animals possess a fuller coat, larger teeth, longer claws, greater muscle development, and the capacity to reproduce. These characteristics of maturity allow the animal to feed itself and its young, protect itself from predators and, under normal conditions, sustain its kind. The animal functions in the manner in which it was created. Similarly, various Scriptures highlight the child-adult comparison/contrast to exhort God's people toward maturity (1 Cor. 13:11; Heb. 5:12–14; 1 John 2:13). God desires for His people to not remain in a juvenile state, but to attain the fullness and flourishing for which He created them.

Childishness is to be put aside (1 Peter 2:1–3). Such "childish" attitudes and behaviors include jealousy, boastfulness, arrogance, rudeness, and other things that destroy peace within Christ's body. The primary attribute of maturity is love, established in a robust relationship between God and His church, and producing a missional movement empowered by the Spirit. There is an apparent interconnectedness of one's spiritual maturity to God's overarching mission. Recognizing this direct correlation between an individual's maturity and fulfillment of God's mission highlights the importance of tending to our spiritual maturity.

Specifically and practically, spiritual maturity brings freedom and nimbleness to the Christ follower. A sense of spiritual agility and awareness begins to develop in their person. Habits begin to form and responses occur without much conscious thinking. The individual becomes captured by a heavenly agenda and progressively releases the priority of the self. A pattern develops of doing the right thing, even when it is uncomfortable and inconvenient.

As alluded to earlier, the maturing person acquires a sturdiness and stability of identity. Their self-understanding and identity sway little when criticism or flattering words come. They still may briefly feel the effect of such words, but these words do not possess the power and influence over their mind and soul as they once did. Whether it is the enticement of the adulterous woman warned about in the book of Proverbs, or the careless and snide comments posted on social media, we are no longer entangled in such rhetoric. This is spiritual growth and evidence of God's transformational work in our lives!

A maturing person also makes decisions driven by biblical values and a sense of God-mindedness, not by impulsive reactions or feelings. For the spiritually mature, the time frame for decision-making often occurs at a different pace. The urgency of the moment does not seem as urgent as it once did. It becomes easier to say "no" or "not right now." Time becomes a friend that allows prayer, reflection, and God's Word to sift a situation or decision. This is the freedom and peace of mind that characterizes mature people we may know and respect.

An appetite for wisdom also develops in those growing in maturity. Such individuals begin to view learning as a spiritual discipline and take on the role of apprentice. There develops a hunger and thirst for the things of God, regardless of the context or medium—whether it is the preaching from the pulpit on Sunday morning, the midweek small group Bible study, the one-on-one mentoring, or daily personal quiet time.

Rare are the mountaintop experiences in our life. Most of life is lived in very ordinary, common, and uneventful moments. This being the case, mature believers know that the Holy Spirit uses these normal, everyday arenas—study, sexuality, work, relationships, and rest (Matt. 5–7)—to carry out His transforming work. Brother Lawrence, the well-known sixteenth-century French monk, practiced the presence of God as he washed dishes in the monastery kitchen.[7] His God-minded and worship-saturated awareness transformed such a typically mundane chore into a faithful act of worship.

The New Testament's portrayal of sanctification almost always involves community. Thus, our picture of spiritual maturity should also include significant relationships with others. There is a level of transparency and vulnerability evident in those who have fostered deep intimacy with the Lord. They willingly allow their attitudes, thoughts, and behavior to be examined by the Spirit. This typically translates in a horizontal direction as well. The same posture of vulnerability and openness is displayed within their inner circle of relationships, as trust is developed. It is in this kind of relational culture, with the Lord and with others, that the sanctifying practices of confession, repentance, accountability, and true knowing are nurtured.

How do pastors and church leaders grow a congregation's spiritual depth and apply a vision of spiritual maturity? Obviously, every congregational culture is different and made up of individuals at varying levels of maturity. But a few practical principles can help this begin to take shape in our churches. First, spiritual maturity develops best in closely connected regular relationships. If the work of maturity is to occur, the individuals involved need to be known intimately by one another (small group, church board, marriage, etc.). Second, our pursuit of maturity develops best in discipleship relationships. This involves intentionality, agreed upon goals, regular mutual engagement, and seeking Christ in all things. Last, it becomes difficult for spiritual maturity to grow in the life of the congregation if the leaders of that congregation are not themselves pursuing spiritual maturity. Pastors and church ministry leaders must exemplify the process of maturity in their own lives if they desire spiritual growth in their people.

CONCLUSION

Over the past few years, I have had the heart-wrenching experience of watching two friends enter glory long before any of us were expecting this to happen. Cancer was the culprit in both accounts. Each of them left this earth with heartbroken spouses and young children. These types of situations surface numerous questions that will not be understood or answered until glory—not least about the goodness of God. In the midst of the dark valley that each of my friends journeyed through, both allowed me and others closest to them to walk with them through it. This was an unexpected but precious gift. We were invited into a sacred space into which very few are welcomed—into their pain and suffering, their doubt, fear, uncertainty, questions; but also into their hope, perseverance, faith, grace-infused effort, trust, and utter dependence on their Savior. I was able to peer into their lives in a way that revealed a maturity and sanctification that seldom is seen, as circumstances of this magnitude tend to expose realities of the human person never anticipated. Their profound trust in Christ provided those of us around them with the opportunity to observe a level of maturity that left a lifelong imprint on our hearts. I will forever be reminded of the faith these friends displayed as I walked alongside them. As I interact with their remaining families today, I am reminded of their legacies and the deep influence each one has had in my life. To this day, they are the clearest and most vivid picture I have of spiritual maturity.

Reflecting on their stories, I am reminded of the steadiness that Christ brings to our lives. God aims to establish rhythms in our lives that weather crisis and tumultuous circumstances. His aim is not our proficiency and productivity, but to expose Christlike maturity that points to a world not yet revealed. By God's grace, my friends acquired hearts, affections, and convictions that fostered faithfulness under the most intense circumstances. Each of them would tell you (and maybe one day they will) that their acquisition of such spiritual maturity was developed over decades of small steps in their daily walk with Christ. However, what I observed over the last few months of their lives was a potent gift and testimony that pointed to the beauty and wonder of our Savior. Let us pursue their example as we seek a life of maturity and lead others in the same, revealing His glory and accomplishing His mission.

NOTES

1. John Calvin, *Institutes of the Christian Religion*, trans. Henry Beveridge (Peabody, MA: Hendrickson, 2008), 6.

2. M. Robert Mulholland, Jr., *Shaped by the Word: The Power of Scripture in Spiritual Formation*, rev. ed. (Nashville: Upper Room, 2000), 41.

3. Michael F. Bird, *Evangelical Theology: A Biblical and Systematic Introduction* (Grand Rapids: Zondervan, 2013), 118.

4. John Koessler, *True Discipleship: The Art of Following Jesus* (Chicago: Moody, 2003), 41.

5. M. Elizabeth Lewis Hall, "Suffering in God's Presence: The Role of Lament in Transformation," *Journal of Spiritual Formation and Soul Care* 9, no. 2 (2016): 219.

6. J. Todd Billings, *Rejoicing in Lament: Wrestling with Incurable Cancer and Life in Christ*, (Grand Rapids: Brazos, 2015), 38.

7. Brother Lawrence, *The Practice of the Presence of God* (Uhrichsville, OH: Barbour, 1998).

Winning in Spiritual Warfare

SAMUEL NAAMAN

The spirit world is a reality recognized by the Bible. Its opening pages begin with spiritual conflict, a conflict that continues throughout Scripture and culminates in a final battle and the creation of a new heaven and earth. This spiritual reality influences every culture and society, although it is more central to some cultures, religions, and worldviews than others. The non-Western worldview recognizes that everything in this world is influenced by an active spirit world. This belief is so animated in some cultures that individuals seek to protect themselves from its influence through amulets, charms, or incantations. Some people attribute illness to a curse or angry ancestral spirits and will seek someone with spiritual authority to heal, deliver, or restore spiritual harmony.

By contrast, the Western worldview takes a more material or scientific approach, so the concept of a spirit world is pushed to the margins. For example, the average Westerner typically attributes illness to medical causes and seeks a scientific solution by going to a physician. This assumption has influenced the Western church, leading to an often diminished understanding and emphasis on the spiritual aspects of life and faith. But even in secular, humanistic Western cultures, people have a curiosity about the unseen, which leads some to fascination with such things as psychics, tarot reading, and inner healing manuals.

Whether acknowledged or not, a real spiritual battle is raging. Many people are held in bondage as their lives and livelihood are destroyed by evil forces that prowl around seeking someone to devour (1 Peter 5:8). Those who engage this spirit world, either out of curiosity or as an integral part of life, acknowledge that there is power in the spirit world; but they naively believe this power is neutral. In exchange for power, people end up tormented by these spirits. And yet God provides a way of escape—a Savior who sets us free from the power and hold of Satan.

It is my desire that Christians will be equipped to fight the spiritual battle that we all face, seeking the help of our Lord Jesus by His Spirit. In this chapter, we will cover several topics of spiritual warfare, and then consider biblical answers to combat this reality in our lives so that we might live in victory, glorifying our Lord Jesus Christ.

BIBLICAL VIEW OF THE SPIRIT WORLD

According to the Bible, a spiritual battle has been ongoing since the creation of this world. It is important to remember that God is in control of the universe. He governs and sustains His creation. We as image bearers are the pinnacle of God's creation, and He is for us, not against us.

The biblical presentation of the spirit world includes angels, both good and evil. Good angels are spirits—supernatural, celestial beings, whose mission is to serve God and His people. Hebrews 1:14 asks, "Are not all angels ministering spirits sent to serve those who will inherit salvation?" (NIV). Evil angels consist of Satan and his angels. The Hebrew word for "Satan," which means "opposer" or "adversary," and "devil" from the Greek word *diabolos,* are used interchangeably in the New Testament. These evil angels proved unfaithful and were driven out of heaven (Rev. 12:7–8). They are called demons or evil spirits (Luke 10:17, 20 NLT), and in the end will be cast "into the eternal fire prepared for the devil and his angels" (Matt. 25:41 NIV).

IN THE OLD TESTAMENT

Satan's fall took place before the creation of the world, and now he opposes all of God's creation, making this world the battleground between him and God (Rev. 12:7–17; see Isa. 14:12–14; Ezek. 28:12–17).[1] The first record of this battle takes place in the garden of Eden (Gen. 3:1–15), describing the weapons Satan used to tempt Eve and the consequences of their encounter. He tempted Eve to partake in what God had forbidden by eating from the tree of the knowledge of good and evil. Satan's first tool was to create doubt. The second tool was to promise that Eve would be like God—an appeal to pride. Eve, with Adam, yielded to the temptation, with the consequence that God's world was subjected to Satan, plunging it into a kingdom of darkness and spiritual alienation from its Creator (Eph. 2:2; Rev. 12:7–17).

The first indication of God's provision for winning this battle is introduced in Genesis 3:15. God promises Eve that from her seed will come someone to crush the head of Satan—the Savior, who inaugurated the kingdom of God by defeating the devil (Heb. 2:14) and bringing salvation and hope to humankind.

The first two chapters of Job give the reader a peek behind the curtain concerning the spiritual reality of the unseen world. Satan challenges God's protection of His people through the character of Job. Satan must ask for God's permission to bring death, destruction, and disaster. God's only stipulation was that he was not to take Job's life. The battle has consequences in the real world, and the book of Job is an example of how to respond when we are under attack from Satan and his forces.

Another example of this spiritual battle is seen in the story of Elisha in 2 Kings 6. Faced with a desperate battle, Elisha's servant believed the situation was hopeless due to the strength of the enemy, what he could perceive considering only the physical world. Elisha told him not to be afraid, since those who were with Israel were more than those who were with the enemy—and God revealed the hills full of horses and chariots of fire, the reality of the spiritual world. Another dimension of spiritual battle is shown in Daniel 10. Daniel was given a vision, and the angel who finally came to explain this vision told Daniel that he had been delayed twenty-one days because he was opposed by the prince of the kingdom of Persia. Through this vision, we see there are spiritual forces that try to prevent God's truth from getting to us. Prolonged prayer and fasting are among the tools we must employ to gain breakthroughs in spiritual warfare. We need not be afraid in our spiritual battles, for God is able and willing to fight our battles if we ask Him.

IN THE NEW TESTAMENT

The New Testament provides more details concerning our spiritual battle. A cosmic war comes full force at Jesus' incarnation. The Scriptures say that Jesus came to set us free from Satan: "The Son of God appeared for this purpose, to destroy the works of the devil" (1 John 3:8). When Herod learned of Jesus' birth, he was enticed by Satan to issue a decree to kill all the young boys in Bethlehem and the surrounding area up to three years of age. This was an attempt by Satan to eliminate Jesus Christ as an infant, putting an end to the plan of salvation for humankind.

At the inauguration of Jesus' public ministry, Jesus was led by the Spirit into the wilderness to be tempted by Satan. The temptation that Jesus went through mirrors the first temptation of Adam and Eve and is the same spiritual battle that we face (Heb. 4:15).[2] The first battleground is in the physical realm. Satan used the human need for food. In the same way, Satan tempts us using basic human needs, such as food, sex, and our desire for material things.

> Do not love the world nor the things in the world. If anyone loves the world, the love of the Father is not in him. For all that is in the world, the lust of the flesh and the lust of the eyes and the boastful pride of life, is not from the Father, but is from the world. The world is passing away and also its lusts; but the one who does the will of God continues to live forever. (1 John 2:15–17)

Jesus used the weapon of Scripture in this battle, which is also our first line of defense. I cannot emphasize enough the importance of knowing the Bible well. As followers of Christ, we must be dedicated to the study of God's Word. We need to have full faith in the inerrancy of the Bible, holding firm the belief that the Bible is relevant in every generation and culture, including our own. Knowing the Bible well is paramount in our ability to stand our ground and not succumb to the attacks of the devil (1 Peter 5:8–9).

The second area of temptation in spiritual warfare comes in an appeal to our pride and identity. Jesus resisted the temptation to elevate Himself through grandstanding. Satan appeals to our insecurities, our feelings of worthlessness, and our shame by always drawing attention to ourselves. What makes Jesus' temptation different than ours is that Jesus, as the Son of God, could legitimately have shown the world His power, but in so doing He would have disobeyed His Father. Again, Jesus' weapon to combat this temptation was Scripture.

The third area of temptation in this spiritual standoff comes from the deep human desire for control and power. As prince of this world, Satan offered to hand over all his kingdom to Jesus, if Jesus would but bow down and worship him (likely a false promise, since Satan is the father of lies, John 8:44). Many people look for power in the unseen world and are willing to give up all they have to obtain it. Once again, Jesus brought Scripture to bear as a weapon to combat temptation; in this He serves as our model. We see that after these encounters with the devil, angels came to strengthen Jesus. Spiritual warfare is a tough battle. Spiritual warfare will take all one's strength to resist, and requires humble dependence on the Lord's power. We cannot avoid spiritual confrontation, for it is an integral part of the Christian life, but we can rely on the Lord's strength and provision to remain faithful and steadfast in the midst of it.

BIBLICAL AND CONTEMPORARY ACCOUNTS OF SPIRITUAL WARFARE

As we read in Luke 4:14–30, Jesus declared war on Satan's kingdom right at the onset of His public ministry. He did this by preaching about the kingdom of God, offering freedom to captives and the oppressed, healing, and proclaiming God's new reign (Acts 10:38). Jesus was turning the upside-down world right side up.

The next event in Luke 4 records a spiritual battle that happened as Jesus was preaching in Capernaum. As He taught in the synagogue, an evil spirit manifested itself, causing a disturbance in the meeting. The evil spirit knew that Jesus had come to destroy Satan and his works, so it pleaded for mercy. Jesus commanded the spirit to be quiet and come out of the man. The spirit obeyed, exiting the man without injuring him. When the people saw this demonstration of God's power over evil spirits, they were amazed, and news of the event spread throughout the area. When we are taking back territory from Satan, such manifestations of evil will occur.

This reminds me of an incident I experienced in Pakistan. Our family was on vacation in Quetta, Balochistan. As was our custom, we attended daily local revival meetings. On one evening, Sister Alice was leading worship. As she prepared to speak, a woman, a nominal Christian, began screaming and foaming at the mouth. Everyone was frightened by the commotion when this woman suddenly levitated off her seat and flew through the air about fifteen feet to where Sister Alice was standing. Alice coolly put down her accordion and held the woman, commanding the evil spirit to leave her. She signaled to the pastor to continue with the service, while she and several other members of the congregation calmly escorted the woman to a side room. After a few minutes they returned, the woman sat down peacefully, and Sister Alice got up to speak as if nothing spectacular had happened. This powerful confrontation demonstrated the truth of the gospel to my younger sister, who consequently gave her life to Christ that evening.

We can draw several principles from this incident. First, we should not look for demons or evil spirits; they will manifest themselves, but we should not seek them out. We see this consistently in Jesus' ministry. satan likes the attention when we look for demons behind every bush, so to speak, or when we ascribe the source of every bad circumstance to him. We live in a fallen world in which bad things happen. Not everything can or should be directly attributed to satanic causation (including temptation). Second, we should never confront demons alone. Spiritually mature people went with Sister Alice to pray against the evil spirits. Jesus wisely sent out the disciples in pairs to heal the sick, raise the dead, cleanse those who had leprosy, and drive out demons (Mark 6:7), so we should not presume to take on the spirit world alone. Third, we must not give evil spirits center stage. Rather, we must focus our attention on the authority of Christ (Luke 10:17–20). When Jesus cast out demons, He commanded silence. Sister Alice took this woman out of the sanctuary, and the service continued. Fourth, spiritual confrontations reveal the power of Jesus Christ in the gospel, and people will be affected by such demonstrations.

Another example of spiritual warfare in Jesus' ministry concerned a physical attack by evil forces (Mark 4:35–5:20). Following a fruitful time of ministry teaching the crowds and healing many demon-possessed and sick, Jesus and His disciples departed and went to the other side of the Sea of Galilee. While they were at sea, evil forces attacked Jesus and the disciples, and a violent storm came up. After this crossing Jesus would confront a legion of demons, so this was an attempt to obstruct Jesus' ministry through fear and possible death. Spiritual warfare can be manifested in the physical realm with flying objects, rattling doors, and other such displays of unexplained phenomena, which seek to interfere, intimidate, or instigate fear. Though Christians from Western countries might not see such blunt incidents of demonic activity, we need to be aware of its subtlety.

My father was once taking an American pastor out for evangelistic meetings in Pakistan. God was blessing the ministry, and many formerly nominal Christians gave their lives fully to the Lord. One night around 3:00 a.m., my father awoke at the sound of the front door rattling. At first, he thought it was his helper with some urgent message. He called the man's name but received no response.

The rattling intensified, but now was accompanied by strange noises. The Lord impressed upon my father that this was a spiritual attack. My father knelt and extended his hand toward the door and began to pray loudly and quote Scripture. By this time, the American pastor was wide awake. My father looked at him and said, "We are being attacked by Satan. He does not want our ministry to be fruitful." Not knowing what else to do, the pastor started to pray for my father by placing his hands on him. My father commanded Satan, "Leave us alone. You have no power over us. We command you in the name of our Lord Jesus to leave this place. We belong to Him." After an intense time of prayer, the door stopped rattling, the noises ceased, and they knew the battle was over. They both prayed and thanked God, and then went to sleep. For this American pastor, it was the first time encountering spiritual warfare and victory in the name of Jesus.

This does not only happen in other countries. Those doing ministry in areas where darkness reigns will encounter spiritual warfare. My colleague, Dr. Roy Oksnevad, did pioneer church planting in Hoboken, New Jersey, in the 1980s. One night he was unable to breathe, as if someone were choking him. His roommate woke from a deep sleep and felt an evil presence in the room. Not knowing what else to do, he immediately began pleading the blood of Jesus over the situation and rebuking Satan, commanding him to leave. Finally, my colleague was released from the chokehold. They discussed what had just happened and then prayed together.

We can draw several principles from these illustrations. First, whenever you seek to bring light in an area that has long been kept in darkness by Satan, there will be outright spiritual warfare. Satan does not readily relinquish his territory without a fight (e.g., Acts 13:6–11; 19:23–31). Next, we remember that Christ already has defeated Satan and his demons by the cross and resurrection. Paul instructs us in 2 Corinthians 10:3–4, "For though we walk in the flesh, we do not wage battle according to the flesh, for the weapons of our warfare are not of the flesh, but divinely powerful for the destruction of fortresses." Third, claiming the blood of Christ is not a formula that automatically makes evil spirits flee. The disciples tried to cast out a demon from a boy unsuccessfully until Jesus came and did it (Matt. 17:14–21). When the seven sons of Sceva, a Jewish chief priest, tried to drive out evil spirits in the name of the Lord Jesus, they were overpowered and beaten (Acts 19:13–16). We will have to pray through the conflict by the authority of Christ until the crisis is over.

The battle with Satan intensified at the Passover feast, just before the arrest and crucifixion of Jesus at the cross. The battle was intense, and the disciples were not exempt. The Bible tells us that Satan entered Judas, one of the twelve apostles, to conspire to hand Jesus over to the temple guards (Luke 22:3). Satan also asked to attack Peter, leading him to deny Jesus (Luke 22:31–34). All the disciples fled from Jesus at His arrest, even after the warning from Jesus not to sleep but to pray, so they would not enter into temptation (Luke 22:40–46). Satan used the crowd to influence Pilate against his better judgment, and he eventually capitulated to the crowd by handing Jesus over to be crucified (Luke 23:1–25). Satan even blinded the eyes of the Jews so they did not recognize the Son of God (John 1:11; 2 Cor. 4:4).

However, Jesus conquered the grave and overcame death. By the blood of Jesus, we are more than conquerors. So we see in Revelation 12:

> Then I heard a loud voice in heaven, saying, "Now the salvation, and the power, and the kingdom of our God and the authority of His Christ have come, for the accuser of our brothers and sisters has been thrown down, the one who accuses them before our God day and night. And they overcame him because of the blood of the Lamb and because of the word of their testimony, and they did not love their life even when faced with death. For this reason, rejoice, you heavens and you who dwell in them. Woe to the earth and the sea, because the devil has come down to you with great wrath, knowing that he has only a short time." (vv. 10–12)

We must remember that no matter how intense the battle, Jesus has already conquered Satan and his evil spiritual forces.

FREEDOM FROM SPIRITUAL BONDAGE

We also see the reality of spiritual warfare in the ministry of the early church, which Jesus established in the wake of His departure to continue His mission and shine the light of the gospel in the midst of darkness (Acts 1:8; 10:38; 26:18). One example is found when Paul and Silas were church planting. They came across a slave-woman who had a spirit by which she could predict the future. In this case, the evil spirit in her recognized that these men were servants of the Most High God. Knowing that this knowledge originated from an evil spirit, Paul commanded the spirit to come out of her. As a result, she lost her ability to predict the future, and her masters were furious at losing their source of income. Subsequently, Paul and Silas were thrown into prison under false charges. A dimension of spiritual warfare is to set people free from their bondage to evil spirits (Acts 16:16–24).

Objects such as religious artifacts, charms, and amulets used to ward off demonic spirits are likely not as familiar to those in Western cultures as in other parts of the world. However, when we minister to people from different religious backgrounds, we need to consider their spiritual heritage and practices. We must address potential spiritual bondage that individuals bring from their Hindu, Muslim, Buddhist, ancestral, folk, or other religious backgrounds. People do not get involved in these activities because they are ignorant or uneducated, but because their worldview includes manipulation of the spirit world. They have no other alternatives for protection from the unseen world than through the use of fetishes, charms, and rituals.

When people do come to know Christ, it is important to address the bondage that these religious symbols create in their lives. Unless these artifacts are renounced and destroyed, thereby setting the person free from their power, these objects will hinder the spiritual growth and life of the new believer. These objects (and corresponding practices) are not neutral. That is why those who practiced sorcery burned their scrolls publicly (Acts 19:19–20). The early church knew this, so a part of their baptismal ritual included a renouncing of Satan and all his works. The destruction of high places, ritual sites, ritual objects, and altars was also a part of God's commands in the Old Testament (Deut. 12:1–4), along with explicit commands against sorcery, divination, or the consulting of spiritual mediums for spiritual guidance (Deut. 18:9–14; Lev. 19:26, 31).

PUTTING ON THE ARMOR OF GOD

Spiritual warfare is acknowledged throughout the epistles in the New Testament. Paul reminds us that we do not fight against flesh and blood, but that we have divine power to destroy strongholds. So then, we do not wage war as the world does (2 Cor. 10:3–4). Our battle is not against philosophies, social agendas, politicians, or the latest trends on social media. Politics is not the savior of our social ills. Our battle is against rulers, authorities, powers of this dark world, and the spiritual forces of evil in the heavenly places (Eph. 6:12). The church needs to speak truth—the Word of Christ—into the myriad of competing voices that claim to have the answers. Many of these voices are not neutral and lead to grave consequences if we follow them. We have seen how Satan used half-truths to deceive Adam and Eve, and Paul reminds us that there are dark forces that continue to lead humanity away from God and into bondage (2 Cor. 11:2–4, 14). Spiritual discernment is necessary among the people of God.

Paul admonishes the Christian to be strong in the Lord and in His mighty power. We must put on the full armor of God so that we can take a stand against the devil's schemes and the powers of darkness in this fallen world (Eph. 6:10–11, 13). Unless Christians live in the victory that God provides, the Christian community will become inept—powerless to speak truth in a world that desperately is looking for direction, deliverance, and hope. In Ephesians 6, Paul describes the spiritual armor that believers must put on to combat the spiritual forces which seek to deceive us.

THE BELT OF TRUTH

Our spiritual war involves truth claims. The exclusivity of truth is no longer tolerated in our culture. The new "truth" is tolerance. It advocates that all religions amount to the same thing and that every opinion has equal value. To maintain a tolerant society, society must be intolerant of intolerance. Confusion is generated by the litany of voices that do not tolerate absolute truth, in contrast to Jesus' claim that He is the truth and the only way to the Father (John 14:6).

In the religious realm, pantheism, broadly understood, includes ancient Eastern religions like Hinduism, Buddhism, and Taoism. Their offspring are such things as the New Age Movement and Scientology. Aberrant religions such as Jehovah's Witness and Mormonism as well as various cults blend biblical wording with unbiblical conclusions that sound appealing but are untrue and deceptive to many. Numerous people and cultural systems are in bondage to Islam. Self-appointed spiritual experts surface and proclaim a belief system of tolerance, claiming that there are no eternal truths, that truth is only what each person feels is right. The fruit of these efforts to mimic God's revealed truth permeates our culture, sometimes duping even believers. Giving in to the message of counterfeit truths has consequences that will affect our spiritual lives. The world seems enamored with the new, while the conventional truth found in Christianity seems old.

In the academic and political realms, we observe the reign of philosophies that reflect utopian ideals, but lack a proper biblical worldview concerning the fall and its effects. As a result, these philosophies only lead to greater division and chaos, and disillusionment when leaders fail to fulfill their promises. The world is fallen, leaders are fallen, and societies are fallen. The only truth that addresses this fallenness is the truth of Scripture. Jesus took our pain and suffering to the cross and rose again. God gives us the power to live through the promised indwelling of the Holy Spirit. Jesus informs us that He who is in us is greater than he who is in the world (1 John 4:4).

THE BREASTPLATE OF RIGHTEOUSNESS

David Wells, in *God in the Wasteland*, reminds the church that every culture makes some sins easier to indulge in and others more difficult. Paul's admonition in Ephesians 6 is to put on the breastplate of righteousness so that we will have the ability to discern how sin is made to look normal and how righteousness is made to look strange.[3] This means that our breastplate of righteousness will put us at odds with predominant cultural values. As American culture drifts further away from its Judeo-Christian moorings, the intensity of the spiritual battle increases. We see a direct consequence to our spiritual life as we continue to allow contemporary cultural values to erode a biblical understanding of righteousness. We end up sitting in judgment of Scripture, thinking that its values are no longer enduring but instead passé. Thus the church mirrors the pervading cultural norms concerning sexuality, marriage, and the accumulation of wealth. The antidote is putting on God's righteousness and living by biblical values.

The Gospel of Peace

A consistent message throughout the Bible is that the peace of God, which surpasses understanding, is part of our new life in Christ (Phil. 4:7). Scripture tells us to live at peace with everyone, as far as it depends on us (Rom. 12:18). We are to be peacemakers in a world of violence and division (James 3:15–18). We are to take this message of peace with God to the lost (Rom. 5:1–2; 2 Cor. 5:18–20).

In *The Invisible War*, Chip Ingram warns that when we advance the kingdom of God, we can expect spiritual attacks to occur in these circumstances especially: (1) spiritual growth, (2) invading enemy territory through evangelism, (3) exposing the enemy with his false ideas and promises, (4) breaking with the world through repentance from long-held patterns of sin and ungodly relationships, and (5) blessing to come, meaning that God soon will do something special to advance His kingdom.[4]

I can give you a personal example to illustrate when we can expect spiritual attacks. My father, Reverend Naaman, a convert from Islam, saw many Muslims come to Christ. Over a period of time he began to receive threatening letters and phone calls from underground Muslim extremists to stop his ministry. They knew he was a former Muslim and were agitated and angry that he was converting many more to Christianity. He was warned that if he did not stop his work, they would kill his son.

My father did not give in to these threats. The result was that on June 2, 1990, my younger brother Obed was gunned down by these Muslim extremists in front of the church. This sent shock waves among the small Christian community. The next day, during the funeral, my father stood up and publicly declared that he had forgiven the killers of his son. Many people were stunned and later asked how he could do this. My father replied, "I have preached on forgiveness for over thirty years. Now is the time to testify to it, if what I preached really is true." This public act of forgiveness bore much fruit, not just among the nominal Christians of that city, but also among Muslims. I have never forgotten my father's words: "Son, we need to practice forgiveness as Jesus forgives all our sins unconditionally." Satan cannot get a foothold when people are on fire with the gospel of peace (Eph. 4:26–27).

The gospel of peace can be costly in a world where evil seems to reign. We cannot let the devil get a foothold in our lives through anger or unforgiveness. This is a spiritual battle that, left unchecked, will devour us (Gal. 5:15). The Scriptures admonish,

> Never repay evil for evil to anyone. Respect what is right in the sight of all people. If possible, so far as it depends on you, be at peace with all people. Never take your own revenge, beloved, but leave room for the wrath of God, for it is written, "Vengeance is mine, I will repay," says the Lord. . . . Do not be overcome by evil, but overcome evil with good. (Rom. 12:17–19, 21)

THE SHIELD OF FAITH

Faith is an extremely important element in spiritual warfare. Satan will do everything to discourage the believer from moving forward in faith. William Carey is famously known for saying, "Expect great things from God; attempt great things for God." Christians are often attacked with self-doubt, thinking they will never accomplish anything for God. Hebrews 11:1 teaches that faith is the certainty in what we hope for and proof about what we do not see. Satan, the accuser of those in Christ (Rev. 12:10), brings an onslaught of accusations: we are hypocrites, we do not have a testimony to share, or no one wants to hear our message anyway. These fiery darts can be extinguished with the shield of faith.

I personally experienced the darts of Satan when a team of us started praying in the 1990s to start a ministry called South Asian Friendship Center in downtown Chicago. We started praying, and I was assailed with many doubts about this venture. Raising funds was difficult since I did not then have connections with churches in the States. The ministry center would need continued support to sustain its work over the years, and resources were few.

But with the shield of faith in hand, the team members stepped out together. We have seen God do many good things in the past twenty-five years. He has used our team to bring a message of hope and salvation to many, and we were able to train many young people who are serving the Lord locally and globally. We have faced intense spiritual warfare, and the team and ministry have had to adapt to changing situations. This account might not sound as dramatic as some presented in this chapter. But spiritual attacks also come in the forms of fundraising challenges, making connections, working with diverse groups, and so on. Christians in Western countries might well deal with attacks in these areas, which will not seem as overt as some examples from other settings. But by faith, the Lord has protected us and kept us in our area of ministry, even in the face of opposition.

THE HELMET OF SALVATION

One way Satan attacks believers is by questioning our position in Christ, causing us to doubt our salvation. Those of us in ministry can testify to the attacks we have endured when Satan used our failures, our areas of struggle, and our wandering thoughts to lead us to question our salvation. This is a particular area of vulnerability for new Christians. The helmet covers the head, where our thoughts reside. We are to have our minds on eternal things (Col. 3:1), conform our minds to what is right, not to the world (Rom. 12:2), and love God with all that we are, including our minds (Matt. 22:37).

Attacks on our salvation can come in another form. We can be tempted to deny our salvation (e.g., Luke 22:31–32; 1 Tim. 1:18–20). This is especially true when faced with suffering for our faith. Revelation 2:10 warns, "Do not fear what you are about to suffer. Behold, the devil is about to throw some of you into prison, so that you will be tested, and you will have tribulation for ten days. Be faithful until death, and I will give you the crown of life" (see 1 Peter 5:9).

We know of situations in which someone converts to Christianity and is harassed or worse. Without the helmet of salvation firmly in place, people may be pressured or manipulated into renouncing their faith rather than live with the consequences of their beliefs. This is not uncommon in areas such as Nigeria, which experiences undisguised spiritual warfare. Jesus made it clear that there is a cost to discipleship (Luke 9:23–27), and we must be vigilant in knowing about and praying for brothers and sisters in extreme circumstances.

THE SWORD OF THE SPIRIT

We mentioned previously the importance of the Scriptures in battling Satan when we considered the temptation of Jesus (Matt. 4). One cannot emphasize enough the importance of not only knowing the basics of the gospel story, but also being so familiar with the Word of God that it is always the basis of our thoughts and reactions.

Increasing biblical illiteracy is not only alarming, but inexcusable considering the armory of study tools we have available to us as well as a plethora of versions of Scripture. In the Western world especially, we have unprecedented opportunity to study Scripture and, even more important, to internalize its truth. Between books, blogs, podcasts, radio, and so on, the Word of God is readily available. However, not all Christians around the world have so much accessibility for various reasons, but other means of being armed with the sword of the Spirit are attainable.

For example, growing up in Pakistan, I learned the importance of the Bible through my family and the lives of many Christians who were not formally educated. Dr. I. D. Shahbaz, a Sikh convert, translated the entire book of Psalms and converted them into songs in Punjabi. These Punjabis did not have any formal biblical training or education, yet they memorized the entire book of Psalms through song! Someone would start the first verse, and the rest followed suit singing the whole chapter. The Psalms spoke profoundly to these uneducated people concerning God's love for them. My father emphasized reading the Bible with Muslims in evangelism because it is so powerful. Throughout my life I witnessed the power of God's Word to save people. Satan does not want us to be familiar with the Bible, or to share it such that people discover the profound truth that God loves them (John 3:16).

PRAYER

We have talked about the necessity of prayer in spiritual warfare. Just before Jesus was to be crucified, He went to the Mount of Olives to pray. He entreated His disciples, "Pray that you do not come into temptation" (Luke 22:40). The disciples fell asleep instead of praying, and as a result, they ran away at the time of Jesus' arrest. Peter, the "rock," would deny three times even knowing Jesus, just as the Lord had predicted. Jesus knew the power of prayer to resist the devil and how easy it is for God's people to capitulate in the heat of battle. Therefore, Paul tells us to pray in the Spirit on all occasions with all kinds of prayer and requests. Through prayer, we stay alert to the devil's schemes (Eph. 6:11, 18–20).

A powerful example of prayer comes from South Korea, where I studied theology. This country experienced a significant spiritual revival after the Korean War. One of the strong components behind the growth of the Korean church is their dedication and devotion to prayer. Almost every church, regardless of denomination, has a "dawn prayer meeting," where people come to the church around 5:00 a.m. for prayer and a short devotion before heading to their jobs. Christians also go to "prayer mountains" for fasting and prayer. God has blessed these fervent prayers, as South Korea has some of the largest churches in the world and is one of the most formidable missionary-sending countries. To overcome the devil, we must remain diligent and focused in our prayer lives. Renewal and revival, both in our personal lives and in the life of the church, are built on the foundation of a solid prayer life.

CONCLUSION

The biblical worldview acknowledges that a spiritual war is taking place in this world and in the heavenlies. Everyone has some understanding of a spiritual reality that is influenced by their own worldview, culture, or religion, including secular and humanistic perspectives. The battleground is over God's creation; and humans, as the crowning work of God's creation, are Satan's targets. Whenever the church advances into Satan's territory, there will be attacks of various kinds.

How can we as believers have victory over Satan in spiritual warfare? From the time of the fall in Genesis until the culmination of human history, we know that God is for us and has provided the tools needed to win this battle. We cannot do it in our own strength. God has provided the armor necessary to stand our ground and remain standing victoriously in the end. We can rest assured that we will always fight an enemy who already has been defeated on the cross by the death and resurrection of our Lord Jesus Christ (Col. 2:15; Heb. 2:14–15), and who someday will face ultimate judgment (Rev. 20:10). So we need not fear. We are encouraged by these words: "Submit therefore to God. But resist the devil, and he will flee from you. Come close to God and He will come close to you" (James 4:7–8a). The Holy Spirit gives us the power needed to daily live a victorious life.

Satan has no ultimate victory over a child of God, nor is he all-powerful. We are covered in Christ's blood, and God sees Christ's righteousness, not our sinfulness. We are His children, His workmanship, and His servants. We live in a fallen world, but with His help, we will always be victorious in this life. May we have total dependence on our Lord to give us boldness as His witnesses and lights to those around us. "The God of peace will soon crush Satan under your feet" (Rom. 16:20).

NOTES

1. Many interpreters see Ezekiel 28 and Isaiah 14 as referring to or alluding to Satan in his pre-fallen state and the circumstances surrounding his fall.

2. Of course, not every sinful temptation we face is directly caused by the devil, as James 1:13–15 describes the source of temptation as rooted in our own sinful desires. Even so, we still must remain on guard against an adversary who seeks our destruction (1 Peter 5:8).

3. David F. Wells, *God in the Wasteland: The Reality of Truth in a World of Fading Dreams* (Grand Rapids: Eerdmans, 1994), 59.

4. Chip Ingram, *The Invisible War: What Every Believer Needs to Know about Satan, Demons, and Spiritual Warfare* (Grand Rapids: Baker, 2006), 118–21.

Ministering to Children

ELIZABETH SMITH

At a certain meeting, two and a half people were converted to Christ. A friend asked Mr. Moody if he meant two adults and a child. "No," said Mr. Moody. The facts were just the opposite; they were two children and an adult. "When a child is led to Christ, a whole life is saved!"[1]

D. L. Moody, the noted nineteenth-century American Evangelist, began his ministry by establishing a Sunday school class in Chicago, Illinois, that intentionally reached children who came from underprivileged homes.[2] Moody's children's ministry grew into a church and challenged the status quo for evangelistic efforts to children. Mr. Moody encouraged children to attend Bible classes, and when they did, rewarded them with candy and pony rides. D. L. Moody was very devoted to reaching children for Christ. Near the end of his life, he said, *"If I could relive my life, I would devote my entire ministry to reaching children for God!"* What a superlative role model D. L. Moody is for today's ministry worker.

The purpose of ministry to children is to call them into a relationship with Christ, which inaugurates their journey of faith formation. The call to salvation is not reserved for adults alone; the gospel call is to be given accurately and clearly so all who are being drawn by the Spirit can respond in faith. Salvation is, at its heart, a response to an invitation that leads to transformation; this invitation is the heart of a children's ministry that glorifies God, expands the kingdom, and edifies the child and their family.

Our philosophy of ministry to children follows our theology and together, they inform the pedagogical theory that directs which methods will be chosen to instruct children in the faith. These understandings inform what we believe about who we are as people within our relationships, especially our families, and how we develop in all human domains throughout our lifespan. We consider how culture influences our beliefs about God and how we function within this world and the church. Theology is the food of the meal, our philosophy of ministry is how the meal is prepared, and our methodology is how the meal is served.

Once theology and philosophy have been ascertained, then methodology can be determined for the most effective ways to instruct children in the things of God. Methodology includes all the ways children can learn: lectures, small group discussions, object lessons, puppets, crafts, songs, skits, meditation. Our methodology ought to avoid pragmaticism and instead choose methods that are effective in reaching the heart of the child. Theology leads to philosophy, which leads to methodology; this is the pattern we must adhere to in order to build an effective, relevant, and God-glorifying children's ministry.

Whatever is believed by the larger church body and taught by the elders is to be used as markers for the ministry to children as well. The doctrines of our faith create both the content and practice of our ministry to children. Knowing what we believe about God is necessary, for we cannot give away to children that which we do not have ourselves.

The following primary questions address the framework for ministry to children and can prepare a theologically informed foundation for this ministry. We follow the directive to make disciples when ministering to children (Matt. 28:19). These questions and their subsequent answers directly affect what type of disciple a child becomes.

- What is the Word of God?
- Who is God?
- How do children come to know God?
- How do children grow in their faith in God?
- What is the role of the child's family in their faith formation?
- What is the role of the church in the discipleship of children and their families?

Theology is inherently practical and necessary to children's ministry. There is danger in putting aside theology to seek solutions to practical issues. Challenges in ministry can become the tyranny of the urgent, pushing aside the study of God and His Word. When this occurs, theology is replaced with hand selecting doctrines and verses that replace a solid system of belief and results in a prooftext for morality. We end up teaching what sounds good instead of teaching the whole counsel of God. The apostle Paul in his farewell to the Ephesians wrote, "For I did not shrink from declaring to you the whole counsel of God" (Acts 20:27 ESV).

WHAT IS THE WORD OF GOD?

It is in God's Word that we learn His character, His law, and His will. Children need to know God and they will learn who God is through His Word. The Bible must be the source of all our definitive knowledge about God and ourselves.

It is only through Scripture that from infancy, children are able to gain wisdom "that leads to salvation through faith which is in Christ Jesus" (2 Tim. 3:15). The author of Deuteronomy pleads with parents to teach the words of Scripture diligently. You "speak of them when you sit in your house, when you walk on the road, when you lie down, and when you get up" (Deut. 6:6–7). The author continues to urge parents to keep the words close at hand: "Tie them as a sign to your hand, and they shall be as frontlets on your forehead. You shall also write them on the doorposts of your house and on your gates" (Deut. 6:8–9). Carrying written religious material was a common Eastern practice in order to keep significant religious teachings constantly in mind. In these verses, parents were to remember the words of God so as to teach them to their children at every opportunity. It is still the message that families and the church adhere to in order to nurture the faith of their children. Scripture "gives understanding to the simple" (Ps. 119:130). As such, ministry to children is to be grounded in biblical instruction; to do otherwise is to not heed the warning given through the parable of the wise and foolish builders (Matt. 7:24–27).

Once God's Word has been understood to have a clear message, it can then be seen as inspired, inerrant, and sufficient. The central messages of the Bible are easily understood and are all we need for a life of faith. It is without error and sufficient because God is the one who inspired every jot and tittle and God never makes anything imperfect. Teaching children that the Bible is like no other book in the world and that it is absolutely true and necessary is a primary building block to their faith. Children must determine where they will get their knowledge. The world will offer them any number of misleading options that their flesh will be tempted to believe. The sooner we establish the Word of God as their authority in life, faith, and service, the sooner we prepare children to know their God and fight off the temptations of the world (2 Peter 1:4), Satan (Eph. 6:11), and their flesh (Rom. 7:18). Just as Jesus used Scripture to combat Satan's attacks, so we can teach children to use Scripture to fight temptation from the evil one (Matt. 4:1–11).

Children must learn to find the Bible reliable to answer their questions about life's spiritual matters and, subsequently, inform their life choices, and find comfort therein. God's words are unchanging in their truth and children can trust that the direction it gives them as children will be the same as when they are adults. Children must learn that reading and studying Scripture is necessary to grow in their relationship with God and that without its wisdom and power, their faith will wither.

Children can delight in learning more about their God and how His holiness, grace, love, mercy, and justice are displayed in their lives. Children can grow wise in serving God through His ordinances, commands, and knowledge of the church.

WHO IS GOD?

A study of God from His Word reveals that God has made Himself known in His attributes, functions, and will. God desires children to know Him. Knowing God in His attributes helps children form a picture of who God is as a being they can know, love, and serve. Knowing God in His functions helps children know what God does within His creation and throughout history. Knowing God's will enlightens children on God's desires and decrees and helps them understand God's plans for them.

God must be portrayed as He portrays Himself. Adults may feel uncomfortable talking about God's anger, wrath, justice, and punishment, but God can only be worshiped when He is known as He truly is. Communicating who God is with sensitivity to the child's age is key to a child's comprehension of who God is. This does not mean, however, that certain attributes of God or His actions against sin are eliminated from the conversations we have with children. The best rule of thumb when discussing God is to tell the truth in love (Eph. 4:15).

A clear understanding of God's holiness includes His inability to tolerate sin and a knowledge of His justice explains His necessary condemnation of it. God is holy and all who wish to dwell with Him must also be holy. This is impossible unless the imputed righteousness of Christ covers the sinner and imputation occurs at the moment a child places their faith in Christ, repenting of their sin. Jesus spoke of sin's punishment (hell) more than any New Testament writer and it is this punishment that we are saved from when we turn to Christ. Jesus is not just a good idea; He is a necessary one, for without Him all perish, including children.

> [Children] have an everlasting inheritance of happiness to attain, and it is that for which you must bring them up. They have an endless misery to escape, and it is that which you must diligently teach them. If you do not teach them to escape the flames of hell, what thanks do they owe you for teaching them to speak and do? If you do not teach them the way to heaven and how they may make sure of their salvation, what thanks do they owe you for teaching them how to get their living a little while in a miserable world? If you do not teach them to know God and how to serve him and be saved, you teach them nothing, or worse than nothing.[3]

God's attributes are best understood as a cohesive system of characteristics, each informing the others in their entirety. God's holiness permeates His love, which works with His just nature, which must be seen in light of His grace. However, in considering them in light of the development of children, certain characteristics are more critical to faith formation at certain ages. As children grow in their faith, they will come to know God more and more.

HOW DO CHILDREN COME TO KNOW GOD?

According to the Scriptures, salvation is through faith alone in Christ alone by grace alone for the glory of God alone (Rom. 5:1–2). This proclamation of the gospel is necessary for a child's soul to be redeemed. Children are born into sin (Ps. 51:5) and out of their own volition, choose to sin (Rom. 8:8); but upon repentance and confession of their sin (Rom. 10:9–10) with faith in Christ by the grace of God, not by works, a child can stand justified before God (Eph. 2:8–9). This is the only path open to a child who wishes to know God.

Children are saved by a work of the Spirit in their lives. The Spirit draws the child to the Father (John 6:44), awakening them to spiritual awareness. With the divine call to their soul, children will turn to Christ and will be justified by God through Jesus. God's inward call produces the regeneration of our soul resulting in repentance of sin and a confession of faith in turning to Christ for redemption. It is then the child is filled with the Spirit, who will indwell the child throughout their life, transforming them into the image of Christ until their day of glorification. This *ordo salutis* (order of salvation) is the same for a child as an adult. Understanding this allows the minister to children to seek to bring understanding to the child of the work of God in their life and their resultant response.

Knowing that salvation is a work of God, prayer for the soul of the child is critical. Whether a ministry's theology is covenant or dispensational, when it comes to a child's placement under the covenant of grace, neither ministry of the gospel presumes that the child is regenerate. The child must come to an acceptance of God's saving grace by their own volition. Charles Spurgeon's mother, Eliza, prayed earnestly for her children often throughout their lives. Charles never forgot how she threw her arms around him and cried out to God, "Oh, that my son might live before Thee!" Charles's soul was pierced and his heart stirred as he considered the witness his mother was bearing before the throne of God on his behalf. Her prayers had such a profound impact on him when he was young that he wrote many years later, "How can I ever forget her tearful eye when she warned me to escape from the wrath to come?"[4]

God sends His spirit to save the souls of men; in the end, God determines salvation. Yet, we must remember, it is often the prayers of the saints that are those means that lead to salvation for the sinner's soul. A responsibility of every children's ministry is to pray earnestly for the souls of the children in their care to be saved.

Praying for God to work, the minister to children can look for signs of the Spirit's movement. Children show signs of the work of the Spirit (Gal. 5:22–23) when they ask questions seeking knowledge of God, feeling penitent over their sin, seeking to praise God, and displaying the fruit of the Spirit. The Holy Spirit will love and show the same interest in the things that the Father and the Son cherish. Therefore, the child will display a work of the Spirit when they themselves love and show the same interest in the things of God. As signs of the Spirit become evident, ministers can initiate discussions, prayer, and Bible studies to nurture the child's fledgling spiritual interest. This is the work of the children's ministry.

Ministers explain key gospel points to the child, including their sin and the need to repent of sin, what Christ has done on their behalf, and the resultant promise of eternal life with the indwelling of the Spirit from the moment of belief. All of these truths can be understood by children in early childhood. How much you communicate at any one time and in what order is dependent upon the questions and readiness of the child. Ask God to give you wisdom and enlighten the heart of the child (Eph. 1:18).

HOW DO CHILDREN GROW IN THEIR FAITH IN GOD?

Children are sponges; they soak up information at every opportunity. They primarily learn through their senses—what they see, hear, touch, taste, and smell. They experience the truth first and then subsequently, as they mature cognitively, understand it. Growing in faith for a child requires an environment that promotes spiritual understanding in a variety of methods. The adults teaching the child control the environment, which includes the physical materials, curricular helps, and their own character disposition when relating with the child.

Before discussing the typically developing child and the normative spiritual formation considerations, every ministry to children should consider the atypically developing child. All children are made in the image and likeness of God and therefore, children of all abilities are of great worth. Children with disabilities need to be included since they have the potential to know and experience God too. God's Holy Spirit can speak to the heart and soul of a child in ways we may not comprehend or fully realize. Limiting the work of God in their life because of a disability or illness does not align with God's call for the church to make disciples of all peoples. Accommodations to lessons, activities, and classroom space is a serious responsibility that ensures a safe and secure environment for children with special needs. Every lesson taught and event planned should be preceded by the question,

How can we reach children with disabilities in our community for Christ in a way that is both welcoming and aimed at fulfilling the Great Commission?

All children, no matter their ability, culture, socioeconomic status, or ethnicity see adults as a testimony for God. Adults are always role models and communicate what faith looks like in the God they say they believe in. If an adult proclaims that God's Word tells the truth and provides direction and comfort for the believer, but the child never sees the adults consistently running to the Word for said helps, then the child will hear one thing (the Bible is sufficient) but believe another (we say the Bible is sufficient but we run to people, other books, and our own self-understanding for direction and comfort). Children are naturally suspicious of the hypocritical adult who claims faith but lives in contrast to their spoken words. Jesus questions the Pharisees on this very thing; "Why do you call Me, 'Lord, Lord,' and do not do what I say?" (Luke 6:46). An adult's hypocrisy is the primary enemy of a child's faith.

Ensuring children understand the gospel message necessitates knowing child development. Essential gospel truths explained through Scripture using simple language with a limited number of words creates an optimal situation for a child's faith formation. Teachers may overcommunicate truth by using synonyms frequently or too many words, which confuses truth and is not helpful to a child's personal application of it. Initially, keeping terms and explanations simple, knowing the child will grow in their understanding as they age and mature, is an essential starting point. As children grow older, adults build on truths children grasp, helping them to know God with increasing intimacy.

Speaking truth to a child's heart means living out the truth that is taught, and to teach intelligibly means to communicate at the level of the child. An adult minister to children must always be considering how the child understands truth. While adults can grasp and wrestle with abstract ideas, children are concrete learners and cannot understand things they cannot see or personally experience. They require tangible, specific explanations, best understood when hands-on experiences are created so they can see and touch what they are trying to understand. Children are not little adults.[5]

Rapidly changing brain structures throughout childhood reflect in a child's ability to form coherent systems of belief as their intellect develops over time and in stages. Developmental psychologist Jean Piaget created the following stage theory for the normative cognitive development throughout the human lifespan.

- **Sensorimotor stage** (infancy)—Children are exclusively aware of what they see and what they are doing, and try through trial-and-error to discover the interactions and relationships between objects. As object permanence develops, a child's memory emerges.

- **Preoperational stage** (preschool through age 7)—Building on early language development, growth in symbolism allows language to mature. Reasoning based on their limited knowledge and intuition produces a lack of logic but the new experience of imagination.

- **Concrete Operational stage** (ages 7–11)—Growing in external awareness, a child's egocentrism diminishes, their autonomy increases, and their concrete reasoning improves logical processing and reality-based conclusions.

- **Post Operational stage** (ages 11 and older)—Hypothetical and abstract reasoning emerges as the consistent, logical use of symbols allows for systematic processing that produces hypothetical possibilities. Relationships between objects and persons and philosophical debates become increasingly possible and of interest to the maturing person.

Two theorists, Lawrence Kohlberg and James Fowler, built on Piaget's cognitive theory and developed moral and spiritual development theories respectively.[6] By noting a child's ability to understand the concepts of same and different, how the relationship of two objects affect one another, the ability to consider what they can only imagine, and their increased ability to comprehend abstract ideas, a child's moral and spiritual development takes on a corresponding pattern of growth. Kohlberg's six-stage theory for moral development portrays a child's motivation to conform or nonconform to social expectations of right and wrong. Knowing these stages helps adults have appropriate expectations regarding a child's obedience and better understand a child's moral reasoning. It also helps the adults choose wisely in both how they reward or punish a child's behavior.

- **Preconventional Stage** (ages 3–7, childhood)
  Stage 1: avoid punishment
  Stage 2: obtain reward

- **Conventional Stage** (ages 8–13, most adolescents and adults)
  Stage 3: desire approval of others
  Stage 4: maintain law and order

- **Postconventional Stage** (adulthood or rarely attained)
  Stage 5: approve mutual benefit
  Stage 6: motivated by individual principles

Erik Erikson, a developmental psychologist and psychoanalyst, developed a psychosocial developmental stage theory that characterizes an age-appointed psychosocial crisis that negotiates a person's biological and sociocultural factors.[7] This eight-stage theory purports that successful negotiation of the crisis results in healthy ego and social development. For children, knowing what they are negotiating in their social and cultural environment explains why certain tasks are critical to their healthy psychological and emotional development. Knowing this allows the adult to encourage, discipline, and relate in ways that maximize the child's social potential. This directly affects how the child sees themselves and their relationship with God.

- **Infancy** (age 1)—trust vs mistrust; basis of hope and faith
- **Early Childhood** (1–3)—autonomy vs shame; basis of an independent will
- **Preschool** (3–5)—initiative vs guilt; formulate a purpose
- **School Age** (5–12)—industry vs inferiority; possess competency
- **Adolescence** (12–18)—ego identity vs role confusion; develop fidelity to self
- **Young Adulthood** (18–40)—intimacy vs isolation; pursue love
- **Middle Adulthood** (40–65)—generativity vs stagnation; distribute care
- **Older Adulthood** (65 plus)—ego integrity vs despair; share wisdom

Another way to understand a child's spiritual development is to delineate God's attributes and doctrines of faith according to what would be most influential to the child in light of their cognitive, moral, and psychosocial development. In a previous work, *God Never Changes . . . But My Family Always Does,* I determine which theological and spiritual truths are of most importance to create a strong theological foundation for faith and life by explaining the different doctrines, attributes, and functions of God in age-appropriate language, paying attention to a child's moral motivations and their psychosocial crises with virtue development.[8]

Infancy: prenatal through 12 months old—A parent/caregiver forms an attachment with their infant that provides the platform for further development. The virtues of faith and hope find their roots when infants are lovingly cared for in a faithful relationship with their parent/caregiver. These doctrines inform the relationship a parent/caregiver has with the infant child: the doctrine of the Trinity, God's faithfulness, and God's love.

- *Knowing God is triune* is to know that God is always in relationship with Himself, always fully present, and always fully aware of the relationship He has with Himself. He does not function apart from relationships.

- *Knowing God is faithful* shows us His constancy in character and function; as such, He is worthy of our complete trust.

- *Knowing God is love* allows us to feel, express, and experience love with God and one another as a sacrificial, all-encompassing, benevolent, and caring love.

Toddler: 2–3 years old—The curiosity of the child, their willful choices, and their need for reassurance are aptly addressed when parents mirror the sovereign authority of God in their home with clear expectations, boundaries, and consequences, bringing security to the child's life. Any authority that is effective must be good; a good parent/caretaker provides guidance in moral choices, develops the child to their greatest potential, and comforts during times of suffering. These doctrines inform the relationship a parent/caregiver has with the toddler: God's sovereignty, God's goodness, and God's graciousness.

- *Knowing God is sovereign* establishes His authority, His power, and His ability to help us; His sovereignty directly affects our moral choices, our faith, and our ability to handle suffering.

- *Knowing God is good* allows us to experience the joy and freedom that comes from obeying and trusting our heavenly Father.

- *Knowing God is gracious* draws us to His mercy and brings us simultaneously to repentance and relief.

Preschool: 3–5 years old—Having developed trust as infants and independence as toddlers, children now expand their imagination as preschoolers. Living in a world with justice promotes righteousness and wisdom, and structured environments promote peace. Advancing a preschooler's understanding of who God is requires us to embrace their own unique creativity and ignite their imagination. Knowing God is holy allows the preschooler to come to an awareness of their own sin and, subsequently, their need for a Savior. These doctrines inform the relationship a parent/caregiver has with the preschooler: God's justice, God as Creator, God's holiness.

- *Knowing God is just* allows us to see authority as having the right to rule, establish what is right and good, possess the ability to determine what is wise and true, and has the power to execute both reward and punishment.

- *Knowing God as Creator* embraces the intentional diversity of humanity, the innate creativity every person possesses, and that God as Creator has every right to tell His creation how to live.

When a child knows they have been fearfully and wonderfully made, they inherently recognize that the role of creator is a position of authority, which is to be acknowledged. Creation is held accountable to the one who has created them. God as Creator is outside of His creation and unchangeable in form and function. This is the immutable transcendent nature of God and allows the child to recognize that their life is not their own to live as they choose and indeed, they are accountable to submit and worship the One outside of themselves. God's right to instruct and demand obedience from His creation is within His right as God. The salvation message begins with this understanding of accountability of the creation to the Creator.

- *Knowing God is holy* leads to a knowledge of the gospel, starting with our need of a Savior due to our sin, the antithesis of God's perfection.

School Age: 6–10 years old—Those school-age children who have placed their faith in Christ are comforted by knowing God goes with them as they expand their circles of relationships at school, the neighborhood, and with more diverse friendships. Learning how to discern truth from falsehood helps children structure their world and understand reality. Seeing work as a divine responsibility changes how children approach their increased responsibilities in academics and at home. Children's emotions are increasingly diverse and expansive during these years. While these emotions influence and inform our thoughts and actions, they need not direct or dictate our behaviors and choices.

These doctrines inform the relationship a parent/caregiver has with the school-age child: God's immanence, God is truthful, God as the giver of both work and emotions.

- *Knowing God is immanent*, always present with His creation, engaging with believers in an intimate, emotional level brings comfort and security as school-age children expand their interaction with the world.

- *Knowing God always tells the truth* allows children to know they can always trust God to guide them in the right way through His promises, His will, His law, and how He has revealed Himself through Christ who proclaimed that He is "the way, the truth and the life" (John 14:6).

- *Knowing God is the author of work* enables children to move to a new level of understanding and ability that allows them to take on more responsibility and ownership of their world.

- *Knowing God is the author of our emotions* helps children enjoy, regulate, and understand all the new emotions they experience, allowing them to inform and influence their choices, but not dictate or demand them.

A systematic understanding of who God is in light of a child's development brings intentionality to how children are being introduced to God. A well thought-through plan of who God is and how He will be explained to children is necessary so they are not left in confusion, but are developing a comprehensive working knowledge of God.

When programming for groups of children as in a church's children's ministry or class, two main questions can be answered that will determine the classroom methods and curriculum chosen: (1) How does a child experience God? and (2) How does a child know God?

In his introduction to *Perspectives on Children's Spiritual Formation*, Michael Anthony, proposes that a child's spiritual formation can be best understood through the matrix created by Urban Holmes, which considers direct experience of prayer and spirituality, and David Kolb's Learning Cycle.[9] Acquiring and processing new information on scales of feeling to thinking and observing to doing creates a quadrant of possible pedagogical environments that explain different paradigms of children's ministry. Anthony depicts spiritual formation of children as "an interactive relationship between . . . experiencing and knowing (God)."[10]

FEELING (ACTIVE EXPRESSION) AND WATCHING/REFLECTION: CONTEMPLATIVE REFLECTIVE

This model is characterized by reflection, meditation, prayer, and storytelling; programming would include contemplation, godly play, and guided imagery. Quiet meditation with God's spirit so as to encounter Him in an awe-filled way strives to go beyond the teaching of biblical information into a purposeful and active pursuit of intimacy with God. This model follows Montessori pedagogical ideals and nurturing a child's faith within their own family and the church; most churches embracing this model adopt a covenantal theology of grace.

FEELING (ACTIVE EXPRESSION) AND ACTIVE PARTICIPATION: MEDIA DRIVEN ACTIVE ENGAGEMENT

The methods of creative expression characterized by high-energy movement and instructional technology (dramatic arts, video, and impacting music) allows children to be in motion and enjoy discovering truth. Teachers in this model are generally optimistic, look for innovative teaching methods, and spend time relating to their students more than studying the Bible to prepare a lesson. Technology and appealing to the culture are highly valued.

Thinking (Cognitive Reasoning) and Watching/Reflection: Instructional Analytic

Spiritual formation is nurtured through a study of God's Word as cognitive reasoning with systematic instruction and memorizing of God's Word are key. Time is spent looking to God's Word for answers to life's spiritual and daily matters, often referring to teachers and parents to confirm their theological interpretations and applications. Study and instruction of God's Word with an emphasis on Bible memorization is common.

Thinking (Cognitive Reasoning) and Active Participation: Pragmatic Participatory

This model uses choreographed singing, dramatic presentations of the Bible, various sensory experiences, and a mild use of technology. Fun is a driving value that encourages children to be actively involved in their learning while looking for practical applications of the Bible. Principles of Scripture with practical application is more important than memorization or exegetical study of the Bible, and learning styles guide the teacher's choice of instructional methodologies. Special needs children are intentionally included.

Determining what instructional methods should be used to instruct a child's faith is determined by which model an instructor adopts. Each model values something different based upon their understanding of how children think and experience God. A variety of auxiliary issues must also be addressed to determine which pedagogical paradigm is adopted:

- Technology Use
- Cultural Sensitivity
- Ethnic Distinctions
- Financial Investment
- Programming Considerations
- Volunteer Training and Availability
- Safety and Security Plans
- Curriculum Choices

Each of these issues are considered in light of the ministry model that has been adopted. The theology of the ministry seen in light of the philosophical considerations always precedes these issues. However, these issues must be discussed as methodologies for religious instruction are determined.

WHAT IS THE ROLE OF THE CHILD'S FAMILY IN THEIR FAITH FORMATION?

Parents are the primary nurturer of a child's faith. The author of Deuteronomy 6 commands parents to teach their children to love the Lord their God with all their heart, soul, and strength. Scripture uses language that tells parents to sharpen their children spiritually, impress the commandments on their heart, and whet the child's appetite for the things of God. Parents are commanded to avoid frustrating their children spiritually, which is a barrier to a child's faith.

It is not new that parents are called to live out their responsibility to parent their children in the faith faithfully. The eighteenth-century leader of America's Great Awakening, Jonathan Edwards, preached a "Farewell Sermon" to his New England congregation. In this last address, which urged the congregants to faithful living, he included these strong admonitions.

> Every Christian family ought to be as it were a little church, consecrated to Christ, and wholly influenced and governed by his rules. And family education and order are some of the chief of the means of grace. If these fail, all other means are likely to prove ineffectual. If these are duly maintained, all the means of grace will be likely to prosper and be successful. Let me now therefore, once more, before I finally cease to speak to this congregation, repeat, and earnestly press the counsel which I have often urged on the heads of families, while I was their pastor, to great painfulness in teaching, warning, and directing their children; bringing them up in the nurture and admonition of the Lord; beginning early, where there is yet opportunity, and maintaining constant diligence in labours of this kind.[11]

How can children's ministry partner with parents to help them fulfill God's mandate for them as disciplers of their children within the home? There are three primary Family Ministry models today: family-integrated, family-based, and family-equipped.

- **Family-Integrated** is intentionally designed to eliminate or minimize any age/stage programs or classrooms; children are not to be separated from their family, especially their parents. Children are with their parents, under their care and direction, during the corporate worship services and gatherings. Intergenerational discipleship is a value that places the responsibility of faith formation within the family, particularly fathers, in which one older generation nurtures and trains up the younger members of the family. Since the family has the responsibility to care for children spiritually, the church is an extension of the family.

- **Family-Based** embraces a church's programmatic structure and uses age/stage classes to nurture and equip the individual members of a family. Each ministry within the church intentionally seeks to find ways that bring generations together and minister to and with the family holistically. Parents are encouraged to get involved in the programs at the church that are developmentally designed for their children as a part of the parent's discipleship of the child.

- **Family-Equipped** provides intergenerational programming within a structure that equips parents as the primary disciplers of their children. Parents are held accountable for their efforts in discipleship. Graduated age/stage programs exist for the individual edification of the members within the family, but they are often structured within a larger goal of having families learn, serve, and worship together.

In addition to choosing a family ministry model that is compatible with the children's ministry, churches and ministries should consider families who experience distress. Such challenges families face are poverty, violence, addiction, abuse, and divorce. Reaching those in our communities who are hurting is a mandate of Scripture. Proverbs 31:8–9 says, "Open your mouth for the people who cannot speak, for the rights of all the unfortunate. Open your mouth, judge righteously, and defend the rights of the poor and needy." Orphans and children who are homeless are to be considered as well. "Pure and undefiled religion in the sight of our God and Father is this: to visit the orphans and widows in their distress, and to keep oneself unstained by the world" (James 1:27).

In the United States, foster care may be a civil program church members could consider as a viable way to reach these children. Providing resources, volunteering respite care, and serving in shelters are all community organizations that partner with churches. Adoption may be an option for some families as well. Families who open their homes to adopt children are served well by churches that support them in both practical and spiritual ways. There are many ways a ministry to children can choose to reach the families in their church and community. An intentional plan with much prayer that embraces the unique characteristics of the ministry can accomplish great feats in the kingdom of God.

WHAT IS THE ROLE OF THE CHURCH
IN THE DISCIPLESHIP OF CHILDREN AND THEIR FAMILIES?

A ministry to children cannot be viewed apart and separate from the local church body. Children who come to faith in Christ are members of this family and as such, have brothers and sisters of the faith. Attending worship services, prayer, and Bible study are all part of being spiritually shepherded, and alongside these normative educational opportunities is the participation in the church ordinances of baptism and the Lord's Supper.

Both ordinances are an expression of the church's theology and are under the direction of the elders and pastors. Parents and children are to be instructed in how the church teaches and encourages participation in the ordinances. No matter whether the child partakes of the ordinance or not, an understanding of the key theological practices of the church matures their faith.

Scripture teaches that all believers have spiritual gifts and the Bible commands all believers to use their gifts for the benefit of the church. If given an opportunity, children can serve in unique and valuable ways within the body. Serving alongside mature believers in the church family encourages the child to see themselves as a part of the kingdom.

Like all believers, when children come to faith in Christ they are transferred from the kingdom of darkness to the kingdom of light (Col. 1:13). The kingdom of light is established by God and He is the sovereign, eternal ruler over all creation (Ps. 103:19). The kingdom of God also refers to the rule God has over our spiritual life that resides in our heart. Repentance is required to enter this kingdom that Jesus declared was not of this world (Matt. 4:17; John 18:36). When we repent, we are born again into it (John 3:3). Children who place their faith in Christ are kingdom kids. They are sons and daughters of the King and in this exalted position, they have acquired a formidable enemy (Satan). Teaching children who they are in Christ, how to fight the temptations of the evil one, and to stand in victory through the inevitable battles of spiritual warfare is the battle cry of every children's ministry. From the youngest ones among us, may we train them up in the way they should go (Prov. 22:6). And in the end, may they come to know, love, and serve God for their whole life.

NOTES

1. D. L. Moody, cited in Jean Piaget, *Science of Education and the Psychology of the Child* (New York: Viking, 1970).

2. "D.L. Moody," n.d., https://www.moody.edu/about/our-bold-legacy/d-l-moody/.

3. Richard Baxter, *The Godly Home*, ed. Randall J. Pederson (Wheaton, IL: Crossway, 2010), 116.

4. Keeper of the Home, "Eliza Spurgeon: Legacy of an Apt and Godly Helper," August 9, 2011, https://www.moody.edu/about/our-bold-legacy/d-1 -moody/.

5. Piaget, *Science of Education and the Psychology of the Child*.

6. Lawrence Kohlberg, *The Psychology of Moral Development: The Nature and Validity of Moral Stages* (San Francisco: Harper & Row, 1984) and James W. Fowler, *Stages of Faith: The Psychology of Human Development and the Quest for Meaning* (San Francisco: Harper & Row, 1981).

7. E.H. Erikson, *Childhood and Society* (New York: Norton, 1950).

8. Elizabeth Smith, *God Never Changes . . . But My Family Always Does* (self-pub., 2019).

9. Michael J. Anthony, "Introduction—Putting Children's Spirituality in Perspective," in *Perspectives on Children's Spiritual Formation: Four Views*, ed. Michael J. Anthony (Nashville: Broadman & Holman Publishers, 2006), 32.

10. Ibid., 33.

11. Jonathan Edwards, *A Farewell Sermon*, Sermon Chapbook Series (Minneapolis: Curiosmith Bookshop, 2011), 56.

Ministering to Teenagers and Leading a Youth Ministry

TIM DOWNEY

We learn to talk as we mimic our parents and others. We attend school for the sole purpose of learning information from others that would otherwise be overwhelming to learn independent of our teachers. We learn to drive as others patiently— and sometimes not so patiently!—teach us in the finer skills of maneuvering three and a half tons of metal at high rates of speed. The list goes on. If we genuinely desire to excel in an area of life, it will typically require the investment of another. Certainly that is true of young people, who have not yet formed all their beliefs and attitudes, and who are looking for others to guide them.

One of the difficult things about ministry, not to mention life in general, is that the future is unknown. The phrase "hindsight is 20/20" is repeated often when people look back on decisions they regret. In effect, had they known then what they know now, they would have done something different. Fortunately, a person can learn from the life experiences and wisdom of others who have gone before them. This chapter will offer a voice of experience, guidance, and hard-earned lessons to support those currently working in youth ministry or seeking to start a youth ministry.

PERSONAL CHARACTER OF A YOUTH MINISTER

There are many characteristics that should define the person who seeks to shepherd students to know and follow Christ. The first of those characteristics is to be a genuine disciple of Jesus. While it may seem obvious that the one who pastors students should be a disciple of Jesus, that fact is frequently assumed rather than investigated. Too often questions regarding the strategy of ministry and chemistry of relational connection drive the decision of who will lead the youth ministry. Being a kid magnet, or "rock star personality," are of little to no importance in the decision of who should shepherd students within a ministry. Characteristics such as those have driven the decision of who is selected for youth ministry positions far too often. Having a magnetic personality can be useful in God's hands but can also often bring the trappings of egotism. A better defining characteristic is having the "fragrance of Christ" (2 Cor. 2:15). That fragrance can be sensed through one who is: Spirit-filled (Eph. 5:18), humble (1 Peter 3:8), biblically grounded (2 Tim. 2:15), respectful of others (1 Peter 2:17), filled with love for one another (1 John 4:7–11), and desiring to serve with no recognition (Gal. 5:13).

The second characteristic that should define a youth pastor is simply having a deep, godly affection for students. Having a godly love for students will enable the youth pastor to persevere during difficult experiences that inevitably come during life and ministry. More importantly, loving students well is key to caring for the whole student. It is not enough to merely indoctrinate students into the faith. Students should have caring adults who will journey with them through the many pains and difficulties of adolescence. Students are hardwired to sniff out leaders who do not genuinely love them. Being a youth pastor in hopes that it will lead to becoming a senior pastor is a tragedy that manipulates students as pawns in a field test. The church should never knowingly allow a person of this mindset to be responsible for the spiritual welfare of students. Surely, there are times when youth pastors will transition from one ministry position to another, but using the position of youth pastor as a goal toward something else, reveals the heart of the potential leader (and church), and a fundamental misunderstanding of youth ministry and the students who comprise it.

Crawford Loritts makes an insightful comment about the character of a leader in his book *Leadership as an Identity: The Four Traits of Those Who Wield Lasting Influence*, when he writes about the necessity of brokenness in the life of a leader. "Brokenness is a conscious, core awareness that you need God in all things. A broken person has come to realize that he is nothing and can do nothing apart from God's presence and enabling power."[1] Brokenness is not a characteristic that we often think of being constant in our lives, yet Loritts' explanation of the word drives at the heart of pride. It is essential for any disciple of Christ to be reminded daily of the need for complete dependence upon the work of the Spirit.

PHILOSOPHY OF YOUTH MINISTRY

When the term *philosophy* is introduced into a conversation about ministry, it tends to be provocative. Some interpret philosophy as something to be wrestled with in the world of academia and of little use in the real world. While philosophical discussions without boundaries can indeed lead to endless contemplation with no realization of actions, this should not prevent healthy discourse regarding the values that drive the ministry. Ministry that seldom or never reviews the values and philosophy that drives those values, will likely be influenced more by trends than truths.

Developing a biblically informed philosophy for youth ministry requires an honest review of the historical account of God's work in and through youth in Scripture. Is the spiritual formation of adolescents demonstrated within the pages of Scripture? A brief overview of key biblical characters during the days of their youth is beneficial to the subject.

Scripture frequently reminds us of the receptivity of youth to God, how they were regularly empowered by God for His purposes, and the importance of the personal investment by adults and spiritual caregivers. Dave Keehn addresses the topic of God's calling to youth:

> Whether you hold onto "Sunday School assumptions" that Samuel was a small child when God called to him or was a Jr. High aged-teenager as Josephus states is of small consequence, either way—God spoke to Samuel, calling him to follow, obey and serve the Almighty God in his youth, not just later when he was an adult. God was not designating Samuel for "assignments to be determined later." When Samuel was "old and gray," he testifies himself that it was from the time of his youth that he was a leader for the people of Israel (1 Sam. 12:2). This word "youth" is *na'uwr*, used to describe "early life." Another example of God calling young people to serve Him is Joshua, who was Moses' aid since "youth" [*běchurowth*] (Numbers 11:28).[2]

Luke tells the story of Jesus as a twelve-year-old "sitting in the midst of the teachers, both listening to them and asking them questions" (Luke 2:46) as He prepared to lead in religious services among the Jewish community at age thirteen. The spiritual mentoring of adolescents by religious leaders and the community at-large has been a historical precedent for several millennia within the Jewish, as well as Christian, cultures.

There are many examples recorded in Scripture of characters like Joseph (Gen. 39), David (1 Sam. 17), Daniel and his friends (Dan. 1), Christ's disciples, who are generally perceived as youth,[3] and likely several of the disciples of Paul, who were responsive to the calling of God during their youth, and as a result, became key characters within God's redemptive plan.

Therefore, as a philosophy of youth ministry is developed, those who are responsible for the spiritual formation of students must appreciate that students in early and middle adolescence are more receptive to God than at any other time in their lives. God often calls youth to be and do things that will require nothing less than absolute surrender to the Spirit. Consequently, youth should be discipled in the faith by spiritually mature adults (which includes parents), who will spiritually invest, challenge, and engage them in significant responsibilities for the sake of Christ's kingdom on earth. To marginalize, isolate, or otherwise assume youth are too immature or incapable, will only create a seedbed for the growth of such unbiblical thinking.

The Great Commission to make disciples and to teach them to obey everything Christ commanded (Matt. 28:18–20), should be the guiding principle of youth ministry. The astute youth pastor will routinely evaluate the strategies that are being utilized within the youth ministry by asking this very honest and weighty question: Are these methods making disciples who obey the teachings of Christ? The Great Commission could be summed up in two memorable points: *ownership* of the faith and *perseverance* in the faith. Ministry to youth would do well to create laser focused approaches that seek to accomplish these two focal points.

While there may be various methods that *intend* to meet the goal of making disciples who own the faith and persevere in the faith, the evaluative lens should always be: is this activity, event, ministry, accomplishing or leading toward the goal? If not, then the wise youth leader will need to make the sometimes difficult, but necessary decision to end such a method, regardless of its popularity to students or leaders. The objective of the youth pastor should be to *make disciples*; not the *making of activities* that seldom produce fruit that remains (John 15:16). Keep in mind, programs are to serve people, not the other way around.

A note of caution regarding the evaluative processes should be made here. Without careful, sincere evaluation, the tendency of any ministry will be toward justification. The drift toward the familiar is innate. Lack of change can be strangely compelling. Proof is found in how often one sits in the same area during a church worship service, drives the same route to work, or holds a toothbrush with the same hand. For example, imagine a youth ministry that has a longstanding precedent of participating in a summer camp. The students always love the event and even bring their friends to it. The gospel is always clearly communicated at camp, great discussions ensue, tears are shed, yet fruit that remains is nearly nonexistent. After camp, there is seldom connection with students and families who are not followers of Christ. Truthfully, the students who are not disciples of Christ are often never seen again, except for the occasional youth event. The typical measurement to use in evaluating this camp may be to merely look at the number of students who attend the camp and the enthusiasm that the camp generates. Instead, the better method of evaluation would be to determine if in fact disciples, who *own* the faith and *persevere* in the faith, are being made through the camp. The use of quantitative metrics in the evaluation of any ministry is perfectly fine, if quantities reveal the qualitative results of making disciples.

PRACTICES OF YOUTH MINISTRY

With a biblical philosophy as a foundation, there are a few essential practices that every youth ministry should consistently employ. Focusing on other, less important practices will, in time, undoubtedly divert the attention of even the most seasoned veteran.

UNDERSTANDING AND ADVOCACY

The need for understanding and advocacy for youth is an essential ingredient within every church. The evidence is scattered throughout every church, on every continent on the globe, where adolescents have been forgotten, marginalized, or otherwise seen as an annoyance. The realization of such faulty thinking is often discovered too late and the church must close its doors due to the dying of its congregants and irrelevancy in the culture.

Every church must persistently seek to understand the unique challenges that each generation of students encounter within the cultures they reside. The church must refuse to presume that the plights of the present generation of students is no different than previous ones. In fact, each generation is facing increasingly multifaceted obstacles due in large part to the ever-growing effects of social media, deconstruction of the family, accessibility of pornography, and the rejection of and animosity toward Christianity and its values within Western culture. Understanding alone is not enough though. In addition, advocacy for students should be one of the principal characteristics within the church. Discovering or creating means by which the church can involve, mentor, and champion the journey of students is an essential ingredient in the overall emotional and spiritual well-being of the adolescent.

DISCIPLESHIP AND MENTORING

Unfortunately, all too often youth ministry in the local church is still relegated to an attractional model that, in fact, is not attractive, not to mention ineffective in making disciples. One of the most troublesome issues with the attractional model in youth ministry is that it leaves the impression that the experience in youth group is what should be expected in the church worship service, leaving students with a sense of disillusionment when they seek to find that model in a church during or after college. There are not very many church worship services that begin with interactive games and end with a fifteen-minute talk that focuses on teen issues.

The primary need, as well as desire, of most students is to have a caring adult in their lives whom they can trust to be mentored by during the challenges of early and middle adolescence. Optimally, the primary person would be a godly parent. In addition to a godly parent, students need other spiritually mature adults who become trusted sources of wisdom and counsel, who often also echo the perspectives of their Christian parents. This support system of godly parents and other adults in the lives of students creates a fertile soil in which seeds can be planted and healthy spiritual fruit can emerge. We see that network of spiritual mentors reflected in the life of Jesus in Luke 2, as mentioned above. Unfortunately, not every student who comes to church has a Christian parent, or a parent who is spiritually mature and willing to invest heavily into their children. Those students must be discipled by caring spiritual surrogates who will love them and invest time and spiritual resources on their behalf. Imagine what would have happened had the early church in Acts had the attitude of "it is too bad that Saul (Paul) does not have godly parents to mentor him in the faith; he might have amounted to something with his background in Judaism." It is unimaginable that Saul would have been left on his own without Barnabas, or someone else, mentoring him in the faith (Acts 9, 11) considering the spiritual climate within the context of the first century church. Within the current post-Christian context of America, students will seldom produce fruit that remains apart from mentoring adults in their lives.

Mentoring, or discipling, can take different forms during the adolescent years. Sometimes the mentor can be a caring adult who simply shows interest in the student. Engaging a student in light conversation by asking about the recital, game, or other interest of the student, or attending an event in which the student has a role communicates significantly to the student. This kind of attention by a trusted thoughtful adult can have lasting influence.

Another type of mentoring could be in the form of attending camp, a mission trip, or other extended event of the youth ministry. These types of investments can often be watershed experiences in the lives of students. During events like these students are more apt to be themselves, rather than seeking to be or act in ways that gain the approval from their peers. Honesty and measured vulnerability by the student are more likely over extended ministry events. These times can often afford meaningful conversations and begin building bridges into the lives of students for years to come. Students do not quickly forget the role that adults play in their lives through these experiences.

Discipleship in the form of small groups or one-on-one meetings is a long-term, intentional type of mentoring. Through meeting weekly, the wise mentor focuses on the following: spiritual training (2 Tim. 3:16–17; Eph. 4:12–15) by studying Scripture with the students; the practice of thoughtful and reflective prayer individually and collectively; the development of iron sharpening relationships (Prov. 27:17) that include accountability and honest communication that flows between the adult and students; and the support of caring relationships where appropriate vulnerability can thrive.

Finally, the wise youth leader should consider apprenticeships, internships, or residencies as opportunities to disciple students who wish to become leaders, either vocationally or avocationally within the church setting. The primary purpose of the apprenticeship should be to develop and disciple young leaders toward becoming mature followers of Christ, who will make disciples. Honing one's skills in homiletics or administrative skills is good, unless being discipled by loving, caring men and/or women of the faith is absent. If the apprenticeship does not produce fruit that lasts (John 15:16), it is of no value. Apprentices should first and foremost be discipled to abide in Christ.

With a clear commitment toward discipleship, apprenticeships can be extremely useful tools in the hands of wise youth leaders when used to develop character, competency, and leadership capacities within the life of a young man or woman of God. These learning environments should be filled with opportunities to learn through active participation in planning, teaching, discipling, and, as appropriate, decision-making. The young mentee should feel some of the weight of the responsibilities they are given, while at the same time provided a safety net by the youth pastor. Note though, that overloading the apprentice with unreasonable or excessive tasks should never be practiced. Help the apprentice to discover and leverage his or her gifts/skills to spread his or her wings in those areas. At the same time, help identify the apprentice's weaknesses and develop a performance improvement plan, and then hold him or her accountable to improve.

One of the keys to success through an apprenticeship is a seasoned youth pastor who will ensure that the mentee is provided with adequate training and stated expectations. Simply assigning a responsibility to an apprentice without training to thrive within the area, is a sign of an inexperienced leader. The knowledgeable leader will take the necessary steps to ensure that the apprentice understands his or her role, responsibilities, and is well prepared to excel. Coupled with training the youth pastor must outline defined boundaries and expectations for the apprentice. Often conflict happens around undefined or misunderstood expectations. The clearer the expectations, the greater the chance of success for the mentee.

WELL-EQUIPPED VOLUNTEERS

Committed, well-equipped volunteers are important to any church. They quite literally carry the load for the ministry. Within the setting of youth ministry, volunteers who understand the developmental characteristics of students, and are fully equipped and capable of engaging with students at a heart level, are literally indispensable. It is nearly impossible for a lone youth pastor to disciple, counsel, equip, and engage in ministry more than eight-to-ten students. At any given time, a group of students might be experiencing depression, divorce of their parents, bullying by peers, anxiety over academics, etc. In addition to the emotional challenges that are consistently present, there is the weight of equipping each of the students in the Word of God and prayer, with an aim toward serving Christ's church to make disciples of others. For these reasons, and many more, volunteer recruitment must be done with excellence. Without question, finding faithful, potentially effective volunteers can sometimes be a significant amount of work. Remember that excellence does not come easily. It is far more difficult to deal with dreadful volunteers than it is to put in the time and work to find and equip ideal volunteers. Hiring is much easier than firing, especially with volunteers.

Before seeking to recruit volunteers, the youth pastor would do well to study the Scriptures to identify the essential characteristics that should be evident in the life of any youth volunteer. While the volunteer may not be an elder as described in the New Testament, it would be wise to consider the elder qualifications as a place to begin making a profile of the qualified volunteer (1 Tim. 3; Titus 1; 1 Peter 5). Seek the counsel of those wiser in the faith, especially veteran youth pastors who have a respected history in the ministry. Once you have developed a profile for the desired volunteer, keep in mind that it is a guideline for potential recruits into the ministry, not a list of requirements. Very few individuals will meet all the characteristics, but good candidates will align with many or even most of the reasonable qualifications.

Once the profile for a volunteer is created, it is time to begin thinking about how to begin to recruit the right person(s). While the typical route would be to simply place an announcement in the weekly church handout, PowerPoint, or make a verbal announcement during the weekend services, a word of caution is needed before using this method. When a general announcement is made asking for people to volunteer to work with students, that means that anyone might volunteer. Just think about that for a moment. Do the students need just whoever is first to volunteer? Absolutely not. So, use extreme caution when making announcements, since one might get more than one is prepared to receive.

The following procedures in the "hiring" process of volunteers may, to some, seem a bit overboard, especially if the youth ministry is in a small church setting. The natural inclination for most leaders is to assume that everyone is well known and there is no need for a formal process in the onboarding of youth volunteers. While the tendency to simply trust everyone is understood (after all these are brothers and sisters in Christ), the current cultural complexities require that churches maintain due diligence in protecting students, as well as the congregation at large. That being stated, require that all candidates complete a thorough application for the volunteer position. If the church does not have a current application to use as a draft, one can easily be found to download online. It is recommended that the application include the following: biographical information, employment history, ministry serving experience, church membership/attendance over the past 5–7 years, names and contact information for three references within the church, and permission to conduct a criminal background check. There are numerous services that are of minimal cost.

Once the application and reference check are completed, set up a time and place to meet with the volunteer candidate to interview them for the position. Even if the candidate is already known, meeting together for the sole purpose to talk over the application and the responsibilities of the volunteer role is extremely important. By setting a formal interview the youth pastor communicates the importance of the role and the weightiness of serving Christ. As you interview the person ask open-ended questions and listen carefully for answers that prompt further questions. Be careful not to ignore those cues. If you allow a person to talk long enough, eventually they will reveal their core values. Knowing the core values of a person is significant when it comes to onboarding people into ministry roles.

A final thought for the interview process may be to consider some sort of profile assessment to aid in the matching of gifts, skills, and abilities to the role within the ministry. There are numerous such assessments available today. A word of coaching regarding the use of assessments would be prudent here. Assessments, regardless of which one, provide nothing more than tendencies based upon the answers provided to questions. While they can be very helpful in providing general inclinations, none of them consider the work of the Spirit in the life of a believer. The Spirit within the life of a Christ follower is powerful. With that in mind, remember that a person's tendency or inclination, is often greatly affected in positive ways by God. Our propensity is to place far too much emphasis on our abilities and resources, and far too little on God's.

LEADING WELL

Near the beginning of this chapter the character of the youth pastor was addressed. Character provides the fertile soil from which the fruit of leading well may emerge. Leading well is more than simply executing best practices from the latest leadership book. There are numerous topics to be addressed within the subject of leadership. Here, we will focus simply on one piece of the puzzle called leadership.

Anyone who is disciplined enough and driven enough can practice leadership methods. While many of those well proven methods can be helpful in leading others, without a heart that loves God and others, a willingness to serve with humility, accept position, and submit to authority, *none* of what the leader does will be of eternal value.

The challenge for anyone who desires to lead is that everyone answers to someone, eventually. Often when we think of leading, we think of the leader who does what she wants, how she wants it, and answers to no one. News flash: Those people eventually either end up in jail or worse. No one gets to call all the shots, and if they do, it is not for long, because sooner or later that person will be corrected, caught, or fired.

Leading well will require understanding and embracing the motto "leading while following" that I have used for years or, as some have called it, "second chair leadership." Leading while following requires that we recognize that if we truly wish to have godly influence for the duration, we must embrace the reality that our ideas are not the best ideas, they are just our ideas. We must embrace that our approaches, designs, strategies, and tactics are not new and they are not the best, at least most of the time. When there is a willingness to step back and serve, especially when it matters most, we place ourselves in a position of trusting God's sovereignty. And when we trust God above our insights, above the decisions of others, we place ourselves in the position of experiencing the hand of God, instead of the genius of man. Every day that is set before us has opportunities to either build trust or destroy trust. What we do in a moment of tension between doing things expeditiously and righteously defines us. What we do reveals the true nature of our heart. Unless we are willing to submit to our authorities we will never develop credibility, which will create a glass ceiling that we will never be able to burst through. Does change need to happen in your church? Change absolutely needs to happen. Every home, church, organization, and life needs change. Yet how we respond in the moment of tension will directly impact whether we even have a voice at the table.

Please understand what is *not* being written here. This is not a plea to never speak up or give an opinion. The youth pastor should absolutely be willing to speak up, stand up, and engage in the conversation. But, while doing so, be mindful that your voice is one of many. Your ideas and opinions may often be good, but they are not the *only* ideas, and they most assuredly are not divinely authoritative. Choose to be a person who leads while following. Choose to submit to the authorities God has placed in your life. Seldom do senior leaders become heretics or morally bankrupt requiring youth ministers to become the prophet crying in the wilderness.

Choose to be a model of humility, service, grace, and love. Decide to be the person who will learn from others with decades more wisdom, and recognize that their ideas are usually not wrong, they are simply a different means to the same end. This can at first be challenging, with practice, it becomes easier in the future.

PLAN OF YOUTH MINISTRY

When referring to the plan of youth ministry, this section will address the curriculum plan rather than the plan of activities. A curriculum plan is the plan of Bible study that is needed for the students. One of the primary responsibilities of the youth pastor is to ensure that correct or sound Bible doctrine (teaching) is being taught to students (Titus 2:1; 2 Tim. 1:13; 1 Tim. 4:16). The youth pastor must prayerfully evaluate the spiritual climate of the students within the care of the church. What do the students need to know about God, the Bible, doctrines, key characters in Scripture, significant stories within the Bible, spiritual life, conduct of a Christian?

Block off a day and gather together key individuals with different perspectives to speak into the youth ministry plan of teaching. Spend time carefully thinking through these types of questions. Afterwards, filter through all that was suggested and synthesize the primary and secondary targets for teaching.

After identifying core teaching content, research Bible study materials that may be purchased online or through a local Christian bookstore. Determine if there are resources in the marketplace that could be used to address specific areas of teaching. There are some resources that are quality products. However, the informed youth pastor will thoroughly read and evaluate those resources prior to using them for teaching the Bible to students.

There are a few primary tests for any Bible study materials to pass before purchasing. First, does the publisher and the specific resource align with the church's theological beliefs? Are there doctrines supported within the material that do not align doctrinally with the church? Second, does the material have a scope and sequence that maps out the teaching of primary doctrines of Scripture, provides a plan of teaching through each book of the Bible, and addresses the primary life issues and concerns of the adolescent? Finally, is the resource easy to follow for the student and the teacher?

Remember, the goal is to teach students the Bible and the truths and principles contained within the Bible that are essential for life change. So, whether the study resources are purchased or written by the youth pastor or someone else capable, choose to stay on target with needs that were pinpointed by the group early in the planning process. Choose not to give in to convenience over content.

PEOPLE OF YOUTH MINISTRY

Students are not the only concern of the youth pastor. There are several different groups within the sphere of youth ministry of a local church. Each group of people noted below must be continually considered and engaged at varying levels. Failure to recognize the significance of each group will have lasting negative consequences.

STUDENTS

Earlier in the chapter advocacy for teens was discussed. With the idea of advocating for students in mind, a very simple and yet fundamental point must be made toward the youth pastor and all those who would seek to serve within youth ministry settings. A genuine, God-honoring love for students is an absolute, indispensable quality for anyone who might aspire to work with students in ministry. Within the leader there must be a heart cry that longs for the student to know Jesus as Savior and Lord, and a determination to walk alongside the student during this stage of life. The leader must understand or be willing to understand the formidable challenges that each student faces, and extend compassion toward them as they walk the path before them.

The youth pastor should never fill a position merely to learn how to be a pastor. Student ministry is not a lab, and students are not lab rats that can be used to practice for "real ministry." Students must be cared for, loved, and mentored in the faith. A constant turnover from one youth pastor to the next should never be the norm. Youth pastors must commit to the church, the students, and most importantly to God to remain faithful despite sometimes challenging people or circumstances.

PARENTS

Once a naïve, young youth pastor who had recently attended a fine Christian college (and did not major in youth ministry) joined a church staff immediately upon graduation. After about a year on staff, the youth pastor identified what he believed to be a significantly needed change in the programming side of the ministry. The youth pastor came to his staff supervisor (me) with his idea of the needed change. He was given permission to begin planning for the change but would first need to communicate with the parents of students what was about to take place. It was not necessary to gain the approval of the parents, but merely inform them of the impending change. Upon hearing this, the young youth pastor exclaimed, "I don't need to tell the parents. This is my ministry and they are my students." You might be smiling at his audacity, but I can assure you, I was not smiling when he said this to me. It was more a look of utter confusion. I then reminded him that the students were the children of the parents and they were not his students. He was then instructed to notify the parents of the change and set up an informational meeting for the parents of students.

Depending upon the demographics of the church served, there is likely a large percentage of families with adolescents represented. One of the key responsibilities of the youth pastor is to provide support to families of teens. More than any other developmental stage of life, parents need all the support than can find during the teenage years. The stages of early and middle adolescence are not only trying for parents, but these years can also be especially difficult for the teens themselves. From hormones to homework, the years between ages eleven to eighteen have the potential to be the most life-altering, for better or for worse. Understanding that tension, for both the parents and the students, is of monumental importance for the youth pastor. The wise youth pastor will do everything possible to support the family unit during these tumultuous years.

One of the responsibilities of any youth pastor is to join with parents and work together to provide teaching in sound doctrine, discipleship environments that produce transformation, and opportunities to serve Christ within the church and around the world. It is essential that every youth pastor fully embrace that the role of Christian parents is to teach their children about God and His commands (Deut. 6:6–7; 11:19), and it is the role of the church to equip students (and others) to do the work of ministry (Eph. 4:12–16). Together youth pastors and parents can be a formidable force to influence the lives of students toward godly futures.

It is worth noting here again that there are many students that belong to local churches without their parents. In these cases, it is equally essential that godly families and youth pastors work together even more intentionally to provide spiritual surrogates for those students who do not have Christian parents. In some communities, this may be more commonplace. Reaching parents and families that are not Christian presents unique challenges that require different tactics. While the approach may need adjusting depending on the demographics, the core principles of discipling, mentoring, caring, and loving students and parents must be key practices. As youth pastors create and sustain healthy partnerships with parents, it is much more likely that there will be many years of productive ministry.

VOLUNTEERS

Developing long-term, godly relationships with the youth ministry volunteers should never be overlooked. Volunteers are the key support systems within any ministry of the church. Creating and sustaining trusting bonds between the leader and volunteers cannot be overemphasized. Spend time having meals together, praying together, and caring for one another. The volunteers of the youth ministry should be extended family for the youth pastor. We have gone on vacations with our volunteers. We have been there when their children were born and when their children got married. We have forged seemingly impenetrable relationships with them over a period of decades. Volunteers should be your greatest ally and vice versa. It has been stated by some that staff should not become too close to volunteers within the church due to the potential of conflict when difficult decisions need to be made. Friendships may interfere with duty to the church. However, nowhere in Scripture is this kind of distancing encouraged. Instead we are commanded to love one another and share our lives together (1 Thess. 2:7–8). From this author's perspective, that is simply the risks of relationships. Lean in, love well, and care well for your volunteers. It will change their lives and yours.

COMMUNITY

Youth ministry is busy. Every day there is someone to meet with, something to plan, a Bible teaching to prepare. Without intentionality it would be quite easy for youth pastors to become isolated from the community where they live. Yet the community is where the youth pastor should be known and seen. While we know that Jesus frequently withdrew to be alone (Luke 5:16), He is most often seen in the Gospels being present with people in the marketplace, the temple, people's homes, amongst people who needed God. So also, the youth pastor must be in the community, serving in schools, connecting with social services, attending athletic games and recitals, going wherever students or their parents might be. Being present in the community and known by the community is one of most beneficial uses of the youth pastor's time.

OTHER YOUTH PASTORS

One of the most rewarding relationships for youth pastors is other youth pastors. They understand the complexities of youth ministry better than other staff, parents, or even a spouse. Other youth pastors are in the trenches with adolescents and parents and can be a breath of fresh air with their keen ability to truly grasp the daily challenges faced. In addition, they can sometimes offer new insight, support, and wise counsel that is often hard to find from others. These relationships can become iron sharpening iron relationships (Prov. 27:17) that help the youth pastor stay focused and not lose hope when difficulties arise. Make it a goal to seek out other youth pastors with similar values and begin building relationships with them. Some of those relationships will last a lifetime!

The Next Youth Pastor

Inevitably, whether in ten years or forty years, a person will leave the position they presently hold. Passing the baton well to one's replacement is one of the humblest acts of service a youth pastor can ever provide for students. Setting up one's successor well will require constructing an efficient system of ministry that comprises excellent people and proven processes. Systems and processes have not been discussed in this chapter, but the book *Management Essentials for Christian Ministries* by Anthony and Estep or Mark DeVries' book, *Sustainable Youth Ministry*, are invaluable resources to use while developing effective systems and processes for youth ministry.

Beyond excellent people and efficient systems, the departing youth pastor can and should prepare the students and parents for the transition, regardless of the reason for departure. Changes are difficult for the students. Emotional and spiritual bonds have been built, and students have difficulty thinking rationally over emotionally. Helping students understand why the transition must take place and how they may benefit from it are pivotal. Coach the students through how they can support the next youth pastor. In preparing the ministry well for transition, we do a great service to the church and the students.

CONCLUSION

The intent of this chapter is to provide some foundational practices for how to effectively minister to teenagers and lead a youth ministry with excellence in the sight of God. The responsibilities of leading a ministry can sometimes seem overwhelming. Often those who lead in youth ministry are in the early stages of adulthood, and their new role can be intimidating. While some insecurity will go away with time, it is essential to remember the encouraging words of Paul to his young mentee, Timothy: "Let no one look down on your youthfulness, but rather in speech, conduct, love, faith, and purity, show yourself an example of those who believe" (1 Tim. 4:12). With inexperience there is the potential to either question ourselves to the point of being immobile, or obsessively control things resulting in pushing others away. A delicate balance of loosely holding things is best understood in Proverbs 16:9, "The mind of a person plans his way, but the LORD directs his steps." God is ultimately in control of His ministry.

NOTES

1. Crawford W. Loritts, *Leadership as an Identity: The Four Traits of Those Who Wield Lasting Influence* (Chicago: Moody Publishers, 2009). 36.

2. Dave Keehn, "Biblical Mandate for Youth Ministry (Part 2): Youth Ministry in the Old Testament," *The Good Book Blog*, Biola University, February 15, 2012, https://www.biola.edu/blogs/good-book-blog/2012/biblical-mandate-for-youth-ministry-part-2-youth-ministry-in-the-old-testament.

3. Otis Cary and Frank Cary, "How Old Were Christ's Disciples?," *The Biblical World* 50, no. 1 (1917): 3–12, https://doi.org/10.1086/475815.

Leading a Young Adults Ministry

KIRK S. BAKER

Every age demographic has its own set of contextual realities to navigate, and each stage of life produces unique dynamics that we must process, learn, or embrace. While this is so, whether we're talking about toddlers learning to walk or retirees exploring where to spend their extra time, young adults are faced with certain areas more acutely during these years of 18 to 30 than at other times of life. They are in one of most transitional and formative junctures they will ever face. Everything is open to being explored—the theology and culture of the church in which they grew up, the type of person they want to marry or if they want to marry at all, discerning educational and career paths, and moving toward financial independence from parents and taking their place in the fully adult world.

In this chapter we'll explore issues of particular interest concerning young adults for the purpose of developing a framework of effective ministry to those in this pivotal stage of life.

AREAS OF DEVELOPMENT

IDENTITY AND IDEALS

The identity of young adults is being solidified and challenged in a variety of ways. The person they thought themselves to be in high school or college is being tested. Whether one was known as a good student or a star athlete, as a rebel or the life of the party, these personas become increasingly exposed, revealing their fragility and instability as a foundation from which to build a solid adult identity. Exploration is common and to be expected, but young adults require helpful examples and conversation partners in their identity formation process.

For example, a young person may want to live a life of service, perhaps helping with relief efforts in developing countries or working in a challenging urban area, but soon discovers the complexities often associated with these ventures. Such tension can become a great opportunity and teacher, or it can drive a person toward discouragement and apathy. Young adults, whose minds are still developing, are therefore becoming aware of the gap between their stated ideals and their functional reality. This creates a unique opportunity and prime avenue for those walking alongside young adults for strategic engagement in their processes of discipleship, mindfulness, and self-discovery in discerning their place and purpose in the world.

RELATIONSHIPS

Relationships during the young adult years seem to be a key area where God is up to transformative work. From roommate situations to dating relationships to leadership opportunities, there are many lessons to be learned in how healthy relationships function. Opportunities are plentiful for leaning into difficult relational tensions and working through them, rather than pulling the plug and walking away when things become difficult.

EDUCATION

Many young adults who attend college begin to ask questions for which they do not yet have answers. This is not only the basis of good education, but it also propels them more deeply into their faith journey. Engaging in higher education as a Christ follower aims not only to provide answers to questions and issues, but to serve as a foundation for faithfulness in all of life. Not least, this foundation must take into account one's desires, affections, and habits, which form the basis for a faithful way of life.

SPIRITUAL CONVICTION

The young adult years serve as a realm where individuals can begin to unpack their spiritual heritage and chart the course ahead. It is healthy to reflect deeply over what we have been given and taught, to appreciate it, and to honestly assess how our spiritual background fits alongside many other options being presented. Congruence with and fidelity to our deeply held beliefs and convictions becomes the priority, rather than simply accepting pat answers or conforming to a kind of rigid behaviorism. The young adult season provides the opportunity to develop a thoughtfully integrated faith, engaging with the world around them.

DISTINCTIVE ISSUES IN THE YOUNG ADULTS YEARS

As well as certain areas of development, the young adult years are a prime time to consider certain issues particularly distinctive to this season of life.

SPIRITUAL RESILIENCE

As stated, these years are a time when many young adults are making decisions about their own beliefs and how they will live them out. Along with that, many will vacillate between spiritual highs or spiritual lows depending on their momentary circumstances and level of maturity. Sustainability in the Christian life requires us to develop a degree of sturdiness and resilience that weathers the bumps and challenges life brings, and effectively navigating patterns of sin and temptation are part of this process. Perfection is not the goal at this stage or indeed at any stage, but helping young adults accurately discern and address the problem strategically is part of the recipe for success.

SEXUALITY

How a person lives out their sexuality reveals much about their spiritual maturity and how they presently process their relationship with God. Sexuality is a critical avenue through which we as Christ followers begin to integrate our confessed faith with our embodiment of that faith in concrete ways. In addition to one's own sexuality, our changing culture presents almost unprecedented challenges to forming a biblical viewpoint on matters of gender. The rapidly changing landscape in what societal mores are not only acceptable but deemed normal requires Christians to be especially informed and able to proactively and lovingly be prepared with a biblical perspective for issues that will inevitably come up within our circles.

From the issues surrounding one's sexual identity to what it looks like to live out one's femininity or masculinity, faithfulness in the realm of gender and sexuality must be pursued. Dialoguing with young adults on issues of sexuality provides significant understanding of their perception of self, God, and others. This generation of young adults is often eager to discuss sexuality, making it a fruitful subject to explore. When engaging in such dialogue, it is especially important that we strive to learn and understand their point of reference as the discussion unfolds. Hearing their concerns, tensions, and convictions will provide a necessary platform for Scripture, theology, and logic to shed further light on the issue. Such conversations, though sometimes marked by tense interpersonal dynamics, can be fruitful when engaged with humility, grace, and love.

PORNOGRAPHY

A proper understanding of sexuality as a gift from God clearly reveals distortions of the divine plan. One of these, pornography, has grown in force and intensity in the lives of young adults and unfortunately is not going to subside anytime soon. Among each of the generational groups, young adults ages 18–24 are the most frequent pornography users. According to recent statistics, almost six in ten young adults (57 percent) seek out pornography daily, weekly, or monthly.[1] This problem must be addressed in a structural and systemic manner (such as the implementation of firewalls, policies, and such).

However, true help in this area needs to incorporate a more holistic solution. Pornography usage reflects more than just a behavioral issue, but rather an issue that is rooted in one's heart, affections, and thought life. Strategies that move young adults toward health and godliness ultimately need to create new habits and patterns of thinking, feeling, and doing.

TECHNOLOGY

Our phones, computers, and electronic devices have become the center of our existence. We seem to have oriented our entire lives around them, such that it seems increasingly difficult, even impossible at times, for us to detach ourselves from our devices in everyday life. Technology is growing in its power to shape our routines and habits and bleeds into other areas such as our thought life and relational health. Its influence has been gaining strength and requires our thoughtful participation to understand its effects especially on young adults in their pursuit of maturity.

VOCATIONAL DISCERNMENT

Students long for ways to see how their academic discipline connects to their faith in Christ. We need to foster ways for college students to be exposed to other Christ followers in their respective disciplines. Entering into discipline-specific conversations and mentoring relationships provides the necessary ingredients to grow the vision for their vocational calling.

ENGAGEMENT WITH THE CHURCH

One of the issues I observe regularly among college students and young adults in general is a weak view of the local church and its purpose. They often fail to recognize the need or reason to be immersed in the fellowship of a local church body on a weekly basis. Many feel that if they have their small group or peer group for fellowship, a podcast of some engaging speaker for teaching, and some popular musical artist on Spotify or other streaming service for worship, then they are all good! Those ministering to this group have an opportunity to help them develop a vision for the local church that goes beyond simply their felt needs and consumer-istic tendencies. The body needs them, and they need the rest of the body.

As helpful as it is to learn the habits, tendencies, and patterns of young adults, the real learning comes by building relationships with them. Young adults care deeply about community and connecting. This means physical presence as well as virtual presence. They desire to do life with others. Entering into their world is the only significant way to truly understand who they are becoming, thus making it possible for us to walk faithfully with them.

A FRAMEWORK FOR SPIRITUAL FORMATION IN YOUNG ADULTS

What do we mean by "spiritual formation"? Spiritual formation is a work of the Holy Spirit, based on the foundation of Christ's finished work, that enables the believer to respond actively to the prompting of the Holy Spirit through the media-tion of the Word of God. Christ is progressively formed in the individual (Gal. 4:19) in the context of regular mutual participation in the Christian community and in self-reflective practices from the moment of conversion until consummation, when the believer is in the presence of the Lord. In summative form, it is the Word of God, the Spirit of God, and the people of God working together for the glory of God. The following are principles that contribute to the spiritual formation of young adults.

Spiritual formation requires understanding the heart. Helping students and young adults understand the dynamics of their heart and affections is critical for the transformation process. The habits they keep and the desires they possess and cultivate determine the lifestyle they adopt. Bringing these underlying factors to the surface can aid awareness, growth, and maturity in the lives of young adults.

Spiritual formation requires us to know and be known. God shows us how true knowing is intended to occur (Gen. 1–2; John 4). The fall of humanity introduced a distorted way of knowing and, throughout Scripture, God beckons us to know Him (as well as one another) the way He knows us. This requires vulnerability and relating in ways that are not normative in our culture. When we begin to know God and each other in the manner He has proposed, growth and maturity are not far behind.

Spiritual formation is embodied and incarnational. Jesus modeled for His followers how to live out their lives. He did not merely teach good ethics or revolutionary ideas, but demonstrated and embodied a way of life for His disciples, showing them what it actually looked like. Throughout the centuries, the process of disciple-making, as foundational for Christian identity and witness, has followed Jesus' example and pattern of how to live faithfully with God and with one another.

Spiritual formation is progressive. Our transformation into the likeness of Jesus does not occur in a linear fashion. We go through many stops and starts, twists and turns along the way. We cannot predict our formational journey, but must lean on the Spirit, the Word of truth, and God's grace as we navigate what life brings. It is often through difficulty and crisis that much of God's transformative work takes place. Ministry with college students and young adults usually entails helping them weather and make sense of these changing and sometimes unforeseeable life occurrences.

Spiritual formation occurs in and through community. While each of us exists as an individual, it is in community that God has placed us for His testimony and glory. In light of the great diversity that exists within the body of Christ and humanity in general, living faithfully in community is messy and often wearisome. However, it is usually through such contexts that God produces His best work.

The reality of the gospel provides the foundation for each of these principles, producing the hope and transformation needed for any progress in the Christian life. As pastor and author Tim Keller reminds us, we are saved by believing the gospel and then we are transformed in every part of our minds, hearts, and lives by believing that gospel more and more deeply as life goes on (Rom. 12:1–2; Phil. 1:6; 3:13–14).[2] The recognition of one's position and standing in Christ is crucial for spiritual growth, especially in the identity-forging young adult years.

COMPONENTS OF MINISTRY TO YOUNG ADULTS

Several components are critical for supporting effective ministry to young adults. Obviously, the particular ministry context—whether a college campus, a local church congregation, or the community around them—will determine how each element is specifically addressed. The items below focus on developing the "whole person" to implement the needed knowledge, skills, and capabilities within a certain context.

- Identity Formation: Young adults will gain a deeper understanding of their identity in Christ and how that identity relates to their spiritual life.

- Relational Formation: Young adults will increase their love and appreciation for others.

- Theological Formation: Young adults will develop the ability to study, discern, and apply truth from the Bible in order to foster a life of faithfulness to God and in relation to others.

- Heart Transformation: Young adults will grow in their ability to assess their spiritual health and engage in practices that promote spiritual growth.

- Missional/Vocational Formation: Young adults will grow in their understanding of Christian mission, in their ability to reach outward in service, and in their discernment and pursuit of vocational calling.

The hope for each young adult is that they bless the world not only through their developing competencies, but through the forming of their very person. The *type* of engineer or teacher one becomes matters much—that is, the character, competence, and integrity that one embodies in such vocational roles. The church is called to fashion young adults who both see the great needs in the world and respond with faithful, sustainable service and care. The goal is not simply to fill a job or professional role in society, but rather to develop leaders who will go about their task or vocation in a way that distinctively reflects the character of Christ. This may look like teaching in a difficult school in an inner-city community where many do not want to go, or building bridges in a developing country where government funding may or may not come through, or serving as a city planner in one of our urban centers while possessing a kingdom mindset. In ministering to young adults, the church seeks to form the kind of person who sees the need and willingly steps into a calling that can bring about faithful change for the common good.

Identification of personal competencies and the latest assessment tools from the business world alone cannot determine a young adult's unique calling. Study, reflection, and the prayers of Scripture directed by the Holy Spirit in the context of the local church remain our most valuable resources. The complexities of our world require creativity, innovation, integration, cross-disciplinary conversations, humility, a fearlessness to fail, and a deep dependency and partnership with those other embodied souls whom the Lord has placed alongside us.

A HOLISTIC VISION OF CARE

All the things we are talking about point to recognizing our holistic nature as created beings. God has fashioned us in His image to be rational, relational, emotional, physical, and spiritual. Neglecting any one of these faculties in our efforts to foster growth and maturity in young adults can truncate progress. Each of these facets of our being speaks in some way to the others. We must remember the interconnect-edness of these realms in order to help and not hinder growth.

For example, when we encounter an individual with an eating disorder, simply focusing on their caloric intake is shortsighted. Instead, we might consider explor-ing their relational patterns, their understanding of identity, their processing of past or present trauma, their emotional sturdiness, and their theology of embod-iment. It becomes readily apparent that providing help and appropriate care in such a situation requires resources and expertise beyond one person's ability. Thus, there is wisdom in partnering with a pastor, clinical therapist, close friends, family members, and/or mentors close to the struggling individual as well.

FOSTER PATTERNS OF CRITICAL THINKING AND DISCERNMENT

Our young adults find themselves at a variety of places spiritually. Some have grown up in the church and have left feeling disillusioned and frustrated. Others have come to faith in Christ recently and are learning to walk spiritually for the first time. Several are questioning the convictions of the church and are longing for someone to connect the dots for them. And all of them are wrestling with signifi-cant questions to make sense of the world in which they live.

It is critical that we take the time to listen to their stories and begin to locate where each individual is positioned in relationship to God, others, and the com-munity at large. Doing this will provide the best opportunity to truly guide them and develop a level of engagement and relationship that can move us further down the path of transformation and growth. Neglecting this season of listening and learning short-circuits the potential establishment of significant relationships.

ENCOURAGE PERSONAL EXAMINATION

A normative practice in the Christian life is to submit our thinking and behav-ior to God's Word. Our culture, as well as the tendencies of our heart, are constantly drawing us toward distorted living. To counteract this ever-present pull toward worldliness, we must adopt gospel-centered habits. Such soul assessment provides clarity for ministry to young adults and helps them foster lifestyle patterns that move them toward Christlike transformation. One author suggests that young adults need to acquire "a complex moral conscience [and become part of] a citi-zenry who can recognize and assess the claims of multiple perspectives and are steeped in critical, systemic, and compassionate habits of mind."[3]

When the people of God had become careless in their relationship with Him, the Lord rebuked them through the prophet Haggai: "Consider [i.e., give careful thought to] your ways!" (Hag. 1:5). He urged them to reflect on their circumstances and to evaluate their careless lifestyle in light of what God had told them. The prophet Jeremiah prays, "You know me, LORD; You see me and examine my heart's attitude toward You" (Jer. 12:3a). And the apostle Paul states that "the one who is spiritual discerns all things" (1 Cor. 2:15).

Self-awareness is a critical quality for young adults to develop as they navigate this season of their lives. These passages can serve as a great help as they dial in to practices promoting wisdom and discernment. Little by little, the aim is for them to acquire greater clarity concerning themselves, their God, those around them, and the context in which they are located.

USE QUESTIONS

Using questions to explore the values and convictions held by young adults is an eye-opening exercise. There are various avenues to venture down to uncover why they believe what they do. First, highlight the inconsistencies or contradictions in their thinking. Begin to gently challenge assumptions and explore gaps or holes in their logic. The goal is not to demand they adopt your view on issues, but to foster thoughtful and charitable engagement with the ideas in play. Help them wrestle through the complexities of life under the authority of Scripture.

Second, help them discern what their habits and practices reveal about their underlying beliefs and values. Often, routine behaviors are acquired without too much thought or reflection. These kinds of questions help to disclose the individual's operational or *lived* theology. They may articulate one thing, but their behavior clearly communicates something different. Discovering these inconsistencies may provide a pathway for growth and greater intimacy with God.

Third, pose questions that create cognitive dissonance to gain further insight. The topic of sexuality and specific lifestyle choices with respect to sexuality can raise this kind of dissonance. For example, many young adults struggle to reconcile the tension between a close friend who has adopted a homosexual lifestyle and what Scripture declares about such a lifestyle. Again, the aim is not to create a divide between you and the young adult, but to foster critical thinking and theological thoughtfulness that moves toward gospel faithfulness.

INVESTIGATE VOICES OF INFLUENCE

Several voices speak into the lives of our young adults, seeking to be influential over beliefs, values, and behaviors.

Some individuals may be drawn to celebrities, with fame and wealth being the guiding light. Others may gravitate toward the professors or philosophers of the day, giving intelligence and knowledge center stage, while some young adults may find technological innovators or entrepreneurs appealing voices to download.

Regardless of what they order off the "menu," much power and influence are given to these voices. To discern and discover the nature of such influential voices, one may find it beneficial to investigate the cultural artifacts that the young adult has adopted. Surveying their technology choices or entertainment portals can fuel profitable conversation toward understanding the heart of many young adults. Life experiences—such as high school, summer camp, athletic teams, dating relationships, jobs, and church—also can offer a deeper understanding of such influencers. Each of these encounters represents a network of shaping forces that marinate one's heart and mind. Ultimately, the main question we must ask is this: What have these voices of influence produced, created, or formed? What outcomes are resulting? What vision of life are they serving or promoting?

CREATE A SUPPORT NETWORK AND RELATIONAL SPACE TO BE KNOWN

The post office in my small, East Coast Canadian town served as a gathering spot for those who lived there. The daily venture to pick up your mail became the place where you received much more than packages and utility bills. It was a place where you were known. It was impossible to leave the premises without having engaged those who knew you as well as several generations of your family. There was something comforting and reassuring in knowing that you were part of a community that extended beyond your immediate family. This reality of being known was a double-edged sword. You had ever-present help and resources for the struggles of life, but you also had the quandary of everyone knowing the minute details of your life—the good and the bad. This was organic accountability at its best.

Part of the relational dynamic present in my small town existed because of the communal narrative each of us represented. Our stories intertwined. We did life among one another, and our close proximity had implications on several fronts. If you treated someone's daughter poorly on your date Friday night, you knew you would see her father in the local hardware store or at the hockey game on Saturday afternoon. This relational context often kept us from sinful choices. This context of being known also created a forced level of reconciliation, growth, and healing when relational breaches or hurtful actions did occur. Such mutual knowledge served as a quasi-built-in transformational tool.

The culture that was created in my small town has left me with a few routines that have helped my spiritual life. For one, I learned that being known is a good thing—that it is even beneficial, as it reflects the way God intended for us to exist.

Transparency, even on a corporate scale, brings a sense of freedom. Being well known in the community is pretty much a given; it is somewhat inescapable and bakes into the community a sense of family. Our small-town culture also taught me how to maintain confidentiality. Amid the deep knowing that we shared, I learned the importance of recognizing what should remain confidential.

Another habit fostered by my small-town upbringing was that of challenge. Challenge became acceptable, encouraged, and even at times expected. It functioned as a built-in tool for growth. As people often were confronted with difficulty or some form of hardship, benefit and blessing sometimes followed—forging health in the community and the individual.

How does this relate to ministry with young adults? Young adults need to develop similar relational patterns. Forming strong relational ties with those around them provides significant growth and potential for transformation. Their maturity and transformation into the likeness of Christ involves their everyday responses to relational experiences.

Young adults thrive when they have a safe place to share their doubts, concerns, questions, and struggles. It is in the context of trusted relationships that we often experience God's care, concern, and compassion. He places individuals in our lives who meet us in our everyday circumstances, tangibly expressing Christ's love for us. This may be listening to someone pour out their heartfelt doubt. It may be giving someone a safe space to ask questions of God, of themselves, or about the world. You may be the recipient of someone's overwhelming grief or graced with someone's potential job prospect. Whatever their particular role, God gifts us people in our lives to help make sense of, navigate, and embrace the various experiences we encounter.

Our relational tendencies are formed over time with a multitude of variables involved. Some play a very significant and primary role, while others affect relational patterns in a minimal way. The type of relational pattern envisioned here is best fostered when certain conditions are met:

> Accept and welcome differentiation.
> Value people but critique ideas.
> Encourage transparency and vulnerability.
> Maintain confidentiality.
> Provide support when needed.
> Build trust and reciprocity.
> Help young adults be seen and known. Recognize who they are, where they reside, and what shapes and influences them.
> Reject the appetite for power, control, and self-amplification.

Practice the spiritual disciplines (prayer, study, fasting, etc.) in community. Cast vision and inspire resilience for the road ahead.

STIMULATE REFLECTION

As we continue to explore a process to engage young adults, building and investing in relationships is essential. Asking the right questions to stimulate reflection can provide a great avenue to discover what God is doing in their lives. The following questions may help us discern where an individual is in relationship to the things of God, as well as how they understand themselves and locate themselves in the world. What is currently happening in his life that God is bringing to his attention? What story anchors her life? Who is God in his life? What is the gospel story? Where is redemption found? Who are they? Who are we? Where did we come from? Why did things go wrong? How can they be put right? How does she orient herself in the world? What part has pain and suffering played in his life? What is she most passionate about? What are his skills? How does he define the good life? What determines success for her? And by what or whose standard do they measure such success?

These questions can serve as catalysts to explore where God is at work in an individual and to discern where they are coming from. Our use of such questions is best implemented in a loving, organic, and humble manner. It is crucial that we evaluate our own motives and relational posture as we participate in this process.

EXPLORE PERSONAL NARRATIVE

I have found that letting young adults tell their stories is a powerful and life-giving practice. It serves as a powerful tool in the process of maturation and spiritual growth. As young adults explore their personal history and attempt to articulate it to those in their community, they begin to understand the integrated pieces of their lives in a deeper way. They may not fully comprehend why God has allowed every detail, but they may begin to make sense of the varied seasons, experiences, and relationships of their lives in a more integrated way.

There are various ways to share these stories. Stories can be told individually, with one person giving their testimony of Christ's work in her life, or by having one of her close friends interview them in a more dialogical format. In either case, those listening are blessed, and a deeper relational connection is forged between the sharer and the listeners. Several *types* of storytelling also can be used. You may invite a new believer to articulate his conversion experience, pointing to God's grace, mercy, and involvement in his life. Or, you could have someone share about their journey through a crisis and how the Lord displayed His faithfulness during such a difficult season. Of particular value for young adults, you might invite a seasoned individual to share their own journey of vocational discernment, or how they navigated their journey into marriage, or how they have persevered in their relationship with the Lord.

Several benefits result from these personal narratives. Hearing stories knits our hearts to the person sharing, often creating empathy and connection. We find ourselves appreciating and valuing the person in a deeper way. Systems and networks of support can be fostered in personal experiences, since our tendency is to find points of connection with our own stories or to connect another's story with those stories we already know. Vision also is cast through use of personal narrative. Whether a young adult is trying to navigate their job prospects, a romantic relationship, or the ethical dilemmas of our day, the story of one further along the path of life is sure to enlighten their own path as well.

Put simply, offering a personal narrative develops a sense of both knowing and being known. God is establishing fellowship with us, as well as fostering our relational intimacy with one another. Additionally, God is revealing more of Himself and creating an increased awareness of His involvement throughout our stories.

FIND ADDITIONAL MENTORS

The support network and relational space to be known is certainly not limited to the professional on a church staff. If you're in such a position, recruit and train those who have an appetite, aptitude, and ability to invest in other young adults. Cast vision for the call to lifelong discipleship and long-term fruit bearing. Help potential mentors envision the future marriages, families, vocational contexts, and ministry opportunities of those in whom they would invest. Of course, not every young adult is willing and/or ready to receive what a mentor has to offer, so invest wisely—exercising discernment and patience as you watch for faithful responses.

GATHERING AND SENDING

One of the themes that runs through the pages of Scripture is the gathering and sending of God's people. We must teach and build this formative, historical rhythm of both gathering and sending into the young adults among whom we minister. The idea of gathering—with God and His people—promotes rest, security, being known by others, and giving attention to the inner life of the heart and mind. This realm functions for the restoration, care, and establishing of our identity in Christ. The sending dynamic, from God and His people, addresses mission, life challenges, adventures into the unknown, and the outward pursuit to engage God's world. This realm functions for our stretching, testing, and strengthening our reliance upon God.

We need to spend time focusing on both realms. Settling too long on the gathering side creates fat souls overly acquainted with comfort and self. Conversely, too much time on the sending side develops fragile souls that cannot faithfully steward the missional endeavors to which God has called us.

Navigating a Crisis of Faith

A familiar narrative in the young adult season of life is experiencing a crisis of faith. Young adults are more prone to such crises due to the unique and transitional season of their lives, presenting many questions and changing circumstances. What does this look like? Usually, it involves previously held beliefs about God and their faith being tested and challenged by competing belief systems or life experiences. As young adults encounter a faith crisis, each of them has experienced different circumstances that have brought them to such a point. So then, it is important to listen well and to discern the root issues beneath the various contextual layers.

Every time I walk with a young adult in their crisis, I learn something. My aim is to build relational trust and to create a safe place for them to be open. I listen to their concerns, doubts, experiences, relationships, fears, and pain. I affirm their personhood, validate their struggle, and help them identify ways that God may be taking them to a deeper level of relational intimacy with Him. This is not a crystal clear or formulaic process, but the goal is to keep walking down this path together. I often see God meet the two of us in the process and ask us both to trust Him more.

The following guidelines and principles can inform our conversations as we help young adults walk through a faith crisis.

- Create a hospitable and safe place to express and surface spiritual doubts and struggles.

- Build relational trust, both individually with you, and corporately with the broader leadership team or community.

- Practice and develop active listening skills to validate and affirm the nature of the concern or crisis.

- Come as a learner and guide rather than a problem solver or one who has all the answers.

- Model thoughtful reflection on God, self, and the world.

- Help the individual explore and reflect on the tension or presenting problem from various perspectives.

- Explore the potential holistic manifestations of the brain-body connection.

- Allow the pace and pathway to develop organically, rather than determining a timeline for progress.

- Maintain relational connection even when the individual steps away from the dialogue process.

- Foster a network of relational connections and resources, beyond just a connection with you.

- Pray for and with the individual, if he or she is open to it.

Certainly the young adult years are key developmental ones for many reasons, but helping a young person see through a dark time in their faith journey will serve them throughout their lives. As has been noted, we do not go through life's challenges in a continuous or straight line, but situations or crises will recur in some form. As you walk with a young person through a rough patch in their faith journey, you'll present them with tools to better handle a future difficult chapter.

FINAL THOUGHTS

As we bring this chapter to its conclusion, let us now recap some of the realities young adults are facing. For example, it has been said that most of our lives are spent at work, so make sure you believe in what you do. A myriad of factors affect the young adult's discovery of vocation in our present-day world, and this vocational search can be a daunting process. Gone are the days when an individual works at the same job and company for forty years. Most young adults today will have several jobs—even careers—that span a variety of skills and contexts.

We may support young adults in two practical ways as they navigate this process. First, we can help them discover the intersection of *the world's deep hunger* on one hand, and *their own deep gladness* on the other.[4] What gifts, abilities, and competency do they possess, and how may they use those strengths to address the significant needs in our world? Second, we can connect them with faithful Christ followers who are serving in the vocation to which they aspire. Wisdom from a seasoned saint who knows the path forward may prove indispensable.

However, people do not suddenly plunge into a job or calling. Leading up to vocational opportunities has been education. The formation of a young adult's educational experience and understanding has been in process from his or her earliest days and has come through a myriad of educational philosophies and practices. Some of these have served students well, while others have not. The church of Christ has a responsibility to help its followers think about and engage in education

"Christianly"—that is, in a manner that reflects a distinctly Christian perspective and commitment. We must make it a priority and goal to model intentionally how one navigates the educational realm with Christlike faithfulness. Such a posture of humility will facilitate genuine learning and help students to pursue academic honesty and integrity in their work.

We previously have highlighted the significance of identity formation in the young adult years. To seek guidance from Scripture in addressing such formation, we may look to Jesus' example. In John's gospel, before Jesus rises to wash the disciples' feet, He articulates some profound statements concerning His identity— namely, that He was sent by the Father and will be returning to the Father. As Jesus ventures out to perform this incredibly humbling act of washing His disciples' feet, the reader is steadied by the source of the gesture. Christ's personhood and identity is secure in the glory from which He came, making this scene all the more shocking. John discloses not only where Jesus is "from" and "where" He is about to go, but also Jesus' purpose and mission while on earth.

Jesus' example here directs us to secure our identity in relationship with God. We observe Jesus lean on both where He has come from and where He is going. Jesus' identity is found in relationship to His Father. As we minister to young adults, we can guide them into an understanding that their lives—their moral grounding and their acts of service—flow from their identity in Christ.

In closing, let us consider that the process of helping young adults move toward spiritual maturity does not simply rely on a formula or set of propositions to be adopted, but rather reflects life organically lived out in community, directed by and in submission to the Word and Spirit of God. There will be moments that perplex us, questions that confuse us, and actions that concern us. Yet through it all, we trust that God has blessed us with the opportunity to walk with these dear ones in building His church and carrying out His mission at this particular time in history. Let us see the immense gift it is to participate in the lives of young adults and to observe the transforming power of Christ at work in them during such a formative season of holistic development.

NOTES

1. Barna Research, https://www.barna.com/research/porn-in-the-digital-age-new-research-reveals-10-trends/.

2. Tim Keller, *Center Church: Doing Balanced, Gospel-Centered Ministry in Your City* (Grand Rapids: Zondervan, 2012), 48.

3. Sharon Daloz Parks, *Big Questions, Worthy Dreams: Mentoring Young Adults in Their Search for Meaning, Purpose, and Faith* (San Francisco: Jossey-Bass, 2000), 10.

4. Frederick Buechner, *Wishful Thinking: A Seeker's ABC*, rev. and expanded ed. (San Francisco: HarperOne, 1993), 118–19.

Ministering to Women

PAMELA MACRAE

Ministry to women in the congregation can be complicated. What kind of pastoral care do women need or want? What is appropriate? How does a pastor or ministry leader respond in order not to neglect women? What is the Christian duty of the leader? Pastors and women who are ministry leaders for women can struggle with how to best care for women in their congregation, and rightly so. The needs are quite varied. Women want guidance and help with the biblical text. They need help with relationships that are to be characterized by love and Christian unity. They want support as they grow in faith and spiritual maturity. In this chapter, we will consider ways to minister effectively to women in the congregation from the perspective of a male pastor, as well as women who are in ministry leadership to women.

PASTORAL MINISTRY TO WOMEN

God calls pastors to shepherd His flock (1 Peter 5:2–3). Their task is to comfort and help sheep who are in the midst of painful and difficult life circumstances. Pastors share sorrows, witness joys, and go after ones who wander from the faith. They lead and guide the flock to restful pastures so they can thrive securely. They feed on the bounty of fertile pastures, find great blessings, and bear much fruit (Jer. 3:15; Ezek. 34; Eph. 4:11).

It is not easy or automatic for God's people to live in unity. Christians are to be on mission together for the gospel of Jesus Christ, but certainly, they need help to grow personally and corporately. God gives shepherds to His people to teach them how to honor one another, live in Christian unity, and consider the other better than themselves (Phil. 2:3–4). They are to bear with one another, prefer the other, and co-labor side by side for the Lord (Rom. 16). They offer spiritual gifts to one another, willingly giving and receiving the blessings of these gifts. Men and women, boys and girls, all work together for God's will and purpose to build up the church while growing into maturity in the fullness of our Lord Jesus Christ (Eph. 4).

SHALOM

The term *shalom* describes how God wants life to be for His people. It means living without fear, timidity, or even a sense of threat. Shalom means a state of peace, as women and men flourish and thrive as God intended. Shalom is meant to be the personal and collective experience of God's people. What exactly does shalom mean? Cornelius Plantinga Jr. provides a helpful description of this peace, or biblical shalom. He writes,

> The webbing together of God, humans, and all creation in justice, fulfillment, and delight is what the Hebrew prophets call *shalom*. We call it peace, but it means far more than mere peace of mind or a cease-fire between enemies. In the Bible, shalom means *universal flourishing, wholeness, and delight*—a rich state of affairs in which natural needs are satisfied and natural gifts fruitfully employed, a state of affairs that inspires joyful wonder as its Creator and Savior opens doors and welcomes the creatures in whom he delights. Shalom, in other words, is the way things ought to be.[1]

Pastors and ministry leaders who shepherd women in the church by offering pastoral care and support are enormously influential in how women in the church thrive and flourish.

JESUS IS THE GOOD SHEPHERD

In other chapters of this volume, we have looked at the call and charge for pastors to be shepherds of God's people. The intention here is not to repeat that content. However, it will be helpful to review two passages that describe shepherds as the basis for understanding how to shepherd well God's flock, and women in particular.

In Ezekiel 34:1–6, God rebuked shepherds who were supposed to take care of His flock, Israel, but instead were neglecting and abusing them. The shepherds fed themselves, not the flock. They ate well and were well clothed in wool and slaughtered the finest animals. They were not taking care of the sick, weak, or scattered sheep. Shepherds severely dominated the sheep. The sheep became food for every beast. Some wandered away from the flock, yet the shepherds did not go find them to bring them back to safety.

In John 10:1–12, Jesus describes someone who enters a sheep pen, not by the door, but by climbing in as a thief or robber. He cannot get the attention of the sheep because the sheep do not know his voice. This thief comes to steal, kill, and destroy (10:10), leaving the sheep vulnerable to wolves who snatch them and scatter them (10:12).

These two passages provide graphic pictures of sheep who are suffering and languishing from neglect and mistreatment. They are bereft of hope, while the shepherds seek their own benefit and well-being. Shepherds, appointed to protect the sheep, tragically end up causing devastation and harm to them instead.

God says in Ezekiel 34 that He will not always allow His sheep to suffer in this manner. Away with the bad shepherds! God declares that He will Himself shepherd His people. He says, "Behold, I Myself will search for My sheep and look after them" (v. 11). "I will care for My sheep and will rescue them from all the places where they were scattered on a cloudy and gloomy day" (v. 12). Do you hear the mournful way God describes the day in which His people were neglected? It was "a cloudy and gloomy day."

God declares through the prophet Ezekiel that He will deliver His sheep. He will search for them. He will care for them and feed them in good pastures, by good streams, where they will lie down in safety. He will bless them. They will be secure and know He is their God and that they belong to Him.

Ezekiel then speaks prophetically of the time when God will send Jesus, who will be the messianic Shepherd who brings showers of blessing with seasons of fruitfulness (34:14–15, 27). There will be a time when His people will "know that I, the LORD their God, am with them, and that they, the house of Israel, are My people. . . . As for you, My sheep, the sheep of My pasture, you are mankind, and I am your God" (34:30–31; see Ps. 100:3).

In John 10, Jesus contrasts Himself as the Good Shepherd with those who pose as shepherds but actually are thieves and robbers. As the Good Shepherd, He is known by His sheep. They hear His voice, and He gives them not only life, but abundant life. It is He who lays down His life for His sheep.

A key point of each passage is that shepherds are required to take care of the sheep. Good shepherds provide what is needed for sheep to experience shalom—that is, abundant life to the fullest extent. Shepherds who neglect the flock are rebuked.

The picture of good and bad shepherds from John 10 and Ezekiel 34 helps clarify what Peter means in 1 Peter 5:1–4 when he charges the elders of the church to shepherd the flock of God among them, not by domineering over them, but as an example. Peter reminds the shepherds that the Chief Shepherd will return, and they will have to answer for how they cared for His flock (see John 21:15–17). They are not the Chief Shepherd. They are the under-shepherds who are to shepherd well all of the flock God has entrusted to them.

This is precisely why pastors must offer loving pastoral care to women. Pastors must shepherd the *whole flock*. No favorites. It is important for the shepherd to know the flock, as well as invite the flock under their care to know them. Jesus did not model selective pastoral care. He did not avoid women. He did not adhere to strict cultural barriers that kept Him away from women. He touched them. He called attention to their devotion. He asked them about their hurts and pain, and ministered deeply to their needs. He met their needs with personal, one-on-one compassion both privately and publicly. And yet, He also modeled boundaries that are instructive for pastoral care.

POTENTIAL BARRIERS FOR THE MALE PASTOR

Cautions associated with pastoral care for women from male pastors are not only extensive, but in many cases, well justified. It is not uncommon for pastors to be warned about the risks of pastoral care to women. Podcasts, articles, blogs, and books alert pastors to the risks of inappropriate pastoral relationships with women, and of course, this makes sense. Who among us does not have stories to tell about respected pastors by whom we felt blindsided when we heard about their abusive or inappropriate relationship with a woman? At some point, most of us have felt overwhelmed by the extent of this problem.

Yet for too long, we have been overcorrecting the situation. While no one disputes that temptations are great and moral failure is more common than we would like, it seems the predominant response is to encourage pastors to take excessive caution in every interaction with women, often to the point of avoidance. This can make it hard for pastors to form healthy relationships or friendships with women. Some pastors, perhaps inadvertently, conclude that women are inherently risky. Therefore, they make very strict rules to avoid any possible hint of impropriety for themselves or their staff. Guidelines govern where and when to talk to women, and whether one-on-one ministry conversations in their office are appropriate. Interestingly, a pastor may routinely refer a woman to a (male) counselor, who has appointments in an office in a professional setting, but somehow it seems questionable or even inappropriate for a pastor to conduct pastoral counseling for a woman in his own office. What message does this unintentionally communicate about the assumed ethical and moral trustworthiness of a pastor, as compared to a counselor?

Sadly, some pastors simply decide to avoid altogether any interaction with a woman other than casual social conversation. They reason that for the sake of the gospel, and to protect their reputation, marriage, and ministry, this is the best way to be above reproach and righteous (1 Tim. 3:1–7). These are worthy concerns.

However, there also is a risk of objectifying women, seeing them primarily as sexual beings. A woman's soul gets pushed into the shadows along with her theological, emotional, and spiritual needs, while her body is elevated as the most important thing about her. The interaction between the pastor and the woman should be informed by the relationship and social structure of shepherd and sheep, pastor and congregant, not predominantly the category of male and female.

Robertson McQuilkin, former professor and president of Columbia International University, is famously quoted as saying, "It is much easier to move to a consistent extreme than to remain in the center of biblical tension."[2] This relates to biblical and theological interpretive issues, but also finds legitimate application more broadly in ministry tensions. It is easier to have fixed rules and decide to avoid altogether any relational ministry to women, than reliance on the Holy Spirit for guidance in discerning what she needs and how God might be asking her pastor to serve her. This does not mean ministry should be impulsive or impetuous. It means the shepherd must know God's Word, and then in both normative and unpredictable situations, trust the Holy Spirit to show how to faithfully minister to women as their shepherd and pastor.

POTENTIAL BARRIERS FOR THE WOMAN MINISTRY LEADER

For women in positions of ministry leadership predominantly focused on ministry to women, there are other tensions as well. Paul teaches in Titus 2 that it is important and essential for women to teach other women. This leaves us with no doubt of the value of women shepherding other women, an important and essential ministry to affirm. Regardless of cyclical debates and questions about the value of specific gendered ministry within the church, it is clear that whether or not it happens through formal programming, women will always find a way to minister to other women, irrespective of where it happens. Stories about the relationship between women in Scripture, such as Mary and Elizabeth (Luke 1) or Naomi and Ruth (Ruth) illustrate the teaching and instruction from Titus 2 about women ministering to and training women. Therefore, the church does well to honor this reality and make space for focused ministry efforts to women by women.

Women who are called and appointed to leadership in ministry to women, yet without formal theological or ministry training, can be tempted to look at their male counterparts and feel insecure or ill-equipped for the work of ministry. Trained pastors can also disregard these same women because of this reality. In recent years, the number of seminary-trained women who have full-time staff positions has increased, but historically, women have served in ministry settings largely out of gifting and without formal theological or ministry training. In fact, historically and globally, this has been the case for many ministry leaders of either gender. Theological education is valuable and should be encouraged, but it is not always available or possible. If someone has not had formal theological training, they are no less legitimate in ministry. Never underestimate how God trains and equips His people to serve Him. It would be a mistake to elevate formal education such that it discredits what God teaches through other means, not least, through the local church. God is not limited in how He uses people with certain gifts, training, or experience. We have only to read Scripture to know that is true.

An issue that often comes up for women is the unique challenge of staffing that can consist largely of volunteers. Not all ministry leaders for women are paid staff. The view that a paid position requires more commitment than a volunteer position misses the importance of a conviction that we are in service to God first, regardless if one is paid or not. It is important to teach and train women who volunteer for this ministry (as for other ministries) to recognize their work on the ministry team as a calling from God into ministry service. Ministry teams are not simply administratively oriented, functioning only when the workload requires action. This would be a mistake. Shepherds and a ministry team function best when there is longevity, team development, and discipleship. Rotating team members may feel appealing for busy women; however, as with other ministry and pastoral staff teams, constant turnover weakens effectiveness. Train women for ministry that is motivated by the Spirit and that reflects the urgency of the gospel (Matt. 28:16–19). Women benefit from consistency and longevity in their leaders.

Another serious barrier can be a lack of respectful funding within the church budget. A church that prioritizes ministry to women will need to provide money for training events, retreats, Bible study, and discipleship curriculum. Typically, one of the largest ministry expenses rises from the need to pay vetted and qualified childcare workers who take care of the children of young mothers while they gather to study God's Word. Without childcare, it is often impossible for women to come to a Bible study. And finally, whenever possible, it is critically important for a woman to be hired as full-time ministry staff. Having a paid staff person to specifically minister to a segment of the congregation signals affirmation, respect, and value.

In churches holding a biblical perspective that the position of senior pastor and elder is reserved for qualified and called men, it is particularly significant for male leadership to support and affirm the value of women in ministry leadership. Not all Christians or churches agree on biblical passages that describe pastoral and elder leadership roles and functions. The authority structures of ecclesial function vary tremendously. However, it is sad and painful when biblical interpretation and ecclesial function become hurtful to relationships, due to attitudes of superiority that provoke some to feel undervalued and dismissed. Leaders not only have a God-given responsibility to affirm and welcome the ministry by and for women in the church, but also must understand that in many situations, they hold the keys that open ministry doors. Not all leadership teams function in the same way. It is the responsibility of leadership to provide what is essential for women to flourish and minister effectively within the church. This includes active support, personal and public encouragement, adequate resources, and a willingness to create space for these ministries. We must not underestimate the importance of affirming a person's calling from God, nor should we hesitate to find ways to develop that call.

More women than we might expect have been wounded and discouraged by pastors who have not made ministry space for them in the church—space where they can thrive with a sense of shalom. When women are not able to receive pastoral support for ministry within the church, for reasons other than a theological position, discouragement can easily set in. Recently a pastor explained that he felt theologically comfortable opening far more doors for ministry leadership and service for women than are currently available in the congregation where he pastors, but felt restricted because he knew a few men in the church who would be offended. However, he made no mention of women in that same congregation who not only were offended, but also deeply discouraged and confused by these limitations. The frustrations women feel may not only be directed toward the pastor and elders, but ultimately toward God Himself, as they wonder what He thinks of them and what He wants them to do. This reaction is key and must not be overlooked. Therefore, a pastor must be careful how he is representing God's heart to women in the church.

Women who provide leadership oversight for ministry to women must come to this work charged by God to care for His flock. Theirs is the ministry of the Great Commission (Matt. 28:16–20), modeled after the Good Shepherd (John 10). Discerning and caring for the needs of women in the church takes wisdom and prayer, trusting God to reveal what is necessary to care well for His sheep. God provides pastoral care from both men and women to women (and men). Jesus is our Good Shepherd, but by God's grace, the Spirit gives gifts to both men and women to shepherd (pastor) His people.

MINISTRY BOUNDARIES

Relational boundaries can be described in three separate categories: rigid, porous, or healthy (wise). A person who has rigid relational boundaries tends to be self-protective, letting very little in or out of their personal space. It is hard to know or be known by someone with rigid boundaries. People with porous boundaries function somewhat indiscriminately, allowing too much in from other people and giving too much out. Finally, a person with healthy, wise boundaries demonstrates godly wisdom and discernment to regulate what gets in and goes out. A person in this category wisely shares and withholds himself or herself, while accepting what the other person is able to offer.

When one ponders how Jesus shepherds, it becomes clear that it is not possible to codify absolute, rigid boundaries. A pastor cannot eliminate pastoral care for women in an effort to be wise and discerning, or even self-protective. On the other hand, we know porous boundaries can set up potentially unhealthy and inappropriate relationships devoid of godly wisdom. No one has to be available for every problem, or give people unquestioned access whenever they ask.

Even Jesus established boundaries when ministering to people's needs. John 2:24 says, "But Jesus, on His part, was not entrusting Himself to them, because He knew all people." Jesus knew the hearts of people and wisely chose whether or not to entrust Himself to them. He modeled a rhythm of life that balanced ministry, rest, and solitude (Mark 6:31–32). In John 20:17, when Mary Magdalene saw Jesus in the garden and clung to Him, He told her not to. He told her to go tell others, even though He knew she wanted more of Him. Jesus did not answer every desire or request, and neither should anyone in ministry.

Yet even in view of the warm invitation to relationship that we see from our Lord, we know that pastors who give too much time or attention may easily become misunderstood. Pastoral care with undisciplined boundaries can move the relationship into unpredictable and emotionally confusing territory, where inadvertent cues may be sent or received. Misunderstanding can happen from innocuous social kindnesses, even when the intentions are pure. When a woman comes to an office for help, there should be appropriate boundaries in place. High moral, emotional, and physical boundaries must be maintained. Every precaution must be in place to avoid unintentional messages.

To be sure, maintaining wise and appropriate ministry boundaries does not eliminate meaningful relationships and pastoral care. Scripture records meaningful relationships that both Jesus and Paul had with women. Neither avoided women. Jesus loved Mary and Martha and enjoyed warm times of fellowship in their home in deeply compassionate and theological ways (Luke 10:38–42; John 11:1–44). He also welcomed women into social settings that were not the cultural norm (Luke 7:40–50; John 12:1–8). Paul writes in Romans 16 about many women with whom he obviously enjoyed a deep relationship and shared meaningful ministry.

It is essential for a pastor to know his own weaknesses and temptations, avoiding anything that would not be wise to offer another person. Some pastors feel the freedom to give a hug in a public place when someone is hurting, but not everyone ministers in the same way. While exercising caution in physical touch is important, realize that it is impossible to make one absolute rule that applies to every situation. Thankfully, the Holy Spirit was given to us to teach us how to be loving shepherds. He is present to help. Godly wisdom often comes in common sense. When in doubt, seek wisdom and help from a wise mentor.

PASTORAL HELP IN MINISTRY STRUGGLES

Philippians 4:2–3 is an interesting and helpful passage about women in the church who need relational help. These verses often come up in discussions about the potential for women in the church to cause problems. Yet in this passage, while Paul addresses a serious dispute between two women named Euodia and Syntyche, he also provides an example of how pastors can support and encourage women who actively minister in the church.

Acts 16 records the story of the birth of the church at Philippi. On Paul's second missionary journey, he went to Philippi, which was a leading city in the district of Macedonia. On the Sabbath, because there was no synagogue in this Roman colony, Paul went to find a place of prayer. Just outside the city gate by the river, he found Lydia, who was a worshiper of God, and a group of women. Paul spoke to the women about the gospel of Jesus Christ, and the Lord opened Lydia's heart to believe. She and her household were then baptized (v. 15). Lydia is thus recognized as the first recorded convert, not only in Philippi, but in all of Europe. We are told in Acts 16:40 that the first gathering location of the church was in her home.

When Paul mentions Euodia and Syntyche in Philippians 4, he includes a few significant descriptors to help us understand some important facts about these women. In verse 3, he says their names are written in the book of life, so we know they are believers. We also know they have wrestled and labored together, in fact, side by side with Paul and other leaders to declare the good news of the gospel. It would also seem they are mature believers in this congregation. As some commentators have suggested, it is quite possible they were part of a core ministry team. What is certain is that they have influence over others for the gospel in the church of Philippi. To miss their importance as fellow workers with Paul for the gospel would be an interpretative error.

From Acts 16 and Philippians 4, we know the names of three women who were influential in the church at Philippi. God used these women, along with other believers, to spread the gospel and build up the church. Such shared experiences can create deep relational bonds. Lydia, Euodia, and Syntyche, who were likely friends, were part of the early formative stages of this church and no doubt thrilled to participate in this new, great work of the Holy Spirit. What excitement!

Two verses provide necessary context to help us understand why Paul singled out Euodia and Syntyche and pled with his "true companion" (likely a leader of the church with whom Paul had served) to help them come to agreement (4:3). Earlier in the letter to Philippi, Paul instructed the church to "conduct yourselves in a manner worthy of the gospel of Christ . . . standing firm in one spirit, with one mind striving together for the faith of the gospel" (1:27). He also asked them to "make my joy complete by being of the same mind, maintaining the same love, united in spirit, intent on one purpose" (2:2). Love and oneness of spirit is crucial for unity. Clearly, this was not the description of the current relationship between Euodia and Syntyche. While the text does not tell us the issue, we can safely assume it was causing problems within the leadership of this church. It certainly was enough of a concern that Paul pointed it out and asks someone described as a loyal yokefellow to help these women who were stuck in a disagreement (4:2–3).

But this passage also points to another important issue. Notice how Paul gets right in the middle of a hard relational situation between two women in the Philippian church. He obviously had to know they were hurting. Most women who experience an ongoing struggle with a friend suffer anxiety, pain, and distress. It was a loving and kind rebuke for Paul to press for resolution.

Our pain, as also was true in their case, affects those around us. It is hard not to notice when good friends are struggling. Paul instructs the leader in the church to take hold of these women to help them resolve their issue. There is an urgency in Paul's request. It was important for their good, but also for the good of the church. Conflicts in a church can grow and tempt friends to take sides. Disunity grows when left unattended and unresolved. By affirming their work as contenders for the gospel together with other leaders, Paul certainly expects this matter to be resolved, so that colaboring efforts for the gospel could continue.

Consider again from these verses the normative relationship Paul models in this passage of men and women laboring together for the gospel. Consider the model of male ministry leaders helping women ministry leaders resolve relational struggles. What help does this example give you in your current ministry setting?

PASTORAL ENCOURAGEMENT

This final section of the chapter offers practical ways pastors can encourage women who serve as ministry leaders for women, and women who are in the congregation. We feel encouragement most deeply when it comes within a relationship characterized by love. Even correction or confrontation, when given from one we know loves us, can lead us to hope and comfort. When we receive direction in places where we feel lost, we are helped. The love of a pastor can strengthen us, and strengthen our service to others and the Lord, but the greatest gift of a pastor is to encourage us to know Jesus Christ. Strong encouragement often makes us feel endeared to the one who gives it. Yet encouragement from a pastor who shepherds well will always focus our gaze to remain fixed on our Lord Jesus.

Providing spiritual nourishment and pastoral care for the flock is central to your calling as a shepherd, but you are not the one who is ultimately responsible for their every need. Many women are eager for Bible study, discipleship, and theological engagement. Women learn through podcasts, books, conferences, and retreats. Encourage women who provide these ministries within your own church, but when not available, encourage women to seek these out from other places. Be ready to interact and listen to what they are learning and offer wisdom and discernment to help them evaluate fidelity to the Scriptures. You will not be the only source of spiritual teaching for the women in your church, but you will be responsible to the Lord to watch over their souls (Heb. 13:17).

Evaluate the gifts of the women in your congregation and, whenever possible, create places for them to be used. Equip women with ministry training and encourage their call by your support. God has always made a way for women to serve, teach, lead, and preach the gospel; and His purpose for women has never changed. Invite the women in your church to talk with you about what they feel God is calling them to do and then see how best to support them in their call.

THEOLOGICAL ENGAGEMENT

There are women in your congregation who are eager for biblical and theological conversation yet have few interlocutors. Pastors may say they are willing to talk, but it is important that they invite conversations. This is especially true with topics that are hard to talk about, such as the view of women in ministry leadership. You will have women in your congregation who have deep and complex feelings on this issue. Make every effort to not avoid this topic simply because there are potentially divisive points of view. Women want to understand what the Bible says. They want to know your position, and the process you went through to arrive at your conclusions. There are differing theological views with a wide scope of applications, which makes it easy to understand why there is so much confusion. Most spiritually mature Christian women are able to dialogue with grace and respect, yet this topic can feel so personal. Ministry leaders do well to look beyond disordered emotions for underlying pain or hurt that is still raw and in process.

This conversation is especially important for women who serve or want to serve in ministry leadership within the church. Such women need to comprehend clearly the church's formal, written positions, along with any normative, yet unwritten positions. Clear boundaries offer freedom within which to work, whereas unclear boundaries may produce feelings of insecurity and the fear of overstepping. The unknown is destabilizing.

Beyond topics related to women in leadership, many theological issues interest women in the church. Initiate conversations with those who are spiritually mature and theologically astute to draw out their thoughts. It is affirming when pastors acknowledge theological depth and show interest in what women know. There can be rich, mutual edification as you share together.

Encourage seminary-level study for women who show an interest in deeper theological knowledge. Perhaps you could express your value in their learning by prioritizing a tuition fund for women. Then, when you have theologically trained women, create a place for them to serve in your church. Even if women are not in official church positions, identify those whose ministry would benefit from ongoing training and theological formation and consider how you will steward those gifts and in what ways women can continue to minister and teach the gospel.

Another way to invite theological engagement is by asking women, both Bible scholars and others, for sermonic input and feedback. Their perspective may help you to see the text from a different angle of vision and think about the text in a new way. They might ask questions you had not thought to ask, or caution you to handle a particular portion of Scripture carefully so you do not inadvertently communicate it in a way that is insensitive to women. While the number of commentaries by women is growing, most available works are by men. Search for sources that will broaden your viewpoint. Be curious about the perspective of a woman and invite her thoughts. It might be intimidating for some women to engage with you on this level, but persist in making your request. Most women, when asked, would be honored and grateful for your interest in their thoughts and feedback.

Their perspective can be especially helpful when your sermon is on a woman in the Bible. Women who have been in Bible study for years have likely studied most of the women in the Bible. If you preach on a woman they have studied at length, but miss important points of her story and conflate her significance, women will notice. It is hard to hear a sermon that fails to acknowledge the depth and richness of what God did in and through her story. When it is so meaningful for women, they want you to notice too. Only casual attention to the text when it is about a woman tempts women to question the depth of your preaching on other portions of Scripture as well.

ACTIVE ENCOURAGEMENT FOR MINISTRY TO WOMEN

Women who are ministry leaders for women sincerely value pastoral interest and support. When you show interest, you signal legitimacy and respect. Because you are considered an "expert," your encouragement and support means far more than other opinions and assessments. Two times when pastoral support is particularly meaningful are when leaders are preparing for ministry, and when direct ministry happens.

The women's leadership team meeting is an important place to visit. Women would likely be very excited to tell you what is happening in the lives of the women they serve. They might appreciate an opportunity to ask questions about ministry situations they struggle to know how to handle. There might be a biblical or theological question they want to discuss, but would hesitate to make an appointment to do so. They might be curious about your hopes for the church or what you sense God is doing in the church body at large. Face-to-face meetings with the ministry team are far more helpful than reading a required monthly report or catching a quick update in an unexpected hallway conversation. When you are physically present, you can hear and see the passion of the women who serve the women in your church. You might become aware of a particular need in the ministry of which you were unaware. Is their budget sufficient? Is there something you can do to provide for the ministry development of the women who serve in your congregation? Might there be a conference you can encourage women to attend, or resources you can make sure they have? The opportunity for your women leaders to engage with other ministry leaders will enlarge their vision for what God can do in ways that perhaps they have never seen before.

This encouragement for pastors to visit leaders' meetings is not to be confused with giving *too much* oversight. It might seem suspicious for the pastor to come often and, albeit perhaps unintentionally, signal a lack of trust in what they are doing. There is no need to visit every week, but it is important to stay in touch regularly! Typically, one or two visits per year is sufficient to learn what is happening and let the women know you value what they are doing. Pastors are special guests, and while women will likely love having you visit, your presence, as an authority figure, could be slightly intimidating. Knowing about the visit ahead of time allows leaders to be prepared and to prepare others for your visit.

Typically, ministry events for women function on a predictable schedule. When there are regular Bible studies or ministry events, stop by to see what is happening. Pray over women as they begin their new Bible study, or praise the Lord with them on their final class day. Fit in with the rhythms of your people. Enjoy and give thanks for what God is doing among women.

When you are in the room where the Bible study happens and can sense the

Spirit at work, you are more apt to praise the Lord publicly for what God is doing. In his letters, Paul always affirmed the good things God was doing in the churches (e.g., 1 Thess. 1; Rom. 1; Col. 1). When we read his accounts, we are encouraged. Likewise, your church will be encouraged when in sermons you mention what God is doing in and through the women in your church.

Another way to encourage and support women in your congregation is to pay attention to Christian women who are influencers. Do the women in your church use a video-driven Bible study? Have you watched sessions or read books by their favorite teachers? It is easy to research current women leaders through social media. Women would be encouraged to know you take that level of interest in their spiritual development by learning about people who matter to them. You might be amazed at the depth of content they commit to studying each week.

The message of Paul in both Romans 16 and Philippians 4 affirms that men and women worked together, which gives biblical precedent for men and women joining together in gospel ministry. If you have the resources available to support a woman on staff to oversee pastoral care of women, her presence and position will affirm the value you have for taking care of the women in your congregation. She also will be an invaluable resource for you, and help you better understand the needs of your congregation. To that end, women should be part of the ministry vision casting for the church, as the Spirit opens their eyes to the needs of people around them. Prioritize the voice of women with others who labor together for the gospel.

Finally, if you know women who are questioning your level of support, initiate conversations that will allow you to understand their concerns and perceptions. This can be a moment of sacred ministry. Perhaps God would have you bring healing and hope to women who may have been hurt by painful situations in the past. Listen empathetically and follow up with thoughtful responses.

CONCLUSION

The task of shepherding a flock can be daunting. Regardless of one's positional, formal or informal pastoral care of women, it is easy to fear falling short. But the call for men and women to shepherd women is to serve as Jesus served and participate in what God is doing in Christ to reconcile the world to Himself (2 Cor. 5:19). There may be many perceived risks, but in reality, this is a place of mutual blessing. God reveals Himself to us through Jesus Christ, who is the cornerstone of the church (Eph. 2). His purpose is to draw people to Himself and to use the church to reveal the multifaceted wisdom of God (Eph. 3). God is at work in the church. The gates of hell cannot overpower it (Matt. 16:18). The call of God to serve in ministry to the church is an immeasurable gift. By His grace, He has given you His Spirit to dwell within you (John 14:16–18), give you power, make you wise, and fill you with faith, hope, joy, and peace (Rom. 15:13). Without Jesus Christ, the gift of being a pastor and shepherd would be a weight too great to bear. But because of Him, you share not only in His suffering, but also in the great joy of being close enough to see what God is doing deep in the hearts of His people (1 Peter 4:13).

Model what Paul described as co-laboring for the gospel in order to dispel any notion that the positional power of a pastor or ministry leader conveys an attitude of superiority. When you show value to those who serve on staff, who serve as lay leaders, and those who presently are too weak to serve, you encourage unity and affirm the places God has purposed for them. Yes, pastoral oversight brings significant responsibility. The task of a shepherd is clear (Ezek. 34). A blessing of the pastorate is that you receive the opportunity to serve others and take care of them. Jesus modeled ministry with humility and servanthood. As He loved and served us, let us love and serve others.

Not everyone is given the privilege and joy of walking with women in the most significant moments of their lives, to speak words of hope and promise over them, and to witness moments when God breaks through and reveals Himself to them. God has given you this gift and responsibility.

> *Now may the God of peace, who brought up from the dead*
> *the great Shepherd of the sheep through the blood of the eternal covenant,*
> *that is, Jesus our Lord, equip you in every good thing to do His will,*
> *working in us that which is pleasing in His sight,*
> *through Jesus Christ, to whom be the glory forever and ever. Amen.*
> HEBREWS 13:20–21

NOTES

1. Cornelius Plantinga Jr., *Not the Way It's Supposed to Be: A Breviary of Sin* (Grand Rapids: Eerdmans, 1995), 10.

2. Christopher R. Little, ed., *Transformed from Glory to Glory: Celebrating the Legacy of J. Robertson McQuilkin* (Ft. Washington, PA: CLC Publications, 2015), 45.

Ministering to Men

BOB MACRAE

Much research over the years has shown that men have been disappearing from local churches in droves since the 1990s. This startling development shows that a robust ministry to men has never been more important among evangelicals.

This chapter will explain how both men and churches can benefit from a men's ministry, as well as a strategy for having a men's ministry that is meaningful and effective. How each individual men's ministry accomplishes this goal may look very different, depending on location, finances, and demographics. Through a clear understanding of the purpose of a men's ministry and seeking wisdom through prayer, leaders can have confidence the Holy Spirit can lead them as to how God will accomplish His purposes through them in their particular context.

THEOLOGICAL FOUNDATIONS

What is the purpose of a men's ministry? Is a men's ministry even a biblical concept? It is important to note that when one looks at Scripture, there are relatively few commandments in the New Testament directed specifically to men. By far, the vast majority of commands are directed not just to men, nor merely to women, but generally to all who desire to follow Jesus. The New Testament contains nearly 700 commands given by Jesus and the writers of the Gospels and Epistles, and commands that apply to a single gender appear only in the Epistles. It would be difficult to find one general command of Jesus in the Gospels that can be targeted to men only. In other words, Jesus' main emphasis was not to teach one how to act like a man or a woman, but how to act as one who desires to follow Him.

For example, in Matthew 28:19–20, followers of Christ are told to "make disciples." This is not a hint, a suggestion, or a preference; it is a command. This is not a command to only men. It is a command to all who are followers of Christ. We are to be disciples who make disciples. Although Jesus never used the word "Christian," if one were to interpret the word properly, a Christian is a disciple or follower of Jesus Christ. Jesus spent His public life of ministry telling and showing His disciples, then and now, what it looks like to be His follower. Disciples are told to be obedient, generous, sacrificial, dedicated, loving, kind, compassionate, lovers of truth, honest, and meek. The characteristics listed in the previous sentence are only a small sampling of the many characteristics, fruit, or descriptions Christ commanded His followers to possess. The list could go on for pages.

By no means do these characteristics make a person a disciple of Christ, but Jesus says they describe the person who is a disciple of His. Paul makes it very clear that one is saved (or becomes a disciple, follower of Christ, or a true Christian) by grace through faith (Eph. 2:8–9). In addition, Paul in the very next verse makes it clear that those people who are saved by faith are created to do good works (Eph. 2:10). These godly characteristics are displayed by a person indwelt by God's Spirit as a consequence of one's life or relationship with God; they are not the cause of the relationship.

PHILOSOPHY OF MEN'S MINISTRY

In light of what has been stated, where does men's ministry fit into the life of the local church or parachurch ministry? Is there a legitimate place for it? The answer to that last question is yes. However, some men's ministries seem to focus most of their attention teaching men how to be men, rather than teaching men how to be a follower of Christ within the context of being men. One might ask, "What is the difference?" The difference, although initially appearing to be subtle, is significant. Jesus was not preoccupied with telling men how to be men or women how to be women. He told them how to follow Him, seek His kingdom above all else, and produce more disciples (Matt. 6:33; 28:19–20). Does that mean there is no distinction between how men and women follow Christ? No, but the distinction is oftentimes not as big as we try to make it.

THE IMPORTANCE AND BENEFITS OF A MEN'S MINISTRY

Often, when studying the Word of God, men can be challenged to discover the characteristics of a godly person with specific application targeting the unique roles that come with being a man. By approaching Scripture this way, churches can share a united purpose and philosophy of making disciples who make disciples for all their ministries, although the implementation of the goal will look different for each specific ministry.

As previously stated, some New Testament commands are given specifically to men and others to women, although these instances are relatively few. Following are a list of commands specifically addressed in the role of being a woman or a man: to **wives,** 1 Corinthians 11:6–7; 14:34–35; Ephesians 5:22–24; Colossians 3:18; to **husbands,** Ephesians 5:25–28, 33; Colossians 3:19; to **fathers,** Ephesians 6:4; Colossians 3:21; to **women,** 1 Timothy 2:11–12; to **men desiring to be bishops/elders,** 1 Timothy 3:1–7; to **men desiring to be deacons,** 1 Timothy 3:8–13; to **older men,** Titus 2:2; to **older women,** Titus 2:3–5; and to **young men,** Titus 2:6–8. While this list of verses is relatively short and needs to be studied, they are relatively few in comparison to the many verses describing the characteristics of what an obedient disciple of Jesus should be, regardless of whether that disciple is male or female.

With the mission of making disciples who make disciples as the primary goal of the church, pastors and leaders of a men's ministry must take advantage of opportunities to not only teach what God's Word instructs believers to do, but also to give practical means of application where men can live out what they have been taught.

Men's ministry is a valuable opportunity for men to be able to talk about their spiritual experience and journey with other men. As men there are often common experiences and challenges to which other men can relate as husbands, brothers, sons, uncles, and grandfathers. These are roles that are unique to men. There is value in learning how to be a Christ follower within those roles, but it must be done without deemphasizing the command that encompasses all others, which is to be a disciple who makes disciples. While learning how to be a better husband is important (particularly for the wives), men's ministries cannot make that the sole or even primary focus, or the main context for illustrations and application during teaching and Bible study because not all men are married.

It is a worthwhile endeavor for men to study the Word of God together. There is always more we need to learn from the Bible. Greater numbers of Christians within the church are more biblically illiterate than in past generations. Many reasons have been considered for this reality: the deemphasizing of Sunday school, an increase in topical rather than expositional preaching, the avoidance of teaching "difficult" passages for fear of offending some listeners, pastors who are too busy with other responsibilities to prepare deeply or pastors who by necessity are bi-vocational, having less time for sermon preparation. Whatever the cause, churches need to evaluate the depth of biblical knowledge amongst their people and strate-gically, through the guidance of the Holy Spirit, assemble a plan for helping mem-bers know what God's Word teaches. Every church won't accomplish this goal in the same way; the main question is: are people being taught the Word of God?

If men are lacking in biblical knowledge, a men's Bible study may be exactly what is needed. Due to work schedules and other responsibilities, this might need to take place early on a weekday morning before work, or early on a Saturday morn-ing. Evenings or later times in the weekend often do not work as well for many men.

Since relationships and friendships are such an important piece of the Christian life, it would be wise to incorporate some small group discussion into the Bible study guided by a trained leader. Many men lack strong friendships marked by spiritual conversations, vulnerability, accountability, and prayer. This does not develop overnight but comes through small group discussion and prayer following a Bible study and has the potential of seeing those relationships develop.

Over time, a short time of prayer could be a great avenue to get more reserved men to open up and share a prayer request or pray out loud. For some men, such behavior could be a first. Becoming familiar with praying out loud in front of trusted friends may be what encourages the man to lead his family in spoken prayer at home.

The trained leader does not need to be seminary-trained, but one who has had been trained and instructed how to ask good questions, how to engage the introverted man, and how to respond to things expressed that are in opposition to the teaching of the Word of God. The leader should love the Lord God with all his heart and show evidence of being a follower of Christ. Discussion questions should be sent out several days in advance so thought and prayer can precede the small group discussion. This also gives time for the Holy Spirit to direct the leader in how best to guide the group. While training does not need to be long, it must be adequate, so the recruited leader is set up for success. Too often people are asked to serve in various roles in the church or outside ministries while providing little to no training. As a result, poor results may cause the volunteer to feel inadequate, even ungifted. He may not lack giftedness, but simply may not have the training to do the job for which he has been recruited. The responsibility for the lack of success is not on the volunteer, but on the leader who recruited him without pro-viding adequate training.

THE INCLUSION OF ALL MEN

SINGLE MEN

When a church has a Bible study for the men, there needs to be a purposeful attempt to include all men within their sphere of influence. Too many times, singles in the church are made to feel incomplete—contrary to Scripture. Both Jesus and the apostle Paul were single, and neither their ministry nor manhood were deficient due to singleness. Paul argued there are advantages for some men to remain single (1 Cor. 7:7–8). Singles should not be made to feel as junior members of a men's ministry or to the overall ministry of any church.

This message toward single men can be subtle when the majority of illustrations or applications are directed to those in marriage relationships. Many men's ministries should let the single man know he is valued and his involvement in the ministry is desired and welcomed.

There are more single men in our culture now than in the recent past. This may be due to more men postponing marriage until older, choosing to be single, being a widower, or being single by divorce or separation. A men's ministry can support and disciple men who have experienced the tragedy of divorce without necessarily advocating for it. Too often, in an effort to look like it is not advocating or supporting certain behaviors, the church can ignore individuals who desperately need support and godly encouragement as they walk a difficult path. Everyone has a different story, and all stories need to be heard. All Christ followers have sin in their lives, and ostracizing men who don't seem to fit into a church's desired checklist can thwart a church's potential for ministry.

PAST OFFENDERS

The only unpardonable sin is the rejection of the gospel. The gospel says anyone can have their sins forgiven and they can stand in an accepted relationship with God through faith in Jesus Christ. This was accomplished on the cross when Jesus paid the penalty for mankind's sins, a penalty of death all humans deserve. Christ's resurrection proved Jesus was indeed the Son of God as He claimed, and that the sacrifice of His life on the cross as payment for the sins of those who believe by faith was sufficient to satisfy the justice of God the Father. The Holy Spirit indwells each believer and is present to guide the child of God in their spiritual growth and development. The gospel is for everyone.

If we believe no sin is unforgiveable, does the church and the men's ministry demonstrate that belief? All mankind needs the forgiveness of God for every sin. When one is released from prison for a crime, can that person find a safe place in a church that would welcome him to worship or investigate the claims of Jesus?

Is the convicted and released rapist or child abuser welcome in our ministries? While certain sins come with lifelong consequences, do we find ways to minister to people with sordid pasts?

Some churches have begun programs allowing former male sex offenders to attend church and be under the watchful care of a trained, accountable, constant male companion. This practice keeps the church from being at risk by leaving an individual with a criminal past alone in the church building risking a repeated offense. While the recidivism of some crimes and behaviors can be statistically high, one cannot assume every offender will be a repeat offender, and therefore there is no ministry that should not welcome such a person. When appropriate safeguards are in place, the church both protects children and other vulnerable church members while welcoming past offenders to worship God, thereby communicating that no sin is beyond the capacity of God's forgiveness.

Former sex offenders and those convicted of similar crimes should never be in the same location as children. A men's ministry may be the best and most appropriate place to welcome such a person. Whether the person has already repented or is curious to investigate if the Bible has anything for him, that person should be welcomed, but with appropriate cautions. Sometimes gospel-centered living brings uncomfortable situations. A church's desire for comfort should never override its mission to reach people and make disciples. A church or ministry must report any offense or suspected criminal offense to the proper authorities, regardless of the position or reputation of the accused.

We must keep in mind that all men have stories and past sins. Even a man who has become a follower of Christ will still struggle with sin on some level. A man can also have a habitual or damaging sin that he fell into after his conversion to Christ. A men's ministry can be an effective place for healing and recovery.

HIGH SCHOOL STUDENTS

There is wisdom in welcoming teenage boys into the men's ministry. Much has been written about the high church dropout rate during the adolescent years. Studies have shown there is less likelihood of youth leaving the church when they have established relationships with adults in the congregation. A men's ministry can be a wonderful way of connecting teenage boys with older men from the church. If a high school graduate leaves for college, enlists in the armed services, or joins the workforce, there is a higher likelihood he will stay connected to his church if adult men are communicating with him in his absence.

STRATEGY FOR MEN'S MINISTRY

Every local church ministry should take the time to evaluate its programs. Activities, events, and programs should fit under one of these descriptive categories: Build, Win, or Equip. In many churches there seems to be an overemphasis on Building events or programs.

BUILDING

Building events are opportunities designed to build into the life of the person who is already a believer. This often can come under the umbrella of church services, Bible studies, Sunday school, and small groups. There is nothing wrong with Building events, in fact a ministry would suffer without them. However, if Winning or Equipping events or programs are absent, the ministry may have a decidedly healthy imbalance.

WINNING

Winning events are designed for the nonbeliever. It is the opportunity to provide an entry point for the man who has not yet chosen to follow Christ. Generally, a man will not make his first entry point to a church through a Bible study. Men may be more prone to attend a ball game, go on a fishing trip, or involve themselves in a father/son or father/daughter event that appears to be fun. The enjoyable activity is the draw.

A desire to see their friends come to Christ should be the motivating factor in inviting unbelievers. Such an event should expose them to the gospel. The degree and depth to which the gospel is shared should depend on how equipped the other men in the ministry are to share the good news with their friends.

An event should not happen merely for something to do. While guests and less mature men may see the event as something fun, ministry leaders should view it as a Winning event. The events and activities should include a presentation of the gospel. This should not be seen as manipulation, but as an expression of love for those still dead in their sins and outside of Christ.

EQUIPPING

There is a need to Equip men to make disciples, and this area is where too many men's ministries may fall short. The purpose of an Equipping event is to train men *how* to do ministry. This could include helping men understand the Win, Build, Equip model of disciple-making that Jesus demonstrated. Men need to know how to share their faith with another man. Some men may need to be taught how to engage unbelievers in general conversation.

MEETING THE SPECIFIC NEEDS OF MEN

Larger churches can offer a wide range of ministries specific to men. For example, larger ministries can focus on recovery or healing from addictions. These might include groups that deal with pornography and sexual addiction, alcohol addiction, drug addiction, grief recovery for those who have lost a spouse or child to death, and divorce recovery. Most churches are not large enough to offer so many specific ministries. If God has placed a disproportionate number of men in a church who are dealing with a specific area themselves, perhaps the Holy Spirit is directing that church to provide a ministry to help men with those struggles.

While most churches cannot provide such specific need-based ministries and support groups, a church and men's ministry must at least be a resource of information so men can be directed to the appropriate help. If that place happens to be another church in the area, one should not avoid giving out information for fear of losing one of their parishioners to the local "competition." A church should not be in the business of competing for members. Rather, leaders should have enough personal security and love for their people to ensure their congregants are getting the best help possible for their specific challenges.

Benefitting from the ministry of another church or organization does not mean a man will leave his home church to join the one with the specific ministry from which he is benefitting. While that could happen, the concern of losing a parishioner should never override the pastor's or leader's desire to see a disciple gain the help he needs to mature in his walk of following Jesus. Such groups and support can fit into the Win or Build distinction.

FURTHER STEPS OF ACTION

For the church that has a good number of men who are biblically literate, another Bible study for the men may not be what is most needed. There comes a point where one needs to quit gathering more information and head knowledge, instead of putting into action, implementing, or applying the knowledge they have already gained. While teaching men (as well as women, youth, and children) how to be a disciple of Jesus should be the driving force of any church, a pastor needs to help his people see and experience opportunities to put faith into practice. The knowledge gained from church services, small groups, Sunday school, and Bible studies need application ministries and opportunities. For men, there are numerous ways this can happen, which naturally fall under the umbrella of a men's ministry.

PRAYER PARTNERS

The Bible is very clear that the older believer is to invest in the younger (Titus 2:2–5). This can happen in a number of contexts. Older teenagers should be welcomed into a men's ministry. An excellent way to do this is to match interested students with men from the church as prayer partners. Prayer requests can be shared via text message or email with a monthly breakfast or meeting for a snack, coffee, or lunch. There need not be a set program so long as the purpose for the partnership is being accomplished.

The goal for such a partnership should not be a top-down relationship, but one where both parties can support each other through prayer. By specifically targeting high school and college-aged men, the church is also being strategic in establishing greatly needed relationships at a particularly vulnerable time in life. If the young man is still in school, the friendship and relationship have a higher promise of success if the prayer partner shows interest in sports, concerts, hobbies, or after-school jobs in which the young man is participating.

BIG BROTHER OR MENTORING PROGRAM

In a time when more and more boys are growing up in homes without dads, a wonderful and necessary ministry men in the church can offer is to young boys. The men can care and invest in these boys in similar fashion to that of a Big Brothers program. Many single moms would love to have a trusted man take their son to a sporting event, go fishing for a morning, play a game, attend the boy's Little League game, or most importantly, take an interest in his spiritual life.

For this ministry, necessary precautions need to be taken to protect the boys from anyone who would take advantage of or abuse a boy. All men in such programs must submit to a background check, attend special training provided by the men's ministry, follow child safety policies, and be held to high accountability by the program coordinator. The men should always let the mother or guardian as well as the program coordinator know what activity they are doing with the boys, where they are going, and when they will return. The program coordinator should keep a written log for every man participating in such a program.

A men's ministry must have a program that establishes wise guidelines and policies, doing everything possible to set up reasonable safeguards with accountability for the sake of a future generation of men, many in desperate need of a mature and godly example in the absence of a father. For example, the boys should not spend the night with their mentors unless it is in the context of a group event involving multiple individuals. Meetings and events should take place in public spaces. Men should never enter a boy's home unless a parent is present, and they are invited. If a boy is driven to the event or place of meeting by the mentor, the ride should be direct without detour. Policies must be made from wisdom and not fear.

MINISTRY OF HELPING

In a time where many families and individuals find themselves in difficult financial situations, many nonemergency projects get put aside. Such projects could include painting the interior and exterior of their home, tree trimming, lawn maintenance, car maintenance, and similar projects. While everyone seems to be busy these days, how much of a blessing would it be to the widow, single mom, or family on a tight budget to have a group of men take care of one of these projects?

Some drive cars that are unsafe because they desperately need new brakes. It often is not a situation of neglect as much because of the financial inability. If a church or ministry had a person designated to receive such requests, that person could coordinate needed repairs.

If such tasks were offered and performed, the opportunity to help people with such services could be announced in the church bulletin, newsletter, email announcements, Facebook, or website enabling people to ask for help easily. If a need is suspected, the ministry should diplomatically inquire as to whether their services could be of help. Such a service ministry is consistent with the Scripture's instruction to care for the widow, particularly when there are no family members available to do so (1 Tim. 5:8).

This type of helping ministry need not be limited to people from within the church. Such services can be used to show the love of Christ to the nonbeliever, as well as communities and public schools with needs and projects not within their budget. Serving opportunities such as these can fall into the Win or Build categories. It could be Win for the men who have been invited to participate but are not yet believers or for the people being served to see the love of Christ.

Another help ministry could be to use retired men to provide rides to doctor's offices, grocery stores, or hair salons for those in need of transportation. Such a small act of kindness can be a wonderful way of showing the love of Christ. It can also be rewarding for the person serving who may be looking for a tangible way to serve God in his older years.

COMMON INTEREST EVENTS

While everything done within a men's ministry should be obvious to those in leadership as to how an event and activity falls into the **Win, Build,** or **Equip** purpose, there are many other activities that can be done that fit within a Win purpose without a lot of imagination. For example, a church may have a men's basketball team, softball team, or provide outings that involve camping or fishing. There should *always* be a justifiable purpose for every ministry. For example, a group of men from the church can get together to go fishing *(an event)*, or a group of men can go fishing and purposely invite men for whose salvation they have been praying *(an event with a purpose)*.

While many men enjoy outdoor activities that involve sports like hunting, fishing, or golf, that is not true of all men. While some would enjoy a Win activity such as going to a football game that involves a tailgating pregame feast, some of the men may be more excited to be able to grill or create their favorite dish. A ministry needs to be careful to not give the impression that all men love the stereotypical "man things" such as hunting and fishing. While there seems to be a rise in gender confusion among some men, particularly amongst those of younger generations, reinforcing such stereotypes may unnecessarily add to the confusion. Men's ministries need to be smart and thoughtful and dependent on the Holy Spirit as to how they define and describe what a man is.

CONCLUSION

As men in the leadership of the ministry are equipped to understand the strategy of a disciple-making ministry, more will be able to see how events can be used to work toward the purpose of making disciples, rather than doing events or activities for the sole purpose of fun, entertainment, tradition, or simply to stay busy. One can have fun and be entertained when purposefully engaging in activities, but the overarching purpose of making disciples can help form the structure that moves a ministry from being simply active to being strategic.

When churches understand the purpose of any ministry is to ultimately be making disciples, churches can look at their niche and demographic and ask God for wisdom as to how to do that best in a men's ministry that considers their unique factors. The idea is not to mirror one ministry after another that has seen success, but to consider how God has called your church to be effective in the setting in which He has placed it.

Ministering to the Aging

DAVID L. WOODALL

INTRODUCTION

The average age of the American population is increasing. According to the United States Census Bureau's 2017 National Population Projections, in the early 2030s the number of older people (age sixty-five and above) will surpass and continue to surpass the number of children (under eighteen) for the first time in the history of the United States.[1] At the same time, the median age of church attenders is also escalating as both life expectancy and life span increase, the elderly maintain better health, and younger people are increasingly rejecting a biblical worldview.[2]

These realities point to the need for churches to have a vibrant and informed ministry to older individuals. The goal of this chapter is two-fold. The first section is devoted to a biblical theology of aging. References to the elderly are placed in their biblical context to articulate a biblical view of aging that should serve as a foundation for ministry in the church. The second section reflects on modern research to identify the unique needs faced by the elderly and to suggest how these needs could be addressed by both the elderly and those who minister to them.

A BIBLICAL THEOLOGY OF AGING

To be human is to experience the passing of time. From the moment of creation, Adam experienced age in the cycles of days, months, and years. And this was good. It was the fall of humanity, however, that introduced the reality of decline into the aging process. Humanity would now experience deterioration during the aging process and eventual death (Gen. 3:13–19). Life would now be a struggle as age increases. In the midst of this struggle, however, humanity retains the image of God (Gen. 5:1–3, James 3:9) and therefore, retains value, significance, and dignity throughout the course of life.

The Bible is full of reminders related to the transitory nature of life (Isa. 40:6–8; Job 9:25–26; Ps. 103:14–16; James 1:10–11; 4:14; 1 Peter 1:24–25). Moses realized this as he experienced the hardships of the wilderness wanderings. A psalm attributed to Moses confesses that God is eternal, but humanity is mortal (Ps. 90:1–3). Corporeal lives are characterized by frailty and brevity (Ps. 90:5–11). The young fighting men who entered the wilderness would die by the age of seventy or eighty (Ps. 90:10). In light of this reality, aging individuals are exhorted not to live in the past but to live in the present time in a pursuit of wisdom (Ps. 90:11–17).

AGING IN THE PENTATEUCH AND HISTORICAL NARRATIVES

The Pentateuch introduced specific nomenclature related to extreme old age and death. Select elderly individuals were "full of years" (Abraham at 175 [Gen. 25:7–8], Jacob at 180 [Gen. 35:28–29], Jehoiada at 130 [2 Chron. 24:15], and Job at 140 [Job 42:16–17]). Select elderly died at a "good old age" (Abraham [Gen. 15:15], Gideon [Judg. 8:32], and David [1 Chron. 29:28]). These phrases are found in the context of experiencing the Lord's blessing for a life well-lived (Gen. 24:1). Great value and importance was placed on individuals who walked with the Lord into advanced age. Abraham began a new calling when he was old (Gen. 12:1–4), and Moses was eighty when he was called (Ex. 7:7). In addition to leaders appointed by God, there were other "elders of Israel" who provided leadership in various situations requiring wisdom (Ex. 3:16, 18; 18:12; 24:1, 9). God often used older adults to accomplish His will in the great turning points of salvation history. There should be no loss of meaning or significance in old age.

The Mosaic law legislated respect for elders. When an elder entered the assembly, the people should stand as a sign of respect for the elder and reverence for God (Lev. 19:32). One characteristic of Israel's rebellion in the days of Jeremiah was the fact that the elders were not shown proper respect (Lam. 5:12). As Israel wandered in the wilderness and entered the promised land, they were (as adults!) to honor their father and mother by their actions, especially through all the hardships that the journey would entail (Ex. 20:12). Those who publicly asserted that they wanted their parents "out of the way" and refused to care for them in old age were guilty of a capital offense (Ex. 21:17; Lev. 20:9).[3] Following the command to honor parents would result in longevity as a nation in the land (Deut. 5:16), but rejection of the command would lead to disaster. Respect and honor for the elderly should be expressed by actions that promote their welfare.

Although there was no legislation on retirement in the modern sense of cessation from work to pursue pleasure, there was an indication that the type of work responsibility sometimes changed with increased age. When the Levites reached the age of fifty, for example, they were no longer involved in the transport of the tabernacle. They still, however, continued to serve in certain age-appropriate activities (Num. 8:23–26). Likewise, the elderly Jesse no longer went off to war (1 Sam. 17:12–13).

The narrative sections of the Old Testament describe two diverse pictures of old age. Some elderly suffered extensively from physical decline; other elderly remained physically strong. Isaac, Jacob, and Eli, for example, had vision loss in old age (Gen. 27:1–2; 48:10; 1 Sam. 3:2), yet Moses was full of strength and clear vision at the age of 120 (Deut. 34:7), and Caleb was strong enough at eighty-five to accomplish strenuous physical activity (Josh. 14:10–11).

Although some elderly people do experience declining health, it is not always accompanied by forms of dementia. The elderly Jacob suffered with sickness, lack of strength, and blindness but was still in full control of his mental faculties when he changed the order of blessings on his grandsons Manasseh and Ephraim (Gen. 48:1–20). At eighty, Barzillai supported David during Absalom's rebellion even while suffering from diminished hearing and taste (2 Sam. 19:31–35). The narrative shows that we dare not view all elderly as useless and lacking mental clarity.[4]

Even though some elderly lived in the past and criticized the present (note the response to the new temple foundations by the elders, Ezra 3:12–13; Hag. 2:3), other elderly like Moses, Joshua, and Caleb were visionary leaders. Older counselors were valued for their insight into the current situation (1 Kings 12:6–8). "The stereotype of intransigent older citizens must be understood as a warning against such behavior, but not as a characterization of old age."[5] Therefore, even though the historical books recognized the harsh realities of physical decline, they continued to embrace the honor and dignity of the elderly encoded in the creation narrative and Mosaic legislation.

AGING IN THE WISDOM LITERATURE

Old Testament wisdom literature gives a proper perspective on the historical narrative concerning old age. The physical appearance of "gray hair" was often used to identify the elderly in contrast to youth (Deut. 32:25, 1 Sam. 12:2). In wisdom literature, it became a symbol for the valued wisdom that came from experience. "The glory of the young is their strength; the gray hair of experience is the splendor of the old" (Prov. 20:29 NLT). The wisdom associated with old age came from a life that was lived out in righteousness. "A gray head is a crown of glory; it is found in the way of righteousness" (Prov. 16:31). In harmony with Mosaic law, elderly parents should be given respect and reverence (Prov. 1:8–9; 20:20; 30:11, 17). "Listen to your father, who fathered you, and do not despise your mother when she is old" (Prov. 23:22). Although not viewed as a promise, those who walked with the Lord experience a long and fulfilling life (Ps. 91:16). "They (the righteous) will still yield fruit in advanced age; they will be full of sap and very green" (Ps. 92:14). Psalm 71 uniquely gives the perspective of a man in old age. In a time of hardship, he stood alone (no family or friends are mentioned) and diminished in physical strength (Ps. 71:9). His enemies interpreted this as a sign that God had forsaken him (Ps. 71:10–11), but the opposite was true. Even as he called on God to "not cast me away at the time of old age" (Ps. 17:9), he reflected with hope and confidence on God's mighty deeds and desired to propagate this theology to the younger generation (Ps. 71:14–21). The elderly are in a unique position to teach the young.

The book of Job, however, qualified this traditional wisdom. Although wisdom did indeed come with age, it was possible for even the elderly to misunderstand a certain situation. Amid Job's personal tragedy, the elder Bildad articulated a traditional wisdom that would hold Job personally responsible for his current misfortune (Job 8:8–10, see 32:7). But Job correctly responded that this "wisdom" did not apply in his situation (Job 12:1–12). Ironically, Elihu spoke truth when he said, "The abundant *in years* may not be wise" (Job 32:9). Ecclesiastes likewise described an old king who was foolish because he no longer listened to others (Eccl. 4:13).

Perhaps the most extensive description of the difficulties related to old age is found in Ecclesiastes 12:1–5. Here the effects of old age are pictured as a storm crashing down on an estate. For example, "Those who look through windows grow dim" (Eccl. 12:3) is most likely a reference to the dimming of eyesight in old age.[6] The physical challenges of aging, however, need not be viewed as pessimistic when connected with the fear of God (Eccl. 12:13). In light of physical changes, youth are challenged to use their vigor to pursue God (Eccl. 12:1). Wisdom literature, therefore, highlights the value of wisdom that comes from age and a life of righteousness. This wisdom, however, must constantly be viewed in light of human limitations.

AGING IN THE GOSPELS AND ACTS

The New Testament affirms and advances the theology of the aging developed in the Old Testament. The Mosaic command to honor parents continued to be in force, and any attempt to get around the command nullified the Word of God (Matt. 15:3–9). It continued even when a relationship with Jesus and the advance of the kingdom rearranged priorities (Matt. 6:33; Luke 14:26).

The unique material in Luke–Acts testified to the value of old age. Luke is very concerned to advance the theology that the good news of salvation in Christ is for all people: social outcasts, Samaritans, women, Gentiles, lepers, and (for the purpose of our study) the elderly. Zechariah and Elizabeth were both "advanced in years" (Luke 1:7, 18, 36) when God miraculously enabled them to conceive and play a significant role in salvation history. Although they had been childless throughout their lives (Luke 1:7, 36), they were known in their later years for their righteous actions and prayer (Luke 1:6). Zechariah continued to serve as a priest even in his old age (Luke 1:8–10). Although Zechariah had his initial doubts about the promised conception, he eventually embraced the theology that "nothing will be impossible with God" (Luke 1:37), and Elizabeth demonstrated great faith in her prayer that recognized the fulfillment of God's promises in the pregnancy of Mary (Luke 1:39–45). God clearly grants dignity and worth to the elderly by working through them in key moments in salvation history.

Luke alone recorded the insight of two righteous elderly individuals. Simeon was not explicitly described as an old person, but the revelation that he would not die before he had seen the Lord's Messiah (Luke 2:26) and his resignation to death after he had done so implied old age (Luke 2:29). He received special revelation by the Holy Spirit, responded to the leading of the Holy Spirit to enter the temple courts (Luke 2:27), and spoke words of praise and prophecy (Luke 2:29–32, 34–35). Anna, on the other hand, was described as very old—at least eighty-four (Luke 2:37). As an elderly person, she functioned as a prophetess, devoted her life to worship, fasting, and prayer, and embraced the new work that God was doing in history (Luke 2:36–38). Both Simeon and Anna embodied the wisdom tradition of the Old Testament and confirmed the dignity and worth of older people as God worked through them.

John has two unique references to elderly people, using them both in terms of comparison to youth. In response to Jesus' statement on the necessity of being born again to gain entrance into the kingdom of God, Nicodemus wondered how someone could be born when they are old (John 3:4). The fact that he stressed old age has led some commentators to suggest that Nicodemus was talking about character change and the inability of older people to change their ways.[7] But this is just another instance of spiritual misunderstanding expressed in terms of a physical impossibility. The reference to an older person was for dramatic effect to highlight the absurdity of this on a physical level.[8]

The second reference to an elderly person in John comes after Peter's restoration to ministry (John 21:15–17). Jesus told Peter, "When you were younger, you used to put on your belt and walk wherever you wanted; but when you grow old, you will stretch out your hands and someone else will put your belt on, and bring you where you do not want to go" (John 21:18). Although the young enjoy freedom and mobility while the elderly are often dependent on others, John explained the saying as a statement related to the kind of death that Peter would experience (John 21:19). The younger Peter would have several years of freedom and mobility, but the older Peter, following our Lord, would suffer crucifixion. The older Peter would stretch out his hands to be nailed to a cross beam, and the beam, so to speak, would be dressed upon him before he was led to the place of execution.[9]

The reference to elders in the Gospels parallels the Old Testament usage and forms a transition to the use of the terms in the Epistles. The biblical text gives no indication of the age of an elder, and the Greek word often translated as "elder" is sometimes used in a comparative sense of an older person in contrast to a younger person (Luke 15:25; John 8:9; Acts 2:17; 1 Tim. 5:1–2; 1 Peter 5:5). In the Synoptic Gospels, the elders always appear in the plural and refer to a group that functioned alongside the official chief priests and scribes. They maintain the "tradition of the elders" (Matt. 15:2; Mark 7:3, 5). Supposedly, this group was selected for their wisdom and therefore granted an advisory role, but, in contrast to Simeon and Anna, they were constantly attacking the ministry of Jesus, especially during His passion (Matt. 16:21). In Acts, these elders oppose both the apostles (Acts 4:1–12) and Paul (Acts 23:14; 24:1; 25:15).

AGING IN THE EPISTLES

The beginning of the church was marked by the pouring out of the Spirit on those who believed in Christ. This happened to all believers regardless of race, social status, gender, or age (Acts 2:17–18; Gal. 3:28; 1 Cor. 12:13). The churches established certain expectations for interaction with the elderly. In harmony with Old Testament theology, parents must be given honor and obedience by children of all ages within the household (Col. 3:20; Eph. 6:1–3). Disobedience to parents was a characteristic of those who were not part of the Christian community (Rom. 1:30; 2 Tim. 3:2). Fathers were to evidence the wisdom of their age by responding to their children in a proper way (Col. 3:21; Eph. 6:4).

Elders—those older in comparison to youth—play a significant role in the New Testament Epistles. Leadership in the church does not automatically come with age. Spiritual qualifications must be observed, and church elders must not be new to Christianity (1 Tim. 3:1–7; Titus 1:6–9). They provide spiritual leadership to the church (James 5:14) and shepherd the flock by being examples (1 Peter 5:1–3). Older people are not without need of instruction. Both older men and women should be taught to live in a certain way (Titus 2:1–3). Younger Christians should not abrogate the authority of elders but should submit to their leadership (1 Peter 5:5). Elders should be given honor (1 Tim. 5:17). They may need correction, but it is a serious thing to bring an accusation against an elder (1 Tim. 5:1, 19–20). Widows are in special need of care, which should be provided by family if possible. If not, widows who met certain qualification should be honored by care from the church (1 Tim. 5:3–10), especially if they are over sixty (1 Tim. 5:9).

Although the fall of humanity has introduced difficulties into the aging process, individuals should redeem the aging process by developing godly character and the acquisition of wisdom that comes from a life of godliness. The Bible speaks with one voice concerning the appropriate attitude that should be granted the elderly: honor, respect, reverence, and an attentive ear to their wisdom. God still works in the lives of the elderly. At the same time, the elderly need to be exhorted to develop spiritually to respond properly to the difficulties faced in old age.

CONTEMPORARY NEEDS OF THE ELDERLY

With a biblical theology of aging as the foundation, this section of the chapter will now seek to identify the unique needs faced by the elderly, view them through the lens of biblical theology, and identify how ministers of the gospel should respond to those needs. The unique needs of the aging fall into five broad categories related to physical, mental, psychological, social, and spiritual needs.

Ministers of the gospel need to beware of their attitudes toward the elderly and identify any thinking that is not in harmony with biblical theology. Dr. Robert Butler, the first director of the National Institute on Aging in the United States, defined ageism as prejudice on the part of one age group toward another age group. He suggests that this attitude might be prevalent toward the elderly in America, "a society that has traditionally valued pragmatism, action, power, and the vigor of youth over contemplation, reflection, experience, and the wisdom of age."[10] The church must reject any sort of utilitarian or pragmatic approach to human worth that might marginalize the elderly.[11] This might be expressed in the attitude that a church of mostly elderly is a church with problems, or in the idea that the focus needs to be on the youth because the future belongs to them, or in the feeling that the elderly are a strain on the resources of the church.

Aging is complex, and the minister of the gospel must resist the urge to lump all elderly individuals into one category. The needs of the "Greatest Generation" are more acute than the needs of Baby Boomers who have benefited from medical, sociological, and technological advancement. The minister of the gospel should honor the elderly at every stage and value their contribution to the church.

PHYSICAL NEEDS

The biblical narrative describes the physical deterioration that takes place during the aging process in a fallen world. As individuals age, they experience a decrease in physical energy, issues with mobility, coordination issues related to time, speed, and accuracy, as well as a decrease in the ability to gather information collected through sight, hearing, taste, and smell.[12] These physical changes come with different rates and intensity. "Many people are not seriously limited by aging even in their 80s. The implication is that normal aging does not produce decrements that require society systematically to exclude older people from participation at the workplace or anywhere else."[13] Churches, for example, should rethink any policy that requires all pastors or elders to retire by seventy or any other arbitrary age.

There are a number of things that a church should do in order to accommodate to the physical limitations of the elderly and thus redeem the physical effects of the fall: handicap accessibility to all essential areas can overcome decreased mobility; increased font size in visual displays and printed material can overcome vision difficulties; and a ministry to transport elderly who cannot or do not wish to drive are just a few suggestions. Each church should address the needs that are unique to their specific congregation.

The church should also develop a biblical view of the physical body that encourages attention to the physical even during (and especially because of) the aging process. Senior adults especially need to keep active, adjusting for physical limitations. Exercise, hydration, rest, diet, and freedom from addictions are all important to combat decline in the aging process. On the other hand, heroic and expensive efforts to cover up the aging process should be reconsidered. A person's identity and value should be found in Christ, not in physical appearance. In the ancient culture of the Bible, the physical marks of aging (especially "gray hair") were properly honored as marks of experience. Today both the elderly and the church should embrace this truth. The church should lead the way in a cultural shift that views the aging physical body as a visual mark of value, wisdom, and experience rather than inadequacy and insignificance. Actions toward the elderly should flow out of this worldview.

Hearing loss increases in direct proportion to aging. About 25 percent of those between sixty-five and seventy-four have disabling hearing loss, and the percentage increases to 50 percent among those who are seventy-five or older.[14] It can take the form of *presbycusis* (age-related difficulty hearing high pitch voices or high-pitch consonants like f, t, th, s and z) or *phonemic regression* (hearing but not understanding).[15] In a study of the advantages and disadvantages of *elderspeak* (unique speech used to communicate to the elderly), Kemper and Harden concluded that reducing grammatical complexity, repeating, and expanding on material resulted in increased comprehension among the elderly, while using short sentences, slow rate of speech and high pitch did not. Some of the latter characteristics can be demeaning to the elderly.[16] Those who preach and teach the Bible to older adults should be aware of these findings.

Why not just wear hearing aids since adequate hearing is necessary for social interaction? Studies show that many older adults reject hearing aids because: (1) quality functional hearing aids are often costly, (2) they are sometimes difficult to use and require help from others, (3) there is often a denial of hearing loss because it happens so gradually, (4) wearing a hearing aid is a mark of aging (which tends to be denied), and (5) wearing a hearing aid is a threat to self-image in a culture where a person with a hearing aid is perceived as incompetent.[17]

As people age, therefore, they should make every effort to care for their physical bodies as a means to fight against the deterioration introduced by the fall. The church can teach a proper view of the physical body, communicate issues of self-identity that are focused on Christ, organize to accommodate physical needs, and act in a way that reflects a biblical view toward the elderly.

MENTAL NEEDS

There has been much research in the last few decades related to the decline of mental capacity as a function of age. Recent conclusions indicate that forgetfulness and decrease in mental function is not necessarily the experience of everyone in old age and that there is a wide variation among people. Some types of thinking, like *crystallized intelligence* (cognitive functions gained by education and experience over a long period of time) remain constant well into the seventies, while fluid intelligence (cognitive functions related to reasoning and problem solving) are more likely to decline earlier.[18] Keeping the mind active through intellectual pursuit into new areas, solving crossword and number puzzles, and engaging in some form of problem-solving will slow down mental decline in this area. Elderly church members should be encouraged to take advantage of all the good resources available to pursue biblical studies or some other form of knowledge.[19] Churches can learn much from elderly members, especially when it comes to their wisdom in crystallized intelligence that comes from education and experience. Encourage them to tell their story and to share in certain situations.

Nor should older people be stereotyped as those who refuse to learn new things, especially as it relates to technology. A Pew Research Center Fact Sheet concludes that use of social media among older adults is increasing and use of social media is more representative of the broader population.[20] Seniors are using social media to connect with family and friends in a significant way. Churches should not hesitate to use technology and social media to minister to the elderly.

There is an increased chance of dementia (or *neurocognitive disorder*, with its symptoms of "difficulties with memory, language, abstract thinking, reasoning, decision-making and problem-solving"[21] as the elderly increase in age (affecting 6–10 percent of those sixty-five and older), but this does not mean that every lapse in memory is a sign of dementia.[22] The Alzheimer's Association has produced a helpful list of early warning signs and symptoms of Alzheimer's (a specific form of dementia) as opposed to something that might be a temporary slip-up. For example, losing track of dates, seasons, and the passage of time is a warning sign of Alzheimer's or another form of dementia, but getting confused about the day of the week only to realize it later is not.[23] A loving community that interacts with the elderly might notice the early signs of dementia and encourage medical help. Do not assume that all elderly have dementia or that the elderly should be dismissed because all old people have impaired thinking skills.

Creativity (defined as "the ability to innovate, to change the environment rather than merely adjust to it in a more passive sense"[24]) is commonly viewed as focused in youth while wisdom (defined as "a broad perspective on life, discerning a larger view of life's meaning than permitted by a hand-to-mouth subsistence"[25]) is focused on old age, and research tends to support this. But creativity is not absent in the elderly. Instead of being based on enthusiasm, creativity in the elderly is based on wisdom gained in reflection on experience and education. Both young and old need to work together in the church to produce creativity that is well rounded.

Elderly individuals, therefore, should continue to explore new areas of learning, problem solving, and creativity. Resisting the temptation to live in the past, they should embrace new technology to connect with family and friends as well as to advance the gospel. Churches should guide the elderly in this area and invite them into ministry to learn from their wisdom and creativity.

PSYCHOLOGICAL NEEDS

Another common negative stereotype related to older people is the idea that personality changes for the worse during the aging process. Although there are certain physical and cognitive changes that might lead to negative personality change with age, there is considerable socio-scientific evidence to suggest that "personality change is more the exception than the rule. People do not typically grow more neurotic with age."[26] Even though they suffer more physically, the elderly do not necessarily become hypochondriacs; even though they are frugal with their money as they navigate retirement budgets, the elderly are not necessarily stingy; apart from extenuating circumstances like physical pain, cognitive change, or difficult life circumstances, the elderly are not necessarily grouchy.[27] All of these are stereotypes that should not be imposed on the elderly as a whole.

Are older people depressed? Although this is a common conception among people of all ages, the Centers for Disease Control and Prevention have found that rates of depression among those 65 and older who interact with community are significantly lower than those of the general population, especially those in the 18–24 age group.[28] This is somewhat surprising in light of all the added challenges related to aging. Studies have found, however, that the elderly who live in assisted living facilities and nursing homes—and especially those who need help with activities of daily living (ADLs) like bathing, dressing, transferring, toileting, and eating—experienced a higher rate of depression.[29]

The church can respond by providing various types of biblical training and emotional support for the elderly that will help them navigate the challenges that are unique to aging. The areas of anxiety unique to the elderly involve issues related to finances, health, stress, death, decreased contact with children, and issues related to loss of possessions, abilities, and relationships.[30] Loss of a job can lead to a loss of identity and social role as seniors feel disconnected from pro-ductivity, worth, and economic power.[31] In order to overcome depression, encourage the elderly to serve others and be involved in volunteer projects. "In the past, senior adults were thought of as requiring help; in this century, seniors will be those giving help."[32] Providing community and support is especially important when the elderly move into assisted living or nursing home situations.

Elderly individuals will experience increased psychological and emotional needs as they increase with age, but this does not need to result in negative person-ality change. The church can help by giving a biblical perspective on issues related to loss and by connecting seniors to ministry and community.

SOCIAL NEEDS

Older adults still have social needs. This contradicts earlier studies that seemed to indicate that as people aged, they tended toward increased *interiority*—becoming more introverted and focused on their inner life.[33] *Disengagement theory* taught that "as people grow older, they withdraw from society. At the same time, society withdraws from older adults, expecting that they will step aside to make room for the younger generation."[34] This thinking now appears to be misleading. Although the size of a person's social network shrinks with the passing of time, the need for social interaction tends to be fixed, and extroverted people do not slide down the slope to introversion. Senior adults still prefer to maintain relationships in their social network.[35] Gerontologist Robert Atchley concluded that "social continuity is an important force that minimizes the effects of physical aging" and that "serious discontinuity in relationship and environments can make the effects of physical aging even worse."[36]

After years of ministry to senior adults, Gallagher identifies several character-istics of this age group, and many of them are social in nature: (1) they love to be with friends and have a great need for a loving and caring church, (2) they love to interact with a caring pastor and church staff, (3) they desire to associate with those who share their beliefs and values, (4) they love to share their experiences and feelings, and (5) they love children and youth.[37] The church, therefore, should not reject older people by thinking that they all prefer to be alone. Church is a won-derful place to maintain the social networks necessary for thriving in advanced years. A little creativity (involving seniors themselves) could easily come up with things like prayers chains, group meeting for lunch or other activities, volunteer work at the church, a visitation ministry, etc.

SPIRITUAL NEEDS

Older adults in the church also face unique spiritual challenges. Hiett and Whitworth suggest that ministry to the spiritual needs of the elderly should focus on four areas: instruction, worship, fellowship, and expression.[38] (1) Senior adults continue to need biblical instruction to help them understand the message of the Bible. Addressing issues related to a biblical theology of aging as well as articulating a biblical perspective on items like death, the eternal state, loneliness, family rela-tionships, and self-esteem will give older adults the context in which to respond to their current situation. (2) Corporate worship in a blended experience that recog-nizes that traditions of the elderly can be very significant. A time of singing hymns and inviting older adults to pray or share from their experience can be a meaning-ful act of worship for everyone involved. (3) The biblical idea of fellowship involves sharing in the common realities of the Christian experience. Although there should be sharing that transcends the boundaries the gender, social status, and age, older adults find it meaningful for their self-esteem to enjoy fellowship with one another in organized activities. (4) Expression has to do with actively being involved in some sort or service or volunteer work. The young minister should not make the mistake of thinking that retired individuals no longer want to be involved in the work of the ministry. Here is how one group expressed their desires to their pastor: "Give us less pity and give us more opportunity, give us the respect not simply for having lived so long, but respect born of what we are and still can be, much more than what we have been; do not count us out; do not put us on the ash heap, wring-ing your hands all the way to the graveyard about our aging miseries."[39]

CONCLUSION

Both biblical imperatives and sociological data should challenge the church to have a compelling vision for ministry to the elderly. This involves acting in a way that shows honor and respect, organizing to meet the unique needs of the elderly, and connecting them to ministry opportunities. When this happens, the church, society, and the elderly themselves will benefit. Studies show that older adults who are involved in a religious community have better physical health, reduced need for health services, a greater sense of well-being, less depression, and greater concern for others.[40] May this be increasingly true of the elderly in our churches.

NOTES

1. United States Census Bureau, "Older People Projected to Outnumber Children for the First Time in U.S. History," www.census.gov/newsroom/press-releases/2018/cb18-41-population-projections.html (accessed March 13, 2018).

2. Samuel Smith, "GenZ is the Least Christian Generation in American History, Barna Finds," *The Christian Post,* www.christianpost.com/news/gen-z-is-the-least-christian-generation-in-american-history-barna-finds.html.

3. Douglas K. Stuart, *Exodus,* NAC (Nashville: Broadman & Holman, 2006), 489.

4. J. Gordon Harris, *Biblical Perspectives on Aging: God and the Elderly* (Philadelphia: Fortress Press, 1987), 47–48.

5. Ibid., 45.

6. Tremper Longman, *The Book of Ecclesiastes,* NICOT (Grand Rapids: Eerdmans, 1998), 270.

7. Merrill C. Tenney, "John" in *The Expositor's Bible Commentary: John and Acts,* ed. Frank E. Gaebelein, vol. 9 (Grand Rapids: Zondervan, 1981), 47.

8. D. A. Carson, *The Gospel According to John,* PNTC (Grand Rapids: Eerdmans, 1991), 190–91.

9. Ibid., 679.

10. Robert N. Butler, "Age-Ism: Another form of Bigotry" *Gerontologist* 9/1 (Winter 1969): 243.

11. Millard J. Erickson, *Christian Theology,* 3rd ed. (Grand Rapids: Baker, 2013), 503–504.

12. Robert Atchley, *Aging: Continuity and Change* (Belmont, CA: Wadsworth Publishing, 1983), 44; Arthur Becker, *Ministry with Older Persons: A Guide for Clergy and Congregations* (Minneapolis: Augsburg, 1986), 51–63; and Jeffrey A. Watson, *The Courage to Care: Helping the Aging, Grieving, and Dying* (Grand Rapids: Baker, 1992), 125–27.

13. Atchley, *Aging,* 64.

14. National Institute on Deafness and Other Communication Disorders, "Quick Statistics on Hearing," www.nidcd.nih.gov/health/statistics/quick-statistics-hearing (accessed December 15, 2016).

15. Joan T. Erber and Lenore T. Szuchman, *Great Myths of Aging* (Oxford: John Wiley & Sons, 2015), 7–8.

16. Susan Kemper and Tamara Harden, "Experimentally Disentangling What's Beneficial about Elderspeak from What's Not," *Psychology and Aging* 14/4 (December 1999): 656–70.

17. Ibid., 9–12.

18. Ibid., 37–42.

19. Examples include the resources in www.biblicaltraining.org and online courses offered by Moody Bible Institute and Moody Theological Seminary.

20. Pew Research Center, "Social Media Fact Sheet," www.pewinternet.org/fact-sheet/social-media/ (accessed June 12, 2019).

21. Erber and Szuchman, *Great Myths,* 46.

22. Ibid., 46–52.

23. Alzheimer's Association, "10 Early Signs and Symptoms of Alzheimer's," www.alz.org/alzheimers-dementia/10_signs.

24. Dean Keith Simonton, "Creativity and Wisdom in Aging" in *Handbook of the Psychology of Aging*, 3rd ed., James E. Birren and K. Warner Schaie, eds. (San Diego: Academic Press, 1990), 320.

25. Simonton, "Creativity and Wisdom in Aging," 320.

26. Erber and Szuchman, *Great Myths*, 66–67.

27. Ibid., 67–77.

28. Ibid., 91–93.

29. Ibid., 91–93.

30. Richard H. Gentzler, Jr. *Aging and Ministry in the 21st Century: An Inquiry Approach* (Nashville: Discipleship Resources, 2008), 37.

31. Becker, *Ministry with Older Persons*, 51–63.

32. David P. Gallagher, *Senior Adult Ministry in the 21st Century* (Loveland, CO: Group 2002), 11.

33. Erber and Szuchman, *Great Myths*, 81.

34. Ibid., 82.

35. Ibid., 82–84.

36. Atchley, *Aging*, 65.

37. Gallagher, *Senior Adult Ministry*, 13–25.

38. Marlin Hiett and Ellen Whitworth, "Understanding Older Adults," *Christian Education Journal* 4/2 (January 1983), 15.

39. Carol Lefevre and Perry Lefevre, eds., *Aging and the Human Spirit* (Chicago: Moody Press, 1981), 88.

40. Harold G. Koenig and Douglas M. Lawson, *Faith in the Future: Healthcare, Aging and the Role of Religion* (West Consholockem, PA: Templeton Foundation Press, 2004), 10–11.

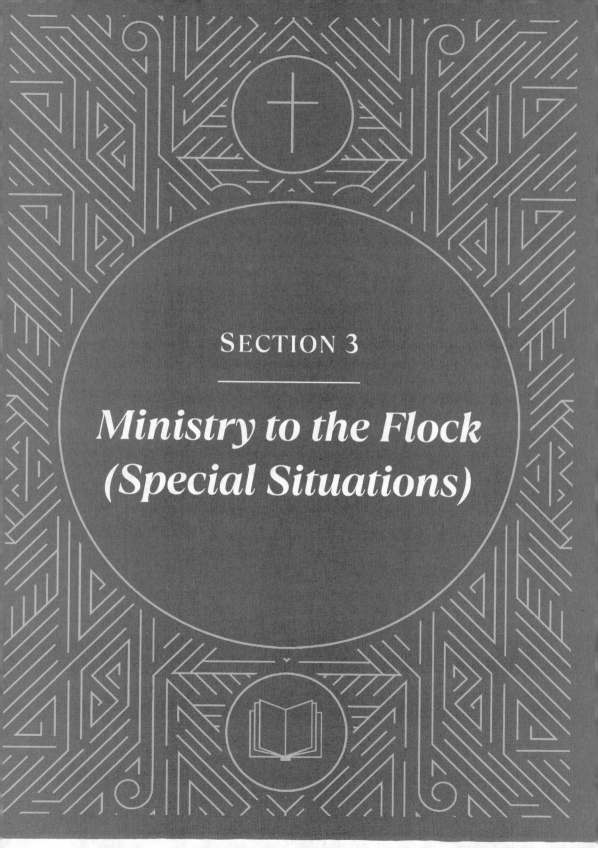

SECTION 3

Ministry to the Flock (Special Situations)

INTRODUCTION

The Pastor's Heart

MICHAEL J. BOYLE

Understanding the heart of a pastor is understanding the heart of a shepherd. David's life was summarized, "So he shepherded them according to the integrity of his heart, and guided them with his skillful hands" (Ps. 78:72). Shepherding requires two things: integrity of heart and skillful hands. Ministry skills are important for pastors and these skills can be learned by them through books, education, or on the job. However, integrity of heart qualifies the pastor for ministry, and this must be managed through self-care. *Integrity* is being ethically sound, upright, and complete. It is the self-care of the pastor's heart that must be maintained throughout his lifetime. He must be aware of the responsibilities, temptations, and risks of ministry so that he can nurture his own heart to successfully carry out his pastoral vocation.

In the previous section, we looked at phases of life that everyone goes through and how the pastor can minister to each one. In Section 3, we will examine some special situations that a pastor faces. Often, these situations involve deep kinds of pain. Because of this, the pastor's soft, warm, caring heart is especially important. Wisdom, compassion, and genuine empathy is needed. Sometimes, there must be a balance between pastoral chastisement and loving acceptance of the congregant—a difficult balance to maintain! In this section, we will look at the special requirements of ministry to the sick, the divorced, the disabled, the abused and exploited, the gender-confused or same-sex attracted, the struggler with mental health issues, and the long-term single or childless person. We will also examine the special challenges of a small church setting. In these cases, the caring heart of the pastor is of utmost importance. According to God, what kind of heart is a pastor supposed to have?

THE RESPONSIBILITIES OF A PASTOR

A pastor's heart is the merging of his pastoral responsibilities and congregational relationships. In Scripture, the apostle Paul pictures this heart through three separate lenses. First, a pastor is **an approved steward** (1 Thess. 2:4–6). He is approved by God. He is set apart and sanctioned by the Lord to serve the church of Jesus Christ. A pastor does not serve his own church and his own people, as if they belong to him. No, rather, he is a steward for the Lord Jesus Christ and a caretaker of His church. How often pastors speak of "my church" when they should be speaking of "Christ's church"!

Second, a pastor is **a nursing mother** (1 Thess. 2:7–8). This *nursing mother* was not the child's birth mother, but the nurse who cared for and even suckled the newborn child. An emotional connection is made by the pastor. Paul describes this ministry as gentle, tender, and caring. According to Paul, a pastor should have a fond affection for his congregation so that these folks become "very dear" to the pastor.

Third, a pastor is as **an imploring father** (1 Thess. 2:9–11). A pastor models for the congregation a godly life. This sets the foundation for him to exhort, encourage, and charge the children under his care to walk in a manner worthy of Christ. This fatherly training involves correction of the congregation as well as encouragement and comfort as needed. The heart of the pastor implores the folks in his church as a good father would his own children.

THE TEMPTATIONS OF A PASTOR

When carrying out pastoral responsibilities, a pastor faces certain temptations. **Pride** is a temptation for a new convert if he were to become an elder in the church. Paul warned that he might "become conceited and fall into the condemnation incurred by the devil" (1 Tim. 3:6). But pride is not restricted to young converts. Wisdom cries out in Proverbs, "The fear of the LORD is to hate evil; pride, arrogance, the evil way, and the perverted mouth, I hate" (Prov. 8:13). Unless they heed the warning of wisdom, all pastors face the temptation of pride. It is one of the greatest temptations a pastor will face. C. S. Lewis observes, "Unchastity, anger, greed, drunkenness, and all that, are mere fleabites in comparison: it was through Pride that the devil became the devil: Pride leads to every other vice: it is the complete anti-God state of mind."[1] Lewis states again in *Mere Christianity*, "For Pride is spiritual cancer: it eats up the very possibility of love, or contentment, or even common sense."[2]

Another temptation a pastor faces is **power**. When the seventy disciples returned and told Jesus about their success and that even the demons were subject to His name, Jesus warned them, "Nevertheless, do not rejoice in this, that the spirits are subject to you" (Luke 10:20a). Privilege and responsibility come when a pastor has authority and power over a congregation. He can be tempted to use and abuse this power. He can find himself rejoicing, celebrating, even bragging about the power he has. Jesus warned that if you are to rejoice, "rejoice that your names are recorded in heaven" (Luke 10:20b).

A third temptation a pastor encounters is **position**. Status and titles are earned and given to pastors. If you make it a point to set apart and be recognized by the title of Pastor, Reverend, Elder, Minister, Preacher, Bishop, or Doctor, it may mean you have succumbed to the temptation of position. There are good reasons to be recognized as such, yet there are also prideful ones. Examine your heart! Jesus warned His disciples, "Beware of the scribes who like to walk around in long robes, and like personal greetings in the marketplaces, and seats of honor in the synagogues, and places of honor at banquets" (Mark 12:38–39). There is an ever-present temptation to seek to be honored, to be seated at head tables, to speak at conferences, and to have numerous followers on social media. But Jesus' warning was not heeded by His disciples. At the Last Supper, "a dispute also developed among them as to which one of them was regarded as being the greatest" (Luke 22:24). Striving to be the greatest is striving for position. But praise God, Peter had learned his lesson by the time he wrote 1 Peter. Of all the titles of position he could have chosen, he referred to himself "as your fellow elder" (1 Peter 5:1a). Then Peter warned his fellow elders not to lead "as domineering over those assigned to your care" (1 Peter 5:3a). Pastors who strive for fame, stature, titles, and reputation are succumbing to the temptation of position.

THE RISKS FOR A PASTOR

Every occupation faces risks. Some risks are obvious, such as those faced by firefighters, first responders, police officers, electricians, and loggers. The pastorate is no different, even though its risks might be more hidden. Recent studies have identified the risks of the pastorate. A surprising danger for pastors is the **spiritual neglect** of their own walk with Christ. To avoid this, pastors must make the Word and prayer a priority in their daily relationship with God. The apostles realized the importance of making the Word and prayer the priority for their ministry. The early church faced the complaint of overlooking the Hellenistic Jewish widows (Acts 6:1). The Twelve stated that they should not "neglect the word of God in order to serve tables" (6:2). To address the problem, they appointed seven men to serve in the church. The apostles concluded, "But we will devote ourselves to prayer and to the ministry of the word" (6:4). Apparently, the apostles neglected Scripture and prayer in order to carry out the ministry. This conflict forced them to reevaluate the use of their time and their priorities. They concluded that they needed to prioritize their personal spiritual disciplines of their walk with Christ in order to carry out their responsibilities of ministry. That is true for pastors today too.

Another risk created by the pastorate is **loneliness**. One sociological study found that "70 percent of pastors do not have someone they consider a close friend."[3] In 2017, pollster George Barna identified that 52 percent of pastors said they have felt lonely or isolated in the last three months.[4] Even though ministry engages the pastor into the lives of so many people, it still creates a place of loneliness, of lacking friendships or deep connections. This places a pastor at risk for temptation, burnout, discouragement, and depression. Not having the support and encouragement of a friend or colleague in ministry makes for a lonely life.

Another often overlooked risk for pastors is **their families**. "When asked whether it's true that their current church tenure has been difficult on their family, two out of five pastors acknowledge it's 'somewhat true' (40%)."[5] Pastors frequently wrestle with the tension of family vs. ministry. Too often, pastors choose ministry over family. They think God will provide for their spouse or children because they are honoring their calling. However, the pastor is responsible for the love and care of their spouse and their children. One of the qualifications of an elder/pastor is that he "manages his own household well, keeping his children under control with all dignity" (1 Tim. 3:4). The pastor must take a day off each week for rejuvenation, and plan vacations and time away from the church with his family.

SELF-CARE FOR A PASTOR'S HEART

The accumulation of the risks, stresses, conflicts, and demands of ministry places the pastor at great risk of **ministry burnout**. According to one study, 45 percent of pastors say they have experienced depression or burnout to the extent that they needed to take a leave of absence from ministry.[6] The Barna Group concurs with this high experience of burnout. They note that three out of four pastors know "at least one fellow pastor whose ministry has ended due to burnout (76%)."[7]

The underlying issue behind pastoral burnout is a burnt-out heart. From King David, we learn that spiritual shepherds must have "integrity of his heart" (Ps. 78:72). From King Solomon, we learn to "watch over [our] heart with all diligence, for from it flow the springs of life" (Prov. 4:23). The word "watch" was used of a watchman on the tower of the city. He was to keep his eye on the horizon for any enemy or danger that may come to cause harm. So too, pastors need to watch over their hearts.

They are to be vigilant in watching for the temptations, the dangers, and the risks that they face and protect themselves from those calamities. Paul gave a similar command to the Ephesian elders: "Be on guard for yourselves and for all the flock, among which the Holy Spirit has made you overseers" (Acts 20:28). Pastors think Paul's priority was for them to "guard the flock." But instead, Paul's first priority was: "Be on guard for yourselves." Every pastor needs to be guarding his heart daily as he enters ministry. This, of course, raises the question, How do I guard my heart?

Like watchmen on the walls, pastors must be aware of the temptations they face that are personal, repetitive, or derived from their family origins. They must also consider the risks that they are taking in their ministry unless they put a stop to these great dangers. But a pastor can also prepare and protect himself by being proactive in his ministry and paying attention to himself.

The Old Testament prophet Elijah learned the importance of self-care from God. Ministering on Mount Carmel, Elijah prepared a sacrifice, called fire from heaven to consume his sacrifice, led the killing of 450 Baal prophets, and outran King Ahab to Jezreel—a distance of about thirty miles! After all this, exhausted and tired from ministry, Jezebel threatened to kill Elijah, so "he was afraid, and got up and ran for his life" (1 Kings 19:3). In his troubles, fears, and self-pity, Yahweh led Elijah to Mount Horeb. There God's caring hand provided Elijah with the four R's that prevent burnout: rest, renewal, realignment, and a relationship (in this case, with Elisha). Like we see with Elijah, self-awareness of potential problems and spiritual practices that provide remedies can prevent ministry burnout, moral failure, or depression.[8] Let us now look at each of the four R's that God has given us.

REST

It is in rest (Hebrew, *shalom*) where the revitalization and rejuvenation of the pastor's calling and passion begins. When God finished His work of creation, He rested on the seventh day. When the disciples returned from extended ministry of preaching, teaching, and casting out demons, Jesus brought them together and said, "'Come away by yourselves to a secluded place and rest a while.' (For there were many people coming and going, and they did not even have time to eat)" (Mark 6:31).

Pastors must do what it takes to get away for some silence and solitude. It may be running, cycling, or sailing. It may be time alone in a coffee shop or library. It may be some time spent in the outdoors at a park, in the mountains, on a path, or by a lake. The point is to get away from people to be alone and rest. Elijah wandered in the wilderness alone for forty days and nights until he came to Mount Horeb (1 Kings 19:8). Pastors need to get away too, sometimes even for extended periods like this. This deep kind of rest will not just happen. This rest needs to be planned and scheduled. This pattern can begin with an annual retreat of three or four days. This allows a pastor to create a plan for some major goals for the next year. A personal retreat day each month can be planned to review how he has been doing spiritually and in his family relationships for the last month and the progress he has made on his major goals. Planning this way helps a pastor to relax, review, and reflect so he may prevent ministry burnout.

RENEWAL

Renewal is a time of refreshment, restoration, and rekindling. It is a time to ask questions. Is your life filled with the things that you are required to do? Does your list consist of preaching, teaching, leading, caring, visiting, praying, and organizing meetings? Renewal is taking a new look at your walk with Christ and making sure it is being cultivated outside of your ministry requirements. When Elijah stood on Mount Horeb, the Lord did not reveal Himself in a mighty way, but He was in "a sound of a gentle blowing" (1 Kings 19:12). This was something new and different for Elijah. No doubt it soothed him to encounter God like this.

Renewal is an excellent time to engage in a new spiritual discipline. There are disciplines of engagement when you take on a deeper challenge: prayer, study, worship, or service; and there are disciplines of abstinence when you intentionally withhold something: silence, solitude, fasting, and meditation. To renew your spiritual walk, practice a new spiritual discipline over a lengthy period of time, expecting the Lord to use it to direct your life and encourage you in your relationship with Him.

REALIGNMENT

With the barrage of activities and demands on your life, a pastor starts losing sight of why he came into ministry in the first place. Pastors are striving to improve their preaching skills, ministry skills, leadership skills, emotional skills. Or they are trying to increase their congregational attendance, their church budget, their missionary support, their outreach into the community. Over time, the pastor wrestles with his own fitness for the ministry he has developed. Elijah also wrestled with his calling, wrapping himself in his mantle to listen to Lord speak to him. This is the same mantle he would throw onto Elisha to call him in the same ministry path. After this meeting with the Lord, Elijah was realigned with his ministry as a prophet of anointing kings and preparing Elisha to serve in his place (1 Kings 19:15–17).

Steps to realign with your calling require time alone again. This is necessary time to review your strengths and weaknesses, gifting, family origins, coping mechanisms, and boundaries. Examine these aspects of your self-awareness. Examine your calling and ministry fitness. You may decide to recommit to the ongoing ministry you have been entrusted to lead, or you may need to step away and look for a new ministry.

RELATIONSHIPS

The pastoral ministry can be one of the loneliest jobs a person could have and one with the fewest friendships. Pastoral colleagues are needed to help identify toxic patterns that might have developed. These true friends can help you determine if you are staying too long in a certain track, if you need to see it through, or look for something else. After all the years that Elijah served alone, the Lord finally assigned Elisha to follow Elijah and minister to him (1 Kings 19:21).

The current pastoral culture of the "Lone Ranger" is not what Jesus promoted. Jesus always sent His disciples out two by two. Likewise, the early church sent missionaries out together: Barnabas and Saul, Paul and Silas, and Barnabas and Mark. The Old Testament is also filled with leaders serving together: Moses and Aaron, David and Jonathan, or Elijah and Elisha.

Ministry friendships require pastors to be proactive to find other pastors of similar circumstances and similar ministries to build meaningful relationships. Because of similar life circumstances and challenges, solo pastors often build better friendships with solo pastors, while multi-staff lead pastors connect with multi-staff lead pastors, and associate pastors build better friendships with other associate pastors. Pastors will learn, "Oil and perfume make the heart glad, and a person's advice is sweet to his friend" (Prov. 27:9). Find another pastor in your town, city, ministry association, or denomination and plan to meet for coffee or a meal on a monthly basis. From this simple habit, a deep friendship may begin.

CONCLUSION

The Lord Jesus Christ has called you to be a pastor. He has gifted you to be a pastor. He wants you to shepherd His people. And as that shepherd, He wants you to be self-aware of the risks and temptations you face.

Many pastors have failed because they lacked integrity of heart. But many have also failed because they lack the skillful hands. In our changing world, you must develop special skills to minister to the divorced, abused, disabled, gender confused, and long-term single or childless. You will also need to navigate small church settings and mental health issues. No pastor is prepared for ministry with just integrity of heart. No pastor is prepared for ministry with just special skills. The prepared pastor has both integrity of heart and skillful hands.

NOTES

1. C. S. Lewis, *Mere Christianity* (New York: Harper One, 1952), 122.

2. Ibid., 125.

3. H. B. London and Neil N. Wiseman, *Pastors at Greater Risk*, rev. ed. (Ventura, CA: Gospel Light 2003), 264.

4. Barna Group, *The State of Pastors: How Today's Faith Leaders Are Navigating Life and Leadership in an Age of Complexity* (Barna Group, 2017), 38.

5. Barna Group, *The State of Pastors*, 37.

6. London and Wiseman, *Pastors at Greater Risk*, 170.

7. Barna Group, *The State of Pastors*, 26.

8. The following summarizes material from Michael J. Boyle, *A Preventative Ministry for Pastoral Burnout: A Study of Elijah in 1 Kings 19* (DMin. diss., Gordon-Conwell Theological Seminary, 2012).

CHAPTER 3.1

Ministering to the Sick and Terminally Ill

HARRY SHIELDS

Listen in on any conversation over lunch, either in the breakroom at work or a sidewalk café, and you will not likely hear much talk about death. Even in the church narthex, congregants will not talk about death and dying. We don't like the subject because we don't know what to say, other than, "You have my sympathies." Or we avoid the subject because we also want to avoid the experience for as long as possible. The same can be said regarding discussion relating to sickness and terminal illness.

However, sickness and death are realities in every community and in every local church. Throughout the history of the church, Christians have been at the forefront of caring for sick and dying people. In the context of war and famine, Christ followers risked their lives to care for the sick and injured. And they did so because their Savior, over and over again, exhibited great compassion for people who were coming to the end of their earthly existence.

One of the ways the church can positively impact a death-denying culture is to minister compassionately to sick and dying people. Every pastor will encounter sickness and death in some context, outside of one's own personal appointment with death. So it is important that one knows how to approach those who have been diagnosed with a terminal disease. By definition, a terminal illness is any end-stage disease that cannot be adequately treated, and is reasonably expected to result in the death of the patient. This term is more commonly used for progressive diseases such as cancer, advanced heart disease, and various forms of dementia. Traumatic events that eventually lead to death are usually not placed under the title of terminal illness. When people are diagnosed with a terminal illness, caregivers will need to think comprehensively. That is, we will have to think about how to care for family members and close friends, not just for the terminally ill patient.

BIBLICAL BASIS

Compassion for people in all circumstances, especially those facing impending death, is rooted in the very heart of God. Psalm 51:1 functions as a prayer of repentance. In this psalm King David could appeal to God for forgiveness because God was a God of abundant mercy. In similar fashion the psalmist likens his dilemma as a hunted man as being entrapped in deep mire. Yet he confidently prays that God will deliver him due to the Father's abundant mercy. In Psalm 103:13–14 David likens God to an earthly father who has compassion on his children. There is no turn away from the needs of His children, because He knows our helplessness and great human need. So for King David, compassion is a way of life, since God Himself is a compassionate God.

The Old Testament prophets also spoke of God's compassion for His people. They saw a future for Israel, even after the Jewish people were hauled off into exile. Isaiah announced that there would be a time of great rejoicing due to God's compassionate work of restoring His people. The prophet asked in Isaiah 49:15, "Can a woman forget her nursing child and have no compassion on the son of her womb?" The implied answer is a resounding no, because God is full of compassion for the afflicted (Isa. 49:13).

The Gospel accounts of Christ's earthly ministry likewise portray a God who is filled with compassion and abounding mercy. In Matthew 9:36 we are told that Jesus saw large crowds coming toward Him. Immediately He had compassion on them, "because they were distressed and downcast, like sheep without a shepherd." More specific to the issue of physical afflictions, Matthew 14:14 records how Jesus had compassion on the approaching crowds and healed their sick.

At least two of Jesus' parables describe the importance of God's people demonstrating compassion. In Luke 10:33, a Samaritan took a huge risk in caring for a man beaten by robbers and left for dead. The parable was initiated when a lawyer asked Jesus what was necessary to inherit eternal life. Jesus was in no way encouraging good deeds as the path to heaven. Rather His point was that if one truly loved God, the God of compassion, one would extend compassion to a person in need.

In Luke 15:2, the religious leaders found it disgusting that one who was purported to be the Messiah would have relationships with sinners. Jesus knew what they were thinking, so He told the well-known story of the prodigal son. The parable describes how an earthly father sees his wayward son far away and runs to him. In spite of the son's sin, the father had compassion on him, and welcomed him home (Luke 15:20–25). Our Lord's point in telling the parable was to reveal what God the Father was like—a God of compassion and rich in mercy. The implication is that Christ followers should be compassionate as well.

The apostle Paul also supports the practice of compassionate responses. In Ephesians 4:32 and again in Colossians 3:12 Paul makes it clear that interpersonal care, especially for those in serious need, was to characterize the new life Christians had in Christ. And the basis of this call to compassion was the redemptive work of Jesus. The finished work of Jesus has made Christ followers alive in Him. We are raised with Him and called to show kindness and compassion to those who are hurting (Col. 3:12).

The biblical evidence is clear: God is a compassionate God, who has given believers new life in Jesus. This new life compels us—not to fear death or hide from its humbling effects—but to face disease and death even as our Savior did. Just as Jesus cared for people, Christians are to minister to the terminally ill with compassionate care.

SIX AREAS WHERE CHRISTIANS CAN IMPLEMENT COMPASSIONATE CARE

VISITING THE SICK AND SHUT-INS

Pastors wear many different hats. They serve by faithfully proclaiming God's Word week after week. They carry out ministry tasks as vision-creators, ministry managers, counselors, and apologists for the faith. But one of the often-neglected ministries related to pastoral life is that of visitation, especially visiting the sick.

Once someone is admitted to the hospital or is homebound due to some sickness, the pastor will usually receive word that a congregant would like a pastoral visit. In addition to training others in the congregation to assist with the task of visitation, pastors and church leaders will want to follow some simple steps of visitation protocol. First, it is always wise to call ahead to the hospital or the person's home to find an appropriate time to visit the congregant. One can always stop by unannounced, but if a patient is in the midst of multiple medical tests, an unannounced visit can quickly become problematic. Second, prior to making the visit, the pastor or church leader will want to select a short passage of Scripture to read during the visit. Selections from the psalms are often best suited for refocusing the patient's thoughts on the love and care of God. Third, after a brief greeting, the one making the visit will want to keep the visit anywhere from thirty to forty minutes in length. Patients tire easily, and as much as they will appreciate a pastoral visit, the time spent with the patient should not be too long. Fourth, it is best not to ask as to what diagnosis has been given, or what concerns medical personnel might have communicated. Allow the patient to volunteer information without a lot of probing on the pastor's part. Fifth, close the time together in prayer. One can learn a great deal about a patient's concerns or even diagnosis by asking, "How might I pray for you today?" After the congregant's response, close the time in prayer. Reassure the patient before leaving that the congregation (not just the pastor) will keep them in prayer. It is also wise before leaving to inquire from other family members how the congregation might help. Many churches have a caregivers' team that assists in providing meals and follow-up visits.

Compassionate Care for the Terminally Ill Patient

When caregivers learn that a parishioner or an acquaintance from the church family is dying, it is important to visit the patient as soon as possible. As stated in the general protocol for visitation, it is always good to make a phone call beforehand to inquire if it is a good time to stop by. People who have recently received notice of a terminal illness are often taken by surprise. Therefore, when preparing to read Scripture, the pastor will want to read passages that remind listeners of God's great love and compassion for them. Psalm 23 and Exodus 2:23–25 can be helpful choices. The point is that one needs to give some thought to what can be read, and how one might approach an offer to pray.

Once an agreed upon time has been established, the pastor or caregiver will want to move from introductory small talk to an inquiry about what the patient is experiencing. The pastor might say, "I understand that you visited the doctor yesterday. Can you share with me what you learned?" The response can be anything from a stoic response to an outburst of tears. Some patients will indicate in word or body language that they do not want to talk. The pastor's role is not to force a discussion but to communicate that one is there to comfort and give support in any way possible.

In her pioneering research among terminally ill patients, Elizabeth Kubler-Ross identified five stages of grief. Perhaps a better way to describe grief is to identify possible responses that a dying person might have. In actuality, patients may not experience all five stages or responses of grief but only one or two.[1] Pastors and caregivers will be wise in knowing the various grief responses that terminally ill patients may have. Many of these responses will seem to be out of character for the person who is suffering. Their questions and ways of responding should not be viewed as personal attacks against the caregiver. Responses may include:

Denial. The person has heard a doctor's diagnosis and the initial response most likely will be shock. However within a short period of time the patient will deny that the diagnosis was accurate. They might suggest that once they get a second opinion everything will be cleared up without any further worries. Penelope Wilcock suggests that it is not helpful to the patient to go along with the denial by suggesting that a second opinion should be sought. However, there is a benefit to this initial response of denial. It serves as a kind of buffer in the struggle to come to grips with the terminal diagnosis.[2]

Anger. The normal human response is to back away from angry people and the fierce words that spew from their mouths. But pastors and caregivers need to realize that anger is another way the patient is trying to cope with the diagnosis. Anger is a way terminally ill people attempt to cope with sadness and fear regarding the uncertainty of what is ahead. Anger is often directed toward God, wondering why He would allow the patient to get sick at this point in their lives. Pastors will want to pray for wisdom in responding to those who exhibit various degrees of anger. After all, plans regarding career and retirement may have been suddenly turned upside down. Therefore, the wise pastor will want to nurture the ability to offer a listening ear. In this initial visit the goal will be to listen and communicate that the pastor and the church care. Later visits can deal with the deep theological issues such as why a good God allows suffering.

Bargaining. Bargaining is the action in word or deed, in which the terminally ill patient tries to appeal to God and others to change the diagnosis to something more positive. Wilcock says, "Bargaining feels like a very busy stage, an almost feverish activity of the soul. The energies of the person seem directed inwards negotiating with God, questioning, coming to terms."[3] A grieving person's body is not only under attack, but his or her faith is under attack as well. So a patient will often try to "do something for God" to see if God will bring about some form of healing. God may very well intervene to restore the sick person. But with skill and appropriate timing, the discerning pastor will want to remind terminally patients that the best is up ahead (see John 14:2).

Depression. In many cases depression characterizes the person's life right up until the time of death. Depression poses many challenges for those involved in pastoral care. They want to make things better, and if possible, reduce the pain. But there are some benefits to what seems like a very negative emotion. After the intense expressions of anger, and the almost hyperactivity related to bargaining, depression allows the patient to enter a form of rest. Again, pastors will not want to force their faith or beliefs on anyone, but a response of depression may allow for times of reading longer passages of Scriptures, especially the Psalms. Depression may open a door for the patient to talk about the past, or to express concern for other family members. So use this response phase to listen and express the great love and knowledge of God for us (see Ps. 139).

Acceptance. Not every patient gets to this final point, but many do. This response may come as a surprise to pastors, friends, and other caregivers. Acceptance, according to Wilcock, can take the form of peace and tranquility. At other times it feels like a kind of remoteness.[4] An important ministry for pastors in this response stage is to allow the patient to reflect on life and the important aspects of the life they have lived.

Grief is a normal response to all kinds of loss in a Christian's life. The apostle Paul reminded the Thessalonian Christians that we do not grieve like unbelievers who have no hope (1 Thess. 4:13). There is always a proper place in the Christian life to shed tears and experience sadness. However pastors and caregivers have a great opportunity to communicate the rich truths of resurrection life to those who grieve.

MINISTRY TO FAMILY MEMBERS OF THE TERMINALLY ILL

Family members of those with terminal diagnoses go through the five responses to grief as well. Spouses of the terminally ill person carry some of the heaviest burdens in the whole process of dying. They take on responsibilities that they may not have had in the past. Children also carry a heavy burden as they watch their parents trying to make decisions and get necessary resources to help the patient. Pastors will want to try to assess the needs of the family and offer loving suggestions. Sometimes a pastor can send emails or make phone calls to family members in other parts of the country. Make sure that permission is given before contacting any other friend or family member. A question might be phrased as, "Mary, may I have your permission to call your son in New York, regarding the doctor's visit today?" Family dynamics are complicated, and pastors don't want to upset those dynamics any more than they already are.

In the late stages of the dying process, decisions have to be made rather quickly. Pastors will want to be available to answer questions. Family members have an innate desire to do the right thing. But they don't always know what the right thing might be. The place to start is to have some idea as to how close one might be to death. People can always rally from a difficult time with taking new medications and therapies. But for the most part, we know that one is getting closer to dying when they have difficulty eating or actually stop eating or drinking on their own. It is not always the case, but those who move closer to death tend to sleep for longer periods of time. It is during these times of uncertainty that pastors can provide important counsel to spouses and children of terminally ill patients.

The goal of all the care that will be offered is to keep the patient comfortable as much as possible. The comfort offered will not only be related to the physical, but to the emotional and spiritual. That is why pastors will want to counsel family members to talk about symptoms and options outside of the hearing of the patient.

People who are dying most likely still have an acute sense of hearing. So have one person stay in the room with the patient and have medical discussions in another room with other family members.

Family members often have not discussed what to do when death is imminent. Medical personnel will begin to talk about treatment options that are unfamiliar to the normal layperson. For this reason, pastors will want to help congregants think about advanced directives that can be helpful when end-of-life issues have to be made. One of the best ways to do this is to introduce congregants to a simple document called "Five Wishes." The document is written in simple language that asks people to declare their intentions for end-of-life decision-making. The "Five Wishes" document enables prospective patients to make their wishes known prior to death actually occurring.[5]

"Five Wishes" provides important information with respect to the following: (1) Who will make health care decisions when the patient can no longer make them; (2) What specific medical treatment does the patient want or not want; (3) How comfortable does the patient want to be; (4) How does the patient want other people, especially family and medical personnel, to treat them; and (5) What does the patient want other family members to know specifically.

In some congregations, parish nurses or physicians will hold information seminars to discuss end-of-life decision-making. During those seminars they will introduce the "Five Wishes" document. After completing the documents, photocopies can be made and kept in secure places in a prospective patient's home. Other copies can be given to a primary-care physician to put into the patient's permanent files. In addition, with the permission of the patient the "Five Wishes" form can be duplicated and transferred to other appropriate medical facilities.

Another way pastors can minister to family members of terminally ill patients is to inform all congregants about the use of *advance directives*. In preparing advance directives, a prospective patient will want to identify one or more individuals who will legally be appointed to make health decisions when an individual no longer can do so on their own. The individuals identified for decision-making responsibility are identified as having power of attorney. Many of these individuals are either spouses, children, or other surviving family members.

There are two basic power of attorney functions. The first one is the power of attorney for health care. When a patient can no longer make a decision regarding medical treatment on their own, the power of attorney for health care will be contacted by medical personnel to make specific treatment decisions. The second function is the power of attorney for property. When a person who is terminally ill and can no longer pay bills or sell property, the power of attorney for property will have the legal empowerment to do so. Of course, both health care decisions and financial decisions are stipulated in an individual's last will and testament. Pastors can provide a significant ministry by encouraging all congregants to engage in the stewardship of preparation—preparing for one's personal wishes when a terminal illness occurs.

HELPING FAMILIES MAKE IMPORTANT TREATMENT DECISIONS

When patients learn that an illness is terminal, the shock goes from the individual to the entire family. It is only a matter of time until all family members begin to grieve. But in the context of grieving, important decisions still have to be made. Whatever recommendations are made, the primary goal will be to keep the patient as comfortable and pain free as possible. A pastor will want to know about treatment options so as to provide counsel to families if requested.

Nutrition and Hydration

The decision to provide nutrition and hydration is one of the most controversial topics in the care of terminal patients. The technique involves inserting a small plastic tube through the nose and into the stomach as a way to provide nutrition when a patient cannot eat on their own. Sometimes the tube is placed under the skin and into the stomach. At first, the procedure would seem to be helpful in keeping someone alive. But there are problems with such procedures. Patients often have diarrhea, which in turn can be a cause for painful bed sores. Some medical personnel believe that the attempt to prolong life is actually a means of increasing one's pain just prior to death. The same can be said for IV hydration methods. In dementia and Alzheimer patients the brain has actually stopped communicating to the need to eat and drink. The disease is never cured because of an IV, so family members need to decide if it has ultimate value.

Dr. John Dunlop cites the fact that dehydration in a patient is not as bad as we might think. The symptom is actually a patient's friend, in that it is one of the most peaceful ways to die, and there is little or no discomfort. Pastors who have a general understanding of artificial feeding techniques can provide invaluable counsel to grieving patients and family members.[6]

Hospitalization

Christianity has greatly contributed to society by establishing hospitals and care centers. Hospitals serve as important institutions in the care and recovery of patients. However, when there is no known cure for a given disease and the patient will be dying, sending that person to the hospital may not be the best thing to do. Hank Dunn cites several reasons for advising family members to not necessarily send a terminally ill loved one to the hospital. He states:

- Hospitalization may actually increase a patient's anxiety level. They end up being in an environment that is not familiar. Routines are different than what they have received at home or in some other familiar facility.

- There is also an increased chance that a patient will get an infection while in the hospital. Infections in turn can cause a host of other problems.

- If the terminally ill patient has dementia, medical staff may be inclined to use sedation or restraints to keep the patient in a room. But this only increases stress and anxiety.

- Hospitals may also be inclined to perform additional testing that is not necessary for the dying patient. Medical testing is what hospitals do, but moving from room to room and test to test only increases a dying person's fears.[7]

Palliative Care

Since comfort care and pain reduction are the two primary concerns for terminally ill patients and their families, caring in the last stages of life can take two different forms. One is palliative care. It is the kind of care that is available to any patient with a serious illness, whether that person is about to die or not. Palliative care is a team approach to treatment, often involving the patient in decisions that are being made. Dunn says that the primary purpose of palliative care is to provide pain and symptom relief with the idea that the patient might return to some type of routine activity. Palliative care, since it is a team approach, emphasizes communication. As a result, doctors meet together to discuss progress and the next steps that might be taken. The focus is on the entire person, not just the disease the person is carrying.[8]

Hospice Care

The second type of comfort care is hospice care. It is very similar to palliative care, but it is employed by terminally ill patients and their families as death seems imminent. And how would a family know if their loved one is near death? The primary signs are that they tend to sleep more and for long periods of time. The dying person stops eating and drinking as time passes.

Hospice care is normally provided by an agency different from the hospital or nursing home where the patient might be residing. In consultation with a medical doctor, a team of nurses and CNAs will come to the patient's residence to provide services prior to his or her death. The philosophy behind hospice care is that everyone has the right to die without pain or discomfort, and to do so with dignity. Hospice staff members work with the family, the family physician, and other caregivers. Dunn identifies several things that will happen once someone is admitted to hospice. Terminally ill cancer patients would no longer receive chemotherapy or radiation treatments. Antibiotics would be slowly withdrawn, unless they are used to reduce pain. Diagnostic tests would be stopped, and feeding tubes would be removed. The purpose in all of these procedures would be to provide comfort for the patient, so that they might die with the greatest amount of comfort possible.[9]

Deciding to withdraw certain medical procedures can create stress for family members who are watching all that is going on. Quite often they will have questions for the medical staff and for pastors. They will wonder if they are doing the right thing. Joe Carter, writing for the Ethics and Religious Liberty Commission of the Southern Baptist Convention, identifies four occasions when the withdrawal of treatment is ethically sound. First, withdrawal of medical treatment is ethically sound when the terminal illness is irreversible. Second, it is ethically sound if the withdrawal of the treatment is not the cause of death. Allowing someone to die is not the same as killing someone. For instance, removing an IV does not cause the death. The patient's terminal disease is the cause of death. Third, the withdrawal of treatment does not mean that care for the patient is being withdrawn. Fourth, withdrawal of nutrition and hydration will be the last medical procedure prior to the person's death.[10]

Some family members will want all types of medical procedures to be employed for as long as possible. Some pastors may disagree with a family's decision to keep prolonging medical treatment, even though it seems obvious the person will not recover. However, pastors have a responsibility to inform about best practices without insisting on those practices.

TRAINING THE CHURCH FAMILY FOR MINISTRY TO THE TERMINALLY ILL

In many congregations a team of caregivers are trained to minister to terminally ill congregants and their families. Visiting the sick and grieving can be one of the most powerful witnesses a local church can make. A pastor has a lot of things to care for in the course of any given week. Preaching will always be an important ministry of the pastorate. However, pastors can speak with their actions just as strongly as they do in their sermons by the way they minister to others.

In addition to teaching people the great doctrines of the faith, pastors will want to equip others to love the terminally ill in Jesus' name. Training in visitation practices is most important. Here are some things that a church's care team will want to remember:

- Train team members to visit the terminally ill in their homes, hospitals, or assisted living facilities. It will be wise to call ahead to make sure the patient is at home, and not traveling to a facility for medical treatments. Have team members set a time with the patient and the family to visit, rather than just dropping in unannounced.

- While visiting, members of the care team should carefully phrase statements. People mean well when they say, "Let me know if there is anything I can do." The problem with such a statement is that it actually puts the burden on the patient or family, who now, in the midst of their grief, have to think about how other people can help. A better approach is to simply do something that will help. For example, a pastor or caregiver might say, "If it's okay with you, I would like to come over and mow your lawn this afternoon." Or a church member might say, "If it's okay with you, I would like to bring a meal over to you tomorrow night. Is there anything I should avoid preparing regarding allergies or personal tastes?" The caregiver might follow the question up with some possible suggestions for a meal. People in the congregation can sign up on a special link on the church's website to provide meals for the family or to help with other household tasks.

- When a caregiver goes to the home for a visit, respect medical personnel who may be at the patient's bedside performing important functions. Wait until they are finished, and then ask the patient if this is a good time to visit. If it isn't, pray for the patient or other family members, and then plan to return on another day. However if the patient is looking forward to the visit, get a chair and move as close as possible to where the person is located. Sometimes terminally ill patients just want another person's presence—without conversation. At other times the patient may enjoy someone singing a favorite hymn or chorus. One of the best activities is to read portions of the Bible. If the patient doesn't know his or her own favorite Bible passage, reading from the Bible can be very comforting. Passages like Psalm 23, Matthew 6:31–34, 1 Corinthians 15:50–58, and Revelation 21:1–4 can be extremely comforting.

- There will be times when terminally ill patients still have the ability to think deeply about life. They may ask questions about God, evil, and suffering. Dr. John Dunlop comments that some caregivers become apprehensive about facing challenging theological questions, but his advice is worth considering. Dunlop suggests that instead of being frightened by the challenging questions of life, take your time in giving an answer. Discussions about life and death do not have to turn into apologetic debates. It is best to sit with the patient and wonder about the wisdom and goodness of God together.[11] Ask the patient what they have pondered about pain and suffering. It is always important to remind others, especially the terminally ill and their grieving family members, that God Himself did not avoid suffering. He allowed the second person of the Trinity, Jesus Christ, to experience great suffering. In addition, suffering and death is the ultimate doorway into an eternity where sin, sickness, suffering and tears will be no more (see Rev. 21:1–4).

Caring for people on the eve of death is no easy task. And certainly pastors cannot do it alone. Therefore, the wise pastor will establish a training class. A class for elders, deacons, deaconesses, and other caregivers clearly demonstrates the love of Christ in practical ways. Teach the care team to pray for the patient, visit the patient, read Scripture to the patient, and perform simple acts of care and support. A church that cares for the sick and dying will develop a God-honoring reputation that draws others in the community to the love of Christ.

COMMUNICATING THE GOSPEL TO THE TERMINALLY ILL

There will be times when pastors and members of the care team will have questions about a patient's spiritual status. Similar to the deeper theological conversations mentioned above, those who visit the terminally ill will have reservations about discussing one's spiritual status. We assume that personal, spiritual beliefs are just that—personal—and others have no right to interfere. Such a conclusion is wrong on two counts. First, it is a denial of our Lord's calling for all of us to go and make disciples (see Matt. 28:18–20). Second, it is a failure to love people regarding the most important issue in all of life, their eternal destiny.

Pastor Terry Rush observes that many Christians have questions about the destiny of someone's soul, but quickly add, "I don't know what to say." Rush suggests three things need to be kept in mind.

First, people want to know God. It's true that no one seeks after God on their own (see Rom. 3:11). However, people dealing with a terminal disease may very well be moved by the Holy Spirit to start asking important questions. When pastors are visiting the terminally ill, they can very kindly ask, "Have you ever given any thought about what will happen after this life ends?" This question can prompt a whole host of other questions and thoughts, because in the shadow of death, people who have been lifelong spiritual rebels may want to know about God.[12]

Second, people who start to seek to understand God and the hereafter also want to know what to do. Here is where knowing the basics of the gospel message are so important. Members of the care team will want to remind the patient that God identifies us all, including the caregiver, as spiritual rebels. We are all justly deserving of the wrath of God (see Rom. 3:23). But the good news in the context of the Bible's bad news is that God took care of our sin problem for us. Remind the patient that Christ did what we could not do for ourselves in satisfying the righteous, holy demands of God (see Rom. 5:10). As the caregiver senses the leading of the Holy Spirit, invite the patient to trust Jesus as their own personal Savior (see Rom. 5:1 and Eph. 2:8–10). After all, ministry to the terminally ill might very well be one the greatest times of spiritual harvest.[13]

Third, terminally ill people want to know what life beyond the grave will be like. Pain and death seem like such horrible things to experience, but the Scriptures give us some clues into the glories of eternity. Remind the terminally ill person that our present sufferings are minimal in comparison to the glory we will experience in eternity. This was the apostle Paul's testimony in view of his own suffering (see 2 Cor. 4:17–18). Use Scripture as the primary tool in pointing people away from their pain to the glories of heaven and eternal life in Jesus.

CONCLUSION

Our culture is a death-denying culture. The average citizen does not want to talk about death, and they want to avoid the experience if at all possible. But we cannot deny death. Scripture affirms that human beings are appointed to die once. After that comes the resurrection, a resurrection for Christians unto eternal life and joy in heaven (Heb. 9:27). These are important truths to remember, especially when family members and friends of our churches and communities are faced with the realities of terminal illness. It is the church that is equipped with truth, love, and compassion to help terminally ill people to die with dignity—the dignity that only Christ can give.

NOTES

1. Penelope Wilcock, *Spiritual Care of Dying and Bereaved People* (Abingdon, PA: Breathing Room Foundation, 2013), 100–106.

2. Ibid., 103–4.

3. Ibid., 104.

4. Ibid., 104.

5. See "Five Wishes," a living will document at https://samaritannj.org/resources/5-wishes-living-will-documents. This document meets the legal requirements for an advance directive in 42 U.S. states and the District of Columbia.

6. John Dunlop, *Finishing Well to the Glory of God: Strategies from a Christian Physician* (Wheaton, IL: Crossway, 2011), 197.

7. Hank Dunn, *Hard Choices for Loving People: CPR, Feeding Tubes, Palliative Care, Comfort Measures, and the Patient with a Serious Illness*, 6th edition, (Naples, FL: Quality of Life Publishing, 2016), 38.

8. Ibid., 27.

9. Ibid., 32.

10. Joe Carter, "When Can Christians Withdraw Life Sustaining Medical Treatment?" The Ethics and Religious Liberty Commission, May 3, 2018, https://erlc.com/resource-library/articles/when-can-christians-withdraw-life-sustaining-medical-treatment.

11. Dunlop, *Finishing Well*, 179.
12. Terry Rush, "What Should We Say to Unsaved, Terminally Ill?" *The Christian Chronicle*, February 1, 2009. https: / christianchronicle.org/what-should-we-say-to-unsaved-terminally-ill.
13. Ibid.

Ministering to the Divorced

HARRY SHIELDS

Preachers are fond of quoting divorce statistics when it comes to delivering sermons on divorce and remarriage. In an article for The Gospel Coalition, Glenn Stanton observed that the idea that Christians divorce at roughly the same rate as nonreligious people, is patently false. He goes on to say that there is great benefit to couples and families when they read the Bible regularly, pray together, and attend church services on a regular basis. Stanton explicitly states, "People who seriously practice a traditional religious faith—whether Christian or other—have a divorce rate markedly lower than the general population."[1] He goes on to say that on the basis of extensive research, conservative Protestants who regularly attend church are 35 percent *less likely* to divorce than those who have no religious affiliation. On the other hand, those who nominally attend church are 20 percent *more likely* to divorce than compared with the secular culture.[2] Those who practice a more vibrant faith, even if it is not distinctly Christian, will also report higher degrees of commitments to their partners, greater marital satisfaction, and lower levels of negative interaction with one's spouse. Therefore, the idea that Christianity reflects the secular culture's experience regarding divorce is simply not accurate.

However that does not mean that pastors can avoid issues like marital unfaithfulness, divorce, and potential remarriage. Pastors need to be prepared to provide pastoral care and counsel to people contemplating or having experienced the trauma of divorce. Almost every family in the church can testify to marital conflict in some part of their extended family, with relatives and friends often forced into taking sides. Pastors are often sought out to provide counsel and perhaps even to officiate at a future wedding. Decision-making in such situations against the backdrop of a divorce is no easy matter. So what is a pastor supposed to do when the congregation is faced with the issue of divorce, ongoing singleness, or even remarriage?

Every pastor will have to develop a theology of marriage, divorce, and remarriage. Far beyond what this chapter can provide, a pastor will need to spend significant time studying the Scriptures and poring over scholarly textbooks on the subject of divorce. Since pastoral counsel of divorced congregants can be fraught with strong emotions—since every family and every congregation has had some experience interacting with divorced people—pastors will need to develop convictions about the topic. Therefore, church leaders need to start their research with both pastoral conviction and pastoral compassion.

Pastoral Conviction

Many discussions on the subject of divorce begin from what might be called moral arguments for or against divorce. They are important, but in reality, there is a better starting point. We need to affirm what we believe about God and His nature. It is God's attributes that should shape what a pastor believes and communicates. For instance, the Bible teaches that God is "faithful and true." That is, whatever God communicates, especially in the Scriptures, is true. He never lies. Everything He says is trustworthy (see John 17:17). So, when God reveals His will about marriage and divorce in the Scriptures, we can trust that everything He says is absolutely true.

In addition to God's truthfulness the Bible teaches about the goodness of God. When we say that God is good, we are saying that God always acts in accordance with what is right, true, and good (1 John 1:5). God cannot do anything that is unholy or unrighteousness. Therefore, whatever God asks of us within the realm of marriage and divorce is for our ultimate blessing. Everything that comes from God, whether in word or deed, is always for our well-being (James 1:17).

Pastors will also want to develop their ministry convictions on the basis of God's love and grace. God does not simply extend love and grace on occasion. The triune God is the personification of love and grace (see 1 John 4:7–8). In spite of the fact that Christians are fallen individuals capable of sinning in any situation, God through the person and work of Jesus Christ extends grace to His people. His grace is the very means by which repentant, believing people can live a whole new life that is honoring to the Savior (Rom. 6:4; Eph. 2:4–10).

As pastors ponder the hard questions of life, and as they give counsel to members of their congregations, they will want to do so out of convictions formulated from the study of God's Word. So, if God speaks *truthfully* through the Scriptures, we can trust what God has revealed about any subject, especially issues related to marriage and divorce. If God is *good* in all His ways, pastors can be certain that wisdom from God is ultimately concerned for the well-being of His people. And if God is full of love and grace, then pastors and counselees can be confident that God can meet them and sustain them no matter what relational traumas they may have experienced. Sometimes pastoral counsel based on God's Word may initially face resistance from those contemplating divorce or those who have experienced divorce. But biblically based instruction can be trusted no matter how people initially receive it.

PASTORAL COMPASSION

In addition to conviction, there is another side of pastoral care and counseling that must also be taken into consideration. Pastors are not doctrinal robots who dispense theological information without any emotional engagement. Pastors deal with people facing real problems in the midst of deep pain. There should always be an spiritual and relational component to caring for people in emotional conflict.

After dealing with her own pain through an unwanted divorce, Laura Petherbridge has been given a unique ministry to counsel separated and divorced individuals. In one of her articles, Petherbridge shared ideas about emotional pain that separated and divorced people experience. For instance, she reminds her readers that divorce is like death. It is the death of a dream and the end of a covenant that was intended to last throughout one's earthly existence. Divorcees often feel betrayed by one that they previously trusted more than anyone else. And for many divorcees there is never 100 percent closure. Every birthday celebration, every graduation, and every wedding of one of the children brings back painful memories. Petherbridge says that in many situations, divorce causes one or both former spouses to dread Sundays. There is a fear, whether real or imagined, that other people are watching and wondering what really happened in the marriage. As a result, some divorcees may abandon their faith for a while or forsake it altogether.[3]

The wise pastor will always want to represent God's perspective on the importance of marriage. But one will also want to consider the pain that people in marital conflict are facing. Without compassion and understanding it will be difficult to encourage people to continue to walk with Christ in pain and suffering. Rather than being a stigma that some people have to bear, divorce can actually be an opportunity for pastors and churches to reach the broken in their time of great need. Therefore, pastors will need to complement their biblical convictions about marriage with Christ-anointed compassion.

THE PASTOR'S ROLE IN MINISTERING TO THE DIVORCED

As stated above, pastoral care to the divorced must be administered through biblical convictions as well as pastoral compassion for people going through deep pain. The remainder of this chapter will focus on two areas of pastoral ministry to people facing various forms of marital conflict: (1) Pastoral Exegesis: the pastor's need to understand and communicate key biblical texts related to marriage, divorce, and remarriage; (2) Pastoral Care: the pastor's role in providing specific forms of care and counsel.

PASTORAL EXEGESIS

When people visit a new church, they will frequently ask about the church's position on a variety of subjects. And if an individual has experienced a divorce in the past, one will want to know what the church believes about divorce and remarriage, as well as what role a divorcee might have in a given church. There are generally three primary positions on the subject. Pastors would do well to be familiar with the various positions in preparation for doing their own research on divorce and remarriage. Then a pastor will need to examine key biblical texts to draw personal conclusions about divorce and remarriage.

Some churches believe that there is no allowance for divorce on any grounds whatsoever. Adherents to this view attempt to harmonize what are known as the *exception clauses* in Matthew 5:31–32 and Matthew 19:9 with similar statements in the gospels of Mark and Luke, where the exceptions are not stated. According to this view a correct reading of Jesus' words should not be the phrase "except for the reason of sexual immorality," but rather "not even in the case of immorality." The key term is the Greek word *porneia*, from which we get the word *pornography*. The term covers various kinds of sexual immorality or unchastity, including though not limited to adultery. This view holds that Jesus was being asked whether "something indecent," that is *porneia*, was the cause Moses was referring to for divorce in Deuteronomy 24. The conclusion often made is that Jesus was telling the Pharisees that they had misunderstood God's intentions, and there was no legitimate cause for divorce at all.[4]

Other churches embrace what might be called the divorce-but-no-remarriage position. According to this position only the death of a spouse would allow for a living spouse to remarry. The idea is that death is the only factor that legitimately dissolves a marriage covenant (see Rom. 7:1–3). The exception clauses in Matthew 5 and 19 are interpreted as causes for a couple to separate, but only for a time. The intended hope would be that during a temporary time of separation, the couple might reconcile. The argument according to this view is that divorce never dissolves a marriage, but only death. Therefore, divorce would be allowable due to *porneia* being discovered, but it would never allow for remarriage, no matter whether one spouse was an innocent party or not.[5]

Still another view reasons that there may be a legitimate allowance for remarriage after a divorce. The argument in this view has a number of variations. However, the essential reasoning is that *porneia* is a legitimate cause for breaking the marriage covenant through a formal divorce. It follows then that in such cases, remarriage is permissible. This view also holds that Paul's argument in 1 Corinthians 7 instructs Christian converts not to divorce their unbelieving spouses. However, if the unbeliever leaves or abandons the marriage, then a legitimate remarriage is permissible, but only to another Christian.[6]

As has already been established, pastors will surely encounter divorced individuals or those contemplating divorce within their congregations. And it has been stated above that pastors must ultimately develop their own personal view on the subject of divorce based on convictions about the nature of God, convictions about the authoritative Word of God, and finally pastoral compassion. So, what are the key biblical texts that might help pastors and churches to establish their own policies on marriage, divorce, and remarriage? Eight passages from the Old and New Testaments should serve as a foundation for pastoral conclusions concerning marriage, divorce, and remarriage.

Genesis 2:24

Pastors and church leaders will need to examine key Old Testament passages within the larger cultural and historical context which Moses wrote. Genesis 2:24 is foundational to all that follows in the Old Testament regarding marriage and divorce. Moses said, "For this reason a man shall leave his father and his mother, and be joined to his wife; and they shall become one flesh." The Genesis account reveals the concept of marriage as a covenant union. Tony Evans writes, "The reason divorce is very hard and very narrow in Scripture is that marriage is a divinely covenanted relationship. It is not just a haphazard ceremony where two people stand before a preacher, say 'I do,' and go on a honeymoon."[7] Commenting on this same concept of ancient covenants, Instone-Brewer observes that the laws and narratives in the Pentateuch were written against the backdrop of Babylon's King Hammurabi. In a world where there were frequent injustices, especially toward women, "These laws did mark the beginning of impartial justice instead of relying on the arbitrary decisions of a ruler or a judge, everyone knew what punishment would be, meted out for each crime, and they also knew what was and wasn't a crime."[8] So, in a world of unjust practices Moses wrote that marriage was a covenant characterized by a one-flesh relationship. This was more than a reference to a sexual union. It meant that, unlike the nations surrounding Israel, a husband could not easily put his wife away and find someone else to marry. They were joined together as husband and wife—no longer two people, but one covenant united couple. Therefore, pastors would do well to read this familiar passage on marriage, keeping ancient culture in mind.

Exodus 21:10–11

At first glance, this text may seem to be irrelevant to contemporary discussions on marriage and divorce. But it reveals insight into the ancient world, as well as the mind of God. Moses wrote, "If he (an Israelite husband) takes to himself another woman, he may not reduce her food, her clothing, or her conjugal rights. But if he will not do these three things for her, then she shall go free for nothing, without payment of money." Apparently, it was understood that Israelite men were able to divorce their wives and remarry. Moses wasn't justifying the practice, but it was clearly assumed that divorce, and most likely adultery, was occurring in Israel—surely also polygamous marriages. But the subtler inference from the text is that there was some agreement that men made with their wives as part of the ancient marriage covenant. That is, the husband was to guarantee that his wife had food, shelter, and conjugal rights. These basic rights were understood by every couple entering into marriage. Shelly concludes that it was part of the "bride price" or "dowry" that a prospective groom paid the father of the bride. This dowry was the usual and customary support a man would provide prior to the marriage.[9] Even if an Israelite man later divorced his wife without cause, or if he entered into a polygamous relationship with a second wife, the first wife had to be cared for. Therefore, behind many of the Old Testament statutes was a provision for the protection of the woman. This reflects God's heart for those in a weaker position.

Deuteronomy 24:1–4

Of all the Old Testament texts that discuss marriage and divorce, Deuteronomy 24 is the one most often cited. The reason for its significance is that it is the same text Jesus is questioned about in Matthew 19. Moses wrote:

> When a man takes a wife and marries her, and it happens, if she finds no favor in his eyes because he has found some indecency in her, that he writes her a certificate of divorce, puts it in her hand, and sends her away from his house, and she leaves his house and goes and becomes another man's wife, and the latter husband turns against her, writes her a certificate of divorce and puts it in her hand, and sends her away from his house, or if the latter husband who took her to be his wife dies, then the former husband who sent her away is not allowed to take her again to be his wife, after she had been defiled; for that is an abomination before the LORD, and you shall not bring sin on the land which the LORD your God is giving you as an inheritance.

There are a variety of interpretations on what Moses was communicating to the people of Israel. But once again the cultural context was important. One must ask, just why did Moses have to write these words, words related to what some commentators refer to as *case law*. The text was designed to clarify existing practices related to marriage and divorce. Moses was again writing against the backdrop of the surrounding nations that had a very open-ended view of divorce. Even more importantly, women who were divorced in the ancient world were treated as little more than a man's private property, to do with them whatever the man wanted. Against this backdrop, Moses was writing words that would in most cases protect a woman from unjust treatment.

The key phrases in the text are "some indecency" (v. 1), and "for that is an abomination before the Lord" (v. 4). It is important to observe that Moses was not trying to delineate the appropriate conditions under which one may divorce and then remarry. Some interpreters argue that this passage affirms the view that divorce is never acceptable to God, and that one is always married to one's first wife. If so, then why did Moses state that a certificate of divorce had to be written, if God did not see it as a legitimate divorce? For those who say that someone who has been divorced and remarries, must then go back to a first spouse cannot possibly draw such a conclusion from this text. They are essentially telling people to use divorce as the corrective to divorce.[10]

Although commentators sometimes try to make the woman the guilty party in this passage, the facts do not support this conclusion. For instance, if the woman was being put away by the husband because she had committed adultery, the Law stated in Deuteronomy 22:22 that the penalty for adultery was execution. So, it wasn't the woman who was at fault, but the husband who decided to divorce her. Feinberg and Feinberg write the following: "We think OT law made this exception because she was 'pushed' into adultery by a first husband who divorced her for 'erwat dabar' (some indecency) and put her on the street with nowhere to turn in that society but to another man."[11] The guilty party was the man, and the subsequent abomination was a woman forced into a situation she didn't want or deserve. So, to protect the woman from harsh injustices, Moses demanded that the husband was to write a certificate of divorce, even though this breaking of the marriage covenant was not God's will. Shelly notes that a husband in ancient Israel could not simply divorce and then reclaim his first wife sometime later. He had to give her a certificate of divorce, which gave her the right to remarry, even though initially she was put in the abominable situation of being pushed out of the marriage, not once but perhaps multiple times.[12] Therefore, Deuteronomy 24:1–4 was a means of protecting the wife from ongoing humiliation.

Malachi 2:10–16

Another text that is often cited for teaching that there are no grounds for divorce, and subsequently no grounds for remarriage is Malachi 2:10–16. The passage is difficult to interpret because of two possible translations for verse 16. Some Bible versions, like the NASB, end with the phrase, "I [God] hate divorce." Other versions translate the Hebrew with the words, "'For the man who does not love his wife but divorces her, says the LORD, the God of Israel, covers his garment with violence" (ESV). Either rendering often draws the conclusion that God so strongly opposes divorce that it is wrong for couples to both divorce and certainly to remarry.

There are two problems with this conclusion. First, the Deuteronomy 24 passage already allows for the possibility of divorce in order to protect a wife from being treated like unwanted property. Second, the context of Malachi 2 reveals that there is something more at the heart of Yahweh's condemnation of the people who had returned from exile. What was condemned was the actions of Israelite men to divorce under every condition imagined so as to take foreign wives as their brides. These men were not divorcing on the basis of Deuteronomy 24 and "some indecency." Rather these men were showing unconscionable faithlessness to their Jewish wives. That is what God hated.[13] Therefore, the text does not give enough information to validate the conclusion that there is no basis for divorce and subsequent remarriage in any and every case. The statement was given in a specific context.

Before looking at important New Testament texts on the subject of divorce, it is important to observe one additional Old Testament passage. It is an important one that helps to answer whether it is ever right for a spouse to pursue a divorce, especially on the grounds of sexual immorality. During the reign of King Josiah, the Lord spoke through the prophet Jeremiah to rebuke the southern kingdom of Judah. The prophet writes, "She (i.e., Judah) saw that for all the adulteries of that faithless one, Israel, I had sent her away with a decree of divorce" (Jer. 3:8 ESV) The reference is to Israel's spiritual adultery. God had kept the marital promises implied in Exodus 21:10–11 and Deuteronomy 24. And yet there was no repentance. So, with respect to the northern kingdom or Israel, God Himself became a divorcer.

By the time of Christ's birth, divorce was a common practice in first-century Judaism.[14] In fact, one rabbinical school, led by rabbi Hillel, taught that Jewish men could divorce their wives for two reasons. The first was for sexual immorality on the part of the wife, and the second was what Hillel referred to as "any cause." Referring to Deuteronomy 24:1, Hillel and his followers noted that Moses used the phrase "because he has found some indecency in her." They wondered why he simply didn't use the term *sexual immorality* (*porneia*). So, they concluded that a man had a right to divorce his wife, either for her sexual unfaithfulness or for "any cause" he deemed appropriate.[15]

Another school of thought, led by rabbi Shammai, took a different approach when teaching on the subject of divorce and remarriage. They argued that the phrase in Deuteronomy 24 referred to sexual immorality alone, and no other cause for divorce was legitimate.[16]

These were the two prevailing Jewish ideas on divorce and remarriage at the time of Christ's birth. Some interpreters believe that it was this "any cause" view for divorce that was behind Joseph's decision to initially divorce Mary, the mother of Jesus. And it was this hotly contested debate that was also thrust upon Jesus in His debates with the religious leaders of His day. However, to draw pastoral and church conclusions about divorce and remarriage, leaders will have to consider what was happening in Matthew 5:31–32 and 19:1–10.

Matthew 5:31–32

A key interpretive marker in the Sermon on the Mount is the phrase "You have heard that it was said . . . But I say to you that . . ." But even prior to Jesus addressing the subjects of anger, lust, and divorce, Jesus made another important statement. He said, "Do not presume that I came to abolish the Law or the Prophets; I did not come to abolish but to fulfill" (Matt. 5:17). By using this phrase Jesus was challenging interpretive distortions that the rabbis and religious leaders of the day were practicing. For instance, religious leaders would say that a person who took the life of one individual was subject to judgment and execution. But Jesus goes one step further in fulfilling the Law before His followers. He said that murder wasn't just a physical act, but a heart issue. If a person hated another individual, whether they committed an actual murder or not, they had essentially killed that person. It was a heart issue. Jesus went on to apply this same heart hermeneutic to the issues of adultery and divorce. Adultery wasn't just a physical act between two people married to other spouses, but it was an issue of lust in one's heart.

So, when one interprets Matthew 5:31–32, it is important to keep in mind that Jesus' purpose was not to render a decision on whether one could remarry after a divorce. He was really getting to the heart of Deuteronomy 24:1–4. For a man to divorce his wife for the "any cause" idea that was prevalent in the first century would really be forcing his wife into an adulterous relationship. Why? It was because the original marriage was the covenant relationship that was sanctioned by God. To put the woman away for "any cause" coming from a corrupt heart would also make the woman guilty of adultery because it would force her out on the street and, of necessity, into the arms of another man.

It is important to keep in mind that Matthew 5:31–32 does not discuss the issue of remarriage. Other texts will better inform pastors and church leaders regarding how to respond to people who desire to remarry. As for Christ's purposes in the

Sermon on the Mount, He wanted His hearers to know that there was more to the Law than simply doing or not doing certain things. Jesus was elevating the covenant of marriage against a frivolous background of dissolving marriages for "any cause." He was showing that true obedience to God was a matter of the heart, not just following or fudging on specific rules.

Matthew 19:1–12 and Mark 10:2–12

As His ministry grew with greater and greater influence, the religious leaders challenged Jesus at every opportunity. In Matthew 19, Jesus returned to the region of Judea, where He was confronted by a group of Pharisees. They asked Him specifically, "Is it lawful for a man to divorce his wife for any reason?" (Matt. 19:3). These religious leaders were trying to draw Jesus into the "any cause" debate mentioned above. But He was not interested in their debate. Instead He takes them back to Genesis 2 and reminds them that God created them as male and female. As a couple they were to leave the authority of each spouse's home and start their own household. In fact, the marriage covenant was so unique in God's eyes that they were to become one flesh—not just two people in a sexual union but with the goal of being one new entity.

The religious leaders apparently weren't satisfied with Jesus' answer, so they pressed the issue. They alluded to Deuteronomy 24, trying to persuade Jesus that Moses *commanded* divorce. But Jesus was quick to respond, reminding them that Moses *allowed* for divorce (Matt. 19:8). The distinction between the terms "commanded" and "allowed" was crucial to what Jesus was trying to communicate. He wanted to show that the real issue was a matter of the heart. Instone-Brewer observes that the term for "hardness of heart" means "stubbornness." In fact, the term appears only one other place in the context of divorce, where Jeremiah warns the people of Judah that He might divorce them as He had done with Israel. So, the prophet appeals to his hearers to "circumcise yourselves to your Lord, and circumcise your hardheartedness."[17] Jesus was saying that this was not the way of God from the beginning of time. He wanted marriages to be permanent. Instone-Brewer writes,

> Jesus says that marriage was not like this "from the beginning" (Mt 19:8). In Eden there was no sin to break up marriages, and therefore there was no need for divorce. But when sin came and marriages started going wrong, Moses "allowed" divorce for broken marriage vows (Mt 19:8). Jesus thought that people were being too quick to divorce, so he reminds them that Moses meant divorce to only occur when there was "hardheartedness"—that is, a stubborn refusal to repent and stop breaking marriage vows.[18]

A quick reading of Mark 10:2–12 has led some readers to believe that the questioning by the Pharisees by Jesus was a simple retelling of the Matthew 19 account. Shelly observes that both Matthew and Mark were careful to include geographical markers. That is, they stated that Jesus "went to the region of Judea and beyond the Jordan" (Mark 10:1). This would have put Jesus in Perea, the very region ruled by Herod Antipas, who left his own wife to marry Herodias. So, the Pharisees were most likely trying to set Jesus up to create conflict between Him and the ruling monarch of the area. Jesus was not one to back away from speaking the truth. Speaking of all people who chose to divorce their mates "without cause," Jesus was saying that when someone, great or small, puts away a spouse for any reason other than adultery (see Deut. 24), they are convicted by the Law of covenant-breaking adultery.[19] For people who say that divorced people who remarry are living in constant adultery can't really validate such claims from this text. It is the act of divorcing one's mate that causes the adultery. So, the text doesn't really address issues or causes surrounding remarriage. Shelly writes,

> In fact, we should always remember that reclaiming one's former mate is the one thing specifically forbidden in Deuteronomy 24:1–4. If you are in a second, third, or fourth marriage today, the call of God to you has nothing to do with getting out of your present relationship and trying to get back with your first mate. It has everything to do with making your present relationship as healthy and divorce-proof as possible.[20]

1 Corinthians 7:1–40

Paul's first letter to the Corinthian church was written about AD 55. The Roman world during the time of Paul's ministry was somewhat hostile to a biblical view of marriage. Sexual immorality was particularly rampant in the city of Corinth. Most Roman young men avoided marriage and fatherhood in order to enjoy as many exploits as possible. In addition, some of the believers in Corinth were pondering the idea that being unmarried might be a more holy status in their service for the Lord. As a result, the believers in Corinth wrote to the apostle Paul to ask a series of questions, one of which was about how a Christian should practice the faith, whether as a single or married person. These questions also contemplated whether it was acceptable for a Christian to divorce. First Corinthians 7 was Paul's response to these questions.

In 1 Corinthian 7:6–9 Paul concedes that it might be best to remain single. However, this was not a rejection of marriage in general. Paul endorsed marriage as a good thing. Instone-Brewer suggests that in verses 1–5 Paul was writing with Exodus 21:10–11 in mind, and subtly reiterating the responsibilities each spouse had to the other marriage partner. That is, spouses were to provide to each other food, clothing, conjugal rights, and faithfulness to one another.[21] Then in verses 10–16 Paul addresses Christians who were married to unbelievers. He tells them they are not to "separate," that is they were not to divorce. If they should choose to divorce, since Roman law allowed for easy divorces, they were to remain unmarried with the hope of reconciliation. The only exception to maintaining the marriage vows was when an unbelieving spouse chooses to leave the marriage. In verse 15 Paul states that if the unbelieving spouse leaves, "let him leave." Then the believer who remains is "not under bondage in such cases, but God has called us in peace."

Conclusions Drawn from the Biblical Texts

The purpose of this overview is designed to help pastors and church leaders make biblically informed decisions as they deal with divorced individuals, who may be contemplating remarriage. First, it must be emphasized that God's ideal is for men and women to enter into marriage and see it as a permanent, earthly relationship. Second, it is also important to realize that both Old Testament and New Testament authors wrote in cultural contexts where divorces occurred on a regular basis in spite of God's ideal for one-man-with-one-woman-for-life. Third, divorce was often allowed to protect the wife, who had few protections in an unjust world (see Deut. 24:1–4). Fourth, if couples are contemplating divorce, Christian spouses specifically should avoid being the cause of the divorce. In addition, they should also seek reconciliation if at all possible. Fifth, the biblical record does not always speak clearly about the possibility of remarriage after a divorce occurs. If it is better for a person to marry than to burn with passion (see 1 Cor. 7:9), then it seems reasonable that it would be better for divorced people to be allowed to remarry, but only marriage to another Christians (see 1 Cor. 7:39).

PASTORAL PRACTICES

It goes without saying that pastors and church leaders will encounter people who are contemplating divorce and the possibilities of remarriage. What are some practical things that pastors and churches might do?

First, it will be important to communicate what a specific local church believes regarding marriage, divorce, and remarriage. Beliefs about these subjects should be in writing as part of the official policy of a local church. But as stated at the beginning of this chapter, pastors will want to bring personal conviction about their views to any discussion with divorced individuals. At the same time, they will want to enter counseling sessions with deep-seated compassion for the people who ask for pastoral care. People will benefit from knowing that a pastor cares about them and is willing to give them a listening ear.

Second, prior to having to talk about the subject of divorce and remarriage, pastors should implement classes and seminars on marriage enrichment. As a strategic part of marriage enrichment, churches will want to offer ministries of marriage mentoring. Young marrieds and couples facing conflict in their marriage will benefit from having another older couple to mentor them. One such ministry is Re/Engage, a ministry where trained couples meet with other couples in a large group/small group format to interact on topics relevant to marriage enrichment. Re/Engage offers both vital information for married couples as well as couple-to-couple accountability (http://marriagehelp.org/).

Third, for individuals who have already experienced a divorce, pastors will want to encourage the possibility of reconciliation if at all possible. But if reconciliation is not possible, divorcees will want to be encouraged to participate in a ministry like DivorceCare. DivorceCare is a thirteen-week class that provides expert advice (usually in the form of a video), as well as group discussion time. The discussion time allows participants to interact on the topic and to share their own personal challenges related to divorce (https://www.divorcecare.org).

Fourth, when an individual or a couple having experienced divorce comes to seek remarriage, the wise pastor will want to encourage caution. Even if a pastor believes that remarriage is a biblical possibility, it is often wise to encourage a divorced person to wait for at least a year after the divorce before contemplating a new marriage.

Fifth, people who have experienced the pain of divorce will not necessarily have the opportunity to remarry for a variety of reasons. What all Christians need—whatever one's marital status—is an opportunity to grow in their relationship with Christ. Small group discipleship ministries offer a place for personal spiritual growth. Some pastors, after studying the biblical evidence, may not feel comfortable officiating at the wedding of people who have been divorced. In such cases, a pastor can still invite divorced individuals into the church's small group ministry. Not only will these individuals grow in their relationship with Christ, but there will be a greater possibility they will feel welcome by a congregation that has a high view of marriage.

NOTES

1. Glenn Stanton, "FactChecker: Divorce Rate Among Christians," The Gospel Coalition, September 25, 2012, https://www.thegospelcoalition.org/article/factchecker-divorce-rate-among-christians.

2. Ibid.

3. Laura Petherbridge, "10 Things I Wish Church Leaders Knew About Divorce," Facts & Trends, August 23, 2018, https://factsandtrends.net/2018/08/23/10-things-i-wish-church-leaders-knew-about-divorce.

4. John S. Feinberg and Paul D. Feinberg, *Ethics for a Brave New World* (Wheaton, IL: Crossway, 1993), 306–7.

5. Ibid., 307–8.

6. Ibid., 308–10.

7. Tony Evans, *Divorce and Remarriage* (Chicago: Moody Publishers, 2012), 10.

8. David Instone-Brewer, *Divorce and Remarriage in the Church: Biblical Solutions for Pastoral Realities* (Downers Grove, IL: InterVarsity Press, 2003), 26.

9. Rubel Shelly, *Divorce & Remarriage: A Redemptive Theology* (Abilene, TX: Leafwood, 2007), 52.

10. Ibid., 57.

11. Feinberg and Feinberg, *Ethics for a Brave New World*, 315.

12. Shelly, *Divorce & Remarriage*, 60.

13. Ibid., 63.

14. Instone-Brewer, *Divorce and Remarriage in the Church*, 55.

15. Ibid., 55–57.

16. Ibid., 57.

17. Jer. 4:4 LXX as quoted in Instone-Brewer, *Divorce and Remarriage in the Church*, 63.

18. Ibid., 63.

19. Shelly, *Divorce & Remarriage*, 103.

20. Ibid., 106.

21. Instone-Brewer, *Divorce and Remarriage in the Church*, 73.

CHAPTER 3.3

Ministry in a Disability Inclusive Congregation

DAWN SOETENGA CLARK

Disability is part of the human condition. Bill Gaventa says, "The question is not whether one will be affected by disability, but when."[1] The Lausanne Committee for World Evangelization, a global movement that mobilizes evangelical leaders to collaborate for world evangelization, estimates that there are over a billion people in the world with various disabilities, and over 80 percent of them live in less developed nations.[2] The United States Census Bureau reports that 19 percent of the population have some type of disability.[3] Yet even though there is a high prevalence of disability, people with disabilities have sometimes been marginalized by society and by the church.

This chapter outlines how people with disabilities and their families can move from the margins and become full participants in the life and mission of the church. It is divided into three basic sections. In the first section, disability is defined by looking at various models of disability. The second presents biblical foundations for inclusive ministry. The last section introduces practical applications that enable ministry staff to create congregations of faith and belonging for people of all abilities.

DEFINING DISABILITY

An individual may experience disability from birth, or the disability may be the result of illness, injury, or accident. The United Nations Convention on the Rights of Persons with Disabilities defines disability in this way: "Persons with disabilities include those who have long-term physical, mental, intellectual or sensory impairments which, in interaction with various barriers, may hinder their full and effective participation in society on an equal basis with others."[4] Disability is long term, and involves the individual's impairments as well as any barriers.

Our worldview impacts how these elements intersect with one another. Philosopher James Sire defines worldview as "a commitment, a fundamental orientation of the heart, that can be expressed as a story or in a set of presuppositions ... about the basic constitution of reality, that provides the foundation on which we live and move and have our being."[5] Cultures or societies have viewed disability in a variety of ways: as a bio-medical issue, a social-cultural issue, a curse, punishment for sin, or even a blessing/gift from God.

Stephanie Hubach, author of *Same Lake, Different Boat*, suggests three predominant views toward disability: the modernist view, the postmodern view, and the biblical view.[6] In the modernist view, disability is seen as being "an *abnormal* part of life in a *normal* world."[7] The focus is on the person's impairment and the limitations that make them different from the acceptable societal norms. Disability is seen as an abnormality that resides within the individual that prevents them from participating in society. This view has also been referred to as the "medical model," since medical intervention and rehabilitation are seen as the pathway for the participation of people with disabilities in society.

In the postmodern view, disability is considered "a *normal* part of life in a *normal* world."[8] Advocates argue that disability is a matter of normal diversity and should be celebrated rather than seen as a tragedy or a reason for devaluing a person and expecting less from them. It is the view that "normal" society has toward disability that is disabling. The emphasis is on what a person *can* do, rather than on what they cannot do. This viewpoint has also been called the "social model" of disability, and it has given rise to the disability rights and disability pride movements.

Both viewpoints have strengths and weaknesses. The medical model encouraged acts of charity and rehabilitation but failed to address societal attitudes that often led to the marginalization, social exclusion, abuse, and death of people with disabilities. For example, nearly 300,000 people with disabilities were euthanized by the Nazi regime in World War II because they were determined to be "useless eaters."[9] The social model focuses on the personal and societal attitudes that often lead to exclusion and lack of equal participation by people with disabilities, but it has sometimes ignored the impairment of the individual, forgetting that "disability is not solely a socially constructed reality. It also involves concrete bodies with involuntary restrictions that can cause discomfort, pain, and frustration of their own accord."[10]

The biblical model allows us to consider the strengths of each of these viewpoints within a biblical framework. In a biblical worldview, disability is viewed as being a "*normal* part of life in an *abnormal* world."[11] Disability can be expected or "normal" in a world that has been radically changed by the fall. When Adam and Eve sinned, God's perfect creation was marred. All of creation experienced the fall's damage, and brokenness has permeated all of life. Now human bodies experience pain, disease, disability, and death. Our societies are marked by broken relationships, conflicts, and wars. When we think about disability, we cannot merely view the impairment of the individual. We also must address personal attitudes, societal attitudes, and unjust systems that are sinful and exclude and demean people with disabilities. The biblical view celebrates the uniqueness of each person as an image bearer of God, while pointing out attitudes and systems that are not in keeping with scriptural principles.

Although Adam and Eve were created as finite and therefore limited human beings, the fall brought impairments to humanity that caused a new level of limitation and difficulty not previously experienced. The biblical model reminds us that in some mysterious way, disability and various impairments are part of God's plan. "Shall what is formed say to the one who formed it, 'Why did you make me like this?' Does not the potter have the right to make out of the same lump of clay some pottery for special purposes and some for common use?" (Rom. 9:20–21 NIV). The Westminster Catechism affirms that God creates every person, regardless of their role or ability level, to "glorify God, and to enjoy him for ever."[12]

This biblical view of disability raises serious questions for the church. Does the church see people with disabilities as fellow image bearers designed to glorify God? How do we support people experiencing disability, as well as address the traditions and practices of the church that may have excluded them? In what ways does the church need to be reformed and transformed so that people with disabilities are welcomed as full participants in the life and mission of the church? With these questions in mind, we turn to the biblical foundations for inclusive ministry.

BIBLICAL FOUNDATIONS

IMAGE OF GOD

Tim was walking down the street with his mother, Ann. He saw a woman pushing a stroller and ran up to her. He peered inside the stroller and excitedly asked his mother to come and see the beautiful baby. As Ann approached the stroller, she observed that the baby had a noticeable disability. His mother had tears streaming down her cheeks, and Ann asked the woman if Tim had said something hurtful. The woman shook her head and remarked that no one had called her child beautiful before. All they ever saw was his disability. Yet Tim, who has Down syndrome, saw a baby, not a disability.

What is your response when you see someone with a disability? Do you see them as someone made in the image of God, or is your initial reaction, "What is wrong with them?" Do you focus on what is lacking rather than what is "excellent or praiseworthy" in the individual (Phil. 4:8)? When the disciples saw the man born blind, they asked Jesus, "Who sinned, this man or his parents?" Yet Jesus answered, "neither . . . it was was so that the works of God might be displayed in him" (John 9:2–3). Our questions often reveal the attitudes of our hearts.

How does the image of God apply to people with disabilities? Thomas Reynolds, author of *Vulnerable Communion*, says that "Christians have often interpreted disability as a distortion of God's purposes, a marring of the image of God."[13] We must acknowledge that every human being bears the effects of the fall, although the brokenness of some is more visible than others. It is an error to think that disability distorts the image of God more than any other type of brokenness.

Through the centuries, theologians have linked various attributes to the image of God, including "intellectual ability, moral purity, spiritual nature, dominion over the earth, creativity, ability to make ethical choices, and immortality."[14] There is a danger for people with disabilities when a particular characteristic, like intellectual ability, is used to define someone as more or less valuable. Secular bioethicist Peter Singer has suggested that a dog or a pig has greater intellectual capacity than a profoundly disabled infant, and he has used that argument to justify terminating the infant's life.[15]

In his article "The Image of God," John Piper argues that the definition of the image of God must be broad, since Scripture doesn't indicate precisely what it is. He offers this definition: "The *imago Dei* is *that in man which constitutes him as him-whom-God-loves*."[16] Divine love is a love that gives. "For God so loved the world, that He **gave** His only begotten Son" (John 3:16). Just as salvation is a gift of God, the *imago Dei*, is a gift God bestows upon all human beings. Jason Whitt, former director of Baylor University's Institute of Faith and Learning, says, "When the *imago Dei* is recognized as a gift . . . an account of being human opens which leaves none as morally questionable. . . . No one because of some inherent quality may be said to be more or less human than another."[17] Disability inclusive congregations see the value and worth of every person.

THE INCLUSIVE COVENANT

God's covenantal promise to Abraham provides a blessing that extends to everyone: "I will bless those who bless you, and the one who curses you I will curse. And in you all the families of the earth will be blessed" (Gen. 12:3). The Abrahamic blessing is fulfilled in Christ Jesus, and receiving this promise is not dependent upon a certain ability level. In the same way that cultural, socioeconomic, and male/female distinctions are not barriers to the unity we experience in Christ, a person's ability level should not be a barrier either (Gal. 3:28).

In the New Testament, the parable of the great banquet specifically invites the marginalized into the kingdom of God. "Go out at once into the streets and lanes of the city and bring in here those who are poor, those with disabilities, those who are blind, and those who are limping" (Luke 14:21). The church's failure to extend this invitation to people with various impairments has been called the "Lost Mandate."[18] For example, according to the International Mission Board of the Southern Baptist Convention, there are approximately 35 million deaf people worldwide, and they are considered among the least evangelized in the world.[19] Disability inclusive congregations are passionate about bringing all people into the kingdom of God, and they do not see disability as a barrier to the unity we have in Christ.

WELCOME AND HOSPITALITY

David's covenant with Jonathan demonstrates how the fulfillment of a covenantal promise leads to welcome and generous hospitality (1 Sam. 20:12–23). When David became king, he remembered his covenant to show kindness to Jonathan's descendants, and bestowed that kindness on Jonathan's son, Mephibosheth, a man crippled in both feet. David fulfilled his covenantal promise by restoring property, providing for Mephibosheth's physical needs, and extending hospitality. Mephibosheth was brought to the king's table and came into relationship with David, the king (2 Sam. 9:6–10).

The New Testament recognizes that hospitality is a mark of a church leader (1 Tim. 3:2) and a practice for all believers (Rom. 12:13). In Hebrews 13:2, we are commanded, "Do not neglect hospitality to strangers." In true Christian hospitality, we love strangers by welcoming their differences and inviting them to join us in fellowship and worshiping Jesus.

However, our welcome in the church has often become distorted. Churches tend to welcome people who are similar or who can provide some obvious advantage to the congregation. James rebuked the early church for this type of favoritism that had the poor person sit off to the side, socially excluded and demeaned (James 2:1–4). In Luke 14, Jesus observed the way people were vying for positions at the banquet table. He told a parable to address our propensity for only offering hospitality to our family, friends, and those of social influence. Jesus exhorts us to invite those who cannot provide us with any social or material gain (Luke 14:12–14). The church of Jesus Christ is not marked by power, control, dominance, and self-importance; rather, it is marked by servanthood. When we have Jesus, we have everything we need for life and godliness (2 Peter 1:3), and our hospitality can be sacrificial and radical. Author Barbara Newman says, "The Church embodies hospitality . . . by treating all as recipients of divine love,"[20] and disability inclusive congregations display a hospitality that embraces each other's differences.

However, people with disabilities have often felt unwelcomed at church. In a 2013 study in the United States, almost one third of families said they left their place of worship because their child or adult with special needs was not included or welcomed.[21] People with disabilities may be seen as disruptions to services or as drains on resources, rather than a gift to the church. Reynolds exhorts us to remember that "blessed *are* the poor, the marginalized, and the weak. Not, blessed *will be* the poor and weak once they get it all together and become acceptable or normal. . . . In the end, rich and poor, righteous, and sinful, women and men, healthy and sick, able-bodied and disabled, are joined together in a relational wholeness constituted by grace."[22]

GRACE AND POWER IN WEAKNESS

When the apostle Paul begged God to remove his thorn in the flesh, God replied by saying, "My grace is sufficient for you, for [My] power is perfected in weakness" (2 Cor. 12:9). The West has an inclination for hero worship and applauds strength, power, and worldly perfection while hiding weaknesses. Christian leaders may be chosen on the basis of their self-assurance and ability. Yet the Bible is filled with examples of God's grace and power being displayed through human weakness. God chose Moses, a man with speech difficulties, to deliver His people from the hand of the Egyptians (Ex. 4:1–17). God chose Gideon, from the tribe of Manasseh, the weakest clan and the least in his family, to lead the Israelites to victory over the Midianites (Judg. 6:11–16). And God empowered Samson to achieve his greatest victory when he was blind and needed someone else to place his hands on the pillars (Judg. 16:25–30). In reality, we are all jars of clay, and the treasure of the gospel is seen more clearly in our weakness and brokenness than in our strength and ability (2 Cor. 4:7).

In 2010, a disability ministry leadership team from College Church in Wheaton, Illinois, took nine teens and adults with intellectual disabilities on a short-term mission trip to France. These adults were accompanied by their parents, most of whom were senior citizens. In a country that aborts most unborn children identified with a disability, these parents testified to the value and worth of their children with disabilities.

This team served alongside a Moody graduate and missionary in France, who directed a community gospel choir. The teens and adults sang with the choir, played instruments, and shared their stories of faith. After one of the concerts, a secular French psychologist said to a team leader, "We do not believe that people with intellectual disabilities are capable of faith, because they cannot make an informed choice. But I have seen the faces of your group. I have seen how important their faith is to them. I have to reconsider my position." God used these men and women, whom the world had often marginalized, to show that faith is not a matter of the intellect but is a gift of God. Once again, "God chose things the world considers foolish in order to shame those who think they are wise" (1 Cor. 1:27 NLT). Disability inclusive congregations humbly rely on God's grace and strength, not human ability.

HEALING AND DISABILITY

Some people with disabilities have been wounded because the church has told them that their disability persisted because they lacked the faith to be healed. God can always cure a person of their impairment, but in His sovereignty, He may not. A biblical and balanced view of healing recognizes the difference between cure and healing.

A person may be considered cured when the condition or impairment is no longer present, but author Thomas E. Reynolds reminds us that "healing means something more fundamental than curing. It means promoting wholeness as well-being"[23] and "becoming able-bodied is not the criterion for membership in the kingdom."[24] The gospel brings healing into the social, psychological, and spiritual areas of our lives, even if the physical impairment remains. When people who have been socially excluded and devalued are then welcomed into the church and called friends, they experience social and psychological healing. When salvation through Christ is received, doubts of God's goodness are replaced with the joy of His presence. When Jesus heals, He brings people back into right relationship with God and the people of God. Joni Eareckson Tada became a quadriplegic because of a diving accident at the age of seventeen, and later founded Joni and Friends, an organization that brings the hope of the gospel to people affected by disability. She said, "As I delighted myself in the Lord, He gave me the desire of my heart—not miraculous healing, but a sweeter, more intimate union with Jesus Christ."[25]

BODY OF CHRIST

Churches are often homogenous places where there are few differences in race, socioeconomic status or ability level. The apostle Paul reminded the proud and triumphant Corinthian church that the body of Christ is made up of people with a variety of gifts, and all the gifts are needed. He used the imagery of the body to explain how unity and relational wholeness are achieved in the church.

In 1 Corinthians 12, Paul describes four truths about spiritual gifts. First, there are varieties of gifts, services, and activities in the body of Christ, and this diversity of gifts is celebrated (1 Cor. 12:1–3). Second, it is the Spirit who distributes and empowers those gifts (1 Cor. 12:11). Third, honor is given to those parts which seem weaker, but are indispensable (1 Cor. 12:22–24). Amos Yong, author of *The Bible, Disability and the Church* says, "Paul's insistence that the members of the body that seem to be weaker are indispensable, is a stinging rebuke to the non-disabled Corinthian elite, a reprimand that is inclusive of marginalized people with infirmities and disabilities even if not limited to them."[26] Fourth, the gifts are given for the common good, not for the exaltation of an individual (1 Cor. 12:7).

Since the Holy Spirit is the giver of the gifts, no one has a reason to boast, and no one needs to be ashamed of the role they have been given in the body of Christ, for "God has arranged the parts, each one of them in the body, just as He desired" (1 Cor. 12:18). The person who has a disability cannot say they do not belong because they are not able-bodied, and the person without a disability cannot say they don't need the person with a disability. In the body of Christ, there is a mutual submission and appreciation of one another, for the body works together to serve Christ, not self-interest. Disability inclusive congregations honor people with disabilities, recognize their role, and support them in utilizing their God-given gifts in the mission of the church.

ADVOCACY

An advocate pleads the cause of the marginalized to another person or group who can provide assistance. The advocate turns compassion into action. The church family that advocates for people with disabilities will stand with them in their struggles and support them in their cause. Zephaniah 3:19 reminds us that God Himself advocates for the marginalized, "Behold, I am going to deal at that time with all your oppressors; I will save those who limp and gather the scattered, and I will turn their shame into praise and fame in all the earth." The love of Christ compels Christians to discern and do something about the causes of injustice that affect people with disabilities.

In 1957, Garfield Baptist Church (now Spring Creek Church) became concerned that children with special needs were being denied a public school education and took action to address that injustice. In 1964, they opened the Shepherds Home and School in Union Grove, Wisconsin,[27] where students with intellectual disabilities were provided with special education services within a biblical framework. The students became an integral part of the Union Grove Baptist Church and often shared their testimonies and led the congregation in worship. In 1975, the Individuals with Disabilities Education Act was passed, and public school education became a right for all children in the United States. However, it is important to note that the Garfield Baptist Church took action to provide education for special needs children a decade before it was mandated by law.

Ginny Thornburgh, former director of the Interfaith Initiative of the American Association of People with Disabilities, describes advocacy as "the fine art of nudging people forward on a path they may not have considered."[28] Disability inclusive ministry opens the eyes of the congregation and community to the needs and gifts of people with disabilities and "nudges" them to advocate in ways that are supportive and beneficial.

CREATING CONGREGATIONS OF FAITH AND BELONGING

Understanding these biblical foundations of disability inclusive ministry is not enough. These foundations must be **applied** if our churches are to become places of faith and belonging for people of all abilities. After exploring what it means to "become known," this section considers four areas of faith and belonging that are typically found in most churches: worship, discipleship, caring through community, and serving. The section concludes with a discussion of ways in which those with disabilities can participate in the church ordinances.

When Dutch theologian Hans Reinders asked pastors about church members who had a disability, "the most frequent response was 'We don't have them.'"[29] Have our churches inadvertently become places, where, upon entering, people with disabilities exclaim, "This place is not for me!"? Nancy Eiesland, author of *The Disabled God,* said, "For many disabled people the church has been a 'city on a hill'—physically inaccessible and socially inhospitable . . . (and) little effort has been made to promote the full participation of people with disabilities in the life of the church."[30]

According to pastor and author Timothy Keller, "The kingdom means bringing the kingship of Christ in both word and deed to broken lives. . . . We must minister to the whole person. We must reconcile people to God, counsel them to emotional wholeness, free them from structures of injustice, and meet physical needs."[31] Congregations of faith and belonging declare the gospel in word and deed to families affected by disability.

BECOMING KNOWN

God has an intimate knowledge of His children. He has redeemed us, called us by name, and declares that we belong to Him (Isa. 43:1). To belong, a person needs to be known. When we only know a person by their disability or challenges, our view of them is very narrow. "Stigma occurs when we name things wrongly. . . . the church is called to give people back their names, to whisper or shout, 'I call you friends.'"[32]

When Micah was going to join the typical kindergarten class in a new church, his mother asked if she could introduce him to the children. The week before Micah joined the class, she brought in his wheelchair and the switches he uses for communication. She explained the equipment and invited the children to climb into the wheelchair and touch the switches. She prepared and read a picture story-book to the children that focused on Micah's strengths and the things that he enjoyed doing, things that any child would enjoy. He just did them differently. The storybook ended with this invitation: "Can we be friends?" Each child was given a copy of the storybook to take home. When Micah joined the class the following week, he received a warm welcome. When people with disabilities become known by their strengths as well as their weaknesses, we open the door to knowing each other as friends.

Friendship can be expressed through respectful language that focuses on the person rather than the disability. Use terms like "a person with a disability" rather than a "disabled person"; an "accessible bathroom or parking space" rather than a "handicapped bathroom or parking space"; and a "person who uses a wheelchair" rather than a "person confined to a wheelchair."[33]

Not only do we need to know people with disabilities, we need to know our own attitudes toward disability. In his book, *There Is No Asterisk,* Dan Vander Plaats argues that people generally experience five stages in their attitude toward people with disabilities: ignorance, pity, care, friendship, and co-laborers.[34] The book provides congregations with a biblical framework for understanding disability and transforming their attitudes.

WORSHIPING IN COMMUNITY

Congregations typically worship together through song, prayer, Scripture reading, communion, and response to the preached Word. What happens when a human body is incapable of offering a verbal prayer? or reading Scripture? or has no voice to sing? When then does worship look like?

Peter has multiple disabilities and comes to church with his parents. He is not verbal, so it's hard to know how much he understands. But one Sunday, when the congregation began to sing, Peter's head started to sway from side to side. He smiled. Then back and forth in his power wheelchair he began moving his body to the music. As the music swelled, so did his movements. As the hymn came to a close, his body stilled and he sat forward, head at his knees. Peter's exuberant worship challenged the complacent worship of those around him.

In the book *Accessible Gospel, Inclusive Worship,* Barbara Newman describes worship as a conversation "where we speak to God and allow God to speak to our lives," and adds that "inclusive worship happens when you factor in everyone's gifts with everyone's needs."[35] For example, people with mobility impairments may not be able to stand or kneel during specific times in the worship service. Using language that focuses on a person's spiritual response instead of their ability to stand or kneel, such as "Let us all honor the Scripture reading in our hearts, and stand as we are able," invites the entire community into worship, not just the able-bodied. The following resources provide information to make worship spaces more accessible and inclusive:

1. "Disability Ettiquette for Ushers and Greeters" provides key tips for welcoming and providing accommodations for various disabilities.[36]

2. The United Methodist Church Annual Accessibility Audit[37] can be used to evaluate a church's physical, architectural, and communication barriers that prevent a person with a disability from being able to participate fully in congregational life.

3. Sensory worship bags[38] and noise-canceling headphones can be useful tools for attendees who have sensory sensitivities and differences. Bags could include fidgets/sensory toys, a coloring page with colored pencils, a laminated social story[39] about the order of service, or a Bible storybook. Display these items at the entrance to the sanctuary.

DISCIPLESHIP THROUGH RELATIONSHIP

Jesus commands us to disciple all people, not just those without disabilities (Matt. 28:19–20). Pastor Josh Moody says, "Discipleship is intentional friendship for the purpose of spiritual growth that is tailor-made for the person being discipled."[40] Effective discipleship is relational and individualizes the message so that it can be clearly understood by the person being discipled (Neh. 8:8). Both elements are needed, especially when discipling individuals with intellectual and developmental disabilities.

The "peer buddy" approach provides relational discipleship for children and teens with disabilities. Joni and Friends has produced a booklet, *Call Me Friend,* that outlines this intentional and relational approach. A child or teen with disabilities is paired with a peer without disabilities and they learn from each other. The peer welcomes the child with a disability into the Bible class and serves as a model and introduces the child to others in the group. The peer learns new ways to communicate the gospel, and the child with a disability experiences increased participation and belonging. Benjamin Conner, author of *Amplifying Our Witness,* says, "When we choose adolescents with disabilities as friends and practice our faith with them, their evocative witness will challenge the way we understand discipleship."[41]

Discipleship also involves effective communication. The church needs to move beyond traditional means of communicating the gospel if it is to make disciples of people of all abilities. Scottish theologian John Swinton says, "There are different ways in which people can come to know Jesus and different ways in which people can hear the call to become his disciples."[42] Multisensory approaches explain the gospel message through sight, sound, touch, and kinesthetic activities. There are now a variety of Bible curricula for all ages that include these approaches and consider the learning styles of people with various impairments.[43] People with visual impairments benefit from tactile and oral approaches. Those with hearing impairments benefit from visuals and sign language. Since individuals with intellectual disabilities learn through seeing, hearing, and doing, practicing the spiritual disciplines will help them grow in faith.

Consider Paul, a teen who faithfully comes to church with his parents. He does not use verbal speech to communicate and has very limited mobility. One day, in order to involve Paul in prayer time, his teachers filled a cloth bag with large, laminated picture cards of food, games, family, church, friends, school, and Jesus. At prayer time, the teacher brought the bag to Paul and he pulled out a picture card. Then as Paul bowed his head, his buddy verbally prayed a simple sentence prayer, "Thank you, God, for church." After Paul took out two cards, the teacher moved to the next person. However, as the teacher moved on, Paul started rocking in his wheelchair. When the teacher brought the bag back to him, he smiled and continued to participate in prayer until there were no more cards in the bag. Teachers need to "think seriously about what a prayer ministry might look like when it includes, recognizes and listens to what might be the weakest members of the Body who may in fact have the strongest voices."[44]

For adults with intellectual disabilities, a church might consider having a discipleship class that can be open to the community. Make sure the adults with disabilities are involved in leading in all aspects of the class, including welcoming members, reading Scripture, leading worship songs, participating in drama, and giving testimonies. Don't make it a class "for" them, but a class "with" and "by" them.[45]

CONGREGATIONAL CARE IN COMMUNITY

Jesus said, "I am giving you a new commandment, that you love one another; just as I have loved you, that you also love one another. By this all people will know that you are My disciples: if you have love for one another" (John 13:34–35). Christian communities are to be characterized by love for one another, a love that bears one another's burdens (Gal. 6:2). This burden bearing is the responsibility of the entire church body, going beyond Sunday morning and occurring throughout the rest of the week. God is faithful to us from first breath to last (Isa. 46:4), and our church families need to demonstrate this same type of faithfulness to one another. In congregational care, we need to recognize "the difference between the need for crisis intervention and the need for assistance or supports. . . . finding the healthy tension point between merciful intervention and family responsibility . . . [and] discerning the equilibrium between independence and dependence in a place called interdependent community."[46]

There are specific times when families may experience crisis and need specific care from their church family. These times may include:

- Receiving the diagnosis of disability
- Hospitalization and complications related to the disability
- Illness of a parent of a child with special needs
- Aging parent who can no longer care for their child
- Loss of employment and extreme financial hardship

During these times, consider forming a circle of support for the person and/or family. These circles should be composed of a few individuals who know the person and the family, as well as other resource people within the church. The role of this group is to understand the needs of the person and/or family, and to communicate those needs to the congregation and connect the family to needed supports. These groups generally function for the duration of the crisis, but the relationships formed during this time can last a lifetime. A helpful resource is the booklet *Supportive Care in the Congregation.*[47]

Individuals and families experiencing disability also benefit from day-to-day support when there is not a crisis. Disability is long-term, and regular support by the church family can help individuals and their families as they learn to navigate a new way of life. Remember to ask a family what types of support would be appreciated. Don't assume you know what a family needs or wants, since what might be a priority to you may not be a priority to them. The following are proactive ways that the church family can support special needs families and build resiliency:

Presence: Offer to accompany a person to a doctor's appointment, a school Individualized Education Plan (IEP) meeting, a residential facility evaluation, or an insurance meeting, and provide support and advocacy for the family. Ask how you can pray for the person and/or their family.

Respite: Provide family members with a break from caregiving by offering to stay with the person with disabilities for a few hours or provide finances for the family to pay for a caregiver of their choosing. Consider holding monthly respite events where the church family provides care and fun activities for the child or adult with disabilities.

Support Groups: Provide meeting space and biblical resources for support groups where individuals with disabilities and their families can connect with others who are on a similar journey.

Practical Helps: Provide occasional meals, house cleaning, yard work, and simple home repairs, so the family can focus on what is most important in their lives.

Financial: Unsolicited financial assistance can be a means of great encouragement to a family. Provide a financial gift during the holidays or at the beginning of the school year through the church benevolence fund. Provide scholarships to allow individuals and/or families to attend special needs camps.[48]

Transportation: Provide families with a list of qualified drivers who would be willing to take them to church, doctor's appointments, or grocery shopping. Consider investing in a wheelchair accessible bus to transport people to church activities.

SERVING AND CONTRIBUTION

The apostle Paul wrote, "We are His workmanship, created in Christ Jesus for good works, which God prepared beforehand so that we would walk in them" (Eph. 2:10). Yong says, "The church is charged not only with inviting people with disabilities into its community, but also with bringing them in and then honoring their contribution."[49] As we welcome the contributions of all people in our congregations, we need to recognize each other's gifts and acknowledge that there are a variety of ways that something can be done.

Michaela is a teenager who lives with autism and Down syndrome. She has difficulty expressing herself verbally. When her mother was asked what Michaela was good at, she replied, "Michaela loves to twirl." During a church Christmas pageant, Michaela was given the role of one of the angels, and she twirled to the singing of "Glory to God in the highest." Her face and actions radiated "glory."

Our goal must be "the reception of each contribution, resulting in the enrichment and edification of others."[50] The biggest barrier to receiving a person's contribution may be a lack of imagination. We can't assume to know how a person can or cannot serve. We need to ask people with disabilities how they might like to serve, and creatively incorporate their gifts into our congregations. In this way our congregations will become places where "everyone belongs and everyone serves."[51]

The church also needs to recognize the unique contribution of those with profound mental disabilities who may contribute more in terms of "being" rather than in "doing." Whitt says, "What if their presence in the community of believers is essential to our coming to understand more of who God is, who we are, and who we are to be? They challenge us in our self-sufficiency, reminding us that to be human is to be dependent. . .their gift to us may be simply presence—being and not doing."[52]

CHURCH ORDINANCES, DISABILITY AND BELONGING

The church ordinances are ways in which congregations typically formalize belonging. Infant baptism has been fairly inclusive of children with disabilities, since this ordinance relies on the confession of faith by their parents. However, for churches that practice believer's baptism, questions arise, particularly regarding baptizing individuals with profound mental disabilities. Baylor University professor Jason Whitt, whose daughter has a profound disability, offers this suggestion:

> Those in the tradition of believer's baptism should baptize persons with profound intellectual disabilities—not all such persons indiscriminately, but those children and adults who are already present in our congregations, the sons and daughters of faithful parents who have included them in the life of the Church . . . there are cases where baptizing one who cannot confess faith is a proper affirmation of that person's place in the body of Christ.[53]

Communion is a time when the community of faith gathers to celebrate what Christ has done for them on the cross. It is a communal event, and barriers to participation need to be addressed and removed when possible. Since an increasing number of people have dietary restrictions and allergies, provide communion elements that are gluten free, dairy free, and dye free. If your tradition involves going forward to receive the elements, ask a person with mobility impairments if they would like assistance in going forward or adjust your practice and have the minister bring the elements to them.

Sometimes the faith of people with intellectual disabilities is minimized, and they are excluded from the Lord's Table because they may not be able to verbally profess their faith. People with cognitive deficits may be able to express their faith better by their actions (James 2:18). One Sunday, George, a young man with Down syndrome, received the communion bread. As the minister said, "This is My body broken for you," George cupped the bread in his hand and gently stroked it. When we share communion with those in our congregation who have dementia, traumatic brain injury, or intellectual disabilities, we remember that Christ, who is our peace, has reconciled "us both to God in one body through the cross" (Eph. 2:16 ESV).

CONCLUSION

Disability inclusive ministry is ministry to, with, and by people with disabilities. It is ministry that is marked by appreciation for the way God has made each person. It is ministry that is rooted in humility and recognizes that all we are and have comes from God. It is ministry that cares for one another in community and sees the image of God in each person. It is ministry that delights in unity and includes the diverse gifts of each person. It is ministry that advocates for and with people facing injustice. It reflects the true body of Christ. A disability inclusive congregation exemplifies Paul's words to the Corinthians, "God has put the body together, giving greater honor to the parts that lacked it, so that there should be no division in the body, but that its parts should have equal concern for each other. If one part suffers, every part suffers with it; if one part is honored, every part rejoices with it. Now you are the body of Christ, and *each one of you* is a part of it" (1 Cor. 12:24–27 NIV).

NOTES

1. William Gaventa, "The Challenge and Power of Location and Role: Pastoral Counseling in the Lives of Children with Disabilities and Their Families," American Association of Pastoral Counselors, *Sacred Spaces* (2014): vol. 6, 56.

2. "Disabilities: An Infographic," *Lausanne Movement*, https://www.lausanne.org/content/disabilities-an-infographic.

3. "Newsroom Archives," *United States Census Bureau*, July 25, 2012, https://www.census.gov/newsroom/releases/archives/miscellaneous/cb12-134.html.

4. "Article 1-Purpose," *United Nations Convention on the Rights of Persons with Disabilities*, https://www.un.org/development/desa/disabilities/convention-on-the-rights-of-persons-with-disabilities/article-1-purpose.html.

5. James W. Sire, *The Universe Next Door*, 4th ed. (Downers Grove, IL: InterVarsity Press, 2004), 17.

6. Stephanie O. Hubach, *Same Lake, Different Boat: Coming Alongside People Touched by Disability* (Phillipsburg, NJ: P&R Publishing, 2006), loc. 453 of 4134, Kindle.

7. Ibid., loc. 401 of 4134, Kindle.

8. Ibid., loc. 428 of 4134, Kindle.

9. "People with Disabilities," *The United States Holocaust Memorial Museum*, https://www.ushmm.org/collections/bibliography/people-with-disabilities.

10. Thomas E. Reynolds, *Vulnerable Communion: A Theology of Disability and Hospitality* (Grand Rapids: Brazos, 2008), 26.

11. Stephanie O. Hubach, *Same Lake, Different Boat*, loc. 453 of 4134, Kindle.

12. "The Shorter Catechism," *The Westminster Standard*, https://thewestminsterstandard.org/westminster-shorter-catechism/.

13. Reynolds, *Vulnerable Communion*, 177.

14. Wayne Grudem, *Systematic Theology* (Grand Rapids: Zondervan, 1994), 442

15. Peter Singer, "Twenty Questions," in *Journal of Practical Ethics*, https://www.jpe.ox.ac.uk/papers/twenty-questions/.

16. John Piper, "The Image of God: An Approach from Biblical and Systematic Theology," Desiring God, March 1, 1971, https://www.desiringgod.org/articles/the-image-of-god.

17. Jason D. Whitt, "In the Image of God: Receiving Children with Special Needs," *Review & Expositor* 113, no. 2 (2016): https://doi.org/10.1177/0034637316638244.

18. Dan'l C. Markham, *The Lost Mandate* (First Edition Design Publishing, Inc., 2012), loc. 750–923 of 4714, Kindle.

19. "Deaf Peoples," *International Mission Board*, https://www.imb.org/deaf/.

20. Barbara Newman, *Accessible Gospel, Inclusive Worship* (Wyoming, MI: All Belong Center for Inclusive Education, 2016) 53.

21. Melinda Jones Ault, Belva C. Collins and Erik W. Carter, 55. Congregational Participation and Supports for Children and Adults with Disabilities: Parent Perceptions," https://pubmed.ncbi.nlm.nih.gov/23360408/, February 2012. Intellectual and Developmental Disabilities. 51(1):48–61.

22. Thomas Reynolds, *Vulnerable Communion*, 222.

23. Ibid., 223.

24. Ibid., 226.

25. Joni Eareckson Tada, *Life in the Balance: Biblical Answers for the Issues of Our Day* (Grand Rapids: Revell, 2010), loc. 111, Kindle.

26. Amos Yong, *The Bible, Disability and the Church: A New Vision of the People of God* (Grand Rapids: Eerdmans, 2011), loc. 1182 of 2272, Kindle.

27. https://www.shepherdscollege.edu.

28. Michael Beates, *Disability and the Gospel: How God Uses Our Brokenness to Display His Grace* (Wheaton, IL: Crossway, 2012), 119.

29. Hans S. Reinders, *Receiving the Gift of Friendship: Profound Disability, Theological Anthopology, and Ethics* (Grand Rapids: Eerdmans, 2008), loc. 5467, Kindle.

30. Nancy Eiesland, *The Disabled God: Toward a Liberatory Theology of Disability* (Nashville: Abingdon Press, 1994), 20.

31. Timothy Keller, *Ministries of Mercy: The Call of the Jericho Road*, 3rd ed. (Phillipsburg, NJ: P&R Publishing, 2015), loc. 1572–76, Kindle.

32. Jean Vanier and John Swinton, *Mental Health*: The Inclusive Church Resource (London: Darton, Longman and Todd, 2014), loc. 836 of 999, Kindle.

33. Dawn Clark, "Honoring the Image of God," The Dignity and Sanctity of Every Human Life Guide," Focus on the Family 2016, 129–30.

34. Dan Vander Plaats, *There Is No Asterisk*, 21, Nook, a joint publication of Disability Matters and Elim Christian Services, 2017.

35. Barbara Newman, *Accessible Gospel, Inclusive Worship* (All Belong Center for Inclusive Education, 2016), 35.

36. Karen Anderson, "Disability Etiquette for Ushers and Greeters," https://dc15e045549f981eb553-9d15bebde1fa4435613-a6c5d5faeb330.ssl.cf2.rackcdn.com/uploaded/d/0e7587824_1531957934_disability-etiquette-for-ushers-and-greeters.pdf.

37. "Audits and Accessibility Badge," Disability Ministries of the United Methodist Church, https://umcdmc.org/resources/accessibility-and-united-methodist-churches/accessibility-audit/.

38. Krista Webb, "Churches Create Autism-Friendly Worship Bags," *Living Lutheran* (blog), April 3, 2016, https://www.livinglutheran.org/2016/04/churches-create-autism-friendly-activity-bags/.

39. "How to Write a Social Story," *Vanderbilt Kennedy Center*, https://vkc.mc.vanderbilt.edu/assets/files/tipsheets/socialstoriestips.pdf. This worksheet explains how to write a social story that can be applied to any setting.

40. Josh Moody, sermon: "The Essential Church," College Church, Wheaton, IL, June 2, 2019.

41. Benjamin T. Conner, *Amplifying Our Witness: Giving Voice to Adolescents with Developmental Disabilities* (Grand Rapids: Eerdmans, 2012), 76.

42. John Swinton, *Becoming Friends of Time: Disability, Timefullness, and Gentle Discipleship* (Waco, TX: Baylor University Press, 2016), 107.

43. "Curriculum Comparison for Adapted Bible Teacher," *Engaging Disability*, 2020, https://engagingdisability.org/wp-content/uploads/2018/10/Curriculum-Comparison-for-Adapted-Bible-Teaching.pdf. This chart provides a brief description and comparison of special needs curriculums for children, teens and adults.

44. Swinton, *Becoming Friends of Time*, 27.

45. Erik W. Carter, *Including People with Disabilities in Faith Communities: A Guide for Service Providers, Families, and Congregations* (Baltimore: Paul H. Brookes Publishing Co., 2007), 34–35.

46. Stephanie O. Hubach, *Same Lake, Different Boat*, loc. 1735 of 4134.

47. *Supportive Care in the Congregation: Providing a Congregational Network of Care for Persons with Significant Disabilities*, https://www.anabaptistdisabilitiesnetwork.org/Resources/ADNotes/Pages/Supportive-Care.aspx.

48. "Camps and Activities," *Nathaniel's Hope*, 2020, https://www.nathanielshope.org/resources/camps/.

49. Amos Yong, *The Bible, Disability, and the Church*, loc. 1393 of 2272.

50. Ibid., loc, 1044 of 2272.

51. Terry A. DeYoung and Mark Stephenson, *Inclusion Handbook: Everybody Belongs, Everybody Serves* (Reformed Church of America, 2013), 1.

52. Jason D. Whitt, "Baptism and Profound Disability," 65, https://www.baylor.edu/content/services/document.php/188185.pdf.

53. Ibid.

CHAPTER 3.4

Ministering to
the Abused and Exploited

ANDREW J. SCHMUTZER AND ASHLEY M. SCHMUTZER

INTRODUCTION

Some epidemics get the attention they deserve and are put down. We usually think
of diseases like the Spanish flu, malaria, measles and, more recently, the pandemic
of COVID-19. As never before, a global community has had to learn to suffer, *globally*. But there are other crises—in fact, much older ones—that should also be called
pandemics: sexual abuse and exploitation, including human trafficking. There is
no vaccine for these ancient evils. Part of being a global community is learning that
some crimes have been going on as long as humanity has existed. Now we are learning that global consequences also require global accountability. This chapter will
address the related, but distinct problems of sexual abuse and exploitation. There
are both similarities and differences. In addition to the standard sociological data
we will also consider these dark evils from a biblical perspective. We will conclude
with some practical ways to address these complex problems.

Survivors of sexual abuse have learned several crushing lessons that can be
hard for the non-abused to understand. These include: "I was betrayed by someone
I trusted," "Healing from abuse is more complex than I anticipated," "Love is about
taking what one wants," "I must do what I have to in order to survive," and "Even
when I did speak up, those closest to me did not believe me." For survivors, there is
a real logic in these statements. These common statements also reflect damage to

the realms of self, community, and faith—the wounds are complex and comprehensive. By creation's design, a holistic sexuality can be holistically damaged.

From a faith perspective, processing the seeming neglect of God can unleash a profound crisis of faith.[1] Tied to abuse is a *spiritual* trauma that can outlast the psychological and social effects. The collateral damage is not only difficult for victims to emerge from, but this traumatic experience makes it difficult for the non-abused to truly comprehend what victims have endured and why most will continue to suffer.

Standard patterns of grieving and healing do not really fit the abuse profile. Contemporary conceptual frameworks for understanding sexual abuse focus on the gendered fluidity of self, fixate on systems of power, and minimize faith altogether. However, a Christian view of sexual abuse must acknowledge the interplay of multiple layers (i.e., personhood, community, and faith). After all, what does healing mean for survivors who feel at odds with their own body? What is the role of community for victims when survivors struggle to trust relationships in general and authorities in particular? What does spiritual maturity look like for victims of incest? How can spiritual formation programs—built on the tenants of Spirit direction, transformation, and community—intentionally include the sexually broken who struggle with personal trauma (= self), much less their anxiety toward leaders (= community), and smoldering resentment toward God (= faith).[2] These are the complex profiles of many in the church. Increasingly, these are also the stories of many men and woman headed for or already in various ministries. Because sexual abuse and human trafficking overlap in numerous ways, our discussion of the damage and paths toward healing will focus on the interrelated domains of personhood foundational to creation design: *self*, *community*, and *God*.

SOBERING STATISTICS OF SEXUAL ABUSE

Research shows that ten is the average age when girls are abused, and eleven for boys. Overall, one in four girls and one in six boys—or at least one-fifth of all children—are sexually abused by age of eighteen.[3] Abuse is so common, it is rare when someone does not know an abused friend or family member. Anonymous surveys (e.g., Washington State Prison) show that between 75 and 95 percent of male inmates in prison were also sexually abused. Yet because of social conditioning and stereotypes, it is widely agreed that males are far less likely to disclose their abuse than females.[4] *Delayed disclosure* in general leaves survivors talking, on average, twenty years after their abuse.[5]

Interfamilial sexual abuse, that is, abuse among families, is a serious problem. In about 93 percent of cases, the victim knows their abuser.[6] One study found that

43 percent of high school boys and young college men reported that they had an unwanted sexual experience and of those, 95 percent stated that a female acquaintance was the aggressor.[7] Yet this is not the standard narrative of Title IX stories. Relatedly, incest accounts for 70 percent of all sexual abuse.[8] Clearly, "stranger danger" is a gross misconception.

Among the standard effects of sexual abuse repeatedly cited in the literature are: affective consequences (e.g., anxiety, anger, depression); psychosomatic effects (e.g., sleep paralysis, headaches, stomachaches, enuresis); and others including hypervigilance, interpersonal problems, sexualized behavior, and aggression.[9] The experience of trauma writes its own neurological sequence on the brain. For this reason—and other complexities—victims of sexual abuse and exploitation are at great risk for re-victimization. Two-thirds of adult rape victims report that they were sexually abused as children. Also common among victims is avoidance effort (e.g., "unsafe" places, baggy clothes); post-traumatic stress disorder (e.g., bedwetting, self-harm); distorted thinking and isolation (e.g., fear of gender expressions, avoiding religious objects); and compulsivity in sexualized behavior (e.g., masturbation and pornography).[10] While this may seem counter-intuitive, this correlation is due in part to brain molding—the result of traumatic abuse.[11]

The degree of damage varies among victims based on factors such as the age the abuse started, the number of perpetrators, duration of the abuse, the nature of the termination, resilience of the victim, presence of supportive family, physical safety, ongoing therapy, and spiritual support. Most victims of childhood abuse and trafficking suffer long-term effects. This chronic state of alert (i.e., hypervigilance) takes a toll on the victim's body with studies showing that sexually traumatized children are 10 to 15 percent more likely to suffer from cancer, heart disease, gastrointestinal problems, liver disease, and diabetes as adults.[12] It is vital to understand that spiritual transformation and healing requires a more comprehensive partnership of trauma theory alongside a biblical anthropology.

DAMAGED REALMS OF PERSONHOOD IN SEXUAL VIOLATION (ABUSE)

To achieve a more integrative healing, one must understand the comprehensive wounding of sexual abuse victims to the unique realms of personhood: *physical*, *relational*, and *transcendent*. To explore this realm-dynamic, the conceptualization of personhood and its interrelated realms can be viewed as follows:

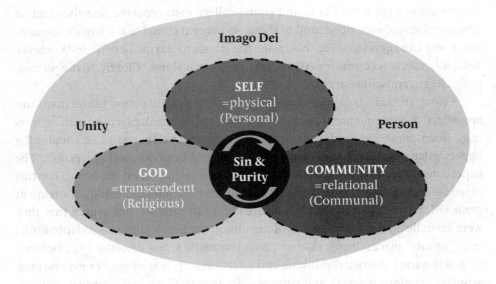

These three realms of personhood are individually definable although they do not function in isolation—they are a unity. Like the components of a multicolored stained-glass window, pieces build a portrait. A soundness is required for the interactive health of each realm within the individual. These are also vulnerable areas of the person. In other words, the corporeal realm can be plundered like a garden; the social realm can be shunned; and the spiritual domain can be utterly confused. Positively, these realms share vibrant *bonds* among them that enable rich communication. Negatively, these are also protective *boundaries,* vital to the health and interaction of each realm.

These boundaries are intended to maintain the holistic order as a human being. Whether in sexual abuse or exploitation, sexual violation is a devasting form of chaos that paralyzes all realms of personhood. As Christian Gostecnik states, "In short, sexuality is and remains the arena where the most important relational configurations play out, and with all their power point to a transcendence and sacredness of interpersonal and family system relationships."[13]

Because of the early violation that is often familial too, sexual abuse uniquely tears down these boundaries that animate the human being as a personal, communal, and spiritual image bearer. Sexual abuse is brutally transgressive. The leader against the led, individual against individual, image bearer against image bearer; it is the human-induced trauma of sexual abuse that makes it uniquely devastating. Because "trauma exists on a continuum," healing sexual abuse must address the spoiling and distortion that now runs throughout these realms.[14] Spiritual formation must now facilitate the personal, social, and theological healing that will be required.

THE IMAGE OF GOD AS BEING-IN-RELATEDNESS

The realms of the personal, communal, and spiritual are uniquely rooted in the theology of creation, particularly surrounding the image of God (Gen. 1:26–28; 9:6). Let us briefly consider each realm and address their interrelationships in light of the effects of sexual violation.

REALM OF SELF: SEXUAL VIOLATION FRACTURES THE UNITY OF PERSONHOOD.

When the Lord speaks to the human beings, He addresses them not as genders, but as *persons* (Gen. 1:26–28). Only as a whole organism is the term "soul" (*nepeš*) even appropriate in creation theology (Gen 2:7). In particular, the Old Testament knows no dualism of body/spirit (e.g., Ps 103:1–2).[15] In various ways, sexual abuse effectively dismembers its victim—it un-creates. Through domination, sexual violation of a person is characterized by humiliation, vulnerability, loss, shame, degradation, a sense of helplessness, and other elements of emotional trauma. *Controlled secrecy* contributes to this distress for victims of both sexual abuse and human trafficking—violation always occurs on the molester's terms. In sexual abuse, even the innate "fight or flight" response is overruled. Complete powerlessness is an initial isolating result common to various forms of sexual violation.[16]

Sexual violation tears apart the *nepeš-wholeness* of a person. As such, sexual abuse *de*-personalizes not simply because it robs, but because it rips out what is intimately connected to the larger fullness of *being*, thus dismantling the symphony of human parts. The victim is abandoned to process the experience in further isolation. Early and progressive "looting" of the body puts the victim's senses on active patrol: defenses are activated, emotions are electrified, physiology is convulsed, and neurobiological information is "recorded"—and all without the spiritual perspective, psychological tools, or social resources to absorb these confusing dynamics. Trying to manage pain in progressive proportions, anger wells up and the victim's personality can fragment; the components of the orchestra no longer play in harmony.[17] Are spiritual mentors and formation programs adequately incorporating the traumatized body (*sōma*) into their practice of ministry? After all, "the integration of sexuality and spirituality is nothing other than the integration of the human being."[18] Assessing our discipleship and church standards requires honest reflection at different levels and, more and more, among several disciplines.

Discipleship ministries may, at times, confuse overcoming sin with ignoring the complex effects of violence. After all, if the old is gone and, the new has come (2 Cor. 5:17), if God no longer remembers our sin (Heb. 8:12), and believers are to think on what is praiseworthy (Phil. 4:8), then what is the believer's warrant to discuss forms of violation including sexual abuse, let alone study it? After all, the thinking may go, even Paul declares that one should "[forget] what is behind" (Phil. 3:13b NIV). However, this sort of stance, for example, does not adequately integrate theology and the psychodynamic disciplines. Further, this perspective does not grasp the complex relational toxins of sin or the long pilgrimage that healing can be. Somatic trauma can live on as *body memory*. So, merely instructing the sexually traumatized to "memorize this Bible passage" is simplistic, even unethical.[19]

Formation programs must seriously explore what redemptive memory and body memory mean for the believer who has experienced trauma. Because redemptive memory is remembering truthfully, Christian programs that claim to heal must not minimize the reality of the *sōma* alongside their biblical commitments to spiritual development, holistic maturity, and social justice. Rather than being a mere "container" in our seasons of grief, the body is a keen participant in meaning, a canny scribe that documents life's horrendous experiences.

REALM OF COMMUNITY: SEXUAL VIOLATION ISOLATES THE "SELF" FROM COMMUNITY.

The creation of humanity resulted from a dialogical act—"Let Us make humankind" (Gen 1:26a);[20] human beings were made *in* community *for* community (Gen. 2:18). Being human ultimately comprises an individual and communal *human being*.[21] Persons and relationships are necessarily linked, for where you find one person you will certainly find another (see Gen 2:18, 23). This truth resonates deeply in the creation account, for once the declaration is made that it is as gendered male and female that God has created human beings the story then speaks of them *only in the plural*.[22]

A core tenant of human creation is being-in-relation.[23] Purpose comes in belonging to an "other."[24] To be human is to be *embodied* in time and space, relating to God and others.[25] Whether through acts of compassion for others or violence against others, embodiment is communicated through performance, and in this way the *sōma* becomes social, a social body.[26]

Abuse, however, poisons person against community. It rends relational ligaments that connect the "who" of personhood to the "what" of embodied life. The connections to one's place in community, and the ability to process social interaction, are severed. Adrift, and with limited ability for protection, the abused "can barely imagine themselves in a position of agency or choice."[27] This is also true of exploitation, such as trafficking. This has long-term effects. Miroslav Volf has made a keen observation:

The self, however, is always a social self, and a wrongdoing intertwines the wrongdoer and the wronged as little else does. For the mistreatment consists not just in the pain or loss endured, but also in the improper relating of the wrongdoer toward the wronged. That improper relating is what we mainly remember as the wrongdoing suffered—and remember it not just with our mind but also with our body.[28]

Sexual abuse persists by seclusion. Through crippling shame and self-loathing, a victim goes through crushing alienation; they can no longer risk the affirmation they desperately need.

A diminished sense of agency and an inability to foster healthy relationships bring further alienation. Crucial to healing this agency is the victim's ability to recognize and regulate their emotions as an agent for oneself. Just as sexual abuse does not occur in a social vacuum, neither can its healing. Part of normalizing the problem of sexual abuse involves listening to victims' stories of suffering and then pulling these victims back into an empathetic community of care. However, relational estrangement can be amplified by a religious environment that promotes an overly personalized faith.

Western Christianity as a whole has emphasized an individual-existential salvation. Eschatologically separated from the communal emphasis of creation, salvation, as it has habitually been played out, has dismissed the physical world and, with it, human embodied sexuality. Alarmingly, a truncated doctrine of salvation can result in a truncated anthropology. In the pietistic worldview, purity and self is lodged in the depths of interiority rather than integrated into a larger relational world.[29] When this happens, biblical healing can fall through unbiblical cracks.

Unfortunately, community may be functionally lost to the victim because community appears neither nourishing nor safe. Healing for victims includes re-actualizing their personhood toward community.[30] Learning to integrate the care and critique of community back into his or her life is a difficult but healing antidote.

REALM OF GOD: SEXUAL VIOLATION MARS CONNECTING METAPHORS FOR GOD.

In the sanctuary of the garden, God is depicted as the attentive father, cosmic king, just protector, master artisan, and gracious provider. The imagery of creation creates a profile of God with metaphorical force writ large.[31] Because metaphors go beyond culture and time, readers are welcomed to look for a correspondence of relations in their own world.[32] It is the reader's own experience that keeps metaphors fresh as worlds merge. God has a rich profile of archetypical images that echo throughout Scripture. He is a midwife (Isa. 66:7–9), mother (Isa. 66:13), parent (Hos. 11:1), and refuge (Ps. 31:2). These are high correspondence metaphors between God, humankind, and community, driven by the two-way traffic of the image of God.[33]

For the sexually violated, their bridging metaphors have also been marred—particularly the nurturing metaphors for God as a father and a protector. For the abused, these are *controlling metaphors*. Like "metaphors among metaphors...they are able to bring coherence to a range of biblical thinking about God; they provide a hermeneutical key for interpreting the whole."[34] When these controlling metaphors are spoiled, the support spanning divine promise and human experience is crushed. For victims of sexual oppression, their operative metaphors are radically distorted. "When the inexpressibility of trauma joins itself to the inexpressibility of the character and nature of God, the crisis for a survivor of faith becomes even more acute."[35] Healing requires finding a new fund of metaphors that re-connect God to His creation and human community.

The loss of controlling metaphors results in losing one's navigational compass. The overwhelming dissonance between the earthly and heavenly father causes many abuse victims to abandon their faith altogether. For the abused, the notion of God as loving parent can be terrifying. If God exists for some survivors, His loving intimacy has been drained off. Hearing other believers praying "Our Father..." only adds to the smothering blanket of frustration of those who feel God never showed up. Terence E. Fretheim admits, "The meaning of a metaphor varies from culture to culture, and even from individual to individual within a single culture. A child, for instance, with a brutal or incestuous father will hear the word 'father' for God with far different ears than I will."[36] When the church is not prepared for this disconnect, it could be ignoring a terrifying reality for up to 20 percent of its congregation—if they are still there.

Controlling metaphors *do* something. They structure life and serve as "grids." They reach into the future, framing meaning of the present. Through metaphor, propositional truth becomes a nurturing ethic as life is filtered and configured.[37] Thus the wrecking of bridging metaphors is the loss of hope. Once damaged, dignity and spiritual reality are forced to limp in a victim's life. The heavenly "father" and His "guardian" angels can become a cruel joke.

With relationships torn socially and spiritually, healing moves a person back toward the design of creation, reconnecting internal spaces and external communities. The sense of the sacred is mediated through the body.[38] So bodies, minds, and souls, through healing, *can* become sanctified spaces again. Adopting the relational view of the image of God, Douglas J. Moo acknowledges, "If we view the 'image of God' as having to do *primarily with the power to form appropriate relationships*—between humans and God, among humans, and between humans and creation—justice can be done to both perspectives."[39] It is right here that one finds the crucial role that spiritual mentors and maturity can have, that is, helping the sexually traumatized "form appropriate relationships," from a biblically integrated perspective.

THE MANY VIOLATIONS OF HUMAN TRAFFICKING

SIMILARITIES AND DIFFERENCES BETWEEN ABUSE AND TRAFFICKING

If sexual abuse is any behavior that exploits a person for one's sexual gratification, human trafficking is forced work in a complex sex industry. While this tragedy may be hidden from a typical local church, exploitation of this type exists and is increasing. "It can happen in any community and victims can be any age, race, gender, or nationality."[40] As such this tragedy is something the church needs to know about. While sexual abuse can include intimidation, bribery, and use of power, it does not entail a business structure for transporting people across national boundaries for economic profit.

There are similarities and differences between sexual abuse and human trafficking. While sexual abuse is, by definition, the abuse of underage youth, human trafficking may use underage youth, but not necessarily. While sexual abuse usually involves one perpetrator acting alone in secrecy, human trafficking relies on a sophisticated network of people—men and women—to shuttle the sex workers around for the advantage of the "bosses." While sexual abuse has no legal consent, there can be a degree of consent and use of passports with human trafficking, but usually under the false pretenses of luring victims to a good job, international adventure, and a better life. Significantly, sexual abuse cuts across all economic lines, ethnicities, and cultures. Human trafficking however, predominantly preys on the poor and socially vulnerable who are easier to exploit. So while sexual abuse does not include trafficking, human trafficking will include various forms of abuse.

THE HORRIFIC SCENARIOS OF TRAFFICKED YOUTH

Statistics vary on numbers of people trafficked around the world for sexual exploitation, but estimates run into the hundreds of thousands and even many millions (some organizations track, in addition to trafficking for sexual exploitation, those pressed into slave labor and/or forced marriages).[41] Human trafficking is the result of complex social, political, and economic problems, and is a fast-growing criminal trade. The sordid network that makes this so lucrative would boggle the mind. Traffickers can make as much money in trafficking women as they can in the drug trade.

The average traffic ring has three to four middle-players. The "transporter" takes the girl or woman and passes her off to someone else. She is then sold to a pimp. The first person in the trafficking chain often knows the victim's family, so often the broader family is betrayed, along with the victim. A job prospect elsewhere is often used as bait, and this plays on the victim's desire to help her own family survive. Motivation to leave home is not hard to come by.

Traffickers know how to pick out vulnerable women. The girls and women want to believe that it is going to be okay. What could be harder than their present state of life? But when the traffickers take away their passports, their options—such as getting away and finding a legitimate job—melt away. Furthermore, these traffickers understand psychology and know how to lure people in. Words such as "abroad" or "big money" are effective among the impoverished.

In the traffic ring, one person *sources*, while another *transports* the women. In human trafficking, a woman can act as a source-agent since a woman can get close to girls and pretend to care about them. Typically, however, even after they realize what's happening, the girls will not run away, since compounds can be gated and houses have bars.

Around the world, standard brothels essentially function like a prison. Upon arrival, the pimps tell the girls that they can work off their purchase price. The price must be worked off. In reality, the girls are faced with a *debt-bondage* that is easily inflated by the pimp. These girls never manage to pay the debt off, and often incur further fines. The implied danger to their families just may be the greatest threat they face—"I know where your children live," they are told. Some stay in sex work to pay for their family's medical bills back home. Many European countries have very lax rules regarding sex work, so thousands are trafficked throughout these countries for prostitution.

But forcing someone to work in prostitution against their will—which this scenario certainly is—amounts to rape. If the local police find trafficked women, they are routinely deported, because they are likely in a given country illegally, and without proper documents. This, in turn, leads to cross-border smuggling (of human lives). That said, sex trafficking can occur in one's hometown, against the victim's will. Ethnic minorities are a very vulnerable group in many parts of the world and therefore experience a greater amount of general discrimination. In these situations, it is the children who often bear the financial burden of caring for their families. Compounding the problems, a person not recognized as a citizen of any country is treated as "stateless." It is not uncommon for these sex workers to routinely take pain killers and use alcohol to make them numb enough to work. It is a brutal fact that anyone with money and, chillingly, some sort of fetish, will pay for sex.

TAKING CONCRETE STEPS

Ironically, many victims of human trafficking may be physically free, but are not psychologically free. Liberating "raids" work if authorities find women chained to their beds, but this does not address the complexities of crushing intergenerational poverty. Yet there are some concrete steps that can be taken to address human trafficking: (1) Confront the issue of demand for sex workers. (2) Face the complexity of structural evil that perpetuates human trafficking. (3) Address change in labor and immigration laws, gender inequality, and access to health care. (4) Foster better legal communication among countries with a history of human trafficking. (5) Focus on programs with substantive aftercare, life skills, and rehabilitation for rescued survivors.

SOME PERSPECTIVES AND PRACTICES FOR HEALING SEXUAL VIOLATION

If pastors and discipleship leaders are going to adequately address the wounds of sexual abuse and human trafficking, we must begin with a richer understanding of embodiment and rituals. Practice and proposition need to be closely enjoined. We will touch on the nature of embodiment from a biblical viewpoint and the contribution of ritual, two elements that interface to bring healing to victims.

BRINGING EMBODIMENT OUT OF THE SHADOWS

Precisely where healing is needed in sexual violation, one may encounter a minimization of the body (*sōma*) as a suspicion of the "flesh" as well as a practical denial of sexual impulses. When this happens, it leaves us with a *disembodied theology* and a great deal of shame.[42] Dallas Willard has lamented that transformation often does not work because it "does not involve the body in the process of transformation." He adds, "One of the ironies of spiritual formation is that every 'spiritual' discipline is or involves bodily behavior."[43] This disembodied theology remains one of the greatest hindrances to the healing of the sexually abused in Christian ministries.

In creation, the human being does not merely *have* flesh and soul, but rather, a person *is* both—transitory yet alive (Gen. 1:26–27; 2:7).[44] The New Testament continues this theme as the body being practically synonymous with the whole personality (Eph. 5:28; Phil. 1:20).[45] In Jesus' Sermon on the Mount, the body is no mere organism; the *sōma* is the self (Matt. 6:25) and helping the person is determined by the ethic of the body's needs (James 2:16). Paul in particular, uses *sōma* as *person*—"sin is not to reign in your mortal body" (Rom. 6:12). Thus, human life, even in the realm of the spirit (*pneuma*), is a somatic existence.[46] Helping the sexually broken heal requires beginning with the most practical of bodily needs they may have.

By creation's design, it is the multifaceted *sōma*—with its ears, eyes, feet, and hands—that opens up a person to dynamic relationships in community The body is designed to be an instrument of communication.[47] This is why the entire person, including the *sōma*, can be deeply "marked" by life's experiences. Our relationship with God is realized *in a body*; when the body is broken and traumatized, so can one's relationship with God be. There is significant *continuity* between earthly and heavenly life that must be manifested in our teaching and goals for maturity. Where rituals are actively used, there is dynamic respect for this spatio-temporal stewardship and its frailty.

USING RITUALS IN HEALING AND TRANSFORMATION

Ritual provides a means for the believing community to discover, enact, and reflect its claims of faith—to extend the presence of God.[48] Ritual brings into being (Lev. 8), restores order (Lev. 13:14, 16), and develops faith (John 9:1–12). If ritualized activity is core to the formation of Christian identity in general (1 Cor. 11:23–26; 12:12–26), it is also crucial to the spiritual transformation of the sexually violated. Theirs is a broken world where the self lives apart from community and is suspicious of God. Here, ritual speaks with dignity for the abused when words cannot or need not be used. For the abused, ritual is restorative because it reconnects life's inner and outer realms, for example, self with community and community with God.

Ritual powerfully intercedes for the *delayed grief* of the abused. For victims of sexual abuse, exploitation, and human trafficking struggling to retain their faith, ritual provides a liturgical forum for engaging the divine in light of one's life experiences. Ritual is capable of laying to rest the "corpse of comprehensive experi-ence." Ritual is also a comforting headstone, welcoming visitation as often as neces-sary. Toward the divine realm in particular, ritual unleashes a creative force for the construction of new relationship and the development of trust.[49] When victims cry out for God to "hear" them, then God breaks loose from His perceived failure and moves closer along a spectrum of redemptive silence and nourishing mystery (see Pss. 13:1–3; 35:17, 22–23; 77:7–9). A foundational starting place is for churches to regularly use lament psalms. The need for lament (psalms) is obvious when people demand that the Lord "hear" (*shema'*) them!—using an imperative toward God! (the opposite of Deut. 6:4, "Hear, Israel!"; see Pss. 17:1; 27:7; 28:2).

The use of rituals in spiritual transformation can bring healing to the sexually broken both inside and outside the church. Some rituals can bring closure to the past—burying a photograph—while others create newness of life for the present—planting a tree—and still others can highlight an eschatological healing. The "self" is no longer defined by its muted history, and community can lend aid with rich interaction with others. Think of the Lord's Table with its broken bread mirrored in His "broken" people. Those who feel abandoned by God can be reoriented to Him (e.g., a drama of "waking" God from His slumber in the boat, Mark 4:35–41). These enactments tied to the realms of life can be powerful rituals for the sexually harmed.

Whether through community intercession or personal petition, ritual carries the rhythms of pain and release through the community and toward God. Rituals do not merely "recite" what is true; they "recalibrate" what is needed by fostering a conversation with God that spans painful breaches in the victim's life. Churches can evaluate themselves: Working alongside therapy, have our programs adequately matched creative practice to textual proposition, addressing the noncognitive needs of victims? Have the victims in our midst been given words to acknowledge their life experience so that they can reenter the faith community in safety, participation, and leadership?

It is the transcending power of metaphor in the earthy drama of ritual that helps generate healing for the sexually traumatized who are struggling to discover our loving God, whatever their faith tradition. So, for example, forgiveness (personal and God's) can be actualized through ceremonial acts at a vespers service; or the use of fasting, reflective music, and body posture can create heightened identification at a drama of the Passion, celebrations of Good Friday, or an Easter service. We must do more to connect these great ceremonies of the redeemed with those who are struggling to hold on to their Redeemer. Is there a better way we can testify to traumatic experience even in corporate worship?

Rituals gather a halo of senses and exercise them redemptively for the needs of the violated that must have nourishing access points to both community and God through "safe" ritual drama.[50] Thus, combining the realms of self, community, and God, ritual performance provides a sense of safety, affirms mutuality of relationships, helps persons cope with transition, practices scriptural application, increases moral sensitivity, creates a sense of predictability, structures the mental world, and maintains contact with the transcendent. Ritual also assists healing by stimulating redemptive agency.

ACKNOWLEDGING VICTIMS' STRUGGLE FOR REDEMPTIVE AGENCY

One of the greatest contributions churches can make to help victims of sexual violence is to create a sense of *redemptive agency* in their lives. Because they were acted upon in ways that "bent" them, victims struggle to harness personal choice. For survivors of sexual trauma, self-agency can be completely foreign. Sexual victims have an "incidental-self" perspective—believing their needs are secondary to all others—and are often *re*-victimized for this reason. They often read Scripture existentially; proposition is a luxury that barely applies to them. For this reason, many victims have a sense of a *text estrangement*, finding that some biblical passages function between maddening and terrorizing. This awareness may increase with healing. For example, consider Romans 12:1 (NLT):

> And so, dear brothers and sisters, I plead with you to give your bodies to God because of all he has done for you. Let them be a living and holy sacrifice—the kind he will find acceptable. This is truly the way to worship him.

To begin with, a command such as "give" can be threatening. "Bodies," however, evokes terror: "If I did have a sense of choice, what is left of my *person* (= "body") that others haven't already taken, threatened, or spoiled?" "Because of all He has done for you" refers to God's redemptive work, but victims of abuse are also likely to feel like victims of faith with these kinds of words—"What did God actually do to stop my abuse?" Moreover, associating "body" with "living sacrifice" is grotesque—"I've already been sacrificed!" "Holy" is over the top. "If God wanted a holy sacrifice, He could have saved this body from its horror." "How can I give what I don't believe I possess any longer?" Finally, "truly . . . worship" can sound both impossible and cruel to victims.

Discipleship and formation programs can help awaken personal agency for the sexually violated by pointing to other texts where, for example, the "servant" himself was "despised," "abandoned," "pierced," and "crushed" (Isa. 53:3a, 5a). Enlivening the text for the traumatized occurs when they find points of connection to their pain. It is the reality of brokenness that victims understand and cling to, and this makes their long journey home possible:

> He was beaten so we could be whole.
>   He was whipped so we could be healed. . . .
> In all their suffering he also suffered. (Isa. 53:5a; 63:9a NLT)

Their trauma means that victims of sexual violence will read Scripture with an interpretation of "self-involvement," and this is what makes them empathetic and capable of being advocates for other "broken" people.

Vital for spiritual transformation, victims must be taught what submitting to the Holy Spirit means in light of their experience. But the language of "submission" will be difficult for survivors. Further, those leading formation programs must also be taught how these tenants of formation "translate" to violated people.

SOME FINAL RECOMMENDATIONS

Guiding the sexually abused in their restoration will require added awareness, interaction, generous dialogue, and retooling of areas in the practice of transformation ministries. Taking embodiment seriously means vigorous effort, for the survivor must shift some emphases toward a more *multivalent* approach of several disciplines in trauma theory, violence, theodicy, spiritual maturity, screening, and mental health for victims. To this end, we can note some basic recommendations for faith ministries and "safe-houses" to more intentionally assist in the healing of the sexually broken.

REGARDING SELF . . .

1. *Help victims redeem their memory for a constructive future.* Harness the insight of victims through support groups made more available and assisted by survivors as well as trained counselors. Sexual victims have a foreshortened or foreboding sense of their future—help them see a new horizon. The non-abused need to understand that most survivors will carry a distinct "limp," but this can be healed into empathy for others.

2. *Help victims develop a sense of self-agency for community life.* Most survivors will remain suspicious of hierarchical leadership. This is due in part to how society toxically divides people into either victim or victimizer. But the raw reality is that multiple things can be true at once. This is why many victims will victimize other people. This is twisted agency, for sure. Regardless, wounds from controlling and narcissistic people have residual effects. Churches and mission agencies need to craft built-in detection techniques to identify and aid men and women with histories of sexual abuse (e.g., written personal sexual histories). Too many victims are drawn to the ministries of abuse and victimization before they've learned to process their own sense of distortions of self and leadership. Healing must precede advocacy. In faith and secular contexts, victims need access to wounded leaders who are sensitive to these complex relational dynamics and can help victims practice a new sense of self-direction.[51]

REGARDING COMMUNITY . . .

3. *Build more healing rituals into formation programs that acknowledge trauma.* Alongside specific types of assessment designed to screen for PTSD, healing rituals can also be built into formation sessions (e.g., role play). These rituals can help incorporate the non-abused into the schema of care that the sexually violated will need in the future ministries. Rituals in these intense sessions would help recalibrate the collapsed distinctions between the subject-object modalities of the

traumatized. In biblical faith, we are all subjects—there are no "object" people. This will allow opportunity to teach and discuss the Christian theology of forgiveness, acceptance, and suffering. Secular society sees everything through a power lens, so realities like forgiveness are shunned as weakness and failure. But formation programs can use the power of storytelling to rehabilitate feelings and raise awareness for justice that dignifies.

4. *Integrate a theology of embodiment into formation and leadership programs.* Dallas Willard is correct: the lack of a robust view of embodiment has left spiritual transformation ill-equipped to address such issues like sexual victimization. As if one must choose between the mind or the body, the role of embodiment and sound theology in formation and discipleship are two parts of the same equation. Sadly, spiritual formation is often presented in an overly "mentalized" fashion. Similarly, let's work with the abused teens in our churches before we write checks for the trafficked in Bangkok. While both are needed, we shouldn't neglect the needs of those struggling to survive in our own community. The need for serious integration has never been greater. Embodiment must also be met in the present and then brought into an eschatology of healing. Some wounded will have to be carried on our backs into glory.

5. *Incorporate the life experiences of victims into the liturgical calendar.* The sexually abused live with a *disenfranchised grief*—their pain needs to be placed in a socially redemptive context.[52] Disenfranchised grief is not corporately mourned, socially supported, or spiritually invited.[53] We cannot just outsource victims of sexual violence to area therapists, never addressing it in our churches, or preferring not to hear painful testimonies. Redeeming the trauma of sexual violence can be aided by employing their stories of suffering in some way, bringing a dignity to a pain long shunned and minimized in the church. Interjecting testimonies, written prayers, drama, lament psalms, and communal silence into the liturgical calendar establishes a vital community witness and spiritual acknowledgment. Spiritual formation for the sexually broken has as much to do with *restoration* as transformation. Noting the absence of opportunity for lament in the contemporary church, Walter Moberly notes:

> Very few hymns express lament and psalms that are used in a modern paraphrase are almost never psalms of lament, but usually psalms of praise. And there is rarely formal liturgical provision for the expression of lament. The virtual exclusion of lament from most Christian worship carries a strong implicit message that such lament has no legitimate place in worship. Yet most congregations most of the time will have someone who is hurting. *It would seem small wonder if some Christians are driven to depression or superficiality, and that others abandon the faith altogether as lacking in integrity and reality.*[54]

REGARDING GOD...

6. *Employ the suffering of God, which fosters transcending connections.* Dietrich Bonhoeffer claimed that "only a suffering God can help."[55] The first emotion of God noted in Scripture was a pained heart toward violence (Gen. 6:6). The exodus from oppression began with a God who sees, hears, knows, and sends rescue for those who are mistreated (see Ex. 3:7–8; Judg. 2:18; Pss. 16:8; 91:15).[56] Further, God Himself even mourns (see Jer. 31:20; 48:30–32, 35–36). Some wounds only find healing in the "scarred Lamb" (Rev. 5:6). This does not spurn the sovereignty of God, but it stresses that in deep suffering there is also the cruciform presence of God that is precious to the broken who are in the midst of indescribable anguish. Nicholas Wolterstorff admits, "Through the prism of my tears I have seen a suffering God. ... Instead of explaining our suffering God shares it."[57] Because God can suffer with people, there is divine tenderness that "stoops" to the realities of complex brokenness (Ps. 113:5).[58] This divine empathy is an *incarnational praxis* that spiritual formation programs and the local church need to actively utilize.

7. *Search for fresh metaphors to help rehabilitate victims' view of God.* New metaphors will take root when victims' experiences of trauma are meaningfully validated in a complete theology that has a human face (see John 4:4–26). Many sexual abuse survivors who are believers desperately need *theological healing.* They've learned never to question God, their parents, or church leaders. These victims quickly side with society that hates all biblical notions of gender, sex, God, and Christianity. But stoking anger does not bring healing. It's time for the church to define and demonstrate what healing means. We know "cure" is not the issue, but this needs to be brought in line with both our theology and practice. Curing isolates causes, healing unites realms. In sexual violation, healing requires the rejuvenation of metaphor, the restoration of the person's communion, with God and His creation. One day the Redeemer of realms will bring all tears and groaning to an end, at *the Great Healing* (Rom. 8:22; Rev. 21:4).

CONCLUSION

The reality of sexual abuse and trauma has been part of the human story since the fall. Victims are in our churches, and it is the church that is uniquely poised to care for these individuals, charged with understanding the deep damage abuse has inflicted, and holding the opportunity for a multifaceted and holistic response.

NOTES

1. Portions of this chapter are from the author's article "Spiritual Formation and Sexual Abuse: Embodiment, Community, and Healing" in the *Journal of Spiritual Formation & Soul Care*, © 2009 by Institute of Spiritual Formation, vol. 2, No. 1, 67–86, Biola University.

2. The publicity of sexual abuse in the Catholic Church over the last few decades clearly illustrates the interconnectedness of these primary realms. This perversion and deceit explains the profound vulnerability and betrayal surrounding sexual abuse. Jennifer Beste notes that by 2006, over 12,895 victims officially reported being abused by Catholic clergy. It has been estimated that in a 52-year period (1950–2002), at least 50,000 young people were abused by priests (J. Beste, "Mediating God's Grace within the Context of Trauma: Implications for a Christian Response to Clergy Sexual Abuse," *Review & Expositor* 105 [2008], 245–46).

3. Shanta R. Dube, R. E. Anda, C. L. Whitfield, et al., "Long-term Consequences of Childhood Sexual Abuse by Gender of Victim," *American Journal of Preventive Medicine* 28 (2005): 430–38. See also http://www.netgrace.org.

4. G. R. Holmes, L. Offen, and G. Waller, "See No Evil, Hear No Evil, Speak No Evil: Why Do Relatively Few Male Victims of Childhood Sexual Abuse Receive Help for Abuse-related Issues In Adulthood?" *Clinical Psychology Review* 17 (1997): 69–88.

5. Sadly, the medical field has not even drawn up clinical best practices when interacting with male survivors of SA. This tacitly reinforces stereotypes that men are the victimizers and, for example, could never be raped themselves. See Les Gallo-Silver, Christopher M. Anderson, and Jamie Romo, "Best Clinical Practices for Male Adult Survivors of Childhood Sexual Abuse: 'Do No Harm,'" *The Permanente Journal* 18 (2014): 82–87.

6. "Stop It Now: The Scope of Child Sexual Abuse Definition and Fact Sheet," https://www.stopitnow.org/faq/the-scope-of-child-sexual-abuse-definition-and-fact-sheet.

7. Bryana H. French, J. D. Tilghman, and D. A. Malebranche, "Sexual Coercion Context and Psychosocial Correlates Among Diverse Males," *Psychology of Men & Masculinity*, March 17, 2014; online publication at http:/dx.doi.org/10.1037/a0035915.

8. Barbara E. Bogorad, "Sexual Abuse: Surviving the Pain," Writing for the American Academy of Experts in Traumatic Stress at http://www.aaets.org/article31.htm.

9. See Felicia Ferrara, *Childhood Sexual Abuse: Developmental Effects Across the Lifespan* (Pacific Grove, CA: Brooks/Cole, 2002); K. Saywitz, A. Mannarino, L. Berliner, and J. Cohen, "Treatment for Sexually Abused Children and Adolescents," *American Psychologist* 55 (2000): 1040–49.

10. Gail Horner, "Child Sexual Abuse: Consequences and Implications," *Journal of Pediatric Health Care* 24 (2010): 358–64.

11. K. A. Kendall-Tackett, L. M. Williams, and D. Finkelhor, "Impact of Sexual Abuse on children: A Review and Synthesis of Recent Empirical Studies," *Psychology Bulletin* 113 (1993): 164–70; also L. Koenig, L. Doll, A. O'Leary, and W. Pequegnat, *From Child Sexual Abuse to Adult Sexual Risk: Trauma, Revictimization, and Intervention* (Washington, DC: American Psychological Association, 2004), 4–5, 33, 37.

12. Doni Whitsett, "The Psychobiology of Trauma and Child Maltreatment," *Cultic Studies Review* 5 (2006): 355; Kirsten Havig, "The Health Care Experiences of Adult Survivors of Child Sexual Abuse," *Trauma, Violence, and Abuse* 9 (2008): 20.

13. Christian Gostecnik, "Sexuality and the Longing for Salvation," *Journal of Religion and Health* 46 (2007): 589.

14. L. J. M. Claassens, D. G. Garber, "First Words . . . Faith Facing Trauma," *Review and Expositor* 105 (2008): 187.

15. Used 755 times, *nepeš* is adequately distinct to be addressed in the vocative for the totality of the human person (i.e., "my life," see Pss 42:5, 11[6, 12]; 43:5), and even a dead corpse! (Lev 21:1; 22:4). See Robert A. Di Vito, "Old Testament Anthropology and the Construction of Personal Identity," *The Catholic Biblical Quarterly* 61 (1999): 217–38.

16. See Linda Hansen Robinson, "The Abuse of Power: A View of Sexual Misconduct in a Systemic Approach to Pastoral Care," *Pastoral Theology* 5 (2004): 395–404.

17. Jennifer Erin Beste writes: "Common mental illnesses include dissociative identity disorder, borderline personality disorder, major anxiety, and depressive episodes. These psychiatric illnesses often lead to chronic suicidality" in *God and the Victim: Traumatic Intrusions on Grace and Freedom* (Oxford: Oxford University, 2007), 53.

18. Kelly M. Murray, J. W. Ciarrocchi, and N. A. Murray-Swank, "Spirituality, Religiosity, Shame and Guilt as Predictors of Sexual Attitudes and Experiences," *Journal of Psychology and Theology* 35 (2007): 223.

19. The attitude of "nothing outside the text" goes beyond *biblical* counseling to a philosophical worldview of *logocentrism* (see K. J. Vanhoozer, *Is There a Meaning in This Text? The Bible, The Reader, and the Morality of Literary Knowledge* [Grand Rapids: Zondervan, 1998], 53–54, 58–60, 64, 77).

20. Bruce C. Birch, et al., *Theological Introduction to the Old Testament* (Nashville: Abingdon, 1999), 49; T. E. Fretheim, *The Pentateuch* (IBT; Nashville: Abingdon, 1996), 74.

21. Cherith Fee Nordling, "The Human Person in the Christian Story," in *The Cambridge Companion to Evangelical Theology*, eds., Timothy Larsen, Daniel J. Treier (Cambridge: Cambridge University Press, 2007), 75.

22. Patrick D. Miller, "Man and Woman: Towards a Theological Anthropology," in *The Way of the Lord: Essays in Old Testament Theology* (Grand Rapids: Eerdmans, 2007), 311; emphasis added.

23. C. F. Nordling, "The Human Person," 72.

24. Ibid., 75.

25. Ibid., 71.

26. A. Strathern, P. J. Stewart, "Embodiment Theory and Performativity," *Journal of Ritual Studies* 22 (2008): 68.

27. Jennifer E. Beste, *God and the Victim*, 51.

28. Miroslav Volf, *The End of Memory: Remembering Rightly in a Violent World* (Grand Rapids: Eerdmans, 2006), 83–84.

29. Robert A. Di Vito, "Anthropology, OT Theological," *The New Interpreter's Dictionary of the Bible* Volume 1: *A–C*, ed. Katharine Doob Sakenfeld; (Nashville: Abingdon, 2006), 1:172.

30. Miroslav Volf, *After Our Likeness: The Church as the Image of the Trinity* (Grand Rapids: Eerdmans, 1998), 83.

31. See Deut. 4:32; Ps. 148:5; Isa. 57:16; Mal. 2:10; Mark 13:19; Eph. 3:9; Col. 1:16; Heb. 12:27; Rev. 4:11.

32. Ian Paul, "Metaphor," in *Dictionary for Theological Interpretation of the Bible*, ed. Kevin J. Vanhoozer (Grand Rapids: Baker Academic, 2005), 509.

33. Terrence E. Fretheim, *The Suffering of God: An Old Testament Perspective* (Overtures to Biblical Theology) (Philadelphia: Fortress, 1984), 10.

34. Ibid., 11.

35. L. J. M. Claassens, D. G. Garber, "Faith Facing Trauma," 188.

36. Terrence E. Fretheim, *The Suffering of God*, 11.

37. William P. Brown, *Seeing the Psalms: A Theology of Metaphor* (Louisville: Westminster John Knox, 2002), 6.

38. M. Gottschall, "Embodiment," in *Handbook of Christian Theology*, eds., D. W. Musser, J. L. Price (Nashville: Abingdon, 2003), 156.

39. Douglas J. Moo, "Nature in the New Creation: New Testament Eschatology and the Environment," *Journal of the Evangelical Theological Society* 49 (2006): 481; emphasis added.

40. US Department of Homeland Security, "What Is Human Trafficking?," https://www.dhs.gov/blue-campaign/what-human-trafficking.

41. "Prayer for an End to Human Trafficking: Human Trafficking Statistics," https://www.worldvision.org/child-protection-news-stories/pray-end-human-trafficking

42. Karen A. McClintock, *Sexual Shame: An Urgent Call to Healing* (Minneapolis: Augsburg, 2001), 28.

43. Dallas Willard, "Spiritual Formation and the Warfare between the Flesh and the Human Spirit," *Journal of Spiritual Formation and Soul Care* 1 (2008): 85.

44. E. Schweizer, "sōma," EDNT 3: 322, *Exegetical Dictionary of the New Testament*, H. Balz and G. Schnieder (Grand Rapids: Eerdmans, 1990–1993).

45. *Greek Lexicon of the New Testament* (BDAG), "sōma," 984.

46. S. Wibbing, "sōma," NIDNTT 1:234, *New International Dictionary of New Testament Theology and Exegesis*.

47. E. Schweizer, "sōma," EDNT 3:323.

48. F. H. Gorman, Jr., "Ritual," *Eerdmans Dictionary of the Bible*, ed. David Noel Freedman (Grand Rapids: Eerdmans, 2000), 1131.

49. Ibid.

50. For a discussion of ritual and forgiveness, see E. A. Gassin, T. A. Sawchak, "Meaning, Performance, and Function of a Christian Forgiveness Ritual," *Journal of Ritual Studies* 22 (2008): 39–49.

51. For example, studies have shown that how a victim's sexual abuse was *terminated* can affect their recovery. Four categories of termination can be identified: (1) the active agent, (2) a sort of termination, (3) third-party intervention, (4) and no story of termination (E. Lorentzen, H. Nilsen, B. Traeen, "Will It Never End? The Narratives of Incest Victims on the Termination of Sexual Abuse," *Journal of Sex Research* 45 [2008]: 168).

52. J. B. Gould, "Spiritual Healing of Disrupted Childhood," *The Journal of Pastoral Care and Counseling* 60 (2006): 263.

53. K. Doka, "Disenfranchised Grief," L. DeSpelder, A. Strickland, eds., *The Path Ahead: Readings in Death and Dying* (Mountain View, CA: Mayfield, 1989), 272.

54. R. Walter L. Moberly, "Lament," *New International Dictionary of Old Testament Theology and Exegesis* (*NIDOTTE*) 4:883–84; emphasis added.

55. Dietrich Bonhoeffer, *Letters and Papers from Prison* (London: Collins Fontana Books, 1953), 164.

56. Even where God has delivered judgment, He may then be pictured as suffering *with* those He's just judged! (e.g., Isa. 54:7–8).

57. Nicholas Wolterstorff, *Lament for a Son* (Grand Rapids: Eerdmans, 1987), 81.

58. When ministering to the sexually violated, one should be cautious of two spiritual extremes: (1) "victory" theologies bent on notions of *cure* rather than *care*, (2) and social stigmas that treat victims with inappropriate stereotypes (i.e., "Well, you know men!"). Both perspectives are driven by fear, lack an adequate integration of theological and psychological understanding, and need more developed notions of transformation to address ongoing healing and problems in victims' lives.

Ministering to the Same-Sex Attracted or Gender Confused

CHRISTOPHER YUAN

In 2015, the US Supreme Court legalized same-sex marriage in all fifty states by a slim 5–4 decision. The *Obergefell* case was certainly a watershed moment in American history; however, it should not have taken anyone by surprise. The ruling simply reflected what most of the country had already believed: that so-called marriage equality was a given, and to oppose it was to be hateful and bigoted. This left a minority of Americans, particularly evangelicals, settling for a new normal.

Unfortunately, this secular trend is not just in the West. It is spreading to the rest of the globe, as developing countries attempt to mimic the "enlightened" modern world's presumed tolerance and acceptance. So how do we, as faithful ministers of the gospel, proclaim the good news in this new normal? How do we better understand sexuality and gender dysphoria biblically and theologically? How can we share Christ and the power of the gospel with those who identify as gay or transgender, or with those who do not so identify yet struggle with same-sex attractions or gender confusion?

MY TESTIMONY: A DIFFERENT DAMASCUS ROAD

You may wonder what authority I have to speak into this topic. This is not just an academic or theological exercise for me, but an issue that is personal and real. Please allow me to tell you a little bit about my own personal conversion story.

In 1993 I announced to my parents I was gay. This led to massive disruption in our family, to put it lightly. Ultimately, this moment became a catalyst that led each of us, one by one, to the Lord. At the time, my unbelieving mother rejected me. We hear the generalization that Christian parents cannot love their gay children and only unbelieving ones can. I experienced the opposite. After my mother became a born-again follower of Jesus, she knew she could do nothing other than love her gay son as God loved her—while we were still helpless, while we were yet sinners, and while we were His enemies (Rom. 5:6–10).

However, with no more secrets, I felt unimpeded to fully embrace "who I was." This new freedom quickly propelled me down a path of self-destruction that included promiscuity and illicit drug use. Certainly, not all gay men go down this road, but it was my reality. Ultimately, I was expelled from dental school in Louisville, moved to Atlanta, and became a supplier to drug dealers in more than a dozen states.

During this time God graciously worked in the lives of my father and mother and brought them both to a saving trust in Christ. My parents did not realize the extent of my rebellion. But in the light of their newfound faith, they knew my biggest sin was not same-sex behavior or involvement with drugs; my biggest sin was unbelief. What I needed more than anything else, through God's gift of grace, was faith to believe and follow Jesus.

My mother began to pray boldly: "Lord, do whatever it takes to bring this prodigal son to You." She did not pray primarily for me to come home to Chicago or to stop my rebellious behavior. Her main request was that God would draw me to Himself and that I would fall into His loving arms as His son, adopted and purchased by the blood of the Lamb.

The answer to her prayers came in an unexpected way: I was arrested for drug dealing. In jail, I experienced the darkest moments of my life when I received the news that I was HIV positive. That night, as I lay in bed in my prison cell, I noticed something scribbled on the metal bunk above me: "If you are bored, read Jeremiah 29:11." So I did and was intrigued by the promise I read there: "'For I know the plans that I have for you,' declares the LORD, 'plans for prosperity and not for disaster, to give you a future and a hope.'"

I read the Bible more and more. As I did, I realized I had placed my identity in the wrong thing. The world tells those of us with same-sex attractions that our sexuality is the core of who we are. But God's Word paints quite a different picture. My true identity is in Jesus Christ alone.

Ultimately, upon my release from jail, I committed to studying and submitting to biblical and theological truth. I applied to and was accepted at Moody Bible Institute and later, seminary. Over time, God has given back the years the locusts had taken away (Joel 2:25). My parents and I now travel around the world as a two-generational ministry, communicating God's grace and God's truth on biblical sexuality. I had the blessing of writing a memoir with my mother about our conversion stories.[1]

In this chapter, we'll discuss the often mislabeled topic of identity, and we'll consider the benefits of applying theological anthropology since a solid theology is essential for a defense of these underlying issues. We'll examine six well-known passages on same-sex behavior, look at God's prescription for our lives—which is holiness—and what it encompasses. We'll explore the pertinent topic of gender identity and dysphoria and take a look at ministering practically to both believers and unbelievers who are same-sex attracted or gender confused.

MISLABELED IDENTITY

When I identified as a gay man, my whole world was gay. All my friends were gay. I lived in an apartment complex that was probably 90 percent gay men. I worked out at a gay gym. I bought groceries at the gay Kroger. My car was from a gay car dealer. Sexuality was the core of my identity, and everything and everyone around me affirmed that.

The issue of sexuality being the basis of one's identity goes beyond incorrect interpretations of Bible passages, bad exegesis, or a low view of Scripture. It is more preliminary than convincing another that same-sex sexual behavior is sinful. Positing that "being gay means this is who I am" reveals a deep philosophical and theological misunderstanding, a faulty presupposition that points to essence, the core of our being.

Matthew Vines, a gay activist, writes that sexual attraction "is simply part of who you are" and "as humans, our sexuality is a core part of who we are."[2] In the conversation around sexuality, this subtle shift from what to who has created a radically distorted view of personhood.

Let us think about this honestly. There is no other sin issue so closely linked to identity. For example, describing someone as a gossiper does not identify who he is but what he does. Describing someone as an adulteress does not identify who she is but what she has done. The same goes for a liar, a cheater, a gambler, or any other moniker we put on a person. But when it comes to sexuality, our current culture says that being gay means this is who one is.

Should the capacity for same-sex attractions really describe *who* a person is at the most basic level? Or rather, should it describe *how* the person is? That is, sexuality should not be who we are, but how we are. Might a failure to distinguish this difference reflect a categorical fallacy that ultimately distorts how we think and live? The terms heterosexual and homosexual turn desire into personhood, experience into ontology. Experience reigns supreme, and everything else has to bow before it. *Sola experientia* ("by experience alone") has won out over *sola Scriptura* ("by Scripture alone"). Genesis 1:27 informs us that we are all created in the image of God. The apostle Paul says that is Christ in whom "we live and move and have our being" (Acts 17:28 NIV). One's identity is not gay, ex-gay, or even straight. Identity is who an individual is in Christ.

BENEFITS OF APPLYING THEOLOGICAL ANTHROPOLOGY

Let us extend the idea of identity to theological anthropology, or the study of humanity as we relate to God. Most of us at some time in our life have asked ourselves: "Who am I?" The teen and young adult years are a key time to examine this question of identity. Adults going through seasons of change such as a midlife crisis or time of loss also question who they are and where they're going. Where do people look to find an answer? For some, self-identity is shaped by family, friends, and culture. Others find their identity in work, sports, or hobbies. And still others, as we've said, find their sole identity in their sexuality, with the encouragement of the world's system.

The answer to "Who am I?" has an impact on how we think, the choices we make, and the relationships we build, which suggests a close relationship between essence and ethics. Who we are (essence) determines how we live (ethics), and how we live determines who we are. If we have a flawed view of who we are, we will have a flawed personal ethic. If we have a flawed personal ethic, we will have a flawed view of who we are. Personhood affects practice, and practice affects personhood.

So, who am I? Who are you? Who are we? This fundamental, ontological question is foundational to wrapping our heads around the topic of same-sex attractions. As a matter of fact, we cannot properly understand human sexuality unless we begin with theological anthropology, the field that seeks to answer the question "Who am I?" through the lens of God's Word.

What aspects of theological anthropology are particularly relevant to the discussion around human sexuality? The image of God (*imago Dei*) and the doctrine of sin (hamartiology)—are both important concepts in systematic theology. You might think, "Why does this matter? I just need something practical to minister to those who are same-sex attracted or gender confused." But there is nothing more practical than good theology. Actually, bad theology leads to apathy, not the other way around. Here are three benefits of beginning with theological anthropology when addressing the issues of homosexuality and transgenderism (identifying as the gender opposite that of one's biological sex from birth).

AVOIDING ARROGANT CONDEMNATION

There is a slight tendency among Christians to view the LGBTQ+ community[3] as the enemy. For example, I sometimes hear people say, "They are ruining our country." Although those who forsake Christ are not making the world a better place, let us not forget that we were once lost ourselves. Sin is what is ruining our country, and the real enemy is the father of lies. Those who identify as LGBTQ+ are also created in God's image, which means every person has value and dignity in God's eyes. We, too, should view people—even sinners—in the same way.

Should we warn people of sin? Of course! And in due time. But what is our tone and our goal? It has been said that D. L. Moody was most qualified to preach about hell because he did it with tears. When we address the topic of same-sex attractions and gender confusion, do we begin with the basis of theological anthropology? Do we view every person being made in the image of God and do all we can to preach the gospel so they can believe, repent, and become a child of God?

INCORRECTLY DIAGNOSING THE SOURCE OF SAME-SEX ATTRACTION

A second benefit of beginning with theological anthropology when addressing homosexuality and transgenderism is that it avoids a common but incorrect diagnosis. Many claim that the primary root causes of homosexuality or gender dysphoria are factors such as an absentee father, domineering mother, or past trauma. In other words, a deficient and imperfect childhood is the culprit behind same-sex attractions or gender confusion.

Certainly, parents can have positive and negative influences on their children; however, influence is not the same as cause. Abuse has grave effects on an individual, but a detrimental life event is not the root of anyone's struggle with sin. For those of you parents who are weighed down with guilt and wondering, "What did I do wrong?" or "How could I have prevented this?" please listen: *It is not your fault.*

Perfect parenting does not guarantee perfect children. Look at Adam and Eve. They had a perfect Father and were raised in a perfect environment, yet they still rebelled. The primary goal of Christian parenting is not necessarily to produce godly children but to be godly parents.

If you are a parent, remember, you are not God. The gifts of faith, sanctification, and eternal life are not for parents to grant—only God revives and redeems. When we rightly remember the biblical doctrine of sin, we realize that any sin (such as same-sex sexual practice or living out in the opposite sex) or any struggle with sin (such as resisting same-sex sexual desire or gender confusion) has only one root cause: original sin. Sin is the problem, and Jesus Christ is God's solution.

Pastor or church leader, if a parent shares with you that their son or daughter identifies as LGBTQ+, the last thing we should do is to place any more undue shame and guilt. There is not a single sin in which we squarely place the sole blame on the shoulders of the parents. Instead of making the same mistake as Job's three friends by giving faulty advice, you should grieve with the hurting parents and remind them that their child is like any other child: a sinner called to surrender everything to Christ.

RESPONDING TO THE "BORN THIS WAY" ARGUMENT

Theological anthropology also helps us address the "born gay" question. Much research has focused on this question, but to date, nothing is conclusive. We are far from determining the answer. But what does Scripture say? How does theological anthropology help us answer this question?

In Psalm 51:5, King David tells us that we are all born into sin. "Behold, I was brought forth in guilt, and in sin my mother conceived me." We all have a sin nature—not a choice—from birth. But this does not mean that someone is born gay. It does mean we are born with a sinful nature and even likely a predisposition for certain sins. But a predisposition is different from a predetermination. Innateness does not mean something is permissible, for being born a sinner does not make sin right.

Despite the lack of scientific evidence, many still believe some people are just born with homosexual attraction. Whether or not this is true, we must point people to a much more fundamental gospel truth. Jesus tells us, "You must be born again" (John 3:7). The old has gone and the new has come. Few truths are more gospel-centric than that. As leaders in the church, we must recognize that for those in the LGBTQ+ community, their main problem is not their sexuality or gender identity. Their main problem is their need to be born again. Only after this has happened can there be an inward transformation of sexual ethics and behavior.

GOD'S PROSCRIPTION: SIX PASSAGES

Having established that our identity is grounded in the *imago Dei* yet tainted by our sinful nature, let us move to the six passages that condemn same-sex sexual behavior: Genesis 19; Leviticus 18:22 and 20:13; Romans 1:26–27; 1 Corinthians 6:9–10; and 1 Timothy 1:10.[4] Romans 1:26–27 tightly grounds its morality and sexuality in Genesis 1–2, the creation. The other five passages are closely interconnected with Leviticus 20:13 as the interpretive background. Leviticus 18:22 and 20:13 most clearly and explicitly condemn same-sex relationships.

A growing number of Christians purport that the Bible has been incorrectly interpreted—and some have gone so far as to label these six the "clobber passages." To call any part of the Word of God a clobber passage reveals a flippant disregard for the holiness and perfection of divine revelation. Although these claims are wrought with bad exegesis and faulty hermeneutics, the main error is not interpreting them in light of the cohesion and interconnectedness of all sixty-six books of the Bible. This is called *canonical intertextuality*. Scripture interprets Scripture, which helps readers avoid misinterpretation. It is easier for false teachers to deconstruct a passage when isolated from the rest of the Bible. But proper exegesis of these passages involves noting the connections to other biblical texts.

Genesis 19 is the infamous story of Sodom's demise. Revisionists—those who claim the Bible does not condemn homosexuality—believe Sodom was *only* guilty of inhospitality or gang rape. They believe this passage does not condemn a monogamous same-sex relationship. Revisionists point out that Sodom's sin as mentioned in Ezekiel 16:49 is more akin to inhospitality, not homosexuality: "Behold, this was the guilt of your sister Sodom: she and her daughters had pride, excess of food, and prosperous ease, but did not aid the poor and needy" (ESV). Their argument continues by bringing up that in every biblical occurrence of Sodom outside of Genesis 19, homosexuality is not specifically mentioned.

This may be true; but ancient Hebrew has no specific word for sex. The Old Testament employs euphemistic language instead, such as "to know" or "to lie with." Hebrew relies on allusions to refer to sex. In Ezekiel 16:50, the prophet continues, "They were haughty and did an abomination before me" (ESV). The combination of two Hebrew words translated as "did an abomination" is an allusion to an important intertextual connection.

The verb "do" (or "commit") with the singular form of "abomination" as a direct object only occurs three times in the Pentateuch (eleven total in the Old Testament).[5] The second and third refer to idolatry (Deut. 13:14; 17:3) and the first occurrence is Leviticus 20:13 (ESV). "If a man lies with a male as with a woman, both of them have committed an abomination." These two Hebrew words in Ezekiel 16:50, "did an abomination," are an intertextual allusion to Leviticus 20:13. Thus the prophet Ezekiel, inspired by the Holy Spirit, was proclaiming that one of the many sins of Sodom—in addition to gang rape and inhospitality—was homosexuality.

The Bible never uses the phrase "did/committed an abomination" to refer to gang rape or inhospitality.

But how do we know whether this law should be followed when there are other Old Testament laws that no longer apply today? Jesus did not come to abolish the law but to fulfill it (Matt. 5:17), and many of the laws concerning what is clean/unclean have been answered in Christ (e.g., Acts 10:9–16). How do we know that a certain Old Testament law carries over into the new covenant? Complexities aside, we most certainly know that the answer is clear when a New Testament author reiterates it. Paul does this not once, but twice, in 1 Corinthians 6:9 and 1 Timothy 1:10.

These two verses in 1 Corinthians and 1 Timothy consist of sin lists. Both include a compound word, *arsenokoitai*, which does not occur anywhere else in the New Testament or before it was written. This compound word was formed by putting together two existing words, *arsen* (male) and *koite* (literally bed, but figuratively sexual intercourse). The Greek translation of the Hebrew Old Testament, called the Septuagint or LXX, was the Bible of first-century Jews and Christians.

Arsenokoitai is an intertextual allusion to *arsen* and *koite* found in Leviticus 18:22 and 20:13 (LXX). As a matter of fact, these two words are right next to each other in Leviticus 20:13 (LXX). As stated above, these two verses in Leviticus most clearly and explicitly condemn same-sex relationships. Paul knew the Corinthian Christians would be familiar with the Septuagint and recognize this clear reference to Leviticus 18:22 and 20:13. By using this compound word, the inspired apostle reaffirmed that this unambiguous proscription against homosexual behavior still stands today.

Romans 1:26–27 is the only passage in the Bible that discusses and condemns women-with-women homosexual behavior. "Women exchanged natural relations for that which is contrary to nature . . . men, too, abandoned natural relations with woman and burned in their desire toward one another, males with males committing shameful acts." Revisionists have done their fair share of attempting to deconstruct and explain Paul's use of "contrary to nature." They claim it is *only* condemning pedophilia or it is *only* condemning men burning with "desire" (1:27) or lust for other men—not a monogamous, mutually loving, same-sex relationship.

But there is no indication this passage is limited to sex with children or youth. Rather, Paul wrote "males with males," and there is no example of a woman committing pedophilia from first-century Jewish or Greco-Roman literature. And to address the other claim about desire or lust, homosexuality is not a sin simply because it involves desire or lust, just as idolatry is not a sin simply because it involves "vile impurity in the lusts of their hearts" (1:24). Both are sinful per se. But the most important mistake is that these two claims miss the perspicuous, intertextual allusions in Romans 1 to Genesis 1.[6]

After a greeting and expressing his desire to go to Rome, Paul frames the first three chapters of his letter to the church at Rome with "the righteous one will live by faith" (1:17). Romans 1:18–32 focuses on the unrighteousness of all humanity (1:18) before shifting to the unrighteousness of the Jews in Romans 2. In Romans 1:18–32, Paul grounds his rebuke in creation; for example, "For since the creation of the world" (v. 20) and "the Creator" (v. 25). The sin of idolatry is contrary to creation/ nature, that is, worshiping "the creature rather than the Creator" (v. 25). For the believers at Rome who read the Septuagint, the interconnection to Genesis would have been clear, with eight references in Romans 1:23, 26–27 to Genesis 1:26–27.

Genesis 1	Romans 1
"human" *anthropos* (Gen. 1:26)	"human" *anthropos* (Rom. 1:23)
"image" *eikon* (Gen. 1:26)	"image" *eikon* (Rom. 1:23)
"likeness" *homoiosis* (Gen. 1:26)	"resembling" *homoima* (Rom. 1:23)
"birds" *peteinos* (Gen. 1:26)	"birds" *peteinos* (Rom. 1:23)
"livestock" *ktenos* (Gen. 1:26)	"animals" *tetrapous* (Rom. 1:23)
"creeping things" *erpeton* (Gen. 1:26)	"creeping things" *erpeton* (Rom. 1:23)
"male" *arsen* (Gen. 1:27)	"men" *arsen* (Rom. 1:27)
"female" *thelus* (Gen 1:27)	"women" *thelus* (Rom. 1:26)

How do these eight references help us better understand the meaning of "natural" and "contrary to nature" mentioned in Romans 1:26–27? Ignoring Paul's intentional references to creation, the meaning could be unclear. However, the eight references to Genesis were not coincidental. Paul continued grounding sinful behavior in creation.

"Natural" is according to God's created order and "contrary to nature" goes against God's created order. Just as idolatry is sinful because it is contrary to creation/nature, homosexuality is sinful because it is contrary to creation/nature. "Unnatural" in Greek is literally "contrary to nature" (*para fusin*). "Natural" is not subjective based on an individual's so-called natural desires, but it is objective based on God's revealed truth in creation.

What is even more phenomenal, Paul's use of *arsen* in verse 27 is connected to *arsenokoitai* from 1 Corinthians 6:9 and 1 Timothy 1:10, which is connected to Leviticus 18:22 and 20:13, which is connected back to Genesis 19 (via Ezekiel 16:50). Revisionists do not recognize the intertextual connections of these six verses. If they did, they would not be revisionists.

GOD'S PRESCRIPTION: HOLINESS

In Romans 1:26–27, Paul grounded sexual ethics firmly in Genesis. Doing so was not novel to the New Testament. In Mark 10 and Matthew 19, Jesus gives what is probably the strongest hermeneutic for biblical sexuality and He establishes it in creation. If you have a loved one who believes the false teaching that homosexuality is not a sin, they will expect you to go over the six above passages, and there is a good chance they will even be better prepared than you. Instead, I would focus on these two parallel passages that articulate Jesus' definition of marriage.

Jesus' Words: Marriage Is Male and Female

In Mark 10:2–9, the Pharisees question Jesus about divorce. The Son of God's response is a forceful rebuke denouncing the practice of dissolving marriage for almost any reason. This shines a light on their hardened hearts (v. 5). As we saw earlier in Romans 1, Jesus similarly grounds His teaching on marriage in the creation narrative:

> "But from the beginning of creation, God created them male and female. For this reason a man shall leave his father and mother, and the two shall become one flesh; so they are no longer two, but one flesh. Therefore, what God has joined together, no person is to separate." (Mark 10:6–9)

Jesus could have quoted from numerous passages to affirm the enduring nature of the marriage covenant, but nothing is more foundational than this Edenic prototype: the covenantal union between Adam and Eve.

God is Lord over marriage because He is the one who joins man and woman together. "No person is to separate" serves as our reminder that divorce runs contrary to God's creation ordinances "from the beginning of creation." Men and women should not undo what God has done. Intentionally breaking up a marriage is in fact an attempt to usurp God. This was Jesus' way of displaying the antithesis between God who joins together and the first-century Jewish men who encouraged separation for essentially any reason.[7]

However, if all Jesus wanted to reaffirm was the indivisibility of marriage, the "one flesh" imagery from Genesis 2:24 would have been sufficient. But Jesus introduces the biblical concept of sexual differentiation from Genesis 1:27, which on the surface does not seem directly relevant: "God created them male and female" (Mark 10:6).[8] Yet for Jesus, it is immensely relevant: there is no marriage apart from the biblical paradigm of male and female. Jesus tethers the creation of "male and female" (Gen. 1:27) to the creation of "one flesh" marriage (Gen. 2:24). This beautifully illustrates that God both differentiates male and female at creation and unites male and female in marriage. Jesus is affirming that when God made male and female, our Creator already had in mind the marital union that followed.

David Gushee, who says he's been described as America's leading evangelical ethics scholar, switched his position on same-sex marriage and now calls for full acceptance of LGBT people in the church. He believes that Jesus in Mark 10 is addressing only divorce and that the passage is irrelevant to the discussion on same-sex marriage.[9]

However, because Jesus includes Genesis 1:27 in Mark 10:6—"God created them male and female"—Gushee's assertion does not hold up to scrutiny. God differentiates the sexes in Genesis 1 and then He unites the sexes in Genesis 2. What Gushee misses is this: the Pharisees' question on divorce becomes subservient to Jesus' teaching on marriage. The Son of God teaches that marriage is both indissoluble and fundamentally male and female.

Another implication of connecting Genesis 1:27 with marriage must not be missed. Not only does this verse establish the reality of sexual differentiation, but more importantly, it is also the key verse from which the doctrine of the *imago Dei* emanates. In other words, Jesus proclaims in Mark 10:6–8 not only that male and female are essential to marriage, but also that marriage points to the image of God—thus bringing together both the nature of marriage and the nature of humanity.

Therefore, from a biblical perspective, marriage is not a basic human or civil right. From God's point of view, sex is not about what adults are free to do with their bodies. "From the beginning of creation," God created marriage to be an indissoluble covenant between "male and female" with a deep correlation to the image of God. Any distortion of marriage—whether divorce, adultery, premarital sex, or same-sex marriage—is not only contrary to God's will but is also an affront to the very image of God.

HOLY SEXUALITY

Both Jesus and Paul ground biblical sexuality in Genesis. Sexual intimacy is reserved for marriage, and marriage is male and female. Does this then mean that heterosexuality is God's standard—*in all its forms*? Heterosexuality constitutes the correct general direction, but does it adequately and fully describe how we all should behave sexually? Our benchmark is Scripture, and everything must be measured by it.

Heterosexuality can be defined as opposite-sex sexual attractions or relations. This definition is exceedingly broad and includes behavior the Bible deems sinful—for example, a man sleeping with several different women, a husband cheating on his wife with another woman, and even a committed monogamous relationship

431

between a cohabiting boyfriend and girlfriend. These three scenarios of heterosexuality may be common, but are without question sinful in God's eyes.

By simply stating that "heterosexuality is right" without qualification, we imply a tacit endorsement of all the sexual immorality listed above. Certainly, marriage between a man and a woman is one type of heterosexual relationship, but it is not representative of all. The broad category of heterosexuality is *not* equivalent to biblical marriage, which is just one expression of heterosexuality.

We have pigeonholed ourselves into the wrong framework for biblical sexual expression: heterosexuality, bisexuality, or homosexuality. It is time to break free from this paradigm and embrace God's vision for sexuality. In our culture of confusion, ambiguity is no longer an option. Instead of affirming what is common, usual, or generally considered normal, we must look precisely at what is biblical. But what other options do we have, you may ask, other than heterosexuality and homosexuality? What we need is a completely new paradigm to represent God's sexual ethic: *holy sexuality*.

Holy sexuality consists of two paths: chastity in singleness and faithfulness in marriage. Chastity is more than simply abstention from premarital sex; it conveys purity and holiness. Faithfulness is more than merely maintaining chastity and avoiding illicit sex; it conveys covenantal commitment. In our common vernacular, "holy" has the sense of pure and morally upright. In Scripture, holiness conveys being set apart and dedicated to God. Holy sexuality should not just mean that we must remain morally pure. But chastity in singleness and faithfulness in marriage also signify that our sexuality must be set apart and dedicated to God.

Both of these paths embody the *only* correct biblical sexual ethic and articulate unambiguously the exact expressions of sexual behavior that God blesses. Too often Christians focus only on marriage but forget about singleness. Case in point—heterosexuality says nothing about chastity in singleness. Yet God blesses both biblical marriage and singleness; one without the other does not sufficiently describe God's will. In a world that blurs the lines of morality into every shade of gray, we must realize that biblical sexuality is black-and-white.

To be honest, I am not really presenting anything new or monumental. From Genesis to Revelation, in the entirety of the biblical witness, only two paths align with God's standard for sexual expression: if you are single, pursue sexual abstinence while fleeing lustful desires; if you are married, pursue sexual and emotional faithfulness to your spouse of the opposite sex also while fleeing lustful desires.

No terminology has accurately represented the biblical standard for sexual expression, which encompasses these two ways of living. While the category of heterosexuality includes some sinful behavior, it also does not clearly include chaste singleness. Therefore, a new phrase is necessary—*holy sexuality*. The purpose of this phrase is to transcend the current secular paradigm of sexual orientation that is unable to point toward God's clear intent for sexual expression.

This term "holy sexuality" is meant to simplify and disentangle the complex and confusing conversation around sexuality. The truth is that God's standard for *everyone* is holy sexuality: chastity in singleness and faithfulness in marriage. Different expectations for different people are not only unfair; they are unbiblical. Instead of determining how we ought to live based on enduring patterns of erotic desires, God's call for *all* humanity, quite simply, is holiness.

Heterosexuality will not get you into heaven and is not the ultimate goal for those with same-sex attractions. God commands us, "You shall be holy, because I am holy" (Lev. 11:45; 19:2; 20:7; 1 Peter 1:16). Because God is holy, He requires His people to be holy as well. Thus, the biblical opposite of homosexuality is not hetero-sexuality—that is not the ultimate goal. The opposite of homosexuality is holiness. As a matter of fact, the opposite of any sin struggle is holiness! Godly marriage and godly singleness are two sides of the same coin. We should stop emphasizing only one without the other. Both are good. Holy sexuality—chastity in singleness and faithfulness in marriage—is God's good standard for *everyone*.

Thus, if you are a leader in the church, stand firm in this truth about holy sexu-ality. Do not waver in the midst of pressures from the culture (external) or from the church (internal). Lovingly and convincingly preach and teach on the beauty of chas-tity in singleness and faithfulness in marriage. Proclaim it full of truth and grace. A high view of holy sexuality will equip your whole congregation, for every person is either single or married. And this foundation will provide hope for those strug-gling not only with same-sex attractions, but anyone fighting daily for their sexual purity. How many parents of wayward children identifying as LGBTQ+ need to be reminded that faith in Christ, which leads to a pursuit of holy sexuality, is the goal?

GENDER IDENTITY AND GENDER DYSPHORIA[10]

The secular world today believes that "gender" is subjective, and even that there are more than two genders. This modern redefinition of "gender" refers to a psy-chological reality independent from biological sex. Gender is now understood as the subjective *self-perception* of being male or female. If we're now saying that *sex* is objective and *gender* is subjective, you would think we would value conforming one's subjective ideas to objective truth. Instead, the opposite is the case: our cul-ture now values altering the objective, physical reality of our bodies to accommo-date the subjective impression of ourselves.

This new form of gnostic dualism separates mind from body and elevates self-understanding as the determiner of personhood—hence the made-up term, *gender identity*. The truth of the matter is this: our sense of self at best describes how we feel, not who we are. In the first chapter of the Bible, God creates the heavens and the earth and fills the earth with living creatures. The crown of creation is *adam*, or man (humankind). And among all the various human characteristics, God highlights one in particular: male and female.

Genesis 1:27 conveys an undeniable connection between "the image of God" and the ontological categories of male and female. Being created in the image of God and being male or female are *essential* to being human. One's sex (male or female) is not simply biological or genetic, just as being human is not simply biological or genetic. *Sex is first and foremost a spiritual and ontological reality created by God.* Being male or female cannot be changed by human hands; sex is a category of God's handiwork, reflecting His original and intended design.

As hard as anyone may try to alter this fact in his or her own body, the most that can be done is artificially remove or augment body parts or use pharmaceuticals to unnaturally suppress the biological and hormonal reality of one's essence as male or female. In other words, society tells us that psychology usurps biology; *what I feel becomes who I am.* When denying physical and genetic reality, we allow experience to supersede essence—and, more importantly, the image of God. Transgenderism is not exclusively a battle for what is male and female, but rather a battle for what is true and real.

So how did we get here? Transgenderism is the fruit of postmodernity. Postmodernism, in which truth is a subjective perception rather than an objective reality, says "You are what you feel." Just as we observed before, experience undergirds our values in today's culture, and everything else must fall in line. It is *sola experientia* ("by experience alone") that comes before *sola Scriptura* ("by Scripture alone").

But God is saying, "You are who I created you to be." The truth is not something we feel; it is not based on our self-perception. In fact, Scripture tells us, "The heart is more deceitful than all else and is desperately sick; who can understand it?" (Jer. 17:9). We cannot trust our own thoughts and feelings, so we need to submit them to God. "Trust in the LORD forever," we are encouraged, "for in GOD the LORD, we have an everlasting Rock" (Isa. 26:4).

Most people's self-perception is congruent with their biological sex. For a small percentage of others, it is not. The mental distress from this dissonance is called *gender dysphoria*. Some choose to identify as transgender male-to-female or female-to-male, in essence elevating psychology over biology.

However, although identifying as an opposite gender is a choice to sin—and going through hormone therapy or surgery is a choice to sin even further—the struggle itself is not. For some, the struggle to resist this sin is very real. Yet as peculiar and unusual as it may be, we must recognize that having unchosen and even persistent thoughts incongruent to one's actual sex is a psychological consequence of the fall—and every believer has areas in which he or she must daily struggle to resist.

Put in this context of human brokenness, one's incongruence between gender and sex may not be as bizarre as many think. Just as giving in to temptation is sinful, while being tempted is not, so giving in to and embracing a fallen and incorrect self-perception of gender is sinful, but the fight is not. Should it surprise us that the deceiver once again whispers to some regarding their sex, "Did God actually say...?" Let us commit to pray for those with gender dysphoria to follow Christ and His truth, rather than follow their darkened minds and the worldly agendas of intersectionality and identity politics.

In our own churches, there are those afraid to confess and seek prayer, lest they be shunned and ridiculed. Let us come around sisters and brothers who do not conform to this world, but are renewing their minds, resisting fallen thoughts of gender dysphoria, and taking every thought captive. Let us all join together as we fight against placing our psychology over our biology. And let us submit it all to God, recognizing that He makes no mistakes.

SHARING CHRIST

Having established the firm foundation of God's truth regarding sexuality and gender identity, now what? As pastors and church leaders, how do we best minister to those wrestling with their sexuality or gender identity? How can we be like Jesus who came "full of grace and truth" (John 1:14)? When Christians discuss same-sex attractions and gender confusion, they often turn to Paul's words from 1 Corinthians 6:9–10.

> Or do you not know that the unrighteous will not inherit the kingdom of God? Do not be deceived; neither the sexually immoral, nor idolaters, nor adulterers, nor homosexuals, nor thieves, nor the greedy, nor those habitually drunk, nor verbal abusers, nor swindlers, will inherit the kingdom of God.

If we only zero in on being "homosexual" and ignore the other eight, we would be missing Paul's point. If we were to reveal the past or even present sins of the heart, no one should inherit the kingdom of God! But I praise the Lord that Paul did not stop there and he goes on in verse 11 to one of my favorite verses in all of the Bible: "Such *were* some of you; but you were washed, but you were sanctified, but you were justified in the name of the Lord Jesus Christ and in the Spirit of our God" (emphasis added).

This is not only good news, it is amazing news! You can be washed, you can be sanctified, you can be justified in the name of Jesus. As church leaders and pastors, our message must be redemptive. We cannot continue simply telling those in the LGBTQ+ community that they are sinners and not tell them about the Savior who saves sinners! It is no wonder the LGBTQ+ community wants nothing to do with Christians—it is because we have not been sharing with them the good news. We have only been sharing the bad news. Let us, church leaders, commit to changing this tragedy and declaring the good news to all!

MINISTERING TO BELIEVERS

Before I share some practical action steps, we must first differentiate between those we hope to minister to. Do they know Christ and embrace His truths about sexuality and gender? If they do, our focus is mentoring and discipleship. However if they do not, then our focus is evangelism and outreach. So let me begin with believers who may experience same-sex attractions or gender dysphoria, but are committed to denying themselves and picking up their crosses daily. If a church member walks into your office and opens up to you, how should you respond?

First, thank them that they trusted you with this very personal matter. Do not freak out. The fact that they opened up to you says a lot about you. Be a good listener and do not assume anything. Most importantly, ask how their faith in Christ fits into their understanding of their sexuality. Ideally, we should hear, "My faith is strong. I am conforming my feelings and desires around my faith and submitting them to Christ." Regrettably, we often hear the opposite.

Second, tell them they are not alone. Christians who are wrestling with their sexuality often believe no one can ever understand them, which is a lonely place to be. Be honest and tell them that you do not know everything there is to know about this issue, but assure them you are committed to walking with them to Jesus. Pastors often tell me that they feel completely unable to help someone who has same-sex attractions or gender confusion simply because they themselves do not struggle with same-sex attractions or gender confusion.

If you think you must experience this same struggle to help someone with same-sex temptations, think again. Such is not true for any other sin! If you know Jesus and have had any victory over sin through Christ, you can help another sinner. As pastors and church leaders, we should be experts at helping sinners to follow Jesus and to go and sin no more—regardless of the variety of sinful behavior.

Third, remind them that their identity needs to be in Christ. This may be the most important point here toward the end of this chapter. I do not know of any other sin issue where we have conflated the sin with personhood or self-identity. As I mentioned before, a liar is not who he is, but what he does. An adulteress is not who she is, but what she has done. And yet some people try to say that "gay" is not what we feel or do, but who we are. No, it is just the opposite. Those who minister should always remember: sexuality is not *who* we are, but *how* we are. Who we are—our identity—is found in Christ.

Fourth, be realistic; do not give false promises. We cannot simply tell our church members to just "pray away the gay." Prayer and reading the Bible are important. However, we must tell our congregations that we do these things not so that difficulties will not come, but so that when they do come—and they will—we will be all the better equipped to remain faithful to God. These spiritual disciplines can help sanctify us. But it is not possible to remove same-sex attractions simply by heaping on prodigious amounts of prayer and Bible study.

Fifth, focus on heart change, not on externals such as how people walk or talk, or how they dress or the length of their hair. Those are not necessarily unimportant things, but we must realize that our goal is not behavior modification. Instead, behavior modification is a result of the most important change, which is an inside-out change of heart as our church members surrender more and more of their lives to Jesus. And heart change is what the gospel is all about.

Sixth, we need to deepen and strengthen bonds within the spiritual family. Many with same-sex attractions long to experience a committed relationship, but recognize that a same-sex relationship is not God's will. What is the best way to meet these legitimate needs for intimacy and community? Can friendship meet these needs? The New Testament establishes something greater and more enduring than friendship.

The answer is found when Jesus points to His disciples and says, "Behold: My mother and My brothers! For whoever does the will of My Father who is in heaven, he is My brother, and sister, and mother" (Matt. 12:49–50). Jesus is not rejecting family; instead, He is elevating something even greater than friends and family—that is, "spiritual family." In other words, the bonds of spiritual family run deeper than those of family and friends.

Spiritual family means that if the church were actually the church, if the family of God were actually the family of God, then being single and not having a physical family would not really matter! Why? Because we would have real family—a family that is eternal. I would have spiritual brothers and sisters to hold me and comfort me and love me and point me to Christ. These things are vital for Christians who wrestle with same-sex attractions or gender dysphoria.

LOVING UNBELIEVERS

But what about unbelievers? How can we encourage our church members to share Christ with their friends or loved ones in the LGBTQ+ community? Are there certain things they should avoid when building a relationship with some of these individuals who do not know Christ? Yes, so let us first begin with those.

Do not compare homosexuality with an addiction or pedophilia or so on. This is not a good way to win people to Christ! Do not use these two words: "lifestyle" or "choice," because it does not feel that way to a LGBTQ+ person. I never used those words before I came to Christ—because I had the wrong identity. I am willing to change my vocabulary for the sake of winning people to Jesus. Do not say, "Love the sinner, hate the sin." Do it, but do not say it. Do not feel you must debate with people or answer every question. Jesus did not. Instead, He would answer in ways that pointed to the kingdom of God (e.g., Luke 20:22–25).

If those are things to avoid, what should you do? Here are some positive and wise action steps I have gleaned from what my parents did when I was a prodigal in a far country.

Pray and fast.

Do battle for people who are unable to intercede for themselves.

Be quick to listen, not quick to speak. If you want others to listen to you, you should listen to them first.

Be intentional. Invite your gay neighbor over for dinner. No, this is not condoning their sin. We should be inviting sinners to dinner—Jesus did!

Be patient and persistent. My parents prayed for eight years—and I know people who have been praying for decades. If God patiently and persistently pursued you, should we not do the same for others?

Be transparent. The best way to proclaim the gospel is to tell your friend who identifies as LGBTQ+ how the gospel has affected your own personal life! Be transparent about what God has taught you and brought you through lately.

Pastors and church leaders, we need to tell our flock that we must live the gospel as well as preach the gospel. I would never have considered the gospel had I not seen the gospel lived out in my parents' lives first. In fact, I did not stop pursuing same-sex relationships because my parents convinced me such relationships were sinful. I stopped because they showed me something better—and His name is Jesus.

God has called you—for such a time as this—to serve the bride of Christ and obey the Great Commission by making "disciples of all the nations" (Matt. 28:18–20). You will more than likely have to deal with this topic, or I should say, have the *privilege* of dealing with this topic. Who better to proclaim God's truth on sexuality and gender identity than you, God's servant? For our job as ministers of the gospel is to show a lost and dying world that whatever they are clinging to—all the fool's gold in the world, fame, money, career, relationships—that not only is following Jesus better, following Jesus is best.

NOTES

1. Christopher Yuan and Angela Yuan, *Out of a Far Country: A Gay Son's Journey to God. A Broken Mother's Search for Hope* (Colorado Springs: WaterBrook, 2011).

2. Matthew Vines, *God and the Gay Christian: The Biblical Case in Support of Same-Sex Relationships* (New York: Convergent Books, 2014), 29, 155.

3. LGBTQ+ stands for lesbian, gay, bisexual, transgender, and queer or questioning. These terms are used to describe a person's sexual orientation or gender identity. The "plus" is supposed to represent other sexual and gender identities. These concepts come from a secular understanding that incorrectly conflates sexuality and personhood.

4. Here are two books for a more in-depth look at these verses: Kevin DeYoung, *What Does the Bible Really Teach about Homosexuality?* (Wheaton, IL: Crossway, 2015); Robert A. J. Gagnon, *The Bible and Homosexual Practice: Texts and Hermeneutics* (Nashville: Abingdon, 2001).

5. "Do/commit" plus "an abomination" (singular direct object) occurs a total of eleven times in the Old Testament: Lev. 20:13; Deut. 13:14; 17:4; Jer. 6:15; 8:12; 32:35; Ezek. 16:50; 18:12; 22:11; 33:26; and Mal. 2:11. Jeremiah's three references are linked to idolatry, specifically child sacrifice (Jer. 32:35). Ezekiel contains four. Besides Ezek. 16:50, two are not specific and one refers to adultery (Ezek. 22:11). Malachi refers to idolatry.

6. Robert A. J. Gagnon, *Bible and Homosexual Practice: Texts and Hermeneutics* (Nashville: Abingdon, 2001), 290–91.

7. John Nolland, *The Gospel of Matthew: The New International Greek Testament Commentary* (Grand Rapids: Eerdmans, 2005), 773.

8. R. T. France, *The Gospel of Mark: A Commentary on the Greek Text* (Grand Rapids: Eerdmans, 2002), 387.

9. David P. Gushee, *Changing Our Mind: A Call from America's Leading Evangelical Ethics Scholar for Full Acceptance of LGBT Christians in the Church* (Canton, MI: Read the Spirit Books, 2019), 83–85.

10. Information in this section is taken from my essay "Gender Identity and Sexual Orientation," The Gospel Coalition, https://www.thegospelcoalition.org/essay/gender-identity-and-sexual-orientation.

Ministering in
a Small Church Setting

MICHAEL J. BOYLE

Most pastors have some experience in a small church, whether they grew up in one, attended one, or even pastored one. When ministering in the small church, a pastor needs to understand how this ministry differs from larger church ministries. There are common practices of all healthy churches, but the ministry changes when you understand that different size churches have different ways of pastoring. The pastor of the small church should understand the uniqueness of a small church, the priorities of the pastor, the pastoral pressures, and the problems facing the small church.

SMALL CHURCHES IN THE BIBLE

When the temple was rebuilt in Jerusalem and the foundation laid, Zechariah asked this rhetorical question of the Lord's work, "For who has shown contempt for the day of small things?" (Zech. 4:10). When this small rebuilt temple was constructed, the Lord was in it and the Lord's eyes were on it. The Lord is not disappointed with small things or small churches.

The church of Jerusalem exploded on Pentecost. "That day there were added about three thousand souls" (Acts 2:41). These were people who had followed Jesus, and many had listened to the words of Jesus over the last three and half years. This was prepared soil for the gospel. But as Paul journeyed and preached the gospel, it was unprepared soil. Large crowds of converted people are not recorded. There is little description of the size of these new churches. It would seem a letter to a city may have covered all the believers in that entire city. As Paul planted churches, we know a few things about them. They all started with new converts. There was not transfer growth. We know in Acts 11 that the scattered believers of Jerusalem planted churches in Antioch. The Philippian church was started with Lydia and her household and a jailer and his family. In the closing lists of several of Paul's epistles, Paul may be identifying some gatherings of believers with the phrase "who are with them" (Rom. 16:14, 15). Paul spoke of the church that met in Aquila and Prisca's home (1 Cor. 16:19) and the church in Nympha's house (Col. 4:15). These would seem to be small churches that meet in homes.

THE SIZE OF CHURCHES

According to the National Congregations Study, the median church in the US has seventy-five regular participants in a Sunday morning worship service. That means that 50 percent of the American churches are seventy-five people in attendance or less. In the same study, they noted that 93 percent of all congregations in America are 400 people or less.[1]

According to the NCS "most congregations (56 percent) are led by a full or part-time solo leader with no additional paid ministerial staff."[2] And "overall, 16 percent of solo or senior pastoral leaders serve multiple congregations, and 34 percent were bi-vocational."[3] This means that most pastors in America pastor small churches. Most pastors serve as solo pastors. And about 50 percent of pastors serve multiple congregations or are bi-vocational. There is a large company of small church pastors. Timothy Keller states, "There is a 'size culture' that profoundly affects how decisions are made, how relationships flow, how effectiveness is evaluated, and what ministers, staff and lay leaders do."[4] Keller identifies that as a church grows larger they will increase in complexity, shift lay/staff responsibilities, increase intentionality, increase redundancy of communication, increase quality of production, increase openness for change, lose members because of changes, structuring smaller, and shift roles of the ministry.[5]

Churches are categorized small (15–200 in attendance), medium (200–400), large (400–800), and larger (800 and more). A megachurch is a larger church with over 2,000 in attendance. According to Keller, each size of church differs in its character, how it grows, and how it crosses the threshold to the next size of church category.[6]

Small church pastors must recognize that small churches and larger churches are different in more ways than just numbers. An apple is a fruit, a peach is a fruit, and a strawberry is a fruit, but they are different. So, too, a small church, medium church, large church, and a larger one are all churches, but they are all different. Pastoring a small church is knowing how it is like all other churches and how it is different.

A unique feature of the small church compared to larger churches is that they are found everywhere. A small church pastor may find himself ministering in a rural community or a small town. But small churches are also found in an urban culture, in a large city, or in the expanding suburbs among the large and mega-churches, and a church may choose to be a small church in any community and function as a house church. Small church pastors have a church size in common but they do not have the same ministry location in common.

PRACTICES OF ALL CHURCHES

All churches are to be a healthy church. A healthy church is **relationally connected** with their worship of God, their love of Jesus Christ, their prayers, their community with one another and the leadership in the church. A healthy church is **emotionally connected** with one another with love, joy, sharing, and caring. A healthy church is **biblically connected** with a devotion to the Word of God for its preaching, teaching, breaking of bread, and making disciples. A healthy church is **experientially connected** through fellowship, meeting the needs of people, discipling one another, having things in common, taking meals together (Acts 2:42–47).

The healthy church will find itself fulfilling the biblical mandate of making disciples. This mandate is unfolded through the book of Acts. The church witnesses to the good news of the gospel (Acts 1). The church embraces people not just from their own town and culture, but from every language, tribe, and nation (Acts 10). The church plants new churches (Acts 11). The church engages in the expanding of the gospel beyond their own town and community and beyond their current influence (Acts 16). And at all times, the church continues "preaching the kingdom of God and teaching things about the Lord Jesus Christ" (Acts 28:31).

THE UNIQUE QUALITIES OF SMALL CHURCHES

Niche Ministry

Small churches oftentimes will have a niche ministry. This will be their specialty. It will be the one thing they do very well. It will be what sets them apart from other small churches. The reason for this is that small churches cannot do everything, but they can do one thing well. Karl Vaters identifies the following small churches as healthy churches by design or by the nature and kind of ministry they are doing. They may be a planting church, training church, house church, retirement community church, countercultural church, impoverished church, transitional church, or a strategically small church.[7] Special attention should be given to the persecuted, which is a small church for reasons different from any other small church. It will function as needed in the country it resides and the type of persecution it faces. It is the one small church that all churches should pray for regularly.

Pastors can help their congregations identify their niche ministry and ministry focus that will make them a contributor to the church of Jesus Christ. The house church will limit its size to under forty. It will multiply as it grows in size to an additional home. The retirement community church will be reaching the aging population of America. It will be the baby boomers—well trained, financially stable, and living in a designated retirement community for people age fifty-five and older.

The impoverished church may have a bi-vocational pastor or a supported pastor funded from outside the church. The congregation may not be able to financially support the pastor. The ministry is for individuals and families with spiritual needs struggling financially.

Chris Kopp is the pastor of Galena Bible Church in Galena, Alaska. He has a niche ministry of training church planters for the villages of Alaska. Pastors join the church for a two-year training program. The training is beyond the ministry tasks of the church. Pastors will be trained in preaching and caring for people, but they will also be trained in hunting and the dressing of animals. The pastors also learn about plumbing, electricity, fixing machines, and home construction. In the native villages, there are no tradespeople to call to fix the things that break in your home, so the church planter is able to serve the community. This is a niche ministry for a small church.

RELATIONSHIPS

The small church is built around relationships. The ministry functions around friendships, family, and neighbors who attend the same church. People join in ministries together because of these close relationships. People will serve and sacrifice in ministries that are not their gifting or their passion because of their relationships with family or friends. A pastor cannot underestimate the importance of these relationships and the strength they bring to the ministry.

When people visit a small church, they expect that they will build friendships and relationships. It is the draw that they can be known by others and that the others will want to know them. People can find programs at bigger churches, but they often cannot find relationships. Even if a small church offers a good program, it is the relationships that bind the ministry together. The pastor is to be aware of the importance of cultivating the congregation's relationship with Jesus Christ, new people, friends, and family because relationships are a key to the life of the church.

CONGREGATIONAL LIFE

The small church is made up of a small group of people. These people have several things in common that make up their congregational life. A pastor of a small church needs to assess and understand these characteristics of their local church.

RELIGIOUS BACKGROUND

Jesus tells the parable of the sower or soils in Luke 8:4–15. In the parable, He identifies four different soils that the seed falls on. In the community of a small church, the pastor needs to assess the soil in which he is pastoring and sowing the seed. It can be sowed "beside the road." In this soil, it will be trampled underfoot and the devil will come and take it away (Luke 8:5, 12). It can be sowed on rocky soil. It will wither away and in the times of temptation fall away (Luke 8:6, 13). He can sow the seed among the thorns. In this case, the seed will be choked with worries and riches and pleasures of *this* life (Luke 8:7, 14). And the final soil is the good soil. In this soil the seed will hold it fast, and bear fruit with perseverance (Luke 8:8, 15).

The soil of the community will have a bearing on the outcome of the ministry. It may slow the process of new believers coming to Christ. It might identify a greater satanic influence in your community. Or it may expose the riches and life pleasures being pursued by your folks. A spiritual assessment will give insight into your community's culture.

The religion of the community will give an understanding of the religious values and convictions of your ministry. In smaller towns in America, it will be defined by the churches in the community: The Roman Catholic church, mainline denominations (Lutheran, Methodist, Presbyterian), evangelical churches, fundamental churches, or charismatic churches. In smaller towns around the world and in larger cities, the ethnicity of the community will define the religion. The religious influence could be Orthodox, Judaism, Islam, Buddhism, Hinduism, or paganism. The religious culture of the community creates a worldview and mindset that the gospel will need to penetrate. This will be an understanding of apologetics and world religions to equip the pastor and church family.

DEMOGRAPHICS

Demographics are the broad strokes that make up the community of the small church. The ethnicity of the community will impact the foods, festivals, and holidays celebrated. It will identify the various customs and practices for weddings, funerals, and other special occasions. The socioeconomics will be impacted by the education level, income level, marital status, occupation, and average size of a family. These elements will provide the unique expressions for worship and ministry based upon their cultural practices and the Christian faith.

CHURCH HISTORY

Every small church pastor needs to be a historian. There are three histories of the church: the church, the denomination/association, and its own town or community. The church history is discovered through the minutes and church documents. The church minutes may expose some problems, discipline, and pastoral leadership. The minutes may give insight into the pastoral leadership over the life of the church. These documents may expose some church conflicts or wounds that have not been addressed that continue to hinder the church. As a pastor, you may bring a healing ministry to the church and an understanding of why the church is the way it is.

The denominational history will explain some basic practices and policies of the church. In denominations and associations of churches, there is usually agreement of doctrine and church governance. This may identify the things that will not change even if you want them to change as a pastor. From the roots of the denomination or association you may be able to draw upon the voice of the founder to move your ministry forward. A leader such as Menno Simon, Martin Luther, or John Wesley may give you a quote that captures the imagination of your congregation for what they could do for Christ.

The history of your community will identify community needs and ministries. This is looking at the history of schools and their sports, the local paper and its stories, and the political arena and its issues. These areas identify the things they celebrate, the needs they have, and the pain of loss. Have there been tragic deaths, tornadoes, hurricanes, floods, or other disasters that people still talk about? These are aspects of life that will be part of your church life as you care and pastor in this town. In a sense, no one escapes the hurt or pain of their own town or community.

LEADERSHIP

All churches need biblical leadership. In the small church, this leadership usually resides in the volunteer leaders of the church and not a paid staff. A pastor serves alongside the church leaders. There are various models of church governance from elder rule, elder led, and congregational. Whichever model your church follows, there are two overarching concepts for church leaders: there is a plurality of leaders who give oversight to the church and the role of the members of the church. With the plurality there is a division of labor. There are some leaders who provide the guidance, direction and leading of the church and some leaders who additionally provide the preaching and teaching of the Word (1 Tim. 5:17).

Even with the plurality of leadership in small church, leadership is from the bottom up. Pastors can cast vision and speak of the future, but in a small church, the congregation must be on board. There is a corporate sense of moving forward. We are all in together. The small church is congregational in nature, practice, communication, and agreement. Larger churches follow the vision and voice of the pastor, while small churches follow the direction of the congregational vote.

PASTORAL PRIORITIES

When the apostles found out that they were neglecting the care of the Hellenistic Jewish widows, they reevaluated the ministry of the early church. They did three things. First, they delegated the care of the widows to a new group of leaders. Second, they devoted themselves to prayer. And third, they devoted themselves to the Word (Acts 6:1–7). All pastors will give attention to prayer and the Word; but other priorities of the small church pastor are pastoral care, building relationships, and paying attention to the details.

Pastoral Care

The pastor of a small church is identified as a shepherd, a lover of the people, and one who cares. He has the opportunity to minister in all the areas of people's lives because of the close relationships that he builds with the congregation. It was the neglect of the widows in Acts 6 that made the apostles review their priorities of ministry. Up until this new growth, the apostles were providing the care for the people. For the solo pastor, the care of the people is not just a priority but a special invitation to join the families of the church in their good times and their bad times. The daily care of the sheep and ministry fills out your schedule and calendar. Whether people call, email, text, Facebook, Instagram, or Twitter, you know what is going on in their daily lives. You find that their different needs require your care and time.

The small church pastor is the primary contact person for the congregation. They call the pastor with any need they may have. The pastor visits the people in the hospital, the shut-ins, and the widows. And this pastoral care allows him to join the families for their celebrations and special services like weddings, birthday parties, graduations, funerals, and baptisms.

And your congregation will ask you to lead in prayer in most settings. You will pray at church potlucks, dinners, meals, and meetings. As much as you assure them that others can pray, they will naturally turn to you and say, "Pastor, could you lead us in prayer." Even in their own homes, they will ask you to lead in prayer before the meal. And you will lead them in this great honor and privilege we have before our God.

As pastor, you are a shepherd of all the people and you provide the personal care to the whole congregation. Your care involves listening, visiting, counseling, and praying with God's people. You join them when they go through difficult trials, temptations, sufferings, and death. You care for them as a spiritual counselor, pastor, and friend encouraging them in their walk with Christ. And as the church grows and new people become part of the church, these ministries change with others providing this care.

RELATIONSHIP BUILDING

Small church ministry is all about relationship building. The opportunity to minister to the various needs in your congregation comes from building a relationship of trust. And that trust opens their hearts for ministry and care. Those meals at church, fellowship times, conversations in the foyer or the parking lot of the grocery store are the places of building relationships. People open up in conversation and about their lives as these relationships deepen. In small churches, congregations join together for ministry, not because of your great vision casting or communication skills, but because of the relationships with one another.

Even the evangelism and outreach in the community is built around relationship building. Again, trust must be developed. This may be drinking coffee together, playing basketball, or working on a community project. But trust opens the door for the gospel. Small churches, small towns, and small communities are all built around relationship building. Invest your time wisely and regularly to build up the church of Jesus Christ by building relationships with God's people and those who desperately need a Savior.

Church relationships are built by cascading communication through every verbal, visual, and social media mediums that will give direction to your ministry. The congregation needs to be reminded regularly where you are going and how you will get there. Communication also gets involved in the nitty gritty part of life. People need to also hear the difficult words "for rebuke, for correction, for training in righteousness" (2 Tim. 3:16) from the mouth of their leader. You will be assured in your ministry by the adage, "Nobody cares how much you know, until they know how much you care." That is the mark of a pastor of a small church.

Communication becomes very personal for small church pastors because they must also be transparent to model the transforming nature of the gospel. After listing an array of sins, Paul concluded, "Such were some of you; but you were washed, but you were sanctified, but you were justified in the name of the Lord Jesus Christ and in the Spirit of our God" (1 Cor. 6:11). Oh, the power of the gospel to know what we were. In a small church, this kind of transparency may be one of the most difficult tasks a pastor faces because of the gossip of a small church.

A pastor models transparency of how the grace of God has worked in his life and how it is currently working in his life. The congregation puts a pastor on a pedestal. Pastors let the people know that they are being sanctified by that same grace that they preach that is working in the lives of their congregation.

OVERSIGHT OF CHURCH DETAILS

In the small church, the pastor functions as the administrator of the church, the executive pastor, or the chief operations officer. It is not an assigned task, but the pastor needs to pay attention to the details of the church: its organization, finances, and spiritual condition.

Organization

Every church has some organization and that organization is codified in written documents. Some of these may be required by law to be registered with the state or government agency. The constitution and bylaws entail the summary understanding of how the ministry will function. The constitution may be a broader and general statement of the organization and how the ministry functions. The bylaws provide the details of how it will all work together. In these documents, the leaders of the church are overseeing the purpose or mission of the church, the doctrinal statement, the qualifications and selection process for leaders and members. Additional components may include the search process for a pastor of the church, church discipline, business meetings, and how to change these documents. In today's culture, the leaders will also need policies or documents for child safety and attenders who may be convicted sexual offenders or registered sex offenders. As the pastor, you need to make sure the church is following these directives and also keep up on changing laws for churches and child safety.

Finances

Oversight of the finances is a fiduciary responsibility of church leaders. This oversight involves the rightful expenses of the church under the direction of church leaders. For legal reasons, the receiving and receipting of gifts must be done in accordance with laws for a nonprofit church or ministry. There is also accountability to the church family for the budget and expenses of the church or the ministry. Financial transparency is a requirement for building trust and open communication with the congregation. As the pastor, you may have to push for openness of communication and being sure finances are being handled appropriately.

Spiritual Condition

Spiritual oversight of the church involves more than the preaching and teaching of the Word. Spiritual oversight extends to the discipleship and the community of the congregation oftentimes built through small groups or one-on-one relationships. Overseeing the "making of disciples of all nations" places evangelism, outreach, and missions as areas of oversight and development for the leaders. To carry this out, as a pastor with your leaders, you need to review the various ministries of the church to see how they are accomplishing the mission of the church and fulfilling their role and function. This oversight is for the children, youth, women, and men of the church.

PASTORAL PRESSURES

MONEY

Small churches breed some common pastoral pressures. Most pastors of small churches face the pressure of money. Working with the leaders, budgets are usually tight. Giving is less than needed. Expenses are higher than expected. Meetings are spent trying to figure out how to cover expenses and increase giving.

The pressure becomes personal for the pastor. As churches tighten budgets, pay increases may not be given. Even regular checks may not be on time. This is especially true in smaller churches and bi-vocational ministries. Budgeting by the church and pastor are important in facing this pressure.

It is important to keep the congregation informed of the needs and to teach about stewardship and giving. Paul wrote, "On the first day of every week, each of you is to put aside and save as he may prosper" (1 Cor. 16:2).

TIME

Time is an ongoing pressure for the pastor of a small church. There are 168 hours for everyone in the week. But for the small church pastor, he is serving alone. No other staff to share the ministry. Funerals, weddings, hospital visits, preaching, teaching, discipleship, leadership development, caring, leading are all his responsibility. And his time must be stretched over ministry and his family. The pressure is real, and this warning is true: "So then, be careful how you walk, not as unwise people but as wise, making the most of your time, because the days are evil" (Eph. 5:15–16).

Making the most of your time is planning the best use of your time. Most pastors meet the ministry demands of their time but miss the family demand of their time. Planning of family time is as important as planning the ministry time. In fact, family time needs to be planned first because ministry will always steal family time; rarely does family time steal ministry time. Plan time with your spouse. Plan time with each of your children. Plan your vacation and then take your vacation.

DISCOURAGEMENT

Small churches do not grow fast. Small churches do not change quickly. Small churches struggle financially. Small church pastors face discouragement. In the fast-paced culture of change and growth, pastors get discouraged because they do not see what they think others are seeing in their ministries. The reading of books, the exploring of church websites, the listening to podcasts, creates an aspiration for more than what the small church will ever be. The idolatry that a larger church will mean a better ministry discourages the heart of the pastor. When small church pastors are discouraged, they need two things. First, they need the peace of Christ. "Do not be anxious for anything, but in everything by prayer and pleading with thanksgiving let your requests be made known to God. And the peace of God, which surpasses all comprehension, will guard your hearts and minds in Christ Jesus" (Phil. 4:6–7). Second, pastors need contentment, "Not that I speak from need, for I have learned to be content in whatever circumstances I am" (Phil. 4:11).

LONELINESS

One of the most difficult pastoral pressures in the small church is loneliness. It is obvious as you are the only person on staff. You are alone. Friendships are made with the leaders and people in your congregation, but missing is another ministry colleague for the husband and wife in ministry. Loneliness unmet over time can lead to discouragement, depression, and ministry burnout.

When Jesus sent His disciples out for ministry, He sent them two by two. Friendships are found throughout the Bible: David and Jonathan, Isaiah and Hezekiah, Josiah and Jeremiah, Daniel and Shadrach, Meshach and Abednego, Jesus and Peter, James and John, and Elijah and Elisha. These friendships were pursued by some and provided by God. Intentionality is required to address loneliness. Reaching out to another pastor, maybe across denominational lines, maybe in another town, but in some way, you need to reach out to build a friendship. Loneliness is real for the small church pastor and ministry friendships provide the companionship needed.

PROBLEMS FACING THE SMALL CHURCH

The small church faces some unique problems. They are not unique—larger churches also face these problems—but small churches provide the soil that allows these problems to take root and grow.

GOSSIP

The small church has fewer people, so gossip does not have to travel very far to take root. The smaller the church, the shorter the distance to reach every person in the church with gossip. Young widows are cautioned that "they go around from house to house; and not merely idle, but also they become gossips and busybodies, talking about things not proper to mention" (1 Tim. 5:13). Gossip goes from person to person and from house to house. The simple process puts small churches at risk. It is talking about things that are not proper to mention. It can be a bad report about a person. It is not good or helpful or edifying.

And unfortunately, the problem with gossip is that it is tasty and irretrievable. "The words of a gossiper are like dainty morsels, and they go down into the innermost parts of the body" (Prov. 18:8). People struggle to resist the temptation of gossip because it is desirable. But the sad part about gossip is that it penetrates the deep parts of the heart to remain and be remembered. The damage from gossip is that it fuels the fire of contention and strife in the church. The goal is to stop the gossip and whisperer. "For lack of wood the fire goes out, and where there is no gossiper, quarreling quiets down" (Prov. 26:20).

RELATED FAMILIES

Related families are not a problem in the church of Jesus Christ. We all want all our family members to know Christ and be part of the family of God. Yet families bring their own baggage with them in life and ministry. For the smaller church, related families can bring their family troubles and conflicts into the church. The number of people affected by this conflict can impact the volunteers serving in every ministry. It can create tensions and quarrels. If the conflict is unresolved or not mediated, the church and ministry will suffer. It impacts the church growth because people in the community know of the family conflict and want to avoid it.

Even when families are walking with the Lord and serving Him faithfully, the size of these families cause others to fear for the ministry of the church. They become afraid that this family makes all the decisions. This family gets all the major roles and responsibilities.

So, whether the related family is doing good or ill, in a small church they can create a distrust or division. Clear attention to family for resolution and reconciliation is necessary. Clear communication of ministry qualifications and requirements cultivate ministry trust.

CHURCH BOSS

People do not need to be leaders to be influencers. They can exert pressure and persuasion by their presence and expressing their opinion. The Church Boss may not be an elected leader of the church. The congregation may highly respect the Church Boss or highly fear the Church Boss. If the Church Boss employs people of the church or does business with them, they may be fearful of losing their job or business, especially if they disagree with him on church matters. Their power may be as a founding member of the church or a child of that family. Or this may be perceived as a large donor to the church. Congregations believe that this person will remove their financial support and the church will be in real trouble.

These influencers can have a positive impact on the church too. They can be supportive of the pastor and leaders. They can be generous financial supporters of the ministry. They can also use their spiritual gifts to serve and build up the saints.

Pastors need to spend time with Church Bosses and the influencers of the church. These can be conversations over a cup of coffee or a meal getting their feedback on future plans and change. The key is to talk with them face to face. And do not be motivated by fear. "There is no fear in love, but perfect love drives out fear" (1 John 4:18). Love them as a sister or brother in Christ.

UNQUALIFIED LEADERS

When a church loses its sense of vision and direction, leaders decide not to lead. The result is an open invitation of "Who wants to serve?" Or a recruitment of "It's pretty easy to be a an elder. It does not take much time and not much to do." Or "It's your turn to serve. It's been three years." Tim Keller comments, "The smaller church by its nature gives immature, outspoken, opinionated and broken members a significant degree of power over the whole body."[8] In any case, small churches can end up with unqualified leaders. And sometimes, filling slots is an attempt to meet the requirements of their constitution and bylaws.

Steps to move toward qualified leaders begins by reviewing the constitution and bylaws. Sometimes churches have adopted constitutions and bylaws from larger churches. These churches need to rewrite their constitution for the size of their church that will have fewer leaders. This may be a solution for any church; reduce the number of leaders to lead. This can help preserve qualified leaders by letting them serve shorter terms with breaks. And if necessary you can put your constitution on hold until you have qualified leaders. In any case it means that leadership training and leadership development must be a priority of the church.

RESISTING CHANGE

The nature of any organism is to grow and change. And the church is an organism. Small churches are resistant to change. They like to hold on to their traditions. They can even become complacent because things are working.

The world around every church is changing. The people are changing. The values are changing. The demographics are changing. So, the small church needs to change.

Since small churches can do one thing well, they need to have a plan for change. Karl Vaters says small churches need to "clear their ministry closets" by following "The Closet Rule." Start by asking the following questions:

- What ministries have ceased to be effective?
- What ministries cost more money, time, or energy than they're worth?
- If we were starting the church today, would we do this?
- What ministries don't fit the mission or vision of the church?
- Can this ministry be refreshed, or should it be ended?
- What are we doing that we wish we didn't have to do?

After this assessment, for each ministry you determine to "renew it," "replace it," or "say goodbye to it."[9]

People respond differently to change. Blanchard and Hodges identify seven reactions people have to change. People feel awkward, so tell them what to expect. People feel alone, so structure activities that create involvement. People will think about what they have to give up, so let people mourn their losses. People think they can only handle so much change, so set priorities on which changes to make. People will be concerned they don't have enough money, time, or skills, so encourage creative problem-solving. People will be at different levels for readiness, so recognize the different risk-takers and early adopters. And finally, people will revert to old behaviors if the pressure is taken off, so keep the people focused.[10]

As the pastor, you will need to walk your congregation through the need to change and the changes. Conversation will go beyond the church leaders. For the families of the church, the stakeholders, and the Church Boss, you will need to plan individual conversations with these folks. Going for a cup of coffee, asking their opinions and thoughts of change will involve them in the thinking process and the influencing of others. In a small church, small conversations pave the way for change because change comes from the bottom up.

CONCLUSION

Ministering in the small church is ministering in a normal church. It is a great privilege. And it is the most common experience of pastors. So, take heart small church pastors. Most churches are small churches. All small churches can be healthy churches. All churches have their own problems. Every church can become a healthy church. All pastors face ministry pressures. And all small church pastors join the company of all pastors who have the privilege of being in an exclusive role of shepherding the followers of Christ in the transforming ministry of the church, that will conform them to the image of God's dear Son, our Lord and Savior Jesus Christ.

So small church pastor, normal church pastor, "Be on the alert, stand firm in the faith, act like men, be strong. All that you do must be done in love" (1 Cor. 16:13–14).

NOTES

1. "American Congregations at the Beginning of the 21st Century," National Congregations Study (2008), http://www.soc.duke.edu/natcong/Docs/NCSIII_report_final.pdf, 5.

2. Ibid., 12.

3. Ibid., 14.

4. Tim Keller, "Leadership and Church Size Dynamics," Gospel in Life, https://gospelinlife.com/downloads/leadership-and-church-size-dynamics.

5. Keller, "Leadership and Church Size," 5–7.

6. Ibid. This is the outline of the article.

7. Karl Vaters, *Small Church Essentials* (Chicago: Moody Publishers), 27–30.

8. Keller, "Leadership and Church Size," 2.

9 Vaters, *Small Church Essentials*, 121–23.

10. Ken Blanchard and Phil Hodges, *The Servant Leader* (Nashville: Thomas Nelson), 66–67.

Ministering to Mental Health Issues

JACOB SANTHOUSE

In providing gifts for His church, God gave His people the necessary tools to pursue healthy lives. One of the most significant assets that God has given us to live healthy lives is each other. Being in community with other believers is a vital part of being healthy and fostering growth in the community. Within that community, counseling can be deployed as a unique tool to care for individuals in a specific way to support them and enable them to live healthy lives serving God to their highest potential. At its heart, counseling comes down to intentionally developing relationships to foster growth in an individual, couple, family, or group. Both pastoral counselors and clinical counselors should take time to understand the role of the other to develop a God-honoring approach to counseling and how they can work together to provide the best possible support for the body of Christ.

BIBLICAL PERSPECTIVE ON MENTAL HEALTH

Understanding the church's role in addressing mental health issues begins with the Bible. When we focus merely on the Bible's larger narrative, it is easy to miss the many biblical references to mental health issues. There are examples that mental health issues were present during Bible times just as they are today. The proper place to begin is to study how the Bible views personhood.

At the heart of a biblical view of the person is the *imago Dei*—God has created all people in His image (Gen. 1:26). Being created in God's image establishes the value and dignity of every person. It makes human beings unique and special among all of God's creation (Gen. 1:20–31). Humans are the only created being who bear the image of God. In Millard J. Erickson's *Christian Theology,* he notes that the designation of being made in God's image makes humans sacred to God.[1] Any approach to serving people, and in this case ministering to mental health issues, should be oriented around recognizing and preserving the value and dignity people as God's image bearers.

While being created in the image of God gives people inherent worth, it does not negate people from experiencing physical and mental issues. Prior to Genesis 3 and the entrance of sin into the relationship between God and humans, Adam and Eve existed in a state of perfection and innocence. They were regularly able to be in the direct presence of God in the garden of Eden (Gen. 3:8). After the fall, all the attributes that set humans apart being created in God's image were distorted. Physically, mentally, and emotionally they no longer functioned in the state of original perfection and relational ease in which God made them (Gen. 3:17–19). This introduced brokenness of the body, both physically through diseases like cancer, heart disease, or blindness and mentally through illnesses such as anxiety, depression, or personality disorders. Acknowledging the reality of the mental issues is fundamental to developing a healthy approach to counseling and mental health.

The Bible provides examples of people who suffered from mental illnesses. David's behavior is described as an act of disguising his sanity (1 Sam. 21:13) and acting as a "an insane person" (1 Sam. 21:14) to fool Achish the king of Gath. Nebuchadnezzar had a loss of mental capacity so that he could no longer rule his kingdom (Dan. 4:33).

Not all the biblical examples are so extreme. King David likely experienced significant depression by his many references to being weary all day, shedding tears, or a life spent in sorrow (Ps. 6:6–7; 31:10; 69:3). Those depressive symptoms combined with a lack of energy, excessive sadness, and not going to war with his troops indicate a current-day diagnosis of depression (2 Sam. 11). Job is another example who it seems would likely qualify for a diagnosis of Post-Traumatic Stress Disorder (PTSD). Job had nightmares (Job 7:14), tried to avoid or forget painful memories (Job 9:27), and felt detached and abandoned by his friends (Job 12:4; 17:6). Even just based on these few examples, it is evident that experiencing issues with mental health is nothing new for humans and was routinely experienced by biblical characters.

DEVELOPING A BIBLICALLY GROUNDED APPROACH TO COUNSELING

Recognizing the presence of mental health issues in Scripture is merely the first step; the next step is to develop an approach to ministering to these mental health issues. Here, the Bible is much less explicit. Nowhere does the Bible say that if someone is experiencing depression or anxiety, they should go see a counselor. However, the Bible does speak to the importance of a relationship with people: after God created Adam, God said, "It is not good for the man to be alone" (Gen. 2:18). God established the importance of people relationally connecting. It seems possible that one of the reasons God established the church was so His people could be part of a fellowship and community of believers (Acts 2:44).

Establishing community implies there must be value in developing relationships with others. Counseling stresses that through intentionally developing relationships with others, it is possible to promote growth and health. Clinical counseling as a profession is based on a concept known as the Wellness model.[2] Wellness asserts that people comprise physical, mental, emotional, and spiritual aspects and in order to effectively work with a person, each of these areas must be addressed. The existence of physical, mental, and spiritual components in humans aligns with the growth of Jesus Christ in His human nature. Luke wrote, "And Jesus kept increasing in wisdom and stature, and in favor with God and people" (Luke 2:52). The biblical affirmation of these distinct aspects demonstrates the importance of ministry to the whole person, and none should be ignored.

In developing a biblically grounded approach to mental health issues, we need to address the true source of healing. This is fundamentally important from a doctrinal standpoint, but also very important for demonstrating how the pastor and the counselor frame their self-understanding. Regardless of who or what tools God uses to bring about health and healing, God is the healer. Paul stated this truth very simply in Colossians 1:16–17: "For by Him all things were created, both in the heavens and on earth, visible and invisible, whether thrones, or dominions, or rulers, or authorities—all things have been created through Him and for Him. He is before all things, and in Him all things hold together." The role of the pastor, counselor, doctor, medication, or any other method that God uses to heal broken people is secondary to God's role. Yet God uses various means to help the hurting, and counselors are an important means of His Healing grace.

Counseling and tools such as medications are among the means God uses to minister healing grace to His people. The integration of a psychological understanding of the brain, the use of medication to treat hormonal or chemical imbalances, and other secular treatments, such as clinical counseling of mental disorders, are a polarizing topic in the church. Sadly, it is not uncommon in the church to hear the argument that the use of secular approaches or the integration of psychological understanding of a mental issue represents a lack of faith or and finds no support in Scripture. This view denies that God created humans with the ability to observe, interpret, and explore His creation in order to better understand how it works. In Psalm 19:1–7, the well-known "The heavens tell of the glory of God" passage, David wrote about how every part of the universe points back to its Creator. The implication is that all truth is God's truth. Such exploration includes the research and science that stands behind psychological understanding and the development of medicines.

Use of our God-given ability to study how the brain functions enables the creation of various medications to support the brain when it is experiencing a deficiency that inhibits full functionality. The Bible identifies God utilizing medical procedures in healing people. Second Kings 20:7 says, "Then Isaiah said, 'Take a cake of figs.' And they took it and placed it on the inflamed spot, and he recovered." There is no question that God healed Hezekiah, but He did it through what was considered—at the time—normal medical means. In 1 Timothy 5:23, Paul tells the young preacher, "Do not go on drinking only water, but use a little wine for the sake of your stomach and your frequent ailments." This seems to be normal instruction for addressing physical needs.

From Scripture, we see that mental health issues are a legitimate struggle for people both inside and outside the church. It is important for church leaders to have a plan for dealing with these mental issues and struggles. Counseling can be a tool to come alongside those who are experiencing mental health problems. Counseling can be incredibly valuable to the whole church community. Though scientific research has been remarkably helpful in developing our understanding of mental illness, it does not require a degree in mental health to support people suffering from mental illnesses. It is a matter of knowing how and when you are able to provide support, and when it is time for you to partner with a trained mental health professional. The following sections will explore specific aspects counseling in a local church ministry setting.

MENTAL HEALTH MINISTRY IN THE CHURCH

Knowing basic counseling skills and when to use them has the potential to be an invaluable asset to your ministry. To utilize them effectively and ethically a few things must be established. It's important to remember that God is ultimately the one who heals, and the counselor has no special power or ability to "fix" the individual. Part of what makes this so important, is that approaching someone with the attitude that "I will fix you" is likely to do more harm than good. Further, adopting a humble approach helps build an environment in the counseling relationship that is more likely to bring about growth in both the counselee and counselor. Leave the roles of healing and judging to God and instead focus on providing safe and loving support. One of the best ways to provide this support is to focus on listening to and reflecting what is said and felt. Be careful not to assume that you know what someone is feeling or what they will say.

Providing church members with mental health support does not start in a counseling session. One of the most significant things a pastor and church leadership can do in supporting those experiencing mental illnesses is to work to destigmatize mental illness. Pastors and church leaders live under a microscope and their beliefs and opinions are often adopted by those they lead. When a church leader shows support for a person and honors the value of the individual struggling with mental illness, it can go a long way toward developing a community in which people who experience mental illnesses are able to thrive. Developing an environment that supports those experiencing mental illness also creates an atmosphere in which counseling can be more effective.

Another way the church can support the mental health needs of the local church is by developing a team approach to addressing mental issues. This enables the church to effectively support not just one suffering member, but many. An effective support team will have a number of different components. The person who provides counseling is only one part of the team. Whenever someone suffers from a mental illness, it affects not only them, but also everyone else in their life. A benefit of the team approach involves having people in the congregation who are willing to come alongside and support the family and loved ones of the individual with the mental issue by seeking to meet their needs.

The other part of the team approach involves networking with local mental health professionals such as licensed counselors or licensed psychologists. There are certain mental illnesses such as extreme depression, anxiety, bipolar disorder, suicidality, and other serious issues where it is vital to be connected to professional resources in the community. Developing this kind of team requires planning. It takes time to network with professionals in the community. If there are mental health professionals within the church body, they can be connecting the church with other professionals in the community and work to develop and train the team.

Taking time to educate the congregation about mental health issues is a necessary early step to take in building the team and preparing the church to be able to support members struggling with mental health. It is also helpful to make church members aware of resources available outside the church. People commonly do not get help because they do not know it is available. The more available support is communicated to the church family, the more likely it is the support will be used.

One practical way to raise awareness can be through partnering with organizations that already provide support such as Celebrate Recovery, Alcoholics Anonymous (AA), or AL-Anon (support group for families of alcoholics). Churches can connect with these organizations by allowing them to use their building to host their meetings. Making such connections can be a great way to provide avenues for additional education and awareness to the church. It also helps the church develop a better idea of the struggles those in the local community face. Allowing these groups to meet in your facility can also provide a gateway for those who are outside of the church to connect with the church family in a meaningful way.

This team approach to mental health issues is beneficial because the burden is shared among many so that no single pastor or leader constantly bears the entire pastoral counseling load. No individual is capable of being sufficiently competent to deal with every issue every person is facing. Attempting to bear the burdens of the entire church congregation alone will result in your pastoral exhaustion and even burnout. Understanding the importance of referral is all part of taking care of yourself and your congregation. It benefits both, which helps both in the long-term.

CONNECTING CHURCHES WITH MENTAL HEALTH RESOURCES

A healthy church community will be able to effectively handle a wide variety of mental health issues; however, there are certain cases where extra support will be required. Having an awareness of what those situations are and having a plan in place for how to handle them is crucial in promoting mental health. The most obvious circumstances that require extra support are those involving serious mental health issues. As already stated, serious issues such as bipolar disorder, anxiety, depression, schizophrenia, or suicidality are just a few of many issues that can benefit greatly from professional attention. One of the problems that often arises in these cases is that the individual is reluctant to pursue proper support. Therefore educating the church community about mental health issues is so important, it increases the likelihood of being aware of the needs of people around us.

When a pastor provides counseling, remembering the value of a team approach with no star players is key to meeting congregational needs ethically. Tangibly, this means making the decision to refer to a professional counselor at times. This means understanding the pride that drives pastors to serve out of the expectation that as pastor it is their responsibility even though there are others more equipped to work with the specific issues. Walking with someone through a severe mental illness is not a solo task. Humbly serving well includes being willing to work within a community that includes pastors, professionals, and others who come together to collaboratively support the needs of the congregation.

The decision to refer someone to a mental health professional can be an incredibly difficult one, and it can be a humbling experience for a pastor. This compounded by the frequent use of clinical jargon and their legally binding agreement for professional counselors to protect the privacy of their clients, referring can also feel like abandonment. In reality, even though it may be a difficult decision, sometimes referring may be in the best interest of the individual. Letting go of our own need to feel important in the process and the supporting from the sidelines can make an enormous difference both in the care the individual receives and in enabling pastors and leaders to take care of themselves. This is a difficult lesson to learn but one that is incredibly freeing and enables the well-disciplined person to work with a greater number of people more effectively.

Referring to mental health support may seem like the church is not providing support, but this is not the case. Seeing a mental health professional is never as effective if the individual does not have a supportive pastor and community. Coming together is more than just a "good idea" though; in Galatians 6:2 Paul wrote, "Bear one another's burdens, and thereby fulfill the law of Christ." Coming together as a congregation and supporting one another through struggles is part of the church's role.

SUPPORTING THE NEEDS OF THE LOCAL COMMUNITY

Being equipped to support mental health issues presents churches with a unique opportunity to minister to the world. From Bible times to now, mental health issues have been a common experience. It is not uncommon for people to look to the church for support. That is why it is so critical that the church respond well to people who come through their doors in pain. Responding well is partially about having a well-developed approach to supporting those with mental illnesses and partially about a willingness to accept the person without judgment. In its approach to mental issues, the hope of the church is that people who look to God's people for mental health support would find much more and stay in the church even after they have found relief from their struggles.

One of the most important connections between the way the church and the world relate through mental health issues is through the opportunity afforded the church in supporting their local community. Individuals dealing with mental issues often look to churches to find support. The church can be a nonthreatening place to pursue support. The willingness people exhibit in looking to churches for support further emphasizes the importance of churches' preparedness in having a plan to support those struggling with mental issues. If people are received well, they stay; if not they move on.

Pastors and church leaders often set the tone for the congregation in how mental issues are perceived and the way individuals experiencing them are treated. Taking the time to pursue knowledge about mental issues and the ways they are treated becomes a key part of being able to effectively support those experiencing them. The moment someone walks through the doors of the church and says, "I've hit rock bottom, I can't go lower, and I've lost everything as a result of my alcohol addiction," it is too late to develop a plan. Therefore, being prepared to support them and directly connect them with resources is vital.

Connecting individuals with support and resources is not the only role of the church. The relationship should not stop after connecting the individual with specific resources. This is where having a well-connected community within the church can also enable the person to connect with someone in the church who is familiar with the issue they are working with and can provide specific support to the individual. Providing support to individuals in this way not only ensures they get the help they need, but it also begins to let them be a part of a community in which they can thrive.

A strong community is secondary to the truth that the church has to offer people. At its heart, the thing that the church truly has to offer those both in and outside of its doors is the hope of the gospel. Viktor Frankl was a Jewish psychiatrist who survived a concentration camp during WWII. In his book *Man's Search for Meaning,* he stated that a man with a "why" can survive any "what."[3] The hope that the church has to offer is a "why" that goes beyond temporary experience. When the church is equipped to handle it and support the mental health needs of those who walk through their doors, it greatly increases the likelihood that the individual will feel supported and become a part of the community.

MENTAL HEALTH AND THE GOSPEL

The worldwide prevalence of mental health issues provides the church with an incredible opportunity to be salt and light for Christ. Not only can the church directly support individuals who are dealing with mental issues, the church can provide a place for people to belong and find healing. The only way the church will effectively be able to do that is being educated about mental illness and how it relates to their beliefs so that they can approach it from a nonjudgmental standpoint that does not ostracize people who are experiencing it.

While welcoming people experiencing mental illnesses does open the door to proclaiming the gospel, it does not mean that the first statement of the church to those experiencing mental illness should be to explain away their issues and present the gospel. If you find someone who is physically dehydrated, your first response is to give them some water, not tell them about Christ, the living water. Starting with the gospel before working to meet their individual needs invalidates their experiences and their struggles. A big part of witnessing through mental health issues is meeting the felt needs of the individual before focusing on their spiritual needs.

This is the basis of a holistic view of the individual. Having a holistic view of the individual is essential in meeting all their needs. Meeting all an individual's needs starts with discovering what their needs are. That is why choosing to listen and care for the individual is the key and the first step in the process supporting those experiencing mental illnesses. When people feel understood and cared for holistically, they will not only recover more quickly, but they are also more likely to be receptive to receiving the good news of the gospel.

The value of the hope that transcends circumstances offered by the gospel for those struggling with mental issues cannot be emphasized enough. In order for it to be well received, it cannot be presented in a superficial "choose this and all your problems will be gone" way. A big part of the hope of the gospel comes from having a purpose that extends beyond personal wants and desires of the individual. As someone who has already experienced this hope, it is important to remember that telling someone to accept or remember the hope of the gospel will not instantly resolve their mental health issues. On the contrary, presenting the gospel in that way is actually more likely to be detrimental than beneficial for both believers and nonbelievers. For example, the experience of depression is marked by a significant loss of enthusiasm, motivation, and hope over a period of time. Telling a clinically depressed person to receive or remember the message of the gospel in order to find hope and resolve their problems will likely not be received. For them to hear the message of the gospel, they have to begin dealing with their depression so that they can actually begin to understand and interact with it.

Knowing the significance of how mental health issues affect people's function is a big part of why the church needs to be informed about these issues. This is where the value of acknowledging mental health issues from the pulpit in the church is so important. The recognition of the legitimacy of mental health issues reduces the stigma people experiencing them feel and decreases the likelihood that they will feel as though they do not belong in the church. It also opens the door to people feeling as though it is acceptable for them to openly talk about their experiences.

The presence of open dialogue around mental health issues within the church not only raises awareness of the issues and needs of the church as a whole, but it also opens the door to having conversations about how faith relates to mental health struggles. This is important not only because members of the church will experience mental health issues regardless of whether or not they openly discuss them, but also because talking about them gives them the opportunity to actually begin the process of healing. The gospel has high potential to be incredibly meaningful to those in the church experiencing mental health issues. The opportunity for this meaning starts with leaders who are willing to start conversations and lead by example.

PRACTICAL SKILLS

Much of this chapter has focused on the attitude that churches should strive for an environment that is supportive for those experiencing mental health issues. This final section transitions into a practical look at tools that can be utilized by pastors, church leaders, and members alike to care for the needs of their congregation. All these skills build on the foundation of listening.

Being a good listener does not require a mental health degree; it requires intentionality and a lot of practice. It also requires a willingness to humbly approach conversations in order to listen and understand rather than to impress or convince. At the most basic level, listening comes down to a willingness to be an ear, not a mouth. All other skills and practices discussed below build on the foundation of choosing to listen before talking. Listening first is essential because it is through the act of listening that the speaker is honored and valued by the listener. It is also only through listening that it is even possible to begin to understand someone else's experience.

For pastors and church leadership, the likelihood of being approached by people who are dealing with mental illness is likely to be a weekly or even daily experience. Being equipped to listen well is an incredibly important skill. In working to develop that skill, one of the most important things to remember is the importance of humility. A humble approach to listening involves using basic counseling skills to be present with and listen to the individual in a way that affirms their inherent value and dignity. Listening in this way causes people to feel not only heard but understood.

While all the following basic counseling skills are useful in working with those who are experiencing mental illnesses, they should be considered useful tools for interacting with anyone. Fundamentally, basic counseling skills involve being attentive to the person both verbally and nonverbally. They involve listening well to hear what is said and to understand what is meant by the speaker. There are three components of basic counseling skills: attending, active listening, and reflecting. When they are used together in conversation, the speaker feels seen, heard, and understood.

ATTENDING

By definition, being attentive to someone indicates that you are paying close attention to them. In a conversation, an attentive person is not thinking about what they are doing tomorrow or what is for dinner. They are listening to every word that is spoken. It is about more than what is said: it involves paying attention to the way the person sits, the speed at which they are talking, and tracking how the parts of the conversation come together to form a whole. However, being attentive is about more than paying attention; it is also about the presence that the listener brings to the room. This means setting distractions aside and focusing wholly on the person. It can mean physically leaning forward into the conversation in a way that communicates "I am engaged, and I value you and the time that we are spending together." The goal of being attentive in conversation is to bring a tangible assurance to the person being counseled that the counselor has shown up to the conversation and is mentally engaged.

ACTIVE LISTENING

As with attending, active listening is used by counselors in every counseling session. It is simply the verbal illustration to the person being counseled that the counselor is engaged in the listening process. There is an internal and external component to accomplishing this effectively. Internally, as a listener, active listening involves working to be aware of personal beliefs and values to understand the impact it may have on the way we understand what is spoken. The internal part of active listening requires taking the time to explore your own beliefs and values so that when issues come up in conversation that create internal tension, it is not jarring.

The other side of active listening is the external side. This is the verbal, tangible way that the listener communicates to the speaker that they are actively tracking the conversation. Simply put, this part of active listening involves asserting the appropriately timed word such as "yeah" or "mm-hmm" when it is appropriate. Engaging in active listening also enables the counselor to easily engage in the next basic counseling skill, reflection.

REFLECTION

Reflection is the basic counseling skill where the active listening and attending skills pay off. Reflection involves listening to what was said by the person, internally synthesizing it to capture its essence, and then briefly paraphrasing it back to them. The purpose of the reflection in listening is twofold. First, it illustrates that as a listener you were attentive and engaged in listening to what was being communicated. Second, it can deepen the understanding of the topic for both the speaker and the listener by lending a different perspective on what was spoken and giving the speaker a chance to clarify what was misunderstood or misrepresented. Reflection is also incredibly valuable because it validates the experience of the speaker.

EMPATHY VERSUS SYMPATHY

Before leaving the practical skills section, there is a common mistake that deserves some attention: failing to establish a clear differentiation between sympathy and empathy. This is one area of confusion people have in listening to one another. Simply put, sympathy is motivated by care of oneself and the other individual, whereas empathy is motivated primarily by care for the other person. Making a sympathetic comment usually helps the speaker feel better, not the person spoken to. Sympathetic comments usually start with an "I am sorry" and also include a "But it really is not that bad, right?" An empathetic comment on the other hand, typically validates the person receiving the comment and requires the person giving it to sit with the discomfort of allowing the other person to sit in their experience of the pain. Empathetic comments usually sound more like "That does sound really painful and difficult." They affirm the statement of the speaker and do not look for a silver lining. A sympathetic comment often simply results in the receiver feeling worse off than they did before. In contrast the cost of the empathetic comment is paid by the caring individual who made the comment, and they must as a result learn to sit within their own discomfort and powerlessness to change the other's situation.

CONCLUSION

Mental illness is a prevalent issue everywhere there are people, and the church is no exception. The existence of mental health issues provides the church with an incredible opportunity to serve the people on their congregation and to be a light in their local community. This requires that they willingly acknowledge the reality and legitimacy of mental health issues, and they actively work to be prepared to support people who are experiencing them in a holistic way: physically, mentally, emotionally, and spiritually. In sum, this means that pastors and church leaders should pursue some education or training in basic counseling skills and should also strive to be connected to local mental health resources. They should work to provide the members of their church with basic knowledge and education regarding mental health issues. They should also look for opportunities to connect and support the ministries and organizations that help those who have mental health needs. And finally, the topic of mental health issues cannot be taboo. When the church comes together in community and openly discusses mental health issues and supports those dealing with them, it enables them to shine a light into their communities that has the potential to change lives.

NOTES

1. Millard J. Erickson, *Christian Theology* (Grand Rapids: Baker, 2013), 473.

2. Jane E. Myers and Thomas J. Sweeney, "Wellness Counseling: The Evidence Base for Practice," *Journal of Counseling and Development* 86, No. 4 (2008): 482-93.

3. Viktor E. Frankl, *Man's Search for Meaning* (New York: Simon and Schuster, 1985), 108.

Ministering to the Long-Term Single and the Childless

KELLI WORRALL

Recent statistics in North America tell two important stories, one about our general society and a second about the church. The first tale describes a society in which singleness and childlessness are both on the rise. In 2018, the United States Census Bureau reported that over 70 percent of adults 18–34 were single, a dramatic increase from 41 percent in 1978.[1] This surge in singleness is likely the result of multiple cultural factors: increasing educational and employment opportunities for both men and women, a desire to pay off debt and gain financial security before tying the knot, a more casual approach to sexual intimacy outside of marriage, the popularity of cohabitation, and a prevalent determination to not make a mistake that will end in divorce—to name a few.

This societal increase in singleness goes hand in hand with a rise in childlessness. In 2017, the percentage of adults in the United States who were living without children had climbed to over 71 percent.[2] Of course, the reasons that North American couples remain childless are also varied and go beyond merely the postponement of marriage. To begin with, an increasing number of Americans are remaining childless by choice, choosing instead to focus on careers and other passions.[3] In addition, the number of couples who struggle with infertility—although down slightly from 2002—was still over 14 percent in 2015.[4]

It is worth noting, as well, that these same trends of a growing single and child-less population can also be observed worldwide and are only expected to continue.[5] These figures provide a descriptive snapshot of our present cultural moment while also foreshadowing a likely trajectory for future generations.

WHO'S IN CHURCH?

In North America, at least, other recent statistics tell a second, parallel story—that of a church where (according to a 2017 study by the Barna Group) only 23 percent of active, churchgoing adults are single.[6] Specific data is unavailable on the percentage of churchgoing adults who remain childless, but it's safe to say that it is far less than the 71 percent represented in the population as a whole. These numbers simply confirm what most of us see when we look around our churches every week: a high proportion of young families, children, and youth, and an underrepresented population of single adults and couples without kids.

This discrepancy is also reflected in the way our churches prioritize everything from staffing to space designation to distribution of funds. In 2014, *Christianity Today* surveyed 2,200 churches from across the United States regarding their budgetary allocations. In the "Program Costs" category, children's and youth ministry received on average the largest piece of the pie at 4 percent of the overall budget.[7] That was double what is commonly earmarked for adult or worship ministry.

David Kinnaman, president of the Barna Group, articulates the rationale behind this heavy focus on children's ministry. "Many religious workers assume that parenthood motivates people to return to their spiritual traditions and to church attendance. This perspective is especially common when it comes to justifying the frequent disengagement among young adults. Sometimes faith leaders go so far as to simply wait for parenthood to occur, when they figure the 'real work' of ministry can begin."[8]

This Barna Group survey, however, also showed that "having children is not an automatic faith-starter for most adults."[9] Many other factors, such as family background and personal faith experiences, have an impact on the choices that young adults make regarding church participation and faith engagement. So while, of course, children's and youth ministry should be an important focus of the church, we ought not unduly target the "young family" demographic. In fact, the Barna study seems to indicate that once young people begin to have children, many of them become so consumed with the work of parenting that faith matters actually take a back seat.[10]

Conversely and ironically, that same Barna survey of single adults revealed a population that is ripe for the harvest. Take the following statistics, for example: "The majority of singles who are not active in or committed to a church are searching for meaning and purpose in life (55%)."[11] Fifty percent of them admit to having emotional pain that they would like to resolve.[12] Forty-five percent of them feel as if something is missing in their lives.[13] Almost two-thirds (65%) are "looking for ways to improve themselves."[14] And perhaps most poignantly, almost one-quarter of them (23%) say that they would be "motivated to go to church if they simply knew that anyone would be welcomed into the church community."[15]

Thus, we have established these important facts:

- Single and childless adults make up a majority of the adult population in the United States (and a growing population around the world).

- The population of most of our churches does not reflect this reality.

- The priorities of most of our churches (staffing, funding, programming, etc.) do not demonstrate a thoughtful, intentional, and effective plan to reach and serve this population.

- Individuals are a part of this population for a myriad of reasons. Adults may be single because of choice or circumstances, divorce, or widowhood. Some would like to be married; others would not. Similarly, couples may be childless by choice. They may be waiting to start a family. They may be struggling with infertility. Or they may have even lost a child. We should not assume a singular, universal narrative.

With this foundational understanding of the cultural and ecclesiastical status quo and presumptive future trends, let us turn to Scripture for a clear understanding of God's view on marriage, singleness, and childbearing.

TOWARD A THEOLOGY OF SINGLENESS, MARRIAGE, AND PROCREATION

Throughout our culture, inaccurate and damaging messages abound regarding the life and status of a single person. Our movies proclaim that a significant other will "complete us," implying that we are not a full person until we find the elusive "one." Popular music idolizes and solicits a version of "love" that is self-satisfying and centers on sex. Advertisements bombard us with products that promise to increase our attractiveness and images by which we can assess our own marital prospects. Indeed, we are so obsessed with and confused about all these things that the very definition of "marriage" has become a matter of political debate.

The pervasiveness of these messages makes it all the more imperative that the church provide a clear voice of truth in this area. Unfortunately, though—perhaps in our well-intentioned efforts to esteem marriage and family—we too often add our own offhanded remarks to the mix, sending strong, though certainly unintended, statements to the unmarried and childless among us. A spouse might be called one's "better half" as though without a partner a person cannot be whole. We claim that parenthood is the "*highest* calling" or that children are "the *greatest* blessing from the Lord," not so subtly sending the message that the couple without children must be "deficiently blessed" or that whatever service God has called a childless adult to must be something "less than" that parent down the row.

Rather than perpetuate the problem, let us commit to being a church that communicates a thorough and biblical understanding of singleness, marriage, procreation, and the community of Christ. Toward that end, we will examine several pertinent passages.

CREATION

In our teachings about marriage and family, we go to the beginning of God's Word to establish our foundation. In Genesis 1, God made humankind in His own image and likeness—to rule over all other creatures (Gen. 1:26). He created both male and female (Gen. 1:27), and He blessed them, saying: "Be fruitful and multiply, and fill the earth, and subdue it" (v. 28). God declared His creation "good."

In Genesis 2, we find a different description of the union between Adam and Eve. In verse 18, God made an interesting pronouncement about His own creation. "Then the LORD God said, 'It is not good for the man to be alone.'" After He had declared every other created entity to be "good," this one thing (man's aloneness) was decidedly *not*. Immediately, God also announced His solution: "I will make him a helper suitable for him." Then, out of the man's rib, God made a woman (Gen. 2:22).

Surely, there is much to learn about God's intention and design for marriage in the study of these two chapters. We can dig into the Hebrew meaning of "suitable helper" to understand the complementary nature of the partnership. We can also study the leave-and-cleave command (Gen. 2:24) to explain the importance of developing a "stronghold" around the union.

However, in his book *Redeeming Singleness*, Barry Danylak makes some important observations about the Genesis account that also help us correctly identify the place of singleness and childlessness in the human experience. First, Danylak points out the different emphases given in chapter 1 versus chapter 2. In Genesis 1, he notes, marriage is implied with the creation of both man and woman, but "marriage" itself is not explicitly named. Also, in Genesis 1, the commission to "be fruitful and multiply" and fill the earth is stated. Interestingly, though, this instruction to procreate is actually *first* given to the sea creatures and birds on the fifth day of creation (Gen. 1:22) and, therefore, precedes any mention of marriage. Danylak explains the significance:

> The procreative mandate is given even *before* human beings are created. It is woven into the very fabric of the created order that God fashioned before human beings were on the earth. What differentiates human beings from the rest of the animal kingdom is not found in the reproductive commission but in the distinctive that they were created in the *image of God* and have an additional mandate to subdue the earth and have dominion over it.[16]

In comparison, the Genesis 2 account actually makes no mention of the act of procreation. Instead, in this chapter, the motivation for the creation of Eve is God's assessment that "it is not good for the man to be alone," so the LORD God makes a "helper suitable for him" (Gen. 2:18). Here, the purpose for the union between Adam and Eve seems to be companionship and support.

According to Danylak, the distinction between these accounts in Genesis 1 and 2 provides a key footing for how we should think about singleness and childlessness, as well as marriage and procreation. "The separation of the two incidents perhaps serves to highlight the author's point that marriage was intended to provide *more* than the mere need to procreate legitimate heirs; it was also the foundation of the new institution of relational support in the human family unit."[17]

In summary, from the creation account, we see the initial command to reproduce—given to *all* of creation, including man and woman. The significance of this procreation mandate will be further developed later in this chapter.

We also see that God created human beings to have fellowship with Him and with one another. As K. A. Matthews writes, "Isolation is not the divine norm for human beings; community is the creation of God."[18] Certainly, this communion can be accomplished in the context of marriage and family. But while marriage as an institution is a mandate in Genesis, entering into a marriage is not mandated for every individual; nor does being married guarantee intimacy with one's partner. The community that God desired to provide can and should also be accomplished in the church.

ADAM AND EVE

The remaining biblical narrative of Adam and Eve further informs our understanding of marriage, singleness, and the role of offspring in the plan of God. In Genesis 3, the fall of Adam and Eve resulted in shame and blame and a severing of communion.

In response, God pronounced a curse on His creation, a curse in which procreation factored significantly. For Adam, the ground would now only produce fruit as a result of his excruciating toil. For Eve, the act of childbirth would now come with pain. And God's judgment on the serpent was hostility between his offspring and the woman's, a hostility that would culminate in Christ crushing sin and death on the cross.

Genesis 4 records the conflict between Adam and Eve's offspring—Cain and his brother Abel—who argued over the acceptability of their respective offerings. The writer of Genesis describes the births of Cain and of Seth somewhat differently.

> Now the man had relations with his wife Eve, and she conceived and gave birth to Cain, and she said, "I have obtained a male child with the help of the LORD." (Gen. 4:1)

> Adam had relations with his wife again; and she gave birth to a son, and named him Seth, for, she said, "God has appointed me another child in place of Abel, because Cain killed him." (Gen. 4:25)

Both times Eve bears a son, "but in the two instances the subject, verb, and object are different."[19] On the occasion of Cain's birth, Eve is the subject of the sentence. "I have obtained a male child." *She* is the actor. The Lord's role is to provide her with assistance.

The account of Seth's birth, however, seems to show a growing understanding of divine sovereignty. Finding this significant, Danylak writes, "This time Eve acknowledges that *God* appointed another offspring."[20] The shift is striking. This time *God* is the subject. He is the mover, the actor, the one in control. And through this child, God will ultimately provide His own Son.

This theme of God alone being the provider of offspring is a central one throughout the book of Genesis and, indeed, the Old Testament as a whole. Repeatedly, God is shown to be the one who opens and closes the womb for His glory, as the outworking of His good plan for His people. Nowhere is this more clear than in His covenant with Abraham.

THE COVENANTS AND ISRAEL

In Genesis 11, we are introduced to Abram (Abraham) and his wife, Sarai (Sarah). In the Hebrew narrative, the way in which a character is first described is key to understanding that character's importance to the story. The first thing we are told about Sarai is that she was unable to conceive (Gen. 11:30).

Immediately following their introduction, Genesis 12 records the call of Abram.

God instructed him to leave his country and his people and go to a new land that God would reveal. This calling came with divine promises, the first of which was progeny. God would make of Abram a great nation that would bless the earth and enjoy God's protection. The second part of the promise was land, which this people would call home.

The fulfillment of these promises, the Abrahamic covenant, did not happen immediately, however. Sarai remained barren, even as God provided land (Gen. 13) and reaffirmed His covenant commitment to Abram. In Genesis 15, Abram expressed his impatience and concern to the Lord.

> Abram said, "Lord GOD, what will You give me, since I am childless, and the heir of my house is Eliezer of Damascus?" Abram also said, "Since You have given me no son, one who has been born in my house is my heir." (Gen. 15:2–3)

In response, God reiterated His promise and His plan—to provide a blood heir for Abram and offspring as numerous as the stars (Gen. 15:4–5), and Abram's immediate response was faith (Gen. 15:6).

Ironically, in the very next chapter, Abram listened to his desperate wife Sarai, who still blamed God for her barren state. The two devised a scheme whereby Abram finally had a son, Ishmael, through a marriage with Sarai's Egyptian maid, Hagar.

Thirteen years later—when Abram was ninety-nine years old—God again appeared to him (Gen. 17:1), reiterating His power over all, and in particular His power over the provision of offspring. After calling Abram to a life of obedience, God once again proclaimed His promises: "You will be the father of a multitude of nations" (Gen. 17:4b) and "I will give to you and to your descendants after you ... all the land of Canaan" (Gen. 17:8).

Later in Genesis 17, God spelled out His specific plan for Abraham—the birth of another son, whose name would be Isaac, and whose mother would be none other than the ninety-year-old Sarah. Soon after that (Gen. 18), Sarah was hiding in her tent and overheard the Lord and His messengers again deliver this announcement. Abraham and Sarah both had the same reaction: they laughed. "Their response underscores the fundamental point: the appointed offspring comes strictly by divine provision; it comes not in any way through the effort of Abraham and Sarah, but despite their efforts."[21]

The themes of marriage and offspring—and God's sovereignty over these matters—continue throughout the book of Genesis and the Old Testament as a whole. Abraham sent his servant to his home country to find a bride for Isaac. Rebekah was clearly the divine choice for Isaac, but she too was barren until Isaac prayed and the Lord responded by providing twins (Gen. 25:21, 24). God promised to continue His covenant relationship with Isaac's son Jacob, providing him with offspring as numerous as the dust, and land to the north, south, east, and west (Gen. 28:13b–15 and 35:10b–12). Providentially, Jacob's wife Rachel, like Rebekah before her, was also barren apart from God's provision.

Later, in Moses's time, the Sinai covenant was given, and spelled out for the Israelites (1) their obligations, (2) God's curses if they turned away from Him, and (3) God's blessings if they obeyed (Ex. 19 and 20; Deut. 28). Marriage and procreation factored into all three of these sections of the "treaty." Notably, *not* included in the stipulations was a command that one must marry or have children. In the blessings section, children were listed as a main aspect of God's provision and reward (Deut. 28:1–4). On the other hand, barrenness was included as one of the curses if one did not obey the voice of the Lord (Deut. 28:15–18).

Danylak draws this conclusion:

> It is thus not difficult to see why it was of utmost importance for each Israelite to marry and beget offspring, for offspring (and thus also marriage) were the *sine qua non* of the individual reception of the covenantal blessings of Sinai. To marry and have offspring was, to an individual, a mark of God's covenantal blessing, and by extension a validation of his obedience to the covenant stipulations. Conversely, to be devoid of children with the result of having one's name "blotted out" of Israel was a mark of his subjection to the covenant curses and by implication a sentence of divine disapproval.[22]

The Davidic covenant (2 Sam. 7) contained several similarities to the Abrahamic. God promised David a great name, a house, descendants, and a kingdom. However, the focus had narrowed from the general blessing of many offspring, to a specific kingdom with messianic foreshadowing.

In summary, during the time of the covenants, God was building His chosen people through the act of procreation. Therefore, being married and having offspring was of utmost importance and a primary way in which God blessed His people.

Also central to these accounts is the truth that human beings do not have ultimate control over their own fertility and progeny. God alone opens and closes the womb for His good purposes.

ISAIAH

The prophecy of Isaiah is full of significant offspring references, beginning with the second verse, where the Lord spoke of His people as "sons I have raised and brought up," sons who have revolted against Him (Isa. 1:2). The main thrust of chapters 1–6 is an indictment of Judah for its failure to obey the commandments of the law, and a part of their judgment would be widowhood and barrenness (3:25–4:1).

To this people, Isaiah was called (Isa. 6). Immediately following the account of his call, we find the narrative of his prophetic ministry to King Ahaz (Isa. 7–12), which includes several descriptions of the child who would one day bring hope. "Behold, the virgin will conceive and give birth to a son, and she will name Him Immanuel" (Isa. 7:14). "For a Child will be born to us, a Son will be given to us . . ." (Isa. 9:6). Over and over, we see the juxtaposition of condemnation and hope—with offspring being central to both.

Later in the book of Isaiah, we find the extended prophecy of the Suffering Servant. The beautiful and beloved passage in Isaiah 53 is central to this.

> But He was pierced for our offenses,
> He was crushed for our wrongdoings;
> The punishment for our well-being was laid upon Him,
> And by His wounds we are healed. (v. 5)

Yet—although He was pierced and crushed—the prophet proclaimed that the Servant would be "lifted up" and "exalted" (Isa. 52:13). The "good pleasure of the LORD will prosper in His hand," and "He will see His offspring" (Isa. 53:10). Michael Rydelnik and James Spencer explain: "Although He was despised and forsaken of men (53:3), the Servant is promised that He will see His offspring (lit., 'His seed'). Normally this term refers to physical progeny, but the context about rejection and the timing of this after His death indicates that the word 'seed' should be taken figuratively for 'followers' (as it is used in Is 57:4)."[23] The Servant would be blessed with *spiritual* offspring as a result of His atoning death. Importantly, this forecasts a broadening view of the growth of God's people, which will no longer happen through progeny alone.

Isaiah chapters 54 and 56 reinforce this point. Isaiah 54 employs the imagery of a single and barren woman who would have offspring more numerous than one married. This passage was addressed to Zion, so "the promise is that God will enlarge and repopulate the land of Israel. . . . Those who had no hope will now experience abundant blessing."[24]

In Isaiah 56, the promise is expanded to the "foreigner" and the "eunuch."

For this is what the LORD says:

> "To the eunuchs who keep My Sabbaths,
> And choose what pleases Me,
> And hold firmly to My covenant,
> To them I will give in My house and within My walls a memorial,
> And a name better than that of sons and daughters;
> I will give them an everlasting name which will not be eliminated.

> Also the foreigners who join themselves to the LORD,
> To attend to His service and to love the name of the LORD,
> To be His servants, every one who keeps the Sabbath so as not to profane it,
> And holds firmly to My covenant;
> Even those I will bring to My holy mountain,
> And make them joyful in My house of prayer.
> Their burnt offerings and their sacrifices will be acceptable on My altar;
> For My house will be called a house of prayer for all the peoples." (vv. 4–7)

Here the prophet indicated that ethnicity and progeny would no longer be the means by which people would receive the Lord's blessing. Instead, individuals would be required to "love the name of the LORD" and "join themselves to [Him]." To the eunuchs who do so, the Lord promised "a name better than that of sons and daughters . . . an everlasting name which will not be eliminated" (Isa. 56:5).

JESUS

When we come to the New Testament, Jesus Himself clearly taught that His followers were joined to Him—not by physical procreation as emphasized in the Old Testament, but by spiritual rebirth. When Nicodemus the Pharisee came to Jesus by night, Jesus told him, "Truly, truly, I say to you, unless someone is born again he cannot see the kingdom of God" (John 3:3). This was a birth of the water and the Spirit—not a biological birth—a difficult and confusing shift for a devout Jew like Nicodemus to understand.

In Matthew 12, Jesus redefined "family" when His own mother and brothers asked to see Him. He responded: "Who is My mother, and who are My brothers?" Then He gestured to His disciples and said, "Behold: My mother and My brothers! For whoever does the will of My Father who is in heaven, he is My brother, and sister, and mother" (Matt. 12:49–50). Certainly, Jesus loved His mother and His brothers. We see that love demonstrated most profoundly when He expressed His care for Mary from the cross (John 19:26–27). But in Matthew 12, Jesus made His focus clear. It was not on physical, familial relationships—but on the kingdom of God.

In Mark 10, Jesus called His disciples to the same kingdom priorities. After His conversation with the rich young man, Jesus proclaimed to His disciples how difficult it was for the rich to enter the kingdom of God. Following Christ must take precedent over the accumulation of wealth. His disciples asked: "Then who can be saved?" (Mark 10:26). And Peter reminded Him of their devotion: "Behold, we have left everything and have followed You" (v. 28). Jesus responded: "Truly I say to you, there is no one who has left house or brothers or sisters or mother or father or children or farms, for My sake and for the gospel's sake, but that he will receive a hundred times as much now in the present age, houses and brothers and sisters and mothers and children and farms, along with persecutions; and in the age to come, eternal life" (vv. 29–30). Following Christ must also take precedent over biological family. But Jesus added a promise—the promise of intimate relationships, a home, and (notably) persecution. Although the road of discipleship would have its struggles, the familial sense of intimacy and home would be regained one hundredfold.

Matthew 19 begins with a conversation between Jesus and the Pharisees regarding marriage and divorce. When the Pharisees inquired about a lawful reason for divorce, Jesus appealed to Genesis and reiterated the high and lasting commitment required of the marriage union, except in the case of immorality. In response to this strict teaching, the disciples proclaimed: "If the relationship of the man with his wife is like this, it is better not to marry" (Matt. 19:10). Jesus replied that there were some "eunuchs" who were thus from birth and others who had been made so by men, against their will. The disciples would have been familiar with both of these types. But Jesus added a third: those who had made themselves eunuchs—by choice—for the sake of the kingdom of heaven, thus approving of His followers who would renounce marriage for the sake of serving Him.

A final teaching of Jesus on the subject of marriage is found in Matthew 22:23–33. In this passage, the Sadducees had come to Him, asking about the state of marriage in the resurrection. Their question regarding seven brothers who all married the same woman in turn was meant to be preposterous and was intended as a trap. But Jesus responded: "You are mistaken, since you do not understand the Scriptures nor the power of God. For in the resurrection they neither marry nor are given in marriage, but are like angels in heaven" (vv. 29–30). And so we learn that marriage is a temporary and earthly institution, but the kingdom of God will last forever.

Of course, all of Jesus' teaching related to the subject of singleness can be understood in light of the fact that Christ Himself remained single throughout His life and had no physical offspring to call His own.

PAUL

The apostle Paul was also single and without physical offspring, and he included in his writings several significant statements that further inform our theology of singleness and procreation.

To begin with, in 1 Corinthians 4:14–15, Paul referred to himself—single and childless—as a spiritual father to the Corinthian church. "I do not write these things to shame you," he writes, "but to admonish you as my beloved children. For if you were to have countless tutors in Christ, yet you would not have many fathers, for in Christ Jesus I became your father through the gospel." The task of "parenting" (mentoring, teaching, admonishing) the next generation to be faithful followers of Christ should not fall *only* to biological mothers and fathers. Rather, all of us who are more mature in the faith play an essential part. (See also Titus 2:1–8.)

Second, in Galatians 3, Paul argued quite severely with his Galatian readers that salvation does not come through progeny or circumcision or the law—but by faith. In verse 7 he says: "It is those who are of faith who are sons of Abraham" (Gal. 3:7). And again, later in the chapter, he writes: "For you are all sons and daughters of God through faith in Christ Jesus. . . . And if you belong to Christ, then you are Abraham's descendants, heirs according to promise" (Gal. 3:26, 29). In other words, the Old Testament blessing that was passed through physical descendants was no longer the means that God would use to grow His people. It is through faith in Christ alone that we now are called "sons" and "daughters."

In his first letter to Timothy, Paul makes a curious statement that does seem, on the surface, to connect salvation and progeny with a surprising twist. The oft-misunderstood 1 Timothy 2:15 reads: "But women will be preserved [the NIV uses "saved"] through childbirth— if they continue in faith, love, and sanctity, with moderation." The limited space of this chapter does not allow for a thorough analysis of this much-debated verse. However, suffice it to say that Paul is here addressing the dangerous deception of particular false teachers who forbid people to marry (1 Tim. 4:3). Paul is affirming the value of family and the woman's significant role; he is *not* resigning them only to this task, nor is he arguing a point of soteriology. Either of those positions would contradict what he elsewhere teaches.

Third, in his letter to the Ephesians, Paul used the imagery of adoption to describe God's relationship with believers.

> Blessed be the God and Father of our Lord Jesus Christ, who has blessed us with every spiritual blessing in the heavenly places in Christ, just as He chose us in Him before the foundation of the world, that we would be holy and blameless before Him. In love He predestined us to adoption as sons and daughters through Jesus Christ to Himself, according to the good pleasure of His will, to the praise of the glory of His grace, with which He favored us in the Beloved. (Eph. 1:3–6)

Whether married or single, the parents of many or none, God has adopted us as sons and daughters through His Son. In his commentary on Ephesians, Klyne Snodgrass writes: "The emphasis on adoption in 1:5 shows that the purpose of election is relational. God, for no other reason than that he is a loving God, chose to adopt people *into his family* through Jesus Christ. *Adoption* is family imagery used to explain the salvation experience, both present (see also Rom. 8:15; Gal. 4:5) and future (Rom. 8:23)."[25]

Finally, we have the most often quoted Pauline passage on the subject of singleness, 1 Corinthians 7. Paul begins the chapter with a strict reminder for married couples—who were undoubtedly tempted by the competing philosophies of asceticism and hedonism that were so prevalent in Corinth at that time. Paul instructed couples to honor their marital relationship and the sexual intimacy that comes with it (vv. 2–5).

Then Paul adds a significant caveat: "But this I say by way of concession, not of command. Yet I wish that all men were even as I myself am. However, each has his own gift from God, one in this way, and another in that" (1 Cor. 7:6–7).

First, Paul was *not* instructing, or even recommending, that everyone should marry or that everyone should remain single. He made that very clear in verse 6. Singleness was his preference, but he recognized that not all would have this "gift."

Second, he calls singleness a "gift" (*charisma*) from God (v. 7). This is the same word that is used in chapter 12 to describe the "manifestation of the Spirit for the common good" (1 Cor. 12:7). These gifts are not limited to what is listed there: wisdom, knowledge, faith, miracles, prophecy, tongues, and interpretation of tongues. Such a gift might last for a season, or it might be manifest for life. It is also important to understand that not all believers who are single have necessarily received this "gift"—just as not all people who have the gift of preaching (for example) preach and not all people who preach have, in fact, received this gift.

In verse 8 of 1 Corinthians 7, Paul addresses the unmarried and widows directly, telling them that "it is good for them if they remain even as I." The language is reminiscent of the creation account ("and God saw that it was good") and of God's assessment of Adam's singleness in Genesis 2:18 ("It is not good for the man to be alone"). Here, Paul is not contradicting God's valuation of Adam's aloneness, nor is he devaluing marriage. However, he *is* intimating that marriage is not the only solution for a person's aloneness—a point that he further develops in chapters 12–14.

Later in chapter 7 (vv. 25–38), Paul returns to the matter of singleness, giving his "opinion" (not a command of the Lord) that—just as the married should remain married—the unmarried should also remain single. And he gives two reasons for this position: the "present distress" and the "trouble in this life."

The exact meaning of "present distress" has been much debated. It could refer to a temporal crisis facing the Corinthian church—financial or cultural. Or it could point ahead to verses 29–31, where Paul warns his readers that "the time has been shortened." Paul may well be suggesting that there is an urgency to the kingdom mission that can best be addressed by a single person.

Finally, in verses 32–35, Paul develops his "trouble in this life" argument. He reasons that attending to the needs of a spouse and children will unavoidably divide one's attention and limit the energy that a Christ follower can give in service to the Lord and to the world.

MINISTERING TO ALL THE CHURCH'S PEOPLE

In light of what Scripture says about singleness and marriage, offspring and child-lessness, what should we do? How can our churches become a place where more singles feel valued and integral to the community? How can we better support couples who struggle (too often silently) with the pain of infertility? How do we best honor, reach, and care for all of the people God has called us to serve?

First, we ought to watch our words. Language matters, and contrary to the popular children's rhyme—"Sticks and stones may break my bones, but words can never hurt me"—words *are* powerful and they *can* hurt. Improving the way we speak about singleness and childlessness will likely need to start with the public communication of our pastors and leaders from the pulpit, but it must also permeate the "pews." We may even need to intentionally train our community on how to better speak life to one another. Here are some practical ideas to consider what we say.

- Be sensitive with the messages we send on certain holidays and occasions that are difficult for those who are hurting. For example, on Valentine's Day we might celebrate all loving relationships—not just romantic ones. On Mother's Day and Father's Day, in addition to acknowledging the mothers and the fathers, we might also honor *all* those who pour into the next generation.

- Do not inadvertently pressure single adults to get married, or childless couples to have children. Asking the "When are you going to . . ." or "Why haven't you . . ." questions are not helpful or kind.

- Similarly, avoid thoughtless jokes. For example, telling a single person, "You're so lucky you . . ." or saying to a childless couple, "You just wait until you have kids . . ." may not be funny to them.

- Do not assume we understand someone's experience or situation. Real people are complex, and life is complicated. As mentioned previously, people are single or without children for a myriad of reasons. Instead, with genuine compassion and mutual care, we should get to know the whole person.

- Do not dismiss grief. When we respond to a miscarriage by saying, "You'll just have to try again," or we try to encourage someone after a breakup by quipping, "There are lots more fish in the sea," we make light of what was likely a very painful loss. Many who are single or childless are processing an immense amount of pain—the death of a dream and the ache of unmet longings. Infertility can also place an immense amount of stress on even the strongest marriage. Each person will move through their healing journey at their own pace, so our churches should be a safe place for the hurting to grieve in their own time and for the downhearted to find hope in the only One who truly satisfies. This walking alongside might look like pastoral counseling or mentorship by well-trained laypeople or the fellowship of a small group or all of these. But, however it happens, it is an important part of caring for the body of Christ.

Second, we need to teach a proper and thorough theology of singleness, marriage, and procreation. This is another place where intentional teaching will likely need to happen. Many people in our churches have an incomplete understanding of what Scripture says about these things, and we place disproportionate value on certain life experiences based on our inadequate knowledge and our cultural biases. A sermon series may be in order. Or a class. Or at least a series of conversations. The biblical content in this chapter can be used to provide a starting place.

Third, we should examine our programs. Building on our theological foundation and biblical understanding, it is wise to revisit some key ministry questions: With whom has God called us to share the gospel? Who is our "Jerusalem"? How many single adults and childless couples live in our community? Are we reaching them effectively? Does our allocation of resources (people, money, time) properly reflect our mission to love them and disciple them in Christ?

In regard to our programming, Brian Kammerzelt, a Moody professor and author of *The Most Eligible Christian*, challenges the church to stop "stratifying ministries along relational lines under any labels."[26] Consider if it is necessary or helpful to have separate groups or classes that only "singles" or "marrieds" or "parents" can attend. To support such segregation, the argument is sometimes given that these segments of the population have different needs. They are at different stages of life. However, all human beings have the same need for fellowship. All Christ followers should be growing in their knowledge of Him and their expression of the Spirit's fruit. And the diversity within a group may actually provide more effective opportunities for members to be "iron sharpening iron" and to "carry one another's burdens." For example, a single woman may appreciate a man's help with automobile maintenance. Young parents may welcome the childcare assistance of a childless couple. And so on.

Fourth, seek out the single and the childless for their input and leadership. We ought not sideline them because of their so-called status. Professor Kammerzelt writes candidly about some of his own experiences: "Spending a life inside Christian culture, I have been asked this question ['Why are you single?'] a few times in interviews for positions of leadership. There are ministry jobs you aren't even eligible for if you are not married. Why is this? What is the fear? ... The interviewers always do their best to hide their motives. They realize the sensitive nature of what they are wanting to know. Despite sincere intentions, the game is obvious, accusatory, and degrading."[27] So, rather than viewing the unmarried and childless with suspicion, let us welcome and honor their experience and gifting and availability to serve (1 Cor. 7:32–35). Let us also keep them accountable to using their gifts for the good of the body and the work of the gospel.

Finally, let us focus our energy on cultivating what Kammerzelt calls "kingdom relationships"—relationships centered on Christ and the cross—throughout our community. "Start propagating the church as a family. **Proactively create a brotherhood and sisterhood among all believers.** Preach this message from the pulpit and at every level of ministry. From children all the way through seniors. Every church should have kingdom relationships training for every newcomer and every leader. We must choose it and protect it at all costs."[28]

May our churches be a place where all people—single and married, parents and those with no children—find a home.

NOTES

1. United States Census Bureau, "Percent Married Among 18-to 34-Year-Olds: 1978 and 2018," November 14, 2018, https://www.census.gov/library/visualizations/2018/comm/percent-married.html.

2. Emily Schondelmyer, "Fewer Married Households and More Living Alone," August 9, 2017, United States Census Bureau, https://www.census.gov/library/stories/2017/08/more-adults-living-without-children.html.

3. Centers for Disease Control and Prevention, "Key Statistics from the National Survey of Family Growth—C Listing," May 7, 2019, https://www.cdc.gov/nchs/nsfg/key_statistics/c.htm#chabitation.

4. Centers for Disease Control and Prevention, "Key Statistics from the National Survey of Family Growth—I Listing," June 20, 2017.

5. Progress of the World's Women, "Families in a Changing World," Global Fact Sheet, New York: UN Women 2019–20, PDF Document, May 31, 2020, https://www.unwomen.org/-/media/headquarters/attachments/sections/library/publications/2019/poww-2019-fact-sheet-global-en.pdf?la=en&vs=0.

6. Joyce Chiu, "A Single-Minded Church," February 9, 2017, https://www.barna.com/single-minded-church/.

7. Brant Henshaw, "How Churches Spend Their Money," Pacific Northwest Conference of the United Methodist Church, December 2, 2014, https://www.pnwumc.org/news/how-churches-spend-their-money/.

8. "Does Having Children Make Parents More Active Churchgoers?," The Barna Group, May 24, 2010, https://www.barna.com/research/does-having-children-make-parents-more-active-churchgoers/.

9. Ibid.

10. Ibid.

11. Chiu, "A Single-Minded Church."

12. Ibid.

13. Ibid.

14. Ibid.

15. Ibid.

16. Barry Danylak, *Redeeming Singleness: How the Storyline of Scripture Affirms the Single Life* (Wheaton, IL: Crossway, 2010), 26.

17. Ibid., 29.

18. K. A. Matthews, "Genesis 1–11:26," *The New American Commentary*, vol. 1A (Nashville: Broadman & Holman, 1996), Logos Bible Software, July 20, 2019, 213.

19. Danylak, *Redeeming Singleness*, 32.

20. Ibid., 33.

21. Ibid., 44.

22. Ibid., 62.

23. Michael Rydelink and James Spencer, "Isaiah," *The Moody Bible Commentary: A One-Volume Commentary on the Whole Bible* (Chicago, IL: Moody, 2014), 1090.

24. Ibid., 1091.

25. Klyne Snodgrass, *The NIV Application Commentary: Ephesians* (Grand Rapids: Zondervan, 1996), 49.

26. Brian Kammerzelt, *The Most Eligible Christian: Rescuing Our Relationships from a Dating-Obsessed Culture* (self-pub., 2020), 60.

27. Brian Kammerzelt, "FAQ: Why Are You Single?," Critique by Creating, August 16, 2012, https://critiquebycreating.com/faq-why-are-you-single-913560d81f54.

28. Kammerzelt, *The Most Eligible Christian*, 59.

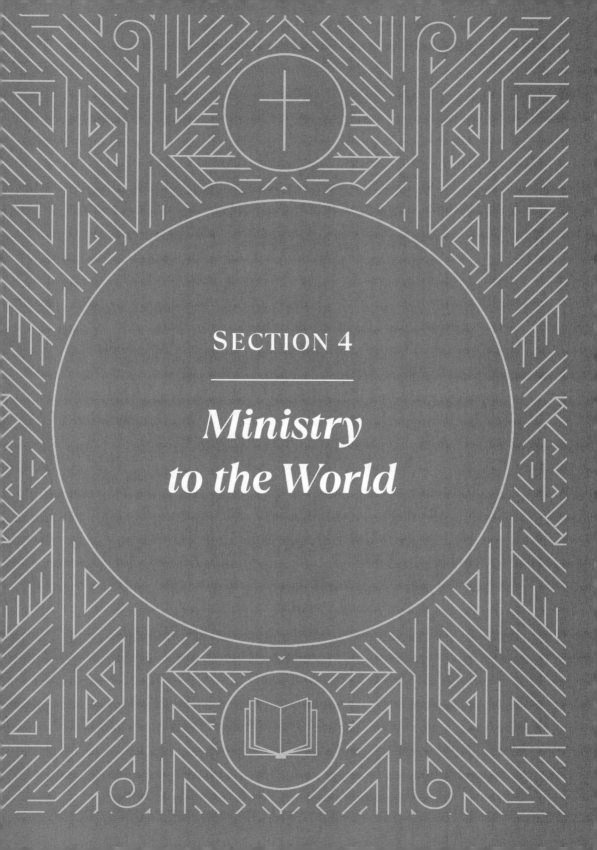

SECTION 4

Ministry to the World

The Gospel Call to the World

KERWIN A. RODRIGUEZ

The church is called to make the gospel known to all people. The Scriptures confirm that God's desire is for all the world to know and worship Him. In His infinite wisdom and grace, He has called the church to proclaim the good news that Jesus is Lord and Savior of the world. Most practicing Christians agree that "being a witness for Jesus" is part of the Christian faith. Yet, many are hesitant to evangelize or fail to take part in missional activities.[1] Despite this hesitancy, the twenty-first century has presented the church with unique challenges and opportunities to faithfully take up this call.

GOD AND THE NATIONS

God's desire for the nations is a consistent thread that runs through all of Scripture. After God scattered the people of Babel across the earth (Gen. 11), He made a covenant with Abram and promised that he would become a great and blessed nation and that, through Abram, "all the families of the earth [would] be blessed" (Gen. 12:3). This promise was important for the Israelites (as well as us) to remember, since the nations were regularly objects of God's wrath rather than God's blessing during much of the Old Testament. For much of Israel's history, she is at war with the nations, under judgment for following after the nations, or being held in captivity by those nations. Most of the prophets look forward to the day of the Lord when the nations will be punished for their wickedness (Joel 3:9; Obad. 1:6; Zeph. 3:6–8).

But there is also something else anticipated by the biblical authors. The psalmists and prophets look forward to the day when "all the ends of the earth will remember and turn to the LORD, and all the families of the nations will worship before [Him]" (Ps. 22:27). According to the Psalms, this reality is proof that there is none like the Lord. "There is no one like You among the gods, O Lord. . . . All nations whom You have made shall come and worship before You, O Lord, and they will glorify Your name" (Ps. 86:8–9). The Lord is worthy to be praised, not just by Israel, but also by all nations and all peoples (Pss. 72:17; 67:2–7).

In Psalm 117, the psalmist invites the nations to praise the Lord because of His lovingkindness (*hesed*). This word is sometimes translated as "covenant loyalty" and is related to God's faithfulness to His people, Israel. But in this short psalm, God's covenant loyalty is the reason for all peoples to praise Him. It is as if the psalmist anticipates a future day when those outside of the covenant people of Israel will be saved and become recipients of His lovingkindness.

The prophets also anticipate a future when the God of Israel extends His lovingkindness to the nations. Jeremiah foresees when Jerusalem will be called "the throne of the LORD, and all the nations will assemble at it, at Jerusalem, for the name of the LORD; and they will no longer follow the stubbornness of their evil heart" (Jer. 3:17). The prophet Micah looks forward to the day when the nations will go to the house of the Lord in His holy city to be taught about His ways so that they might walk in His paths (Mic. 4:2). Through Zechariah, the Lord declares that there will be a time when "many nations will join themselves to the LORD . . . and will become My people" (Zech. 2:11). Isaiah declares that this will happen through the Servant of the Lord who will return Israel back to the Lord and will be "a light of the nations so that [the Lord's] salvation may reach to the end of the earth" (Isa. 49:5–6). This Servant is none other than Jesus, whose life, death, and resurrection would be the means of redemption for both Israel and all the world (Acts 26:23; Rom. 15:8–12).

According to the New Testament, Jesus is the Messiah of Israel and Savior of the world (Luke 2:10–11). He instructs His disciples to preach the good news "in His name to all the nations, beginning from Jerusalem" (Luke 24:47) and gives them the Holy Spirit, so that they might be His empowered witnesses "in Jerusalem and in all Judea, and Samaria, and as far as the remotest part of the earth" (Acts 1:8). Just as the Father sent the Son, so Jesus sent His disciples into the world to bring the good news of God's salvation to all (John 20:21). And the church stands with the disciples and receives Jesus' command to "go therefore and make disciples of all the nations, baptizing them in the name of the Father and the Son and the Holy Spirit, teaching them to observe all that I commanded you" (Matt. 28:19–20 ESV).

Like the Old Testament, the New Testament envisions a future day when all peoples will worship the Lord. In his revelation, John writes that he saw

> a great multitude which no one could count, from every nation and all the tribes, peoples, and languages, standing before the throne and before the Lamb, clothed in white robes, and palm branches were in their hands; and they cried out with a loud voice, saying "Salvation belongs to our God who sits on the throne, and to the Lamb." (Rev. 7:9–10)

Until that day, the church is called to be a vehicle for the proclamation of God's salvation to all peoples. Each passing generation must take up the call. And each generation must do so as new challenges and opportunities arise.

THE GOSPEL CALL TO A CHANGING WORLD

One significant change in the twenty-first century has been the growth of nonreligious people in the North America and Western Europe. A recent study concluded that nearly 80 percent of all churches in the United States are plateaued and declining. The same study stated that while "Protestant evangelicals remain the largest religious group" in the United States, those who identify as religiously unaffiliated have increased significantly in recent years. Western Europe has seen a similar demographic change. According to Pew Forum, the percentage of people who identify as Christians has declined and "the net losses for Christianity have been accompanied by net growth in the numbers of religiously unaffiliated people."[2]

These shifts may be the cause of some Christian hesitancy to share the gospel. Millennials and Gen Zs represent the populations with the largest percentage increases in religiously unaffiliated and atheists.[3] They also demonstrate the greatest reluctance to share their faith with others. According to Barna, nearly half of Christian millennials believe it is "wrong to share one's personal beliefs with someone of a different faith in hopes that they will one day share the same faith." In a different study, researchers discovered that 65 percent of millennials believed "people are more likely than in the past to take offense if they share their faith."[4]

Christians who are reluctant to share their faith might be surprised to discover that unchurched people are more open to conversations about faith than we might expect. According to the study conducted by Barna, more than one in five non-Christians expressed an interest in exploring the Christian faith.[5] Another report, conducted by the Billy Graham Center Institute and Lifeway Research, found that "79 percent of unchurched people are fine with a friend talking about their faith if they value it."[6] Overwhelmingly, non-Christians prefer to explore faith through relational conversations.

A second major change is the significant number of migrants around the world. In 2016, it was estimated that 244 million people lived outside of their birth countries. This figure is triple the total in 1960. In 2013, almost 70 percent of international migrants lived in the United States, Canada, and European countries. The majority of international migrants live in the United States.[7] Wesley Granberg-Michaelson has noted, "The influx of immigrants particularly since 1965 has made the United States the most religiously diverse country in the world."[8]

For many Christians, migration patterns have brought them closer to "the world" than ever before. The task of sharing the gospel to the world can be done locally. As Charles Rijnhart wrote, "The unreached are among us, not actually unreachable at all."[9] Sharing the gospel to the ends of the earth could mean sharing the gospel with someone in your community. This is challenging, of course. According to one research study, "Evangelicals are less comfortable than other groups in conversation with people they consider significantly different from themselves."[10] Some might even feel more comfortable ministering to "the other" when they are "out-there" rather than next door. So, what happens when a migrant becomes a member of our community? Will we take up the call to share our faith in Jesus?

There is, however, a strong possibility that the migrant neighbor is a Christian. While Christianity might be decreasing in North America and Western Europe, it has seen tremendous growth in the Global South and East. Philip Jenkins contends that over the last century, "the center of gravity in the Christian world has shifted inexorably from Europe, southward, to Africa and Latin America, and eastward, toward Asia."[11] There are significantly more Christians who reside in the Global South and East (Africa, Latin America, and Asia) than the Global North (North America and Europe).[12]

One implication of this is that the number of missionaries from the Global South and East has increased significantly. Dorcas Cheng-Tozun writes, "This is the first time . . . that the world has seen so many missionaries from Asia, Africa, and Latin America crossing national borders."[13] As Samuel Escobar wrote, "Christian mission in the twenty-first century has become the responsibility of the global church."[14] The global church ought to pray that God would continue to empower His church to proclaim the gospel with clarity and boldness to the ends of the earth. Despite the realities of our changing world, the church must remain consistently committed to our call to make the gospel known to all people.

This section, "Ministry to the World," will provide insights for the church to continue its mission in ever-changing contexts. Chapters will examine topics such as: the church and its mission, evangelism, the Great Commission, planting and revitalizing churches, and will include special topics in gospel ministry such as urban ministry, contextualization in different cultures, and evangelism to Jewish people. It is our desire that these chapters may provide insight and inspiration for bold and faithful gospel ministry.

NOTES

1. Barna Group, *Reviving Evangelism: Current Realities That Demand a Vision for Sharing Faith*, 2019, 45.

2. Pew Research Center, "Being Christian in Western Europe," May 29, 2018, https://www.pewforum.org/2018/05/29/being-christian-in-western-europe/.

3. Rick Richardson, *You Found Me: New Research on How Unchurched Nones, Millennials, and Irreligious Are Surprisingly Open to Christian Faith* (Downers Grove, IL: IVP Books, 2019), 35–36, and Barna Group, "Gen Z: The Culture, Beliefs and Motivations Shaping the Next Generation," 2018.

4. Barna Group, *Reviving Evangelism*, 47–48.

5. Barna Group, 66.

6. Richardson, *You Found Me*, 58–59.

7. Michael Dimock, "Global Migration's Rapid Rise," Pew Trusts, Summer 2016, https://www.pewtrusts.org/en/trend/archive/summer-2016/global-migrations-rapid-rise.

8. Wesley Granberg-Michaelson, *From Times Square to Timbuktu: The Post-Christian West Meets the Non-Western Church* (Grand Rapids: Eerdmans, 2013), 80.

9. Charles Rijnhart, "The World's Least Reached Are on Our Streets," *Lausanne Global Analysis* 9, no. 6 (November 2020), https://lausanne.org/content/lga/2020-11/the-worlds-least-reached-are-on-our-streets.

10. Barna Group, *Reviving Evangelism*, 49.

11. Philip Jenkins, *The Next Christendom: The Coming of Global Christianity*, 3rd ed. (New York: Oxford University Press, 2011), 1.

12. Todd M. Johnson, "The 100-Year Shift of Christianity to the South," Gordon Conwell Theological Seminary, October 9, 2019, https://www.gordonconwell.edu/blog/the-100-year-shift-of-christianity-to-the-south/.

13. Dorcas Cheng-Tozun, "What Majority-World Missions Really Looks Like," *Christianity Today*, August 26, 2019, https://www.christianitytoday.com/ct/2019/august-web-only/what-majority-world-missions-really-looks-like.html.

14. Samuel Escobar, *The New Global Mission: The Gospel from Everywhere to Everyone* (Downers Grove, IL: InterVarsity Press, 2003), 12.

Understanding
the Church and Mission

KERWIN A. RODRIGUEZ

Here are two foundational questions for congregants and ministers alike: What is the nature of the church, and what is her mission? Congregants may attend a local church as a matter of Christian obligation without considering what their identity as part of the universal church means about them or why they gather each week with a local congregation. Ministers may be a little more attentive to these questions than some in their congregation, but find themselves struggling to articulate a direction for the local church they lead that aligns with the overall mission of the universal church. Clarity on these matters is needed and instructive for Christian leadership and practice.

THE NATURE OF THE CHURCH

What is the church? The church is the worldwide, multiethnic community that has been redeemed and gathered together by God. Its members have been reconciled to God in and through Christ and united by the Spirit of God for the purpose of being sent into the world to announce the good news of God. Admittedly, this definition is lengthy. While other definitions may be more concise, this one attempts to emphasize the triune God's activity in drawing individuals together to form a community of faith called to a particular purpose. It may be helpful to break the definition down to understand the nature of the church more clearly before expanding on the universal church's particular purpose, or mission.

FOR ALL PEOPLE

First, as stated above, the church is a multiethnic community, meaning that the universal church is made up of people from every nation, tribe, and tongue. The gospel of Luke and the book of Acts prepare us for this reality. When the angels appeared to the shepherds at Jesus' birth they announced "good news of great joy which will be for *all the people*" (Luke 2:10, emphasis added). Then when Mary and Joseph took the baby to Jerusalem, Simeon saw Him and declared, "My eyes have seen Your salvation, which you have prepared *in the presence of all the peoples*: a light of revelation for the *Gentiles*, and the glory of Your people *Israel*" (Luke 2:30–32). At the close of Luke's gospel, Jesus said to His disciples, "So it is written, that the Christ would suffer and rise from the dead on the third day, and that repentance for forgiveness of sins would be proclaimed in His name *to all the nations*, beginning from Jerusalem" (Luke 24:46–47).

The book of Acts begins with Jesus about to ascend into heaven. Before He departed from His disciples, He commissioned them to be His witnesses "both *in Jerusalem* and *in all Judea, and Samaria*, and *as far as the remotest part of the earth*" (Acts 1:8). So it should not surprise readers that Acts recounts how the gospel goes out to all the peoples of the earth.

THROUGHOUT THE WORLD

In the earliest days after Jesus' ascension, the gospel spreads and the Holy Spirit comes upon people. They gather together and are "of one heart and soul" (Acts 4:32). From this group emerges Joseph, also known as Barnabas, who was "a Levite of Cyprian birth" (Acts 4:36). The primary focus of Acts 4:32–37 is the unity of those who were gathered together in the Spirit, but the detailed characterization is not insignificant. Barnabas was from the island of Cyprus in the Mediterranean Sea, a ways from Jerusalem, and his role likely foreshadows the spread of the gospel to the rest of Asia Minor.

As a result of persecution, the church is scattered throughout Judea and Samaria (Acts 7–8:1). After preaching the gospel throughout Samaria (Acts 8:4–25), Philip is sent to the road that goes down from Jerusalem to Gaza where he encounters an Ethiopian eunuch. Philip shares the gospel with him and baptizes him. Again the characterization of the eunuch as an Ethiopian is not incidental. The gospel is spreading throughout the world and reaching all the peoples of the earth. By the time we meet Barnabas again, he is joined by Saul (later called Paul) and they are commissioned to preach the gospel throughout Greece.

FROM ALL WALKS OF LIFE UNITED

The passages highlighted in Luke–Acts focus primarily on the spread of the gospel to all peoples and throughout the nations. But the gospel's reception among all people also extends to what Orlando Costas calls "all walks of life." Indeed, the church is "a multitude of men and women from all walks of life, without distinction of race, nationality, economic and educational background. It is a community gathered from every tribe, tongue and nation."[1] One of the beautiful realities experienced by the gospel is that Christ's work extends to all people regardless of sex, ethnicity, and class. Truly all are one in Jesus and receive the identity as God's children (Gal. 3:28).

Paul attributes the unity of the church to the Holy Spirit. He explains to the church in Corinth that "by one Spirit we were all baptized into one body, whether Jews or Greeks, whether slaves or free, and we were all made to drink of one Spirit" (1 Cor. 12:13). Despite ethnic, social, and cultural differences, members of the body "are being built together into a dwelling of God in the Spirit" (Eph. 2:22). The beautiful reality of this community is that its members are "called out of the world into one body and granted a distinctive identity . . . [they are] *one* in spite of their significant social differences."[2] That is how Ruth Padilla DeBorst describes a certain local congregation in Argentina. And what is true of that congregation is true of the universal church as well. Truly, the church "is granted unity by the life-giving Spirit, who extends bridges across linguistic, ethnic, and social differences."[3] In the Spirit, the body of Christ can experience unity, fellowship, and work together "for the faith of the gospel" (Phil. 1:27).

Since members of the body of Christ are being "built together into a dwelling of God in the Spirit" (Eph. 2:22), they can "[stand] firm in one spirit [and strive] together for the faith of the gospel" (Phil. 1:27). The Holy Spirit serves as a source of power and unity for the members of Christ's body. Not only are members joined together by the Spirit, they are also energized to work out the gospel in their own lives, with one another, and in the work God commissions them to do. The Holy Spirit is a guide into truth and godly wisdom (John 16:13; 1 Cor. 2:10–16), leads Christians in godly living (Gal 5:18–25), and is a source of power for Christian witness (Acts 1:8).

REDEEMED AND RECONCILED

This multiethnic community, which has been gathered by God, is also a redeemed community. The concept of redemption originates in the story of Israel. Redemption holds together two concepts: liberation and belonging. Israel was liberated by God from their slavery in Egypt "with an outstretched arm, and with great judgments" (Ex. 6:6). The Lord is the one "who brought [Israel] out of the land of Egypt and redeemed [Israel] from the house of slavery" (Deut. 13:5). This act of liberation resulted in Israel belonging to God as His people. Nehemiah remembers God's act of redemption in his prayer to the Lord and calls Israel "Your servants and Your people whom You redeemed by Your great power and by Your strong hand" (Neh. 1:10). According to the Old Testament, when God rescued Israel from slavery in Egypt, it was in fulfillment of His covenant promise to Abraham (Gen. 17:4–7). As a result, Israel became His people and He became their God.

The New Testament draws on the story of Israel's redemption to refer to the church. Through faith in Christ, all who believe are justified by "His grace through the redemption which is in Christ Jesus" (Rom. 3:24). Paul explains in Romans 9 that God has called His people not only from the Jews but from the Gentiles too. He supports this point by quoting the words of the prophet Hosea: "I will call those who were not My people, 'My people,' and her who was not beloved, 'Beloved.' And it shall be that in the place where it was said to them, 'you are not My people,' there they shall be called sons of the living God" (vv. 24–26). In Galatians Paul refers to the church (both Jewish and Gentile believers of Christ) as those who have been redeemed from the curse of the law. Therefore they are recipients of the blessing of Abraham (Gal. 3:13–14) and receive adoption as children of God (Gal. 4:5).

The apostle Peter also uses Old Testament language to refer to the church as the redeemed people of God. "But you are a chosen people" he reminds believers (1 Peter 2:9). If Israel's story of redemption was liberation out of Egypt into a new home, then the church's story of redemption is liberation out of darkness into light. The church has been delivered from spiritual bondage and captivity and into the spiritual freedom of divine adoption (Heb. 2:14–15). Like Israel, the redeemed church now belongs to God and is known as God's people. As Peter writes, "For you once were not a people, but now you are the people of God" (1 Peter 2:10). So, the New Testament church is the redeemed people of God in and through Christ.

Returning to our definition, the church's members are those who have been reconciled to God in and through Christ and united by the Spirit of God. Those who belong to the church have "peace with God through our Lord Jesus Christ" (Rom. 5:1). Christ died for sinners so that those who were enemies of God "were reconciled to God through the death of His Son" (Rom. 5:10) and have peace with Him, having been presented before God as "holy and blameless and beyond reproach" (Col. 1:20–22).

Reconciliation with God also means that individuals are called to be reconciled with others. In Christ, Christians have peace and are brought together as one body, reconciled both to God and one another (Eph. 2:13–22). As N. T. Wright notes, "The church is first and foremost a *community*, a collection of people who belong to one another because they belong to God, the God we know in and through Jesus."[4] As such, those who belong to one another are called to care for one another and to love and forgive one another.

SENT FOR A PURPOSE

Thus far, we have tried to summarize all that God has done in redeeming and gathering the church. And yet, there is at least one more thing that must be said about the nature of the church. God saves and then He sends. The church is redeemed and gathered by God for the purpose of being sent into the world. Indeed, it is right to conclude that God saves and then sends His people for a particular purpose.

According to Peter, the people chosen and gathered "for God's own possession" has been chosen and gathered to "proclaim the excellencies of Him who has called you out of darkness into His marvelous light" (1 Peter 2:9). In his letter to Titus, Paul describes the church as the people Jesus redeemed for Himself who are "eager for good deeds" (Titus 2:14). Similarly in his letter to the church in Ephesus, Paul calls those who have been saved through faith God's "workmanship," who are "created in Christ Jesus for good works" (Eph. 2:10). So we can summarize the biblical description this way—namely, that those who are redeemed and reconciled to God are gathered together and called the church. The church's members, united and energized by the Spirit, are then sent into the world by God for a particular purpose.

This may be obvious to some readers. It is generally accepted that the church has a purpose. But the real question remains, what exactly *is* that purpose? We now turn our attention to answering this question and describing the mission of the church.

THE MISSION OF THE CHURCH

The mission of the church is to bear witness to the gospel through proclamation and teaching, and through good works toward one another and those outside of the faith. The church, then, carries the gospel to the world through verbal expression and also embodies the gospel to the world through action. Together, word and deed express the good news that Jesus is Lord and has brought about redemption through His life, death, and resurrection. The church bears witness to this gospel in all that it says and does.

THE MISSION SIMPLY STATED

In its simplest expression, this is why the church exists. The church consists of members who have been transformed by the gospel and then are compelled to give public expression to that transformation. In this section, we'll discuss aspects of the mission, and then its fulfillment, which is through both verbal proclamation and actions.

The witnesses of the mission: To be a witness is to affirm or attest to something about which one has personal knowledge or experience. Those who are part of the body of Christ can bear witness to the gospel because they have personally experienced the transformation of the gospel. And then, miraculously through its proclamation and practices, the church offers "a taste of truth: a personal experience of the gospel."[5] So the church "is the place not only where the gospel is heard but also where it is seen. For the meaning of the gospel can ultimately be learned only through a demonstration of what the proclamation means in practice."[6]

Jesus referred to His disciples as witnesses on a few occasions. Before His death, He promised that they would testify about Him. While He ate with His disciples in the upper room before His death He said to them, "When the Helper comes, whom I will send to you from the Father, namely, the Spirit of truth who comes from the Father, He will testify about Me, and you are testifying as well, because you have been with Me from the beginning" (John 15:26–27). Then, as He was about to ascend to heaven, Jesus again promised that the Spirit would empower the disciples and they would be His witnesses in their own neighborhoods and all throughout the world (Acts 1:8). After Pentecost, the apostles referred to themselves as witnesses who were commissioned to testify as to who Jesus is (Acts 10:42).

Members of the church today are disciples of Christ too. They also are filled by the Spirit and are called to testify to the Savior who provides forgiveness of sins (Acts 5:31–32).

Origin of the mission: Perhaps it should not be taken for granted that the church has actually been given a mission. How do we know that the church is a sent community? Some have argued that the mission of the church is rooted in the mission of God. David M. Gustafson writes, "Mission originates with the triune God—Father, Son, and Holy Spirit. . . . Mission is not first and foremost an activity of the church but an attribute of God; God is missional." If God's mission "is to establish his reign on earth as it is in heaven," then the church's mission "is an outworking of the mission of God in the world."[7] Christopher J. H. Wright points out, "The mission of the church flows from the mission of God and the fulfillment of God's mandate." He continues, "The mission is God's. The marvel is that God invites us to join in."[8]

The mission in the grand narrative: God's "mission" is understood primarily by considering the Bible's grand narrative. The narrative begins with God's creation, followed by the problem of human sin and God's promise to restore His creation (Gen. 3:15). The rest of the narrative is the unfolding of God's plan of redemption that culminates in the person and work of Jesus Christ, through whom God's creation experiences redemption and hope for new creation. According to Wright, this entire narrative affirms "that there is one God at work in the universe and in human history, and that this God has a goal, a purpose, a mission that will ultimately be accomplished by the power of God's Word and for the glory of God's name. This is the mission of the biblical God."[9]

Throughout the narrative, God invites humanity to serve as participants in His work. The first humans are invited to work and keep the garden (Gen. 1–2). After the fall, God calls Israel to be His people and promises to bless the world through them (Gen. 12:1–3; Ex. 19:5–6). When Israel fails to keep her covenant with the Lord, God sends His Son, Jesus, to restore Israel *and* bless the world (Matt. 1:21–23; Luke 1:16–17, 54–55; 2:10–11; John 1:29). And after His resurrection, Jesus says to His disciples, "Peace be to you; just as the Father has sent Me, I also send you" (John 20:21). As Wright puts it, "Jesus entrusted to the church a mission that is directly rooted in his own identity, passion and victory as the crucified and risen Messiah."[10]

The mission given: Several New Testament passages provide evidence for the church receiving a commission from Jesus. Most familiar to discussions concerning the mission of the church are the so-called Great Commission passages, where Jesus' words to His disciples are understood as an invitation for all of the church (Matt. 28:16–20; Luke 24:44–49; Acts 1:8). Other passages are also relevant, such as those in which Jesus invites His followers to understand themselves in relation to the rest of the world as sources of blessing or as a counter-community shaped by cruciform values (Matt. 5:13–16; Luke 6:27–38; John 15:18–19). These we will consider more carefully below. For now, they demonstrate that Jesus commissioned His followers to bear witness or testify to who He was and what He accomplished in His life, death, and resurrection.

FULFILLING THE MISSION

The first part of our definition for the mission of the church stated that gospel witness occurs through proclamation and teaching. Through the practice of evangelism, preaching, and teaching, the church proclaims the gospel and produces disciples of Jesus Christ. At the end of the gospel of Matthew, the disciples arrive at a designated place in Galilee to meet Jesus. When they see Him they fall down and worship. Then Jesus says to His disciples,

> "All authority in heaven and on earth has been given to Me. Go, therefore, and make disciples of all the nations, baptizing them in the name of the Father and the Son and the Holy Spirit, teaching them to follow all that I commanded you; and behold, I am with you always, to the end of the age." (Matt. 28:18–20)

The importance of these words are heightened by at least two things. First, they are the concluding words of the gospel of Matthew. Second, they contain an explicit command to the disciples from the resurrected Jesus. Before the command, Jesus' own authority is well established. As soon as the disciples see Him, they fall down and worship Him. Jesus Himself attests to His own authority by stating that *all authority* has been given to Him. Jesus is the Son of God, and the disciples are commanded by Him to proclaim the good news about Him to all the earth. Grammatically, the primary command in the passage is to make disciples of all the earth, that is, to win people. How will they make disciples? By baptizing them—an act that denotes repentance and new life with and in the triune God—in the name of the Father, Son, and Holy Spirit, *and* by teaching them to follow all that Jesus commanded. Jesus' final command to His disciples is straightforward: make disciples by proclaiming the gospel in all the earth so that all who hear might believe Jesus is Lord and by teaching the faith to all who believe. In other words, the church will make disciples first by sharing the good news of God's redemption through Jesus Christ and inviting hearers to respond in faith (Rom. 10:8–11).

Second, the church will make disciples by teaching the faith, or as Jesus instructs, by teaching all that He commanded. Conversion, winning people, is only part of the disciple-making task. The church must also instruct Christ followers concerning all that He commanded so that they might be faithful and full of understanding. For this reason, after Pentecost, the newly baptized believers "were continually devoting themselves to the apostles' teaching" (Acts 2:42).

We can draw additional insight from the apostle Paul's understanding of ministry. He spoke of his own mission as proclamation for the purpose of cultivating disciples into the image of Christ. Paul describes himself as a minister who was commissioned by God to preach the Word of God and proclaim Christ through admonition and teaching so as to "present every person complete in Christ" (Col. 1:23–29). And when Paul instructs Timothy, he reminds him to "preach the word" and to "do the work of an evangelist" so as to "fulfill your ministry" (2 Tim. 4:2–5). Ministers who are called to serve the church do so, at least in part, through verbal proclamation: preaching, evangelizing, and instructing.

"Win People"

Some have suggested that disciple-making is a sufficient understanding of the mission of the church, and that any attempt to enlarge the mission distracts the church from its real task of sharing the gospel and discipling believers. According to this view, the mission of the church should be defined narrowly as proclaiming the gospel and making disciples. That is, simply "to win people to Christ and build them up in Christ."[11] Verbal proclamation is both the priority and the essential task given to the church by Jesus Christ. As another proponent of this view warns, "Nothing must obscure the church's central obligation to preach the gospel."[12]

Positively, the narrow view of the mission of the church focuses on prioritizing the verbal proclamation of the gospel. The acts of preaching, evangelism, teaching, and even worship take on a necessary prioritization. Romans 10:13–15 reminds us,

> For "Everyone who calls on the name of the Lord will be saved." How then are they to call on Him in whom they have not believed? How are they to believe in Him whom they have not heard? And how are they to hear without a preacher? But how are they to preach unless they are sent? Just as it is written, "How beautiful are the feet of those who bring good news of good things!"

One draw for the view that the mission of the church should be limited to proclamation is its appeal to the Great Commission passages described above. As we noted, at least one of these passages contains an explicit command from Jesus to the disciples. Additionally, that these commands come at the end of at least one gospel account (Matt. 28:16–20) validates the command's importance to the apostles' mission as witnesses to and followers of Jesus.

For those who hold this view, the mission of God and the mission of the church are distinct. God is the One who saves, restores, and re-creates the world, and the church bears witness to Him rather than cooperates with Him.

This can be a helpful perspective since some might inadvertently believe that the church can fully restore the world and completely undo the effects of sin on our world. However, members of the body of Christ can also engage in good works for a different reason. Rather than believing their works can do what only God can do—save, restore, and re-create—Christians should understand their good works can bear witness to God's redemptive work. Scripture indicates that God redeems His people to serve as living demonstrations of the transformation and restoration that He has done and will do in His creation (Rom. 8:16–23; 12:1–2; Eph. 4:17–5:2; 1 Peter 2:12).

"Do Good Works"

So, what about good works? Almost every Christian writer or commentator acknowledges that the Bible commands good works. Even those who insist on a limited definition of the mission of the church acknowledge that the Bible commands faith in action. They agree that the Scriptures command "every church to look outside itself, exercise love beyond its doors, and give generously to those in need." And yet, they are also careful to describe such actions as "salt-and-light *opportunities*" instead of "do-this-list-or-you're-sinning *responsibilities*."[13] In the viewpoint of these Christians, doing good deeds are demonstrations of one's individual faith. Good works, they posit, are commanded to individual Christians rather than the church as a whole. The church's mission, from this perspective remember, is to preach the gospel and make disciples. The distinction being made is that the church as an institution is called to disciple-making, while doing good works would be the mission of individual Christians.

The problem with these distinctions is that Scripture does not actually make them. The church described in Scripture is a community of individuals gathered together. Whenever individual Christians obey scriptural commands to do good works, they are doing so as members of "one body" empowered by "one Spirit" (Eph. 4:4).

The fact is, Scripture describes the church as a community with distinct values called to do good works. When the crowds gathered to hear Jesus' teaching on the hills near Galilee, Jesus addressed His disciples and instructed them concerning the values of the kingdom of heaven (Matt. 5:1–7:29). The values expressed in this teaching are countercultural. For example, the Beatitudes name as blessed those who would have been dismissed or disregarded in society, and Jesus invites His disciples to love their enemies and to practice obedience to the law of God as children of God (Matt. 5:44–48).

Most notably Jesus calls His disciples "the salt of the earth," the "light of the world," and "a city set on a hill." Each of these metaphors serves a similar but complementary function. Salt is distinctive. Whether its function is to preserve or provide flavor, it is notable for its distinctive saltiness. Light is also distinctive in contrast to darkness. A city on a hill is distinctive in its elevated position and, since it is elevated, the city can be seen by all. Jesus is calling His followers to live in the world as counteragents who carry the countercultural values He is preaching. When Jesus' followers live distinctively they will be like salt and light, and like a city on a hill. To live as followers of Jesus is to live in contrast to a world of darkness. And when followers live according to these distinctive values, the unbelieving world will see their good works and will be prompted to glorify God because of them (Matt. 5:13–16; 1 Peter 2:12). Paul draws on these metaphors in his letter to the Philippians when he calls the church to live as "children of God above reproach in the midst of a crooked and perverse generation, among whom you appear as lights in the world" (Phil. 2:15).

Several passages describe Jesus' followers as a distinctive community from the world with unique values and practices. Christians are to forgive radically by forgiving enemies (Luke 6:27–38) and forgiving repeatedly (Matt. 18:21–35), just as God forgave us. Christians are called to give generously, especially to those who are in need and cannot return the favor (Luke 14:12–14). Christians are also called to show mercy and kindness to all people, including those who are our enemies (Luke 10:25–37; Rom. 12:20). In doing these things, the church bears witness to the rich grace, mercy, and love of God, which has been made known in Christ. The church is the redeemed and reconciled community of God, and the good works we do are visual representations of God's reign in the world. The church is called to be "a good place in which the good news of reconciliation in Christ is exhibited in bodily form. . . . a place that practices and thus exhibits the reign of God."[14]

These good works take on various forms. Good works include acts of individual righteousness. Members of the body of Christ are called to be people of integrity and strong character. Christians are called to be honest, free from deceit and malice (Eph. 4:22; 1 Peter 2:1). They are called to abstain from sexual sin and strife (Rom. 13:13; 1 Peter 2:11). Through the Christian's upstanding moral behavior, unbelievers may see their actions and glorify God (1 Peter 2:12). But these are not the only kinds of good works that members of the body of Christ are called to practice.

Christians do good works when they love one another in the body of Christ. Jesus commanded His disciples to love one another and said that all people will "know that you are My disciples: if you have love for one another" (John 13:34–35). Christians are called members of "the household of the faith" (Gal. 6:10) and members of "God's household" (Eph. 2:19; 1 Tim. 3:15). A consequence of being called into the family of God is to participate in fellowship with one another. Put another way, it is to have life in common with other believers (Acts 2:44–46). So members of the household of God are called to do good to other members by serving one another. Practically speaking, this most often takes place in local congregations. Christians meeting together in a local congregation demonstrate mutual love and service by praying for one another, listening to, and encouraging one another. Local congregants also serve one another compassionately by caring for each other's physical and financial needs, ensuring that those who are vulnerable or have the greatest needs in the community are provided and cared for.

Finally, the church is called to do good works to those who are outside of the faith as well (Gal. 6:10; 1 Thess. 5:15). Historically, the church has been a countercultural community by advocating for those who are most vulnerable in society. Whether it is advocating for the poor, orphans, or refugees, the church has understood that these acts of mercy and justice are expressions of their belief in the nature, character, and redemptive action of God in Jesus Christ.[15] The church has also believed that engaging in such acts are expressions of Christian love: love of God and love of neighbor (Mic. 6:8; James 1:27). The Christian love ethic is one that extends not just to those who are easy to love, but even to those who are strangers and enemies (Heb. 13:2; Rom. 12:20).

PROCLAIM *AND* DO GOOD

That the church would engage in such activities, both locally and globally, should not diminish the centrality of the gospel. On the contrary, such acts validate our belief in the good news of Jesus Christ. Quite simply, the church is called to bear witness to the gospel. Through verbal proclamation and good works, the church expresses and demonstrates that God has brought about redemption in and through the death, burial, and resurrection of Jesus Christ our Lord. As David Gustafson writes,

> We do not merely speak of God's mercy toward us in the gospel but embody mercy in our care of others (Matt. 5:7). As we declare God's forgiveness in Jesus Christ, we forgive those who have sinned against us (Matt. 18:21–35). As we speak of Jesus's sacrificial love for the world, we love others, even our enemies (Matt. 5:43–48; James 2:8). As we speak of Jesus Christ, whose atoning death reconciled us to God, we practice the ministry of reconciliation, being reconciled with others—even those different from us—and exhort others to be reconciled with God (Matt. 5:23–24; 2 Cor. 5:18). Such demonstrations of the gospel do not undermine the centrality of the gospel message but adorn it and "make the teaching about God our Savior attractive" (Titus 2:10).[16]

This priority of proclamation does not, however, negate the church's responsibility as an alternative community that embodies the gospel through good works. As René Padilla famously liked to say, evangelism and social action are "two wings of a plane." Both "word and deed are inextricably united in the mission of Jesus and his apostles, and we must continue to hold both together in the mission of the church." Padilla affirmed the prioritization of verbal proclamation, since "the widest and deepest human need is for a personal encounter with Jesus Christ." Still, he argued that good works should not be "a mere addendum to mission" because "they point back to the kingdom that has already come and forward to the kingdom that is yet to come."[17]

John Stott also insisted on a more comprehensive definition for the mission of the church while prioritizing evangelism as the most important task for the church. He argued that the Great Commission to make disciples should be held together with the Great Commandment to love our neighbor. He wrote,

> If we truly love our neighbor, we shall without doubt share with him or her the good news of Jesus. How can we possibly claim to love our neighbor if we know the gospel but keep it from them? Equally, however, if we truly love our neighbor we shall not stop with evangelism. Our neighbor is neither a bodiless soul that we should love only their soul, nor a soulless body that we should care for its welfare alone, nor even a body-soul isolated from society. God created the human person, who is my neighbor, as a body-soul-in-community. Therefore, if we love our neighbor as God made him or her, we must inevitably be concerned for their total welfare, the good of their soul, their body, and their community.[18]

CONCLUSION

Given the nature and mission of the universal church, local churches must prioritize the gospel in all they do. Local churches must not forsake the preaching and teaching of the gospel. Nor should local churches forsake embodying the gospel in action. Each local church should be strategic and contextually sensitive in determining how it will go about embodying the gospel in action, specifically in light of its community needs and the resources God has given to them. Whenever and wherever possible, church leaders should encourage and empower members to understand their calling individually and corporately to engage in gospel witness for the glory of God.

NOTES

1. Orlando E. Costas, *The Church and Its Mission: A Shattering Critique from the Third World* (Wheaton, IL: Tyndale House Publishers, 1974), 35.

2. Ruth Padilla DeBorst, "Church, Power, and Transformation in Latin America: A Different Citizenship Is Possible," in *The Church from Every Tribe and Tongue: Ecclesiology in the Majority World*, ed. Gene L. Green, Stephen T. Pardue, and Khiok-Khng Yeo (Carlisle, Cumbria, UK: Langham Global Library, 2018), 47.

3. Ibid., 48.

4. N. T. Wright, *Simply Christian: Why Christianity Makes Sense* (New York: HarperOne, 2010), 210.

5. Kevin J. Vanhoozer, *Faith Speaking Understanding: Performing the Drama of Doctrine* (Louisville: Westminster John Knox Press, 2014), 56.

6. Ibid., 170.

7. David M. Gustafson, *Gospel Witness: Evangelism in Word and Deed* (Grand Rapids: Eerdmans, 2019), 17.

8. Christopher J. H. Wright, *The Mission of God: Unlocking the Bible's Grand Narrative* (Downers Grove, IL: InterVarsity Press, 2006), 67.

9. Ibid., 64.

10. Ibid., 66.

11. Kevin DeYoung and Greg Gilbert, *What Is the Mission of the Church?: Making Sense of Social Justice, Shalom, and the Great Commission* (Wheaton, IL: Crossway, 2011), 63.

12. Mark Dever, *The Church: The Gospel Made Visible* (Nashville: B&H Academic, 2012), 82.

13. DeYoung and Gilbert, *What Is the Mission of the Church?*, 193.

14. Vanhoozer, *Faith Speaking Understanding*, 178.

15. See Christine D. Pohl, *Making Room: Recovering Hospitality as a Christian Tradition* (Grand Rapids: Eerdmans, 1999), and Joshua W. Jipp, *Saved by Faith and Hospitality* (Grand Rapids: Eerdmans, 2017).

16. Gustafson, *Gospel Witness: Evangelism in Word and Deed*, 103.

17. C. René Padilla, *Mission Between the Times: Essays on the Kingdom*, 2nd rev. and updated ed. (Carlisle, Cumbria, UK: Langham Partnership, 2013), 206–10.

18. John Stott and Christopher J. H. Wright, *Christian Mission in the Modern World*, updated and expanded (Downers Grove, IL: InterVarsity Press, 2015), 29.

Evangelizing the Lost

MARY CLOUTIER

Romans 3:23 states that "all have sinned and fall short of the glory of God," and a few chapters later the writer emphasizes that "the wages of sin is death" (Rom. 6:23a). These two brief passages remind every believer of our commonality in sin, lostness, and desperate hopelessness apart from Christ. And yet, each person is created in God's image (Gen. 1:26), and "God so loved the world, that He gave His only Son, so that everyone who believes in Him will not perish, but have eternal life" (John 3:16). This is what we call the gospel, the *good news*, of Jesus Christ.

This word "gospel" is a translation of the Greek *euangelion*, from which we derive the words "evangelist," "evangelize," and "evangelism." In the Bible, this Greek word was used to describe a joyful message (Matt. 4:23; 9:35), as well as the central doctrines or teachings of the gospel (e.g., 1 Cor. 15:1–8).

God's Word offers us a vivid account of His creation of the world, the fall of humanity, and God's promise of salvation through His Holy One, the Redeemer and Messiah, Jesus Christ. The gospels of Matthew, Mark, Luke, and John affirm that Jesus fulfilled messianic prophecies and was God incarnate, yet He was rejected and despised by many who were looking for the promised Messiah. Having been crucified, buried, and resurrected from the dead on the third day, Jesus paid the price of our sins and freed us from the sentence of death. Before returning to the Father, He commissioned His followers to preach the gospel of the kingdom and to make disciples of all the nations (Matt. 28:18–20). His disciples would be empowered by the Holy Spirit and serve as His witnesses "as far as the remotest part of the earth" (Acts 1:8), and ultimately, Christ's redeemed ones "from every nation and all the tribes, peoples, and languages" will gather before the throne and the Lamb, singing His praises in unison (Rev. 7:9–10).

As we receive Christ's commission to preach the gospel and make disciples, let us seek to understand its rootedness in Scripture and grasp key concepts and questions that will help us join wholeheartedly and confidently in His kingdom work.

THE BASICS OF THE GOSPEL

Gospel bearers are those who have heard and believe in salvation through Jesus Christ, and then *proclaim the gospel message to others*. The first bearers were heavenly messengers who announced Messiah Jesus' conception and birth. As His ministry began and advanced, faithful persons who saw or heard of Jesus passed on this good news to others that the Messiah had come. Three days after His crucifixion, heavenly messengers announced the good news of Jesus' resurrection to several faithful women, who then shared it with the apostles (Luke 24:1–10), who in turn spread the word throughout the world (Acts 1:8). To this day, and until Christ returns, gospel messengers must proclaim the good news to the lost (Matt. 24:14). While some evangelize vocationally, most believers share their faith with others in their daily lives—with family, friends, coworkers, and other acquaintances.

THE MESSAGE AND THE RESPONSE

The gospel message includes God's love of humanity and His provision of a Savior, whose death and resurrection fulfill the hope and promise of eternal life to those who believe in Him (John 3:16). With the good news, we must also tell the bad news: all persons are separated from God, due to sin (Rom. 3:23). God's Word tells of the coming judgment (Rom. 2:16) and that sinners are condemned to death (Rom. 6:23). However, the gospel communicates the power of God for salvation to everyone who believes (Rom 1:16).

Jesus told His listeners to *repent* and *believe* in the gospel (Mark 1:15) and explained to Nicodemus that he must be born from above, or *born again*, of water and the Spirit (John 3:3–5). The gospel requires a response of faith and obedience (1 Peter 4:17; Heb. 4:2, 6), and the early believers further made their faith public through baptism (Acts 8:12). We read that the Corinthian believers *received* the gospel and *stood in it* (1 Cor. 15:1). The most important response to the gospel is to "go and tell" it to others (Matt. 28:6–8), the proclamation that began at the empty tomb and will continue until Christ returns.

WHERE TO TAKE THE MESSAGE AND TO WHOM

Jesus proclaimed the gospel of the kingdom in all the villages and cities of Galilee (Matt. 4:23; 9:35). He preached the gospel among the poor (Matt. 11:5), but also among the wealthier classes (Luke 7:36; 19:1–5). He communicated the good news to individuals and groups, men and women, Jews and non-Jews (e.g., Matt. 15:21–28).

Jesus set for us an example to reach the lost at every level of society and in every community of our diverse world. We must communicate the gospel across geo-political boundaries, sending message-bearers and missionaries to places where people have not yet heard the gospel. We also can share the gospel through communication channels that transcend national boundaries—using radio or television, the internet, podcasts, and printed materials. In sharing the gospel, we must translate the message into the relevant languages, contextualizing the message to make it meaningful and understandable to the hearers.

At the birth of Jesus Messiah, the angel announced to the shepherds that the good news would be for *all the people* (Luke 2:10). Jesus confirmed the prophecies that the good news was for *the humble, the brokenhearted, the captives, and the imprisoned* (Isa. 61:1). Jesus said that this gospel would be preached in *the whole world* as a testimony to *all nations* (Matt. 24:14), and Peter affirmed that the gospel was for both *Jews and Gentiles* (Acts 15:7–9).

Because of God's love for all peoples, whom He has created in His image, we must continue to seek ways to communicate the gospel message to *all peoples* of the earth, including those of other beliefs, ethnicities, national identities, social or economic classes, or any other kinds of distinction.

THE GOOD NEWS: FORETOLD AND FULFILLED

The fall of humanity: One can trace the gospel back to Genesis, coming on the heels of God's righteous judgment. His promises and prophecies to the Jewish people throughout the Old Testament demonstrated that the good news ultimately would be revealed and fulfilled in their Messiah. Although the Jewish people were a people specially set apart by God, He clearly foretold that the Gentile nations also would be included in this plan of salvation.

The earliest indication of the gospel comes immediately after the fall, when Eve was deceived by the serpent and, along with Adam, disobeyed God's command. Pronouncing the consequences of this sin, God declared that He would make enemies of the woman's descendants and the serpent's offspring: "He shall bruise you on the head, and you shall bruise Him on the heel" (Gen. 3:15). This prophecy is fulfilled in Christ's victory over Satan. Jesus, by His death, destroyed Satan's power of death and his enslavement of humankind (Heb. 2:14–15).

The covenant with Abraham: In Genesis 12:1–3, God promises Abram, later renamed Abraham, that he will be a great nation, that his name will be great, and that he will be a blessing. In Abraham, all the families of the earth would be blessed. Though God's blessings were for Abraham's people, the Hebrews, this blessing eventually would extend to the Gentile nations, by way of the Jewish people and their promised Messiah (Ps. 67; Isa. 49:6; 52:10).

The birth of the Messiah: The Gospels relate the extraordinary events heralding the birth of Messiah Jesus, tying them directly to the messianic prophecies of the Old Testament. Heavenly and earthly messengers would bear the good news of salvation for God's people and for the nations.

In Luke 1:13–17, an angel of the Lord communicated to Zechariah that his wife, Elizabeth, would bear a son who would fulfill the prophecies of the one sent to prepare the way for the Lord (Mal. 4:5–6). An angel of the Lord told Mary, a virgin, that she would conceive and give birth to the Holy One, the Son of God (Luke 1:30–35). An angel also confirmed to Joseph that Mary was bearing a child conceived by the Holy Spirit (Matt. 1:20–21), fulfilling the prophecy that a virgin would give birth to the Messiah (Isa. 7:14). Faithful men and women bore testimony that Mary's baby was indeed the Messiah, including Elizabeth (Luke 1:39–45), the shepherds (Luke 2:8–18), Simeon (Luke 2:25–32), and Anna (Luke 2:36–38). The birth of the Jewish Messiah was also communicated to non-Jewish magi, who followed the star and traveled a great distance to worship this Child (Matt. 2:1–12).

These accounts affirm Jesus' identity as the Son of God, the Jewish Messiah, and the promised Redeemer. Scripture shows that those who heard gave praise to God, and many went on to tell the marvelous *good news* to others.

GOSPEL WITNESS AND THE TRINITY

The Gospels reflect the interaction of Father, Son, and Holy Spirit as Jesus begins His earthly ministry. In this, Jesus is both the embodiment and fulfillment of the gospel message. Perhaps one of the clearest passages about role of each person of the Trinity comes at Jesus' baptism. As John baptized Him, the heavens opened, the Holy Spirit descended on Jesus like a dove, and God the Father spoke from heaven: "You are My beloved Son; in You I am well pleased" (Mark 1:9–11).

Throughout His ministry, Jesus emphasized that He was doing the Father's work on earth: "The Son can do nothing of Himself, unless it is something He sees the Father doing; for whatever the Father does, these things the Son also does in the same way" (John 5:19).

Jesus was sent by the Father and given authority; likewise, He sent His disciples to preach the gospel and make disciples (Matt. 28:18–20; John 20:21). Jesus called out to Simon and Andrew, who were fishermen, "Follow Me, and I will have you become fishers of people" (Mark 1:17). Jesus called two more fishermen to be His disciples, James and John, who immediately left their nets and followed Him (vv. 18–20). Here, Jesus indicates that His disciples are not merely followers and learners, but they also will *draw others* into God's kingdom through the gospel message.

In Matthew 10, Jesus gave His disciples authority to drive out demons and heal diseases, yet they would be vulnerable and dependent on the hospitality of the communities where they traveled and preached. Jesus told them how to respond if they were welcomed or rejected by a community (vv. 11–14). He warned that they would be arrested and mistreated (vv. 16–18), but promised them the intervention of God's Holy Spirit to guide them in these circumstances (vv. 19–20). Serving as His gospel bearers would cost them their comfort, their relationships, their possessions, and even their very lives (Mark 8:35; 10:28; Matt. 24:9). Yet, Jesus assured them that any loss, sacrifice, or persecution will be more than recompensed in the life to come (Mark 10:29–31).

Jesus traveled throughout Galilee, teaching in the synagogues, proclaiming the gospel, and healing those suffering from disease and disability (Matt. 9:35), His extraordinary ministry confirming His identity as the promised Messiah (Isa. 61:1–2; Matt. 11:2–6; Luke 4:16–21). While the poor, the lame, the sick, and the demon-possessed recognized Jesus' authority and His deity (Luke 4:31–36, 41), Jewish religious leaders opposed Him (Luke 6:6–11; 20:1). He reiterated that He and the Father were one and work in concert (John 10:30; 14:10).

Jesus told His disciples of the coming baptism of the Holy Spirit, a promise from God to them (Acts 1:4–5). The Holy Spirit would empower them to be His witnesses in Jerusalem, Judea, Samaria, and to the remotest areas of the earth (Acts 1:8). This was fulfilled on the day of Pentecost, described in Acts 2, when the Holy Spirit enabled them to speak in diverse tongues, which were understood by the vast crowds of "devout men from every nation under heaven" (Acts 2:5). Peter then declared this event as the fulfillment of prophecy in Joel (Acts 2:14–21; see Joel 2:28–32), and explained how Jesus' crucifixion and resurrection fulfilled the prophecy of David regarding the Messiah (Acts 2:29–36; see Ps. 16:8–11; 110:1). Peter's hearers responded with remorse, asking what their response should be (Acts 2:37). Peter instructed them to repent and be baptized in the name of Jesus Christ for the forgiveness of their sins; they would then receive the gift of the Holy Spirit (v. 38).

Peter added that this promise was for them, their children, and for "all who are far away, as many as the Lord our God will call to Himself" (v. 39).

GOSPEL WITNESS IN ACTS

We see in these early accounts of gospel witness that the Lord God not only prepared people's hearts to receive the gospel, but also directed His servants toward them, to communicate the message. This is evident in Phillip's encounter with the Ethiopian eunuch (Acts 8:26–38) and in Peter's encounter with the faithful Gentile Cornelius (Acts 10). The *sending* role of the Holy Spirit is evident in Acts 13:1–4, as the church in Antioch set apart, commissioned, and sent out Barnabas and Saul, in obedience to the Spirit's command. The Holy Spirit sometimes gave warning to gospel bearers of coming difficulties and dangers (Acts 11:27–30; 20:23; 21:4, 11), and directed where they should go or not go (Acts 16:6–10).

Jewish believers were astonished to see Gentiles come to faith and similarly receive the outpouring of the Holy Spirit *as Gentiles* (Acts 10:44–45). At the Jerusalem Council (Acts 15:4–9), Peter defended the legitimacy of the Gentiles' faith, arguing against the imposition of Jewish laws and traditions, and affirming their common salvation through the grace of the Lord Jesus (v. 11).

In these passages, we see that early believers sometimes wrongly anticipated who would believe and whom God would save. We are not immune to this same error of presumption—that is, expecting God to reject particular groups of unsaved persons or expecting them to reject His gospel message. Given that we cannot know who will believe and be saved, we must purpose to share the gospel message with all peoples, as Jesus commanded (Mark 16:15–16).

The book of Acts also shows that people often came to faith in Christ as part of a *collective* (or *group*) *response*. In Acts 16, God opened Lydia's heart to respond to Paul's message, resulting in the baptism of her entire household (vv. 14–15). Silas and Paul's faithful witness in prison resulted in the conversion of the jailer, along with his entire household (vv. 30–34).

Those bearing the good news must not overlook the impact of the *collective response* to the gospel or minimize the impact that a given *space* or *circumstance* can have on the sharing of the gospel message. We recall that God gives us opportunities "for such a time as this" (Est. 4:14), recognizing His authority over circumstances and people to bring about His will and to communicate His message.

These accounts in the book of Acts help us in the present-day church to receive Jesus' Great Commission with full confidence that His Holy Spirit will likewise fill us, empower us, give us boldness and discernment, and enable us to communicate the gospel where and to whom He sends us. Pastors and teachers can prepare disciples for the great joys and challenges of sharing the gospel by offering a rich and thorough study of Acts.

THE GOSPEL PLAINLY SPOKEN

It is the Holy Spirit who gives the gospel message its power and authority (Acts 4:31; 1 Thess. 1:5). Paul asserted that Jesus Christ had sent him to preach the gospel, "not with cleverness of speech, so that the cross of Christ would not be made of no effect" (1 Cor. 1:17), for this message "is foolishness to those who are perishing, but to us who are being saved it is the power of God" (v. 18). Paul communicated the gospel without trickery or distortion and by openly proclaiming the truth (2 Cor. 4:2b). He recognized that the gospel is "veiled to those who are perishing" (v. 3) because Satan has blinded their minds (v. 4). In contrast to the darkness of sin and unbelief, God makes His light shine in our hearts "to give the Light of the knowledge of the glory of God in the face of Christ" (v. 6). Such belief, Paul asserts, must necessarily lead one to speak—to testify about Christ—that the gospel might spread to many, for the glory of God (vv. 13–15).

Knowing that Satan blinds and deceives unbelievers, a believer must be prepared and willing to communicate the gospel clearly and boldly, expecting that many will turn away or even against them, because they remain in darkness. For those who respond positively to the gospel, all glory, thanksgiving, and praise should be directed to God, for He alone causes His light to shine in the hearts of those previously blind in unbelief.

Very few of us feel fully qualified or capable to communicate the gospel effectively to others. Even though commissioned by Jesus Christ to share this good news throughout the world, we often feel that we lack the ability to adequately communicate such a wondrous, mysterious, and precious message. The Holy Spirit enables believers to communicate the gospel message simply and clearly. Even a plain-spoken, humble person can powerfully convey the saving grace of Jesus Christ, without a high level of education or eloquent speech.

FALSE GOSPELS

Paul asserted that the gospel he preached was not of human invention; he had neither received it from man, nor was he taught it, but he had "received it through a revelation of Jesus Christ" (Gal. 1:11–12). He warned believers about tolerating those who preached "another Jesus," "a different spirit," and "a different gospel" than he preached to them (2 Cor. 11:4). He was worried that, like Eve, they would be deceived by Satan and led astray in their minds (v. 3). Paul was alarmed that the Galatian believers were quickly deserting the gospel of Christ for another, perverted gospel (Gal. 1:6–7). He warned them not to accept another gospel contrary to what they had already received, even if preached by an angel from heaven (v. 8); and he condemned those preaching a false gospel (v. 9).

Today, we also must be vigilant to preach the gospel of Jesus Christ, remaining true to Scripture, even while communicating it relevantly and understandably to our hearers. Both the preacher and the hearer must check to confirm the message accords with Scripture, just as the Bereans did when they heard Paul preach (Acts 17:11). Such discernment comes from faithful study of God's divine Word and sensitivity to the guidance of His Holy Spirit.

PUT INTO GOD'S SERVICE

We sometimes wonder how we can be worthy to share the gospel when we have lived a sinful and disobedient life. Paul acknowledges this very discrepancy in 1 Timothy 1:12–16 to illustrate both his own unworthiness and Christ's transforming work in his life. The Lord *put him into service* (v. 12) and entrusted him with the gospel, not because of Paul's worthiness but because of Christ's saving work in his life. Paul described himself as "a blasphemer and a persecutor and a violent aggressor" (v. 13a). In spite of this, Paul received God's mercy because he had "acted ignorantly in unbelief" (v. 13b). Paul's life was transformed by the Lord's abundant grace and His gift of faith and love in Christ (v. 14).

Paul's next words should humble and motivate every believer who seeks to lead others to the gospel of Christ: "It is a trustworthy statement, deserving full acceptance, that Christ Jesus came into the world to save sinners, among whom I am foremost. Yet for this reason I found mercy, so that in me as the foremost sinner Jesus Christ might demonstrate His perfect patience as an example for those who would believe in Him for eternal life" (1 Tim. 1:15–16). This is the testimony of every saved sinner! We share the gospel out of gratitude, recognizing both the greatness of our own sin and the surpassing greatness of God's grace to us in Christ.

Paul instructed Timothy not to be ashamed of the testimony of Christ Jesus, but to join him in "suffering for the gospel according to the power of God, who saved us and called us with a holy calling, not according to our works, but according to His own purpose and grace, which was granted to us in Christ Jesus from all eternity" (2 Tim. 1:8–9).

Paul's epistles make it clear that we share the gospel because of what Christ has accomplished in us, and we are examples of His transformative and restorative work in our lives. He entrusts us with the gospel and enables us to communicate it boldly and clearly to others, for His glory. If we understand that God entrusts all believers to share the gospel message with humility, yet without shame, on the basis of Christ's saving work in us, then we can expect there will be responses of great joy and belief, as well as great opposition and unbelief. Many will hear and respond to God's offer of saving grace, but many others will reject the message and even violently oppose or seek to silence the message.

PRACTICAL APPLICATION

God appoints and sends out believers to share the good news, whether to their own communities or to distant peoples. For countless generations, through salvation in Christ Jesus, God has transformed sinners and blasphemers into sons and daughters and entrusted them with the precious gospel message, commissioning them to preach it until Christ's return. As stated before, "gospel" comes from *euangelion*, a Greek description for a joyful message. A proclaimer of this good news is an evangelist. The word "evangelist" might call to mind a professional speaker at a revival, but any believer sharing the good news is called to evangelize. Since the New Testament times, men and women of every generation, status, and nation have joined in the effort to promote and perpetuate the gospel message, as Jesus commanded His followers.

PREPARING GOSPEL BEARERS

We know that the gospel must be preached from the end of our block all the way to the ends of the earth. This calls for gospel bearers who faithfully proclaim the gospel close to home as well as those who are able and willing to travel great distances and face challenging circumstances. The church (that is, the body of believers in Jesus Christ) must train, prepare, equip, send out, and sustain such gospel bearers through material and prayer support, even as the early church did in the New Testament.

The foundation for any training or equipping is God's Word, which will make us fully capable and equipped for every good work (2 Tim. 3:16–17). The local church can further build on this foundation by making use of current training courses or curriculums and materials for personal evangelism, particularly those that encourage believers to put into practice what they have learned. Of course, many believers find that God gives them opportunities for conversation with unbelievers in the midst of their daily lives and routines. While training can prepare us with the confidence to share the gospel message effectively, we often find that the opportunity to share it comes at times and in ways that we least expect it. Our readiness, then, is in our attentiveness to the Holy Spirit, who prepares the heart of the unbeliever, just as He provides the message and opportunity for the believer to share the gospel. We can ask the Lord for the opportunity and for the right words to say in such a situation (Col. 4:2–6).

In the workplace or in the marketplace, it is often our conduct, our demeanor, our work ethic, and our treatment of others that indicate that we are followers of Jesus Christ—whether or not we speak it. While many secular environments prohibit or discourage "proselytizing," our coworkers and close acquaintances will sometimes initiate a conversation because of the difference they see in our lives or attitudes. These are the God-given opportunities to share our hope in Christ, in both gentleness and respect (1 Peter 3:15), and to serve as God's ambassadors, that others may also be reconciled to God (2 Cor. 5:20).

Jesus tells us, "There is joy in the presence of the angels of God over one sinner who repents" (Luke 15:10). In the same way, the local church can find a way to celebrate each new believer. A church might light a candle on the altar each time a new person comes to faith, encouraging the congregation to actively share their faith during the week, as well as to share the joyous news whenever a family member, friend, or coworker comes to faith in Jesus Christ.

Some believers are called by God into a full-time vocational ministry of evangelism. Church leadership can help believers discern God's call on their lives regarding vocational ministry, but should be prayerful and discerning as they recommend and support them to that end. Some churches have encouraged mature believers toward formal seminary training and have even paid their expenses as a means of training up workers for the harvest and then sending them into the fields (Matt. 9:37–38). The church can participate in the ministry of such individuals through financial support, prayer, regular accountability, and practical care. Paul affirmed that their vocation is worthy of remuneration (1 Cor. 9:14) and urged believers to support the saints through prayer and petition (Eph. 6:18–20). He also set an example for regular communication and accountability between gospel messengers and the churches who support them.

Through the centuries, Christ's "sent ones" have left their homes and homeland to settle among peoples foreign to them and to the gospel. Dying to self, they have dwelt among their host cultures, learning the language, preaching the gospel, and eventually translating Scripture into the language of the people. Such preservation of the local language conveys both love and respect, incorporating these peoples into what Revelation describes as a multitude "from every nation and all the tribes, peoples, and languages" (Rev. 7:9).

COMMUNICATING THE GOSPEL

There are countless ways to share the gospel message of Jesus Christ, and the believer should be able to communicate—comfortably and clearly—the basic truths found in Scripture. Here are some effective communication mediums for sharing the gospel message, particularly in a community or public setting:

Scripture: It is good to memorize key Bible passages that help us to explain some basic elements of the gospel: (1) God's love for us, (2) the reality of sin and its consequences, (3) Jesus' death on the cross for our sins, (4) Jesus' resurrection from the dead, (5) forgiveness and salvation by grace and through faith alone, and (6) the gift of eternal life through Christ.

Printed materials: Many find that they can share the gospel message more efficiently through the use of printed materials, which can be a tool for conversation or given to others in passing to be read later. While some question the effectiveness of this kind of evangelism, many thousands of people have come to a saving knowledge of Jesus Christ because they received and read the material shared with them. These materials help the reader understand the gospel, using Scripture and prompts to lead one to pray to receive Christ, and a good opportunity to include the contact information for a local church, so that the seeker or new believer may find more information, as well as fellowship, with a local body of believers. It also is important to evaluate the printed material for a correct and clear presentation of the gospel, avoiding those whose message is unclear, deceptive, misleading, manipulative, or distorted.

Illustrations: Since many people are visual learners, it is also useful to offer vivid and tangible illustrations of the gospel message. Methods such as mimes, skits, visual aids, and chalk talks (when the presenter draws a picture to illustrate the message as they speak), often draw a crowd of people who are curious and willing to watch and listen, though many will walk away without engaging in conversation.

Creative illustrations help the hearer and observer better understand the gospel message. Children are particularly responsive to the Wordless Book and can easily learn and retell the gospel message to their friends. The best visual aids are those that can be easily reproduced in an everyday setting or conversation. Some believers learn to share the gospel by drawing an illustration on a napkin, such as the Bridge Illustration, which can be readily accessed online. The EvangeCube is another visual tool.

Storying: Christians can share the gospel by telling stories from the Bible or from Christian history. Many cultures respond best to oral presentations of the gospel, and this type of presentation can be adapted and contextualized for each unique listener or audience. Cultures that are nominally literate or preliterate can easily respond to the storytelling method and just as easily reproduce it in the countless retellings of the message.

Personal Testimony: While some unbelievers may reject the gospel message, they often are drawn to our *personal testimony*, the personal story of how God redeemed us from lostness and sin, and transformed our lives, giving us hope, joy, and assurance of salvation. Oftentimes they see evidence of God's work in our life. The believer can prepare a concise yet compelling testimony, which will both illustrate God's redeeming work in their own life and encourage the hearer to consider the claims of the gospel for themselves.

Church leaders and teachers should encourage believers to prepare their testimony (many recommend a short version of five minutes or less), and can offer guidance in how to improve it for clarity. Because personal testimonies serve to inspire and reinforce our faith, church groups also should create opportunities for members to share them with fellow believers for mutual edification and encouragement.

Hospitality: While many nonbelievers would not readily enter a Christian church or seek out the message of the gospel, they often will respond to genuine friendship and gestures of hospitality. Christians may use hospitality as a way to establish and deepen a friendship, perhaps eventually gaining the trust and listening ear of the nonbeliever. Friendly conversation and a meal is the best way to reach those whose cultures value hospitality and relationship. This approach allows the believer to welcome the stranger (Matt. 25:35; Heb. 13:2), as if we were ministering to Jesus Himself. Persons once hostile or indifferent to the gospel have responded in faith because of such demonstrations of warmth, love, and friendship.

One of the best examples of hospitality is to invite international students or workers for a meal or recreational activity. Many churches invite internationals to holiday celebrations, both to welcome them and help orient them into some of our local customs and traditions. This initiative of course can be reciprocated, wherein we also become hearers and learners of their culture.

Mercy: Believers should offer mercy and care to those in need, particularly those who are hungry, thirsty, imprisoned, unclothed, ill, or suffering (Matt. 25:31–46). As with hospitality, this ministry allows for a tangible expression of Christ's love, hope, and healing. It was this kind of loving, tender care that a Christian nurse offered to a deathly ill Cambodian girl whose family was fleeing persecution and temporarily housed in a refugee camp. Though they did not speak each other's language, the young girl knew in her heart that the nurse's kindness and devoted care came from her Christian God. The girl eventually recovered, and came to a saving knowledge of Jesus Christ. She never knew the nurse's name and could not convey that she, too, had become a believer in Christ. However, this Cambodian girl is now herself a missionary nurse sharing faith, hope, and healing in Christ's name in another Asian nation. She credits her faith to the unknown nurse, whose mercy and devoted care pointed her to the Savior.

Many churches can reach out to newly arrived immigrants and refugees who are settling in and adapting to their new community. Such efforts can combine both mercy and hospitality, as we show sensitivity, friendship, respect, and generosity in a genuine and consistent way. Though their needs will vary and their "openness" to new neighbors might take time, we can seek the guidance of the Holy Spirit for wisdom and sensitivity as we extend to them our sincere welcome, friendship, and care.

WHAT OUTCOME CAN WE EXPECT?

It is the work of the Holy Spirit to convict the hearer of their lostness in sin, their need to repent, and their need for salvation in Christ Jesus. We cannot push, demand, manipulate, or force a person to respond positively to the gospel, but we must nevertheless communicate the gospel in a way that is meaningful, understandable, and compelling to them.

Those sharing the gospel with unbelievers should not assume that the hearers who walk away have not heard or responded to the message. One Chicago businessman stopped to listen to a young adult courteously preaching the gospel to passersby on his way home from work. After a few minutes he continued on his way, but felt convicted by the message. When he arrived home, the man shared the gospel with his wife and told her of his desire that they have a right relationship with God. The two knelt together and prayed for salvation. The young "preacher" never knew that the Lord had used his message to penetrate the hearts of this husband and wife. Yet this story still is told and retold by their children's children, who trace their family's heritage of faith and Christian service to the message of that earnest and faithful young man may years before.

GUIDING NEW BELIEVERS IN A FAITH RESPONSE

The apostle Paul taught that "if you confess with your mouth Jesus as Lord, and believe in your heart that God raised Him from the dead, you will be saved; for with the heart a person believes, resulting in righteousness, and with the mouth he confesses, resulting in salvation" (Rom. 10:9–10). This passage indicates that a new believer's outward response makes known the reality of what has occurred in their heart.

It is for this reason that many speakers or preachers of the Word offer their hearers an opportunity to respond to the gospel message in a church service, audibly or visibly affirming their faith in Jesus by raising their hand or coming forward for prayer. This is often called an "altar call," though not necessarily involving a formal altar or space. Various church traditions employ different ways of inviting hearers to respond such as indicating their desire on a card.

Once a person indicates an interest in accepting Christ, someone—a minister, a friend, whoever is leading the person—typically will guide the respondent in the "sinner's prayer," which enables the individual to verbally confess their understanding that they are a sinner in need of a Savior, that they believe in Jesus' death on the cross for their sins and in His resurrection, and to ask forgiveness for their sins, that they might have eternal life in Jesus. While some Christian traditions have formal written confessional statements, many new believers simply pray from the heart in their own words, expressing their sincere trust and dependence on Jesus Christ. Often the new believer is encouraged to share their faith with others, which serves as both a confession of their own faith (Rom. 10:9) and a gospel witness to others.

GOSPEL WITNESS TODAY: TWO STORIES OF TRANSFORMING FAITH

Isaiah 55 describes God's rich mercy and offer of salvation. The Lord sees that His Word will not return empty; it will accomplish what He desires, and succeed in His intended purpose (v. 11). As believers faithfully share the good news among the nations, their hearers join in its transmission. New believers often are "on fire" to share the good news of what God has done in their lives! The joy of salvation and the burden to share this life-giving message to those we love compels us to find ways to capture their hearts and minds with the gospel. Those closest to us will often note the changes they see in us and marvel at the transformation. This opens the way to tell of God's transforming work of grace in us and our freedom from sin and shame through Jesus Christ.

A close friend and former Muslim, "J," tells of his previous scorn for Christians and his repeated mockery of Oumarou, a Christian friend who gently and persistently witnessed to him about Christ. In the end, it was Oumarou's patience, long-suffering, and his unconditional love that drew "J" to saving faith in Jesus. When "J" shared his new faith with family members, his mother, as a faithful Muslim, followed the prescribed treatment for an *infidel* and secretly poisoned his food. Unaware, "J" ate the poisoned food but did not die. His mother was astounded and gave herself to the Christian God who saved her son from certain death. "J" has since entered into full-time medical ministry in a country far from his home. His familiarity with Islam helps him better communicate the truth of the gospel message in a way that Muslims can understand and in a way that shows respect, compassion, and concern for their physical well-being as well as for their soul. God's gracious and saving work in his own life compels "J" to reach the lost Muslim peoples with the salvation message of Jesus Christ.

In another part of the world, a witch doctor invited a local pastor to her home to ask questions about the transformation she saw in her two young grandchildren. The woman was an animist, believing in and serving the spirits of her region and people. As a witch doctor, she had secret powers unknown to the rest of her community. This secret knowledge and power ensured that the community respected her status and role; she could bless or curse them, and could call on the spirits to communicate hidden knowledge about them. She was the most feared and dangerous person in the community—the medicinal expert and the religious authority among them.

One day, the children of her village were invited to a public place where they received gift boxes, a special message about Jesus Christ (the greatest gift of all), and an invitation to come to a local Christian church later that week. The witch doctor allowed her two grandchildren to participate in the event and later marveled at the many toys and useful items they received in the gift boxes. Because of her grandchildren's enthusiasm, the woman gave them permission to attend a local Sunday school. Each week, the children came home, happily singing songs and relating the stories they heard from the Bible. It was this change in them that caused her to reflect and to invite the pastor into her home to ask him questions: Where did the gifts come from? Who was this Jesus? Why do you love my grandchildren so much? What makes them so happy?

The pastor then was able to relate the gospel message to her in their tribal language. Being a member of the same community, he knew her power and status as a witch doctor, but he also knew that she was in bondage to Satan. Hearing the message, the woman prayed to receive forgiveness for her sins and accepted the salvation found only in Jesus Christ.

The most moving evidence of her new life and faith, however, was witnessed by her whole community when she brought out her many charms, amulets, and fetishes—all the things that gave her secret knowledge, status, and power, and all of which enslaved her to Satan—and burned them in full view of the villagers. This woman's dramatic conversion was overwhelming evidence of God's sovereignty over the unseen forces and principalities they so feared. It was a mighty display of His unconditional love and forgiveness—expressed through those who filled gift boxes for children they would never meet; then through a faithful community of believers who shared the boxes and the message with the children of their village; then through the enthusiastic children whose joy baffled their grandmother; and then through the pastor who clearly and boldly told her of the Savior who died for her sins, that she might have eternal life.

JOINING THE LORD IN PREACHING THE GOOD NEWS . . . THE BEST NEWS

God often uses a whole constellation of people, loosely connected and working together to join in the sharing of the gospel message. God gives each of us opportunity to be a part of His work, but He is the one who causes the growth (1 Cor. 3:5–9). Today, any one of us may be used by God to participate in this interconnected constellation of believers who give, go, pray, support, teach, train, intercede, host, transport, build, and share in many other ways to ensure the communication of the gospel both in our own community and to the ends of the earth. We might not know this side of heaven the effect showing hospitality to a neighbor, participating in a Bible study, or corresponding to someone incarcerated will have. But we can be gospel bearers in countless ways—evangelists—sharing the good news of Christ.

Reliable accounts have come forth showing that God sometimes reveals Himself to nonbelievers in dreams or visions, especially in areas of the world that are culturally hostile to the gospel. However, He generally communicates the gospel through His timeless Word—the Bible—and through the verbal witness of believers throughout the world who proclaim that Word. The message of the gospel is fully trustworthy and compelling. Those of us who have heard the good news and have the assurance of salvation are commissioned to go and to tell the good news to others.

The individual believer and the collective church have a great privilege in joining the Lord in the preaching of the gospel of Jesus Christ. Given the primary role of the gospel in the ministry of the church, we must purpose to train, equip, encourage, and engage believers in sharing their story of faith and in relating the vital message of Jesus Christ to others. While Scripture warns that many will reject the message and even persecute gospel messengers, our confidence is in the presence and leading of the Holy Spirit, who will prepare both the messengers and the hearers of the gospel message.

Jesus declared that this gospel will be preached in the whole world, to all nations, and then the end will come (Matt. 24:14). His Great Commission, given in Matthew 28:18–20, was not limited to His first disciples, but rather commands all generations of Christ followers to share the gospel message—baptizing and teaching those who believe to obey all that Christ commanded, until He returns.

Let us then faithfully and joyfully be prepared and eager witnesses to the gospel that has transformed our own lives. Let us make use of every opportunity, following the Spirit's leading, to do our part in carrying the gospel, the good news . . . the very best news.

CHAPTER 4.3

Doing Urban Ministry

EMANUEL PADILLA

The world is changed, not changing. In 1965, four years before Neil Armstrong walked on lunar soil, Dr. Martin Marty published a booklet about the mission of the church in which he makes two claims: (1) The new environment for Christian mission is urban, and (2) The basic reality of urban life is its secularity.[1] Nearly sixty years later, we are living in the world Dr. Marty anticipated.[2]

In 2018, the United Nations reported an estimated 55 percent of the world's population lived in urban areas. There were 548 cities with at least one million inhabitants, accounting for a fifth of all people. By 2030, they projected that number will balloon to 706.[3] The number of cities is not the only significant figure; cities also grew in population size. In 1970, just five years after Dr. Marty's book, there were only two "megacities" (cities of at least ten million people), New York and Tokyo. In 1990, there were 10. By 2013, there were 28. In 2018, there were 33. Some of these cities are larger in population than most countries. Mexico City, with roughly 20 million people, has more people than over 180 countries in the world today.[4]

Many pastors read these statistics as distant realities. Their congregation, they counter, belongs to the 45 percent of the populace that exists in a rural environment. The skills necessary for urban places are not yet required for their ministry context. However, the line between rural and urban is blurring, and the makeup of the most rural communities is changing as urban people are pushed farther out by powerful economic—and spiritual—forces. The effects of cities reverberate outward to surrounding regions, so it is no longer possible for rural pastors to ignore or distance themselves from the influence of the city. They do so at great risk to their congregational ministry.

529

This chapter is an overview of the skills necessary for ministry to the urban world. Prior to reviewing practical skills, we define the city and what it does. To minister to this world, church leaders must first understand it. The second section of the chapter is an abbreviated biblical theology of the city that also undergirds these skills. This will cover the two major visions of humanity and urban places presented in the biblical narrative. Having established a biblical vision of the city and a proper understanding of its function, the final portion of this chapter presents a praxis for urban ministry. Urban ministry requires a complex combination of theological, ministerial, and urbanist skills, so much of what is presented here is introductory. Where possible, suggested resources have been included for further study.

WHAT IS THE CITY?

This question appears unduly philosophical, but the answer is often debated. Statisticians, urban planners, and politicians each develop a definition fit for their causes, "right in [their own] eyes" (Judg. 17:6). For instance, the United Nations report cited earlier includes an entire page defining the parameters of a city. *CityLab*, a publication covering a wide variety of urban issues, recently published a run of articles attempting to distinguish urban from suburban and rural.[5] Even within the suburban classification, there is a variety of definitions. Therefore, those doing urban ministry must also define what they mean by *urban* and *city*. For pastors, it is natural to begin definitions by first recalling the backgrounds of words, and Dr. Marty provides a succinct etymology for both words. He writes:

> Urban life recalls the Latin background of our language in the term *urbs*. To most thinkers this word represents "the world man builds for himself." It is the largely physical side of man's own creation. "Urban" refers to the form or the structure of life. It is, so to speak, the apartment that man has to furnish.
>
> The word "city," . . . carries the memory of the Latin *civitas*, a word that immediately throws the idea of civilization into . . . minds. *Civitas* refers to the psychic or mental and spiritual side of man's world. It implies not the form of the city but the activity in the city. It does not represent the furnished apartment but the working and thinking of the people who live in the apartment.[6]

A definition of the city needs to account for these two dimensions. The city is both the world that humanity chooses to build as their home and the spirit with which they relate to it, each other, and transcendent realities like goodness, truth, and beauty. The *urban*, meaning the conglomeration of buildings, streets, parks and plazas—the furnishings in the human apartment—is an agent in service to the *city*. It supports the city in forming the minds and spirits of its people. When defining realities that are abstract, instructors will often use images and metaphors to help students gain a clearer understanding. The church, for instance, is described as a "body" (1 Cor. 12:12–26) or a "spiritual house" (1 Peter 2:5) by Paul and Peter respectively. The two dimensions of the city can similarly be summarized in a set of metaphors.

THE CITY AS NODE

People are increasingly incorporating smart devices in their homes (i.e., smart televisions, refrigerators, tablets). These devices are connected via a node, a point of network connection. A Wi-Fi router, for instance, is a node that can redistribute internet access to devices connecting to it. A city, like a Wi-Fi router, is a node, but instead of distributing network connection, it distributes cultural power. A city is a *node* of cultural power. Cities house most of the systems, institutions, and production mechanisms necessary for human flourishing. Political legislation is written in the city. Cultural trends begin in the city. Economic enterprise is run from the city; even farmers travel into the city for their market. Resources are collected in cities and redistributed to surrounding regions. Still, there is a greater function than these that the urban setting enables.

Daniel Burnham, the principal planner responsible for Chicago's city plan, identified the city as "an iconographic reservoir that is capable of inspiring belief in the larger social body and in one's duty to it."[7] Burnham identifies the physical dimension of the city, the urban dimension, as an important influence on the different systems housed therein. For Burnham, the place itself matters. "Things make [people] just as much as [people] make [things]."[8] The force of this formative power is applied to both individuals and societies, and this clarifies the nature of the urban world. Urban places shape societal life. Ralph Turner, in a prophetic voice, writes, "If the city is the world which man created, it is the world in which he is henceforth condemned to live. Thus, indirectly, and without any clear sense of the nature of his task, in making the city man has remade himself."[9]

French philosopher Jacques Ellul reinforces this idea when he suggests that cities are capable of spiritual influence.[10] Ancient Greek philosopher, Lycurgus, claimed the city was the only unit of government capable of establishing a relationship with the individual strong enough to make it (the city) a formative agent.[11] In other words, the city is of greater influence on the character of its people than the state or nation. Since cities are increasingly interconnected like nodes in a system, people in New York, Tokyo, Mexico City, and London are likely to have more in common with each other than with the nonurban citizens in their own countries.[12]

The statistics cited earlier further clarify the degree of influence and reach of the urban world. In 2010, Edwin Heathcote observed that cities like Lagos were growing rapidly, absorbing smaller cities and suburbs in their growth. He observed that these bigger "metacities" needed greater connectivity, and he writes, "Digital networking has not, as was forecast, led to a decline in the city. Rather, it has led to an urbanisation of the rest of the planet."[13] Internet and media communication have catalyzed the development of the human apartment, the urban world. The increased influence and growth of the city is perceived by some as a blessing and by others as a threat. This will be explored further later in the chapter.

THE CITY AS FIRE

In her classic book, *The Death and Life of Great American Cities*, Jane Jacobs uses a different metaphor to define the city. For Jacobs, a city is a large field in darkness being illuminated by scattered fires of varying sizes, each representing intense, diverse, and complex human community. As the community works for mutual support and benefit, they give shape to the field around them; their life together brilliantly reveals the necessary form for the space they coinhabit. As the community teems with the flourishing of a diverse people, a city is born. It is important to acknowledge that this fire is intended to benefit the citizen; it is meant to illuminate a good way of living. For Jacobs, this metaphor served as a critique for modern urban planning and its emphasis on expert planners. The city, Jacobs proposes, is the outworking of everyday citizens pursing life together. The pursuit of this good life is the end enabled by the city; the good life is supposed to be revealed by this fire, this fellowship of citizens cooperating to meet their shared needs. These image reveals three basic functions for the city that can now be explored in the next question.

WHAT DOES THE CITY DO?

First, cities are places of human advancement.[14] Human advancement simply means that cities are not full of poor people because they "make poor people, but because cities attract poor people with the prospect of improving their lot in life."[15] The density of the city enables the flourishing of several groups. For instance, migrants and refugees often seek and find a semblance of refuge from oppressive economic and/or political forces in the city.

Second, cities are places for technological advancement. This is also a product of the city's density. Historically, the city introduces new complexity to roles and occupations for community members. Unlike its predecessor, the village, "the city effected . . . a command over long distance transportation, an intensification of communication over long distances . . . an outburst of invention along with a large scale development of civil engineering, and, not least, it promoted a tremendous further rise in agricultural productivity."[16] The first recorded biblical city reflects this kind of advancement. The children of Cain are the first city-dwellers, and they developed musical instruments, metal works, and are the first herders (Gen. 4:21–22). In addition to diversity, the malleability of the urban environment also contributes to its ability to foster technological advancement. The urban environment, as is visible in most cities, is continually under construction, shifting and changing to accommodate the complex needs of the society.

Third, cities are places that enable human cooperation. Recent trends like coworking spaces rely on the potential creative power produced by the interactions of diverse, technologically adept communities. According to Edward Glaeser, "Americans who live in metropolitan areas with more than one million residents are, on average, 50 percent more productive than Americans who live in smaller metropolitan areas."[17] This is true broadly in the world environment, as is seen when many private corporations plant offices and headquarters in major global cities like Toronto and London. Cities make the cooperation of large and complex institutions manageable by providing the infrastructure, people capital, and economic systems necessary to carry out their work.

Of course, these three functions of the city can and generally do become corrupted. The city can enable systems for human oppression, the development of technologies that result in human harm, and the cooperation of a society that sustains a city that resembles Babylon, a significant biblical image for the depraved city. Urban sociologist Robert Park's warning is worth taking to heart: if the city is the home humanity builds, it is the world humanity is condemned to live in together. Therefore, pastors and their congregations should consider the cities they, along with their neighbors, are making and sustaining. They should especially consider the theological implications of the gospel and the cities they make.

THEOLOGY OF THE CITY

The city reflects a duality in its nature as it does in its dimensions. Like its human architects, the city is corrupted but not fully consumed by sin. The city is both a place of great prosperity and of severe poverty. It is home to institutions that promote peace, and it is the setting for acts of appalling violence. Cities are filled with millions of people, yet many citizens experience loneliness and depression. How can this duality be accounted for theologically? Does the Bible give us a vision for the city that avoids the simplification that construes nature as good and the city as wicked? If it does provide a more complex vision, how does this vision shape the

533

way believers understand and engage the city? In this next section, we present a biblical theology of the city that pursues answers to these questions.

THE CITY IN GENESIS, EXODUS, AND EXILE

There are three important, early checkpoints to consider when studying the story of the Bible and the way it paints cities: (1) Genesis, (2) Exodus, and (3) Exile. Throughout the narrative, the Bible uses two pictures for the city: Babylon and Jerusalem. These get introduced in Genesis, early in the narrative, and serve as archetypes by which all cities are shaped. To develop a biblical theology of the city, one needs to understand the origin of Babylon and Jerusalem, the story arc between them, and the way God's people relate to both. The selected checkpoints provide brief snapshots for each of these thematic elements, and they also shape a praxis for urban ministry. Given the way the rural mythology shaped Christian perspectives of the city over the last sixty years, these themes need correction as they are studied.

Genesis

The book of Genesis introduces Babylon and Jerusalem as major characters in the biblical story. After the flood, Genesis repeats an established pattern. Noah plants a vineyard (an echo of the garden), and the Lord reissues the cultural mandate (Gen. 9:1–20). Moving quickly through the story, the reader encounters the next biblical city in Genesis 11. Without the Lord's favor and in full rebellion, the people gather to make another city. Their pride is in full view. It is common for readers to think that building a city at all was their sin, but the truth is that the *telos* (i.e., purpose) of the city was the real problem. The people wanted to build a city that would give them a new identity and mark their glory as the great makers of the tower. Rejecting the Lord, they started a building project with the expressed purpose of making a name for themselves. Genesis 11 is the introduction of the first biblical image for the city, Babylon. From this passage forward, Babylon serves as the symbol of man's rejection and war against the Lord's Kingship.

Immediately after the incident at Babel, Scripture turns its focus to Abram. On his pilgrimage, Abram is introduced to Melchizedek, the king of Salem and priest of God Most High (Gen. 14:18). "Salem" is the early representation of Jerusalem, the city that displays God's rightful rule and the place of His dwelling.[18] In the story of Abram's encounter with Melchizedek the reader is introduced to the second important image of the city in the Bible, Jerusalem. Babylon is the representation of humanity's evil intention; Jerusalem is the idealized city where God's High Priest, in the order of Melchizedek, will reign as King. Jerusalem is a city of blessing and abundance. Later in Scripture the reader is told that Abram left Ur on pilgrimage, looking not for a farm or garden, but for the city designed and built by God (Heb. 11:10). Like Abraham, the father of faith (Rom. 4:16–17), God's people are called on pilgrimage to seek the city that is to come (Heb. 13:14).[19] The promise of Scripture is that the Lord provides a city for those who thirst and hunger on their pilgrimage (Ps. 107:4–7). The story of the Bible moves from Eden to Babylon and from Babylon to Jerusalem.

Exodus and Exile

The exodus was a significant part of ancient Israel's history and identity.[20] It shaped their understanding of God and His works of salvation.[21] In fact, every occurrence of salvation in the Bible is written as an echo of the exodus, a "new exodus," a repetition of the pattern set in Egypt. During the exodus, God's people are given a new blueprint for life. Indeed, they are given new life completely. Israel is gifted wisdom for the building of a society undergirded not by a lust for mastery, but by service to a life-giving God. The people are instructed to remember Egypt, to rehearse the story, and to live as people who were once slaves. The act of remembrance is meant to shape Israel's societal life, guiding their relationship to strangers, the poor, and the weak. Israel becomes a counterculture, a light to surrounding nations, that reflects the giving love of God. The Law imagines a posture of restraint for God's people, resisting the temptation to dominate the weak, and it highlights the call to live a life distinct from the patterns of Babylon.

Israel failed to develop this counterculture. The early chapters of Jeremiah record a history of priests, shepherds, and prophets disobeying God's instructions. The entire nation's crimes are summarized in two statements: (1) They disowned their God, and (2) replaced Him with other gods (2:13). The leaders were corrupt, and the people were wayward, leading to rampant injustice (Jer. 6:10; 7:5–20, 30–31). Israel did not build the nation, much less the Jerusalem God intended. Instead, they built a mirror-image of Babylon, following the plans for a city built on *libido dominandi*, the lust for mastery.[22] What was ruling Babylon was in them too. God's people were more Babylonian than they were citizens of Jerusalem, and after many warnings, they were cast out from the city of God. The marvel of the exile, however, is God's instruction to Israel: "Seek the welfare of the city where I have sent you into exile, and pray to the LORD on its behalf; for in its welfare you will find your welfare" (Jer. 29:7 ESV).[23]

In his first letter to the scattered church, Peter ties these two biblical themes (Exodus and Exile) together to identify the church and motivate an ethic of restraint and good work (1 Peter 2:11–12). He merges the sojourner and exile identity as a hendiadys—a figure of speech where two words are joined to present a single idea—and from that new identity he instructs the diaspora to resist the overindulgence common to the culture. Instead, he invites them to live good lives and do good work in the sight of nonbelievers. These instructions reflect the life produced by both major OT themes. The exodus creates a form of separation, a resisting of the world's Babylonian pattern. The exiled people of God, however, are called to seek shalom for their corrupted homes. Peter encourages a non-innocent, redeemed people to live in Babylon as *simul justus et peccator,* or simultaneously righteous and sinner. As redeemed sinners, resist evil. As non-innocent exiles, do good. This two-pronged missiology summarizes a healthy philosophy of urban ministry.

A PRAXIS FOR URBAN MINISTRY

This chapter introduced a more complete image of the city, defining it as a node of cultural power. Modern cities mirror the two biblical archetypes (Babylon and Jerusalem) while embodying neither fully. To minister effectively in this complex cultural matrix of brokenness and beauty, Christians need to (1) remember Peter's ethic of restraint and good work and (2) nurture the key elements of a thriving city. Before discussing these further, readers must adopt a distinction within the local congregation. Tim Keller divides the urban congregation into two categories: organized and organic.[24] The organized church consists of pastors, staff, and other official leaders of the congregation. The primary role of this group is evangelism and the discipleship of believers. While these leaders provide a gospel-infused vision for life and ministry, the organic church is the primary vehicle for engaging the city. The organic church consists of lay members working in the variety of systems and institutions of the city. The organized church supports the work of the organic church by caring for their spiritual needs and helping them integrate the gospel and their work.

INTEGRATION OF FAITH AND WORK (PETER'S ETHIC)

Pastors should devote more attention to preparing and mobilizing their congregations toward the active integration of their faith and work. While all Christians are instructed to share the gospel when given the opportunity, this is about preparing Christians to do their vocational work with excellence. It means the pursuit of a distinctly Christian character in the work being done. It also means preparing them to resist the sinful habits of the city as they work within it. In modern cities, this is especially important because pastors are typically marginalized from many of the public and powerful functions of the city. Christian leaders and pastors are relegated to specialized roles as spiritual leaders guiding people in private worship.

In his own day, Dr. Marty observed that the modern city "cut off" the church from "the kinds of decisions in which basic life . . . is affected and formed."[25] He notes that many conservative Christians accepted this new place in the city, suggesting "that the only responsibility of the Christians toward the environment is to rescue and snatch people out of it."[26] These same sincere Christians, observes Marty, "then turn around to criticize most vocally the secularizing of life to which they abandoned society and its people."[27] Instead, Marty proposes a different way of engaging Babylon with the Christian message. He suggests the Christian laypeople—architects, teachers, farmers, artists, marketers, chefs, and bankers—are the necessary workers. They must carry on the Christian mission and lead the exodus from Babylon to Jerusalem. "They will be effective from the human way of speaking to the degree that they penetrate the varieties and definitions of urban life."[28]

NURTURING A THRIVING CITY

The distinction between organized and organic church is crucial when assessing where to focus ministry efforts. The myriad of interconnected crises related to violence, racism, economic disparity, health, and other complex problems overwhelm the effort of any single church. We learned this during the COVID-19 pandemic as congregations worked to support under-resourced communities; problems embedded in the city fabric require systematic and sustained effort that go beyond the means of congregational life. Therefore, church leaders need a framework for measuring the health of their city and assessing which areas require more focused attention. By identifying areas of need, organized leadership can mobilize their congregations toward essential service.

The Institute for Advanced Studies in Culture at the University of Virginia published a series of reports in which they identified six key dimensions or areas to a thriving city. The challenge of measuring these keys is that they are both product of and essential for a healthy city. There is a cyclical quality to them, so the IASC chose to refer to these keys as "endowments." An endowment commonly refers to a fund that is gifted or donated to a cultural institution or school. These funds usually continue to earn interest or other additional gains that enable the creation of new openings for advancement (e.g., new scholarships, open faculty positions, etc.). By using this term metaphorically to refer to the key dimensions of a thriving city, the IASC is suggesting that these keys require work to create and maintain opportunities for flourishing. The endowments are both gift and reward, product and resource.

According to the findings of the IASC, the health of a city is measured according to these six endowments: truth, goodness, beauty, prosperity, well-ordered justice, and sustainability. These six dimensions of flourishing "form the most recognizable horizons of human experience and the building blocks" of human thriving.[29] They also mark the key points of emphasis for urban ministry. Within each endowment, researchers from a variety of community organizations and disciplines reported on over 3,000 indicators of health.[30] There is not sufficient space to review the reports/indicators for each endowment, but a few examples reveal the unique opportunities available to a congregation enabling their laypeople to work with excellence in all sectors of city life.

The Truth (Human Knowledge and Learning)

The truth endowment is about educational systems and the key indicators for measuring educational health in a city. Several indicators mark whether a city has quality education including graduation rates, reading levels, student-teacher ratios, class size, and others. The reports on these indicators also reveal that the endowments are interconnected. Improving the quality of education in the city has correlated outcomes for economic and social life. The same is inversely true. Measures of prosperity—another endowment dimension—impact the quality of education in the city. A Chicago nonprofit called My Block, My Hood, My City (M3) illustrates the complex service approach necessary to address the truth endowment well. Urban congregations can learn from M3 to complexify their ministry approach—making use of the wide variety of skills, professions, and disciplines present in the laity—and address an endowment such as truth in a way that has compounding positive effects on other endowment areas.

M3 provides youth from under-resourced neighborhoods with "an awareness of the world and opportunities beyond their neighborhood."[31] Partnering with local schools, M3 takes students on educational explorations (i.e., tours) "focused on STEM, Arts & Culture, Citizenry & Volunteerism, Health, Community Development, Culinary Arts, and Entrepreneurism." Their goal is to "boost educational attainment in spite of the poverty and social isolation" faced by these students. The results are remarkable. According to their website, students who take educational trips between the ages of 12–18 are 57 percent more likely to earn a college degree or do postgraduate work. By engaging students in other sectors of city life, M3 improves the likelihood of increased education for these students.

Organizations like this one reveal the simple yet creative ways that congregations can influence a dimension of health for the city while creating other positive effects. IASC refers to this as a virtuous cycle, a pattern of thriving that multiplies as improvements in one area create reciprocal benefits in other endowments. There is a second lesson to be learned from M3. Urban ministry requires collaboration across a diverse community of people.[32] The tours offered by M3 require partnerships between cultural centers, restaurants, donors, school principals, and other nonprofits willing to provide excursions and student volunteer opportunities.

These tours are an integration of an array of people working in a variety of sectors. Likewise, the local congregation is an organic connection between peoples from diverse sectors of the city. By inviting laity to imagine creative partnerships, leaders can start virtuous cycles based on the skills and work areas of their congregants. The question of which ministry should be the focus is not always a matter of financial resources but of personnel within the church.

The Beautiful (Creativity Aesthetic and Design)

The beauty endowment is about aesthetic quality and the key indicators for measuring placemaking in a healthy city. Placemaking is a collaborative process in which political agencies, nonprofits, businesses, artists, activists, and communities work together to reshape the built environment for the thriving of local neighborhoods. Very few congregations consider this an essential element of ministry. One exception is the Christian Cultural Center in New York City. To address the escalating gentrification of Brooklyn, Pastor A. R. Bernard helped members of the congregation start a nonprofit that would oversee a $1.2 billon housing development.[33] In partnership with a developer and working with the city's existing policies, the church is working to build an 11-acre "Urban Village" equipped with a performing arts center, local retailers, affordable housing, and everything necessary for a walkable community. This example is intentionally astounding. Many congregations do not have the resources for such an undertaking. Still, all congregations can and should engage in acts of placemaking and beautification.

Organizations like the Project for Public Spaces (PPS) lead the way in advocacy for healthy practices of placemaking, and they propose a series of measured, small scale improvements that greatly increase the health of a place. Missiologist Sean Benesh helpfully calls these small scale projects "tactical or guerrilla urbanism projects."[34] Benesh is referring to active involvement in local neighborhood improvements done in partnership with the community. For instance, David Doig, President of the Chicago Neighborhood Initiative, said in an interview that one of the best ways to reduce crime in a community is to plant gardens.[35] Local Chicago artist, Theaster Gates, restored his late father's home and turned it into a gathering place for artists. This became the central hub for what is now a budding economic center for a southside Chicago neighborhood that was in severe decline. These are just two examples of small scale placemaking, but excellent examples of believers placemaking can be found in many cities.[36]

These anecdotes demonstrate the wide array of needs individual believers and congregations can meet based on the occupational skills among the laity. The work of Canaan Community Church, in Englewood (a south side Chicago neighborhood) serves well as a final example. Canaan had urban farming experts within their congregation and mobilized them to partner with and instruct other congregations in developing urban farms and forms of Community Supported Agriculture (CSA). These churches created a network that provided produce to families in the local community relying on these farms. This was a work of placemaking and sustainability, but it also addressed food distribution injustice; these congregations were in communities identified as food deserts. Pastors leading urban-centric congregations must know the skills of the congregation and empower them to address the complex problems of the community, especially when these problems are the product of Babylonian injustice.

The Just and Well-Ordered (Political and Civic Life)

Global news reports show modern cities around the world are stages for protests about injustice built into political systems. Of all the endowments, the area of political and civic arrangement is the most emotionally freighted. Because of this baggage, believers need the organized church to lead and shape pursuits of justice. Pastoral leaders must reimagine their discipleship pedagogies to include justice as a central theme. They must develop intercultural competence and historically informed race consciousness in those under their care. With courage, they should lead their congregations in advocacy for those marginalized by the political order. N. T. Wright argues that the church is, by definition, "the single, multiethnic family . . . energized by God's Spirit; and . . . called to bring the transformative news of God's rescuing justice to the whole creation."[37] To live into this identity, the church needs reimagined spiritual formation programs.

The discipleship methodology of the local congregation needs a component of historical informed race consciousness. That is, members of the congregation need to learn about the historic and present dynamics that formed and built the social structures of their city. Daniel Burnham, cited earlier as the primary architect responsible for Chicago's first city plan, believed his version of Chicago would be ideal. His work would go on to be cited by Chicago Mayor Richard J. Daley, who referred to Burnham's plan as his favorite book, as he proposed urban redevelopment plans in the late 1950s that drastically marginalized black and brown communities.[38] To effectively minister, congregations must know histories like these histories of urban renewal, redlining, and other practices of injustice that scar their city. This needs to be built into the discipleship of the believer.

NEIGHBORHOOD MAPPING AS A PASTORAL DISCIPLINE

To help congregations identify the endowments to target, Pastors should add to their skills the methods of ethnographers. Moreover, because the six endowment areas have several indicators of health, some difficult to discern by using data alone, pastors must learn to listen to their communities for that which data cannot reveal. Specifically, pastors must learn to map their neighborhoods. This is an essential skill that many seminary-trained pastors do not develop while in their programs. It is, however, common to the church-based training of black and brown ministry leaders. In a recent webinar, Pastor José Humphreys explained that one of his main methods for identifying ministry needs, learned from the tradition of Latino congregations, is to walk his neighborhood, recording the prayers and needs of people on the block.[39] Neighborhood mapping begins with listening, listening profoundly to community needs.

Neighborhood mapping is a scalable skill. In its simplest form, the pastor keeps a journal record of observations he makes as he walks his community. Pastors keep consistent beats, or designated trails; they walk according to a repeated schedule. This allows the minister familiarity with a portion of their neighborhood and culturally significant points therein. A more complex neighborhood map includes records of foot traffic, interviews with local residents, analysis of the makeup of the community, and other more complex forms of data collection and analysis. The goal, whether in simple or complex analysis, is to develop the knowledge of a participant observer, one who knows the community from experience. As pastor Humphreys noted, the consistency of walking and praying with the community connects the minister to the life rhythm of their local neighborhood. Several excellent resources exist to help pastors practice and develop this skill.[40] By using these social science skills, understanding the occupational gifting of the laity in their local congregation, and grading the indicators of health in the six endowment areas for their local city, ministers begin to shape an effective urban ministry praxis; they are better equipped to discover the opportunities to bear witness to shalom in their community.

CONCLUSION

The urban world is not a place to escape or idolize. It is a place in need of faithful love for the sake of all the people affected by it. Because of the city's reach and power, this chapter advocates for an urban-centric ministry philosophy for those in and out of the city. This, however, must include a cautionary word. This chapter is not suggesting the church is called or expected to transform culture in any grandiose or triumphalist manner. In fact, the reflections on the endowments imply the need for more concentrated acts of transformation carried out by local congregations. Small acts of culture-making should not be considered insignificant. The congregation should start with its own locale and pursue initiatives based on the skills of the laity. As Jeremiah told the exiles, "Seek the welfare of the city where I have sent you into exile, and pray to the LORD on its behalf; for in its welfare you will find your welfare" (Jer. 29:7 ESV). A poem by Wendell Berry is an appropriate benediction. He writes:

> Because we have not made our lives to fit
> our places, the forests are ruined, the fields eroded,
> the streams polluted, the mountains overturned. Hope
> then to belong to your place by your own knowledge
> of what it is that no other place is, and by
> your caring for it as you care for no other place . . . [41]

NOTES

1. Martin E. Marty, *Babylon by Choice: New Environment for Mission* (New York: Friendship Press, 1965).

2. Portions of this chapter were previously published at the author's blog, www.worldoutspoken.com. Used by permission.

3. *The World's Cities in 2018* (UN, 2018), http://digitallibrary.un.org/record/3799524.

4. Richard Florida, *Atlas of Cities*, ed. Paul Knox (Princeton: Princeton University Press, 2014), 140.

5. "When Suburbia Got Complicated," *Bloomberg*, December 21, 2018, https://www.bloomberg.com/news/articles/2018–12–21/what-we-learned-about-american-suburbs-this-year.

6. Marty, *Babylon by Choice*, 10.

7. Kristin Schaffer, "Fabric of City Life" in Daniel H. Burnham and Edward H. Bennett, *Plan of Chicago*, ed. Charles Moore (New York: Princeton Architectural Press, 1993), xiii, emphasis added.

8. Daniel Miller, *Stuff* (Cambridge, England: Polity Press, 2009).

9. Ralph H. Turner, ed., *Robert E. Park on Social Control and Collective Behavior: Selected Papers*, 2nd ed. (Chicago: Phoenix Books, 1969), 3.

10. Jacques Ellul, *The Meaning of the City*, repr. (Eugene, OR: Wipf & Stock Pub, 2011), 9.

11. Burnham and Bennett, *Plan of Chicago*, xii.

12. Timothy Keller, *Center Church: Doing Balanced, Gospel-Centered Ministry in Your City* (Grand Rapids: Zondervan, 2012), 155.

13. Edwin Heathcote, "From Megacity to Metacity," *Financial Times*, April 6, 2010, https://www.ft.com/content/e388a076–38d6–11df-9998–00144feabdc0.

14. The three points in this section are from Sean Benesh, *Blueprints for a Just City: The Role of the Church in Urban Planning and Shaping the City's Built Environment* (Portland, OR: Urban Loft Publishers, 2015).

15. Edward Glaeser, *Triumph of the City: How Our Greatest Invention Makes Us Richer, Smarter, Greener, Healthier, and Happier* (New York: Penguin Books, 2012), 70.

16. Lewis Mumford, *The City in History: Its Origins, Its Transformations, and Its Prospects* (New York: Harvest Books), 30.

17. Edward Glaeser, *Triumph of the City*, 7–8.

18. Psalm 76:2 connects the two names.

19. Interestingly, in his history of the city, Lewis Mumford suggests that the earliest cities were destinations of religious pilgrimage.

20. Ronald S. Hendel, "The Exodus in Biblical Memory," *Journal of Biblical Literature* 120, no. 4 (2001): 601.

21. Otto Alfred Piper, "Unchanging Promises: Exodus in the New Testament," *Interpretation* 11, no. 1 (January 1, 1957): 4.

22. See the discussion in Mumford, *The City in History*, 160. Mumford comments on Augustine's discussion in *City of God* about humanity's self-love and the *libido dominandi*. Mumford notes that many of the cities of the ancient world grew into their full form on the parasitism of surrounding areas and the use of slaves. He argues that capital

cities like Babylon expanded by imposing required tributes and "by bringing about a negative symbiosis based on [the] terrified expectation of destruction and extermination," and all the cities after it harbor this base abuse of power. Cities can and often are the places of great injustice, severe violence, and deep-seated inequality.

23. The word translated "welfare" is the biblical word *shalom*. "In the Bible, *shalom* means universal flourishing, wholeness and delight—a rich state of affairs in which natural needs are satisfied and natural gifts fruitfully employed, . . . Shalom, in other words, is the way the world should be" (Cornelius Plantinga Jr, *Not the Way It's Supposed to Be: A Breviary of Sin* [Grand Rapids: Eerdmans, 1996], 10).

24. Keller, *Center Church*, 294.

25. Marty, *Babylon by Choice*, 61.

26. Ibid., 62.

27. Ibid.

28. Ibid., 63.

29. "Human Ecology Framework," *Thriving Communities Group*, accessed December 17, 2020, https://thrivingcitiesgroup .com/our-framework.

30. These reports continue to be added to expand as more research is being developed. See https: //thrivingcitiesgroup .com/indicator-explorer for more information.

31. "How MBMHMC Works," My Block, My Hood, My City, https: //www.formyblock.org/how-it-works-1/.

32. Diversity here refers to diverse occupations, skills, and expertise. This is not a reference to racial or ethnic diversity.

33. "The Urban Village—World Outspoken," https: //worldoutspoken.com/podcasts/urban-village-project/.

34. Benesh, *Blueprints for a Just City*, 16.

35. Interview with author.

36. For more examples listen to *The Embedded Church* podcast hosted by Dr. Eric Jacobsen and urban planner Sarah Joy Proppe (https://www.embeddedchurch.com/).

37. N. T. Wright, *Simply Christian: Why Christianity Makes Sense* repr. ed. (New York: HarperOne, 2021), 200.

38. Adam Cohen and Elizabeth Taylor, *American Pharaoh: Mayor Richard J. Daley—His Battle for Chicago and the Nation*, repr. (Boston: Back Bay Books, 2001), 216.

39. José Humphreys, "Doing Church en el Barrio" (webinar), World Outspoken, May 17, 2021, www.worldoutspoken .com/webinars.

40. See John Dr Fuder, Ray Bakke, and Bob Lupton, *Neighborhood Mapping: How to Make Your Church Invaluable to the Community*, new ed. (Chicago: Moody Publishers, 2014). See also Sean Benesh, *The Urban Cartographer's Toolkit: How to Map, Study, Exegete, Analyze, and Understand Your Neighborhood* (Portland, OR: Intrepid, 2021).

41. Wendell Berry, *This Day: Collected & New Sabbath Poems* (Berkeley, CA: Counterpoint, 2014), 305.

Contextualizing the Gospel in Different Cultures

ANONYMOUS

This chapter is about contextualizing biblical truth—or how biblical truth is made meaningful in a certain context.[1] More specifically, contextualization involves using familiar cultural material to carry truth to specific people in specific places "in terms that do not seem strange to them"[2] so it has its intended effect and pleases God.

Examples of contextualization include the Ghanaian poet Afua Kuma calling Jesus the "the Sword Carrier"[3] and Gbaya Christians from Cameroon and Central African Republic calling Jesus their *Soreh-ga-mo-kee*, that is, the cool tree that brings healing and *shalom*.[4] It is also the Yupik Eskimo Church discerning whether the traditional *yurak* dance, a dance with connections to Shammanism, can be used for worship or if it invites evil spirits or stirs feelings and memories that draw congregants back to beliefs from which Christ delivered them.[5]

Often contextualization has been thought of only for remote places.[6] It is sometimes assumed that when ministering in a culture outside one's own, one must "contextualize" the gospel, whereas at home one simply preaches and applies the gospel. The reality is that "preaching" and "applying" are contextualization. We contextualize just as much "at home" as we do anywhere, just more or less consciously. For a couple of decades, gospel expressions like the "four spiritual laws," the Wordless Book, and phrases like "just accept Jesus into your heart" were common contextualizations—though not always recognized as such by those of us for whom late twentieth-century American evangelicalism was home.

Wherever we are, at home or abroad, biblical truth comes to us through many familiar means, such as:

- words such as "for God so loved the world";
- metaphors and analogies: "living water";
- symbols: the cross;
- rituals: church services;
- art: *The Prodigal*;
- music: Handel's *Messiah*;
- food: the Lord's Supper and fellowship around dinner tables;
- architecture: church buildings that draw our gaze upward;
- people and their examples: Kathy, Bob, Ellie, Sarah, John, Bill, Ruth, Paul, and others;
- communities: where people find identity and belonging;[7]
- . . . and many other means.

These are contextualizations that carry truth into the cultural stories we live by (and live in), lead us to the biblical story,[8] and invite us to redirect our faith from our story to God and His Word—forcing us to decide what, or whom, we trust more.

Jesus' contextualization of the gospel for the rich young ruler didn't fit in the young man's story of salvation by keeping some of the laws. Rather it forced him to decide whether to sell all or not—whether to trust in Jesus' story or his own (Luke 18). By keeping his wealth, he forfeited "many times as much at this time and in the age to come, eternal life" (Luke 18:30). The economics of his story left him excluded and sad.

Contextualization is based on the belief that God was contextualizing when He inspired the biblical authors. For example, the Pentateuch was written in a covenantal form common in ancient times. The stories, poetry, and proverbs throughout Scripture were contextual forms of communication and were loaded with metaphors relevant to the intended audiences. When teaching about the dynamics between His Word and human hearts, Jesus said to an agrarian audience, "a farmer went out to sow his field . . ." and then explained His contextualization of the Word and various human responses (Matt. 13). He called fishermen to be "fishers of men" (Matt. 4); and required the rich young ruler to "sell all" (Luke 18).

The four Gospels were contextualized for various audiences, each using vocabulary and emphasizing themes relevant to particular groups. Acts can be thought of as the story of the contextualization of the gospel from Jew to Gentile.[9] And, as Acts records how the gospel spread to the urban centers, the agricultural metaphors so common in the Gospels fade, and language of merchants, philosophers, soldiers, athletes, and lawyers are used.[10] The epistles are contextualized letters, written to specific groups of people in specific places about specific issues they were facing.

Scripture uses literary forms familiar in particular ancient contexts to carry eternal truth that can be communicated effectively in other words.[11] That is, it is contextualized revelation that can be recontextualized. For example, we recontextualize Jesus' words about thorns in the parable of the sower by talking about the seductive power of the corporate ladder. Though our contextualization can be effective, it never has the status of Scripture. Faithful contextualization doesn't replace Scripture but is used alongside it—while always inviting those we are teaching to study the Scripture themselves.

Contextualization is also based on the belief that Scripture not only authorizes but commands continual contextualization through preaching and teaching—and also through obedience and loving one another (2 Tim. 4:1ff; Matt. 28:18–20; 5:16; 1 Peter 2:12; 1 Tim. 4:12; Titus 2:7; James 1:22). Contextualization cannot be separated from the one(s) contextualizing. The greatest act of contextualization was the incarnation of Jesus: "the Word became flesh and dwelt among us" (John 1:14). Taking the form of a human, He used a body, language, and behavior interpreted in a specific cultural context to make God known in our context. He has commanded us to follow His example (Phil. 2:1–11).

This embodied contextualization continued with Paul who became as a Jew to win the Jews and a Greek to win the Greeks (1 Cor. 9:20). It continued with the Thessalonians as the Lord's message "rang out" everywhere through the example of their "contextualized faith," that is, through their turning from local idols in Thessaloniki to serve the living God (1 Thess. 1:8). It continues with us. Our lives are contextualized expression of Christianity.

Contextualization is an inevitable and intense test of our love and commitment to truth—as well as of our humility. Often people who are passionate about the Lord, His Word, and making His Word clear also have strong convictions around the authority of the Bible and the importance of remaining true to Scripture and sound doctrine. Interestingly enough, sometimes this passion and these convictions can be used to sabotage our witness.

We cannot preach or discuss the Word without using terms familiar in our context. And yet this can lead to error. Knowing this, and wanting to make the gospel clear while also faithfully "guarding the flock" (2 Tim. 1:13–14), people can too quickly accuse each other of confusing or perverting the gospel by how they contextualize it to make it clear. This is evident in the many divisions and arguments within the church. Since our lives and relationships in the church contextualize the gospel by example, when Christians fight, accuse, and divide, the embodied contextualization undermines the message we're trying so hard to make clear. On the other hand, unity between believers contextualizes the truth of the Word by providing evidence, as Jesus said, that we are His disciples, that He came from the Father, and that the Father loves us (John 13:35; 17:23). If actions don't speak louder than words, they certainly cast doubt on them.

Ultimately, according to Scripture, effective communication of the Bible depends on the power of the Word (Isa. 55; Heb. 4) and the work of the Spirit of God (1 Cor. 1–2). The Spirit of God is active through the whole process, He opens eyes (1 Cor. 2), and yet has left us to do a lot of hard work requiring "intense effort"[12] to handle the word of truth correctly (2 Tim. 2:15). That's why Paul could have complete confidence in the power of the gospel (Rom. 1) and that the word of Christ generates faith (Rom. 10) and yet did all he could do to become a Jew to Jews and a Greek to Greeks (1 Cor. 9)—using Jewish cultural material when preaching to Jews (Acts 13) and Greek cultural material when preaching in Athens (Acts 17). Contextualization is the means through which the Spirit works.

This chapter is an attempt to shed light on contextualization, lay out guidelines for faithful contextualization,[13] and make a plea for engaging with one another in humility and love—while not losing our passion or compromising the convictions we hold that honor the Lord.

COMPONENTS AND A PROCESS

There are a few components to the process of contextualization that are simple to identify and yet complex as they work together. These are:

- The Spirit of God, who superintends it all.

- The specific truth the Spirit intends to communicate.

- The biblical story in which that truth functions—the story that Genesis through Revelation tells.

- The inscripturated cultural settings and materials the Spirit of God used to reveal God and His story through the enculturated biblical writers to all people, everywhere, and for all time.[14] An example of this is first-century Corinth, the language and metaphors contained in the Epistles of Paul to the Corinthians (1 and 2 Corinthians), and Paul himself.

- Us, the enculturated people, in whom contextualization happens and who actively contextualize for others.

- Our cultural settings and overarching stories of how life works, that is, our worldviews.

- The cultural material used to preach or teach or demonstrate biblical truth in any cultural setting.

In brief, the process involves interpreting the truth in each context while trusting God and the Bible to judge all of our interpretations.

Basic questions that guide this process are:

- What does the Scripture say through its original cultural material and story?

- How do I interpret that in my current cultural material and cultural story? What do I associate with that message that awakens or mutes my conscience? Opens me or shields me from the point? Clarifies or confuses?

- How do I communicate that meaning to others in their cultural material and cultural story? What will they likely associate with the message as they hear it?

- How do I allow the Lord and His Word to judge all of this and bring necessary correction to me and others—listening to the Spirit's voice and not hardening my heart (Heb. 3)?

One way to organize the process of contextualization is around three interpretations, three stories, and three concerns. First, we interpret what the Bible teaches (a passage or topic) in the cultural material used in the biblical story. Second, we interpret how we understand that truth in our cultural material as it functions in our cultural story. Third, we find cultural material to carry the meaning into the cultural story of those we're teaching and interpret how the truth functions in their cultural story. The first concern is that the contextualization doesn't overshadow or displace the truth. Second is that it doesn't lead to syncretism. Third is that it pleases God.

If we ignore any of the three stories, contextualization often fails because of ignorance and often subtle arrogance. For example, if I ignore your story, I'm likely assuming ours are the same and end up imposing mine on you. If I ignore my story, I'm likely assuming that mine is the same as the Bible's and am neither open to being corrected by the biblical story nor the possibility that your story might be more biblical than mine and that I perhaps have more to learn from you than you do from me. If I ignore the biblical story, or don't keep taking fresh looks at it, I'm likely assuming that mine is the biblical story and fall into the same traps.

For example, the words of Romans 3:24, "δικαιούμενοι δωρεὰν τῇ αὐτοῦ χάριτι" are unfamiliar to most for until translated, "justified freely by His grace (NIV)."

When translated, the legal analogy brings understanding to those who can relate to a legal system and feel guilt. However, most legal systems usually don't offer justification by grace—never through the death of the son of the Judge. This isn't a part of our story of how life works and so gets our attention, draws us in to consider the larger story, invites us to redirect our faith from our story to God and His Word and, in fact, forces us to a decision.

Among people on the Kwahu mountain ridge in rural Ghana, fear of evil spirits is part of their daily lives. The prospect of being declared righteous is lost in the story they live by because fear overwhelms feelings of guilt. Instead, stories from the Bible about the power of Jesus over spirits in Capernaum give them hope that Jesus might have power over the *mmoatia* (local spirits) (Mark 1). What is heard from the Gospels is contextualized into local cultural metaphors:

> Jesus blockades the road of death
>> with wisdom and power.
> He, the sharpest of all great swords
>> has made the forest safe for the hunters.
> The *mmoatia* He has cut to pieces;
>> He has caught *Sasabonsam*
> and twisted off its head.[15]

This description of Jesus doesn't fit their story of how life works and so it gets their attention, draws them in to consider the larger story, invites them to redirect their faith from their story to God and His Word, and requires a decision. The stakes are high. If Jesus isn't "the sharpest of all great swords" it may cost them their lives.

Among groups as seemingly disparate as Al-Shabaab recruits in Kenya to North American millennials and others in a post-Christian context, hospitality often speaks more clearly than words. Guilt is often not felt as intensely as a lack of belonging. Contextualizing the gospel to these groups is a blend of welcoming them into our homes and families, giving them a place to belong, and speaking truth—but welcoming must lead.[16] In this case, hospitality and welcoming become a highly contextualized living expression of the gospel that also validate or invalidate words.

The grace of God in the story of God includes deliverance from fear, restoration of honor, place of belonging, freedom from guilt, and everything else the Bible teaches, so these contextualizations are not replacing the legal analogy of justification, but complementing it.[17] Not all of us come to Christ through the same passage or analogy but are introduced to the grace of God through one of multiple doors. Once inside, we begin a lifetime journey of exploring its breadth and depth.

WHY BOTHER?

Why bother with contextualization—why not just "preach the Word" as Paul told Timothy (2 Tim. 4:2)?

First, Paul, inspired by the Spirit, was contextualizing when he told Timothy to preach the Word. He used the contextual idiom "itching ears" and the cultural ideas of a "drink offering," a fight, race, and "crown of righteousness." But isn't the Word powerful enough without our added contextualization? This is a misleading question because obeying Paul's words requires one to contextualize. The correction, rebuke, and encouragement "with great patience and careful instruction" Paul commanded require explanations and examples that make sense in one's context. It's not that the Word is not powerful enough without our contextualization, but that the Word is powerful in one's context through contextualization.

BECAUSE CONTEXTUALIZATION HAPPENS

Contextualization happens. It's what happens in our minds when we encounter biblical truth.[18] It's unavoidable. As soon as we think a thought or use language we are contextualizing—since thought categories and words grow out of a context. We cannot, not contextualize because we live in a context and a context lives in us. When we hear the word "tree," one person may think of an elm and another might think of a palm. "Tree" is given meaning in our contexts. Similar variations occur with words like "sin," "forgiveness," "sacrifice," "grace," and every other idea. If a person steps out of her town, or continent, the context in her mind comes with her because she can't step out of herself. Interpreting biblical truth in the context of one's mind, contextualization, is always happening.

We also contextualize everything we actively communicate. We use the language, tone, and style appropriate for the context. For example, a person talks one way to his good friend around the dinner table and another way to a board of directors around the conference table. People adapt to the context.

When we simply quote verses of Scripture verbatim, two layers of contextualization have been used: first from God to the original manuscripts of the Bible and then from those to the version of the Bible we're quoting.[19] Even simply emphasizing some verses over others is contextualization. Emphasizing verses that describe salvation in terms of power or belonging draw Tibetans from folk Buddhism[20] while verses describing salvation in legal terms can leave them confused.[21]

When we explain or apply Scripture we're adding layers of contextualization. Explaining "grace" as "God's riches at Christ's expense" was a common way to attempt to bring simple clarity to a deep concept in a memorable way in a Midwest

American evangelical church. Applying "do not steal" requires contextualization since bringing my family into your garden and eating our fill would be stealing in Chicago, but not in rural Zambia. Using everyday examples and analogies is contextualization. Calling Jesus our "Grinding Stone" illumines the person of Christ in a Ghanaian context.[22] Calling the Bible an "owner's manual" or a "love letter" is an attempt to contextualize.

To borrow the title of an excellent article, "we contextualize more than we think."[23] Contextualization involves what happens in the minds of those who receive it. There is an interplay between active and passive contextualization. While we consciously try to contextualize for others, we're being contextualized.

For example, this chapter is published in the *One Volume Seminary* from Moody Bible Institute which, it's anticipated, will mostly be read by a certain audience, so this chapter is contextualized for that audience. At the same time, the reader's perceptions of Moody color his or her perceptions of this chapter. Those perceptions set some parameters around the chapter's meaning and purpose. So, while this chapter is contextualized for its audience, the audience is contextualizing this chapter, that is, reading it in the context of "Moody."

We are walking messages,[24] playing a role, sometimes unaware, that's interpreted and influences the meaning of what we're trying to communicate.[25] You may not know me, but you know something about me since I'm writing for this volume. The more you get to know me the more who you perceive me to be will affect how you understand what I write. Knowing me better may lend credibility or suspicion to what I've written. It may bring clarity or confusion, reveal integrity or hypocrisy.

Therefore, a major concern of contextualization is how we are being interpreted and how that affects the interpretation of the message we're trying to communicate. The first concern of how we're being interpreted is who we really are. Character has as much to do with contextualization as the cultural materials used.

We interpret what we encounter through the context of our experience. Words trigger or activate memories of experience—sometimes bodily responses—so that much more is loaded onto the term than a dictionary definition.[26] These memories of experiences and emotions (and emotional reexperiences), connect with other ideas and familiar metaphors, bring people to mind, create responses, and alter our understanding. The English word "party," for example, triggers memories of a wholesome occasion such as a special birthday to some, while it refers to getting drunk and sexual encounters to others, triggering regret or reigniting temptation. When I hear "father" I might feel loved and trust while someone else feels forsaken and anger. Reading that we are "slaves of God" affects some deeply, requiring them to dissociate that from their experience of slavery while others have to imagine an experience of slavery to make it meaningful. To some the cross invokes gratefulness, praise, and an experience of peace, while to others, fear, and still to others rage! The gospel is often tainted in the minds of those who have been burned by a church. Christianity is considered the "white man's religion" by many—and the Bible, a weapon. So in contextualization we must explore what "load" the term, metaphor, or practice carries—and what memories, associations, and emotions it is likely to trigger in others.

On the other hand, some learned the gospel in a church building through their childhood, surrounded by real people they knew, people who loved them and cared for them—people striving to faithfully live out what the Word of God taught. I grew up in such a church. The church was full of people in all stages of life. I saw faithful believers grow old and die. Funerals were common. For me the gospel was taught and embodied by real people I watched live and die in faith. These people remain some of the faces of biblical truth to me—shaping how I understand it. This was an early contextualization of Christianity for me.

Andrew Walls wrote, "No one ever meets universal Christianity in itself: we only ever meet Christianity in a local form and that means a historically, culturally conditioned form."[27] As no one encounters *uncontextualized Christianity*, no one encounters an uncontextualized Christian or an uncontextualized gospel. Christians have bodies, histories, and are bound in the interpretations of others— that is, bound in the roles they are perceived to play in the interpreters' stories. A gospel without words, metaphors, or the examples of people, would not just be unintelligible, it wouldn't be.

In a sense, we're imprisoned in contextualization. But being imprisoned in context isn't a bad thing. Another way of saying that is that we are part of creation. Creation is our context and so contextualization is part of the goodness of creation—part of His plan. God spoke to us through biblical writers who contextualized as they wrote the inspired texts.[28] Then others used cultural materials of other places to communicate in those places until someone used the cultural materials of our groups and communicated to us. Now we continue the work. Our contextualization is actually recontextualization. We are part of a contextualization chain that God started and will continue until the last "nation" hears.

Since contextualization happens, it isn't something we should do, but something we're doing. Since we cannot, not contextualize—the only question is whether we do it intentionally or not. There are good reasons to choose to be intentional.

TO UN-MUTE CONSCIENCES

Through our contexts the Bible opens our eyes, awakens our consciences, convicts us, and calls us to faith. In this way our contexts serve us. Our contexts can also mute our consciences so there's no reaction if what is normalized becomes the Christian standard. Those of us who wear fine clothes, undergarments, and feast sumptuously while throwing beggars a buck or two don't feel the story of the rich man and Lazarus because equivalent affluence has been normalized, even celebrated, and we think the warning is just for the more affluent. The rich man of Luke 16 might have looked at the "rich fool" who built bigger barns in Luke 12 as the one in danger—who might have looked at Solomon with all of his wives and horses to justify his barns.

To Avoid Words That Have Lost Their Loads

Well-known words carry biblical meaning without understanding. Meaning can fall off words over time without us noticing. Examples can be as basic as "love," "idolatry," "holiness," "sin," and "glorifying God." One generation may wax eloquent unpacking the rich biblical idea of holiness while another struggles to define it apart from Christianese they can't define. And words can become hosts to popular cultural ideas that eat away at the original biblical meaning while we're not paying attention. Holiness is associated with popular ideas of ways to dress, speak, spend Sundays, and whole movements within American Christianity. If I've heard "holiness" all my life and it morphs into just a few cultural practices, I'm not understanding the biblical idea of "holiness." There is a need for recontextualization, a kind of reloading of the biblical meaning onto the cultural carriers of meaning being used.

To Avoid Syncretism

Various metaphors have been used to define syncretism including the ideas of corruption, distortion, and dilution.[29] Syncretism is pictured as something we may fall into in our attempt to contextualize well—"alas in leaning over to speak to the modern world, we have fallen in."[30]

If we frame syncretism relationally before God rather than just conceptually before theology, we cross the line of syncretism when we displease God. Anything that leads us away from allegiance to Christ, His Word, and His body displeases Him. Thinking of it this way, syncretism is more like spiritual adultery (James 4). In the extreme, it may be a "different gospel" (Gal. 1:6). Syncretism is communication that alters the meaning of the truth of the Bible to the point it is no longer true and displeases God.

Avoiding syncretism involves avoiding it at home and elsewhere. We may feel safer not intentionally contextualizing—believing that we're just staying closer to the Word. However, we may be staying closer to our contextualized understanding of the Word, which is vulnerable to syncretism we can't see. René Padilla says,

Those who object to the contextualization of the gospel out of fear of syncretism must take into account a greater danger: precisely when there is no conscious reflection as to the form that obedience to the lordship of Jesus Christ must take in a given situation, conduct is most likely to be determined by the culture instead of by the Gospel.[31]

An example of this might be a syncretized understanding of authority—a subtle redefinition by our contemporary Christian circle formed more by a democratic society than by the Bible—that allows us to begin to think that God is "subject to the people" and we are entitled to judge His ways.

To Carry The Burden

Finally, since contextualization is unavoidable and challenging, we either take more of the burden on ourselves by intentionally contextualizing, or make others take it on themselves. Contextualizing, therefore, is a matter of love.

THE CHALLENGES IN CONTEXTUALIZING

It can be helpful to imagine contextualization as a process on several continuums that involve degrees of correctness, tension, uncertainty, and danger. This process triggers emotions—which explains the sometimes-fierce debates and conflict that surround it. There's much at stake.

One continuum relates to controversy. Degrees of controversy are usually related to the perceived distance from the biblical idea and proximity to a false idea. There is always risk. New Testament writers contextualized with words borrowed from Greek religion and philosophy like μυστήριον (mystery) (Eph. 3:4); μεταμορφόω (transformation) (Rom. 12:2); and λόγος (word) (John 1:1)—leaving potential for the biblical meanings to be confused with their pagan meanings.[32]

In "We Contextualize More Than We Realize," Craig Blomberg discusses examples of contextualization on a continuum from least to most controversial. In this general order he discusses translation, the redemptive analogy of Don Richardson's *Peace Child*, C. S. Lewis's Aslan and the White Witch, *The Great Divorce*, C5 evangelism, using offensive language in sermons, God as Mother, the use of local deity names for the God of the Bible, and "getting high on the big J."[33]

Another continuum is that of irrelevance to syncretism. Leslie Newbiggin frames these as opposite dangers, saying, "if one is more afraid of one danger than the other, one will certainly fall into the opposite."[34] A similar continuum is that of "under-contextualization" to "over-contextualization."[35] Under-contextualization is driven by a high view of Scripture and a lack of awareness of our own contextualized understanding. This leads to the assumption that what we believe doesn't need to be contextualized. So we seek to preserve the tradition we have learned because we believe the truth is most safely found there—whether or not people in the community understand it.

Over-contextualization is driven by a high view of culture—so much so that it is privileged above Scripture. This assumes that a concept from Scripture is so foreign that it must be changed to be true to the message of Scripture in a particular context. There are varying degrees of this. Most extreme is removing an idea from the biblical story because it is unbelievable or offensive—like removing the idea of final judgment. Another is removing offensive biblical concepts and replacing them with other biblical ones, like replacing "Son of God" in Muslim contexts with "Messiah."

Replacing biblical concepts with similar contextual metaphors—like arrangements on a musical theme—falls somewhere in the middle. For example, the Bible reveals Jesus contextually as the "Lion of the tribe of Judah." C. S. Lewis contextualized the character of Christ for late twentieth-century Britain in his creation of Aslan. Afua Kuma contextualized Jesus into rural Ghana as the Lion of the grasslands.[36]

If contextualization is thought of as a continuum from "under-contextualized" to "over-contextualized," then syncretism lies on both ends of the continuum due to uncritically using either "my" old cultural categories or "their" new ones. Neither running to what is new nor retreating to what is old is safe.

SOME GUIDELINES TOWARD FAITHFUL CONTEXTUALIZATION

Bathe the process of contextualization in prayer and meditate in Scripture daily. Much is at stake and we see through a glass darkly. Therefore, we need the One who sees everything, completely understands, and is in authority over all things. We also need the Scripture to be saturating our minds since we yield to its story as the authoritative story.

Remain humble. Though Scripture can be recontextualized, our recontextualizations are fallible because they are our interpretive work. Even when they are accurate, they can be fruitless in a particular person's life since, as Jesus taught, truth can still be stolen, starved, and choked (Matt. 13).

Love one another. If our contextualizing includes fighting and division, our intended message is undermined. Since contextualization includes everything about us, not just what we say, ungodly behavior becomes a part of our message. It infects it with hypocrisy and makes it less credible.

Be humbly ready for controversy. Controversy surrounds contextualization because distorting the gospel, misleading people, and judgment are possible. Slippery slopes exist, but not every slope is slippery. No one has studied the Bible and every context exhaustively, and yet commitment and emotion drive many of us to think that we know enough of the complexities of many situations to render judgment—often from a distance.

Contextualizing from a distance is next to impossible, so immerse yourself as much as possible in the cultural context you're contextualizing for. The more that we experience in a place, the more cultural material we'll have available and the more of that cultural story we'll understand. Learn as much as possible about the lived realities of the people involved. Explore, among other things, the history, politics, sociocultural context, and economics of the community. Talk to people—practitioners, local people, and local sages. Gather stories. Stories usually reveal more than direct answers to questions. They tend to show the depth and breadth of definitions. The dominate narrative will emerge as you gather many stories from people's lives. Listen carefully.

Ask God for healthy relationships with wise people that can collaborate with you. Contextualization done alone is at best weak and more likely misguided.

Be careful that the contextualization doesn't become syncretism. Throughout the process, identify the borders between contextualization and syncretism. Be attuned to signals that you are in danger of syncretism. Criteria for faithful contextualization can be summarized in a few questions:

- Does the contextualization reinforce the biblical story or alter it?[37]

- Do our lives, the process, and the contextualizations have the marks of the leading of the Spirit?

- Is it affirmed by the wider Christian community?

- Does it bear fruit?

Signals we may be in danger of syncretism include:

- Ignoring or rejecting a passage of the Bible, perhaps in order to protect our contextualization.

- Straining to redefine or reinterpret a passage in the Bible based on extrabiblical evidence such as cultural understandings of the biblical context today, read back into the Bible.

- Stretching or compromising the biblical idea to fit the local context.

- Remaining comfortable in our sin.[38]

- Making our contextualizations more prominent in our interpretations, threatening to overshadow or displace the terms, concepts, and metaphors of the Bible. In other words, the voice of Christ must be louder than ours. The voice of Scripture must be louder than ours.[39]

- Finding ourselves building our theologies, ethics, and expectations on our contextualization while ignoring passages of Scripture that nuance or challenge our contextualization. Contextualization approximates meaning, so nuance and clarification of the similarities, differences, and weaknesses of the contextualization are usually needed.

Above all, throughout the process of contextualization, ask the Lord to use His Word to judge both your story and theirs—allowing the Bible and its story to have the authoritative voice. The goal is for our stories to be transformed into a faithful cultural version of the biblical story so faith is generated and God is pleased.

CONCLUSION

Because at each point of interpretation there is possibility of misinterpretation, contextualization is daunting. The presence and work of the Spirit, the need for "accurately handling the word of truth" (2 Tim. 2:15), and Paul's example of "to the Jews I became as a Jew" (1 Cor. 9:20) intersect in wise contextualization in which we can be humbly confident. This confidence is nourished by revelation through Isaiah that the Word of God will "accomplish the purpose for which it has been sent"—couched in the contextualized metaphors of the rain and the snow watering the earth and bringing forth fruit (Isa. 55:10–11).

NOTES

1. Gailyn Van Rheenen, "Syncretism and Contextualization: The Church on a Journey Defining Itself" in *Contextualization and Syncretism: Navigating Cultural Currents.* Evangelical Missiological Society Series no. 13, ed. Gailyn Van Rheenen (Pasadena, CA: William Carey Library, 2006), 4.

2. Stanley H. Skreslet, *Picturing Christian Witness: New Testament Images of Disciples in Mission* (Grand Rapids: Eerdmans, 2006), 121.

3. Kwame Bediako, "Cry Jesus! Christian Theology and Presence in Modern Africa" in *Jesus and the Gospel in Africa: History and Experience*, Theology in Africa Series (Maryknoll, NY: Orbis, 1993), 13.

4. Dean Flemming, *Contextualization in the New Testament: Patterns for Theology and Mission* (Downers Grove, IL: IVP Academic, 2005), 299.

5. For an excellent example of this see John Ferch, "Towards an Indigenous Theology of Worship in Alaska" in *Majority*

World Religions: Theologizing from Africa, Asia, Latin America, and the Ends of the Earth, Evangelical Missiological Society Series no. 26, ed. Allen Yeh and Tite Tiénou (Littleton, CO: William Tyndale Publishers, 2018), 184–200.

6. Musimibi R.A. Kanyoro, "Called to One Hope: The Gospel in Diverse Cultures" in *New Directions in Mission and Evangelization*, ed. James A Scherer and Stephen B. Bevans (Maryknoll, NY: Orbis, 1999), 139.

7. Jayson Georges and Mark D. Baker, *Ministering in Honor Shame Cultures* (Downers Grove, IL: IVP Academic, 2016), loc. 3117.

8. I'm using *stories* as a simplified synonym for worldviews.

9. Flemming, *Contextualization in the New Testament*, 309.

10. Skreslet, *Picturing Christian Witness*, 128.

11. Lamin Sanneh develops this in *Translating the Message: The Missionary Impact on Culture* (Maryknoll, NY: Orbis, 2009).

12. J.P. Louw and Eugene Albert Nida, *Lexical Semantics of the Greek New Testament: A Supplement to the Greek-English Lexicon of the New Testament Based on Semantic Domains*, vol. 1. (Atlanta: Scholars Press, 1996), 661.

13. Paul Hiebert coined the term "critical contextualization." I'm expanding that by calling it wise or faithful contextualization since I am looking at more than methodology.

14. I'm using enculturation to mean being shaped by your original culture. See A. Scott Moreau, ed., *The Evangelical Dictionary of World Missions* (Grand Rapids: Baker Academic, 2000), 309–10.

15. Christiana Afua Gyan (or Afua Kuma), *Jesus of the Deep Forest: Prayers and Praises of Afua Kuma*, English translation of original Twi texts (Accra, Ghana: Asewmpa Publishers, 1981), 17f, in Bediako, "Cry Jesus!," 15.

16. This draws on David Kinnaman and Gabe Lyons, *Good Faith* (Grand Rapids: Baker Books, 2016), 135, and from research conducted by the author in Nairobi and presented at the Evangelical Missiological Society National Meeting, Dallas Texas, September 2017, and at the Academy for Evangelism in Theological Education, South Bend Indiana, June 2018.

17. Georges and Baker, *Ministering in Honor Shame Cultures*, 3300.

18. Paul G. Hiebert, *The Gospel in Human Contexts: Anthropological Explorations for Contemporary Missions* (Grand Rapids: Baker Academic, 2009), 14.

19. Craig Blomberg, "We Contextualize More Than We Realize" in *Local Theology for the Global Church: Principles for an Evangelical Approach to Contextualization*, ed. Matthew Cook, Rob Haskell, Ruth Julian, and Natee Tanchanpongs (Pasadena, CA: William Carey Library, 2010), 47.

20. James E. Morrison, "Contextualizing the Gospel in the Fear-Power World of Folk Buddhists" in *International Journal of Frontier Missiology*, 36:2 (April–June 2019): 69–75.

21. Georges and Baker, *Ministering in Honor Shame Cultures*, loc. 2678.

22. Bediako, "Cry Jesus!" 14.

23. Blomberg, "We Contextualize More Than We Realize," 37–56.

24. Kosuke Koyama, *Water Buffalo Theology* (Maryknoll, NY: Orbis, 1974), 125.

25. David J. Bosch, "The Vulnerability of Mission" in *New Directions in Mission and Evangelization 2: Theological Foundations*, ed. James A. Scherer and Stephen B. Bevans (Maryknoll, NY: Orbis, 1994), 821.

26. Joseph Shaules, *The Intercultural Mind: Connecting Culture, Cognition, and Global Living* (Boston: Nicholas Brealey Publishing, 2015), loc 3157.

27. Andrew F. Walls, *The Missionary Movement in Christian History: Studies in the Transmission of the Faith* (Maryknoll, NY: Orbis, 1996), 235.

28. Blomberg, "We Contextualize More Than We Realize," 40–43. For a longer treatment of how biblical writers contextualized, see Flemming.

29. Natee Tanchanpongs, "Developing a Palate for Authentic Theology" in *Local Theology for the Global Church: Principles for an Evangelical Approach to Contextualization*, ed. Matthew Cook, Rob Haskell, Ruth Julian, and Natee Tanchangpongs (Pasadena, CA: William Carey Library, 2010), 110–11.

30. Flemming, *Contextualization in the New Testament*, 320, citing Stanley Hauerwas and William Willimon, *Resident Aliens* (Nashville: Abingdon, 1989), 27.

31. René C. Padilla, "Contextualization of the Gospel," *Journal of Theology for Southern Africa* 4 (1978): 26.

32. Flemming, *Contextualization in the New Testament*, 298.

33. Blomberg, "We Contextualize More Than We Realize," 37–55.

34. Lesslie Newbigin, *A Word in Season: Perspectives in Christian World Missions* (Grand Rapids: Eerdmans, 1994), 67.

35. David J. Hesselgrave, "Syncretism: Mission and Missionary Indeed?" in *Contextualization and Syncretism: Navigating Cultural Currents.* Evnagelical Missiological Society Series 13, ed. Gailyn Van Rheenen (Pasadena, CA: William Carey Library, 2006), 80–82ff.

36. Bediako, "Cry Jesus!" 8.

37. Flemming, 300.

38. Ronaldo Lidóro, "A Biblical Theology of Contextualization" in *Global Mission: Reflections and Case Studies in Contextualization for the Whole Church,* Globalization of Missions Studies, ed. Rose Dowsett (Pasadena, CA: William Tyndale Library, 2011), 20–21.

39. Dean Flemming, "Paul the Contextualizer," in *Local Theology for the Global Church: Principles for an Evangelical Approach to Contextualization,* ed. Matthew Cook, Rob Haskell, Ruth Julian, and Natee Tanchanpongs (Pasadena, CA: William Carey Library, 2010), 16.

Planting a New Church

ERIC RIVERA

In 2012, God placed upon my wife, Erikah, and me, the clear call to plant a church in Chicago. The task before us felt daunting and many fears flooded our minds. We often asked, *Are we capable of doing this? Is God really calling us to this? Will the plant fail? From where will the funding come? Where do we begin?* At that time, a friend of mine handed me an article written by Tim Keller titled, "Why Plant Churches?," which set us on a trajectory to plant The Brook in 2013.

In his article, Keller made the provocative argument that the continual planting of healthy churches is the single most crucial strategy for reaching people with the gospel and reviving existing churches. He writes, "Nothing else—not crusades, outreach programs, parachurch ministries, growing megachurches, congregational consulting, nor church renewal processes—will have the consistent impact of dynamic, extensive church planting."[1] These words have helped fuel global church planting in varying contexts since.

At the heart of church planting is the spread of the gospel, the making of disciples, and the accomplishing of God's mission in the remotest and darkest communities. It is more than launching a Sunday morning service in a new area. Church planting is reaching a neighborhood with the gospel and gathering a community of believers who make disciples, practice the Lord's Supper and baptism, pray, worship, and teach the Bible, are governed by elders, and practice church discipline.

However, what is true of global missions is also true of church planting. Namely, that the harvest is still plentiful and the workers are still few (Matt. 9:37–38). Simply put, the church needs more planters. The shortage of church planters can be attributed to a variety of reasons including fear of failure, feelings of inadequacy, uncertainty about calling, lack of funding, and the absence of vision for planting.

In this chapter, I will provide a biblical and theological defense for church planting demonstrating that it is in line with the character of God and the testimony of Scripture. In addition, I will present the indispensable trifold foundation for a church planter to be a person of character, calling, and competency. Character is forged by a consistent walk with Jesus. Calling is an inward and outward work done by the Holy Spirit and affirmed by the local church. Competency points to the many moving parts included in the church planting work. In this section I will discuss the practical components and "how-to" of church planting. These insights will give direction for planting healthy and transformational churches in cities, suburbs, and rural communities everywhere.

BIBLICAL FOUNDATIONS FOR CHURCH PLANTING

The biblical foundations for church planting begins in God's desire to save people and the commissioning of His people to proclaim the gospel. From the fall of Adam in Genesis 3 to the victory of the second Adam in the Gospels, God shows Himself to be the ultimate missionary. When sin entered the world through Adam and Eve, humanity became separated from God and in need of redemption. The effects of sin in biblical history are evident throughout the pages of Scripture. But sprinkled throughout the Old Testament timeline is the hope of Messiah. God continually pursues His lost and rebellious sheep near and far, Jew and Gentile alike.

Joel the prophet, commissioned by God, tells the people of Judah to repent and turn to the Lord (Joel 2:12–13). God pursues the broken even while His people were exiled in Babylon. He sends a message of redemptive hope through Jeremiah to the Jewish communities walking in darkness (Jer. 29). He uses Jonah to call the Ninevites—Gentiles in a wicked city—to repent although their hearts were further from God than Nineveh was from Jerusalem (Jonah 3:4–5). In the Old Testament landscape, God frequently extends His mighty hand to bring salvation to sinners. As the Psalmist says, "May God be gracious to us and bless us and make his face to shine upon us, that your way may be known on earth, your saving power among all nations" (Ps. 67:1–2 ESV).

God's missionary ambition continues with the opening of the New Testament. The Gospel writers present God incarnate, Jesus Christ, who came to do what no one but God could do, to "save His people from their sins" (Matt. 1:21). As with the Old Testament prophets, God was not content letting people die in their sin. Rather, He Himself came down and made a way for salvation.

Jesus said that the disciples would receive power when the Holy Spirit comes (Acts 1:8). The Spirit is the great companion that empowers us to fulfill the Great Commission. God is concerned with building His church by the power of the Spirit beginning in Jerusalem, then to Judea and Samaria and ultimately to the ends of the earth. From Pentecost onward, the New Testament is like a church planting documentary.

Named and unnamed men and women enter cities and communities with the sole intention of planting a church through the proclamation of the gospel. When they were moved by persecution, "those who were scattered went about preaching the word" (Acts 8:4 ESV) leading to the starting of churches in cities like Antioch (Acts 11:26). From Antioch Paul and Barnabas were commissioned as missionaries and continued the church planting work in cities like Lystra, Iconium, and Ephesus (Acts 13:1–2; 14:23; 20:17). And so, the gospel spread throughout the Roman Empire with church plants forming in many cities.

From Scripture, we can conclude that God has a plan to advance the gospel through starting churches not only from Jerusalem to Rome, but from Chicago to Kiev, New York to New Delhi, San Francisco to São Paulo, and Seoul to Bangladesh. The church is the people of God whose saving faith is in Jesus. When the gospel spreads, churches will be birthed.

THE CHARACTER OF A CHURCH PLANTER

Before reviewing the nuts and bolts of church planting, it is imperative to understand the foundational importance of godly character. Giftedness does not constitute readiness for the task of church planting. When someone attempts tasks that their gifting is capable of but exceeds their character, they can attain earthly success but lose their spiritual identity in the process.

The character of a planter consistently reminds him that he serves for the glory of God and the fulfilling of the Great Commission. The personal life of a planter keeps in mind that a dying world is watching and temptation surrounds him. Far too many leaders have succeeded in pleasing man with their talents and displeasing God with their lives.

While Paul tells Timothy to fan into flame the gift God had given him (2 Tim. 1:6), he also tells him to persist in keeping a close watch over his life and his doctrine (1 Tim. 4:16). Church planters are wise to cultivate their spiritual gifts but not to do so at the neglect of their doctrine and personal integrity.

Church planters are pastors and pastors find their character job description in 1 Timothy 3:1–7 and Titus 1:5–9. No pastor reflects these qualities perfectly nor does any pastor reflect these qualities by his own willpower and self-discipline. Personal integrity is part of the Holy Spirit's sanctifying work in the Christian's life. Followers of Jesus in turn die to their old self daily allowing the Spirit to forge their character. This happens through a consistent walk with Jesus, communing with Him in prayer, feasting upon the Scriptures, walking in obedience, and experiencing the fires of adversity. In the same way, church planters need to possess a battle-tested character.

Few things will make someone feel as inadequate and exposed as the uncertainty that awaits the various stages of starting a new church. There are mighty mountaintops where people come to faith in Jesus, prayers are being answered, and households are being transformed. There are the vulnerable valleys where it seems that things are not working, people are straying, and your life is under a microscope.

Spiritual attack is real and every church planter will feel it. But when one walks with Jesus and allows the Spirit to form his character, God will fortify the believer's faith to resist the temptations of jealousy, fear, lust, selfish ambition, and pride. And when the planter sins, the Spirit of God is there to call him to repentance. The character of Christian ministers is an integral part of their ministerial fruitfulness, and church planters are no exception.

THE CALLING OF A CHURCH PLANTER

Many people long to know God's will for their lives because with that calling comes a clear purpose and meaning for each day. It answers the question, Why am I doing what I do? In the same way, every church planter must believe that he is called to this task of starting a new church. If he is not called by God to church plant, he will not survive as a planter because the highs and lows of ministry will bring him back to the drawing board asking, "Why am I doing this?" With a firm calling comes a confident answer to that important question.

When God calls a person to plant a church, He often communicates in three different ways to make that calling clear to the planter. First, there is the internal advocacy of the Holy Spirit confirming this calling. Second, there is the affirmation of the local church that can attest to the calling. Third, there are denominational and network assessments that help in the discerning process. For married church planters, a fourth necessary voice God speaks through in discerning this calling is the church planter's spouse.

THE ADVOCACY OF THE HOLY SPIRIT

Every church planter must have a strong sense that God has called him to this task because of the inward testimony of the Holy Spirit. Some have described the Spirit's witness as a "holy discontent." It can be classified as "holy" because the Spirit has placed within the called Christian an unshakable sense that God wants him to spread the gospel and fulfill the Great Commission through starting a new church. It can be considered a "discontent" because the Spirit has placed a longing in his soul to accomplish this task. It is the kind of longing that will not settle for anything else. The Holy Spirit often forges this holy discontent in the church planter's heart when he sees the brokenness of his community and knows that Jesus is what every person in that community ultimately needs and longs for.

This holy discontent for the prophet Jeremiah looked like an overwhelming sense that he had to deliver God's message because it would be like a fire in his chest were he to try to hold it in (Jer. 20:9). For the apostle Paul, it looked like his spirit being provoked at the sight of idols in the city of Athens (Acts 17:16). For Philip it was the insistence to explain the gospel through Isaiah to the Ethiopian eunuch (Acts 8:30). The Holy Spirit confirms the calling of many by placing within them an unquenchable passion to do something. For the planter, that something is planting the gospel in a dark place with the goal of raising up a community of faith that will make disciples and spread the truth of Jesus.

THE AFFIRMATION OF THE LOCAL CHURCH

Not only is one's calling discerned by the advocacy of the Holy Spirit, but is also made clear by the affirmation of the local church. In Acts 13:1–3, the leaders in the church in Antioch were immersed in prayer and fasting when the Holy Spirit said to them to set apart Paul and Barnabas for global church planting. At that point, the local church affirmed God's call on their lives and sent out two of their best leaders.

Someone who is not presently involved with and invested in the local church will find it difficult to receive affirmation in this calling. Local church leaders must know a potential planter before they can affirm his calling. Through relationship with the church, they can observe church planters' integrity, personal life, ministry effectiveness, giftedness, and calling. The church should be best positioned to see a potential planters' track record in their character, as a leader, in the pulpit, with evangelism, and in making disciples and say, "We affirm this person's calling to plant."

THE ASSESSMENT OF A NETWORK OR DENOMINATION

Most networks and denominations use a church plant assessment tool to best discern if a person has the ministry giftedness, character, and ministerial experience needed to lead a successful church plant. These assessment tools are able to come alongside the local church and the planter in the discernment process. They are often made up of detailed interviews, retreats, and questionnaires/tests.[2]

While these networks and denominations may not personally know a planter as well as a local church, their assessors are often comprised of experienced church planters and network leaders who have journeyed alongside of many churches. Thus, they bring with them invaluable experiential knowledge and can be both an informed and unbiased voice of wisdom. When it comes to discerning one's calling to church plant, the potential planter would be wise to seek being assessed to assist in determining if church planting is really for him.

THE AGREEMENT OF YOUR SPOUSE

For some spouses, the church planting idea is exhilarating. They are eager to see the vision unfold and anticipate with excitement the journey ahead. There are other spouses who are terrified at the idea of church planting. The fear of failure, change, loneliness, and inadequacy will feel like too much to bear.[3] It is no secret that ministry in general can be hard on families. Oftentimes spouses and children feel like their lives are under a constant microscope even as they experience the pressures of ministry. Church plant families will also experience these tensions as they manage their own expectations and those of others.

A husband and wife exploring church planting will need to take time praying together aiming to be a couple that will collectively answer the call to plant. If the spouse is not ready to enter into the church plant journey, that is a clear indicator that more time is needed and the church planting process should be put on hold. Husbands and wives have to be on the same page when it comes to accepting the call to start a church. While the process of coming to agreement may delay pursing this calling, it will prove to be the right choice in comparison to forcing the matter without the support of one's spouse.

THE COMPETENCY OF A CHURCH PLANTER

While the calling to begin a new church is inextricably linked to the pastoral calling, church planters are also starters. They have an entrepreneurial bent about them. They must know how to vision something, create it, and gather people to buy in to that vision. In this section we will specifically look at the "how to" of starting a church rather than the general qualities of being a pastor.

LOCATION, LOCATION, LOCATION

The most popular phrase in real estate is "Location, location, location," referring to the most important consideration in pricing and purchasing a home. The same can be said with church planting. The location of the church plant determines the vision and strategy for that plant. While every church must make its aim to glorify God and make disciples, the strategy for accomplishing that aim will differ—sometimes dramatically—from one neighborhood to the next.

Choosing where to plant a church is the biggest decision a planter will make. For this reason, the first step in selecting the potential region, city, town, and community is, like the church of Antioch in Acts 13, to take part in extended time of prayer and fasting. Church planting is a God-sized vision, which makes calling upon Him to lead and direct from the very beginning the right place to start.

BECOME A STUDENT OF YOUR COMMUNITY

After prayer and receiving clarity from God on a general location, begin to research what that community is like from a demographic and socioeconomic standpoint. The church planter must become a student of the place he believes God has led him to plant.[4] He should know the ethnic breakdown along with the median age and income. He should also get a pulse of the religious affiliation of those in the neighborhood and discover if there are other churches in the community. These studies will give the planter the 10,000-foot view of his community.

As helpful as demographic studies are, they do not replace the value of physically stepping into that community. "Exegeting the community is about making an effort," says John Fuder. "You're going to have to roll up your sleeves and get dirty. It's going to cost and it's going to hurt. You have to get out of the ivory tower and into the trenches."[5] One of the best ways to get in the trenches is to go on a prayer walk in the community and lay eyes on the peoples, places, names, and faces of those who live there. As the planter and whoever he is able to bring on board with the church plant walk the community, they should ask God to give them a heart of love and compassion for the people they see and the eyes to see their spiritual, emotional, and felt needs.

As the church plant team enters into a community, they would benefit greatly from setting up interviews with local leaders like the alderman, town mayor, police captain, school principals, and park directors asking them questions about the community while taking the posture of a learner. These interviews will assist in learning the "burden" of the community. The church plant team will likely see common themes and needs emerge, such as quality education, community safety, extracurricular activities for children and youth, racism and ethnic tensions, poverty, teen pregnancy, affordable housing, or services for the elderly.

When a church planter exegetes his community, he will better understand what makes the neighborhood tick, its pressure points, and the things it celebrates.[6] Beyond helping the planter discern if this community is where God has called him to be, these are all details that will allow the planter to form a better idea of what a community is like, how to contextualize the gospel in that community, and how a new church might make a tangible difference there.

The more planters spend time in their community, the more their love and affection for the people around them will grow. This will cause the church to be thoughtful and intentional about its interactions in the neighborhood. In his book *Mi Casa Uptown*, Rich Pérez describes the socioeconomic transitions taking place in Washington Heights, New York, where he pastors Christ Crucified Fellowship, the church he planted in 2011. He grieves some of the changes taking place in his community represented by the closing of local corner stores called bodegas.

These bodegas serve the lowly in the community, carry a rich cultural identity, and represent the heritage of migrants who worked hard to establish a life in the neighborhood. "Bodegas help us," writes Pérez, "the second generation, whose future is here, to build empathy for people on the margins—the foreigner, the stranger trying to make a home and leave a legacy for his children, the people who deeply know what the margins feel like."[7] Pérez possesses a sincere love for the people of Washington Heights through learning people's hurts and fears, joys and smiles, hopes and longings. Likewise, planters must know the heartbeat of people in their community.

RECRUITING A TEAM

No church planter possesses all the necessary qualities for starting a church by his own abilities. He must recruit a core group of people who will leverage their gifts and collectively be an effective team in the church planting process. This core team should be on board with the vision of the church plant and share a collective burden for the community. Ideally, everyone on the church plant team should live in close proximity with the neighborhood in mind, if not in the neighborhood altogether. This team could help define and refine the vision along with creating and leading systems to accomplish the ministry strategy. This team's level of collective gifting and readiness to serve can provide an exciting and dynamic contribution to the church plant from its infancy.

DEVELOPING A VISION FRAME

Once the church planter has prayed, identified the location to plant, studied the community, and begun recruiting a team it is now time for him to bring definition to the vision God has placed on his and his team's heart. In his book *Church*

Unique, Will Mancini speaks of a "vision frame" where each side of the frame represents four important aspects of the vision of the church, with the center part of the frame representing the vision proper.[8]

On the right side of the vision frame is the mission statement, which answers the question, What are we doing? In its simplest terms, the mission of the church plant is the God-given mandate for that church that will remain mostly unchanged over time. This is best expressed by finishing the statement, "This church will glorify God and make disciples by . . . " The mission of the church should be creative, reflective of the church's heartbeat, and expressive of what the church believes God is calling them to do. For example, our mission statement at The Brook in Chicago is, "The Brook exists to glorify God and make disciples by leading the thirsty to the water of life." While making disciples and glorifying God is core for every church's existence, The Brook specifically sees their community as one that is parched and aims to reach people who "thirst" and lead them to Jesus who satisfies their longings. Our mission then reflects our community using the language of water, which is also present in the church's name.

On the left side of the frame are the church's values, which answers the question, Why are we doing it? These core values are the things that motivate the mission of the church. For example, a church that wants to cultivate a family feel in the church by sharing meals together might put "hospitality" as one of its core values. Or a church that wants to see its members grow in their desperation for and communion with God might put "thirsty prayers" as one of their core values.

The bottom of the frame is the church plant's strategy for accomplishing the mission. The strategy answers the question, How are we doing it? It is essentially the road map for how the church will accomplish its mission and vision. One important strategy the church plant must clarify is how it intends to make disciples. Some churches leverage one-on-one discipleship strategies, while others may opt for small groups, life groups, or missional communities, and still others might use Sunday school classes or something similar. Another important strategy to consider is how the church plant intends to spread the gospel in their community. Will they do so through open-air evangelism, relational evangelistic strategies, missional communities, or outreach events? Every strategy will have its strengths and weaknesses and it is up to the planter and his team to craft a strategy that is faithful to the gospel, contextualized, effective, and relevant.[9]

At the top of the frame are the measures or marks for determining the effectiveness of the plant. The measures answer the question, When are we successful? Some qualities of effectiveness can be difficult to measure; however, every church plant must make a plan for determining if they are truly accomplishing what they set out to achieve. Are new connections with unbelievers being made? Are people coming to faith in Jesus? Are people growing in their discipleship and increasingly surrendering more of who they are to the lordship of Jesus? The measures of a church may be as simple as counting and tracking numbers. The church may look for tangible marks such as how many people in the church have connected with lost people? How many people are currently involved in community groups? How many new people did the church connect to serve in a ministry area last quarter? How many people are gathering for our Sunday morning service? How many people have been baptized this year? These measures force the church plant to think strategically as the church begins and then to make an honest assessment of what is going well and what needs refinement after the church begun to meet publically.[10]

At the center of the vision frame is the vision proper. It is the big picture direction that has to do with clear goals and milestones as it answers the question, Where is God taking us? There are three essential components of an effective church vision, the first of which is that it must be clear and concise. Someone once said of vision that if it is a mist in the pulpit, it is a fog in the pew. That is to say, if the vision is not clear to the vision caster, it will be even murkier to the recipients. Likewise, if it is long and complex, it will be forgotten. The second essential component to an effective vision is that it must be compelling. A leader who has no one following them is someone who is simply taking a walk. A good vision stirs people's hearts and persuades them to join in what God is doing. Thirdly, an effective vision must be catalytic. Is there something dynamic taking place putting the vision into motion, or is it static lacking a sense of direction? A catalytic vision creates movement toward the direction God wants the church to go.

CHURCH PLANTING *FOR* OR *FROM* THE HARVEST

A helpful distinction the church planter must consider is whether or not the church plant will aim at planting for the harvest or planting from the harvest. Churches that plant for the harvest generally gather a large number of believers who then go into a community to engage it with the gospel. This model has the strength of beginning with a larger amount of people but has the disadvantage of the church being mostly composed of believers who have transferred from one church to join a new one. On the flip side, a church plant that plants from the harvest begins with a smaller core group of people who aim at making the church increase through evangelism, gathering people from the plentiful harvest. This strategy has the advantage of multiplying disciples where no disciples previously were. It has the disadvantage of beginning the church planting work with a smaller group of people.

ON MISSION IN THE PLENTIFUL HARVEST

Every community has places where people gather. A church plant team should view those spaces as mission fields. These are locations in a neighborhood where the church plant team can meet people, serve, and connect. Those gathering spaces include but are not limited to the local elementary and high schools, college campuses, local park districts, coffee shops, shopping malls, sports leagues, and libraries.[11] The more church planters spend time in their community the more the tangible and felt needs, which are springboards to share the Christ, become clear.

For example, The Brook, a church in Chicago, identified Bell Park as a mission field in its community. People from the church spent months getting to know families at the playground, in park programs, and on the ball fields. Through their interactions, they learned of the community need to see an athletic program for children. The Brook proceeded to begin a baseball league that was able to reach nearly 100 kids in its first three seasons. Coaches in the league were men from the church who were on mission with their teams. Several families came to faith in Jesus and were baptized in the first couple of seasons as a direct result of the baseball league.

LAUNCHING THE CHURCH

As the church planter and the core team labor in the community, they must also create systems for the church before it launches. These central systems include kids' ministry, nursery, finance structure, a connections team, facilities team, a worship team, and a plan for Sunday morning hospitality. These systems are crucial for internal organization, creating a dynamic space for Sunday morning worship, and integrating new visitors to the church.

The new church will need a meeting space that accommodates the immediate needs of the church and allow for the attaining of some of the early vision components. Ideally, the best meeting spaces will be accessible, visible, customizable, and affordable. Accessibility has to do with how easy it is for someone to get there. Clear street names, parking, and fewer stairs make a space more accessible. Visibility is increased, for example, where the location is allowed to have adequate signage. Customizable spaces allow churches to turn a room into a nursery or kids' classroom, or allow for arranging a space to make it conducive for a worship service. Last, a meeting space should be affordable. Many locations quickly become pricey and impair a church's ability to flourish in other areas because of the financial facility commitments. Some common gathering spaces that planters have opted to use are storefront locations, school auditoriums, movie theaters, or occupied church buildings after hours.

Before a church publicly launches, some church plants opt for preview services where they give the community a small sample of what the church will be like a few months before it begins. These preview services also put the newly formed systems to the test and gives time for the new church to tweak them accordingly.

As a date is set for the church to launch, the core team will need to spread the word into the community. Mass mailers, passing out fliers door-to-door, targeted social media ads, outdoor signage, personalized invitations, and newspaper ads are a few ways churches can promote the opening of the new church to their community. Above all, the core team must saturate all these efforts in prayer.

The day the new church becomes public is an exciting and terrifying moment. Months and even years of prayer and hard work have gone into the forming of the plant. The church plant team has to manage expectations. Someone once said that planters overestimate what will take place in one year and underestimate what God can do in three years. In other words the planter needs to have a sober view of what the opening months may look like but keep working and dreaming in the process.

FUNDING THE CHURCH PLANT

Every church plant needs adequate financial backing to accomplish its intended goals. Some planters will strategically choose to be bi-vocational as part of their evangelistic strategy or because of the socioeconomic context in which they plant. For others who will seek to be a full-time church planter, they will need to recruit a team of financial partners to support the plant until it is capable of being self-funding through giving. While some will enjoy the support-raising process and calling people to be generous, many will find this to be difficult. It is important for the church planter to keep in mind that God will enable that which He wills. If God has truly called the planter to plant a church, He will also provide what is needed for the plant however God sees fit. Furthermore, God has already begun to prepare people's hearts to be generous for a God-sized vision like the one behind planting a new church.

In the early stages of the church planting process, the planter should craft a general budget for the first two years of the church. This will give the planter and his supporters a clear understanding of the church's financial need and allow for talking points as he meets with churches and proposed supporters. As financial partners pray and give to the church plant, God will use these men and women in profound ways.

GETTING A FRONT ROW SEAT

Not every story that comes from a church plant will be a win or a success story. Even though some church plants will sputter and not take root, others will grow and flourish in their due season. And what is true in both circumstances is that the church universal is in good hands because it is in God's hands. Jesus said He would build His church and that the gates of hell would not prevail against it (Matt. 16:18). The church is Jesus' church. It does not belong to any pastor in general or church planter in particular. It belongs to Jesus, the Chief Shepherd, who has gladly entrusted His church to local church pastors inviting them to this adventure.

Church plants are like roller coasters with their highs and lows, twists and turns. They will feel emotionally exhausting at one point and exhilarating at another. What is true on each occasion, though, is that church planters get to have a front row seat to see God's mighty works. Planters will see God renew purpose for singles and reconcile marriages. They will witness people place their faith in Jesus and be baptized. They will see the Spirit of God comfort Christians who suffer in the most difficult times. They will also experience God's financial, emotional, and relational provisions at different times and in various ways.

NOTES

1. Tim Keller, *"Why Plant Churches,"* Redeemer City to City, January 1, 2002, redeemercitytocity.com.

2. Some tests can include Myers-Briggs Type Indicator, DiSC Assessment, Prepare/Enrich, Riso-Hudson Enneagram Type Indicator, StrengthsFinder, APEST, and various spiritual gift tests.

3. See Christine Hoover, *The Church Planting Wife: Help and Healing for Her Heart* (Chicago: Moody Publishers, 2013).

4. There are a variety of online tools that will help learn these facts in the United States such as https://www.census.gov, https://missioninsite.com, and https://demographics.coopercenter.org

5. John Fuder, *Neighborhood Mapping: How to Make Your Church Invaluable to the Community* (Chicago: Moody Publishers, 2014), 89.

6. John Fuder provides ten tips to exegete the community: 1. Go as a learner; 2. Seek out an informant (i.e., person of peace who lives in and is knowledgeable about the community); 3. Build a relationship with people in the community; 4. Use an interview guide; 5. Analyze your data; 6. Filter through a biblical worldview; 7. Expand into the broader community; 8. Network available resources; 9. Determine what God is calling you to do; 10. Continually evaluate, study, and explore. See *Neighborhood Mapping*, 21–23.

7. Rich Perez, *Mi Casa: Learning to Love Again* (Nashville: B&H Publishing, 2017), 44.

8. Will Mancini, *Church Unique: How Missional Leaders Cast Vision, Capture Culture, and Create Movement* (San Francisco: Jossey-Bass, 2008).

9. See Ed Stetzer's series of helpful articles on church planting models: https://www.christianitytoday.com/edstetzer/2015/july/finding-right-church-plant-model-introduction-to-church-mod.html.

10. See Dave Ferguson, *Keeping Score: How to Know if Your Church Is Winning* (Exponential Resources, 2014).

11. For more on viewing your community as a mission field, see Jeff Vandersteldt, *Saturate: Being Disciples of Jesus in the Everyday Stuff of Life* (Wheaton, IL: Crossway, 2015).

Revitalizing a Struggling Church[1]

MARK JOBE

Many churches today are declining or barely surviving in communities that have the greatest need of the life-giving presence of Jesus. Though a few churches here and there are growing and expanding rapidly, most are not. The US growth rate of church attendance is not keeping up with population growth. Many local congregations are barely hanging on, living perpetually in a state of slow yet steady decline. This shouldn't be the case. If at all possible, struggling churches should be thrown a lifeline. If that doesn't happen, we will lose two vital things: sacred history and sacred space. Revitalized churches represent an opportunity to recapture a sacred heritage as new congregations become vibrant and life-changing communities once more.

WHAT IS LOST WHEN CHURCHES DIE OUT?

SACRED HISTORY

It is more than just physical assets that are lost each time a church building is closed and converted into residential housing, a strip mall, a high-rise condo, or an agricultural field. Often, the institutional memory of that congregation disappears with the closing of the building. The people who can still recall the church's early days begin to die and move away. In the final years, there is a blurred recollection of the names, events, and themes that laid the foundation for that church. The records, photos, and archives are often trashed or scattered throughout individual members' households, never to be pieced together again. These are chapters in the story of redemption that most history books will never mention. What a loss!

Unless we are connected to our past, we will not fully understand the present. Although the book of Acts ends with chapter 28, the ongoing story of the church represents Acts 29, 30, 31, 32 . . . .104, 105, 106 . . . and on and on. This story must be continually retold. Pastors should be ardent students of church history—not just from ancient times or the Reformation, but more recent church history too. We must appreciate the saints who have paved our way, whether they wore Roman togas or skinny jeans. All sacred history is important because it speaks about God's work. Losing a church means losing a part of "His story."

Sacred Space

In our fast-paced, ever-changing world, "sacred space" is being rapidly displaced by "secular space." Houses of worship once held positions of prominence and were central to the life and development of communities. Some people have argued that church buildings are a detriment to progress of Christianity and the vestiges of paganism. In their book *Pagan Christianity?*, Frank Viola and George Barna make this point:

> Most of us are completely unaware of what we lost as Christians when we began erecting places devoted exclusively for worship. The Christian faith was born in believers' homes, yet every Sunday morning, scores of Christians sit in a building with pagan origins that is based upon pagan philosophy. There does not exist a shred of biblical support for the church building. . . . By doing so, they have supported an artificial setting where they are lulled into passivity and prevented from being natural or intimate with other believers.[2]

There is some truth here, but it is overstated. I agree that the church is not a building but a people set apart by God to accomplish His purposes. Growing up in Europe, I have seen firsthand the irony of ornate cathedrals that are full of tourists but have a scarcity of worshipers. However, I have also come to appreciate the value and significance of sacred space. It's worth preserving.

Many of these struggling churches were once centers of spiritual life and community development. Once these places have been torn down, it is very difficult to obtain zoning for churches again. Four years ago, the church I led purchased an 84,000-square foot building in Chicago to house one of our growing congregations. It was an immense struggle with community leaders, city planners, politicians, and building commissioners to convert this former warehouse into ministry space. Part of the challenge is that church buildings are taken off the property tax rolls. Most politicians have a deep aversion to losing tax money.

Another downside of losing sacred space is that many of these older church buildings are located in unchurched yet highly strategic communities. Often, they are found in gentrified neighborhoods where most 20 to 30-year-old professionals are not actively looking for a church venue. Other times they are found in inner-city neighborhoods where the social and economic needs are the greatest and the resources are scarcest. Or they are found in rural areas where the distances between residences are greater, so churches are harder to reach. Typically, these old church buildings are not found in communities where congregations are thriving and new churches are being planted. Losing such precious sacred space to secular space is like losing a strategic fort on the edge of the new frontier.

WHAT IS KILLING OUR CHURCHES?

Why have these older churches lost their steam? What has happened that has left so many churches struggling and on life support? There is no simple answer to this question. Multiple factors are contributing to the decline of historic urban and rural churches. Here are some of the top factors:

1. THE POST–WORLD WAR II CREATION OF THE SUBURBS

Dramatic demographic trends shifted the residential location of major population groups after World War II. The creation of the suburbs moved many young families away from their family neighborhoods to the outer perimeters of the city. The families that grew up in older churches—families that would have been the natural successors to the previous generation—instead moved away in droves from inner-city and rural churches.

2. CHANGING WAVES OF ETHNIC MIGRATION

As many white middle class families moved out of the city, waves of immigrants were moving in. The cities became the first stop for most initial waves of migration from Europe, Central America, and Asia. This created a strange situation. The older churches continued to embody the culture of the founding group, even though the ethnic makeup of the surrounding neighborhood had dramatically changed. This original culture is sometimes maintained by people who have been at the church for many years and remember when the religious culture was thriving. The result is stagnation or inwardly focused congregations that don't connect with the community.

3. Growing Gentrification of Many Neighborhoods

As a semi-urban lifestyle gains in popularity, many of the neighborhoods close to a city's downtown area have experienced profound gentrification in the last few decades. The urban young professionals buying homes and renting condos in these communities have drastically altered the composition of the neighborhood, as well as the real estate value of the homes. Most of these young professionals are not inclined to attend a traditional neighborhood church. The community around these historic churches may be bustling with economic vitality, night life, and trendy cafés, while at the same time they are desperately struggling with religious life. Most traditional neighborhood churches have had a hard time reaching this segment of the population that often surrounds their sacred space.

4. Natural Life Cycles of Churches

It is no secret that local churches have a life span and natural cycle of existence. Data shows that most churches begin to decline about twenty years into their existence. A church must intentionally and deliberately reinvent itself in order to engage its new surroundings if it plans to continue to grow. Unfortunately, many historic urban churches have had a difficult time reinventing themselves as they have begun to decline. So too, many rural churches stagnate as their traditional, countryside life gives way to modern development. Dramatic changes in urban and rural landscapes, new economic pressures, non-visionary leadership, and tradition-bound power brokers are some of the contributing factors to this lack of adaptation.

5. Deficiency in the Way We Think about Sacred Space

Most evangelicals have viewed church buildings in a utilitarian way: as mere real estate to be used for worship, though not important in and of itself. Whenever the neighborhood started to change, Protestant churches would typically sell their property to an ethnic minority and move farther out to the suburban expansion. In contrast, the Catholic Church has had a much more deeply rooted theology of place. Instead of selling their buildings, they have historically brought in a priest who spoke the language of the new immigrant group and began holding Mass in the new language. This accounts for the strong Catholic presence in many migrant and ethnic neighborhoods. There is much we can learn from this approach!

Terry Bascom describes the hard journey of a declining church this way:

> Increasingly unable to speak to non-Christians, an inwardly focused church begins to decline, due simply to the natural processes of some people moving away and others passing away. As the church declines, those who remain become worried about sustaining the programs they all enjoy. They may reach out, but ineffectively: unable to understand the needs and desires of a secular culture that

has changed, they meet with little success and much disappointment, especially because the driving force of the outreach is to find people who will sustain current programs; it is not to discover what new programs they can initiate to reach the un-churched on behalf of Christ.

With a continually decreasing membership come decreasing human resources. The remnant population ages, its energy declines and the church's unfilled needs increase. Programs are cut or scaled back. Each lost program means the church is less attractive to people on the outside, though, and increases the possibility of members leaving for more vibrant churches that can provide better options. Eventually, when the church can no longer maintain itself, financially or in terms of human commitment, it goes up for sale. And when it does, some other up-and-coming community of faith moves in. Or, the church is razed and replaced by a commercial building and a parking lot.[3]

Unfortunately, it is a fact that if the church real estate is especially valuable, land developers tend to end up with the property. Is this what we want? Should the churches of Jesus Christ be handed over to secular businesses? Or is there a better way?

A THEOLOGY OF RESTART

There is something vital about "redemption" in the DNA of all that God does. The word *redeem* means "to buy back" or "to set free by paying a ransom." This concept involves the idea of ownership and original purpose. When God operates in redemptive mode, He purchases back His things and restores them to their original intent. Jesus is the ultimate agent of redemption. He is called the second Adam. In Genesis 3, we see that the first Adam really messed things up and launched the human race onto the wrong path. But Jesus came to buy back a people for Himself and restore the life trajectories for which they were intended. Restarting a historic sacred space has a prophetic edge with a redemptive twist. The process of redemption begins with a building and congregation that have lost their ability to fulfill their original purpose. There is something incredibly powerful about seeing a sanctuary restored and the pews packed once again with worshiping saints.

In the biblical story of Isaac reopening his father Abraham's wells, we can see several parallels to restarting older churches. Genesis 26:18 tells us that "Isaac reopened the wells that had been dug in the time of his father Abraham, which the Philistines had stopped up after Abraham died, and he gave them the same names his father had given them" (NIV). In the arid desert of the Middle East, water wells represented life-giving places. This is why Jesus used the imagery of a well and water to symbolize His life-giving presence (John 4:1–42). The restarting of historic churches can be viewed as similar to Isaac's quest to reopen his father's ancient wells. Following are five ways that opening old wells has contemporary application to church restarts.

1. THE OLD WELLS HAD A HISTORY THAT WAS IMPORTANT AND SYMBOLIC TO THE NEXT GENERATION.

It may have been more practical to dig new wells, but Isaac chose to reopen the wells of his father for some of the same reasons we should do church restarts today. The wells represented a history that was dear to the community. They symbolized a past that Isaac honored, even though they weren't currently being used to maximum capacity. This was his way of showing that what his father had started may have been on pause, but it was not obsolete.

2. THE OLD WELLS STILL HAD THE PHYSICAL STRUCTURE BUT WERE NO LONGER FUNCTIONING FOR THEIR INTENDED PURPOSE.

Many churches have buildings and sanctuaries that are in good condition but barely being used. The pews are in place, the pulpit is intact, and the nursery still has cribs, but the bubbling overflow of disciple-making has now stopped or has trickled down to mere spiritual drops. A restart allows the buildings to be used again for their intended purpose. Sure, they may need to be fixed up. Yet many sanctuaries can, with the right input, become places of worship and community life once more.

3. THE OLD WELLS NEEDED FRESH ENERGY, A LOT OF WORK, AND A CLEAR VISION TO MAKE THEM USEFUL AGAIN.

Isaac had become a respected and prosperous leader of his clan. Under his guidance, it would take a crew of his energetic young men with a lot of stamina and clear focus to make those old wells work again. I imagine that some of the workers did not understand why Isaac was wasting his time on those old wells when they could have been digging brand-new ones with updated technology. Some of his diggers probably mumbled about the waste of time and money those old wells represented. But Isaac understood the significance of these ancient sources of life. He was willing to invest all this energy because he knew the outcome would be worth it.

4. THE OLD WELLS BECAME PLACES OF DOUBLE BLESSING BECAUSE THEY PROVIDED FRESH WATER IN A HISTORICALLY SIGNIFICANT PLACE.

When the wells were finally opened, they became a source of double blessing. Isaac chose the original names that his father, Abraham, had given the wells many years earlier. This was his way of honoring the past and building on his father's legacy. From then on, whenever the shepherds came to get water, they would drink at a new yet ancient well. They would enjoy not only the water, but the memory of all the past shepherds who had come to this very place. The fresh water of a new well was drawn from a place with deep roots and ancient history. Both of these factors are blessings to those who partake.

5. THE OLD WELLS WERE ONLY PART OF THE PLAN FOR PROVIDING WATER TO A GROWING FLOCK.

Isaac reopened his father's old wells, but he also dug new wells to accommodate his growing flock. Though the old wells were important, they were limited in scope and number. Restarting older churches can be an important part of the plan that God has called us to. However, it is also appropriate to be actively engaged in planting new churches that are not part of a restart. These new plants happen in schools, rentals halls, and other secular spaces. For a few hours a week, they are converted into sacred space. Restarts and church plants are both needed to fully water the flock of God.

THE PROCESS: HOW DO WE RESTART CHURCHES TODAY?

Although no single formula can fit every situation, here are the nine key steps that often happen in the process of a church restart.

1. DIVINE CONNECTIONS: BEING WATCHFUL FOR OPPORTUNITIES

A forward-thinking pastor should always be on the lookout for a revitalization possibility. It takes wise discernment, because each revitalization will need the breath of God and favor from on high to become a healthy disciple-making community of believers. Nevertheless, looking for ways of restarting historic churches and planting new ones is important because the church is at the center of God's strategy to bring His kingdom to this world. The Ukrainian megachurch pastor Sunday Adelaja puts it this way in his book *Church Shift*:

> Church has never been the focus of the Great Commission, but it has always been the most important tool for carrying out the Great Commission. The church is the primary vehicle God uses to train people so they know how to find their Promised Land and rule in their nations. Church is the headquarters, but the battles are not fought at headquarters. They are fought in the field.[4]

Whenever possible, as led by the Holy Spirit, pastors should be open to a revitalization project. This is because the local congregation of believers is the vehicle for societal transformation and the propagation of the gospel message around the world. The Christian church is the organism that Jesus brought to life through the Holy Spirit and set in motion for that very purpose.

2. Breathing Hope: Initial Contact

More often than not, restart opportunities will come to a pastor from churches that reach out for help. To whom do such churches typically reach out? A church with a good name and a ministry that operates with integrity is usually their focus. However, many of these churches will not necessarily come asking for a restart. They might just be looking for counsel or exploring survival ideas. Sometimes they might be seeking potential pastors for their struggling church. That is when a watchful pastor can explain that there could be other options for their future.

The most important element in the initial contact is to infuse hope. Many older leaders have been struggling for so long that they are tired and pessimistic about the future of the church. The pastor of the healthy church should seek to fan the flame of hope in these initial conversations. Help these weary warriors start thinking beyond survival to what a thriving, life-changing ministry would look like once again in that building. Allow their tired souls to dream again and breathe the fresh air of faith and expectation.

The initial contacting person will often be an older individual who has been at the church for many years. Thus, they might be suspicious of your suggestions about a restart or protective of their members and church property. They intuitively feel how vulnerable their church is. Deep inside, they know that difficult change is coming. Most of these initial conversations are not with leaders whose arms are open wide, saying "Come and save us; we have been waiting for you!" So do not mistake their cautious, suspicious, and protective posture as a closed door. Initially, they are just asking the question, "Can you help us?" Then they ask the next question, "Can we really trust you?" Only after that can they ask, "Is a restart possible?"

3. Presenting Dreams: Exploring a New Future

At this point, if openness exists toward a restart, a face-to-face meeting is needed with key decision-makers of the church. This often consists of four or five individuals in their 70s or 80s who have been a part of the church for a long time. The purpose of this meeting is to say, "Here is another option to consider. A restart may or may not be right for you." Be sure to move slowly. Do not push. Instead, just make a gentle offer and let them respond.

In a meeting like this, be sure to tell your story. Share your heart for the neighborhood in which the church exists, and of course, your passion for Christ Himself. Before discussing any details of a restart, you want them to know who you are and what you believe. If you don't have a track record to point to, you can simply tell them the dream you have and point to others who are doing it.

4. OPEN HAND: THE COURTING TIME

Once the struggling church has expressed interest in exploring the restart option, it is time to go into a courting phase. It is important that during this season both parties are candid and honest about who they are and how they operate. Try to keep in mind the image of an open hand. The pastor should remind his team during this season not to get ahead of themselves, but just to keep the church's hand wide open. Once anyone starts grabbing things from the other church and closing their hand around it, pitfalls are set in the path to success. The better posture is to be willing at any time to walk away from the negotiation table, blessing the church and its leaders as you go. You do not want to grasp anything that is not God's best plan for your church or for theirs.

Now would be a good time to invite the original church's leaders to visit your worship services, talk to your leaders, examine your statement of faith, review your constitution, check out your references, and ask any questions they would like of you. Take ample time to get to know them. You might even be asked by the original church to lead their worship services for a few weeks while they are making up their minds. In such cases, you can bring in your worship team and preach the sermon at their site as everyone tests the waters.

5. THE MARRIAGE: MAKING A DECISION

The courting period will usually last from three to six months. Normally the leadership council, board of elders, or deacon board will need to decide whether or not this is right for the church. Often this decision comes down to an inner core of long-term leaders in the church. They are revered figures whom others trust for their insights and longevity. If they are convinced this is the right decision, the rest of the congregation will usually follow.

During this decision-making process, be careful not to take on the role of salesman. Your job is not to sell this idea, but to be honest and thorough in presenting an option that may or may not be right for them. It is the Lord who must make this happen if it is going to work. This approach provides great freedom to everyone. You don't have to focus on convincing their flock, persuading their leaders, or manipulating an outcome. Just the opposite. Make it clear that you have come by invitation only. Decide firmly—then convey it often—that you will not step into this process unless the church formally invites you to partner with them in pursuing a restart.

According to the struggling church's constitution or bylaws, they will probably have to take a congregational vote that requires a certain percentage of agreement to move forward. At this juncture, it is important to consult a not-for-profit attorney so that the church goes about the decision-making process in an ethical and legal way.

6. Fusion of the Old and New: Creating a Launch Team

The wisest course—and one you will regret if you do not pursue it—is to never initiate any merger activity until the legal documents have been signed. It is very risky to move forward on a merge without the legal documents in place. But once those documents have become valid, the union is permanent, and progress can begin. It is much like a marriage: after a time of informal courting, you make a public commitment and determine to make it work no matter what. There can be no bail-out options if the restart is going to succeed. Both sides must enter this covenant with a mentality of long-term commitment.

The first order of business is to create a launch team that has a combination of people from the original church and the new one. The launch team will seek to get the church ready for the grand opening. The best launch team will be composed of high-capacity executive leaders from your church and the key faith-filled leaders from the original church. This team is usually no more than six to seven people. The launch team will need to meet almost weekly leading up to the grand opening.

Note that in preparation for the grand opening, the launch team and leadership staff will be working on various fronts simultaneously. This crunch time tends to generate the most tension and misunderstandings, so be sure to navigate it with extra care and caution. And bathe the process in much prayer.

7. The Remodeling of the Building

Older buildings may require a significant facelift before the grand opening. Often these important updates will include:

- Updating the public bathrooms

- Remodeling the central worship space (which may include building a new stage, installing new carpet or seating, or updating the lighting)

- Upgrading the audiovisual technology: speakers, sound board, projector, screens, etc.

- Installing high-quality new signage on the exterior of the building

- Sprucing up the appeal of the nursery and children's ministry area

- Enhancing the exterior landscaping for a clean, fresh look

• Painting most of the interior of the building with contemporary colors

Remodeling the existing building is by far the most labor-intensive and costly aspect of the launch preparation. To do it right, make sure you hire a general contractor and an interior decorator to help in this process. In the long run, these individuals will save you a lot of time and headaches.

It may be the case that some original members do not appreciate these costly upgrades to the building. Don't be surprised if, after investing significant sums of money in building renovation, the older members complain, "We liked it better the way it was." Be gentle with these folks. Change is always hard, especially for those who have been at the church a long time. It may help if you give them a few of the underlying reasons why the decisions were made.

8. Blending the Relationship between the Original Congregation and the New Church

The original congregation and the new arrivals need opportunities to blend and begin to feel like one. There are many ways to accomplish this, but here are four suggestions:

1. For a few weeks after the merger, share a meal after the morning worship service, at which everyone is invited to stay and mingle. You might find it is better to cater an inexpensive meal rather than take a potluck approach, so that both groups have time to interact instead of being busy with food preparation. The goal is relationships, not gourmet cooking.

2. Have the whole merged congregation meet on a Saturday evening for a prelaunch time of preparation. Original members and new people can come together to organize the grand opening. Everyone should wear a name tag and break up into small groups to introduce themselves. Then the actual launch will not feel like strangers pretending to know each other.

3. Organize a couple of work days on the new building. In light of the remodeling suggested above, there will be plenty of work to do. Invite the original members and new core people to come together to help prepare the building for the grand opening. There is nothing like working together on shared tasks to create a bonding experience.

4. Continue to have worship services in the revitalized church building; but a month or two before the grand opening, change the service time and format. It is important to create a sense of newness as well as continuity. These new rhythms need to be tried and tested before the formal launch.

9. THE LAUNCH

The launch team will need to be made up of people who can make things happen and have a positive influence on both the new attenders and original members. Here are some of the key ministries that should be up and running by the time of the grand opening:

- Worship and Tech Team
- Teaching Team
- Children's Ministry
- Small Groups
- Assimilation Team
- Prayer Team

As you make the launch, remember that your job has not just finished. Quite the contrary, it has just begun. The purpose of all your work has not been to take two congregations and successfully merge them into a happy new club, but to make this new church into a bastion of gospel outreach in the neighborhood and beyond. It is important that as you remodel the building and prepare the people for change that you not neglect your primary call of reaching unbelievers in the community. Generating community awareness during the ongoing process of the restart must be a top priority.

HEALTHY RESTARTS REQUIRE G.R.A.C.E.

When a church makes a priority of being open to restarting older congregations, it forces that church to redefine some of its values. Maintaining these values will be important for the integrity of the restart process. Here are five key values that will help a church approach each potential restart with Christian "G.R.A.C.E." This list is not exhaustive, yet it represents the right outlook by which a church can properly steward its opportunities before God.

GO LOOKING FOR GOD'S ACTIVITY

Active attention to the work of the Lord is a wise part of any church's philosophy of ministry. The pastor and congregational leaders should always be asking, "What is God doing and how can we cooperate?" It is tempting to lay your plans before God and pray, "Lord, please bless this plan of ours." But the place of greatest fruit and lasting impact is in the center of God's work, not human initiatives that head off in their own direction.

You may be asking, "What do you mean by 'looking for God's activity'?" It is nothing other than intentionally looking around to discern the people and places where God is obviously at work. Learn to ask, "Lord, are You trying to get our attention or move us in a new direction?" This may show up as a burst of Christian conversions in a certain community; the convergence of multiple conversations around the same topic; or some unusual open doors to do a new ministry. All of it boils down to learning to hear God's movement and the whispers of His Spirit.

At times when I am working in my home office, I can hear my wife moving about the house. I might not know what room she is in or what exactly she is doing, but I know she is there. When I want to find her, I just listen for her sounds and call out her name, and I find her quickly. In a similar way, pastors must learn to develop an ear for what God is doing. Look for His moving, then call upon His name, and you will end up in the middle of His workings.

RESIST SPIRITUAL COLONIALISM

Religious colonialism has done more to harm the essence and progress of Christianity than probably any other force. A person with a colonial mentality arrives on the scene with the assumption that God has not been present until the colonizer's arrival. Though you may not ever invade a foreign land, "spiritual colonialism" does the same thing. It despises the previous workings of God, believing that one's own brand of the faith is superior to any other. The colonizers think only their story is the real story of Christianity. Cults and Christian denominations alike have often told their story as if Christianity was non-existent or severely flawed until their founder arrived on the scene to be the true representative of God on earth. They believe that their little man-made kingdom is at the center of the universe.

Instead, be humble. When considering a restart, remember that God might have been at work in that community long before you were born or your denomination or church existed. Learn the story of God's work in that place, resisting the temptation to become its hero or savior. Be generous with the history of those who came before you. The former generations of that struggling church form part of the "cloud of witnesses" that is now cheering you on.

APPROACH OPPORTUNITIES WITH HANDS WIDE OPEN

A restart is not necessarily the best option for every struggling church. Rather, the restart is one of multiple options that could be pursued. God may have a better plan that does not include your church's intervention. This attitude will allow you to approach each potential restart with an open hand. You might even want to pray that God would slam the doors shut if moving forward would not bring glory to the name of Jesus. There is incredible freedom when you leave the ultimate decision to God and don't try to grasp, manipulate, contrive, or push people into a decision that they are not walking into willingly. Never agree to a restart unless you are invited by the congregation and leadership team to do so. And if they end the process, be wise enough to release it, for that might have been God's will all along.

CONSIDER WHETHER OR NOT THIS WOULD BE A KINGDOM WIN

Ultimately, the question you should be asking is, Will this decision be a win for the kingdom of God, the name of Jesus, and the spread of His gospel? Avoid anything that smells of nasty prolonged battles, tangled messes, or embittered people. The energy spent on battles for control or in-house fighting will take away from the energy needed to do the real work of the ministry. Some church leaders would rather close a struggling church than ask for help or change their traditions. In such cases, let them close their doors with dignity. Not every failing church should be restarted. Wisdom requires you to discern whether the restart would be, all things considered, a kingdom win.

EXPECT GOD TO MOVE WITH RESURRECTION POWER

As Christians, we should always move forward with the assumption that God's supernatural power will be needed to bring about a true resurrection. This will require faithful people—in both churches—who are diligently seeking the face of God. Christian Schwarz, in his book *Natural Church Development*, says:

> The point separating growing and non-growing churches, those which are qualitatively above or below average is . . . "Are the Christians in this church 'on fire?' Do they live committed lives and practice their faith with joy and enthusiasm?" Since there are significant differences in this area between growing and declining churches, we called this quantity characteristic "passionate spirituality."[5]

There is no substitute for "passionate spirituality" when it comes to restarts. They require a people who have learned to pursue God with full desire and seek His presence and power. A church restart will only be successful when people marked by the holy fire of God are behind it.

NOTES

1. This chapter is adapted from "God Was Already Here: Restarting Sacred Spaces," by Mark Jobe, 2012, Mark Jobe, MultiplicityNetwork.org and NewLifeChicago.org.

2. Frank Viola and George Barna, *Pagan Christianity? Exploring the Roots of Our Church Practices* (Carol Stream, IL: Tyndale Momentum, 2012), 42.

3. Terry Bascom, "Restart: New Life for the Dying Church," https://web.archive.org/web/20090626060724/http://www.congregationalist.org/Archivesold/May_01/Basscom.html.

4. Sunday Adelaja, *Church Shift* (Lake Mary, FL: Charisma House, 2008), 10.

5. Christian A. Schwarz, *Natural Church Development* (St. Charles, IL: ChurchSmart Resources, 2003).

Fulfilling
the Great Commission

TIMOTHY R. SISK

In 1792, William Carey wrote an eighty-seven-page book titled *An Enquiry into the Obligation of Christians to Use Means for the Conversion of the Heathens* in which he argued that the Great Commission (Matt. 28:19–20; Mark 16:15; Acts 1:8) was still the responsibility of the church. There were some in those days who maintained that the commands given by Jesus Christ were only applicable to the early disciples and thus no longer binding on the church. Carey's book, however, was influential in moving the church from its slowness concerning the global proclamation of the gospel, to taking the command of our Lord seriously. Carey's writings and his life serve as a significant historical marker of the church recapturing its responsibility and privilege to make disciples of all nations.

Despite the significant increase in the number of missionaries being sent since the time of Carey, two statistics reveal that the church still has much to do if it is to fully obey the command of Christ and fulfill the Great Commission.

- According to research on the status of global Christianity by Gordon Conwell Seminary, more than 28 percent of the world's population has no access to the gospel. This means over 2.2 billion people have no Bibles from which they can read the Jesus story and no churches or missionaries in their area from whom they can hear the good news.[1]

- Ramesh Richard notes that more than 95 percent of the world's pastors, the leaders of Christ's church, are undertrained.[2]

These two statistics alone highlight the need for every church to enthusiastically embrace its Great Commission responsibility.

Pastors must prayerfully consider how they should be involved in making the gospel known to the unreached and teaching and training local ministers who can lead the global church. The purpose of this chapter, therefore, is to focus on some key areas that will assist pastors and the churches they serve in further engaging with their responsibility for making disciples in all nations by laying a biblical foundation for intentional involvement in fulfilling the Great Commission; assessing the church's current level of involvement; and offering concrete steps for further engagement in completing the mandate of our Savior.

BIBLICAL FOUNDATION FOR FULFILLING THE GREAT COMMISSION

In AD 1095, Pope Urban II preached an impassioned sermon that summoned Christians to wrest control of Jerusalem from the hands of the Muslims. With the promise of both the remission of sins and earthly and heavenly rewards, he sought to stir the crowd to take up arms against those he called enemies of the cross. Pope Urban concluded his fervent plea with a thunderous shout of "God wills it!" That phrase became the rallying cry of the bloody Crusades that followed.

God wills it? Really, Pope Urban? God wills that kind of brutal, senseless slaughter? One would be hard-pressed to find anyone today who would defend the Crusades as God's will. Furthermore, as one reads church history, one is repeatedly troubled as to how God's name has been so carelessly attached to the selfish ploys of mankind. Wars have been waged, millions of dollars have been squandered, and countless hundreds of thousands of human lives have been physically and emotionally destroyed, all in the name of God.

Even today, we are not immune to our own "God wills it" kind of moments. Local churches make plans to build multimillion-dollar buildings and proclaim, "God wills it!" TV evangelists preach healing and prosperity for all: "God wills it!" Secretly we all think that our personal lives should be lived happily ever after. Surely God wills that!

There is always that danger that our stained motives will cause us to declare something is God's will, when in fact it may be just our own selfish craving. That is why the words of Peter in his second letter are so helpful in revealing to us God's will: "The Lord is not slow about His promise, as some count slowness, but is patient toward you, not wishing for any to perish but for all to come to repentance"

(2 Peter 3:9). Paul echoes this same sentiment when he states that God "wants all people to be saved and to come to the knowledge of the truth" (1 Tim. 2:4).

God's will is that no one should perish: neither Americans nor Africans, not Hindus or Muslims, not Indians or Incas. So, what do we do about this desire . . . this will of God? We could ignore it. We know that is what God wants, but we have our own plans and our own desires. We could nibble around the edges of it . . . a little here and a little there . . . just enough to relieve a good case of evangelical guilt. Or we could, with great intentionality, take to heart what our heavenly Father desires. We could wholly commit ourselves to those who have no access to the gospel by going to them and by assisting someone else to go, so that the light of the gospel shines in every part of this globe. We can be confident based on Scripture that God wills that.

As a young married twentysomething, Ray read a book on money management, and its warnings about financial debt scared him to death. Since that time, he and his wife of many years have heeded those warnings and have stayed away from incurring financial debt. However, as followers of Jesus, the Bible teaches that we are all debtors, not to a credit card company or a bank, but we owe something to the 7.7 billion people of this world.

In Romans, Paul writes: "I am under obligation both to Greeks and to the uncultured, both to the wise and to the foolish" (Rom. 1:14). In other words, no one is left out. As Christians we are debtors to our friends, and we even have an obligation to those we detest. We owe a debt to those who look and talk like us and to those we have never met, whose language we cannot understand, and who come from a completely different culture. As followers of Jesus, we are debtors to people in Tokyo and Teheran. We are debtors to the tribes that live along the Amazon River and the tribe that lives in Cleveland. What do we owe them? We owe them a hearing of the gospel of Jesus Christ, the good news that there is forgiveness and hope in Jesus. That is why our churches should be wholeheartedly supporting missions and sending missionaries, because according to the Bible, we have a debt that needs to be paid.

ASSESSING YOUR CURRENT INVOLVEMENT

If we truly believe the above passages and seek to obey them, then that belief should be demonstrable in the way in which we invest the resources that God places in our hands. As you contemplate leading your church into taking proactive steps in fulfilling the Great Commission, the initial step you take should be that of honestly assessing your current level of involvement. What are you currently doing as a church to fulfill the Great Commission? Is playing a role in the fulfillment of the

Great Commission a priority in the church you serve? The danger is that often we claim to deeply believe in fulfilling the Great Commission, but the reality is we are concretely contributing very little to its fulfillment.

There are several simple ways to assess a church's values. What we talk about, pray for, teach, and preach are one set of indicators. Review the sermons preached in the church over the last year. Observe the announcements in your weekly bulletins. Listen to the corporate prayers in your worship services. If the teaching and preaching about the Great Commission, if prayer for laborers across the globe occupies little of corporate worship time, if our announcements are focused on us and our activities, then that is often an indicator that we have failed to prioritize global disciple-making. If an outsider listened to the sermons, prayers, and announcements in your church, would they conclude the Great Commission is a priority?

How a church stewards its financial resources regarding the Great Commission is another indicator of the value it places on missions. Generally, a person's bank statement will reveal what they value. The same can be said about a church. In a survey of churches in the United States, Lifeway Research found that the average church invests only 5 percent of its budget to missions and evangelism.[3] While the Bible does not give us a set percentage of what a church should invest in fulfilling the Great Commission, 5 percent is woefully insufficient given the importance and immensity of the task before us. Look at your church's budget and ask, "Does our giving to missions reflect the priority it is given in Scripture?"

Another tool that can be helpful is an assessment that Advancing Churches in Missions Commitment (ACMC) created to assist churches in evaluating their current level of involvement in missions. This tool can both help you understand your current level of involvement while also giving you goals for how your church can increase its future commitment and activity to the fulfillment of the Great Commission.

LEADING A GREAT COMMISSION-FOCUSED CHURCH

CHURCH LEADERSHIP

After visiting over 500 churches, a missiologist observed that if church leaders are excited about and committed to the Great Commission, then the church will reflect such commitment and enthusiasm. However, if the leaders of the church are lukewarm toward sacrificial engagement in global disciple-making, or if playing a significant role in fulfilling the Great Commission is not a priority to the leaders, then the church generally reflects that as well.

This reality places a significant amount of responsibility on the pastor and leaders of the church to actively prioritize the Great Commission. Without attention and nurture from the church leaders, missions will get lost in the pile of other good and well-meaning activities. In the swirl of church programs and activities (building projects, counseling, Sunday morning worship service planning, children's and youth ministry, committee meetings, etc.), it is easy for the "unknown lost" to slip off the radar. Therefore, church leaders must ground themselves in the Bible's teaching concerning the "lostness" of humanity, the importance of the Great Commission, and the great need and responsibility of the congregation.

Church leaders should take opportunity to visit missionaries and to personally encounter the great needs around the world. The vision church leaders will catch from such exposure will translate into greater enthusiasm in leading the church in its biblically mandated responsibility. The apostle Paul experienced something like this when he walked the streets of Athens. "Now while Paul was waiting for them in Athens, his spirit was being provoked within him as he was observing that the city was full of idols" (Acts 17:16). Paul was surrounded by all the idols in Athens and that eyewitness experience kindled a fire of compassion in his heart for the lost. Because those types of in-person experiences are so powerful, churches should provide funds and time away to allow their leaders the opportunity to walk the streets of cities and villages where the most unreached of the world reside and to feel the spiritual need that exists there.

TEACHING AND PREACHING

A new missionary family had recently arrived in Bolivia and on a Friday night they decided to go to what the Bolivians called the Feria. It was a huge outdoor market with many rows of booths packed with thousands of people. Since the family had only been in Bolivia for three weeks, they could not understand the sales pitches of the folks hawking their wares, but nonetheless was a marvelous taste of a slice of Bolivian culture. That is . . . it was marvelous until they realized that Katie, their seven-year-old daughter was no longer beside them. She had just been there. They had paused to watch an artist painting and then she was gone. Lost in that swarm of humanity.

Lost is a gloomy word. Whether you have lost a game, lost your keys, lost in the stock market, or lost a family member, it is a discouraging word. It gives one a huge sense of emptiness. Bible readers encounter the world lost many times.

One day Jesus was sitting around with a crowd of the outcasts, the nonreligious people who would never frequent the temple. The religious folks could not believe that Jesus would even talk with such people much less eat with them. They were people like the greedy traitors called tax collectors and prostitutes. It was in that setting that Jesus told three stories all having to do with something lost: a lost sheep, a lost coin, and a lost son. He told those stories to those "outcasts" to drive home the reason He had come to earth. Jesus stated: "For the Son of Man has come to seek and to save that which was lost" (Luke 19:10). Christ's love for the lost caused Him to sacrifice His exalted place in heaven and to give His life on the cross on our behalf so we could be saved.

Matthew records how on another occasion the crowds were swarming Jesus. He observed that Jesus, "seeing the crowds, felt compassion for them, because they were distressed and downcast like sheep without a shepherd" (Matt. 9:36). Jesus saw this needy group of people and instead of being irritated with all their needs, He was moved with compassion. It all had to do with how He saw them.

Do you ever wish you could buy some eyeglasses for people that would cause them to see the world or a certain issue the way you see it? Maybe you are having an argument with your spouse or your child or a colleague at work and you just cannot get them to see your point of view. So, you hand them these imaginary glasses and when they put them on, they immediately see the situation just as you see it.

As followers of Jesus, as the body of Christ, we are called to put on Jesus glasses, to see the world, to see people as Jesus sees them. Remember, the crowd that surrounded Jesus that day was not there to do something for Jesus. These were needy people, diseased people, people who wanted Jesus to do something for them. But instead of shunning them for their wretched condition, ignoring them or isolating Himself from these needy people, Jesus had compassion on them.

How do we see the crowds? Because the eyes by which we see people determines how we will treat them. Are they dirty sinners, nuisances, enemies, terrorists, illegals? Or do we see them as Jesus does, as harassed, helpless, sheep without a shepherd in need of the Good Shepherd? When we see people with Jesus' eyes we will be moved not only with compassion, but also moved to action.

That is why pastors and church leaders must constantly keep the lost before their congregations. It is easy to focus our preaching and teaching primarily on the everyday problems of the congregation and ignore the multiple passages in the Bible that highlight the needs of the lost of this world. Therefore, it is vital that we dedicate an appropriate amount of our teaching and preaching each year to help the congregants see the world with Jesus' eyes. Based on your earlier assessment of your preaching schedule, commit to including teaching and preaching on the fulfilling the Great Commission in your sermon calendar. Help your congregation see the world with Jesus' eyes. When you do, they will be moved with compassion and they will pray more, give more, and go more so that the Great Commission can be completed.

BALANCING JERUSALEM, JUDEA, SAMARIA AND THE ENDS OF THE EARTH

In Luke's recording of the Great Commission in Acts, Jesus stated: "But you will receive power when the Holy Spirit has come upon you; and you shall be My witnesses both in Jerusalem, and in all Judea, and Samaria, as far as the remotest part of the earth" (Acts 1:8). This statement by Jesus seems to indicate that disciples are to concurrently be witnesses to people who are like us and nearby (Jerusalem), people who are unlike us and nearby (Judea and Samaria), and people who are unlike us and far away (the remotest part of the earth). As a congregation of disciples of Jesus, the church too needs to consider being a witness to each one of these people groups.

People Like Us Nearby

The gospel writers recorded and preserved almost fifty stories that Jesus told while He was on earth. One of the parables of Jesus was about a certain rich man and Lazarus (Luke 16). This rich man had everything—the finest clothing and the best of food. However, right outside the gate of his home lay Lazarus, covered in sores. He just lay there, too sick to sit up, too weak to even shoo the dogs away and keep them from licking his putrid sores. Later, we learn that the rich man knew Lazarus, which means the man at his gate was no mere stranger. Even then, the rich man refused to help.

The opportunity for this rich man to obey the commands of God and help meet the needs of a fellow human was right there at his gate. Every day as he left his house and returned home, he had to walk right by the starving and sick Lazarus. The rich man did not have to look to some far away land for a way to obey God, it was right there at his gate and even then, he refused to help.

Who are the people at your church's gate that your church needs to serve in the name of Christ? We miss the message of Acts 1:8 if we solely seek to win the lost who reside thousands of miles from us. While we must not forget those far across the seas, we must also not forget those right at our gate. Fulfilling the Great Commission starts at home (Jerusalem).

People Unlike Us Nearby

According to data from Insider Higher Education, there are more than 1.1 million international students studying in universities and colleges in the United States.[4] They come to study business and management, engineering, math, and computer science. Many of these students come from countries where traditional missionaries cannot go. They come from places like China, Saudi Arabia, and India, and they will return to their countries as leaders, people of influence in their societies and areas of expertise.

As you can imagine, these students come to the US often not knowing anyone, the language, or the customs. The food and culture are strange, so it can be an extremely lonely and difficult adjustment. However, that provides followers of

Jesus Christ the opportunity to obey Scripture and practice hospitality. By welcoming these students, helping them get settled, getting to know them, and caring for them, the church can impact their lives.

Many of these international students have never spent time with a true follower of Jesus. The Joshua Project states that 81 percent of Muslims, Buddhists, and Hindus do not personally know a Christian.[5] The only understanding they have of a Christian is what has been communicated through the media or their religious leaders. In a survey of Muslims who have come to Christ, they stated that the most influential factor that caused them to consider Jesus was the lifestyle of Christians they got to know.

As your church ponders how to fulfill the Great Commission, realize that thousands of the most unreached people have come to your city as international students. So, consider volunteering at the international student office of your local college or university. Mobilize your church to practice hospitality and welcome these students. If these 1.1 million students come to the United States and then return to their home country without spending time with a Christian and hearing the good news of Jesus, we as the church of Jesus Christ have missed a golden opportunity. International students are just one example of the possibilities of the church reaching out to people who are unlike us but nearby (Judea and Samaria).

Depending on where you live, it is possible that there are people nearby who speak another language and are of a different ethnicity and culture. As Christians, instead of ignoring or worse, resenting the presence of people who are equally made in the image of God and for whom Christ died, we must lovingly welcome and show compassion toward them. In the Old Testament, Israel was often instructed to "welcome the stranger." As a church, we must reject societal trends that demonize the "other," but instead must be the neighbor that Jesus called us to be (Luke 10).

People Unlike Us Far Away

Traditionally, as the church sought to take the gospel to those who were far away, missionaries were recruited, trained, and supported so that they could go and live among those they were seeking to reach. However, there are some today who argue that the day of sending missionaries cross-culturally has passed. While globalization has made it easier to travel and communicate across the globe, nothing replaces human presence. The incarnation of Christ argues the necessity of the bodily presence of witnesses. Jesus stated, "As the Father has sent Me, I also send you" (John 20:21). Jesus was sent physically to this earth to walk, touch, care for, and give of His life for the lost. To fulfill the Great Commission, the church will continue to need those who go to live among the most unreached places of this world.

NURTURING AND SENDING MISSIONARIES

Every church should strive to be a sending church, that is a church that sends "homegrown" cross-cultural missionaries. For this to happen however, a church must be intentional about teaching and encouraging congregants to prayerfully consider global disciple-making. Creating an environment that nurtures a global ethos is not something that happens naturally. Our natural inclination is to think of "Jerusalem" and the needs in our immediate vicinity. To get the church to consider "Judea, Samaria and the remotest parts of the earth" will require that the leadership of the church proactively lift the eyes of the congregation so that they see the needs of the world (John 4:35).

Pastors and church leaders must continually be sensitive to how the Holy Spirit is working in the lives of the congregants. Identifying those with a passion for the lost and who are gifted in areas that can be utilized in cross-cultural ministry is key. Assisting those with a desire to serve cross-culturally with theological and ministry training is another important step in the life of a church as it seeks to be a "sending" church.

Sending Long-term Missionaries

Depending on your church's denominational affiliation there are multiple ways in which a church can financially support missionaries. Some denominations have programs in which the churches pool their funds to support denominational missionaries. Independent churches can work with mission agencies partnering with other churches to support global disciple-makers. The goal is that the church is giving sacrificially so that all can hear, because where we spend our money is an indicator of where are heart is. Jesus stated: "For where your treasure is, there your heart will be also" (Matt. 6:21).

As mentioned earlier, the average church in the United States gives 5 percent of its annual funds to missions and evangelism. For the Great Commission to be fulfilled, we need to see churches raise this level significantly. While it might not be possible for a church to go from 5 percent to 35 percent in a year, annual increases in missions and evangelism spending are necessary to fulfill the Great Commission.

There is some debate as to the best methodology for supporting missionaries. Some churches choose to support fewer missionaries for greater amounts of money. Other churches choose to support a greater number of missionaries for smaller amounts. There are advantages and disadvantages to both methods.

The advantage to supporting fewer missionaries with greater amounts of funds is that a deeper relationship can be forged, and the missionary family becomes part of the church family. The disadvantage is that if a church supports just a few missionaries, the focus of the church's missionary vision will be narrowed both geographically and in the type of ministries the church supports.

If the church chooses to support more missionaries with lesser funds, the advantage is that with multiple missionaries the church's vision both geographically and ministry-wise can be very broad. The disadvantage is that churches that support many missionaries often do not have the opportunity of getting to know all their missionaries well. Since the Bible does not mandate a given methodology, it seems best to allow each church to determine its own philosophy of missionary support.

The church also needs to consider the locations of where the missionaries they support are being deployed. According to Global Frontier Missions, only one out of every forty missionaries is serving among the most unreached people groups of the world.[6] Another way to frame the distribution of missionaries is to consider that only 2.4 percent of the missionaries are serving among the nearly 2.2 billion people who have never been exposed to the gospel. For these reasons, it is vital that the church consider the priority of the most unreached and proactively seek to assist those who are going to such people groups.

Sending Short-term Missionaries[7]

Short-term missions (STM) have grown significantly over the last sixty years from hundreds of short-term missionaries who went out annually in the 1960s, to currently well over a million who take short-term mission trips annually. This phenomenal growth has taken place, not only because of globalization, but because many mission agencies and local churches sensed this "new" strategy might be instrumental in raising up long-term servants and a means to provide missionaries and national churches with additional laborers. As a result, mission agencies and churches have invested a great deal of both human and financial resources to provide STM opportunities to their constituents.

While the investment of resources and the numbers participating in STM have swelled, caution must be exercised in the use of this methodology. Concerns about this methodology include:

- Costs: The amount of money used to fund STM is enormous, surpassing at least a billion dollars annually. Is this the most prudent way to spend such large sums of donations?

- "Amateurization" of missions: Churches will sometimes send short termers to work in other cultures that they would never allow them to do in their own local church. Often, the majority of STM teams are populated by those with limited foreign language ability, limited ministry experience, and limited cross-cultural awareness. Please, do not send your "B" team to the mission field.

- STM trips are more likely to increase ethnocentrism: While we often think that exposing people to other cultures will increase cultural sensitivity, the opposite is often true. Social scientists point out that short-term exposure to other cultures tends to increase ethnocentrism (the belief that one's culture is superior to all other cultures).

- Promotes a "quick fix" mentality: STM can give the impression that the work of global disciple-making can be accomplished in a matter of days or weeks.

While acknowledging the concerns of STM, the possible benefits of this methodology must also be considered:

- Source of long-term servants: Every semester, there are students who enroll at Moody Bible Institute that are headed into missions because of their participation in a STM trip. The concern however, with some mission agencies, is the "return on investment" they are currently seeing. While the number of STM participants has increased dramatically over the last two decades, growth in the number of long-term missionaries as a result of a STM experience has not increased. Some of this could be solved by churches and agencies being more selective as they form STM teams. Instead of an open invitation to join a STM team, what if churches prayerfully selected members of the team based on the needs of the ministry and spiritual gifting and long-term service potential of the participant?

- Increased prayer and giving: Roger Peterson argues that his post-STM trip surveys indicate that STM participants give more and pray more for missions. First-hand exposure to the needs of the world, can serve as a catalyst to spur believers toward greater global engagement.[8]

- Spiritual growth of the participant: In surveys conducted among Christian university students who participated in a STM trip, "I grew spiritually" and "I learned more about God and His church" are consistently top responses.[9]

- Encouragement of national believers and missionaries: My own experience as a missionary in Japan points to this as being a significant benefit of STM. In nations where there are so few believers, STM participants that meaningfully engage with national believers and long-term missionaries have a wonderful opportunity to minister to and encourage the "receivers."

While some are calling for a moratorium on STM trips, it seems best to incorporate changes that can be instituted that may shrink the numbers, but ultimately increase the effectiveness of STM. So, if your church decides to incorporate this methodology, ask yourself the following questions:

- Who is really benefiting from STM trips? If the answer is primarily the STM participants, then that should be cause for caution and reconsideration of the trip. Are we truly helping the "receivers" or are we adding to their workload and expending resources for the sake of the short-term missionary's personal growth and enjoyment?

- Do our STM trips foster dependency? Missionaries and agencies who host STM trips often scramble to find "work" for the team to do while they are in country. Sometimes the "work" that is performed is something that the local congregation could and should be doing. Creating dependency is one of the significant issues that has negatively impacted missions. We do not want to foster such dependency via STM.

- How do we integrate lessons learned into long-term change/results? Behavioral scientists tell us that long-term change generally happens with long-term exposure. Can we structure the STM experience so that while the team may only be on-site for a limited amount of time, their involvement in training, prayer, and follow-up would extend over a longer period so that lasting change may take root?

Along with interacting with these questions, visit the website https://soe. org/, which promotes a code of best practice for short-term mission practitioners. Understand that while STM can play a role in a church's mission strategy, it must not be the sum of it.

PRAYER

Our public and corporate prayers indicate our priorities. One of the ways you can prioritize missions in your church is by intentionally praying for issues related to the Great Commission in your worship services. Pray corporately for:

- One of the missionaries your church supports. Show a video clip of the missionary's work, read highlights from their latest newsletter or video conference them. Then spend time praying for them.

- An unreached people group. Use a resource like "Operation World" or the "Unreached of the Day" from Joshua Project. Highlight an unreached people group each week to lift the eyes of your congregation toward the needs and opportunities of global disciple-making.

CREATING A GREAT COMMISSION CHURCH

One of the ways to create a global ethos in the church is to have an annual missions conference or special Sundays set aside for missions emphasis. There are multiple websites that can help with the logistics of planning a missions conference or a missions emphasis Sunday. The key to success is for the pastor and church leaders to wholeheartedly promote and support the effort.

For those churches that do not have a tradition of holding such special events, mission agencies can be helpful in coming alongside a local church to plan and implement a conference or a special Sunday. Identify a missions agency, which the church aligns with theologically and methodologically, and enlist their help in promoting the Great Commission. These agencies have years of experience and multiple resources (e.g., human and media) that can assist you in promoting missions. These agencies often have literature, media, and experienced missionaries who can come to your church and challenge the church to greater involvement.

Promotion of the Great Commission should not be limited to just an annual conference or a special Sunday. It is imperative that the church continually keep the needs of the world before the congregation. This can be done in multiple ways: offering courses that focus on the needs of the world, joining with other churches to participate in a Perspectives course at Operation World, making books and literature available, which contain a global focus, and showing video clips of the work of missions around the world during the announcements are just a few ways in which to keep the Great Commission at the forefront of the mission of the church.

CONCLUSION

Since the publication of William Carey's book in 1792, the church has made significant progress in its efforts to fulfill the Great Commission. However, with 2.2 billion people who are still unreached with the gospel and 250 babies being born each minute, the task given to us by Jesus remains immense. Therefore, prayerfully consider how you can lead your church to a deeper commitment to global disciple-making by laying a biblical foundation for your intentional involvement in fulfilling the Great Commission, assessing the church's current level of involvement, and taking concrete steps for further engagement in completing the mandate of our Savior.

NOTES

1. https://gordonconwell.edu/wp-content/uploads/sites/13/2019/04/StatusofGlobalChristianity20191.pdf.

2. https://lausanne.org/best-of-lausanne/95-pastors-untrained.

3. Church Law and Tax, How Churches Spend Their Money, churchlawandtax.com, USA, August 28, 2014.

4. https://www.insidehighered.com/quicktakes/2019/04/23/international-student-numbers-us-decline.

5. https://joshuaproject.net/assets/media/handouts/status-of-world-evangelization.pdf.

6. https://globalfrontiermissions.org/gfm-101-missions-course/state-of-the-world-the-task-remaining/.

7. Material in this section has been taken from Timothy R. Sisk, "Short-Term Missions: Moving Forward," *Japan Harvest Magazine*, Spring 2018, japanharvest.org.

8. D. P. McDonough and R. P. Peterson, *Can Short-Term Mission Really Create Long-Term Missionaries?* (Minneapolis: STEM, 1991), 3.

9. I. Beckwith, "Youth Summer Missions Trips: A Case Study" (PhD diss., Trinity Evangelical School, 1991). See also: D. E. Wilson, "The Influence of Short-Term Missions Experience on Faith Maturity" (DMin diss., Asbury theological Seminary, 1999).

Outreach to the Jewish Community[1]

MICHAEL RYDELNIK

In my observation, Gentile Jesus followers who genuinely want to share their faith with lost people are somewhat reluctant when it comes to Jewish people. When believers hear a Jewish person say, "Oh, I'm Jewish!" all too often they back off, as if Jewish people have a spiritual inoculation against ever hearing about Jesus or as if being Jewish meant they did not need Jesus. Those believers who forge ahead and explain their faith are often frustrated by their own ineffectiveness at communicating the gospel to Jewish people. As a result, there is a tendency to relegate Jewish evangelism to Jewish believers in Jesus or to professional Jewish outreach agencies. Nothing could be further from God's heart for the Jewish people. This chapter is designed to help believers overcome their hesitancy in communicating the good news with Jewish people and provide some insights into more effective outreach to God's chosen people. It will examine Jewish people as an American ethnic group, consider a biblical basis for Jewish evangelism, present the most common barriers to effective communication with Jewish people, offer some basic principles of faith sharing with Jewish people, and finally, observe some of the approaches taken to reach Jewish people.

JEWISH PEOPLE IN AMERICA

In 1654, twenty-three Portuguese Jewish people, fleeing the Inquisition, arrived in New Amsterdam (later renamed New York), becoming the first Jewish people in the New World. Today, there are 6.9 million Jewish people in the United States.[2] Throughout the colonial period, Jewish people came to America sporadically as entrepreneurs, merchants, and traders. But the first significant migration of Jewish people to the United States took place between 1840 and 1860 when about 250,000 arrived. Coming predominantly from Germany, these middle-class immigrants settled throughout the Midwest and worked as shopkeepers and artisans. They came seeking greater freedom and found it.

The greatest influx of Jewish people into the United States took place between 1880 and 1920, when a tidal wave of Jewish immigrants arrived from Eastern Europe, primarily Russia. Fleeing anti-Semitic restrictions, pogroms (organized violent attacks on Jewish communities condoned by the government), and intense poverty, two-and-a-half million Jewish people made their way to the *goldeneh medina* (golden land, the term Eastern European Jews used for the United States) to find freedom, opportunity, and safety. Most settled in major urban centers with more than half going to New York City, where they worked as street peddlers, tailors, and shopkeepers. The children of these immigrants took advantage of American opportunity and within a generation became teachers, lawyers, doctors, and business owners. Today, about one in fifty United States citizens is Jewish. Most Jewish people have congregated in major urban centers, with the New York metropolitan area having the largest population of 2,170,000 Jewish people.

Estimated Top Six Jewish Population Centers in the United States[3]

New York Metropolitan Area	2,170,000
Los Angeles Area	685,000
South Florida	535,000
Baltimore/Washington Area	415,000
Philadelphia Metropolitan Area	310,000
Chicagoland	295,000

Jewish people remain a distinct ethnic minority within the United States.[4] However, despite Jewish people continuing to identify as Jews, religious devotion to and affiliation with Judaism is decreasing. According to the Pew Research Center's

2013 study of the Jewish community, only 10% of the Jewish population identifies with Orthodox Judaism, the most observant and traditional branch. Further, 18% prefer the less rigorous conservative branch of Judaism while 35% favor the liberal Reform branch. Another 30% do not identify with any branch of Judaism at all. Moreover, 22% of Jewish people see themselves as having no religion and only identify as Jews because of their ancestry or ethnicity. The nonreligious group is even higher among millennials, with 32% claiming to be nonreligious Jews.

American Jews tend to be less religious than the American public. Fewer Jews say that they attend religious services weekly or that they believe in God than the general population. In fact, only 26% of American Jews say Judaism, their religion, is very important in their lives, compared with 56% of the public who believe their religion is very important. The only exception in this regard is among the small percentage of Orthodox Jews, who are more committed to their religion than other religious groups in America. Nevertheless, 46% of Jewish people consider being Jewish as very important to them.

Just 19% of the Jewish adults surveyed say observing Jewish law *(halakha)* is essential to what being Jewish means. Further, most Jews believe a person can be Jewish even if that person works on the Sabbath or does not believe in God. Still 78% of Jewish people will attend a Passover Seder and 60% fast on Yom Kippur. Also, despite the declining religiosity of the American Jewish community, still 60% say a person cannot be Jewish if he or she believes in Jesus as the Messiah. Thus, it seems that for most Jewish people, believing in Jesus is still considered a form of cultural suicide.

American Jews hold to such varying degrees of religious observance and maintain such a wide variety of religious beliefs, it is hard to classify their theological position. Michael Medved, a media critic and an Orthodox Jew, writing in *Commentary* some time ago, still aptly summarizes the faith of the modern American Jewish community: "The chief distinguishing characteristic of most American Jews is not what they do believe, but what they do not believe. They do not believe in Jesus as the messiah. Period. End of sentence, end of story."[5]

Religiously, the Jewish community, while by and large resistant to faith in Jesus, is becoming more secularized and assimilated than ever before. However, the American Jewish community continues to exhibit some distinctive tendencies. For example, the Jewish community continues to be highly educated. According to the Pew study, "Jews have high levels of educational attainment. Most Jews are college graduates (58%), including 28% who say they have earned a post-graduate degree. By comparison, 29% of U.S. adults say they graduated from college, including 10% who have a post-graduate degree. Additionally, American Jews are represented as professionals, entrepreneurs, corporate managers, and academics, at a proportionally higher percentage than their population would anticipate."[6]

This brief description of the American Jewish community is reflective of the world Jewish community as well. For example, Israeli Jews are disproportionately secular and also educated at levels far higher than the rest of the Middle East. The secular and educated profile is also true for the Jewish people of France, Great Britain, and especially Russia.

Despite the growing secularization of the Jewish community, Medved maintains that "the deep seated and nearly universal Jewish resistance to claims of the divinity of Jesus will ensure that even the most engaged and energized sort of Christian evangelism will yield few outright converts."[7] Is he correct, or is there an opportunity for Jesus followers to reach their Jewish friends with the good news that Jesus is the Jewish Messiah? Most believers still approach Jewish people as if they were part of a closed, highly religious, tightly organized, community. By understanding the shift to secularization and communicating with that in mind, believers could very well see a greater responsiveness to the gospel on the part of the increasingly secularized and intermarried Jewish community. But is Jewish evangelism still part of the church's mandate? It is to this question we now turn.

A BIBLICAL BASIS FOR JEWISH EVANGELISM

Even beyond the Great Commission (Matt. 28:16–18), the Scriptures indicate that God has a special mandate for Jewish evangelism. Two key verses in the book of Romans particularly demonstrate God's continuing concern for a specialized outreach to the Jewish people.

First, Romans 1:16 is essential for establishing a biblical basis for Jewish evangelism. Unfortunately, believers too often misquote it by cutting off the final clause. Paul wrote, "I am not ashamed of the gospel, for it is the power of God for salvation, to everyone who believes, *to the Jew first and also to the Greek.*"

Interpreters have taken the final phrase of this verse in a variety of ways. Some have held to a *historical* view, arguing that the gospel was formerly offered to the Jews, but it is presently being offered to the Gentiles. There are several problems with this interpretation. To begin with, although the gospel was given to the Jewish people first, it nevertheless continued to be offered to Jewish people after it was given to the Gentiles. Second, if Paul had meant the historical view, he would not have used the Greek word *proton* (first). Instead, he likely would have chosen the Greek word *proteron* which means "formerly."[8] Third, this view implies that the word "first" is to be taken in a chronological sense. However, Romans 2:9–10 uses *proton* with a nonchronological meaning: "There will be tribulation and distress for every soul of mankind who does evil, for the Jew first and also for the Greek, but glory, honor, and peace to everyone who does what is good, to the Jew first and also to the Greek." Clearly Paul does not mean that "tribulation and distress" and "glory, honor, and peace" will come to the Jewish people before the Gentiles. Since Paul is not using the word "first" in a chronological sense in Romans 2:9–10, it is unlikely that he required a chronological sense in Romans 1:16.

Other interpreters have taken the phrase "to the Jew first" in a *methodological* sense. This view mistakenly takes the verse as an evangelistic strategy and method for world evangelization. According to this position, wherever the gospel is preached around the world, it must first be presented to the Jewish people. This interpretation is weak for several reasons. To start with, it relies on taking the word *first* in a chronological sense, just as the historical view does. Moreover, Romans 1:16 describes the nature of the gospel, not a mode of proclamation. In other words, it tells what the gospel is, not how to present it. Finally, it seems impractical and illogical to evangelize Jewish people fully in every given community before proceeding with Gentile evangelism.

It is best to take "to the Jew first" in an *elective* sense, meaning that the Jewish people are the elect or chosen people of God and therefore the gospel is preeminently a Jewish message. This view is strong for the following reasons: First, according to the standard Greek lexicon, the word *proton* should be translated "above all" or "especially" in this context.[9] Second, this translation would fit with Romans 2:9, in which Paul states that condemnation will come to all nonbelievers, but "especially" to the Jewish people because of their privileged status as chosen people. Third, it conforms to the overall argument of Romans, which recognizes the equality of Jews and Gentiles but also the elective priority of the Jewish people (see Rom. 9–11, particularly 11:29). Noted commentator John Murray explains Romans 1:16 this way:

> The power of God unto salvation through faith has primary relevance to the Jew, and the analogy of Scripture would indicate that this peculiar relevance to the Jew arises from the fact that the Jew had been chosen by God to be the recipient of the promise of the gospel and that to him were committed the oracles of God. Salvation was of the Jews (John 4:22, see Acts 2:39; Rom. 3:1–2; 9:4–5). The lines of preparation for the full revelation of the gospel were laid in Israel and for that reason the gospel is preeminently the gospel for the Jew. How totally contrary to the current attitude of Jewry that Christianity is for the Gentile but not for the Jew.[10]

Simply stated, the gospel was, is, and always will be a preeminently Jewish message. The gospel was promised to the Jewish people by Jewish prophets; it was established by a Jewish Messiah; it was proclaimed by Jewish apostles. Even though the gospel was designed for all people, it was particularly prepared for the Jewish people, whether they accept it or not.

The second verse, Romans 11:11, gives both present and future hope to Jewish people. In this verse, Paul began by asking rhetorically if the Jewish people had "stumbled so as to fall"? The answer he gives is a resounding, "No!" His point was that Jewish people, despite their rejection of Jesus, have not fallen headlong so they could not get up again. Their stumbling was not beyond recovery. Paul's argument was that Jewish people are still savable.

This hope for Jewish people is evident in two ways in Romans 11. First, Paul argues that Jewish rejection of Jesus is not final. At the end of Romans 11, Paul maintained that when the fullness of the Gentiles has come, Israel's partial hardening will cease. All the Jewish people alive at that time will turn to Jesus as their Messiah. This national acceptance of Jesus precedes the second coming of the Messiah, at which time, "all Israel will be saved" (Rom. 11:26).

Second, Paul argued that Jewish rejection is not total. At the beginning of Romans 11, Paul has argued that there will always be a remnant in the present day. As proof that God has not rejected Israel (despite their national rejection of Jesus), Paul argued that God has always worked through a remnant. Just as a remnant of 7,000 Israelites did not bow to Baal in the days of Elijah (Rom. 11:1–4), so there is "at the present time, a remnant according to God's gracious choice" (Rom. 11:5). God's faithfulness to the Jewish people is evident in that in every generation of the church age, there has always been a segment of the Jewish people who have trusted in Jesus as their Messiah and Redeemer. Paul was an illustration of this in his day (v. 1) just as Messianic Jews are examples of this truth at the present time.

Having established that Jewish people are savable, Paul explained how God will go about reaching Jewish people. He argued that their transgression (the national rejection of Jesus) has brought salvation to the Gentiles. God's purpose in doing this was to make Jewish people jealous.[11]

The phrase *to make them jealous* means to make people desire what rightfully belongs to them by giving it to someone else. An example of this is in 1 Corinthians 10:22 where the same word is used of God. That verse speaks of Christians worshiping in pagan temples, thus provoking God to jealousy. Believers, who rightfully belong to God, were making Him jealous, because they were worshiping someone else. With this meaning of the phrase in mind, it is easy to understand the point of Romans 11:11. God gave the gospel to the Gentiles with the express purpose of making Jewish people jealous, so that they would want it back for themselves.

Paul was saying that Jewish people are still savable and God wants to use Gentile believers to reach them. Max Reich, formerly professor of Jewish studies at

Moody Bible Institute, has paraphrased Romans 11:11: "To make the Jewish people's mouths water for the salvation which Gentiles have found in the Jewish Messiah!"

When I was in graduate school, I was trying to learn if there were any consistent characteristics in the way Jewish people came to believe in Jesus. So, I studied the published faith stories of 200 Jewish followers of Jesus to see if there were any significant faith patterns among Jewish people. One of the most surprising patterns I discovered was that 92% of Jewish believers in Jesus had their first contact with the gospel through a Gentile who showed them love. God does indeed want to save Jewish people, and He wants to use Gentiles to reach them.

So, should Gentile followers of Jesus present the gospel to the Jewish people? As long as the Great Commission stands, the answer must be yes. Nevertheless, that is not the only reason to communicate the good news to our Jewish friends. It is plain from Romans 1:16 that the gospel is a message especially and preeminently designed for Jewish people. Moreover, from Romans 11:11, it is evident that one of God's foremost purposes in bringing Gentiles to salvation is to make Jewish people want what the Gentiles have received.

Since this is God's purpose and plan, why is so little being done to reach Jewish people? The next section will address the reasons Gentiles are so reluctant to fulfill their special mandate for Jewish evangelism.

THE BARRIERS TO JEWISH EVANGELISM

Gentile believers have not taken up their special mandate for Jewish evangelism for countless reasons. Unfortunately, these include anti-Jewish attitudes and theological dispositions. However, those are not the basic reasons believers do not communicate their faith to Jewish people. I have found that Gentiles are reluctant to discuss the Messiah Jesus with Jewish people because they are fearful. These fears form the essential barriers that must be overcome to reach Jewish people with the good news of Messiah Jesus.

The first barrier to Jewish evangelism is *a fear of wasting time and effort*. Many have the perception that Jewish people are blind to the gospel and therefore unreachable. People ask, "Why waste our precious time and our limited resources for an effort that will have little or no payback?" They are guided by the principle that outreach efforts should be restricted to more responsive people.

This is an unfortunate and invalid fear for several reasons. First, God has called us to the work of evangelizing the world regardless of response. We are not just to obey when we are guaranteed a willing hearer. Even Jesus, in His earthly ministry, came to His own and His own did not receive Him. Every believer would agree that the Lord Jesus was correct in going to the lost sheep of the house of Israel.

Second, the whole idea of a unique judicial blindness for Israel is questionable. Romans 11 does indeed say that Israel was hardened. But the Scriptures also say that every lost person has a blindness to the gospel (1 Cor. 2:14). Nowhere do the Scriptures say that Israel's blindness is greater than any other nonbelieving person. Moreover, the church must also accept some responsibility for helping cause Israel's unbelieving blindness because of the tragic history of Christian anti-Semitism. Finally, the Scriptures do assure a measure of success in Jewish evangelism, promising there will always be a remnant of Jewish people who will believe (Rom. 11:4). Jesus' followers should be faithful to God's mandate for Jewish evangelism regardless of their fear of being unsuccessful.

Gentile Christians are also reluctant to interact with their Jewish friends about the Messiah because of their *fear of an unpleasant situation*. Most Gentile believers are aware that Jewish people generally do not believe in Jesus. Having read the Gospels and Acts, these believers conclude that just as Jesus, Peter, and Paul faced unpleasant opposition to their messages, so will they. They do not want to offend their Jewish friends or deal with an angry reaction from them. But is this valid?

Generally Jewish people do not react angrily when their Gentile friends discuss Jesus with them because they expect Gentiles to believe in Jesus. If approached gently, Jewish people will usually consider the words of their friends, even about Jesus. Even those Jewish people who are disinterested will politely decline to discuss it. Surprisingly, many Jewish people are much more interested than their friends anticipate. Most people, including the Jewish people, are naturally curious and want to learn about other faiths. Some Jewish people are even searching spiritually and will be quite open to consider spiritual truth if people will be bold enough to present it.

Gentile Jesus followers often have a third reluctance in witnessing to Jewish people: *a fear of Jewish knowledge of the Bible*. Too often believers have the mistaken notion that Jewish people know the Scriptures inside out and can quote it in Hebrew. They fear that if they present the gospel to their Jewish friends that unanswerable Jewish objections will be raised. So, they conclude it is best not even to engage their Jewish friends in a discussion of the Bible.

This impression about Jewish knowledge of the Scriptures is simply inaccurate. Most American Jews, as already noted, are quite secularized. Most do not know biblical Hebrew. Even those who have a degree of Jewish education often do not know the Bible very well. Generally Jewish people are amazed at the knowledge that Gentile Christians have of the Jewish Scriptures[12] (Rom 3:2). Believers should not fear Jewish knowledge of the Scriptures.

THE PRINCIPLES OF JEWISH EVANGELISM

Once believers decide that they have a biblical mandate for Jewish evangelism, they are often stymied by their own perceived lack of ability. "I wouldn't even know what to do!" they exclaim. Yet there are some basic principles that every person can follow that will make for an effective witness to Jewish people.

To begin with, believers must have a genuine love for Jewish people. Jewish people have been repulsed from the message of the Messiah Jesus because of the hateful anti-Semitism that has existed in the church. Many Christians object that real believers could not have been anti-Jewish. Sadly, that is simply not true.[13]

Foundational to the church's history of anti-Semitism was the false deicide charge, the belief that the Jewish people are solely and perpetually guilty for the murder of Christ and as such, they as a people are the murderers of God. Sadly, this untrue allegation has done more to advance hatred of the Jewish people throughout church history than anything else. It is particularly galling because the New Testament does not teach this infamous charge in any way.[14]

In the Eastern tradition, for example, the most significant church father, John Chrysostom (344–407), known as the golden-mouthed preacher, wrote eight homilies against the Jews, which are without peer in the whole realm of anti-Jewish literature. A brief sample of his poison tongue follows:

> The Jews are the most worthless of all men. They are lecherous, greedy, rapacious. They are perfidious murderers of Christ. They worship the devil, their religion is a sickness. The Jews are the odious assassins of Christ and for killing God there is no expiation possible, no indulgence or pardon. Christians may never cease vengeance, and the Jew must live in servitude forever. God always hated the Jews. It is incumbent upon all Christians to hate the Jews.[15]

Christian anti-Semitism was also evident in the Western church, in the writings of Augustine. Considered by many to be the greatest theologian of the ancient church and perhaps of all time, both Roman Catholic and Protestant traditions look to him as their theological patron. He developed the theory of the Jews as a "witness people" to explain their continued existence. Allegorizing the story of Cain and Abel, with Cain representing the Jews, according to this theory, the Jewish people were marked by God when they murdered Christ. Hence, they cannot be destroyed but their dispersion and misery serve as testimony of their evil and of Christian truth.[16]

Martin Luther (1483–1546), the father of the Protestant Reformation, vehemently attacked the Jewish people in his work *Of the Jews and Their Lies*. There he wrote,

What then shall we Christians do with this damned rejected race of Jews, since they live among us and we know about their lying and blaspheming curses. We cannot tolerate them if we do not wish to share in their lies, curses and blasphemy . . . (we must) set their synagogues on fire, and whatever does not burn up should be covered or spread over with dirt so that no one may ever be able to see a cinder of stone of it . . . in order that God may see that we are Christians . . . Their homes should likewise be broken down and destroyed . . . They should be deprived of their prayer books and Talmuds . . . their rabbis must be forbidden to teach under the threat of death. Let us drive them out of the country for all time . . .[17]

These are just three examples of two thousand years of hatred. It has been so severe, that Jewish people fully expect contemporary Christians to harbor a vile prejudice against them. What an amazing surprise to Jewish people when Gentile believers openly express concern and compassion for them. The believer's model of love is Paul, the apostle to the Gentiles. He loved his own people so much, that had it been possible, he would have gone to hell, if that would have made it possible for the Jewish people to experience God's love in Messiah (Rom. 9:1–3).

Jewish people will greet simple acts of kindness, such as sending a Passover or a Rosh Hashanah card, with surprise and appreciation. When Christians express solidarity with the Jewish community in standing against anti-Jewish attitudes and actions, Jewish people will be amazed and grateful. Once, former New York City mayor Ed Koch was asked why Jewish voters so appreciated Republican Al D'Amato. His reply was "Jews love a non-Jew who loves them more than they love a Jew."[18] Reversing the Christian tradition of hatred with love will build a platform from which true followers of Jesus may speak to Jewish people about Jesus the Messiah.

A second principle of Jewish evangelism is that believers must live a distinctive lifestyle before the Jewish people. Too often, Jewish people observe Jesus followers and wonder what is different about their faith. By demonstrating a transformed life, believers can attract Jewish people to the message of the Messiah. I have a friend in Israel who is blonde, blue-eyed, and Gentile as they come. Not only has she gained a hearing by her genuine love for Jewish people, but she has provoked sufficient jealousy merely by openly living for the Lord in a genuine way. For example, on a kibbutz one day, she was asked, "What's different about you? Your faith seems so real and makes such a difference in your life." We can have the same question asked of us, by allowing people to see our changed lives so they can glorify our Father in heaven.

A third important principle is for believers to have a sincere respect for the Jewishness of the gospel. Too often, both Christians and Jews forget that faith in Jesus as the Messiah is rooted in promises given to the Jewish people. Jesus said, "Salvation is from the Jews" (John 4:22). Paul agreed when he said that the gospel is pre-eminently to the Jewish people (Rom. 1:16). His respect for the Jewish roots of Christianity is seen in this description of the Jewish people in Romans 9:4–5, "Israelites, to whom belongs the adoption as sons and daughters, the glory, the covenants, the giving of the Law, the temple service, and the promises; whose are the fathers, and from whom is the Christ according to the flesh, who is over all, God blessed forever. Amen."

Not only is the gospel Jewish, so is Jesus the Messiah. Once, when I was visiting in a retirement village, a Jewish woman objected to my faith in Jesus. She said it was for Gentiles not Jews. I read her the first verse of my (Yiddish) New Testament, which describes Yeshua, the son of David and the son of Abraham (Matt. 1:1). She looked at me in shock and said, "You mean He's really Jewish!" That Jesus is the greatest Jew who ever was is one great truth that we must communicate over and over to Jewish people.

A fourth principle of Jewish evangelism is that believers must develop sensitivity to Jewish concerns. This should be particularly evident in the symbols and speech that are used when communicating. For example, Crusaders brutally murdered Jewish people throughout Europe under the sign of the cross during the Crusades. Believers today should be especially careful to avoid using this symbol, which has come to represent hatred to Jewish people, rather than love. Of course, that is not to say that we ought to avoid the message of the Messiah Jesus' atonement. Rather, avoid using the symbol and substitute the word "tree" for the "cross," as in "Messiah died on the tree."

Sensitivity involves using terms that are understandable to Jewish people. For example, most Jewish people are not aware that the word "Christ" is the Greek form for the Hebrew word *Messiah*. Most Jewish people think that "Christ" is a last name (Joseph Christ, Mary Christ, Jesus Christ). Since Jewish people generally do understand the concept of the Messiah, using the word Messiah instead of Christ communicates far better. The following chart lists some words that communicate more understandably and are less offensive to Jewish people.

Don't Say	Do Say
Christ	Messiah
Jesus[19]	Yeshua
Cross	Tree
Church	Congregation
Saved	Forgiven, Redeemed
Savior	Redeemer

Don't Say	Do Say
Old Testament	Scriptures, Tenach
Convert, Conversion	Become a follower of Yeshua
Christian (noun)	Follower of Yeshua
Christian (adjective)	Biblical, Scriptural
Jews	Jewish people
Converted Jew	Messianic Jew; Jewish follower of Yeshua
Died for sins	Atoned for sins
Baptism	Immersion
New Testament	New Covenant

For many Jewish people the name of Jesus alone has become offensive. Therefore, using His Hebrew name can sometimes minimize the offense. The one word of caution is to make sure the Jewish person knows who you mean when you say Yeshua. A believer might say, "When we speak of Jesus, I would like to use His Hebrew name Yeshua. This is the name He was always called by His family and friends."

Believers should not only be sensitive with speech, but with our attitudes as well. Too often Gentile Christians betray stereotypical but untrue attitudes about Jewish people. False perceptions of Jewish wealth, appearance, personality style, or any other stereotype should be rejected completely, not just avoided in conversation.

Followers of Jesus should also become sensitive to Jewish history. The Jewish experience in history has shaped Jewish perspectives about life. We must be aware of the false deicide charge, the Crusades, the Inquisition, expulsions from European countries, forced conversions to Christianity, pogroms, and assorted other anti-Jewish acts and libels, particularly those propagated by the church. When we talk to Jewish people about Jesus, although we must never compromise or be fearful, we must be sensitive to the way Jewish people feel.

Another principle of Jewish evangelism is that believers must be informed about Jewish barriers to belief. One stumbling block to faith is that Jewish people often believe that once they believe in Jesus, they will no longer be Jewish. Nothing could be further from the truth. In the New Testament, Jewish people always remained Jewish when they believed. Even today, when Jewish people become atheists or agnostics or even practice Zen, they remain Jewish. If Jesus really fulfilled the messianic prophecies of the Scriptures, then He is the Jewish Messiah. If that is so, then the most Jewish faith a person can have, is to believe in Him.

Another barrier to belief is that Jewish people often question the reason anyone might believe in Jesus altogether. The simplest approach is to explain that the Messiah was foretold in the Scriptures and then show how Jesus of Nazareth fulfilled those Scriptures. We must root our faith in the Hebrew Scriptures if Jewish people are going to believe in Jesus. The Bible contains many prophecies of the Messiah and their fulfillment by Jesus. The following chart contains some basic ones of which believers should be aware.

A Survey of Messianic Prophecy[20]

Messiah's Birth	Prophecy	Fulfillment
Messiah would be born in Bethlehem.	Micah 5:2	Matthew 2:1
Messiah would arrive by the 1st century.	Genesis 49:10	Galatians 4:4
Messiah would be born of a virgin.	Isaiah 7:14	Matthew 1:23
Messiah would be born with a divine nature.	Isaiah 9:6	John 1:1–2
Messiah's Life		
Messiah would perform miracles.	Isaiah 35:5	Matthew 11:3–6
Messiah would proclaim good news.	Isaiah 61:1–2	Luke 4:16–21
Messiah would be rejected by His own people.	Isaiah 53:3	John 1:11; 7:5
Messiah's Death		
Messiah would die before the Roman destruction of Jerusalem.	Daniel 9:26–27	Luke 19:43–45
Messiah would die as an atonement for sin.	Isaiah 53:5–6, 11–12	2 Corinthians 5:21
Messiah would die by crucifixion.	Psalm 22:16	Matthew 27:35; John 19:18, 31–37

MESSIAH'S RESURRECTION	PROPHECY	FULFILLMENT
Messiah would see life after death.	Isaiah 53:10	Matthew 28:1–10
Messiah would not decay in the grave.	Psalm 16:10	Acts 2:24–32
MESSIAH'S RETURN		
Messiah will be recognized by Israel as the Pierced One at His return.	Zechariah 12:10	Matthew 23:39
Messiah will establish a righteous reign from the throne of David in Jerusalem.	Isaiah 9:7 Amos 9:11–15	Revelation 19:11–16; 20:4

A third block to Jewish faith in Jesus is that many Jewish people find it hard to understand the idea of Jesus dying for their sins. Therefore, it is important to explain the sacrificial system of the Hebrew Bible. Those sacrifices foreshadowed the exchange of life that God would provide through the death and resurrection of Jesus. It is vital to show that substitutionary atonement is not a new concept of the New Testament but one that was anticipated in the Hebrew Scriptures.

Every person is different and may come up with different barriers to belief. Regardless, believers must be ready to help Jewish people hurdle these walls so they can make a reasonable spiritual decision.

Finally, believers must develop holy boldness in raising the issue of Jesus with Jewish people. Do not allow fear and intimidation to take over. The best way to overcome intimidation is by using your sense of humor and the other person's curiosity. For example, a Gentile friend of mine named Gus would frequently tell a Jewish person that the folks in his congregation believed Genesis 12:3. Very often the Jewish person would ask what that verse said. Then Gus would respond, with true surprise, that he was amazed that a Jewish person did not know what was in the Torah. When his Jewish friend would insist on being told what was in this passage, Gus would then, and only then, explain the Abrahamic covenant. Before too long, they would be discussing how that covenant found its ultimate fulfillment in the coming of the Messiah.

Gus was a master at provoking curiosity with a smile and a laugh at the same time. Believers would become more effective in all kinds of evangelism, not just Jewish evangelism, by learning to raise their spiritual flag in a friendly and funny way.

It is still not enough to know how to share with a Jewish person or even to speak up when the opportunity presents itself. Believers who want to reach Jewish people must be intentional in their strategies. Here are some practical steps to take to reach out to Jewish people in reality and not just theory.

PRACTICAL STEPS IN JEWISH EVANGELISM

If anyone wants to reach Jewish people with the good news of the Messiah Jesus, it is essential to *get into the path of the Jewish community*. That means finding where Jewish people are and going there also. The purpose is to establish genuine friendships with Jewish people. Then, presenting the Messiah Jesus is the normal outgrowth of a friendship, not a result of targeting a person or group. When I was in graduate school in Dallas, I took courses in the Jewish adult education programs sponsored by the area synagogues and Jewish organizations. Later, in whichever city I lived, I joined the Jewish Community Center and worked out, played basketball and racquetball, and made friends with other people there. One of my former students joined all sorts of Jewish community activities and Israel support groups and as a result she made friends with many Jewish people, including community leaders. If we are going to communicate the good news to Jewish people, we need to become friends with them first.

A second step in reaching out to Jewish people is to identify with the Jewish community. It is easy for Gentile followers of Jesus to forget that there are Jewish people around them and to neglect identifying with them. One strong Bible believing church in a community with a large Jewish population had virtually ignored their Jewish neighbors for years. They had presumed that the Jewish people around them did not want to have any relationship with this church. Then someone had the idea to put up professionally made signs in front of the church every year at major Jewish holidays. They were simple; for example, one was "A Happy and Sweet Passover to our Jewish Friends and Neighbors!" The same kinds of signs were posted at the fall Jewish High Holy Days and at Chanukah. Almost immediately, the church began to receive letters from Jewish people and even drop-ins from Jewish neighbors, thanking the church for this simple gesture. After two years of doing this, the local Jewish Community Center sponsored an open night, just for the members of this church and invited everyone to join the JCC.

This sort of identification is not limited to whole churches. Individual believers can send Jewish holiday cards to their Jewish neighbors, friends, and acquaintances. Also, greeting cards can be sent when a Jewish acquaintance has a life cycle event, like a baby boy's circumcision or a baby girl's naming, a Bar Mitzvah or Bat

Mitzvah, or a wedding. This shows our Jewish friends that we appreciate them and are not expecting Jewish people to stop being Jewish.

Another practical Jewish outreach strategy is to partner with local Jewish ministries and messianic congregations. Once we have made friends with Jewish people and taken steps to identify with them, we will have opportunity to raise a flag and present the message of Messiah Jesus to them. Nevertheless, many Jewish people, even if spiritually interested, will wonder if it is realistic for a Jewish person to believe in Jesus as the Promised One. To help them see that there are many Jewish people who believe in Jesus as the Messiah, it would be valuable to invite the enquiring Jewish friend to visit a messianic congregation or a local Jewish ministry Bible study. If they agree to visit, they will meet other Jewish followers of Yeshua the Messiah and even hear the good news explained in a Jewish way. Working together with Jewish ministries and messianic congregations is a great way to help Jewish friends see that it is possible to believe in *Yeshua* and still be Jewish.

A more challenging but also more rewarding step that can be taken is for a local church to program for Jewish ministry. One megachurch in the Chicago area discovered that there was a significant number of Jewish seekers attending their contemporary services. They also found that while these Jewish people were intrigued with the messages and music of the church, they were finding it hard to make a spiritual decision. So, the church decided to hold a number of "side-door" events specifically for Jewish people. These included holding Chanukah parties, Passover Seders (meals), and intermarriage workshops. Out of these events, the church formed a Jewish-seeker Bible study group, that addressed the questions and concerns of Jewish seekers. As a result of these intentional efforts, numerous Jewish people made decisions for the Lord.

An additional but surprising step that can be taken is to invite Jewish people to a special event at a local church. For example, the growing secularization of the Jewish community has made many Jewish people more willing to celebrate Christmas as a cultural event. If a local congregation is holding a special Christmas service or program, this would be an ideal time to invite a Jewish friend to come along. Also, if a church is holding a biblical marriage seminar or child rearing program, that could be the kind of event that Jewish people would be interested in attending. Although we always want to be sensitive, it is wise to develop holy boldness and ask your Jewish friends if they might be interested in joining you at this kind of church program.

God is truly working in bringing the Jewish people. Just as Paul wrote, at the present time, there is a remnant of Jewish people coming to faith in their Messiah Jesus "according to God's gracious choice" (Rom. 11:5). In fact, in the last fifty years, more Jewish people have believed in Jesus than in the entire previous history of the church. We just need the holy boldness and practical wisdom to reach out to them.

CONCLUSION

Although much is happening in Jewish ministry, much more remains to be done. Someone once wrote, "For 1800 years, certainly for most of that time, Jews have not been given an opportunity to know what Christianity is, or to know what the Christ means. The ignorance of the Jew concerning Christianity condemns not the Jew, but Christendom." What makes this statement even more potent is that it was not spoken by a Jewish evangelist but by Rabbi Stephen S. Wise, who certainly did not believe in Jesus. Regardless, his words are true. If believers would accept their mandate to reach Jewish people with the good news, many more Jewish people would indeed come to know Jesus, their promised Messiah.

NOTES

1. This article is adapted from Michael Rydelnik, "Outreach to the Jewish Community: The Principles and Possibilities" in *A Heart for the City: Effective Ministries to the Urban Community*, John Fuder, ed. (Chicago: Moody Publishers, 2005), 275–93. Used with permission.

2. The source of this is the Jewish Virtual Library, which derived its statistics from Ira M. Sheskin and Arnold Dashefsky. "United States Jewish Population, 2018," in Arnold Dashefsky and Ira M. Sheskin, eds. American Jewish Year Book, 2018, 251–347, https://www.jewishvirtuallibrary.org/largest-jewish-populated-metropolitan-areas-united-states, accessed 7/27/19.

3. Ibid.

4. This description of American Jewry is derived from *A Portrait of Jewish Americans: Findings from a Pew Research Center Survey of U.S. Jews* (Washington, DC: Pew Research Center, 2013).

5. Michael Medved, "What Do American Jews Believe?" *Commentary* (August, 1996), https://www.commentarymaga-zine.com/articles/what-do-american-jews-believe/ accessed 7/27/2019.

6. *A Portrait of Jewish Americans*, 15.

7. Medved, "What Do American Jews Believe?"

8. F. D. Moule, *An Idiom Book of New Testament Greek*, 2nd ed. (Cambridge: London University Press, 1959), 98; Friedrich Blass and Albert Debrunner, *A Greek Grammar of the New Testament and Other Early Christian Literature*, trans. and rev. by W. Funk (Chicago: Chicago University Press, 1961), 34.

9. Walter Bauer, W. F. Arndt, and F. W. Gingrich, eds., *A Greek-English Lexicon of the New Testament and Other Early Christian Literature* (Chicago: Chicago University Press, 1979), 726.

10. John Murray, *The Epistle to the Romans*, vol. 1 (Grand Rapids: Eerdmans, 1973), 28.

11. God has many purposes in saving people with the most important being to glorify Himself. However, the Greek syntax is clearly a purpose clause, showing that one of God's purposes is to provoke jealousy among the Jewish people.

12. Jewish people call the Old Testament the TaNaK. The three Hebrew consonants comprising the word signify the Old Testament's three divisions: T for Torah (the Pentateuch); N for Neviim (Prophets); K for Ketuvim (Writings).

13. For a thorough discussion of Christian anti-Semitism, see Edward Flannery, *The Anguish of the Jews* (Mahwah, NJ: Paulist Press, 1985), 28–55.

14. For a refutation of the deicide charge, see Michael Rydelnik, "Who Are the Christ-Killers?," *Moody Monthly* 86, no. 2 (October 1985), 38–42. Also, Michael Rydelnik, *They Called Me Christ Killer* (Grand Rapids: RBC Ministries, 2005).

15. John Chrysostom, *Homilies Against the Jews* 4.1; 6.1, 3-4.

16. See Augustine, *Ennaratio on Psalm 58:1, 22; 56:9; Epistles 137.16; Reply to Faustus 13.10.*

17. Martin Luther "Of the Jews and Their Lies," *Luther's Works*, vol. 47, ed. Helmut H. Lehman (Philadelphia: Muhlenberg, 1970), 269–72.

18. Michael Kramer, "Battling Al: Is D'Amato Unbeatable?" *New York Magazine* (January 27, 1986), 28.

19. For many Jewish people the name of Jesus has become a great offense. Therefore, using His Hebrew name can sometimes minimize the offense. The one word of caution is to make sure the Jewish person knows who you are speaking of when you say Yeshua. A believer might say, "When we speak of Jesus, I would like to use His Hebrew name Yeshua. This is the name He was always called by His family and friends."

20. For a thorough explanation of the issues related to messianic prophecy and expositions of virtually all the passages considered messianic, see Michael A. Rydelnik and Edwin A. Blum, eds., *The Moody Handbook of Messianic Prophecy* (Chicago: Moody Publishers, 2019).

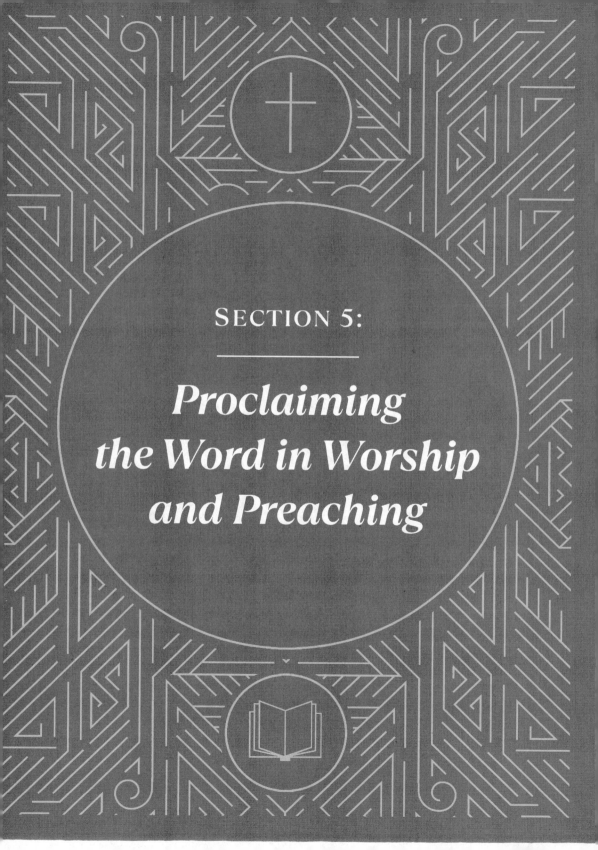

SECTION 5:

Proclaiming the Word in Worship and Preaching

INTRODUCTION

Proclaiming Jesus in Word-Centered Worship

LAURIE L. NORRIS

THE CENTRALITY OF THE WORD IN CHRISTIAN WORSHIP

The church's outward mission is to proclaim the gospel of Jesus Christ to those in need of salvation. However, the church also has an *internal* mission to proclaim Jesus among the people of God. While we are called to go *out* and "make disciples of all the nations," we also are called to baptize these new believers in the confession of Christ and impart to them all the teachings of Christ (Matt. 28:19–20). As the body of Christ meets together for corporate worship, they gather around the Word of God as the centerpiece of communal expression. They do this through the Word read and preached, the Word enacted through baptism and the Lord's Supper, and the Word proclaimed musically. Church leaders must grasp the essential nature of this Word proclaimed *for* the church.

What Is the Word?

When we speak of the "Word," we speak of the eternal Word or *logos* of God (Isa. 40:8; 1 Peter 1:23–25), revealed through God's spoken and written word as recorded in Scripture, and most fully revealed in the person of Jesus Christ, the Word made flesh (John 1:1). We receive the word of Christ, imparted by the Spirit of Christ, in all of its biblical, canonical fullness; and we partake together of this Word in our corporate worship. The eternal Word, embodied in Christ, was written for the ongoing instruction and proclamation of the church.

WORSHIPING IN THE WORD

Christian worship wholly submits to the authority of God's Word and encounters God through this Word. This is the "living and active" Word of God that summons, scrutinizes, and sustains our faith—the "double-edged sword" that performs open surgery on our hearts (Heb. 4:12). While the Word itself is inspired, inerrant, and authoritative in its very substance, Frank Senn rightly observes, "As God's self-communication, the word of God calls forth an encounter with the Person of God himself. One cannot encounter without responding in faith and hope, in fear and love. The preaching of the word is sacramental, because it conveys Christ himself."[1] That is to say, we do not separate the word of Christ from the person and work of Christ. The communication of God's Word leads us to a personal encounter with the triune God of Scripture. This Word convicts, comforts, and confronts. This Word reveals, redeems, and renews. This Word both saves and sustains. This Word, which goes out from the mouth of God, never returns empty; rather, it unfailingly fulfills the work He intends it to accomplish (Isa. 55:11). The very word of Christ by which all things were created (Gen. 1; John 1:1–3; Col. 1:16; Heb. 1:3) now makes us a new creation in Christ.

The earliest expressions of Christian worship reflected this essential commitment to the Word in various forms, as the Scriptures were read and sung, and the teachings of Christ orally rehearsed and physically enacted among those gathered around the shared meal. The reading, preaching, and singing of Scripture closely intertwined. Note, for example, the Word-centered focus of corporate worship in 1 Corinthians 14:26: "When you assemble, each one has a psalm, has a teaching, has a revelation, has a tongue, has an interpretation. All things are to be done for edification." Paul even describes the Lord's Supper as a form of proclamation (1 Cor. 11:26). While certain aspects of corporate worship developed and formalized over time, as the early church grew and expanded, this ministry of the Word continued to be the central focus of worship for all those who faithfully gathered in one place to glorify the name of Christ.

Such focus on the Word of God also later became a foundational tenet of the Reformation; this emphasis represented a return to those Word-centered priorities and practices of the early church. Herman Wegman writes, "The great reformers of the church in the West ordered worship according to one important principle: the holy scripture, the word of God, which they placed at the heart of church life."[2] Senn further explains,

> Worship was to conform, in one way or another, to scripture; scripture was to be read in public worship in the language of the people; sermons were to be preached on the scripture readings; and liturgical practices were to be judged according to biblical norms. This was the great concern of liturgical reform

among the reformers. If *sola fide* became the principle on which personal life was based, *sola Scriptura* became the principle by which liturgical life was formed.[3]

For Martin Luther in particular, this was no abstract or impersonal principle. Rather, Luther understood the Word of God as "first and foremost God's self-communication, and therefore God's self-disclosure." As such, "The word of God is always an event."[4] This Reformation emphasis on the Word resulted in a careful exposition of the biblical text in its context as central to the corporate worship and catechesis of the church.[5] When Christians assembled for worship, they gathered to feast on the Word of God. So too, we presently swim in the currents of that rich tradition, faithfully proclaiming Christ through a focus on His enduring Word in our gathered assembly.

IMPLICATIONS OF A WORD-CENTERED FOCUS
FOR PREACHING AND PUBLIC READING

Our recognition of the absolute authority of God's Word necessarily shapes our philosophy of preaching. Such preaching submits wholly to the biblical message for the church's instruction and exhortation. The preacher faithfully seeks to discern—through diligent study and dependence on the Spirit—the exegetical and theological message of the biblical text in its context, and then seeks to communicate this message in relevant and appropriately contextualized ways for a present audience.[6] We refer to this as "expository" preaching, wherein the point of the text ultimately becomes the point of the sermon. With theological sensitivity and nuance, the preacher carefully constructs a bridge between the world of the biblical text and our contemporary context.

In such an approach, the preacher stands under, not over, the biblical text and consistently ministers the very words of God. While the Spirit certainly works through the personality of the preacher, the preacher is ultimately the herald of another's message, "provid[ing] a living voice for the living Word" as God's words come through the preacher's mouth.[7] The people of God need a steady diet of God's Word, not merely those of the preacher. Since the goal is a direct encounter with the living God through the living Word of God, the substance of every sermon must be that very Word. Scripture should saturate the sermon. This is why Paul exhorts Timothy to "preach the word; be ready in season and out of season; correct, rebuke, and exhort, with great patience and instruction" (2 Tim. 4:2).

The beauty of this approach is that it lets God speak. The power of expository preaching ultimately resides in the Spirit of God working through the Word of God that He inspired. As Paul declares in 1 Thessalonians 2:13, "For this reason we also constantly thank God that when you received the word of God which you heard from us, you accepted it not as the word of mere men, but as what it really is, the word of God, which also is at work in you who believe." Renowned preacher Bryan Chapell rightly concludes, "[God's] Spirit uses the Word itself to fulfill his saving and sanctifying purposes. . . . God infuses his Word with his own spiritual power." It is "the Word preached"—not "the *preaching* of the Word"—that "accomplishes heaven's purposes." [8] Only when preachers faithfully disclose God's Word can they say with utmost authority and confidence, "Thus says the Lord!"

The public reading of Scripture also plays a central role in the church's worship, as evidenced in the earliest accounts of Christian assembly. God's Word is to be *heard*, a beautiful truth often sadly eclipsed in our present world. This public reading of Scripture may occur directly in concert with the Word of God preached. In some contexts, it involves the use of a lectionary that provides a system of readings for the church. These readings, from which the sermon may derive, draw from both Old and New Testaments.

IMPLICATIONS OF A WORD-CENTERED FOCUS FOR CONGREGATIONAL SINGING

A close connection also exists between the Word and song in corporate worship. The Word that is read and preached is also sung. The people of God have always been a singing people, proclaiming the worth of their God through musical expression. In keeping with the patterns of Jewish synagogue worship, the earliest Christians expressed their praise and prayer through the sung (or chanted) word, and especially the psalms and other biblical songs as the source and content of their lyrics. Their central focus was on the Word of God expressed in song, as a means to proclaiming Christ.[9] Some primitive hymns, often credal in content, were even included in the New Testament writings (e.g., Phil. 2:6–11; Col. 1:15–20; 1 Tim. 3:16). Imagine what the neighbors thought as they heard these words arising from a house church meeting next door!

We see this intimate connection between Word and song most explicitly in Paul's instruction to the Ephesians and Colossians. He writes that believers should speak "to one another in psalms and hymns and spiritual songs, singing and making melody with your heart to the Lord" (Eph. 5:19). In Colossians 3:16, he writes, "Let the word of Christ richly dwell within you, with all wisdom teaching and admonishing one another with psalms, hymns, and spiritual songs, singing with thankfulness in your hearts to God."

Singing in the church not only proclaims Christ together through the sung word but also through the expression of unity within Christ's body. This was a point of emphasis in the early church. Ignatius of Antioch declared in the early second century, "Therefore in your agreement and harmonious love, Jesus Christ is sung. Become a choir, one by one, so that being harmonious in love, taking up the song of God in unison, you may sing to the Father with one voice through Jesus Christ, so that he may both hear you and perceive . . . that you are the members of his Son."[10] So then, through song in corporate worship, we proclaim Christ among the people of God by reinforcing the preached Word, instructing the church in Christian doctrine, and expressing the unity of Christ's body.

IMPLICATIONS OF A WORD-CENTERED FOCUS
FOR BAPTISM AND COMMUNION

Preaching and singing both involve the human voice. But since Christianity was based on Christ's bodily incarnation, the actions of the human body also mattered in the early church. The church's observance of baptism and the Lord's Supper enacted the living presence of the Word within the community, as believers identified with the death and resurrection of Christ through the initiating waters of baptism, and together received the sustaining nourishment of Christ through the bread and cup of communion. These observances are not separate from the ministry of the Word; rather, they are the natural extension and culmination of it. The reading, preaching, and singing of God's Word invite and prepare the church of Christ to participate in that very Word, to encounter Jesus Christ Himself through these practices, which He explicitly ordained for the church. So then, Paul writes of the Lord's Supper in 1 Corinthians 11:26, "For as often as you eat this bread and drink the cup, you proclaim the Lord's death until He comes." Through these actions, the church declares the death and resurrection of Jesus Christ, demonstrates their washing of new birth and communal union in Jesus Christ, and partakes of the gracious provisions of the new covenant bestowed through Jesus Christ, the eternal Word made flesh.

CONCLUSION

In addition to fulfilling the Great Commission, the church has an "internal" mission to proclaim Jesus among the people of God. This is the Word proclaimed *for* the church, as the centerpiece of corporate Christian worship. Church leaders must never forget this holy mission.

In light of this commitment, the following chapters will offer extended reflection and instruction on various aspects of corporate worship that pertain to the faithful proclamation of God's Word. These chapters will consider the worship service more broadly, with respect to the role of liturgy and essential elements of corporate worship; the nature, role, and use of sacred music in the worship service; and the incorporation of art and technology in its various forms as vehicles for corporate worship. Subsequent chapters will explain both the significance and essential aspects of baptism and the Lord's Supper, the two ordinances established by Christ for the church. The final chapters will provide direction for the entire preaching process—from the exegesis and interpretation of a biblical text (and the accompanying spiritual preparation of the preacher), to the structure and development of the sermon, to the application of the message for a particular audience, culminating with principles for effective delivery.

These chapters together point us toward one goal: the ongoing proclamation of Jesus Christ among the gathered members of His body. The eternal Word of God, incarnated in Jesus Christ and written down for our instruction, is the substance of our corporate worship. We encounter the living God through the living Word of God—a Word that is read, preached, sung, enacted, and embodied in faithful worship together by the people of God.

NOTES

1. Frank Senn, *Christian Liturgy: Catholic and Evangelical* (Minneapolis: Fortress, 1997), 306–07.

2. Herman Wegman, *Christian Worship in East and West: A Study Guide to Liturgical History*, trans. Gordon Lathrop (New York: Pueblo, 1985), 297.

3. Senn, *Christian Liturgy*, 299.

4. Ibid., 303.

5. Ibid., 306–07. According to Senn, Luther's earliest prescription was that "a Christian congregation should never gather together without the preaching of God's Word and prayer, no matter how briefly."

6. See Haddon Robinson, *Biblical Preaching: The Development and Delivery of Expository Messages*, 2nd ed. (Grand Rapids: Baker, 2001), 21.

7. John Koessler, *Folly, Grace, and Power: The Mysterious Act of Preaching* (Grand Rapids: Zondervan, 2011), 18.

8. Bryan Chapell, *Christ-Centered Preaching: Redeeming the Expository Sermon*, 2nd ed. (Grand Rapids: Baker Academic, 2005), 26, 27. See also John Piper, *The Supremacy of God in Preaching*, rev. ed. (Grand Rapids: Baker, 2015).

9. Andrew B. McGowan, *Ancient Christian Worship: Early Church Practices in Social, Historical, and Theological Perspective* (Grand Rapids: Baker Academic, 2014), 111.

10. Ignatius to the Ephesians, 4.1–2.

CHAPTER 5.1

Thinking about Church Music

BRIAN LEE

INTRODUCTION

Although the origins of this quote are unclear, it has been said that "writing about music is like dancing about architecture." It is difficult to put into words sounds that are intended to communicate, express, and often transcend what words merely cannot on their own. The word "music" comes from the Greek *mousa*, which is where the intransitive verb form "muse" comes from: to become absorbed in thought, or to think about something carefully and thoroughly. But when considering church music, one must not only think carefully and thoroughly, but also biblically, theologically, and practically. Not to do so would negate the meaning of muse due to the absence of careful and thorough thought, or to "a-muse." The people of God, in our idolatry and sin, have often been in a posture of amusement in our worship before the Creator of heaven and earth, whether it be in music, scholarship, leisure, or our very lives.

With this in mind, it is a daunting task to encapsulate in one chapter all the Scripture, millennia of history, and centuries of traditions in thinking carefully and thoroughly about church music today. The main goal of this chapter is to provide some practical applications in music ministry while offering a few larger biblical perspectives on music itself. It is important to acknowledge from the onset that the Word of God and music are not in competition with one another. From God's breath speaking or "singing" into creation that caused vibrations and sounds as the heavens and earth were created in Genesis 1 to the songs in worship that will happen one day among God's people in the book of Revelation, music and God's words are interchangeable as the revelation of Jesus Christ (Rev. 1:1). From entire books of the Bible that are musical texts (Psalms, Habakkuk, Song of Solomon) to the numerous songs or canticles of God's people throughout the Old and New Testaments (the Song of Moses in both Deuteronomy and Revelation, Mary's Song in Luke; the "hymn of Christ" in Colossians 1:15–20, which is said to have been lyrics to a song of faith in the early church), music is embedded into the Word of God. It has been a primary language or languages of worship for the people of God and His church through the ages since the time of Jubal, who was "the father of all those who play the lyre and pipe" at the time when people "began to call upon the name of the LORD" (Gen. 4:21, 26), and those in Christ will continue to sing and call upon His name into eternity. In thinking about church music, we will examine it from three perspectives: the musicians, called to be both appointed and anointed by God; the music, reflecting God's glory; and the message, the centrality of *maranatha*, as the main song and cry of God's people in music and worship.

THE MUSICIANS: APPOINTED, ANOINTED, AND ALLOWANCE

In the opening seconds of a video produced by the Ethnomusicology and Arts Group of SIL International, ethnomusicologist Dr. Brian Schrag outlines what an arts consultant is in the context of different cultures. The arts consultant is someone who works alongside local singers, actors, dancers, and storytellers; researches a community's performing arts and then sparks artistic creation and strives to reach mutual spiritual and social goals with that local community. In many ways, this outlines the significant role and duty a music director, music pastor, or worship leader has in a church community. This person should be a leader who knows who the skilled musicians (singers and instrumentalists) are in a congregation while working alongside them, and also leads and sparks artistic creation in the music and worship of the church. Together, they strive to reach an understanding of how music and worship can function and be fruitful in a local congregation that must first be a fellowship of believers faithful to the Word of God, know Christ, and live Spirit-filled lives before music and worship can flourish to the glory of God.

It is said that the role of a music ministry leader demands more administrative duties than musical responsibilities. Dr. Yongmin Kim, an experienced church music leader and a music professor and director of the Moody Chorale at Moody Bible Institute, says that the role is often about 60 percent administration, 40 percent music related. A myriad of administrative responsibilities can be mentioned, but perhaps one of the most significant is the identifying and understanding of which members in the congregation have both the musical skill and spiritual maturity to be involved in music ministry. This is seen in the life of King David, who appointed both ministers of song and music before the Lord for the worship of His people: "Now these are the ones whom David appointed over the service of song in the house of the LORD, after the ark rested there. They were ministering in song in front of the tabernacle of the tent of meeting until Solomon's building of the house of the LORD in Jerusalem; and they served in their office according to their order" (1 Chron. 6:31–32). Moreover:

> He appointed some of the Levites as ministers before the ark of the LORD, to celebrate and to thank and praise the LORD God of Israel: Asaph the chief, and second to him Zechariah, then Jeiel, Shemiramoth, Jehiel, Mattithiah, Eliab, Benaiah, Obed-edom and Jeiel, with musical instruments, harps, and lyres; also Asaph played loud-sounding cymbals, and Benaiah and Jahaziel the priests blew trumpets continually before the ark of the covenant of God . . . with them were Heman and Jeduthun, and the rest who were chosen, who were designated by name, to give thanks to the LORD. (1 Chron. 16:4–7, 41)

This appointing and identifying by name in understanding who the musicians are requires an assessment of three important categories: musical skill, spiritual character, and personal commitment.

MUSICAL SKILL: APPOINTING

It is often forgotten that David was not only a shepherd, warrior, and king, but he was also a skilled musician (1 Sam. 16:16–18). Being a skilled church musician today is both a heritage from King David and a mandate to value both God-given talent and human diligence in the training and development of musical skill in the life of the church. During David's leadership, there was communication and collaboration between David and the Levites in appointing Chenaniah as the one in charge of the singing because of his level of skill: "Then David spoke to the chiefs of the Levites to appoint their relatives as the singers, with musical instruments, harps, lyres, and cymbals, playing to raise sounds of joy. So the Levites appointed . . . to lead with lyres tuned to the sheminith. Chenaniah, chief of the Levites, was in charge of the singing; he gave instruction in singing because he was skillful" (1 Chron. 15:16–22). Musicians were set apart for service because of their skill under David's leadership:

> Moreover, David and the commanders of the army set apart for the service some of the sons of Asaph, Heman, and Jeduthun, who were to prophesy with lyres, harps, and cymbals . . . who prophesied in giving thanks and praising the LORD. . . . All these were under the direction of their father to sing in the house of the LORD, with cymbals, harps and lyres, for the service of the house of God. . . . Their number who were trained in singing to the LORD, with their relatives, all who were skillful, was 288. (1 Chron. 25:1–7)

Each church community must determine what that level of skill should be relative to their local context, whether it is for the music ministry staff or volunteer musicians from the congregation. While many churches have the resources and opportunity to hire a person with formal musical education and training, some do not have that privilege or blessing, especially in smaller churches or parts of the world where the church is being persecuted. Nevertheless, as seen in both the example of David's leadership and in the psalms (Ps. 33:3 and others), there is a biblical basis and command for having skilled musicians serve the church. Many churches expect that a prerequisite in hiring a lead pastor is evidence of biblical, theological, and pastoral education and training. Similarly, there should be an expectation for those in music ministry leadership that their musical talent and skill has been developed and nurtured through education and training, while understanding that the music and worship of any church fellowship is ultimately fruitful because of the presence of God, faithfulness to Christ, and the filling of the Holy Spirit (Eph. 5:18, 19).

For volunteer musicians in a congregation, church leadership must determine what the skill level should be for someone to participate in the music ministry. Therefore, it is important to have an audition/interview process to best discern if an individual could serve musically and in what capacity. A singer or instrumentalist in a worship team of fewer members can be far more exposed than a singer in a larger choir or instrumentalist in a church orchestra. Having an audition not only allows for a clearer assessment of the level of musical skill for the ministry leader, but it also inherently communicates the importance of skill to the individual and church community. Requiring an official but simple form that a person fills out before an audition helps communicate this value of skill, and it can also inform the church about what musical training and experience a particular member has, along with what specific instruments they play, or what their vocal range is. The audition should be centered around a prepared solo or verse that demonstrates an individual's overall musical sound and ability. But also allow time for other musical skills to be demonstrated. These skills can include sight-reading, playing by ear, improvisation, knowledge in how to modulate from one key to another, rhythmic ability, collaborative/ensemble aptitude, and other practical skills.

SPIRITUAL CHARACTER: ANOINTING

It goes without saying that the spiritual character and maturity of a church leader or volunteer should be significantly important, and it should be no different for those in music ministry. At the same time, it can be easy to assume falsely that those in ministry are living lives of humility and holiness simply because of their training, activity, position, and outward appearance. As fallen people, musicians and artists can be prone to not giving all the glory and honor to God Himself, but to the music itself, to traditions or modern trends, to personal preference in musical genre or worship styles, to other agendas, or ultimately to ourselves. The mere presence of worship music or church musicians does not necessarily mean that God Himself is present or that He is glorified or pleased with our musical sacrifice. Throughout the Bible, the gathering of God's people and their offerings, in particular from priests, prophets, kings or judges, are either accepted and pleasing to Him, or they are utterly rejected and unacceptable in His sight. Amos describes how God says to His people, "Take away from Me the noise of your songs; I will not even listen to the sound of your harps" (Amos 5:23), among many other warning and examples throughout Scripture.

But how does one gauge spiritual maturity and character? In many ways, musical skill, education, and experience can be measured more objectively. Nevertheless, there must be an effort made to prayerfully discern the spiritual character of any music leader or volunteer musician as those who will be proclaiming the Word through music on a given Sunday. Often, the presence of God's Word and prayer in one's life indicates a mature faith in Christ. While an audition demonstrates musical skill, an interview that coincides with the audition can help a church determine whether an individual has the spiritual maturity to be in a music ministry role. Questions that speak into a person's knowledge of the Bible and how music and worship ought to be understood from a biblical worldview can help in this discernment. Even having an individual prepare a statement or answer specific questions related to a biblical understanding of music and worship or other theological truths can be helpful. This can certainly be more significant for those seeking roles in music ministry leadership (worship leader or music director, for example), where leading and discipling others and speaking in a worship service is part of the position. Be open to having Spirit-led worship pastors and leaders, music directors, and other music ministers proclaiming God's truth and His Word in a worship service through music or a prophetic Word, and for those appointed and anointed leaders to potentially disciple the musicians who serve under them.

On the other hand, there is also a potential danger in having a worship leader or musician being viewed as the one responsible for imparting truth, or somehow seen as the most important person in creating an "atmosphere" of worship. As mentioned earlier, it is easy for style, relevance, performance, and a personality of a worship leader or musician to take precedence over the truth of God's Word or His glory and presence. The primary goal for worship leaders and church musicians is to be faithful: faithful to Christ the Bridegroom, faithful to the Word, faithful to the leading and power of the Holy Spirit, faithful in the musical gifts and skills given to them by God. By God's grace, musicians in the church must be held to the same character standards as other church leaders: godly men and women who know Christ, are

Spirit-led, and continuously filled with the Spirit, and who humbly seek and pursue God's presence through lives of prayer and delighting in God's Word (Ps. 1:2).

PERSONAL COMMITMENT: ALLOWANCE

Along with the importance in finding church musicians who are musically skilled and spiritually mature, there is also the challenge in finding people who are willing to give up their time to serve. Therefore, it is important to prayerfully and thoughtfully create an environment of professionalism and spiritual nourishment in rehearsals, meetings, and any forms of communication within a music ministry. It can be an opportunity to attract skillful musicians who can serve, but perhaps who are initially unwilling because of other personal commitments and a minimal allowance of time for the church. Having each rehearsal conducted with preparation and efficient use of time can help create an environment of professionalism. More importantly, the presence of God's Word and prayer at a rehearsal or gathering offers opportunities for discipleship and spiritual nourishment: prayers of gratitude and bearing one another's burdens within a worship team or choir rehearsal can often be a place where church members find a primary small group or core community within a church fellowship. And while the primary goal should never be to include as many people as possible, there can also be both a practical and an eternal value in having more people involved. This can help with scheduling conflicts, and guard against burnout while fostering faithful practice and service, stewardship of God-given musical gifts. Additionally, it gives those involved opportunities for discipleship and spiritual growth. Furthermore, having more people involved can potentially allow for a true generational and ethnic diversity that is not merely external or manufactured, but one that has the potential to honor God and offer a glimpse to the multitude that will worship the Lamb of God before the throne as found in the book of Revelation. This reminds us that one of the most significant roles of a church community and music leader is to identify and understand which members of a congregation could (musical skill) and should (spiritual maturity) be involved with the music ministry. Take time to study, search, audition, interview, communicate, and build relationships with the musicians in the church who are called to be skilled, Spirit-filled, and willing to serve the Lord and others joyfully through music ministry.

THE MUSIC: REFLECTING GOD'S GLORY

The end of the Bible depicts music and song that reflect God's glory: Revelation speaks of God's people with "harps of God in their hands" singing both the song of

Moses and the song of the Lamb (Rev. 15:2–4), along with other music to be sung, played and heard before the throne of God and the Lamb who was slain. Throughout God's Word, there are a plethora of specific verses, chapters, and books connected to song and music, including a picture of God singing over his chosen people on that day: "The LORD your God is in your midst, a mighty one who will save; he will rejoice over you with gladness; he will quiet you with his love; he will exult over you with loud singing" (Zeph. 3:17 ESV).

God's glory is also sounded out and seen in all its majesty, color, and variety in the beginning of the Bible and the story of creation. It was through God speaking, His breath, His "singing" that created the heavens and earth. Genesis 1 can be described as a song that expresses lyrical verses and repeating choruses such as "And God said," "let there be," and "God saw that it was good." But for a worship service to be musically good on a given Sunday, it must overcome challenging circumstances that are different from almost all other musical experiences: the congregation represents participants who typically do not know the musical selections before the start of the service, are completely unrehearsed, and are at best, amateur musicians. And the music is supposed to reflect the glory of God. Acknowledging and understanding these congregational conditions can help music leaders to simultaneously sing/play skillfully and lead the people clearly. There are four main musical elements in which this can visibly and audibly be represented: rhythm, melody and pitch, timbre, and dynamics. But the most significant element in the music is not the music itself, but what it sets, supports, and gives melody to: the song lyrics.

SONG LYRICS

Although instrumental music without words can play an effective and practical role in the music of the church, much of what the church does is music through the singing of words. Studies indicate that people are more prone to remember words, phrases, lessons, or stories when they are set to music. And while the importance of prayer, the ministry of the Word, or the Eucharist in a worship service cannot be overstated, music without words can play a vital role in not only enhancing those elements in a service, but also for carrying out those very purposes and elements in worship.

The words of a hymn or spiritual song are often prayers, calling upon the name of the Lord in praise, thanksgiving, or petition. And as saints are encouraged to pray the Scriptures, our singing enables us to do so. Song lyrics taken directly from Scripture or rooted in God's Word can be prophetic in proclaiming biblical truth, doctrine, and the testimony of Jesus, "for the testimony of Jesus is the spirit of prophecy" (Rev. 19:10). Therefore, it is important to discern and choose songs with texts that are directly from or rooted in Scripture: words that are true, express sound doctrine, and have eternal beauty. It must also be remembered that whether words are spoken or sung, the people of God are to approach His throne with care in the words that are used. Having freedom in Christ and having the Holy Spirit dwell in us does not mean that we are to take our worship casually or carelessly, for the Bible says: "Guard your steps as you go to the house of God, and approach that to listen rather than to offer the sacrifice of fools; for they do not know they are doing evil. Do not be quick with your mouth or impulsive in thought to bring up a matter in the presence of God. For God is in heaven and you are on the earth; therefore let your words be few. For the dream comes through much effort, and the voice of a fool through many words" (Eccl. 5:1–3). Speaking or singing words without thoughtfulness, without purpose, or with excess is to be avoided because God commands us to use caution when approaching Him and warns us in this passage about being hasty or impulsive in His presence, lest we fall into the trap of amusement or entertainment in both our corporate and private worship.

The Word of God also shows us how song lyrics can express praise for His saving works. One example is Moses and the people of Israel singing a song of praise after God delivered them out of Egypt and across the Red Sea: "I will sing to the LORD, for He is highly exalted; / The horse and its rider He has hurled into the sea. / The LORD is my strength and song, / And He has become my salvation; / This is my God, and I will praise Him; / My father's God, and I will extol Him" (Ex. 15:1–2), later sung by Aaron's sister Miriam with all the women who went out with tambourines and dancing. The Bible commands us to sing the psalms (Col. 3:16; Eph. 5:19), which contain laments, praises, and the prophetic truth of Christ in both the first advent and the second one to come. Furthermore, there are numerous psalms and references to the psalms throughout the Bible that instruct us to sing praises to God for who He is and what He has done. Often, these songs are sung in direct correlation with the saving work of the Lord. It can be worthwhile to find time in worship to use music and song as praise following a reading of Scripture, testimony, message, sacrament, prayer, or any part of the service that tells a narrative of God's faithfulness and salvation. Furthermore, when choosing what songs will be sung in a worship service, it is important to discern and understand where the text comes from and what type of text it is: are the song lyrics taken directly from passages or verses from the Bible? If not, what passages of the Bible or biblical truth or doctrine do they communicate? While the content of the song text is important, one can also read aloud verses from God's Word before, during, or after music is played or sung. And while there is certainly a time and place for non-biblical texts or beautiful poetry to be sung in a worship service, let us also remember the supremacy and the authority of God's Word, for it was God's speaking ("and God said") in Genesis 1 that had power and intercession in beauty and truth in His creation. It is the living, imperishable, and enduring Word of God that is supreme, for "all flesh is like grass, and all its glory is like the flower of grass. The grass withers, and the flower falls off, but the word of the Lord endures forever" (1 Peter 1:23–25; Isa. 40:6–8).

RHYTHM

Rhythm in music is the measurement of time or duration in a given moment (one note), a musical phrase, or the general pace and timing over large sections. The story of creation in Genesis 1 has a certain rhythm and groove. It happens in a continuum of time with clear boundaries between evening, morning, and from one day to the next. In the same way, music happens in a continuum of time that can have a certain rhythm and groove that is either clear to the people participating or unclear, unstable, or tainted. The simple choice of what tempo (speed of the beat) a worship team or song leader decides can either make or break a particular singing of a song: too fast a tempo, and the singability of a tune and the message of the text can be lost. Too slow, and the congregation cannot sustain phrases while the music sounds sluggish and stodgy. Generally speaking, the tempo of a hymn or worship song should be chosen based on the natural or spoken rhythm of the lyrics, highlighting the primary importance of the message of the text. One way this can be determined is by speaking or reciting the text only, allowing for its natural poetic meter and pace to be felt and heard by the music leader. Clarity of rhythm also connects to the ability of a congregation to sing together in time. Whether it is a song leader up front who is conducting the congregational choir or the rhythm section of a worship team, it is important for a clear tempo to be established. For the singers who lead up front, it is important to be on the same page with one another and the congregation regarding the rhythm of the melody: this is often challenging when there are more highly syncopated rhythms in a more contemporary worship song or in a hymn that has different traditions or versions. The pursuit of musical clarity and detail is both duty and delight, as faithful musicians strive to understand and reflect God's clear, detailed beauty in His creation through music.

MELODY AND PITCH

Singing or playing in tune or on pitch is certainly an important aspect in reflecting God's design and beauty through music. One could say that God's creation in Genesis 1 was perfectly in tune and in harmony with the Creator and with its surroundings. But a common error of judgment that worship leaders often make is the selection of a key in which the melodic range of a particular song is difficult for most people to sing. When this happens, the decision of key is often made based on the origins or traditions of a worship song or hymn, the personal preference of the song leader or musicians, or an arbitrary decision without much thoughtful planning and intent. The determining factor of which key to set a song in should be based on the melodic range of a given song (not necessarily based on a fixed key): a song's highest note and lowest pitch in the melody. Most songs of faith have a melodic span of about an octave, although some of the more modern songs can have a wider range based on its original context or use. Nevertheless, the highest note of the melody should usually not exceed the pitch D (fourth line of the treble clef for female voices, the D above the staff in bass clef for male voices). Occasionally, it may be acceptable or even desirable to go slightly higher: some worship leaders prefer setting a key that allows a bit of discomfort in the upper range as it may promote a certain volume and enthusiasm in singing out ("Make a joyful noise unto the LORD!"). But any key set too high or too low for the sake of the personal range or preference of a worship leader can be detrimental in the musical output and "tuning" of the congregation.

Whether it is from a lead vocalist or instrumentalist such as a keyboard player, the melody must be clearly heard by the congregation so that it fosters good ensemble and collaboration by all involved, which is a challenge in an unrehearsed environment. Furthermore, new or unfamiliar songs should either be taught with time and intent or be presented with limited harmony so that the congregation can clearly hear the melody in the moment of singing. The melody plays a vital role in many musical experiences, as it is often what people remember from a particular musical work. Its compatibility with the text is also an important factor in assessing whether it is a "good" tune or not. Be sure to select tunes that are simple for most to sing and remember, but ones that are also musically beautiful and intriguing: some of the most beloved songs of faith, both older and newer, have both a deep and rich meaning of the texts that are expressed through the beauty and makeup of a wonderfully crafted melody.

TIMBRE

There is an immense variety and beauty in God's creation. Genesis 1 talks about living things that are created "each according to its kind," whether it is vegetation, plants, fruits, trees, and the creeping things and beasts of the earth. There is also contrasting images and sounds one might imagine in the creation of light and darkness, sea and dry land, heaven and earth, sun and moon, male and female. There is the grand and majestic alongside the small and intimate, each with its own unique beauty and design. Music in worship can reflect all of this, albeit in our fallen and sinful nature as a shadow of what is to come. Nevertheless, music can express the immense variety and beauty, the juxtaposition of sounds, textures, dynamics, ranges, and other musical expressions that can point to the beauty of God's creation and to the beauty of our eternal destiny when all things will be restored through Christ. And while every musical element can express these realities, it is musical timbre—tone color and combination of voices and instruments—that perhaps most vividly does so.

"A symphony must be like the world: it must contain everything," stated Gustav Mahler, an Austrian composer from the late Romantic era who composed nine complete symphonies that elevated the scope of the symphonic form and expanded the possibilities of sound for an orchestra. It is in the symphony orchestra where the variety, scope, and world of sound is unsurpassed in a real musical sense: the possibilities of grand and intimate, high and low pitches, the array of textures and colors, reflect the created world and its different kinds. Of course, most churches do not have the capacity or personnel to have a symphony orchestra as part of a worship service each week, let alone all. Nevertheless, there can be an effort made for the music to value this type of reflection of Genesis 1 through what kind of instruments and voices exist, are implemented, and in what combination for any worship service. And while it is of declining use in most churches, the organ has the capacity to serve in this way for many churches. The array of volume levels, sounds and instruments, textures and colors are all capable in the organ, which is why Mozart deemed it the "king of instruments." In churches where an organ is not available or used, understanding how best to express "a world of sound" with acoustical or electronic instruments and amplification can help in expressing the plethora of sounds, textures, and colors that are part of the beauty of God's creation.

But the primary musical timbre of God's people over the ages has been the human voice. Men and women singing a new song, a joyful noise, and praises to the Lord with or without instruments can also convey the beauty of God's creation and His eternal truth through texted melody and music. And like the organ, the presence of church choirs seems to be declining in most churches. One must remember that the true choir or worship team in a church is the congregation itself, as the people lift their voices and call upon the Lord. Nevertheless, similar to the value of the instrumentalists or the rhythm section of a worship team giving a foundation for the congregation, a choir can also function in helping lead an unrehearsed congregation to sing well: to sing more clearly, more fervently, more beautifully. One might even say that it is biblical to have a choir regardless of worship tradition or musical style, as many of the psalms were written "to the choirmaster," which indicates the importance of choirs in worship and liturgy. But practically, when the congregational choir is represented in the smaller church choir itself, it is of value both musically and in congregational participation and provides more musical and spatial cohesiveness to the service.

MARANATHA: THE SONG OF GOD'S PEOPLE

Although this Aramaic word is found only once in the Bible (1 Cor. 16:22), *maranatha* was used as a greeting, a creed, and as liturgy in the early church. But it also captures what has been the central hope and prayer of God's people over the ages since the beginning, when people began to call upon the name of the Lord. And the musical message and cry of the saints must be rooted in *maranatha* because it is a word centered in Jesus Christ.

Depending on the context or how the word is spoken and read, it has three different meanings: the Lord has come (past), the Lord will come again (future), and Lord, come (present). It is centered in Christ, the Alpha and Omega, who is Lord of all creation and who has come to His people in the first advent about 2,000 years ago, and who will come again as the Scriptures prophetically proclaim countless times. But the message and meaning of *maranatha* also expresses the need for God's people to humble ourselves before Jesus, bow at His feet in holy fear like the apostle John in the book of Revelation, and acknowledge our brokenness, weakness, sin, and absolute dependency for Jesus to come and be with us. The prophetic message of *maranatha* expresses God's past, present, and future truth both clearly and urgently.

Because of the centrality of Christ and the prophetic nature of *maranatha*, the music of the saints must reflect that reality. One only needs to look at the book of Psalms, the songbook of the Bible, to see this. The Psalms in many ways is "the Book within a book." It is the gospel in lyrical and musical form. There are psalms proclaiming that the Lord has come in the past through his creation, His presence, and works to His people in the wilderness during the exodus. There are psalms that proclaim that the Lord is coming: predicting both the birth of Jesus when the Word became flesh, but also pointing to the second Advent when the Lord will come again and restore His kingdom on earth (from Zion/Jerusalem/Israel to the nations) and make all things new. But the music of the psalms also expresses our need for the Lord in the present: when God's people are broken, hurting, or under threat like King David was when he was in the wilderness, the song of God's people must be rooted in the *maranatha* cry, prayer, and call as the psalms are.

There are several practical applications when pursuing the message of *maranatha* in a music ministry. One central application is the choice of song lyrics, which has already been discussed earlier in the chapter. It is important to discern and choose songs with lyrics that express the centrality and presence of Christ past, present, and future, mirroring what the psalms do both as a whole and within individual chapters. Another application in proclaiming the *maranatha* message is during seasons of the church calendar. Two main opportunities for a church to musically lean into each year are during the Lent and Advent seasons. Lent offers the opportunity for a church to sing songs that express our brokenness, sin, and need for the Lord to come now to heal and forgive us, and share in music that proclaims that He has come—His birth, death on the cross, and that He has risen from the dead. Advent is a season of waiting for the Lord to come, not just for His birth in Bethlehem, but also for the coming Day of the Lord that the Scriptures point to. These weeks and seasons of the church calendar not only provide an opportunity for a church to use music to proclaim and express the *maranatha* message in more significant and impactful ways, but it also reminds us to pursue this central message each Sunday in the music and worship of the church.

CODA

The most important application of the *maranatha* message is for the people of God to live it, both as individuals and as the body where Christ is the head (Col. 1:18; Eph. 5:23). Not only should the music of the church reflect this central message, but musicians and all who sing His praises (for the people of God are commanded to sing), must live lives that reflect the headship of Christ.

One must not start thinking or musing about a topic, music or otherwise, with the topic itself, lest it become wisdom from our own eyes (and ears). Music and corporate worship that is pleasing unto the Lord is a result of the people of God fearing the Lord in reverence and repentance, humbling ourselves before Him, crying out for His presence in our brokenness and singing songs of thanksgiving for what He has done and what He will do "in that day," and ultimately because of the Lord's steadfast love, mercy, and grace. Indeed, He is the One from whom all blessings flow.

Leading Worship in the Local Congregation

RYAN J. COOK

INTRODUCTION

Every Sunday around the globe, Christians gather together for corporate worship. They have been doing so week in and week out for the last two thousand years. Pastors and other church leaders are often called on to oversee and direct these gatherings. This raises some important questions. When the church gathers, what kinds of things should they be doing? How can one tell if a worship service was a successful one or not? What criteria for success should be used? What is the purpose of these gatherings?

Many churches tend to one of two errors in trying to answer these questions. They either rely on tradition, or resort to pragmatism. That is, some churches simply keep doing what they have always done without much reflection as to why. Or they take a third, more pragmatic approach—whatever attracts the most people must be best. Any of these approaches fall short of a biblically grounded, historically informed, and culturally appropriate basis for congregational worship. This is not a minor issue. The habits we form through our weekly congregational worship shape how we view God, His Word, our sense of mission to the world, and our understanding of the body of Christ. In short, corporate worship plays a critical role in our discipleship.

Perhaps this is why Scripture is so clear that God cares deeply how His people worship. A large percentage of the Pentateuch comprises instructions for how and where Israel was to worship. As Israel's history unfolded, God was often frustrated with the nation's failure to worship properly. In Isaiah, God laments, "These people come near me with their mouth and honor me with their lips, but their hearts are far from me. Their worship of me is based on merely human rules they have been taught" (Isa. 29:13 NIV).[1] Indeed, some of Paul's strongest warnings concerned abuses in corporate worship (1 Cor. 11:27–30). At least one reason why God takes corporate worship so seriously is because it plays an important role in shaping the character and identity of the worshiper. The psalmist warned Israel against making idols for just this reason: "Those who make them [idols] will become like them, everyone who trusts in them" (Ps. 115:8).

The goal of this chapter is to articulate a biblical theology of corporate worship, to reflect on how the church has practiced worship through its history, and to build a theologically informed foundation for contemporary corporate worship.

WHAT IS CORPORATE WORSHIP?

According to English dictionaries, the word "worship" primarily means "the feeling or expression of reverence and adoration for a deity."[2] This expresses well how most people understand the term today. This default understanding of worship can lead to the mistaken idea that worship leaders are responsible for orchestrating an experience that leads the congregation to encounter God. However, the Bible is clear that we do not initiate worship. God is the initiator. He invites us to worship Him and we respond. As Constance Cherry reminds us, "We do not begin by thinking about ourselves and what *we* want out of worship. Nor do we evaluate worship based entirely on what we receive from it. Rather, we consider who God is and God's expectations for worship."[3]

God's expectations for worship are found in Scripture. The Bible has a wide range of words and expressions for worship that help define the concept more precisely. We can categorize the biblical teaching on worship under three headings: worship as physical gestures, worship as corporate ritual, and worship as attitude.[4]

WORSHIP AS PHYSICAL GESTURE

The most common words for worship in Hebrew and Greek are verbs that literally denote prostration, or lying down on the ground before God.[5] The psalmist calls the community to worship in this way: "Come, let's worship [prostrate ourselves] and bow down, let's kneel before the LORD our Maker" (Ps. 95:6). The same idea of prostration for worship is used by Paul (1 Cor. 14:25).

Of course, there are other physical gestures called for in worship (e.g., clapping, dancing, waving arms). But it is striking that the most common word for worship in the Bible is a term that denotes bowing to the ground. This indicates something about the way in which we approach God. We approach Him as an inferior before a superior. Prostration is a gesture of humility, respect, and awe. Additionally, the fact that a word related to a physical gesture is central to the meaning of worship indicates that worship includes not only our minds and hearts, but our bodies as well.

WORSHIP AS CORPORATE RITUAL

The overwhelming majority of texts devoted to worship describe it as an activity of the community. When God delivered Israel out of Egypt, it was so that His people could participate in worship (Ex. 3:12). Large sections of the Pentateuch describe the weekly and annual calendar for corporate worship (Ex. 12–13; 23:10–19; 34:18–26; Lev. 16; 23; 25; Num. 9:1–14; 28–29; Deut. 16). In the New Testament, the church was born as a community at worship during Pentecost (Acts 2). Instructions concerning worship in the Epistles assume a corporate context (e.g., 1 Cor. 11–14).

When the church gathers in worship, it is more than just a group of disconnected individuals who happen to be in the same building and singing the same songs.[6] Rather, we gather, "being diligent to keep the unity of the Spirit in the bond of peace. There is one body and one Spirit, just as you also were called in one hope of your calling; one Lord, one faith, one baptism, one God and Father of all who is over all and through all and in all" (Eph. 4:3–6). Corporate worship involves the believing community gathering at God's invitation to respond in a unified way to praise, thank, bless, confess, petition, lament, and testify to God based on how He has revealed Himself in Scripture and what He has done for us in salvation.

WORSHIP AS ATTITUDE

Biblical worship also requires an appropriate attitude, or disposition. Merely going through the proper rituals has never been enough. God desires a life that is devoted to Him. In Psalm 24, David asks, "Who may ascend onto the hill of the LORD? And who may stand in His holy place?" and responds, "One who has clean hands and a pure heart, who has not lifted up his soul to deceit and has not sworn deceitfully" (vv. 3–4). When Moses summarized God's primary requirements for Israel's worship, he emphasized that Israel was to love God and serve Him with "all your heart" (Deut. 10:12–13). The author of Hebrews encourages the church to worship God "with reverence and awe; for our God is a consuming fire" (Heb. 12:28–29).

This brief analysis of how the Bible talks about worship supports David Peterson's definition of biblical worship as "approaching or engaging with God on the terms that he proposes and in the manner that he makes possible. It involves honouring, serving and respecting him, abandoning any loyalty or devotion that hinders an exclusive relationship with him. . . . [W]orship is more fundamentally faith expressing itself in obedience and adoration."[7]

This chapter is primarily concerned with corporate worship. Another way of describing this is "liturgy." The word "liturgy" itself comes from a Greek word meaning a "service of a formal or public type" (*leitourgia*).[8] For some, the word "liturgy" conjures up images of high church with formal and elaborate rituals. However, the word itself simply refers to what a community does together to worship God. Every church has a liturgy whether they know it or not. This chapter is designed to help us think theologically and practically about how to lead a congregation in corporate acts of worship, or its liturgy.

HOW TO DETERMINE BIBLICAL WORSHIP: REGULATIVE PRINCIPLE VERSUS NORMATIVE PRINCIPLE

It is clear that modes of worship changed throughout Scripture. Think of the difference in worship practice between Abraham and Solomon, or Samuel and Daniel. In the Old Testament, believers worshiped at altars, in the tabernacle, at the temple, and in exile.[9] The death and resurrection of Jesus also brought significant changes in the way believers worshiped in the New Testament. Given all these diverse practices, what does it mean to have biblical worship?

Historically the church has framed this debate as the regulative versus normative principle in corporate worship. The regulative principle asserts that a church should only engage in activities that the Bible explicitly commands.[10] While those who espouse the regulative principle debate exactly how to apply it, the basic philosophy behind it is fairly clear. This view was held by John Calvin and the Puritans.[11]

Other parts of the church have held to the normative principle. That is, the church is free to include any practice as long as it is not forbidden in Scripture.[12] This view has been espoused by Anglican and Lutheran churches.

Both views raise important questions. For the regulative principle, it is difficult to discern exactly how corporate worship was practiced during the New Testament church era. There is also the significant issue of cultural context. Even if we said the same words and did the same actions as the first-century church, it would likely mean something quite different in a twenty-first-century North American context. For the normative principle, one of the main questions is, How do we incorporate new elements into a corporate worship service without allowing them to crowd out ones Scripture clearly enjoins us to include?

Perhaps the wisest course is to find a middle way between the normative and regulative principles. Our worship practices should be biblically/theologically grounded.[13] That is, they should be based on clear emphases in Scripture, both Old and New Testaments. But there is room for diversity in what those practices look like based on our own cultural location and theological tradition.

BIBLICAL THEOLOGY OF CORPORATE WORSHIP

The biblical material related to worship is vast. For the purpose of this discussion, I have organized the material under the following three headings: Sacred Space, Sacred Time, and Sacred Acts.[14]

SACRED SPACE

God is present everywhere. However, the Bible is clear that in certain places, God reveals Himself in a unique and powerful way. The places where encounters like this occur become holy, or sacred space.[15] At creation, God placed Adam and Eve in a garden and had regular fellowship with them there (Gen. 2–3). After Adam and Eve's sin, they were exiled from the garden and access to God's presence (Gen. 3:24). As a result, sacred space was centered on altars where God would accept the worship of His people (e.g., Gen. 12:8; 22:1–19; 26:25). The concept of sacred space comes to its climax in the Old Testament with the building of the tabernacle and temple.[16]

The tabernacle was also patterned after the garden of Eden.[17] In essence, the tabernacle was a small piece of heaven on earth. Imagine an ancient Israelite walking past the intricately woven curtains to enter the tabernacle. It would feel like they had stepped into a new realm, where God dwells. Standing between the court of the tabernacle and the actual tent of meeting was an altar. This would have reminded ancient Israel that it is only through atonement for sin that one could approach the presence of God. The temple retained and enhanced these same features.

For ancient Israel, God used sacred space to teach Israel in profound ways. First, it was an incarnational way of relating to God. That is, the temple/tabernacle recognized that we are embodied creatures. It gave ancient Israel a way to relate to God in space and time. Second, the space itself taught Israel truths about their relationship with God. Namely, if God can be present in the tabernacle/temple, He also could be absent, and Israel would experience the pain of exile. The space illustrated that sin was a barrier between them and God physically. It reminded Israel that atonement was necessary to progress into God's presence. The tabernacle also taught Israel about the danger of idolatry. The tripartite structure of the tabernacle was similar to many Canaanite shrines. One striking difference was that in those shrines, the holy of holies would house an idol as the focus of veneration. The holy of holies in the tabernacle had no such object. This would have been a regular reminder that idol worship and worship of Yahweh were incompatible. Finally, the temple/tabernacle also gave Israel a glimpse of the pre-fallen world and a glimpse of the eschaton, where the focus is God's presence with His people (Rev. 21–22).

In the New Testament, Jesus embodied God's presence on earth. As John tells us, in Jesus "the Word became flesh, and dwelt [tabernacled] among us" (John 1:14). Jesus was a kind of walking temple.[18]

After Pentecost, Paul taught that the church is the body of Christ indwelt by the Holy Spirit (Eph. 2:19–22). In this way, Christians are like the temple (1 Cor. 6:18–20). Because of this, there are no instructions for what a Christian meeting place is supposed to look like. The focus is on the people who are indwelt by the Spirit, not on the geographical location of a place of worship. Nevertheless, the eschatological hope of the New Testament is that God will once again dwell with humanity in a physical space in the new heavens and new earth (Rev. 21–22). At that time, "the throne of God and of the Lamb will be in it, and His bond-servants will serve Him; they will see His face, and His name will be on their foreheads" (Rev. 22:3–4).

SACRED TIME

On the fourth day of creation, God said, "Let there be lights in the vault of the sky to separate the day from the night, and let them serve as signs to mark sacred times, and days and years" (Gen. 1:14 NIV). One of the reasons God created the universe in the way that He did was so that the sun, moon, and stars could be used to "mark sacred times"—that is, so that we would know when we should worship.

The Old Testament sets aside weekly and annual times for worship. During the creation week, God Himself modeled a Sabbath. The word "sabbath" means "to cease, stop, rest, celebrate."[19] In doing this, God created a pattern of work and worship. At Sabbath, Israel was to stop and remember. They were to remember that God was their Creator and Redeemer (Ex. 20:11; Deut. 5:15). Their identity was not found in their work, but in their relationship with God. It was a time when everyone was to cease their labor—men, women, children, servants, and animals (Ex. 20:10).[20]

For ancient Israel, the Sabbath had several important functions in their understanding of worship: (1) Sabbath reminded Israel that it was not human work that provides us with security and identity. Rather, God is our Creator, Redeemer, and Provider. (2) Sabbath was a time to have compassion on the poor. Israel was to remember that they were once slaves in Egypt, and so not to treat others harshly (Deut. 5:15). (3) Sabbath was a sign of God's covenant with Israel (Ex. 31:12–17).[21]

In addition to a weekly Sabbath, the Old Testament outlines annual feasts for the community to celebrate. These include Passover, Firstfruits, Festival of Weeks, the Day of Atonement, Festival of Tabernacles, and Purim (Lev. 23; Est. 9:26–28). God also outlined non-annual festivals for Israel to celebrate, including the Year of Jubilee and Sabbatical Year (Lev. 25). At the Year of Jubilee, debts would be canceled and property restored to any Israelites who had sold their inheritance due to economic hardship, while the Sabbatical Year allowed the land to rest and the yield of the land to be given to the poor (Lev. 25:4–6). These festivals provided breaks in the year, which were focused on God. They were regular, dramatized events that reminded people how God had provided (e.g., Firstfruits), rescued (e.g., Passover), and dealt with sin (e.g., Day of Atonement). They instilled in children an understanding of redemptive history (Deut. 6:20–25). And they provided a way to care for the poor of the land (Lev. 25).

In the New Testament, the apostles continued to meet weekly on the Sabbath (Acts 13:14; 16:13; 17:1–2). However, as the church loosened its ties to Judaism, the primary day of worship shifted to the first day of the week in honor of the day Jesus rose from the dead. This shift can be seen in the New Testament itself (1 Cor. 16:2; Rev. 1:10).[22] The early church quickly embraced the wisdom of weekly times of corporate worship punctuated by yearly festivals to commemorate what God had done (e.g., the equivalents today of Christmas, Good Friday, Easter, and Pentecost).

SACRED ACTS

God instructed His people to engage in many activities as a part of worship. Prayer was always a central element. The prayer of ancient Israel was informed by the rich laments, praises, and thanksgivings of the Psalter (e.g., 2 Chron. 20:21).[23] The New Testament likewise enjoins God's people to sing "with psalms, hymns, and spiritual songs," along with offering prayers for all people (Col. 3:16; 1 Tim. 2:1). Singing was clearly an important part of worship for the New Testament church. There are songs embedded within the New Testament itself (e.g., Luke 1:46–55; 68–79; Phil. 2:6–11). The apostle Paul encouraged the church in Ephesus to sing as a corrective to the mental and sensual darkness their culture surrounded them with (Eph. 4:17–5:19).[24] Singing also powerfully demonstrates the unity of the church, not just rationally (i.e., we believe the same things), but bodily by the whole congregation unified together in praise.

The public reading of Scripture was a central feature of Old Testament worship. Moses required the Levites to read the entire Torah before all Israel every seventh year at the Festival of Booths (Deut. 31:9–13; Neh. 8:9–18). The reading of the Torah was also required at covenant renewal ceremonies (Josh. 8:30–35). The neglect of reading Scripture in worship led to devastating consequences for Israel (2 Kings 22–23; 2 Chron. 34–35). Public reading of Scripture continued to be the usual practice in the New Testament church (1 Tim. 4:13; Rev. 1:3). In addition to reading Scripture, worship leaders also interpreted and applied it to the congregation as a part of worship (e.g., Ezra 7:10; 2 Tim. 4:1–2).

Sacrifice was one of the most central elements of Old Testament worship. Sacrifice was a way of demonstrating that sin needed to be atoned for through a blood sacrifice. This is illustrated especially well in the Day of Atonement sacrifice (Lev. 16). In addition to making atonement for sin, sacrifices were ways of giving to God, showing thanks for what the Lord had done, and celebrating in the presence of God. As a specific type of offering, tithes were also an important part of worship. Tithes provided the financial support for priests who worked at the temple, provided for the poor, and expressed the worshiper's dependence upon God.[25] In the New Testament, believers celebrate the perfect sacrifice for sin, Jesus (Rev. 5:9). In addition, Paul reminds believers that they are to be a "living and holy sacrifice" as an act of worship (Rom. 12:1). While the tithe is not directly imposed in the New Testament, believers collect money for the poor as part of their worship and support church leaders (1 Cor. 16:1–4; 2 Cor. 8:1–9:15; 1 Tim. 5:17–18).

A BRIEF AND SELECTIVE HISTORY OF CORPORATE WORSHIP

Corporate worship has been practiced in a bewildering variety of ways over the millennia. Numerous debates have emerged regarding everything from the meaning of Communion to the date of Easter. Nevertheless, some understanding of how the church has practiced worship provides insight into how Christians have attempted to faithfully apply Scripture to corporate worship and helps us understand why we worship the way we do today. For this selective history of corporate worship, we will examine several moments in the history of the church: the early church (through the fourth century), the medieval church, the Reformation church, and American frontier worship.[26]

THE EARLY CHURCH

The New Testament does not outline for us what a typical church service was like. In fact, the earliest written description of a church service in the Bible is an abysmal failure that Paul needs to correct: "In the following directives I have no praise for you, for your meetings do more harm than good" (1 Cor. 11:17 NIV). Because of this, we have to carefully read the New Testament and accounts of the early church fathers to gain a sense of what early Christian worship was like. In addition to the Old Testament and practice of Jesus, the early church's worship was guided by two quite different institutions—the synagogue and the Greco-Roman meal. These two institutions influenced Christian worship related to the preaching of the Word and the practice of Communion, respectively. At times these institutions also served as a kind of negative influence. That is, Christians adopted practices that clearly distinguished them from the synagogue or a Greco-Roman meal.

Jesus regularly taught in and worshiped at a synagogue (Matt. 4:23; 9:35; Luke 4:15). The early church also continued to attend the synagogue, often using worship there as an opportunity to proclaim Jesus as the Messiah (Acts 9:20; 13:26–35; 14:1; 17:10–12; 18:4). The similarity to early Christian worship was striking enough that at least one early Christian assembly was called a synagogue (James 2:2).

Synagogue practices were diverse, depending on the region, but they included the following: reading of the Torah and Prophets, instruction and sermons, and communal prayer.[27] Since many people in ancient times were either illiterate or could not afford to own books, being taught from the Scriptures meant hearing them read aloud. This was followed by discussion and instruction from the passages read. Scripture could be read and commented on by a variety of members of the congregation, illustrated well by the practice of Jesus and Paul (Luke 4:16–21; Acts 13:14–16).[28] All these practices were used by the early Christian community. In fact, a passage in Acts 20 gives insight into biblical teaching at a worship service. On a Sunday, the Christians in Troas gathered "to break bread" (20:7). After this, Paul spoke for so long that a young man fell out of a window being overcome by sleep (20:9). Some have seen this as evidence of a long sermon. However, the word used for Paul's teaching (*dialegomai*) indicates that it was more of a conversation, or discussion (20:7, 9). Here we get a picture of Christians gathering around a meal and discussing Scripture long into the night.

There is also evidence for a more formal sermon. The book of Hebrews is often understood as the transcription of a sermon. Some of Paul's letters were also intended to be read aloud in churches and likely mimicked a familiar sermonic form (Col. 4:16).

The earliest description of Christian worship also involves a meal (Acts 2:42). These meals were not a social event added to worship, like a potluck, but were the regular form of Christian gathering. Jesus Himself had commanded the disciples to continue practicing what we call the Lord's Supper (Luke 22:19). As Christianity gained converts from the Gentile world, the Greco-Roman meal influenced Christian gatherings. Greco-Roman meals took place in a dining room with a U-shaped table. An outline of a typical night included washing of hands, offering an opening prayer or hymn and libation, the meal proper, mixed wine brought with entertainment and/or conversation.[29] Some of these elements are discernable in early Christian worship.

There are also clear differences from a Greco-Roman meal. Most strikingly, Christians allowed believers from every social status, slave and free, to share table fellowship. Also, one of the distinctive marks of early Christian worship was the holy kiss (Rom. 16:16; 1 Cor. 16:20; 2 Cor. 13:12; 1 Thess. 5:26). Kissing was primarily associated with familial relationships. Early Christians viewed one another as family. Thus, along with the practice of calling one another "brother" and "sister," they included this familial greeting. This was countercultural enough that some early Roman observers accused Christians of incest.

Singing and music was certainly a part of early Christian worship (Eph. 5:19; Col. 3:16; James 5:13). The earliest Christian songs comprised scriptural texts (including Psalms), traditional hymns, and some original compositions. We do not know musically what they sounded like. Interestingly, there was a lively debate regarding the use of instruments in worship. Clearly, instruments are used in Scripture, but in Greco-Roman society certain musical instruments were associated with pagan worship. Because of this association, many historians do not think the early church included instrumental music.[30]

In the second century, Justin Martyr described a typical worship service. It is worth quoting at length.

> On the day called Sunday there is a gathering together in the same place of all who live in a given city or rural district. The memoirs of the apostles or the writings of the prophets are read, as long as time permits. Then when the reader ceases, the president in a discourse admonishes and urges the imitation of these good things. Next we all rise together and send up prayers. When we cease from our prayer, bread is presented and wine and water. The president in the same manner sends up prayers and thanksgivings, according to his ability, and the people sing out their assent, saying the "Amen." A distribution and participation of the elements for which thanks has been given is made to each person, and to those who are not present they are sent by the deacons. Those who have means and are willing, each according to his own choice, gives what he wills, and what is collected is deposited with the president. He provides for the orphans and widows, those who are in need on account of sickness or some other cause, those who are in bonds, strangers who are sojourning, and in a word he becomes the protector of all who are in need (*First Apology* 67).[31]

There are several elements in this description worth highlighting: (1) Selections from both the New Testament and the Old Testament were read aloud. This was critical because few Christians would have had access to a copy of the Bible, so this was the primary way it was learned. (2) A leader gave a sermon encouraging the "imitation of these good things" they had just read. (3) Corporate prayer was practiced as a response to the reading of Scripture. (4) Communion was practiced in the form of a meal with bread and mixed wine. (5) As a part of worship, a collection was taken for the poor, orphans, widows, prisoners, the sick, strangers, and others in need.

As the Christian faith exploded in the third and fourth centuries, corresponding changes occurred in the way that Christians worshiped together. Instead of meeting in smaller groups in homes for an evening banquet, they began to meet on Sunday morning in larger buildings designated for the purpose. Communion became no longer part of an actual meal, but was served as a token meal with small portions of bread and wine. These changes were driven by the practical difficulty of managing a much larger Christian population.[32]

While many changes took place in Christian worship during these early centuries, several consistent elements stand out: Sunday assembly, significant readings from Scripture with singing of psalms, a sermon, prayers of intercession, the kiss of peace, partaking of the Lord's Supper, and collection to support the poor and needy. Some parts of the Christian worship service were culturally influenced, while other parts were countercultural. The worship service was a way to give thanks for what God had done in Christ, to have fellowship with one another, to provide teaching, and to care for the poor.

THE MEDIEVAL CHURCH

The medieval liturgy is more developed and complex than the early church, but many of the same elements can be found in it. The service was broken into two parts: Liturgy of the Word and Liturgy of the Upper Room. The emphasis was clearly on the latter. The climax of the service was the Eucharist. An outline of pre-1570 Roman liturgy is found in Figure 1.

Figure 1: **Pre-1570 Roman Liturgy**[33]

LITURGY OF THE WORD	LITURGY OF THE UPPER ROOM
Choral Introit	Offertory
Kyrie ("Lord have mercy")	Preparation of the Elements
Gloria ("The Lord be with you . . .")	Salutation (*Sanctus* and *Benedictus*)
Collect(s)	Eucharistic Prayer
Old Testament Reading / Antiphonal Chant	Words of Institution / Call for Holy Spirit to Change Elements
Epistle Reading / Gradual (Psalm singing)	Lord's Prayer
Alleluia	Kiss of Peace
Gospel Reading	Fraction
Sermon	*Angus Dei*
Nicene Creed	Communion
Dismissal of Noncommunicants	Collect followed by Benediction

After a call to worship, the liturgy commences with the *Kyrie*. In this prayer, the congregation is reminded of their inability to come into God's presence on their own merits. Thus, a prayer for God's mercy is necessary. Following this was the *Gloria*, a pure expression of praise as a response to the cry for mercy. It demonstrates that mercy has been granted. Then came Scripture reading with selections from both testaments and the Gospels. Following the short sermon was a recitation of the Nicene Creed, which summarized the church's Christian confession. The high point in the service came in the Liturgy of the Upper Room. This was seen as a response to the Word portion of the service. The congregation would give their offering, pray, partake of the Lord's Supper, and be dismissed with a benediction.

Much of this is a natural outgrowth of early Christian worship. However, there were some problems in medieval worship that a brief examination of the liturgy does not expose. The service was spoken in Latin; thus the vast majority of worshipers could not understand what was being said. Worship for them was more of a mystical experience with the high point being the changing of the bread and wine into the body and blood of Christ (i.e., transubstantiation). The church became the institution that guarded and dispensed grace; this led to some abuses, including the selling of indulgences. Nevertheless, there are some positives to medieval worship, such as its use of art and architecture to capture the imagination. It included many elements in its worship that are well-grounded in Scripture and in the practice of the early church.

THE REFORMATION CHURCH

Corporate worship in the Reformation period was primarily a reaction to and attempt to purify Roman Catholic worship as practiced in the medieval era. The Reformers responded to medieval Roman worship in one of three ways. Lutherans tended to be more conservative in liturgical reform. They attempted to purify and reform worship, while retaining much from the medieval form. The most significant changes to worship related to Luther's belief in the priesthood of all believers and in the once-for-all sacrifice of Christ on the cross. This conviction led to the service being conducted in the language of the people instead of in Latin. Also, the music was not sung only by a choir, but by the whole congregation. Luther also replaced the offering before the Lord's Supper with a prayer for the congregation, to avoid any potential confusion that people were purchasing grace.[34] Finally, Luther added the Aaronic blessing as the closing benediction (Num. 6:24–26).

The radical wing of the Reformation represented by Anabaptists provided the most significant changes to corporate worship.[35] They brought a new freedom to forms of worship with an emphasis on being Spirit-led.[36] They rejected the notion that certain places, people, or things were sacred. For example, they only allowed the words from the Gospels or 1 Corinthians to be read during the Lord's Supper. They gathered in homes instead of church buildings or cathedrals. In essence, they did away with most rituals. A few Anabaptist leaders even included singing in the list of rituals to be banned. They agreed with Luther's theology of the priesthood of all believers, but took this a step further, rejecting any form of an official clergy. The ultimate example of how drastically this could change congregational worship can be seen with the Quakers. When Quakers gather for worship, they sit and wait for the Spirit to move before doing anything. Sometimes they have long periods of silence; then someone will be moved to pray, or sing, or read Scripture, or preach.

John Calvin and his followers attempted to purify worship through having fixed elements in the worship service, but providing freedom in the way these elements were arranged and expressed. Holding to the regulative principle, Calvin discerned four primary elements in worship from Acts 2:42: the Word, prayer, the meal, and alms.[37] Based on this foundation, Calvin developed the liturgy seen in Figure 2.

Figure 2: **Calvin's Liturgy**[38]

Liturgy of the Word	Liturgy of the Upper Room
Scripture Sentence (e.g., Psalm 121:2)	Collection of Alms
Confession of Sin	Intercessions
Psalm Sung	Apostles' Creed
Ten Commandments	Words of Institution
Prayer of Illumination (with Lord's Prayer)	Exhortation
Scripture Reading	Consecration Prayer
Sermon	Communion
	Psalm Sung
	Thanksgiving Prayer
	Aaronic Blessing

The Liturgy of the Upper Room (or what is often called "Communion") was only celebrated quarterly through the year, and thus the majority of services entailed only the Liturgy of the Word. The opening sentence welcomed the congregation to worship. The confession of sin reminded the congregation of the need for grace and forgiveness. Calvin introduced singing psalms as an important part of worship. He hired gifted poets and musicians to set the psalms to music.[39] The high point and focus of the service was the sermon.

Despite all its diversity, there are some common elements in Reformation worship. The preaching of the gospel became a central focus. In general, the Liturgy of the Word replaced the Liturgy of the Upper Room as the primary focus of the service. Congregational participation became much more prominent with the service now in the language of the common people. A revised understanding of the meaning of the Lord's Supper and baptism brought changes to those elements of the service. Music also continued to be a point of significant concern in worship, albeit a contentious one. Some Reformers forbade singing, while others allowed the singing of psalms, and others allowed the singing of new songs.

FRONTIER WORSHIP

Following the Reformation was rapid growth in changes to how Christians worshiped,[40] and one of the most significant developments from America was the influence of frontier worship.[41] In the aftermath of the War of Independence, there was a push for the country to expand west of the Appalachian Mountains. This created a significant issue for churches, namely, how to minister to a largely unchurched population scattered over enormous distances of thinly settled countryside. One institution that arose to meet this need was the camp meeting. These meetings would call together everyone from a whole region for several days of preaching, prayer, and singing; the songs were simple and easy to learn. This type of worship was designed to make converts of unbelievers. Those who were changed by these camp meetings then founded their own churches, or brought many of the elements of camp meetings into their local church.

Camp meetings were generally held in three parts: a song service using popular music, a sermon, and an invitation for conversion. This led to major liturgical changes that crossed denominational lines and paved the way for the great revivalists of the next century. Some of the changes this introduced into particularly evangelical churches were as follows: (1) Corporate worship functioned primarily as a form of mission, or evangelism. (2) Music gained a real importance in corporate worship and served a practical function, that is, to draw people in and prepare them for repentance and conversion. (3) The liturgical calendar was replaced by a more pragmatic one.[42] Many evangelical services today are the descendants of this more popular style of worship.

This survey has been selective and focused primarily on the church in Europe and North America. However, even this brief analysis helps one to understand how corporate worship has developed into its present-day practice. The history of Christian worship has been one of a continual interaction of three forces:

(1) a desire to stay faithful to the biblical text; (2) the influence of tradition; and (3) changes in the cultural context, in which new needs arise. There is a continual necessity to reflect theologically on how and why the church worships the way it does. This is one of the ways the church should be always reforming so that it can faithfully honor God and form mature followers of Christ in the time, place, and tradition it inhabits.

BUILDING A THEOLOGY AND PRACTICE OF CORPORATE WORSHIP

What should corporate worship look like today? Certainly some corporate worship is going to look quite different from others depending on the cultural context. But even given this diversity, it is still possible to outline a story arc to worship that captures well the biblical pattern and that can be adapted to different cultural settings.[43] This story arc has four movements: gathering, word, table/response, and sending.[44] This section will outline the general purpose for each of these movements and describe possible elements in the service to include in them. How these elements are actually practiced may necessarily be adjusted depending on the cultural context of a church's community. In most cases, the suggestions offered are not a matter of right versus wrong, but of good practices versus better, or better versus best.[45]

Gathering

The story arc of worship begins with God. He invites us to worship Him. Scripture is clear that we can only come to worship at God's invitation because He has created a way for us. The first words spoken in a service are the most important for highlighting this truth. Thus, a service begins with a call to worship. Think of the different tone set by opening a service with "Good morning, glad you could make it!" versus "Come let us worship and bow down. Let us kneel before the Lord our God, our maker!" How we frame the service affects how the congregation understands the purpose and function of worship. As James Smith puts it, "In contrast to a worship service that vaguely begins when the music starts playing and parishioners slowly saunter in to join the crowd, a worship service that begins with the Call to Worship has already received a word from the God who is active in worship and who *wants* us there."[46] There are many ways of expressing this truth at the beginning of a service, either through song, reading of Scripture, a statement by a worship leader, or a congregational reading.

The typical response to God's invitation is one of praise! We can celebrate who God is and what He has done to make worship possible. This is usually done through song, but added to this can be reading from Scripture or a congregational responsive reading. The tone in this section should be one of joy, awe, and reverence.

Confession is also an important part of the gathering. We need to be reminded of our sin and of the forgiveness we have available in Christ. Confession can be expressed through a set prayer, through Scripture reading (e.g., Ps. 51), or through a time of silent prayer. This is an essential part of the story arc of worship. God calls us to worship and we acknowledge our unworthiness (Isa. 6:5). However, we are not left with the guilt of our sin. The confession should move to a time where forgiveness in Christ is proclaimed! If we lose this part of worship, there are consequences: "To be called to confession week after week is to be reminded of a crucial chapter of the gospel story. What is lost when we remove this . . . [is] an important *counter*-formative aspect of the gospel that pushes back on secular liturgies of self-confidence that, all week long, are implicitly teaching us to 'believe in yourself.'"[47] This embodies well the Old Testament aspect of worship that confronted cultural idolatries in worship.

Another important element in the gathering is the congregational greeting. We greet one another as brothers and sisters in Christ. In the New Testament, this aspect of worship was the holy kiss. While many societies would not find it appropriate to literally obey this command, it is important to express the unity we have in Christ as a church family.

Other elements that could be included in the gathering portion of a service are the reading of a creed or affirmation of faith, testimonies, or responsive readings—that is, practices that express God's invitation and our response.[48] Our confession of sin, assurance of forgiveness, expression of unity in Christ, and praise to God all counter false narratives that our culture proclaims to us.

WORD

Listening to Scripture read and interpreted has been a key component to corporate worship since the time of Moses. The emphasis in this portion of the service is to hear from God as He addresses us through His Word. As a congregation, we can prepare for this through a prayer of illumination. This can be a set prayer, an extemporaneous prayer by the worship leader, a song, or a verse of Scripture. For example, one could read from Isaiah, "The grass withers, the flower fades, but the word of our God stands forever" (40:8). Or one could sing a song such as "Speak, O Lord."[49]

This is also an appropriate time to read Scripture. While public reading of Scripture has historically been a central part of worship, in recent years evangelical churches have gotten away from this practice. One study found that evangelical churches on average spend less than 2 percent of the service reading the Bible.[50] This forms a striking contrast to the 9 percent of the service given over to announcements. Reading Scripture publicly is an opportunity to involve members of the congregation to lead a portion of the service.[51] In addition to prayer and reading Scripture, the sermon, or homily, is a vital element of this portion of the service, which is addressed elsewhere in this volume.

TABLE/RESPONSE

Now that we have heard from God, it is appropriate for the congregation to respond. The celebration of the Lord's Supper is one important way to respond. This can be administered in several different ways.[52] The Lord's Supper is a way to remember what Christ has done for us, to celebrate our current unity in Christ, and to look forward to His imminent return.

In addition to the Lord's Supper, we can respond to the Word through giving to the poor. This response to worship has deep roots throughout Bible times and historic practice of the church. Songs and prayers of thanksgiving are also appropriate ways to respond. This part of the service may be adjusted depending on the content of the sermon. Some passages of Scripture encourage a response of repentance or confession. Others encourage a response of commitment or dedication. The content and tone of the primary passage should dictate the most appropriate tone and content of the response. It is helpful to think of this as a conversation. In the Word, God has spoken. Now, we get a chance to respond to what God has said.

SENDING

The final movement of the service is the sending. Just as God is the one who called us to gather in worship, God is also the one who sends us out into the world empowered for mission. While this is a brief part of the service, it is vital in framing how the congregation views itself and its relationship with God and the world.[53] The sending is composed of two elements: the benediction and the charge.[54] One of the primary duties of a priest in the Old Testament was to pronounce God's blessing over the congregation (Deut. 10:8; 21:5). The Lord Himself gave Aaron the words to use in the blessing of His people, "The Lord bless you, and keep you; the Lord cause His face to shine on you, and be gracious to you; the Lord lift up His face to you, and give you peace" (Num. 6:24–26). This was the way in which God's name was put on the people of Israel (Num. 6:27). A benediction is not a prayer. It is not directed to God, but to the congregation, and it pronounces and asks for God's blessing over His people. God's blessing is not something to be desired for personal safety, comfort, or well-being. Rather, God's blessing is designed to empower His people to accomplish His mission. Blessing is for a purpose.

The charge is also an important part of closing a service. It is a reminder to the congregation of who they are and what the Lord has called them to do. That this has historically been a central component to corporate worship can be seen from the fact that services in Latin were called a "Mass." This comes from the Latin phrase *mitto miss,* meaning, "you are sent."[55] The emphasis in the charge is to "Go." Both the benediction and the charge come together in the Great Commission (Matt. 28:19–20).[56]

There are many ways in which to carry out this twofold task of sending. The benediction and charge could be written specifically to tie into the sermon or Scripture reading for the day. The congregation can be summoned to a moment of silence to reflect on what the Lord has called them to do. One can ask other members of the congregation to pronounce the benediction (e.g., children blessing the adults of the church).[57] As we leave the service, we are reminded that God has a mission in which He has called us to participate. We are also reminded that we are not alone in our task. We are surrounded by brothers and sisters in Christ and empowered by His Spirit. We are sent with God's blessing and presence with us.

CONCLUSION

Leading the congregation in worship is a high and holy task. Thankfully we are blessed to have significant guidance from Scripture and the history of the church on how to do this well. The main message of this chapter is to be intentional about what is included and excluded in a service. Worship gatherings should be biblically grounded, historically informed, and culturally relevant. The four movements in a service (gathering, word, table/response, sending) may look significantly different in varying cultural contexts. However, the underlying theology and goals of each movement should be the same. The habit of regular meeting for corporate worship is one of the primary ways a congregation is shaped in their relationship with God, other believers, and the world. Because it is so central to discipleship, it is worthy of careful study and intentional practice.

NOTES

1. Failure to worship God appropriately was also the primary reason for the destruction of the first temple and exile to Babylon (2 Kings 21:10–15). At least four people in the Bible were put to death by God because of their improper worship: Nadab and Abihu (Lev. 10:1–2), and Ananias and Sapphira (Acts 5:1–11).

2. Catherine Soanes and Angus Stevenson, eds. *Concise Oxford English Dictionary* (Oxford, UK: Oxford University Press, 2004), electronic edition.

3. Constance Cherry, *The Worship Architect: A Blueprint for Designing Culturally Relevant and Biblically Faithful Services* (Grand Rapids: Baker Academic, 2010), 4.

4. Daniel Block, *For the Glory of God: Recovering a Biblical Theology of Worship* (Grand Rapids: Baker Academic, 2014), 8–22.

5. The Hebrew term is the verb *sagad*. The Greek counterpart is *proskuneō*. In Hebrew, the word is often accompanied by the prepositional phrase "to the ground" or "with the nose to the ground" (Block, *For the Glory of God*, 12). Some of these passages include Genesis 18:2; 24:52; Ruth 2:10; and 1 Samuel 25:23.

6. Cherry, *The Worship Architect*, 13.

7. David Peterson, *Engaging with God: A Biblical Theology of Worship* (Downers Grove, IL: IVP, 1992), 283.

8. *Greek-English Lexicon of the New Testament and Other Early Christian Literature, 3rd Edition (BDAG)*, 591. This term is used in the New Testament (e.g., Luke 1:23; Heb. 8:6; 9:21).

9. The patriarchs built altars at various places and sacrificed to God individually (e.g., Gen. 12:8; 22:1–19; 26:25). After the exodus, God revealed a new apparatus for worship that included Levitical priests, the tabernacle, proscribed sacrifices and offerings, and a liturgical calendar (e.g., Ex. 25–31; 34–40; Lev. 1–9). During the reign of Solomon, the locus of God's presence in Israel transitioned to the temple in Jerusalem (1 Kings 8). After the destruction of the temple, congregational worship had to adjust to a new kind of existence in exile.

10. The regulative principle was classically defined by John Girardeau: "A divine warrant is necessary for every element of doctrine, government and worship in the church; that is whatsoever in these spheres is not commanded in Scriptures, either expressly or by good and necessary consequences from their statements is forbidden." (John Lafayette Girardeau, *Instrumental Music in the Public Worship of the Church* [Richmond, VA: Whittet & Shepperson, 1888], 9).

11. For a more nuanced discussion of various shades of the regulative principle, see Michael Farley, "What Is 'Biblical' Worship? Biblical Hermeneutics and Evangelical Theologies of Worship," *Journal of the Evangelical Theological Society* 51 (2008): 591–613.

12. Gregg Allison defines the normative principle in this way: "The church is free to incorporate any elements into its worship unless Scripture either explicitly or implicitly prohibits them." See *Sojourners and Strangers: The Doctrine of the Church* (Wheaton, IL: Crossway, 2012), 429.

13. My view would be similar to the "biblical-typological" approach described in Farley, "What Is 'Biblical' Worship," 602. The strength of this approach is that it includes significant engagement with both the Old and New Testament texts related to corporate worship.

14. This outline is taken from Tremper Longman III, *Immanuel in Our Place: Seeing Christ in Israel's Worship* (Phillipsburg, NJ: P&R, 2001). He also includes the category of "Sacred People."

15. Leland Ryken et al., *Dictionary of Biblical Imagery* (Downers Grove, IL: InterVarsity, 2000), 748.

16. In Exodus, God outlined clear and detailed instructions for the building of the tabernacle. A close reading of these texts confirm several important points: (1) the tabernacle was God's idea (Ex. 25:1–9); (2) it was based on His revelation (Ex. 25:9); (3) God empowered the builders (Ex. 31:1–11); and (4) it was a place where God agreed to meet His people.

17. There were cherubim woven into the veil that separated the holy of holies from the holy place and on the outer curtains of the tabernacle, just as cherubim guarded the entrance to the garden after the fall (Gen. 3:24; Ex. 26:1, 31). The description of the menorah also uses tree imagery similar to the garden (Gen. 2–3; Ex. 25:31–40).

18. This can be seen in some of Jesus' miracles. When He touched lepers, they became clean (Matt. 8:2–4). He also forgave sins and declared that He was the only way to gain access to the Father (John 14:6), things that could previously only be accomplished in the temple.

19. *Hebrew and Aramaic Lexicon of the Old Testament (HALOT)*, 1407.

20. Israel was not a society where the wealthy and powerful could have a day of leisure while everyone else still worked, ensuring productivity. The Sabbath was for all.

21. Block, *For the Glory of God*, 275.

22. While Paul commanded the church at Colossae to "let no one pass judgment on you in questions of food and drink, or with regard to a festival or a new moon or a Sabbath" (2:16 ESV), the church is commanded to not forsake regularly meeting together (Heb. 10:24–25).

23. Some psalm titles also indicate use in corporate worship, e.g., Psalms 30 and 92.

24. Steven Guthrie, "Singing in the Body and in the Spirit," *Journal of the Evangelical Theological Society* (2003): 633–46.

25. For a detailed and thorough description of sacrifices and tithes in the Old Testament, see Block, *For the Glory of God*, 247–70.

26. For a more robust history of worship, see James F. White, *A Brief History of Christian Worship* (Nashville: Abingdon, 1993); Geoffrey Wainwright and Karen Westerfield Tucker, *The Oxford History of Christian Worship* (Oxford, UK: Oxford University Press, 2006).

27. Lee Levine, *The Ancient Synagogue: The First Thousand Years*, 2nd ed. (New Haven, CT: Yale University Press, 2005), 145–69.

28. See Andrew B. McGowan, *Ancient Christian Worship: Early Church Practices in Social, Historical, and Theological Perspective* (Grand Rapids: Baker Academic, 2014), 68–72.

29. For a more detailed description see McGowen, *Ancient Christian Worship*, 20–25; Dennis E. Smith, *From Symposium to Eucharist: The Banquet in the Early Christian World* (Minneapolis: Fortress, 2003).

30. McGowen, *Ancient Christian Worship*, 112–24.

31. Justin Martyr, "How We Christians Worship," trans. Everett Ferguson, *Christian History Magazine* 37 (Carol Stream, IL: Christianity Today, 1993), https://www.christianitytoday.com/history/issues/issue-37/how-we-christians-worship.html.

32. Andrew McGowan helpfully describes what worship was like in the fourth century based on detailed sources from Augustine's church at Hippo. The service began with the clergy greeting the congregation with "The Lord be with you." The congregation stood for the entire service and was divided by gender. Scripture was then read from both the Old and New Testaments, concluding with a reading from the Gospels. This reading was done by designated ministers, followed by a sermon. At this point in the service, prayers were offered by a deacon for the community. The prayer for the Eucharist was said, and the community responded with an "Amen." After partaking of the bread and wine, the kiss of peace was offered. See *Ancient Christian Worship*, 60–62.

33. Chart adapted from Bryan Chapell, *Christ-Centered Worship: Letting the Gospel Shape Our Practice* (Grand Rapids: Baker Academic, 2009), 23.

34. Chapell, *Christ-Centered Worship*, 35–41.

35. For an excellent overview of this diverse movement, see William R. Estep, *The Anabaptist Story* (Grand Rapids: Eerdmans, 1975).

36. White, *A Brief History of Christian Worship*, 108.

37. Chapell, *Christ-Centered Worship*, 42–43.

38. Adapted from Chapell, *Christ-Centered Worship*, 23–24.

39. Charles Garside Jr., "The Origins of Calvin's Theology of Music: 1536–1543," *Transactions of the American Philosophical Society* 69 (1979): 1–36.

40. Two of the most significant changes not discussed in this chapter are the rise of Methodism and Pentecostalism.

41. This term comes from James White, *A Brief History of Christian Worship*, 142–77. This section is based on his careful analysis. For some criticism of his approach, see Lester Ruth, "Divine, Human, or Devilish? The State of the Question on the Writing of the History of Contemporary Worship," *Worship* 88 (2014): 290–310.

42. While Christmas and Easter were kept, other new elements entered: Memorial Day, Mother's Day, Ministry Fair day, Thanksgiving, and remnants of the weeklong revival services.

43. This plotline has been truncated by traditions associated with frontier worship, including many seeker-sensitive approaches. See the discussion in James K. A. Smith, *You Are What You Love: The Spiritual Power of Habit* (Grand Rapids: Baker Academic, 2016), 103–10.

44. Smith, *You Are What You Love*, 95–96; Cherry, *The Worship Architect*, 35–52.

45. For this section, I happily acknowledge my debt to Constance Cherry's book *The Worship Architect*. The experience and research she collected has served as the foundation for my discussion here.

46. Smith, *You Are What You Love*, 96, emphasis original.

47. Ibid., 97, emphasis original.

48. For several helpful ideas, see Cherry, *The Worship Architect*, 59–60.

49. Keith and Kristyn Getty, "Speak, O Lord," recorded 2006 on *In Christ Alone*, Getty Music, 2006, CD.

50. Constance Cherry, "My House Shall Be Called a House of . . . Announcements," *Church Music Workshop* (January–April 2005): 29–35.

51. There are many articles and blogs that can help the worship leader run this aspect of the service well. For an example, see https://worship.calvin.edu/resources/resource-library/ten-tips-for-reading-scripture-in-public-worship/.

52. Another chapter in this volume details specifics regarding this portion of the service.

53. Cherry, *The Worship Architect*, 112–13.

54. Ibid., 113.

55. Ibid.

56. The Great Commission charges the follower of Jesus to "go, therefore, and make disciples," but it also includes a blessing: "Behold, I am with you always, even to the end of the age" (Matt. 28:19–20).

57. Cherry, *The Worship Architect*, 118.

Cultivating the Creativity, Messages, and Media of Your Community

BRIAN KAMMERZELT

What comes to mind when you think of "ministry media"? What do you think of? Is it church social media posts and sermon video aids? Is it radio networks and Christian bookstores? Is it liturgical practices and devotional materials? Do you have a high or low view of ministry media as a concept? The term *ministry* should bring to mind the highest ideal of creativity. If it doesn't, then all the more reason for us to pursue ministry media that matters. That is, to pursue media that is made as an act of worship, free from modern technique, biases, business practices, or market pressures—a form of media as pure and unfettered reality revealing creativity. What's at stake is nothing less than the pure message of the gospel and the broader realm of ministry communication—messages that minister (attend to the needs of others) in an infinite variety of creative ways.

Creative communication is a central dimension of Christian life and practice. We are a people given a story, gifted a medium, commissioned with a message, and imbued with creativity. What is praise and worship if not communications? In this regard, the modern church is in exceptional biblical company.

The Bible begins with God's intrinsic creative nature (Gen. 1). We are created in the image of a creative God (Gen. 1:26). Our cultural mandate is to cultivate and care for all God has created for us (Gen. 1:28). Unable to create from nothing, we work with what God has given us (Gen. 1:29). Our creative work is to take part in caring for and cultivating the earth (Gen. 2:15). Sin let entropy into the created order and therefore God's creation must be constantly revived (Gen. 4:6). God establishes this motif by communicating lasting meaning through symbolic creative beauty (Gen. 9:13–16).

We have been entrusted with this divine creation and creativity (Ps. 8:6). Our innate expressions of this creativity are revealed throughout Scripture in expansive mediums—from music to fine metal working (Gen. 4:21–22).[1] Our work is commissioned to have meaning beyond its utility (Ex. 28). These creative media expressions and their meanings are naturally shared and used to guide others (Ex. 15:20). This creativity and skill is not merely of our own nature as image bearers, but may be amplified by the Holy Spirit to accomplish God's design (Ex. 35:30–35). We also mediate our human, and often broken, experiences within our cultural forms (1 Sam. 18:6–7). Our craftsmanship and architecture matters because of what it communicates (1 Chron. 17, 22).

We are instructed to sing to God (1 Chron. 16:23). Our most primal and universal medium, music is at the center of key moments in life throughout the narrative of God's people: in meaningful relationships (Gen. 31:27; Luke 15:25); in significant ceremonies (2 Sam. 15:10; 1 Kings 1:39); in public celebrations (2 Sam. 6:5); to comfort and push back the darkness (1 Sam. 16:23); even when our songs become corrupted in our fallenness (Ex. 32:17–19). Jesus, Our Savior, sings intentionally with His community (Matt. 26:30; Mark 14:26). Likewise, His followers return the gift of song to God and in doing so minister to others (Acts 16:25).

We follow the one who is God perfectly imaged in our human context: Yeshua the Nazarene; Jesus of the Bible; the medium and the message of God (John 1:1–18).[2] The Son of Man[3] is introduced to us as the son of David (Matt. 1).[4] Beyond shepherd or ruler (1 Sam. 17:34; 2 Sam. 5), the progenitor of our Savior was an author, songwriter, poet, and musician (1 Sam. 16:15–18; 2 Sam. 23).[5]

Great communicators and artists populate the Bible as central characters: Isaiah was a poetic historian and creative orator (2 Chron. 32:32; Isa. 6:6–8); Solomon was a brilliant poet, songwriter, and writer of wisdom (1 Kings 4:29–34); The writer of Job applied the styles of a play, a novel, and of poetry (Job 3:1–27:23; 1:1–2:13; 38:1–42:6); Jeremiah lamented in poetry and prophetic drama (Jer. 8:18–9:6); Ezekiel and Hosea were creative orators and engaged prophetic drama (Ezek. 3:16–19; 7; Hos. 1); Most of the minor prophets wrote poetry (Joel 1–3; Amos 1–2; Obad. 1; Mic. 1; Nah. 1; Hab. 1; Zeph. 1); Jonah chose short story and poetry to tell his tale (Jonah 1:1–2; 2:2–9).

When we consider that the New Testament contains frequent quotations or allusions to the Psalms—which are songs, poetry, and creative expression—it is clear that these forms were vitally important for the apostles' self-understanding and critical for their worship and life of devoted obedience to Jesus. As such, the New Testament cannot be separated from the meaning rooted in the soil of the Psalms. Clearly, the New Testament writers saw themselves as living the drama of the Psalter, now brought to a stunning conclusion and given incredible and unforeseen depth of meaning in the person of Jesus.

Throughout the New Testament the people of God respond in poetry and song. Significantly, Luke records Mary's Magnificat (Luke 1:46–56) in our introduction to the incarnation. The mother of Jesus performs her own sung words in response to the blessing bestowed upon her. This song is a poetic verbalization of praise as a worshipful and prophetic reaction directly linking the history and character of God to the incarnation of God through her in Jesus Christ. Her specific words are a radical cultural expression in any context. We see again that the meanings embedded in lyric, poetry, and the medium of song are a central way that those living within the unfolding of the incarnation could express themselves and interpret their experience as part of the ongoing drama of God's activity in the world. Likewise, remembrance and community in common song, expressed in corporate singing to God, and grounded in the Psalms, is considered natural and expected practice (Rom. 15:9; 1 Cor. 14:15; Eph. 5:19; Col. 3:16; James 5:13; Rev. 5:9).

The gospel itself means "good news," which is a story to be communicated to all who will hear (Mark 16:15). The New Testament writers took up the spoken and written word in a multitude of forms: Matthew wrote a narrative that changed him as he composed it;[6] Mark wrote in memoir of Peter's self-denouncement (Mark 14:66–72);[7] Luke wrote a two-part biography; John wrote a creative nonfiction version of the gospel from the intimate understanding he shared with Jesus Himself;[8] Paul wrote beautiful, poetic, and elucidating letters; the writer of Hebrews wove the testaments together in creative grandeur, showing that Jesus is supreme over all; John wrote the illustrative, epic, dramatic finale to the canon—an apocalyptic revealing through language that situates us in time and space as we learn to hope for eternity.

Ever the craftsman, Jesus blended imagination, illustration, and style into His life and teaching at every turn. This blend resulted in the most meaningful, memorable, and transformative ministry messages, parables, and moments. Ultimately, at the center of the cross, at the height of Jesus' suffering, at the moment Christ bore the full weight of our sin, simple lyrics of lament from Psalm 22:1 were cried out, "My God, my God, why have you forsaken me?" That Jesus chose a lyric from the songs of David for this moment of ultimate pain should be enough to reassure us of the importance of media that ministers.

There simply is no narrative of God's work in the world without creative communication. The Bible is a physical compilation of mediums recorded and gifted to us. Equally so is the community of Christ followers as a culturally expressive, living memory, and eternal storage medium of ultimate meaning. Our message is the gospel (1 Cor. 15:3–4) and that specific testimony is to be backed by media that glorifies God and ministers to others in an infinite variety of creative ways.

MINISTRY MEDIA MATTERS

We were created to create. The expression of our collective ideals and their embodiment in material form externalizes as art, music, dance, plays, architecture, stories, speech, and other forms we call media. These forms create a mediated, symbolic reality. The influential media theorist James W. Carey makes a strong connection between our media and our reality.

> Reality is, above all, a scarce resource. . . . The fundamental form of power is the power to define, allocate, and display this resource. Once the blank canvas of the world is portrayed and featured, it is also preempted and restricted. Therefore, the site where artists paint, writers write, speakers speak, filmmakers film, broadcasters broadcast is simultaneously the site of social conflict over the real. . . . A critical theory of communication must affirm what is before our eyes and transcend it by imagining, at the very least, a world more desirable.[9]

As cocreators in the making of meaning that points to the ultimate reality—One that is making all things new, One that is the way out of the dark, One at work countervailing entropy and holding all things together (Col. 1:17)—we must take our communications, art, media, and technology seriously. Modern media possess nearly unrivaled influence over an individual's identity and reality. Due to the immense culture-making potential of art and media, ministry communicators must be among the most theologically trained and biblically grounded. The complexities of crafting theologically accurate messages using classic and modern media should not be underestimated.

As such, there is no good way to simply *add* arts and technology to an existing community's style of worship. In fact, thinking in additive language makes it all the more likely we won't achieve what we are hoping to accomplish. That is not how meaningful communications, media, and art happens. We need a fully inclusive, theological approach to our communicative efforts. Simply put, everything communicates—not just a spoken sermon or corporate music. From the preaching to the melody, to the lyrics, to the space, to the tech, to the way we position our bodies—everything communicates together in interrelationship to create the meaning of our messages.

The seminal media critic Marshall McLuhan made this point many times, later remembered by his son, Eric McLuhan:

> He was continually amazed at the reluctance, often the downright refusal, of people to pay attention to the effects of media, and at their hostility to him for what he revealed. They included those, clergy and lay, who enthusiastically embrace the latest technologies without regard for their effects. Such people are blindly eager to make the Mass or the sacraments, or the congregation the content of each new gadget or technology that comes along—in the interest of "bringing the Church up to date" and "making the Church relevant." They are quite innocent of the power of these forms to transform their users—innocent but not guiltless.[10]

When asked, "As a Christian, have you examined the effects that such a context has on the Church and, more precisely, on faith?" McLuhan answered, "I would prefer that most questions of that sort be dealt with by theologians, but they do not seem to be interested."[11]

THE MAKING OF MEANING

As natural communicators, everyone has a model for or perspective on communications and culture whether we recognize it or not. This perspective is shown in what we make. The way we understand what communications is and how it works or happens affects the content we create and the messages we make. Our communications theory affects our creativity. Theory shapes actuality. Theology drives praxis.

We apply our theology and communications theory every day. So, if our communications do not result as intended, then maybe we should look more deeply at what we believe. If nothing affects our reality as much as our communications, then we must take particular care that our theology and communications practices line up. To do this we begin with a commitment to a cohesive order:

Jesus > Bible > Theology > Communication Theory > Communication Practices

Unfortunately, given our place in communications history, many of us find ourselves merely applying existing modern techniques and best practices (usually borrowed from other fields such as entertainment or marketing) to our ministry messages without first properly aligning those practices to our theology and ultimately to the message and person of Jesus. Without clear biblical and theological connectivity, our messages will never mean what they were meant to. Our starting point cannot be about production values or better techniques for transmitting to an audience if our ministry media is to matter and minister in the way it is meant to. A distinct theology of communications, media, and art, as well as an accompanying framework for creating ministry media, is vital before employing any specific communications practices in a given community.

A COMMON MODEL FOR COMMUNICATIONS THEORY AND THEOLOGY

This is the Common Model for Communications Theory and Theology. Rooted in fundamental theological, historical, anthropological, biological, sociological, and psychological observations about human cultures and messages, the common model works broadly in any context, culture, or belief system. However, this model is completely theological in its function (as any good theory should be).

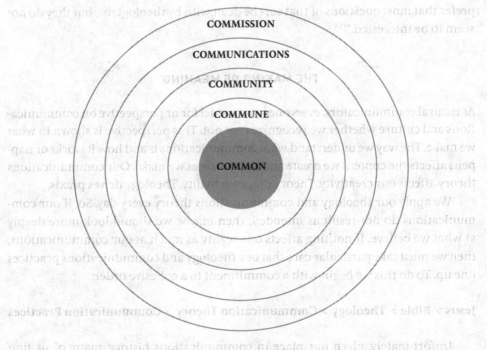

There is more than a verbal tie between the words "common," "commune," "community," and "communication"—all words with their roots in the same notion, "to make common." We come together around what we hold in common. In that, we begin to commune with one another around that common center. From that communion a community and its identity are formed. When a community begins to express its identity and beliefs, it externalizes in forms we recognize as communications (art and media). The communications of any given community have an innate reason for being, a purpose to accomplish—a commission. The result is expressions of every kind flowing from a common center of shared understanding and like-mindedness that creates cultural meaning.

The theological implications of the above should be readily apparent. The common model will not only aide in generating theologically accurate, meaningful ministry messages, but it can also ensure the cohesive order required. If there is a question about our communications, we should look to our community, and ultimately to our common center: Jesus. Likewise, we cannot let our attempts to accomplish our commission override or become detached from our communion, unrepresentative of our community, or not reflective of Jesus. What we believe about who Jesus is will affect the nature of our community and by extension our communications.

OUR COMMON CENTER

Our common center? Jesus Christ. We want to point to that truth and experience that meaning through the public witness of our communities in whatever forms we can. In John 14, Jesus proclaims that He is the way, the truth, and the life. The Greek word for "the truth" equally means "the reality." Jesus Himself is the better reality being made known. Not His words, but His person is The Way. Ministry media as reality revealing creativity is ultimately revealing Christ. He is who we are "to make common." All that we make must point to our common center, revealing the Truth to be Jesus Christ Himself.

In Jesus Christ, there is no distance or separation between medium and message. He is the one example where the medium and the message are fully one and the same. "In the beginning was the Word . . . " (John 1:1). What is the story all about? How is the story to be told? Simply, the Word (Heb. 1:2). From the very beginning God told the story with the Word (Gen. 1:1–3). In the Word all things are held together (Col. 1:15–20). Reality itself is bound by the Word.

God did not ultimately reveal Himself through projections or delivered doctrines, but by entering into human history and accompanying His people. The difference between transmission and transformation is Jesus Christ. Without Him at the center, whatever communications practices we choose will not ultimately matter. From Him flows our communications and ministry media to accomplish our Great Commission. Only then is the church a communion of love, a community of believers, and an agent of reconciliation.

What does this look like in practice? Jesus' first instructional words of ministry were an unconditional invitation, "Come and see" (John 1:39). From word one, it wasn't about convincing others to listen; it was about inviting them to see for themselves. In the same way, the Samaritan woman (John 4:28–30), whom Jesus chose to first fully reveal Himself as Christ and the beginning of His revelation beyond the Jewish people, spoke the first missionary words: "Come and see . . . Could this be Messiah?" Ministry media can function as an unfettered invitation for the world to come and see the Savior we bear witness to.

Can our Christology really shape our choices about art and technology in ministry? Let's use one of the most recent technological media marvels (as of this printing) as an example, virtual reality. Should we have virtual reality church services? "No!" might be the reaction. Why not? "Jesus was incarnate on earth so therefore we too must be physically present with others" may be the reasoning. Just that quickly we go from what we believe about Jesus Christ to a position on a specific modern medium in just two moves. Our theology can and should drive our media choices.

THE ESSENCE OF OUR COMMUNION

Christian theology is fully communal in nature. As children of the triune God we should both seek and provide insight into why communion is so vital. God clearly intends for us to have meaningful relationships. We were made in His image of communion—Father, Son, and Holy Spirit (Matt. 28:19)—beautifully distinct, yet perfectly unified. God desires a relationship with us and has gone to unfathomable lengths to communicate to us through Christ in order to make that relationship possible (John 3:16; Phil. 2:8). This intersects for us wherever two or more are gathered in His name, "I am there in their midst" (Matt. 18:20). Thus we come into the same space as Jesus in His name by our common union in Christ. In this way, we become integrated by the Spirit as one unified body (Eph. 4:4–6). A fundamental truth throughout Scripture is that we become like whatever or whomever we worship (Ps. 115:4–8), and it is impossible to effectively communicate to others something that we are not ourselves (Luke 6:43–45).

To find each other and share is one of our most fundamental human impulses. Communion literally means sharing, or more specifically, the sharing of intimate thoughts and feelings on a mental or spiritual level. The intimacy of our sharing is what generates meaningful human interaction and that meaning transforms the interaction into communion. We know through our personal experiences within relationships that connections can speak volumes more than any words. In turn, those connections are overwhelmingly the inspiration for our media. Our

Christian relationships in the context of the gospel shape us most deeply. So, if everything communicates, then perhaps communing speaks to us the loudest.

What we do when together is what makes up the essence of our communing. What the church decides to participate in as we congregate is what we call liturgy, most simply translated as "the work of the people." This work is itself a type of medium and thereby transcends mere interpersonal communications or isolated technical execution of media. Something truly special is made possible in the ritual of the church gathering and communing—something held together and communicated via our liturgies.

Every congregation has a liturgy whether it is called that or not. All church practice is by nature communication: art and media (sermons, songs, public speaking, sacraments, dramas, rituals, bulletins, call-and-response, video, audio) and the basis of our public doxology. Therefore, liturgy is the bonding agent, the cellular root of all ministry communications. If we are talking about church production styles, then we are talking about liturgy, and if we are talking about liturgy we are talking about theology (doxology). Again, our practices must follow our theology so that those practices represent our theology. A proper theology of communications (especially when applied to the local church) is far more than a combination of old and new. More than the best of tradition and transmission, more than stylistic preferences, it is the complex interaction of material and immaterial spaces; of orality and electricity; of humanity and deity. The practices of a church are rituals that reaffirm our unity and the gospel of Christ. Likewise, ministry media can function as rich, meaningful experiences that remind us who we are, call us to serve God, and revive us to respond to that call.

THE CHARACTER OF OUR COMMUNITY

When our communing grows in numbers, structure, and time we become a community. Christocentric community should take on a unique character from the distinctively meaningful relationships and identity that form us. If we follow Christ's example and begin our messaging with "Come and see," there must be something the hearer may come to see. What they see there communicates in concert with any messages or worship heard within. Therefore, the character of our community shapes the meaning of our messages and is itself a primary kind of ministry media. Any real theology of communications is an ecclesiology of community.

God intends to image forth His kingdom through His beloved community: the reconciled and transformed body of Christ. We are to be the realization of divine love in lived social relation (John 13:34–35). The wonder (Acts 2:22) and power

(Rom. 1:16) of the gospel is not meant to be in a metaphorical sense or in spirit. The church is to physically, actively, and creatively represent a new reality being made known.[12] We are to live as if the world is already as it will one day be: "on earth as it is in heaven" (Matt. 6:10).

As such, a church community is a message for better or worse. Just as it is between individuals, it is with groups: the personal medium is vastly more powerful than the message of the conveyed words. Obviously the meanings of our transmitted messages are overwhelmingly affected by the degree to which they are represented in lived reality. Transmitted messages, no matter how excellent and compelling, without physical representation are simply not complete communication. God's perfect design for communications prioritizes the localized environment of worship and cultural production as the vehicle for the gospel message to be lived out. The local church should be a primary way meaning gets into us, into our culture, and from there into our creative expressions.

The church community is a living ecosystem, being experienced. Not a production or a performance, not a fantasy or false reality. These experiences are what we live. They are what we remember. When we experience together, we remember together, we recreate reality together, we rebuild, we repair entropy's spiritual effects. In this way, the role of the church is *anamnesis*—meaning a lived memory. The local church (and by extension the Holy Spirit) has its own type of storage medium in itself as God's chosen agent of connection, transfer of meaning, and interpretative guide. The printed Bible is not our only media, and it certainly doesn't fully communicate absent the Holy Spirit and the church.

The Sunday gathering should be awakening people anew each week to the grand purpose we were created for (2 Peter 1:3–8), the ministry of reconciliation we are called to (2 Cor. 5:11–21), and the kingdom we now live within (John 17:16). The Sunday gathering does not merely instruct the church how to go back to the broader culture and simply manage or do better at it. Instead, we are invited into a new beloved community immune from the pressures of the world because of the shared identity and reality we possess in Christ.

What does this look like in practice? Jesus formed a radically new kind of community around Him that shattered and inverted the world's existing categories—one that was an invitational, prayerful, missional, didactic, dialogical, sacrificial, inclusive, challenging, cross-cultural, countercultural, restorative, otherworldly, God-centered, people on the move. The character of His community communicated as much about who He was as His messages (Luke 15:2; 7:34).

THE NATURE OF OUR COMMUNICATIONS

As a community externalizes its ideals, the fruit of its communing manifests in cultural forms we recognize as communications—art, music, dance, plays, architecture, sculptures, stories, speech. We have been gifted with the ability to make most anything into a medium. From a scribbled line to a global web of technology, if we can imbue it with meaning that others can later retrieve, then whatever it is can become media—be it online social networks or community quilts, digital production and projection or bulletins and flannelgraphs, fine art or all the ordinary communications tools.

This means that, historically, every liturgy, sculpture, song, sermon written or preached, devotional and curriculum, building and decoration, everything in our museums—all of it is ministry media. These artifacts are extensions of the localized Christian community and the storehouses of meaning for the church. Ministry media matters. It has always mattered deeply, and now in the "mediated age" it matters more than ever.

Every culture produces recognizable forms of communications, art, technology, and media. Our communication is our culture and there is no culture without communication. Communications and culture are inextricably linked. In this way, there is no such thing as communicating *to* a culture. We are a part of a given culture by the act of communicating within it. At that moment we are cocreating and negotiating meanings. Here again is why we cannot merely add art and technology to our existing practices—at least not without risking a separation of those messages from their meaning, turning participants into audiences, audiences into attenders, and attenders into consumers.

We now have an immense array of media technologies available to us, as well as exposure to a global library of art and media styles that spans human history. However, a right theology of communications must be useful and relevant in any time, in any language, and in any manner of poverty or wealth. While we may have the resources to employ all forms of media technology, we must be certain that our techniques don't distract from the message, corrupt the message, or become the message.

In our efforts to use media to proclaim the gospel and minister to the needs of others, the challenge we face is that we can often be too eager to adopt technology for its potential to amplify our reach without recognizing the consequences the technologies and media can have on a culture. If communication is our culture, then our media can be seen as part of our cultural ecosystem. These media environments are more difficult to see, and therefore all the more reason we must navigate them with proper theology.

As technology, it is tempting to view things like audio, video, or internet technologies as nothing more than neutral vehicles. Or culturally, it is tempting to interpret one type of technology or one style of expression as either solution or corruption. Both are a misunderstanding of how communications work—putting undue focus on the specific technology or style and not enough on those we are communicating with and the meanings created in interrelationship with media. Our media are not just technical amplifiers, but more like extensions of ourselves, our emotions, our concepts, and even our central-nervous systems. A technology may be neutral with respect to its moral intent but is far from neutral in its effect on a message and meaning. The technology shapes and communicates.

That is to say, technological change is not additive but ecological. A new medium in the living ecosystem does not add something to the community; it changes everything. This clearly has immense implications for the life of the church. This theologically informed media ecology puts us in a position to shape the time and space we live in by offering new or different ways of communicating—new environments—that can then change the nature of those we come in contact with and the culture we are a part of. It gives us eyes to see what and how cultural artifacts may bring about flourishing.

The communications practices of our church communities should grow organically out of the lives and culture they are in while free to incorporate and remix the expressions of the global church. Therefore, a theology of communications may not be able to define a specific practice for us, but it must certainly determine the nature of what we are to be communicating.

What does this look like in practice? Jesus' life, message, death, resurrection, ascension, and intercession is the good news. The gospel itself models not just the great lengths God went to in order to enter our environment and communicate with us for our transformation. The gospel also exemplifies the complexity of complete communications when seen in its biblical and historical entirety. Simply reflect on the symbolic meaning of that brutal-turned-beautiful piece of technology, the cross.

Can a theology of communications actually make choices about art and technology in church? Applying a theology of communications simply begins with knowing what the meaningful forms of communications, art, and technology are to the culture of a given community. Then that group already knows which forms of expression they should be investing in. While there are fundamental communication practices and established styles, they can be expressed in an infinite variety of creative ways. This will look different from one culture to another. As with most things in ministry, looking to the people in a church is always more powerful than searching for the latest self-professed guru's advice or chasing perceived success strategies of other communities.

THE QUALITY OF OUR COMMISSION

A community and the message it represents is not complete without purpose, a mission. To give a community a mission is to commission them to that purpose. That commission originates from their common center. The message cannot be rightly interpreted without knowing its reason for being or who sent it.

The quality of our commission is affected by the nature of our modern electric mass communications technologies. The electric message has no body, no being. Our media literally "dis-incarnates" us from our messages and our meanings. The incarnate example of Jesus means a disincarnate world should be of great concern to the church. Jesus communicated via intimacy with obedience to the Father, which provided the basis for His communication with us and therefore is the basis for our witness—embodied, grounded, and missional.

To do so means our ministry communications must also serve to (re)ground us into this present reality and realign us to God's redemptive purpose. Our reality is consistently broken down by people who are lost physically and spiritually due to the natural, unceasing decay of the created order; reality then must constantly be repaired. One of the ways we combat this breakdown is through our communications and by extension our art and media. In this way, we produce, maintain, repair, and transform the ways we understand and experience reality. Therefore, we need to relentlessly speak truth into existence and into each other's lives in an infinite variety of creative ways.

Or more specifically, to revive or wake up! That is what revival is—waking up to a better reality being made known. We are all to keep at the unceasing work of rebuilding to the best of our small capacity, confident we are a part of something infinitely, unstoppably greater than ourselves. We make a statement about what can and should be by our creating. In other words, we critique by creating. Our critique of the breakdown of the world should be entirely creative. In this way we make better thoughts, attitudes, beliefs, and even our identity and reality possible by speaking them into existence (Matt. 5:13–16). More than that, through creativity we make something else vital possible—invitation. No person or culture can change without the invitation to put aside one way for a better way. Unfettered creation, invitation, and inclusion—this is the rhythm of revival.

Ultimately the invitation into a better, truer reality is a call to repentance and alignment with God's intended purpose through Christ. The good news undoes all falsehoods and invites us into truth that is far greater. Change comes through greater creativity, accompanied by an invitation to participation. That means that we ought not walk away from the world, but should have the courage to invite God's redeeming presence into it and expose the darkness:

For you were once darkness, but now you are light in the Lord; walk as children of light. . . . all things become visible when they are exposed by the light, for everything that becomes visible is light. For this reason it says,

> "Awake, sleeper,
> And arise from the dead,
> And Christ will shine on you." (Eph. 5:8–14)

Can our missiology really shape our choices about art and technology in church? To illustrate, what is the visual representation of a community? How would one best illustrate or describe it to someone who has never heard of church? What are we inviting them into? If a video was made of a church's ministry, what would it reveal? Would it be images of electric lights or sacrificial servants? Would it be a story or a promotion? Would the viewer feel welcomed or unrepresented? Or how much time does the average person spend looking at a screen vs. a physical person while in church? Are they listening to preaching or watching a disembodied, projected message?

CONCLUSION

More technological tools are available for ministry than ever before. Likewise, the issues surrounding media use in ministry have become increasingly complicated and costly. Few understand how media affects a message or a community. Some fall into the trap of using it "just because it is there." Others avoid important expressions because they seem out of reach or unfamiliar. Seemingly more and more screens, wires, amps, and lighting are finding their way into churches, while at the same time trends suggest a generation shifting away from media-saturated styles of worship. Fortunately, a theology of communications can go a long way toward demystifying media's power and simplifying the extent to which media matters to any given cause, community, or context.

Here are three principles for application in today's church:

1. Enlist theologically trained media artists and creative directors in the church as worship leaders. Never underestimate the complexities of crafting theologically accurate messages using media that has the intended reception. The reasons for choosing one media form over another or how a medium changes a message by its very nature requires skilled caretakers of the message to guide the creative process. Find these content creators and empower them to cultivate the creativity of the community. Think of the worship leader role to encompass the entirety of the community's communications (not just music) in ways that are shaped by a theology of communication.

2. Draw from the stories and experiences of the community. Rather than looking for examples from popular culture (Christian or otherwise) reclaim the power of testimonies and bond it with the power of media. The narrative that God is weaving in a specific space and place should be the driving force behind a media philosophy. This roots media decisions in the ethos and praxis of a community. Testimony is organic, natural, and often simply needs to be recorded and shared. All honest and healthy communities have compelling stories of God at work to testify.

3. Do not feed the consumers. Within a consumer culture it is easy to fall (even unintentionally) into the business of entertaining congregants or marketing messages. As receivers of media it is easy to fall into the habits of merely consuming—diffusing the impact via choosing to be entertained—rather than being open to what God would say through the messages. It would be better to have no media in a church than to perpetuate passive consumption patterns.

Above all, remember that everything communicates. Resist the urge or pressure to follow trends or utilize every possible medium. Media use should be simple, if not invisible, and make sense to the community and the world around it. Aim communications to radiate outward from the common center of Jesus Christ and the gospel. In doing so, all media will point back inward to that central identity.

NOTES

1. Are modern technological tools made of metals and sand fresh forms of "tools of bronze and iron"?

2. See also John 14:9; Col 1:15; Col 3:10; Heb 1:3; Rev. 1:12–16.

3. Matt. 20:28; 8:20; 9:6; 11:19; 16:13; 18:11; 20:28; 24:27; Mark 8:38; Luke 18:8; John 1:51; 5:27; 6:53; 12:23; 13:31; Acts 7:56; Rev. 1:13.

4. Also Matt. 12:23; 25:22; 21:9; Mark 10:48; 12:35; John 7:42; Rom. 1:3; 2 Tim. 2:8; Rev. 5:5.

5. Seventy-five of the Psalms are attributed to David.

6. Eugen Rosenstock-Huessy, *The Fruit of Lips: Of Why Four Gospels?* (Eugene, OR: Wipf and Stock Publishers, 1978), 23. Eugen is referencing the perspective difference evident between Matthew 1:1, 21, and the way he writes in chapter 28.

7. Ibid., 33–34.

8. Ibid., 35.

9. James W. Carey and G. Stuart Adam, *Communication as Culture, Revised Edition: Essays on Media and Society* (New York: Routledge, 1992), 87–88.

10. Eric McLuhan, Introduction to Marshall McLuhan, *The Medium and the Light: Reflections on Religion and Media* (Eugene, OR: Wipf & Stock Pub, 2010), xxiii.

11. Ibid, 45.

12. Brian Kammerzelt, "3. Be Agents of Change," The Just Life, September 13, 2010, https://thejustlife.org/3-be-agents-of-change-59b46667af53.

Baptizing a Christian

ERIC MOORE

THEOLOGICAL FOUNDATION

One does not have to read too far into the New Testament to realize that baptism plays a significant role in the life of God's people. In the gospel of Mark, we see that "John the Baptist appeared in the wilderness, preaching a baptism of repentance for the forgiveness of sins" (Mark 1:4). John was preparing the people for the coming of the Messiah. Although this baptism was important and served a key purpose in the life of Israel, it is different from the believer's baptism that was inaugurated after Christ rose from the dead.

Jesus stated in Matthew 28:18–20, "All authority in heaven and on earth has been given to me. Therefore go and make disciples of all nations, baptizing them in the name of the Father and of the Son and of the Holy Spirit, and teaching them to obey everything I have commanded you. And surely I am with you always, to the very end of the age" (NIV). This baptism was not in preparation of the coming of the Messiah, but it was to identify with the death, burial, and resurrection of the Messiah.

John the Baptist was a transitional figure. He was a bridge between the Old and New Testament. His baptism was for the purpose of preparation of the Messiah. Once Jesus Christ completed His mission on earth, there was no longer a need for John's baptism. This is evident in Acts 19. Paul asks a group of individuals about the type of baptism they had received. They responded that they had received the baptism of John. To that, Paul replied, "John baptized with the baptism of repentance, telling the people to believe in Him who was coming after him, that is, in Jesus" (Acts 19:4–5).

Since John proclaimed that his baptism was for the repentance of sin (Luke 3:3), it might seem strange that Jesus approached John to be baptized by him. This even confused John, so he stated that he needed to be baptized instead by Jesus. Of course, Jesus, who was sinless, had no need to repent. Jesus chose to be baptized for at least three reasons. First, He wanted to identify with the people. Although He did not need to repent, He identified with sinners who did. Second, His baptism symbolized what He would experience later in His life and ministry. Just as a believer in Jesus Christ looks back to the cross, Jesus was looking forward to the cross He would bear for the sins of the world. Third, it was the commissioning of His earthly ministry.

When Jesus came up out of the water, three remarkable things occurred. The heavens opened, the Holy Spirit descended upon Him as a dove, and God the Father spoke from heaven. Any of these events would be significant in and of themselves; however, all three make a resounding statement. The heavens opening alludes to the dream of Jacob where he envisioned angels ascending and descending into heaven (Gen. 28:10–16). In fact, Jesus told Nathaniel that he would see the heavens open and angels ascending and descending upon the Son of Man (John 1:49–51).

The Holy Spirit descending upon Jesus demonstrated the glory of God resting upon the Son. Jesus was being anointed by God for the task that lay ahead of Him. God, the Father proclaimed His approval of His Son by stating, "This is My beloved Son, in whom I am well pleased" (Matt. 3:17). The Father's approval identified Him as the one sent by God. He was the prophet that Israel had been waiting for (Deut. 18:18). All three members of the Trinity were clearly present and in approval of the commissioning of Jesus for His earthly ministry. This event is the connection that bridges the gap of John's baptism and the believer's baptism. Jesus was baptized under the old system but with the new liberty of grace in mind.

VIEWS ON BAPTISM

There are differing views on baptism. In fact, Thomas Schreiner wrote, "When a matter like baptism has been debated for so long without consensus among Christians, it is tempting to conclude that further discussion is fruitless."[1] The three views of baptism that dominate the Protestant landscape are infant baptism of the children of the covenant, baptismal regeneration, and believer's baptism.

INFANT BAPTISM

In this view, baptism is a sign of the covenant in its fulfillment just as circumcision was the sign of that covenant in the time of promise. Its primary function is not to symbolize our response to the promise of the gospel, but to signify and seal the gospel to which we are called (by the word and the symbol) to respond in lifelong faith and repentance. This is as applicable to infants as it is to others without compromising its significance.[2] Congregational, Presbyterian, and Reformed churches tend to espouse this view of baptism.

BAPTISMAL REGENERATION

Those who hold the view of baptismal regeneration believe that baptism saves the person being baptized. The person might be an infant or an adult. Often, 1 Peter 3 is quoted to regarding the justification of this view:

> The patience of God kept waiting in the days of Noah, during the construction of the ark, in which a few, that is, eight persons, were brought safely through the water. Corresponding to that, baptism now saves you—not the removal of dirt from the flesh, but an appeal to God for a good conscience— through the resurrection of Jesus Christ, who is at the right hand of God, having gone into heaven, after angels and authorities and powers had been subjected to him. (vv. 20–22)

It is believed that just as in the days of Noah, eight were saved through the water, the same is true today. Noah was a prophetic representation of what God was going to do when He conveyed His promise to His people through His Word in baptismal form.[3] God saves through faith by the means of baptism.

Martin Luther, in his *Short Catechism*, asks the following question in his section on the sacrament of holy baptism: "How can water do such great things?" He answers, "It is not the water indeed that does them, but the word of God which is in and with the water, and faith, which trusts such word of God in the water."[4]

BELIEVER'S BAPTISM

Believer's baptism is the view that a person is baptized after he has placed his faith in the person and work of Jesus Christ for salvation. Romans 6 states, "Or don't you know that all of us who were baptized into Christ Jesus were baptized into his death? We were therefore buried with him through baptism into death in order that, just as Christ was raised from the dead through the glory of the Father, we too may live a new life" (Rom. 6:3–4 NIV).

As the apostle Paul lays out his argument for living a sanctified life, he reminds his readers that those who are in Christ had symbolically died with Christ when they were baptized. Paul closely connects baptism with the salvation experience in verse 4, but it is not a cause of salvation. Baptism depicts that aspect of the Christian's conversion that unites him to Christ, especially to Christ in His death. It is an outward expression of saving faith and the solemn symbol of dying with Christ.[5]

Baptism tends to be one of the first acts of obedience after salvation. Once a person has placed his faith in the person and work of Jesus Christ, the most natural next step is to be baptized. This is made clear in the encounter that Philip had with the Ethiopian eunuch in Acts 8. Philip has the wonderful opportunity to share the good news of Jesus Christ with the Ethiopian statesman. He had come to Jerusalem for the Passover and was in the process of returning home. When Philip preaches the gospel to him, the question that proceeds from his mouth is, "Look! Water! What prevents me from being baptized?" (Acts 8:36–38).

The Ethiopian eunuch demonstrated that the first step of obedience is an act of faith. It showed that he wanted to identify with Jesus. Therefore, it is a good idea to teach the person who is getting baptized the significance of water baptism as stated in the first two paragraphs of this section.

BAPTISMAL QUESTIONS

NUMBER OF BAPTISMS

One of the questions that often arises when a person has accepted Christ at an early age and then rededicates his life to Jesus later in life is whether they should get re-baptized. Some Christian denominations argue that if a person believes that he lost his salvation and is coming back to the Lord in faith, then the person should consider being re-baptized. If one believes in eternal security, then there is no need to be re-baptized if one made a clear profession of faith as a young person. The person was living in a backslidden state but had not lost his salvation. So, a rededication of the heart is probably all that is needed. However, if the person had not truly trusted Jesus for salvation earlier in his life, then baptism is the natural next step in following Christ.

WATER BAPTISM VS. SPIRIT BAPTISM

New believers are often confused about the relationship between water baptism and the baptism of the Holy Spirit. Although this chapter does not address the baptism of (by or in) the Holy Spirit directly, it needs to be addressed for the purpose of clarity. The passage in Scripture that generally prompts this confusion is Acts 8. The good news of Jesus Christ had begun to spread out of Jerusalem to Judea and Samaria just as Jesus predicted. The Samaritans began to place their faith in Jesus Christ for salvation. Prior to this, the Jews and the Samaritans had very little to do with one another. Jews would travel around Samaria to get from Judea to Galilee. Peter and John were sent from the young church in Jerusalem to get a firsthand account of what was happening in this region.

When Peter and John arrived, they prayed for the Samaritan believers. They prayed that they might receive the Holy Spirit. According to Acts 8:16–17, the reason they prayed this prayer was because "the Holy Spirit had not yet come upon any of them; they had simply been baptized in the name of the Lord Jesus. Then Peter and John placed their hands on them, and they received the Holy Spirit" (NIV). This would appear on the surface to indicate that a person can be saved and yet not be "baptized, filled or indwelt" with the Holy Spirit. Thus, the confusion of the new believer.

There are two key things to know about Acts. First, Acts is a transitional book. It provides a narrative of how the church was birthed and established. It tells the story of what transpired between the time of Jesus' resurrection and the establishment of Jew and/or Gentile churches. In fact, it is the narrative of Acts 1:8, "But you will receive power when the Holy Spirit has come upon you; and you shall be My witnesses both in Jerusalem, and in all Judea, and Samaria, and as far as the remotest part of the earth." Second, Acts is descriptive as opposed to being prescriptive. The book of Acts tells us "what happened." It does not tell us what "should happen" in the church. The general and Pauline Epistles provide that instruction for us.

As a descriptive and transitional book, this section of Scripture shows us "how" God united the Jewish Christians with the Samaritan Christians. Peter and John had the wonderful privilege of observing the same Holy Spirit that rested on Jesus and the same Holy Spirit that filled them be received by the Samaritans. The Lord delayed the receiving of the Holy Spirit for the purpose of uniting two groups of people in Jesus Christ.

Today, water baptism is an external picture of Spirit baptism. When a person places her faith in Jesus Christ for salvation, the Holy Spirit of God indwells the believer (Rom. 8:9) and she is baptized in the Spirit (1 Cor. 12:13). There is no need to try to coordinate the two baptisms or wait for the Spirit's baptism. Nor does one have to get baptized by water to receive the Holy Spirit. At the moment of salvation, the Holy Spirit does His work. Then, at the appropriate time, the internal work of God is depicted through the external sign of baptism.

IN WHOSE NAME?

Another concern for those who are getting baptized or have recently been baptized is the formula that is to be pronounced over them as they are being baptized. This concern is usually the result of reading what Jesus stated in Matthew 28:19, "Go, therefore, and make disciples of all the nations, baptizing them in the name of the Father and the Son and the Holy Spirit." This passage would indicate that a pronouncement should be something along the lines of, "I baptize you in the name of the Father and the Son and the Holy Spirit." This fits with what Jesus told His apostles to do.

However, when we look Acts, there is no such formula being stated regarding baptism. In fact, on several occasions another statement is commonly used surrounding the baptismal event. Acts 8:16 speaks of individuals being baptized in the name of the Lord Jesus. In Acts 10:48, Peter ordered that Cornelius and his family be baptized in the name of Jesus Christ. In Acts 19:5, the disciples of John the Baptist believed and were baptized in the name of the Lord Jesus.

From passages like these some have concluded that the formula to be pronounced over the person being baptized is more in accord of, "I baptize you in the name of the Lord Jesus Christ" (or a variant of this; Lord Jesus, Jesus Christ or Jesus). This has caused some confusion and encouraged some previously baptized individuals to be re-baptized with the "correct" formula.

Several things need to be addressed regarding this issue. First, there is no confusion on the part of Jesus and the apostles. If anybody understood what Jesus meant, it would be the first-century apostles who heard directly from the risen Savior. Second, nowhere in the New Testament do we have a step-by-step instruction manual on the necessary ingredients of an acceptable baptismal event. Third, there is no place in Scripture where we observe an apostle or anyone else reciting a formula during a baptism.

So how do we reconcile the two sets of passages? In Matthew 28, Jesus was directing His apostles to continue the process of making disciples. They were to do so by going, baptizing, and teaching. As Jesus was returning to His Father in heaven, He would send the Holy Spirit to lead, comfort, and empower them. The name of the Father, Son, and Holy Spirit communicated the tri-unity of God; three in one. The collective authority of the triune God would be with them as they moved out to make disciples for Jesus.

The statements in Acts regarding water baptism and the name of Jesus refer to the reason for which the individual was baptized. A person's name stood for his character. This is true with regard to Jesus' name. A person who was baptized in the name of Jesus was a person who identified with Jesus and believed the purpose for which Jesus came. They identified with His death, burial, and resurrection. The character of Jesus was trustworthy and therefore, they identified with Him in baptism.

In fact, there may have been no formula pronounced during the early church's baptism ceremonies. It was more important that the person understood why they were getting baptized than it was that a formula was pronounced. The formula was probably more for the observers than the individual being baptized. They should already know why and in whom they are being baptized. Therefore, the matter of using a single or threefold name at the moment of water baptism should be left to the discretion of individual churches.

BAPTISMAL PRACTICES

BAPTISM CLASS

It is helpful if the minister has a class to explain the significance and the logistics of the baptismal event. There are a few things that should be addressed in the class. First, it is an opportunity to make sure (to the best of the pastor's ability) that the individual who desires to be baptized is a genuine believer in Jesus Christ. The course itself is an excellent tool for evangelism. Often a person will come to the class because they think that baptism saves them, or they think getting baptized will please God, or they think baptism is the right thing to do. It is good that he or she has a desire to be baptized, but the desire is often for the wrong reason. In this class, the minister has an open door to present the gospel.

After the person's spiritual state has been established, the significance of the event should be thoroughly explained. Normally, this will include an explanation to the person receiving baptism, and to their parent(s) if they are young, about why a person gets baptized.

First, the minister would do well to show in Scripture the connection between faith and baptism. He should clearly show that water alone or a church ritual has no bearing on a person's spiritual status before God. Salvation is a matter of faith. What is done in the water of baptism is an outward sign of inner faith.

Second, baptism is commanded by our Lord and Savior Jesus Christ. In Matthew 28:18–20, Jesus states, "All authority has been given to Me in heaven and on earth. Go, therefore, and make disciples of all the nations, baptizing them in the name of the Father and the Son and the Holy Spirit, teaching them to follow all that I commanded you; and behold, I am with you always, to the end of the age." Although Jesus does not explain the purpose of baptism in this statement, it establishes that this is something that the Lord desires His disciples should practice. It is a command by which believers demonstrate their obedience to His lordship in their life. Obedience does not save, but this is an obedient step of faith on the new believer's part.

Third, water baptism identifies the new believer with the death, burial, and resurrection of Jesus Christ. Just as Jesus died for the believer's sin and rose from the grave, demonstrating His power over death, the believer in Jesus has also died with Christ and been resurrected to a new life in Him. Paul stated,

> Or do you not know that all of us who have been baptized into Christ Jesus have been baptized into His death? Therefore we have been buried with Him through baptism into death, so that, just as Christ was raised from the dead through the glory of the Father, so we too might walk in newness of life. For if we have become united with Him in the likeness of His death, certainly we shall also be in the likeness of His resurrection. (Rom. 6:3–5)

No matter which tradition the minister follows, a class on baptism will help the participant or their parents understand the significance of the occasion.

BAPTISMAL SERVICE

When it comes to the actual baptism service or event, there are several variables to consider. As stated earlier, there is no prescribed way to hold a baptismal service. However, there are some standard practices that could be of benefit to the officiant.

Many churches will hold a separate service specifically for the individuals being baptized. Often this is an early morning service before the normal worship service or in the afternoon afterwards. The purpose of this stand-alone service is to focus all the attention on the individuals being baptized. These types of baptismal services are often held on Sunday. However, some churches will have an annual outdoor baptism at a lake or pool during the warmer months in addition to what is normally done during the year at the church facility. This is often viewed as one of the highlights of the church's calendar. In some ways it connects the church with the outdoor baptismal event of Jesus.

Other churches integrate the baptismal event into the normal worship service. Usually this is accomplished by either eliminating an aspect of the service such as the "meet and greet" and replacing it with the baptism. The benefit of this is that more witnesses attend. As the church grows numerically, more members will be available to welcome the new believers into the family of God. On the other hand, it can be rushed due to the need to keep the worship service moving.

Many churches will give those being baptized the opportunity to give their testimony just prior to being baptized. During the baptism class, the candidate is coached to keep the testimony short (two to three minutes) and to state the key aspects of how he or she came to faith in Jesus Christ and why they have chosen to be baptized. This accomplishes three things. First, it reminds the candidate why he or she is about to be baptized. Second, it informs the congregation of how God has been working in this individual's life and how He might be working in the lives of others. Third, it is a witness to any unbelievers in attendance. Candidates should be encouraged to invite unsaved friends, neighbors, coworkers, and family members to the event. There are churches who do not allow the candidates to share. However, this might be an aspect of baptism that should be considered.

In more traditional churches, the minister or clergy performs the actual baptism. If he is assisted, it is normally by another clergy member. However, some churches have moved away from this practice. The minister still oversees the process, but he is often assisted by a family member such as the mother or father of a child. Or he is assisted by a friend or family member responsible for the individual placing their faith in Jesus Christ. As the Bible is silent about who is to perform the baptismal act, many have used this freedom to invite other believers in Christ whom God has used to play a part in the person's spiritual growth to participate.

As with any practice, the liberty can be taken too far. Every occurrence of baptism in Scripture is performed by a believer in Jesus Christ. There are not instances of an unbeliever baptizing a believer. So, one must take caution if an unbelieving parent wants to participate in the event. With this said, it will be left to the discretion of the ministerial official. He may feel that as long as he is overseeing the event, the parent can participate. On the other hand, he may feel it is inappropriate. Either way, this should be discussed in the baptismal class.

Logistically, there are a few things that should be considered. In more traditional settings, a baptismal robe is often worn for the purpose of uniformity and modesty. In our contemporary church culture, the formality is often lifted. With this comes the potential for an unintentional lack of modesty. Often this is because baptism is a onetime event for the candidate, so they are not experienced with what it will do to the appearance of their clothing. This is why it is important for the minister to instruct both women and men on the proper clothing to wear.

Simple instructions about practical matters are helpful, such as the need to bring a towel to the baptismal event. If the baptism is held at the church, then towels can be provided. If it is at a park, pool, or lake, then the candidate should be encouraged to bring one. Remember that once the candidate is immersed in the water, clothing becomes clingy, and white clothing is for all practical purposes transparent. This should be addressed prior to baptism.

Another item of discussion is the position and assistance of the candidate in the baptismal process. It is normally assumed (incorrectly) that a smaller person cannot baptize a larger individual. This is not the case. The water is a friend and gives great support to the one doing the baptizing. As long as the candidate provides a relatively stiff body and a place to hold, the mechanics of baptism are fairly simple. The candidate and the baptizer should enter water that is just above the waist if possible. The candidate should cross his arms across his chest or pinch his nose with one hand and grab his arm with his other hand. The baptizer should place one hand firmly on the candidate's back. The other hand should grip one of the candidate's folded arms. At the proper time the baptizer should push the candidate backwards into the water. After the candidate is fully immersed, he should be pulled upward. The water will help him to stand up.

In some cases, the candidate will choose to be baptized face forward. Once again, there is no step-by-step process laid out in Scripture. So, this option is available for those who are afraid of the water and would like to see themselves enter the water.

A question that has been posed is, "Can somebody get baptized if there is not enough water in an area?" Although a situation might occur where this is a real concern, this is usually not the case. However, in that situation water should probably be used symbolically in the ritual.

PROPER AGE

Often parents are concerned about the proper age for their child to be baptized. Parents who are zealous for their child to be in good standing with the Lord may want their child baptized as soon as they have trusted in Christ. Others do not want to act too hastily because the baptism may happen too early in the child's spiritual development. Some churches delay the baptism of any child to the age of twelve. The rationale is that a twelve-year-old has enough reasoning to understand why he wants to be baptized. But should this be a hard and fast rule to adhere to? It is easy and clean, but not necessarily the best.

When children were brought to Jesus "so that He might lay His hands on them and pray," the disciples tried to stop them. But Jesus' answer was "Leave the children alone, and do not forbid them to come to Me; for the kingdom of heaven belongs to such as these" (Matt. 19:13–14). Children were brought to Jesus. A causal reading might imply that the parents were responsible for the children coming to Jesus. However, Jesus' response suggests that the children wanted to come to Jesus and not that the parents brought them. "Leave the children alone" and "Do not forbid" implies that the children were coming on their own. If a child has a clear understanding of who Jesus is and what He has done for him or her, there seems to be no reason to hinder them being baptized. Now a mother or father may want to delay baptism for other reasons, but the reason should not be made primarily because of the age of the youth.

CHURCH MEMBERSHIP

Some churches have membership policies that preclude a person who has not been baptized from formally joining their local church. This is a church practice based upon the constitutional guidelines of that local assembly of believers. The Bible itself does not have a policy on this subject.

Jesus instructed His followers to make disciples (Matt. 28:19). The disciple-making process includes baptism. If placing one's faith in Jesus Christ places Him into the universal church and the local church is to reflect that reality, then the details of when water baptism happens (before or after joining a local church) is moot. The question is whether the person is following Christ. If they are following Christ, then baptism will be a natural step in the growth process of the believer.

CONCLUSION

There are many significant moments in the life of a pastor. He is often the first one (outside of the immediate family) at the hospital when a child is born. He is often the last one at the cemetery when a loved one is put to rest. Often, he is the one called when a dear church member falls ill. Couples will even change their wedding date just to have their beloved pastor perform the ceremony. All these events are unique and special in their own way. However, there is nothing like baptizing a new believer. It is a blessing to participate in this momentous step of faith for this individual. To experience the joy that exudes from the face of the believer as he or she rises out of the water is one of the greatest highlights of being a pastor.

NOTES

1. Thomas Schreiner and Shawn Wright, *Believer's Baptism: Sign of the New Covenant in Christ* (Nashville: B&H Publishing, 2006), 67.

2. David Wright, *Baptism: Three Views* (Downers Grove, IL: IVP Academic, 2009), 104.

3. Robert Kolb, *Understanding Four Views on Baptism* (Grand Rapids: Zondervan, 2007), 91.

4. Martin Luther, *Small Catechism* (St. Louis: Concordia Publishing House, 1971), 17.

5. Michael Rydelnik and Michael G. Vanlaningham, eds. *The Moody Bible Commentary* (Chicago: Moody, 2014), 1753.

CHAPTER 5.5

Celebrating
the Lord's Supper

GREGG QUIGGLE

For I received from the Lord that which I also delivered to you,
that the Lord Jesus, on the night in which He was betrayed, took bread;
and when He had given thanks, He broke it and said,
"This is My body, which is for you; do this in remembrance of Me."
In the same way He took the cup also after supper, saying,
"This cup is the new covenant in My blood; do this, as often as you drink it,
in remembrance of Me." For as often as you eat this bread
and drink the cup, you proclaim the Lord's death until He comes.

1 CORINTHIANS 11:23–26

These words written by the apostle Paul in 1 Corinthians are repeated in millions of churches throughout the world every Sunday. They are used as part of the four practices shared by virtually all branches of Christianity: the public reading of Scripture, preaching from the Bible, baptism, and Communion. Communion or Eucharist, although it is referred to by various terms, perhaps most popularly as the Lord's Supper, is one of the central and distinctive services of Christianity. Not only is it referenced by Paul, but it appears in all four Gospels. In addition to the various New Testament texts that describe the practice, both Christian and non-Christian documents testify to its widespread practice among early believers. Its practice among Christians was so well-known that enemies used it to accuse Christians of cannibalism. As Christianity spread and developed, disagreements about the meaning, purpose, value, and even the name of Communion developed. These disagreements became so intense they are one of the fundamental reasons for the existence of many Christian denominations. This became particularly apparent during the development of what we today call "Protestantism" during the sixteenth century in Europe. Most people today are shocked to learn that during this time period, the number one cause for execution was one's view of Communion or baptism.

In this chapter we will seek to survey various understandings of Communion. To accomplish this, the chapter is divided into four parts. First, is a brief survey of the establishment of Communion in Scripture. Second, the longest portion, will be given to explaining difference between various churches' understanding of Communion. Third is a look at the various methods used by different churches. Finally, the chapter will end with a summary and conclusion.

THE ESTABLISHMENT OF COMMUNION

SURVEY OF MOVEMENTS

It is necessary to introduce briefly some of the people and movements we will reference in this chapter. While the names of Martin Luther and John Calvin are quite familiar, such is not the case for Ulrich Zwingli or the believers known as Anabaptists. Zwingli lived at the same time as Luther. While Luther was seeking to reform the church in Germany, Zwingli was attempting similar changes in the Swiss city of Zurich among the German-speaking Swiss citizenry. Most scholars trace what we call Reformed Churches or the Reformed Tradition primarily to Calvin but also to Zwingli. The Anabaptists got their name from insisting on adult baptism. The name comes from their practice of baptizing again adults who had been first baptized as infants. They were seeking to re-create what they saw as the pure Christianity of the New Testament church. They are the forerunners of Mennonites, Amish, and many Baptist and Brethren churches.

We will also briefly mention the Eastern Orthodox Church or simply the Orthodox Church. These churches are distinct from the Roman Catholic Church. While there are some similarities, they have their own unique doctrines and traditions. Like Protestants they reject the idea that the pope is the head of the church on earth. The largest number of modern-day devotees are in Russia.

BIBLICAL PASSAGES

Most Christians trace Communion's origin to what is commonly referred to as the Last Supper. Jesus brought His disciples together for the last time before His death, and they shared a meal. Matthew describes it this way in his gospel:

Now when evening came, Jesus was reclining at the table with the twelve. And as they were eating, He said, "Truly I say to you that one of you will betray Me." Being deeply grieved, they began saying to Him, each one: "Surely it is not I, Lord?" And He answered, "He who dipped his hand with Me in the bowl is the one who will betray Me. The Son of Man is going away just as it is written about Him; but woe to that man by whom the Son of Man is betrayed! It would have been good for that man if he had not been born." And Judas, who was betraying Him, said, "Surely it is not I, Rabbi?" Jesus said to him, "You have said it yourself."

Now while they were eating, Jesus took some bread, and after a blessing, He broke it and gave it to the disciples, and said, "Take, eat; this is My body." And when He had taken a cup and given thanks, He gave it to them, saying, "Drink from it, all of you; for this is My blood of the covenant, which is being poured out for many for forgiveness of sins. But I say to you, I will not drink of this fruit of the vine from now on until that day when I drink it with you, new, in My Father's kingdom." (Matt. 26:20–29)

In addition to Matthew's account, this event is also recorded in the other three Gospels: Luke 22:7–38; Mark 14:12–25; and John 13:1–17:26. As was shown above, Paul also recounts the event in 1 Corinthians 11:23–28. Taken together, these passages provide the basic framework and elements for the practice of Eucharist or Communion.

The gospel accounts reference the Passover as the backdrop for the Last Supper. The parallels between Communion and Passover are striking. The Passover is the means whereby the people of Israel remember the Lord bringing them out of bondage in Egypt. In Exodus 12, the Lord instructs them to kill a lamb and smear the blood on the doorposts of their dwelling. This blood provided protection for the firstborn male of Israel. The lamb was to be eaten along with bread. The Israelites were instructed to use no yeast in preparing the meal, thus the bread would be unleavened.

At the Last Supper, Jesus passed out the cup and made the revolutionary declaration that His blood will provide forgiveness of sins (Matt. 26:28). By this statement Jesus asserted that the temporary solution to sins provided by body and blood of animals will now be definitively dealt with by His body and blood, the body and blood of God incarnate. Communion proclaims this good news. Christians remember and proclaim Christ's atoning death in every Eucharist or Communion service.

The texts found in all four Gospels outline the basic components of Communion or Eucharist. Wine is tied to the blood of Christ and bread represents the body of Christ. It is also clear that one of the purposes is to remember Christ and His work. The other purpose is a proclamation that Jesus is the solution to sin and death. Although the text mentions wine, many evangelical churches have chosen to use unfermented grape juice rather than wine out of desire to avoid consuming alcohol. One of the more notable illustrations of this belief is Thomas Welch (1825–1903). Welch, a staunch Wesleyan Methodist teetotaler, was the founder of one the most famous brands of unfermented grape juice—Welch's.

There are two other important Communion texts. First is John 6:51–59. Jesus is teaching in the context is the feeding of the five thousand. After the miracle, Jesus interprets its meaning:

> "I am the living bread that came down out of heaven; if anyone eats from this bread, he will live forever; and the bread which I will give for the life of the world also is My flesh."

> Then the Jews began to argue with one another, saying, "How can this man give us His flesh to eat?" So Jesus said to them, "Truly, truly, I say to you, unless you eat the flesh of the Son of Man and drink His blood, you have no life in yourselves. The one who eats My flesh and drinks My blood has eternal life, and I will raise him up on the last day. For My flesh is true food, and My blood is true drink. The one who eats My flesh and drinks My blood remains in Me, and I in him. Just as the living Father sent Me, and I live because of the Father, the one who eats Me, he also will live because of Me. This is the bread that came down out of heaven, not as the fathers ate and died; the one who eats this bread will live forever."

Some have argued that this teaching of Jesus is a reference to the Lord's Supper. Others maintain it should not be used to develop an accurate understanding of the Supper. This is a widely debated text and engaging it is beyond the scope of this chapter. However, if one is to try to make this a Communion text, there are two issues that must be addressed. First, the event in John 6 is well before the account of the Lord's Supper. Second, there are some key linguistic differences. Many commentators have pointed out that if John wanted to write John 6 in such a way to draw a reader's mind toward the Communion table, he (and Jesus) would have used different words. This means he leaves out some "key words" that are closely associated with Communion in other Lord's Supper passages. The most important is the word "body" (the Greek word is *soma*). If we look back at the texts we have noted, 1 Corinthians 11:24, Matthew 26:26, Mark 14:22, and Luke 22:19, all four of these Communion passages use the word *soma* or body. However, in John 6, John records Jesus using the word "flesh" (*sarx*). The word "body" is conspicuously missing throughout the chapter. If the point of the text is eucharistic, why would Jesus not use the same word He uses at the Lord's Supper?

A second text is 1 Corinthians 10:16: "The cup of blessing that we bless, is it not a participation in the blood of Christ? The bread that we break, is it not a participation in the body of Christ?" (ESV). This text is less disputed. It is widely accepted this is a reference to Communion, however what it teaches about Communion is debated. We will explore this later.

VARIOUS VIEWS OF UNDERSTANDINGS OF COMMUNION

MASS, EUCHARIST, OR COMMUNION?

Churches in liturgical traditions, Lutheran, Anglican/Episcopalian, Roman Catholic, and Orthodox, often refer to this service as Eucharist. Eucharist comes from the Greek word *eucharista,* which means "thanksgiving." It is the term used by Matthew, Mark, and Luke in their telling of the Last Supper. It also appears in the form of a verb in Paul's account.

In the Roman Catholic Church, Eucharist is part of the Mass. Mass comes from the Latin phrase "*Ite, missa est.*" It means, "go, you are sent," and reflects the Latin liturgy practiced by the Roman Church. These are the last words of the priest or deacon at the end of the service. The Mass consists of two parts: the liturgy of the Word and the liturgy of the Eucharist. The liturgy of the Word revolves around Scripture readings, a short sermon, and prayers. The Eucharist portion revolves around the consecration and distribution of bread and wine. Some Lutheran and Anglican/Episcopalian churches may also use the term "mass." While the Lutheran and Anglican/Episcopalian service follows the pattern of the Roman Church, their understanding of what happens to the elements in Eucharist is different. The Orthodox Church follows roughly the same pattern as the Roman Catholic Mass. It is often referred to as the Divine Liturgy rather than the Mass, as Mass refers to the Latin-based service. Another difference between Orthodox and Roman Catholic is the type of bread used. The Orthodox church uses leavened bread, Roman unleavened.

Other Christian churches use terms like "Communion" or the "Lord's Supper." Generally, they are less liturgical and do not practice Communion every week. These churches usually describe Communion as an ordinance rather than a sacrament. They also tend to view the elements differently than the those who use the term "Eucharist."

ORDINANCE OR SACRAMENT?

Another area of disagreement is whether Communion should be viewed as an ordinance or sacrament. An ordinance is simply a decree from a divine figure. In this case, Jesus, the Son of God, decrees that His followers are to observe this ritual. The purpose of this ordinance is to symbolically reenact the gospel, that is, the life, death, burial, resurrection, and return of Jesus Christ. The ordinance exists as a means to remind us of Christ's work on our behalf. By comparison, a sacrament is a religious ritual or ceremony that imparts grace to the recipient. The Roman Catholic and Orthodoxy denominations believe there are seven sacraments; baptism, chrismation in Orthodoxy/confirmation in Roman Catholicism, Eucharist, holy orders, holy unction, marriage (holy matrimony), and penance (confession). Protestants who believe in sacraments contend there are only two sacraments: baptism and Communion.

Protestants who use the term "sacraments" believe the sacraments are able to impart grace, an ability that comes from the relationship of the sacrament to Scripture. They see sacraments as an extension of Scripture, a way to make the promises of the Bible tangible and personal. So, for example, "Eucharist" is another way to make the promises of Jesus, that His body is broken for us and blood shed for us, very personal and real. Perhaps one of the better ways to illustrate this is to compare taking a sacrament to hearing a sermon. In a sermon the promises of God found in the Scriptures are proclaimed generally to a group. Sacraments are received individually and involve one's taste, touch, and smell. In both a sermon and a sacrament, the Word of God is proclaimed, but by different vehicles.

The Protestant Reformer John Calvin is particularly helpful on this point. In his famous work, *The Institutes of the Christian Religion*, Calvin describes a sacrament as "an external sign, by which the Lord seals on our consciences his promises of good-will toward us, in order to sustain the weakness of our faith, and we in our turn testify our piety towards him, both before himself, and before angels as well as men."[1] Calvin is arguing that the sacraments are God's accommodation to our weakness. While the promises of Scripture are stable and certain, our faith is weak. In Communion or Eucharist, the concept of the shed blood and broken body of Christ are made real and tangible by bread and wine. So, God gives us bread and wine to support our faith. They function to reinforce God's promises to us.

Protestants also believe that the impact the sacraments have on the recipient is solely dependent on faith. Receiving God's Word, whether in sermon or sacrament is only ultimately effective if one believes the promise. Merely knowing what the Bible says does not make one a Christian. One must believe the Bible. The power of a sermon or sacrament to change one's life is not in the sermon or sacrament itself. It is in the promise of the Scriptures received in faith by the recipient. However, one cannot believe what one does not know. Sacraments are the means whereby we know. Paul puts it this way in Romans 10:14, "How then are they to call on Him in whom they have not believed? How are they to believe in Him whom they have not heard? And how are they to hear without a preacher?" In the sacrament of Eucharist, the believer is reminded again of the truth, Jesus gave His body and blood for them. But they must believe this proclamation. Hebrews 11:6 captures this basic Protestant belief, "without faith it is impossible to please him, for whoever would draw near to God must believe that he exists and that he rewards those who seek him" (ESV).

How sacraments function as a means of grace is somewhat different in Roman Catholicism. The key distinctive of the Roman Church is the concept of *ex opere operato*. It is a Latin phrase meaning "by the very fact of the actions being performed."[2]

The point is that the sacraments have inherent power and have effect precisely because God's power is in them. Roman Catholics acknowledge that the benefits of the sacrament can vary according to inner disposition of the person receiving it, but ultimately it is about the sacrament itself. The Orthodox accept the concept of "*ex opere operato*" in the sense that the sacrament's worthiness is not a function of the worthiness of the minister or the recipient.

This concept of "*ex opere operato*" has become extremely important recently as a result of the tragedy of pedophilia among Roman Catholic clergy. Specifically, if it later becomes apparent my priest was engaged in pedophilia, was the Eucharist I received from the priest valid? "*Ex opere operato*" addressed this question. As we have seen, the validity of the sacrament is not determined by the morality of the priest. But it does raise another difference between Protestants and Roman Catholic sacramentalists. Specifically, what makes a sacrament valid?

Protestant sacramentalists generally believe that for a Eucharist to be valid, it must be administered by an ordained minister and be tied to the promises of Scripture. To illustrate, Christians meeting together, drinking wine, and eating crackers does not constitute a Eucharist, even if they are talking about Jesus. The purpose of ordination in these traditions is to grant to individuals the right to preach and administer sacraments. We previously saw the connection between preaching and sacraments, both being forms of proclaiming Scripture. It follows then that if one is ordained to preach, they are also ordained for sacraments.

Consequently, Scripture and ordained ministers are necessary for the Eucharist to be valid.

For the Roman Catholic Church, ordination is also required. The difference comes in the role of the institutional church in validating the sacrament. Canon 841 of the Roman Church's Canon Law states, "Since the sacraments are the same for the whole Church and belong to the divine deposit, it is only for the supreme authority of the Church to approve or define the requirements for their validity." Protestants maintain only the Bible has that authority.

A wide variety of Protestants are opposed to the sacramentalist's position. These generally include Baptists, Brethren, Mennonites, Pentecostals, Free Churches, Bible Churches, and independent churches. These traditions reject any concept of sacrament, preferring the term "ordinance." Communion for these Protestants is not a means of grace, rather it is an act done in response to the command of Jesus.

While churches who view Communion as a sacrament tend to practice it weekly, these churches usually practice Communion either once a month or once a quarter. Some of these churches also allow for Communion to be practiced without the presence of clergy. Many of these churches emphasize the role Communion plays in unifying the congregation in their common belief. In this way "Communion" is seen as primarily being between the participants.

THE RISEN CHRIST AND THE BREAD AND WINE

Another major area of disagreement involves the nature of the elements in Communion. Specifically, what relationship, if any, does the risen Christ have to the elements in Communion? The Roman Church holds to transubstantiation. The Orthodox Church has a similar belief, although they object to the term "transubstantiation." This teaching is that when the elements are consecrated, the bread and the wine are miraculously transformed into the literal body and blood of Christ. This is true despite the fact the bread and wine keep the appearance of regular bread and wine. In other words, when an ordained priest blesses the bread of the Lord's Supper, it is transformed into the actual flesh of Christ even though it has the same taste, color, and smell as bread. The same is true for the cup. When the wine is blessed, it is transformed into the blood of Christ, even though its taste, smell, and appearance remain unchanged. What is critical is the concept of transformation. This means that after the transubstantiation, neither bread nor wine remain in the elements.

> Consequently, especially for the Roman Church, it follows that the Mass is a sacrifice. They describe it as a sacrifice "offered in an unbloody manner". In the Mass, the Roman Church argues that in essence the sacrifice of the cross is made present to the recipient. Further, they maintain this represented sacrifice is propitiatory. That is, there is an atoning component to the Mass.[3]

This understanding of Eucharist, which included ideas like transubstantiation, sacrifice, and *ex opera operato* were central to much of the debate in the Reformation. Those who would eventually become known as "Protestants" would reject these ideas. However, it also became evident that Protestants would not come to an agreement among themselves either. Indeed at least three different Protestant views would emerge in the sixteenth century. Specifically: real presence espoused by Luther, spiritual presence promoted by Calvin, and the symbolic/memorial view of Zwingli and the Anabaptists.

Luther, in his book *The Babylonian Captivity of the Church* (1520), vigorously attacks both transubstantiation and the concept of the Eucharist as an "unbloody" sacrifice. Luther agreed with the Roman Church that Christ is truly present in the elements of the Eucharist. However, he rejected Rome's concept of transubstantiation.

For Luther, the concept of transubstantiation was too dependent on the philosophical argument of figures like Aristotle. And the Roman Church argued that after consecration, bread and wine were no longer present. Finally, transubstantiation allowed for the Eucharist to be understood as a sacrifice.

In place of transubstantiation Luther argued for real presence. Although some have described Luther's position as "consubstantiation," that probably is not the best way to describe it. In fact, Luther never used that word or believed the true corporeal presence of Christ is "in, under, and with" the elements of bread and wine. Here is how he expressed it in his *Larger Catechism*: "It is the true body and blood of our Lord Jesus Christ, in and under the bread and wine which we Christians are commanded by the Word of Christ to eat and to drink. . ."[4] There is a vagueness to this definition that is deliberate. Luther believed that mystery and paradox are part of the Christian faith. That is not to say faith violates reason, rather it cannot be totally grasped by the human mind. Luther was not concerned to explaining how Jesus can be present with His body and blood under bread and wine. As he put it, "We say the Sacrament is bread and wine, but not mere bread and wine, such as are ordinarily served at the table, but bread and wine comprehended in, and connected with, the Word of God."[5] Two points are evident. First, the connection of the elements to the Word of God defines the elements. Second, Luther is more interested in calling people to believe Jesus' words, "This is my body" than he is getting them to fully understand them.

John Calvin argues for a kind of spiritual presence. This also has a mystical aura to it. He writes of the individual going up to heaven rather than Christ coming down into the elements. For Calvin, when the believer receives the bread and wine, the Holy Spirit causes them to be raised into the heavenly realm where they commune or feed on the risen Christ. They are strengthened and refreshed in their faith.[6]

The reformer of Zurich, Ulrich Zwingli, articulates a third position. Although there are some nuances that differentiate them, this position would also be embraced by a group known as Anabaptists. Mennonites, Amish, some Brethren, and Baptists trace themselves to this group.

At the core of Zwingli's position is his belief that the Bible taught the elements in Communion were simply signs. By that he meant they function to communicate a meaning that is not the sign itself. There is no real presence. That is not to say he denies any presence, but Christ's presence is a function of the individual's contemplation or memory. What he is saying is there is no presence of Christ tied to the elements.

Anabaptists joined Zwingli in rejecting real presence. However, their rejection was even more radical. Anabaptists dropped the term "sacrament" in favor of "ordinance." While Zwingli would assert a spiritual presence based on contemplation of faith, Anabaptists would argue for a pure memorial view. The Swiss Brethren issued a statement of belief in 1527 called the Schleitheim Confession. It describes the Lord's Supper as the breaking of "one bread in the remembrance of the broken body of Christ" and the drinking of the cup "as a remembrance of the shed blood of Christ."[7] There is no other reference to the nature of the elements in the confession. Bread and wine are symbols, nothing more, whose purpose is to remind us of what Christ has done. This shared remembrance then is the basis of our communion with each other.

This memorial view produced a much simpler form of Communion. Anabaptist Communion services are described as the pastor simply tearing out and passing out a piece of bread for each congregant. When everyone had a piece, the minister would take a piece for himself and eat it. The congregation would then eat their piece. After this was completed, the pastor would take a cup or bottle of wine and take a drink. It would then be passed around for the others. There was no special blessing or consecrating of the elements.

Anabaptists also emphasize the horizontal nature of Communion. By that I mean they see the purpose as unifying the congregation.[8]

SERVING COMMUNION OR EUCHARIST

As we have seen, views on sacraments or ordinances are central and distinctive to the beliefs of many denominations. Many of you may be members of a particular denomination that has specific instructions how a Communion service is to be run and how the elements of Communion should be served.

In the Roman Church, because of their understanding of the role of the church and doctrines like *ex opere operato* and transubstantiation, the priest controls the serving of the Eucharist. They alone can consecrate the elements. This is generally done on an altar and then distributed to the congregants. After the elements are consecrated, the congregants come forward to receive the elements. If it is a large congregation, the priest may be assisted by deacons.

The Orthodox Church also emphasizes the role of the priest. They practice what is called "intinction." In intinction, the bread and wine are combined and taken together. Some argue this is a continuation of an ancient practice. Others say it illustrates unity by having the body and blood consumed simultaneously. Finally, some simply point to it as the most efficient manner to practice Communion. In the case of the Orthodox Church, the bread and the wine are mixed and then served by the priest directly into the mouth of the recipient using a spoon. Another distinction of the Orthodox tradition is their serving of Communion to infants. Infants who have been baptized and confirmed in the Orthodox Church can receive Holy Communion.

A few other denominations practice intinction. In those cases, the bread is dipped into the wine or juice. It is important to note that in the Orthodox Church and Roman Catholic Church only the priest may dip the bread into the wine, whereas among Protestants the congregants may dip the bread.

Many Protestant churches begin Communion by reading the text from Corinthians cited at the beginning of the chapter. Some follow this text by doing what some people refer to as "fencing the table." Essentially, this means reminding the congregants to examine themselves and warning of the profound implications of taking Communion in a state of unrepentant sin. At this point, the issue of whether Communion is open or closed/close comes into play. Open means the church allows anyone who is a believer to participate in the taking of the elements. Closed or close means Communion is restricted to either members of that congregation or members of that denomination. In some churches that emphasize close Communion, the service is held at a different day or time than normal worship. In a few churches, Communion is combined with foot washing, meaning the members wash each other's feet as part of the service.

If you are free to use multiple methods, following are some common practices used by churches. Generally, these are used by churches that see Communion as solely a memorial service. One method is to have the Communion elements served to the congregation while they are seated. In this case, laypeople from the congregation service the elements. For the bread, plates of crackers or torn pieces of bread are prepared. Similarly, trays of small cups of juice or wine are prepared. These are often placed on a table at the front of the church. The pastor or pastors sit behind the table facing the congregation. The Corinthians text is read, and the pastor explains the process. The pastor will explain whether Communion is open or closed. If it is closed, he will encourage nonbelievers or those who are not members of that church/denomination to refrain from taking the elements.

At this point, those serving will come forward to take the elements. They will then pass them throughout the congregation. Some churches have the elements held by each member until all are served. Then following a prayer and/or the reading of Luke 22:19, "This is My body, which is being given for you; do this in remembrance of Me," the congregation eats the bread at the same time. This symbolizes the people as all being united in Christ. Alternately, some churches pray or read the Luke text before the elements are passed out and instruct the congregants to partake of the elements individually as they receive them. This is to symbolize the personal nature of our relationship with Christ. Finally, some churches do both; that is, they will have the congregants take the bread individually, and then have them wait to take the cup together.

Protestant churches that tend to see Communion as a sacrament usually have Communion served by the pastor or priest. If the congregation is large, sometimes other leaders of the church assist in serving. By doing this they are emphasizing that Communion is an extension of the preaching/teaching office. In these denominations, what separates the clergy from the laypeople is the right to teach or preach. Since they see Communion as a form of preaching, it must be administered by an ordained pastor.

In these cases, the people come forward to receive the elements from the pastor or priest. If it is a large congregation, after the pastor says a few words and/or prays, the elements are given to the elders or deacons. They stand at the end of each aisle. The congregants then come forward by rows to receive the elements. When they reach the pastor or priest, the bread is placed either in the hands of the congregant or they open their mouth, and the pastor places it on their tongue. In the case of the cup, the congregant again goes forward, and the pastor tips the cup so they can drink. The pastor wipes the cup and turns it after each congregant drinks.

For churches that tie Communion closely to the Passover, unleavened bread is used. Others use bread or crackers. As mentioned earlier, many churches use unfermented grape juice. This is for two reasons. First is a commitment to the prohibition of alcohol. Second is out of respect for recovering alcoholics among the congregation.

Some churches will have the congregation sing a hymn together or have hymns played as the elements are being passed. Other will have a time of quiet for silent prayer. Some may have silence after one of the elements and a hymn or chorus played during the second element.

CONCLUSION

In Communion, the church proclaims that Jesus Christ shed His blood and gave His body on account of our sins. The innocent paid for the guilty. This is the core of our faith. This is truly the gospel, good news to be proclaimed to all.

It is also clear this is a serious matter. We began by recalling Paul's words in 1 Corinthians 11. Let me now remind you of the following verses. "But a person must examine himself, and in so doing he is to eat of the bread and drink of the cup. For the one who eats and drinks, eats and drinks judgment to himself if he does not properly recognize the body. For this reason many among you are weak and sick, and a number are asleep" (1 Cor. 11:28–30). God takes this so seriously that according to Paul some in Corinth had died from mistreating Communion.

This does not mean we should avoid Communion. We have seen how the word "Eucharist" comes from the Greek *Eucharista*, which means "thanksgiving." So, while it is solemn, it is also a cause for celebrating Christ's work for us. Further, Jesus did not establish Communion so that we could avoid it. The taking of Communion is a divinely ordained practice. God established it because He knew we need to be constantly reminded and encouraged by Christ's work for us. One wonders how many Christians have been hobbled in their walk with Christ by neglecting to partake of this gift.

It can be easy to get lost in all these detailed arguments. Sometimes when faced with all these disagreements one is tempted to simply say this is all too complicated. But Jesus commanded His people to remember Him through bread and wine. It is good for our souls and binds us with our brothers and sisters in Christ. Sadly, it is too easy to forget what Christ has done for us. We need to be reminded again and again. When you lead your people in this service you are calling them to remember the essence of our faith. It is a remarkable privilege. So, brothers and sisters, Christ bids us come to His table in solemnity and thanksgiving. Let us be faithful stewards of this good gift from God!

NOTES

1. John Calvin, *Institutes of the Christian Religion*, trans. Henry Beveridge, 4.14.1.

2. The *Catechism of the Catholic Church* explains it in the following manner: "This is the meaning of the Church's affirmation that the sacraments act *ex opere operato* (literally: 'by the very fact of the action's being performed'), i.e., by virtue of the saving work of Christ, accomplished once for all. It follows that "the sacrament is not wrought by the righteousness of either the celebrant or the recipient, but by the power of God." From the moment that a sacrament is celebrated in accordance with the intention of the Church, the power of Christ and his Spirit acts in and through it, independently of the personal holiness of the minister. Nevertheless, the fruits of the sacraments also depend on the disposition of the one who receives them." *Catechism of the Catholic Church*, 2nd ed. (Washington, DC: United States Catholic Conference, 2019), 1128.

3. Here is how the current Catholic catechism puts it: "[1365] Because it is the memorial of Christ's Passover, the Eucharist is also a sacrifice. The sacrificial character of the Eucharist is manifested in the very words of institution: 'This is my body which is given for you' and 'This cup which is poured out for you is the New Covenant in my blood.' In the Eucharist Christ gives us the very body which he gave up for us on the cross, the very blood which he 'poured out for many for the forgiveness of sins.'"

"[1366] The Eucharist is thus a sacrifice because it re-presents (makes present) the sacrifice of the cross, because it is its memorial and because it applies its fruit: [Christ], our Lord and God, was once and for all to offer himself to God the Father by his death on the altar of the cross, to accomplish there an everlasting redemption. But because his priesthood was not to end with his death, at the Last Supper 'on the night when he was betrayed,' [he wanted] to leave to his beloved spouse the Church a visible sacrifice (as the nature of man demands) by which the bloody sacrifice which he was to accomplish once for all on the cross would be re-presented, its memory perpetuated until the end of the world, and its salutary power be applied to the forgiveness of the sins we daily commit."

"[1367] The sacrifice of Christ and the sacrifice of the Eucharist are one single sacrifice: 'The victim is one and the same: the same now offers through the ministry of priests, who then offered himself on the cross; only the manner of offering is different.' 'And since in this divine sacrifice which is celebrated in the Mass, the same Christ who offered himself once in a bloody manner on the altar of the cross is contained and is offered in an unbloody manner. . . this sacrifice is truly propitiatory.'"*CCC, 1365, 1366, 1367.*

4. Martin Luther, *Large Catechism*, part 5, marginal number 8.

5. Ibid., part 5, marginal note 9.

6. Calvin, *Institutes*, 4.17.32

7. *Schleitheim Confession*, Article III.

8. This is seen at the end of the statement on Communion in the Dordrecht Confession of 1632. This statement is one of the most important documents for the Mennonite church. It reads: "We also confess and observe the breaking of bread, or Supper, as the Lord Christ Jesus before His suffering instituted it with bread and wine, and observed and ate with His apostles, commanding them to observe it in remembrance of Him; which they accordingly taught and practiced in the church, and commanded that it should be kept in remembrance of the suffering and death of the Lord; and that His precious body was broken, and His blood shed, for us and all mankind, as also the fruits hereof, namely, redemption and eternal salvation, which He purchased thereby, showing such great love toward us sinful men; whereby we are admonished to the utmost, to love and forgive one another and our neighbor, as He has done unto us, and to be mindful to maintain and live up to the unity and fellowship which we have with God and one another, which is signified to us by this breaking of bread." *Dordrecht Confession of Faith*, Article X.

Interpreting Scripture for Preaching

RYAN COOK

The pastorate is a complex and demanding calling. In any given week one may be asked to manage a board meeting, visit shut-ins, provide marriage counseling, reach out to a wayward teenager, resolve conflict between church members, help plan for the next community outreach, and/or conduct a funeral. This is all important and necessary work. However, none of those activities should take away from the primary calling of a pastor, to "preach the word" (2 Tim. 4:2). This involves understanding the Bible well and being able to call the church to faithfully respond to it. In an early manual for pastors on hermeneutics, Augustine began, "There are two things on which all interpretation of Scripture depends: the mode of ascertaining the proper meaning, and the mode of making known the meaning when ascertained."[1] He recognized two skills needed for pastors: a proper methodology to understand the meaning of Scripture, and skill at communicating and applying its message. This may sound rather straightforward, but both parts of the previous sentence require serious reflection.

The Bible is a large and diverse book. It is written in three different languages over a period of some 1,500 years by authors who differed widely in education, temperament, and cultural context. These authors wrote in diverse genres to different audiences for different purposes. To understand the Bible well is a task that requires a significant level of study and research.

The contemporary audience is also important to understand. Sermons are not preached to an abstract group of listeners, but to particular people living in particular communities. Give attention to understanding the context of the audience. One may then envision what it would look like for a particular group of people to respond to the Bible faithfully. For example, what would it look like for a particular church to respond faithfully to Abraham's offering of Isaac (Gen. 22), or Paul's Damascus road experience (Acts 9), or the Sermon on the Mount (Matt. 5–7)?

These are not the only important factors to consider. Augustine also recognized that interpreting the Bible for preaching was more than just mastering the content of the Bible and communicating it clearly. He understood that the preacher's own character and relationship with God were essential. He states, "The soul must be purified that it may have power to perceive that light, and to rest in it when it is perceived . . . For it is not by change of place that we can come nearer to Him who is in every place, but by the cultivation of pure desires and virtuous habits."[2] In other words, it is not enough to understand what Scripture says and preach it, one must also believe it and be changed by it. The preacher who believes Scripture and "rests" in it will have a better grasp of how to interpret and apply Scripture for the church.

This chapter cannot cover all of the necessary elements for a robust hermeneutic for preaching, but should be seen as an introductory guide. It is organized under three main headings: Regular Practices for Biblical Interpretation, Engaging the Text, and Engaging the Audience. The first heading answers the question, How can I become the kind of person who interprets and applies Scripture well? The second heading provides a practical approach to understanding the Bible. The final heading engages questions about contemporary significance and application.

REGULAR PRACTICES FOR BIBLICAL INTERPRETATION

An observer of contemporary American culture once wrote, "It is rare to find a piece of journalism, of political rhetoric, or even of academic writing that clearly evidences the struggle to express the truth 'about what it is to be human and hungry in a fallen world full of wonders.'"[3] This is especially true in preaching, where sermon writing can become simply another task to check off the list. How does one continue to wrestle honestly with the meaning of Scripture and its significance for the contemporary church week after week? What the interpreter brings to the text of Scripture matters. Part of growing and keeping fresh as an interpreter of Scripture is to intentionally engage in practices, or life-habits that will enable you to bring the right kinds of knowledge, experience, and perspective to the text of Scripture.

PRAYER

Mature biblical interpretation flows from a life grounded in prayer. Theologian Brevard Childs put it this way, "Prayer is an integral part in the study of Scripture because it anticipates the Spirit's carrying its reader through the written page to God himself."[4] We do not read and preach from Scripture simply to mine it for historical information or to impress our listeners with our grasp of the historical-cultural context (as important and essential as that is). Rather, prayer reminds us that when we read Scripture we are engaging with the Author, with God Himself. A life of prayer is one way we can take off our sandals in recognition that Scripture is holy ground. Prioritizing time in prayer as a part of the exegetical process is essential, the more so because it is easy minimize or ignore.

READING SCRIPTURE

Nothing can replace having a good, detailed grasp of Scripture as a whole. Augustine believed that the first rule to follow in seeking to interpret the Bible is, "to know these books, if not yet with the understanding, still to read them so as to commit them to memory, or at least so as not to remain wholly ignorant of them."[5] The reason why this is so important is that it helps the reader have a clear grasp of the story of the Bible as a whole. It immerses one in the language and imagery of Scripture and helps one interpret difficult passages in light of passages that have a more transparent meaning.

There is no other way of acquiring this kind of knowledge than regular and repeated reading of Scripture. There are many helpful Scripture reading plans available for free online. For example, the nineteenth-century Scottish pastor Robert Murray M'Cheyne put together a popular reading plan that takes the reader through the New Testament and Psalms twice a year and the Old Testament once. This requires reading about four chapters a day. The Kingdom Bible reading plan created by Jason DeRouchie has the reader work through the Psalms twice each year and all other books of the Bible once. It also has the reader in both the Old and New Testament each day. Both of these reading plans can be easily found through an online search. These are two of many helpful reading plans available. The overall goal is to be saturated in Scripture. As a young pastor Jonathan Edwards committed to the important task of knowing Scripture well in this way, "Resolved: To study the Scriptures so steadily, constantly, and frequently, as that I may find, and plainly perceive, myself to grow in the knowledge of the same."[6]

GENERAL READING

The preacher is required to stand before a diverse audience and speak about the weightiest topics in life: God, suffering, relationships, death, sin, salvation, hope, joy, and judgment to name just a few. They are called to do this week after week in an engaging and compelling way. This is a prodigious task. One great help is to engage in a plan of general reading.[7] That is, reading done not for the sake of specific research for a sermon, but to help one become a more rounded person in general. There are no rules about the right way to go about this. I will provide one example of a general reading plan that can serve as a guide.

Each day, read a portion of one ancient and one modern theologian, or book of biblical scholarship. It is helpful to read ancient authors for a number of reasons. Their books are normally still in print because they have an enduring value and speak to universally important topics. They also are mostly written from a pre-Enlightenment context. This often provides a helpful perspective that is very difficult to find elsewhere. There is a lifetime of wisdom to be mined from writers like John Calvin, Martin Luther, Augustine, Anselm, and Irenaeus among many others.[8] Modern theologians or biblical scholars are helpful in that they keep one up to date with current research and reflect on how the Bible addresses issues in contemporary culture.[9] To keep this kind of reading manageable, block out one fifteen- to twenty-minute space in the morning and one in the afternoon. At this rate, one will be able to read many books in a year. Scripture tells us that God has gifted the church with teachers (1 Cor. 12:28); reading widely can help one benefit from many of God's gifted servants from both today and from ages past.

In addition to reading theological works, regular reading of novels, biographies, poems, journalism, and short stories can be both a joy and a great help in sermon writing. Novelists and poets write movingly about universal aspects of being human. For example, the tension between law and grace is powerfully narrated in *Les Misérables*. The insidious nature of greed and the pain of exile can be felt in John Steinbeck's *The Grapes of Wrath*. To reflect on the nature of love and its distortions, one could hardly do better than C. S. Lewis's *'Till We Have Faces*. An additional benefit to reading quality literature is that these writers model how to use language effectively, which is so critical in good preaching. This kind of reading allows one to be tutored and shaped by writers who know how to use the English language best. A helpful reading list of these kinds of books can be found in Cornelius Plantinga's *Reading for Preaching*, or Leland and Philip Ryken's *Pastors in the Classics*.[10]

Prayer, saturation in Scripture, and a plan of general reading are all important habits to cultivate. They will help you bring a wealth of wisdom and experience to any given biblical text. Mature biblical interpretation is not just a skill to be learned and mastered, but requires attentiveness to God, His Word, language, and to the lived reality of the congregation.

ENGAGING THE TEXT

The goal of this section is to provide a practical method for studying a passage for preaching. Interpreting the Bible is not always a linear process, nevertheless, it is possible to logically describe several discrete steps one would need to move through to be prepared to write a sermon.

CHOOSE THE UNIT OF TEXT

The first requirement is to choose the text to preach from. It is possible to choose a large unit of text, even an entire book, for a single sermon. One could preach on the book of Job as a whole, or the Joseph story in its entirety in one sermon (Gen. 37–50). However, it is usually best to pick a more manageable unit of Scripture. The unit of text should have a clear beginning and ending point. These are determined differently depending on the genre.

In narrative texts, the smallest unit of text to be preached on should be the episode, or pericope. Episodes in narrative texts are determined by looking for the following:

1. Introductory or concluding formula. These are statements that either prepare the reader for the following episode, or summarize and conclude an episode. These features can be illustrated by examining Abraham's offering of Isaac in Genesis 22. Genesis 22:1 provides a clear opening statement, "After these things, God tested Abraham." This provides a break with the previous episode and serves as a kind of heading for what follows. The question then becomes, Where does the episode end? Verse 19 provides the reader with a clear concluding statement. Additionally, verse 20 provides another opening statement, "Now after these things . . ." This indicates that the episode should be considered Genesis 22:1–19.

2. Shifts in character, geographical location, or temporal framework. Each of these items can be used to discern a new episode. For example, Exodus 3 records Moses's encounter with God at the burning bush. However, the scene does not conclude at the end of chapter 3. The geographical location, characters, and temporal framework are all carried into chapter 4. However, in 4:18 the narrator says, "Moses went back to Jethro his father-in-law and said to him . . . " This narrates a change in location and time as well as the addition of a character. Thus, the episode of Moses at the burning bush should be considered Exodus 3:1–4:17. One must remember that chapter and verse divisions are late, medieval additions to the biblical text. At times, they divide the text at the wrong places.

In epistles, the primary unit of thought is the paragraph. In this genre, one should look at changes in topic, argumentation, tone, or other linguistic cues. For example, in 1 Corinthians 7–16, Paul introduces each new topic with a heading.

In 7:1 he states, "Now concerning the matters about which you wrote . . ." Then, in 8:1 he continues, "Now concerning food offered to idols." This would indicate that 1 Corinthians 7:1–40 is all addressing a singular topic. It is certainly possible to preach on a smaller paragraph within that unit, but the unit itself needs to be studied holistically.

Other times, an epistle might carry a grammatical feature through a section and provide a clear indication of a unit. For example, 1 John 1:6–2:2 contains three pairs of conditional sentences, "If we say we have fellowship with him . . . If we walk in the light . . . If we say we have no sin . . . If we confess our sins. . . ."[11] Similarly, changes in tone can mark a new section in an epistle. There is an abrupt shift in James 5:1 where the author turns to address the wealthy, "Come now, you rich . . ." Then, in verse 7, James shifts back to addressing his main audience, "Be patient, therefore, brothers." This indicates that 5:1–6 should be seen as a discrete unit.

Each genre has its own way of signaling natural breaks in a passage. For the Psalms, the main unit is the strophe. For the prophets, it is the oracle. For legal material, it is a series or collection.[12] In each of these genres, the kinds of observations and questions illustrated in the discussion of narrative and epistles will be helpful. An additional help is to analyze a passage in several different Bible translations. Bible translations provide headings and paragraph divisions. Analyzing where translations differ in their divisions often provides a helpful perspective on the issues involved in choosing a passage.

EXAMINE THE LITERARY CONTEXT

The second requirement is to acquire a clear sense of the flow of the book being studied and how the specific passage fits into it. For smaller books, like Galatians, Ruth, or Joel, it is possible to read the entire book through. For larger books, like Isaiah, it might be difficult to read through the book in its entirety in one sitting. In this case, find a good commentary with a detailed outline, or summary of the book. Knowing where and how a passage fits into the larger context will often provide important insights into its meaning.

For example, it is important to know that God's testing of Abraham (Gen. 22) comes near the end of the Abraham cycle (11:27–25:11). After Genesis 22, Abraham does not speak to God again and God does not speak to Abraham. It thus serves as a kind of climax to the Abraham narrative. Also, Genesis 22:1–19 and Genesis 12:1–3 have shared vocabulary and themes. Genesis 22 can be profitably understood as a kind of counterpoint to God's call of Abram in Genesis 12. In John's gospel, the episode of Nicodemus meeting Jesus at night is intentionally contrasted with His conversation with the woman at the well (John 3–4). These episodes mutually illuminate one another and observations from this kind of study would be lost if each episode was considered independently. As a final example, consider 1 Corinthians 15, Paul's magnificent chapter on the resurrection. There is a reason why this chapter comes near the very end of the book and not at the beginning. It serves as a kind of climax to the book and provides a helpful perspective from which to consider all of the other issues he has addressed.

READ, READ, READ—AND OBSERVE

Once you have a good grasp of the literary context, return to your passage and read, read, read! Nothing can replace a detailed knowledge of the words and flow of the passage. As you read, note questions and make observations. Look for repeated words and themes. Describe the tone of the passage—is it calm and reasoned, impassioned and imperative, or reflective and meditative? Note questions related to the culture and background, the meaning of particular words, and the overall purpose of the passage. If you have facility with the original languages, translate your passage and note questions related to the grammar and syntax. If you do not have access to the original languages, read the passage in at least three different translations and note differences. At the end of this process you should have a long list of observations and questions related to your passage.

RESEARCH

At this point, it is time to do some research. Commentaries are the single most helpful source to consult. Especially important are commentaries that will engage with the original language, provide helpful background information, and interact with important secondary literature.[13] This kind of study will not only help answer some of the questions you already have, but will also raise new questions and provide you with perspectives on the passage that you may have missed in your own reading and observations.

The observations and questions you raised about the passage may require you to engage in word studies, or additional research on particular cultural or historical questions. This may require consulting theological wordbooks, Bible atlases, Bible handbooks, and/or Bible dictionaries. It is important to note that different genres of Scripture often require different kinds of background information and research.[14] For example, expository texts like the Epistles and prophetic oracles often require one to analyze the precise context in which they are written. Who was the author? Who was the audience? What particular issues are being addressed? This is key to understanding specific commands in these genres. This kind of background information accounts for why James can say, "Abraham believed God, and it was counted to him as righteousness' . . . You see that a person is justified by works and not by faith alone" (2:23–24 ESV). Whereas Paul says, "For if Abraham was justified by works, he has something to boast about, but not before God. For what does the Scripture say? 'Abraham believed God, and it was counted to him as righteousness'" (Rom. 4:2–3 ESV). Paul and James seem to be using the same passage of Scripture to make opposite points. However, when one understands the different issues they are addressing to their different audiences, the alleged contradiction disappears. Knowledge of the author, audience, and circumstances are vital to understanding these passages rightly.

For other genres it is either not possible, or not as important to understand the precise historical context. For example, the book of Job speaks meaningfully even though we do not know who the author was, or the exact time period in which it was written. Those kinds of issues do not impact the interpretation of the book significantly. The same is true for books like Proverbs and Ecclesiastes. For these kinds of texts, a more general understanding of the cultural context is important.[15]

SUMMARIZE ORIGINAL MEANING

Once the research on the passage has been completed, it is time to start focusing your study and reflection. One useful exercise is to summarize your passage in a paragraph.[16] Use past tense verbs to summarize what your passage meant to its original audience. As an example of this, consider Genesis 12:1–3.

While a full exegesis of this passage is not possible in the scope of this chapter, I will highlight some pertinent historical and contextual factors for this passage, then demonstrate a summary. Genesis 12:1–3 comes at an important juncture in the book of Genesis. Genesis 1–11 has narrated creation and the fall (Gen. 1–3). As a climax to the narrative of the fall, God indicated that He would be at work to address the reality of sin (Gen. 3:15). However, humanity continues to spiral downward: Cain killed Abel, Lamech boasted of violence (Gen. 4:23–24), the whole earth had become corrupted (Gen. 6:5). The flood represented a potential new beginning; however, soon after Noah and his family left the ark, Noah had his own "fall" (Gen. 9:20–29). The culmination of this section comes in the narrative of the Tower of Babel where all of humanity unite in pride and hubris (Gen. 11:1–9). All of this raises a question for the reader, How is God going to resolve this issue? How is He going to be at work in the midst of a corrupt world? Genesis 12:1–3 provides the beginning of an answer to that question. Being able to place this passage in its larger context is vital to a correct understanding.

Examining the passage itself, a few observations are important to note: (1) YHWH speaks directly to Abram. We do not know exactly how. There is no explicit relationship between YHWH and Abram before this. Abram is also not introduced with a description of his righteousness as Noah was earlier in Genesis (Gen. 6:9). (2) God commands Abram to leave behind three things: his country, his kindred, and his father's house. A study of these terms indicates that the terms narrow in focus from the general to the specific, culminating in the leaving behind of his extended family and his *Beth-Ab*, or his closest relatives. One must understand the significance of this in the ancient world. There was no police state. Safety and security came from being connected to a kinship group. God is asking Abram to leave that behind. (3) Abram must make this sacrifice without knowing exactly where he was going; God would show him at the right time (12:1). (4) God makes a promise that Abram would have a great name, that he would be protected by God, and that all the families of the earth would be blessed through him (12:2–3). The reference to a "great name" harkens back to the Tower of Babel episode where the people said, "Come, let's build ourselves a city, and a tower … and let's make a name for ourselves; otherwise we will be scattered abroad over the face of the whole earth" (11:4). Here the people desired to achieve lasting significance and safety by banding together in opposition of God's command after the flood to disperse and fill the earth (9:7). Abram's call can be seen as the counterpoint to this. God declares that He will make Abram's name great and will be his source of safety and security apart from his land and kinship group. Additionally, this calling of Abram has implications for the entire world. Somehow, Abram leaving his homeland and having offspring that would become a great nation would be a blessing to the world. (5) The final observation to make is that the narrator highlights some important facts: Sarai is childless (11:30) and Abram is seventy-five years old (12:4).

Based on this brief examination of the context, a summary of Genesis 12:1–3 would read something like this, "As a response to the crisis of the fall and its aftermath, God called Abram to leave behind his homeland and his family to live in a land God would show to him. God also promised Abram that He would make him into a great nation even though he was elderly and had no children. Since Abram was leaving his source of protection behind, God promised that He would be Abram's protection. God Himself would bless those who blessed Abram and curse those who tried to harm him. Finally, God would use Abram's obedience to become a source of blessing for the entire world." The goal in this section is to summarize clearly the main thrust of the passage in its context.

ENGAGING THE AUDIENCE

It is not enough to clearly understand and communicate what a passage of Scripture meant to its original audience. The preacher must wrestle with the question, What is the significance of this passage for today? For some passages, this question seems rather straightforward. For example, Jesus commanded His disciples to "love your enemies and pray for those who persecute you" (Matt. 5:44). This would indicate that if I have an enemy, I should love and pray for them. For other passages, it is more difficult to ascertain the significance of the passage for today. For example, the apostle Paul commands Timothy to "do your best to come to me soon . . . when you come, bring the cloak that I left with Carpus at Troas, also the books, and above all the parchments" (2 Tim. 4:9, 13 ESV). It is not possible to literally obey the commands in this passage, so what is its significance for the believer today? How can that significance be ascertained? Answering these questions involves a two-step process: Formulating theological principles and contextualizing these principles.

FORMULATING THEOLOGICAL PRINCIPLES

Once the meaning of a passage is understood, a helpful question to ask is, What is the author trying to *do* with this passage? That is, what were the author's goals in communicating this portion of Scripture? The goal of any individual passage should fit into the larger purpose or goal of the book as a whole.

As a specific example, let's continue to reflect on Genesis 12:1–3. This passage fits into the larger goal of the book of Genesis as a whole. Allen Ross describes the purpose of Genesis in this way: "Genesis provides the historical and theological basis for God's covenant with his people . . . the central theme of Genesis is the provision of a divine covenant with Abraham and his descendants with its promises to make them the people of God, heirs of the land of Canaan, and a blessing to the world."[17] The book of Genesis was written to help Israel understand who God is, His relationship with the world, what went wrong in the world, and how they were a part of His plan to address it. Genesis 12:1–3 helps to achieve that goal in a specific way. Any theological principles formulated should align with the purpose of the book as a whole.

Understanding the message of a passage and how it fits into the overall purpose of the book enables one to articulate underlying theological principles in the passage.[18] Grant Osborn describes three ways we can determine a theological principle in a biblical text: (1) the principle "might be stated directly in the text, as in 'love your neighbor as yourself' (Lev. 19:18; Mk 12:31). (2) In historical portions it might be implied on the basis of the text's explicit interpretation of the event . . . (3) It may apply indirectly in terms of general principles rather than the specific situation."[19]

For Genesis 12, the third option is the only one possible. God's commands in Genesis 12:1–3 do not directly apply to the believer today. No modern reader lives in Haran, so being called out of Haran is not possible. Most modern readers do not live in a *Beth-Ab* ("father's house") with the same social structure today, and so could not leave that behind either. From this passage, God is not calling a believer today to leave their homeland behind and go to an unspecified place that He will show them. So, one must look to more general theological principles that the passage is teaching. These principles should flow from the meaning of the passage and align with the author's purpose.

One list of principles from Genesis 12:1–3 could look like this: (1) God uses people to further and carry out His mission to the world; (2) God often uses people that one would not expect. In this case, God called a geriatric, barren couple and declared He would make a great nation out of them. So, God uses people to carry out His mission in the world, but paradoxically He often uses rather unlikely people; (3) God makes big promises in helping to fulfill His mission to the world. Abram and Sarai were forced to live in the tension between God's promises and their lack of fulfillment for most of their lives; (4) God equips people with what they need to obey His call. In this case, God promised Abram protection; (5) God has a worldwide mission and Abram and his descendants are a part of that mission. From them, all the nations of the world will be blessed. These principles fit with the overall purpose in Genesis. Moses was trying to help Israel understand who God was and their identity as descendants of Abraham. It is important to note that the theological principles are not more important than the text of Scripture itself. These principles provide a way to structure a sermon that reflects on the significance of a passage, but are not a substitute for the passage.

FORMULATE THE PREACHING IDEA

The purpose of a sermon is not merely to summarize the meaning of a passage, or even expound on its theological principles in the abstract. Rather, a sermon should bring a passage of Scripture to bear on a particular congregation. One way to accomplish this is to formulate a preaching idea. Haddon Robinson defines the preaching idea in this way: "The statement of a biblical concept in such a way that it accurately reflects the Bible and meaningfully relates to the congregation."[20] It is important to note that a single passage may be preached in different ways. There is not one preaching idea that could encompass all of the theological principles listed above. Rather, there are several different preaching ideas one could formulate from Genesis 12:1–3 that would each be a faithful exposition of the passage. This is not to say that any preaching idea will do. It certainly is possible to have the wrong preaching idea from a passage. The preaching idea should be clearly connected to and grounded in the passage. It also should connect meaningfully to the congregation. Ideally, it should be short and memorable.

One example of a preaching idea from Genesis 12:1–3 could be, "God is different than you think." This sermon would reflect on the nature of God and specifically what this passage reveals about Him. The fact that God works through people to carry out His mission to the world is perhaps a different strategy than most of us would choose. This kind of a sermon would resonate well with a congregation that may think they have God all figured out. Another example of a preaching idea from this passage could be, "God's promises provide hope for the world." The sermon could talk about the lavish promises made to Abram and how Abram had to live in the tension between promise and fulfillment, or lack thereof. This is certainly a situation believers find themselves in today. This theme fits Genesis 12 into its canonical context. Another preaching idea could be, "Who would you choose to start a movement that will change the world? Not who you think!" This idea is rooted in the fact that the narrator has told us that Abram is elderly and that Sarai is barren. These are not the people one would expect to be historically significant. This message could be used to encourage a congregation that significance in ministry is dependent upon God, not on the skill or qualifications of His servants.

All of these can be faithful preaching ideas. It takes wisdom to know what preaching idea should be used in a given context. The preaching idea should be used to help bring the congregation into the world of the text, an engagement that can cause real transformation.

CONTEXTUALIZATION

Once the theological principles and the preaching idea have been formulated, they need to be contextualized for a specific audience. A preacher does not simply communicate theological principles and ideas, but brings those principles to bear in the life of a congregation. The preacher must wrestle with the question, What would it look like to faithfully respond to this part of Scripture today? This process is called contextualization, or application. Grant Osborne defines contextualization in this way, "Contextualization is that dynamic process which interprets the significance of a religion or cultural norm for a group with a different (or developed) cultural heritage."[21] In other words, the Bible was originally written to people who were living in a different cultural context. The challenge for the preacher is to understand how to respond faithfully to a passage of Scripture today, in a very different cultural context.

At times the primary application of a passage will be to think differently about God, or ourselves, and/or others. Other times, an application may require a change in behavior. For example, one might need to call a congregation to "love their enemy" (Matt. 5:44). Or to flee from sexual immorality (Heb. 13:4). One may need to specify just what each of these commands means in today's context, but the main response is to live in a different way. Other times application may inspire hope or deepen faith.

It is often helpful to think of various segments of the congregation when writing the application portion of a sermon. What would it look like for an elderly couple to respond faithfully to this portion of Scripture? For a stay-at-home mom? For a junior high student? For someone who just lost their job? Intentionally thinking about groups of people in the congregation may help inspire a more specific application. At times, the primary application of an application may be simply a call to faith. For example, the best way to apply a passage like Genesis 12:1–3 is not primarily to call people to leave their homeland, or to volunteer for a ministry they have been afraid to, or any specific behavioral change. Rather, it should call the congregation to believe in the kind of God who would call Abram.

CONCLUSION

In this brief introduction to biblical interpretation for preaching, there are three main areas to highlight. Faithful interpretation of Scripture begins with the interpreter. The interpreter should be dependent upon God, a person of prayer, and one who is intimately familiar with the whole of Scripture. The interpreter should have a deep well of experience to draw from. This experience comes not only from life, but from the wealth of experience that can be mined through reading. Secondly, the interpreter should carefully study the meaning of a passage in its original context. They should have a clear understanding of what the author was doing with the passage under investigation. Finally, the interpreter should reflect carefully on how their audience could respond faithfully to this passage of Scripture. This is a difficult, demanding, and deeply rewarding task worth of our best thinking, research, and communication.

NOTES

1. Augustine, *On Christian Doctrine*, 1.1.

2. Ibid., 1.10.10.

3. Ellen Davis, "Teaching the Bible Confessionally in the Church" in *The Art of Reading Scripture*, eds. Ellen Davis and Richard Hays (Grand Rapids: Eerdmans, 2003), 15. For the final line, she cites Barbara Brown Taylor, *When God Is Silent* (Cambridge, MA: Cowley, 1998), 110.

4. Brevard Childs, *Biblical Theology in Crisis* (Philadelphia: Westminster, 1970), 219.

5. Augustine, *On Christian Doctrine*, 2.9.14.

6. Jonathan Edwards, *The Works of Jonathan Edwards*, vol. 1. (Edinburgh: Banner of Truth Trust, 1974), lxiii.

7. See, Cornelius Plantinga Jr.'s discussion of a general reading plan in the preface to *Reading for Preaching: The Preacher in Conversation with Storytellers, Biographers, Poets, and Journalists* (Grand Rapids: Eerdmans, 2013).

8. A helpful list of ancient authors and recommend reading can be found at www.ccel.org.

9. Lists of modern theologians and biblical scholars can be found in many places. One good place to start is to read books on *Christianity Today*'s book award lists. Reviews of many standard commentaries, reference works, systematic theologies, and reference works can be found at www.bestcommentaries.com.

10. Cornelius Plantinga Jr., *Reading for Preaching: The Preacher in Conversation with Storytellers, Biographers, Poets, and Journalists* (Grand Rapids: Eerdmans, 2013); Leland Ryken, Philip Ryken, and Todd Wilson, *Pastors in the Classics: Timeless Lessons on Life and Ministry from World Literature* (Grand Rapids: Baker, 2012).

11. Example from Dean Deppe, *All Roads Lead to the Text: Eight Methods of Inquiry into the Bible* (Grand Rapids: Eerdmans, 2011), 2.

12. For a helpful discussion of the main genres in Scripture, see chapters 9–10 in William W. Klein, Craig Blomberg, and Robert L. Hubbard, *Introduction to Biblical Interpretation* (Nashville: Thomas Nelson, 2004).

13. www.bestcommentaries.com has a helpful ranking system for commentaries along with recommendations for each book of the Bible.

14. John Goldingay, "What Is Involved in Understanding a Passage from the Bible?" in *Key Questions about Biblical Interpretation: Old Testament Answers* (Grand Rapids: Baker, 2011), 5.

15. For additional help regarding this section, see the chapter on "Hermeneutics" in this volume.

16. See J. Scott Duvall and J. Daniel Hays, *Grasping God's Word: A Hands-On Approach to Reading, Interpreting, and Applying the Bible*, 3rd ed. (Grand Rapids: Zondervan, 2012), 42.

17. Allen Ross and John N. Oswalt, *Cornerstone Biblical Commentary: Genesis, Exodus*, vol. 1 (Carol Stream, IL: Tyndale House Publishers, 2008), 10.

18. See Grant Osborne, *The Hermeneutical Spiral: A Comprehensive Introduction to Biblical Interpretation*, 2nd ed. (Downers Grove, IL: InterVarsity, 2006), 441–46.

19. Ibid., 443. Osborne is summarizing from J. Robertson McQuilkin, *Understanding and Applying the Bible: An Introduction to Hermeneutics* (Chicago: Moody Publishers, 1983), 258–65.

20. Haddon Robinson, *Biblical Preaching: The Development and Delivery of Expository Messages*, 3rd ed. (Grand Rapids: Baker Academic, 2014), 75.

21. Grant Osborne, *The Hermeneutical Spiral*, 410–11.

Structuring a Sermon

LAURIE L. NORRIS

A sermon is like the tip of an iceberg—much of the work that creates it remains hidden beneath the surface but is essential to the process. How does the preacher move from study to sermon? This can be a daunting question. Having worked faithfully through the exegetical-theological process, the preacher has wrestled with the biblical text, outlining its argument and analyzing its details, seeking to grasp its meaning both historically and universally for the people of God. This careful and in-depth study has yielded the fruit of a singular "big idea" or "central proposition" that synthesizes and encapsulates the theology of a given passage. Put simply: What is the point of this passage?[1]

FROM EXEGESIS TO HOMILETICS

Once the passage has been thoroughly understood, the sermon enters a new stage of development. The process begins to shift from exegesis to homiletics. The sermon now comes into clearer focus, as the preacher engages in bridge-building between two worlds: the world of the biblical text and the world of the present-day hearer.[2] We now ask, What is the point of this passage *for this particular audience*? What is the point of this sermon? While stage one focused on the text, stage two directs attention toward the audience. With theological sensitivity, we move from biblical exegesis to audience exegesis. Like an hourglass that has narrowed from broad ideas to a more particular focus, so now the preacher homes in on a specific audience and begins to shape the sermon. This chapter will provide a general overview of guiding principles for constructing the message.

PURPOSE OF THE PASSAGE

The first step in moving from text to sermon requires identifying the purpose of a given passage. Why is this passage here? What is the distinct contribution of this pericope within its more immediate and canonical context? What is the author (both human and divine) doing or trying to accomplish in this text among the original recipients? What question is the author answering? What behavior is he encouraging or confronting? By looking at the author's emphases and contextual cues, we seek to articulate his central purpose in writing. Once the overarching purpose of the *text* has been identified, we consider the needs of our own audience. More specifically, we consider what our listeners share in common with the original audience.

On this point, Bryan Chapell's work provides helpful direction. Chapell introduces the concept of the "fallen condition focus."[3] This refers to **a human problem or burden addressed by specific aspects of a biblical text.** The "fallen condition" describes the reality of life in a fallen, sin-cursed world: a problem of belief, a pattern of sin, a point of temptation, an experience of suffering. It then addresses God's remedy for that condition and our appropriate response. This fallen condition focus helps serve as a theological bridge to the present audience, as the preacher seeks appropriate alignment between the purpose of the text and the purpose of the sermon. This is the "sweet spot" in preaching, when the intended purpose of the original passage most closely aligns with the purpose of the sermon.

As the sermon addresses the very condition the passage was written to address, so the preacher invites the biblical text to do that same work in us today. Although specific circumstances may change with time and culture, the underlying issues we face are not so dissimilar. We struggle with the same doubts, the same fears, the same temptations. We are called to pursue the same kind of perseverance in the face of opposition, the same kind of holiness, the same kind of love for God and neighbor. The packaging changes, but the substance of our condition remains the same. So then, God's Word remains *always* relevant and speaks with undiminished power and authority to our circumstances today, just as it did millennia ago. God's Word poignantly addresses every need of the human heart. How, then do we discern both the universal and particular needs of our contemporary audience?

AUDIENCE ANALYSIS

The question of purpose requires another step. While in alignment with the biblical text, the sermonic purpose is aimed at a particular audience and rhetorical situation. This requires audience analysis. Here, we exegete people, not the text. This is a skill often neglected by preachers in their preparation process. Unfortunately, those who hold the Scriptures in highest regard may fall most readily into such neglect, due to a prioritizing of God's Word. Hours of faithful labor in biblical exegesis may eclipse equally faithful labor in discerning the needs of the listeners. This does not reflect the heart of expository preaching, which holds together a focus both on text and audience. Yes, God's Word is the center of and authority for expository preaching. But that Word is also directed toward a specific group of people. What do they need to hear? How will they hear it? How should they respond to it in their particular life circumstances?

Such a focus on the audience does not diminish the authority and centrality of Scripture in this process. Quite the opposite: Concern for the audience reflects the absolute priority and necessity of the biblical text. Because this is God's living Word, true food and nourishment for our souls, we do everything possible to help its reception (1 Cor. 9:19–23). Of course, the Spirit ultimately will convict, direct, and transform the hearer, but the preacher expends every effort to communicate that Word with clarity and sensitivity—bringing that authoritative, timeless, and transforming Word to bear on a particular people in a particular time facing particular circumstances.

Imagine investing hours of careful preparation on a gourmet, multicourse meal, only to find that your dinner guests have food allergies that prohibit consumption of most items on your menu! How foolish the host would feel, how futile in their efforts. A good host always seeks to understand the digestive needs, preferences, and limitations of invited guests. Why, then, do we expect something less in the preparation of a sermon for the people of God to consume and digest? How much more is at stake than an evening meal! After all the time spent laboring over the passage, like a good meal, the preacher must take that next step of laboring over the audience. What needs to be said? How will the hearers likely hear that message? How must the preacher rethink, reword, or reframe that message to ensure the best chance of mutual understanding?[4]

Here, the developmental questions become an especially useful tool: What does it mean? Is it true? What difference does it make?[5] These questions help to bridge the gap between text and audience by identifying necessary spheres of explanation, validation, and relevance. What is needed for the audience to rightly understand, believe, and apply the biblical text? Audience analysis seeks to anticipate and address these questions in advance of delivering the sermon. What might interfere with communication? What questions might clutter the communication channel or create potential barriers to understanding? What underlying beliefs might hinder receptiveness or even generate resistance (even that "operational" or lived theology that sometimes confronts or contradicts our stated beliefs)? Where might confusion occur? Does the preacher come to the sermon with presuppositions that must be laid on the table for the sake of clarity? Does the audience fully understand why they need to hear this sermon, why they need to consume this feast, which the preacher has so faithfully and painstakingly prepared for them? These are the kinds of questions that the preacher addresses in studying not only the passage, but the people. Identifying an audience's felt need does not *determine* the sermon's purpose, for certainly our felt needs can be misguided (as anyone with small children knows). However, felt needs may help the preacher *discern* how best to address the underlying needs. God's Word ultimately determines the purpose, but preachers walk through the door of felt need. God's Word is worthy of that wholehearted effort.

Some needs are universal, reflecting creation ideals and expressing the human condition in all times and places. Other needs are more particular. The preacher considers, for example, the audience demographics (age, gender, marital/family status, level of education, socioeconomic status, culture, race/ethnicity, etc.), their spiritual condition, and their corporate identity. Entire books engage this subject more fully, from various angles, and the upcoming chapter on application will dig more deeply into these questions. But the point here is simple: The preacher must strive to know and understand the audience as part of the preparation process. This honors, rather than diminishes, the central place of God's Word in expository preaching.

PURPOSE OF THE SERMON

So then, based on this analysis, we return to the question of the sermon's purpose. Recognizing, of course, the Spirit's agency in this process in ways not limited to the preacher's intended sermonic purpose, the preacher should have a sense of urgency in delivering the message. Why are you preaching this message? Based on your careful exegesis of this text, what is your sermon intended to accomplish? At what primary target are you aiming? Does your desired outcome emphasize the mind, the affections, or a specific behavior? What is the proper response to this portion of God's Word, for this audience, in light of their present condition and circumstances? This stated purpose will constrain the preacher's focus from beginning to end, like a laser beam. It also will serve as a gatekeeper for the preacher in making those hard choices about what to include and exclude (one of the most painful parts of preaching!). Like a sieve that filters out the clutter, the purpose enables the preacher to identify necessary content and to remove extraneous content that does not ultimately serve the purpose.

In submission to the Spirit, preachers need to know the driving purpose of their sermon. They cannot say *everything*. So, as the old adage goes, if you aim at nothing, you will hit it every time. A point in every direction is no point at all.

THE HOMILETICAL IDEA

Once the sermonic purpose has been clearly identified, the preacher articulates a "Big Idea" for the sermon (the central proposition or preaching idea) that reflects this underlying purpose with crystal clarity. The big idea of the biblical text over which the preacher has labored will become the essence of the sermon. This is a fundamental distinctive of expository preaching—that the central point of the biblical text becomes the central point of the sermon. As H. Grady Davis has stated succinctly in his classic book *Design for Preaching*, "[A] well-prepared sermon is the embodiment, the development, the full statement of a significant thought."[6] This concept of the big idea need not deny the complexity and multivalence of Scripture, which may resemble a stained-glass window more than a singular pane. Good preaching surely brings out the beauty and complexity of the biblical text. That said, even the individual panes of a stained-glass window come together to form a larger, unified image that conveys an overall message. So then, good preaching attends to the unifying theological message, but does so without simplistic reductionism. The sermon submits to the text in its primary focus, even while addressing various textual emphases and pastoral concerns for a particular audience.

The preacher should frame the big idea with the audience in mind, using contemporary, concise, and memorable language to encapsulate the entire passage preached. Sermons often miss their intended target for lack of clarity and lack of unity. That is, they do not have a clear point, or they have made too many points. However, the sermon is not simply a collection of disparate details derived from the preacher's hours of study. The big idea serves as an incisive and lucid summary sentence that ties the sermon together as a meaningful, unified, and coherent whole, leaving no confusion in the listener's mind about the point of the sermon, as faithfully distilled from the passage at hand. In many cases, this sentence will take the force of the imperative mood, to indicate a proper response to the word preached and a direction for its application. For example, in a sermon on 2 Corinthians 12:7–10 (Paul's "thorn in the flesh"), we might say: "Embrace your weakness as 'ground zero' of Christ's grace and power." Or, summarizing the message of David's penitential psalm in Psalm 51: "What you confess about the Lord's character will determine the character of your confession." Formulating that clear and concise statement often proves one of the most challenging steps in the entire process.

STRUCTURING THE SERMON

At this point, the preacher considers how best to organize the sermon. The sermon's structure will reflect the content of the message, the flow of the passage, and the specific purpose for the audience. Structure addresses some of these concerns: How early to introduce the big idea, how to develop the big idea, and how to support the big idea. What structure will best accomplish the sermon's stated purpose?

OUTLINING THE SERMON

Some preachers may find it helpful to write out an initial, rough manuscript to gain a general sense of the sermon's direction. However, a preaching outline is paramount for the preparation process, especially regarding clarity. Outlines enable the preacher to see the message and its argument with precision. Outlines provide a skeleton for the sermon, that is, a necessary structure that gives form to the message. The outline should not function like a straitjacket for the preacher, forcing the preacher into linear structures that may or may not fit the genre of the passage or the preacher's cultural context. Rather, the outline should make the preacher *clearer*.

Outlines force the preacher to plan their words, to craft their message for greatest clarity and coherence, and to consider what parts of the message need more (or less) development. They reveal logical gaps in the argument and imbalances in the content. Outlines assist the preacher in making intentional choices about what to include and exclude, and how best to order that material once selected. This material involves both macro structures, as well as development within each movement of the sermon.

MANUSCRIPTING THE SERMON

Some preachers choose to move from initial sermon outline to a final sermon manuscript. Manuscripting the message prompts more careful attention to the sermon's overall flow of thought, smoothness of connections, clarity of argument, and choice of language—both in beauty and economy of language. The value of concise style for sake of clarity applies to both writing and speaking.[7] A sermon manuscript will force the preacher to wrangle with words, to seek precision both in what to say and how best to say it. The goal is oral clarity. Oral clarity means writing for the ear, not for the eye. It means cutting excess verbiage, clutter, and circuitous or passive, indirect constructions. It means giving our sermons a strong edit. It also means avoiding unnecessary complexity in the structure of one's argument. In writing out the sermon, the preacher seeks simplicity. Simplicity is not *simplistic*, but it communicates the profound truth of God's Word in language that is clear, understandable, and accessible for the listener.

SERMON DEVELOPMENT

The sermon's overall structure typically takes one of two basic logical forms: deductive or inductive. These structures relate to the placement and development of the big idea.

Deductive Sermon

A deductive structure will introduce the big idea *in full* early in the message. The rest of the sermon will develop and support this big idea. In such sermons, the preacher shows their homiletical hand by giving the big idea up front (and maybe the main points of the sermon as well). The focus here is clarity. A proposition is stated, then explained, proved, and/or applied.[8] Consider the illustration of a puzzle. In a deductive message, the preacher will show the audience the picture on the box, then turn attention to the pieces that form such a picture.

Inductive Sermon

An inductive structure, by contrast, will withhold the big idea until the end. This generates a sense of mystery, discovery, or suspense. In this case, the preacher will build the puzzle picture piece by piece. The picture on the front of the box will come into view only as the pieces intersect. A problem is posed, then later resolved. A question is raised, then later answered. A subject with multiple complements unfolds, respectively, with each subsequent move. A story is told, and its message disclosed only through the climax and resolution of its narrative plot. Inductive sermons can have a disarming effect on the listener, leading the audience on a journey of discovery from one premise to the next, until a conclusion (i.e., the big idea) is drawn. Such progressive revelation of the argument proves beneficial when an audience is prone to resist or outright reject the sermon's central proposition. Rather than putting an audience on the defensive, an inductive structure invites the audience into a process of deliberation that forces them to wrestle with the preacher's final conclusions. While such deliberation may not result in agreement, it does result in meaningful engagement with the message. In other words, if the preacher has made a compelling case for premises A and B, then the listener must also consider the merits of conclusion C.

Inductive and Deductive Sermons

Some sermons reflect elements of both inductive and deductive structures. In an inductive-deductive (or, semi-inductive) sermon, the message begins inductively, but the big idea surfaces mid-message and is developed deductively thereafter. The structure will depend on when the preacher deems it best to introduce the sermon's central idea.

729

Whether one selects an overall deductive or inductive arrangement to structure the sermon, the goal of clarity remains paramount. An inductive structure should not result in obscurity or needless complexity. If anything, an inductive sermon requires more clarity in direction, because the listeners do not know where they are going. They must follow the preacher step by step, as the argument progressively unfolds. As a blindfolded individual depends upon a trusted guide for clear directions and signals where to stop, where to step, and where to turn, so must the preacher provide clear direction for the audience in following each twist and turn of the sermon. The choice of structure contributes to the clarity of message.

SERMONIC SHAPE

Within these two primary ways of developing a sermon, the more particular form and flow of the sermon will vary, depending on the nature of the content and needs of the audience. The preacher may reorder some elements of the passage in a logical sequence for preaching. For example, the outline may employ a temporal framework to organize certain theological ideas (such as salvation past, present, and future). It may arrange the items in a list by grouping them together in a more conceptual framework. It may synthesize or consolidate the content to cover breadth of material. Or it may reorder the premise and conclusion in the text to build more tension in the sermon and develop a more inductive argument. This must be done with care so that the preacher remains faithful to the text.

Cyclical passages, in which the biblical author circles back to similar points, may invite a more conceptual arrangement of the material for preaching, both to emphasize the central message of the passage and to avoid unnecessary redundancy that may disrupt the sermonic flow or progress in thought. This would apply, for example, to preaching some psalms or portions of the Johannine gospel and letters. Other passages will demand a closer, more exact following of their logical progress to faithfully communicate the author's rhetorical action. For example, some sermons will strictly adhere to the argument of a didactic text, while others will reflect the narrative plot form of the biblical text in their sermonic shape. Biblical preaching respects not only the content of God's Word, but also the form in which God has communicated that content—that is, the particular literary genre of a text. Sensitivity to literary genre as narrative, poetry, prophecy, apocalyptic, epistle, etc., should influence the preacher's choice of sermonic form.[9] The preacher should "feel with" the biblical text in discerning the shape of the sermon for a particular audience.

SERMONIC MOVEMENTS

Having determined the overall structure and shape of the sermon, the preacher must next consider the particular movements of the sermon and how best to flesh them out.[10] The imagery of moves conveys organic movement and progress in keeping with the sermon's flow. The preacher does not simply state main points; rather, the preacher moves fluidly from one point to the next, connecting ideas with seamless ease. This occurs by using clear main points, supporting points, and transitions.

MAJOR MOVEMENTS

Major movements, or so-called main points, of the sermon form the body of the sermon. The content and progress of main points will reflect the various logical structures discussed above, in keeping with the particular thrust of the passage and purpose of the sermon. Not every sermon will call for three coordinate points that form a parallel list. A sermon might move from premise to conclusion or problem to solution. It might move from exegetical analysis to theological reflection, and finally, to present application. In any case, each main point should serve as a necessary building block to the sermon's central message and unifying idea.

Such movements also divide the sermon into manageable units of thought for the listener. Rather than overwhelm the audience with large blocks of material, the preacher seeks to organize and distribute that material in smaller sections that fully develop each point. The preacher should strive for balance of content, both in the number and length of moves. Too few points will lead to dense content that is difficult to digest. Too many separate points, however, will lead to shallow and underdeveloped material that leaves the listener with an unsated appetite and many unanswered questions. Too many points may undermine the unity of the message. The sermon should feel like a unified whole, not a series of disconnected points. The number of major moves should be appropriate for the passage (not forcing or imposing an alien structure upon the text), for the audience, and for the length of sermon. As the old saying goes, less is more. The preacher should make fewer points but may need to work hard to develop them fully. That is, *one should say more about less*. Sometimes a disproportionately *long* main point actually contains two propositions and should become two points, whereas a disproportionately short main point may fit better as a sub-point within another move. Attention to such details aids clarity of communication and flow of argument.

Each major move of the sermon should begin with a clear summary statement (main point) that encapsulates the content of the move in a simple sentence and singular point. The preacher should strive for direct, precise, and memorable language, avoiding passive and circuitous sentence constructions that diminish force and clarity. Wording should strive for contemporary relevance and present significance, personally addressing the audience with the "Today!" of the biblical text. When appropriate (i.e., not forced or wincingly trite), one should consider using various forms of parallel wording, sentence structure, sound, or alliteration for main points, to reinforce clarity and memory.

BUILDING A MOVE

Having identified these major divisions, the preacher must now fully develop the content for every move of the sermon. As Haddon Robinson aptly wrote, the sermon outline needs to put on flesh.[11] This step involves the **explanation**, **illustration**, and **application** of the biblical text to support each main point. We do this in continued submission to the Word of God—not imposing our own agenda on the passage or ignoring difficult or "inconvenient" portions of the text—but faithfully proclaiming the Word in ways that bring the text to light and life for the audience.

Explanation

Here, we revisit the "Developmental Questions": What does it mean? Is it true? What difference does it make? These questions serve the preacher well in structuring the message and in determining what content to include for the listeners to understand, believe, and apply the Word preached. The preacher is careful to engage directly with the biblical text. What words, grammatical constructions, or concepts require explanation? Are there any textual difficulties that should be addressed? What does the text *mean*? What elements of the historical and cultural background need to be unpacked for the listener to enter the world of the text? The preacher should weave such content into the sermon in engaging ways. Explanation of the text should not sound like a technical commentary. Rather, it should stir our interest and deepen our awe for the richness of God's Word; it should bring the world of the text to life.

With respect to belief, what significant interpretive decisions need validation? What proofs might support the preacher's claim? What kind of theological validation is required in moving from the biblical text to present day application for a contemporary audience? The question of belief goes beyond cognitive agreement or mental assent. It extends to "operational theology," that is, our lived theology. Powerful preaching seeks the Spirit's conviction in addressing the audience's underlying beliefs. It surfaces and confronts the frequent disconnect between our stated and lived belief—that is, the truth we mentally and verbally affirm, yet practically deny. For example, we believe God is sovereign in our circumstances, but how does this belief show up in our response to a financial crisis or relational conflict? Do we *really* believe this? What does my life—my thoughts, words, and actions—reveal about my belief? The preacher seeks to dislodge the audience from a place of complacent comfortability and draw them into a posture of submission to God's Word. Such preaching exposes our hearts, delves more deeply into the crevices of doubt, and confronts our misplaced affections and sinful motivations. Such preaching rouses a new recognition of our need for this divine Word. It invites the listener to cry out with fresh awareness, "Lord, I believe; help my unbelief!" (Mark 9:24).

Supporting Material

The preacher will judiciously select supporting materials to explain, validate, illustrate, and apply the biblical text for a particular audience. This can take many forms: repetition and restatement, necessary explanatory material, use of factual information (statistics, data, etc.), definition, quotations, biblical narration, examples, and illustrations.[12] What does the audience need for understanding? For example, definitions clarify what words mean and do *not* mean. By taking time to define key words and concepts, the preacher can avoid unnecessary misunderstanding and remove potential barriers for communication.

The preacher should use factual information carefully and credibly, without misrepresenting or manipulating the data. Similarly, the sermon should not sound like a research paper, citing one source after another. Quotations should be used sparingly, representing recognized and credible sources. Preachers need to discover and develop their own voice—learning to internalize the message and craft it for a particular audience, to labor over the "best" language for greater beauty and clarity and not simply rely on the wording of others.

Illustrations

Illustrations support the sermon in multiple ways. By painting a picture for the listener, they show, not only tell, the preacher's point. Illustrations can clarify (explanation), strengthen our belief (validation), and/or show us the lived implications of a point (application). Some illustrations can do all three of these simultaneously. In this sense, illustrations can do some heavy lifting for the preacher. Illustrations may be brief, like an analogy or striking word picture. These will occur with frequency throughout the sermon. Other illustrations are more extended and developed (e.g., stories). For the sake of clarity, balance, and overall impact, the preacher should avoid overloading each move with more than one substantive illustration.

In selecting illustrations, the preacher must discern what best supports the point. Illustrations should not draw attention to themselves or compete with Scripture; the goal is not to entertain. Rather, illustrations should be woven into the message in a way that directs greater attention to the passage preached. In this way, illustrations serve the biblical text, functioning like stage lights to illuminate the "main act," that is, the living and authoritative Word of God. So then, the preacher must clearly connect the illustration to its point, driving home the illustration with full force to its logical conclusions.

How unfortunate and anticlimactic to spend significant time building up an illustration that languishes at third base and never quite makes it to home plate. Illustrations should clearly and *explicitly* make the point they are intended to support. Some illustrations may even recur thematically throughout the message or serve as bookends between beginning and end. The preacher must consider both the potential gains and losses of each illustration: How closely will certain members of the audience relate to the illustration? How many people will the illustration hit, and with how much force?[13] Whom might it exclude? Will the illustration potentially alienate or offend some, while connecting with others? How much explanation will the illustration require? How much investment of time will the illustration take? Is that investment worth the point it makes? Such questions will guide the preacher in selecting illustrative material that effectively serves the message.

Application

So then, in building a move, the preacher will flesh out the main point by explaining and illustrating a portion of God's Word, all the while drawing the listener back to the biblical text. But there is one more step. As appropriate to the sermon's overall structure and argument, and with sensitivity to the Spirit, the preacher also seeks to apply each main point to the audience in meaningful, personal, and specific ways that reflect an appropriate theological extension of the biblical text for a contemporary context. God's Word always elicits a response from the hearer, and so the preacher must always seek to lead God's people toward such response. This reflects the sermon purpose, discussed above.

The preacher must never shy away from the divine imperative explicit or implicit in the text. As we see in the New Testament Epistles, indicatives lead to imperatives. This is the "therefore" of Scripture. Those who now enjoy union with Christ must live out that union in distinctive ways that mark out their holy identity, both individually and corporately. Preaching in the imperative—that is, calling people to a faithful response—avoids moralism because it clearly presents the "why" and "how" of obedience as grounded in God's provision and enablement, not our own righteousness. In applying the text, the preacher must do no less than does Scripture itself, bringing God's revealed will to bear on specific people in a specific context facing specific circumstances and challenges.[14] The preacher invites the listener into a transforming encounter with the living Word of our triune God.

TRANSITIONS

Transitions create seamless flow throughout the message. They occur between major divisions of the sermon, but also within those divisions. They move the listener logically from one idea to the next, reminding the listener of what has come before and preparing the listener for what lies ahead. Like a door on its hinges, they point backward and forward. Transitions will vary in length and content depending on their function in the argument. How does one idea relate to the other? For example, is the preacher making a simple connection between ideas ("and")? Or is the preacher drawing a more complex inference ("if . . . then")? Such transitions do not emerge in the moment of delivery. Rather, they reflect the preacher's own clarity and progress of thought in the preparation process. This requires careful planning.

Transitions should feel smooth, not stilted. Consider the difference between a novice and experienced driver operating a manual transmission ("stick shift") vehicle. Unlike the novice driver, whose movements are jerky, disjointed, and abrupt, the experienced driver will accelerate with seeming ease, smoothly and almost imperceptibly shifting in and out of each gear. Similarly, experienced preachers will naturally *lead* their listeners from one idea to the next. Their movements will flow.

Transitions clarify the argument by demonstrating how ideas relate to one another. Transitions provide repetition and restatement of main points, and they also signal the listener to prepare for new developments in the sermon. The absence of clear and consistent transitions produces confusion, frustration, and uncertainty in the listener, akin to driving down a long stretch of highway without any clear road signs or mile markers to orient your location or gauge your progress. Similarly, transitions function like road signs in the sermon. Sometimes they signal a major exit and/or on-ramp between larger moves; other times they simply indicate the specific "mile" within a move. In either case, they clarify the listener's present "location" in the sermon. That is, they prevent the listener from getting lost! Transitions serve as sermonic signage. They also contribute to the overall unity of the message by tying together the various parts in relation to the whole.

INTRODUCING AND CONCLUDING THE SERMON

INTRODUCTIONS

Introductions capture the listeners' attention and establish expectations for the sermon. Against a barrage of competing voices that vie for our fleeting attention, the preacher invites the audience to "tune in," as it were, to a particular radio station and "tune out" all other competing frequencies to hear the Word of God preached in this present moment. The introduction should *introduce* the message, preparing the soil and planting the seeds of the sermon that will grow from beginning to end. (Note: The sermon introduction should not be confused with the occasional "pre-introduction," which introduces the preacher, but not the sermon.)

The preacher first captures attention through an opening image (an illustration, probing question, quotation, etc.) and then connects that image to a particular audience need. Surfacing and developing audience need for the message stirs the appetite of the listeners and prepares them to partake of the meal that awaits them through the preaching of God's Word. What question will the sermon answer? What problem will it address? What need will it meet? These questions naturally lead into the next step: introducing the subject and/or big idea of the sermon. Put simply, what will this message be *about*? The degree of disclosure and specificity on this point will depend on whether the preacher has chosen an inductive or deductive development for the message (see above).

Once the subject of the sermon is raised, the preacher will introduce and read the biblical text, in the light of its original context. This passage will be the substance of the sermon, the "meal" of the message. Here, the preacher establishes the sermon's authority as grounded in the biblical text, bringing audience needs and questions into a fresh encounter with the timeless and authoritative Word of God. Finally, the preacher will preview the message by laying out a "road map" that orients the audience to the sermonic journey that awaits them. What is the central question being addressed, and how will they reach the destination? This may involve a preview of the sermon's main points or a more general, conceptual overview of the sermon's structure. Either way, the preacher offers needed direction for the listener and signals a clear transition between the introduction and body of the message.

CONCLUSIONS

Conclusions serve two primary purposes: to review the message and call for a response. That is, they summarize the main points and big idea of the sermon and invite the listeners to respond appropriately to the word of the Lord. Application should not make its first appearance in the conclusion. Rather, the conclusion should drive home those points of relevant application already made in the body of the sermon. In the conclusion, the preacher will seek the unity of the message, tying together loose ends, encapsulating the argument, and relating the sermon's multiple points back to the overarching big idea.

The preacher should avoid introducing new ideas in the conclusion that distract the listener and detract from the sermon's focus.[15] New ideas raise new questions that the preacher does not have time to address or develop. Such questions redirect the listener's attention in ways that can undermine the entire message. This is the time, with laser focus and precision, to conclude the message *already* preached. The conclusion should move the listeners toward true closure. This means avoiding the "crash and burn" ending, that is, an abrupt ending for which the listener feels unprepared. This also means avoiding the "false conclusion" (i.e., circling the runway and failing to land the plane) and/or re-preaching one's entire sermon in the conclusion (or worse yet, in the closing prayer!). Preachers instead should seek a smooth landing that begins with a gradual descent and touches down with finality. For the sake of the listener, well-planned conclusions avoid both extremes of abruptness and aimlessness.

To close the sermon, the preacher may leave the audience with a final image or illustration, a memorable quotation, or an inciting question. The preacher might even come full circle, returning to the sermon's opening image or telling "the rest of the story." But most importantly, the preacher will call the listeners to respond to the central imperative of the text, to take the next step of obedience, to reorient their misplaced affections, to be doers of the Word and not hearers only (James 1:19–25). These are the preacher's final words, the words most likely to reverberate in the minds and memories of the listeners. As such, they should be the preacher's most personal and passionate plea—a fervent and compelling appeal that holds nothing back, contending for faithfulness among the people of God and casting a hopeful vision for what such faithfulness looks like in our daily lives.[16]

CONCLUSION

The process of moving from exegesis to sermon demands spiritual sensitivity and selectivity, both in discerning the audience need and in framing the message with respect to overall structure and particular content. In submission to the Spirit of Christ, the preacher must wrestle with the necessity of what to say and how best to say it, standing under the biblical text and refusing to compromise its message. The mountain of preparatory work becomes the proverbial "tip of the iceberg" in preaching—that is, the culmination of a long and intensive process consolidated in sermonic form. The final message represents the fruit of much prayerful labor: prayer for the Spirit's guidance in rightly understanding and handling the word of truth, prayer for spiritual wisdom to discern the needs of the listeners and communicate accordingly, and prayer for *oneself* to faithfully incarnate the word of God preached.

Preaching is a spiritual task, in which God works directly through His Word and His Spirit to confront and transform. While the preacher is a necessary conduit for the message, the preacher's words ultimately serve the authoritative word of

God. That is the goal: to bring people into direct contact with the eternal and living Word of our triune God, so that they might know, love, and obey Him more fully. As Duane Litfin rightly observes, expository preaching "plugs the audience into the Word of God" and gives them a "direct experience with Scripture."[17] Throughout this process, the preacher must always remember that ultimate source of authority and power for the message: the Spirit of God working through the Word of God among the people of God.

NOTES

1. Most Evangelical writing on expository preaching in recent decades is indebted to Haddon W. Robinson's *Biblical Preaching: The Development and Delivery of Expository Messages*, 3rd ed. (Grand Rapids: Baker Academic, 2014). His influence, both explicitly and implicitly, will be felt throughout this chapter, even when not cited directly. That said, many of these principles also reflect ancient canons of rhetoric and principles of communication that do not originate with Robinson.

2. For this analogy of the sermon as a bridge, see John R. W. Stott, *Between Two Worlds: The Art of Preaching in the Twentieth Century* (Grand Rapids: Eerdmans, 1982), 135–78.

3. Bryan Chapell, *Christ-Centered Preaching: Redeeming the Expository Sermon*, 2nd ed. (Grand Rapids: Baker Academic, 2005), 48–57.

4. Max Warren described this process as "quadruple-thinking," that is, "thinking out what I have to say, then thinking out how the other man will understand what I say, and then re-thinking what I have to say, so that, when I say it, he will think what I am thinking!" (*Crowded Canvas: Some Experiences of a Life-Time* [London: Hodder & Stoughton, 1974], 143).

5. Robinson, *Biblical Preaching*, 49–66.

6. H. Grady Davis, *Design for Preaching* (Philadelphia: Muhlenberg, 1958), 20. For further rationale concerning the "big idea" in preaching, see Robinson, *Biblical Preaching*, 17–23.

7. See the classic work by William Strunk Jr. and E. B. White, *The Elements of Style*, 4th ed. (New York: Macmillan, 2000).

8. Robinson, *Biblical Preaching*, 78–85.

9. See, for example, Jeffrey Arthurs, *Preaching with Variety: How to Re-create the Dynamics of Biblical Genres* (Grand Rapids: Kregel, 2007). With respect to preaching narrative *as narrative*, see esp. Steven D. Mathewson, *The Art of Preaching Old Testament Narrative* (Grand Rapids: Baker, 2002).

10. For the language of sermonic "movement," see Winfred Omar Neely, "Sermons That Move," in *The Moody Handbook of Preaching*, ed. John Koessler (Chicago: Moody, 2008), 324–34.

11. Robinson, *Biblical Preaching*, 97.

12. Ibid.

13. This refers to what is known as the "ladder of abstraction." The lower one goes down the ladder of abstraction, the more concrete and specific the message. This touches fewer members of the audience, but does so with greater force. The higher one goes up the ladder of abstraction, the more people one touches, but with lesser force. The preacher must move up and down this "ladder" to achieve both inclusion and impact. Ideally, the preacher will find a common rung of shared experience at the lowest level of abstraction that hits the most people with the greatest force.

14. For more in-depth discussion of application in the sermon, see the following chapter on "Applying the Sermon" by Kerwin Rodriguez.

15. Robinson, *Biblical Preaching*, 132.

16. On introductory and concluding elements, see Robinson, *Biblical Preaching*, 119–32.

17. Duane Litfin, *Public Speaking: A Handbook for Christians*, 2nd ed. (Grand Rapids: Baker, 1992), 339.

CHAPTER 5.8

Delivering a Sermon

WINFRED NEELY

Are you a biblical preacher? Are you an expository preacher? Does the biblical text shape and determine how you communicate Scripture? Are there standards that help us come to a better self-understanding about where we are located in the hermeneutical and homiletical landscape as preachers?

Reflecting on these questions, respected "teacher of preachers" Haddon Robinson wrote, "Expository preaching at its core is more a philosophy than a method. Whether we can be called expositors starts with our purpose and with our honest answer to the question: 'Do you, as a preacher, endeavor to bend your thought to the Scriptures, or do you use the Scriptures to support your thought?'"[1]

Robinson's question is perceptive, but let's extend his observation. The preacher's self-identification as an expositor must also begin with an honest answer to a similar question: Do you, as a preacher, endeavor to bend your sermonic delivery to the Scripture? That is, do you allow the text under consideration to be the principal factor in determining not only what you preach, but also *how* you preach the textual *what*?

Implicit in our additional questioning is the realization that generally our idea of an expository preacher—or the nature of an expository sermon—may be too narrow. Introducing the term "expository" limits the nature of the message to explanation, when in fact biblical preaching involves more than explanation. A preacher may faithfully communicate the "what" of the text, and yet inadvertently do injustice or maybe even violence to the text by separating the textual "what" from its stylistic, rhetorical, and emotional moorings in message delivery.

MERGING THE WHAT AND THE HOW

We understand expository preaching to be more than the explanation of a text; it is also, as much as possible, the reproduction of the full-orbed textual and genre dynamics in message delivery. Thus, we conclude that yes, sermonic delivery at its core is more a philosophy than a method. The expository message agrees with the text in content, in structure, in mood, in pathos, in tension management, in rhetorical and stylistic dynamics, and in purpose. Thus, it follows that how we understand and treat message delivery is also a factor in determining if one is an expositor in the broader sense of the term.

For example, Walter Liefeld has noted that the tone, emotional colors, and energy of Paul's words in the letter to the Galatians are important, laying the foundation for how the letter should be preached.[2] Consider the impact of the emotion and energy that flows just from this sampling of compelling words from the first chapter of the epistle: amazed, quickly, deserting, disturbing, distort, accursed, persecute, destroy, zealous (vv. 6, 7, 8, 9, 13, 14). Imagine a sermon in which the preacher exposits the facts of the passage—the "what"—while not attending to the "how." In that scenario, Liefeld rightly states, "The expositor of Galatians who only gives a cool, logical explanation of justification by faith has evacuated the epistle of its impact."[3]

Paul uses a series of rhetorical questions in Galatians 3:1–5, beginning with attention-getting words: "You foolish Galatians, who has bewitched you?" He continues, "Did you receive . . .?" "Are you so foolish?" "Did you suffer . . . in vain?" "Does He who provides you . . .?" Paul is emotional. He is frustrated. He is baffled. His use of these rhetorical questions "carries an emotional communication as well as a logical one."[4] Certainly this passage—and numerous others in Scripture—need not be diminished by a delivery devoid of the emotion and power the writer intends.

We can summarize these introductory remarks succinctly:

> In the delivery of the sermon, the preacher should communicate the content of the text *and* reproduce the rhetorical and emotional dynamics of the text in question.

In the preaching moment, the textual content (the what) should merge with the textual form (the how) in the embodied delivery of the sermon. This union constitutes expository/biblical preaching in the broad sense of the idea. Thus, in the delivery of the message, the preacher should strive not only to communicate the content of the text, but also to reproduce the rhetorical dynamics from the text in the delivery of the message as in the examples from Galatians above. We strive for a text-shaped message delivery.

The remainder of this chapter will explore how the preacher merges content and form in the preaching moment. However, before we move to strategies of form and content, we will first consider the value of oral preparation and rehearsal with respect to sermonic delivery.

THE VALUE OF REHEARSAL

Haddon Robinson, who shaped students of biblical preaching for fifty years, encouraged preachers to practice before they preach:

> The minister should rehearse his sermon before he delivers it. Rehearsal tests the structure of the message. Rehearsal also enhances style. As he practices, the preacher may find a phrase that illuminates an idea in a particularly effective way. Rehearsal also improves delivery. A professional actor would not think of going before an audience without first going over his material orally—usually many times—to be sure that it comes to him easily. How can it be spoken so that it will be clear? When should he increase his force, vary his rate, change his pitch, or pause to let a line sink in? While a preacher is more than an actor, he should not be less. Effective delivery must be practiced since the minister cannot think about it much as he speaks.... Beginners will profit from rehearsing with a full voice while standing before a mirror and using a tape recorder.[5]

Oral preparation and message rehearsal improve sermonic delivery in the preaching moment. Some years ago, the preaching faculty of Moody Bible Institute made message rehearsal a student requirement in its preaching classes. Each student was required to be a part of a rehearsal group, comprising three or four students from the class; the purpose of the group was to listen to one another's messages and offer critique and constructive observations. The rehearsal group interacted with these sermons before the student presented the message to the class.

Faculty observed that after message rehearsals were made a requirement in our preaching classes, the overall delivery of the sermons improved. Moreover, students who were a part of the rehearsal group witnessed an interesting phenomenon. They watched the student's sermon improve through the rehearsal. When the student preached the sermon in class, the students in the rehearsal group expressed their delight in watching the student preacher grow in the process, and in some cases witness dramatic improvement in the message delivery. The big takeaway for the students and for us on faculty in this department was this: diligent rehearsal improves message delivery, and rehearsal (including rehearsal with others) is a valuable lifelong discipline and practice.

Important as oral preparation and rehearsal are, however, they do not necessarily result in the merging of the "what" and "how" of the text. That nuanced task requires an exegetically informed oral preparation and message rehearsal, which takes into consideration the rhetorical dynamics, word order, and syntactical contours of the text. Such a rehearsal improves the holistic delivery of the sermon and moves the preacher closer to the merging of the "what" and the "how" in the message delivery.

The exegetically informed preparation for message delivery will occur in two stages. We will devote the remainder of this chapter to explaining these two stages of preparation for message delivery.

We'll first discuss oral preparation—oral shape—which includes pacing, moves, voice. Then we'll move to connecting the oral shape of the message with physical embodiment—facial expressions, gestures, and communicative movement.

ORAL PREPARATION

The purpose of the first stage of rehearsal is to weave oral preparation into the message preparation process from start to finish.

Ideally, if you plan your preaching schedule and have a preaching calendar, you will know weeks or even months in advance what the text for the upcoming Sunday will be. But whatever your planning method, once you have selected the text that will be the basis for your upcoming message, practice reading that text aloud during the week before the next stage of rehearsal when you'll connect the oral shape of the message with physical embodiment. *Do not underestimate the value of this step.* As you study the passage, pay attention to word order, note the shifts in pace, feel the texture of the words in your text, allow yourself to experience the pathos of the text, and journey along the path of the text's emotional curve. Note well Liefeld's observation (emphasis added):

> We tend to think that recourse to emotion is a human device for homiletical manipulation. I would like to suggest that more properly this *emotional dimension can and should be drawn from Scripture itself as part of the exposition.* This will both keep us from missing what Scripture contains and caution us against introducing emotional aspects to our sermon that are not appropriate to the passage being expounded.[6]

As you read the text, try to reproduce verbally the textual dynamics in your reading of the passage during the week. Use a recording device. Listening to ourselves as preachers is a humbling and vulnerable discipline. To this day, despite years of experience, I still approach this discipline of self-critique with a measure of apprehension, but this effort is invaluable and one of the ways we continue to grow as preachers.

As you listen to yourself, ask yourself this question: Does my reading reproduce the textual dynamics of the passage? If not, why not? Your goal is for your reading in the sermonic moment to be an exegetically informed oral interpretation of the text.

Writing about exegetically informed reading of a passage in the sermonic moment, Ian Pitt-Watson observed, "The reading of Scripture should be a high point in the service. . . . I carefully rehearse every word of Scripture that I shall read. All I have learned in my exegetical work goes into that reading. A word wrongly stressed or a sentence wrongly inflected can distort Scripture, and that is a serious matter. Good reading is a fruit of good exegesis."[7] Pitt-Watson then provides us with some sound homiletical counsel:

> Read narrative as if you had just been an eyewitness of the events recorded; read poetry as poetry and delight in its rhythms and parallelisms. Read familiar passages as if they had never been heard before. Reflect the mood of the passage—joy or grief, love or anger. . . . Sometimes one hears preachers (who should know better) read Scripture as casually as they might a telephone book.[8]

In the history of biblical preaching, thoughtful listeners have appreciated the public reading of Scripture by preachers such as John Henry Jowett, Gardner C. Taylor,[9] and G. Campbell Morgan. Congregants who heard Morgan preach were said to have learned more from his reading of a biblical text than they learned from another speaker's explanation of that same text!

Narrative Pacing

After nearly twenty years of training and coaching student preachers at Moody Bible Institute, I have observed that some beginners preach at the speed of light, and others preach at donkey-and-buggy pace, both imposing their natural vocal paces onto the text. This is a problem because it detracts from the message. The remedy is growth and verbal stretching on the part of these speakers in order to be faithful to Scripture in message delivery.

Preachers should adapt their pace to the pace of the narrative under consideration. For example, consider Genesis 22. In verse 2, the narrator arranges the phrases in a way to slow down the narrative. The narrator could have just dropped the bombshell: "Take your son and offer him as a burnt offering." Instead, the phrases in between the opening summons and the command to offer Isaac slow the narrative down: "Take your son." "Your only son." "Whom you love." Then, as the narrative progresses, the pace gradually increases with a rapid flurry of verbs in verses 9 and 10: "came to the place, built the altar, arranged the wood, bound his son, laid him on the altar, reached out with his hand, and took the knife to slaughter his son." The pace is rapid, with the tension reaching its climax when Abraham takes the knife! The preaching pace should reflect the narrative's buildup in pace and tension. In short, when the narrative pace slows down, the preacher should slow down. When the narrative pace increases, the preacher's pace should increase.

Even though the preacher will not always read the entire narrative in the sermon, the preacher should practice reading the narrative as a whole in order to reproduce the narrative shifts in pace in the delivery of the sermon.

Sometimes biblical narrators employ "narrative lingering." This delaying tactic is not merely slowing the pace for its own sake; it is a deliberate lingering for teaching purposes. For example, notice how Moses lingers in Genesis 3:6 (emphasis added): "When the woman *saw* that the tree was good for food, and that it was a *delight* to the eyes, and that the tree was *desirable* to make one wise, she took some of its fruit and ate." Why does Moses linger here? Why does he encourage us to slow down and linger here? Because as we linger here with the Spirit of God, we observe and feel the seductive power and process of temptation at work before the fatal step of "taking" transpires (Gen. 3:6d). The one forbidden fruit seems to offer so much, but it is a lie. Lingering in the context of this narrative makes this clear. In the delivery of the message, the preacher should linger where the narrator lingers. The lingering is not merely a delay tactic, but rather a redemptive lingering in view of life transformation. As the narrative lingering of Genesis 3:6 shows, the reproduction of the "how" is more than stylistics; it is pedagogical, theological, and redemptive in its aim.

If your text is a narrative, you typically should not engage in a verse-by-verse exposition. Within the time constraints of the church service, handling of some narrative texts such as 1 Kings 11 (43 verses long) requires creative narration and select reading. (It is also wise to respect the time parameters adopted for message length. Men and women who are not in the service because they are on security or involved in children's ministry operate within time constraints. If preachers habitually go over the allotted time to preach, they place an unnecessary burden on those who serve in other areas during the service.)

How should the select reading be determined in a narrative? In order to move toward a merger in their delivery, preachers should take their clues from the narrator. Sometimes in Old Testament narratives, the narrator will stop the action in order to describe a person or a place. The narrator might also pause to provide a theological evaluation of the action. For example, at the end of 2 Samuel 11, the account of David's actions against Uriah the Hittite, the narrator breaks from the action. Where the narrator does this to make a comment is a good place for the preacher also to stop the creative narration and say something like the following:

"Notice how the narrator takes a break in the action to make sure we get the important point at the end of verse 27: 'The thing that David had done was evil in the sight of the LORD.'"

In order for the "what" and "how" of this comment to be merged in the preacher's delivery, the reading should be an exegetically informed oral interpretive reading.

REHEARSAL OF SERMONIC MOVES

Language is linear. That is, language, no matter one's cultural context, is composed of a series of rhetorical units. Since the linearity of language is universal, every sermon has a linear dimension and is composed, as David Buttrick puts it, of a series of "rhetorical units." Buttrick identifies these units as "moves."[10] Our concern here is the connection between move development in expository messages and oral preparation. As I have noted in *The Moody Handbook of Preaching*, move development in messages based on the New Testament letters and other similar prose genres includes the following: (1) *stating* and *restating* the main point, (2) *illustrating* or *exemplifying* some aspect of the portion of Scripture that supports the main point, (3) *reading* the portion of Scripture that supports the main point, (4) *applying* the main point to contemporary life, and (5) *reviewing* the main point and transitioning to the next move.[11]

As you develop the move, word the move in a way that you would say it. Go over each component orally. As you consider the pastoral needs of your listeners, determine what elements of the text require explanation. As you do this, visualize your audience. Imagine that you are in conversation with them. As you write down your explanations, verbalize each word. Use simple and concrete language in your explanations, and capture the texture of the terms vocally. Go over the explanations orally. As you weave oral preparation into move development, keep in mind that you may have the tendency to tell stories and communicate illustrations with excitement, energy, imagination, and pathos, but you might tend to *explain* the passage with little or no energy at all. You want to explain the text with equal pathos and energy, varying your vocal dynamics and highlighting the significance of the text through oral interpretation.

It is important to note that we are not saying that you do not reference the text prior to the reading in the move. Instead, when you state, restate, explain, and then illustrate the main point or some element of it, your listeners have more information about the portion of Scripture under consideration in the move. As a result, they are prepared for a richer interaction with the portion of Scripture that supports the main point.

Rehearse the reliving and the relating of examples and illustrations. If you come across a quotation you might include in a move, read that quotation aloud.

Practice the pacing, slowing down and speeding up for interpretive purposes. Vary your pitch. A monotone delivery is lethal to the life of the sermon, practically driving it into cardiac arrest. As you write out the applications, go over them orally. As you write out the introduction and conclusion, go over them orally.

THE VALUE OF VOICE IN BIBLICAL PREACHING

The importance of the preacher's voice in biblical preaching cannot be overemphasized. The expositor must develop their vocal range so that their vocal dynamics are tied organically to the biblical text. If we are truly expositors of the Bible, the inspired text, we must allow the text to take our voices where the Holy Spirit wants to take them. We will not be able to serve some of the dynamics inherent in biblical texts with a limited vocal range. We must use our imagination to experience the emotion and passion of the passage and then allow our voices to move in tandem with the text and the emotions, pathos, and energy of the passage.

An audience can listen to a dull voice for only a few minutes. If our listeners are falling asleep or bored, we need to ask ourselves, "Is my voice putting them to sleep?"[12] The communication of God's Word should be a vocally rich experience—not because the preacher's voice draws attention to itself, but because the Holy Spirit uses the preacher's vocal range to help listeners see and notice fresh vistas of truth in the passage![13] As Pitt-Watson reminds us, "Slovenly speech is unacceptable in the pulpit, so be prepared to make the lips, teeth, and tongue really work hard. That is what gives intensity to the spoken word, especially words quietly spoken."[14] And he's right.

PHYSICAL EMBODIMENT

The purpose of the next stage of rehearsal is to connect the oral shape of the message with physical embodiment—facial expressions, gestures, and communicative movement. The congregation does more than listen to the preacher; they see and notice the preacher's facial expressions, the ethos of the eyes, the smiles (cold smiles, sarcastic smiles, insecure smiles, haughty smiles), and the preacher's movements. Listeners hear and see the preacher. We have some uncomfortable news for some of you. The prayer that some preachers offer to God at the beginning of their sermons—"Lord, hide me behind the cross"—is well-intended, but uninformed. In two thousand years of church history, the Lord has never responded to this prayer in the affirmative. God does not hide the preacher behind the pulpit or on the platform! People see and observe the preacher. Thus, everything that the preacher does in the actual delivery of the sermon matters. In short, the instrument is not just the preacher's voice. The instrument is the preacher as an embodied person, whose total self is the instrument in the preaching moment.

BENEFITS OF REHEARSAL WITH THE COMPLETED MANUSCRIPT

Even if you preach without notes or do not use a manuscript, or even if you use one or the other, it is a good exercise to write out a full manuscript of the sermon. Whether it's the use of a manuscript, notes, or a few words written down, no substitute exists for internalizing the sermon for the following reasons.

Clarity: The diligent preacher will reap several benefits at this level of preparation. Rehearsal with a manuscript will help you become aware of elements in the message that still may not be clear. For example, years ago I rehearsed a particular message with a completed manuscript. I sensed that a section in one of the moves was not clear. For some reason, I convinced myself that this unclear section would work. The following Monday in our staff evaluation of the Sunday service, which included my sermon, one of the staffers asked me, "Pastor Neely, what did you mean when you said such and such?" I thought, *Wow, that was the part of the message that was not clear to me in my own rehearsal.* If it is not clear to us, how can we expect a muddy section in our manuscript to be clear to our listeners? As one familiar preaching adage rightly concludes, "A mist in the pulpit is a fog in the pew." Rehearsal with a complete manuscript may flag elements of the message that are not clear.

Better Wording: At this stage of rehearsal, better wording will come to you as you go over the manuscript. Sometimes you may find yourself in a creative zone as the Spirit of God brings better and more memorable wording to you. The Spirit will bring to your mind slices of life from your past that may serve as pertinent examples and illustrations.

Deeper Message Internalization: Weaving oral preparation into message preparation helps the preacher internalize the message. Rehearsal with a completed manuscript will help you deepen the internalization of the message. As you weave oral preparation into the message preparation process, keep in mind that something deeper than memorizing a manuscript must occur. Your goal is to internalize the message, to make it a part of your soul, so that the message comes out of your heart. Two of my former students put it this way: "Having had an extra two days to rehearse and fine-tune my presentation, I was able to rely less on a memorized manuscript and engage more with an internalized truth, which made the presentation feel more natural and less scripted" (Alex Gowler). "I realized the importance of internalizing a sermon even if I have notes or a manuscript; internalizing brings the preacher into the sermon" (Micah Boerckel).

OWNING THE PREACHING SPACE

Use physical movement in a way that is communicative.

In messages based on biblical narratives, connect strategic movement to geography and places in the story. In order to do this well, determine where these places are on your platform or preaching space. For example, if you preach a message on Ruth 3, where is the walled city of Bethlehem? Where will you locate the threshing floor? Where is the pile of grain where Boaz slept? Determine in advance where you will physically locate these places. As you relive and relate the story when you are in Bethlehem, move to the part of the platform where you have decided to locate Bethlehem. Do the same with the threshing floor and the place where the pile of grain is located. This kind of strategic movement ties your movements to geography and enhances the sermonic presentation. Some transitions do not involve a change in geographical location. In such cases, instead connect strategic movement to major plot shifts or psychological developments in the story.

In messages based on epistolary literature, use your physical movement to indicate to your listeners where you are in the moves. Link your physical movement to the logical progress of move development. When you begin another move, shift to another part of the platform.

THE COMMUNICATIVE POWER OF GESTURES

Message content and the emotional curve of the biblical text should guide the way you gesture during the preaching event. A gesture is any physical motion used to communicate ideas and emotional responses. Competent preachers use gestures to emphasize elements of the message and to nuance ideas and concepts. If you say the same thing with your arms folded, or clasping your hands, or opening your arms wide, these gestures will nuance the communication in dramatic and different ways.

Gestures do a number of things. Broad gestures put the preacher at ease. Gestures capture attention and arouse interest.[15] Through gestures, listeners are able to feel what the preacher feels. Gestures are a vital part of biblical preaching, and the wise preacher does not underestimate their communicative power. Timothy Gura and Charlotte Lee observe, "Responsiveness is such an important factor in the total process of communication that you would do well to work on gestures conscientiously during rehearsal periods."[16]

In order to develop competence in the use of gestures and separate them from idiosyncratic movements, the speaker should rehearse in front of a mirror. This will help make him or her aware of personal mannerisms that may hinder the clear communication of God's Word.

We all bring our idiosyncratic body movements to the preaching moment.

These grow out of our personalities. As such, they are not gestures per se because they are not communicative. Instead, they actually get in the way of our message by inadvertently drawing unnecessary attention to ourselves and diverting direction away from the message. For example, some preachers habitually tilt their heads to the right or the left. Some preachers point their toes to the floor and move their feet in awkward ways. Some preachers move backward and forward on their heels, shifting their bodies up and down. What is interesting about this phenomenon is that these speakers are not aware of these movements. When they watch themselves in a recording, most are appalled at these movements and deeply concerned that these mannerisms actually hindered their communication of God's Word.

THE POWER OF EYE CONTACT

One of the key ways a preacher is able to connect deeply with listeners and cultivate trust—indeed, perhaps the most important form of nonverbal communication—is eye contact. Eyes communicate emotions and attitudes, and are gateways to a preacher's world. Do not stare at your listeners but do make eye contact with them. See them. Really look at them. And make sure you look at and scan every section of the congregation as you preach.

USE OF THE HANDS

Next to the face, the most communicative part of the body is the hands. We may use our hands to point to something and to express welcome. We may use our hands to show how we repel or reject ideas. We may make a fist to show anger or determination. It is hard to overestimate the communicative power of the hands.

Since the hands are the second most communicative part of the body, preachers need to make full use of the most effective forms of amplification that free up the hands for communicative purposes.

VARYING VOCAL DYNAMICS

The following elements of vocal delivery should be exegetically informed, as discussed earlier in this chapter.

Pitch: Pitch is movement of the voice up and down the scale. Vary your pitch. Make sure that when you go up in volume, you go down in pitch. This will keep the voice from cracking, and the vocal sound will be more resonant. Remember that delivery in a monotone is deadly to the message and results in audience boredom. Avoid flatlining your delivery.

Punch: Punch is variation in volume and force. Using a wide range of volume, from loud to soft, will enhance delivery. Keep in mind that you do not need to scream. Due to advances in technology and the use of amplification devices, speakers today do not have to yell to be heard. Your emphasis will come through variety. Sometimes intensity can be as effective as volume. We remind young preachers that the power is in the lightning and not in the thunder.

On the other hand, some preachers will never raise their voices. They say "God" or "Jesus" or talk about His death and resurrection, mention His ascension to glory, discuss His present session at God's right hand, and point us to the promise of the Lord's second coming in ways that lack vigor and power. We encourage these preachers to add some *oomph*—that is, some vocal energy and volume—to their delivery.

Progress: Progress is the rate of delivery, the speed at which a person speaks. Be flexible in your rate. Use a faster pace for the less important details. Use a slower pace for key assertions and ideas. A very slow rate gives a very strong emphasis. Again, the text should play the primary role in determining sermonic rate (see the earlier discussion on Narrative Pacing).

Dramatic Pause: The dramatic pause refers to purposeful and informed silence in the preaching moment. By use of the dramatic pause, the preacher allows space and time for a thought to sink deeper into the minds of listeners. For example, if we read the narrator's comments about David's actions in 2 Samuel 11—"The thing that David had done was evil in the sight of the LORD" —and then pause dramatically for a few seconds, we make space for the narrator's assessment to have more impact on the listeners.

The dramatic pause is a strategic way to manage tension in the message. For example, if the preacher says something like this: "What is the point? What is the big takeaway for us today?" and then pauses, both the questions and the pause build tension and heighten interest. The rhetorical result is the preacher communicates the big idea in a more powerful way. It is a pedagogical principle that learning takes place at the point of felt tension. The dramatic pause is useful in tension management for pedagogical purposes.

A long dramatic pause—three to five seconds, which seems like an eternity in the preaching moment—heightens tension, communicates the emotional content of ideas, and indicates a change of direction in the message. The dramatic pause captures attention and arouses interest. We know through empirical evidence the attention-arousing power of the dramatic pause. And we concur with Buttrick's observations:

> Studies indicate that, after a pause, audiences are alert; their attention level is high, they hear well. Such heightened attention will last for a few sentences after the pause before, gradually, attention will relax. Thus, wise speakers know that they only have a few sentences—perhaps three—in which to focus attention and to establish what it is they will be speaking.[17]

Thus, the skillful use of the dramatic pause is not merely rhetorical, but an expression of care and concern for God's people.

ATTENDING TO CULTURAL PREACHING CONTEXTS

In the preaching moment, the preacher also needs to consider the cultural context of the preaching event. While the preacher must be faithful to the text in the sermonic delivery, this does not mean that the preacher should not take audience dynamics into consideration. For example, an American preaching in the UK may want to be more conscious of volume. Americans have a tendency to be too loud for the British context. In some English-speaking Chinese contexts, the audience will not respond with the kind of verbal affirmation (such as "amen") that we may see in some African American contexts. Instead, Chinese listeners affirm the message by listening closely; this is obvious in body language, tears, audience lean, laughter, smiles, and other forms of nonverbal audience response.

The preacher must adjust delivery to the cultural context in question. Audiences should not have to adjust to the delivery style of the preacher. Preachers should desire to develop the delivery competences that will allow them to preach effectively in their own cultural contexts, as well as in other cultural contexts.

THE INDISPENSABLE FOUNDATION: PRAYER

Your preaching ministry will never rise above the power of your personal prayer life. For that reason, from a posture of humility not of legalism, spend an hour in prayer before you preach. Then rehearse the message on your knees before the Lord. You will consequently have more power in your delivery. The Holy Spirit will grant you more insight, and He Himself will fuel your passion for the truth of the message! As John Stott said so compellingly,

> It is on our knees before the Lord that we can make the message our own, possess or re-possess it until it possesses us. Then when we preach it, it will come neither from our notes, nor from our memory, but out of the depths of our personal conviction as an authentic utterance of our heart.... We need to pray until ... the fire burns in our heart, and we begin to experience the explosive power of God's Word within us.[18]

In this connection between preaching and prayer, we want to encourage you to deepen and enlarge your prayer life. Spiritual power in biblical exposition is the result of a powerful life of prayer! Cultivate the habit of spending an hour in prayer daily. Here is the challenge: If you spend one hour in prayer daily for the next year, a year from now your life will be more powerful in the biblical sense, and there will be a marked difference in your preaching. Your preaching will have the touch of that intangible heavenly presence and power.

CONCLUSION

Preachers should not separate the "what" of the text from the "how" of the text. The union of the textual "what" and the textual "how" is a literary and homiletical marriage that we should cherish and celebrate in our preaching. As we work and strive to grow as biblical communicators, may this chapter be used to help us all deliver messages that truly communicate the "what" and the "how" of the text under consideration.

NOTES

1. Haddon W. Robinson, *Biblical Preaching: The Development and Delivery of Expository Messages*, 3rd ed. (Grand Rapids: Baker Academic, 2014), 5.

2. Walter L. Liefeld, *New Testament Exposition* (Grand Rapids: Zondervan, 1984), 85–87.

3. Ibid., 87.

4. Ibid., 85.

5. Haddon W. Robinson, *Biblical Preaching*, 205–06

6. Liefeld, *New Testament Exposition*, 87.

7. Ian Pitt-Watson, *A Primer for Preachers* (Grand Rapids: Baker, 1986), 90.

8. Ibid.

9. Several years ago, I listened to a recording of the late Gardner Taylor's reading of Luke 3:1–6. The reading was masterful, vocally rich, interpretive, and so powerful that I can still hear his voice as I think about how he read this passage.

10. David G. Buttrick, *Homiletic Moves and Structures* (Philadelphia: Fortress, 1987), 22–23.

11. Winfred Omar Neely, "Sermons That Move," in *The Moody Handbook on Preaching*, ed. John Koessler (Chicago: Moody, 2008), 324–34.

12. Patsy Rodenburg, *The Actor Speaks: Voice and the Performer* (New York: Palgrave Macmillian, 2000), 180.

13. Through reading Patsy Rodenburg's books on the use of the voice in acting, my insight into the importance of vocal range in preaching was deepened. My thoughts in this paragraph were derived from her thoughts about the use of vocal range when working with texts in plays. I connected her thoughts on vocal range with the text of Scripture. For more in-depth reading about the use of the voice, consult Patsy Rodenburg, *The Actor Speaks* and *The Right to Speak: Working with the Voice* (2nd ed.; New York: Methuen Drama-Bloomsbury, 2015).

14. Pitt-Watson, *A Primer for Preachers*, 93.

15. In his day, John Henry Jowett was one of the most effective and competent expositors in the English world. He was also a delight to watch. Those who watched him remarked that he was the master of graceful gestures.

16. Timothy Gura and Charlotte I. Lee, *Oral Interpretation*, 12th ed. (New York: Routledge, 2010), 123.

17. Buttrick, *Homiletic Moves and Structures*, 37.

18. John R. W. Stott, *Between Two Worlds* (Grand Rapids: Eerdmans, 1982), 201.

Applying the Sermon

KERWIN A. RODRIGUEZ

"So will My word be which goes out of My mouth;
It will not return to Me empty, Without accomplishing what I desire,
And without succeeding in the purpose for which I sent it."
ISAIAH 55:11

Fundamentally, preaching addresses people with the Word of God. This means that preachers are concerned with being both biblical and attentive to the lived situation of the people listening. These two worlds, the world of the text and the world of the listener, stand far apart in the minds of listeners. The preacher's task is to proclaim how the Scriptures direct the lives of people in accordance with who God is and what He is doing. This proclamation, then, serves as an invitation for the receiving community to participate in the world remade by the gospel. Preaching that is faithful to both the text of Scripture and the context of its receivers will be primarily concerned with helping listeners "conform their lives—their heads, hearts, and hands—to what Scripture shows God to be doing to renew all things in and through Jesus Christ."[1] The whole person is addressed by Scripture and by its proclamation.

Application in the sermon is the move toward the listener to make explicit the ways the receiving community can respond to the preached Word. It is not an easy move. In fact, Haddon Robinson warns, "More heresy is preached in application than in Bible exegesis."[2] How then, does one apply the Scriptures without misusing the Scriptures? The task requires wisdom from God. It also demands careful attention to the ways biblical texts convey meaning and deep understanding of the receiving community addressed in the sermon. This chapter will provide insight on sermon application so that the preacher might more effectively invite listeners to be transformed by the preaching of God's Word.

SCRIPTURAL FOUNDATIONS FOR APPLICATION

Scriptural Authority

Application in the sermon depends first on the very nature of its source material, the Scriptures. The Bible is the Word of God. As the Word of God, it serves to reveal who God is, what God has done, and what God is doing in the world. But the Scriptures do not merely convey information about God, they also do something with their words. The psalmist describes the law of the Lord as perfect and affirms that the Scriptures restore the soul, make the simple wise, and enlighten the recipients of the Word (Ps. 19:7–8). When the apostle Paul encourages Timothy to continue in the "sacred writings," he affirms that the Scriptures are "breathed out by God" (ESV) and "profitable" (2 Tim. 3:16). Perhaps it is time for preachers to consider how the inspiration of Scripture and its profitability serve our understanding of its authoritative nature.

For many, the inspiration of Scripture primarily refers to its authoritative nature, narrowly defined by its truthfulness and reliability. Evangelicals affirm that "the Bible, including both the Old and New Testaments, is a divine revelation."[3] Though we can speak of the human authors of these texts, God is its ultimate author.[4] The authority of the Scriptures is tied to the authority of ultimate author, God. These doctrinal statements are important and helpful descriptions of the nature of the biblical text, but we must go a step further.

The Scriptures are not just authoritive because they belong to God; they are authoritative because they make divine authoritative claims on its hearers. To affirm the authoritativeness of Scripture is not just to affirm its truthfulness, but to affirm its purpose. Kevin Vanhoozer writes, "God commissions just these texts to play a vital and authoritative role in the plan of salvation whereby the triune Lord communicates his light (knowledge), life (redemption) and love (fellowship)."[5] So then, the Scriptures are authoritative because they are the true revelation of God, which God Himself uses for the formation of its hearers. Paul states the purpose this way: the Scriptures are "profitable for teaching, for reproof, for correction, and for training in righteousness, so that the man of God may be complete, equipped for every good work" (2 Tim. 3:16–17 ESV). Summarizing the divine purpose of God's revelation, Vanhoozer continues, "The purpose of Scripture is both to inform us about Christ and to form Christ in us ... Scripture renews our minds, reorients our hearts and revitalizes our imaginations."[6]

SCRIPTURAL MEANING

Scripture then, is authoritative because it is divinely inspired and divinely purposed for the formation of its readers. Before we turn toward sermon application specifically, we should consider scriptural meaning. Jeannine Brown defines meaning "as the complex pattern of what an author intends to communicate with his or her audience for purposes of engagement, which is inscribed in the text and conveyed through use of both shareable language parameters and background-contextual assumptions."[7]

The practice of application presupposes biblical meaning as something "inscribed in the text" and "intend[ed] . . . for purposes of engagement." Scripture does something to its reader. Whenever the preacher attempts to apply the Scriptures, the attempt should be rooted in the ways the Bible addresses its reader.

Some preachers talk about the sermon as "hearing a word from the Lord." So long as this "word" is ground in what the biblical text *says* and *does* (central idea and purpose), the word we hear from Scripture is a prophetic, wise, and re-scripting word. Each adjective describes how Scripture addresses its readers.

SCRIPTURE ADDRESSING THE READER

A PROPHETIC WORD

Scripture addresses readers as a prophetic word. The prophets in the Bible were called and sent by God to "call the people back to their covenant relationship with Yahweh."[8] As a messenger of God, the prophet uniquely represented God to those addressed by His word. The true prophet was so closely aligned to the interests of God that his words were almost indistinguishable from the words of God (Jer. 1:9).

Several descriptions have been offered to characterize prophetic speech. One characterization helpful for the present discussion is prophetic speech as "a truth-telling, hope evoking word."[9] Each of these adjectives are relevant. First, prophetic speech as a "truth-telling" word highlights that the word functions as truth confronting falsehood. The true prophet of God spoke out against the worship of false gods (Isa. 1:29; 57:1–13) and the inauthentic piety of the people of God (Isa. 58:1–14). In doing so, the prophetic word confronted people to repent by turning from their falsehood to worship the one true God.

The second adjective "hope evoking" is also important. Not every prophetic word evoked hope, since much of prophetic speech was a word of judgment. Still, prophetic speech as a whole looked forward to the Lord's deliverance. This hopeful word is a comfort for the people of God since it reassures them that God is faithful to His people and will surely deliver her (Isa. 40:1–5).

So then Scripture as a prophetic word both tears down and builds up (Jer. 1:10). It confronts readers with their sin and calls him or her to repent of falsehoods. It also offers hope by leading the reader to see and hope in God as faithful deliverer.

A WISE WORD

Scripture addresses readers as a wise word. Wisdom literature has a practical disposition. It offers direction for all of life. In Scripture, the guidance it offers is grounded in one's relationship to God. Knowledge and wisdom begin with the fear of the Lord. From there, individuals receive spiritual insight into all areas: interpersonal relationships, finances, work, and even the fate of the wicked and the righteous.

According to wisdom literature, one's perspective and practice is reordered by one's relationship to God so that the wise person follows the way of the Lord. This way of the Lord is marked by justice, righteousness, and equity (Prov. 1:2–3). Unlike the fool, the wise person is diligent and prudent. Throughout wisdom literature, it is apparent that wisdom is acquired. The simple can become wise by responding positively to wisdom's invitation to life properly ordered (Prov. 8). In the New Testament, wisdom comes from God (James 1:5–6) and Scripture has the power to "make you wise for salvation" (2 Tim. 3:15).

Scripture then, offers a wise word. It offers an invitation to reorder one's life according to the ways of God, the Creator and ruler of the world. This wise way applies to all of life and rejects the sort of compartmentalization that separates "sacred" affairs from "practical" ones.

A RE-SCRIPTING WORD

Scripture addresses readers as a re-scripting word. Readers engaged with Scripture discover that it serves as a kind of script. The Bible acts like a script because "each part of Scripture contributes to our understanding of the whole theodrama, both the meaning of what God has said/done and what we must say/do in response."[10]

The analogy of Scripture serving as a "script" can be confused when we assume that each part is to be performed "word for word." The suggestion that the Bible addresses people as a re-scripting word does not suggest that the Bible intends listeners to emulate all of the characters and their actions. As Vanhoozer notes,

> Scripture gives us not a script in the narrow sense of the term—a detailed template for speech and action-but in the broader sense of a collection of authoritative scenarios that serve as lessons, positive and negative, for us (1 Cor. 10:6–11). We are to speak and act in situations today *as* faithful prophets

and apostles did in theirs . . . What is on offer is not merely information to be mastered but concrete wisdom to be deployed in a variety of situations.[11]

Why is the word offered by the Bible a re-scripting word? It is a re-scripting word because when readers engage with the Scriptures, they come with their own script, a competing worldview that informs one's belief, values, and practices. When readers are addressed by God through His Word they discover an alternative way of understanding, being, and living in the world.[12] The reader finds in Scripture the charge to reject conforming to the patterns of the present evil age and instead to be transformed by the renewal of one's mind (Rom. 12:2).

Scripture reading is an invitation to engage with the Spirit's work to transform and renew one's mind. Ideally the faithful reader will be open to the invitation and find one's way of understanding, being, and living altered.

The text speaks to its readers by offering a prophetic, wise, and re-scripting word. When the preacher-interpreter identifies the purpose of the text and moves toward developing the purpose of the sermon, these three descriptors will be helpful to identify what the text is saying and doing. After careful exegesis, the preacher can ask how the text intends to form the implied reader. Does the text offer a prophetic word that confronts the reader in their falsehoods and evoke hope in God's faithfulness and promised deliverance? Does the text offer a wise word that instructs and invites the reader to practically follow the way of the Lord? Does the text offer a re-scripting word that deconstructs the reader's beliefs, values, and practices and proposes a new way of understanding, being, and doing?

Engaging the task of understanding the meaning of Scripture in this way, will make developing sermon applications easier. As noted above, careful attention to biblical meaning is only one half the equation. Sermon application also demands deep understanding of one's receiving community. Let us turn our attention from exegeting Scripture to exegeting our listeners.

UNDERSTANDING YOUR LISTENERS

Some ministers preach to the same listening community every week. Others are itinerant preachers, preaching to strangers at a conference or as a guest speaker in a church. Regardless of one's familiarity with the individual members of the listening audience, preachers must do all they can to understand who is listening to the sermon. In his book *Folly, Grace, and Power,* John Koessler notes that the preacher exercises the priestly function of representing and advocating for the people.[13] He writes, "Like the priest, the preacher does not stand apart from those who hear but is called from among them in order to sympathize with them (Heb. 4:15)."[14]

Representation and advocacy in our biblical preaching first requires understanding. Preachers must be attentive to the needs and lived realities of their listeners by understanding them demographically, culturally, and pastorally.

DEMOGRAPHICALLY

Understanding the demographic of your audience is perhaps the most basic level of understanding, yet it is an essential starting point. Preachers must answer the question: Who am I speaking to? All audiences have some kind of demographic diversity. And yet, preachers craft sermon applications as if all members of the audience are the same. Novice preachers tend to project their own life situations onto their listeners. Even experienced preachers make the same mistake. Talk with a single person in your church and you will hear their disappointment that applications are almost always directed toward married individuals. Understanding one's audience demographically provides a helpful starting point so that the preacher is able to identify commonalities and differences among the listening group. It also encourages the preacher to construct sermon applications that address the diverse life situations of a particular audience.

Imagine your listeners sitting in front of you. How would you describe the group demographically?

- How many of them are male or female?
- What is the age or generational makeup of the group?
- What about the racial and ethnic identities represented in the audience?
- Are there any single, divorced, or widowed people?
- Do many of the individuals in the audience have children?
- What is the average age of their children?
- What about the education level of the various individuals in the group?
- What kind of work do they do?

One could be even more descriptive by dividing the audience into even more specific subgroups.

- For example, can those who are single be divided into individuals who are in a committed relationship and those who are looking to be in one?

- If there are professions held in common, might there be other subdivisions within that category? For example, say there are a number of individuals who are teachers in the congregation.

- Can these teachers be divided into Christian school teachers and public school teachers? Or for other professions, can professionals be divided by whether they are self-employed or employed by an organization?

These descriptions and subdivisions become helpful tools for the preacher to craft specific applications. The exercise is not meant to be exhaustive, rather it encourages ministers to think concretely about the lives of their listeners. As one homilitician notes, preachers should consider these subcategories in order "to see if your biblical truth shows up in some situations."[15] The goal is not to provide an application for every unique situation, but to consider how one can tailor applications throughout the sermon to address the varied situations of one's audience with specific direction.

CULTURALLY

If our understanding of the people we minister to ended at the level of demographics, it would be rightly labeled as superficial. A minister must go deeper by understanding their listeners culturally. Definitions of culture vary and almost every definition is preceded by the admission that defining the concept is difficult due to its complexity. Andy Crouch offers a concise definition of culture as "what we make of the world."[16] This succinct definition communicates more than its length indicates. One thing Crouch's definition highlights is the meaning dimension of culture. Ultimately humans are making sense of the world.

Other definitions focus on the observable aspects of this sense making. These definitions conceive of culture as a "lived worldview." Vanhoozer, for example, defines culture as "the lens through which a vision of life and social order is expressed, experienced, and explored."[17] Homiletician Matthew D. Kim similarly defines culture as "a group's way of living, way of thinking, and way of behaving in the world."[18] These definitions are not necessarily at odds with one another. However one defines the complex concept, it is important to observe that culture both communicates and orients the way we view ourselves, others, and the world.

Complicating things even further is that an individual's cultural identity is also complex. Individuals do not belong to a single cultural group. Instead individuals inhabit various cultural and subcultural groups. Each person's social identity is shaped by various cultural factors. Our making sense of ourselves, others, and the world is shaped by such things as race, ethnicity, gender, location, and religious history. Each individual can be shaped by these factors in different ways, but everyone's sense making and lived worldview is informed by these cultural factors to some degree or another.

The faithful preacher's task is difficult. It requires the development of cultural intelligence. Kim rightly argues, "It is in the purview of *every* preacher to understand and appreciate *everyone's* cultural nuances, to move them forward in their sanctification process in becoming more Christlike in their maturity."[19] The skill of cultural intelligence takes cultivating. Preachers should invest time and energy to learn how culture informs both life and ministry practice. Thankfully several helpful resources are accessible.[20] Kim recommends the following actions to deepen understanding in a diverse community,

> (1) reading books that include the literature and historical experiences of a different culture; (2) engaging in participant-observation by attending events and activities of a particular culture, participating as much as possible, and jotting down notes of what you have learned; (3) conducting focus-group interviews to ask questions about a select group of individuals and their cultures; and (4) spending time with congregants from various contexts, especially in their natural environments such as in their homes and in other cultural settings.[21]

Cultural understanding matters. It provides insight to the ways our listeners make sense of the world. For the purposes of preaching and ministry, this "sense making" is expressed in the form of beliefs, values, and habits. Preachers ought to be able to describe how their listeners view themselves, others, and the world around them according to the narratives their cultural identity provides. Additionally, preachers should note how these narratives shape the formation of beliefs, values, and habits of their listening community.

Pastorally

We have noted that understanding the audience demographically asks, "Who am I speaking to?" Understanding the audience culturally asks, "How do my listeners make sense of themselves, others, and the world?" Understanding the audience pastorally asks, "What are they going through at the moment?" This question is perhaps the most personal and requires sensitivity to the pressing needs and experiences of the receiving community.

Preachers who have a personal connection with his or her audience are at an advantage in this regard. Local church pastors are typically aware of painful experiences or hopeful developments in people's lives. They are more likely to know when individuals experience loss, or when relationships are in conflict. They also know when prayers have been answered and the community is rejoicing because of God's provision. Sermons can become personal encounters between God and His people when the preacher mediates between the two, voicing laments and expressing praise in response to the community's experiences. "The preacher enters into the joys and sorrows of those to whom he or she preaches."[22]

Pastoral preaching requires wisdom from God and attentiveness to those who are in need. Preaching can offer a timely word that heals painful wounds or affirms redemptive moments. When preparing sermons, pastors will hold out the lives of their people before God as an act of love and concern. In doing so, pastors hope to provide insight or comfort for those who are entrusted into their care. Pastoral preaching is an act of love. It echoes the love the apostle Paul had for the church in Thessalonica. Paul writes, "But we proved to be gentle among you. As a nursing mother tenderly cares for her own children, in the same way we had a fond affection for you and were delighted to share with you not only the gospel of God, but also our own lives, because you had become very dear to us" (1 Thess. 2:7–8).

In addition to love, pastoral preaching arises out of a deep sense of empathy and an awareness of the responsibility one has for the community one speaks for and to. For the celebrated Gardner C. Taylor, the King James rendering of Ezekiel 3:15 captured the experience of the preacher well. "I came to the exiles who lived at Tel Abib near the Kebar River. And there, where they were living, I sat among them for seven days—overwhelmed."[23] While preachers are commissioned by God to give a word to the people, they are often most effective when they remember they were called from among the people. Preachers are not just heralds, but first-hand witnesses to the work and power of God. Like Paul, the preacher declares, "For I handed down to you as of first importance what I also received" (1 Cor. 15:3a). Preachers can speak with empathy because they have experienced pain and joy and have received words from God that bring comfort and strength. The authentic experience of the preacher can be a deep resevoir from which to draw commonalities between the preacher and the listening community. Alcántara observes, "When people learn that the preacher is a fellow sojourner through the hardships and heartaches of human existence, they lean forward and pay attention."[24]

It would seem that itinerant preachers are at a disadvantage. Can a visiting preacher or a conference speaker understand and preach pastorally in the same way a rooted preacher can? The answer is both no and yes. It is true that a pastor has the tremendous benefit of living, observing, and experiencing life within a particular community over long periods of time. There is a potential for personal connection and attentiveness that cannot be overstated. Still, itinerant preachers can preach pastorally as well.

Pastoral preaching is fundamentally a disposition of shepherding through preaching. One does not have to know all of the intimate details of the congregation's life to be able to speak honestly, lovingly, and empathetically. As long as itinerant preachers approach the task of preaching as shepherds, they can be sensitive to ways biblical texts address real life situations that include disappointments and triumphs, loss and blessing, and pain and joys. All preachers, whether local or itinerant, ought to avoid abstract appeals. All preachers should offer specific and concrete applications that can be "seen" by the audience when offered by the preacher. Listeners can imagine how the biblical text can become manifested in their own lives.

DEVELOPING THE SKILL FOR APPLICATION

CONSIDER YOUR OWN LIFE

Some preachers are better at application than others. This should not excuse preachers who are not naturally inclined toward crafting good application in the sermon. All preachers should be concerned with developing the skill for applying the text. This skill begins with the preacher's consideration of his own life. Preachers should learn to apply the Scriptures to themselves. Cecilio Arrastía, the celebrated Cuban homiletician reminds preachers, "If preaching is to make others vibrate with the power of the Gospel, it is [necessary] that those who preach experience their own vibrations. If the message doesn't produce fear and trembling in the proclaimers, it is impossible to produce that effect in the listeners."[25]

As preachers prepare sermons, they should spend time reflecting on their own lives, prayerfully asking God to reveal how they can be transformed by His Word. This spiritual practice of self-reflection will not only result in spiritual growth in the preacher, it will also produce more thoughtful, honest, and effective applications in the sermon. As Gregory I wrote, "[The preacher's] voice more easily penetrates his listeners' hearts when his way of life commends what he says. Thus, what he enjoins by speaking he helps by showing how it is to be done."[26]

SPEND TIME WITH PEOPLE

A second habit that will develop the preacher's skill for crafting applications is to spend time with people. Live life with and among the people of God. Latino/a theologians refer to this as attending to *lo cotidiano,* the daily lived experience. The underlying assumption about preaching is that it speaks to "daily struggle" (*la lucha*). Preachers, then adopt the habit of accompaniment, the practice of regularly walking with the people and being in community with the people. The listening community should not be an afterthought during sermon preparation. Time spent with the people can be just as valuable as time spent in the study exegeting the text. Some preachers might even consider dialoguing with a small group from the listening community as a part of the sermon development process. Preachers can meet with community members to discover insights about the passage and can later debrief after the sermon to evaluate whether the sermon was effective in connecting God's Word with their lived experiences.

APPLYING THE SCRIPTURES IN THE SERMON

It is appropriate here to provide a few specific directions for applying the Scriptures in the sermon. These seven directions can provide preachers guidance for developing sermon applications that are both faithful to the text of Scripture and the context in which the preacher preaches.

IDENTIFY THE FUNCTION OF TEXT

Recall the passage's central idea and purpose and ask whether this passage is providing a prophetic word, a wise word, and/or a re-scripting word. Readers will remember that Scripture functions prophetically when it confronts false worship and practices and calls the listening community to faithfulness and hope in God. Scripture offers a word of wisdom by inviting hearers to pursue the way of the Lord. And Scripture is a re-scripting word when it deconstructs the hearer's way of life and offers an alternative way of life in accordance with God's redemptive actions and purposes.

Take a sermon based on Luke 22:24–30 for example. In the passage, an argument arose between Jesus' disciples about which of them was the greatest. Ironically, the argument arose after the Passover feast in the upper room and Jesus' declaration that one of them was going to betray Him (Luke 22:7–23). When He overheard the argument, Jesus admonished them and declared that the greatest among them is the one who serves. What is the function of this passage? The passage offers a re-scripting word in that Jesus prescribes an alternative way of life for His disciples, one that elevates the one who serves over the one who is served. For both the disciples and listeners today, the passage subverts our assumptions about what and who is "great."

KNOW THEIR CIRCUMSTANCES

Consider your specific audience and reflect on how their lives are affected by the passage in light of the passage's central idea and purpose. How might specific individuals in the audience be informed and transformed by the biblical text? While there may be a general application that can be naturally drawn from the passage, think about your listeners' particular needs. One way to do this is to think of your audience according to two axes: Are they able and are they willing? Some in your audience may lack the know-how or resources to faithfully respond to the sermon. Rather than tell the audience what they must do, name tools, or helps for doing it. The second question refers to heart motivation: are they willing? Some may have the resources but lack the motivation. These individuals may need application that highlights the consequences for failing to obey the passage or may be moved by highlighting the results of faithful obedience.

ADDRESS ALL PEOPLE

When crafting application, make sure to address all of the person. Applications can easily be limited to behaviors. Individuals are told they must stop certain actions and practice new ones. Faithful preachers will recall that biblical texts form individuals wholistically. The Word addresses the head, heart, and hands of a person. Some preachers are most comfortable offering behavioral applications. "This passage tells us to do this or stop that." And it is true, faithful obedience to the Scriptures involves right action. But application can and should be pointed in other directions. In addition to asking how the passage directs the actions of my listeners, preachers can add, How does this passage address the beliefs, values, and motivations of my listeners? The broader question is, How does this passage invite the listener to faithful life in Christ? And faithful life in Christ includes right thinking and doing. Preachers can also consider whether the listener will object to the Word being offered? Perhaps the application offered is a response to an emotional or rational objection the listener offers.

CONSTRUCT VARIED APPLICATIONS

Applications can be thought of as examples or case studies. Since all audiences are diverse, preachers should present a variety of ways in which people can be addressed and formed by the passage. Recall the various demographic and cultural subdivisions that can be present in a community. Develop sermon applications that include multiple subgroups. While constructing applications ask, How can this application be contextualized for the single person or the stay-at-home mother? What would this application look like in the life of an teenager or an elderly person? The core application may be the same, but examples from the perspective of different groups in your congregation can make the sermon more effective. Relatedly, offer applications for both individuals and the whole community. This can be especially effective when preaching in a local church context. The question can extend beyond how this informs and transforms *me* to how this text informs and transforms *us* as a community. Does this passage address the collective church body? Perhaps the sermon inspires a collective project or outreach or a change in how the community understands its collective mission.

APPLY FROM THE TEXT

Ensure that your applications are fitting moves from the text. In other words, make sure that applications are reasonably derived from the biblical text's meaning and purpose. Preachers ought to practice caution when constructing sermon application. In some ways applications really are implications of the text rather than explicit commands directly lifted from the passage. As such, preachers must be careful to verify that applications are fitting extractions from the passage's central idea and purpose.

WEAVE INTO THE SERMON

Consider where you will include applications throughout the sermon. Sermon application should be naturally intertwined with the other parts of the sermon rather than give the impression that it has been added on at the end like an appendix to the sermon materials. At the very least, application should serve as natural bookends at the beginning and end of the sermon. Preachers will recall that one of the characteristics of an effective introduction is that it surfaces the needs of the listener in connection to the sermonic theme or central idea. The conclusion of the sermon should serve as the preacher's final appeal to the listener and provides an opportunity to connect the text to the life of the listener. Additionally, the preacher should consider where application may fit within the body of the sermon. Some sermons may be more inclined toward explicit application in each move within the body, while other sermons may be better served to limit application to the final move. Narrative sermons, for example, may fall into this category. Instead of applying each move directly, the preacher may consider how he or she can imply points of connection throughout the narrative retelling and resolve the needs surfaced at the beginning of the sermon in the final developmental move before offering a final appeal in the conclusion.

DEPEND ON THE HOLY SPIRIT

Give room to the Holy Spirit to work in you and your listeners. You may be surprised that God works to address your listeners in ways you could not have imagined or foreseen. Preachers should diligently work at crafting relevant application, but they should also remember that the Spirit will speak to individuals in deeply personal ways without us having addressed their particular need. Trust that the Spirit is the one who is primarily acting in the preaching event. Both the preacher and listening community should come to the sermon with the expectation that God, the Spirit, will speak. We must be ready for God to give a word to His congregation. The sermon is primarily a word from God. While we prepare ourselves and our sermons in order to be effective, ultimately we entrust ourselves, our sermons, and the people listening to the Spirit's care each time we preach.

CONCLUSION

The preacher is God's servant, empowered by the Spirit to communicate life-giving messages. The sermon has power because it is in some sense a word that belongs to God. God has chosen preaching as a means of bringing life into the hearts and minds of our listeners. Like the prophet Ezekiel, faithful preachers of God's Word hold on to the promise that God's proclaimed Word has the power to open graves and cause the dead to come to life (Ezek. 37:1–14). Preachers have been entrusted with an incredible task. Paul asks, "How are they to hear without a preacher? And how are they to preach unless they are sent? Just as it is written, 'How beautiful are the feet of those who bring glad tidings of good things'" (Rom. 10:14b–15)!

Faithful biblical preaching is applicational preaching. "Application gives expository preaching purpose."[27] This kind of preaching acknowledges that as long as it strives to be faithful to the message and purposes of God's Word, it will inevitable seek to produce transformation in the lives of its hearers.

NOTES

1. Kevin J. Vanhoozer, "Scripture and Theology: On 'proving' Doctrine Biblically," in *The Routledge Companion to the Practice of Christian Theology*, ed. Jim Fodor and Mike Higton (New York: Routledge, 2015), 141.

2. Haddon Robinson, "The Heresy of Application," Preaching Today, n.d., https://www.preachingtoday.com/books/art-and-craft-of-biblical-preaching/interpretation-and-application/heresy-of-application.html.

3. Jonathan Armstrong, "On the Revelation of God," in *Standing Firm: The Doctrinal Commitments of Moody Bible Institute*, ed. Bryan O'Neal and John Jelinek (Chicago: Moody Publishers, 2019), 45.

4. Steven H. Sanchez, "On the Authority of Scripture," in *Standing Firm: The Doctrinal Commitments of Moody Bible Institute*, ed. Bryan O'Neal and John Jelinek (Chicago: Moody Publishers, 2019), 55.

5. Kevin J. Vanhoozer, "True Pictures: What Every Pastor Should Know About Biblical Truth and Interpretation," in *Pictures at a Theological Exhibition: Scenes of the Church's Worship, Witness and Wisdom* (Downers Grove, IL: IVP Academic, 2016), 78.

6. Ibid., 79.

7. Jeannine K. Brown, *Scripture as Communication: Introducing Biblical Hermeneutics* (Grand Rapids: Baker Academic, 2007), 48.

8. Grant R. Osborne, *The Hermeneutical Spiral: A Comprehensive Introduction to Biblical Interpretation*, rev. and expanded ed. (Downers Grove, IL: IVP Academic, 2006), 260.

9. Walter Brueggemann, "Holy Intrusions of Truth and Hope," in *God's Word and Our Words: Preaching from the Prophets to the Present and Beyond*, ed. W. Hulitt Gloer and Shawn Boyd (Eugene, OR: Pickwick Publications, 2019), 1.

10. Kevin J. Vanhoozer, *Faith Speaking Understanding: Performing the Drama of Doctrine* (Louisville: Westminster John Knox Press, 2014), 245.

11. Ibid., 246.

12. Walter Brueggemann, *The Word Militant: Preaching a Decentering Word*, 1st ed. edition (Minneapolis: Fortress Press, 2008), 26.

13. John Koessler, *Folly, Grace, and Power: The Mysterious Act of Preaching* (Grand Rapids: Zondervan, 2011), 95–97.

14. Ibid., 96.

15. Donald Sunukjian, *Invitation to Biblical Preaching: Proclaiming Truth with Clarity and Relevance* (Grand Rapids: Kregel Ministry, 2007), 113–14.

16. Andy Crouch, *Culture Making* (Downers Grove, IL: InterVarsity Press, 2013), 23–24.

17. Kevin J. Vanhoozer, Charles A. Anderson, and Michael J. Sleasman, eds., *Everyday Theology: How to Read Cultural Texts and Interpret Trends Cultural Exegesis* (Grand Rapids: Baker Academic, 2007), 26.

18. Matthew D. Kim, *Preaching with Cultural Intelligence: Understanding the People Who Hear Our Sermons* (Grand Rapids: Baker Academic, 2017), 5.

19. Ibid., 17.

20. J. Brian Tucker and John Koessler, *All Together Different: Upholding the Church's Unity While Honoring Our Individual Identities* (Chicago: Moody Publishers, 2018); Soong-Chan Rah, *Many Colors: Cultural Intelligence for a Changing Church* (Chicago: Moody Publishers, 2010); Matthew D. Kim, *Preaching with Cultural Intelligence: Understanding the People who Hear our Sermons* (Grand Rapids: Baker Academic, 2017); Intercultural Development Inventory, https://idiinventory.com/.

21. Kim, *Preaching with Cultural Intelligence*, 19.

22. Jared Alcántara, *Learning from a Legend: What Gardner C. Taylor Can Teach Us about Preaching* (Eugene, OR: Cascade Books, 2016), 92.

23. Ibid., 89.

24. Ibid., 21.

25. Cecilio Arrastía, *Teoría y Práctica de La Predicación* (Miami: Editorial Caribe, 1993), 36–37. Translated to English from Spanish.

26. Gregory the Great, *The Book of Pastoral Rule*, trans. George E. Demacopoulos (Crestwood, NY: St Vladimir's Seminary Press, 2007), 51.

27. Haddon W. Robinson, *Biblical Preaching: The Development and Delivery of Expository Messages*, 3rd ed. (Grand Rapids: Baker Academic, 2014), 10.

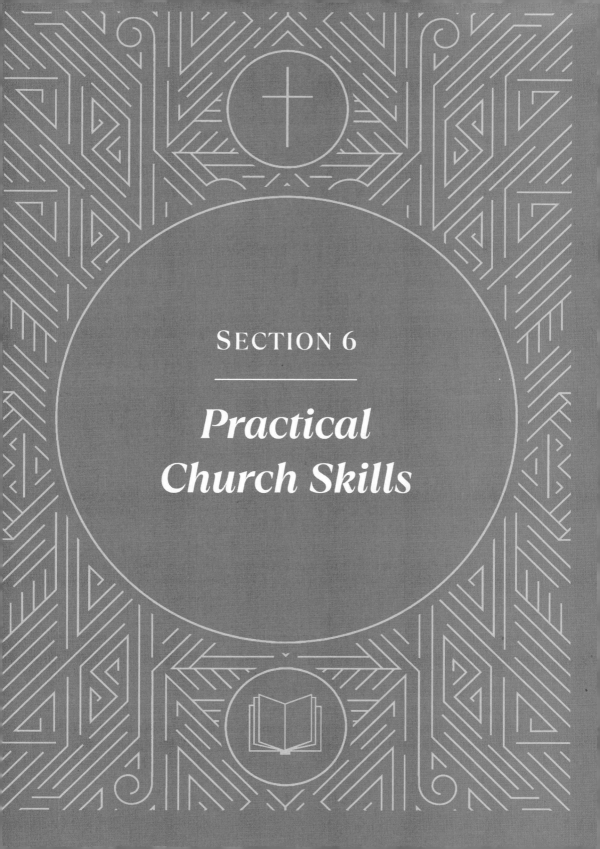

SECTION 6

Practical Church Skills

The Personal Integrity of the Pastor

KERWIN A. RODRIGUEZ

Many Christians know what it feels like whenever a well-known pastor's name is attached to a scandal made public. Sadly, it is a regular occasion. One doesn't have to search long to find a recent story about a fallen pastor who, despite having great charisma and talent, resigned or had to be removed from a ministry position for an act of impropriety. A pastor who is skilled and well-liked might be easy to recognize, but a minister of strong character and personal integrity ought to be the standard.

Character refers to a person's inner, moral qualities. It is what *truly makes* a person. No inner, moral quality can be more important or significant for pastoral work than the quality of integrity. To be a person of integrity is to be an honest and morally upright person. A person of integrity demonstrates consistency in his or her actions, beliefs, and values both publicly and privately. For the Christian minister, integrity is rooted in one's relationship to God and the indwelling of the Spirit and is motivated by a call as servants of the gospel.

Integrity is vital in every part of the pastor's ministry. Often, the pastor is aware of how important it is to maintain integrity in the more visible parts of church life. Yet integrity is just as necessary in the little things, the day-to-day duties that a pastor must carry out. In this section, we will look at some of those practical skills: leadership development, conflict management, member assimilation and discipline, basic Bible teaching, premarital counseling, presiding at weddings and funerals, and of course, financial matters. Integrity must characterize all aspects of ministry, from the pulpit to the back office. What does biblical integrity look like?

And what insights have God's people offered us through the ages? By being aware of God's high standard—and the potential pitfalls out there—the pastor can live with integrity in every part of his ministry.

AN EMPHASIS WORTH RETURNING TO

The church has emphasized character for much of its history. In his work *On Christian Doctrine,* Augustine explains that the moral life of the preacher should be valued over rhetorical strategies and skill. He writes, "Whatever may be the majesty of the style, the life of the speaker will count for more in securing the hearer's compliance." He later exhorts the minister to "let his manner of living be an eloquent sermon in itself."[1] To Augustine, character was more important than skill.

John Chrysostom also understood the importance of the life of the minister. In his *On the Priesthood,* he explains that an individual ought not become a minister "unless he possesses a robust and exceedingly vigorous character."[2] In the sixth century, Gregory the Great also esteemed character when he wrote that minister's ought to live in a manner that serves as an example in life more than just words. The minister who is called to "speak the highest things is compelled by the same necessity to exhibit the highest things. For that voice more readily penetrates the hearer's heart, which the speaker's life commends, since what he commands by speaking helps the doing of by showing."[3]

Lest one think a minister's personal character and integrity only mattered to the early church fathers, one could point to other historical figures like Charles Spurgeon who instructed future ministers on its importance. In his collection of lectures to his students, Spurgeon exhorts, "Let the minister take care that his personal character agrees in all respects with his ministry." He warns of the minister who is duplicitous and lacks integrity:

> We do not trust those persons who have two faces, nor will men believe in those whose verbal and practical testimonies are contradictory. As actions, according to the proverb, speak louder than words, so an ill life will effectually drown the voice of the most eloquent ministry. After all, our truest building must be performed with our hands; our characters must be more persuasive than our speech. . . . Too many preachers forget to serve God when they are out of the pulpit, their lives are negatively inconsistent.[4]

Space prohibits further examples, but the point is clear: ministers have long exhorted other ministers to pay attention to their personal lives because character matters. And yet, despite these exhortations, there continues to be a need to warn against the devaluing of character for ministers.

One author argues that character has been devalued in contemporary society since at least the twentieth century when society shifted from a culture of character to a culture of personality. In *Quiet*, Susan Cain writes that prior to the shift, "The ideal self [in the culture of character] was serious, disciplined, and honorable. What counted was not so much the impression one made in public as how one behaved in private.... But when they embraced the Culture of Personality, Americans started to focus on how others perceived them."[5] After interviewing an evangelical minister, Cain warns, "Many evangelicals [have] come to associate godliness with sociability."[6]

In light of this warning, it should be stressed again: character and personal integrity matter for pastoral ministry. More than the skills one can learn from training and especially more than one's charisma, seasoned and aspiring ministers should remember that the Lord "stores up sound wisdom for the upright [and] is a shield to those who walk in integrity" (Prov. 2:7).

INTEGRITY ACCORDING TO THE SCRIPTURES

Throughout the Old Testament the idea of integrity is linked to faithfulness, righteousness, and honesty. A key Hebrew word that is occasionally translated "integrity" is the word *tamim*, which can mean without blemish, complete, sincerely, undefiled, or upright.

The word is used to describe Noah (Gen. 6:9) and Abraham (17:1). It is also used to call the people of God who are to serve the Lord with sincerity and faithfulness (Josh. 24:14). Throughout the wisdom books, individuals who walk with integrity are blessed by God (Ps. 84:11; Prov. 10:9; 20:7; 28:19). The psalmist exclaims in Psalm 15 that only the one "who walks with integrity and works righteousness" can abide in the presence of the Lord. The rest of the psalm links integrity with truthful speech and a rejection of dishonest gain. Likewise Proverbs 11 contrasts dishonesty with integrity. The dishonesty of a false balance "is an abomination to the LORD" (11:1) but the Lord delights in "a just weight." The upright are guided by their integrity and will be delivered (11:4, 6, 8), while the crooked will be destroyed (11:3, 5, 6, 8). According to the Old Testament, men and women of God are to walk in integrity, and such a way of life is marked by righteousness and honesty.

In the New Testament, various terms are used to convey the idea of a person or minister who walks in integrity. These words are usually translated as "faithful," "sincere," "blameless," and "incorruptible." One such word used to express the concept of integrity by the apostle Paul is *pistos*, typically translated "faithful." Paul used the word frequently to describe his own ministry (1 Tim. 1:12) or the ministry of other co-laborers as a *faithful* service to God and the church (1 Cor. 4:17; Col. 4:7, 9;

Eph. 6:21). For Paul, the minister's *faithful* service mattered for two reasons: (1) ministers were stewards of God and (2) ministers were models for the church of God.

The first reason can be seen in a few different passages. For example, in 1 Corinthians 4:1–4 Paul identifies himself and his co-ministers as "stewards of Christ and stewards of the mysteries of God." As stewards it is essential that they be "found trustworthy," otherwise they would make poor stewards. Stewards carried the message of the one who sent them, and their success depended upon whether the one who sent them could trust them to accomplish the task *and* whether the recipients of the message could trust them to deliver the message faithfully. For Paul it is most important that the Lord find him to be a trustworthy steward. This motivation ensures that the minister remain faithful to his or her call since it is ultimately God who judges the minister and examines one's hearts. Rather than work for the approval of men, the minister who is entrusted with the gospel works having already been approved by God and expecting to be examined by God (1 Thess. 2:4). Paul is assured time and time again by this fact. In a later correspondence with the church in Corinth, Paul writes, "For our proud confidence is this: the testimony of our conscience, that in holiness and godly sincerity, not in fleshly wisdom but in the grace of God, we have conducted ourselves in the world, and especially toward you" (2 Cor. 1:12).

So then, the church does not stand as judges or approvers of the stewards of the gospel, but as witnesses of their faithfulness. When the pastor is a faithful minister of God, the church sees an example from which to model their own faithful practice. Paul's hope and prayer is that this sermonic life results in the church's own faithful and worthy walking of the gospel (1 Thess. 2:10–12). According to Paul, their example in ministry has been one that is devout, upright, and blameless. In other words, Paul and his co-ministers were men and women of integrity! It is for this reason that Paul sets his own life and the lives of his companions before the church (Phil. 3:17), so that they may also live faithful and blameless before God.

Paul instructs Timothy and Titus to view their own ministries this way too. He urges Timothy to show himself as an example "in speech, conduct, love, faith, and purity" (1 Tim. 4:11–12). Later in the letter he repeats, "Pay close attention to yourself and to the teaching; persevere in these things, for as you do this you will save both yourself and those who hear you" (1 Tim. 4:16). Paul instructs Titus to give the same instruction to young men so that they might show themselves "to be an example of good deeds [in all things]" (Titus 2:7).

According to the Old and New Testament, believers and especially ministers of the gospel should be men and women of integrity. Their lives should be above reproach in all areas since their ministry is a stewardship from God and an example to others who are watching.

TEMPTATIONS AND PITFALLS FOR MINISTERS OF THE GOSPEL

Every Christian should "be on the alert [since the] adversary, the devil, prowls around like a roaring lion, seeking someone to devour" (1 Peter 5:8), but a minister's challenge is unique. Given the nature of pastoral work, ministers face burnout and stress and are often susceptible to temptations that test a minister's integrity. Three particular temptations deserve brief mention.

MINISTERIAL DISHONESTY

Today, preachers often feel as though they are competing for their congregation's attention and appreciation. Every Sunday morning some pastors feel inadequate knowing that some in the congregation are comparing their sermon with the latest from the popular preacher whose sermons are available as a podcast or video stream. On top of that, ministers are often overburdened and are responsible for too many things, leaving the task of preparing sermons inconceivable. So what does a busy pastor do? A preacher might be tempted to take someone else's sermon and preach it as their own. Pastors ought to be aware of the serious potential consequences for such actions. Many pastors have lost their jobs for preaching other people's sermons. Worse, the act of sermon stealing lacks integrity. It is wrong. Preachers can be on alert against this temptation by taking protecting their time for study and preparation and crediting those who aided in the formation or constructing of the sermon in the bulletin or published materials on the sermon or by casually noting that another preacher came up with the phrase or illustration.[7]

Another similar temptation for ministers is to falsify accomplishments or credentials. Either due to feelings of inadequacy or as a strategy for professional advancement, some ministers add experiences or education to their resumes or suggest in public comments that they have done more than they actually have. This too demonstrates a lack of integrity. Attending a university or graduate school is not the same thing as graduating from said school. Experiences should be described honestly in speech and writing.

FINANCIAL IMPROPRIETY

Ministers can also fall prey to the temptation of financial impropriety. In both small and large churches, pastors ought to be open about financial budgets including pastoral salaries. Additionally, churches should ensure that other trustworthy individuals are involved in the receiving and accounting of church finances. More will be stated in a later chapter on this issue.

PERSONAL FAILINGS

Most instances of pastoral failings can be linked to a personal failing. A minister resigns or is removed when it is found out that the minister had been involved in a pattern of sin. Sometimes the sin is sexual, an affair or sexual harassment against someone in the community. Other times the sin is a consistent pattern of verbal abuse, manipulation, or bullying of other church staff or ministry members. Whenever these failings occur, the damage is far-reaching. Victims of abuse or harassment can sometimes be ignored or ostracized while the church tries to deal with the shock of the pastoral failing and looks for someone to blame for the trauma the congregation feels afterward. Family members of the minister can also feel abandoned as they navigate the in-between space of congregant and relative. And church members can feel deeply affected even if they had little or no involvement in the incidents.

PRACTICING INTEGRITY

How then should ministers deal with the temptations ministers face and avoid the pitfalls that have befallen so many? First ministers should remember that while they are ministers of the gospel, they are recipients of it as well. The minister ought to view him or herself as a sinner redeemed by the mercy and grace of God. They too should heed the words of Paul and daily seek to walk in accordance with the Holy Spirit that now indwells us (Rom. 8; Gal. 5:16, 25).

Second, ministers ought to practice disciplines and habits to cultivate their spiritual lives. The minister ought to regularly practice the foundational habits of Scripture reading and prayer. Let it never be said of any pastor that they seldom find time to take in God's Word for themselves. As Augustine once shared, "When I unpack the [Scripture], I [am] breaking open bread for you. What I [give] you is not mine. What you eat, I eat. What you live on, I live on."[8] Ministers should also engage in other traditional spiritual disciplines such as fasting and meditation and practice the habit of unplugging from social media.

Third, ministers should engage in personal accountability and ministry partnership. Ministry can be isolating and lonely. Pastors often feel as if they don't have anyone they can talk to about their personal struggles or insecurities. It is critical that pastors find individuals who can serve as accountability partners. It is usually recommended that these individuals not be members of the church where a pastor serves. Relatedly, pastors should find others who can be co-laborers in their ministry. This can take the form of a ministry team in a local congregation or a group of community pastors who come together to share ideas, offer encouragement, and even pray for one another whenever ministry challenges or personal issues arise.

Ministers are stewards of God. As such every minister ought to attend to the cultivation of their Christian character so that they can walk in integrity in all areas of life. While ministry skills are important, nothing is more vital than the faithfulness and trustworthiness of the pastor.

NOTES

1. Augustine, *On Christian Doctrine*, 4:27–29.

2. St. John Chrysostom, *On the Priesthood*, 5:51.

3. Gregory the Great, *Pastoral Care*, chapter 6.

4. Charles Spurgeon, *Lectures to My Students* (Peabody, MA: Hendrickson Press, 2010), 18.

5. Susan Cain, *Quiet: The Power of Introverts in a World That Can't Stop Talking* (New York: Crown Publishing Group, 2012), 21.

6. Ibid., 70.

7. For further discussion on sermon plagiarism, see Scott M. Gibson, *Should We Use Someone Else's Sermon?* (Grand Rapids: Zondervan, 2008).

8. Quote attributed to Augustine in Thomas G. Long, *Preaching from Memory to Hope* (Louisville: Westminster John Knox Press, 2009), 40.

Leading People

CRAIG HENDRICKSON

"Leadership is influence."[1] This pithy quote made famous by John Maxwell has gained significant popularity among those reflecting on the nature of leadership over the last few decades. Indeed, it may be one of the more popular definitions used in ministry leadership courses as future pastors and ministry leaders begin to reflect on the nature of their own leadership. This leads to an important question, then—Is it true? Is leadership primarily one's ability to influence another person or group? On the one hand, yes. At its core, leadership is about using influence to lead others, and in this sense, everyone is a leader. Parents, for example, shape their children's character daily, whether through positive reinforcement, modeling, or discipline. Spouses influence each other regularly through the words we say or do not say, or the actions we do or do not do to one another. Coworkers influence one another whenever they are assigned a task or project to complete together. Friends and neighbors give advice, provide a listening ear when the other is suffering, help with tasks, and provide other means of relational, emotional, or psychological support for one another. Name a relationship, and there is influence being utilized. Understanding this can be empowering, as it reminds each of us that we are in fact leaders, that we are important to others, even if we do not see it in ourselves.

There is a shortcoming with this definition, however, especially as it relates to those of us who are called to lead God's people in some way. It does not speak to the issue of how we use our influence, and to what end. Adolf Hitler, after all, was incredibly influential. The problem is that he used his influence over the German people to start the largest global conflict that the world has ever seen, and to carry out the largest documented genocide in history. We also hear all too often how pastors abuse their authority through manipulation, coercion, or sexual impropriety to satisfy their egos, agendas, or illicit desires. The result is often a trail of broken individuals and congregations left to figure out how to heal and move forward without their once-trusted leader. How a leader uses his or her influence, then, as well as the objective they pursue with that influence, is crucial to practicing healthy and effective leadership.

How might we understand the nature of spiritual leadership, then? And what does it mean to lead God's people in various ministry settings? In the rest of this chapter, we will answer these questions by reflecting theologically on three essential aspects of spiritual leadership in Christian ministry settings: (1) self-leadership, (2) relational leadership, and (3) visionary leadership. Accomplishing this will help those God has entrusted to lead His people better understand how we can steward this role well.

THE NATURE AND PRACTICE OF SPIRITUAL LEADERSHIP

Research carried out over the last several decades has consistently shown that credibility is the foundation of effective leadership. Why? Because leadership is a relationship between two or more people built on trust. Whether you are the pastor of a church, the leader of a nonprofit or parachurch ministry, or leading a business or an organization, the people you are leading need to trust you; trust that you will always have their best interests at heart; that you will never put your own self-interest above theirs or the ministry. They need to trust that you will make the right decisions when called on so that their church, ministry, or organization can grow, thrive, and adapt when necessary. Trust is a crucial component in the leader-follower relationship and provides a key component for credibility.

As you might infer, then, credibility is a multifaceted concept. It involves competency, but just as importantly, also involves character. Extensive research conducted over the past thirty-five years by James Kouzes and Barry Posner supports this claim, with honesty, forward-looking, inspiring, and competent topping the traits that followers most admire in their leaders.[2] What this demonstrates is that the majority of us admire and willingly follow leaders who are trustworthy, clearly communicate the direction we are headed, inspire us to be more, and who demonstrate an ability to do the job well. As we discuss what it means for pastors and ministry leaders to lead God's people throughout the rest of this chapter, then, we will begin with the character of the leader, which can be cultivated by intentional practices relating to self-leadership.

SELF-LEADERSHIP

According to Steve Brown, self-leadership is the prerequisite for leading others well.[3] Why? Without learning how to lead themselves well, leaders cannot lead others well. They can easily become distracted or consumed by their own personal failures, struggles, or sin. They can put their focus in places where it does not belong, causing them to miss opportunities God may be presenting them with. All too often, it can also cause them to miss how their own self-serving motivations or blind spots may be negatively impacting those they are seeking to influence. An example from the ministry of a pastor named Carl illustrates this well.

When Carl was just beginning his pastoral career, he was full of self-confidence. He had just left a successful career in another field, and believed he had the necessary skills to lead his church into some significant change as an assistant pastor. As part of a large ministry team in a church that had been declining for several years, he believed that he had the answers necessary to help the church become much more effective and begin to grow again. There was a problem, however. Steve, the senior pastor, appeared blind to the best way to go about ushering in much needed change. This inevitably led to weekly arguments between Carl and Steve in the staff meeting that left the entire team feeling discouraged. The frustration on both sides grew to the point that there was almost no interaction between them during the rest of the week.

As his frustrations grew, Carl contemplated leaving the ministry. Before taking this drastic step, though, he instead decided to deal with the situation by pouring himself into the ministries he was leading. If Steve wouldn't listen, then perhaps modeling how to get it done properly with his own team could show him the way forward. Carl soon ran into a problem, however. On his own team, he began to face some significant resistance from Jamie, one of his young leaders. Almost every week, Jamie would grind the team meeting to a halt with his combative attitude and resistance to any idea Carl or the other team members had. He was convinced that he knew the best way to move forward, and that Carl and the others were simply being held back by useless traditions and disconnection from the culture. Carl's frustration with Jamie continued to grow, until he finally told Jamie that he either needed to stop disrupting his meetings or find another ministry to serve with.

The conversation seemed to serve its purpose initially, but two weeks later, Jamie disrupted the meeting again. Instead of engaging in an argument with Jamie once again, however, Carl did not immediately respond to Jamie's pushback. In that moment, he sensed the Holy Spirit speaking directly to him: "Carl, you are Jamie." As he sat there stewing in his frustration, Carl suddenly realized that he had grossly misinterpreted what was going on. Instead of thorns in his side, he realized that Jamie and Steve were instead God's provision in his life to refine his own character flaws. But, because he had been so busy focusing on Jamie and Steve as problems, he hadn't taken the time to look at his own role in the conflicts. Accordingly, it took several frustrating months for him to realize that his arrogance and overreliance on his perceived leadership skills had contributed toward a conviction that he alone had the answers. The result? He didn't listen to others input well, and accordingly, his ministry relationships and leadership effectiveness suffered.

Carl's story highlights the necessity of self-leadership well. With better self-leadership, he may have recognized his own contribution toward the conflicts he was consistently embroiled in. He might then have made necessary adjustments to his attitude and practice of leadership much sooner, saving himself, Steve, and both of his teams a great deal of frustration. Carl is not alone, however. Many of us have been taught that leadership is a set of skills to practice or traits to embody. Accordingly, we have neglected important practices that cultivate self-awareness and character.

Jesus models another way for us, however. Jesus did not primarily lead His disciples from a base of skills or competencies. Instead, He led from a sense of intimacy and dependence on God that cultivated a clear understanding of His messianic mission, as well as the limitations imposed by His humanity. Consider, for example, an episode in Capernaum early in Jesus' ministry. Jesus had spent much of the day preaching and casting out demons (Mark 1:21–28), and the rest of the evening doing healing and deliverance ministry at Simon's mother-in-law's house in Capernaum (Mark 1:29–34). Likely tired after a long day of ministry, Jesus finally succumbs to His fatigue and goes to sleep for a few hours. Before anyone in the house is awake, however, Jesus gets up early the next morning to spend some time with His Father in prayer (Mark 1:35). It seems that in spite of the urgency of any ministry business still undone, or the desire to celebrate the previous days miracles with His disciples, Jesus has more important business to address . . . connecting with His Father and tending to His own soul.

The disciples, of course, do not realize where He is or what He is doing. So they immediately set out set out to find Him and bring Him back (Mark 1:36–37). Upon finding Him, they immediately let Jesus know that He is not where He is supposed to be, and that everyone is looking for Him (Mark 1:36–37). Not always being one for social conventions, however, Jesus gives them an answer they are not expecting . . . no (Mark 1:38). Instead, with an air of certainty and confidence, He informs them that He needs to leave to resume His ministry in other nearby towns, which is actually what God has sent Him to do.

Jesus here demonstrates a way of engaging in ministry that is counterintuitive for those of us who are driven by results, performance, and often ego. Instead of submitting to the wishes of His followers by returning to town to perhaps heal those still waiting on Him, or to celebrate the previous days' ministry highlights, He resists the temptation to please His followers and moves on to other ministry opportunities. This begs the question—how is He able to withstand the pressure He is facing to serve the immediate needs of those around Him? Jesus was the Son of God, after all. Could He not have easily performed a few more healings in Capernaum before moving on to preach and do ministry in the nearby towns? Could He not have taken some time to celebrate and revel in all that God had done the day before? While the answer to these question would seem to be yes, something else needs to be considered. Jesus was not just fully God; He was also fully man. Accordingly, He was vulnerable to some of the same temptations faced by many leaders today . . . the temptation to substitute ministry for spirituality, which can lead to fatigue and burnout; the temptation to get lost in the tyranny of the urgent, which can cause us to lose sight of the bigger picture when facing pressure from others; and the temptation to please others, which can cause us to function outside of our call, competence, and capacity. Yet, Jesus does not give in to these temptations. Instead, He stands resolute, reaffirms His understanding of His Father's call on His life, and reengages His ministry of preaching and teaching throughout Israel.

Jesus' courageous decision in the face of both internal and external pressures He must have been facing are instructional for us. If we wish to lead others well according to His call on our lives and within our human limitations, we need to lead ourselves well. One of the ways we can do this is by regularly practicing what Peter Scazzero calls slowing down for loving union.[4] In the midst of the busyness of life and ministry, Jesus makes the intentional decision to take the time He needs with His Father. He likely realizes that as His fame grows, the demands on Him will increase significantly. Because of this, He needs the strength to withstand the pressure to meet others' expectations so that He will not say yes to every opportunity that comes His way, but can instead live more fully into the calling God has placed on His life. In other words, Jesus models here for us how to say good nos in service to our higher yes.

Jesus' courage to meet this challenge seems to flow directly from His intentional time and intimacy with God. Notice that when Jesus is faced with His disciples' sense of urgency as He emerges from His time with God, He calmly and confidently tells them that instead of doing what they ask, they are going to move on to other opportunities for ministry. Jesus' time with God seems to have given Him the clarity and confidence in the nature of His messianic mission to withstand what for many of us, would be enormous pressure to acquiesce. Many of us, for example, may have given in for fear of letting others down. This, of course, is one of the great temptations for ministry leaders—succumbing to the lie that our worth hinges on our popularity . . . on what others think of us. Consequently, we consistently say yes to the demands placed on us to the point where we have no time for God or for rest, which when left unchecked can lead to significant fatigue and ultimately burnout.

Another way we can lead ourselves well is by taking a weekly Sabbath. In our production and results-oriented culture, Sabbath has become something of a lost art in the church, even among many clergy. Many of us justify our lack of Sabbath-keeping as necessary for the work of the church. We tend to forget, however, that God Himself took a Sabbath after His creation work was completed (Gen. 2:2–3). We must ask ourselves, then: If the infinite, immortal, all-powerful God of the universe felt it necessary to rest after His work was completed, how much more necessary is it for us to rest?

Still others justify ignoring Sabbath by pointing out that Jesus never repeats the command, so it is no longer binding in the new covenant. When we assert this, however, we conveniently forget that Jesus kept Sabbath throughout His earthly ministry (Mark 1:21; Luke 4:16; 13:10); yet He does so in a way that seems to reframe it. In the Old Testament, Sabbath is instituted for God's people as a day of rest and worship (Ex. 20:10; Lev. 23:3). It serves as a sign of the covenant between God and His people, and is meant to remind His people of their unique relationship with Him (Ezek. 31:13). In one of Jesus' confrontations over Sabbath with the Pharisees, however, Jesus says, "The Sabbath was made for man, and not man for the Sabbath" (Mark 2:27). While Jesus is primarily seeking to remove many of the impossible human standards that had been added to Sabbath regulations over the centuries here, He is also subtly highlighting something else . . . Sabbath is a gift, not a burden. And, as a gift, it is meant to help us thrive in our relationship with God, with others, and even with ourselves. When we slow down long enough to simply be with God, or as the translators of the New American Standard Bible put it, when we "stop striving" (Ps. 46:10), the created order is restored. God retakes His rightful place on the throne as we surrender control of our lives and ministries, as well as the results of our labors, to Him. It is in this act of surrender that we are freed from the burden of responsibility for outcomes. We are also freed to release others from that same responsibility, and because of it, we can all live more fully into who God has created us to be.

Yet, there are two more benefits that Sabbath provides to those in leadership. When we are rested and more deeply connected to God, we tend to treat those around us better and make better decisions. When we are consistently running on empty, it is easy to lose patience with those we interact with. When we are exhausted, it is easy to make rash decisions without all of the pertinent data. Time and time again we see that the results of these decisions are often unhelpful at best, and catastrophic at worst, which can ultimately cut into a leader's credibility.

When we are rested, however, we significantly lower the chance of either of these issues happening.

Evidence for this comes from an unlikely source for ministry leaders. Surgeon Atul Gawande shows how the use of checklists and pause points during surgery—before anesthesia, before incision, and before leaving the operating room—can reduce mistakes and save lives.[5] Each pause point is designed to be long enough for members of the team to make basic checks, like confirming the patient's identity at the beginning, or checking for all the needles and sponges at the end. While it might not seem like pausing for a few minutes would make a difference, the results are striking. For example, starting in the spring of 2008, eight hospitals began using Gawande's checklist. Within months, the rate of major complications for surgical patients had fallen by 36 percent, while deaths fell 47 percent. It is no wonder, then, that Gawande also urges people in other professions to use pause points for their jobs as well. Pause points provide an opportunity to stop, think about what you are about to do, and make a good decision based off of all available information. In the case of a ministry leader, they provide an opportunity to recenter ourselves in God's presence so that we can remain connected to the source of our wisdom, which can ultimately lead to better outcomes in our decisions.

While Sabbath-keeping and slowing down for loving union provide a key foundation for leading oneself well, there is also a third practice that is vital if we are to lead others well. We need to allow others to speak lovingly, truthfully, and courageously into our lives. We see Jesus model this for us repeatedly in His earthly ministry. He corrects His disciples when they misunderstand the nature of leadership and authority and begin seeking positions of power and prestige (Matt. 20:20–28). He corrects them again when they begin to get full of themselves after their success in the mission field (Luke 10:17–20). Yet, He also gently restores Peter so that he can once again take a position of leadership in the young church after He ascends to heaven (John 21:15–20; Acts 1:9). Jesus' goal in these interactions is to mature His disciples; to help them become aware of their faulty, sinful motives and behaviors so that they can repent and become the Christ-centered leaders He is calling them to be. He realizes that if this is going to happen, He needs to speak directly into their lives so that they can discern and address what they likely cannot see on their own—what Peter Scazzero calls our shadow.[6]

According to Scazzero, our shadow is the damaged, but mostly hidden part of who we are that can manifest in sin or other dysfunctional behaviors. It is often caused by a wound of some kind, like childhood abuse, abandonment, betrayal, heartbreak, or other forms of relational hurt or trauma. It can be caused by unmet sinful desires, which drive us toward destructive behaviors like pornography, substance abuse, or narcissistic tendencies. It can even be the dark side of a strength, like significance, which can cause us to always pursue the next bigger, better challenge that promises us with the results or validation we desire. When left unchecked, our shadow undermines the best of who we are and hinders our ability to serve others well.

As we invite trusted companions to ask us difficult questions and point out impure motives that might not be obvious to us, then, we allow them to fulfill an important function in our lives. Mentors, leadership coaches, counselors, denominational leaders, ministry colleagues, or trusted friends can observe things about our behavior we might not see, and give us insights into our hearts that we might not discover on our own (Prov. 27:17). "The heart is more deceitful than all else and is desperately sick" (Jer. 17:9) after all. Because of this, we need those with wisdom to ask us the difficult questions and tell us hard truths (Prov. 27:6), to guide us (Prov. 12:15), and to ultimately help us understand ourselves in ways that can transform not just who we are, but our relationships as well. The result is a leader who is surrendered to the work of God in their life, who when the hard work is continually engaged in, will develop the character necessary to make good decisions, treat others well, and ultimately, be trusted by others. In other words, they will have credibility.

RELATIONAL LEADERSHIP

What should be readily apparent by now, is that when it comes to credibility, character matters. It does not stop there, however. Credibility also involves competencies. This, of course, raises a natural question . . . Which competencies are most important to lead God's people well? While we cannot hope to address all of the competencies that make an effective leader in the space remaining, we can briefly discuss some of the most relevant by reflecting theologically on key findings from more than fifty years of Gallup research on leaders and followers. According to Tom Rath and Barry Conchie, the most effective leaders invest in their own and other people's strengths and surround themselves with good people and maximize their team.[7]

Think about a time in your work and/or ministry environment when you were most engaged and fulfilled. Chances are fairly high, according to Rath and Conchie, that the reason for your high level of engagement is that you were utilizing your strengths . . . the best of who you are and what you have to offer.[8] Research conducted by Gallup over the last several decades has consistently demonstrated this, with higher levels of engagement, productivity, self-confidence, and even pay when employees are aware of and utilize their strengths in their work environments.[9] While this may seem like pop psychology to some, it highlights a basic truism for almost all leaders . . . we want to be put in a position to thrive and succeed in our ministry roles. Think, for example, about the last job or ministry position that you applied for. Did you look over the role description and say to yourself, "This position requires me to do quite a few functions and tasks that I am absolutely terrible at. Yes, this is the job I've been looking for!" Of course not. When looking for a job, especially one in ministry, we all want a position that is meaningful, that aligns with how we perceive God's call in our lives, that allows us to use our spiritual gifts and strengths, and that allows us to bring our best in service to Christ and His people on a daily basis. We realize, of course, that no job is perfect . . . even in ministry. But we do want to put ourselves in a position where we can utilize our primary gifts, strengths, and passion most of the time.

One implication of this for those called to lead God's people, is that if we are going to lead others effectively, we need to structure our roles primarily around our spiritual gifts and strengths, not our deficiencies. Otherwise, we risk increasing our own frustration and ineffectiveness, while at the same time hindering other gifted people from contributing the way God has designed them. Paul tells the Corinthians that the Spirit of God gives manifestations of the Spirit to His people for the common good (1 Cor. 12:7), and that each person's gifts are indispensable to the health of the church (1 Cor. 12:12–26). When we function outside of our own gifts, and consequently prevent others from functioning in theirs as we operate where they could be instead, what we might be saying to God is, "I know better than You do what we need." Or possibly, "You haven't given us who we need to do effective ministry here." Either way, we are functioning out of fear or pride . . . or both. On the one hand, it is the height of arrogance to tell God that we know better than He does what we need to do effective ministry. On the other, it is from the depths of fear that we doubt His resources. Instead, God is inviting us to trust Him, and His plan for our ministries, by believing that He has given us who and what we need to do effective ministry for His glory. It is the responsibility of ministry leaders then, to make sure that we are utilizing our spiritual gifts and strengths for the common good.

Utilizing our own gifts and strengths is not enough, however. We also need to make sure that those following our leadership are aware of and operating in their giftedness, strengths, and passion as well. Otherwise, they too will become frustrated and disengaged from their own roles as paid ministry staff or volunteers. This means that a primary task of leading people effectively is identifying what they do well, putting them in a position to do it, and developing them so that they can do it to their fullest potential. Paul reminds the church at Ephesus that the main task of those He has gifted to lead His church is not to do ministry. Instead, it is to equip His people to do ministry (Eph. 4:11–12). Why? Paul says that this is the way to build up and unify the church so that she can reach her full potential in

Christ (Eph. 4:12–13). Doing so helps a church move from immaturity to maturity, better reflecting our relationship to Christ and with one another (Eph. 4:14–16). This interdependence with one another ultimately helps our ministry team maximize our strengths and gifts for more effective and fruitful ministry.

The problem, of course, is that this biblical principle contradicts the prevailing view that many congregants have of their pastors . . . that they are the paid professionals called to do the ministry of the church. In our highly consumeristic culture, pastors are expected to meet congregants' needs by attending to visitation, pastoral care, preaching and teaching multiple times during the week, administration and finance, leadership development, podcasting, and anything else necessary to keep the church, and the members, growing and functioning. This, as the saying goes, is why we pay you, pastor. To make matters worse, many pastors actually foster this view because it meets their own ego needs. The problem, of course, is when pastors and congregants buy into this culturally formed view, the pastor, and the church herself, become nothing more than religious commodities to consume.[10] When left unchecked, this places an incredible strain on leaders who do not have the gifts or abilities to meet all of these needs. This eventually leads to overdependence on the leader, potential burnout for the leader, and frustration on all sides as everyone is left unsatisfied.

The solution to this problem is to resist this cultural value, and instead, develop capable and qualified leaders who can utilize their gifts and strengths and contribute toward the work of ministry. This approach is promoted by Paul in his letters to the churches in Corinth and Ephesus, and is modeled in his own life and ministry as he mentors Silas, Timothy, and others through his writings (Acts 15:40–16:5; 1 and 2 Tim.). Perhaps even more importantly, however, Jesus models this approach for us throughout His ministry. The Gospels center much of their content on the personal ministry of Jesus, which includes several stories highlighting His intentional approach toward developing His disciples. Jesus realized that His earthly ministry would last only a relatively short period of time, and that for His church to thrive after His departure, He would need to develop capable leaders who could reproduce themselves in others. Because of this, He first called people to follow Him (Luke 5:1–11, 27–32). He then spent time walking with them, ministering with them, and observing them, until He chose some to lead (Luke 6:12–16). After modeling ministry to them for a time, He then sent them out to do ministry (Luke 10:1–11), and upon their return, He coached, corrected, and encouraged them (Luke 10:17–24). Finally, He empowered and released them into their ministries as those who would bear witness to His identity and works as the Messiah (Acts 1:8).

Within this collection of stories, we see a large part of Jesus' emphasis in His earthly ministry—train up those who would carry on His work in His name long

788

after He was gone. As those seeking to follow Jesus' example, then, should we not also make this a significant part of our ministries as well? None of us, after all, are immortal. We will all move on at some point from our current or future ministries, whether by choice to pursue another call (or retire), or by the choice of others if we are not leading competently. It serves us and our ministries well, then, to invest in the development of those God has entrusted to our care. This begs the question of course, of how? Drawing on the relationship between Barnabas and Saul/Paul in the book of Acts, Gary Mayes suggests a four-phase approach toward developing leaders that also draws on principles from Jesus' approach discussed above: (1) seeking out, (2) sponsoring in, (3) serving together, and (4) sending off.[11]

At various times in the early church's development, God worked in some powerful ways. One such time was in the city of Antioch after the disciples fled the persecution brought on by the stoning of Stephen (Acts 7). As the gospel began to spread to the Greeks and large numbers were converted, the church in Jerusalem decided to send Barnabas to investigate (Acts 11:19–24). After seeing all that God was doing, he realized that a zealous young man with whom he had a relationship could be very useful to build up the fledgling church in this situation—Saul. Barnabas immediately heads off to Tarsus, finds Saul, and brings him back, where together they taught and strengthened the growing church for a year (Acts 11:25–26). Notice that Barnabas doesn't take the task on by himself. Nor does he sit back and wait for some dynamic teacher to miraculously appear. Instead, he assesses the situation, realizes that there is a gifted young man who can contribute to God's work in their midst, and seeks him out intentionally.

This is also the invitation God gives to those of us called to lead God's people in specific locations around the globe. Just as Barnabas sought out Saul, and Jesus sought out the disciples, so should we seek out those God is calling to serve alongside us in ministry as well. We are not to sit on our hands and wait for promising young leaders to seek us out. Instead, we should always have our spiritual eyes open to identify promising young men and women whom God has called and gifted to serve with us in ways that complement our gifts and strengths, and ideally, offset our weaknesses. Doing so not only strengthens our ministry and increases our impact for God's glory, but it gives young leaders the opportunity to discover, use, and develop gifts they may not even realize they have for the common good (1 Cor. 12:7). It also allows our ministries to function as the healthy, growing bodies Paul says they are (1 Cor. 12).

There are times, however, when a young leader may not be trusted by others in the ministry. They may have a questionable past or have made some mistakes. Perhaps they've brought an unfavorable reputation with them from another ministry or from their life before Christ. It is at times like this when a more seasoned leader, one with relational and spiritual authority, needs to step in on behalf of the emerging leader and sponsor them in. Not on a whim, or simply out of the hope that they are different now, and definitely not out of desperation to fill a role. That rarely ends well. But out of trust born from relationship.

This was the case with Saul, who had spent a great deal of time building up hostility and fear among those in the Jerusalem church by persecuting them vigorously (Acts 8:1–3; 9:1–2). So, when faced with exclusion from the Jerusalem church because of this history of antagonism and violence, it took someone who knew him and believed in him enough to sponsor him in. We see Barnabas again take the initiative here, advocating for Saul's character resulting from his encounter with Jesus (Acts 9:26–28). The result? Well, definitely not a revival. In fact, the Hellenistic Jews in the city end up trying to kill him as he preaches the gospel fearlessly and force him to leave (Acts 9:29–30). But this early foundational experience with Barnabas and the Jerusalem church laid the groundwork for Saul's later service with Barnabas in Antioch, and what would eventually become a lifetime of faithful service throughout the known world.

We see in these early episodes of Barnabas and Saul's relationship the beginning of Mayes's third phase—serving together. After seeking him out and sponsoring him into ministry at both Jerusalem and Antioch, Barnabas serves with Saul for a full year in Antioch (Acts 11:26), and much longer in the mission field. They are then sent by the church together to Judea with financial support for the church during a famine (Acts 11:27–30), back to Antioch with John Mark (Acts 12:25), and ultimately to the Gentiles for an extended mission together (Acts 13:1–14:28). During this time they enjoy an incredibly fruitful ministry together throughout Asia Minor, planting churches and leading many to Christ.

Interesting to note in Luke's narrative, is that early in their ministry together, Luke primarily refers to the pair as Barnabas and Saul (Acts 11:25–26, 30; 12:25; 13:2), perhaps indicating the nature of their relationship as mentor and mentee. This would be natural, as Barnabas is likely mentoring Saul during this time, perhaps even teaching him how to tone down some of his brashness. But in the middle of their journey we see a transition . . . Saul, who now becomes known as Paul, seems to become more prominent in the relationship when Luke refers to them as Paul and his companions (Acts 13:13). From this point on, he primarily refers to them as Paul and Barnabas (Acts 13:42–43, 46, 50; 14:1, 3, 23), and perhaps it is during this narrative that we see a case of the pupil surpassing the teacher.

Paul's development in this narrative prepares the soil for the last phase—sending off. It is often inevitable in ministry that as young leaders develop more fully into their giftedness and gain a clearer sense of God's call in their lives, we need to release, or send them, into their next phase of service. Sometimes it can be within our ministries with increased responsibilities and autonomy, where they have room to exercise their gifts and contribute to the ministry's effectiveness. Other times, however, it requires a physical sending off into other forms of fruitful ministry that God is calling them to. We see this specifically play out in the case of Paul and Barnabas when they have a conflict over whether to take John Mark with them on their next missionary journey. Unable to resolve the issue, they go their separate ways, each now engaging in the ministry they feel God calling them to (Acts 15:36–40).

We never want to see a ministry split due to a conflict. Sometimes, however, these types of separations are necessary so that young leaders who have developed their giftedness and clarified their sense of call can reach their full potential for God's glory. Like Paul and Barnabas, remaining together might contribute toward conflicts as both leaders try to operate in their giftedness, determine the best course of action, or even who should serve on their team. This is especially true when the ministry vision God has given to each doesn't fully line up anymore. It is at this time that it might be wise to commission and send the leader into their next season of ministry somewhere else before conflict emerges. This allows them to continue to develop and exercise their gifts in pursuit of their God-given vision, while also allowing you to continue to develop the next group of leaders who can contribute to your ministry. In this way, we follow Paul's exhortation to raise up faithful leaders who will also be qualified to teach and develop others (2 Tim. 2:2), while also ensuring the continuing faithfulness and fruitfulness of our own ministries moving forward.

VISIONARY LEADERSHIP

Finally, leading others effectively requires understanding what our followers need. After honesty and trust, which we have already discussed at length, the next two traits that followers most admire in leaders according to Kouzes and Posner are forward-looking and inspiring.[12] What this means is that leaders need to be able to motivate those they lead to pursue a clear and compelling vision of the future for the ministry. But this is more than just seeking a vision in your prayer closet and communicating it to others. This is the Moses on the mountaintop approach to leadership that depends entirely on God communicating His will to one anointed leader. While this is certainly a biblical approach and can be effective for a time with the right kind of charismatic leader,[13] it is an Old Testament approach that appeals most often to those from hierarchical cultures who believe that God speaks primarily to and through the senior pastor or key ministry leader. For those leading people from today's generations in the West that value more flattened models involving participation and shared leadership, however, this style of top-down leadership is much more challenging. It also suggests that the Spirit only speaks to one person in a given ministry, which runs counter to the model displayed in the early church that often led through a plurality of leaders who had all been given the Spirit of God (Acts 11; 15).

Cultivating a shared vision for the future then, involves enlisting others in the process to build around common ideals and values. This can be done with any number of approaches, including formal systemwide processes like Appreciative Inquiry,[14] or creating listening groups with as many members as possible to discern God's will together through prayer, dialogue, and theological reflection.[15] But, it can also occur through more informal processes like holding conversations with a breadth of key stakeholders inside and outside of the ministry. The specific approach taken matters less than ensuring that as many people as possible from all key constituencies in your ministry feel heard and involved in the process. The result of this type of process will be a shared vision from God that becomes ours—not yours. The leader's role then becomes communicating God's vision for the ministry as clearly as possible and as often as necessary, to ensure that collectively, we continue moving toward God's preferred future for our ministry. And this after all, is exactly where we want to be—collectively following the Spirit of God toward a future centered in God's will.

NOTES

1. John Maxwell, *Developing the Leader Within You 2.0* (Nashville: Harper Collins Leadership, 2019), 1.

2. James M. Kouzes and Barry Z. Posner, *The Leadership Challenge: How to Make Extraordinary Things Happen in Organizations*, 6th ed. (Hoboken, NJ: John Wiley & Sons, 2017), 31.

3. Steve A. Brown, *Leading Me: Eight Practices for a Christian Leader's Most Important Assignment* (Burlington, ON: Castle Quay Books, 2015), 18.

4. See Peter Scazzero, *The Emotionally Healthy Leader: How Transforming Your Inner Life Will Deeply Transform Your Church, Team, and the World* (Grand Rapids: Zondervan, 2015).

5. Atul Gawande, *The Checklist Manifesto: How to Get Things Right* (New York: Picador, 2011).

6. Scazzero, *Emotionally Healthy Leader*, 51–80.

7. Tom Rath and Barry Conchie, *Strengths Based Leadership: Great Leaders, Teams, and Why People Follow* (New York: Gallup Press, 2008), 2–3.

8. Ibid., 15.

9. Ibid., 14–17.

10. See Paul Metzger, *Consuming Jesus: Beyond Race and Class Divisions in a Consumer Church* (Grand Rapids: Eerdmans, 2007).

11. Gary Mayes, *DNA of a Revolution: 1st Century Breakthroughs That Will Transform the Church* (Anaheim Hills, CA: Long Wake Publishing, 2013), 65–82.

12. Kouzes and Posner, *Leadership Challenge*, 31.

13. Craig S. Hendrickson, "Using Charisma to Shape Interpretive Communities in Multiethnic Congregations," *Journal of Religious Leadership* 9 no. 2 (2010).

14. Mark Lau Branson, *Memories, Hopes, and Conversations: Appreciative Inquiry, Missional Engagement, and Congregational Change,* 2nd ed. (Lanham, MD: Rowman & Littlefield. 2016).

15. Alan J. Roxburgh, *Missional Map-Making: Skills for Leading in Times of Transition* (San Francisco: Jossey-Bass, 2010).

Developing Elders and Future Church Leaders

ERIC MOORE

Leadership in the church is a critical issue. The success of any organization depends upon having good leadership at the helm. It is no different in the church of Jesus Christ. In many ways, the leadership in the church is different from leadership in business or politics. However, in some ways it can be very similar. Normally, when we think of church leadership, we look at what the Bible calls "elders." The term "elders" has several connotations associated with it. First, a person who is advanced in years is referred to as an elder. Second, but not always, an elder or older person is associated with wisdom. Because of his experience in life, he can guide or speak into circumstances that others have not experienced. Both aspects of this term help to define a biblical elder. Third, an elder is generally associated with a family. He is usually the patriarch of a family, clan, or tribe.

UNDERSTANDING ELDERSHIP

OLD TESTAMENT PERIOD

In the Old Testament, elders were individuals who led Israel and are spoken of as sitting at the gate. Proverbs 31 speaks of the virtuous woman's husband sitting at the gate of the city (Prov. 31:23). In Lamentations, Jeremiah grieves over the fact that elders are gone from the city gates (Lam. 5:14). The city gates in the Old Testament were the place where business was transacted, and civic laws were enforced. In the book of Ruth, Boaz approached the kinsmen redeemer at the city gate to seek the rights to marry Ruth (Ruth 4:1). The transaction was conducted at the gate in front of the city's elders making the transaction official. The elders who first appear in Scripture are surprisingly Hebrew and Egyptian. As Joseph is heading to Israel to bury his father, Jacob (Israel), Genesis tells us, "And Joseph went up to bury his father: and with him went up all the servants of Pharaoh, the "elders" of his house, and all the elders of the land of Egypt" (Gen. 50:7). So, elders is not a purely Hebrew concept. However, God used it to direct the affairs of Israel as early as the days of Moses (Ex. 3:16). The Lord told Moses, "Go and gather the elders of Israel together and say to them, 'The LORD, the God of your fathers, the God of Abraham, Isaac, and Jacob has appeared to me, saying, "'I am indeed concerned about you and what has been done to you in Egypt."'"

God often held the elders responsible for the spiritual well-being of the nation. In Numbers 11, God told Moses to gather seventy elders around the tabernacle (Num. 11:16). The Lord would speak to the nation through these select individuals. In turn, they were to help lead the people under Moses's direction.

INTERTESTAMENTAL PERIOD

After the closing of the Hebrew Old Testament, there was a period of time often called "the 400 years of silence." It is called this because no word from God was recorded between the closing of the book of Malachi and the Gospels. It is generally believed that during this period, synagogue worship began in Judea.[1] Local assemblies of Jews would gather in towns on the Sabbath to read Scripture and worship. The synagogue system was firmly in place when Jesus began His ministry. Throughout the Gospels, Jesus enters these facilities and teaches the people. Some respond positively and others don't. In these synagogues, elders oversee the organizational and spiritual affairs of congregants. Any city or town that had ten Jewish men who wanted to organize a synagogue was free to do so.[2] Although the specific functions of elder varied from synagogue to synagogue, it has been assumed that the council of elders (presbyters) was the chief governing board of a congregation.[3]

NEW TESTAMENT PERIOD

Early Church

In the New Testament, Jesus, called a group of twelve men to accompany Him on the mission given to Him by God, the Father. These twelve individuals were considered His disciples. They walked with Jesus. They were sent out to act as ambassadors of the faith. They even had the ability to heal on occasion. As Jesus approached the time of His crucifixion, He changed their title to "apostles." They were to be the caretakers of the faith after Jesus would leave this earth to return to His Father in heaven. In many ways, these apostles set the standard for the elders of the church.

The church in Jerusalem was primarily of Hebrew heritage. As a result of the Holy Spirit's coming at Pentecost and the gospel being preached, a significant number of Jews came to faith in Jesus Christ. This new faith needed leadership. It was natural for these newly converted Jewish people to connect the current leadership with leadership of their past. With the birth of the church came the title "elders" to recognize leaders in the church. In Acts 15, the term is first associated with the church.

A group of individuals had come to Antioch and began to cause division over the issue of circumcision. Paul and Barnabas went to the church in Jerusalem to resolve the issue. Acts 15:2 tells us, "And after Paul and Barnabas had a heated argument and debate with them, the brothers determined that Paul and Barnabas and some others of them should go up to Jerusalem to the apostles and elders concerning this issue."

It is not clear if "the apostles and elders" are the same individuals or if these are two distinct groups of people or even a mixture of both. However, the first church installed a group of leaders called by the title of elders. Those who held this office were responsible for a major decision regarding the ethical direction of the church. Inherent in this responsibility is that the individual needed to be a person of good character, spiritually mature and a man of faith.

The apostle Paul lays out the character traits of an elder in the Pastoral Epistles, particularly in 1 Timothy 3:2–7:

> An overseer, then, must be above reproach, the husband of one wife, temperate, self-controlled, respectable, hospitable, skillful in teaching, not overindulging in wine, not a bully, but gentle, not contentious, free from the love of money. He must be one who manages his own household well, keeping his children under control with all dignity (but if a man does not know how to manage his own household, how will he take care of the church of God?), and not a new convert, so that he will not become conceited and fall into condemnation incurred by the devil. And he must have a good reputation with those outside the church, so that he will not fall into disgrace and the snare of the devil.

A short definition of each of these qualities is worth exploring. *The Moody Bible Commentary* explains these character traits this way:

> Above reproach is the overarching qualification, further spelled out by what follows. Husband of one wife indicates that an elder cannot be involved in extramarital relationships, something common in the first-century Greco-Roman world. The phrase does not, however, automatically disqualify a divorced man since Scripture allows for divorce (and remarriage) under certain circumstances without God considering it sin. Temperate ("clear-headed in one's judgments")

and prudent ("self-controlled," "serious" about his life and ministry) show how the candidate relates to himself, respectable ("well ordered") and hospitable toward others. Able to teach indicates his competence with the Word of God and provides one of the hints in this passage about an overseer's function. A candidate for office of overseer must demonstrate a pattern of moderation in the use of alcohol and the expression of anger.

The inability to manage ("to lead, preside over"; "rule") his children or household disqualifies him from serving as an elder. This parenthetic statement demonstrates that congregational management involves nurture.

Church leadership requires spiritual maturity. The word translated new convert was often used in contemporary Greek writings to refer to something newly planted. Spiritual neophytes should not be appointed to church office because they are especially vulnerable to spiritual conceit. Reputation is literally "testimony." It is not enough for a church leader to be well thought of by those within the assembly. Unlike the previous verse, which pointed to Satan as a cautionary example, the snare of the devil refers to a trap laid by the devil for the leader, as the devil tempts him to become proud about his position of importance in the church. God is opposed to those who are proud (James 4:6), and people will not hold them in high regard (James 4:10).[4]

A similar list of qualifications is found in the first chapter of the Book of Titus. Paul informs Titus,

> I left you in Crete, that you would set in order what remains and appoint elders in every city as I directed you, namely, if any man is beyond reproach, the husband of one wife, having children who believe, not accused of indecent behavior or rebellion. For the overseer must be beyond reproach as God's steward, not self-willed, not quick-tempered, not overindulging in wine, not a bully, not greedy for money, but hospitable, loving what is good, self-controlled, righteous, holy, disciplined, holding firmly the faithful word which is in accordance with the teaching, so that he will be able both to exhort in sound doctrine and to refute those who contradict it. (Titus 1:5–9)

The first group of elders in the church of Jerusalem may have been selected from Jesus' extended group of disciples. In Luke, Jesus sends out seventy disciples (Luke 10:1–2). These individuals are in addition to the twelve. At Pentecost, 120 followers of Jesus were in the upper room praying (Acts 1:15). Later in the book of Corinthians, Paul shares that five hundred followers of Jesus saw Him after His resurrection (1 Cor. 15:6). It is believable that among these individuals were men whose character matched the qualities listed in the Pastoral Epistles.

Expanding Church

However, the situation may have been different when it came to establishing elders in predominantly Gentile churches. Prior to the trip to Jerusalem by Paul and

Barnabas to meet with the elders, the two of them had embarked upon a journey through Asia Minor to share the gospel and establish churches in the region. They preached the gospel in the towns of Salamis and Paphos on the island of Cyprus. The duo preached and saw people converted in Perga in Pamphylia, Antioch in Pisidia, Iconium, Lystra, and Derbe. After arriving in Derbe, they returned to Lystra, Iconium, and Antioch to establish leadership among the Christians. Acts 14:21–23 states that "they returned to Lystra, to Iconium, and to Antioch, strengthening the souls of the disciples, encouraging them to continue in the faith, and saying, 'It is through many tribulations that we must enter the kingdom of God.'" When they had appointed elders in every church, having fasted and prayed, they commended them to the Lord in whom they had believed.

How were Paul and Barnabas able to establish elders in these churches so quickly? The first missionary journey did not take more than two years.[5] One theory is that the initial elders were primarily of Hebrew heritage or Gentiles converted to Judaism. Paul's method of gospel proclamation was to preach first in the synagogue. From there he would branch out into the community. We see this in Acts 17:1–2, "Now when they (Paul and Barnabas) had traveled through Amphipolis and Apollonia, they came to Thessalonica, where there was a synagogue of the Jews. And according to Paul's custom, he visited them, and for three Sabbaths reasoned with them from the Scriptures." When Jews believed the message, they were more likely to reflect godly character traits than the average Gentile as Gene Getz argues,

> Since there were a number of committed Jews and devout Gentiles in these cities, these men who responded to the Gospel would have grown quickly in their faith. And when Paul and Barnabas returned to these churches, we can be sure they looked for these men.[6]

Of course, a supernatural work of the Holy Spirit may have helped Paul and Barnabas in choosing the right men for this position, though the biblical text doesn't supply us with that information. We can safely assume they sought men with the character traits listed in 1 Timothy and Titus.

On Paul's third missionary journey, he desired to meet with the elders of the church at Ephesus. We don't have a record of when elders were established at this church, but we know that Paul spent three years teaching, preaching, and discipling at Ephesus (Acts 20:31). During this time, he established elders in the congregation, which is clear from Acts 20. Paul had left Ephesus due to a riotous situation stirred by the preaching of the gospel. Although he was physically distant from the church, Paul remained spiritually and emotionally attached to the ministry. He desired to help it to continually thrive for the cause of Christ. On Paul's way back to Jerusalem for the feast of Pentecost, he requested a meeting with the church elders at Ephesus in the city of Miletus. Paul's words to the elders give us a glimpse of what Paul expected out of the elders. As he tells them that they will never see him again, the apostle instructs them to do the following:

> "Be on guard for yourselves and for all the flock, among which the Holy Spirit has made you overseers, to shepherd the church of God which He purchased with His own blood. I know that after my departure savage wolves will come in among you, not sparing the flock; and from among your own selves men will arise, speaking perverse things to draw away the disciples after them. Therefore, be on the alert, remembering that night and day for a period of three years I did not cease to admonish each one with tears. And now I entrust you to God and to the word of His grace, which is able to build you up and to give you the inheritance among all those who are sanctified. I have coveted no one's silver or gold or clothes. You yourselves know that these hands served my own needs and the men who were with me. In everything I showed you that by working hard in this way you must help the weak and remember the words of the Lord Jesus, that He Himself said, 'It is more blessed to give than to receive.'"
>
> When he had said these things, he knelt down and prayed with them all. (Acts 20:28–36)

This passage assigns several responsibilities to the elders. First, there is a need to protect the flock and themselves from false doctrine. This implies that elders must be students of the God's Word and know how to apply it to everyday life. Second, they need to constantly be alert for those who would deceive the people of God. In fact, they need to take notice of one another, not in a suspicious manner, but in the sense of knowing that nobody is above the need to be evaluated. Third, they should be diligent workers for the cause of Christ and not for greed. Finally, they should be open-handed with what God has given them to steward. It is more blessed to give than receive.

CONTEMPORARY PERIOD

One of the more controversial elements regarding elders in our contemporary society is the gender of the individual. In the Old Testament, as stated earlier in this chapter, an elder was a male. He was generally older and more mature, but he was born a male. In our contemporary culture, the issue of being qualified to lead has taken the main stage. In a society where women are qualified to lead Fortune 500 organizations in areas of banking, finance, law, marketing, and manufacturing, it seems primitive to exclude women from the top positions of leadership in the local church. As a result, many have sought to redefine eldership to any adult who demonstrates the qualities or characteristics listed in 1 Timothy and Titus. It is often stated that the New Testament culture was a male-dominated society and the selection of a woman elder was not possible. But in enlightened society, some argue that these restrictions should be lifted to allow the best qualified to fulfill these roles. This is usually supported by Galatians 3:28, "There is neither Jew nor Greek, there is neither slave nor free, there is neither male nor female; for you are all one in Christ Jesus." An objective exegesis of this verse clearly shows that the meaning is not that genders are nullified, but that all are accepted equally in Christ. Thus, it does not negate roles given to men and women in the church structure.

Although, the argument for female elders is compelling from a sociological viewpoint, it falls short exegetically. First is the actual definition of the term elder. The core meaning of the word means older man.[7] Second, every time that it is used in Scripture, it refers to a man. Third, we have no examples of women serving as elders in the Bible. Fourth, in the book of Revelation the example of the twenty-four elders all represent men (twelve patriarchs of Israel and the twelve disciples). The overall bent of Scripture seems to imply that God's desire is for a man to fulfill this role. That said, there is nothing in Scripture that remotely implies that men are better, smarter, or more qualified for the role. The reason seems to be wrapped up in the creation order of humanity (1 Tim. 2:12).

This does not mean that God will not elevate women to leadership positions when needed. The example that is often cited from the Old Testament is Deborah, who was a judge in Israel during the time of the judges. She was clearly a civic and spiritual leader giving guidance to men (Judg. 4:4–7). To deny this is to deny what is clearly presented in Scripture. However, this seems to be the exception to the rule, not the rule. In the New Testament, there are women who follow Jesus, such as Joanna and Susanna (Luke 8:1–3). There are woman leaders mentioned in the early church as well. Philip had four daughters who were prophetesses (Acts 21:8–9). Priscilla and her husband, Aquila, traveled with Paul and discipled Apollos in Ephesus (Acts 18:1–26). Phoebe served as a deaconess in Rome (Rom. 16:1). We have examples of women leaders in Scripture, but no examples or mandates for women elders.

The question is then asked, "How then should women serve?" The Bible addresses the specific areas where women can teach. The Bible makes it clear that older women are to teach the younger (Titus 2:3–5). This implies that the older women are more mature and can impart their wisdom on to those who desire to learn from them. The role of teaching is often associated with authority, which would imply that women can lead women. It is also clear that women can teach and lead children. The real question is whether women can lead or teach men. In this case, each local assembly will need to address the extent of the prohibition of women having authority over a man (1 Tim. 2:12). In one assembly the congregation may see this as an absolute. In other words, under no circumstance should a woman teach in a mixed seating of men and women. In another assembly, the church may feel that a woman may speak in a mixed setting on "Mother's Day" or a "Woman's Day" celebration. The speaker has been given authority to speak by the leadership of the church. In another church, a woman may be ordained as an associate pastor so long as she is under the male elder board and a male senior pastor. How this works out in each local church will look different for each assembly.

ELDER DEVELOPMENT

Church leadership should consider specific men for the position of elders before the leadership is ever approached about the position by those men. In other words, the church leadership should be asking themselves, "Do these individuals have the character traits that would make for a good elder?" Although the Bible tells us, "If any man aspires to the office of overseer, it is a fine work he desires to do" (1 Tim. 3:1), the church leadership should be considering men all the time. This means before the aspirations of the man have been clearly articulated, the leadership should have taken note of the individual's spiritual development. If the church leadership is "always considering," then once a person expresses his aspiration to the position of an elder, there is a unanimity of agreement.

However, there should be a desire in the man's heart for the role. The last thing we want to do is appoint a man to a position of spiritual leadership if there is no desire or aspiration for the position. In fact, the term "aspires" in 1 Timothy 3:1 means "to stretch out," "reach after," to "yearn for." His aspirations for the position should be clearly expressed. These aspirations will be articulated in word, but also in his deeds.

The practice of "always considering" helps when approached by others who are not under consideration. From time to time, a person may aspire to eldership who lacks the necessary character traits needed to fulfill the role. His rationale behind the aspirations are not necessarily rooted in Scripture. He may be a good candidate for future consideration, but presently is spiritually immature and needs more discipling in the things of God. Church leaders should be prepared to share why he will not be considered for eldership at this time and provide a possible pathway to the office in the future if leaders believe this is an option.

CAUTIOUS QUALIFICATIONS

Because people can be swayed by culture, decisions on candidates for eldership in a local church can be influenced more by the culture than by biblical standards. So here are a few things that do not automatically qualify one for the elder board.

Win at All Costs

A go-getter is a person who is driven to make things happen. He loves to see things get done. If given a challenge, he will complete it on time and under budget. As a result, he has probably been elevated in his company to a significant position and has done well for himself. There is nothing wrong with this person being an elder, but ministry is not only about product. Examine him carefully. Does he meet the biblical qualifications? Is he able to teach sound doctrine? Is he able to love and serve people?

The Over Empathizer

An empathizer is the person who tends to listen to the complainer in the group. At first glance, this person seems to have a good heart and shows concern about the neglected or the one who is left behind. It is good to have empathy for those who are suffering. However, it is not good for an organization that needs to move forward to continually side with the disgruntled individuals who are against change in the organization. Make sure you examine a person's balance between empathizing with others and embracing the church's vision.

The Reminiscer

This person thinks the church was ideal in the past and reminisces often. They seem godly, but their hearts are captive to a craving for safety and security. New ideas will be questioned, and old programs will be hailed as the best way to move forward. What worked in the past should work now. Make sure that a commitment to the old ways is not confused with a commitment to God's way.

Energizer Bunny

The world loves the excited visionary who has great plans and dreams for the church. The excitement is contagious. His enthusiasm for the things of the Lord is impressive. Unfortunately, the enthusiasm is often for the latest cultural trend being integrated into the church. He loves fads. New is in, old is out. When others share why a particular technology or ministry cannot be brought into the church, his enthusiasm fades. Often, it will turn to resentment. Soon people will begin to wonder what you did to kill his enthusiasm for the Lord.

One Agenda Man

Often, a passionate person will join the church. It is good to be passionate. But it is better when that passion aligns with the church's vision for ministry. However, that is not always the case. A person who is only focused on his pet project is not a good elder candidate. This person may be covering selfishness with a veneer of self-righteousness toward a cause where he can be a hero.

These individuals and others who have an agenda that is not God's are the reason Paul instructed Timothy not to appoint people to leadership quickly. Choosing the right people for leadership takes time. Since it takes time, we need to be patient. Our challenge is to find and develop humble, godly men for eldership in our congregations.

QUALIFICATIONS FOR ELDERS

Disciples

Jesus told His disciples, "Go therefore and make disciples" (Matt. 28:19). The key to developing an elder pipeline is to have and maintain a good discipleship process. From this pool of qualified men growing in their walk with the Lord Jesus Christ that elders should arise.

The first step in raising up faithful elders is selecting the mature men. Many a pastor has become frustrated because he has spent countless hours pouring into a person only to be let down or disappointed in the outcome. This risk cannot be eliminated. Just look at Jesus and Judas. Judas spent three years with the Master and still rejected Him and His mission. Pastors are not immune. However, there are some things that can help in choosing the individuals with the right qualifications.

Bobby Harrington and Alex Absalom list four traits when looking for people to invest in.[8] The first trait is **availability**. Is the individual someone who makes the time to be available for helping lead the church? In a culture that is consumed with "being busy," does this person make his spiritual growth a priority? Are they willing to eliminate lesser things from their life to grow in the things of Christ? This can be determined by asking the person to meet with you for four to six weeks for Bible study at a time that is somewhat a stretch. This may be an early morning video conference or breakfast. This will help determine if this is a priority in his life.

The second trait is **faithfulness**. Is the individual somebody who is already serving in the church? If not, then you might want to pass on him unless there are some other intangibles that you have observed that make it worth the risk. If he is serving, is he faithful to the task? What do others say regarding his responsibilities? Is he somebody others go to for advice or is he the one always asking for advice? Is he a leader or a follower? Is he wise or naïve? All these questions should be examined before you venture into a leadership development plan with him.

The third trait is **teachability**, which is a synonym for the vital trait of elder that must typify a godly elder. It is important that church leaders know the Word of God, but it is more than just knowledge of the Bible. It is also the receiving of this knowledge. Is this somebody who is eager to grow in the things of the Lord?

Often self-taught Bible students and Bible college/seminary trained students can come with a sense of arrogance regarding their knowledge of God's Word. A good disciple comes to a teaching event knowing that he can learn from anyone and is open to what God might teach him.

The fourth trait is **reliability**. Is this person somebody who you can depend on? Is this person on time? If not, does he call to say that he will be late? Is he somebody who does what he says? Psalm 15:4 states that a man of integrity "swears to his own hurt and does not change" (ESV). Does this man follow through on tasks to the very end or does he bail after the initial excitement of a project is over?

A person doesn't have to be perfect in every area, but these are key characteristics worth evaluating if you are going to invest your life in a person who will be a leader in your church.

Discipleship

Once a man has been identified as a strong potential candidate for eldership, a discipleship plan should be developed. This may be leading the men through a Bible reading program. It could be working through a systematic theology studying the major doctrines of Scripture. Another option is to read books about Christian leadership and discuss them.

The length of this development plan should allow you to evaluate the individuals in a variety of situations and settings. It should not be so long that the individuals involved begin to feel as if nothing is being accomplished. There should be at least three requirements of those who participate in the discipleship process. First, they must commit to the full process. It is important to let them know that this will last for a certain duration of time. Second, if there is a group of elders candidates, members of the group must be committed to each other over the same period of time. Third, whatever is shared in confidence in the group stays in confidence. Finally, they must commit to leading their own group once the present group ends.

This development plan and these three requirements will accomplish two things. First, it will help determine who really wants to grow in Christian leadership. And second, it develops a pipeline of leadership in the church. Only a handful of the individuals may actually become elders, but many will become leaders of ministries within the church. A pool of potential elders will likely arise from this group.

Use of Technology

One of the challenges in our culture is the availability of time. So many sources of information vie for our attention. Not only are we busy, but our jobs are global, which means we can be physically in another country on any day of the week. This challenges our notion of discipleship. Discipleship used to mean meeting once a week or twice a month at a physical location for food, fellowship, accountability, and prayer. This is tougher to accomplish with so many moving parts in each of our lives. This is where we need to begin to use technology to our advantage.

Physical gatherings should still be planned, but optional technology to remotely participate in the gathering should be made available at every meeting. Physical attendance should be expected and required, but in case of circumstances beyond the participant's control remote access should be provided. Most workers, especially the younger generation, communicate by media on a regular basis. This should be integrated into the discipleship process.

In addition, meeting times and days should be agreed upon and published for the next six months to a year. This gives the participants the opportunity to arrange their schedule to make these gatherings. This also communicates the importance of these meetings.

Without promoting one curriculum over another, there are a number of good video series that can help develop our leaders. A combination of personal instruction along with video is a good mix. In fact, if the material can be streamed, this will help participants who cannot make the meeting. The missing member can watch the streamed material on his media device at an alternate time and connect with the group in the next session as you review the previous material.

Training

Candidates should be placed into temporary leadership positions in the church for three purposes. The first is for the existing leaders to evaluate their leadership style and effectiveness. The last thing you want is to put a poor leader in a key position that will cause harm to the church. However, you must be able to observe how a person leads.

Second, this gives the individual experience leading within the church. Corporate leaders are not always the best leaders in a volunteer organization. Although the goals can be similar, often the soft skills of leadership are different. This helps the person to learn to lead by influence and not by position or power.

Third, this gives the congregation the opportunity to view the individual in a leadership role and to give feedback to existing leadership. Those who are being led will be able to provide valuable information regarding the person's strengths and weaknesses. As a leader, you will only be able to evaluate the person from the top down. Members will be able to provide insight from the bottom up.

After the training phase is completed, the governmental process needs to be completed. Each church has their own constitution or operating procedures when it comes to ordaining or installing elders. This needs to be officially accomplished and documented.

After this, the individual or individuals should be presented to the congregation in an official capacity. This may be a separate ceremony or during the normal worship service. The main thing is that the church body is aware of the process and the official office of the new elder.

CONCLUSION

The other day, I happened to be reading the first few verses of Acts 16. Paul had embarked on his second missionary journey with Silas. When they arrived in Lystra, the text says, "And a disciple was there, named Timothy, the son of a Jewish woman who was a believer, but his father was a Greek, and he was well spoken of by the brothers and sisters who were in Lystra and Iconium. Paul wanted this man to leave with him" (Acts 16:1b–3a).

Prior to Paul ever mentoring Timothy, he was well spoken of not only in Lystra but in Iconium as well. Paul took note of what God was already doing in Timothy's life. Today, there are Timothys in our midst too. Our job is to identify them, work with them, and appoint them. It might take some time to develop our leadership dream team, but let's start where we are. Every journey worth taking begins with the first step.

NOTES

1. Lee I. Levine, *The Ancient Synagogue: The First Thousand Years*, 2nd ed. (New Haven, CT: Yale University Press, 2005), 432.
2. Leon Wood, *Survey of Israel's History* (Grand Rapids: Zondervan, 1986), 371.
3. Levine, *Ancient Synagogue*, 433.
4. Michael Rydelnik and Michael G. Vanlaningham, eds. *The Moody Bible Commentary* (Chicago: Moody Publishers, 2014), 1899.
5. John McKay, *Paul: His Life and Teaching* (Grand Rapids: Baker Academic, 2003), 61.
6. Gene Getz, Brad Smith, and Bob Buford, *Elders and Leaders: God's Plan for Leading the Church: A Biblical, Historical and Cultural Perspective* (Chicago: Moody Publishers, 2003), 70.
7. *Presbuteros.*
8. Bobby Harrington and Alex Absalom, *Discipleship That Fits: Five Kinds of Relationships God Uses to Help Us Grow* (Grand Rapids: Zondervan, 2016), 186–87.

Managing Conflict

CRAIG HENDRICKSON

If there is one truism in life, it is that you will have conflict. For those leading a church or ministry, this is especially true, as leaders are called to lead people . . . broken people . . . people with emotional wounds . . . people with dreams, desires, and values that often conflict with those of others. And this inevitably leads to conflict . . . sometimes with the leader, and sometimes with one another. Leaders are also called to lead these same broken people with conflicting agendas to places they may have never been to, and quite often, do not necessarily want to go. It is one thing, for example, to say we value outreach as a ministry; it is quite another to sacrifice resources or existing programs focused on church members to invest in that outreach to others. It is one thing to say we value diversity. It is another to give up your deeply held preferences for a particular worship style for the benefit of others. The truth, then, is that if you are going to lead God's people, you need to be prepared to deal with conflict regularly, and consequently, deal with it well.

In this chapter, we will discuss how leaders can effectively manage, and ultimately, resolve conflict in a healthy, biblical way. We will begin by defining conflict and discussing common causes of the conflicts we face. We cannot, after all, resolve what we do not understand. Accomplishing this, we will explore different examples of conflict in Scripture, paying special attention to how Jesus and God's people experienced and dealt with conflict. In doing so, we will discover God's deeper purpose for conflict in our lives and ministries, and identify principles informing how we might resolve those conflicts well.

THE NATURE AND CAUSES OF CONFLICT

Let's be honest for a moment; conflict can be scary. Conflicts threaten relationships, threaten a ministry's health and effectiveness, and can even threaten pastor's jobs when not dealt with properly. Conflict can cost those involved a great deal. So, for some of us, it is easier to avoid it altogether. Or, to simply hope it will go away. But conflict rarely goes away. When conflict is ignored, it simply goes under the surface and emerges later. But, even if a particular conflict does not reappear, there is usually another conflict waiting to materialize in its place. Because of this phenomenon, it is helpful to understand what conflict is and why it occurs.

There are many definitions of conflict; too many to mention here. Norm Sawchuck, for example, defines conflict as "two or more objects aggressively trying to occupy the same space . . . two persons each trying to have his/her 'own way' regarding an important decision."[1] In a shorter, simpler definition, Ken Sande proposes that conflict is "a difference in opinion or purpose that frustrates someone's goals or desires."[2] While these definitions provide some helpful understanding into the nature of conflict, they ultimately fall short because not all conflicts are about important decisions or frustrated goals. Instead, conflict is multifaceted and can be caused by many different factors arising from complex human interactions. Folger, Poole, and Stutman present a more nuanced understanding of conflict, suggesting that it is "the interaction of interdependent people who perceive incompatible goals and interference from each other in achieving those goals."[3] This is a more helpful definition for our purposes, because it situates conflict within social interactions between people who have differing perceptions of their reality; especially relating to their desired outcomes and apparent resistance from the other party. This focus on perception is important, as it highlights the importance of communication and social interpretation when conflict occurs in a relational and/or ministry setting.

This understanding of the importance of perception gives us insight into many of the reasons that conflict transpires in ministry settings. One of the most common causes is that of unmet expectations. This happens most often when there is a lack of clarity about what is expected in a given situation or with a task to be performed. But it can also happen due to a second cause—poor communication. Think about how often you have been in an argument and said something like, "That's not what I said!" Or perhaps an email or text you sent was not as clear as you thought it was, and the person receiving your communication did not do what you asked. Miscommunications happen all the time in relationships.

A third cause of conflicts relates to unclear roles and power relationships. When the boundaries of power and responsibilities have not been fully clarified, disputes can erupt. Fourth, with all of the complexities that make up individual personalities, conflicts can occur simply because of different temperaments or attitudes. We've all been there—that person just grinds you the wrong way, and eventually, you lose your patience. Fifth, conflicts of interest between individuals or groups can arise when there is chronic disagreement between parties. For example, perhaps the seniors and young adults in a church have been wrestling for control over the style of worship for years. Finally, whenever change is introduced into a ministry setting, stress and anxiety increases. New staff, new programs or systems, ending a long-running program, changing from pews to seats, or other large or seemingly small changes that are important to people can cause unexpected conflict.

When these types of conflicts occur, it is easy to become frustrated or discouraged. Some, after all, might seem petty or insignificant, while others may seem like they will never go away. When that happens, it is easy for a pastor or ministry leader to get tempted to walk away. According Barna research, unresolved conflict is actually one of the leading contributors to pastors leaving the ministry.[4] There are many reasons for this, but one is because of a misunderstanding of God's purpose in conflict. Before we turn our attention to developing conflict resolution skills, then, it is important to understand how conflict functions in Scripture, so that we might better understand what God's purpose may be for those conflicts.

CONFLICT IN SCRIPTURE

When one reads the Bible, it could easily be said that it is all about conflict. From the very beginning . . . from the story of the fall (Gen. 3), through the conflict between brothers resulting in Abel's death (Gen. 4); to the numerous accounts of family strife in Abraham's family tree (Gen. 12–50), to the extended conflicts between Israel and Egypt (Ex. 1–14) and Israel and the Philistines (1 Sam. 17); from enmity between David and Saul (1 Sam. 18–28), to repeated confrontations between Jesus and the Pharisees (Matt. 23); throughout the development of the early church in Jerusalem (Acts 4:1–8:3), into the mission field (Acts 14–15), and in several of Paul's letters (1 Cor., Gal. 2); and ultimately, to the very end culminating in the final battle between God and the devil to usher in the new heavens and the new earth (Rev. 20); conflict saturates the pages of Scripture. This, of course, is a depressing and incomplete reading of Scripture; one that leaves out the overarching story of a loving God relentlessly working to redeem His fallen, sinful creation, culminating in the Christ event. Yet, because of sin's effects, it is no wonder that the narratives of Scripture are full of stories of selfishness, greed, covetousness, jealousy, and other sinful desires that result in repeated conflicts. The question becomes, then, what can we learn from instances of conflict in the Bible that might inform both our understanding of and engagement with conflict? To answer this question, we will briefly survey select episodes in the life and ministry of Jesus, as well as among Israel and the early church.

JESUS AND CONFLICT

As we take a closer look at Jesus' life and ministry, we quickly realize through His words and actions that He had an interesting, even unexpected relationship with conflict. From the very onset of His public ministry, when He took a whip to the money lenders and vendors in the temple courts (John 2:13–16; see Matt. 21:12–16) and began to reframe Jewish religious practice, we see that Jesus had no problem initiating conflict when it served His purposes. We also see in Luke's depiction of the beginning of Jesus' public ministry that He had no problem avoiding, or perhaps more aptly, not dealing with conflict when it didn't suit His immediate purpose (Luke 4:23–30). Yet, we also see when conflict develops in other instances, once between His disciples (Matt. 20:20–28) and another time with a woman caught in adultery (John 8:3–11), that He deals with it directly and resolves it. It is obvious that Jesus' approach toward conflict is not simply go "be reconciled to your brother" (Matt. 5:23–24), as many of us might assume it would be. Instead, it is varied and diverse, adapting to the needs in the situation.

What can be learned from this? First, resolving conflict requires discernment, not a one size fits all approach. Christians in North America often tend to focus our approach to conflict on one or two passages—Matthew 5:21–26 and/or Ephesians 4:26–27. We use these passages to inform a sense of urgency to go directly to those we have a conflict with to reconcile as quickly as possible in all situations. While this is often helpful in reconciling strained or broken relationships, Jesus demonstrates that it might not always be appropriate. Some conflicts are better left to another time, especially those that are not urgent or all that serious, or in Jesus' case, when addressing an explosive situation directly might lead to a worse outcome. Others might require a more indirect approach, especially when dealing with someone with different cultural values and practices (more on this later). If reconciliation is the goal in conflictual situations (Matt. 5:21–26), then discernment is needed.

Second, conflict is not something to shy away from; rather, a leader can actually initiate it when the situation calls for it. Similar to Jesus' cleansing of the temple, conflict can often surface values and practices that are hindering the church's mission and fellowship, and possibly people's access to God. In this way, conflict is actually desirable in a change situation, as long as the leader is equipped to manage it. When a leader initiates conflict at the right time in the right way, then, it can lead to positive outcomes that eliminate barriers to God's mission, and instead enhance a ministry's ability to participate in it.

Third, conflict can move in a constructive or destructive direction depending on your response to it. Although we realize that God's sovereign plan was in effect, Jesus could have easily ended His public ministry just after it began if He decided to deal directly with the enraged crowd in Nazareth. Instead, He deals with the situation with wisdom and He survives the crowd to continue His ministry. Likewise, His approach toward the religious leaders trying to trap Him with the adulterous woman produced positive outcomes, both for the woman who received forgiveness, and for Him. How we engage conflict matters and will ultimately determine whether the situation is transformational for those involved.[5]

CONFLICT AMONG GOD'S PEOPLE

While there are many examples to choose from, there are four instances of conflict among God's people that are particularly helpful for thinking through how we might approach conflict in our ministries as leaders. The first is in Exodus 18:13–23, which might be best described as a pre-conflict passage. In this story, Moses's father-in-law, Jethro, corrects Moses for trying to be sole arbiter and judge over the entire nation, warning him that continuing to do so would likely burn him out (Ex. 18:17). He also intimates that the people might already be frustrated with him, as many are waiting in line all day to see him (Ex. 18:14). To address both of these issues, he suggests teaching the people how to live and follow Yahweh well, and to appoint wise leaders with good character as judges under him to share the load (Ex. 18:20–23).

The next three episodes all occur in the life of the early church. The first is an example of ethnic division and inequality in the church, as the Hellenistic Jewish widows were being overlooked in daily food distribution (Acts 6:1–7). The solution arrived at by the apostles is to restructure their ministry system, appointing seven Hellenistic Jewish deacons to oversee the process so that they could stay devoted to other spiritual matters. The second instance is another episode relating to ethnic unity, with a sharp division arising over whether to require Gentile believers to be circumcised and obey the Mosaic law to ensure their salvation and inclusion in the church (Acts 15:1–5). After a protracted dialogue (Acts 15:6–18), a resolution is reached, and the only restrictions imposed are to preserve ritual purity so that ongoing table fellowship can continue between Jewish and Gentile believers (Acts 15:19–21). Through both instances, there is transformation of the parties involved—the first leading to increased missional vitality in the church (Acts 6:7), and the second to great joy and ministry fruitfulness (Acts 15:30–35). The third instance, however, brings no immediate resolution or apparent transformation. In fact, there is a ministry split after a conflict occurs between Paul and Barnabas over whether to include Mark on their upcoming missionary journey (Acts 15:36–41). While Paul and Barnabas both seem to go on to fruitful ministry with their partners, both go their own way into the mission field; their relationship at least temporarily fractured.

What do these occurrences of conflict, resolution, and nonresolution have to say to us? They again remind us that conflict can be either constructive or destructive. When handled well, conflict is a window of opportunity . . . to learn new insights, grow, or to envision a new future. As both cases of ethnic division in the early church demonstrate, key issues and tensions can be surfaced, and ministry organizations can reevaluate and clarify their goals and mission. In the cases of Moses and Jethro and the division over food distribution in the Jerusalem church, new and creative ideas for organizational structure and programs can emerge, and trust can be deepened. When conflict is not handled well, however, there can be destructive consequences. The case of Paul and Barnabas's dispute demonstrates that ministries can split or lose personnel, and individuals can be damaged and relationships broken. When this happens, relational or organizational trust can erode, learning opportunities can be missed, and a view to God's redemptive work in the situation can be lost.

We also see the importance of bringing parties together to dialogue, pray, and seek God's wisdom until they reach a transformational and mutually beneficial outcome. The clearest example of this is when the future of Gentile inclusion in the church is in question in Acts 15. Throughout this extended process, they share testimonies of God's redemptive work among the Gentiles (Acts 15:4, 12), leaders in the church engage in extended dialogue together whereupon they reflect on their past experiences of God working among both them and the Gentiles (Acts 15:6–13), and they reflect on Scripture (Acts 15:14–18). This process of seeking God and pressing into one another in what must have been tense discussions due to the serious nature of the dispute (Acts 15:2) and significance of the outcome, ultimately allowed them to clarify the issues and work out a win-win outcome. Together, they gained clarity on God's will for the life and mission of the church, and because of it, the church adapted and thrived (Acts 15:22–35).

Third, the issues of ministry reorganization with Moses and Gentile inclusion in the early church required the effective listening, humility, and willingness to adapt. Conflicts are never resolved simply through talking at one another. They are resolved when both parties are willing to listen to one another to discern what God might be doing in the situation. Moses listened and accepted the wise correction from his father-in-law with humility, and ultimately reorganized Israel's entire judicial system because of it. The parties involved regarding Gentile inclusion in the church listened to one another and to God through tense discussions, resulting in new clarity about God's will for ethnic unity in the expanding church.

Fourth, preparing our ministries to handle conflicts biblically and faithfully can increase the potential for constructive outcomes. Jethro does not just tell Moses to assign capable men to judge the people; he also instructs him to teach the people all of God's decrees for how they should do life together (Ex. 18:20–21). This essential preemptive work can pay off in the long run for every ministry and relationship. When people understand God's will for their lives and how He would have them deal with conflicts when they arise, demands on leaders are reduced and they are able to focus on other important tasks.

Finally, never give up on broken relationships. As much as anything else, God desires His people to be reconciled and unified so that we can experience the life He designed us for, and so the world will see and believe in His Son (Matt. 5:24; John 17:20–23). While we are not told if Paul and Barnabas ever reconciled, the implication is they may have as we do know from other New Testament accounts that Paul and Mark did. After seeing no ministry use for Mark because of his past desertion in the mission field (Acts 15:38), Paul changes his mind at some point and specifically requests his presence because of his usefulness later in his ministry (2 Tim. 4:11). The two are also together at least twice more during key points of Paul's ministry to the Gentiles (Col. 4:10; Philem. 23–24), with evidence through the language used that they developed an ongoing and meaningful relationship (Philem. 23–24).

We could continue mining the Scriptures for insights, but by now the point should be clear. God desires to transform His people through the conflicts we face and has given us clear instruction and guidance in His Word on how we can experience it. In the next section, then, we will lay out a biblically informed approach toward conflict resolution that leaders can utilize in their relationships and their ministries.

PRINCIPLES & PRACTICE OF TRANSFORMATIONAL CONFLICT RESOLUTION

As we have discussed, every conflict presents an opportunity. Whether that opportunity results in positive outcomes in the life of a leader and his or her ministry depends how it is addressed. The key, then, is for leaders to prepare themselves and their ministries to address conflict constructively. The most effective way to do this is to be proactive rather than simply reactive. To be proactive requires getting in front of conflict before it occurs through preparation—individually and corporately. This occurs first by collaboratively developing a biblically informed philosophy of conflict resolution with their teams. It also occurs by training their leaders and people with the necessary skills to resolve conflict effectively and transformationally. Finally, leaders should collaboratively develop and agree to a conflict covenant with their team that can hold everyone accountable to a biblical approach to reconciliation.

PHILOSOPHY OF CONFLICT RESOLUTION

The heart of a meaningful philosophy of conflict resolution needs to be a theological understanding of conflict. While this can be complex due to the differing approaches to conflict present in Scripture—some that were discussed earlier in this chapter—and the many different biblical passages where conflict occurs, there is one theological concept that needs to remain in the center of any philosophy of conflict resolution—reconciliation. Before a leader and his or her team discuss approaches, skills, and even their preferred biblical passages to inform their approach, what needs to be held rock solid in the center is a theology of reconciliation. Reconciliation, after all, is at the heart of Jesus' words to His disciples when He tells them to "go and be reconciled" to the person/people with a grievance against them (Matt. 5:24 NIV). Reconciliation is at the heart of the gospel (2 Cor. 5:17–21) and is God's desire for His people as well. As we live reconciled to one another, we demonstrate and testify to the world about God's goodness, as well as His ability to transform and heal what was broken by sin.

With reconciliation at the center, the leader and his or her team needs to also agree about what other biblical passages should be included. These will vary from ministry to ministry and from culture to culture, as certain scriptural stories, concepts, and commands may be more appropriate for particular contexts. Remember, for example, that the approach Jacob took when resolving his longstanding conflict with his brother Esau was to send a gift through mediators, not to approach him directly in a one-on-one conversation (Gen. 32–33). This differed from the approach we see in Acts 15, where the disputing parties worked through their conflict in the gathered assembly through dialogue, prayer, and theological reflection.

Further, the cultural lenses we bring to the interpretive task also shape how we read particular passages. Many in the West, for instance, tend to read Jesus' exhortation to go and be reconciled (Matt. 5:24) as a command to approach those we are in conflict with directly and work it out in face-to-face conversation. We often do this by drawing on Jesus' words to go and show someone engaging in sin their fault directly, then before two or three witnesses, then before the entire church if they will not listen (Matt. 18:15–17). When doing so, however, we often fail to recognize that this exhortation is given in the context of church discipline regarding someone who is sinning, not for resolving conflict with that person. In fact, experience would tell us that confronting someone in their sin may actually lead to conflict with that person, not resolve it. By conflating these two ideas, then, we inadvertently combine two commands from Jesus that are addressing two separate issues into one uniform approach for addressing conflict that is not natural to either text in their contexts.

In contrast to this understanding, those from more indirect and/or shame-based cultures read the same exhortation to go and be reconciled as a call to make amends with their brother or sister using their own culturally appropriate means of conflict resolution, such as third-party mediation, gift-giving, or more indirect means of communication so as not to bring further shame on the individual. In their context, these approaches actually protect and preserve the relationship, whereas a more direct approach might actually introduce shame and further harm the relationship.[6] We need to realize then, that our preferred approach to conflict is often more informed by our culture, our family upbringing, and sometimes even our own preferences, fears, and dysfunction than by Scripture. Consequently, while we need to inform our philosophy of conflict resolution with relevant biblical passages for our context, we need to keep reconciliation at the center, as this goal is what should drive all of our efforts.

A second facet of any meaningful philosophy of conflict resolution is immediacy. Both Jesus (Matt. 5:21–26) and Paul (Eph. 4:26–27) speak to the importance of quick resolution when it comes to conflict. Why? Because there are harmful consequences for all parties involved when conflict goes unaddressed. Jesus warns that there can be both spiritual and legal costs associated with unresolved conflict. Similarly, Paul highlights the spiritual and emotional price to be paid, noting that our unresolved anger gives the enemy a foothold in our lives that can ultimately be destructive. This does not, of course, undo what was said earlier about times when discretion and discernment are needed when deciding how to deal with conflict. It does, however, highlight that when there is a relational break of some kind, especially one characterized by anger, resentment, or bitterness, it needs to be addressed as quickly as possible to restore the relationship to a state of peace for the good of all involved.

This leads to a third important aspect of a philosophy of conflict resolution—collective agreement on an approach toward conflict resolution. This will be discussed more in-depth in the following section, but for now it will suffice to highlight that there needs to be agreement by those on a ministry team, and ultimately within a ministry, how they will deal with conflict when it arises. This may be fairly straightforward when a ministry comprises people from primarily one cultural group. It becomes more complex when leading in an intercultural setting. An intercultural setting requires understanding the different cultural values present relating to conflict and authority, as well as a mutually agreed upon approach that is not informed solely by the dominant culture's values. This will take time, but through a commitment to and engagement with one another, a diverse leadership team can come to an agreement that can be clearly communicated and taught to the congregation or members of the ministry organization.

Finally, your ministry's philosophy of conflict resolution should communicate your view toward and desired outcome from conflict. That is, how do you collectively understand the purpose of conflict, as discussed earlier in this chapter, and what do you see as God's purpose through it? Doing so provides an eye toward the future of God's transformative purposes in conflict and anchors the difficult work of conflict resolution in hope. Hope, after all, is what pushes us to endure and stay together when times are difficult (1 Thess. 1:3).

SKILLS AND APPROACHES TOWARD CONFLICT RESOLUTION

Agreeing on a comprehensive philosophy of conflict resolution is just the first step in preparing your team and ministry to deal with conflict constructively. It also involves training them to live out this philosophy in their daily lives and ministry. The tendency of many leaders is to believe that their job is complete once they teach biblical concepts of conflict resolution. This is just the beginning, however. Just as in good preaching, specific application is needed along with the communication of biblical truth; otherwise, most people are not able to translate abstract theological ideas into daily practice. In the case of conflict resolution, this means that specific skills often need to be learned to apply these ideas well. Further, many are also not aware how their own preferred conflict style, often learned in their family and culture of origin, can hinder or facilitate constructive outcomes from conflict. It is important, then, to train people in the strengths and weaknesses of their preferred style, as well as when those styles may create challenges relating to the nature of the conflict being faced, or the culture of the person/group that the conflict is with.

CONFLICT RESOLUTION SKILLS

While space will not allow for a full treatment of all the necessary skills for resolving conflict constructively, we can identify and briefly discuss four of the most essential. The first is listening well. Duane Elmer notes the importance of seeking understanding through inquiry before we form judgments or blame others; separating facts from fiction, incomplete information, feelings, and interpretation; and the importance of frequently acknowledging and summarizing what the other party is saying to ensure accuracy of understanding for those embroiled in conflict.[7] This can only occur when we take a posture of listening for understanding, rather than listening to formulate our response.

This is where an approach called active listening becomes useful. Active listening places both parties in a posture of listening rather than talking (James 1:19–20). It helps facilitate clear communication as each party in turn summarizes what they have heard the other party say in their own words, and then asking if this is the correct understanding of what has just been communicated. Using this approach alternately between involved parties enhances accurate communication between those involved, and enables fuller understanding of the issues at stake. It also allows both parties to separate fact from fiction as they suspend judgment on one another until deeper understanding is achieved.

A second important skill flows directly from application of the first—empathy. While empathy is thought by many to be synonymous with sympathy, it is actually the ability to understand and share the feelings of another. In the case of conflict resolution, this is a critical skill as it allows the listener to put him- or herself in the other's place and appreciate his or her feelings and perspective on the matter.[8] When one can identify and communicate the emotion beneath the words to the other party, it communicates deeper understanding, and can often facilitate a more meaningful interaction. It demonstrates concern for the person by helping them feel truly heard, while also enabling the listener to enter into the other's experience in a way that they might be able to identify with. This may in turn foster some type of common ground, or bridge, that was previously missing.

A third skill, or posture, is affirming the relationship. When facing conflictual situations, many fear an irreparable break in the relationship, which is why some choose to avoid conflict altogether. Before entering into a resolution process, then, it is important to first consider how much stress the relationship can bear when choosing your approach, or, whether you should step back for a time or even let the issue go completely. It is then important to affirm the relationship, to clearly communicate how you feel about the person and that you are addressing the issue because of how much you value them. You can then proceed to share the nature of the issue from your perspective, and your desire to resolve it and repair the relationship. As you do, it is important to remember to address behaviors rather than the person or their motivation. If you do sense defensiveness or tense emotions in the words or posture of the other while you are sharing, remember to back up and reassure them of your friendship and desire to understand.[9] But, even if you do not, you should still reaffirm the relationship after you share, reminding them that the reason you are sharing is because of your value for the friendship.

Finally, you must always be prepared to demonstrate flexibility. Remember, the goal is reconciliation, and the best way to accomplish this is to find a win-win resolution where both party's interests are served through a process that is characterized by integrity and fairness.[10] This will sometimes require employing a conflict style different from the one you are most comfortable with . . . a topic we will briefly discuss next.

CONFLICT STYLES

One of the most widely used conflict instruments since its development in 1974 is the Thomas-Kilmann Instrument, also known as the TKI Conflict Styles assessment. The purpose of the TKI is to help those who take the assessment identify their preferred conflict style, recognize the strengths and weaknesses of that style, and determine the situations where their style can be used appropriately and effectively. Further, it helps those assessed identify the preferred styles of others, and guard against getting locked into utilizing only their preferred style in all situations. Just as Jesus used different approaches toward conflict when the situation dictated, so are leaders called to discern and utilize the appropriate style in different situations as well.

According to the TKI, there are five primary styles, or approaches to dealing with conflict: (1) competitive, (2) collaborative, (3) compromising, (4) accommodating, and (5) avoiding. Those who are competitive seek to win at all costs and are always thinking about the next argument to defeat their opponents. This approach can be helpful when speed for the decision is key or others on the team lack the expertise to make a decision, but it can also be unhelpful, or even harmful when the issue is complex, team members possess a high degree of competence, or when both parties are equally powerful. Collaborators, on the other hand, seek win-win solutions that will satisfy the goals and desires of both parties. This approach can be time-consuming and is not helpful when an immediate decision is needed or when other parties do not have adequate problem-solving skills, but when issues are complex, a synthesis of ideas is needed, or when both parties possess resources needed to reach a solution, this approach can be extremely effective.

The compromising style seeks solutions by having both parties give something up, essentially splitting the difference. This approach works well when a temporary solution is needed for a complex issue, but consensus cannot be reached because the goals of both parties are mutually exclusive. The problem is that it often leaves both parties unsatisfied, and does not work well when one party holds more power than the other or the problem is complex enough to need collaboration and problem-solving. The accommodating style also creates a level of dissatisfaction, but only with one party. This approach is characterized by a party willing to sacrifice their own goals and agenda for the perceived good of the relationship, and will often make it seem like everything is fine. This approach is not helpful when the issue is important to you or the other party is in the wrong, but it can be productive when the issue is more important to the other party, you are in a position of weakness, or preserving the relationship is more important the issue in question.

The last approach is typified by avoiding the issue. When dealing with an avoider, you may not even realize there is an issue. Avoiders often feel it is hopeless to even address the issue, and will do their best to escape from the situation without even acknowledging there is an issue. As we saw earlier in the example of Jesus, there are times when avoiding conflict can be helpful, such as when the negative effects outweigh the positives, a cooling off period is needed, or if the issue is simply trivial. On the other hand, it is often extremely unhelpful, especially when the issue is important to you, immediate attention is needed, or you are responsible for a decision.

Learning how to utilize each of these styles can help a leader become much more effective at addressing conflict. Better understanding their own preferred style can help them recognize why some of their conflict situations may not have been resolved as they had hoped. Considering other's preferred styles can help a leader better recognize how and why their team members or followers respond the way they do in conflicted situations. Teaching others to recognize and utilize different styles when the situation calls for it can help those in your ministry engage conflict more constructively more consistently, which will ultimately provide better outcomes for yourself and for your ministry.

CONCLUSION

This chapter has by no means provided all of the necessary knowledge and skills to resolve all of the conflicts you are likely to face in your ministry. It has, however, provided the necessary foundation to launch you forward on a journey toward constructively engaging the conflicts you are sure to face as you lead your ministry toward God's preferred future for you. Recognizing that God desires to use conflicts profitably in our lives and ministries can change our perspective and approach toward those conflicts. We can face them courageously, rather than avoid them out of fear or uncertainty. Identifying how Jesus and God's people engaged the various conflicts they faced can inform helpful principles and practices for our own ministries as we seek to honor God in the conflicts He allows us to face. And, finally, recognizing the different ways that we need to approach various conflict situations can strengthen our ministries by better positioning us to experience the transformation that can result from conflict handled well. Conflict is an inevitability for every leader and ministry; the better prepared you are to handle it, the more likely you are to experience God's redemptive power in and through your ministry.

NOTES

1. Norm Sawchuck, *Managing Conflict in the Church: Understanding & Managing Conflict*, vol. 1 (Indianapolis: Spiritual Growth Resources, 1983), 35.

2. Ken Sande, *The Peacemaker: A Biblical Guide to Resolving Personal Conflict* (Grand Rapids: Baker Books, 2004), 24.

3. Joseph P. Folger, Marshall Scott Poole, and Randall K. Stutman, *Working through Conflict: Strategies for Relationships, Groups, and Organizations* (New York: HarperCollins, 1997), 4.

4. See Barna Group, *The State of Pastors* (Ventura, CA: Barna Group, 2017).

5. See John Paul Lederach, *Preparing for Peace: Conflict Transformation Across Cultures* (Syracuse, NY: Syracuse University Press, 1995).

6. Duane Elmer, *Cross-Cultural Conflict: Building Relationships for Effective Ministry* (Downers Grove, IL: IVP Academic, 1993).

7. Ibid., 180–81.

8. Ibid., 181.

9. Ibid., 180–81.

10. Ibid., 181.

CHAPTER 6.4

Assimilating, Disciplining, and Restoring Members

GERALD W. PETERMAN

Our chapter addresses three interrelated, complex, and very important issues. We phrase these issues as questions: First, are those regularly attending a local congregation integrated into the life of that body so there can be giving and receiving of service, guidance, and encouragement? That is, is there *membership*? Second, when there are failures—and we all fail—is there an appropriate redemptive response, whether gentle or firm? That is, is there *discipline*? Third, since failures involve breaches of trust, can trust be regained so that giving and receiving can be enjoyed again? That is, is there *restoration*?

Each topic raises complex issues of debate in our twenty-first century. We will first treat a few preliminary issues that are relevant to membership, discipline, and restoration before moving to specific issues regarding each.

WHAT IS THE CHURCH?

Some of the challenges regarding membership, discipline, and restoration can be minimized when believers understand the nature of the church. The church is not a vendor, a store, or a lodge; it is not the PTA, the Lions Club, or an Alcoholics Anonymous support group, though all these are valuable and important. In a highly consumer-oriented society, we are often tempted to view the church as a retailer with whom we transact for our benefit. We choose to patronize the congregation

821

that gives us the most return on our investment of time or money. Such a view, which needs consistent correction, often leads to rather loose connections to the local congregation.

Although there are some similarities with other social groups, the church is not a club. It is a redeemed community of brothers and sisters (Matt. 18:5; Mark 3:35; Rom. 8:29) with a commission from the Redeemer (Matt. 28:18–20; Luke 24:46–47). Since the church has a commission from the Lord, it must take that commission very seriously (which is not to say the commission is without adventure and enjoyment). The commission to make disciples is carried out by disciples. The disciple-making process requires the whole community to strive together for a common goal (Phil. 1:27–28). To help us further comprehend what the church is, we will look at three images from the New Testament.

First, the local church is *God's people.* Businesses, towns, ethnic groups, and families have people; each people group is associated with or for something in particular. So Paul tells Titus that our Lord Jesus Christ "gave Himself for us to redeem us from every lawless deed, and to purify for Himself a people for His own possession, eager for good deeds" (2:14). That is, although God is certainly the Creator of every man, woman, and child, not every person is among God's people by redemption. From Titus, we see the twofold purpose of Christ's death for us: purification and good works. Peter likewise calls Christians "a chosen people, a royal priesthood, a holy nation, a people for God's own possession, so that you may proclaim the excellencies of Him who has called you out of darkness into His marvelous light" (1 Peter 2:9).

Our good works will adorn the gospel; they are not themselves the gospel. Certainly the gospel, when rightly embraced, will also be lived; it is enacted and bears fruit. Yet the gospel is not works or lifestyle; the gospel is proclaimed with words (Acts 9:20; 1 Cor. 2:13). And good works will make the good news appealing (Matt. 5:16; Phil. 2:15; Titus 2:10). This lifestyle is not necessarily about making *one's local congregation appealing.* We must avoid the subtle temptation to see this as about our own congregation's prestige or growth. To state it negatively, if we engage in honorable behavior, there will be no opportunity for those outside to find fault (1 Tim. 6:1; Titus 2:5; 2 Peter 2:2). This is one of the reasons the church carries out discipline among its members, to safeguard those good works that should adorn the gospel and to discourage those works that would disparage gospel witness. After all, our Lord's commission means making disciples and teaching them to observe all He commanded (Matt. 28:20).

The second image is the local church as a *house or household.* Regarding this, Paul writes to his coworker, giving instructions about Timothy's ministry in Ephesus:

> I am writing these things to you, hoping to come to you before long; but in case I am delayed, I write so that you will know how one should act in the household of God, which is the church of the living God, the pillar and support of the truth. (1 Tim. 3:14–15)

We will return to these verses below; for now, we focus on the term "household." In the New Testament we have in mind the terms *oikos* (house) or *oikeios* (member of the household). The first is often translated literally as "house" or "home" (Matt. 9:6; Mark 2:1; John 11:20), but sometimes as "family" (1 Tim. 5:4) or "descendants" (Luke 1:27). Similarly, the second term gets translated as "those of the household" (Gal. 6:10; Eph. 2:19; 1 Tim. 5:8).

This is not exclusively a New Testament conception; the background is from the Old Testament. As early as Exodus 16:31, the descendants of Jacob were known as "the house of Israel," and we find the label dozens of times afterward (e.g., Num. 20:29; Josh. 21:45; Isa. 5:7). It refers to the people of God as one large family, with God as their Father (Isa. 64:8).

The house is not a building, but an association of people, often linked by kinship. This bond or association is presupposed when we hear Jesus ask, "Who is My mother, and who are My brothers? . . . whoever does the will of My Father who is in heaven, he is My brother, and sister, and mother" (Matt. 12:48, 50). Similarly, Paul repeatedly calls congregations brothers and sisters (as in Rom. 1:13; 1 Cor. 1:10; 2 Cor. 1:8; Gal. 1:2). Just as the literal household of parents and children continues to exist while its members are physically scattered over the course of any day, so Paul's instruction concerns behavior of the household members while gathered or when scattered. When Paul teaches the Ephesians, he mentions that they are members of God's household (2:19). Wherever we are, we represent this family.

Returning to 1 Timothy 3, Paul says the church is "the household of God, which is the church of the living God, the pillar and support of the truth" (v. 15). Philip Towner rightly comments that the two terms "pillar" and "support" "depict the church, in the combative setting of heresy, as existing to provide a powerful and steadfast support for 'the truth.'"[1] As a household, the local congregation has the task and privilege of proclaiming and living by the truth as God's representatives. One of the many amazing things about the God of the Bible is that He most often works through His people! From Adam and Eve, to Ruth and Boaz, to Mary and Joseph—He works through people. Further, when Paul says he writes so that people will know how to conduct themselves in the household of God, the issue is certainly not restricted to a couple of hours on Sunday morning. We should understand "in the household of God" to mean "as one who belongs to God's family." Those in God's family represent Him and His family wherever they happen to be.

The third image is the local *church as a body*. In both 1 Corinthians and Romans we see Paul illustrate how the church works by using the metaphor of the body: "For just as the body is one and yet has many parts, and all the parts of the body, though they are many, are one body, so also is Christ" (1 Cor. 12:12; see also Rom. 12:4–5). The various parts work in unique ways, and that uniqueness is good for the whole (1 Cor. 12:8). We are, together and individually, agents through whom God works. We do our best work when we are united, knowing our own skills and gifts so that we contribute what is necessary and helpful to overall thriving. In such an environment, new attendees or recent converts should be urged to join and to see the benefits of joining—for themselves, for the entire community, and for the advance of the gospel.

ASSIMILATION

In light of these reflections on the nature of the church, assimilation—that is, bringing people into formal connection with a congregation through membership—can be seen as an exciting, challenging, and wise process. We consider three aspects of this process below: loving attraction, commitment to one another, and consistent clarity and teaching.

LOVING ATTRACTION

Assimilation has parallels with dating: there are two parties, apprehensive perhaps at first, seeking to find out whether a long-term relationship will work. There is exploration, learning about each other, and deciding if such things as backgrounds, perspectives, and goals will mesh into a life together. So also with assimilation there needs to be conversation and learning about both parties. Not every new attendee needs to be assimilated, but at least there should be this process of mutual exploration. What are the backgrounds represented? What are the expectations and desires? What are the theological perspectives? What are the gifts and skills? What are the unique factors that could contribute to a mutually beneficial relationship? This exploration needs to occur intentionally yet genuinely, patiently yet not necessarily slowly.

With assimilation, we should think about making the congregation inviting. This will involve many things. Newcomers and recent converts will find such things as love, support, instruction, correction, guidance, family fellowship, and opportunities for service and for worship. To draw a phrase from the introduction, *giving and receiving* are important. One finds friendship, thus receiving support; and one gives time, talent, and work, thus joining our Lord's mission.

COMMITMENT TO ONE ANOTHER

A local congregation is very much a "one another" entity (more on this later). People are there for each other; they are participants, not observers. We dare not treat church membership as an issue of numbers. We must treat it as a relationship and a partnership. At the risk of being redundant, we must all fight against a consumerist or individualist mentality and strive to understand how God wants us to relate and to function together. Assimilation involves a kind of commitment—a commitment that works in both directions—between the individual and the congregation. When we use the word "commitment," we understand that we all have multiple commitments in life, and each looks different—for example, a worker's commitment to a company, a parent's commitment to a child, and a husband or wife's commitment to each other. How do we know that the local church should involve mutual commitment, and how do we define or understand the commitment? Commitment is seen in a couple of ways.

First, we consider briefly Matthew 18:15–20 and 1 Corinthians 5:1–5 (which we revisit later). In both cases, we observe that the one who needs correction is accountable to the congregation, and vice versa. So Jesus says, "Tell it to the church"; and Paul says, "When you are assembled." Both passages presuppose there is commitment and accountability within the local church, though neither passage uses these particular terms—that is, a relationship with mutual obligations.

Second, we can see evidence of this commitment in the many commands of the New Testament that involve "one another." Restricting ourselves to just a few of these commands from the New Testament letters, we see:

- So then we pursue the things which make for peace and the building up of one another (Rom. 14:19).

- Be kind to one another, compassionate, forgiving each other, just as God in Christ also has forgiven you (Eph. 4:32).

- Let the word of Christ richly dwell within you, with all wisdom teaching and admonishing one another with psalms, hymns, and spiritual songs, singing with thankfulness in your hearts to God (Col. 3:16).

- Therefore, encourage one another and build one another up, just as you also are doing (1 Thess. 5:11).

- Be hospitable to one another without complaint. As each one has received a special gift, employ it in serving one another as good stewards of the multi-faceted grace of God (1 Peter 4:9–10).

What conclusions shall we draw? Relationships in the congregation can be enjoyable (hopefully they will be!), but they are not simply casual. We are in the business of disciple-making. Everyone, at one time or another, needs support, help, correction, encouragement, instruction, and guidance. Likewise, each individual should experience close relationships where there can be sharing of joys, heartaches, challenges, and prayer requests. That is part of the "one another" process of which Scripture speaks.

If new attendees have this perspective, they should be invited—indeed lovingly, but strongly encouraged—to formalize this relationship with membership. Here is where a membership covenant can be very helpful, when it clearly establishes mutually agreed upon standards of behavior and structures of accountability within a local church body, drawing all such standards from Scripture. A covenant formally sets out the expectations for the individual member toward the congregation and vice versa, including but not limited to such things as prayer, attendance at corporate worship, economic support, discipline, care, and guidance.[2]

Admittedly, some individuals strongly oppose such covenants, seeing them as an abuse of pastoral authority, and/or contrary to Jesus' command to make no oath (Matt. 5:34–36), believing that such a covenant brings in another mediator between the individual and God. Others view such a covenant as helpful in providing guidance for discipleship and in maintaining good church order.[3] This writer is cautiously supportive. In our litigious age, these covenants can help protect all those involved. Again, since it spells out *mutually agreed upon standards of behavior and structures of accountability*, it gives assurance to all, from the senior leadership to the newest member.

CONSISTENT CLARITY AND TEACHING

Some of the challenges regarding membership can be alleviated when believers of a local congregation not only know the nature of church, but they hear it explained often. It is important that new and old members alike understand the benefits of church membership and its corresponding responsibilities. We all need regular reminders that we are God's people, His household, and the body of Christ; we need to learn of the many facets, tasks, privileges, and responsibilities associated with being His church. Likewise, the task of correction should presuppose consistent and specific—not vague—communication about such matters. We must not blindside people with standards or procedures that we have not articulated clearly and consistently. Just as parents lovingly and clearly establish family expectations, so the leaders of the congregation should do the same.

These things are difficult in our age. Just over a hundred years ago, most people lived on the farm or in a close-knit rural community.[4] It was a different cultural context. Now we go to jobs thirty to sixty hours a week, sometimes also commuting several hours a week. Often we have few significant relationships. Our jobs, for the most part, focus on matters of skill. One shows up, does the work, and that is that. There may be some issues that involve character, such as being on time, being a collegial worker, or having a good attitude. But unless one steals from the company, character does not typically become a focus.

The situation is very different, however, with respect to the local congregation. As we saw above, the local congregation is like a family. Each person represents the household, is attached to the household, and affects the household in all that one does. Whether these are issues of skill or issues of character, everything matters.

DISCIPLINE

PRELIMINARY ISSUES

Discipline has its background in the Old Testament. The house of Israel—one large kinship group—needed to maintain obedience in order to be a light to the nations, to serve as a royal priesthood and holy people in the midst of the world (Ex. 19:6). Not only that, but correction was often good for all involved: for those corrected, for the community, for the witness to the world, and for the glory of God. In the Old Testament we find several instructive examples of discipline (e.g., Lev. 19:17; Deut. 13:12–16; 17:1–6; 19:16–19; Josh. 7:1–24; Ezra 9–10).

Particularly helpful is Nehemiah 5:1–13. Nehemiah is serving as governor of Judah with a group of Jews who have returned from Babylonian exile. Sadly, many of the poor among them are suffering economic hardship to the point of selling their children into slavery (v. 5)! One cause is exploitation: the richer among them are making high interest loans to these poorer brothers, in disobedience to the law of Moses (v. 7; for laws against interest, see Ex. 22:25; Deut. 23:19). Nehemiah heard and rebuked the creditors, who restored the items that had been exacted from the poor (vv. 12–13). The correction administered brings at least three benefits: first, the wealthy were brought to obedience to God; second, the poor gained respect and material possessions; third, God was glorified by the community's new fellowship.

We often associate the word "discipline" with some sort of drastic and formal—and perhaps painful—correction or guidance. It is unfortunate, however, that this is the first thing that comes to mind when thinking of church discipline. As said before, low levels of guidance, encouragement, and correction should be happening all the time in the "one-another" ways discussed earlier. At one level, sin is inevitable, and therefore also hurts. On this side of the new heaven and the new earth, we all fail. We would hope that, if our brother or sister sins and we speak to the individual in private (or the reverse), that our correction will be heard and well received (Matt. 18:15). But in the rare instance of correction not being heard and the situation reaching the level of "tell it to the church" (Matt. 18:17), we should ask about general teaching to guide our approach. The following principles are important to consider when dealing with these more severe cases:

First, we always approach discipline with humility, not with pride or self-righteousness—constantly watching ourselves, lest authority be abused. Paul encourages and warns: "Brothers and sisters, even if a person is caught in any wrongdoing, you who are spiritual are to restore such a person in a spirit of gentleness; each one looking to yourself, so that you are not tempted as well" (Gal. 6:1).

Second, we grieve; we suffer together. That is, we have the emotional reaction that fits the events. Discipline is not about rage or vindictiveness. When Paul addresses the instance of immorality at Corinth he says, "You remain arrogant and have not mourned instead, so that the one who has practiced this deed might be removed from among you" (1 Cor. 5:2, author's translation). Notice that grief or mourning is the posture the congregation should have in the face of such immorality. The grief is corporate, not private. Grief is natural when damage is done, reputation is shattered, relationships are broken, and the moral purity of both the individual and the congregation are lost.

Third, we always work with patience and gentleness, not demanding quick transformation. We all know that transformation is a slow, up and down process. Let us keep in mind the Golden Rule: "Treat people the same way you want them to treat you" (Matt. 7:12). When we fail, we want others to help us recover, and also to be patient with us! Likewise Paul says, "We urge you, brothers and sisters, admonish the unruly, encourage the fainthearted, help the weak, be patient with everyone" (1 Thess. 5:14).

Fourth, and closely related to the third point above, correction requires sensitivity to other people's suffering. In all things, from habitual malicious gossip to marital infidelity, the presenting problem is almost never one thing; our lives are too complex for that. In all cases, there will be a history—with layers of pain that can include loneliness, grief, depression, anger (the righteous kind or the unrighteous kind), unresolved conflict, abuse, betrayal, and various kinds of relational breakdown. Along with needed correction, we must not forget to weep with those who weep (Rom. 12:15). Discipline and restoration will involve engaging suffering and being emotionally connected, just as our Lord wept over the coming judgment of Jerusalem, even though the judgment was deserved (Luke 19:41). This can be sensitive and highly emotional, and appropriately so. On the other hand, we must not engage in emotional reasoning—that is, thinking with our feelings instead of thinking with Scripture and spiritual wisdom, as is common today. Nevertheless, one needs emotional intelligence when treating painful situations.

Fifth, as often as is practical, while being discreet and guarding each other's honor, we should not work alone in this process but rather work with others—with witnesses, with counselors, with the congregation, and not with isolated power. Perhaps excommunication is called for, that is, removal of the individual from the fellowship and all that such removal entails (no access to corporate worship, to Communion, to Christian friendship, to the teaching of Scripture; see 1 Cor. 5:2). If excommunication is necessary, however, let us rely on the wisdom of the congregation in appropriate, circumspect ways, not just that of a few elders or one pastor.

Sixth, no one is exempt. From oldest to youngest, from newcomer to church leader, all are accountable. As Paul informs us, even elders (and by implication pastoral staff) are not exempt from this process of discipline and restoration (1 Tim. 5:19–21).

Seventh, we carry out discipline with godly courage. These days, careful biblical discipline is rare. Conflict is common. Anger, bitterness, and alienation are common. But redemptive biblical confrontation for the purpose of repentance and restoration is uncommon. We seem to be afraid of confrontation, worrying about hostility from others, or dreading being shamed on social media. The possibility of lawsuits frightens us. We have drunk of the perspective of our age that says there is no objective truth. Our culture speaks loudly about "tolerance" and not "judging" others, and we listen. Thus, we are tempted to compromise biblical principles to avoid messy or difficult conversations. Furthermore, the complex task of discipline and restoration is hard work. We are often too lazy to undertake it. May God have mercy on us, especially as leaders in the church, so that we carry out discipline with courage that is guided by the Holy Spirit.

CARRYING OUT DISCIPLINE

We will treat three basic questions concerning church discipline. First, what are the goals of discipline? Second, what are the issues or situations that call for action, that is, for discipline? Third, how is such discipline to be administered?

What Is the Goal of Discipline?

The goal of discipline is repentance and restoration. Restoration will be discussed in more detail below. For now, we note that the offending individual must come to the painful realization that their actions were sinful and harmful to self, to others, and to the local congregation, and consequently turn from their previous habits. This genuine repentance needs to demonstrate genuineness through appropriate fruit (Matt. 3:8).

Regarding restoration of the individual, when Jesus gives His prescription about confronting a brother who sins (Matt. 18:15), He mentions that if the brother listens, then you have gained your brother. "Listen" here is more than just hearing words; it is like the "hear" or the "listen" we find in John 8:47: "The one who is of God hears the words of God" (see Luke 9:35; John 10:8; Acts 3:22). It is a receptive and repentant hearing. The hearer confesses the wrong. Now there can be restored fellowship; there has been a restoration where previously there was alienation.

Similarly, when Paul discusses discipline in 1 Corinthians 5, he mentions the salvation of the guilty man—explaining that excommunicating him was done in hopes that the man's spirit will be saved in the day of the Lord (v. 5). Regarding this case, we mention two things. First, in our twenty-first-century Western society we are incredibly individualistic and impersonal, and thus can easily miss what Paul is saying. In the first-century world, people did not have cellphones, online banking, email, food delivery to the door, entertainment by internet, or the self-checkout at the supermarket. What they had was real, live people; people and relationships were incredibly important. One's social group was one's safety net; it provided all one's needs. Being cut off from your social group was dangerous and frightening, as we see in the fear of the former blind man's parents when they know the potential of being cut off from the synagogue (John 9:22). Thus, the threat of being put out of the congregation (1 Cor. 5:2) was extremely serious and especially for those who had left their prior social-religious community to follow Christ. Do we promote in our churches the kind of community life that makes the potential loss of such community truly devastating?

Second, Paul gives the goal here: salvation. Paul assumes that salvation is not assured when the individual is in persistent, serious sin. All of us sin, of course (2 Chron. 6:36; Eccl. 7:20; James 3:2). We must always remember that we are saved by God's grace, not by our obedience (Eph. 2:8–9). But the habit of serious moral error should bring into question our assurance, in our own hearts and in the view of the community. If we persist in such error, we have no reason to be assured, and nor do others.

So then, we want to bring individuals back from transgression and restore them to discipleship, love, kindness, obedience, fellowship, camaraderie, and community (Gal. 6:1). The motivation or goal of discipline is never vindictive or harsh. The goal is never merely to display authority or to vent one's own anger or the congregation's sense of anger and betrayal—even though these feelings might rightly exist. There may be instances where a particular individual's transgression brings great pain and embarrassment to the body. But we dare not pursue discipline for the sake of vindictiveness.

What Issues Call for Discipline?

Our second question pertains to the kinds of issues that call for discipline. In this regard, we would do well to follow the New Testament as closely as is contextually feasible for us. Searching the Scripture yields the following criteria:

1. Unrepentance: Matthew 18 references a brother or sister sinning (or sinning against another individual). No particular sin is specified. But our Lord says we must confront with gentleness in the hopes that there will be repentance. In this particular case, when the situation escalates to potentially bringing the issue before the church, the issue now has become hard-heartedness (unrepentance) rather than whatever transgression initially caused the confrontation.

2. Factiousness: Paul tells Titus to warn a factious person once and then twice. Factions, that is, schisms or competing groups, are deadly to the community and to the love of the congregation. They undermine "the unity of the Spirit in the bond of peace" (Eph. 4:1–6). So, this is something to be taken quite seriously for the health of everyone. After a first and second warning, if there is no repentance or change, the individual is to be shunned (Titus 3:10; see Rom. 16:17). Under this heading we can also place the spreading of contrary doctrine (see 1 Tim. 6:3–5). On the one hand, such false teaching should be stopped (Titus 1:10–11); but on the other, Paul implies that such teaching leads to factions and strife (1 Tim. 6:5).

3. Undisciplined Busybody Activity: Another example Paul mentions is undisciplined church members. Paul reminds the Thessalonians that when he was with them, he worked hard to support himself, in part to give them an example to imitate (2 Thess. 3:7). One reason he writes is that he knows of certain Thessalonians who are not following his instructions. He says, "For we hear that some among you are leading an undisciplined life, doing no work at all, but acting like busybodies" (3:11; see 1 Tim. 5:13). The busybody, or meddler, gets into other people's affairs—probably the affairs of a wealthy patron—and so are "entangling themselves in issues that were properly none of their concern."[5] Almost certainly such entanglements caused conflict and took the focus off the gospel. Paul's response is clear: "Now we command you, brothers and sisters, in the name of our Lord Jesus Christ, that you keep away from every brother or sister who leads a disorderly life and not one in accordance with the tradition which you received from us" (2 Thess. 3:6).

4. Serious Moral Error: Previously we mentioned 1 Corinthians 5, where a man of the congregation is known to be sleeping with his father's wife. For our topic, Paul has insightful and important teaching, asserting that the Corinthian church continues in its arrogance or in being "puffed up" (see 1 Cor. 4:6 ESV). The Corinthians are awash with spiritual pride because of their leaders, their giftedness, and their knowledge (see 1:29–31; 4:6–7, 18–19; 5:6; 8:1; 13:4), thinking that they are godly, spiritual, and uniquely blessed by God. Even knowing of the man's behavior, the congregation continues in such arrogance.[6] The apostle says that instead they should have mourned the sin in their midst, so that the man would be put out of the congregation. Again, we see confirmation that discipline is not to be done out of vindictiveness or anger, but rather out of mourning—that is, something precious has been lost, and we grieve the situation.

In review, we should be careful to base discipline on New Testament examples, rather than simply on our feelings or our memories of past discipline. Scripture gives us examples of serious moral error. Similar to 1 Corinthians 5, Paul mentions those who are "lovers of self, lovers of money, boastful, arrogant, slanderers, disobedient to parents, [and] ungrateful" (2 Tim. 3:2–5a). He exhorts Timothy to "avoid such people as these" (3:5b). We also find a habit of undisciplined life that meddles in others' affairs (also condemned in 1 Tim. 5:13). Serious and sad are a hard-heartedness with lack of repentance (Matt. 18:15–17), and the causing or facilitating of factions, such as seen in Romans 16:17. These last two sins become especially serious when they continue even in the face of gentle correction.

How Do We Administer Discipline?

Our third question concerns how discipline is to be carried out. There are many variables to take into consideration. Referring again to the key passages mentioned earlier, we see that as often as possible, discipline should start at a low level with much gentleness and as little force as necessary. So, a private, one-on-one conversation will often be the first action to take, as Jesus mentioned in Matthew 18:15. Assuming that there is no confession or repentance, then further action is needed. The same principle, however, applies to the next step: we should use as little force as possible. So Jesus mentions taking along one or two witnesses to encourage, to pray for, and to exhort the individual toward recognition of the problem and toward seeking change (Matt. 18:16).

At this point, if there is no recognition or change, the matter should be brought to the whole congregation. Again, the goal is not to vent or to bring private issues into the public. Rather, we would bring the matter to the whole congregation so that the wisdom of the body can speak to the issue (and not simply the insight of the two or three witnesses), and so that the guilty party can see the seriousness of the issue. The gathering of the whole body might not be feasible in a megachurch or even a congregation with multiple services. Wisdom is needed. But essential is the collective insight of a large group that knows the individual. Finally our Lord says, "If he refuses to listen even to the church, he is to be to you as a Gentile and a tax collector" (Matt. 18:17; see 1 Cor. 5:2–5). That is, there is still opportunity for change! Every appeal has been made prior to enforcing the most severe consequence, that is, excommunication—here described as treating the unrepentant as an outsider (Gentile or pagan and a tax collector).[7]

In navigating these situations, one would profit from consulting the case studies found in Jonathan Leeman's book *Church Discipline: How the Church Protects the Name of Jesus*. The book covers a variety of scenarios, which are quite instructive for those in church leadership. And, of course, some practical outworking of the church discipline process will be influenced by the congregation's established structure of church governance, within their more particular ecclesial context.

RESTORATION

As emphasized throughout this chapter, the ultimate goal of church discipline is restoration. Put simply, restoration means the individual is welcomed back into the fellowship of the community, acknowledged as a brother or sister in Christ who is following Jesus in discipleship. Of course, the timing and circumstances for such restoration will require accountability and wisdom. How should it be accomplished? While a few places in the New Testament letters provide guidance for discipline, they do not provide us any examples or specific instruction on how to restore. There are, however, places we can go for guidance. Three things are important: repentance, forgiveness, and trust. Since we looked at repentance above, we will focus on forgiveness and trust.

FORGIVENESS

With sin and correction, there has been hurt; thus forgiveness is needed. Only the specific circumstances can dictate who must forgive, whether an individual, several people, or the whole congregation. But forgive we must, for Paul charges us, "Be kind to one another, compassionate, forgiving each other, just as God in Christ also has forgiven you" (Eph. 4:32; see Matt. 6:15). We should be known as forgiving people since God has already forgiven us (Matt. 18:23–35). When we forgive, we release the offender from the debt owed to us; we do not require vengeance or restitution. Forgiveness is both a one-time event (we decide to forgive) and ongoing affirmation (we reaffirm our commitment both to forgive and to live like it). Forgiveness can be one-sided; that is, we can grant this release even if the offender does not repent or acknowledge wrong (Mark 11:25). Concerning forgiveness, there are many common myths that need to be dispelled. Here we mention only two:

1. Forgiveness is the same as reconciliation: It is not. Forgiveness can be one-sided, but reconciliation is two-sided. Reconciliation requires repentance and ongoing transformation in order for the parties to come back together in trusting fellowship. This takes time; much patience is needed. We examine trust below.

2. *When I forgive, I must also forget:* We must not. When we forget what people have done, we actually forget who they are. We only know their character from their patterns of past actions. Forgiveness does not require forgetting; indeed, at times forgetting would be foolish. If we discover that the treasurer has been embezzling money from the church, the person needs to be forgiven, *and removed from service.* But if we forget the person's evil habit, we run the risk of making the horrible mistake of returning the worker to the previous task. We should keep in mind that forgiving another person does not change that person's habits. Habits can change—for God has mercy—through repentance, appropriate restitution, and ongoing discipleship.

TRUST

With sin, correction, and hurt, there has been a loss of trust; we need time to regain it. One can honestly grant forgiveness to another while still needing time for trust to be restored. Trust is based in character; we trust someone when we learn through observation that the person is trustworthy. We come to see trustworthiness over the course of time. Although the passage deals with qualifications for elders, and so does not address instances of sin and restoration directly, we will take some guidance from 1 Timothy 3. Paul says,

> An overseer, then, must be above reproach, the husband of one wife, temperate, self-controlled, respectable, hospitable, skillful in teaching, not overindulging in wine, not a bully, but gentle, not contentious, free from the love of money. He must be one who manages his own household well, keeping his children under control with all dignity . . . And he must have a good reputation with those outside the church. (vv. 2–4, 7)

Few of these requirements treat history; most concern character. One must discern that the candidate for elder has proper character. Although there is no guarantee, several years of good behavior in the past (that is, good character), are the best predictors of future faithfulness.

How does one discern character? We do not discern it quickly by way of a job application, a questionnaire, or a résumé. Sadly, one cannot simply accept the word of the one who claims to be trustworthy. We discern character through careful observation over the course of weeks, or months, or perhaps even years. Note that Paul implies research is needed for discerning character. That is, to conclude that the candidate for elder has a good reputation with those outside the church (3:7), we must ask those outside the church!

We compare the above discernment with the discernment needed when an individual is being restored to the congregation. The person's prior place in the congregation will determine how much trust is needed for full restoration. Low levels of responsibility require lower levels of trust, and higher levels, more trust. If a pastoral office or specific ministry tasks are involved, the congregation needs to see that there has been transformation. Transformation does not equal perfection; none of us has attained that. Let us keep in mind that *genuine* obedience can be present even when that same obedience is not *perfect*. On this side of glory, no one's obedience or love is perfect, yet Paul can describe the Philippians as obedient (2:12) and the Thessalonians as those who love (1 Thess. 3:12). May God grant us to find such obedience and love.

Gardens need proper soil preparation, careful planting, protection from pests and from invading weeds, and tender care and guidance for the plants to flourish. As God's household, it is similar with a congregation. Careful assimilation/membership, discipline, and restoration are necessary for the church to thrive.

NOTES

1. Philip H. Towner, *The Letters to Timothy and Titus* (Grand Rapids: Eerdmans, 2006), 275.

2. For helpful discussion, see Matt Schmucker, "Membership Matters—What Is Our Church Covenant?" March 1, 2010, 9Marks, https://www.9marks.org/article/membership-matters-what-our-church-covenant/.

3. For the first view, see Wade Burleson, *Fraudulent Authority: Pastors Who Seek to Rule Over Others* (Independently published, 2017); for the second, see Bethlehem Baptist Church Staff, "The Meaning of Membership and Church Accountability," revised February 2001, Desiring God, https://www.desiringgod.org/articles/the-meaning-of-membership-and-church-accountability.

4. Generally, population has been shifting from rural to urban and suburban areas for many years. See https://www.pew socialtrends.org/2018/05/22/demographic-and-economic-trends-in-urban-suburban-and-rural-communities/.

5. Gene L. Green, *The Letters to the Thessalonians*: The Pillar New Testament Commentary (Grand Rapids: Eerdmans, 2002), 351.

6. In part, we follow the translation of David E. Garland, *1 Corinthians* (Grand Rapids: Baker, 2003), 155: "How, then, can you still be puffed up?"

7. D. A. Carson, "Matthew," *The Expositor's Bible Commentary*, vol. 9, ed. Tremper Longman III and David E. Garland (Grand Rapids: Zondervan, 2010), 456.

Teaching a Bible Lesson

PETER WORRALL

At seventeen, I had a keen spirit, but no training. Because of this, I stuck to the manual—religiously. I taught at my aunt and uncle's Sunday school. I started by asking students questions about that morning's topic, and they typically responded enthusiastically from their own experience. Then I read the Bible story aloud, as their concentration began to wane. Next, I asked some basic questions related to the text—questions of comprehension, which they sometimes could answer and often could not. And finally, I gave them the printed curriculum worksheet, which they were to complete and bring back the following week for a prize. Only one of them usually did.

I was faithful in my commitment—albeit naïve and unprepared—and I believe that the Lord used those Bible studies to teach that group of young people, at least to a certain degree. However, as far as I know, only one of those individuals is still in church. Not only that, but I taught that study in the same way that I had been taught growing up in my church. I believe I am the only one my age from my home church who is still actively involved in a church.

So what happened? What was wrong with our model?

AN ACCURATE WORLDVIEW

Just a couple of years after that teaching experience, I went to university, and studied theology with a liberal Catholic professor who did not believe in a transcendent God. She mocked my biblical faith. She advocated pushing God into one small corner of life and, instead, leaning into the strength of community. She taught us revolutionary theology, and the only time we picked up the Bible was to destroy the book of John. By the time I graduated, I could reason my way *out* of the faith better than I could defend it. Of the twelve evangelical Christians who started our course, only I and one other remained as believers. The rest had left the faith.

In addition to studying theology, I also trained as an elementary education teacher. At the time, I assumed that these studies in education had very little to do with my theology, faith, or church. As far as my teaching career was concerned, I saw myself as responsible for mathematics and language arts, not the Bible.

Without even realizing it, I had developed a secular worldview—where "Christian things" and "the world's things" did not intersect. Just as my professor had suggested, my theology was being pushed into a corner, and I became more and more comfortable in "the world." My lifestyle choices also reflected that reality. I was still a Christian, but as soon as I graduated from university, I went off to Japan to seek my fortune and teach in their public school system. My thoughts of God were passionate but infrequent. I wanted to live this life to the full, and I only considered God when Sunday came around or I got into an argument about His existence. The rest of my life was "God-free."

After a couple years of living out this secular mindset, I could no longer ignore the Holy Spirit's conviction. How could the God I *said* I believed in have so little to do with my life? I left Japan and the comfortable life I had built there and went to Pakistan to teach in a missionary school. There, God continued to work on my heart until—at the age of twenty-eight—I went to seminary to learn more about Him and His Word.

In my seminary coursework, God began to show me the errors in my thinking. At the core of my distortions had been a faulty view of Scripture and the idea that there exists a "God space" *and* a "secular space." It was revolutionary for me to realize that there is no such divide. The secular space in my thinking and my life was gradually eradicated as I saw more and more of the world as sacred. The "God-of-the-gaps" expanded out of the space where I had tried to contain Him, and I understood that He is Lord of all.

While I was in seminary, I met my wife, Kelli, who wrote and edited Bible curriculum for a Christian publisher. From Kelli, I learned that even Bible curriculum writers do not always read and interpret Scripture in the most appropriate or effective ways. Too often, their starting place is a principle or truth they want to teach. Then they turn to Scripture and search for a passage that might reinforce their point. Do we want to teach kids to be courageous? Let's tell them the story of David and Goliath. Do we want students to give their money generously to the Lord? How about studying the widow who gave her last two copper coins? In this way, some curriculum writers read into the Bible what they want to see and simply use it to support their own—albeit good and important—ideas. The term for this is "eisegesis," and there are several problems with this approach.

First, when taken out of context, the Bible ceases to function as it was intended and is made to say what we want it to say. Second, the Bible memory verses included in such lessons rarely come from the actual passage of study. Certainly, it is important to memorize Scripture. However, memorizing fewer verses and understanding them deeply and in context has greater value. Third, this approach can reduce the Bible to just another moral book—a list of dos and don'ts. Yes, the Bible does contain beneficial rules, but it is so much more than that. A Muslim, Buddhist, or even atheist could just as easily have written some of the curriculum we saw coming out of various Christian publishing houses. Such curriculum focuses on soliciting better behavior, but people behave better in all kinds of traditions. Based on such a reading of Scripture, what would make the Christian tradition any different?

As my wife and I looked at several Bible curriculum products and even wrote a few studies in a freelance capacity, we became increasingly concerned and increasingly passionate about the need for Bible teaching that stays true to the text and allows God's Word to teach in the way it was intended.

THE THREE-LEGGED STOOL

Before we start to color in the details, let us consider a bigger picture. I was a teacher for many years before I heard someone discuss the "three-legged stool." It took even more years for me to realize the full implications of this concept.

As parents, obviously, we have responsibility for our children. In their development, we are one leg in their educational process. Parents are entrusted with children from God, and we ought to raise them in godly ways. This means bringing God into all areas of our family life. Deuteronomy 6:6–7 provides a model: "These words, which I am commanding you today, shall be on your heart. And you shall repeat them diligently to your sons and speak of them when you sit in your house, when you walk on the road, when you lie down, and when you get up." Every day, throughout the day, we must turn our eyes, and our children's eyes, to the Lord.

The second leg of the stool is the school. Sadly, school, television, and video games are increasingly "God-less" environments. From kindergarten through high school, children will spend 15,000 hours in school. Such immersion in an atmosphere that marginalizes God usually has an effect. Having regular conversations with our children about the obvious issues, such as evolutionary theory or sexual purity, certainly is a starting place. However, this matter is much more pervasive.

The "null curriculum" (learning from what is *not* taught) speaks volumes to children's developing worldview. They will not likely see God as relevant to their math or science or literature or art. They will not likely understand that God is necessary for every area of life—indeed, for life itself.

Homeschooling and Christian schooling can provide a strong alternative. However, some homeschool curriculum or Christian schools do not do much better than public schools at teaching a biblically integrated worldview. Rather, they propagate a similar problem by providing a Bible lesson for one hour each day, while still leaving God out of the rest of the curriculum.

The third leg of the stool is the church. The church plays an important role in providing Bible training and discipleship for its members. However, a Sunday school or youth group cannot provide all of the spiritual and biblical input that a student needs. If parents do not mentor at home, and the school is silent about God, spending one or two hours at church each week will not provide an adequate foundation in faith—especially when children spend a good amount of that time playing games and eating snacks.

These principles are as important for adults as children. In many seminary doctoral programs in education, adults are prioritized over the teaching of children. They talk about how we emphasize the need to be more engaged and active with adults, but assume a passivity with children. However, as we see from Jesus' own example, what marks good teaching is common whether we teach adults or children.

So, what more can a church do?

TEACHING A BIBLE LESSON

Most of us would like the job of Bible teaching to be simple. We want to purchase a packaged curriculum, read through the materials, cut out a few tools, buy a few supplies, and march into our classroom ready to share with our eager students exactly what the leader's guide tells us. Better yet, we want to pop in a video to which the students can sing and dance along. We are happy to let a video share some helpful points and lead us in memorizing a Bible verse or two. Then all we need to do is pass out a coloring page and maintain crowd control.

However, for reasons we have already discussed, teaching a solid Bible lesson is not easy. It takes some time and training. In the Bible, we read of God calling and equipping people to teach His Word. The transformative power of Scripture in our lives and the lives of our students is well worth every bit of effort.

So, where do we start? We begin by *choosing a section of Scripture for our study*. I am partial to tackling a whole book of the Bible from start to finish. However, addressing a particular subject and selecting passages that address that topic can work as well, as long as each passage is studied and taught in its proper context. If the students you are teaching are unbelievers or new to the faith, I would advise beginning with the book of Mark. It is the first of the Synoptic Gospels, and it contains many words of Jesus. If your students know Jesus, I think it is good to start at the beginning of God's Word, with Genesis. Based on your knowledge of the students, prayerfully seek the Lord's will regarding where in the Bible to begin your study.

Second, commit to *reading the passage.* Read the first few times with an open mind—not trying to dissect it or dig into the details. Do not rush ahead to decipher what it means or come at the passage with preconceived ideas about its meaning. Let it speak for itself, and see what is truly there. Read to grasp the overall flow of the passage. Ask yourself questions of the text, drawing from the actual words and concepts in the text. After the final time of reading it through, articulate what you think it means.

Third, after you have read the passage a few times, *read through one or two Bible commentaries.* Do not only choose commentaries that reinforce your own understanding or interpretation. It is good practice to seek out other viewpoints; doing so can expand and challenge your ideas. Sometimes we are unaware of various ways in which a passage can be understood. Reading a commentary can expose us to other possible interpretations.

Fourth, *look up any difficult words or unfamiliar place names* in a Bible dictionary or a Hebrew or Greek lexicon. You do not need to know Greek or Hebrew to comprehend what the passage is saying. The lexicon will identify and explain key words. Also, consult a map of the ancient world or a Bible atlas to gain understanding of where the passage took place. Biblical events happened in real places, and the location of each event had important implications for the narrative. In addition, the recipients of a New Testament epistle may have been wrestling with issues or obstacles peculiar to their space. Taking these few steps to pursue the background of a passage can make unfamiliar names intelligible and provide essential insight into the context.

Fifth, after reading through the passage and doing this background work, the next step is *to discern what the passage is saying.* We begin by articulating the "textual" or "big idea."[1]

Each passage tends to have one big idea that it is communicating, though it may also contain subthemes that we can and should teach. While a teacher may find and communicate good truth from a text that is not the "textual idea," the "textual idea" best conveys the purpose for which the passage was written and should be communicated as the central point or message of the text.

The best big ideas are specific to the passage (and context of the passage) being studied. This idea should identify the audience, the attitude or behavior that needs to change, and the context for that change. For example, the statement "Love people" could broadly apply to numerous passages in Scripture. However, in the context of Romans 12, we could focus on this big idea: "People are to love each other in a Romans context—whether Jewish or Gentile—while accepting all spiritual gifts."

Consider 1 John 4:7–21, another passage about love, but also with a particular emphasis. A more specific big idea for this text may read, "Christians overwhelmed by heretical teaching should love one another with a love from God that expels all fear." Such an idea is rooted in the text, and can be narrowed down even further to make it more specific. In this way, the big idea best expresses the purpose for which the passage was written and the specific situation it was intended to address. One of the good things about this level of specificity is that each passage has a reason for existing. In this case, that includes a focus on the false teaching faced by the readers of John's epistle.

Sixth, once you have identified the textual big idea, you *derive the main teaching point(s)*.[2] To determine the main teaching point, ask this key question: "What about this message is relevant and applicable to the students I teach?" Our first inclination as teachers might be to think in terms of the head, or mind. We might focus on what our students should *know* or how they should *think* differently. These cognitive dimensions of learning are certainly important. However, the heart and hands must be equally considered. The questions, How should my students *feel*? and What should my students *do*? are just as important. In educational literature, these three modes, or domains of learning, are described in terms of the "head, heart, and hands"; or, "cognitive, affective, behavioral"; or, "concepts, attitudes, skills." Some educators omit the affective domain of learning altogether because they claim it cannot be measured. However, such concern for measurement should not dictate the Bible teacher's choice in learning objectives. The head, heart, and hands sum up a person's entire being. If we teach for heart change, that should be included in our objectives.

By way of example, let us look at a biblical passage and identify some potential teaching objectives. In a study of Mark's gospel, we would start at chapter 1.

> The beginning of the gospel of Jesus Christ, the Son of God,
> just as it is written in Isaiah the prophet:
>
> "Behold, I am sending My messenger before You,
> Who will prepare Your way;
> The voice of one calling out in the wilderness,
> 'Prepare the way of the Lord,
>
> Make His paths straight!'"

> John the Baptist appeared in the wilderness, preaching a baptism of repentance for the forgiveness of sins. And all the country of Judea was going out to him, and all the people of Jerusalem; and they were being baptized by him in the Jordan River, confessing their sins. John was clothed with camel's hair and wore a leather belt around his waist, and his diet was locusts and wild honey. And he was preaching, and saying, "After me One is coming who is mightier than I, and I am not fit to bend down and untie the straps of His sandals. I baptized you with water; but He will baptize you with the Holy Spirit." (Mark 1:1–8)

What do we observe? First, it is the "beginning of the gospel." Some commentators say this refers to the whole book of Mark; other commentators believe it only points to this particular passage. I take "beginning of the gospel" to mean the whole book. Thus, our passage (Mark 1:1–8) is "The Beginning of the Beginning," as it were.

The subject of the passage is John the Baptist. The passage is about him, and he is doing the action. From the subject, we can discern the textual big idea. What is John the Baptist *doing*? What action is he taking? "John the Baptist prepares the way for Jesus, who is greater." However, John the Baptist also appears in the other Gospels. So, for greater specificity, we should ask: Is there anything distinct about *this* passage? In Mark 1, we note Isaiah's prophecy concerning John. He is dressed like Elijah from the Old Testament (see 2 Kings 1:8), and his mission is to bear testimony that someone far greater than he is coming. Yes, all four Gospels give testimony about John and his importance, but here in Mark 1, the emphasis is on comparing John and Jesus, finding Jesus to be greater.

From the textual big idea of "John the Baptist prepares the way for Jesus, who is greater," we move to the main teaching point(s). Why must my students know this truth? This does not change the truth of the passage, but rather considers how the passage is appropriate and applicable to the audience. How does the passage change our thinking? What about our hearts and our actions? Sometimes the main *cognitive* teaching point is simply the same as our textual big idea. In this case, for example: "John the Baptist prepares the way for Jesus, who is greater." However, we also need to consider the desired behavioral and affective outcomes. How should we *act*? What should we *do*? The fact that Jesus is greater means He is to be worshiped above all. The fact that He is greater means He is to be lifted up. In this way, both the heart and the hands respond appropriately to the truth of the passage. While several valid teaching points may come from a particular passage, it is better to choose one main point and teach it well than to aim at several points and spread the lesson thin.

When we have our textual big idea and our main teaching points, we know where we are going. Now we must plan how to get there.

LESSON PLANS

Teachers lay out lessons in lesson plans. In general, all lesson plans have at least three parts. The lesson must start with something that reorients the students from their present mindset. You may have been thinking about this lesson for a while and may be motivated to teach it—but your students rarely share your enthusiasm. An "initiating set" will take the students from the plane where they are dwelling and—all things being equal—bring them into yours. The body of the lesson will flow well, once the students are oriented. Finally, a closure or a review will highlight key information and check for its reception.

An investigative lesson does not tell the students the meaning outright. An investigative lesson provides clues, which students must recognize and investigate. If students genuinely inquire about the meaning of the text, the lesson will follow a certain progression, but students will see the path forward less clearly than if you had told them the meaning up-front. Student learning unfolds as a process of guided self-discovery. For ease of planning, the format developed by Madeline Hunter, who was an established authority in lesson plan writing,[3] is commonly used and covers the following areas:

1. Anticipatory Set (Focus). As the students come into the class, what will you do to orient them toward your objectives? How will you get their attention on your ideas?

2. Purpose (Objective). Why are you teaching the lesson? How will you instruct the head, heart, and hands of your students to be different as a result of the lesson's aim?

3. Input. What is the big idea of the lesson? Why are you teaching this today? What new knowledge or skill should the student leave with?

4. Modeling. How will you work through the ideas of the passage as an example for your students? Where have you seen these ideas communicated well? Use these examples to educate your students.

5. Guided Practice. Have the students work through problems that come from the material. They should do this under your supervision and with your correction. As students grow older, partner with them rather than simply tell them. Participate toward solved life circumstances, but also highlight the challenges of applying the text.

6. Checking for Understanding. Review the material in a setting where you are present to check and correct the students' examples. This should be formative. In other words, you are not looking to award a grade for the work, but rather to fine-tune their skills to show they understand the concepts.

7. Independent Practice. Give the students work to do on their own. Let them wrestle with the concepts and show they understand your objectives.

8. Assessment. The assessment mentioned here is summative. In other words, students should know everything by now, and you should assess whether they know it. How effective has your teaching and their learning been?

9. Transfer. A weakness in North American education is the lack of transfer. We must apply the truth in various contexts. Consider, for example, the command to love. We're commanded to love God with all our being. We're told to love our neighbor, including the foreigner among us. In the parable of the good Samaritan, Jesus illustrated a rather surprising definition of who showed love to a neighbor in a practical way. In the Epistles, we're instructed many times to love one another in the church, honor others above ourselves, be at peace with everyone if at all possible.

We can adapt this model for Sunday school. First, orient the students to the lesson. Deal with extra ideas and influences that the student must leave behind. You can think of these things as distractions. You want to have a stimulation that brings students into the present with you, such as a good question or illustration. This is called the "hook" because it hooks the student out of their present state of mind and grabs their attention. It is also called the "initiating set" since it starts off the lesson. Once the class is asking a question the biblical text can answer, present the information given by the text. Read the passage and explain its meaning. This is a teacher task, but the task should transition to see whether students have comprehended the basic meaning. Once students have received the content, they should be encouraged to clarify, refine, expand, and process their understanding in collaboration with one another, under the teacher's clear direction. Then the students are ready to be individually accountable for personal comprehension. Unfortunately, often pastors and teachers do not assess whether their parishioners or students have comprehended anything. When evaluating a student, the assessment should be appropriate to the material presented. For example, in learning the principle of love, students should demonstrate whether they actually love more as a result of reading the text and how. It is not sufficient simply to write "love" on a piece of paper.

The final task of effective Bible teaching is to reinforce these principles throughout the year. Learning should not stop with the completion of a unit. Rather, we must revisit our lessons to reinforce the learning experience.

These steps reflect the most basic lesson plan. Some lesson plans, however, take a more inquiry-based approach to learning. Such an approach emphasizes essential questions that drive student learning. The popular literature in this area comes from Grant Wiggins and Jay McTighe, who recommend that you think about the focus of your lesson and then plan in a backward fashion.[4] You begin with the big ideas or desired skills, which are sometimes referred to as "essential questions" or "understandings." Next, you consider what would evidence that understanding. Third, you plan your lesson. This fits with more of an inquiry-based approach. The important thing in inquiry is what you ask the students, not what you tell them. Of course, the outcome of the lesson must be identified, as people can get off-topic easily. However, if they focus, students will inquire and ask questions about the passage—inviting students to more directly take initiative and participate in their learning.

LESSON CONTENT AND TEACHING METHODS

One Tuesday night when I was eighteen, I arrived at my church with a bowl of water and some stuffed toys. I was teaching a Bible lesson on Daniel—to a group of adults. My students have likely forgotten the lesson by now, but I have not. I remember it because, at the time, I thought it was a terrible failure. What was I thinking, trying to use children's methods with adults?

I know now that I could have changed some things to be more effective that night many years ago, but I also know—from my years of education training—that I was actually on the right track. Many of the methods that we use to teach children work equally well with adults. Both children and adults can and should be taught creatively and actively. This may involve experimentation—some trial and error—and we should feel free to make mistakes in the process. We should also remember that teaching creatively does not mean that we dumb down the content. It does mean that we, as teachers, become students of our students. We study them to learn how they learn best. Some methods will work well for some students, and other techniques will work better for others.

Howard Gardner's Theory of Multiple Intelligences can help us understand how students learn in many different ways. Gardner first outlined his theory in his 1983 book *Frames of Mind: The Theory of Multiple Intelligences.*[5] Varied understandings of what constitutes intelligence influence our particular lesson aims and teaching objectives. Several years ago when I was teaching fifth grade, I had to give a very smart boy a B in physical education. He was getting As in all his other subjects, but he just was not applying himself in our gymnastics unit of phys ed. His mother was not happy when she saw the B. She was even more upset that it counted toward his grade point average. When I would not change the grade, this mother was compelled to work with her son. Over the next couple months, he worked hard in gymnastics and improved his grade as a result. This reflects a difference in kinds of intelligences.

Howard Gardner has identified several different types of intelligence that people possess, both children and adults. His original list included the following types of intelligence: verbal-linguistic, logical-mathematical, bodily-kinesthetic, visual-spatial, musical-rhythmic, interpersonal, and intrapersonal. A few years later, Gardner added existential intelligence and naturalistic intelligence to the list. Even now, the list is not necessarily complete or fixed. As teachers, we must continue to look for the diverse and individual ways our students learn. While considering multiple intelligences is important in any classroom, it is essential when we teach the Bible at church. Our Bible lessons may be the only Bible training that some of our students receive, so we must present biblical truth in a way that connects personally to them.

Dr. Kathy Koch in *8 Great Smarts* explains these concepts for working with children as word smart, logic smart, picture smart, music smart, body smart, nature smart, people smart, self-smart.[6] Koch credits Gardner's studies, explaining to parents and teachers that everyone is smart in at least one way. Understanding which of the intelligences is prevalent in a child or an adult is paramount to effective teaching.

Let us consider how each of these intelligences can help us design our teaching methods when it comes to teaching the Bible. To connect with a student who is linguistically intelligent (word smart), we may have our students write a poem or work with the alphabet in some way. For our lesson on Mark 1, we could ask the students to write a story about how they have shared their faith like John the Baptist. Alternatively, we could have them write a poem about how John the Baptist would feel when Jesus arrived on the scene. For our students with logical-mathematical intelligence (logic smart), we could include mathematical activities in their processing of the story. Students could count and list the number of prophecies that Jesus fulfilled throughout the book of Mark.

We often relegate bodily-kinesthetic intelligence (body smart) to gym class. However, we can get students moving in any location. And we can have them talk as they move. Getting students to walk outside the church can provide a different setting, or playing a game can reinforce a truth that is being taught. For our lesson on Mark 1, these students would love to feel some camel hair. They could also collect "locusts and wild honey" that we have hidden around the room, and in this way can "become John the Baptist." This helps our students step out of their world and into the world of the Bible. While they are hunting, you could discuss the following questions with them: Why would John the Baptist wear camel hair? Would you like to wear camel hair? Why or why not? Why would he eat locusts and wild honey? What would they taste like? Would you eat that? What if there were plenty of locusts? What if there were few?

Our students with visual-spatial intelligence are very aware of our teaching space. Anything we do to decorate the room will appeal to them. If we are starting our series from the book of Mark, we would do well to put some things on the walls that will enhance our lessons: maps of Israel and pictures of the area, for example. Our visual-spatial (picture smart) students will also enjoy any art projects we design, as we invite them to draw or create something in response to the story.

Teachers of young children often use music in the classroom to good effect. In kindergarten, we sing songs to teach students the days of the week, the parts of the body, the months of the year, the books of the Bible, addition and subtraction, and anything else we can put to a melody. However, we wrongly assume that, as we get older, we cannot learn from our singing. In doing so, we miss the opportunity to enjoy the power of music and to appeal specifically to our students with rhythmic-musical intelligence (music smart). I believe that the use of songs for learning can and should extend into adult life. Our passage in Mark 1 could become a song. We could write the song ourselves and teach it to our students. Alternatively, we could ask them to help write the song with us, or in small groups. We also could find worship songs that reinforce our textual big idea—the greatness of Jesus— and we could sing those songs with our students by way of application. Why should our worship songs not also be instructive songs? As the Scriptures use songs to instruct God's people, why would we not also teach through song?

Students with interpersonal intelligence (people smart) enjoy interacting with their classmates about the truths of a lesson. To engage best our interpersonally intelligent students, we should provide opportunities for conversation in the classroom. Give students a few minutes to meet in pairs or small groups to discuss the passage and answer questions together. Provide a worksheet or talking points. Of course, most students enjoy such talking times, but these students in particular feel they have learned when they have talked.

Students can also help us as teachers. They are able to see how the truths of a lesson relate to people. They are keenly aware of how people are feeling in the group and can connect with them personally. Many pastors and teachers I have met love the biblical text and have a high verbal-linguistic intelligence. However, they are less proficient in communicating the truth of the text to the hearts of their students. This is not necessarily a failure on the part of the pastor or teacher; it just means that individuals with interpersonal intelligence need to be part of a team. The passage from Mark 1 can and should be applied in a specific way to the lives of the students in our classroom. Our students with interpersonal intelligence can help us answer the question: Why does the truth of this passage matter to each one of us?

Of Dr. Gardner's seven initial intelligences, we have saved the most personal for last. People who are unwilling to be changed themselves cannot effectively change the world. To that end, intrapersonal intelligence (self-smart) looks at the Bible passage and asks, "How do I need to change? How does this passage change me?" Our intrapersonal learners will appreciate quiet time alone with their thoughts. When encountering Mark 1, we might talk with students about how we are preparing the world to meet Jesus. Students might journal in response to this question: How would I compare to John the Baptist? Our own reflection as a teacher, and the reflection we encourage in our students, should go heart deep and not be a superficial flight at 30,000 feet. Our initial answer might be, "I am not doing anything (or much) to prepare the world for Jesus, and that matters to me." A subsequent question could be: Who can I reach, and how?

Our answers to these questions should be revisited in future weeks. We should not teach our students week-by-week without cultivating any lasting relationship. Following up with our students and caring for their ongoing growth is a significant part of a teacher's role.

We also may have students in our classroom who exhibit the two additional intelligences: naturalistic intelligence and existential intelligence. Our students who are strong in naturalistic intelligence will appreciate the ways in which any Bible story relates to the created world. The events in the Bible happened in a real place and real time. In most (if not all) biblical stories, some aspect of the created world has significance. We best serve our naturalistic learners when we allow them to experience that significance firsthand. These learners are similar to kinesthetic learners in their appreciation for the tactile, so similar teaching methods (as previously described) may be effective with them, especially if done outside.

Finally, students with strong existential intelligence will want to discuss foundational, intuitive, big-picture questions: Where do we come from? Why are we here? Does the earth have a purpose? What will happen to us in the future? We serve these students well when we provide periodic overviews to remind them of the bigger picture. These students also enjoy summarizing a series or looking at a topic from a different angle or point of view. In our lesson on Mark 1, we might ask the class, "What would have been the point of prophecy in the Bible?" or, "If you had to prepare people for someone's arrival, what would you do?" Let students voice their own questions. Certainly, as the teacher you will need to monitor these conversations, but do not see them necessarily as rabbit trails. Our existentially intelligent students especially will benefit from being able to connect each lesson to the rest of the world.

Remember, a person probably has more than one intelligence. It is possible to imagine someone with all of them. Students in some contexts have learned to suppress their intelligence, so good teachers may even contribute to a student's ongoing self-discovery process.

A final word about teaching to the "multiple intelligences": While each of the intelligences *can* be addressed when teaching any passage, we will not have time to address all intelligences in every lesson. For each lesson, we should choose a few that will connect best to our students. Choose what best communicates the textual big idea and helps to accomplish your main teaching points. If possible, mix it up from lesson to lesson. If you do a kinesthetic activity one week, try a musical exercise the next. Keep notes on which methods seem to work best with your students. It requires additional planning, but you may even want to try setting up several stations in your room—with each station providing an experience for a different type of learner. Then allow students to choose which station they want to visit. However you decide to implement your understanding of the multiple intelligences, be patient with yourself and with your students. Do not aim for perfection. Aim for authentic and engaging encounters with Scripture.

ASSESSMENT

"Oh no! Not assessment!" I can hear you silently scream as you read this heading.

However, yes. Assessment.

Whether we are teaching high school calculus or the book of Galatians at our church, it is important for us as teachers to evaluate how well we have done with our teaching and how students have performed in their learning. If we are assessing our students' comprehension of content, a simple pencil and paper test might suffice. We could ask them to write out the main point of the passage we studied last week. We could have students list the characters from a biblical narrative we taught them a few months back. We could have our youth group members recall the textual big idea from each lesson in our series.

However, assessment of our Bible teaching must go further and deeper than that. Yes, the content is important, but the goal of Bible teaching is not simply the transfer of knowledge. The goal is life change. Obviously, assessing life change is much more difficult. Difficult—but not impossible. Through careful observation and intentional conversations and even planned application exercises, we will have the joy of seeing our students grow and become more like Christ.

As you consider assessment, also remember these important points: (1) Heart and life change is the work of the Holy Spirit. We are simply His co-teacher, His human ambassadors. Do not take on more of this responsibility than is yours to carry. (2) True and lasting life change often takes time. Do not grow impatient with the process. You might be planting seeds that someone else will harvest. (3) We are fighting a spiritual battle. Pray often for your students and with your students. This is the greatest privilege of a teacher.

For our lesson on Mark 1, here are a few ways that we might assess student learning. First, we might observe whether or not the students express enthusiasm when we worship together in response to the lesson and the truth that Jesus is greater. This may be our affective teaching point. Enthusiasm is an emotion. If our students demonstrate enthusiasm for their Savior in response to an encounter with this passage, we can give glory to God. If, on the other hand, we see that students are lackluster and distracted in their worship, perhaps they have not yet developed the enthusiasm of the passage.

In response to Mark 1, it is one thing to write down that I will try to be more enthusiastic in preparing the way for Jesus, and another thing to evidence that enthusiasm in concrete ways. This does not necessarily mean the lesson was a failure. The lesson may have been a success because you now have evidence (thanks to assessment) that students do not actively share their faith. Now, you have the basis for an emphasis on evangelism.

GOOD BIBLE TEACHING

If the Bible is taught in the above style, student learning will reflect a genuine encounter with the actual message of Scripture. Certain passages will make more sense when taught in context, but students still may struggle to understand some passages. If the struggle is presented genuinely, this can serve as a great exercise for students to realize both the vastness of Scripture and their own finite understanding. There is so much in God's Word for us to examine!

Approach Bible study as an adventure where God is leading you into more of Him. If it becomes a laborious study for you, it will be laborious for your students. When the text is hard, communicate how you have struggled with it. When the text encourages you, communicate your sense of God's goodness and presence. Enjoy studying the Bible, and communicate the Bible to others from that sense of enjoyment.

I also believe, as an educator, that the church should talk more about education and support families in their educational choices. Yes, education can be a tricky topic. It involves everyone, including our children. Most parents have strong and deeply rooted views on child-rearing, and perhaps no subject is closer to our heart. Perhaps for this reason, many pastors are happy to stay silent on the issue—taking a hands-off approach and leaving educational decisions entirely to the parents. Education, however, is a foundational and essential part of how we, the church, train and mentor the next generation. So then, as we consider how to teach a Bible lesson, we do so recognizing the immense importance and gravitas of the task before us.

CONCLUSION

In this chapter, we have covered a rudimentary analysis of how to teach an effective Bible lesson. We do this by first carefully reading and studying the passage—not approaching the passage with a preconceived notion of what it says. We then must communicate and engage the passage with all the vigor of one committed to reaching every kind of learner with the living Word of God. To this end, vary the way you relate the main ideas, using different teaching modes to communicate effectively with different intelligences. Finally, assess what you have communicated to see if the teaching was effective. Improve what is lacking, and praise the Lord for what goes well. Most importantly, pray that your students' relationship with God will continue to grow!

NOTES

1. This is the "exegetical big idea." Exegetical means the idea comes out of the text and is not inserted into it. The passage, not the interpreter, dictates the specific idea and its context.

2. This is the "pedagogical idea"—that is, the idea you will teach.

3. For Madeline Hunter's lesson plans look at https://www.csun.edu/sites/default/files/Holle-Lesson-Planning.pdf. You will see a comprehensive explanation of the plan in the notes.

4. Grant Wiggins and Jay McTighe, *Understanding by Design*, 2nd ed. (Alexandria, VA: ASCD, 2005).

5. Howard Gardner, *Frames of Mind: The Theory of Multiple Intelligences* (New York: Basic Books, 1983).

6. Kathy Koch, *8 Great Smarts: Discover and Nurture Your Child's Intelligences* (Chicago: Moody, 2016).

CHAPTER 6.6

Conducting
Premarital Counseling

DANIEL GREEN

Premarital counseling is widely considered to be good preparation for the considerable challenges of a marital relationship. The goal of this article is to provide some general principles for such counseling, and to suggest some specific sessions that should be included. The latter will be dealt with in detail.

GENERAL PRINCIPLES

The counselor's church should have essential guidelines for couples who wish to get married. Such guidelines should be followed by the counselor. If for any reason he is hesitant, he should not accept the counseling responsibility. He should lovingly but honestly tell the couple why he cannot lead the preparation, and how they might grow to a place where getting married is more advisable. Once he is satisfied that the couple has an adequate spiritual foundation for their relationship, he may proceed.

The counselor should be very positive with the couple that has come looking for good marriage preparation. They have made a good choice to be married, and another good one to prepare well for it. The counselor should be enthusiastic and encouraging. He should let the couple know that he will do all that he can to help them get prepared for this exciting stage in their lives.

One practical challenge to the process is that many couples have already decided to get married, and many have even set a date and chosen a venue. The counselor should not be pressured by such premature plans. He should inform the couple that he will not continue counseling, or perform a wedding, if he feels uncomfortable with their chances of having a healthy marriage. He may wish to reserve his commitment until he has gotten to know the couple and has conducted the first counseling session.

The goal of marriage should be stressed throughout the counseling sessions. Here it should be stated that wedded bliss is not the mark. Rather, sanctification is the ultimate goal of the union, as is true of all Christian relationships. As has been suggested by one author, holiness, not happiness, should be the goal of Christian marriage.

The pastor who is helping a couple get ready for marriage should not feel alone, neither should he accept total responsibility for the couple's preparation. Others may be enlisted to help. Experienced couples with good marriages and adequate training may be called upon to help. Young couples may be matched with more mature ones during the preparation period, with the anticipation that these relationships will last beyond the nuptials.

The couple themselves bear the main responsibility for their preparation. Thus, they should take the time seriously, read recommended books together, and complete homework assignments. The counselees should agree with the counselor's expectations before any of the sessions begin.

Although there are many good books about marriage, caution is called for here. There can be too many books assigned during the preparation period. Time, expense, and the academic ability of the couple need to be considered. The pastor is probably more prone to reading than many of his parishioners. He will need to choose carefully among a small number of titles that will be included in the sessions.

The time allotted for each session also needs to be reasonably limited and well-planned. The possible time that could be spent on each session far exceeds what makes good sense. Ninety minutes per session is probably a good limit. Thus, the counselor should prioritize the questions of the couple and the issues that he thinks are most important. He will need to trust the couple to prepare well in advance as well as relying on any reading that he assigns to help him communicate essential material.

The counselor should make one-page handouts for the couple. They should be simple and biblical. They will probably contain some of the material described below, but can also include other information that the pastor thinks may be relevant to the people in his congregation. These pages may be emailed to the couple before each session, sent in a packet, or given directly to the couple after a given session so that they may prepare for the next one.

At the end of each session, the pastor should briefly summarize what was covered that day, pray for the couple, and give a brief introduction to the next session.

SPECIFIC SESSIONS

There is no set number of meetings, approved approach, nor exact content, stipulated in Scripture. It is up to each counselor to set forth a schedule of topics to be covered. Below is a suggested set of sessions that have proven helpful to those wanting to prepare for wedlock. Before each session, the participants should work through the material individually, and then talk through the information together, before meeting with the counselor who will guide them through the lessons. The suggested specific sessions set forth here are (1) backgrounds and personality analysis; (2) marriage purpose and roles; (3) communication and conflict; (4) balancing the budget; (5) permanence and priorities; and (6) sexual intimacy. There should be about one month between sessions. It cannot be overly stressed that the counselor should believe in the lessons that he chooses. Thus, the sessions described below are only suggestive.

SESSION ONE: BACKGROUNDS AND PERSONALITY ANALYSIS

There is an abundance of personality tests available to be taken online or in person. Among the most popular are the DiSC, Enneagram, Myers-Briggs Type Indicator, and the Taylor-Johnson Temperament Analysis. Each has individual tests and scoring. Most have statistical information on what personality types are most compatible, and what the various strengths and challenges are when persons of various personality types marry. The counselor needs to invest the necessary time and perhaps training to establish a preference for a test. This is the one that he should assign for the couple to use. Before the first session with the counselor, the couple should complete the test and submit the results to him. He should take adequate time to examine the results to prepare for discussion with the couple. He should lead with positive indications and follow with any concerns that he may have.

It is wise to involve the parents of the couple in the process where possible. One way to do this is to ask each set of parents to write you, the pastor, a letter titled, "Why we appreciate (fiancé's name) becoming our daughter-in-law/son-in-law." The results can help the counselor discern certain family dynamics. Where there are multiple sets of parents, the couple may decide who is asked to complete the task. It is important that the parents be assured that their potential in-law will not see the letter. This may free them to write a more forthright response.

A question that may be asked is, "What originally attracted you to your fiancé?"

This should stimulate some discussion. Hopefully there is something here beyond the expected answer of physical attributes. Another helpful question is, "What are the most important things that you have in common?" These two questions, together, may help the counselor discern the depth of the relationship.

Asking the couple for lists also gives them a chance to think about their relationship. For instance, "Give 12–15 reasons that you want to marry_____." This may help the person consciously state what they have simply felt before. A good matched request is "List 12–15 things that you have going for you that will make your marriage work."

Finally, you can get the couple to think about their family backgrounds. Your lesson may include the invitation to describe the personalities of each parent, and how they related to each other as the counselee grew up. How did they divide responsibilities? How did they settle disagreements? Another helpful exercise is to have them describe their relationship with each parent. Each of these questions may seem simple, but they may provoke a great deal of discussion and thought. It is possible that they have never considered their family backgrounds from any sort of objective perspective. The counselee may experience considerable discomfort at times, or may be quite capable of examining his family background without their feelings taking over. The counselor should be sure to ask each of the counselees to think about what they have learned from their parents, both good and bad.

SESSION TWO: PURPOSES AND GOALS OF MARRIAGE

The couple may be assigned a book to be read and discussed before, and during, the counseling session. A suggestion is *Each for the Other: Marriage as It's Meant to Be* by Chapell and Chapell.[1] Open-ended questions, such as "What was the point you two discussed the most?" or "Were there any new things that you learned?" may help stimulate conversation. Naturally, the counselor should read any text that he recommends, to be sure that he is comfortable with its content.

There are some important biblical passages to consider, such as Genesis 1:27–28; 2:18–25; and Ephesians 5:22–33. Each of these can be read, with discussion questions included.

For Genesis 1:27–28, the emphasis should be on the purpose of humankind. The text is clear that both male and female are created in the image of God, and that both are required for a biblical marriage. The last statement alone may stimulate quite a bit of discussion. Two purposes for marriage are expressed here: bearing children and ruling for God. Again, each of these items can engender discussion. One of the purposes of the couple is "to rule." Thus, the couple is to push back against a spiritually declining culture. They have a purpose beyond themselves. Helpful questions for the study time may include, "What do these verses say about the purposes of humankind?," "Who is created in the image of God?," and "What does this say about the potential of the male and female?"

Genesis 2:18–25 is a beautiful text that yields abundant insight for marriage. A helpful question may be, "What is involved in a biblical marriage?" The answer is companionship, complementary roles, leaving and cleaving. Each of these phrases is loaded with practical import. The counselor should let the couple determine the direction of the discussion, as long as they stay within the boundaries of the text. Besides the biblical requirements, their society and the government have expectations too. The couple can be asked what they are. This is a good time to deal with the marriage license and the required signings of documents. A crucial question is "What does it mean 'to leave father and mother'?'" It is likely that Old Testament couples lived in very close proximity to their parents and were still able to fulfill this expectation.

Interestingly, it says that a *man* should do this. It is, perhaps, stereotypic to say that the female is prone to cling to her parents. The man may do so as well. The point is that the couple is to now become a separate unit. This independence has implications for finances. Will they expect to receive, or accept, monetary aid from their parents? Will they live in the home of one of their parents? How will these issues affect their unity? What principles and boundaries will they set?

Does their ability to "leave" reflect on their readiness for marriage? Some of the same considerations apply to arguments, which will probably arise between the two. How much, if any, will be shared with parents? What relationship will be prioritized, the one with the mate, or the existent one with parents? A good practical question is how each will "protect" his mate emotionally from potentially overreaching parents. It usually works best if there is a predetermined conviction to represent the interests of one's mate rather than one's parents.

There needs to be give and take with regard to how much time will be spent at the homes of each of the in-laws. Has the couple discussed this issue? What is the comfort level of each? Where will holidays be spent? Thanksgiving and Christmas often come with unwritten family expectations. How much time will be devoted to siblings? Sometimes there are complex scenarios due to divorce and remarriage or remarriage after the death of one's parent. Although there is no rule that applies to every couple, they do need to have a preliminary set of convictions that work for them. A couple in premarital counseling does not need to solve all of these dilemmas, but an awareness of such issues should make for some good conversations.

Ephesians 5:22–33 does not promise happiness to all that obey its precepts, but it does tell a couple-to-be how to please God in the execution of their roles. This, too, is an important aspect of counseling. Pleasing God, not themselves, is important. They need to work together for His pleasure, not simply to have a harmonious relationship. This passage raises the sometimes-controversial issue of the submission of a wife to her husband. It is critical here to explain what the term means and does not mean. The husband is to lead the relationship according to this passage. The submission is not mutual, in the sense of both partners having the same leadership privileges and responsibilities. The husband needs to lead by initiative and example. He is to love her as Christ loves the church. He is to sacrifice his desires for her. Submission does not imply inferiority. There is even submission between the members of the Trinity. Jesus submits His will to the Father (John 14:31). Likewise, the wife is to respond to the husband's leadership by honoring his position and following his initiative. A good lesson plan should include a number of questions like, "What does submission mean?" "Under what circumstances might it be difficult?" and "Under what circumstances would submission be wrong?" The main responsibility of the pastor here is to get the couple talking about the issue, not to straighten out all their thinking in one appointment.

Not only is the husband to lead the marriage in terms of general initiative and personal sacrifice, but he is also to lead it spiritually. He is to prioritize the spiritual growth of his wife (Eph. 5:27). Here the pastor can suggest some ways that the husband can initiate times of Bible reading or prayer for the couple.

The couple should be taught that their relationship is to reflect the relationship of Christ and the church to others. The husband's love and initiative should reflect that of the Father, and the wife's respectful submission should reflect that of the church. Thus, the couple's children, friends, and acquaintances would be able to see what an intimate spiritual relationship looks like.

A very challenging lesson like this one demonstrates the wisdom of having only one session a month. The material needs to be mulled over, discussed, maybe even debated. This will take some time. There may be a degree of disagreement over the demands of the various passages. Hopefully, in time, the couple will come to agreement on the major issues.

This session, like others, may be closed in prayer for the overall preparation process. If the pastor allows the couple to pray out loud, he may also be able to further access their spiritual maturity.

SESSION THREE: COMMUNICATION AND CONFLICT

Communication may be the single most important element in marital health. Learning to truly listen and understand each other is essential. The Bible is replete with passages about good listening and healthy interaction. Among passages that might be assigned to read, in order, are Proverbs 15:1; 18:2, 6–7, 13; 15:28; 17:28; 12:25; and 16:13; James 3:1–12; Ephesians 4:25–32; Colossians 3:12–17. At the beginning of the session, the counselor can open the time to discussion of any passage that was especially interesting to the couple. This may take a large portion of the session. The power of words to build and destroy, the willingness to solve problems and forgive, and the general kindness and friendliness that should characterize all relationships can be discussed. Be sure to discuss what it means to "not let the sun go down on your anger" (Eph. 4:26). Another critical discussion is how words should be used, or limited, during a conflict. What statements should be out of bounds? The couple should share with each other what would be particularly hurtful to them. Here, the counselor may share, or illustrate from his own experience, the sort of words that might be particularly wounding.

Questions can be asked of the two people in turn. For instance, "Describe the potential that words have to destroy your relationship." This will probably not be hard for them to do. They may even have a recent example to share. Another effective question is, How do rejection, passivity, and pride effect conversation? At any place in the session, the couple may get deeply involved in thought and talk. They should generally be allowed to finish their processing as learning is taking place.

The couple needs to hear about *reflective listening*. This practice can greatly enhance a relationship. It involves one person speaking to another, and the second person repeating back the message in their own words. The first person then makes corrections to this understanding. Then the listener can try again. As many rounds can be tried until the speaker is satisfied with the listener's understanding. After this is explained to the couple, there can be a practice exercise. The female counselee can tell the man something important and see if he is able to repeat it to her satisfaction. As in the description above, they can keep trying until they get it right. Normally the male will need a lot more practice at this than the female. Once they have completed this exercise, you can talk with them about it. Tell them what you think they did well and how they could improve their practices and attitudes. If the couple can successfully integrate this into their communication pattern, they have an excellent chance to effectively connect.

Once this critical practice has been advanced, other, more individual, questions can be answered. "Truthfully speaking, how much praise do you need, and how do you like it expressed," is a most revealing inquiry. Here, you may need to probe as the counselees may be hesitant to answer. They may also be willing to tell one another something that they do not want to say in front of you. That is okay. You can suggest that they be sure to tell each other the answer. This touches the well-known concept of love languages. Most people like to hear some genuine praise from people that they love. Their partners may have been raised in environments where such praise was not present. Thus, it is a skill to be learned. Another personal question might have to do with how they like to be treated when they are ill. Some want a great deal of attention; others wish to be left alone. There is no right and wrong answer to these questions. They are simply preferences that their futures mates should know.

SESSION FOUR: BALANCING THE BUDGET

The use of money can be a great stressor in a relationship. Agreeing on a good plan for its utilization is a big accomplishment for a couple-to-be. Thus, establishing good principles, and a sound scheme for implementation is an important responsibility.

The couple should be assigned to write as detailed a budget as they can, assuming the amount of money that they can reasonably expect to have at their disposal. A book like *The Complete Financial Guide for Young Couples* by Larry Burkett should be read as an excellent guide.[2] The percentages suggested for each item should be followed. The couple should include the amount of money that they expect to spend on major items like car payments, clothing, entertainment, food, giving, housing, insurance, rent, student loans, transportation, taxes, and vacations. It is sometimes a good exercise to visit a local grocery store to figure out how much food costs. Have the couple calculate the expense of groceries for two weeks. Typically overlooked items in a budget are expenses for coffee, cosmetics, and snacks. It is very important that they work with money available after taxes, that is the net available, rather than the gross. The counselor should read the proposed budget quite critically, looking especially for the tendencies to use unrealistic percentages and leave items unaccounted for. There should be giving, investing, and saving in every budget. Money that is going to be spent regularly may be put into standard mailing envelopes. When money is taken out, it may be recorded on the outside of the envelope for future evaluation. When the money is gone, no more can be spent on that item until the next paycheck. The couple needs to establish an emergency fund that holds about three months of expenses. If the budget is not realistic, the counselor needs to reject it and send the couple back to the table to work out the deficiencies.

As part of the session, Scripture should be read and studied. Important passages to be read in order are Proverbs 10:2; 28:6; 22:7; 3:9–10; 11:24–26; 19:17; 23:4–5; 30:7–9; 1 Timothy 6:7–10; Matthew 6:24–33; 2 Corinthians 8–9. A list of major principles should be kept. The reading and discussion of these passages should yield a lot of insight.

A good discussion might start with the importance of money in present society. How does this compare or contrast with biblical teaching? What are the benefits and limitations of money? How dependable is money? How should it be used?

There are a number of practical issues that need to be discussed. Who will supervise the budget and bills? Typically, one person of the two is better at managing money. This is the person who should keep close track of the agreed-upon budget. Watching over finances can be delegated by the leader of the home. A male can delegate but is still responsible before God for final decisions. Will there be one bank account, or will both parties do their own banking? The former is easier for accountability, the latter is often more convenient. Whatever is decided, transparency and honesty are critical. Who will calculate and pay taxes? While both may gather pertinent documents, one will be responsible for the final calculations. Since both people are required to sign the official documents, both should be fully satisfied with the preparation. Sometimes it is worth it to hire a professional to do the preparation. Although this will result in another expense, the couple is free from any tension that might otherwise come between them. Will the individuals get personal allowances? If so, how much will they receive? The amount should be realistic, as the mates are sure to spend some money on themselves. How these allowances are spent may be one area where there does not need to be accountability to the other.

Thoughts about borrowing money and indebtedness should be discussed. Debt is a major pressure on a marriage and should be avoided as much as possible. People who owe large amounts of money are not free (Prov. 22:7). Certain items are usually too expensive to pay for out of pocket. Such purchases may be cars, homes, and student loans. A good rule of thumb is not to borrow on depreciating items. Most young couples cannot afford to buy an automobile with cash. Loans for autos should also be for the shortest affordable term. Buying a good preowned vehicle is often wise as the new owners will enjoy reduced cost and be able to have a dependable car. Borrowing money to purchase a home can easily be defended as the long-range value appreciation, tax breaks, and pleasure of ownership make it wise. The shorter the term of payment and the lower the interest, the wiser is the purchase. The monetary return on a good education is well-documented. It pays to get a college degree, even if some debt is incurred. Apart from these exceptions, debt should be strongly resisted. Luxury and pleasure items should not be allowed to bust the budget. Large credit card debt reveals that a couple is living far above the level that their income justifies. If credit cards are used, they should be paid off monthly. All charges should be known to, and approved by, both partners. If the couple cannot manage them well, they should not be used. Discipline is required of partners that love each other and want to protect their relationship.

SESSION FIVE: PERMANENCE AND PRIORITIES

This lesson will focus on the ideal of a permanent marriage and then on a number of important issues related to a long-term relationship. Here the couple should discuss their desires and dreams for their family.

Few couples enter a marriage thinking that they will get a divorce, but many do. Therefore, it is wise to do some study on the subject. There are a number of passages that should be read and considered. Among them are Genesis 2:18–25; Deuteronomy 24:1–4; Hosea 1–2; Malachi 2:14–16; Matthew 19:1–9; Mark 10:1–12; Luke 16:18; 1 Corinthians 7:10–16; and Leviticus 18. Many of these are difficult to interpret. The counselor should have studied each one and have a conviction as to what they mean. Naturally, he will guide the couple toward the position that he, or his church, holds. There is a wide range of views among those who hold a high view of Scripture. Some do not allow for any divorce or remarriage at all. At the other end of the spectrum are those who believe that if a person becomes a believer all past situations are effectively erased and the person is free to remarry. The evangelical consensus (majority) view is that divorce is not acceptable biblically except in the cases of unrepentant adultery and desertion by an unbeliever, with remarriage being permitted in both cases. A number of questions can be asked of the couple, and/or included on the preparation sheet. Among these is "What is God's will for a marriage?" This is an open-ended question that can be taken in a number of directions. "How does the phrase 'one flesh' in Genesis 2 relate to the question of permanence in marriage?" is another thought-provoking question. Two summary questions might be "What is God's overall attitude on divorce from the Old Testament?" and "What do the gospel passages teach on the subject?" The couple might be asked to summarize their scriptural convictions on divorce and remarriage. Discussion of this important matter will ideally serve to increase the couple's determination to stay together even in difficult situations.

At this point the session may turn more toward their desires and dreams for the future. Even these should be grounded in Scripture, reading Deuteronomy 6:6–7; Psalm 127; and Ephesians 6:1–4. They should be asked about their perspective on having and raising children. Some couples do not want children because they are self-absorbed or afraid of the type of world such a child would experience. The first can be gently challenged on their view, and the second can be comforted and encouraged that God would help them raise well-adjusted kids in any environment. A major point is that if they have children, the parents should value them very highly and mentor them patiently to follow the Lord on their own. The couple can be challenged as to what a good spiritual environment for their child might look like.

Childcare should be discussed. How will the children be raised? Will the mother work outside of the home? Is a "Mr. Mom" scenario biblical? Such questions may stimulate a lot of discussion and can be upsetting. This is a great opportunity for you to mentor them and help them to adopt a biblical model. Remember that this may be the first time that they have been asked to discuss these issues. Try to refrain from lecturing and listen to how they try to work out this matter.

"How many children would you like to have?" is an inquiry sure to stimulate discussion. If one wants two and the other three, they are close to agreement. However, if one wants one and the other wants five, there is a lot of discussion to be had. Again, the counselor's place is to help moderate the discussion, not to make decisions. Both parties should be encouraged to state their views and give reasons for holding them. The couple also needs to think about how children will affect their relationship, and how time should be prioritized. How will the couple maintain their relationship? How will extended family be involved in raising their kids? Yet another question related to priorities is "How much money would you like to have?" This will touch on whether the mother will work outside the home, how many hours per week the couple is willing to work, and whether or not they are willing to be away from home for business travel.

By encouraging discussion about a number of these challenging issues, the counselor will lead the couple toward a more mature relationship.

SESSION SIX: THE SEXUAL RELATIONSHIP

The couple may be assigned *Intended for Pleasure*, by Ed Wheat.[3] Wheat was a Christian medical doctor who wrote a book that is both physiologically correct and intensely practical. Time has not decreased its worth. The material is also available by audio and e-book.

The counselor should recognize that this an unusually sensitive subject. Some counselees, especially females, may not be comfortable discussing all aspects of this intimate topic. At some point the counselor may wish to connect the female with another trusted and trained woman in the congregation with whom she may discuss certain details. Another possible approach is to have the couple do the assignment together, and then meet with the counselor for an appointment that will be directed by the counselees' questions. The pastor should avoid questions that probe too deeply. Other couples may be comfortable with a very open discussion of sexual matters. An easy way to find out is to ask them at the end of session five, or have the male call the pastor and declare how he and his fiancée would like to approach the discussion time. Assuming that the couple is open to frank discussion, the session may be conducted as follows:

This appointment may begin with questions from the couple. The counselor should be emotionally prepared for any question and should not express shock or surprise. Open discussion may set the stage for decades of a good relationship with the counselees. Even though many couples may be sexually experienced, the reading may expose them to new information.

A helpful, open-ended, question is "What impression did the reading leave with you regarding the sexual relationship?" This lets the couple express themselves and allows the pastor to discern their needs.

Have the counselees read the Song of Solomon in a modern translation that indicates when the male and female, respectively, are speaking (the ESV, HCSB, and NIV all have this feature). Have them answer some questions like, "How does the groom express his love to the bride?" Similarly, "How does the bride express herself to the groom?" "What features about their lovers do they emphasize?" They should list specific biblical references and characteristics that are praised and then say how this should affect the way that they speak intimately to one another, and what they learn with respect to the sexual relationship.

Also have them read Proverbs 5:15–23. Ask them to identify God's attitude toward sex, with references from the text. They may also be asked to compare the teaching of this passage with Song of Solomon. Does it add anything?

A third important passage is 1 Corinthians 7:1–5. Most couples readily see that sexual relations should be a regular part of a marriage. It is also apparent that they should not be a special reward. What may not be as obvious is the several parallels in the passage. Both have duties to one another. The husband has as much responsibility to satisfy his wife sexually as she does to satisfy him. The woman does not have complete control of her body, nor does the male have complete control over his body. They should not abstain from sexual relations for long periods of time while using spiritual practices as an excuse. They need to understand that regular sexual relations help safeguard them from spiritual attacks from Satan.

There should be an opportunity to summarize God's attitude toward sex. It is very positive and the counselor should be sure that they recognize this.

A very sensitive matter may be raised by the counselor during this meeting. Most couples will want to have a frank talk about any previous sexual experiences with other partners. If this conversation has not already taken place, it probably should. This will protect them from any embarrassing surprises at a later date. The names of former partners may be mentioned, especially if the persons are in the same geographic area. It is wise not to share many details.

When these sessions are complete the pastor and the couple may turn their attention to the wedding ceremony.

CONCLUSION

Premarital counseling is an important part of pastoral oversight and mentoring. By following the course outlined above, or modifying it according to his preferences, a pastor help may prepare a young couple for a successful marriage.

NOTES

1. Bryan Chapell with Kathy Chapell, *Each for the Other: Marriage as It's Meant to Be* (Grand Rapids: Baker Books, 2006).

2. Larry Burkett, *Complete Financial Guide for Young Couples* (Colorado Springs: David C. Cook, 2005).

3. Ed Wheat, *Intended for Pleasure* (Grand Rapids: Fleming H. Revell, 2003).

Conducting
a Wedding Ceremony

CHRIS RAPPAZINI

INTRODUCTION

The wedding ceremony is often a highlight in a couple's life and can be one of the best parts about your ministry. In this chapter we will briefly cover what the Bible says about marriage and wedding ceremonies; however, much of the chapter will cover the many details of conducting a wedding rehearsal and ceremony that every officiant needs to know.

WHAT DOES THE BIBLE SAY ABOUT MARRIAGE?

Our foundation for understanding marriage is rooted in our commitment to the Bible as the only authoritative guide for our faith and practice.[1] Many Scripture passages speak to the meaning, purpose, and practice of marriage; however, since this chapter focuses on conducting a wedding ceremony, I will only highlight a few aspects about what the Bible says about marriage.

Scripture helps us think theologically about the commitment two people make toward one another and God. Beginning in Genesis, God ordained marriage as an institution and covenantal relationship between a man and woman whom God alone unites (Gen. 1:27–28). Husband and wife are to leave their fathers and mothers and become "one" in the new bond created (Gen. 2:23–24; Matt. 19:4–6).

The marriage is to be a lifelong commitment (Eccl. 9:9; Prov. 5:18) where the husband and wife are to mutually submit, serve, love, and respect one another (Eph. 5:21–33). In marriage, husbands and wives commit to be sexually faithful to one another (Ex. 20:12; Lev. 18–20; Heb. 13:4). Adultery appears to be the only biblically acceptable reason for divorce (Matt. 5:32) but all marriages should strive for reconciliation, provided there is a safe environment for both people. The ideal marriage relationship mirrors God's unconditional love He has for His people (Isa. 54:5; 62:5). God does not ordain everyone to marry (1 Cor. 7:1–40), but for those who are, it is a blessing from the Lord that helps sanctify His people into become more holy (1 Peter 1:16).

WHAT IS A WEDDING CEREMONY?

Very little in Scripture is written on wedding ceremonies themselves. Traditionally, Christian wedding ceremonies can be traced back to the first century.[2] Most likely, Christian wedding ceremonies were modeled after Jewish wedding ceremonies (John 2:1–12). Throughout the ages, ceremonies adapted to reflect what was culturally acceptable. In general, most Christian wedding ceremonies were presided over by the priest or minister and consisted of liturgy and a sermon.

In recent years, ministers have been faced with the decision on whether or not they will officiate a given ceremony. For instance, should a minister marry any Christian couple? Only a couple who is a member of the church? Nonbelievers? A believer and a nonbeliever? Same-sex couples? The minister's family and/or friends? It is important for all ministers to think biblically and theologically on these matters and have their position approved by the church or denominational leadership. Having one's views known and clearly articulated could save the pastor, and the church, from any future conflict, as well as legal trouble.

A Christian wedding ceremony is a worship service where two people declare their union together in front of their friends and family. Similar to a Sunday morning worship service, the service is to ascribe worth, honor, and glory to God. Contrary to popular belief, the ceremony is not about displaying the bride's dress, showcasing the couple's romantic love story, or simply being a precursor to the reception party. First, and foremost, a Christian wedding ceremony is a time where people gather to worship God for the great things He has done. Unfortunately, not everyone in society would agree. However, as a minster to God's people, it is your job to teach people why the couple chose to have a Christian wedding ceremony.

HOW TO CONDUCT A CHRISTIAN WEDDING CEREMONY

The day has almost come. The bride and groom can see the finish line of their ongoing engagement and months, sometimes years, of wedding planning. However, wedding day is just the beginning. It is the foundation of a covenant the couple is making with one another and with God. They are about to launch into a bond that no amount of premarital counseling could ultimately prepare them for. A minister is helping them establish a point in their relationship that they can constantly reflect as the time they said, "Yes!" to one another. They are about to enter into a challenging journey and the officiating minister has the opportunity to shepherd that special moment and help them start off on the right path.

In reality, while the minister is focusing on the covenant they are about to make, thousands of other thoughts are swirling around the couple's minds. The minister is thinking about bringing an uplifting message from the Scriptures, but the couple is thinking about the pictures and reactions they will get on social media. The minister is focused on the beautiful union of marriage, but the couple is trying to keep their parents from fighting. The minister is concentrating on the vows, the couple is daydreaming about a honeymoon. The minister wants the Holy Spirit to be present, but the couple may be missing loved ones who are absent. Face it, during the wedding week, the one who is the most levelheaded and has the appropriate perspective of what is taking place, is the officiating minister. His task is to remind the couple and everyone else, the real reason they are gathered. This undertaking begins during the wedding week at the wedding rehearsal.

THE WEDDING REHEARSAL

It is important to rehearse the wedding a day or two before the ceremony to make sure everyone is on the same page. Most likely, the bride, groom, their families, and friends have been at the venue decorating all day. They are probably exhausted, running on adrenaline or fumes, and have been so focused on the minor details that they need someone to remind them of the big picture. That someone is the minister.

After the officiating minister has been introduced to all the key participants, it is important for him to say a word or two in front of everyone. Gather everyone together and pass out a template of the order of the service. The minister can then use this moment to introduce himself, explain his relationship to the bride and groom, the importance of a marriage commitment, and remind all that the purpose of a wedding service is to glorify God. Spending a few moments addressing everyone does several things. First, it demonstrates that the minister is the leader of the worship service. Even if the couple hired a wedding planner, the minister was asked to be in charge of the ceremony. It is important that everyone, including the wedding planner, know who is leading the ceremony.

After introductions and a brief word about the purpose of a ceremony, it is important to cover the ceremony's logistics. Perhaps begin by placing people where they will be during the ceremony. Since the minister probably does not know all the details, he may need some help. Once everyone is in place, then let everyone know that the first thing you will rehearse is how the wedding party will exit. This may seem odd to do first, but the law of primacy says that people usually remember most what is done first. Then once everyone has left the stage, or the front of the room, and is in the lobby area, you can practice the processional. Now everyone knows where he or she is to stand.

After the processional, the wedding party is in place, and the bride has been walked down the aisle, you will want to practice the Giving of the Bride. The person giving the bride away most likely has never had to give away his daughter before. This can often times be a very emotional experience. This is why rehearsing this part of the ceremony is important.

Next, review the order of the service. If any parts, such as special music, Scripture reading, etc., need to be rehearsed, it might be good to do so at rehearsal. Special elements such as Communion, foot washing, and unity candles do not need to be rehearsed in full, but it might be wise to have those participating know where and how these elements will be done. After running through the order of service, have the party practice the recessional and the processional, just so everyone (including those overseeing music) is coordinated.

Always pray before and after the rehearsal. Why is this important? First, this invites the Holy Spirit into this worship service and puts everyone under His submission. Second, it reminds participates of the One who is being worshiped and glorified during the service. Finally, the beginning prayer communicates that the officiating minister has been designated as ceremony leader, and the closing prayer signals when he is handing over the responsibilities to someone else.

THE WEDDING REHEARSAL DINNER

After the wedding rehearsal is over, the minister's job is not done. Typically, the officiant is invited to the rehearsal dinner. The minister should use dinnertime to get valuable, personal information about the bride and groom from their families and wedding party to include in the sermon. This is also a time when deep, meaningful conversations can take place about God, life, and marriage. Do not be shy about presenting the gospel, praying with people, or sharing a biblical worldview on topics that arise in conversations.

Check with all the parents to see how they are doing and ask them what their child was like when they were younger. Simple questions like this accomplish at least two things. First, it helps the officiant fulfill his role as a pastor. Sure, he was hired to officiate the wedding, but he is a pastor at heart. Parents, and even grandparents, are coming to grips with the fact that their little one has grown up. Listening to their fears, worries, and questions about their child's unforeseen future can be powerful. They may also be reflecting on their own wedding day and marriage, which could reveal old wounds if the marriage did not work out or if their spouse is deceased. Obviously, the young couple needs your prayers and God's guidance, but so do their parents and grandparents. Be their pastor, too, even if it is just for a couple of days.

Second, sometimes these conversations give you examples of their son or daughter's interests as a child. Store those details or illustrations in your mind or write them down. You could then use that information in the wedding sermon introduction.

The pastor will also want to check in with the bridesmaids and groomsmen. They may not be going through the same emotions as the parents, but it is possible that siblings, cousins, or friends have feelings other than joy for the bride or groom. They may be feeling selfish, envious, jealous, lonely, angry, or have questions about God's timing in their own lives. The minister should not try to solve all these issues at this time. However, it is wise to be aware that these emotions might be present in some of the folks present.

After checking in with the bridesmaids and groomsmen, if appropriate, I like to ask them to help me finish my sermon. I explain that I want to make the sermon personal and ask something like, "Since you know_____ best, what are some fun things you think are vital for their new spouse to know as they enter into marriage together?" Try your best to write down their responses, which could vary from, "Her favorite candy is gummy worms" to "Don't expect her to function properly in the morning without her avocado toast and mocha coffee" or "He is a die-hard Tigers fan, so game day is a big deal."

Additionally, try to gain an understanding as to what the bride or groom's friendship means to those in the wedding party. Perhaps ask a question like, "What are some of the best qualities about _____?" Gathering this information and using it in the wedding sermon will make it unique and specific for not just the bride and groom, but for all the guests.

TIPS FOR THE WEDDING REHEARSAL

- Dress business casual.

- Arrive early and help where needed.

- Bring a pen and paper, tablet, or smartphone to quickly jot down names and notes. There is too much to remember, so make sure you can write them down.

- Print a template of the ceremony and give it to everyone at the rehearsal (including the people in charge of technology).

- Bring masking tape to mark places on the floor so everyone knows where to stand.

- Ask the bride and groom for the marriage license and envelope with correct mailing address.

WEDDING DAY

The day has finally come. Premartial counseling is over, rehearsal and accompanying dinner are complete, and two people are about to take vows that have a lifelong impact. Even though people have been getting married for generations, no two weddings are the same. A person's culture, family, friends, generation, past relationships, and spirituality, as well as the geography, weather, and venue can influence the ceremony. Nonetheless, God has called you a pastor to shepherd a couple during one of their most important moments in life. It is both an honor and an incredibly challenging task.

After arriving at the church or venue, the pastor should visit with the bride, maid-of-honor, groom, best man, parents, and wedding coordinator to see how the day has been. Keep in mind, no wedding is perfect and there might well be drama. One of a minister's tasks is to be the calming presence and rational thinker. He should encourage people to remember that the day is about how the bride and groom have chosen to glorify God with their commitment to one another. Rarely do wedding days go exactly as planned—but that is okay. Teach people that God is still in control and as long as the bride, groom, and you are there, the wedding can take place. A good way to remind people of this is through prayer. Beginning with the bride and the people with her, try to steal a few moments to pray for her. Perhaps invite others there to pray for her as well. Then go to the groom's dressing room and do the same.

THE WEDDING CEREMONY

It is beneficial to have the entire order of service scripted because there are too many distractions and elements of a wedding to keep straight. Having a detailed description of everything that will transpire will put a minister's mind at ease and help him focus on everyone's emotional and spiritual temperaments.

There are countless ways to conduct a wedding ceremony. At its core, a wedding ought to be both biblical and personal. A basic wedding ceremony template looks like this:

WEDDING CEREMONY TEMPLATE
Prelude
Seating of Grandparents and Parents
Processional
Ring Bearer and Flower Girl
Entry of the Bride and Father
Welcome and Greeting, Prayer
Giving of the Bride
Scripture Reading/Song(s)
Sermon
Exchange of Vows
Ring Exchange
Pronouncement and the Kiss
Recessional
Dismissal

It's wise to plan the worship ceremony with the bride and groom during one of the last premarital counseling sessions. This way, with the pastor's help, they are able to make it memorable and God-honoring. Following are suggestions on various aspects of the wedding ceremony.

Welcome and Greeting, Prayer

People will sense the mood of the service from the minister's welcome. Since this is a day to celebrate God's goodness and providence, welcome people with a huge smile and happy tone. Weddings are supposed to be joyous occasions, and people will notice the minister's attitude. He should feel free to make it light-hearted and welcoming. A quick use of humor can lighten the mood quickly. This is also an opportunity for the minister to explain how he knows the couple and begin to tell their story. At this point, he may want to address the couple, but really he is welcoming attendees to a worship service. He could say something like, "Nearly five years ago, these two people standing before you met at a coffee shop. They were total strangers. But after some time they became friends and then fell in love. Today, they are meeting here to declare to God their commitment to one another. And they wanted to make sure you were here to witness this very special occasion. They are so thankful you all could make it. Welcome!" Then follow with a simple prayer.

Sermon[3]

Many pastors use the same sermon for every wedding ceremony they officiate. However, that does a disservice to both the couple and the Lord. It is easier to use the same sermon repeatedly, but pastors can do better. Does it take more time, effort, and creativity to write a new sermon for every wedding you officiate? Yes. But be different. Make each worship service honoring to God by giving your very best in creating a sermon that is both biblical and personal.

Even though each sermon needs to vary, the structure of wedding sermons may be similar. While other aspects of the service is directed to everyone in the service (procession, welcoming, songs, pronouncement, presentation, recessional) the sermon is specifically geared toward the couple. The minister should use the sermon to speak directly to the couple while remembering that everyone else is listening. Therefore, the sermon could begin by reminding the couple how their relationship started and grew. This makes it personal for them and their guests. Or perhaps a minister could begin by talking about their childhood and their relationship with their parents. (This is when you can use the background research from the rehearsal dinner.) Use some of the comments from the bridesmaids and groomsmen for transitions and humor. This makes the message specific to the couple and engaging.

After the sermon's introduction, transition to the Bible and the pastor's encouragement and advice for the couple. This portion need not be long, but it does need to be biblical. To make it personal, an officiating minister might use the meaning of the couple's names or something interesting about them that can be linked to the Scripture passage. This takes some creativity, and usually a concordance, but it makes the sermon both personal and biblical.

Once he has landed on a passage of Scripture that connects to the couple, the minister must unpack the main idea of that passage. Using sound exegetical skills, discover the subject (What is the author talking about?) and complement (What is the author saying about what he is talking about?). Then, combine your subject and complement and write down the exegetical idea. Essentially, the exegetical idea is one sentence that encompasses the main idea of the passage. Next, shape the exegetical idea into a shorter and more memorable preaching idea.[4] The preaching idea ought to be repeated several times throughout the sermon.

One final, critical element to include in wedding sermons is the importance of a marriage that centers on Jesus Christ. Marriages and weddings can omit Jesus from ever making an appearance. But as a follower of Jesus and advocate for the Holy Spirit, we honor God with our lives, marriages, and ministry by making Him our foundation. There will be unbelievers and people with broken marriages at every wedding. They may be offended to hear about God's role in a marriage. But as a minister of God's Word, it is incredibly important for marriages to revolve around Christ and His commandment to love one another (John 15:12). Therefore, whenever you have the opportunity, exhort people to put Christ at the center of their marriage.

A Few Principles to Remember Writing a Wedding Sermon

- Make it personal. If the sermon can be repeated in multiple wedding ceremonies, it is not specific enough. Get creative and use the couple's name, occupations, hobbies, or background and connect it to Scripture.

- Make it biblical. After connecting the couple to some aspect of Scripture, expound upon the truth of the Scripture.

- Make it memorable. Be sure the sermon has a clear, memorable idea that is connected to the biblical text. Repeat the idea so the couple, as well as guests, can apply the idea to their marriage and life.

- Make the sermon concise. The length of a wedding sermon varies depending on culture, but it is usually much shorter than a typical Sunday morning sermon. My wedding sermons are usually between eight and twelve minutes, so use discernment when determining the length of the sermon.

Exchange of Vows and Rings

The exchange of vows and wedding bands express and symbolize the couple's commitment to one another. In preparation for the ceremony, ask the bride and groom how they would like this part of the service to be conducted. Some couples write their own vows. Others prefer traditional vows. Either is acceptable; however, review the vows with the couple, usually in a premarital counseling session, so they know the meaning behind their words. During the ceremony, it is helpful to explain the meaning behind the different elements.

Special Elements (Unity Display, Communion, Foot-washing, etc.)

Couples are getting more and more creative on how they want to display their commitment to one another. They are often seeking ways to make special moments and memorable experiences. There is no problem with these expressions; however, make sure the couple has the right motive behind any special element that is included. Understanding why the couple chose to add a special element will also help the minister introduce that portion of the ceremony.

Presentation and Dismissal

Even though the dismissal may seem straightforward, there are several important details to remember. People are taking cues from the officiant. When he presents the couple for the first time as husband and wife, the tone should be celebratory. Encourage those in attendance to clap and cheer.

After the wedding party has exited, people need directions on what is next. Before the service, make known any specific requests from the wedding party or coordinator. It is also helpful to announce the location of the reception and the time it will begin. Usually, the recessional is implemented with music, so the minister will want to coordinate with those doing the music to play gently during final announcements. Finally, try to make your last words uplifting and exciting. Perhaps something like, "Let's keep rejoicing all night! Let the celebration continue!"

Wedding License

Sometime after the ceremony, be sure to have the newly married couple sign the wedding license. In God's eyes they are already married, but in the state's eyes a wedding license needs to be signed and mailed. Every state's procedures differ so it is *extremely* important to understand the laws of the state(s) where the wedding is being conducted. Research the laws months in advance in case there is any paperwork that needs to be filed beforehand.

After the wedding license is signed, immediately put it in a stamped and addressed envelope and drop it into the nearest mailbox on the way home. Do not wait days to send in the marriage license as many states have only a few days in which it can be postmarked.

Tips for the Wedding Ceremony

- Dress in culturally appropriate ways.

- Be on time and prepared.

- Purchase a small binder used specifically for weddings. Print your notes so you can easily find your place and will not be turning the pages constantly.

- Turn your phone off (maybe ask others to turn their phones off too).

- Carry a tissue or handkerchief in your pocket (usually for the groom).

- Print vows on nice paper, or print sections of the sermon, and give it to the bride and groom after the wedding. This also makes a great one-year anniversary gift.

- Write down details about the reception that need to be communicated at the end of the service.

- Be professional but not too serious.

CONCLUSION

A Christian wedding ceremony ought to be both biblical and personal. God appoints ministers to lead a service that honors Him. But each wedding ceremony needs to be unique because every couple you marry is different. Observing and listening to the couple, their family, and friends will help a pastor discern how God wants him to officiate the worship service. When he aims at crafting a service that is both scriptural and distinct, a minister creates special memories that last a lifetime and glorify God.

NOTES

1. Moody Bible Institute: Positional Statement on Human Sexuality, https://www.moodybible.org/beliefs/positional-statements/human-sexuality/.

2. Abraham E. Millgram, *Jewish Worship* (Philadelphia: The Jewish Publication Society of America, 1971), 326–30.

3. A terrific resource for writing a wedding sermon is Scott Gibson, *Preaching for Special Services* (Grand Rapids: Baker, 2001).

4. Haddon W. Robinson, *Biblical Preaching: The Development and Delivery of Expository Messages,* Third edition (Grand Rapids: Baker, 2014).

CHAPTER 6.8

Conducting a Funeral

DANIEL GREEN

God-honoring funerals are an important part of a pastor's ministry duties. People are typically in their most vulnerable state and stand in need of the comfort the gospel brings. It is an opportunity for the pastor to wield the good news in a way that shines light into darkness for unbelievers and reminds followers of Christ of the certain hope they have beyond this life.

In this essay, there are two main sections: considerations for conducting a funeral and steps to conducting a funeral. Under each of the main sections, there are numerous items that should be given thought.

CONSIDERATIONS FOR CONDUCTING A FUNERAL

THEOLOGY

The pastor is the resident theologian for a funeral, and he needs to think carefully about how the service is structured, and how the content is delivered. A Christian funeral should not be an incautious celebration. Death represents a terrible failure for the human race. God created human beings for His glory, but they sinned and were alienated from Him (Gen. 3:1–24). Paradise was lost. The original environment had been one of health in every way: spiritual, physical, and emotional. There were no human deficiencies of body or mind. The fellowship between God, Adam, and Eve was perfect and unbroken. When the first couple sinned, the results were immediately devastating and universal. Death entered the world and spread to all people (Rom. 5–12). All aspects of the human being were affected (Eph. 4:17–19).

Thereafter, the passing of a loved one has caused deep sorrow for survivors (John 11:32–36). It's clear that death is not the way it is supposed to be.

It is appropriate for survivors to mourn deeply for their loss of someone dear to them. Tears, fear, shock, and remorse are typically present. A funeral service should provide the living with an opportunity for reflection and positive change (Eccl. 7:2) and should give everyone a chance to think about the brevity of life and the importance of serving the Lord well while on earth (Ps. 90). Since God has built humans with a need for evaluation of present life, a period of quiet during the service is always appropriate.

But a Christian funeral should not be morbid. The believer has overcome death through accepting Christ as personal Savior. The Good Shepherd has given His life for the deceased believer (John 10–11). Upon death he has passed spiritually immediately into the presence of the Lord Jesus (2 Cor. 5–6). To die and be with Christ is better than to live on earth, no matter how fruitful life and ministry might be here. To die is not the end of life, but the beginning of a new phase. It is to know Christ better than ever before. For the follower of Christ, it's not death to die.

The believer who has passed away has entered something far better (Phil. 1:20–26). He has entered immediately into a world of unimaginable pleasure, unlike any earthly experience (1 Cor. 2:9). The Father's deep desire for lasting fellowship with the believer will be fulfilled. There will be no more sorrow, pain, or death. All physical maladies will vanish, and there will be no more emotional struggles. All grief will have passed (Rev. 21:3–4). Heaven is the place that Christ went to prepare for the Christian to live forever (John 14:2–3). The believer will be with Jesus in heaven, in intimate quarters, with immediate access to the Son. Physically, he will follow Christ in a resurrection that will transform his body and signal final victory over death (1 Cor. 15:50–58). Thus, believers may comfort one another when the earthly life of a fellow believer ends (1 Thess. 4:13–18). Thus, his body and spirit will be eternally joined.

WHAT ABOUT THE BODY?

The treatment of the human body is also a matter of theological significance. The question of whether the deceased should be buried traditionally, or cremated, is widely asked. Evangelicals have historically discouraged cremation, seeing it as disrespectful to the human body. The body that will be resurrected is based on the same body that we live in on earth. God will transform it at the resurrection of the believer, fitting it for heaven (1 Cor. 15:50–53). Therefore, it is reasoned, no deliberate action that decomposes the body should be taken. The practice has also been discouraged since it has been associated with non-Christian religions. Buddhists sometimes practice it, and it is the preferred choice of traditional

Hindus. These Eastern religions teach that humans are one with the cosmos in a way that Christianity doesn't, and the practice of scattering cremated ashes in the air or water symbolizes this.

However, the discussion has broadened more recently. Cremation is significantly less costly. In addition, there are many countries in the world where there is simply not enough land to bury everyone in the traditional way. Thus, there are social justice issues, along with the stewardship of money and land. Some believe that resources are too precious to be spent on traditional burial. Money should be spent on the basic needs of the living and land should be used for crops and housing, these advocates say. Some also wish to donate organs or their whole bodies for scientific research, with cremation to follow.

Christians have no unified position on the matter of cremation. It is deemed acceptable by some Anglicans and Baptists. While Catholics have traditionally discouraged the practice, it is presently approved if the ashes are properly contained and not scattered. It is prohibited in Eastern Orthodoxy and Orthodox Judaism.[1] It seems best to leave the matter to the conscience of the individual believer, who should make his wishes known to significant others while living. Pastors should have liberty to express their convictions while preaching, advising, or participating in services.

PARTICIPATING ORGANIZATIONS

The involvement of organizations outside of the church are sometimes also important in a funeral. Will military rights be accorded? In the United States, military veterans are often eligible for honors at their funerals. This may include a rifle salute, and/or the presentation of a flag to the significant others of the deceased. Such participants are highly respectful of the occasion and should be welcomed. Military personnel will gladly yield to the wishes of the family and pastor as to when such honors should be accorded.

Sometimes the deceased has belonged to a controversial organization such as the Free Masons, who wish to participate in the service. Since the organization promotes some non-Christian ideas such as unusual teachings about the order of Melchizedek and strongly enforced secret orders, it is best for pastors to refuse cooperation. It may be best to suggest another time when the organization can conduct its rites. This could be at the funeral home during a time outside the formal service. Such should be decided by the funeral home personnel and scheduled at their convenience. If the pastor has freedom to speak with believing family members about his convictions, he may be able to stay out of the picture completely.

SPIRITUAL STATUS

What if the deceased person is not a Christian? The spiritual status of the deceased should be discussed only where there is a fair certainty that they have gone to heaven. There is nothing to be gained by commenting negatively on the person who has passed away. This is true in both public and private settings. Neither should a deceased person who has not followed Christ on earth now be pronounced as in heaven. This would be a breach of professional ethics. When the deceased is not well-known by the minister, generalities are in order. It may be said that the one who has died was loved by his family and appreciated in the community. It may also be stated that if the person could speak to the survivors today, he would wish for them to trust Christ as Savior.

LIFE ENDING CIRCUMSTANCES

Similarly, any socially questionable ending to a life should be addressed very delicately, if at all. There may have been a suicide, drug overdose, altercation with law enforcement, death from AIDS, or some other difficult circumstance. One should keep in mind the living in such instances. They should not be further injured or embarrassed by unnecessary comments. Most such situations are too complex to be completely understood, and comments delivered during a short message are bound to be inadequate and, perhaps, offensive. There is no need for the pastor to act as spiritual judge in such situations.

SPECIAL CIRCUMSTANCES

In the case of a death of an infant or other person who was mentally unable to give assent to faith, wise judgment should be exercised. Strong convictions and accompanying emotions will likely be present among the attenders. Some may believe that the Bible is clear that such persons will be in heaven (2 Sam. 12:23) or that persons who could not believe will not be held responsible for their lack of profession in Christ. Others are concerned about the responsibility for the original sin of all persons, the unlikelihood of all such persons being elect and/or pronouncement of salvation on those who have not trusted in Christ. The pastor needs to be aware that there are arguments for and against the likelihood of such persons being in heaven. It is probably best not to express certainty in either direction. It is theologically safer to speak of God's sovereignty (Eph. 1:11), justice (Ps. 11:7), goodness (Nah. 1:7), and love (Rom. 8:35–39).

Some families may wish to have some sort of service for miscarried babies. This kind of request is certainly theologically consistent and should be honored. There may be a simple memorial, or a burial on private property if the fetus is in possession. The pastor should be willing to give some reflection on life and death, the sorrow of loss, and deep disappointment. Such presence and careful words will honor the family and help them in their time of loss. Legal requirements should be researched and observed.

Formal services should not be performed for animals. They are not a part of creation for whom Christ died. Perspective should be kept by pastor and parishioner. While remembrance of loved animals may be helpful to the family, the pastor should think twice about his involvement.

STEPS TO CONDUCT A FUNERAL

DECIDING WHETHER OR NOT TO ACCEPT THE SERVICE

If the deceased is a member of the congregation in good standing there is, practically speaking, no reason not to participate in the service. In fact, such participation may be an unstated expectation, or even a contractual obligation. But some situations may give the minister pause. The deceased may be a relative of a parishioner not known by the pastor. This would force the message and overall approach to the service to be very general. The funeral may be too great a distance from the pastor's home and thus too taxing a trip.

The funeral may also be for a congregant who is under church discipline or notably discontent. To offer services for someone who was in rebellion would certainly not be obligatory and could be quite stressful emotionally. The pastor will need to exercise his judgment before accepting an invitation and should seek the counsel of church leaders or other trusted pastors.

ANTICIPATING A CONGREGATIONAL NEED

There is no good reason for the pastor's overall ministry to suffer due to an expected funeral. Many funerals can be anticipated when the deceased has been seriously ill or weakened due to advanced age. Other church business can be taken care of in advance. Extra work can be devoted to sermon preparation in the weeks leading up to the death. Or another staff pastor may be assigned to the funeral.

Another option is to have a trusted visiting preacher be on call for a Sunday sermon after a week when the pastor has been occupied with the special needs related to a death in the congregation. Pastoral calls can be made to the debilitated person to help them prepare for their departure. This preparation may include a mate and children. Once a death has occurred, the planning of the funeral begins.

INITIAL CONTACT WITH FAMILY

It is very important to contact surviving family as soon as possible after the death of a parishioner. Some will need immediate emotional and spiritual care.

In such cases, a pastor should leave other tasks quickly and proceed to the family's home. Normally, survivors will not be alone. In a case where a woman will be by herself, it is wise for the pastor to take another person with him. This initial visit should be relatively short. Condolences should be given, Scripture read, and prayer offered. There may also be an opportunity to meet some family members. Some bereaved persons will not want a personal visit, preferring to mourn in private at first. In such a case the pastor should use the phone wisely. He can still offer sympathies and may also be able to read Scripture and pray. Other methods of communication such as email and texting may also be employed if deemed appropriate. The pastor should take mental notes during this initial contact as to the emotional and spiritual condition of the bereaved. In either scenario, a time should be set for a meeting with the funeral director the next day.

INFORMING THE CHURCH TEAM

The church funeral team needs to be informed immediately when someone in the church dies. As soon as the initial meeting with the family has concluded, they should be given more specific information. The members and responsibilities may vary according to the size of the church. In a larger congregation there may be professionals assigned to the task. In most churches, however, there will be a large group of laypersons involved. There will probably be a soloist and musicians with whom the pastor works regularly in such services, and who can be trusted to perform professionally and follow proper protocol for the occasion. The funeral home will be able to recommend a soloist if needed. There may be some sort of funeral chairperson to inform, who will be able to contact other important parties—those who will prepare the church building, the prayer chain leader, and the hostess for any reception or dinner after the interment. All procedural elements should be clearly described in church documents, along with any costs for facility use, food, and other expenses.

MEETING WITH THE FUNERAL DIRECTOR

The pastor should arrive to the funeral home at least thirty minutes in advance of the bereaved to spend time with the funeral director. The director should be considered an important colleague at the service. He is an experienced professional and is in his element. The pastor should readily defer to his judgment in all cultural and procedural matters. Together, the pastor and the funeral director can exchange thoughts about the situation and come to an agreement as to how any particularly challenging situations might be handled. The director may know more family history than the pastor and may be able to share some helpful information. He will also have much experience in assessing various situations and family dynamics.

Once the bereaved arrives, there will be business to complete. An order of service will be developed. There is often a set sequence that the funeral home follows unless the pastor requires that it be changed. Most of the time, the usual sequence be followed as long as there is sufficient time allotted for the message. The bereaved are often quite concerned with the eulogy, and their wishes should be followed if possible. The eulogizers may not be polished speakers, but they are present because of a close relationship with the deceased. Their performance is not the responsibility of the pastor. It is fine for the pastor to give counsel and input to the service, but he should also cooperate with family wishes wherever possible.

During this meeting the question of traditional burial versus cremation will certainly be raised. If a traditional burial is chosen, caskets will be shown. These will vary greatly in price. This is a family matter that does not vitally concern the pastor. If he is consulted, he should be wary of giving expensive advice. He might want to say that any of the caskets would be more than suitable. Once the family chooses a unit, the pastor should keep any negative thoughts to himself.

There may also be opportunity to address spiritual matters or family conflicts. Sometimes family members may not have spoken in years, but now need to communicate for the service to be planned. The pastor needs to be a wise and gentle mediator in such cases. He should not be a go between, relaying what one alienated party desires to say to the other party. With prayer and wise intercession, however, he may be able to effect a conversation or even a reconciliation.

VISITATION BEFORE THE SERVICE

Sometimes there will a visitation on the eve of the funeral service. Discuss with the funeral director the practices of your church community and culture. Some communities have family services that the pastor leads following the visitation. Depending on the practices of the church, it is a courtesy to at least stop by the visitation for a few minutes. This will provide an opportunity to check on the status of the survivors and meet some people from the community who will not be present for the service the next day. It is also a good idea to greet the funeral director and make any last-minute adjustments he might suggest.

There may also be a more formal visitation on the day of the funeral. On such occasions there may be a receiving line of close relatives standing together. It is best if the pastor lets his presence be known without intruding. The family may wish for him to join them in the line. If requested, he should surely comply. He is being included as an important part of the family and will be introduced to many relatives and acquaintances who will hear his message later that day. Another scenario may have the close relatives sitting at the front of the room, receiving visitors. In this case, the pastor may wish to pass through the line with others before the service. The pastor may be asked if the deceased is presentable. He should always answer yes as the funeral directors will have done their best to make everything acceptable.

THE FUNERAL SERVICE

The Elements

A funeral's elements of the funeral may vary according to local traditions, culture, preferences of the pastor or of the bereaved family. Usually, the order will be general greeting and offering of condolences by the pastor, the reading of the obituary by the pastor, song (solo, group, or congregational), prayer, eulogy, sermon, prayer, announcements, dismissal. These may be varied, however.

Order of Service

The funeral director will have provided the pastor and all attendees with an order of service when they enter the room. The casket should be closed at this time. Normally, the pastor will give brief introductory remarks, followed by a solo, eulogy, and message. This order may vary according to the traditions of the area.

Before the Service

The pastor should contact each participant before the service so they know exactly when they will present, and how long they have to do so. Eulogizers in particular may be prone to emotion, exaggeration, and lack of time consciousness. This should not be the concern of the pastor unless the presentation is excessively long.

The Message

The message should usually not be more than twenty minutes in duration. The text for the message may be selected from such passages as John 10:1–11, John 14:1–6, 1 Corinthians 15:50–58, or 1 Thessalonians 4:13–18. It should be primarily a message of hope focused on the living, not on the deceased. There may not be any occasion in the pastor's ministry when he will have the opportunity to preach the gospel to more people who are lost. The gospel of salvation should be clear, and the tone of delivery positive. The message should do no unnecessary harm.

The Conclusion

Once the funeral service proper is concluded, the pastor will often be the one to give instructions for additional gatherings. He should be clear about the location of the interment, and who is expected to be present. Sometimes the family wishes for this aspect of the funeral to be private, sometimes all funeral attendees are welcome. He should also be clear about the time and location of any luncheon to follow. He may then dismiss the audience. He should remain until the last visitor has departed, at which time he will meet at the casket with the funeral director. This is a time to be certain that any valuables, including jewelry and mementos, be removed from the deceased or casket, and returned to the family.

THE INTERMENT

The Casket

The pastor will normally ride in the lead car, which bears the casket, while close family will follow in another official car. This will give him an opportunity to talk with one of the funeral directors. This is valuable time as the driver will likely be an important colleague for many years. He may also need to hear the gospel himself. Once at the interment site, the pastor should proceed to the rear of the hearse, where he will meet the pall bearers. They may need basic instructions about carrying the casket, which may be heavy. He will lead them to the site of the interment. He should double-check with the funeral director to be sure which site is for the deceased as there may be several open on a given day. He should lead at a pace that considers the group as a whole. Once there, the director will help the pall bearers situate the casket on the equipment that will lower it into the ground. The closest relatives of the deceased will be seated near the casket, probably under a shelter.

The Service

The pastor should stand at the head of the casket and remain in charge of this part of the service. If military rights are to be accorded, this will normally be the time for them. There may be a rifle salute. A flag may be folded by military personnel and presented to the closest relative. At this point the pastor may make a few very brief comments from appropriate passages of Scripture that were not used for the funeral message. Prayer should be offered.

The Burial

Before the casket is lowered into the ground survivors may wish to say some last words. The attendees may then be dismissed for the luncheon. The pastor will stay behind until the casket has been lowered into the grave. He may then ride back with the funeral director for the meal. While it is not his place to invite the funeral directors, it is assumed that they may attend the meal. If it seems that there has been an oversight, he should feel free to invite the directors to attend.

THE LUNCHEON

Prayer

The luncheon should be opened in thanksgiving for the food. It may be best for a church elder to pray, since the pastor may be delayed at the grave site. The prayer should be kept simple, and not be a rehash of matters already addressed. A member of the funeral committee may also give some general directions about the meal.

Purpose

A funeral luncheon can serve several helpful purposes. It is a courtesy for persons who have traveled a great distance to pay their respect to the deceased. They are given a good meal, a place to rest for a while, a respite from the financial and emotional commitment to attend the service. It may also serve as a reunion of sorts. Family that may not have seen each other for a long time are brought together. While it may seem inappropriate to mingle and exchange personal information at the funeral, such a gathering can bring balance to the day. Dying is part of life that goes on for everyone else. There will doubtless be some reminiscing about the person who died. Stories can be exchanged. Perspectives on the person's life can be given that others had not considered. Survivors may feel honored by what is shared. Such a gathering can also strengthen surviving family and friends. They can catch up on their lives, observe the growth and maturity of children, and support each other in grief. Words of comfort and comforting hugs provide great consolation for many. Sometimes the meal will be an introduction to other more general gatherings in days to come.

Pastoral Ministry

For the pastor, this luncheon presents an unusually good opportunity to meet friends and family of the deceased. He should determine beforehand not to spend this time with parishioners whom he already knows. Instead, he should try to meet family and friends of the deceased that he does not know. He won't likely be viewed as an intruder, but as a welcome part of each table. There may be some intimate conversations that open the way for sharing the gospel, or future pastoral care. He may learn new facts about the deceased and his family. This is not a time to force the gospel on people, but a time to trust God for whatever conversation may arise. Attendees will appreciate good listening. While the pastor does not need to be the last one on site, he should not be in a hurry.

Funeral Team

Such an occasion is also an opportunity for the funeral team at the church to serve and grow together. All members should be as informed as possible about the details of the meal. They should arrive promptly at the venue, ready to work. Each person should have as their goal to help the family and friends of the deceased. The food should be well-prepared and presented, the tables properly set, and the meeting room clean as possible. Small talk should be kept to a minimum. Some of the team will be among the last to leave the scene, having overseen a meticulous cleaning of the site.

Keeping the Congregation Informed

Most congregations and cultures are communal enough to care a great deal about the welfare of their members. It is therefore wise leadership that keeps the flock appraised of the status of those who are ill or suffering from terminal illness. They may be mentioned in announcements or prayer. When a death occurs, there should be clear and specific information posted in the various church communications: website, Facebook, and email prayer lists. This should include, at minimum, the time of visitations and the service. If the funeral is already scheduled by the time of a Sunday service, a formal announcement might be made from the pulpit. In the case of unexpected, or unusually tragic, circumstances, the pastor may want to take a few minutes during a Sunday morning service to address the congregation.

Finances

Every church will have its own practices and provisions for the funeral services. Some may make it a benefit of membership with the facilities and luncheon provided for the family. Other churches may have expenses for the family. Financial matters should be explained in a document that may be given to the deceased's family at the proper time. In some situations, there will be a financial obligation for facility use, or food.

Pastoral Communication

The pastor should be sure to thank the workers publicly and privately. In most churches a mention of the funeral at the first Sunday service after the funeral, and a thanks to everyone that helped is appreciated. The minister should also write a personal note of thanks to the leader of the church funeral team with the assumption that it will be passed on to the members.

PROFESSIONAL APPEARANCE AND DEMEANOR

A funeral is a formal affair, and the pastor should be dressed well for the occasion. Even where dress codes have been significantly relaxed, he should wear a suit and tie. All clothing should be clean, pressed, and dry-cleaned if necessary. All buttons should be fastened. Shoes should be dark and polished. Colors should generally be subdued. Black or dark blue suits are best with a white or light blue shirt. A tie may have some color but should be conservative. Styles should be traditional rather than novel. Appropriate dress is necessary in a cold climate or inclement weather.

The demeanor of the officiant needs to be calm. This is not a time for uncontrolled weeping or show of emotion. Such may be expressed in private before or after the funeral, but the pastor needs to have self-control during the service in order to discharge his duties and help others do so. He should not be involved in joking or horse play before, during, or immediately after the service. While others may have moments of lightheartedness or hilarity, it is important for the pastor to be conservative in his expressions. The most sensitive people at the services need to be respected. He will lose nothing by being conservative but may lose respect, and even cause resentment, if he is not.

BUSINESS ASPECTS

In many contexts it is customary for the pastor to receive compensation for services rendered. This may be a line item on a funeral home's list of expenses. In such a case, some official from the home will give the pastor a check or tell him that one will be arriving in the mail. In some situations, families of the deceased will prefer to give the pastor cash or a check personally. The pastor should not inquire of a family about any anticipated honorarium. They may have forgotten or have not yet decided as a group what to do. Remuneration should not be his motive for serving the family (1 Peter 5:4). He will need to report any honorarium as taxable income.

AFTERCARE FOR SURVIVORS

Spouses of the deceased will likely suffer quite considerably. They will need to experience the classic emotions of denial, anger, bargaining, depression, and acceptance. The pastor may coach the survivor through the stages or may refer to a trusted Christian therapist. He should be active in the continuing oversight and care of the bereaved. A period of significant mourning should be expected, but unusually poor progress in adjustment would call for considerate intervention, and perhaps discussion with family members as to the welfare of the widow/widower.

Phone calls and emails will usually be welcomed. These may be daily at first, then several times a week, tapering off to weekly and monthly as time passes. A yearly contact, near the anniversary of the death, is often greatly appreciated. In the case of a female survivor, church deaconesses, or other women should be enlisted to visit the bereaved in her home, and to undertake a general schedule of care. The pastor and others in the church should not hesitate to mention the deceased in front of the mate. This may trigger sorrow or tears, but the mention is almost always appreciated.

Children who lose a father, or especially a mother, are vulnerable emotionally. They are sometimes ignored in the effort to console bereaved mates. They, too, need care. Few will have the emotional maturity to deal adequately with their considerable grief. Sometimes they will even suffer neglect as a surviving parent struggles to adjust. The children may act out in ways that are unusual for them. The pastor should prepare youth workers and Sunday school teachers for this possibility. Like their parents, they should be encouraged to talk, and assured that they will be cared for by God, family, friends, and the church. The church may arrange for persons of the gender of the deceased to befriend the child (men with boys, women with girls) and include them in significant church-related activities.

FINAL WORDS

Funerals are one of the greatest opportunities you will have as a pastor to shepherd God's people and to share the gospel. Plan ahead for people to meet the Savior for comfort or salvation. Pray for your ministry, words, and care for the family. And be sure to direct all people to the great Shepherd and Savior, Jesus Christ. Above all, hold the gospel high.

CONCLUSION

When the pastor begins to conduct funerals, he need not be intimidated. By following the steps outlined here, in the two major sections of the article, he may be assured that he will not be overlooking major components of a funeral service. As he gains experience, he will become more effective in the administration of this important rite.

NOTE

1. "13 Different Religious Perspectives on Cremation," Everplans (accessed July 1, 2019).

Handling Finances

GERALD PETERMAN

In the modern world, as in the ancient, money is a sensitive subject. Let's admit it. Issues of greed, privacy, manipulation, embarrassment, pride, mismanagement, fraud, anxiety, misunderstanding, power struggles, and abuse come up right away. The news often reports about churches and financial scandal. We need sound instruction grounded in Scripture to guide our thinking and to guard the reputation of the gospel and the church. In the following pages we have two sections: first we treat broad principles to cover all our dealing with finances; and second, we deal with guidance on specific issues.

BROAD PRINCIPLES

TRUSTING GOD AND NOT MONEY

Despite how obvious it seems, we must not take this principle for granted, for it is an outworking of the gospel. Though a simple exhortation, it is hard to live by, no matter the level of one's income. It can be especially difficult when pastoral staff feel a unique burden concerning the congregation's finances. Further, although Bible knowledge is very important, we should not think that having it somehow exempts us from such temptation.

Contentment, commanded by John the Baptist (Luke 3:14) and exemplified by Paul (Phil. 4:11; see also 1 Tim. 6:6–8), is a spiritual virtue. It will not grow on its own, it must be cultivated. On the other hand greed, which is idolatry (Eph. 5:5; Col.

3:5), is like a weed. It can spring up anywhere and so is a constant temptation. Let's listen to these reminders:

> "If I have put my confidence in gold, and called fine gold my trust, if I have gloated because my wealth was great, and because my hand had obtained so much.... That too would have been a guilty deed calling for judgment, for I would have denied God above." (Job 31:24–28)

> Do not trust in oppression, and do not vainly rely on robbery; if wealth increases, do not set your heart on it. (Ps. 62:10)

> "How you boast about the valleys! Your valley is flowing away, you backsliding daughter, who trusts in her treasures, saying, 'Who can come against me?'" (Jer. 49:4)

> Instruct those who are rich in this present world not to be conceited or to set their hope on the uncertainty of riches, but on God, who richly supplies us with all things to enjoy. (1 Tim. 6:17)

The God who promised to supply all our needs (Phil. 4:19; Matt. 6:30–33) will provide for His church as well; there will certainly be times when we do not—at least not immediately—*understand* how He will do so. But we can *trust*.

Tithing

What should be our perspective on tithing? As an elder or pastor in our congregation, we might be tempted to command the people to tithe (give 10 percent) of their income; in doing so we will be implicitly treating the 613 commandments of Moses as if they are obligatory for Christians today. We assert that the books of Moses are the inspired and inerrant word of God and are therefore profitable (2 Tim. 3:16). On the other hand, we do not work with the perspective that Mosaic legislation is obligatory for Christians. The subject requires serious thought. In what follows we have two broad sections:

First, are Christians required to obey Moses? I think we can all agree that to a certain extent they are not. For instance, few if any Christians make three trips to Jerusalem per year for the mandatory feasts (Ex. 34:23–24; Deut. 16:16); parents do not make a habit of executing rebellious children (Deut. 21:18–21); and most of us are not too concerned about encountering our neighbor's lost livestock (Deut. 22:1–3). But what about other laws? Since the topic is complex and whole books are written on it, we cannot engage in lengthy discussion.[1] We conclude, negatively, that we should not treat the commandments of Moses is if they are covenant regulations for Christians, and positively that there are principles in Moses from which we should learn. How does this work out in practice? By way of example, let us return to the three laws above. We can draw these conclusions:

- Though three trips to Jerusalem are not required of Christians, God's people should enjoy a calendar where there are important days of assembly for celebration and for remembering what God has done through history and in their own lives.

- We do not execute rebellious children, but we should keep in mind that egregious sin within the family of God is dangerous and must be addressed with seriousness, even if it means putting the person out of the congregation (see 1 Cor. 5; this topic is treated in chapter 6.4, "Assimilating, Disciplining, and Restoring Members").

- Whether or not we own livestock, we see from Deuteronomy 22 that the principle is not "finders keepers, losers weepers." What does not belong to us does not belong to us. If we find what does not belong to us, love means we search for the owner or at very least keep it safe until the owner comes looking for it.

We come now to our second portion regarding the Law. What commands about economic giving do we find in the law of Moses? Restricting ourselves just to the tithe legislation in the Pentateuch, we discover that there were three tithes:

The Levitical Tithe: "To the sons of Levi, behold, I have given all the tithe in Israel as an inheritance, in return for their service which they perform, the service of the tent of meeting" (Num. 18:21). We see here the principle of "the laborer is worthy of wages" (Luke 10:7; more on this later). Furthermore, the Levites must tithe on the tithe they receive, giving it to Aaron (Num. 18:26). Since one cannot tithe on what one cannot measure, the Levitical Tithe cannot be the same as the Poor Tithe or the Festival Tithe. As we will see below, neither one of those was measurable by the Levites.

The Poor Tithe: "At the end of every third year you shall bring out all the tithe of your produce in that year, and shall deposit it in your town. And the Levite, because he has no portion or inheritance among you, and the stranger, the orphan, and the widow who are in your town, shall come and eat and be satisfied" (Deut. 14:28–29). Later we find the same tithe described this way: "When you have finished paying all the tithe of your produce in the third year, the year of the tithe, then you shall give it to the Levite, to the stranger, to the orphan, and to the widow, so that they may eat in your towns and be satisfied" (Deut. 26:12–13). How will the needy access this food? It is stored locally. Probably we find the same type of operation with the storehouse tithe of Malachi 3:10. Since the Poor Tithe is eaten in local towns, it cannot be the same as the Festival Tithe, which is eaten in Jerusalem.

The Festival Tithe: We cite a paragraph from Deuteronomy:

"You shall certainly tithe all the produce from what you sow, which comes from the field every year. You shall eat in the presence of the LORD your God, at the place where He chooses to establish His name, the tithe of your grain, your new wine, your oil, and the firstborn of your herd and your flock, so that you may learn to fear the LORD your God always. But if the distance is so great for you that you are not able to bring the tithe, since the place where the LORD your God chooses to set His name is too far away from you when the LORD your God blesses you, then you shall exchange it for money, and bind the money in your hand and go to the place which the LORD your God chooses. And you may spend the money on whatever your heart desires: on oxen, sheep, wine, other strong drink, or whatever your heart desires; and there you shall eat in the presence of the LORD your God and rejoice, you and your household. Also you shall not neglect the Levite who is in your town, for he has no portion or inheritance among you." (Deut. 14:22–27)

This tithe was taken to the place of worship—which was later established as Jerusalem—and enjoyed there. Note that at least two requirements of this festival are joy and sharing, both done because of one's covenant attachment to the God of Israel.

These three tithes all had to do with agricultural products—with what comes from the flock, field, vineyard, and orchard. There were some in the Old Testament period who did not make their income primarily from agriculture but from wages. So we read at Leviticus 19:13, "You shall not oppress your neighbor, nor rob him. The wages of a hired worker are not to remain with you all night until morning." There is, however, nothing in Scripture about tithing on wages. In part this explains our Lord's rebuke saying, "Woe to you, scribes and Pharisees, hypocrites! For you tithe mint and dill and cumin, and have neglected the weightier provisions of the law: justice and mercy and faithfulness" (Matt. 23:23). Probably most Pharisees living in Jerusalem worked at a profession other than farming, such as working as a professional scribe or making tents as Paul did (Acts 18:3).

From this all-too-brief look at the tithe, we can apply the following principles to the modern church. Our regular members and regular attenders should be giving regularly for the following three reasons: First, ministry should be supported, and it should be supported for the glory of God and for the good of the receiver. Similar to the Levites, we have a relationship of giving and receiving. That is, the Levites were due compensation because of their work (Num. 18:21). So also those who labor in preaching, teaching, and the like are due compensation because of their work. Whether we give 10 percent, or more, or less, our laborers need to be supported so they can give themselves fully and freely to the Lord's work. We will discuss this again later (Partnership with Other Believers).

Second, we should take care of one another, especially our poor. Again, we will look into this later when we discuss a benevolence fund. But certainly the Poor

Tithe—along with the crops left in the field, Leviticus 19:9–10—went to the poor, the widow, the alien, and the Levite (Deut. 14:28–29). These were all vulnerable people within Israel. The local congregation, likewise, should be concerned about its economically vulnerable people.

Third, there was the Festival Tithe. This tithe was used for a time of worship, feasting, and enjoyment before God, thanking Him for His provision and having fellowship with one another. One does not need to think too far to realize that we can apply this principle to supplying people in our local congregation with a place to meet and resources they can use together to celebrate God's goodness, doing so with mutual love, with joy, and—of course—with food.

PARTNERSHIP WITH OTHER BELIEVERS

What is the relationship between the full- or part-time staff and the givers in a congregation? What word best describes the relationship? The word is "partnership"—translating the noun *koinonia*—drawn largely from Philippians as the apostle Paul describes his relationship with the congregation that he planted (Acts 16:11–40). This small letter matters since Paul's typical financial policy was to support himself through tentmaking (Acts 18:3) and not accept compensation while on site with a particular congregation (2 Cor. 11:7–12; 12:13–15; 1 Thess. 2:5–9; 2 Thess. 3:6–12). Furthermore, only the Philippians supported Paul economically while he was in other parts of the Roman world proclaiming Christ. We learn this fact from his acknowledgment of the supplies they sent while Paul was under house arrest in Rome (Acts 28:30).[2] He says (using this time the verb of *koinonia*):

> You yourselves also know, Philippians, that at the first preaching of the gospel, after I left Macedonia, no church shared with me in the matter of giving and receiving except you alone; for even in Thessalonica you sent a gift more than once for my needs. (Phil. 4:15–16)

Paul uses a unique phrase early in Philippians, when he reports that one of his grounds for thanks to God and one of the sources of his joy is the Philippians' partnership with him in the gospel (again, *koinonia*). The partnership "includes their support but also takes into account their prayers for him (1.19), their own witness in Philippi (1.27-8, 2.15), their suffering with him (1.30) and their taking part in his affliction (4.14)."[3] Almost certainly this means that both he and they are suffering for and also advancing the gospel. On the other hand, he brought them the gospel and supports them spiritually through his prayers (Phil. 1:9–11) while they support him economically. They were partners; while one may be mostly preaching and teaching and another mostly supporting economically, nevertheless they both partook of the gospel, and were working together for its advance. They had different primary tasks but both he and they were on the same mission.

Finally, partnership is worship. We have often been told, and rightly, that giving to our local church is worship. But how is it worship? Is it giving to God? Philippians is one of the best places to begin answering these questions. They sent Paul support multiple times (4:15–16). How does he describe the latest gift he received? In this way: "I have received everything in full and have an abundance; I am amply supplied, having received from Epaphroditus what you have sent, a fragrant aroma, an acceptable sacrifice, pleasing to God" (4:18). This is worship language from the Old Testament (Lev. 2:2; 3:5; 4:11; 6:8; 8:21; Num. 15:3–7; 18:17; 28:6–8). We can compare Hebrews 13:16: "And do not neglect doing good and sharing [again, *koinonia*], for with such sacrifices God is pleased." We worship when we joyfully give to support those in ministry and to bless the poor among us.

TRANSPARENCY AND ACCOUNTABILITY

Ministers must handle church finances transparently and establish systems of accountability. Such systems will help protect everyone. Paul treats this issue in 2 Corinthians 8–9. The chapters are unique being wholly given to encouraging the Corinthians to bring to completion their earlier commitment to the collection, mentioned also at 1 Corinthians 16:1–4. Over the course of several years Paul worked to take up this collection for "the poor among the saints in Jerusalem" (Rom. 15:26). Working with Paul was Titus, a coworker of Paul well-known to the church (2 Cor. 2:13; 7:6–14; 8:6). We can learn much as we listen in to his instructions; we will pay particular attention to 2 Corinthians 8:18–21:

> We have sent along with [Titus] the brother whose fame in the things of the gospel has spread through all the churches; and not only that, but he has also been appointed by the churches to travel with us in this gracious work, which is being administered by us for the glory of the Lord Himself, and to show our readiness, taking precaution so that no one will discredit us in our administration of this generous gift; for we have regard for what is honorable, not only in the sight of the Lord, but also in the sight of other people.

We want the same things that Paul wanted. Whenever we are handling the generous offering of God's people, we want to carry out the task in a way that will not discredit the work or ministry. Rather, we want all we do to be seen as honorable, first in the sight of God, but also before people. And these people will include the givers and all those who watch the administration of monies who are not givers. How should this be done? Again following Paul's example we should see that the workings are divided up between people who are skilled, known, and trusted because of their good character. A degree in accounting is not required but might be helpful; past conviction for extortion does not ban someone forever, but we must be very cautious. There should be multiple workers who can hold each other accountable and each must be known, respected, and skillful. We suggest at least three individuals, with no two being from the same family; after an agreed term of service, they should be replaced by others who serve.

Assuming one passes a plate or a bag on Sunday morning, then, as we mentioned earlier, we should follow the same principles we found with Paul and the collection. So as to have checks and balances and avoid suspicion, multiple people should be involved, each one with strong character and a good reputation. Each individual or family's giving should remain confidential.

We believe it is important that paid church staff not know how much people are giving or even whether they are giving (see Thinking about Budgeting below), though of course those handling the offering and keeping giving records must know. For staff with such knowledge the temptation would be to befriend the rich or generous giver (Prov. 14:20) or express disappointment with those who do not give—whether expressed knowingly or not! We do not need that kind of potential problem in our pastoral relationships.

SPECIFIC TOPICS

THINKING ABOUT BUDGETING

Before we delve into the budget, let us talk about the end of life. When one of our loved ones has lived a long life, it can at times be difficult to let go. That is normal. Oddly, at times, the difficulty is exacerbated by the demand for a miracle that will extend life. Sadly, at times, this makes things more stressful, not less. That is, some folks might find that letting a loved one die is very difficult because a miracle is being expected from God.

Please do not misunderstand. Of course, sometimes God heals and works miracles. He is involved! But we should all admit that if this kind of miraculous intervention were His typical way of working, not many people would die. Yet, as we look around we see that just about everybody does. Until our Lord's return, death has become typical.

Why this talk about death? It introduces the first of two subjects for this small section on budget. First, our approach to budgeting should ask what is typical about congregations and their income. Certainly God can work outside the typical and miraculously bring income. I have seen it happen! Nevertheless, in our default mode of operation, we should not expect our income to be extraordinary, but rather to be typical. And if that is the case, we need to know what is typical for giving among Christians. A natural place for us to go is the book *Passing the Plate*.[4] The authors draw on a massive amount of data from American Christians covering a great variety of denominational backgrounds. Here a few key issues are summarized:

1. About 20 percent of American Christians give nothing at all; nothing to charities and nothing to church.

2. Among those who do give, the mean average is around 3 percent of pretax income.

3. Among regular church attenders, the most generous 5 percent contribute about half of total giving.

4. American Christians with higher incomes typically do not give more as a percentage of their income.

5. While per capita income increased over the twentieth century, giving as a percentage of income went down.

Let us not be like Peter and assume that because of our great leadership and inspiring teaching, our congregations will prove to be more faithful, more courageous, and so more generous. Rather, we should start simply. How many regular attenders and/or giving units do we have? What do the demographics of the congregation tell us about estimated average income? Assuming 20 percent give nothing, we can then multiply the rest by 3 percent to arrive at an approximate figure for yearly income.

Second, what are the priorities of our funding? Beyond the three needs discussed above (paying workers, supporting the vulnerable, and making resources available for community and worship gathering), how does one choose ministry funding? It is a tough decision. The question is largely an issue of the congregation's vision statement and ministry location. For some ministry to single mothers will be vital; for others job training for members will take higher priority; for still others world mission will be at or near the top of the list. We are all limited; there is not enough time, energy, or money to serve every need we might hear of.

Third, how will we spend what we do have? While budgeting for the small and for the large church can vary tremendously, there are general principles. We draw these from Karl Vaters, who has done a very helpful series on financial issues. He blesses us with "9 Principles for Creating an Annual Budget in a Small Church" from his blog *Pivot: Innovative Leadership from a Small Church Perspective*. We give the nine points from Vaters's blog (in quotation marks) along with a few other comments, some more, some less.

1. "Don't spend more money than you bring in": That should be obvious; we should not overspend at home or at church. Overspending is not faith; it is foolishness.

2. "Set aside money every month for annual bills": In the midst of regular monthly bills the ones that come due quarterly or yearly can be forgotten. Instead, put them on the schedule so they can be anticipated and planned for.

3. "Underestimate your income": We looked at this above. Of course, if one has last year's income figures to draw on, one does not need to create a number. But better to be surprised by more than expected than the reverse.

4. "Overestimate your outgo": Prices go up. What about utility and insurance costs? Again, it is better to have a long-range plan than to be surprised.

5. "Anticipate seasonal fluctuations": We will spend a bit more time here. It is typical for giving to go up at the end of the year and to drop in the summer. What should be done? Let us remember Proverbs 6:6–8: "Go to the ant, O sluggard; consider her ways, and be wise. Without having any chief, officer, or ruler, she prepares her bread in summer and gathers her food in harvest" (ESV). In other words, we should anticipate, make the best use of the season, and plan.

We might minimize seasonal fluctuation if we have people automate their giving. Many different automated giving platforms are available. Most claim, correctly, that automated giving yields more consistent income. On the one hand, many people are accustomed to automating their bills, so it would not be a massive shift for them to automate giving. Automated giving often proves to supply a church with steadier income, smooth out the ups and downs of seasons, and even increase overall giving. Consequently, there are predictions being made that in the next few years passing a plate will completely disappear from our local meetings.

On the other hand, should something be done just because it can be done? A parallel to this is the common practice of large churches with multiple campuses having one location with live preaching with the other sites getting the message on a video screen. What does this practice say about our theology of assembly and teaching? About how we understand proclamation? In a similar manner, we should ask what automated giving does to worship? How we want giving to be integrated as worship into our assembly as an act of worship and service? Each congregation should ponder these questions.

Finally comes the question of fees and security. Is automated giving safe? Will the online giving platform charge our congregation fees? Of course, if people give cash there can be a security issue as well. Doubtless there will be decisions made with various conclusions and different kinds of churches. But we should keep in mind that with automated giving a price might be paid—pun intended—of losing the in-person element of giving as worship.

6. "Start an emergency fund": Our furnace stopped working on the coldest day of an Illinois January; and, of course, it was the weekend! This is not the time to wonder how it will be repaired or replaced. An emergency fund is needed and preferably it should have six months of income.

7. "Include an ongoing building maintenance plan": Assuming that there is a building, it needs to serve others as well as possible and can only do so when properly maintained.

8. "Design the budget with the people who have a stake in it": The budget must be a joint effort. Solo wisdom will not work here. Who are the stakeholders? The youth workers, the nursery staff, and the cleaning staff all need a voice along with others. As Vaters says, "Not only will you get a more accurate understanding of what's needed, you'll get more cooperation from the ministry members when their concerns have been acknowledged."

9. "Factor finances into *how* you'll do a ministry, not *if* you'll do a ministry": Long-range planning is essential. Certainly there is a time for first things first. Proverbs 24:27 says, "Prepare your work outside; get everything ready for yourself in the field, and after that build your house" (ESV). In an agricultural society the field and the flock provide food and clothing for those in the house. But we do not want money to run the ministry but the other way around.

For more information, I highly recommend *Budgeting for a Healthy Church* as a very practical resource.[5]

THINKING ABOUT BENEVOLENCE

The church is not engaged in a nationwide war on poverty. Certainly, to be a neighbor, one will be called on to be compassionate to others, often making a financial sacrifice (as the Good Samaritan did, Luke 10:25–37). While we must be ready to help all people (Luke 6:35), local congregations are especially obligated to those in the household of faith (Gal. 6:10; Rom. 12:13). Thus, in keeping with emphases we find deeply rooted in the Old Testament, a congregation should care for its own who are disadvantaged (e.g., Ex. 22:22; Isa. 1:17; Ps. 146:9; Jer. 22:3). In both Testaments, widows are emblematic of the vulnerable. The "orphan" and the "widow" appear eleven times in Deuteronomy alone (e.g., 10:18; 14:29; 16:11); and Luke, with his well-known concern for the vulnerable, narrates how the early church addressed the needs of widows (Acts 6:1–6).

Concerning the care of widows, we have a very instructive paragraph in 1 Timothy 5:3–18. From it we find the following principles, which can be broadly applied to helping not only widows but all those economically needy within a congregation:

First, the primary caregiver is family. Paul mentions family three times (5:4, 8, 16) and the care that those younger show to those older is described as a "return" (5:4), that is, in social reciprocity terms, it is giving back to those who have given to you. This way of showing honor accords with the teaching of Jesus (Matt. 15:4–6).

Second, it appears that work is not an option, although it is not explicated here. The age requirement hints in that direction. Leviticus 27:3–7 seem to be assuming that past sixty one's strength significantly declines. On the basis of Paul's instruction in 2 Thessalonians 3:6–13, it is best to assume that when one can work, then one takes care of one's own needs. Our age is less dependent on manual labor and so work options might be available.

Third, when it is clear that no family is available to help and work is not an option, it is the congregation's role. A level of care is not specified; one might guess food, clothing, and shelter (1 Tim. 6:8). This will be a burden (1 Tim. 5:16)—that is, an obligation—that the congregation will gladly carry.

Fourth, those helped must be believers with proven character. Paul stresses this; summarizing 5:3–18 we find the following: (1) "*having been* the wife of one man" is the same sort of expression we find describing elders in 3:2 (the husband of one wife). Rather than an issue of history, the issue is character; the expression means she was faithful to her husband.[6] (2) A list of godly traits and habits is given, including hoping in God, regular prayer, hospitality, good works, helping those in distress, and foot-washing. All these talk of character, giving types of behavior one expects, not a mandatory checklist. Of course, the behavior expected or forbidden can vary from age to age and culture to culture. Perhaps in the twenty-first-century West foot-washing is not so crucial.

Fifth, the congregation keeps a record of those whom it assists (5:9). Qualified widows are "put on the list." That is, they are enrolled or catalogued (*katalego*). We find this word in the New Testament only in 1 Timothy. It implies some sort of official program with record keeping. For the dignity of those supported, it is best to keep these records confidential.

Finally, before moving on, we can apply the principles found in 1 Timothy 5 to our broader church community. We love our brothers and sisters. How do we help those who want to work but who are unemployed or underemployed? Each congregation will need to approach these needs in ways feasible for them, but we offer two ideas:

1. Congregations can partner with local businesses and other community organizations to provide counseling, encouragement, basic economic needs, and job training. Compare the perspective developed by Jobs for Life: "We believe God created everyone to work. He designed all of us with gifts and talents to subdue and steward the earth through work. We find our purpose, meet our economic needs, and worship God through our work."[7]

2. Congregations can create a microfinance fund, making available low-interest loans. For those who cannot get credit elsewhere, the fund is used to empower them to create their own businesses.[8] This option need not be seen as disjunctive from short-term help and job training. Indeed, bringing these together can create powerful results.

For further guidance one might see the Sample Benevolence Policies that are available.[9]

THINKING ABOUT STAFF, SALARIES, AND COMPENSATION

Among many things that can be said, five are crucial. *First,* is there a need for new staff? The answer might be that the ministry can be done by the people. After all, pastors and teachers equip the body to do the ministry (Eph. 4:11–12). Is a specially trained person required for ministry need? Is the new ministry in line with our church's vision or ministry plan? Is there room in the budget or are the givers willing to support the hire? If, after prayerful consideration, we answer these questions in the affirmative, a new hire is probably best.

Second, we have often heard the cruel joke about how the elder board set the pastor's salary very low and then said, "Well, pastor, you'll just need to trust God." Surely it is not the case, however, that the pastor must trust God while others do not. We all must trust, if for no other reason than wealth is uncertain (1 Tim. 6:17) and hard work, while tending toward wealth, does not guarantee security (Prov. 23:4–5).

Third, according to Paul, pay in response to work is a right (*exousia*, which is not a common meaning for him). He claims the right not to work, that is, not to labor at tasks other than preaching, teaching, prayer, and counsel (1 Cor. 9:4–6, 12). And this "expectation of support is not predicated on status, but on work carried out for the benefit of others."[10] Nevertheless, someone's rights imply someone else's responsibilities. Those blessed by the ministry are obligated to support the ministry. Similar is Galatians 6:6, which says, "The one who is taught the word is to share all good things with the one who teaches him." As in Philippians 4, Paul here uses the verb of *koinonia*, "share," a term that we often find in financial contexts (Rom. 12:13; 15:26; 2 Cor. 8:4).[11]

Fourth, discussing the compensation for elders, Paul asserts that "the laborer is worthy of his wages" (1 Tim. 5:18). That is, pastoral compensation is about social reciprocity. Because the Christian worker has taught, planned, managed, prayed, and counseled, this laborer has the right to compensation in return. Paul applies the same principle to himself in 1 Corinthians when he asks, "If we sowed spiritual things in you, is it too much if we reap material things from you?" (9:11). Here "material things" are financial support.[12] The clear answer to this rhetorical question is: "No, it is not 'too much.' It is completely right!" To rephrase it, because the church staff has labored, the congregation has the obligation to support them.

Fifth and last, how do we establish an appropriate salary? This can be a challenging question, and we dare not leave the answer to our feelings or to anecdotal evidence. On the one hand, from the perspective of the church board or finance team, most of the work has been done for us by ChurchSalary.com. The website asks for all the relevant information such as the ministry position, zip code, level of experience and education, church size, overall church budget, and the like. It also takes into account "local cost of living information, retirement and debt calculators, non-ministry job comparisons" as well.[13] After ChurchSalary provides a salary number, the leadership can ponder its application in their context. On the other hand, from the perspective of the minister, one might start with "How Should Pastors Approach the Salary Question?" on The Gospel Coalition website.[14]

THINKING ABOUT BUILDINGS AND BUILDING CAMPAIGNS

While buildings are often taken for granted, the gospel should guide thoughts and planning about property and buildings. The issue is not what will accrue to the church's reputation or to the staff's prestige or convenience. Although he is not speaking about buildings, Don Carson's warning holds true: "The lust for recognition can attack theology students, pastors, and seminary teachers alike."[15] Again, facilities are not about recognition. The issue is what is best for the advance of the gospel in the local community and around the world. This is the principle with which Paul works when, on the one hand, he asserts that he has the right to be supported (1 Cor. 9:4–11), and on the other hand explains that he has not used this right because—in his view—using the right would hinder the gospel (9:12).

Keeping these things in mind, questions should be asked about building or expanding facilities: Are we currently getting the most out of the space we have? Would it be cheaper or more cost effective to own (compared to renting)? Will building have a positive impact on the community we serve—both those within and outside the congregation? Will our ministry vision best be followed with a building? If we need a mortgage, will payments not be a burden that keeps us from other ministry opportunities (we suggest that total debt be no higher than twice annual income)? Do our regular givers fully support taking on debt? Assuming these questions are answered affirmatively, it is time to establish a building committee to consider all the details involved.

CONCLUSION

Our discussion has been brief; there is far more that could be said. And one might ask, "What about stewardship?" Typically all Christian discussion of money and possessions is put underneath the rubric of stewardship. The terms "steward" and "stewardship" are sometimes used in the New Testament regarding finances (Luke 12:42; 16:1–8), but more often they appear with respect to stewarding the gospel, spiritual truth, or spiritual gifts (e.g., 1 Cor. 4:1–2; 1 Peter 4:10). We think about a local congregation's finances then, so the elders or the pastoral staff become the stewards of the congregation's finances as Paul describes the elders as stewards of the household of God (1 Tim. 1:4; Titus 1:7).

RESOURCES

Alcorn, Randy. *Money, Possessions, and Eternity*. Carol Stream, IL: Tyndale House, 2003.

Baker, David L. *Tight Fists or Open Hands? Wealth and Poverty in Old Testament Law*. Grand Rapids: Eerdmans, 2009.

Blomberg, Craig. *Neither Poverty nor Riches: A Biblical Theology of Possessions*. Downers Grove, IL: InterVarsity Press, 2000.

Croteau, David A. *Tithing after the Cross: A Refutation of the Top Arguments for Tithing and a New Paradigm for Giving*. Gonzalez, FL: Energion Publications, 2013.

Getz, Gene. *Rich in Every Way: Everything God Says About Money and Possessions*. Brentwood, TN: Howard Books, 2004.

Jamieson, Janet T. and Philip D. Jamieson. *Ministry and Money: A Practical Guide for Pastors*. Louisville: Westminster John Knox Press, 2009.

Jeremiah, David. *Stewardship Is Lordship*. San Diego: Turning Point, 2004.

Johnson, Luke Timothy. *Sharing Possessions: What Faith Demands*. Grand Rapids: Eerdmans, 2011.

MacArthur, John. *Whose Money Is It, Anyway? A Biblical Guide to Using God's Wealth*. Nashville: Word, 2000.

Peterman, G. W. *Paul's Gift from Philippi: Conventions of Gift Exchange and Christian Giving*. Cambridge: Cambridge University Press, 1997.

Potts, S. L. *How to Not Be a Broke Pastor: The Definitive Guide for Understanding and Maximizing the Benefits from Your Pastoral Compensation*. BrokePastor Press, 2017.

Powell, Mark Allan. *Giving to God: The Bible's Good News About Living a Generous Life*. Grand Rapids: Eerdmans, 2006.

Quiggle, James D. *Why Christians Should Not Tithe: A History of Tithing and A Biblica Paradigm for Christian Giving*. Eugene, OR: Wipf and Stock, 2009.

Rosner, Brian. *Greed as Idolatry: The Origin and Meaning of a Pauline Metaphor*. Grand Rapids: Eerdmans, 2007.

Witherington III, Ben. *Jesus and Money: A Guide for Times of Financial Crisis*. Grand Rapids: Brazos, 2010.

NOTES

1. Among many others, see Greg L. Bahnsen, *Four Views on Law and Gospel* (Grand Rapids: Zondervan, 2010); Thomas R. Schreiner, *40 Questions about Christians and Biblical Law* (Grand Rapids: Kregel, 2010); James D. Quiggle, *Why Christians Should Not Tithe: A History of Tithing and a Biblical Paradigm for Christian Giving* (Eugene, OR: Wipf & Stock, 2009).

2. Gerald Peterman, "Philippians," *The Moody Bible Commentary*, Michael Rydelnik and Michael Vanlaningham eds. (Chicago: Moody Publishers, 2014), 1857.

3. G. W. Peterman, *Paul's Gift from Philippi: Conventions of Gift Exchange and Christian Giving* (Cambridge: University Press, 1997), 100.

4. Christian Smith and Michael O. Emerson, with Patricia Snell, *Passing the Plate: Why American Christians Don't Give Away More Money* (Oxford: University Press, 2008), 29–56. The authors use several sets of data from the years 1993–2006 (see 231–36).

5. Jamie Dunlop, *Budgeting for a Healthy Church: Aligning Finances with Biblical Priorities for Ministry* (Grand Rapids: Zondervan, 2019).

6. See William D. Mounce, *Pastoral Epistles* (Nashville: Thomas Nelson, 2000), 287; and I. Howard Marshall, *The Pastoral Epistles* (London: T&T Clark, 1999), 594.

7. "Or Misison and Vision," Jobs for Life, https://www.jobsforlife.org/about.

8. For example see https://www.faithdriveninvestor.org/microfinance, https://www.twelvechurches.org/micro-loans .html, and also Brian Fikkert and Russell Mask, *From Dependence to Dignity: How to Alleviate Poverty through Church-Based Microfinance* (Grand Rapids: Zondervan, 2015).

9. For example see "Sample Benevolence Policy from the Evangelical Council on Financial Accountability at https://www.ecfa.church; "Benevolence Policy Tips for Churches" at www.clergyfinancial.com; and "Developing a Church Financial Benevolence Ministry that Meets or Exceeds IRS Guidelines from the State Convention of Baptists in Ohio, at https://www.scbo.org.

10. Roy E. Ciampa and Brian S. Rosner, *The First Letter to the Corinthians* (Grand Rapids: Eerdmans, 2010), 402.

11. Thomas R. Schreiner, *Galatians* (Grand Rapids: Zondervan, 2010), 368.

12. Eckhard J. Schnabel, *Der erste Brief des Paulus an die Korinther* (Wuppertal, Germany: R. Brockhaus Verlag, 2006), 490.

13. See https://www.churchlawandtax.com/salary/start/.

14. Jeff Robinson, "How Should Pastors Approach the Salary Question?," The Gospel Coalition, September 19, 2018, https://www.thegospelcoalition.org/article/pastors-approach-salary-question/.

15. D. A. Carson, "The Trials of Biblical Studies" in *The Trials of Theology: Becoming a 'Proven Worker' in a Dangerous Business*, Andrew J. B. Cameron and Brian S. Rosner, eds. (Fearn, Scotland: Christian Focus Publications, 2010), 116.

Acknowledgments

A project of this size could not have been possible without the contributions and support of many others. We are grateful to our colleagues, the faculty of Moody Bible Institute and Moody Theological Seminary, whose classroom teaching and ministry inspired this project. To the authors who contributed chapters, thank you. In addition to your many responsibilities in service to the Institute, you made space to contribute to this work because of your commitment to equip the church.

We also are grateful to Moody Publishers and those who conceived of, supported, and promoted this project. We are especially indebted to Bryan Litfin for his guidance, leadership, creativity, and support. Special thanks to Randall Payleitner, Connor Sterchi, and the talented team of editors at Moody Publishers: Kevin Mungons, Pam Pugh, and Jeff Robinson.

We are most grateful to our spouses: Meloday (Michael), Bob (Laurie), and Meredith (Kerwin) for their encouragement and patience. Without your love, support, and attentive proofreads, our participation in this project would not have been possible.

Finally, we want to give thanks to our Lord Jesus Christ and the Holy Spirit for providing encouragement, strength, and a unifying collaboration with our colleagues through this process.

SCRIPTURE INDEX

921

SUBJECT INDEX

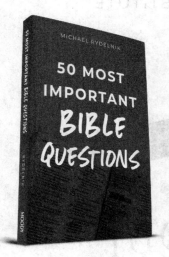
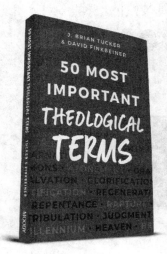

Seminary is an important step toward ministry—but only when you make the most of it.

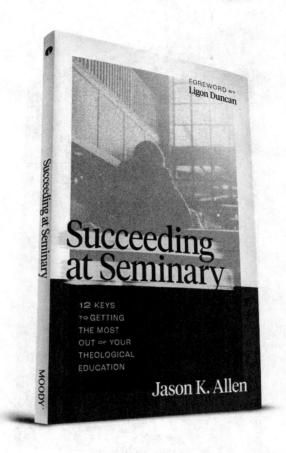

Prepare for your calling and make the most of your theological training with *Succeeding at Seminary*. You'll learn how to select the right institution and weigh the pros and cons of online or in-person classes. You'll also receive tips for developing rapport with peers and professors and get insights for how to navigate a work, study, and family-life balance to help you survive the rigors of advanced theological learning.

978-0-8024-2632-1 | also available as an eBook

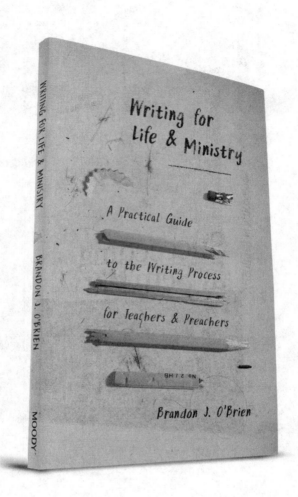